D1108553

A Treasury of the

THEATRE

Volume Three

MODERN BRITISH AND AMERICAN DRAMA
FROM OSCAR WILDE TO ARTHUR MILLER

Revised Edition, Edited by

JOHN GASSNER

SIMON AND SCHUSTER, NEW YORK

ALL RIGHTS RESERVED INCLUDING THE RIGHT OF REPRODUCTION IN WHOLE

OR IN PART IN ANY FORM

COPYRIGHT, 1935, 1940, 1950, 1951, BY SIMON AND SCHUSTER, INC.

THIS VOLUME IS REVISED AND EXPANDED FROM THE ORIGINAL

"A TREASURY OF THE THEATRE" EDITED BY BURNS MANTLE AND JOHN GASSNER

PUBLISHED BY SIMON AND SCHUSTER, INC., ROCKEFELLER CENTER

1230 SIXTH AVENUE, NEW YORK 20, NEW YORK

SECOND PRINTING

MANUFACTURED IN THE UNITED STATES OF AMERICA

The editor and publishers of A TREASURY OF THE THEATRE are grateful to the following publishers, playwrights, and translators for permission to reprint many of the plays in this volume:

To George Bernard Shaw and Dodd, Mead & Company, Inc., for their consent to the inclusion of *Candida* by George Bernard Shaw. Copyright 1898 by Herbert S. Stone and copyright renewed in 1926 by Dodd, Mead & Company, Inc., New York.

To Charles Scribner's Sons for their consent to the inclusion of *The Admirable Crichton* by James M. Barrie. Reprinted from *The Admirable Crichton* by James M. Barrie; copyright 1918 by James M. Barrie, 1946 by Peter Llewelyn Davies; used by permission of the publishers, Charles Scribner's Sons.

To Charles Scribner's Sons for their consent to the inclusion of *Escape* by John Galsworthy. Copyright 1926 and published by Charles Scribner's Sons, New York.

To G. P. Putnam's Sons for their consent to the inclusion of *The Workhouse Ward* by Lady Gregory. Copyright 1909 by Lady Gregory. Reprinted from *Seven Short Plays* by Lady Gregory. Published by G. P. Putnam's Sons, New York.

To Random House, Inc., for their consent to the inclusion of *Riders to the Sea* by John Millington Synge.

To The Macmillan Company and Sean O'Casey for their consent to the inclusion of *The Plough and the Stars* by Sean O'Casey. Copyright, 1926, by Sean O'Casey. By permission of The Macmillan Company, publishers, 60 Fifth Ave., New York.

To Doubleday & Company, Inc., for their consent to the inclusion of *The Circle* by W. Somerset Maugham. Copyright 1921 by Doubleday & Company, Inc., New York.

To Coward-McCann, Inc., and R. C. Sherriff for their consent to the inclusion of *Journey's End* by R. C. Sherriff. Copyright 1929 by R. C. Sherriff. Published by Coward-McCann, Inc., New York. No amateur or professional performance of any kind may be given without permission in writing from Samuel French, Inc., 25 West 45th Street, New York.

To Doubleday & Company, Inc., for their consent to the inclusion of *Blithe Spirit* by Noel Coward. Copyright 1941 by Noel Coward, reprinted by permission of Doubleday & Company, Inc., New York.

To Random House, Inc., and Eugene O'Neill for their consent to the inclusion of *Anna Christie* by Eugene O'Neill. Coyright 1922 by Eugene O'Neill. Published by Random House, Inc., New York.

To Random House, Inc., and Eugene O'Neill for their consent to the inclusion of *The Hairy Ape* by Eugene O'Neill. Copyright 1922 by Eugene O'Neill. Published by Random House, Inc., New York.

To Harcourt, Brace and Company, Inc., and Maxwell Anderson and Laurence Stallings for their consent to the inclusion of *What Price Glory?* by Maxwell Anderson and Laurence Stallings, from *Three American Plays,* copyright 1926 by Maxwell Anderson and Laurence Stallings. Published by Harcourt, Brace and Company, Inc., New York.

To Longmans, Green & Company and Maxwell Anderson for their consent to the inclusion of *Elizabeth the Queen* by Maxwell Anderson. Copyright, 1930, by Longmans, Green & Company, New York.

To Rinehart & Company, Inc., and Marc Connelly for their consent to the inclusion of *The Green Pastures* by Marc Connelly. Copyright, 1929, by Marc Connelly. Published by Farrar & Rinehart, Inc., New York.

To Coward-McCann, Inc., and Thornton Wilder for their consent to the inclusion of *Our Town* by Thornton Wilder. Copyright 1938, by Coward-McCann, Inc. (Text used is that of the 1938 Coward-McCann Library edition.) *Caution:* All rights strictly reserved. Inquiries regarding any kind of performance should be addressed to Harold Freedman, 101 Park Avenue, New York.

To Random House, Inc., and Clifford Odets for their consent to the inclusion of *Golden Boy* by Clifford Odets. Copyright 1937 by Clifford Odets. Published by Random House, Inc., New York.

To Random House, Inc., and Lillian Hellman for their consent to the inclusion of *The Little Foxes* by Lillian Hellman. Copyright 1939 by Lillian Hellman. Published by Random House, Inc., New York.

To Harcourt, Brace and Company, Inc., and William Saroyan for their consent to include *My Heart's in the Highlands* from *Three Plays* by William Saroyan. Copyright, 1939, 1940, by Harcourt, Brace and Co., Inc. *Caution:* Professionals and amateurs are hereby warned that *My Heart's in the Highlands*, being fully protected by copyright, is subject to royalty. All rights, including professional, amateur, motion picture, talking motion picture, radio broadcasting, television, recitation, public reading, are strictly reserved. All applications for the right to give stock and amateur production of this play should be made to Samuel French, of 25 West 45th Street, New York 19, or Samuel French, of 7623 Sunset Blvd., Hollywood 46, Calif., or in Canada to Samuel French (Canada) Ltd., 480 University Avenue, Toronto.

To Random House, Inc., and Tennessee Williams for their consent to the inclusion of *The Glass Menagerie* by Tennessee Williams. Copyright 1945 by Tennessee

Williams and Edwina D. Williams. Published by Random House, Inc., New York.

To The Viking Press, Inc., and Arthur Miller for their consent to the inclusion of *Death of a Salesman* by Arthur Miller. Copyright 1949 by Arthur Miller. Reprinted by permission of The Viking Press, Inc. *Caution:* Professionals and amateurs are hereby warned that *Death of a Salesman,* being fully protected under the copyright laws of the United States of America, the British Empire, including the Dominion of Canada, and all countries in the International Copyright Union, is subject to royalty. All rights, including professional, amateur, motion picture, recitation, lecturing, public reading, radio broadcasting, and the rights of translation into foreign languages, are strictly reserved. Particular emphasis is laid on the question of reading, permission for which must be secured from the author's agent in writing. Inquiries on all rights (except amateur rights) should be addressed to MCA Management, Ltd., 598 Madison Avenue, New York 22. The amateur acting rights of this play are controlled exclusively by the Dramatists Play Service, Inc., 14 East 38th Street, New York 16, without whose permission in writing no amateur performance of it may be given.

CAUTION:

All the plays listed above are fully protected under the copyright laws of the United States of America, the British Empire including the Dominion of Canada, and all other countries, members of the Copyright Union. All rights including professional, amateur, motion picture, recitation, public reading, radio broadcasting, televised performance, and the rights of translation into foreign languages are strictly reserved in their present form. These plays are for the reading public only. All inquiries for such rights must be addressed to the copyright owners. Also see special cautions under acknowledgments.

TO

HALLIE FLANAGAN DAVIS

for her service to the American theatre

TO

HALLIE FLANAGAN DAVIS

for her service to the American theatre

CONTENTS

PREFACE

THE READER who lights upon the present volume of *A Treasury of the Theatre* will, I hope, enjoy its contents and find it a useful introduction to the subject of modern drama in English. The survey moves from the eighteen-nineties, when the insurgents Oscar Wilde and Bernard Shaw infiltrated the Victorian theatre, to the middle of the present century, when playwrights as different as Noel Coward and Arthur Miller occupied London and New York playhouses.

This volume is a complete and independent unit. The reader should know, however, that it is the third part of a three-volume *Treasury of the Theatre,* which traces the history of the drama from its beginnings in classic Greece to our own times. The immediate forerunner of the present section is *A Treasury of the Theatre: From Henrik Ibsen to Jean-Paul Sartre,* which introduces us to the modern drama in continental Europe.

The over-all design of our *Treasury* precludes the inclusion of most of the ephemeral plays with which we are all familiar. Nor does it invite any special indulgence in the urbane intimacies usually favored in discussions of the latest stage productions of London's West End and Manhattan's Broadway. That I have not legislated against humor or felt any particular obligation to solemnity is attested by the representation of such congenial playwrights as Wilde, Shaw, Barrie, Maugham, and Saroyan in this collection. But our perspective in this book is that of history, and an attempt to maintain it has been made in the introductions to the subdivisions and the plays. The volume is, in effect, a combined anthology and history of the modern English, Irish, and American drama.

The modern drama in English is almost entirely a twentieth-century product. In 1900 the platitude that a substantial part of the modern drama has been composed in our language would have been a startling exaggeration. Before then, only England, among the English-speaking countries, had some approximations of Ibsen drama, and even the English playwrights, with the sole exception of Bernard Shaw, lagged far behind continental playwrights in dealing with the imperatives of modern thought. As Irwin Edman has pointed out, there is a "time lag" in the cultural life. Literature lags behind developments in science and philosophy, and the theatre lags behind literature. Men of letters are apt to arrive at an intellectual position long after it has been taken for granted, if not indeed after it has already been abandoned, by scientists and philosophers. The men of the theatre, working in a medium that requires instant popular approval, make discoveries that have already been ventilated by the novelists. Although the "time lag" could also be discerned in continental Europe (Balzac and Stendhal antedated Ibsen by nearly half a century), it was more pronounced in the English-speaking theatre to the same degree that British and American fiction lagged behind European fiction.

The English-speaking theatre's slow progress, nonetheless, proved to be advantageous in some respects. It might be argued that the phlegmatic English temperament and American pragmatism were deterrents to the wild excesses of naturalism and expressionism in continental Europe, and that the volatile and poetic spirit of the Irish disposed Ireland's dramatists against arid realism. But in all probability British and American playwrights escaped experimental excesses mainly because they attained to modernism too late to be overwhelmed with evangelical passion for any particular dramatic style or theory. Even Bernard Shaw's large claims for the "drama of ideas" were tempered by common sense and by interest in the drama as entertainment.

The playwrights were not the grimmest of naturalists reveling in sordid and depressing detail because naturalism was no longer novel when it arrived on English and American shores. Nor were they wholly subjugated by the "Maeterlinckéd sweetness" of poetic symbolism and the later frenzies of expressionism because the *symbolistes* and the *expressionists* had already passed their trial period on the European continent when they crossed the English Channel and the Atlantic Ocean. With respect to naturalism's claims to holding the mirror up to nature, most of our English-speaking dramatists had had time to realize, with Logan Pearsall Smith, that "All mirrors are magical mirrors; never can we see our faces in them." With respect to suggestive symbolism, they had had time to discover that suggestions and nuances are apt to be lost in an auditorium of more than a few hundred seats occupied by audiences longer than half an hour. There was a difference between the Marie Laurencin style of depersonalization affected by the young Maeterlinck in the eighteen-nineties and the vigorous poetic dramas of a Synge or the shrewd whimsies of James M. Barrie after 1900. As T. S. Eliot was to write many years after Maeterlinck's early work had become a faded memory, "Synge wrote plays about characters whose originals in life talked poetically, so he could make them talk poetically and remain real people. The poetic prose dramatist [such as Maeterlinck] who has not this advantage has to be too poetic." And even Barrie fortified his elfin spirit occasionally with hard Scottish sense.

As for modern innovations in theatre art, while there was much to be learned about stage production and scenery from the continent, it was an advantage to have had European stage directors and scenic artists make the first experiments in dramatic style. While profiting from their triumphs, British and American theatre artists could also profit from their mistakes. It was no great loss even to have the home-grown Ellen Terry's son, Gordon Craig, try his most far-flung scenic visions abroad, so long as a substantial residuum could be usefully employed by British and American scene designers such as Paul Shelving, Robert Edmond Jones, and Lee Simonson. From Granville-Barker's Court Theatre Shakespearean productions in 1912 to the work of Peter Brooks in his mid-century staging of *Measure for Measure* at Stratford and *Ring Around the Moon* in London, English stage direction has had strong claims to distinction. By 1950, indeed, the English theatre's sense of style could not be surpassed anywhere. And many a theatrical miracle could also be attributed by then to the Abbey Theatre's early productions and to the staging of plays in America by such directors as Arthur Hopkins, Jed Harris, and Philip Moeller, as well as by such successors as Elia Kazan, Harold Clurman, and Robert Lewis.

We may not, of course, overlook the limitations to which the English-speaking drama and theatre have been subject. Each English-speaking country appears to have qualified dramatic creativeness in its own special way. It has long been evident that Irish playwrights have been apt to rely too much on native charm, that British playwrights have tended to be as mild as they have been suave, and that American playwrights have often been somewhat callow, as well as erratic. And on the whole it may be said that the English-speaking theatre world has been deficient, for better or worse, in satirical relentlessness and metaphysical turns of mind. Stage production in England and America, besides, has too often favored surfaces, and the actor has tended to rely on his personality rather than on his art. He has tended to be an individualist astray and, to that degree, has often failed to create a complete individual on the stage.

Still, after all the debits and credits have been balanced, it is an inescapable conclusion that the modern theatre between 1900 and 1950 would have been a decidedly poorer institution without the contribution of the English-speaking countries. The English stage has to its credit the supreme dramatist of the century, Bernard Shaw. The Irish theatre will always be remembered for the two playwrights, Synge and O'Casey, who had bells in their throats while many contemporaries shouted or groaned themselves hoarse. The American stage has a strong claim to impressiveness with O'Neill, whose wrestlings with the time-spirit were titanic and whose very stammerings were detonations. From the special talent of these men, and from that of their colleagues in occasional achievements up to the advent of Arthur Miller's *Death of a Salesman* in America, came work that, if surely less deep than a Sophoclean well and less dazzling than a Shakespearean sunburst, was, nevertheless, often stirring or stimulating. High comedy was fairly well served by British and American wits, while poetic drama and tragedy were encompassed in Ireland, England, and America about as well as it has been possible to achieve poetic and tragic art in our century. The intellect was mobilized for defensive and offensive maneuvers, even if no major victories were won except when Shaw was in the field. The heart was deployed with some breadth and intensity, and the spirit found employment in some honorable capacities.

These contentions could have been more thoroughly substantiated in the present volume if the number of plays could have been doubled without dislocating the paper industry and unbalancing the *Treasury*'s survey of the world theatre. But a volume representing the work of Shaw, Synge, O'Casey, Galsworthy, O'Neill, Wilder, Williams, and Miller should give some indication of the range and power of the theatre that came into being when Victorianism receded in England, when the insurgent Irish spirit found a channel to the stage, and when American vigor finally cut a swathe through modern dramatic literature.

J. G.

June 1951

Modern Drama in England and Ireland

Modern Drama in England and Ireland

The two major events to take place since the early eighteen-nineties in the English-speaking theatre across the Atlantic were the modernization of the British drama and the birth of the Irish theatre. The two developments occurred within a decade of each other, and each came as the climax of efforts to meet a strongly felt need. England had yet to develop an effective modern drama at the beginning of the eighteen-nineties; Ireland had yet to create a theatre of national character at the start of the twentieth century. Both nations were faced with the challenge of modern times, and, fortunately, both could look to Continental Europe for inspiration.

Beginning with the eighteen-fifties, indeed, Englishmen had reason to be envious when they looked across the narrow stretch of water that separated them from the Continent. They saw, first, a European theatre increasingly supplied after 1850 with a drama overdidactic but concerned with facts of contemporary life, when composed by the younger Dumas, and commonplace in thought but vigorously objective, when written by Emile Augier. By 1879, moreover, it was evident that a giant had arisen in the north. Ibsen, the Norwegian iconoclast, was challenging the old order in both society and the theatre with *A Doll's House*. Simultaneously, Zola was spreading the gospel of a new dramatic art that would be as concerned with reality and as free from artifice as the great novels of the century. A new stage, energetic and forthright, was making its presence felt. By 1890, in fact, the Continent possessed an impressive body of social and psychological drama irradiated by the modern mind and spirit. Ibsen had by then added *Ghosts, An Enemy of the People, The Wild Duck, Rosmersholm, The Lady from the Sea,* and *Hedda Gabler* to the modern repertory. The irascible but provocative genius August Strindberg, also from the north, had contributed *The Father, Comrades, Miss Julie,* and *The Creditor.* Henry Becque, in Paris, had delivered two witheringly honest studies of reality, *The Vultures* and *The Parisian Woman.* The Russian theatre was moving toward a profoundly human realistic drama after Tolstoy's *The Power of Darkness,* written in 1886. The German theatre had discovered Gerhart Hauptmann in 1889. Moreover, a "free theatre," dedicated to modernism, was gaining a following in Paris and Berlin; André Antoine had established his Théâtre Libre in 1887, and Otto Brahm his Freie Bühne in 1889. Both theatres were producing significant studies of society and character. Could the theatre in England remain insulated from the modern world to which the nation had made so many contributions in industry, science, and thought?

By 1900, moreover, a new art theatre had arisen in Europe, a theatre dedicated to the recovery of imagination and poetry or poetic nuance. Symbolist and neoromantic drama—written by newcomers such as Maeterlinck and Rostand, and even by those pioneers of realism Ibsen and Strindberg—brought spiritual power and enchantment to the stage. A second challenge faced the British Isles. Could England and Ireland succeed in serving beauty as well as truth?

Before either truth or beauty could be served, however, the stage in England had to shed its contented insularity and the stage in Ireland had to be placed on firm foundations. Considerable exertion would be necessary on the part of progressive dramatic critics, playwrights, actors, and stage producers in the British Isles. The magnitude of the task can be realized today only by casting a backward glance at the Victorian period.

VICTORIAN DRAMA

If it is too much to say that British drama was an arid waste between the time of Sheridan and the advent of Wilde and Shaw, there is no doubt that the theatre in England suffered a century of decline between 1780 and 1880 except for the triumphs of certain great actors, chiefly in Shakespearean drama. England, once the soil of distinguished dramatists, not to mention the greatest of all dramatists, failed to develop a single playwright of real importance. Sentimental comedy, strongly favored by the growing middle classes, who frowned upon levity and demanded moral uplift, supplanted the wit of Jonson, Congreve, Gay, and Sheridan. At best, the comic muse was served by farces devoid of any sort of distinction except facility in pandering to complacent minds. And tragedy, the high art in which England had once excelled, was displaced by romantic thrillers accompanied by background music, giving currency to the term "melodrama."

The theatre remained almost exclusively in the hands of hack writers until the last quarter of the century. It was dedicated to melodrama, farce, adaptations of plays by second-rate Continental authors, and spectacles—except, of course, for Shakespearean plays, which were, however, mangled by the actor-managers. The nadir was reached in the mid-Victorian period, which experienced many social and intellectual stirrings in directions other than that of playmaking. The theatre, dependent upon the patronage of the average man and generally promoted by average men hungry for a profit, lagged far behind science, social thought, and even the novel. Darwin, Huxley, Mill, Carlyle, Arnold, Ruskin, Dickens, Thackeray, George Eliot, and Emily Brontë were fully active at the time. The greatness of mid-Victorian literature lay in its protest against the prevailing thought and conduct. But the theatre, complacently on good terms with its public, would have no traffic with the critics of society; it gave no indication, in fact, of being aware of their existence for many decades. As late as 1879, Matthew Arnold could lament with absolute justice that "in England we have no modern drama at all." The date is significant; it was the year of Ibsen's *A Doll's House.*

If we are to comprehend the significance of the battle waged and won for a modern drama in England, we must understand the "Victorian Compromise" reflected and served by the theatre. The Victorians had made some excellent adjustments between reality and social convenience, and these were not to be publicly questioned by young people, irresponsible artists, or mere entertainers. In politics and in society, the adjustment was, as the historian Carlton J. H. Hayes declared, "between democracy and oligarchy, whereby the bourgeoisie enjoyed political rights and left the lower classes to shift for themselves. It was tacitly assumed that if a man was poor, it was due either to his own fault or to inexorable economic laws." In time, the suffrage was extended, especially by the Second Reform Bill of 1867; in time, too, social legislation bettered the condition of the laboring classes. But class distinctions could not be removed by fiat, and social legislation continued to be frowned upon by the average middle-class and upper-class mind, leaving much work for reformers and a great deal of provocation for Bernard Shaw's wit and indignation even in the twentieth century.

The average Victorian, frightened by the rise of scientific and skeptical thought, raised his defenses of convention higher than ever and endeavored to make them as impregnable as possible. Manners, sentiment, family life, the rearing of children, public education, morals, and religion were fortified against invasion by the modern spirit; and the strength of the fortifications may be measured by the great efforts that men such as Bernard Shaw and Samuel Butler had to make to breach them. A bargain was struck with religion, so that it would not interfere with business. And a bargain was struck with Darwinism, so that man might still enjoy a divine dispensation while using the Darwinian theory of "the struggle for existence" in nature as justification for unrestricted competition in society.

At the same time, improvement could be discerned in the evolution of society, assuring the Victorian gentleman that a divine purpose was at work. Optimism became a cult as England acquired more and more wealth and industry continued to make remarkable advances. Tennyson, taking his cue from the growing railway system, saw society in 1842 "spinning down the ringing grooves of change." Commerce was also binding the nations together, and he felt moved to express popular expectations of a "Parliament of man" and a "Federation of the world," held in "fretful awe" by the "common sense of most." England had a constitutional government which did not interfere very much with private behavior and business. "Liberalism" prevailed in the land. And it was a central doctrine of the Liberal party that so long as government refrained from interfering with the natural law of supply and demand and with the liberty of the individual, even in the case of child labor, all would turn out for the best, thanks to reason and self-interest. One need not be disturbed by the way of the world. Robert Browning's Pippa, in 1841, was blissfully certain that "God's in his heaven—all's right with the world."

In "wandering between two worlds, one dead, the other powerless to be born," Matthew Arnold was the exceptional man. The average Victorian was prepared to make the best of all the worlds open to him. Arnold was disturbed by the conflict between science and religion, but the ordinary man, having made a convenient distinction between the weekday and Sunday, found no reason to be distressed. Arnold was appalled by the "Philistinism" of the materialistic middle classes, and Carlyle thundered against the "dismal science" of *laissez-faire* economics. But Arnold could be ignored as an intellectual and a snob; Carlyle, as a dyspeptic or a prophet. If the Victorian needed a symbolic public figure, he had the best one of all at Windsor Castle, and she would never let him down. The good Queen remained loyal to the memory of Prince Albert and to the teachings of her tutors. She forbade smoking on the premises, recommended a whipping for advocates of "women's rights," and was "not amused" by the sallies of Gilbert and Sullivan. She was a monument—as solid as Nelson's statue—to the unwavering virtue of the race.

Even Victoria's poet laureate, however, came to realize that "the old order changeth, yielding place to new." Tennyson's optimistic view of the age, expressed in *Locksley Hall,* in 1842, actually changed to the refrain of "Chaos! Cosmos!" in *Locksley Hall Sixty Years After,* in 1886. The political stirrings grew more pronounced; the intellectual currents, more tempestuous. The voices of Carlyle and Arnold could be heard louder in the land and were joined by other voices. John Henry Newman and others clamored against a religion of accommodation. Ruskin condemned a society notable for the ugliness of its cities and factory towns. "There is no Wealth," he declared, "but life; life, including all its powers of love, of joy, of admiration. That country is the richest which nourishes the greatest number of noble and happy human beings." So spoke the professor of art at Oxford whose reverence for beauty became a social passion, leading him to spend the whole of his fortune of two hundred thousand pounds on the creation of a model industrial community, the Guild of St. George, in 1871. An esthetic revolt, which had been taking shape since 1848, when Dante Gabriel Rossetti founded the Pre-Raphaelite Brotherhood, reinforced the moral protests with its call for art *versus* utility and refined pleasure *versus* grubbing for money. The poets—Rossetti, Swinburne, and others—became "fleshly" when they were not directly involved with social problems. And "art for art's sake," whether supported by the Pre-Raphaelites and Walter Pater or promoted by the later artistic rebels of the eighteen-nineties, was itself a protest. The campaign being waged was the same as that of the philosophers and social thinkers, whose tools were logic and statistics. The poets were contemporaries of John Stuart Mill, then writing in behalf of feminine emancipation and elaborating his "utilitarian" philosophy of "the greatest good for the greatest number," and of Karl Marx, then drafting his *Das Kapital* in the British Museum.

A new dispensation came to the theatre, slowly and unsteadily, it is true, and with many accommodations, but with increasing effect. The story of the progress of the stage has a familiar ring by now, but each advance had the startling effect of an air-raid siren when modernity seemed little short of disastrous to the guardians of convention.

In rapid summary, we may take note of the coming of new dramatists, of their struggle for acceptance by the theatrical managements, and of their growing success with audiences. The first advances were tentative and qualified, hedged about with circumspection; the later ones were brazen and captured attention with the vigor of their assault on conventional behavior and sentiment.

THE FORERUNNERS OF MODERN DRAMA

Credit is usually given first to the mid-Victorian playwright T. W. Robertson, who was something of a prodigy to his age because he took realistic notice of the "cash nexus," or money consideration, in personal relationships such as love and marriage. His first important piece, *Society,* appeared in 1865 at the successful comedienne Marie Wilton's little Queen's Theatre, in London. Conventional in plot, with the hero winning love and fortune at the end, *Society* nevertheless inched toward the modern drama. Characters spoke openly of the significance of money in life and in marriage, calling marriage "a union mutually advantageous," and regarding "honor" as synonymous with "not being bankrupt." Tom Robertson's *Caste* (1867), although feeble in characterization, took notice of the subject implied by its title. It is true that Robertson accepted the stratification of society and deplored social climbing. But he was the first British playwright to look at the life around him and present some of its facets on the stage, although he is apt to be remembered most often for favoring the use of real doorknobs in realistic scenery. Late in the eighteen-eighties, the young Bernard Shaw, then England's most outspoken drama critic, could still treat him with respect, because it was not until two decades after the production of *Caste* that a playwright was to go

beyond Robertson in veracity and concern with contemporary realities.

The interim is notable only for the plays and libretti of W. S. Gilbert, a professed political conservative who nevertheless possessed a genius for making breaches in the Victorian barricade. Especially in his collaborations with Arthur Sullivan, beginning in 1878 with *H. M. S. Pinafore,* this irrepressible humorist played gadfly to Victorian society in a manner as pointed as it was enchanting. But Gilbert-and-Sullivan musical comedy, delightful as it is, was a special department, requiring an almost freakish talent and a genius for poetic nonsense. The Savoy operettas, although they may have left reverberations in the spacious brain of Shaw and in the smaller ones of other British playwrights, could not revitalize the nonmusical stage.

It was the European theatre that accelerated the still lagging rate of progress. In the eighteen-nineties, the French sources, upon which English playwrights and managements had relied for much of their material, began to disappear. The English theatre could not possibly adapt and stage for its public the pungent naturalistic plays of Zola, Becque, and their followers; it had to rely upon home-grown products. At the same time, the British playwrights could not remain entirely impervious to developments abroad. In 1873, Edmund Gosse had drawn attention to Ibsen in a widely read magazine article, and a translation of Ibsen's *Emperor and Galilean* appeared in 1876. A questionable adaptation of *A Doll's House* was performed in 1884. William Archer translated *Pillars of Society* in 1880 and published it in 1888, and Karl Marx's gifted daughter, Eleanor Marx-Aveling, followed suit with translations of *Ghosts* and *An Enemy of the People.* A volume containing the latter three plays appeared in England in 1888. It sold well and attracted a good deal of attention. The following year, Archer's painstaking, if hardly inspired, translation of *A Doll's House* was produced at the Novelty Theatre in London, with the well-known Shakespearean actress Janet Achurch as Nora. The play had a good run and aroused much controversy in the press. *Pillars of Society* had a single performance about a month later. In 1890–1891, a five-volume edition of Ibsen's plays was published in England; it contained all his prose plays from *The Vikings* to *Hedda Gabler* and was, in fact, the first collection of his works to be published anywhere. *The Lady from the Sea* appeared in two separate translations in 1890; a biography of Ibsen was published at about the same time; and Shaw delivered a celebrated lecture on "Socialism in Ibsen" before the Fabian Society in July 1890. The following year, *Rosmersholm* was produced at the Vaudeville Theatre in London and was roundly denounced in the newspapers. *Ghosts* was scheduled for public presentation, only to draw suppression from the censor. It was given a private performance, however, by the Independent Theatre on March 13, 1891, and was defended in print by Archer. At about the same time, Shaw expanded his Fabian lecture into the famous book-length essay *The Quintessence of Ibsenism*. Then *Hedda Gabler* won success at the Vaudeville Theatre, where it was produced by the actress-manager Elizabeth Robins, who played Hedda. Finally, in 1893, the Independent Theatre, the experimental venture of J. T. Grein which had introduced Shaw to the theatre a year before with *Widowers' Houses,* successfully revived *Ghosts*. The battle for Ibsenism was won.

Now it was up to the British playwrights to make the most of the victory. Shaw did. But there were circumspect, long-practicing playwrights who took profitable advantage of the altered situation in the British theatre by expediently compromising. They forged no thunderbolts like Ibsen's but gave imitations of them that provided novelty without danger. Today their work seems mild enough to make us wonder what the shouting they provoked was all about. In the 'eighties and the 'nineties, however, their work was very "advanced," except to Shaw, then functioning as a dramatic critic, who was able to penetrate beneath the surface of their pretensions to courage.

The first of the pseudo Ibsenites was Henry Arthur Jones (1851–1929), a crusty but well-intentioned gentleman of the stage who considered himself a pioneer. Jones, who had won early success with the usual pabulum, had become sufficiently conscious of Ibsenism in 1884 to collaborate (with Henry Herman) on an adaptation of *A Doll's House* and to write *Saints and Sinners,* a play then considered a slashing attack on Philistinism. Although it was a melodrama of seduction, injured innocence, and ultimately triumphant virtue, Jones's drama exposed religious hypocrisy with its story of the persecution of an upright pastor by members of his congregation. In 1889, Jones reviewed the subject of marriage with more than ordinary severity, in *The Middleman*. As late as 1896, he shocked his public by showing a clergyman in the toils of illicit passion, in *Michael and His Lost Angel,* although the play ended in repentance and expiation on the part of the clerical hero. With *Mrs. Dane's Defence,* produced in 1900, Jones still thought himself bold, because he had drawn a more or less sympathetic portrait of a woman with a "past." In a few earlier plays, climaxed by two well-written comedies of manners, *The Liars* and *Dolly Reforming Herself,* he had tilted a lance at British foibles and insincerities. For a man of sharp temperament and good intentions, Jones was remarkably sensible of an obligation to please the public and to offend it as little as possible. Late in life he wrote Brander Matthews that, although he had created some ninety plays and had helped to move things along, only four or five times had he been able to write the play he "should have written if the conditions of the English theatre had been as easy for the dramatist as they are today."

Equally willing to move with the tide of the new realism and equally resolved not to let it sweep him out to sea was Jones's contemporary Arthur Wing Pinero, who ultimately achieved a baronetcy for his facile playwriting. After composing successful farces in the 'eighties, none more charming than *The Magistrate* (1885), he too became speciously progressive, and again it was the fallen-woman theme that gave a British playwright some semblance of modernity. Pinero's *The Second Mrs. Tanqueray* was produced in 1893 and heralded as a work of remarkable realism by the British public, which had as yet only small acquaintance with the modern drama. A woman with a past was Pinero's heroine, and he went so far as to sympathize with her efforts to rehabilitate herself by marriage to a gentleman. The only fly in the ointment was the fact that Pinero proceeded to show that the effort was doomed to faiiure. He was not entirely unconvincing and he was comparatively free from sentimental tear-shedding; he gave the impression that inexorable fate was working itself out in the real world and in a real character. Between ventures into comedy of manners such as *The Gay Lord Quex,* Pinero composed a number of additional social and character studies, *The Notorious Mrs. Ebbsmith* (1896), *Iris* (1901), and *Mid-Channel* (1909)— plays that might have seemed moderately advanced if Shaw had not already delivered himself of *Candida, Mrs. Warren's Profession,* and *Man and Superman*. The truth is that Pinero retained a quite Victorian mind to the very end. Only his comedy *The Thunderbolt* (1908) suggested the capacity for critical scrutiny that characterizes a truly modern playwright, and even here Pinero relied on the hoary device of a lost will to energize his action. As long ago as 1895, Shaw called Pinero "a humble and somewhat belated follower of the novelists of the middle of the nineteenth century," and this opinion seems even more justified today than it did then.

Pinero, along with Jones and others, might have been described by phrenologists as a man endowed with a large bump of reverence. It was an anatomical feature entirely absent in Wilde and Shaw, who were able to bedevil society with their irreverence. Pinero and Jones wrote a number of "problem plays," but these were cautious and narrowly circumscribed excursions into the modern world. They belonged to the age of Dumas *fils* and Augier rather than to the world of Ibsen and Shaw. This is so not only because Pinero and Jones adhered to the "well-made play" formula of plot construction but because, to paraphrase George Meredith, they fiddled harmonics on the strings of domesticity. The gifted professor-critic Gilbert Norwood did not depart greatly from the truth when he wrote that "your pseudo-advanced writer invariably reveals his caliber by this assumption that the 'Problem play' must treat of marital infidelity; there is only one sin—the Decalogue has become a monologue."

SHAW AND THE MODERN THEATRE

The first playwright to aerate the British theatre was Oscar Wilde, even though he brought something less than a serious interest and intention. Plays were for him a ready means of augmenting his income and discharging his exuberance, so that he was content with conventional plots and trashy formulas of playwriting. But his delight in baiting society and his irrepressible wit made him the first brilliant writer of comedy of manners after Sheridan—if it is not indeed with Sheridan's seventeenth-century masters, Wycherley and Congreve, that we must associate him. Wilde first shocked British sensibilities with the decadent biblical one-acter *Salomé,* originally written in French for Sarah Bernhardt; in the same year (1892), he wrote *Lady Windermere's Fan,* the first of three problem plays which made thesis drama something more than an exercise in moralization—a word that Wilde would have dreaded beyond all words. In *Lady Windermere's Fan,* as well as in *A Woman of No Importance* (1893) and *An Ideal Husband* (1895), Wilde blasted away with a carefree air at Philistinism and social hypocrisy. "A man who moralizes is usually a hypocrite, and a woman who moralizes is invariably plain," says his Cecil Graham, in *Lady Windermere's Fan.* In the three problem plays, Wilde himself indulged in some moralizing, but only at the expense of conventional morality. Like George S. Kaufman and his colleagues in the American theatre of the nineteen-twenties, Wilde, who anticipated the "wisecrack" on a more literary level, was able to serve convention and sophistication in the same breath. The plot satisfied the ordinary requirements of playgoing while the acid of mocking commentary dissolved conventionality in the play and in the playgoer. Finally, in 1895, Wilde wrote the gayest farce in the English language, *The Importance of Being Earnest.* Farce is usually the very antithesis of drama of ideas. This was not the case here, since the epigrams in conjunction with the extravagant complications comprised a perfect reversal of Victorian principles. Wilde upset the Victorian apple-cart, and so great were his skill and good humor that he made his public enjoy watching the apples roll.

If his incorrigible laziness and ill-fated quarrel with the Marquess of Queensbury had not interfered with his career, Wilde might have continued to entertain the British public in ways to which it had not been accustomed for a century or more. His disappearance from the theatre, however, was less than calamitous, for Shaw was now at hand with greater intellect and energy—in fact, with an alto-

gether superior equipment for exorcising the ghost of Victorianism. This was, however, only one of the tasks Shaw imposed on himself. Iconoclast and prophet, humorist and social critic, this emigrant from Ireland subsumed all previous and contemporary efforts to modernize the British stage, giving British drama a status that will not easily diminish so long as his plays are read and performed.

Shaw's achievement stems for the most part from the unique quality of his genius, from his mastery of language, and from the marvelous play of his mind on the human scene. He had a dialectical skill given to few men who have written dramatic literature, a flair for showmanship, a feeling for acting and stagecraft, and an ability to make even discussion vibrate with drama—qualities which were not always apparent to Shaw's contemporaries. His genius consisted also in a capacity for characterization and in an intense sincerity, both of which were often overlooked or minimized by his early critics. Shaw's individuality, already the subject of many books, cannot be summarized briefly without being miserably shortchanged, and the savor of his special creativeness cannot, indeed, be transcribed by criticism that does not help itself generously to his own words. But what is easily enough established for the purpose of a perspective on theatrical history is the nature of Shaw's contribution to the rise of a modern drama in England, or, for that matter, elsewhere in the Western world.

Achieving a modern drama was never a simple matter of filling plays with realistic details of background and conduct. If it had been, Dumas *fils* and Augier, Jones and Pinero, and any number of other second-rate playwrights of our time would be modern and important. Like Ibsen, Shaw was aware that realism of detail was less important than the application of intelligence to reality. Any conscientious observer can supply the facts, but only an acutely intelligent person can interpret them incisively and significantly—and only a talented person can make drama of them. The true realist in Shaw was the thinker, not the reporter.

Like Ibsen too, but in a livelier spirit, Shaw was able to sublimate the *facts* of society and of individual conduct into *ideas.* He brought analysis and discussion into the drama of the period after 1890 and gave pre-eminence to the drama of ideas, doing this equally well in tragedy, comedy, and extravaganza. There have been only four types of comedy in the world: Aristophanic comedy, comedy of manners, romantic comedy, and comedy of ideas. All but the last were the creation of past ages. Comedy of ideas is the only modern contribution to the history of high comedy, and it is largely Shaw's creation.

Shaw opened the gates of the theatre to a flood of challenging new ideas. When he entered the theatre he brought with him Schopenhauer, Nietzsche, Samuel Butler, Lamarck, Henry George, Karl Marx, the Webbs, and other redoubtable figures who were shaping modern thought and life. He made the discursive drama possible and often triumphant, which is no small accomplishment. Nor was it an unimportant one, since it enabled the drama to keep abreast of happenings beyond the footlights. In an age of unprecedented dissemination of ideas and of growing conflicts in which these ideas played significant parts, Shaw's achievement came to be appreciated more and more; it amounted to a vitalization of playwriting beside which the contributions of writers such as Jones and Pinero shrank into insignificance. Even Ibsen had not kept abreast of the modern world to the same degree.

According to Shaw, an Ibsen play consisted of *exposition, situation,* and *discussion.* Whether or not this was an accurate analysis of Ibsen's dramaturgy, it applied well enough to Shaw's plays and to those of some of his disciples, especially Granville-Barker. Freely construed, the Shavian dramaturgic formula serves, in any case, to point up for us an important cleavage between the new drama and the old. The old, tried, and indeed still often practiced formula may be said to be: exposition, development (with a view to knotting situations into a major complication or crisis), and resolution or dénouement (literally, the disentangling or untying of the plot). Substitute the principle of exposition, situation, and discussion, and the result is a type of drama that prevails less by hypnotizing its audience than by enlightening or at least stimulating it to mental activity. The latter theory of writing is obviously the very opposite of Wilkie Collins' prescription for storytelling: "Make 'em laugh; make 'em weep; make 'em wait." Factitious suspense vanishes in truly modern drama. Asked whether he would care to set down three rules for playwriting, Oscar Wilde facetiously declared, "The first is not to follow the methods of Mr. Henry [Arthur] Jones, and the second and third are to the same effect." Although Wilde, for whom plot was a mere convenience, himself followed Jones's methods in most plays, his quip sums up the dramaturgic revolt of Shaw and many other moderns, from Becque and Ibsen to Saroyan and Brecht.

To employ "exposition, situation, and discussion," well exemplified by Shaw in such diverse pieces as *Candida, Man and Superman,* and *Saint Joan,* one would need a "new" kind of dialogue and a "new" logic. The dialogue must possess sparkle and intellectual vigor—qualities not of course really new when we remember Aristophanes, Shakespeare, Molière, and other worthies, but fresh in idiom and content. Wilde summed up a distinction between the old and new styles of dialogue when a crash of scenery interrupted a rehearsal of his comedy *A Woman of No Importance.* Stopping the rehearsal, Wilde told the company, "Ladies and gentlemen. Pray, don't be alarmed. The crash you have just heard is merely some of Mr. Jones's dialogue that

has fallen flat." As for logic, it is true that so competent a guardian of the trusty old craftsmanship as Pinero once declared, "Cause—effect! Cause—effect! Two of the most substantial parts of the fabric which go to make up a fine play are logic and intuition. Without logic you cannot construct a play. Without intuition you cannot write it." Nevertheless, the logic Pinero had in mind was not the logic of Shaw and his successors. Pinero meant only the credible motivation of behavior within the play or the cohesion of successive situations and actions within the boundaries of a plot. The Ibsen-Shaw school added a logic of social reality. It implicated the *world of the characters and not merely the world of the play*—that is, it considered the milieu from which human beings acquire their manners and beliefs, their problems, their social status and livelihood, and their ideas. The modern use of logic involved, in addition, the free play of critical reason on habitual life and thought, the pleasure of keen argument, the delight in the exchange or conflict of opinions. Logic, in short, was a drab servant in the older theatre. It was a bright mistress or clever wife in the new theatre. And Shaw was a past master of the art of dialectics—which means, for theatrical purposes, that he found drama in ideas. It is not surprising that his work seemed undramatic to those who found drama only in bedroom situations.

Shaw, we may say in conclusion, also discovered a new poetry for the theatre, although members of the old guard found it the very antithesis of poetry. In a superficial sense, they were right. The dialogue was athletic, intellectual prose instead of prose dressed in the gaudy furbelows of Victorian stage conversation. The point of view was often mundane, for the dramatist claimed an interest in sociological fact and insisted on an underlying economic situation. He penetrated into the painfully prosaic substructure of the superstructure of manners and morals. "Karl Marx," Shaw declared on the occasion of one of his many birthdays, "made a man of me," and Shaw was bent upon proving this in his plays, as well as in his prefaces and tracts, assigning a decisive role to economics in works as diverse as *Widowers' Houses, Mrs. Warren's Profession, Pygmalion,* and *Major Barbara.* Shaw brought politics, too, into the theatre—not romantic flourishes against tyranny, which were as old as Schiller and the young Goethe, nor the superficial politics of intrigue successfully used in Scribe's classic *The Glass of Water* (which even Nazi Germany found innocuous enough to certify for production), but politics in the serious sense in which it was used by Plato and Aristotle, Metternich and Disraeli, Marx and Lenin —and Shakespeare. This kind of political thought, a hard and cold reality whether it appears in the great discussion between Warwick and the Bishop, in *Saint Joan,* or in the decisions of King Magnus, in *The Apple Cart,* was prose to those who confused sentiment with poetry. Shaw was the last person in the world whom the Victorians would have called a poet.

How one could nevertheless claim for him the title of poet can be seen in Shaw's fine artistry: his cadences, imagery, and power of metaphor; his brilliant precision, which recalls Dryden, even as his full-throated rhetoric recalls the King James Bible, Bunyan, and Milton; his moral passion, without which he held life was not worth living; and, for all his glitter of jibe and paradox, his greatheartedness. The analyst, realist, and wit was also a man of prophetic disposition who was convinced, with his Father Keegan of *John Bull's Other Island,* that "every dream is a prophecy: every jest is an earnest in the womb of Time." Somehow, through discursive writing, handsprings of argument, bouts with history, collusions with the "Life Force," and the rest of his sleight of hand, Shaw managed to transform modern reality into vision and passion. In all his vocal masquerade through the disenchanting forest of fact, one could hear Father Keegan's profession of faith: the dream of "a country where the State is the Church and the Church the people: three in one and one in three"; "a commonwealth in which work is play and play is life: three in one and one in three"; "a temple in which the priest is the worshipper and the worshipper the worshipped: three in one and one in three"; "a godhead in which all life is human and all humanity divine: three in one and one in three"—in short, the dream of the poet, with or without the benefit of economics and dialectics.

More significantly than any of his contemporaries, Shaw revealed the possibilities of a poetry of prose in the theatre. Laying claim to nothing more than lucidity of thought and expression, Shaw nonetheless demonstrated that statement can be imaginative and incandescent. In this respect, too, he epitomized a fact of modern literature—namely, the un-Victorian realization that poetry is not synonymous with ornamentation. It was a realization inherent in the verse of Robert Frost, T. S. Eliot, and the later Yeats, and it was also a characteristic feature of such diverse plays as those of Chekhov, Pirandello, Lorca, and Eliot. Genuine poet-playwrights of the past had, of course, instinctively adhered to the principle that poetry was essence, not decoration; this is as apparent in the pages of Sophocles and Racine as in those of later writers such as the Ibsen of *Peer Gynt.* But the prettifying of sentiment and evasion of reality had been a chronic obsession of the playwrights challenged by Ibsen and Shaw, resulting in a pseudo poetry of both verse and prose and therefore in pseudo literature. In Shaw's writing, prose was good prose (none better had been written in English after Swift); and when it became metamorphosed into poetry, it was honest poetry. That has been the ideal of all true modernists of the drama; it is largely what we mean when we say it is characteristic of the modern stage that playwrights began once more to write plays that could qualify as literature. For this reason, as well as because their work had a content of thought, playwrights began to be pre-eminent in the theatre instead of playing roles secondary to those of actors and managers. In this respect, too, Shaw epitomized a new dispensation. No other playwright who was not also a stage director or actor claimed as much authority and had as much to say about the production of his plays. What passed for an idiosyncrasy, if not for vanity and arrogance, in Shaw was actually a portent of the modern playwright's arrival at voting age in the theatre.

Finally, it is plain that Shaw revealed a capacity for imagination that only poets possess. He could re-create history imaginatively in such plays as *Caesar and Cleopatra, Androcles and the Lion,* and *The Devil's Disciple.* He could employ fantasy with fine effect, in the Don Juan episode of *Man and Superman,* in the epilogue of *Saint Joan,* and in less successful plays. He was never reluctant to invent unlikely situations whenever his agile mind needed a fable. Nor did he hesitate to employ symbolism, notably in *Heartbreak House.* For a man who stressed the bleak realities of economics and practical politics, he took singular liberties with commonplace fact. As a thinker, Shaw took great pride in his "realism." As an artist, however, he refused to allow himself to be fettered to realistic technique and style. He retained the right to be buoyant, free, and inventive; and there was joyous creativity in his blood and sinew. He played the prophet and imp at will, and sometimes he was both. He struck a sober attitude or cut a fanciful caper, and in either case scored a point. Shaw, in short, was the master of reality and not its slave. In this respect, as well as in the wide range of his artistry, he belongs to the small number of dramatists to whom true greatness can be attributed.

THE OTHER MODERNISTS

Not everything that constitutes the modernity of Shaw's drama could be found in the modernity of his fellow playwrights. Shaw's work stood, and still stands, as the summation of their separate and fragmentary contributions to the British theatre. It has been convenient here to touch upon his multifaceted work as the measure of many of the individual efforts that add up to the modern British drama. But it was through the accumulation of plays by others as well as by Shaw between the eighteen-nineties and the beginning of the First World War that England acquired a modern stage. It took some time before Shaw's plays, barred by censorship and by the British commercial managements and opposed by conservative critics and playgoers, could win a large audience. And it took years before Shaw proved as acceptable to the great public as several of his fellow playwrights, whose merit was more transparent. Time has dealt as harshly with them as it has been kind to Shaw, despite their early success. They were more modest in their ventures and claims, more cautious, or more congenial, and consequently more persuasive.

There were, before 1914, a few writers such as Jones, Pinero, and C. Haddon Chambers who continued to take cautious steps in the new direction— and the steps began to add up. There were also the minor Shaws. One of these was the short-lived Stanley Houghton (1881–1913), whose *Hindle Wakes* presented a poor girl refusing to be made honest by a rich weakling after an illicit week end. (Insisting on a "single standard," she explains to right-thinking people that she doesn't care for the man any more than "a fellow cares for any girl he happens to pick up.") Another moderate Shavian was St. John Hankin (born in 1860 and a suicide in 1909), whose *Last of the De Mullins* concerns a woman who defies her family's code of honor by rejecting the father of her illegitimate child and going into business. Also a Shavian was the brilliant actor and producer (later a superb Shakespearean critic) Harley Granville-Barker (1877–1946), who wrote incisive, if not always engrossing, attacks on Victorian convention such as *The Madras House* (1910) and antiromantic dramas such as *The Voysey Inheritance* (1905) and *Waste* (1907).

England also acquired its twentieth-century quota of naturalists and writers of new problem plays with a naturalistic coloring. Elizabeth Baker contributed an affecting drama of lower-middle-class life, *Chains* (1909), to show how "little men" are entrapped by environment and fateful circumstances. Githa Sowerby, three years later, provided the powerful middle-class drama *Rutherford and Son,* set in the home of a domestic tyrant and old-fashioned industrialist. Writers of one-act realistic plays also began to multiply, the best of them being Harold Brighouse. The growing cities, especially Manchester, provided much matter for slices of life from twentieth-century industry.

At the other extreme stood the dramatists of country life, no longer painting idyllic pictures but taking note of the harsher aspects of the countryside from Yorkshire to Scotland, sometimes employing unlovely dialects, sometimes noting the effects of industrialization. And combining the starkest naturalism with eerie feeling, producing a kind of "Gothic naturalism," the poet John Masefield sublimated village naturalism, actually as old as George Crabbe's eighteenth-century verse tales, into the near masterpiece *The Tragedy of Nan,* in 1908. It was a brutal drama that belongs to the genre of peasant naturalism best realized in Tolstoy's *The Power of Darkness.* It treated country life in the spirit of Hauptmann and of Erskine Caldwell, exposing its meanness. But it was also more richly charged with poetic power than the plays of those who, like Stephen Phillips, James Elroy Flecker,

Gordon Bottomley, Lascelles Abercrombie, and John Drinkwater, tried to revive the poetic drama in England with historical and legendary subjects.

Present, besides, was John Galsworthy (1867–1933), the strongest and most admired social naturalist, who cast aside a lyric talent (visible in the long story *The Apple Tree*) in order to serve truth and conscience. Beginning with *The Silver Box,* Galsworthy exposed the inequities in British life with dogged persistence, but also with gentlemanly equanimity and detachment. His claims as a naturalist rested on his fidelity to colloquial dialogue, his firm grasp of character, and his willingness to see all sides of a question. This equableness, apparent from his first plays (*The Silver Box,* in 1906, *Joy,* in 1909, and the class-conflict drama *Strife,* in 1910) to his last completed play (*Escape,* in 1929), tended to diminish the force of his writing and was perhaps more a limitation than a virtue. But at the time of their first productions, when their subjects and analyses were fresh, Galsworthy's plays made the British theatre a living force. And beneath the moss that has since then gathered on some of them still lies some vital undergrowth. Galsworthy was appreciated, and can still be respected, for the solidity of his dramaturgy, for his restraint and discipline, and for the authenticity of his characters. "A human being," he declared, "is the best plot there is. . . . He is organic. And so it must be with a play." Galsworthy was no more of an iconoclast in dramaturgy than he was in opinion. He wrote, "A good plot is that sure edifice which slowly rises out of the interplay of circumstance on temperament, and temperament on circumstance, within the enclosing atmosphere of an idea." He could not have expressed his intention better. It is plain that he acknowledged the force of ideas in the theatre. It is also evident that he was not bent upon creating a new kind of drama and refrained from breaking the mold of plot. But he made the old kind of drama sufficiently better, sufficiently more persuasive and lifelike, to make it seem significantly new in a theatre largely devoted, then as now, to fabrication rather than to life.

It would have been too much to expect that the British public (or, for that matter, any public) could subsist exclusively on the sober realism of the British playwrights. England continued to produce musical pieces, farces, and light comedies—pleasantries, indeed, of all kinds, whose modernity lay on the surface. Even in this airy world there were, however, capers of less than Victorian circumspection, and the master who cut them best was James M. Barrie, who was idolized by the public and seen in perspective only by the discriminating few. Sentimentalist though he was, he was also an ironist of sorts before 1914. A cynic at heart, he had a good eye for the starch in a stuffed shirt, as may be noted in *The Twelve-Pound Look, The Admirable Crichton,* and *What Every Woman Knows.* With these pieces, as well as with that most "escapist" of plays *Peter Pan,* this idiosyncratic son of a Scottish weaver played the agile imp and prankster in the years before the First World War. Shaw the gadfly still stings. Barrie seems a rather tired Puck these days. But Puck too had his role to play in the early years of this century.

NEW THEATRE FOR OLD

With Shaw leading the procession and the others marching or mincing behind, then, the British stage came of age before 1914.

The Independent Theatre, founded in 1891 as a small subscription organization with the help of the critic William Archer, could produce plays "privately" and was therefore free from censorship by the Lord Chamberlain's office. After its production of Ibsen's *Ghosts,* the Independent Theatre discovered Shaw as a playwright when Grein asked him to write a play for the organization and Shaw obliged by completing *Widowers' Houses* (originally intended as a collaboration with Archer). Satirizing Grein's enemies, Archer asked derisively, "Who is this Dutchman who dares to be dissatisfied with our honest, healthy, comfortable, fat, and flourishing drama?" But Grein enjoyed the support of some significant figures in the British world: George Meredith and Thomas Hardy among the novelists, Pinero and Jones among the playwrights, Frank Harris, A. B. Walkley, and Shaw among the journalists.

Seven years of intermittent activity was all that the Independent Theatre enjoyed. But when it closed, in 1897, it had twenty-six productions to its credit. By that time Shaw had completed *The Philanderer, Mrs. Warren's Profession, Arms and the Man, You Never Can Tell,* and *Candida.* As Shaw has written, "the search for native dramatic masterpieces, pursued by Mr. Grein with the ardor and innocence of a foreigner, was so complete a failure that at the end of 1892 he had not produced a single original piece of any magnitude by an English author." After 1897, the acuteness of "this humiliating national emergency" was over, but by then the Independent Theatre had expired.

Henceforth the West End, London's Broadway, was to prove more congenial to the modernists and the experimental groups were to grow in power in influence. Two years after the demise of Grein's little theatre, the Stage Society of London came into being. Founded for the purposes of experimental production and evasion of the British censor, the Stage Society gave Sunday-night performances of plays by Shaw, Ashley Dukes, and European playwrights, some of which were subsequently moved to London's West End. Next came the gallant little repertory companies. The Birmingham Repertory Theatre arose in 1907 with amateur actors, including the playwright John Drinkwater. Six years later, the group opened its own theatre, which had the dis-

tinction of being the first theatre in England specially built for repertory. Subsidized by Sir Barry Jackson, it operated without thought of profit and with experimental zeal. Birmingham became the first British city to have its own civic theatre. In 1929, Jackson opened the Malvern Festival with a Shaw program, including the world *première* of *The Apple Cart.* Jackson was extremely generous in supporting his convictions; when he presented all five parts of *Back to Methuselah,* its astounded author, Shaw, asked him, "Jackson, are you certain your wife and children are insured?"

Important, too, was the Manchester Repertory Theatre, founded in 1908 by Miss A. E. F. Horniman (1860–1937), the generous patroness of the stage who four years earlier had enabled the Irish National Theatre Society to establish its permanent home in Dublin, the Abbey Theatre. Her outstanding early discovery was the young genius Stanley Houghton, who did not live long enough to carry his talent to its full promise. The first fruits of the theatre in Manchester were pictures of North-country life, naturalistic dramas for the most part. (The Manchester style of drama continued to exert an influence for a long time; as late as 1935, England's best unemployment drama, *Love on the Dole,* reflected that influence.) In 1913, the Manchester group introduced one of the best-known English naturalistic dramas, *Jane Clegg,* written by St. John Ervine, of Ulster county, with Dame Sybil Thorndike as the slum heroine who finally drives out her ne'er-do-well scapegrace of a husband.

Enlightened commercial enterprise must also be credited with advancing the drama and stagecraft. Especially important was the career of Granville-Barker as co-manager, director, and actor of the Court Theatre in London, founded in 1904. Under the management of Granville-Barker and Vedrenne, the Court Theatre housed thirty-two productions within three years; eleven of these were plays by Shaw. It was also Granville-Barker who presented Galsworthy's first social drama *The Silver Box,* in 1906, and who gave Masefield's *The Tragedy of Nan* its first professional production. Granville-Barker continued his far-reaching career at the Savoy Theatre, giving modern productions of Shakespearean plays there between 1912 and 1914. He modernized stagecraft and it was he who gave America its first important lesson in artistically trim and expressive stage art, when he played a New York season at Wallack's Theatre in 1915–1916. A recital of facts such as these makes a dull chronicle for those who have no memories or vivid descriptions at hand. But every effective production of a good play is an eventful experience, and the English theatre, always blessed with excellent actors who became still better under superior direction, abounded in such experiences by the time the First World War closed the formative phase of theatrical modernism in England.

ENGLISH DRAMA AFTER 1918

Thereafter, the story of British drama can be summarized rather briefly. The battle for modernism was won; with some notable exceptions, the fruits were meager. Shaw's labors brought forth *Heartbreak House* (written during the war but first produced in 1920 by the Theatre Guild of New York) and his masterpiece *Saint Joan* (1923). A number of other plays which were not up to his highest standards were still better than a good deal of the work of his contemporaries. Galsworthy continued to write until a few years before his death in 1933. He created one of his best-written and most deeply felt plays, *Loyalties*, in 1922, and seven years later, a veritable summary of his works, *Escape*, appeared; he gave nothing else of consequence to the stage. James M. Barrie began to succumb in 1916, the year of *A Kiss for Cinderella*, to his saccharinity and fancy, managing only to bring things to an elfin boil in *Dear Brutus*, in 1917, and to produce a questionable excursion into mysticism, *Mary Rose*, three years later. Nothing of importance came from other prewar writers, and the effect of the first global holocaust was negligible in the theatre except for Shaw's *Heartbreak House* and for *Journey's End* (1929), by a new writer of promise, R. C. Sherriff. Sherriff's later work, however, proved disappointing. John Drinkwater apparently had shot his bolt with *Abraham Lincoln*, in 1919. A scattering of poetic drama appeared but was wholly unimpressive except for the work of the expatriate from St. Louis and Harvard, T. S. Eliot, who provided *Murder in the Cathedral* (1935) and *The Cocktail Party* (1949).

The harvest in serious drama was painfully meager: a few plays of less than major proportions —Sutton Vane's *Outward Bound;* Rudolph Besier's biographical romance *The Barretts of Wimpole Street;* Gordon Daviot's *Richard of Bordeaux;* and Laurence Housman's *Victoria Regina.* Social conscience during the economic depression of the 'thirties yielded Ronald Gow and Walter Greenwood's *Love on the Dole,* based on a novel by the latter, and a few plays by J. B. Priestley, such as *The Inspector Calls.* Democratic fervor inspired two superior but hardly pre-eminent dramas: Emlyn Williams' *The Corn is Green* and Terence Rattigan's *The Winslow Boy.* Robert Nichols and Maurice Browne proved prescient in 1928 with their imaginative atom-bomb drama, *Wings over Europe,* without however, splitting the atom of humdrum realistic drama, which evidently offers greater resistance than uranium. Clemence Dane wrote a fairly moving play, *A Bill of Divorcement* (1921), and a highly original drama, *Come of Age* (1934). And Mordaunt Shairp, along with plays of far less merit, wrote a distinguished drama of sybaritism, *The Green Bay Tree.*

In one field, however, the British theatre remained pre-eminent: in comedy—and farce—of manners. Somerset Maugham, who took playwriting less seriously than he did fiction writing, came to the fore with the scintillating satire on snobbery *Our Betters* (1917), the clever problem comedy *The Constant Wife* (1923), and the wise play *The Circle* (1921). C. K. Munro, who also wrote a sharp but amateurish antiwar play, *The Rumor,* produced one piece of clever entertainment, *At Mrs. Beam's.* Winnie the Pooh's laureate, A. A. Milne, contributed a few pieces of pleasant foolery, such as *Mr. Pim Passes By, The Truth About Blayds,* and *The Dover Road.* Frederick Lonsdale, who had started on his career in 1908, continued to write brittle comedies such as *The Last of Mrs. Cheyney,* and St. John Ervine, who had written powerful realistic drama between 1913 and 1915 (*Jane Clegg* and *John Ferguson,* the play that saved the infant Theatre Guild in 1920), revealed a talent for polished comedy in *The First Mrs. Frazer,* in 1928. Ashley Dukes, better known as a critic and adapter of German expressionist drama, contributed an original romantic comedy, *The Man with a Load of Mischief* (1924). John Van Druten used the British "public school" to advantage in his comedy of adolescence, *Young Woodley* (1925), but rounded out his career as a welcome American citizen, with such plays as *The Voice of the Turtle* and *I Remember Mama,* in the nineteen-forties. Benn Levy, later Labor parliamentarian as well as husband of the actress Constance Cummings, contrived good fun, especially with the tart farce *Springtime for Henry* (1931). Dodie Smith provided gentle entertainment in such pieces as *Autumn Crocus* and *Call It a Day,* in the nineteen-thirties.

The roster of British comedies can be continued, indeed, almost interminably without establishing more than that British urbanity remained steady in a world that gyrated into a second world war and—miraculously—out of it. Even the very serious-minded J. B. Priestley proved more successful with an antic disposition, in *The Good Companions* and *Laburnum Grove,* than when he aired liberal or socialist sympathies. A crusty humorist, James Bridie (Dr. Mavor to his Scottish patients), wrote charmingly and wisely and is the most original humorist to have arisen in the nineteen-thirties. He favored whimsies, such as *The Black Eye, Tobias and the Angel,* and *Susannah and the Elders.* And topping all these playwrights in clever theatricality, Noel Coward bounded into the British theatre with suavity occasionally poisonous, wit often just brazen enough to provoke laughter instead of offending, and cynicism that always fell short of challenging anyone's conviction or intellect.

It is apparent that England relied heavily on its humorists, and their worldly-wise writing was an accomplishment that the English treasured in bad times as well as good. Perhaps these comedies, notable for their gayety and literate dialogue, afforded an assurance that intelligence and a civilized attitude could be maintained even in times of stress. Sometimes, as in some Noel Coward comedies, there was even defiance in the writing, as though the English prided themselves on being unintimidated by the weight of serious problems. Sometimes, as in the work of Maugham, a genial cynicism gave the impression that Britons could not be frightened because they knew the way of men and women too well to expect something better than could be had. And sometimes, as in the plays of Bridie, the English theatre was philosophically resigned to human contradictions and follies. If these qualities did not give rise to a particularly exciting theatre, they nevertheless helped produce a civilized one, preferable, in some respects, to the frantic Central European and the devoutly utilitarian Russian theatre after 1920.

The British theatre, which began somewhat reluctantly to modernize itself with Wilde and Shaw, moved toward the mid-point of the twentieth century somewhat tired by the struggle with momentous crises. Some playwrights turned to religious drama, and a few of their plays—notably Eliot's *Murder in the Cathedral,* Dorothy Sayers' *Zeal of Thy House,* and Christopher Hassall's *Christ's Comet*—were exquisitely written and noble in spirit. A few writers, most notably Auden, Isherwood, and Spender, tried to create a "left-wing" poetic drama. But the rest of the dramatists avoided social and spiritual encounters. They were almost invariably adroit, but they were content to be amiable and urbane.

THE "CELTIC RENAISSANCE" IN THE THEATRE

It occurred to the excellent poet and gentleman William Butler Yeats in 1899 that it was high time for his native Ireland to have a national drama and stage. A little later, a frail young man of English descent, John Millington Synge, waited in a Parisian apartment for his genius to germinate. "You will never create anything by reading Racine," Yeats told him and urged him to go to the Aran Islands off the west coast of Ireland to reacquaint himself with his people. Synge heeded his friend's advice, and so Ireland acquired her first resident dramatist. Ireland had, it is true, contributed playwrights such as Farquhar, Goldsmith, Sheridan, Wilde, and Shaw to the English theatre. But Ireland had had no real theatre of its own since the Middle Ages.

In the eighteen-nineties, its hopes for home rule aroused by the career of its leader, Charles Stewart Parnell (1846–1891), Ireland began to experience a cultural renaissance. After 1890, with Parnell's career ended, home rule suffered a crushing setback and Ireland's political struggle was sublimated into cultural activity. A Gaelic League was founded in 1893 with the express purpose of promoting the study of the Gaelic language and its ancient literature; scholars such as the poet Douglas Hyde began to write in the old language and urged others to follow suit. Even George Moore, the expatriate novelist, made the attempt. The rich ore of Irish legend began to be mined by Hyde, Yeats, "Æ" (George W. Russell), and others. The Irish Literary Society came into full bloom. The dramatic activity with which Europe was teeming inspired the Irish literati to envisage a national theatre. It would be an art theatre, like the free theatres that had promoted the cause of Ibsen and Ibsenism, and even more like the new art theatres founded by such proponents of stylized stagecraft as Gordon Craig, who was better heeded on the Continent than in England.

In his youth, Yeats, who was ultimately to prove himself one of the most modern of modern poets, was a romanticist. He belonged to the literary generation of the eighteen-nineties which exalted "art for art's sake" in reaction to realism in art and materialism in society. In the "mauve" 'nineties, he became one of the founders of the Rhyming Club of London, which counted William Morris, William Ernest Henley, Arthur Symons, and Lionel Johnson among its fellows. Moreover, Yeats was acquainted with the French symbolists, notably with Paul Verlaine, the poet, and with Maurice Maeterlinck, the prime symbolist among dramatists. Neither a nationalist nor an Irish Catholic, Yeats owed his allegiance to art rather than to Irish politics in those days; he was converted to nationalism chiefly by his esthetic interests, because he found in Ireland a rich source for romantic beauty and poetic speech. Ireland may have lacked the sophistication of the literary circles in Paris and London to which Yeats was accustomed; but even that was an advantage, since fresh poetic emotion was more apt to be aroused by the still rather primeval Irish countryside than by the industrial cities of England and the Continent. Yeats's early one-act play *The Land of Heart's Desire* (1894) was drawn from the folk imagination of Ireland, and the contagion of Irish patriotism soon accentuated his romanticism. In the one-act drama *Kathleen ni Houlihan,* he expressed the call of patriotism in poetic Maeterlinckian terms, Ireland being symbolized by a wizened woman whose account of her injuries ("strangers in her house," and her "four beautiful daughters"—Ireland's four provinces—taken from her) finds a champion in a young man. Yeats continued writing plays in this vein and later, interestingly, in the style of the Japanese Noh play, creating a new, if narrowly limited, poetic drama in the English tongue.

Yeats's enthusiasm for an Irish theatre won the support of the socially prominent Lady Gregory and of her affluent neighbor Edward Martyn, a devout Catholic who enthusiastically espoused Ibsen and an ardent nationalist famous for raising a furor by opposing the recruiting of Irish volunteers for the Boer War. Yeats also attracted George Moore, more French and English than Irish but important because of his social prominence and because his naturalistic novels had already given him prestige

Yeats's enthusiasm bore fruit, and on May 8, 1899, the Irish Literary Theatre made a stormy debut in the "Ancient Concert Rooms" of Dublin. Devout and patriotic Irishmen protested vehemently against the production of Yeats's play about a woman's sacrifice of her soul for starving people, *The Countess Cathleen,* as an insult to the Faith and to Irish womanhood. But English reviewers wrote of it favorably, and the Irish Literary Theatre opened a second season with a piece by George Moore and a fantastic drama, *Maeve,* by Edward Martyn.

At this time the productions were given with actors imported from England, and the enterprise could be viewed virtually as an offshoot of the British movement toward a modern theatre. George Moore's social drama *The Strike at Arlingford* had been an early Independent Theatre production in England, and so had Yeats's *The Land of Heart's Desire* (1894). Ireland, moreover, still had no company of actors, although Irish players were growing in number and the brothers Frank and William G. Fay were touring with a small but brilliant company. Yeats saw a performance of theirs and was sufficiently impressed to turn his *Kathleen ni Houlihan* over to them. On April 2, 1902, with P. J. Kelly and Dudley Digges in their ranks, the Fay players presented Yeats's play and a piece by "Æ" before a wildly enthusiastic audience. Encouraged by this reception, they formed the National Dramatic Society, with Yeats as president, and concluded their season with several other productions. In 1902, they presented two more poetic pieces by Yeats (*The Hour Glass* and *The King's Threshold*), Lady Gregory's *Twenty-Five,* Padraic Colum's *Broken Soil,* and the first of Synge's short masterpieces, *In the Shadow of the Glen.* Within half a year, the company, now augmented by the remarkable Sara Allgood, was riding the crest of a wave of popularity that carried it to London and won it the patronage of the generous Miss Horniman. The group lost P. J. Kelly and Dudley Digges in America when it played at the St. Louis Exposition, in 1904, but in that year, in spite of criticism by extreme Irish zealots who had rioted at the performance of Synge's one-acter, the National Dramatic Society became Ireland's national theatre. Miss Horniman supplied the funds for a playhouse erected in Abbey Street, Dublin, and promised a subsidy to keep the nascent organization in operation for a term of ten years. Over the protest of suspicious chauvinists, the company received a patent and the Abbey Theatre was born.

Henceforth the Abbey was the focal point of dramatic writing in Ireland, and with good reason, since this theatrical company became one of the most distinguished in the world, developing an art of ensemble and an aptitude for authentic performance excelled only by the Moscow Art Theatre and the Théâtre du Vieux Colombier.

The poets continued to write and had, indeed, their quota of productions at the Abbey. But the Irish drama that really made the Abbey Theatre and the Irish dramatic movement effective was essentially a folk art, combining realism of environment and character portrayal with the poetic colloquial dialogue and temperament of Ireland. Irish drama, in its first phase, was a fusion of realistic and neo-romantic or symbolist elements, with sometimes one and sometimes the other dominant. That the Irish drama suffered considerable limitation because too many of its writers turned their backs on Ibsen and the drama of ideas is unquestionably true. The fact was noted vigorously by Ireland's great genius, James Joyce, who inveighed against Celtic mysticism. (Joyce's own play, *Exiles,* written in 1914, was Continental drama and had nothing in common with the prevailing national style.) Yet Lady Gregory's formula, taken from Aristotle, "To think like a wise man but express oneself like the common people," prevailed sufficiently to produce work of more than provincial distinction. This was true in spite of the supersaturation of playwriting with Celtic folklore and with Irish charm. Lady Gregory herself contributed no profundity, but brought peasant drama to the Abbey between 1906 and 1907 with one-act masterpieces such as the delightful comedy of crotchety old age *The Workhouse Ward* and the little tragedy of patriotism *The Gaol Gate.* And Lady Gregory's example resulted in a deluge of peasant drama written by George Fitzmaurice, Padraic Colum, William Boyle, and others. Even the least significant of their plays were steeped in humor, in local color, and in a sense of reality, although they do not qualify for any great importance to the world theatre. Most important of all, the local-color movement brought forth the genius of Synge.

Synge, who gave the English-speaking theatre its greatest one-act tragedy, *Riders to the Sea,* in 1904, also supplied its outstanding folk comedy, *The Playboy of the Western World,* in 1907. He was lost to the Abbey by 1909, when he died of cancer in his thirty-eighth year. But Synge left a legacy in these two works that helped to sustain for decades Ireland's claim to an important place in the twentieth-century drama. Nor did he fall greatly below his high standard with the rollicking farce *The Tinker's Wedding,* the folk comedy *In the Shadow of the Glen,* the symbolic drama *The Well of the Saints,* and the uncompleted romantic tragedy *Deirdre of the Sorrows,* which he did not live to see produced. "All art," he wrote in his preface to the published version of *The Playboy of the Western World,* "is a collaboration, and there is little doubt that in the happy ages of literature, striking and beautiful phrases were as ready to the story-teller's or the playwright's hand as the rich cloaks and dresses of his time. I got more aid than any learning could have given me from a chink in the floor of the old Wicklow house where I was staying, that let me hear what was being said by the servant girls in the kitchen." Synge was fully aware of his debt to Ireland and he repaid it handsomely, even though Irish superpatriots responded to most of his efforts with violent demonstrations.

There was, however, an understandable reason for the indignation of these nationalists, foolish though it may seem to us today. They sensed a mocking temper in his plays—and they were right. Synge would have been a minor playwright like most of his colleagues, if he had not possessed a questing and somewhat skeptical temperament. He did not deal ostensibly with modern questions, yet his outlook was critical. He did not favor the modern drama of ideas, yet was modern in his skepticism. Above all, he was a serious artist for whom the question of national touchiness was irrelevant. He was writing at heart not for the national movement but for eternity, expressing his conviction in the preface to *The Tinker's Wedding* (a farce that treated a priest altogether too cavalierly for the Ireland of his day), when he wrote that "the drama, like the symphony, does not teach or prove anything." He did not wish to go out of fashion, like the realistic theatre's "analysts with their problems, and teachers with their systems," but proposed to be perennial, like "the blackberries on the hedges." Whether he might have gone beyond his intention if he had lived long enough to exhaust his rural material cannot be ascertained, although it is true that he was planning to write a drama of city slum life shortly before his death. In any case, this descendant of Cheshire Englishmen and creator of Irish drama was an exquisite artist who sublimated peasant drama into universal drama. Without presenting the modern conflicts and discussions that characterize much of the modern drama, he proved himself a modern dramatist. His work can be located midway between twentieth-century naturalism and symbolism. His greatest claim to modernity lay in his ability to transmute common life into a natural, seemingly effortless poetry.

O'CASEY AND IRISH MODERNISM

Rural material did become subject to the law of diminishing returns after Synge's death, although the peasant continued to supply Irish drama with some moving or hilarious plays, such as Seumas O'Kelly's tragedy *The Shuiler's Child,* Lennox Robinson's delightful comedy *The White-headed Boy* (1916), and George Shiels's *The New Gossoon* (1930). For some fifteen years, indeed, the Abbey Theatre lacked a playwright of major standing, until it presented Sean O'Casey's *Juno and the Paycock* in 1924. Between 1911 and 1915, it is true, St. John Ervine did turn out drama of a different order from that of the Celtic ruralists: *Mixed Marriage* (a drama of class and religious conflict in Belfast), *Jane Clegg,* and *John Ferguson.* But, although he took charge of productions at the Abbey in 1915, he was an Ulsterman and British at heart, and he left Ireland with a tart one-act farewell, *The Island of Saints, and the Way to Get Out of It.* In 1909, the year of Synge's death, Lord Dunsany made his debut at the Abbey with his sharp one-act play *The Glittering Gate,* but his imagination was better stimulated by the Orient than by Ireland. He was to win adherents in the little theatres of the English-speaking world with bizarre pieces such as *The Gods of the Mountain* (1911) and *A Night at an Inn* (1916). A Maeterlinckian symbolist but also a thrillmonger, Dunsany attracted much attention. Yet it can hardly be maintained that he has any significance for either the European or Irish theatre.

Ireland, nevertheless, was fortunate in being able to produce a dramatist of first rank after the First World War, something that cannot be said for England proper. O'Casey's artistry linked him with the Abbey's first great period, insofar as he proved himself as fully capable of turning common life into poetry as Synge. And like his distinguished forerunner, O'Casey became a master of language. But it was with a new realism that O'Casey made a distinctive contribution to Irish, as well as to world, drama. His realism was not nourished on the soil but was thrust up from the cobbled streets of Dublin in the midst of the city poor. He gave Ireland its first true proletarian drama in the two masterpieces *Juno and the Paycock* and *The Plough and the Stars.* And what is perhaps more important to the perspectives of dramatic art, O'Casey introduced a fresh sympathy, a critical spirit, and an awareness of twentieth-century conflicts into the poetry of speech and mood already sufficiently ingrained in Irish drama. The spirit of Synge seemed to have merged with the spirit of Ibsen and Shaw in O'Casey's Abbey Theatre plays. This was eventful not only for Dublin but for the rest of the English-speaking world, which acquired two plays of major distinction, as well as a third which was estimable, if less remarkable, *The Shadow of a Gunman.* Rising to the occasion, the Abbey Theatre gave the three plays superb productions between 1923 and 1926, and henceforth O'Casey was acknowledged one of the outstanding dramatists of the century. For the Abbey, too, these productions were significant. How great a departure they were for a theatre that had been rather grudging in its reception of critical social drama will be best realized if we recall that the Abbey did not get around to producing *A Doll's House* until 1923! For a short period, the Abbey stood once more in the front lines of modernism.

O'Casey's next plays, although still Irish in essence, came to be identified with the English theatre. Rejected by the Abbey, his pacifistic and semi-expressionistic drama *The Silver Tassie* (1929) was first produced in London, with Charles Laughton as the hero. Settled in London, O'Casey then gave England the wholly symbolic drama *Within the Gates* (1933), not the most substantial of his plays but a noble composition that was welcome in a period of receding exaltation in the British theatre. His next play to have its *première* in Dublin, *Red Roses for Me,* a poetic class-conflict drama, came many years later, in 1943.

The Irish drama after O'Casey's break with the Abbey would have been exceedingly meager but for the advent of Paul Vincent Carroll, an Irish schoolmaster residing in Glasgow. The best of Carroll's plays, *Shadow and Substance* (1934) and *The White Steed.* both charged with critical spirit, were unflattering to Irish life but once more called attention to Ireland as the seedbed of good dramatists. With help from Denis Johnston, the highly original author of *The Moon in the Yellow River* (1931), and others, the Irish drama continued to be moderately fruitful in the nineteen-thirties; and a number of new dramatic efforts in the next decade indicated that playwriting was still germinating.

THE FUTURE OF ENGLISH AND IRISH DRAMA

The Abbey suffered new periods of decline after 1926 and underwent several reorganizations. Eire, now an independent state, left its national theatre somewhat less than independent in the selection of plays, and this may account for some of the difficulties in finding and encouraging talent. The Abbey, moreover, experienced the rise of rival theatres in Dublin, notably the Gate Theatre, founded in 1928 by Hilton Edwards and the actor-director-dramatist Micheal MacLiammoir. The Gate departed from naturalistic stagecraft and adopted more modern methods of staging than those practiced by the Abbey. It presented stylized dramas, both home grown and imported. In time, another kind of drama, imaginative in a Continental manner and evocative of modern complexities, might arise from the modernism of the Gate. As the century reached its mid-point, Irishmen could look forward to another spurt of interesting playwriting.

Englishmen, who had grown accustomed to expecting help in the theatre from Ireland, could hope for a similar revival in the drama as they went about putting their house in order after the Second World War. England by then had embarked upon a policy of giving financial assistance to its noncommercial theatres, mainly outside London, but it was not yet certain that any drama of transcendent merit was on the verge of blossoming as a result of the government's unprecedented effort to smile benignly on the stage. England had enjoyed up to 1950 some sixty years of modern drama, a good part of it contributed by Irish-born writers. Some satisfaction could be taken in this fact. Whether the second half of the century would breed another Shaw, O'Casey, Barrie, or Galsworthy could not be foretold. Much would depend upon the state of the world, a changed world in which England was no longer the wealthy ruler of a mighty empire. If the seams of the globe did not burst entirely in the age of atomic energy, there might be hope for the drama in an England diminished in size and power. The little city-state of Attica had produced immortal dramatic literature. Size and political strength in a nation are fortunately not indispensable to the creative spirit. Intellect and greatheartedness are. And these qualities, manifested in England during the crisis of Hitler's *Blitz* and again when the country had settled down to solving its postwar problems, might come to the aid of British theatre in the unpredictable years to come.

This much was certain by 1950: England was intent upon giving the theatre every opportunity to enlarge itself and to move in new directions, even if these were not yet definable. An Arts Council was encouraging noncommercial productions, touring companies were visiting the provinces in increasing number, and many provincial theatres which had been converted to motion-picture houses before 1939 had been reconverted to the uses of the drama. Even the powerful commercial management of H. M. Tennent Ltd. had established a nonprofit division at the old Haymarket Theatre, and the Old Vic, famous for the quality of its production of classics, was becoming a national theatre. Even the creation of a poetic drama was receiving encouragement in London, at the small Mercury Theatre directed by Martin Browne. Most important of all, playwrights were beginning to deepen their content and to refine their artistry.

It was significant that Terence Rattigan, who had turned out froth before the war and soufflés such as *O Mistress Mine* during it, was writing plays such as *The Winslow Boy,* a tribute to the cause of civil liberty, and *The Browning Version,* a long one-act psychological drama. Much was expected from the actor-dramatist Emlyn Williams, who had followed *The Corn Is Green* with the imaginative drama of a messianic visitation in a Welsh village, *The Wind of Heaven,* and from the young playwright Peter Ustinov, who had been displaying a Chekhovian vein of characterization since 1942, when his study of Russian *émigré* life, *The House of Regrets,* was produced. J. B. Priestley had begun to interlace his dramas of social conscience with imagination; Christopher Fry, the young author of *The Lady's Not for Burning* and *Venus Observed,* was on the way to creating scintillating verse drama; and T. S. Eliot had finally succeeded in writing a modern poetic drama, *The Cocktail Party,* that was completely stageworthy even in the commercial theatre. Martin Browne called his Mercury Theatre a "poet's workshop," and more young writers could be expected to work in it. Perhaps the best sign was the fact that the Arts Theatre Club in London, which produced Fry's poetic plays and subsidized new playwrights, had by 1950 gained a membership of 20,000. England appeared to be on the eve of a renovation of its drama.

Oscar Wilde

(1854–1900)

Casting a backward glance at his destroyed career in the book he wrought out of his prison experiences, *De Profundis*, Oscar Wilde wrote, "I took the drama, the most objective form known to art, and made of it as personal a mode of expression as the lyric or the sonnet; at the same time, widened its range and enriched its characterization." Although the second part of the statement is now open to question, this proud assumption of a beaten man, when it was written, was not far enough from the truth to be seriously challenged. Certainly, as Burns Mantle wrote, "the drama as a personal mode of expression was definitely influenced by Oscar Wilde."

Born in Dublin on October 16, 1854, of brilliant and socially prominent parents, Oscar Wilde began to reveal his talents at an early age. The precocious lad, whose later abnormality may have had its origins in his mother's fondness for dressing him as a girl, made an enviable record at Magdalen College, Oxford. He became a distinguished student of the classics and also won the Newdigate Prize for poetry. Among the admiring teachers and friends of his undergraduate years were such leaders in the world of art as John Ruskin, then Slade Professor of Art, and Walter Pater.

After traveling in Italy and Greece, Wilde came to London, where a book of his poetry and his melodrama *Vera, or the Nihilists* were published. Thereafter, supported in high society by his wife's ample fortune, Wilde became the most lionized wit in England. Regarding himself as an "apostle of the beautiful," he raised the slogan of estheticism and put his preachment into practice with such extravagance that he shocked his social inferiors and amused his equals. George Du Maurier caricatured him in *Punch,* and Gilbert and Sullivan aroused merriment at his expense in *Patience.* Wilde, however, remained undisturbed, and continued to wear his motley: the knee breeches, black silk stockings, velvet jacket, flowing tie, and sunflower, to which he owed the innocent part of his notoriety.

Unfortunately, Wilde, who fancied himself a latter-day Greek, did not confine his cultivation of decadence to peccadilloes that could bear the light of day. He lapsed into a coarse sensualism and indulged in perverse sexual practices. Consequently, the Marquess of Queensbury, father of the poet Lord Alfred Douglas, with whom Wilde had struck up a close friendship, became suspicious of him. Wilde made the mistake of bringing a suit of slander against the Marquess, who had insulted him publicly, and unsavory revelations at the trial in 1895 outraged public opinion. Wilde was prosecuted and sentenced to two years at hard labor in Reading Gaol. Although prison life evoked two of his best writings, *The Ballad of Reading Gaol* (1898) and *De Profundis* (published after Wilde's death, in 1905), it left him a broken man. He spent his last years in Paris in a state of progressive physical deterioration and died in straitened circumstances on November 30, 1900.

More important than his artificial early verse and his decadent novel *The Picture of Dorian Gray* (1891) were the comedies in which Wilde exhibited his talent for witty conversation. In addition to writing the febrile melodrama *The Duchess of Padua* and the powerful, if decadent, one-act drama *Salomé* (1892), he turned out three comedies and a farce: *Lady Windermere's Fan* (1892), *A Woman of No Importance* (1893), *An Ideal Husband* (1895), and *The Importance of Being Earnest* (1895). In the estimation of the pioneering critic of the British stage William Archer, Wilde became "the most exquisite stylist that had written for the stage since Congreve"; according to another critic, his "light, elegant comedies were unsurpassed in wit and epigrammatic brilliance since Sheridan."

Wilde's epigrams were, however, more than polished gems. They were clever inversions of conventional opinion and often barbed comments on British society. The play of repartee, moreover, was supplemented by situations and portraits of society people that showed a critical faculty heretofore revealed in British drama only by Shaw. Wilde even fancied himself a writer of problem plays, and he may be associated by the historian of literature with such writers of Continental thesis drama as Dumas *fils* and Augier. He differs from these earlier writers only in his mastery of drawing-room comedy —that is, in his lightness and grace, although these qualities remained unsupported by genuine characterization and good dramaturgy, of which there is a considerable amount in the work of Augier. In substance, *Lady Windermere's Fan* treated the "fallen woman" with sympathy and directed considerable criticism at the holier-than-thou attitude of Victorian women of good society. In *A Woman of No Importance,* Wilde castigated the social set; in *An Ideal Husband,* he examined political reputations.

Curiously for a man bent upon publicizing himself as an arch-esthete, Wilde left the dream world of estheticism when he turned to the drama. Directly or indirectly, Wilde, who revealed a sharp intelligence in his volume of criticism *Intentions* (1891) and in his essay *The Soul of Man under Socialism,* added some fibre to the drama. In *Lady Windermere's Fan,* he spun out an intrigue and developed it with plot contrivances that playwrights had long found useful. Lady Windermere suspects her husband of carrying on an intrigue with a woman of shady reputation, Mrs. Erlynne, who turns out to be her mother. Seeking revenge in the Victorian tradition, Lady Windermere goes to an admirer's apartment, leaving her fan there. In order to save her daughter's reputation, Mrs. Erlynne claims the fan and thereby foregoes all chances of winning her way back into good society. Sentiment is thus served, especially as Mrs. Erlynne never reveals her identity to her daughter. But in the course of the play, Wilde has also struck at the snobbish superiority of the daughter. Victorian prudery is satirized by means of the situation and of such coruscating epigrams as "Wicked women bother one. Good women bore one. That is the only difference between them."

Anticipating Maugham's *Our Betters* in *A Woman of No Importance,* Wilde satirized the American habit of knocking at the gates of the British aristocracy and took pains to show that British society was a shallow affair at best. It is doubtful that even Shaw delivered a better broadside against the gentry than "the English country gentleman galloping after a fox—the unspeakable in full pursuit of the uneatable." A society of hollow and useless people where one can live down "anything except a good reputation" is what Wilde shows us in *A Woman of No Importance;* the society is made tolerable only by evidences of wit in the speakers, which no one would make the mistake of attributing to them rather than to Wilde himself. The ghost of Congreve would have chuckled to hear Mrs. Allonby tell her friends that her husband was a promissory note and that she was tired of meeting him. But when the play was written, even its wit was less remarkable than the fact that Wilde should have exposed fashionable society and conventional notions to scorn.

In *An Ideal Husband,* Wilde even tried his hand at political drama. He contrived a story in which an important government official, who made his fortune by selling a state secret, is nearly blackmailed into promoting a wildcat scheme for building a worthless canal. If Wilde showed no particular brilliance when he dealt with life beyond the drawing room, his subject matter itself was an advance over the old-fashioned theatre in England, particularly since he was free from Victorian sanctimoniousness. His ideas were shallow, but he evinced some respect for ideas as a force rather than as a conversational convenience. A character in *An Ideal Husband* declares, "All thought is immoral. Its very essence is destruction. If you think of anything, you will kill it. Nothing survives being thought of."

Still, Wilde's slipshod plots were distinctly detrimental to his most ambitious comedies; for "problem plays," which these works suggested, his plots were too contrived and perfunctory. General opinion holds, therefore, that he was most successful in the pure farce *The Importance of Being Earnest.* "It still stands," Burns Mantle wrote in 1935, "as the play that most perfectly illustrates the particular brilliance that he brought to the theatre. . . . It accepted the dare of competition represented by the Pineros and Joneses by following the pattern of their drawing-room comedies in developing a super-farce that was witty as well as literate and as finished in its writing as it was extravagant in its absurdities." Here he could give free rein to sprightly fantastication, and his characterization did not have to meet the requirements of credibility. Contrivance being a virtue rather than a vice in farce, Wilde succeeded in turning flippancy into a fine art.

Wilde was evidently confident when he wrote *The Importance of Being Earnest* that his skill had not failed him. Asked the day before the *première* whether he expected his play to succeed, he replied, "My dear fellow. The play *is* a success. The only question is whether the audience will be a success." The audience was. George Alexander, the actor-manager, had chosen an ideal cast for his celebrated St. James's Theatre production. Nevertheless, the play was withdrawn in the same year (1895) when Wilde lost his libel suit against the Marquess of Queensbury. For years, no producer dared revive the play. But a revival in the season of 1909–1910 was highly successful, as were John Gielgud's 1939 production in London and his 1947 production in New York.

"In matters of grave importance," Wilde had quipped in his farce, "style, not sincerity, is the vital thing." If one hesitates to apply this aphorism to moral questions, it nonetheless works perfectly for this stage piece. "Played sincerely," Brooks Atkinson commented after seeing the Gielgud production, *"The Importance of Being Earnest* would be intolerable—probably impossible. But played purely as style without sincerity it shows genius for the theatre, which has always provided a gay haven for wits and iconoclasts." Whatever the limitations we may ascribe to the work, it is to the theatre that it belongs, wholly and without the slightest sign of fatigue. Properly performed, it reveals, as Atkinson noted, a "hard, lucid, metallic artifice—very modern in materials despite the age of the tradition."

BIBLIOGRAPHY: Brooks Atkinson, *Broadway Scrapbook* (pp. 280–283), 1947; John Mason Brown, *Seeing More Things* (pp. 215–220), 1948; George Jean Nathan, *The Theatre Book of the Year 1946–1947* (pp. 328–331), 1947; Hesketh Pearson, *Oscar Wilde, His Life and Wit,* 1946; Edouard Roditi, *Oscar Wilde,* 1947; Ernest Short, *Theatrical Cavalcade* (pp. 51–54), 1942.

THE IMPORTANCE OF BEING EARNEST

By Oscar Wilde

CHARACTERS

JOHN WORTHING, J.P.

ALGERNON MONCRIEFF

REV. CANON CHASUBLE, D.D.

MERRIMAN (*Butler*)

LANE (*Manservant*)

LADY BRACKNELL

HON. GWENDOLEN FAIRFAX

CECILY CARDEW

MISS PRISM (*Governess*)

THE SCENES OF THE PLAY

ACT I.

Algernon Moncrieff's Flat in Half-Moon Street, W.

ACT II.

The Garden at the Manor House, Woolton.

ACT III.

Drawing-Room of the Manor House, Woolton.

Time—The Present.

Place—London.

ACT I.

SCENE: *Morning-room in* Algernon's *flat in Half-Moon Street. The room is luxuriously and artistically furnished. The sound of a piano is heard in the adjoining room.*

[Lane *is arranging afternoon tea on the table, and after the music has ceased,* Algernon *enters*]

ALGERNON: Did you hear what I was playing, Lane?

LANE: I didn't think it polite to listen, sir.

ALGERNON: I'm sorry for that, for your sake. I don't play accurately—anyone can play accurately—but I play with wonderful expression. As far as the piano is concerned, sentiment is my forte. I keep science for Life.

LANE: Yes, sir.

ALGERNON: And, speaking of the science of Life, have you got the cucumber sandwiches cut for Lady Bracknell?

LANE: Yes, sir. [Hands them on a salver]

ALGERNON: [Inspects them, takes two, and sits down on the sofa] Oh! . . . by the way, Lane, I see from your book that on Thursday night, when Lord Shoreman and Mr. Worthing were dining with me, eight bottles of champagne are entered as having been consumed.

LANE: Yes, sir; eight bottles and a pint.

ALGERNON: Why is it that in a bachelor's establishment the servants invariably drink the champagne? I ask merely for information.

LANE: I attribute it to the superior quality of the wine, sir. I have often observed that in married households the champagne is rarely of a first-rate brand.

ALGERNON: Good Heavens! Is marriage so demoralizing as that?

LANE: I believe it *is* a very pleasant state, sir. I have had very little experience of it myself up to the present. I have only been married once. That was in consequence of a misunderstanding between myself and a young woman.

ALGERNON: [Languidly] I don't know that I am much interested in your family life, Lane.

LANE: No, sir; it is not a very interesting subject. I never think of it myself.

ALGERNON: Very natural, I am sure. That will do, Lane, thank you.

LANE: Thank you, sir. [Lane *goes out*]

ALGERNON: Lane's views on marriage seem somewhat lax. Really, if the lower orders don't set us a good example, what on earth is the use of them? They seem, as a class, to have absolutely no sense of moral responsibility.

[Enter Lane]

LANE: Mr. Ernest Worthing.

[Enter Jack. Lane *goes out*]

ALGERNON: How are you, my dear Ernest? What brings you up to town?

JACK: Oh, pleasure, pleasure! What else should bring one anywhere? Eating as usual, I see, Algy!

ALGERNON: [Stiffly] I believe it is customary in good society to take some slight refreshment at five o'clock. Where have you been since last Thursday?

JACK: [Sitting down on the sofa] In the country.

ALGERNON: What on earth do you do there?

JACK: [Pulling off his gloves] When one is in town one amuses oneself. When one is in the country one amuses other people. It is excessively boring.

ALGERNON: And who are the people you amuse?

JACK: [Airily] Oh, neighbors, neighbors.

ALGERNON: Got nice neighbors in your part of Shropshire?

JACK: Perfectly horrid! Never speak to one of them.

ALGERNON: How immensely you must amuse them! [Goes over and takes sandwich] By the way, Shropshire is your county, is it not?

JACK: Eh? Shropshire? Yes, of course. Hallo! Why all these cups? Why cucumber sandwiches?

Why such reckless extravagance in one so young? Who is coming to tea?

ALGERNON: Oh! merely Aunt Augusta and Gwendolen.

JACK: How perfectly delightful!

ALGERNON: Yes, that is all very well; but I am afraid Aunt Augusta won't quite approve of your being here.

JACK: May I ask why?

ALGERNON: My dear fellow, the way you flirt with Gwendolen is perfectly disgraceful. It is almost as bad as the way Gwendolen flirts with you.

JACK: I am in love with Gwendolen. I have come up to town expressly to propose to her.

ALGERNON: I thought you had come for pleasure? . . . I call that business.

JACK: How utterly unromantic you are!

ALGERNON: I really don't see anything romantic in proposing. It is very romantic to be in love. But there is nothing romantic about a definite proposal. Why, one may be accepted. One usually is, I believe. Then the excitement is all over. The very essence of romance is uncertainty. If ever I get married, I'll certainly try to forget the fact.

JACK. I have no doubt about that, dear Algy. The Divorce Court was specially invented for people whose memories are so curiously constituted.

ALGERNON: Oh! there is no use speculating on that subject. Divorces are made in Heaven—[Jack *puts out his hand to take a sandwich. Algernon at once interferes*] Please don't touch the cucumber sandwiches. They are ordered specially for Aunt Augusta. [*Takes one and eats it*]

JACK: Well, you have been eating them all the time.

ALGERNON: That is quite a different matter. She is my aunt. [*Takes plate from below*] Have some bread and butter. The bread and butter is for Gwendolen. Gwendolen is devoted to bread and butter.

JACK: [*Advancing to table and helping himself*] And very good bread and butter it is, too.

ALGERNON: Well, my dear fellow, you need not eat as if you were going to eat it all. You behave as if you were married to her already. You are not married to her already, and I don't think you will ever be.

JACK: Why on earth do you say that?

ALGERNON: Well, in the first place girls never marry the men they flirt with. Girls don't think it right.

JACK: Oh, that is nonsense!

ALGERNON: It isn't. It is a great truth. It accounts for the extraordinary number of bachelors that one sees all over the place. In the second place, I don't give my consent.

JACK: Your consent!

ALGERNON: My dear fellow, Gwendolen is my first cousin. And before I allow you to marry her, you will have to clear up the whole question of Cecily. [*Rings bell*]

JACK: Cecily! What on earth do you mean? What do you mean, Algy, by Cecily! I don't know anyone of the name Cecily.

[*Enter* Lane]

ALGERNON: Bring me that cigarette case Mr. Worthing left in the smoking-room the last time he dined here.

LANE: Yes, sir. [Lane *goes out*]

JACK: Do you mean to say you have had my cigarette case all this time? I wish to goodness you had let me know. I have been writing frantic letters to Scotland Yard about it. I was very nearly offering a large reward.

ALGERNON: Well, I wish you would offer one. I happen to be more than usually hard up.

JACK: There is no good offering a large reward now that the thing is found.

[*Enter* Lane *with the cigarette case on a salver. Algernon takes it at once.* Lane *goes out*]

ALGERNON: I think that is rather mean of you, Ernest, I must say. [*Opens case and examines it*] However, it makes no matter, for, now that I look at the inscription, I find that the thing isn't yours after all.

JACK: Of course it's mine. [*Moving to him*] You have seen me with it a hundred times, and you have no right whatsoever to read what is written inside. It is a very ungentlemanly thing to read a private cigarette case.

ALGERNON: Oh! it is absurd to have a hard-and-fast rule about what one should read and what one shouldn't. More than half of modern culture depends on what one shouldn't read.

JACK: I am quite aware of the fact, and I don't propose to discuss modern culture. It isn't the sort of thing one should talk of in private. I simply want my cigarette case back.

ALGERNON: Yes; but this isn't your cigarette case. This cigarette case is a present from someone of the name of Cecily, and you said you didn't know anyone of that name.

JACK: Well, if you want to know, Cecily happens to be my aunt.

ALGERNON: Your aunt!

JACK: Yes. Charming old lady she is, too. Lives at Tunbridge Wells. Just give it back to me, Algy.

ALGERNON: [*Retreating to back of sofa*] But why does she call herself little Cecily if she is your aunt and lives at Tunbridge Wells? [*Reading*] "From little Cecily with her fondest love."

JACK: [*Moving to sofa and kneeling upon it*] My dear fellow, what on earth is there in that? Some aunts are tall, some aunts are not tall. That is a matter that surely an aunt may be allowed to decide for herself. You seem to think that every aunt should be exactly like your aunt! That is absurd! For Heaven's sake give me back my cigarette case. [*Follows* Algernon *round the room*]

ALGERNON: Yes. But why does your aunt call you her uncle? "From little Cecily, with her fondest love to her dear Uncle Jack." There is no objection, I admit, to an aunt being a small aunt, but why an aunt, no matter what her size may be, should call her own nephew her uncle, I can't quite make out. Besides, your name isn't Jack at all; it's Ernest.

JACK: It isn't Ernest; it's Jack.

ALGERNON: You have always told me it was Ernest. I have introduced you to everyone as Ernest. You answer to the name of Ernest. You look as if your name was Ernest. You are the most earnest-looking person I ever saw in my life. It is perfectly absurd your saying that your name isn't Ernest. It's on your cards. Here is one of them. [*Taking it from case*] "Mr. Ernest Worthing, B 4, The Albany." I'll keep this as a proof your name is Ernest if ever you attempt to deny it to me, or to Gwendolen, or to anyone else. [*Puts the card in his pocket*]

JACK: Well, my name is Ernest in town and Jack in the country, and the cigarette case was given to me in the country.

ALGERNON: Yes, but that does not account for the fact that your small Aunt Cecily, who lives at Tunbridge Wells, calls you her dear uncle. Come, old boy, you had much better have the thing out at once.

JACK: My dear Algy, you talk exactly as if you were a dentist. It is very vulgar to talk like a dentist when one isn't a dentist. It produces a false impression.

ALGERNON: Well, that is exactly what dentists always do. Now, go on! Tell me the whole thing. I may mention that I have always suspected you of being a confirmed and secret Bunburyist; and I am quite sure of it now.

JACK: Bunburyist? What on earth do you mean by a Bunburyist?

ALGERNON: I'll reveal to you the meaning of that incomparable expression as soon as you are kind enough to inform me why you are Ernest in town and Jack in the country.

JACK: Well, produce my cigarette case first.

ALGERNON: Here it is. [*Hands cigarette case*] Now produce your explanation, and pray make it improbable. [*Sits on sofa*]

JACK: My dear fellow, there is nothing improbable about my explanation at all. In fact it's perfectly ordinary. Old Mr. Thomas Cardew, who adopted me when I was a little boy, made me in his will guardian to his grand-daughter, Miss Cecily Cardew. Cecily, who addresses me as her uncle from motives of respect that you could not possibly appreciate, lives at my place in the country under the charge of her admirable governess, Miss Prism.

ALGERNON: Where is that place in the country, by the way?

JACK: That is nothing to you, dear boy. You are not going to be invited. . . . I may tell you candidly that the place is not in Shropshire.

ALGERNON: I suspected that, my dear fellow! I have Bunburyed all over Shropshire on two separate occasions. Now, go on. Why are you Ernest in town and Jack in the country?

JACK: My dear Algy, I don't know whether you will be able to understand my real motives. You are hardly serious enough. When one is placed in the position of guardian, one has to adopt a very high moral tone on all subjects. It's one's duty to do so. And as a high moral tone can hardly be said to conduce very much to either one's health or one's happiness, in order to get up to town I have always pretended to have a younger brother of the name of Ernest, who lives in the Albany, and gets into the most dreadful scrapes. That, my dear Algy, is the whole truth pure and simple.

ALGERNON: The truth is rarely pure and never simple. Modern life would be very tedious if it were either, and modern literature a complete impossibility!

JACK: That wouldn't be at all a bad thing.

ALGERNON: Literary criticism is not your forte, my dear fellow. Don't try it. You should leave that to people who haven't been at a University. They do it so well in the daily papers. What you really are is a Bunburyist. I was quite right in saying you were a Bunburyist. You are one of the most advanced Bunburyists I know.

JACK: What on earth do you mean?

ALGERNON: You have invented a very useful younger brother called Ernest, in order that you may be able to come up to town as often as you like. I have invented an invaluable permanent invalid called Bunbury, in order that I may be able to go down into the country whenever I choose. Bunbury is perfectly invaluable. If it wasn't for Bunbury's extraordinary bad health, for instance, I wouldn't be able to dine with you at Willis' to-night, for I have been really engaged to Aunt Augusta for more than a week.

JACK: I haven't asked you to dine with me anywhere to-night.

ALGERNON: I know. You are absolutely careless about sending out invitations. It is very foolish of you. Nothing annoys people so much as not receiving invitations.

JACK: You had much better dine with your Aunt Augusta.

ALGERNON: I haven't the smallest intention of doing anything of the kind. To begin with, I dined there on Monday, and once a week is quite enough to dine with one's own relatives. In the second place, whenever I do dine there I am always treated as a member of the family, and sent down with either no woman at all, or two. In the third place, I know perfectly well whom she will place me next, to-night. She will place me next Mary Farquhar, who always flirts with her own husband across the dinner-table. That is not very pleasant. Indeed, it is not even decent . . . and that sort of thing is enormously on the increase. The amount of women in London who flirt with their own husbands is perfectly scandalous. It looks so bad. It is simply washing one's clean linen in public. Besides, now that I know you to be a confirmed Bunburyist I naturally want to talk to you about Bunburying. I want to tell you the rules.

JACK: I'm not a Bunburyist at all. If Gwendolen accepts me, I am going to kill my brother, indeed I think I'll kill him in any case. Cecily is a little too much interested in him. It is rather a bore. So I am going to get rid of Ernest. And I strongly advise you to do the same with Mr. . . . with your invalid friend who has the absurd name.

ALGERNON: Nothing will induce me to part with Bunbury, and if you ever get married, which seems to me extremely problematic, you will be very glad to know Bunbury. A man who marries without knowing Bunbury has a very tedious time of it.

JACK: That is nonsense. If I marry a charming girl like Gwendolen, and she is the only girl I ever saw in my life that I would marry, I certainly won't want to know Bunbury.

ALGERNON: Then your wife will. You don't seem to realize, that in married life three is company and two is none.

JACK: [Sententiously] That, my dear young friend, is the theory that the corrupt French Drama has been propounding for the last fifty years.

ALGERNON: Yes; and that the happy English home has proved in half the time.

JACK: For heaven's sake, don't try to be cynical. It's perfectly easy to be cynical.

ALGERNON: My dear fellow, it isn't easy to be anything now-a-days. There's such a lot of beastly competition about. [The sound of an electric bell is heard] Ah! that must be Aunt Augusta. Only relatives, or creditors, ever ring in that Wagnerian manner. Now, if I get her out of the way for ten minutes, so that you can have an opportunity for proposing to Gwendolen, may I dine with you to-night at Willis'?

JACK: I suppose so, if you want to.

ALGERNON: Yes, but you must be serious about it. I hate people who are not serious about meals. It is so shallow of them.

[Enter Lane]

LANE: Lady Bracknell and Miss Fairfax.

[Algernon goes forward to meet them. Enter Lady Bracknell and Gwendolen]

LADY BRACKNELL: Good afternoon, dear Algernon, I hope you are behaving very well.

ALGERNON: I'm feeling very well, Aunt Augusta.

LADY BRACKNELL: That's not quite the same thing. In fact the two things rarely go together. [Sees Jack and bows to him with icy coldness]

ALGERNON: [To Gwendolen] Dear me, you are smart!

GWENDOLEN: I am always smart! Aren't I, Mr. Worthing?

JACK: You're quite perfect, Miss Fairfax.

GWENDOLEN: Oh! I hope I am not that. It would

leave no room for developments, and I intend to develop in many directions.

[Gwendolen and Jack sit down together in the corner]

LADY BRACKNELL: I'm sorry if we are a little late, Algernon, but I was obliged to call on dear Lady Harbury. I hadn't been there since her poor husband's death. I never saw a woman so altered; she looks quite twenty years younger. And now I'll have a cup of tea, and one of those nice cucumber sandwiches you promised me.

ALGERNON: Certainly, Aunt Augusta. [Goes over to tea-table]

LADY BRACKNELL: Won't you come and sit here, Gwendolen?

GWENDOLEN: Thanks, mamma, I'm quite comfortable where I am.

ALGERNON: [Picking up empty plate in horror] Good heavens! Lane! Why are there no cucumber sandwiches? I ordered them specially.

LANE: [Gravely] There were no cucumbers in the market this morning, sir. I went down twice.

ALGERNON: No cucumbers!

LANE: No, sir. Not even for ready money.

ALGERNON: That will do, Lane, thank you.

LANE: Thank you, sir. [Goes out]

ALGERNON: I am greatly distressed, Aunt Augusta, about there being no cucumbers, not even for ready money.

LADY BRACKNELL: It really makes no matter, Algernon. I had some crumpets with Lady Harbury, who seems to me to be living entirely for pleasure now.

ALGERNON: I hear her hair has turned quite gold from grief.

LADY BRACKNELL: It certainly has changed its color. From what cause I, of course, cannot say. [Algernon crosses and hands tea] Thank you. I've quite a treat for you to-night, Algernon. I am going to send you down with Mary Farquhar. She is such a nice woman, and so attentive to her husband. It's delightful to watch them.

ALGERNON: I am afraid, Aunt Augusta, I shall have to give up the pleasure of dining with you to-night after all.

LADY BRACKNELL: [Frowning] I hope not, Algernon. It would put my table completely out. Your uncle would have to dine upstairs. Fortunately he is accustomed to that.

ALGERNON: It is a great bore, and, I need hardly say, a terrible disappointment to me, but the fact is I have just had a telegram to say that my poor friend Bunbury is very ill again. [Exchanges glances with Jack] They seem to think I should be with him.

LADY BRACKNELL: It is very strange. This Mr. Bunbury seems to suffer from curiously bad health.

ALGERNON: Yes; poor Bunbury is a dreadful invalid.

LADY BRACKNELL: Well, I must say, Algernon, that I think it is high time that Mr. Bunbury made up his mind whether he was going to live or to die. This shilly-shallying with the question is absurd. Nor do I in any way approve of the modern sympathy with invalids. I consider it morbid. Illness of any kind is hardly a thing to be encouraged in others. Health is the primary duty of life. I am always telling that to your poor uncle, but he never seems to take much notice . . . as far as any improvement in his ailments goes. I should be much obliged if you would ask Mr. Bunbury, from me, to be kind enough not to have a relapse on Saturday, for I rely on you to arrange my music for me. It is my last reception and one wants something that will encourage conversation, particularly at the end of the season when everyone has practically said whatever they had to say, which, in most cases, was probably not much.

ALGERNON: I'll speak to Bunbury, Aunt Augusta, if he is still conscious, and I think I can promise you he'll be all right by Saturday. You see, if one plays good music, people don't listen, and if one plays bad music people don't talk. But I'll run over the program I've drawn out, if you will kindly come into the next room for a moment.

LADY BRACKNELL: Thank you, Algernon. It is very thoughtful of you. [Rising, and following Algernon] I'm sure the program will be delightful, after a few expurgations. French songs I cannot possibly allow. People always seem to think that they are improper, and either look shocked, which is vulgar, or laugh, which is worse. But German sounds a thoroughly respectable language, and indeed, I believe is so. Gwendolen, you will accompany me.

GWENDOLEN: Certainly, mamma.

[Lady Bracknell and Algernon go into the music-room, Gwendolen remains behind]

JACK: Charming day it has been, Miss Fairfax.

GWENDOLEN: Pray don't talk to me about the weather, Mr. Worthing. Whenever people talk to me about the weather, I always feel quite certain that they mean something else. And that makes me so nervous.

JACK: I do mean something else.

GWENDOLEN: I thought so. In fact, I am never wrong.

JACK: And I would like to be allowed to take advantage of Lady Bracknell's temporary absence . . .

GWENDOLEN: I would certainly advise you to do so. Mamma has a way of coming back suddenly into a room that I have often had to speak to her about.

JACK: [Nervously] Miss Fairfax, ever since I met you I have admired you more than any girl . . . I have ever met since . . . I met you.

GWENDOLEN: Yes, I am quite aware of the fact. And I often wish that in public, at any rate, you had been more demonstrative. For me you have always had an irresistible fascination. Even before I met you I was far from indifferent to you. [Jack looks at her in amazement] We live, as I hope you know, Mr. Worthing, in an age of ideals. The fact is constantly mentioned in the more expensive monthly magazines, and has reached the provincial pulpits I am told: and my ideal has always been to love some one of the name of Ernest. There is something in that name that inspires absolute confidence. The moment Algernon first mentioned to me that he had a friend called Ernest, I knew I was destined to love you.

JACK: You really love me, Gwendolen?

GWENDOLEN: Passionately!

JACK: Darling! You don't know how happy you've made me.

GWENDOLEN: My own Ernest!

JACK: But you don't really mean to say that you couldn't love me if my name wasn't Ernest?

GWENDOLEN: But your name is Ernest.

JACK: Yes, I know it is. But supposing it was something else? Do you mean to say you couldn't love me then?

GWENDOLEN: [Glibly] Ah! that is clearly a metaphysical speculation, and like most metaphysical speculations has very little reference at all to the actual facts of real life, as we know them.

JACK: Personally, darling, to speak quite candidly, I don't much care about the name of Ernest . . . I don't think that name suits me at all.

GWENDOLEN: It suits you perfectly. It is a divine name. It has a music of its own. It produces vibrations.

JACK: Well, really, Gwendolen, I must say that I think there are lots of other much nicer names. I think, Jack, for instance, a charming name.

GWENDOLEN: Jack? . . . No, there is very little music in the name Jack, if any at all, indeed. It does not thrill. It produces absolutely no vibrations. . . . I have known several Jacks, and they all, without exception, were more than usually plain. Besides, Jack is a notorious domesticity for John! And I pity any woman who is married to a man called John. She would probably never be allowed to know the entrancing pleasure of a single moment's solitude. The only really safe name is Ernest.

JACK: Gwendolen, I must get christened at once— I mean we must get married at once. There is no time to be lost.

GWENDOLEN: Married, Mr. Worthing?

JACK: [Astounded] Well . . . surely. You know that I love you, and you led me to believe, Miss Fairfax, that you were not absolutely indifferent to me.

GWENDOLEN: I adore you. But you haven't proposed to me yet. Nothing has been said at all about marriage. The subject has not even been touched on.

JACK: Well . . . may I propose to you now?

GWENDOLEN: I think it would be an admirable opportunity. And to spare you any possible disappointment, Mr. Worthing, I think it only fair to tell you quite frankly beforehand that I am fully determined to accept you.

JACK: Gwendolen!

GWENDOLEN: Yes, Mr. Worthing, what have you got to say to me?

JACK: You know what I have got to say to you.

GWENDOLEN: Yes, but you don't say it.

JACK: Gwendolen, will you marry me? [*Goes on his knees*]

GWENDOLEN: Of course I will, darling. How long you have been about it! I am afraid you have had very little experience in how to propose.

JACK: My own one, I have never loved anyone in the world but you.

GWENDOLEN: Yes, but men often propose for practice. I know my brother Gerald does. All my girl-friends tell me so. What wonderfully blue eyes you have, Ernest! They are quite, quite blue. I hope you will always look at me just like that, especially when there are other people present.

[*Enter* Lady Bracknell]

LADY BRACKNELL: Mr. Worthing! Rise, sir, from this semi-recumbent posture. It is most indecorous.

GWENDOLEN: Mamma! [*He tries to rise; she restrains him*] I must beg you to retire. This is no place for you. Besides, Mr. Worthing has not quite finished yet.

LADY BRACKNELL: Finished what, may I ask?

GWENDOLEN: I am engaged to Mr. Worthing, mamma. [*They rise together*]

LADY BRACKNELL: Pardon me, you are not engaged to anyone. When you do become engaged to some one, I, or your father, should his health permit him, will inform you of the fact. An engagement should come on a young girl as a surprise, pleasant or unpleasant, as the case may be. It is hardly a matter that she could be allowed to arrange for herself. . . . And now I have a few questions to put to you, Mr. Worthing. While I am making these inquiries, you, Gwendolen, will wait for me below in the carriage.

GWENDOLEN: [*Reproachfully*] Mamma!

LADY BRACKNELL: In the carriage, Gwendolen!

[Gwendolen *goes to the door. She and* Jack *blow kisses to each other behind* Lady Bracknell's *back.* Lady Bracknell *looks vaguely about as if she could not understand what the noise was. Finally turns round*]
Gwendolen, the carriage!

GWENDOLEN: Yes, mamma. [*Goes out, looking back at* Jack]

LADY BRACKNELL: [*Sitting down*] You can take a seat, Mr. Worthing. [*Looks in her pocket for note-book and pencil*]

JACK: Thank you, Lady Bracknell, I prefer standing.

LADY BRACKNELL: [*Pencil and note-book in hand*] I feel bound to tell you that you are not down on my list of eligible young men, although I have the same list as the dear Duchess of Bolton has. We work together, in fact. However, I am quite ready to enter your name, should your answers be what a really affectionate mother requires. Do you smoke?

JACK: Well, yes, I must admit I smoke.

LADY BRACKNELL: I am glad to hear it. A man should always have an occupation of some kind. There are far too many idle men in London as it is. How old are you?

JACK: Twenty-nine.

LADY BRACKNELL: A very good age to be married at. I have always been of opinion that a man who desires to get married should know either everything or nothing. Which do you know?

JACK: [*After some hesitation*] I know nothing, Lady Bracknell.

LADY BRACKNELL: I am pleased to hear it. I do not approve of anything that tampers with natural ignorance. Ignorance is like a delicate exotic fruit; touch it and the bloom is gone. The whole theory of modern education is radically unsound. Fortunately in England, at any rate, education produces no effect whatsoever. If it did, it would prove a serious danger to the upper classes, and probably lead to acts of violence in Grosvenor Square. What is your income?

JACK: Between seven and eight thousand a year.

LADY BRACKNELL: [*Makes a note in her book*] In land, or in investments?

JACK: In investments, chiefly.

LADY BRACKNELL: That is satisfactory. What between the duties expected of one during one's lifetime, and the duties exacted from one after one's death, land has ceased to be either a profit or a pleasure. It gives one position, and prevents one from keeping it up. That's all that can be said about land.

JACK: I have a country house with some land, of course, attached to it, about fifteen hundred acres, I believe; but I don't depend on that for my real income. In fact, as far as I can make out, the poachers are the only people who make anything out of it.

LADY BRACKNELL: A country house! How many bedrooms? Well, that point can be cleared up afterwards. You have a town house, I hope? A girl with a simple, unspoiled nature, like Gwendolen, could hardly be expected to reside in the country.

JACK: Well, I own a house in Belgrave Square, but it is let by the year to Lady Bloxham. Of course, I can get it back whenever I like, at six months' notice.

LADY BRACKNELL: Lady Bloxham? I don't know her.

JACK: Oh, she goes about very little. She is a lady considerably advanced in years.

LADY BRACKNELL: Ah, now-a-days that is no guarantee of respectability of character. What number in Belgrave Square?

JACK: 149.

LADY BRACKNELL: [*Shaking her head*] The unfashionable side. I thought there was something. However, that could easily be altered.

JACK: Do you mean the fashion, or the side?

LADY BRACKNELL: [*Sternly*] Both, if necessary, I presume. What are your politics?

JACK: Well, I am afraid I really have none. I am a Liberal Unionist.

LADY BRACKNELL: Oh, they count as Tories. They dine with us. Or come in the evening, at any rate. Now to minor matters. Are your parents living?

JACK: I have lost both my parents.

LADY BRACKNELL: Both? . . . That seems like carelessness. Who was your father? He was evidently a man of some wealth. Was he born in what the Radical papers call the purple of commerce, or did he rise from the ranks of the aristocracy?

JACK: I am afraid I really don't know. The fact is, Lady Bracknell, I said I had lost my parents. It would be nearer the truth to say that my parents seem to have lost me . . . I don't actually know who I am by birth. I was . . . well, I was found.

LADY BRACKNELL: Found!

JACK: The late Mr. Thomas Cardew, an old gentleman of a very charitable and kindly disposition, found me, and gave me the name of Worthing, because he happened to have a first-class ticket for Worthing in his pocket at the time. Worthing is a place in Sussex. It is a seaside resort.

LADY BRACKNELL: Where did the charitable gentleman who had a first-class ticket for this seaside find you?

JACK: [*Gravely*] In a hand-bag.

LADY BRACKNELL: A hand-bag?

JACK: [*Very seriously*] Yes, Lady Bracknell. I was in a hand-bag—a somewhat large, black leather hand-bag, with handles to it—an ordinary hand-bag in fact.

LADY BRACKNELL: In what locality did this Mr. James, or Thomas, Cardew come across this ordinary hand-bag?

JACK: In the cloak-room at Victoria Station. It was given to him in mistake for his own.

LADY BRACKNELL: The cloak-room at Victoria Station?

JACK: Yes. The Brighton line.

LADY BRACKNELL: The line is immaterial. Mr. Worthing, I confess I feel somewhat bewildered by what you have just told me. To be born, or at any rate bred, in a hand-bag, whether it had handles or not, seems to me to display a contempt for the ordinary decencies of family life that remind one of the worst excesses of the French Revolution. And I presume you know what that unfortunate movement led to? As for the particular locality in which the hand-bag was found, a cloak-room at a railway station might serve to conceal a social indiscretion— has probably, indeed, been used for that purpose before now—but it could hardly be regarded as an assured basis for a recognized position in good society.

JACK: May I ask you then what you would advise me to do? I need hardly say I would do anything in the world to ensure Gwendolen's happiness.

LADY BRACKNELL: I would strongly advise you, Mr. Worthing, to try and acquire some relations as soon as possible, and to make a definite effort to produce at any rate one parent, of either sex, before the season is quite over.

JACK: Well, I don't see how I could possibly manage to do that. I can produce the hand-bag at any moment. It is in my dressing-room at home. I really think that should satisfy you, Lady Bracknell.

LADY BRACKNELL: Me, sir! What has it to do with me? You can hardly imagine that I and Lord Bracknell would dream of allowing our only daughter—a girl brought up with the utmost care—to marry into a cloakroom, and form an alliance with a parcel? Good morning, Mr. Worthing!

[Lady Bracknell *sweeps out in majestic indignation*]

JACK: Good morning!

[Algernon *from the other room, strikes up the Wedding March.* Jack *looks perfectly furious, and goes to the door*]

For goodness' sake don't play that ghastly tune, Algy! How idiotic you are!

[*The music stops, and* Algernon *enters cheerily*]

ALGERNON: Didn't it go off all right, old boy? You don't mean to say Gwendolen refused you? I know it is a way she has. She is always refusing people. I think it is most ill-natured of her.

JACK: Oh, Gwendolen is as right as a trivet. As far as she is concerned, we are engaged. Her mother is perfectly unbearable. Never met such a Gorgon . . . I don't really know what a Gorgon is like, but I am quite sure that Lady Bracknell is one. In any case, she is a monster, without being a myth, which is rather unfair. . . . I beg your pardon, Algy, I suppose I shouldn't talk about your own aunt in that way before you.

ALGERNON: My dear boy, I love hearing my relations abused. It is the only thing that makes me put up with them at all. Relations are simply a tedious pack of people, who haven't got the remotest knowledge of how to live, nor the smallest instinct about when to die.

JACK: Oh, that is nonsense!

ALGERNON: It isn't!

JACK: Well, I won't argue about the matter. You always want to argue about things.

ALGERNON: That is exactly what things were originally made for.

JACK: Upon my word, if I thought that, I'd shoot myself. . . . [*A pause*] You don't think there is any chance of Gwendolen becoming like her mother in about a hundred and fifty years, do you, Algy?

ALGERNON: All women become like their mothers. That is their tragedy. No man does. That's his.

JACK: Is that clever?

ALGERNON: It is perfectly phrased! and quite as true as any observation in civilized life should be.

JACK: I am sick to death of cleverness. Everybody is clever now-a-days. You can't go anywhere without meeting clever people. The thing has become an absolute public nuisance. I wish to goodness we had a few fools left.

ALGERNON: We have.

JACK: I should extremely like to meet them. What do they talk about?

ALGERNON: The fools! Oh! about the clever people, of course.

JACK: What fools!

ALGERNON: By the way, did you tell Gwendolen the truth about your being Ernest in town, and Jack in the country?

JACK: [*In a very patronizing manner*] My dear fellow, the truth isn't quite the sort of thing one tells to a nice, sweet, refined girl. What extraordinary ideas you have about the way to behave to a woman!

ALGERNON: The only way to behave to a woman is to make love to her, if she is pretty, and to someone else if she is plain.

JACK: Oh, that is nonsense.

ALGERNON: What about your brother? What about the profligate Ernest?

JACK: Oh, before the end of the week I shall have got rid of him. I'll say he died in Paris of apoplexy. Lots of people die of apoplexy, quite suddenly, don't they?

ALGERNON: Yes, but it's hereditary, my dear fellow. It's a sort of thing that runs in families. You had much better say a severe chill.

JACK: You are sure a severe chill isn't hereditary, or anything of that kind?

ALGERNON: Of course it isn't!

JACK: Very well, then. My poor brother Ernest is carried off suddenly in Paris, by a severe chill. That gets rid of him.

ALGERNON: But I thought you said that . . . Miss Cardew was a little too much interested in your poor brother Ernest? Won't she feel his loss a good deal?

JACK: Oh, that is all right. Cecily is not a silly, romantic girl, I am glad to say. She has got a capital appetite, goes for long walks, and pays no attention at all to her lessons.

ALGERNON: I would rather like to see Cecily.

JACK: I will take very good care you never do. She is excessively pretty, and she is only just eighteen.

ALGERNON: Have you told Gwendolen yet that you have an excessively pretty ward who is only just eighteen?

JACK: Oh! one doesn't blurt these things out to people. Cecily and Gwendolen are perfectly certain to be extremely great friends. I'll bet you anything you like that half an hour after they have met, they will be calling each other sister.

ALGERNON: Women only do that when they have called each other a lot of other things first. Now, my dear boy, if we want to get a good table at Willis', we really must go and dress. Do you know it is nearly seven?

JACK: [*Irritably*] Oh! it always is nearly seven.

ALGERNON: Well, I'm hungry.

JACK: I never knew you when you weren't. . . .

ALGERNON: What shall we do after dinner? Go to a theater?

JACK: Oh, no! I loathe listening.

ALGERNON: Well, let us go to the Club?

JACK: Oh, no! I hate talking.

ALGERNON: Well, we might trot round to the Empire at ten?

JACK: Oh, no! I can't bear looking at things. It is so silly.

ALGERNON: Well, what shall we do?

JACK: Nothing!

ALGERNON: It is awfully hard work doing nothing. However, I don't mind hard work where there is no definite object of any kind.

[*Enter* Lane]

LANE: Miss Fairfax.

[*Enter* Gwendolen. Lane *goes out*]

ALGERNON: Gwendolen, upon my word!

GWENDOLEN: Algy, kindly turn your back. I have something very particular to say to Mr. Worthing.

ALGERNON: Really, Gwendolen, I don't think I can allow this at all.

GWENDOLEN: Algy, you always adopt a strictly immoral attitude towards life. You are not quite old enough to do that. [Algernon *retires to the fireplace*]

JACK: My own darling!

GWENDOLEN: Ernest, we may never be married. From the expression on mamma's face I fear we never shall. Few parents now-a-days pay any regard to what their children say to them. The old-fashioned respect for the young is fast dying out. Whatever influence I ever had over mamma, I lost at the age of three. But although she may prevent us from becoming man and wife, and I may marry someone else, and marry often, nothing that she can possibly do can alter my eternal devotion to you.

JACK: Dear Gwendolen.

GWENDOLEN: The story of your romantic origin, as related to me by mamma, with unpleasing comments, has naturally stirred the deeper fibers of my nature. Your Christian name has an irresistible fascination. The simplicity of your character makes you exquisitely incomprehensible to me. Your town address at the Albany I have. What is your address in the country?

JACK: The Manor House, Woolton, Hertfordshire.

[Algernon, *who has been carefully listening, smiles to himself, and writes the address on his shirt-cuff. Then picks up the Railway Guide*]

GWENDOLEN: There is a good postal service, I suppose? It may be necessary to do something desperate. That, of course, will require serious consideration. I will communicate with you daily.

JACK: My own one!

GWENDOLEN: How long do you remain in town?

JACK: Till Monday.

GWENDOLEN: Good! Algy, you may turn round now.

ALGERNON: Thanks, I've turned round already.

GWENDOLEN: You may also ring the bell.

JACK: You will let me see you to your carriage, my own darling?

GWENDOLEN: Certainly.

JACK: [*To* Lane, *who now enters*] I will see Miss Fairfax out.

LANE: Yes, sir.

[Jack *and* Gwendolen *go off.* Lane *presents several letters on a salver to* Algernon. *It is to be surmised that they are bills, as* Algernon, *after looking at the envelopes, tears them up*]

ALGERNON: A glass of sherry, Lane.

LANE: Yes, sir.

ALGERNON: To-morrow, Lane, I'm going Bunburying.

LANE: Yes, sir.

ALGERNON: I shall probably not be back till Monday. You can put up my dress clothes, my smoking jacket, and all the Bunbury suits . . .

LANE: Yes, sir. [*Handing sherry*]

ALGERNON: I hope to-morrow will be a fine day, Lane.

LANE: It never is, sir.

ALGERNON: Lane, you're a perfect pessimist.

LANE: I do my best to give satisfaction, sir.

[*Enter* Jack. Lane *goes off*]

JACK: There's a sensible, intellectual girl! the only girl I ever cared for in my life. [Algernon *is laughing immoderately*] What on earth are you so amused at?

ALGERNON: Oh, I'm a little anxious about poor Bunbury, that's all.

JACK: If you don't take care, your friend Bunbury will get you into a serious scrape some day.

ALGERNON: I love scrapes. They are the only things that are never serious.

JACK: Oh, that's nonsense, Algy. You never talk anything but nonsense.

ALGERNON: Nobody ever does. [Jack *looks indignantly at him, and leaves the room.* Algernon *lights a cigarette, reads his shirt-cuff and smiles*]

ACT II.

SCENE: *Garden at the Manor House. A flight of gray stone steps leads up to the house. The garden, an old-fashioned one, full of roses. Time of year, July. Basket chairs, and a table covered with books, are set under a large yew tree.*

[Miss Prism *discovered seated at the table.* Cecily *is at the back watering flowers*]

MISS PRISM: [*Calling*] Cecily, Cecily! Surely such a utilitarian occupation as the watering of flowers is rather Moulton's duty than yours? Especially at a moment when intellectual pleasures await you. Your German grammar is on the table. Pray open it at page fifteen. We will repeat yesterday's lesson.

CECILY: [*Coming over very slowly*] But I don't like German. It isn't at all a becoming language. I know perfectly well that I look quite plain after my German lesson.

MISS PRISM: Child, you know how anxious your guardian is that you should improve yourself in every way. He laid particular stress on your German, as he was leaving for town yesterday. Indeed, he always lays stress on your German when he is leaving for town.

CECILY: Dear Uncle Jack is so very serious! Sometimes he is so serious that I think he cannot be quite well.

MISS PRISM: [*Drawing herself up*] Your guardian enjoys the best of health, and his gravity of demeanor is especially to be commended in one so comparatively young as he is. I know no one who has a higher sense of duty and responsibility.

CECILY: I suppose that is why he often looks a little bored when we three are together.

MISS PRISM: Cecily! I am surprised at you. Mr. Worthing has many troubles in his life. Idle merriment and triviality would be out of place in his conversation. You must remember his constant anxiety about that unfortunate young man, his brother.

CECILY: I wish Uncle Jack would allow that unfortunate young man, his brother, to come down here sometimes. We might have a good influence over him, Miss Prism. I am sure you certainly would. You know German, and geology, and things of that kind influence a man very much. [Cecily *begins to write in her diary*]

MISS PRISM: [*Shaking her head*] I do not think that even I could produce any effect on a character that, according to his own brother's admission, is irretrievably weak and vacillating. Indeed, I am not sure that I would desire to reclaim him. I am not in favor of this modern mania for turning bad people into good people at a moment's notice. As a man sows so let him reap. You must put away your diary, Cecily. I really don't see why you should keep a diary at all.

CECILY: I keep a diary in order to enter the wonderful secrets of my life. If I didn't write them down I should probably forget all about them.

MISS PRISM: Memory, my dear Cecily, is the diary that we all carry about with us.

CECILY: Yes, but it usually chronicles the things that have never happened, and couldn't possibly have happened. I believe that Memory is responsible for nearly all the three-volume novels that Mudie sends us.

MISS PRISM: Do not speak slightingly of the three-volume novel, Cecily. I wrote one myself in earlier days.

CECILY: Did you really, Miss Prism? How wonderfully clever you are! I hope it did not end happily? I don't like novels that end happily. They depress me so much.

MISS PRISM: The good ended happily, and the bad unhappily. That is what Fiction means.

CECILY: I suppose so. But it seems very unfair. And was your novel ever published?

MISS PRISM: Alas! no. The manuscript unfortunately was abandoned. I use the word in the sense of lost or mislaid. To your work, child, these speculations are profitless.

CECILY: [Smiling] But I see dear Dr. Chasuble coming up through the garden.

MISS PRISM: [Rising and advancing] Dr. Chasuble! This is indeed a pleasure.

[Enter Canon Chasuble]

CHASUBLE: And how are we this morning? Miss Prism, you are, I trust, well?

CECILY: Miss Prism has just been complaining of a slight headache. I think it would do her so much good to have a short stroll with you in the park, Dr. Chasuble.

MISS PRISM: Cecily, I have not mentioned anything about a headache.

CECILY: No, dear Miss Prism, I know that, but I felt instinctively that you had a headache. Indeed I was thinking about that, and not about my German lesson when the Rector came in.

CHASUBLE: I hope, Cecily, you are not inattentive.

CECILY: Oh, I am afraid I am.

CHASUBLE: That is strange. Were I fortunate enough to be Miss Prism's pupil, I would hang upon her lips. [Miss Prism glares] I spoke metaphorically. —My metaphor was drawn from bees. Ahem! Mr. Worthing, I suppose, has not returned from town yet?

MISS PRISM: We do not expect him till Monday afternoon.

CHASUBLE: Ah yes, he usually likes to spend his Sunday in London. He is not one of those whose sole aim is enjoyment, as, by all accounts, that unfortunate young man, his brother, seems to be. But I must not disturb Egeria and her pupil any longer.

MISS PRISM: Egeria? My name is Lætitia, Doctor.

CHASUBLE: [Bowing] A classical allusion merely, drawn from the Pagan authors. I shall see you both no doubt at Evensong.

MISS PRISM: I think, dear Doctor, I will have a stroll with you. I find I have a headache after all, and a walk might do it good.

CHASUBLE: With pleasure, Miss Prism, with pleasure. We might go as far as the schools and back.

MISS PRISM: That would be delightful. Cecily, you will read your Political Economy in my absence. The chapter on the Fall of the Rupee you may omit. It is somewhat too sensational. Even these metallic problems have their melodramatic side.

[Goes down the garden with Dr. Chasuble]

CECILY: [Picks up books and throws them back on table] Horrid Political Economy! Horrid Geography! Horrid, horrid German!

[Enter Merriman with a card on a salver]

MERRIMAN: Mr. Ernest Worthing has just driven over from the station. He has brought his luggage with him.

CECILY: [Takes the card and reads it] "Mr. Ernest Worthing, B 4 The Albany, W." Uncle Jack's brother! Did you tell him Mr. Worthing was in town?

MERRIMAN: Yes, Miss. He seemed very much disappointed. I mentioned that you and Miss Prism were in the garden. He said he was anxious to speak to you privately for a moment.

CECILY: Ask Mr. Ernest Worthing to come here. I suppose you had better talk to the housekeeper about a room for him.

MERRIMAN: Yes, Miss.

[Merriman goes off]

CECILY: I have never met any really wicked person before. I feel rather frightened. I am so afraid he will look just like everyone else.

[Enter Algernon, very gay and debonair]
He does!

ALGERNON: [Raising his hat] You are my little Cousin Cecily, I'm sure.

CECILY: You are under some strange mistake. I am not little. In fact, I am more than usually tall for my age. [Algernon is rather taken aback] But I am your Cousin Cecily. You, I see from your card, are Uncle Jack's brother, my Cousin Ernest, my wicked Cousin Ernest.

ALGERNON: Oh! I am not really wicked at all, Cousin Cecily. You mustn't think that I am wicked.

CECILY: If you are not, then you have certainly been deceiving us all in a very inexcusable manner. I hope you have not been leading a double life, pretending to be wicked and being really good all the time. That would be hypocrisy.

ALGERNON: [Looks at her in amazement] Oh! Of course I have been rather reckless.

CECILY: I am glad to hear it.

ALGERNON: In fact, now you mention the subject, I have been very bad in my own small way.

CECILY: I don't think you should be so proud of that, though I am sure it must have been very pleasant.

ALGERNON: It is much pleasanter being here with you.

CECILY: I can't understand how you are here at all. Uncle Jack won't be back till Monday afternoon.

ALGERNON: That is a great disappointment. I am obliged to go up by the first train on Monday morning. I have a business appointment that I am anxious . . . to miss.

CECILY: Couldn't you miss it anywhere but in London?

ALGERNON: No; the appointment is in London.

CECILY: Well, I know, of course, how important it is not to keep a business engagement, if one wants to retain any sense of the beauty of life, but still I think you had better wait till Uncle Jack arrives. I know he wants to speak to you about your emigrating.

ALGERNON: About my what?

CECILY: Your emigrating. He has gone up to buy your outfit.

ALGERNON: I certainly wouldn't let Jack buy my outfit. He has no taste in neckties at all.

CECILY: I don't think you will require neckties. Uncle Jack is sending you to Australia.

ALGERNON: Australia! I'd sooner die.

CECILY: Well, he said at dinner on Wednesday night, that you would have to choose between this world, the next world, and Australia.

ALGERNON: Oh, well! The accounts I have received of Australia and the next world, are not particularly encouraging. This world is good enough for me, Cousin Cecily.

CECILY: Yes, but are you good enough for it?

ALGERNON: I'm afraid I'm not that. That is why I want you to reform me. You might make that your mission, if you don't mind, Cousin Cecily.

CECILY: I'm afraid I've not time, this afternoon.

ALGERNON: Well, would you mind my reforming myself this afternoon?

CECILY: That is rather Quixotic of you. But I think you should try.

ALGERNON: I will. I feel better already.

CECILY: You are looking a little worse.

ALGERNON: That is because I am hungry.

CECILY: How thoughtless of me. I should have remembered that when one is going to lead an entirely new life, one requires regular and wholesome meals. Won't you come in?

ALGERNON: Thank you. Might I have a buttonhole first? I never have any appetite unless I have a button-hole first.

CECILY: A Maréchal Niel? [Picks up scissors]

ALGERNON: No, I'd sooner have a pink rose.

CECILY: Why? [Cuts a flower]

ALGERNON: Because you are like a pink rose, Cousin Cecily.

CECILY: I don't think it can be right for you to talk to me like that. Miss Prism never says such things to me.

ALGERNON: Then Miss Prism is a short-sighted old lady. [Cecily puts the rose in his button-hole] You are the prettiest girl I ever saw.

CECILY: Miss Prism says that all good looks are a snare.

ALGERNON: They are a snare that every sensible man would like to be caught in.

CECILY: Oh! I don't think I would care to catch a sensible man. I shouldn't know what to talk to him about.

[They pass into the house. Miss Prism and Dr. Chasuble return]

MISS PRISM: You are too much alone, dear Dr.

Chasuble. You should get married. A misanthrope I can understand—a womanthrope, never!

CHASUBLE: [With a scholar's shudder] Believe me, I do not deserve so neologistic a phrase. The precept as well as the practice of the Primitive Church was distinctly against matrimony.

MISS PRISM: [Sententiously] That is obviously the reason why the Primitive Church has not lasted up to the present day. And you do not seem to realize, dear Doctor, that by persistently remaining single, a man converts himself into a permanent public temptation. Men should be careful; this very celibacy leads weaker vessels astray.

CHASUBLE: But is a man not equally attractive when married?

MISS PRISM: No married man is ever attractive except to his wife.

CHASUBLE: And often, I've been told, not even to her.

MISS PRISM: That depends on the intellectual sympathies of the woman. Maturity can always be depended on. Ripeness can be trusted. Young women are green. [Dr. Chasuble starts] I spoke horticulturally. My metaphor was drawn from fruits. But where is Cecily?

CHASUBLE: Perhaps she followed us to the schools.

[Enter Jack slowly from the back of the garden. He is dressed in the deepest mourning, with crape hat-band and black gloves]

MISS PRISM: Mr. Worthing!

CHASUBLE: Mr. Worthing?

MISS PRISM: This is indeed a surprise. We did not look for you till Monday afternoon.

JACK: [Shakes Miss Prism's hand in a tragic manner] I have returned sooner than I expected. Dr. Chasuble, I hope you are well?

CHASUBLE: Dear Mr. Worthing, I trust this garb of woe does not betoken some terrible calamity?

JACK: My brother.

MISS PRISM: More shameful debts and extravagance?

CHASUBLE: Still leading his life of pleasure?

JACK: [Shaking his head] Dead.

CHASUBLE: Your brother Ernest dead?

JACK: Quite dead.

MISS PRISM: What a lesson for him! I trust he will profit by it.

CHASUBLE: Mr. Worthing, I offer you my sincere condolence. You have at least the consolation of knowing that you were always the most generous and forgiving of brothers.

JACK: Poor Ernest! He had many faults, but it is a sad, sad blow.

CHASUBLE: Very sad indeed. Were you with him at the end?

JACK: No. He died abroad; in Paris, in fact. I had a telegram last night from the manager of the Grand Hotel.

CHASUBLE: Was the cause of death mentioned?

JACK: A severe chill, it seems.

MISS PRISM: As a man sows, so shall he reap.

CHASUBLE: [*Raising his hand*] Charity, dear Miss Prism, charity! None of us are perfect. I myself am peculiarly susceptible to draughts. Will the interment take place here?

JACK: No. He seems to have expressed a desire to be buried in Paris.

CHASUBLE: In Paris! [*Shakes his head*] I fear that hardly points to any very serious state of mind at the last. You would no doubt wish me to make some slight allusion to this tragic domestic affliction next Sunday. [Jack *presses his hand convulsively*] My sermon on the meaning of the manna in the wilderness can be adapted to almost any occasion, joyful, or, as in the present case, distressing. [*All sigh*] I have preached it at harvest celebrations, christenings, confirmations, on days of humiliation and festal days. The last time I delivered it was in the Cathedral, as a charity sermon on behalf of the Society for the Prevention of Discontentment among the Upper Orders. The Bishop, who was present, was much struck by some of the analogies I drew.

JACK: Ah, that reminds me, you mentioned christenings I think, Dr. Chasuble? I suppose you know how to christen all right? [Dr. Chasuble *looks astounded*] I mean, of course, you are continually christening, aren't you?

MISS PRISM: It is, I regret to say, one of the Rector's most constant duties in this parish. I have often spoken to the poorer classes on the subject. But they don't seem to know what thrift is.

CHASUBLE: But is there any particular infant in whom you are interested, Mr. Worthing? Your brother was, I believe, unmarried, was he not?

JACK: Oh, yes.

MISS PRISM: [*Bitterly*] People who live entirely for pleasure usually are.

JACK: But it is not for any child, dear Doctor. I am very fond of children. No! the fact is, I would like to be christened myself, this afternoon, if you have nothing better to do.

CHASUBLE: But surely, Mr. Worthing, you have been christened already?

JACK: I don't remember anything about it.

CHASUBLE: But have you any grave doubts on the subject?

JACK: I certainly intend to have. Of course, I don't know if the thing would bother you in any way, or if you think I am a little too old now.

CHASUBLE: Not at all. The sprinkling, and, indeed, the immersion of adults is a perfectly canonical practice.

JACK: Immersion!

CHASUBLE: You need have no apprehensions. Sprinkling is all that is necessary, or indeed I think advisable. Our weather is so changeable. At what hour would you wish the ceremony performed?

JACK: Oh, I might trot around about five if that would suit you.

CHASUBLE: Perfectly, perfectly! In fact I have two similar ceremonies to perform at that time. A case of twins that occurred recently in one of the outlying cottages on your own estate. Poor Jenkins the carter, a most hard-working man.

JACK: Oh! I don't see much fun in being christened along with other babies. It would be childish. Would half-past five do?

CHASUBLE: Admirably! Admirably! [*Takes out watch*] And now, dear Mr. Worthing, I will not intrude any longer into a house of sorrow. I would merely beg you not to be too much bowed down by grief. What seem to us bitter trials at the moment are often blessings in disguise.

MISS PRISM: This seems to me a blessing of an extremely obvious kind.

[*Enter* Cecily *from the house*]

CECILY: Uncle Jack! Oh, I am pleased to see you back. But what horrid clothes you have on! Do go and change them.

MISS PRISM: Cecily!

CHASUBLE: My child! my child! [Cecily *goes towards* Jack; *he kisses her brow in a melancholy manner*]

CECILY: What is the matter, Uncle Jack? Do look happy! You look as if you had a toothache and I have such a surprise for you. Who do you think is in the dining-room? Your brother!

JACK: Who?

CECILY: Your brother Ernest. He arrived about half an hour ago.

JACK: What nonsense! I haven't got a brother.

CECILY: Oh, don't say that. However badly he may have behaved to you in the past he is still your brother. You couldn't be so heartless as to disown him. I'll tell him to come out. And you will shake hands with him, won't you, Uncle Jack? [*Runs back into the house*]

CHASUBLE: These are very joyful tidings.

MISS PRISM: After we had all been resigned to his loss, his sudden return seems to me peculiarly distressing.

JACK: My brother is in the dining-room? I don't know what it all means. I think it is perfectly absurd.

[*Enter* Algernon *and* Cecily *hand in hand. They come slowly up to* Jack]

JACK: Good heavens! [*Motions* Algernon *away*]

ALGERNON: Brother John, I have come down from town to tell you that I am very sorry for all the trouble I have given you, and that I intend to lead a better life in the future. [Jack *glares at him and does not take his hand*]

CECILY: Uncle Jack, you are not going to refuse your own brother's hand?

JACK: Nothing will induce me to take his hand. I think his coming down here disgraceful. He knows perfectly well why.

CECILY: Uncle, do be nice. There is some good in everyone. Ernest has just been telling me about his poor invalid friend, Mr. Bunbury, whom he goes to visit so often. And surely there must be much good in one who is kind to an invalid, and leaves the pleasures of London to sit by a bed of pain.

JACK: Oh, he has been talking about Bunbury, has he?

CECILY: Yes, he has told me all about poor Mr. Bunbury, and his terrible state of health.

JACK: Bunbury! Well, I won't have him talk to you about Bunbury or about anything else. It is enough to drive one perfectly frantic.

ALGERNON: Of course I admit that the faults were all on my side. But I must say that I think that Brother John's coldness to me is peculiarly painful. I expected a more enthusiastic welcome, especially considering it is the first time I have come here.

CECILY: Uncle Jack, if you don't shake hands with Ernest I will never forgive you.

JACK: Never forgive me?

CECILY: Never, never, never!

JACK: Well, this is the last time I shall ever do it. [Shakes hands with Algernon and glares]

CHASUBLE: It's pleasant, is it not, to see so perfect a reconciliation? I think we might leave the two brothers together.

MISS PRISM: Cecily, you will come with us.

CECILY: Certainly, Miss Prism. My little task of reconciliation is over.

CHASUBLE: You have done a beautiful action to-day, dear child.

MISS PRISM: We must not be premature in our judgments.

CECILY: I feel very happy. [They all go off]

JACK: You young scoundrel, Algy, you must get out of this place as soon as possible. I don't allow any Bunburying here.

[Enter Merriman]

MERRIMAN: I have put Mr. Ernest's things in the room next to yours, sir. I suppose that is all right?

JACK: What?

MERRIMAN: Mr. Ernest's luggage, sir. I have un-packed it and put it in the room next to your own.

JACK: His luggage?

MERRIMAN: Yes, sir. Three portmanteaus, a dress-ing-case, two hat-boxes, and a large luncheon-basket.

ALGERNON: I am afraid I can't stay more than a week this time.

JACK: Merriman, order the dog-cart at once. Mr. Ernest has been suddenly called back to town.

MERRIMAN: Yes, sir. [Goes back into the house]

ALGERNON: What a fearful liar you are, Jack. I have not been called back to town at all.

JACK: Yes, you have.

ALGERNON: I haven't heard anyone call me.

JACK: Your duty as a gentleman calls you back.

ALGERNON: My duty as a gentleman has never interfered with my pleasures in the smallest degree.

JACK: I can quite understand that.

ALGERNON: Well, Cecily is a darling.

JACK: You are not to talk of Miss Cardew like that. I don't like it.

ALGERNON: Well, I don't like your clothes. You look perfectly ridiculous in them. Why on earth don't you go up and change? It is perfectly childish to be in deep mourning for a man who is actually staying for a whole week with you in your house as a guest. I call it grotesque.

JACK: You are certainly not staying with me for a whole week as a guest or anything else. You have got to leave . . . by the four-five train.

ALGERNON: I certainly won't leave you so long as you are in mourning. It would be most unfriendly. If I were in mourning you would stay with me, I suppose. I should think it very unkind if you didn't.

JACK: Well, will you go if I change my clothes?

ALGERNON: Yes, if you are not too long. I never saw anybody take so long to dress, and with such little result.

JACK: Well, at any rate, that is better than being always over-dressed as you are.

ALGERNON: If I am occasionally a little over-dressed, I make up for it by being always immensely over-educated.

JACK: Your vanity is ridiculous, your conduct an outrage, and your presence in my garden utterly absurd. However you have got to catch the four-five, and I hope you will have a pleasant journey back to town. This Bunburying, as you call it, has not been a great success for you. [Goes into the house]

ALGERNON: I think it has been a great success. I'm in love with Cecily, and that is everything. [Enter Cecily at the back of the garden. She picks up the can and begins to water the flowers] But I must see her before I go, and make arrangements for another Bunbury. Ah, there she is.

CECILY: Oh, I merely came back to water the roses. I thought you were with Uncle Jack.

ALGERNON: He's gone to order the dog-cart for me.

CECILY: Oh, is he going to take you for a nice drive?

ALGERNON: He's going to send me away.

CECILY: Then have we got to part?

ALGERNON: I am afraid so. It's a very painful parting.

CECILY: It is always painful to part from people whom one has known for a very brief space of time. The absence of old friends one can endure with equanimity. But even a momentary separation from anyone to whom one has just been introduced is almost unbearable.

ALGERNON: Thank you.

[Enter Merriman]

MERRIMAN: The dog-cart is at the door, sir. [Algernon looks appealingly at Cecily]

CECILY: It can wait, Merriman . . . for . . . five minutes.

MERRIMAN: Yes, miss.

[Exit Merriman]

ALGERNON: I hope, Cecily, I shall not offend you if I state quite frankly and openly that you seem to me to be in every way the visible personification of absolute perfection.

CECILY: I think your frankness does you great credit, Ernest. If you will allow me I will copy your remarks into my diary. [*Goes over to table and begins writing in diary*]

ALGERNON: Do you really keep a diary? I'd give anything to look at it. May I?

CECILY: Oh, no. [*Puts her hand over it*] You see, it is simply a very young girl's record of her own thoughts and impressions, and consequently meant for publication. When it appears in volume form I hope you will order a copy. But pray, Ernest, don't stop. I delight in taking down from dictation. I have reached "absolute perfection." You can go on. I am quite ready for more.

ALGERNON: [*Somewhat taken aback*] Ahem! Ahem!

CECILY: Oh, don't cough, Ernest. When one is dictating one should speak fluently and not cough. Besides, I don't know how to spell a cough. [*Writes as* Algernon *speaks*]

ALGERNON: [*Speaking very rapidly*] Cecily, ever since I first looked upon your wonderful and incomparable beauty, I have dared to love you wildly, passionately, devotedly, hopelessly.

CECILY: I don't think that you should tell me that you love me wildly, passionately, devotedly, hopelessly. Hopelessly doesn't seem to make much sense, does it?

ALGERNON: Cecily!

[*Enter* Merriman]

MERRIMAN: The dog-cart is waiting, sir.

ALGERNON: Tell it to come round next week, at the same hour.

MERRIMAN: [*Looks at* Cecily, *who makes no sign*] Yes, sir.

[Merriman *retires*]

CECILY: Uncle Jack would be very much annoyed if he knew you were staying on till next week, at the same hour.

ALGERNON: Oh, I don't care about Jack. I don't care for anybody in the whole world but you. I love you, Cecily. You will marry me, won't you?

CECILY: You silly you! Of course. Why, we have been engaged for the last three months.

ALGERNON: For the last three months?

CECILY: Yes, it will be exactly three months on Thursday.

ALGERNON: But how did we become engaged?

CECILY: Well, ever since dear Uncle Jack first confessed to us that he had a younger brother who was very wicked and bad, you of course have formed the chief topic of conversation between myself and Miss Prism. And of course a man who is much talked about is always very attractive. One feels there must be something in him after all. I daresay it was foolish of me, but I fell in love with you, Ernest.

ALGERNON: Darling! And when was the engagement actually settled?

CECILY: On the 14th of February last. Worn out by your entire ignorance of my existence, I determined to end the matter one way or the other, and after a long struggle with myself I accepted you under this dear old tree here. The next day I bought this little ring in your name, and this is the little bangle with the true lovers' knot I promised you always to wear.

ALGERNON: Did I give you this? It's very pretty, isn't it?

CECILY: Yes, you've wonderfully good taste, Ernest. It's the excuse I've always given for your leading such a bad life. And this is the box in which I keep all your dear letters. [*Kneels at table, opens box, and produces letters tied up with blue ribbon*]

ALGERNON: My letters! But my own sweet Cecily, I have never written you any letters.

CECILY: You need hardly remind me of that, Ernest. I remember only too well that I was forced to write your letters for you. I wrote always three times a week, and sometimes oftener.

ALGERNON: Oh, do let me read them, Cecily?

CECILY: Oh, I couldn't possibly. They would make you far too conceited. [*Replaces box*] The three you wrote me after I had broken off the engagement are so beautiful, and so badly spelled, that even now I can hardly read them without crying a little.

ALGERNON: But was our engagement ever broken off?

CECILY: Of course it was. On the 22nd of last March. You can see the entry if you like. [*Shows diary*] "To-day I broke off my engagement with Ernest. I feel it is better to do so. The weather still continues charming."

ALGERNON: But why on earth did you break it off? What had I done? I had done nothing at all. Cecily, I am very much hurt indeed to hear you broke it off. Particularly when the weather was so charming.

CECILY: It would hardly have been a really serious engagement if it hadn't been broken off at least once. But I forgave you before the week was out.

ALGERNON: [*Crossing to her, and kneeling*] What a perfect angel you are, Cecily.

CECILY: You dear romantic boy. [*He kisses her, she puts her fingers through his hair*] I hope your hair curls naturally, does it?

ALGERNON: Yes, darling, with a little help from others.

CECILY: I am so glad.

ALGERNON: You'll never break off our engagement again, Cecily?

CECILY: I don't think I could break it off now that I have actually met you. Besides, of course, there is the question of your name.

ALGERNON: Yes, of course. [*Nervously*]

CECILY: You must not laugh at me, darling, but it had always been a girlish dream of mine to love some one whose name was Ernest. [Algernon *rises,* Cecily *also*] There is something in that name that seems to inspire absolute confidence. I pity any poor married woman whose husband is not called Ernest.

ALGERNON: But, my dear child, do you mean to say you could not love me if I had some other name?

CECILY: But what name?

ALGERNON: Oh, any name you like—Algernon, for instance. . . .

CECILY: But I don't like the name of Algernon.

ALGERNON: Well, my dear, sweet, loving little darling, I really can't see why you should object to the name of Algernon. It is not at all a bad name. In fact, it is rather an aristocratic name. Half of the chaps who get into the Bankruptcy Court are called Algernon. But seriously, Cecily . . . [Moving to her] . . . if my name was Algy, couldn't you love me?

CECILY: [Rising] I might respect you, Ernest, I might admire your character, but I fear that I should not be able to give you my undivided attention.

ALGERNON: Ahem! Cecily! [Picking up hat] Your Rector here is, I suppose, thoroughly experienced in the practice of all the rites and ceremonials of the church?

CECILY: Oh, yes. Dr. Chasuble is a most learned man. He has never written a single book, so you can imagine how much he knows.

ALGERNON: I must see him at once on a most important christening—I mean on most important business.

CECILY: Oh!

ALGERNON: I sha'n't be away more than half an hour.

CECILY: Considering that we have been engaged since February the 14th, and that I only met you to-day for the first time, I think it is rather hard that you should leave me for so long a period as half an hour. Couldn't you make it twenty minutes?

ALGERNON: I'll be back in no time. [Kisses her and rushes down the garden]

CECILY: What an impetuous boy he is. I like his hair so much. I must enter his proposal in my diary.

[Enter Merriman]

MERRIMAN: A Miss Fairfax has just called to see Mr. Worthing. On very important business, Miss Fairfax states.

CECILY: Isn't Mr. Worthing in his library?

MERRIMAN: Mr. Worthing went over in the direction of the Rectory some time ago.

CECILY: Pray ask the lady to come out here; Mr. Worthing is sure to be back soon. And you can bring tea.

MERRIMAN: Yes, miss. [Goes out]

CECILY: Miss Fairfax! I suppose one of the many good elderly women who are associated with Uncle Jack in some of his philanthropic work in London. I don't quite like women who are interested in philanthropic work. I think it is so forward of them.

[Enter Merriman]

MERRIMAN: Miss Fairfax.

[Enter Gwendolen]

[Exit Merriman]

CECILY: [Advancing to meet her] Pray let me introduce myself to you. My name is Cecily Cardew.

GWENDOLEN: Cecily Cardew? [Moving to her and shaking hands] What a very sweet name! Something tells me that we are going to be great friends. I like you already more than I can say. My first impressions of people are never wrong.

CECILY: How nice of you to like me so much after we have known each other such a comparatively short time. Pray sit down.

GWENDOLEN: [Still standing up] I may call you Cecily, may I not?

CECILY: With pleasure!

GWENDOLEN: And you will always call me Gwendolen, won't you?

CECILY: If you wish.

GWENDOLEN: Then that is all quite settled, is it not?

CECILY: I hope so. [A pause. They both sit down together]

GWENDOLEN: Perhaps this might be a favorable opportunity for my mentioning who I am. My father is Lord Bracknell. You have never heard of papa, I suppose?

CECILY: I don't think so.

GWENDOLEN: Outside the family circle, papa, I am glad to say, is entirely unknown. I think that is quite as it should be. The home seems to me to be the proper sphere for the man. And certainly once a man begins to neglect his domestic duties he becomes painfully effeminate, does he not? And I don't like that. It makes men so very attractive. Cecily, mamma, whose views on education are remarkably strict, has brought me up to be extremely short-sighted; it is part of her system; so do you mind my looking at you through my glasses?

CECILY: Oh, not at all, Gwendolen. I am very fond of being looked at.

GWENDOLEN: [After examining Cecily carefully through a lorgnette] You are here on a short visit. I suppose.

CECILY: Oh, no, I live here.

GWENDOLEN: [Severely] Really? Your mother, no doubt, or some female relative of advanced years, resides here also?

CECILY: Oh, no. I have no mother, nor, in fact, any relations.

GWENDOLEN: Indeed?

CECILY: My dear guardian, with the assistance of Miss Prism, has the arduous task of looking after me.

GWENDOLEN: Your guardian?

CECILY: Yes, I am Mr. Worthing's ward.

GWENDOLEN: Oh! It is strange he never mentioned to me that he had a ward. How secretive of him! He grows more interesting hourly. I am not sure, however, that the news inspires me with feelings of unmixed delight. [Rising and going to her] I am very fond of you, Cecily; I have liked you ever since I met you. But I am bound to state that now that I know that you are Mr. Worthing's ward, I cannot help expressing a wish you were—well, just a little older than you seem to be—and not quite so very alluring in appearance. In fact, if I may speak candidly——

CECILY: Pray do! I think that whenever one has anything unpleasant to say, one should always be quite candid.

GWENDOLEN: Well, to speak with perfect candor, Cecily, I wish that you were fully forty-two, and more than usually plain for your age. Ernest has a strong upright nature. He is the very soul of truth and honor. Disloyalty would be as impossible to him as deception. But even men of the noblest possible moral character are extremely susceptible to the influence of the physical charms of others. Modern, no less than Ancient History, supplies us with most painful examples of what I refer to. If it were not so, indeed, History would be quite unreadable.

CECILY: I beg your pardon, Gwendolen, did you say Ernest?

GWENDOLEN: Yes.

CECILY: Oh, but it is not Mr. Ernest Worthing who is my guardian. It is his brother—his elder brother.

GWENDOLEN: [Sitting down again] Ernest never mentioned to me that he had a brother.

CECILY: I am sorry to say they have not been on good terms for a long time.

GWENDOLEN: Ah! that accounts for it. And now that I think of it I have never heard any man mention his brother. The subject seems distasteful to most men. Cecily, you have lifted a load from my mind. I was growing almost anxious. It would have been terrible if any cloud had come across a friendship like ours, would it not? Of course you are quite, quite sure that it is not Mr. Ernest Worthing who is your guardian?

CECILY: Quite sure. [A pause] In fact, I am going to be his.

GWENDOLEN: [Enquiringly] I beg your pardon?

CECILY: [Rather shy and confidingly] Dearest Gwendolen, there is no reason why I should make a secret of it to you. Our little county newspaper is sure to chronicle the fact next week. Mr. Ernest Worthing and I are engaged to be married.

GWENDOLEN: [Quite politely, rising] My darling Cecily, I think there must be some slight error. Mr. Ernest Worthing is engaged to me. The announcement will appear in the Morning Post on Saturday at the latest.

CECILY: [Very politely, rising] I am afraid you must be under some misconception. Ernest proposed to me exactly ten minutes ago. [Shows diary]

GWENDOLEN: [Examines diary through her lorgnette carefully] It is certainly very curious, for he asked me to be his wife yesterday afternoon at 5.30. If you would care to verify the incident, pray do so. [Produces diary of her own] I never travel without my diary. One should always have something sensational to read in the train. I am so sorry, dear Cecily, if it is any disappointment to you, but I am afraid I have the prior claim.

CECILY: It would distress me more than I can tell you, dear Gwendolen, if it caused you any mental or physical anguish, but I feel bound to point out that since Ernest proposed to you he clearly has changed his mind.

GWENDOLEN: [Meditatively] If the poor fellow has been entrapped into any foolish promise I shall consider it my duty to rescue him at once, and with a firm hand.

CECILY: [Thoughtfully and sadly] Whatever unfortunate entanglement my dear boy may have got into, I will never reproach him with it after we are married.

GWENDOLEN: Do you allude to me, Miss Cardew, as an entanglement? You are presumptuous. On an occasion of this kind it becomes more than a moral duty to speak one's mind. It becomes a pleasure.

CECILY: Do you suggest, Miss Fairfax, that I entrapped Ernest into an engagement? How dare you? This is no time for wearing the shallow mask of manners. When I see a spade I call it a spade.

GWENDOLEN: [Satirically] I am glad to say that I have never seen a spade. It is obvious that our social spheres have been widely different.

[Enter Merriman, followed by the footman. He carries a salver, tablecloth, and plate-stand. Cecily is about to retort. The presence of the servants exercises a restraining influence, under which both girls chafe.]

MERRIMAN: Shall I lay tea here as usual, miss?

CECILY: [Sternly, in a calm voice] Yes, as usual. [Merriman begins to clear and lay cloth. A long pause. Cecily and Gwendolen glare at each other]

GWENDOLEN: Are there many interesting walks in the vicinity, Miss Cardew?

CECILY: Oh, yes, a great many. From the top of one of the hills quite close one can see five counties.

GWENDOLEN: Five counties! I don't think I should like that. I hate crowds.

CECILY: [Sweetly] I suppose that is why you live in town? [Gwendolen bites her lip, and beats her foot nervously with her parasol]

GWENDOLEN: [Looking round] Quite a well-kept garden this is, Miss Cardew.

CECILY: So glad you like it, Miss Fairfax.

GWENDOLEN: I had no idea there were any flowers in the country.

CECILY: Oh, flowers are as common here, Miss Fairfax, as people are in London.

GWENDOLEN: Personally I cannot understand how anybody manages to exist in the country, if anybody who is anybody does. The country always bores me to death.

CECILY: Ah! This is what the newspapers call agricultural depression, is it not? I believe the aristocracy are suffering very much from it just at present. It is almost an epidemic amongst them, I have been told. May I offer you some tea, Miss Fairfax?

GWENDOLEN: [*With elaborate politeness*] Thank you. [*Aside*] Detestable girl! But I require tea!

CECILY: [*Sweetly*] Sugar?

GWENDOLEN: [*Superciliously*] No, thank you. Sugar is not fashionable any more. [Cecily *looks angrily at her, takes up the tongs and puts four lumps of sugar into the cup*]

CECILY: [*Severely*] Cake or bread and butter?

GWENDOLEN: [*In a bored manner*] Bread and butter, please. Cake is rarely seen at the best houses nowadays.

CECILY: [*Cuts a very large slice of cake, and puts it on the tray*] Hand that to Miss Fairfax. [Merriman *does so, and goes out with footman. Gwendolen drinks the tea and makes a grimace. Puts down cup at once, reaches out her hand to the bread and butter, looks at it, and finds it is cake. Rises in indignation*]

GWENDOLEN: You have filled my tea with lumps of sugar, and though I asked most distinctly for bread and butter, you have given me cake. I am known for the gentleness of my disposition, and the extraordinary sweetness of my nature, but I warn you, Miss Cardew, you may go too far.

CECILY: [*Rising*] To save my poor, innocent, trusting boy from the machinations of any other girl there are no lengths to which I would not go.

GWENDOLEN: From the moment I saw you I distrusted you. I felt that you were false and deceitful. I am never deceived in such matters. My first impressions of people are invariably right.

CECILY: It seems to me, Miss Fairfax, that I am trespassing on your valuable time. No doubt you have many other calls of a similar character to make in the neighborhood.

[*Enter Jack*]

GWENDOLEN: [*Catching sight of him*] Ernest! My own Ernest!

JACK: Gwendolen! Darling! [*Offers to kiss her*]

GWENDOLEN: [*Drawing back*] A moment! May I ask if you are engaged to be married to this young lady? [*Points to* Cecily]

JACK: [*Laughing*] To dear little Cecily! Of course not! What could have put such an idea into your pretty little head?

GWENDOLEN: Thank you. You may. [*Offers her cheek*]

CECILY: [*Very sweetly*] I knew there must be some misunderstanding, Miss Fairfax. The gentleman whose arm is at present around your waist is my dear guardian, Mr. John Worthing.

GWENDOLEN: I beg your pardon?

CECILY: This is Uncle Jack.

GWENDOLEN: [*Receding*] Jack! Oh!

[*Enters Algernon*]

CECILY: Here is Ernest.

ALGERNON: [*Goes straight over to Cecily without noticing anyone else*] My own love! [*Offers to kiss her*]

CECILY: [*Drawing back*] A moment, Ernest! May I ask— are you engaged to be married to this young lady?

ALGERNON: [*Looking round*] To what young lady? Good heavens! Gwendolen!

CECILY: Yes, to good heavens, Gwendolen, I mean to Gwendolen.

ALGERNON: [*Laughing*] Of course not! What could have put such an idea into your pretty little head?

CECILY: Thank you. [*Presenting her cheek to be kissed*] You may. [Algernon *kisses her*]

GWENDOLEN: I felt there was some slight error, Miss Cardew. The gentleman who is now embracing you is my cousin, Mr. Algernon Moncrieff.

CECILY: [*Breaking away from* Algernon] Algernon Moncrieff! Oh! [*The two girls move towards each other and put their arms round each other's waists as if for protection*]

CECILY: Are you called Algernon?

ALGERNON: I cannot deny it.

CECILY: Oh!

GWENDOLEN: Is your name really John?

JACK: [*Standing rather proudly*] I could deny it if I liked. I could deny anything if I liked. But my name certainly is John. It has been John for years.

CECILY: [*To* Gwendolen] A gross deception has been practised on both of us.

GWENDOLEN: My poor wounded Cecily!

CECILY: My sweet, wronged Gwendolen!

GWENDOLEN: [*Slowly and seriously*] You will call me sister, will you not? [*They embrace.* Jack *and* Algernon *groan and walk up and down*]

CECILY: [*Rather brightly*] There is just one question I would like to be allowed to ask my guardian.

GWENDOLEN: An admirable idea! Mr. Worthing, there is just one question I would like to be permitted to put to you. Where is your brother Ernest? We are both engaged to be married to your brother Ernest, so it is a matter of some importance to us to know where your brother Ernest is at present.

JACK: [*Slowly and hesitatingly*] Gwendolen— Cecily—it is very painful for me to be forced to speak the truth. It is the first time in my life that I have ever been reduced to such a painful position, and I am really quite inexperienced in doing anything of the kind. However I will tell you quite frankly that I have no brother Ernest. I have no brother at all. I never had a brother in my life, and I certainly have not the smallest intention of ever having one in the future.

CECILY: [*Surprised*] No brother at all?

JACK: [*Cheerily*] None!

GWENDOLEN: [*Severely*] Had you never a brother of any kind?

JACK: [*Pleasantly*] Never. Not even of any kind.

GWENDOLEN: I am afraid it is quite clear, Cecily, that neither of us is engaged to be married to anyone.

CECILY: It is not a very pleasant position for a young girl suddenly to find herself in. Is it?

GWENDOLEN: Let us go into the house. They will hardly venture to come after us there.

CECILY: No, men are so cowardly, aren't they? [*They retire into the house with scornful looks*]

JACK: This ghastly state of things is what you call Bunburying, I suppose?

ALGERNON: Yes, and a perfectly wonderful Bunbury it is. The most wonderful Bunbury I have ever had in my life.

JACK: Well, you've no right whatsoever to Bunbury here.

ALGERNON: That is absurd. One has a right to Bunbury anywhere one chooses. Every serious Bunburyist knows that.

JACK: Serious Bunburyist! Good heavens!

ALGERNON: Well, one must be serious about something, if one wants to have any amusement in life. I happen to be serious about Bunburying. What on earth you are serious about I haven't got the remotest idea. About everything, I should fancy. You have such an absolutely trivial nature.

JACK: Well, the only small satisfaction I have in the whole of this wretched business is that your friend Bunbury is quite exploded. You won't be able to run down to the country quite so often as you used to do, dear Algy. And a very good thing, too.

ALGERNON: Your brother is a little off color, isn't he, dear Jack? You won't be able to disappear to London quite so frequently as your wicked custom was. And not a bad thing, either.

JACK: As for your conduct towards Miss Cardew, I must say that your taking in a sweet, simple, innocent girl like that is quite inexcusable. To say nothing of the fact that she is my ward.

ALGERNON: I can see no possible defence at all for your deceiving a brilliant, clever, thoroughly experienced young lady like Miss Fairfax. To say nothing of the fact that she is my cousin.

JACK: I wanted to be engaged to Gwendolen, that is all. I love her.

ALGERNON: Well, I simply wanted to be engaged to Cecily. I adore her.

JACK: There is certainly no chance of your marrying Miss Cardew.

ALGERNON: I don't think there is much likelihood, Jack, of you and Miss Fairfax being united.

JACK: Well, that is no business of yours.

ALGERNON: If it was my business, I wouldn't talk about it. [*Begins to eat muffins*] It is very vulgar to talk about one's business. Only people like stockbrokers do that, and then merely at dinner parties.

JACK: How you can sit there, calmly eating muffins, when we are in this horrible trouble, I can't make out. You seem to me to be perfectly heartless.

ALGERNON: Well, I can't eat muffins in an agitated manner. The butter would probably get on my cuffs. One should always eat muffins quite calmly. It is the only way to eat them.

JACK: I say it's perfectly heartless your eating muffins at all, under the circumstances.

ALGERNON: When I am in trouble, eating is the only thing that consoles me. Indeed, when I am in really great trouble, as anyone who knows me intimately will tell you, I refuse everything except food and drink. At the present moment I am eating muffins because I am unhappy. Besides, I am particularly fond of muffins. [*Rising*]

JACK: [*Rising*] Well, that is no reason why you should eat them all in that greedy way. [*Takes muffins from* Algernon]

ALGERNON: [*Offering tea-cake*] I wish you would have tea-cake instead. I don't like tea-cake.

JACK: Good heavens! I suppose a man may eat his own muffins in his own garden.

ALGERNON: But you have just said it was perfectly heartless to eat muffins.

JACK: I said it was perfectly heartless of you, under the circumstances. That is a very different thing.

ALGERNON: That may be. But the muffins are the same. [*He seizes the muffin-dish from* Jack]

JACK: Algy, I wish to goodness you would go.

ALGERNON: You can't possibly ask me to go without having some dinner. It's absurd. I never go without my dinner. No one ever does, except vegetarians and people like that. Besides I have just made arrangements with Dr. Chasuble to be christened at a quarter to six under the name of Ernest.

JACK: My dear fellow, the sooner you give up that nonsense the better. I made arrangements this morning with Dr. Chasuble to be christened myself at 5.30, and I naturally will take the name of Ernest. Gwendolen would wish it. We can't both be christened Ernest. It's absurd. Besides, I have a perfect right to be christened if I like. There is no evidence at all that I ever have been christened by anybody. I should think it extremely probable I never was, and so does Dr. Chasuble. It is entirely different in your case. You have been christened already.

ALGERNON: Yes, but I have not been christened for years.

JACK: Yes, but you have been christened. That is the important thing.

ALGERNON: Quite so. So I know my constitution can stand it. If you are not quite sure about your ever having been christened, I must say I think it rather dangerous your venturing on it now. It might make you very unwell. You can hardly have forgotten that someone very closely connected with you was very nearly carried off this week in Paris by a severe chill.

JACK: Yes, but you said yourself that a severe chill was not hereditary.

ALGERNON: It usedn't to be, I know—but I daresay it is now. Science is always making wonderful improvements in things.

JACK: [*Picking up the muffin-dish*] Oh, that is nonsense; you are always talking nonsense.

ALGERNON: Jack, you are at the muffins again! I wish you wouldn't. There are only two left. [*Takes them*] I told you I was particularly fond of muffins.

JACK: But I hate tea-cake.

ALGERNON: Why on earth then do you allow tea-cake to be served up for your guests? What ideas you have of hospitality!

JACK: Algernon! I have already told you to go. I don't want you here. Why don't you go?

ALGERNON: I haven't quite finished my tea yet, and there is still one muffin left. [Jack *groans, and sinks into a chair.* Algernon *still continues eating*]

CURTAIN

ACT III.

SCENE: *Morning-room at the Manor House.* Gwendolen *and* Cecily *are at the window, looking out into the garden.*

GWENDOLEN: The fact that they did not follow us at once into the house, as anyone else would have done, seems to me to show that they have some sense of shame left.

CECILY: They have been eating muffins. That looks like repentance.

GWENDOLEN: [*After a pause*] They don't seem to notice us at all. Couldn't you cough?

GWENDOLEN: They're looking at us. What effrontery!

CECILY: They're approaching. That's very forward of them.

GWENDOLEN: Let us preserve a dignified silence.

CECILY: Certainly. It's the only thing to do now.

[*Enter* Jack, *followed by* Algernon. *They whistle some dreadful popular air from a British opera*]

GWENDOLEN: This dignified silence seems to produce an unpleasant effect.

CECILY: A most distasteful one.

GWENDOLEN: But we will not be the first to speak.

CECILY: Certainly not.

GWENDOLEN: Mr. Worthing, I have something very particular to ask you. Much depends on your reply.

CECILY: Gwendolen, your common sense is invaluable. Mr. Moncrieff, kindly answer me the following question. Why did you pretend to be my guardian's brother?

ALGERNON: In order that I might have an opportunity of meeting you.

CECILY: [*To* Gwendolen] That certainly seems a satisfactory explanation, does it not?

GWENDOLEN: Yes, dear, if you can believe him.

CECILY: I don't. But that does not affect the wonderful beauty of his answer.

GWENDOLEN: True. In matters of grave impor-

tance, style, not sincerity, is the vital thing. Mr. Worthing, what explanation can you offer to me for pretending to have a brother? Was it in order that you might have an opportunity of coming up to town to see me as often as possible?

JACK: Can you doubt it, Miss Fairfax?

GWENDOLEN: I have the gravest doubts upon the subject. But I intend to crush them. This is not the moment for German scepticism. [*Moving to* Cecily] Their explanations appear to be quite satisfactory, especially Mr. Worthing's. That seems to me to have the stamp of truth upon it.

CECILY: I am more than content with what Mr. Moncrieff said. His voice alone inspires one with absolute credulity.

GWENDOLEN: Then you think we should forgive them?

CECILY: Yes. I mean no.

GWENDOLEN: True! I had forgotten. There are principles at stake that one cannot surrender. Which of us should tell them? The task is not a pleasant one.

CECILY: Could we not both speak at the same time?

GWENDOLEN: An excellent idea! I nearly always speak at the same time as other people. Will you take the time from me?

CECILY: Certainly. [Gwendolen *beats time with uplifted finger*]

GWENDOLEN AND CECILY: [*Speaking together*] Your Christian names are still an insuperable barrier. That is all!

JACK AND ALGERNON: [*Speaking together*] Our Christian names! Is that all? But we are going to be christened this afternoon.

GWENDOLEN: [*To* Jack] For my sake you are prepared to do this terrible thing?

JACK: I am.

CECILY: [*To* Algernon] To please me you are ready to face this fearful ordeal?

ALGERNON: I am.

GWENDOLEN: How absurd to talk of the equality of the sexes! Where questions of self-sacrifice are concerned, men are infinitely beyond us.

JACK: We are. [*Clasps hands with* Algernon]

CECILY: They have moments of physical courage of which we women know absolutely nothing.

GWENDOLEN: [*To* Jack] Darling!

ALGERNON: [*To* Cecily] Darling! [*They fall into each other's arms*]

[*Enter* Merriman. *When he enters he coughs loudly, seeing the situation*]

MERRIMAN: Ahem! Ahem! Lady Bracknell!

JACK: Good heavens!

[*Enter* Lady Bracknell. *The couples separate in alarm. Exit* Merriman]

LADY BRACKNELL: Gwendolen! What does this mean?

GWENDOLEN: Merely that I am engaged to be married to Mr. Worthing, Mamma.

LADY BRACKNELL: Come here. Sit down. Sit down immediately. Hesitation of any kind is a sign of mental decay in the young, of physical weakness in the old. [*Turns to* Jack] Apprised, sir, of my daughter's sudden flight by her trusty maid, whose confidence I purchased by means of a small coin, I followed her at once by a luggage train. Her unhappy father is, I am glad to say, under the impression that she is attending a more than usually lengthy lecture by the University Extension Scheme on the Influence of a Permanent Income on Thought. I do not propose to undeceive him. Indeed I have never undeceived him on any question. I would consider it wrong. But of course, you will clearly understand that all communication between yourself and my daughter must cease immediately from this moment. On this point, as indeed on all points, I am firm.

JACK: I am engaged to be married to Gwendolen, Lady Bracknell!

LADY BRACKNELL: You are nothing of the kind, sir. And now, as regards Algernon! . . . Algernon!

ALGERNON: Yes, Aunt Augusta.

LADY BRACKNELL: May I ask if it is in this house that your invalid friend Mr. Bunbury resides?

ALGERNON: [*Stammering*] Oh, no! Bunbury doesn't live here. Bunbury is somewhere else at present. In fact, Bunbury is dead.

LADY BRACKNELL: Dead! When did Mr. Bunbury die? His death must have been extremely sudden.

ALGERNON: [*Airily*] Oh, I killed Bunbury this afternoon. I mean poor Bunbury died this afternoon.

LADY BRACKNELL: What did he die of?

ALGERNON: Bunbury? Oh, he was quite exploded.

LADY BLACKNELL: Exploded! Was he the victim of a revolutionary outrage? I was not aware that Mr. Bunbury was interested in social legislation. If so, he is well punished for his morbidity.

ALGERNON: My dear Aunt Augusta, I mean he was found out! The doctors found out that Bunbury could not live, that is what I mean—so Bunbury died.

LADY BRACKNELL: He seems to have had great confidence in the opinion of his physicians. I am glad, however, that he made up his mind at the last to some definite course of action, and acted under proper medical advice. And now that we have finally got rid of this Mr. Bunbury, may I ask, Mr. Worthing, who is that young person whose hand my nephew Algernon is now holding in what seems to me a peculiarly unnecessary manner?

JACK: That lady is Miss Cecily Cardew, my ward. [Lady Bracknell *bows coldly to* Cecily]

ALGERNON: I am engaged to be married to Cecily, Aunt Augusta.

LADY BRACKNELL: I beg your pardon?

CECILY: Mr. Moncrieff and I are engaged to be married, Lady Bracknell.

LADY BRACKNELL: [*With a shiver, crossing to the sofa and sitting down*] I do not know whether there is anything peculiarly exciting in the air in this particular part of Hertfordshire, but the number of engagements that go on seems to me considerably above the proper average that statistics have laid down for our guidance. I think some preliminary enquiry on my part would not be out of place. Mr. Worthing, is Miss Cardew at all connected with any of the larger railway stations in London? I merely desire information. Until yesterday I had no idea that there were any families or persons whose origin was a Terminus. [Jack *looks perfectly furious, but restrains himself*]

JACK: [*In a clear, cold voice*] Miss Cardew is the granddaughter of the late Mr. Thomas Cardew of 149, Belgrave Square, S.W.; Gervase Park, Dorking, Surrey; and the Sporran, Fifeshire, N.B.

LADY BRACKNELL: That sounds not unsatisfactory. Three addresses always inspire confidence, even in tradesmen. But what proof have I of their authenticity?

JACK: I have carefully preserved the Court Guide of the period. They are open to your inspection, Lady Bracknell.

LADY BRACKNELL: [*Grimly*] I have known strange errors in that publication.

JACK: Miss Cardew's family solicitors are Messrs. Markby, Markby, and Markby.

LADY BRACKNELL: Markby, Markby, and Markby? A firm of the very highest position in their profession. Indeed I am told that one of the Mr. Markbys is occasionally to be seen at dinner parties. So far I am satisfied.

JACK: [*Very irritably*] How extremely kind of you, Lady Bracknell! I have also in my possession, you will be pleased to hear, certificates of Miss Cardew's birth, baptism, whooping cough, registration, vaccination, confirmation, and the measles; both the German and the English variety.

LADY BRACKNELL: Ah! A life crowded with incident, I see; though perhaps somewhat too exciting for a young girl. I am not myself in favor of premature experiences. [*Rises, looks at her watch*] Gwendolen! the time approaches for our departure. We have not a moment to lose. As a matter of form, Mr. Worthing, I had better ask you if Miss Cardew has any little fortune?

JACK: Oh, about a hundred and thirty thousand pounds in the Funds. That is all. Good-bye, Lady Bracknell. So pleased to have seen you.

LADY BRACKNELL: [*Sitting down again*] A moment, Mr. Worthing. A hundred and thirty thousand pounds! And in the Funds! Miss Cardew seems to me a most attractive young lady, now that I look at her. Few girls of the present day have any really solid qualities, any of the qualities that last, and improve with time. We live, I regret to say, in an age of surfaces. [*To* Cecily] Come over here, dear. [Cecily *goes across*] Pretty child! your dress is sadly simple, and your hair seems almost as Nature might have left it. But we can soon alter all that. A thoroughly experienced French maid produces a really marvelous result in a very brief space of time. I remember recommending one to young Lady Lancing, and after three months her own husband did not know her.

JACK: [*Aside*] And after six months nobody knew her.

LADY BRACKNELL: [*Glares at Jack for a few moments. Then bends, with a practised smile, to* Cecily] Kindly turn round, sweet child. [Cecily *turns completely round*] No, the side view is what I want. [Cecily *presents her profile*] Yes, quite as I expected. There are distinct social possibilities in your profile. The two weak points in our age are its want of principle and its want of profile. The chin a little higher, dear. Style largely depends on the way the chin is worn. They are worn very high, just at present. Algernon!

ALGERNON: Yes, Aunt Augusta!

LADY BRACKNELL: There are distinct social possibilities in Miss Cardew's profile.

ALGERNON: Cecily is the sweetest, dearest, prettiest girl in the whole world. And I don't care twopence about social possibilities.

LADY BRACKNELL: Never speak disrespectfully of society, Algernon. Only people who can't get into it do that. [*To* Cecily] Dear child, of course you know that Algernon has nothing but his debts to depend upon. But I do not approve of mercenary marriages. When I married Lord Bracknell I had no fortune of any kind. But I never dreamed for a moment of allowing that to stand in my way. Well, I suppose I must give my consent.

ALGERNON: Thank you, Aunt Augusta.

LADY BRACKNELL: Cecily, you may kiss me!

CECILY: [*Kisses her*] Thank you, Lady Bracknell.

LADY BRACKNELL: You may also address me as Aunt Augusta for the future.

CECILY: Thank you, Aunt Augusta.

LADY BRACKNELL: The marriage, I think, had better take place quite soon.

ALGERNON: Thank you, Aunt Augusta.

CECILY: Thank you, Aunt Augusta.

LADY BRACKNELL: To speak frankly, I am not in favor of long engagements. They give people the opportunity of finding out each other's character before marriage, which I think is never advisable.

JACK: I beg your pardon for interrupting you, Lady Bracknell, but this engagement is quite out of the question. I am Miss Cardew's guardian, and she cannot marry without my consent until she comes of age. That consent I absolutely decline to give.

LADY BRACKNELL: Upon what grounds, may I ask? Algernon is an extremely, I may almost say an ostentatiously, eligible young man. He has nothing, but he looks everything. What more can one desire?

JACK: It pains me very much to have to speak frankly to you, Lady Bracknell, about your nephew, but the fact is that I do not approve at all of his moral character. I suspect him of being untruthful.

[Algernon *and* Cecily *look at him in indignant amazement*]

LADY BRACKNELL: Untruthful! My nephew Algernon? Impossible! He is an Oxonian.

JACK: I fear there can be no possible doubt about the matter. This afternoon, during my temporary absence in London on an important question of romance, he obtained admission to my house by means of the false pretense of being my brother. Under an assumed name he drank, I've just been informed by my butler, an entire pint bottle of my Perrier-Jouet, Brut, '89; a wine I was specially reserving for myself. Continuing his disgraceful deception, he succeeded in the course of the afternoon in alienating the affections of my only ward. He subsequently stayed to tea, and devoured every single muffin. And what makes his conduct all the more heartless is, that he was perfectly well aware from the first that I have no brother, that I never had a brother, and that I don't intend to have a brother, not even of any kind. I distinctly told him so myself yesterday afternoon.

LADY BRACKNELL: Ahem! Mr. Worthing, after careful consideration I have decided entirely to overlook my nephew's conduct to you.

JACK: That is very generous of you, Lady Bracknell. My own decision, however, is unalterable. I decline to give my consent.

LADY BRACKNELL: [*To* Cecily] Come here, sweet child. [Cecily *goes over*] How old are you, dear?

CECILY: Well, I am really only eighteen, but I always admit to twenty when I go to evening parties.

LADY BRACKNELL: You are perfectly right in making some slight alteration. Indeed, no woman should ever be quite accurate about her age. It looks so calculating. . . . [*In meditative manner*] Eighteen, but admitting to twenty at evening parties. Well, it will not be very long before you are of age and free from the restraints of tutelage. So I don't think your guardian's consent is, after all, a matter of any importance.

JACK: Pray excuse me, Lady Bracknell, for interrupting you again, but it is only fair to tell you that according to the terms of her grandfather's will Miss Cardew does not come legally of age till she is thirty-five.

LADY BRACKNELL: That does not seem to me to be a grave objection. Thirty-five is a very attractive age. London society is full of women of the very highest birth who have, of their own free choice, remained thirty-five for years. Lady Dumbleton is an instance in point. To my own knowledge she has been thirty-five ever since she arrived at the age of forty, which was many years ago now. I see no reason why our dear Cecily should not be even still more attractive at the age you mention than she is at present. There will be a large accumulation of property.

CECILY: Algy, could you wait for me till I was thirty-five?

ALGERNON: Of course I could, Cecily. You know I could.

CECILY: Yes, I felt it instinctively, but I couldn't wait all that time. I hate waiting even five minutes for anybody. It always makes me rather cross. I am not punctual myself, I know, but I do like punctuality in others, and waiting, even to be married, is quite out of the question.

ALGERNON: Then what is to be done, Cecily?

CECILY: I don't know, Mr. Moncrieff.

LADY BRACKNELL: My dear Mr. Worthing, as Miss Cardew states positively that she cannot wait till she is thirty-five—a remark which I am bound to say seems to me to show a somewhat impatient nature—I would beg of you to reconsider your decision.

JACK: But my dear Lady Bracknell, the matter is entirely in your own hands. The moment you consent to my marriage with Gwendolen, I will most gladly allow your nephew to form an alliance with my ward.

LADY BRACKNELL: [*Rising and drawing herself up*] You must be quite aware that what you propose is out of the question.

JACK: Then a passionate celibacy is all that any of us can look forward to.

LADY BRACKNELL: That is not the destiny I propose for Gwendolen. Algernon, of course, can choose for himself. [*Pulls out her watch*] Come, dear, [Gwendolen *rises*] we have already missed five, if not six, trains. To miss any more might expose us to comment on the platform.

[*Enter* Dr. Chasuble]

CHASUBLE: Everything is quite ready for the christenings.

LADY BRACKNELL: The christenings, sir! Is not that somewhat premature?

CHASUBLE: [*Looking rather puzzled, and pointing to* Jack *and* Algernon] Both these gentlemen have expressed a desire for immediate baptism.

LADY BRACKNELL: At their age? The idea is grotesque and irreligious! Algernon, I forbid you to be baptized. I will not hear of such excesses. Lord Bracknell would be highly displeased if he learned that that was the way in which you wasted your time and money.

CHASUBLE: Am I to understand then that there are to be no christenings at all this afternoon?

JACK: I don't think that, as things are now, it would be of much practical value to either of us, Dr. Chasuble.

CHASUBLE: I am grieved to hear such sentiments from you, Mr. Worthing. They savor of the heretical views of the Anabaptists, views that I have completely refuted in four of my unpublished sermons. However, as your present mood seems to be one peculiarly secular, I will return to the church at once. Indeed, I have just been informed by the pew-opener that for the last hour and a half Miss Prism has been waiting for me in the vestry.

LADY BRACKNELL: [*Starting*] Miss Prism! Did I hear you mention a Miss Prism?

CHASUBLE: Yes, Lady Bracknell. I am on my way to join her.

LADY BRACKNELL: Pray allow me to detain you for a moment. This matter may prove to be one of vital importance to Lord Bracknell and myself. Is this Miss Prism a female of repellent aspect, remotely connected with education?

CHASUBLE: [*Somewhat indignantly*] She is the most cultivated of ladies, and the very picture of respectability.

LADY BRACKNELL: It is obviously the same person. May I ask what position she holds in your household?

CHASUBLE: [*Severely*] I am a celibate, madam.

JACK: [*Interposing*] Miss Prism, Lady Bracknell, has been for the last three years Miss Cardew's esteemed governess and valued companion.

LADY BRACKNELL: In spite of what I hear of her, I must see her at once. Let her be sent for.

CHASUBLE: [*Looking off*] She approaches; she is nigh.

[*Enter* Miss Prism *hurriedly*]

MISS PRISM: I was told you expected me in the vestry, dear Canon. I have been waiting for you there for an hour and three-quarters. [*Catches sight of* Lady Bracknell, *who has fixed her with a stony glare.* Miss Prism *grows pale and quails. She looks anxiously round as if desirous to escape*]

LADY BRACKNELL: [*In a severe, judicial voice*] Prism! [Miss Prism *bows her head in shame*] Come here, Prism! [Miss Prism *approaches in a humble manner*] Prism! Where is that baby? [*General consternation. The* Canon *starts back in horror.* Algernon *and* Jack *pretend to be anxious to shield* Cecily *and* Gwendolen *from hearing the details of a terrible public scandal*] Twenty-eight years ago, Prism, you left Lord Bracknell's house, Number 104, Upper Grosvenor Street, in charge of a perambulator that contained a baby, of the male sex. You never returned. A few weeks later, through the elaborate investigations of the Metropolitan police, the perambulator was discovered at midnight, standing by itself in a remote corner of Bayswater. It contained the manuscript of a three-volume novel of more than usually revolting sentimentality. [Miss Prism *starts in involuntary indignation*] But the baby was not there! [*Everyone looks at* Miss Prism] Prism, where is that baby? [*A pause*]

MISS PRISM: Lady Bracknell, I admit with shame that I do not know. I only wish I did. The plain facts of the case are these. On the morning of the day you mention, a day that is forever branded on my memory, I prepared as usual to take the baby out in its perambulator. I had also with me a somewhat old but capacious handbag in which I had intended to place the manuscript of a work of fiction that I had written during my few unoccupied hours. In a moment of mental abstraction, for which

I never can forgive myself, I deposited the manuscript in the bassinette, and placed the baby in the handbag.

JACK: [*Who has been listening attentively*] But where did you deposit the handbag?

MISS PRISM: Do not ask me, Mr. Worthing.

JACK: Miss Prism, this is a matter of no small importance to me. I insist on knowing where you deposited the handbag that contained that infant.

MISS PRISM: I left it in the cloak-room of one of the larger railway stations in London.

JACK: What railway station?

MISS PRISM: [*Quite crushed*] Victoria. The Brighton line. [*Sinks into a chair*]

JACK: I must retire to my room for a moment. Gwendolen, wait here for me.

GWENDOLEN: If you are not too long, I will wait here for you all my life.

[*Exit* Jack *in great excitement*]

CHASUBLE: What do you think this means, Lady Bracknell?

LADY BRACKNELL: I dare not even suspect, Dr. Chasuble. I need hardly tell you that in families of high position strange coincidences are not supposed to occur. They are hardly considered the thing. [*Noises heard overhead as if someone was throwing trunks about. Everybody looks up*]

CECILY: Uncle Jack seems strangely agitated.

CHASUBLE: Your guardian has a very emotional nature.

LADY BRACKNELL: This noise is extremely unpleasant. It sounds as if he was having an argument. I dislike arguments of any kind. They are always vulgar, and often convincing.

CHASUBLE: [*Looking up*] It has stopped now. [*The noise is redoubled*]

LADY BRACKNELL: I wish he would arrive at some conclusion.

GWENDOLEN: This suspense is terrible. I hope it will last.

[*Enter* Jack *with a handbag of black leather in his hand*]

JACK: [*Rushing over to* Miss Prism] Is this the handbag, Miss Prism? Examine it carefully before you speak. The happiness of more than one life depends on your answer.

MISS PRISM: [*Calmly*] It seems to be mine. Yes, here is the injury it received through the upsetting of a Gower Street omnibus in younger and happier days. Here is the stain on the lining caused by the explosion of a temperance beverage, an incident that occurred at Leamington. And here, on the lock, are my initials. I had forgotten that in an extravagant mood I had had them placed there. The bag is undoubtedly mine. I am delighted to have it so unexpectedly restored to me. It has been a great inconvenience being without it all these years.

JACK: [*In a pathetic voice*] Miss Prism, more is restored to you than this handbag. I was the baby you placed in it.

MISS PRISM: [*Amazed*] You?

JACK: [*Embracing her*] Yes . . . mother!

MISS PRISM: [*Recoiling in indignant astonishment*] Mr. Worthing! I am unmarried!

JACK: Unmarried! I do not deny that is a serious blow. But after all, who has the right to cast a stone against one who has suffered? Cannot repentance wipe out an act of folly? Why should there be one law for men and another for women? Mother, I forgive you. [*Tries to embrace her again*]

MISS PRISM: [*Still more indignant*] Mr. Worthing, there is some error. [*Pointing to* Lady Bracknell] There is the lady who can tell you who you really are.

JACK: [*After a pause*] Lady Bracknell, I hate to seem inquisitive, but would you kindly inform me who I am?

LADY BRACKNELL: I am afraid that the news I have to give you will not altogether please you. You are the son of my poor sister, Mrs. Moncrieff, and consequently Algernon's elder brother.

JACK: Algy's elder brother! Then I have a brother after all. I knew I had a brother! I always said I had a brother! Cecily—how could you have ever doubted that I had a brother? [*Seizes hold of* Algernon] Dr. Chasuble, my unfortunate brother. Miss Prism, my unfortunate brother. Gwendolen, my unfortunate brother. Algy, you young scoundrel, you will have to treat me with more respect in the future. You have never behaved to me like a brother in all your life.

ALGERNON: Well, not till to-day, old boy, I admit. I did my best, however, though I was out of practice. [*Shakes hands*]

GWENDOLEN: [*To* Jack] My own! But what own are you? What is your Christian name, now that you have become someone else?

JACK: Good heavens! . . . I had quite forgotten that point. Your decision on the subject of my name is irrevocable, I suppose?

GWENDOLEN: I never change, except in my affections.

CECILY: What a noble nature you have, Gwendolen!

JACK: Then the question had better be cleared up at once. Aunt Augusta, a moment. At the time when Miss Prism left me in the handbag, had I been christened already?

LADY BRACKNELL: Every luxury that money could buy, including christening, had been lavished on you by your fond and doting parents.

JACK: Then I was christened! That is settled. Now, what name was I given? Let me know the worst.

LADY BRACKNELL: Being the eldest son you were naturally christened after your father.

JACK: [*Irritably*] Yes, but what was my father's Christian name?

LADY BRACKNELL: [*Meditatively*] I cannot at the present moment recall what the General's Christian name was. But I have no doubt he had one. He was eccentric, I admit. But only in later years. And that was the result of the Indian climate, and marriage, and indigestion, and other things of that kind.

JACK: Algy! Can't you recollect what our father's Christian name was?

ALGERNON: My dear boy, we were never even on speaking terms. He died before I was a year old.

JACK: His name would appear in the Army Lists of the period, I suppose, Aunt Augusta?

LADY BRACKNELL: The General was essentially a man of peace, except in his domestic life. But I have no doubt his name would appear in any military directory.

JACK: The Army Lists of the last forty years are here. These delightful records should have been my constant study. [Rushes to bookcase and tears the books out] M. Generals . . . Mallam, Maxbohm, Magley, what ghastly names they have—Markby, Migsby, Mobbs, Moncrieff! Lieutenant 1840, Captain, Lieutenant-Colonel, Colonel, General 1869, Christian names, Ernest John. [Puts book very quietly down and speaks quite calmly] I always told you, Gwendolen, my name was Ernest, didn't I? Well, it is Ernest after all. I mean it naturally is Ernest.

LADY BRACKNELL: Yes, I remember that the General was called Ernest. I knew I had some particular reason for disliking the name.

GWENDOLEN: Ernest! My own Ernest! I felt from the first that you could have no other name!

JACK: Gwendolen, it is a terrible thing for a man to find out suddenly that all his life he has been speaking nothing but the truth. Can you forgive me?

GWENDOLEN: I can. For I feel that you are sure to change.

JACK: My own one!

CHASUBLE: [To Miss Prism] Lætitia! [Embraces her]

MISS PRISM: [Enthusiastically] Frederick! At last!

ALGERNON: Cecily! [Embraces her] At last!

JACK: Gwendolen! [Embraces her] At last!

LADY BRACKNELL: My nephew, you seem to be displaying signs of triviality.

JACK: On the contrary, Aunt Augusta, I've now realized for the first time in my life the vital Importance of Being Earnest.

TABLEAU

CURTAIN

George Bernard Shaw

(1856–1950)

The modern English drama began to achieve importance when the critic George Bernard Shaw reworked a manuscript he had written with another critic, William Archer, and presented it in 1892 to the experimental Independent Theatre of J. T. Grein under the title *Widowers' Houses*. Thereafter, Shaw enriched the theatre with play after play, his work becoming the most significant collection of modern dramatic literature by a single playwright.

A neighbor of Oscar Wilde in Dublin, Shaw descended upon London in 1876 as the "upstart son of a downstart father," after having worked for a time in a Dublin real-estate office. He brought with him a haphazard education, some training in music, acquired from his family, and an inordinate appetite for knowledge. His mother, who had found her life with an alcoholic husband unbearable, had preceded her son to London and was teaching music there; she was thus able to assist the young Shaw with her earnings. Supplementing his allowance with hack literary work, Shaw proceeded to round out his informal education, concentrating on the social sciences.

He fell first under the spell of Henry George's single-tax program and then under the influence of Marxism. In time, he became a pillar of the socialist Fabian Society, a formidable soapbox orator, and a successful Labor party candidate for municipal office. Thus he laid the groundwork for his appraisal of man as an economic and political animal and of society as a decrepit organism which required the ministrations of socialism.

Meanwhile, Shaw continued his literary pursuits, turning out a number of discursive novels between 1880 and 1883. Although these had little merit, they were excellent finger exercises for his satiric and conversational talent and may be regarded as overtures to the brilliant social critique in his dramatic work. In addition, Shaw soon acquitted himself ably as a critic of music and of the drama. Although his criticism was erratic, it was astonishingly virile and scintillating; scorning the theory of art for art's sake as untenable, he called for a living relationship between the arts and society. Progressive artists such as Wagner and Ibsen found an effective champion in his reviews and in his books *The Perfect Wagnerite* and *The Quintessence of Ibsenism*. His collected reviews, *Dramatic Opinions and Essays*, although occasionally highhanded and sometimes obtuse (as in the review of *The Importance of Being Earnest*), comprise the most distinguished body of dramatic criticism in English since the death of John Dryden. Finally, Shaw sallied into the theatre with plays of his own.

His first contribution, the naturalistic comedy *Widowers' Houses*, was an exposé of slum conditions and of the mercenary landlordism that battened on them. That it struck the stage like a thunderbolt was inevitable. Although Henry Arthur Jones had already written a realistic problem play, *Saints and Sinners* (1884), and although Jones and Arthur Wing Pinero were soon to add other studies of the social scene, such as the former's *Michael and His Lost Angel* and the latter's *The Second Mrs. Tanqueray*, Shaw's first contribution was of a different order. Jones and Pinero were by inclination and intention compromisers, and their promotion of the realistic or the social drama was mild and tentative. Shaw, on the other hand, penetrated deeply into issues, spoke his mind freely, and gave no quarter.

Shaw's *Mrs. Warren's Profession* (1898) exposed the economic basis of prostitution and the hypocrisies of an upper-class society that drew profits from exploitation of labor in the sweatshops—a newer kind of immorality than commercialized lechery. His *Major Barbara* (1905) proved a blunt indictment of philanthropy as a mere façade for a profit-minded social order responsible for the very miseries it tries to alleviate. Although in his later plays he departed from strictly realistic problem drama, Shaw continued to express himself uncompromisingly about the larger issues of the twentieth century. He wrote wisely about British imperialism and Ireland, in *John Bull's Other Island;* about the futility of the old war-ridden social order, in *Heartbreak House;* about the failure of the Ramsay MacDonald brand of parliamentary socialism, in *The Apple Cart;* about the hopelessness of the situation in Europe on the eve of the Second World War, in *Too True to Be Good;* and about the coming of fascism and revolution, in *On the Rocks.* Even in these plays his polemics were edged with wit, and he performed some dazzling somersaults while delivering them.

For a long time, English critics professed to dismiss Shaw as a clever and paradoxical mountebank. Indeed, he began early to evince a talent for comic improvisation that had not been approximated since the death of Molière. But even his lighter exercises—those in which he did not concern himself directly with economic and political problems—were serious in aim. His second play, *Arms and the Man,* deflated military glory; *The Devil's Disciple* and *Captain Brassbound's Conversion* subjected heroism to provocative examination; *Candida, The Philanderer, You Never Can Tell,* and *Getting Married* brought domestic relations into his field of observation; *Man and Superman* gave incisive treatment to love and the biological drive. Throughout these and other plays Shaw maintained a brilliant barrage against traditional obfuscations and pretensions. Representative was his satire *Pygmalion,* in which the difference between a cockney flower girl and a duchess is dismissed as a matter of economics and of accomplishments obtainable with a little training.

Shaw's range proved altogether remarkable. In the writing of imaginative drama, he revealed a staggering virtuosity with the vitalistic fantasia *Back to Methuselah,* which also entertained the comic idea that men make a mess of this world because they do not live long enough to develop any sense. In the two historical pieces *Caesar and Cleopatra* and *Saint Joan,* he practically changed dramatic horizons. *Caesar and Cleopatra* was a wholly modern historical comedy; *Saint Joan* combined spiritual exaltation with the apparatus of historical materialism to a degree that has not yet been even remotely approached by other playwrights. And if it is true, as it has been charged, that many of Shaw's characters were simply mouthpieces, it is indisputable that he proved himself a master of characterization whenever he cared to exercise that art. Caesar is a brilliant portrait of a whole man and genius; the saints in Shaw's comedy of early Christianity, *Androcles and the Lion,* are supremely human; Barbara and Undershaft, in *Major Barbara,* are memorable; *Candida* is one of the outstanding character dramas in the English language.

In view of these achievements and of this versatile master's influence on the theatre as a social philosopher and as the virtual creator of modern comedy of ideas, it is difficult to pigeonhole him. He has been inconsistent in his thinking and in his panaceas, oscillating in different plays between socialist idealism and superman-worship, between a passion for social democracy and faith in a dictatorship of the intelligent. Nevertheless, he has pursued one main objective—that of building the "good society," the City of God on earth. Perhaps the best description of his dramatic genius is to be found in Ludwig Lewisohn's estimate of him, made as early as 1915: "Mr. George Bernard Shaw is a writer of comedy with a tragic cry in his soul. In the middle ages he would have been a great saint, appalled at the gracelessness of men's hearts, militant for the kingdom of God. Today he is a playwright, appalled at the muddle-headedness of the race, a fighter for the conquest of reason over unreason, of order over disorder, of economy over waste." "The real joke," Shaw himself reminded us, "is that I am earnest."

"The real joke" is, however, somewhat more complicated, for the earnestness of the would-be reformer lost its sociological character as soon as Shaw's creative imagination came into play. There was thrust upon the stage a personality the antithesis of our conception of a reformer with a blueprint for society. On one hand, Shaw revealed a spirit highly responsive to the nobility and loneliness of exceptional people and painfully aware of human contradictions that social "uplift" cannot alter. On the other, he displayed a volatile imagination that invariably carried him beyond the pulpit into regions of pointed fantastication and theatrical invention. In short, the creative spirit, the Life Force which he celebrated, had its way with Shaw, and found in him a ready collaborator.

In *Candida,* Shaw's dramatic talent is more uniform than in any other play except *Saint Joan,* for his approach to playwriting has been in many instances regrettably haphazard. Here his mastery of characterization is beyond dispute; his heroine is a completely modern and remarkably rounded person —she is Ibsen's Nora grown up and self-possessed. Comic technique and a fundamental seriousness are so ably fused in this work that it may rightly be regarded as one of the masterpieces of high comedy. Social issues such as the emancipation of women and the exploitation of labor are present, but they are subordinated to the interest in Candida's character. Finally, this comedy has the virtue of coming to instant life on the stage.

Shaw once wrote, "When you get accustomed to my habit of mind, you will not find me such bad company. But please do not think you can take in the work of my long life-time at one reading." This is true both of his plays and of his nondramatic writing. But, though they bear rereading, the plays are almost crystalline in their clarity. And more than most of them, *Candida* reveals its substance to normal eyesight—and without the need of sociological hairsplitting. Even "the secret in the poet's heart," which Marchbanks takes with him on his exit into the night, is no conundrum. Neither the profoundest nor the most provocative of Shaw's plays, representing, as Burns Mantle noted, "a compromise of the radical with the conformist dramatist," *Candida* simply represents its author at the peak of his ability to transfigure traditional material for the modern mind.

Composed in 1894, *Candida* belongs to a group of dramas that Shaw called "Pleasant Plays." But its pleasantness does not lie in the conventional reassurance that a marriage can be invulnerable; it is the gay wisdom impacted into this domestic comedy that makes it pleasant. If the tradition of marriage is upheld, it is not on traditional grounds but on modern terms, free of social hypocrisy and self-delusion. In the process of dramatic complication and discussion, the principals achieve self-knowledge, which, being a portable commodity, can also be taken out of the domestic forum. And here Shaw, now playing the Ibsenite with suavity, was serving substantially the same principle of self-realization that Ibsen proposed as an objective. Candida, remaining true to her nature and need, finds self-realization in keeping her marriage intact; she also teaches Marchbanks to know himself and to live in conformity with that knowledge. Marchbanks' secret, well described by Eric Bentley although better demonstrated by Shaw himself, "is the secret of Shaw the Outsider who is the real Insider, the man who is strong enough to leave the homestead and live with himself and his vision."

Against the opinion that *Candida* is a triumph of character comedy—although one could hardly fail to think so when an actress such as Katharine Cornell plays the Reverend Morell's wife—we may set A. B. Walkley's quizzical impression when he saw the play at the Court Theatre in April 1904. "Fantasy," wrote that scintillating critic, "has its place in the theatre, as well as realism, and that is one reason why the theatre has room for Mr. Bernard Shaw. His method of travestying life is to eliminate from it everything but the pure intelligence. . . . We are such stuff as dreams, not manuals of logic, are made of. 'Why did I love my friend?' asks Montaigne, and gives the only true answer: 'Because it was he, because it was I.' By systematically ignoring this all-important side of life, all its subconscious and unconscious elements, by representing life in general and love in particular as based upon ratiocination, Mr. Shaw obtains most amusing results." Walkley proceeds to question Shaw's reduction of the main drama to discussion and to the rational conclusions of Candida, finding the external reality of the char-

acters amusingly at variance with "the internal fantasy of their actions." We may reply that the characters, especially Candida, merely articulate in rational terms what they must feel for irrational reasons; and that this is the way of real people whose cortex is in good working order. And we may propose a reason different from Walkley's, if perhaps no less facetious, for the humor of the play, apart from the amusing situation: the incongruity of sense in a senseless world is a rich source of comedy. In any case, there is warrant for believing that Shaw would think so, if he were pressed to account for the main source of his humor. As usual, however, Walkley scored a point in his critical crotchet. Our respect for *Candida* as a character comedy and the amazement of those who are surprised that Shaw should have been capable of writing one must not obscure the fact that it *is* a comedy of ideas.

BIBLIOGRAPHY: Eric Bentley, *Bernard Shaw,* 1947; Bentley, *The Playwright as Thinker* (pp. 137–157, 162–172, 186–189), 1946; G. K. Chesterton, *George Bernard Shaw,* 1909; John Gassner, *Masters of the Drama* (pp. 591–616), 1940, 1945; Archibald Henderson, *Bernard Shaw: Playboy and Prophet,* 1932; James Huneker, *Iconoclasts* (pp. 233–268), 1905; Hesketh Pearson, *G.B.S.: A Full-Length Portrait,* 1942; A. B. Walkley, *Drama and Life* (pp. 214–250), 1908; Edmund Wilson, *The Triple Thinkers* (pp. 220–265), 1938; S. Winstén, ed., *G.B.S. 90,* 1946.

CANDIDA

By George Bernard Shaw

ACT I.

A fine October morning in the northeast suburbs of London, a vast district many miles away from the London of Mayfair and St. James', much less known there than the Paris of the Rue de Rivoli and the Champs Elysées, and much less narrow, squalid, fetid and airless in its slums; strong in comfortable, prosperous middle-class life; wide-streeted, myriad-populated; well-served with ugly iron urinals, Radical clubs, tram lines, and a perpetual stream of yellow cars; enjoying in its main thoroughfares the luxury of grass-grown "front gardens," untrodden by the foot of man save as to the path from the gate to the hall door; but blighted by an intolerable monotony of miles and miles of graceless, characterless brick houses, black iron railings, stony pavements, slaty roofs, and respectably ill-dressed or disreputably poorly-dressed people, quite accustomed to the place, and mostly plodding about somebody else's work, which they would not do if they themselves could help it. The little energy and eagerness that crop up show themselves in cockney cupidity and business "push." Even the policemen and the chapels are not infrequent enough to break the monotony. The sun is shining cheerfully; there is no fog; and though the smoke effectually prevents anything, whether faces and hands or bricks and mortar, from looking fresh and clean, it is not hanging heavily enough to trouble a Londoner.

This desert of unattractiveness has its oasis. Near the outer end of the Hackney Road is a park of 217 acres, fenced in, not by railings, but by a wooden paling, and containing plenty of greensward, trees, a lake for bathers, flower beds with the flowers arranged carefully in patterns by the admired cockney art of carpet gardening and a sandpit, imported from the seaside for the delight of the children, but speedily deserted on its becoming a natural vermin preserve for all the petty fauna of Kingsland, Hackney and Hoxton. A bandstand, an unfinished forum for religious, anti-religious and political orators, cricket pitches, a gymnasium, and an old-fashioned stone kiosk are among its attractions. Wherever the prospect is bounded by trees or rising green grounds, it is a pleasant place. Where the ground stretches flat to the gray palings, with bricks and mortar, sky signs, crowded chimneys and smoke beyond, the prospect makes desolate and sordid.

The best view of Victoria Park is from the front window of St. Dominic's Parsonage, from which not a single chimney is visible. The parsonage is a semi-detached villa with a front garden and a porch. Visitors go up the flight of steps to the porch: tradespeople and members of the family go down by a door under the steps to the basement, with a breakfast room, used for all meals, in front, and the kitchen at the back. Upstairs, on the level of the hall door, is the drawing-room, with its large plate glass window looking on the park. In this room, the only sitting-room that can be spared from the children and the family meals, the parson, the Reverend James Mavor Morell, does his work. He is sitting in a strong round-backed revolving chair at the right hand end of a long table, which stands across the window, so that he can cheer himself with the view of the park at his elbow. At the opposite end of the table, adjoining it, is a little table only half the width of the other, with a typewriter on it. His typist is sitting at this machine, with her back to the window. The large table is littered with pamphlets, journals, letters, nests of drawers, an office diary, postage scales and the like. A spare chair for visitors having business with the parson is in the middle, turned to his end. Within reach of his hand is a stationery case, and a cabinet photograph in a frame. Behind him the right hand wall, recessed above the fireplace, is fitted with bookshelves, on which an adept eye can measure the parson's divinity and casuistry by a complete set of Browning's poems and Maurice's Theological Essays, and guess at his politics from a yellow-backed Progress and Poverty, Fabian Essays, a Dream of John Ball, Marx's Capital, and half a dozen other literary landmarks in Socialism. Opposite him on the left, near the typewriter, is the door. Further down the room, opposite the fireplace, a bookcase stands on a cellaret, with a sofa near it. There is a generous fire burning; and the hearth, with a comfortable armchair and a japanned flower-painted coal scuttle at one side, a miniature chair for a boy or girl on the other, a nicely varnished wooden mantelpiece, with neatly moulded shelves, tiny bits of mirror let into the panels, and a traveling clock in a leather case (the inevitable wedding present), and on the wall above a large autotype of the chief figure in Titian's Virgin of the Assumption, is very inviting. Altogether the room is the room of a good housekeeper, vanquished, as far as the table is concerned, by an untidy man, but elsewhere mistress of the situation. The furniture, in its ornamental aspect, betrays the style of the advertised "drawing-room suite" of the pushing suburban furniture dealer; but there is noth-

ing useless or pretentious in the room. The paper and paneling are dark, throwing the big cheery window and the park outside into strong relief.

The Reverend James Mavor Morell is a Christian Socialist clergyman of the Church of England, and an active member of the Guild of St. Matthew and the Christian Social Union. A vigorous, genial, popular man of forty, robust and goodlooking, full of energy, with pleasant, hearty, considerate manners, and a sound, unaffected voice, which he uses with the clean, athletic articulation of a practised orator, and with a wide range and perfect command of expression. He is a first-rate clergyman, able to say what he likes to whom he likes, to lecture people without setting himself up against them, to impose his authority on them without humiliating them, and to interfere in their business without impertinence. His well spring of spiritual enthusiasm and sympathetic emotion has never run dry for a moment: he still eats and sleeps heartily enough to win the daily battle between exhaustion and recuperation triumphantly. Withal, a great baby, pardonably vain of his powers and unconsciously pleased with himself. He has a healthy complexion, a good forehead, with the brows somewhat blunt, and the eyes bright and eager, a mouth resolute, but not particularly well cut, and a substantial nose, with the mobile, spreading nostrils of the dramatic orator, but, like all his features, void of subtlety.

The typist, Miss Proserpine Garnett, is a brisk little woman of about 30, of the lower middle class, neatly but cheaply dressed in a black merino skirt and a blouse, rather pert and quick of speech, and not very civil in her manner, but sensitive and affectionate. She is clattering away busily at her machine whilst Morell *opens the last of his morning's letters. He realizes its contents with a comic groan of despair.*

PROSERPINE: Another lecture?

MORELL: Yes. The Hoxton Freedom Group want me to address them on Sunday morning. [*Great emphasis on "Sunday," this being the unreasonable part of the business*] What are they?

PROSERPINE: Communist Anarchists, I think.

MORELL: Just like Anarchists not to know that they can't have a parson on Sunday! Tell them to come to church if they want to hear me: it will do them good. Say I can only come on Mondays and Thursdays. Have you the diary there?

PROSERPINE: [*Taking up the diary*] Yes.

MORELL: Have I any lecture on for next Monday?

PROSERPINE: [*Referring to diary*] Tower Hamlets Radical Club.

MORELL: Well, Thursday then?

PROSERPINE: English Land Restoration League.

MORELL: What next?

PROSERPINE: Guild of St. Matthew on Monday. Independent Labor Party, Greenwich Branch, on Thursday. Monday, Social-Democratic Federation,

Mile End Branch. Thursday, first Confirmation class —[*Impatiently*] Oh, I'd better tell them you can't come. They're only half a dozen ignorant and conceited costermongers without five shillings between them.

MORELL: [*Amused*] Ah; but you see they're near relatives of mine, Miss Garnett.

PROSERPINE: [*Staring at him*] Relatives of yours!

MORELL: Yes: we have the same father—in Heaven.

PROSERPINE: [*Relieved*] Oh, is that all?

MORELL: [*With a sadness which is a luxury to a man whose voice expresses it so finely*] Ah, you don't believe it. Everybody says it: nobody believes it—nobody. [*Briskly, getting back to business*] Well, well! Come, Miss Proserpine, can't you find a date for the costers? What about the 25th?: that was vacant the day before yesterday.

PROSERPINE: [*Referring to diary*] Engaged—the Fabian Society.

MORELL: Bother the Fabian Society! Is the 28th gone, too?

PROSERPINE: City dinner. You're invited to dine with the Founder's Company.

MORELL: That'll do; I'll go to the Hoxton Group of Freedom instead. [*She enters the engagement in silence, with implacable disparagement of the Hoxton Anarchists in every line of her face.* Morell *bursts open the cover of a copy of* The Church Reformer, *which has come by post, and glances through Mr. Stewart Hendlam's leader and the Guild of St. Matthew news. These proceedings are presently enlivened by the appearance of* Morell's *curate, the Reverend Alexander Mill, a young gentleman gathered by* Morell *from the nearest University settlement, whither he had come from Oxford to give the east end of London the benefit of his university training. He is a conceitedly well intentioned, enthusiastic, immature person, with nothing positively unbearable about him except a habit of speaking with his lips carefully closed for half an inch from each corner, a finicking articulation, and a set of horribly corrupt vowels, notably ow for o, this being his chief means of bringing Oxford refinement to bear on Hackney vulgarity.* Morell, *whom he has won over by a doglike devotion, looks up indulgently from* The Church Reformer *as he enters, and remarks*] Well, Lexy! Late again, as usual.

LEXY: I'm afraid so. I wish I could get up in the morning.

MORELL: [*Exulting in his own energy*] Ha! ha! [*Whimsically*] Watch and pray, Lexy: watch and pray.

LEXY: I know. [*Rising wittily to the occasion*] But how can I watch and pray when I am asleep? Isn't that so, Miss Prossy?

PROSERPINE: [*Sharply*] Miss Garnett, if you please.

LEXY: I beg your pardon—Miss Garnett.

PROSERPINE: You've got to do all the work to-day.

LEXY: Why?

PROSERPINE: Never mind why. It will do you good to earn your supper before you eat it, for once in a way, as I do. Come don't dawdle. You should have been off on your rounds half an hour ago.

LEXY: [*Perplexed*] Is she in earnest, Morell?

MORELL: [*In the highest spirits—his eyes dancing*] Yes. I am going to dawdle to-day.

LEXY: You! You don't know how.

MORELL: [*Heartily*] Ha! ha! Don't I? I'm going to have this day all to myself—or at least the forenoon. My wife's coming back: she's due here at 11:45.

LEXY: [*Surprised*] Coming back already—with the children? I thought they were to stay to the end of the month.

MORELL: So they are: she's only coming up for two days, to get some flannel things for Jimmy, and to see how we're getting on without her.

LEXY: [*Anxiously*] But, my dear Morell, if what Jimmy and Fluffy had was scarlatina, do you think it wise—

MORELL: Scarlatina!—rubbish, German measles. I brought it into the house myself from the Pycroft Street School. A parson is like a doctor, my boy: he must face infection as a soldier must face bullets. [*He rises and claps* Lexy *on the shoulder*] Catch the measles if you can, Lexy: she'll nurse you; and what a piece of luck that will be for you!—eh?

LEXY: [*Smiling uneasily*] It's so hard to understand you about Mrs. Morell—

MORELL: [*Tenderly*] Ah, my boy, get married—get married to a good woman; and then you'll understand. That's a foretaste of what will be best in the Kingdom of Heaven we are trying to establish on earth. That will cure you of dawdling. An honest man feels that he must pay Heaven for every hour of happiness with a good spell of hard, unselfish work to make others happy. We have no more right to consume happiness without producing it than to consume wealth without producing it. Get a wife like my Candida; and you'll always be in arrear with your repayment.

[*He pats* Lexy *affectionately on the back, and is leaving the room when* Lexy *calls to him*]

LEXY: Oh, wait a bit: I forgot. [Morell *halts and turns with the door knob in his hand*] Your father-in-law is coming round to see you. [Morell *shuts the door again, with a complete change of manner.*]

MORELL: [*Surprised and not pleased*] Mr. Burgess?

LEXY: Yes. I passed him in the park, arguing with somebody. He gave me good day and asked me to let you know that he was coming.

MORELL: [*Half incredulous*] But he hasn't called here for—I may almost say for years. Are you sure, Lexy? You're not joking, are you?

LEXY: [*Earnestly*] No, sir, really.

MORELL: [*Thoughtfully*] Hm! Time for him to take another look at Candida before she grows out of his knowledge. [*He resigns himself to the inevi-table, and goes out.* Lexy *looks after him with beaming, foolish worship.*]

LEXY: What a good man! What a thorough, loving soul he is!

[*He takes* Morell's *place at the table, making himself very comfortable as he takes out a cigarette*]

PROSERPINE: [*Impatiently, pulling the letter she has been working at off the typewriter and folding it*] Oh, a man ought to be able to be fond of his wife without making a fool of himself about her.

LEXY: [*Shocked*] Oh, Miss Prossy!

PROSERPINE: [*Rising busily and coming to the stationery case to get an envelope, in which she encloses the letter as she speaks*] Candida here, and Candida there, and Candida everywhere! [*She licks the envelope*] It's enough to drive anyone out of their senses [*Thumping the envelope to make it stick*] to hear a perfectly commonplace woman raved about in that absurd manner merely because she's got good hair, and a tolerable figure.

LEXY: [*With reproachful gravity*] I think her extremely beautiful, Miss Garnett. [*He takes the photograph up; looks at it; and adds, with even greater impressiveness*] Extremely beautiful. How fine her eyes are!

PROSERPINE: Her eyes are not a bit better than mine—now! [*He puts down the photograph and stares austerely at her*] And you know very well that you think me dowdy and second rate enough.

LEXY: [*Rising majestically*] Heaven forbid that I should think of any of God's creatures in such a way! [*He moves stiffly away from her across the room to the neighborhood of the bookcase*]

PROSERPINE: Thank you. That's very nice and comforting.

LEXY: [*Saddened by her depravity*] I had no idea you had any feeling against Mrs. Morell.

PROSERPINE: [*Indignantly*] I have no feeling against her. She's very nice, very good-hearted: I'm very fond of her and can appreciate her real qualities far better than any man can. [*He shakes his head sadly and turns to the bookcase, looking along the shelves for a volume. She follows him with intense pepperiness*] You don't believe me? [*He turns and faces her. She pounces at him with spitfire energy*] You think I'm jealous. Oh, what a profound knowledge of the human heart you have, Mr. Lexy Mill! How well you know the weaknesses of Woman, don't you? It must be so nice to be a man and have a fine penetrating intellect instead of mere emotions like us, and to know that the reason we don't share your amorous delusions is that we're all jealous of one another! [*She abandons him with a toss of her shoulders, and crosses to the fire to warm her hands*]

LEXY: Ah, if you women only had the same clue to Man's strength that you have to his weakness, Miss Prossy, there would be no Woman Question.

PROSERPINE: [*Over her shoulder, as she stoops,*

holding her hands to the blaze] Where did you hear Morell say that? You didn't invent it yourself: you're not clever enough.

LEXY: That's quite true. I am not ashamed of owing him that, as I owe him so many other spiritual truths. He said it at the annual conference of the Women's Liberal Federation. Allow me to add that though they didn't appreciate it, I, a mere man, did. [*He turns to the bookcase again, hoping that this may leave her crushed*]

PROSERPINE: [*Putting her hair straight at the little panel of mirror in the mantelpiece*] Well, when you talk to me, give me your own ideas, such as they are, and not his. You never cut a poorer figure than when you are trying to imitate him.

LEXY: [*Stung*] I try to follow his example, not to imitate him.

PROSERPINE: [*Coming at him again on her way back to her work*] Yes, you do: you imitate him. Why do you tuck your umbrella under your left arm instead of carrying it in your hand like anyone else? Why do you walk with your chin stuck out before you, hurrying along with that eager look in your eyes—you, who never get up before half past nine in the morning? Why do you say "knoaledge" in church, though you always say "knollledge" in private conversation! Bah! do you think I don't know? [*She goes back to the typewriter*] Here, come and set about your work: we've wasted enough time for one morning. Here's a copy of the diary for to-day. [*She hands him a memorandum*]

LEXY: [*Deeply offended*] Thank you. [*He takes it and stands at the table with his back to her, reading it. She begins to transcribe her shorthand notes on the typewriter without troubling herself about his feelings. Mr. Burgess enters unannounced. He is a man of sixty, made coarse and sordid by the compulsory selfishness of petty commerce, and later on softened into sluggish bumptiousness by overfeeding and commercial success. A vulgar, ignorant, guzzling man, offensive and contemptuous to people whose labor is cheap, respectful to wealth and rank, and quite sincere and without rancor or envy in both attitudes. Finding him without talent, the world has offered him no decently paid work except ignoble work, and he has become, in consequence, somewhat boggish. But he has no suspicion of this himself, and honestly regards his commercial prosperity as the inevitable and socially wholesome triumph of the ability, industry, shrewdness and experience in business of a man who in private is easygoing, affectionate and humorously convivial to a fault. Corporeally, he is a podgy man, with a square, clean-shaven face and a square beard under his chin; dust colored, with a patch of gray in the centre, and small watery blue eyes with a plaintively sentimental expression, which he transfers easily to his voice by his habit of pompously intoning his sentences*]

BURGESS: [*Stopping on the threshold, and looking round*] They told me Mr. Morell was here.

PROSERPINE: [*Rising*] He's upstairs. I'll fetch him for you.

BURGESS: [*Staring boorishly at her*] You're not the same young lady as hused to typewrite for him?

PROSERPINE: No.

BURGESS: [*Assenting*] No: she was younger. [*Miss Garnett stolidly stares at him; then goes out with great dignity. He receives this quite obtusely, and crosses to the hearth-rug, where he turns and spreads himself with his back to the fire*] Startin' on your rounds, Mr. Mill?

LEXY: [*Folding his paper and pocketing it*] Yes: I must be off presently.

BURGESS: [*Momentously*] Don't let me detain you, Mr. Mill. What I come about is private between me and Mr. Morell.

LEXY: [*Ruffily*] I have no intention of intruding, I am sure, Mr. Burgess. Good morning.

BURGESS: [*Patronizingly*] Oh, good morning to you. [*Morell returns as Lexy is making for the door*]

MORELL: [*To Lexy*] Off to work?

LEXY: Yes, sir.

MORELL: [*Patting him affectionately on the shoulder*] Take my silk handkerchief and wrap your throat up. There's a cold wind. Away with you.

[*Lexy brightens up, and goes out*]

BURGESS: Spoilin' your curates, as usu'l, James. Good mornin'. When I pay a man, an' 'is livin' depen's on me, I keep him in his place.

MORELL: [*Rather shortly*] I always keep my curates in their places as my helpers and comrades. If you get as much work out of your clerks and warehousemen as I do out of my curates, you must be getting rich pretty fast. Will you take your old chair?

[*He points with curt authority to the arm chair beside the fireplace; then takes the spare chair from the table and sits down in front of Burgess.*]

BURGESS: [*Without moving*] Just the same as hever, James!

MORELL: When you last called—it was about three years ago, I think—you said the same thing a little more frankly. Your exact words then were: "Just as big a fool as ever, James?"

BURGESS: [*Soothingly*] Well, perhaps I did; but [*with conciliatory cheerfulness*] I meant no offence by it. A clorgyman is privileged to be a bit of a fool, you know: it's on'y becomin' in his profession that he should. Anyhow, I come here, not to rake up hold differences, but to let bygones be bygones. [*Suddenly becoming very solemn, and approaching Morell*] James: three year ago, you done me a hill turn. You done me hout of a contrac'; an' when I gev you 'arsh words in my nat'ral disappointment, you turned my daughrter again me. Well, I've come to act the part of a Cheristhin. [*Offering his hand*] I forgive you, James.

MORELL: [*Starting up*] Confound your impudence!

BURGESS: [*Retreating, with almost lachrymose deprecation of this treatment*] Is that becomin' language for a clorgyman, James?—and you so par-tic'lar, too?

MORELL: [*Hotly*] No, sir, it is not becoming language for a clergyman. I used the wrong word. I should have said damn your impudence: that's what St. Paul, or any honest priest would have said to you. Do you think I have forgotten that tender of yours for the contract to supply clothing to the work-house?

BURGESS: [*In a paroxysm of public spirit*] I acted in the interest of the ratepayers, James. It was the lowest tender: you can't deny that.

MORELL: Yes, the lowest, because you paid worse wages than any other employer—starvation wages—aye, worse than starvation wages—to the women who made the clothing. Your wages would have driven them to the streets to keep body and soul together. [*Getting angrier and angrier*] Those women were my parishioners. I shamed the Guardians out of accepting your tender: I shamed the ratepayers out of letting them do it: I shamed everybody but you. [*Boiling over*] How dare you, sir, come here and offer to forgive me, and talk about your daughter, and—

BURGESS: Easy, James, easy, easy. Don't git hinto a fluster about nothink. I've howned I was wrong.

MORELL: [*Fuming about*] Have you? I didn't hear you.

BURGESS: Of course I did. I hown it now. Come: I harsk your pardon for the letter I wrote you. Is that enough?

MORELL: [*Snapping his fingers*] That's nothing. Have you raised the wages?

BURGESS: [*Triumphantly*] Yes.

MORELL: [*Stopping dead*] What!

BURGESS: [*Unctuously*] I've turned a moddle hem-ployer. I don't hemploy no women now: they're all sacked; and the work is done by machinery. Not a man 'as less than six-pence a *hour*; and the skilled 'ands gits the Trade Union rate. [*Proudly*] What 'ave you to say to me now?

MORELL: [*Overwhelmed*] Is it possible! Well, there's more joy in heaven over one sinner that repenteth—[*Going to* Burgess *with an explosion of apologetic cordiality*] My dear Burgess, I most heartily beg your pardon for my hard thoughts of you. [*Grasps his hand*] And now, don't you feel the better for the change? Come, confess, you're hap-pier. You look happier.

BURGESS: [*Ruefully*] Well, p'raps I do. I s'pose I must, since you notice it. At all events, I git my contrax asseppit (accepted) by the County Council. [*Savagely*] They dussent 'ave nothink to do with me unless I paid fair wages—curse 'em for a parcel o' meddlin' fools!

MORELL: [*Dropping his hand, utterly discouraged*] So that was why you raised the wages! [*He sits down moodily*]

BURGESS: [*Severely, in spreading, mounting tones*] Why else should I do it? What does it lead to but drink and huppishness in workin' men? [*He seats himself magisterially in the easy chair*] It's hall very well for you, James: it gits you hinto the papers and makes a great man of you; but you never think of the 'arm you do, puttin' money into the pockets of workin' men that they don't know 'ow to spend, and takin' it from people that might be makin' a good huse on it.

MORELL: [*With a heavy sigh, speaking with cold politeness*] What is your business with me this morning? I shall not pretend to believe that you are here merely out of family sentiment.

BURGESS: [*Obstinately*] Yes, I ham—just family sentiment and nothink else.

MORELL: [*With weary calm*] I don't believe you!

BURGESS: [*Rising threateningly*] Don't say that to me again, James Mavor Morell.

MORELL: [*Unmoved*] I'll say it just as often as may be necessary to convince you that it's true. i don't believe you.

BURGESS: [*Collapsing into an abyss of wounded feeling*] Oh, well, if you're determined to be un-friendly, I s'pose I'd better go. [*He moves reluctantly towards the door.* Morell *makes no sign. He lingers*] I didn't hexpect to find a hun-forgivin' spirit in you, James. [Morell *still not responding, he takes a few more reluctant steps downwards. Then he comes back whining*] We huseter git on well enough, spite of our different opinions. Why are you so changed to me? I give you my word I come here in pyorr (pure) frenliness, not wishin' to be on bad terms with my hown daughrter's 'usban'. Come, James: be a Cheristhin and shake 'ands. [*He puts his hand sentimentally on* Morell's *shoulder.*]

MORELL: [*Looking up at him thoughtfully*] Look here, Burgess. Do you want to be as welcome here as you were before you lost that contract?

BURGESS: I do, James. I do—honest.

MORELL: Then why don't you behave as you did then?

BURGESS: [*Cautiously removing his hand*] 'Ow d'y' mean?

MORELL: I'll tell you. You thought me a young fool then.

BURGESS: [*Coaxingly*] No, I didn't, James. I—

MORELL: [*Cutting him short*] Yes, you did. And I thought you an old scoundrel.

BURGESS: [*Most vehemently deprecating this gross self-accusation on* Morell's *part*] No, you didn't, James. Now you do yourself a hinjustice.

MORELL: Yes, I did. Well, that did not prevent our getting on very well together. God made you what I call a scoundrel as he made me what you call a fool. [*The effect of this observation on* Burgess *is to remove the keystone of his moral arch. He becomes bodily weak, and, with his eyes fixed on* Morell *in a helpless stare, puts out his hand appre-hensively to balance himself, as if the floor had suddenly sloped under him.* Morell *proceeds in the same tone of quiet conviction*] It was not for me to quarrel with his handiwork in the one case more than in the other. So long as you come here honestly as a self-respecting, thorough, convinced scoundrel, justifying your scoundrelism, and proud of it, you are welcome. But [*and now Morell's tone becomes formidable; and he rises and strikes the back of the chair for greater emphasis*] I won't have you here sniveling about being a model employer and a converted man when you're only an apostate with your coat turned for the sake of a County Council contract. [*He nods at him to enforce the point; then goes to the hearth-rug, where he takes up a comfortably commanding position with his back to the fire, and continues*] No: I like a man to be true to himself, even in wickedness. Come now: either take your hat and go; or else sit down and give me a good scoundrelly reason for wanting to be friends with me. [Burgess, *whose emotions have subsided sufficiently to be expressed by a dazed grin, is relieved by this concrete proposition. He ponders it for a moment, and then, slowly and very modestly, sits down in the chair* Morell *has just left*] That's right. Now, out with it.

BURGESS: [*Chuckling in spite of himself*] Well, you are a queer bird, James, and no mistake. But [*almost enthusiastically*] one carnt 'elp likin' you; besides, as I said afore, of course one don't take all a clorgyman says seriously, or the world couldn't go on. Could it now? [*He composes himself for graver discourse, and turning his eyes on* Morell *proceeds with dull seriousness*] Well, I don't mind tellin' you, since it's your wish we should be free with one another, that I did think you a bit of a fool once; but I'm beginnin' to think that p'raps I was be'ind the times a bit.

MORELL: [*Delighted*] Aha! You're finding that out at last, are you?

BURGESS: [*Portentously*] Yes, times 'as changed mor'n I could a believed. Five yorr (year) ago, no sensible man would a thought o' takin' up with your ideas. I hused to wonder you was let preach at all. Why, I know a clorgyman that 'as bin kep' hout of his job for yorrs by the Bishop of London, although the pore feller's not a bit more religious than you are. But to-day, if henyone was to offer to bet me a thousan' poun' that you'll end by bein' a bishop yourself, I shouldn't venture to take the bet. You and yore crew are gettin' hinfluential: I can see that. They'll 'ave to give you something someday, if it's only to stop yore mouth. You 'ad the right instinc' arter all, James: the line you took is the payin' line in the long run fur a man o' your sort.

MORELL: [*Decisively—offering his hand*] Shake hands, Burgess. Now you're talking honestly. I don't think they'll make me a bishop; but if they do, I'll introduce you to the biggest jobbers I can get to come to my dinner parties.

BURGESS: [*Who has risen with a sheepish grin and accepted the hand of friendship*] You will 'ave your joke, James. Our quarrel's made up now, isn't it?

A WOMAN'S VOICE: Say yes, James.

[*Startled, they turn quickly and find that* Candida *has just come in, and is looking at them with an amused maternal indulgence which is her characteristic expression. She is a woman of 33, well built, well nourished, likely, one guesses, to become matronly later on, but now quite at her best, with the double charm of youth and motherhood. Her ways are those of a woman who has found that she can always manage people by engaging their affection, and who does so frankly and instinctively without the smallest scruple. So far, she is like any other pretty woman who is just clever enough to make the most of her sexual attractions for trivially selfish ends; but* Candida's *serene brow, courageous eyes, and well-set mouth and chin signify largeness of mind and dignity of character to ennoble her cunning in the affections. A wisehearted observer, looking at her, would at once guess that whoever had placed the Virgin of the Assumption over her hearth did so because he fancied some spiritual resemblance between them, and yet would not suspect either her husband or herself of any such idea, or indeed of any concern with the art of Titian. Just now she is in bonnet and mantle, laden with a strapped rug with her umbrella stuck through it, a handbag, and a supply of illustrated papers.*]

MORELL: [*Shocked at his remissness*] Candida! Why—[*Looks at his watch, and is horrified to find it so late*] My darling! [*Hurrying to her and seizing the rug strap, pouring forth his remorseful regrets all the time*] I intended to meet you at the train. I let the time slip. [*Flinging the rug on the sofa*] I was so engrossed by—[*returning to her*]—I forgot—oh! [*He embraces her with penitent emotion*]

BURGESS: [*A little shame-faced and doubtful of his reception*] How orr you, Candy? [*She, still in* Morell's *arms, offers him her cheek, which he kisses*] James and me is come to a unnerstandin'—a honorable unnerstandin'. Ain' we, James?

MORELL: [*Impetuously*] Oh, bother your understanding! You've kept me late for Candida. [*With compassionate fervor*] My poor love: how did you manage about the luggage?—how—

CANDIDA: [*Stopping him and disengaging herself*] There, there, there. I wasn't alone. Eugene came down yesterday; and we traveled up together.

MORELL: [*Pleased*] Eugene!

CANDIDA: Yes: he's struggling with my luggage, poor boy. Go out, dear, at once; or he will pay for the cab; and I don't want that. [Morell *hurries out.* Candida *puts down her handbag; then takes off her mantle and bonnet and puts them on the sofa with the rug, chatting meanwhile*] Well, papa, how are you getting on at home?

BURGESS: The 'ouse ain't worth livin' in since you left it, Candy. I wish you'd come round and give the **gurl a talkin' to. Who's** this Eugene that's come with you?

CANDIDA: Oh, Eugene's one of James's discoveries. He found him sleeping on the Embankment last June. Haven't you noticed our new picture [*pointing to the Virgin*]? He gave us that.

BURGESS: [*Incredulously*] Garn! D'you mean to tell me—your hown father!—that cab touts or such like, orf the Embankment, buys pictur's like that? [*Severely*] Don't deceive me, Candy: it's a 'Igh Church pictur; and James chose it hisself.

CANDIDA: Guess again. Eugene isn't a cab tout.

BURGESS: Then wot is he? [*Sarcastically*] A nobleman, I s'pose.

CANDIDA: [*Delighted—nodding*] Yes. His uncle's a peer—a real live earl.

BURGESS: [*Not daring to believe such good news*] No!

CANDIDA: Yes. He had a seven-day bill for £55 in his pocket when James found him on the Embankment. He thought he couldn't get any money for it until the seven days were up; and he was too shy to ask for credit. Oh, he's a dear boy! We are very fond of him.

BURGESS: [*Pretending to belittle the aristocracy, but with his eyes gleaming*] Hm, I thort you wouldn't git a piorr's (peer's) nevvy visitin' in Victoria park unless he were a bit of a flat. [*Looking again at the picture*] Of course I don't 'old with that pictur, Candy; but still it's a 'igh-class, fust-rate work of art: I can see that. Be sure you hintroduce me to him, Candy. [*He looks at his watch anxiously*] I can only stay about two minutes.

[*Morell comes back with Eugene, whom Burgess contemplates moist-eyed with enthusiasm. He is a strange, shy youth of eighteen, slight, effeminate, with a delicate childish voice, and a hunted, tormented expression and shrinking manner that show the painful sensitiveness that very swift and acute apprehensiveness produces in youth, before the character has grown to its full strength. Yet everything that his timidity and frailty suggests is contradicted by his face. He is miserably irresolute, does not know where to stand or what to do with his hands and feet, is afraid of Burgess, and would run away into solitude if he dared; but the very intensity with which he feels a perfectly commonplace position shows great nervous force, and his nostrils and mouth show a fiercely petulant wilfulness, as to the quality of which his great imaginative eyes and fine brow are reassuring. He is so entirely uncommon as to be almost unearthly; and to prosaic people there is something noxious in this unearthliness, just as to poetic people there is something angelic in it. His dress is anarchic. He wears an old blue serge jacket, unbuttoned over a woolen lawn-tennis shirt, with a silk handkerchief for a cravat, trousers matching the jacket, and*]

brown canvas shoes. In these garments he has apparently lain in the heather and waded through the waters; but there is no evidence of his having ever brushed them.

As he catches sight of a stranger on entering, he stops, and edges along the wall on the opposite side of the room]

MORELL: [*As he enters*] Come along: you can spare us quarter of an hour, at all events. This is my father-in-law, Mr. Burgess—Mr. Marchbanks.

MARCHBANKS: [*Nervously backing against the bookcase*] Glad to meet you, sir.

BURGESS: [*Crossing to him with great heartiness, whilst Morell joins Candida at the fire*] Glad to meet you, I'm shore, Mr. Morchbanks. [*Forcing him to shake hands*] 'Ow do you find yoreself this weather? 'Ope you ain't lettin' James put no foolish ideas into your 'ed?

MARCHBANKS: Foolish ideas! Oh, you mean Socialism. No.

BURGESS: That's right. [*Again looking at his watch*] Well, I must go now: there's no 'elp for it. Yo're not comin' my way, are you, Mr. Morchbanks?

MARCHBANKS: Which way is that?

BURGESS: Victawriar Pork Station. There's a city train at 12:25.

MORELL: Nonsense. Eugene will stay to lunch with us, I expect.

MARCHBANKS: [*Anxiously excusing himself*] No—I—I—

BURGESS: Well, well, I shan't press you: I bet you'd rather lunch with Candy. Some night, I 'ope, you'll come and dine with me at my club, the Freeman Founders in Nortn Folgit. Come, say you will.

MARCHBANKS: Thank you, Mr. Burgess. Where is Norton Folgate—down in Surrey, isn't it? [*Burgess, inexpressibly tickled, begins to splutter with laughter*]

CANDIDA: [*Coming to the rescue*] You'll lose your train, papa, if you don't go at once. Come back in the afternoon and tell Mr. Marchbanks where to find the club.

BURGESS: [*Roaring with glee*] Down in Surrey—har, har! that's not a bad one. Well, I never met a man as didn't know Nortn Folgit before. [*Abashed at his own noisiness*] Good-bye, Mr. Morchbanks: I know yo're too 'ighbred to take my pleasantry in bad part. [*He again offers his hand*]

MARCHBANKS: [*Taking it with a nervous jerk*] Not at all.

BURGESS: Bye, bye, Candy. I'll look in again later on. So long, James.

MORELL: Must you go?

BURGESS: Don't stir. [*He goes out with unabated heartiness.*]

MORELL: Oh, I'll see you out. [*He follows him out. Eugene stares after them apprehensively, holding his breath until Burgess disappears.*]

CANDIDA: [*Laughing*] Well, Eugene. [*He turns with a start and comes eagerly towards her, but stops ir-*

resolutely as he meets her amused look] What do you think of my father?

MARCHBANKS: I—I hardly know him yet. He seems to be a very nice old gentleman.

CANDIDA: [*With gentle irony*] And you'll go to the Freeman Founders to dine with him, won't you?

MARCHBANKS: [*Miserably, taking it quite seriously*] Yes, if it will please you.

CANDIDA: [*Touched*] Do you know, you are a very nice boy, Eugene, with all your queerness. If you had laughed at my father I shouldn't have minded; but I like you ever so much better for being nice to him.

MARCHBANKS: Ought I to have laughed? I noticed that he said something funny; but I am so ill at ease with strangers; and I never can see a joke! I'm very sorry. [*He sits down on the sofa, his elbows on his knees and his temples between his fists, with an expression of hopeless suffering*]

CANDIDA: [*Bustling him good-naturedly*] Oh, come! you great baby, you! You are worse than usual this morning. Why were you so melancholy as we came along in the cab?

MARCHBANKS: Oh, that was nothing. I was wondering how much I ought to give the cabman. I know it's utterly silly; but you don't know how dreadful such things are to me—how I shrink from having to deal with strange people. [*Quickly and reassuringly*] But it's all right. He beamed all over and touched his hat when Morell gave him two shillings. I was on the point of offering him ten. [Candida *laughs heartily.* Morell *comes back with a few letters and newspapers which have come by the midday post*]

CANDIDA: Oh, James, dear, he was going to give the cabman ten shillings—ten shillings for a three minutes' drive—oh, dear!

MORELL: [*At the table, glancing through the letters*] Never mind her, Marchbanks. The overpaying instinct is a generous one: better than the underpaying instinct, and not so common.

MARCHBANKS: [*Relapsing into dejection*] No: cowardice, incompetence. Mrs. Morell's quite right.

CANDIDA: Of course she is. [*She takes up her handbag*] And now I must leave you to James for the present. I suppose you are too much of a poet to know the state a woman finds her house in when she's been away for three weeks. Give me my rug. [Eugene *takes the strapped rug from the couch, and gives it to her. She takes it in her left hand, having the bag in her right*] Now hang my cloak across my arm. [*He obeys*] Now my hat. [*He puts it into the hand which has the bag*] Now open the door for me. [*He hurries up before her and opens the door*] Thanks. [*She goes out; and* Marchbanks *shuts the door*]

MORELL: [*Still busy at the table*] You'll stay to lunch, Marchbanks, of course.

MARCHBANKS: [*Scared*] I mustn't. [*He glances quickly at* Morell, *but at once avoids his frank look, and adds, with obvious disingenuousness*] I can't.

MORELL: [*Over his shoulder*] You mean you won't.

MARCHBANKS: [*Earnestly*] No: I should like to, indeed. Thank you very much. But—but—

MORELL: [*Breezily, finishing with the letters and coming close to him*] But—but—but—but—bosh! If you'd like to stay, stay. You don't mean to persuade me you have anything else to do. If you're shy, go and take a turn in the park and write poetry until half past one; and then come in and have a good feed.

MARCHBANKS: Thank you, I should like that very much. But I really mustn't. The truth is, Mrs. Morell told me not to. She said she didn't think you'd ask me to stay to lunch, but that I was to remember, if you did, that you didn't really want me to. [*Plaintively*] She said I'd understand; but I don't. Please don't tell her I told you.

MORELL: [*Drolly*] Oh, is that all? Won't my suggestion that you should take a turn in the park meet the difficulty?

MARCHBANKS: How?

MORELL: [*Exploding good-humoredly*] Why, you duffer—[*But this boisterousness jars himself as well as* Eugene. *He checks himself, and resumes, with affectionate seriousness*] No: I won't put it in that way. My dear lad: in a happy marriage like ours, there is something very sacred in the return of the wife to her home. [Marchbanks *looks quickly at him, half anticipating his meaning*] An old friend or a truly noble and sympathetic soul is not in the way on such occasions; but a chance visitor is. [*The hunted, horror-stricken expression comes out with sudden vividness in* Eugene's *face as he understands.* Morell, *occupied with his own thought, goes on without noticing it*] Candida thought I would rather not have you here; but she was wrong. I'm very fond of you, my boy, and I should like you to see for yourself what a happy thing it is to be married as I am.

MARCHBANKS: Happy!—your marriage! You think that! You believe that!

MORELL: [*Buoyantly*] I know it, my lad. La Rochefoucauld said that there are convenient marriages, but no delightful ones. You don't know the comfort of seeing through and through a thundering liar and rotten cynic like that fellow. Ha, ha! Now off with you to the park, and write your poem. Half past one, sharp, mind: we never wait for anybody.

MARCHBANKS: [*Wildly*] No: stop: you shan't. I'll force it into the light.

MORELL: [*Puzzled*] Eh? Force what?

MARCHBANKS: I must speak to you. There is something that must be settled between us.

MORELL: [*With a whimsical glance at the clock*] Now?

MARCHBANKS: [*Passionately*] Now. Before you leave this room. [*He retreats a few steps, and stands as if to bar* Morell's *way to the door.*]

MORELL: [*Without moving, and gravely, perceiving now that there is something serious the matter*]

I'm not going to leave it, my dear boy: I thought you were. [Eugene, *baffled by his firm tone, turns his back on him, writhing with anger.* Morell *goes to him and puts his hand on his shoulder strongly and kindly, disregarding his attempt to shake it off*] Come: sit down quietly; and tell me what it is. And remember: we are friends, and need not fear that either of us will be anything but patient and kind to the other, whatever we may have to say.

MARCHBANKS: [*Twisting himself round on him*] Oh, I am not forgetting myself: I am only [*covering his face desperately with his hands*] full of horror. [*Then, dropping his hands, and thrusting his face forward fiercely at* Morell, *he goes on threateningly*] You shall see whether this is a time for patience and kindness. [Morell, *firm as a rock, looks indulgently at him*] Don't look at me in that self-complacent way. You think yourself stronger than I am; but I shall stagger you if you have a heart in your breast.

MORELL: [*Powerfully confident*] Stagger me, my boy. Out with it.

MARCHBANKS: First—

MORELL: First?—

MARCHBANKS: I love your wife.

[Morell *recoils, and, after staring at him for a moment in utter amazement, bursts into uncontrollable laughter.* Eugene *is taken aback, but not disconcerted; and he soon becomes indignant and contemptuous*]

MORELL: [*Sitting down to have his laugh out*] Why, my dear child, of course you do. Everybody loves her: they can't help it. I like it. But [*looking up whimsically at him*] I say, Eugene: do you think yours is a case to be talked about? You're under twenty: she's over thirty. Doesn't it look rather too like a case of calf love?

MARCHBANKS: [*Vehemently*] You dare say that of her! You think that way of the love she inspires! It is an insult to her!

MORELL: [*Rising quickly, in an altered tone*] To her! Eugene: take care. I have been patient. I hope to remain patient. But there are some things I won't allow. Don't force me to show you the indulgence I should show to a child. Be a man.

MARCHBANKS: [*With a gesture as if sweeping something behind him*] Oh, let us put aside all that cant. It horrifies me when I think of the doses of it she has had to endure in all the weary years during which you have selfishly and blindly sacrificed her to minister to your self-sufficiency—you [*Turning on him*] who have not one thought—one sense—in common with her.

MORELL: [*Philosophically*] She seems to bear it pretty well. [*Looking him straight in the face*] Eugene, my boy: you are making a fool of yourself—a very great fool of yourself. There's a piece of wholesome plain speaking for you.

MARCHBANKS: Oh, do you think I don't know all that? Do you think that the things people make fools of themselves about are any less real and true than the things they behave sensibly about? [Morell's *gaze wavers for the first time. He instinctively averts his face and stands listening, startled and thoughtful*] They are more true: they are the only things that are true. You are very calm and sensible and moderate with me because you can see that I am a fool about your wife; just as no doubt that old man who was here just now is very wise over your Socialism, because he sees that you are a fool about it. [Morell's *perplexity deepens markedly.* Eugene *follows up his advantage, plying him fiercely with questions*] Does that prove you wrong? Does your complacent superiority to me prove that *I* am wrong?

MORELL: [*Turning on* Eugene, *who stands his ground*] Marchbanks: some devil is putting these words into your mouth. It is easy—terribly easy—to shake a man's faith in himself. To take advantage of that to break a man's spirit is devil's work. Take care of what you are doing. Take care.

MARCHBANKS: [*Ruthlessly*] I know. I'm doing it on purpose. I told you I should stagger you.

[*They confront one another threateningly for a moment. Then* Morell *recovers his dignity*]

MORELL: [*With noble tenderness*] Eugene: listen to me. Some day, I hope and trust, you will be a happy man like me. [Eugene *chafes intolerantly, repudiating the worth of his happiness.* Morell, *deeply insulted, controls himself with fine forbearance, and continues steadily, with great artistic beauty of delivery*] You will be married; and you will be working with all your might and valor to make every spot on earth as happy as your own home. You will be one of the makers of the Kingdom of Heaven on earth; and—who knows?—you may be a pioneer and master builder where I am only a humble journeyman; for don't think, my boy, that I cannot see in you, young as you are, promise of higher powers than I can ever pretend to. I well know that it is in the poet that the holy spirit of man—the god within him—is most godlike. It should make you tremble to think of that—to think that the heavy burthen and great gift of a poet may be laid upon you.

MARCHBANKS: [*Unimpressed and remorseless, his boyish crudity of assertion telling sharply against* Morell's *oratory*] It does not make me tremble. It is the want of it in others that makes me tremble.

MORELL: [*Redoubling his force of style under the stimulus of his genuine feeling and* Eugene's *obduracy*] Then help to kindle it in them—in me—not to extinguish it. In the future—when you are as happy as I am—I will be your true brother in the faith. I will help you to believe that God has given us a world that nothing but our own folly keeps from being a paradise. I will help you to believe that every stroke of your work is sowing happiness for the great harvest that all—even the humblest—shall one day reap. And last, but trust me, not least, I will help you to believe that your wife loves you and is happy in her home. We need such help, Marchbanks: we need it greatly and always. There are so many things to make us doubt, if once we let our understanding be troubled. Even at home, we sit as if in camp, encompassed by a hostile army of doubts. Will you play the traitor and let them in on me?

MARCHBANKS: [*Looking round him*] Is it like this for her here always? A woman, with a great soul, craving for reality, truth, freedom, and being fed on metaphors, sermons, stale perorations, mere rhetoric. Do you think a woman's soul can live on your talent for preaching?

MORELL: [*Stung*] Marchbanks: you make it hard for me to control myself. My talent is like yours insofar as it has any real worth at all. It is the gift of finding words for divine truth.

MARCHBANKS: [*Impetuously*] It's the gift of the gab, nothing more and nothing less. What has your knack of fine talking to do with the truth, any more than playing the organ has? I've never been in your church; but I've been to your political meetings; and I've seen you do what's called rousing the meeting to enthusiasm: that is, you excited them until they behaved exactly as if they were drunk. And their wives looked on and saw clearly enough what fools they were. Oh, it's an old story: you'll find it in the Bible. I imagine King David, in his fits of enthusiasm, was very like you. [*Stabbing him with the words*] "But his wife despised him in her heart."

MORELL: [*Wrathfully*] Leave my house. Do you hear? [*He advances on him threateningly*]

MARCHBANKS: [*Shrinking back against the couch*] Let me alone. Don't touch me. [Morell *grasps him powerfully by the lapel of his coat: he cowers down on the sofa and screams passionately*] Stop, Morell, if you strike me, I'll kill myself: I won't bear it. [*Almost in hysterics*] Let me go. Take your hand away.

MORELL: [*With slow, emphatic scorn*] You little sniveling, cowardly whelp. [*Releasing him*] Go, before you frighten yourself into a fit.

MARCHBANKS: [*On the sofa, gasping, but relieved by the withdrawal of* Morell's *hand*] I'm not afraid of you: it's you who are afraid of me.

MORELL: [*Quietly, as he stands over him*] It looks like it, doesn't it?

MARCHBANKS: [*With petulant vehemence*] Yes, it does. [Morell *turns away contemptuously.* Eugene *scrambles to his feet and follows him*] You think because I shrink from being brutally handled—because [*with tears in his voice*] I can do nothing but cry with rage when I am met with violence—because I can't lift a heavy trunk down from the top of a cab like you—because I can't fight you for your wife as a navvy would: all that makes you think that I'm afraid of you. But you're wrong. If I haven't got what you call British pluck, I haven't British cowardice either: I'm not afraid of a clergyman's ideas. I'll fight your ideas. I'll rescue her from her slavery to them: I'll pit my own ideas against them. You are driving me out of the house because you

daren't let her choose between your ideas and mine. You are afraid to let me see her again. [Morell *angered, turns suddenly on him. He flies to the door in involuntary dread*] Let me alone, I say. I'm going.

MORELL: [*With cold scorn*] Wait a moment: I am not going to touch you: don't be afraid. When my wife comes back she will want to know why you have gone. And when she finds that you are never going to cross our threshold again, she will want to have that explained, too. Now I don't wish to distress her by telling her that you have behaved like a blackguard.

MARCHBANKS: [*Coming back with renewed vehemence*] You shall—you must. If you give any explanation but the true one, you are a liar and a coward. Tell her what I said; and how you were strong and manly, and shook me as a terrier shakes a rat; and how I shrank and was terrified; and how you called me a sniveling little whelp and put me out of the house. If you don't tell her, I will: I'll write it to her.

MORELL: [*Taken aback*] Why do you want her to know this?

MARCHBANKS: [*With lyric rapture*] Because she will understand me, and know that I understand her. If you keep back one word of it from her—if you are not ready to lay the truth at her feet as I am—then you will know to the end of your days that she really belongs to me and not to you. Good-bye. [*Going*]

MORELL: [*Terribly disquieted*] Stop: I will not tell her.

MARCHBANKS: [*Turning near the door*] Either the truth or a lie you must tell her, if I go.

MORELL: [*Temporizing*] Marchbanks: it is sometimes justifiable.

MARCHBANKS: [*Cutting him short*] I know—to lie. It will be useless. Good-bye, Mr. Clergyman.

[*As he turns finally to the door, it opens and* Candida *enters in housekeeping attire*]

CANDIDA: Are you going, Eugene? [*Looking more observantly at him*] Well, dear me, just look at you, going out into the street in that state! You are a poet, certainly. Look at him, James! [*She takes him by the coat, and brings him forward to show him to* Morell] Look at his collar! look at his tie! look at his hair! One would think somebody had been throttling you. [*The two men guard themselves against betraying their consciousness*] Here! Stand still. [*She buttons his collar; ties his neckerchief in a bow; and arranges his hair*] There! Now you look so nice that I think you'd better stay to lunch after all, though I told you you mustn't. It will be ready in half an hour. [*She puts a final touch to the bow. He kisses her hand*] Don't be silly.

MARCHBANKS: I want to stay, of course—unless the reverend gentleman, your husband, has anything to advance to the contrary.

CANDIDA: Shall he stay, James, if he promises to be a good boy and to help me to lay the table?

[Marchbanks *turns his head and looks steadfastly at* Morell *over his shoulder, challenging his answer*]

MORELL: [*Shortly*] Oh, yes, certainly: he had better. [*He goes to the table and pretends to busy himself with his papers there*]

MARCHBANKS: [*Offering his arm to* Candida] Come and lay the table. [*She takes it and they go to the door together. As they go out he adds*] I am the happiest of men.

MORELL: So was I—an hour ago.

ACT II.

The same day. The same room. Late in the afternoon. The spare chair for visitors has been replaced at the table, which is, if possible, more untidy than before. Marchbanks, *alone and idle, is trying to find out how the typewriter works. Hearing someone at the door, he steals guiltily away to the window and pretends to be absorbed in the view.* Miss Garnett, *carrying the notebook in which she takes down* Morell's *letters in shorthand from his dictation, sits down at the typewriter and sets to work transcribing them, much too busy to notice* Eugene. *Unfortunately the first key she strikes sticks.*

PROSERPINE: Bother! You've been meddling with my typewriter, Mr. Marchbanks; and there's not the least use in your trying to look as if you hadn't.

MARCHBANKS: [*Timidly*] I'm very sorry, Miss Garnett. I only tried to make it write.

PROSERPINE: Well, you've made this key stick.

MARCHBANKS: [*Earnestly*] I assure you I didn't touch the keys. I didn't, indeed. I only turned a little wheel. [*He points irresolutely at the tension wheel*]

PROSERPINE: Oh, now I understand. [*She sets the machine to rights, talking volubly all the time*] I suppose you thought it was a sort of barrel-organ. Nothing to do but turn the handle, and it would write a beautiful love letter for you straight off, eh?

MARCHBANKS: [*Seriously*] I suppose a machine could be made to write love-letters. They're all the same, aren't they?

PROSERPINE: [*Somewhat indignantly: any such discussion, except by way of pleasantry, being outside her code of manners*] How do I know? Why do you ask me?

MARCHBANKS: I beg your pardon. I thought clever people—people who can do business and write letters, and that sort of thing—always had love affairs.

PROSERPINE: [*Rising, outraged*] Mr. Marchbanks! [*She looks severely at him, and marches with much dignity to the bookcase*]

MARCHBANKS: [*Approaching her humbly*] I hope I haven't offended you. Perhaps I shouldn't have alluded to your love affairs.

PROSERPINE: [*Plucking a blue book from the shelf and turning sharply on him*] I haven't any love affairs. How dare you say such a thing?

MARCHBANKS: [*Simply*] Really! Oh, then you are shy, like me. Isn't that so?

PROSERPINE: Certainly I am not shy. What do you mean?

MARCHBANKS: [*Secretly*] You must be: that is the reason there are so few love affairs in the world. We all go about longing for love: it is the first need of our natures, the loudest cry of our hearts; but we dare not utter our longing: we are too shy. [*Very earnestly*] Oh, Miss Garnett, what would you not give to be without fear, without shame—

PROSERPINE: [*Scandalized*] Well, upon my word!

MARCHBANKS: [*With petulant impatience*] Ah, don't say those stupid things to me: they don't deceive me: what use are they? Why are you afraid to be your real self with me? I am just like you.

PROSERPINE: Like me! Pray, are you flattering me or flattering yourself? I don't feel quite sure which. [*She turns to go back to the typewriter*]

MARCHBANKS: [*Stopping her mysteriously*] Hush! I go about in search of love; and I find it in unmeasured stores in the bosoms of others. But when I try to ask for it, this horrible shyness strangles me; and I stand dumb, or worse than dumb, saying meaningless things—foolish lies. And I see the affection I am longing for given to dogs and cats and pet birds, because they come and ask for it. [*Almost whispering*] It must be asked for: it is like a ghost: it cannot speak unless it is first spoken to. [*At his normal pitch, but with deep melancholy*] All the love in the world is longing to speak; only it dare not, because it is shy, shy, shy. That is the world's tragedy. [*With a deep sigh he sits in the spare chair and buries his face in his hands*]

PROSERPINE: [*Amazed, but keeping her wits about her—her point of honor in encounters with strange young men*] Wicked people get over that shyness occasionally, don't they?

MARCHBANKS: [*Scrambling up almost fiercely*] Wicked people means people who have no love: therefore they have no shame. They have the power to ask love because they don't need it: they have the power to offer it because they have none to give. [*He collapses into his seat, and adds, mournfully*] But we, who have love, and long to mingle it with the love of others: we cannot utter a word. [*Timidly*] You find that, don't you?

PROSERPINE: Look here: if you don't stop talking like this, I'll leave the room, Mr. Marchbanks: I really will. It's not proper.

[*She resumes her seat at the typewriter, opening the blue book and preparing to copy a passage from it*]

MARCHBANKS: [*Hopelessly*] Nothing that's worth saying is proper. [*He rises, and wanders about the room in his lost way, saying*] I can't understand you, Miss Garnett. What am I to talk about?

PROSERPINE: [*Snubbing him*] Talk about indifferent things. Talk about the weather.

MARCHBANKS: Would you stand and talk about indifferent things if a child were by, crying bitterly with hunger?

PROSERPINE: I suppose not.

MARCHBANKS: Well: *I* can't talk about indifferent things with my heart crying out bitterly in its hunger.

PROSERPINE: Then hold your tongue.

MARCHBANKS: Yes: that is what it always comes to. We hold our tongues. Does that stop the cry of your heart?—for it does cry: doesn't it? It must, if you have a heart.

PROSERPINE: [*Suddenly rising with her hand pressed on her heart*] Oh, it's no use trying to work while you talk like that. [*She leaves her little table and sits on the sofa. Her feelings are evidently strongly worked on*] It's no business of yours, whether my heart cries or not; but I have a mind to tell you, for all that.

MARCHBANKS: You needn't. I know already that it must.

PROSERPINE: But mind: if you ever say I said so, I'll deny it.

MARCHBANKS: [*Compassionately*] Yes, I know. And so you haven't the courage to tell him?

PROSERPINE: [*Bouncing up*] Him! Who?

MARCHBANKS: Whoever he is. The man you love. It might be anybody. The curate, Mr. Mill, perhaps.

PROSERPINE: [*With disdain*] Mr. Mill!!! A fine man to break my heart about, indeed! I'd rather have you than Mr. Mill.

MARCHBANKS: [*Recoiling*] No, really—I'm very sorry; but you mustn't think of that. I—

PROSERPINE: [*Testily, crossing to the fire and standing at it with her back to him*] Oh, don't be frightened: it's not you. It's not any one particular person.

MARCHBANKS: I know. You feel that you could love anybody that offered—

PROSERPINE: [*Exasperated*] Anybody that offered! No, I do not. What do you take me for?

MARCHBANKS: [*Discouraged*] No use. You won't make me real answers—only those things that everybody says. [*He strays to the sofa and sits down disconsolately*]

PROSERPINE: [*Nettled at what she takes to be a disparagement of her manners by an aristocrat*] Oh, well, if you want original conversation, you'd better go and talk to yourself.

MARCHBANKS: That is what all poets do: they talk to themselves out loud; and the world overhears them. But it's horribly lonely not to hear someone else talk sometimes.

PROSERPINE: Wait until Mr. Morell comes. He'll talk to you. [*Marchbanks shudders*] Oh, you needn't make wry faces over him: he can talk better than you. [*With temper*] He'd talk your little head off.

[*She is going back angrily to her place, when, suddenly enlightened, he springs up and stops her*]

MARCHBANKS: Ah, I understand now!

PROSERPINE: [*Reddening*] What do you understand?

MARCHBANKS: Your secret. Tell me: is it really and truly possible for a woman to love him?

PROSERPINE: [*As if this were beyond all bounds*] Well!!

MARCHBANKS: [*Passionately*] No, answer me. I want to know: I must know. *I* can't understand it. I can see nothing in him but words, pious resolutions, what people call goodness. You can't love that.

PROSERPINE: [*Attempting to snub him by an air of cool propriety*] I simply don't know what you're talking about. I don't understand you.

MARCHBANKS: [*Vehemently*] You do. You lie—

PROSERPINE: Oh!

MARCHBANKS: You do understand; and you know. [*Determined to have an answer*] Is it possible for a woman to love him?

PROSERPINE: [*Looking him straight in the face*] Yes. [*He covers his face with his hands*] Whatever is the matter with you! [*He takes down his hands and looks at her. Frightened at the tragic mask presented to her, she hurries past him at the utmost possible distance, keeping her eyes on his face until he turns from her and goes to the child's chair beside the hearth, where he sits in the deepest dejection. As she approaches the door, it opens and Burgess enters. On seeing him, she ejaculates*] Praise heaven, here's somebody! [*And sits down, reassured, at her table. She puts a fresh sheet of paper into the typewriter as Burgess crosses to* Eugene]

BURGESS: [*Bent on taking care of the distinguished visitor*] Well: so this is the way they leave you to yourself, Mr. Morchbanks. I've come to keep you company. [*Marchbanks looks up at him in consternation, which is quite lost on him*] James is receivin' a deppitation in the dinin' room; and Candy is hupstairs educatin' of a young stitcher gurl she's hinterusted in. She's settin' there learnin' her to read out of the "'Ev'nly Twins." [*Condolingly*] You must find it lonesome here with no one but the typist to talk to. [*He pulls round the easy chair above fire, and sits down*]

PROSERPINE: [*Highly incensed*] He'll be all right now that he has the advantage of your polished conversation: that's one comfort, anyhow. [*She begins to typewrite with clattering asperity*]

BURGESS: [*Amazed at her audacity*] Hi was not addressin' myself to you, young woman, that I'm awerr of.

PROSERPINE: [*Tartly, to* Marchbanks] Did you ever see worse manners, Mr. Marchbanks?

BURGESS: [*With pompous severity*] Mr. Morchbanks is a gentleman and knows his place, which is more than some people do.

PROSERPINE: [*Fretfully*] It's well you and I are not ladies and gentlemen: I'd talk to you pretty straight if Mr. Marchbanks wasn't here. [*She pulls the letter out of the machine so crossly that it tears*] There, now I've spoiled this letter—have to be done all over again. Oh, I can't contain myself—silly old fathead!

BURGESS: [*Rising, breathless with indignation*] Ho! I'm a silly ole fat'ead, am I? Ho, indeed [*Gasping*] Hall right, my gurl! Hall right. You just wait till I tell that to your employer. You'll see. I'll teach you: see if I don't.

PROSERPINE: I—

BURGESS: [*Cutting her short*] No, you've done it now. No huse a-talkin' to me. I'll let you know who I am. [Proserpine *shifts her paper carriage with a defiant bang, and disdainfully goes on with her work*] Don't you take no notice of her, Mr. Morchbanks. She's beneath it. [*He sits down again loftily*]

MARCHBANKS: [*Miserably nervous and disconcerted*] Hadn't we better change the subject. I—I don't think Miss Garnett meant anything.

PROSERPINE: [*With intense conviction*] Oh, didn't I though, just!

BURGESS: I wouldn't demean myself to take notice on her.

[*An electric bell rings twice*]

PROSERPINE: [*Gathering up her note-book and papers*] That's for me. [*She hurries out*]

BURGESS: [*Calling after her*] Oh, we can spare you. [*Somewhat relieved by the triumph of having the last word, and yet half inclined to try to improve on it, he looks after her for a moment; then subsides into his seat by* Eugene, *and addresses him very confidentially*] Now we're alone, Mr. Morchbanks, let me give you a friendly 'int that I wouldn't give to everybody. 'Ow long 'ave you known my son-in-law James here?

MARCHBANKS: I don't know. I never can remember dates. A few months, perhaps.

BURGESS: Ever notice anything queer about him?

MARCHBANKS: I don't think so.

BURGESS: [*Impressively*] No more you wouldn't. That's the danger in it. Well, he's mad.

MARCHBANKS: Mad!

BURGESS: Mad as a Morch 'are. You take notice on him and you'll see.

MARCHBANKS: [*Beginning*] But surely that is only because his opinions—

BURGESS: [*Touching him with his forefinger on his knee, and pressing it as if to hold his attention with it*] That's wot I used ter think, Mr. Morchbanks. Hi thought long enough that it was honly 'is opinions; though, mind you, hopinions becomes vurry serious things when people takes to hactin' on 'em as 'e does. But that's not wot I go on. [*He looks round to make sure that they are alone, and bends over to* Eugene's *ear*] Wot do you think he says to me this mornin' in this very room?

MARCHBANKS: What?

BURGESS: He sez to me—this is as sure as we're settin' here now—he sez "I'm a fool," he sez; "and

yore a scounderl"—as cool as possible. Me a scounderl, mind you! And then shook 'ands with me on it, as if it was to my credit! Do you mean to tell me that that man's sane?

MORELL: [*Outside, calling to* Proserpine, *holding the door open*] Get all their names and addresses, Miss Garnett.

PROSERPINE: [*In the distance*] Yes, Mr. Morell.

[Morell *comes in, with the deputation's documents in his hands*]

BURGESS: [*Aside to* Marchbanks] Yorr he is. Just you keep your heye on him and see. [*Rising momentously*] I'm sorry, James, to 'ave to make a complaint to you. I don't want to do it; but I feel I oughter, as a matter o' right and dooty.

MORELL: What's the matter?

BURGESS: Mr. Morchbanks will bear me out: he was a witness. [*Very solemnly*] Your young woman so far forgot herself as to call me a silly ole fat'ead.

MORELL: [*Delighted—with tremendous heartiness*] Oh, now, isn't that exactly like Prossy? She's so frank: she can't contain herself! Poor Prossy! Ha! Ha!

BURGESS: [*Trembling with rage*] And do you hexpec me to put up with it from the like of 'er?

MORELL: Pooh, nonsense! you can't take any notice of it. Never mind. [*He goes to the cellaret and puts the papers into one of the drawers*]

BURGESS: Oh, *I* don't mind. I'm above it. But is it right?—that's what I want to know. Is it right?

MORELL: That's a question for the Church, not for the laity. Has it done you any harm, that's the question for you, eh? Of course, it hasn't. Think no more of it. [*He dismisses the subject by going to his place at the table and setting to work at his correspondence*]

BURGESS: [*Aside to* Marchbanks] What did I tell you? Mad as a 'atter. [*He goes to the table and asks, with the sickly civility of a hungry man*] When's dinner, James?

MORELL: Not for half an hour yet.

BURGESS: [*With plaintive resignation*] Gimme a nice book to read over the fire, will you, James: thur's a good chap.

MORELL: What sort of book? A good one?

BURGESS: [*With almost a yell of remonstrance*] Nah-oo! Summat pleasant, just to pass the time. [Morell *takes an illustrated paper from the table and offers it. He accepts it humbly*] Thank yer, James. [*He goes back to his easy chair at the fire, and sits there at his ease, reading*]

MORELL: [*As he writes*] Candida will come to entertain you presently. She has got rid of her pupil. She is filling the lamps.

MARCHBANKS: [*Starting up in the wildest consternation*] But that will soil her hands. I can't bear that, Morell: it's a shame. I'll go and fill them. [*He makes for the door*]

MORELL: You'd better not. [Marchbanks *stops irresolutely*] She'd only set you to clean my boots, to save me the trouble of doing it myself in the morning.

BURGESS: [With great disapproval] Don't you keep a servant now, James?

MORELL: Yes; but she isn't a slave; and the house looks as if I kept three. That means that everyone has to lend a hand. It's not a bad plan: Prossy and I can talk business after breakfast whilst we're washing up. Washing up's no trouble when there are two people to do it.

MARCHBANKS: [Tormentedly] Do you think every woman is as coarse-grained as Miss Garnett?

BURGESS: [Emphatically] That's quite right, Mr. Morchbanks. That's quite right. She is corse-grained.

MORELL: [Quietly and significantly] Marchbanks!

MARCHBANKS: Yes.

MORELL: How many servants does your father keep?

MARCHBANKS: Oh, I don't know. [He comes back uneasily to the sofa, as if to get as far as possible from Morell's questioning, and sits down in great agony of mind, thinking of the paraffin]

MORELL: [Very gravely] So many that you don't know. [More aggressively] Anyhow, when there's anything coarse-grained to be done, you ring the bell and throw it on to somebody else, eh? That's one of the great facts in your existence, isn't it?

MARCHBANKS: Oh, don't torture me. The one great fact now is that your wife's beautiful fingers are dabbling in paraffin oil, and that you are sitting here comfortably preaching about it—everlasting preaching, preaching, words, words, words.

BURGESS: [Intensely appreciating this retort] Ha, ha! Devil a better. [Radiantly] 'Ad you there, James, straight.

[Candida comes in, well aproned, with a reading lamp trimmed, filled, and ready for lighting. She places it on the table near Morell, ready for use]

CANDIDA: [Brushing her finger tips together with a slight twitch of her nose] If you stay with us, Eugene, I think I will hand over the lamps to you.

MARCHBANKS: I will stay on condition that you hand over all the rough work to me.

CANDIDA: That's very gallant; but I think I should like to see how you do it first. [Turning to Morell] James: you've not been looking after the house properly.

MORELL: What have I done—or not done—my love?

CANDIDA: [With serious vexation] My own particular pet scrubbing brush has been used for black-leading. [A heartbreaking wail bursts from Marchbanks. Burgess looks round, amazed. Candida hurries to the sofa] What's the matter? Are you ill, Eugene?

MARCHBANKS: No, not ill. Only horror, horror, horror! [He bows his head on his hands]

BURGESS: [Shocked] What! Got the 'orrors, Mr.

Morchbanks! Oh, that's bad, at your age. You must leave it off grajally.

CANDIDA: [Reassured] Nonsense, papa. It's only poetic horror, isn't it, Eugene? [Petting him]

BURGESS: [Abashed] Oh, poetic 'orror, is it? I beg your pordon, I'm shore. [He turns to the fire again, deprecating his hasty conclusion]

CANDIDA: What is it, Eugene—the scrubbing brush? [He shudders] Well, there! never mind. [She sits down beside him] Wouldn't you like to present me with a nice new one, with an ivory back inlaid with mother-of-pearl?

MARCHBANKS: [Softly and musically, but sadly and longingly] No, not a scrubbing brush, but a boat—a tiny shallop to sail away in, far from the world, where the marble floors are washed by the rain and dried by the sun, where the south wind dusts the beautiful green and purple carpets. Or a chariot—to carry us up into the sky, where the lamps are stars, and don't need to be filled with paraffin oil every day.

MORELL: [Harshly] And where there is nothing to do but to be idle, selfish and useless.

CANDIDA: [Jarred] Oh, James, how could you spoil it all!

MARCHBANKS: [Firing up] Yes, to be idle, selfish and useless: that is to be beautiful and free and happy: hasn't every man desired that with all his soul for the woman he loves? That's my ideal: what's yours, and that of all the dreadful people who live in these hideous rows of houses? Sermons and scrubbing brushes! With you to preach the sermon and your wife to scrub.

CANDIDA: [Quaintly] He cleans the boots, Eugene. You will have to clean them to-morrow for saying that about him.

MARCHBANKS: Oh! don't talk about boots. Your feet should be beautiful on the mountains.

CANDIDA: My feet would not be beautiful on the Hackney Road without boots.

BURGESS: [Scandalized] Come, Candy, don't be vulgar. Mr. Morchbanks ain't accustomed to it. You're givin' him the 'orrors again. I mean the poetic ones.

[Morell is silent. Apparently he is busy with his letters: really he is puzzling with misgiving over his new and alarming experience that the surer he is of his moral thrusts, the more swiftly and effectively Eugene parries them. To find himself beginning to fear a man whom he does not respect afflicts him bitterly]

[Miss Garnett comes in with a telegram]

PROSERPINE: [Handing the telegram to Morell] Reply paid. The boy's waiting. [To Candida, coming back to her machine and sitting down] Maria is ready for you now in the kitchen, Mrs. Morell. [Candida rises] The onions have come.

MARCHBANKS: [Convulsively] Onions!

CANDIDA: Yes, onions. Not even Spanish ones—

nasty little red onions. You shall help me to slice them. Come along.

[*She catches him by the wrist and runs out, pulling him after her.* Burgess *rises in consternation, and stands aghast on the hearth-rug, staring after them*]

BURGESS: Candy didn't oughter 'andle a peer's nevvy like that. It's goin' too fur with it. Lookee 'ere, James: do 'e often git taken queer like that?

MORELL: [*Shortly, writing a telegram*] I don't know.

BURGESS: [*Sentimentally*] He talks very pretty. I allus had a turn for a bit of potery. Candy takes arter me that-a-way: huse ter make me tell her fairy stories when she was on'y a little kiddy not that 'igh [*Indicating a stature of two feet or thereabouts*]

MORELL: [*Preoccupied*] Ah, indeed. [*He blots the telegram, and goes out*]

PROSERPINE: Used you to make the fairy stories up out of your own head?

[Burgess, *not deigning to reply, strikes an attitude of the haughtiest disdain on the hearth-rug*]

PROSERPINE: [*Calmly*] I should never have supposed you had it in you. By the way, I'd better warn you, since you've taken such a fancy to Mr. Marchbanks. He's mad.

BURGESS: Mad! Wot! 'Im too!!

PROSERPINE: Mad as a March hare. He did frighten me, I can tell you just before you came in that time. Haven't you noticed the queer things he says?

BURGESS: So that's wot the poetic 'orrors means. Blame me if it didn't come into my head once or twyst that he must be off his chump! [*He crosses the room to the door, lifting up his voice as he goes*] Well, this is a pretty sort of asylum for a man to be in, with no one but you to take care of him!

PROSERPINE: [*As he passes her*] Yes, what a dreadful thing it would be if anything happened to you!

BURGESS: [*Loftily*] Don't you address no remarks to me. Tell your hemployer that I've gone into the garden for a smoke.

PROSERPINE: [*Mocking*] Oh!

[*Before* Burgess *can retort,* Morell *comes back*]

BURGESS: [*Sentimentally*] Goin' for a turn in the garden to smoke, James.

MORELL: [*Brusquely*] Oh, all right, all right. [Burgess *goes out pathetically in the character of the weary old man.* Morell *stands at the table, turning over his papers, and adding, across to* Proserpine, *half humorously, half absently*] Well, Miss Prossy, why have you been calling my father-in-law names?

PROSERPINE: [*Blushing fiery red, and looking quickly up at him, half scared, half reproachful*] I—— [*She bursts into tears*]

MORELL: [*With tender gayety, leaning across the table towards her, and consoling her*] Oh, come, come, come! Never mind, Pross: he is a silly old fathead, isn't he?

[*With an explosive sob, she makes a dash at the door, and vanishes, banging it.* Morell, *shaking his head resignedly, sighs, and goes wearily to his chair, where he sits down and sets to work, looking old and careworn.*
Candida *comes in. She has finished her household work and taken off the apron. She at once notices his dejected appearance, and posts herself quietly at the spare chair, looking down at him attentively; but she says nothing*]

MORELL: [*Looking up, but with his pen raised ready to resume his work*] Well? Where is Eugene?

CANDIDA: Washing his hands in the scullery—under the tap. He will make an excellent cook if he can only get over his dread of Maria.

MORELL: [*Shortly*] Ha! No doubt. [*He begins writing again*]

CANDIDA: [*Going nearer, and putting her hand down softly on his to stop him, as she says*] Come here, dear. Let me look at you. [*He drops his pen and yields himself at her disposal. She makes him rise and brings him a little away from the table, looking at him critically all the time*] Turn your face to the light. [*She places him facing the window*] My boy is not looking well. Has he been overworking?

MORELL: Nothing more than usual.

CANDIDA: He looks very pale, and gray, and wrinkled, and old. [*His melancholy deepens; and she attacks it with wilful gayety*] Here [*pulling him towards the easy chair*] you've done enough writing for to-day. Leave Prossy to finish it and come and talk to me.

MORELL: But——

CANDIDA: Yes, I must be talked to sometimes. [*She makes him sit down, and seats herself on the carpet beside his knee*] Now [*patting his hand*] you're beginning to look better already. Why don't you give up all this tiresome overworking—going out every night lecturing and talking? Of course what you say is all very true and very right; but it does no good: they don't mind what you say to them one little bit. Of course they agree with you; but what's the use of people agreeing with you if they go and do just the opposite of what you tell them the moment your back is turned? Look at our congregation at St. Dominic's! Why do they come to hear you talking about Christianity every Sunday? Why, just because they've been so full of business and money-making for six days that they want to forget all about it and have a rest on the seventh, so that they can go back fresh and make money harder than ever! You positively help them at it instead of hindering them.

MORELL: [*With energetic seriousness*] You know very well, Candida, that I often blow them up soundly for that. But if there is nothing in their church-going but rest and diversion, why don't they try something more amusing—more self-indulgent? There must be some good in the fact that they prefer St. Dominic's to worse places on Sundays.

CANDIDA: Oh, the worst places aren't open; and even if they were, they daren't be seen going to them. Besides, James, dear, you preach so splendidly that it's as good as a play for them. Why do you think the women are so enthusiastic?

MORELL: [Shocked] Candida!

CANDIDA: Oh, I know. You silly boy: you think it's your Socialism and your religion; but if it was that, they'd do what you tell them instead of only coming to look at you. They all have Prossy's complaint.

MORELL: Prossy's complaint! What do you mean, Candida?

CANDIDA: Yes, Prossy, and all the other secretaries you ever had. Why does Prossy condescend to wash up the things, and to peel potatoes and abase herself in all manner of ways for six shillings a week less than she used to get in a city office? She's in love with you, James: that's the reason. They're all in love with you. And you are in love with preaching because you do it so beautifully. And you think it's all enthusiasm for the kingdom of Heaven on earth; and so do they. You dear silly!

MORELL: Candida: what dreadful, what soul-destroying cynicism! Are you jesting? Or—can it be? —are you jealous?

CANDIDA: [With curious thoughtfulness] Yes, I feel a little jealous sometimes.

MORELL: [Incredulously] What! Of Prossy!

CANDIDA: [Laughing] No, no, no, no. Not jealous of anybody. Jealous for somebody else, who is not loved as he ought to be.

MORELL: Me!

CANDIDA: You! Why, you're spoiled with love and worship: you get far more than is good for you. No: I mean Eugene.

MORELL: [Startled] Eugene!

CANDIDA: It seems unfair that all the love should go to you, and none to him, although he needs it so much more than you do. [A convulsive movement shakes him in spite of himself] What's the matter? Am I worrying you?

MORELL: [Hastily] Not at all [Looking at her with troubled intensity] You know that I have perfect confidence in you, Candida.

CANDIDA: You vain thing! Are you so sure of your irresistible attractions?

MORELL: Candida: you are shocking me. I never thought of my attractions. I thought of your goodness—your purity. That is what I confide in.

CANDIDA: What a nasty, uncomfortable thing to say to me! Oh, you are a clergyman, James—a thorough clergyman.

MORELL: [Turning away from her, heart-stricken] So Eugene says.

CANDIDA: [With a lively interest, leaning over to him with her arms on his knee] Eugene's always right. He's a wonderful boy: I have grown fonder and fonder of him all the time I was away. Do you know, James, that though he has not the least sus-

picion of it himself, he is ready to fall madly in love with me?

MORELL: [Grimly] Oh, he has no suspicion of it himself, hasn't he?

CANDIDA: Not a bit. [She takes her arms from his knee, and turns thoughtfully, sinking into a more restful attitude with her hands in her lap] Some day he will know—when he is grown up and experienced, like you. And he will know that I must have known. I wonder what he will think of me then.

MORELL: No evil, Candida. I hope and trust, no evil.

CANDIDA: [Dubiously] That will depend.

MORELL: [Bewildered] Depend!

CANDIDA: [Looking at him] Yes: it will depend on what happens to him. [He looks vacantly at her] Don't you see? It will depend on how he comes to learn what love really is. I mean on the sort of woman who will teach it to him.

MORELL: [Quite at a loss] Yes. No. I don't know what you mean.

CANDIDA: [Explaining] If he learns it from a good woman, then it will be all right: he will forgive me.

MORELL: Forgive!

CANDIDA: But suppose he learns it from a bad woman, as so many men, especially poetic men, who imagine all women are angels! Suppose he only discovers the value of love when he has thrown it away and degraded himself in his ignorance. Will he forgive me then, do you think?

MORELL: Forgive you for what?

CANDIDA: [Realizing how stupid he is, and a little disappointed, though quite tenderly so] Don't you understand? [He shakes his head. She turns to him again, so as to explain with the fondest intimacy] I mean, will he forgive me for not teaching him myself? For abandoning him to the bad women for the sake of my goodness—my purity, as you call it? Ah, James, how little you understand me, to talk of your confidence in my goodness and purity! I would give them both to poor Eugene as willingly as I would give my shawl to a beggar dying of cold, if there were nothing else to restrain me. Put your trust in my love for you, James, for if that went, I should care very little for your sermons—mere phrases that you cheat yourself and others with every day. [She is about to rise]

MORELL: His words!

CANDIDA: [Checking herself quickly in the act of getting up, so that she is on her knees, but upright] Whose words?

MORELL: Eugene's.

CANDIDA: [Delighted] He is always right. He understands you; he understands me; he understands Prossy; and you, James—you understand nothing. [She laughs, and kisses him to console him. He recoils as if stung, and springs up]

MORELL: How can you bear to do that when— oh, Candida [with anguish in his voice] I had rather you had plunged a grappling iron into my heart than given me that kiss.

CANDIDA: [*Rising, alarmed*] My dear: what's the matter?

MORELL: [*Frantically waving her off*] Don't touch me.

CANDIDA: [*Amazed*] James!

[*They are interrupted by the entrance of* Marchbanks, *with* Burgess, *who stops near the door, staring, whilst* Eugene *hurries forward between them*]

MARCHBANKS: Is anything the matter?

MORELL: [*Deadly white, putting an iron constraint on himself*] Nothing but this: that either you were right this morning, or Candida is mad.

BURGESS: [*In loudest protest*] Wot! Candy mad too! Oh, come, come, come! [*He crosses the room to the fireplace, protesting as he goes, and knocks the ashes out of his pipe on the bars.* Morell *sits down desperately, leaning forward to hide his face, and interlacing his fingers rigidly to keep them steady*]

CANDIDA: [*To* Morell, *relieved and laughing*] Oh, you're only shocked! Is that all? How conventional all you unconventional people are!

BURGESS: Come: be'ave yourself, Candy. What'll Mr. Morchbanks think of you?

CANDIDA: This comes of James teaching me to think for myself, and never to hold back out of fear of what other people may think of me. It works beautifully as long as I think the same things as he does. But now, because I have just thought something different!—look at him—just look! [*She points to* Morell, *greatly amused.* Eugene *looks, and instantly presses his hand on his heart, as if some deadly pain had shot through it, and sits down on the sofa like a man witnessing a tragedy*]

BURGESS: [*On the hearth-rug*] Well, James, you certainly ain't as himpressive lookin' as usu'l.

MORELL: [*With a laugh which is half a sob*] I suppose not. I beg all your pardons: I was not conscious of making a fuss. [*Pulling himself together*] Well, well, well, well, well! [*He goes back to his place at the table, setting to work at his papers again with resolute cheerfulness*]

CANDIDA: [*Going to the sofa and sitting beside* Marchbanks, *still in a bantering humor*] Well, Eugene, why are you so sad? Did the onions make you cry?

[Morell *cannot prevent himself from watching them*]

MARCHBANKS: [*Aside to her*] It is your cruelty. I hate cruelty. It is a horrible thing to see one person make another suffer.

CANDIDA: [*Petting him ironically*] Poor boy, have I been cruel? Did I make it slice nasty little red onions?

MARCHBANKS: [*Earnestly*] Oh, stop, stop: I don't mean myself. You have made him suffer frightfully. I feel his pain in my own heart. I know that it is not

your fault—it is something that must happen; but don't make light of it. I shudder when you torture him and laugh.

CANDIDA: [*Incredulously*] I torture James! Nonsense, Eugene: how you exaggerate! Silly! [*She looks round at* Morell, *who hastily resumes his writing. She goes to him and stands behind his chair, bending over him*] Don't work any more, dear. Come and talk to us.

MORELL: [*Affectionately but bitterly*] Ah no. I can't talk. I can only preach.

CANDIDA: [*Caressing him*] Well, come and preach.

BURGESS: [*Strongly remonstrating*] Aw, no, Candy. 'Ang it all!

[Lexy Mill *comes in, looking anxious and important*]

LEXY: [*Hastening to shake hands with* Candida] How do you do, Mrs. Morell? So glad to see you back again.

CANDIDA: Thank you, Lexy. You know Eugene, don't you?

LEXY: Oh, yes. How do you do, Marchbanks?

MARCHBANKS: Quite well, thanks.

LEXY: [*To* Morell] I've just come from the Guild of St. Matthew. They are in the greatest consternation about your telegram. There's nothing wrong, is there?

CANDIDA: What did you telegraph about, James?

LEXY: [*To* Candida] He was to have spoken for them to-night. They've taken the large hall in Mare Street and spent a lot of money on posters. Morell's telegram was to say he couldn't come. It came on them like a thunderbolt.

CANDIDA: [*Surprised, and beginning to suspect something wrong*] Given up an engagement to speak!

BURGESS: First time in his life, I'll bet. Ain' it, Candy?

LEXY: [*To* Morell] They decided to send an urgent telegram to you asking whether you could not change your mind. Have you received it?

MORELL: [*With restrained impatience*] Yes, yes: I got it.

LEXY: It was reply paid.

MORELL: Yes, I know. I answered it. I can't go.

CANDIDA: But why, James?

MORELL: [*Almost fiercely*] Because I don't choose. These people forget that I am a man: they think I am a talking machine to be turned on for their pleasure every evening of my life. May I not have one night at home, with my wife, and friends?

[*They are all amazed at this outburst, except* Eugene. *His expression remains unchanged*]

CANDIDA: Oh, James, you know you'll have an attack of bad conscience to-morrow; and I shall have to suffer for that.

LEXY: [*Intimidated, but urgent*] I know, of course, that they make the most unreasonable demands on you. But they have been telegraphing all over the place for another speaker: and they can get nobody but the President of the Agnostic League.

MORELL: [*Promptly*] Well, an excellent man. What better do they want?

LEXY: But he always insists so powerfully on the divorce of Socialism from Christianity. He will undo all the good we have been doing. Of course you know best; but— [*He hesitates*]

CANDIDA: [*Coaxingly*] Oh, do go, James. We'll all go.

BURGESS: [*Grumbling*] Look 'ere, Candy! I say! Let's stay at home by the fire, comfortable. He won't need to be more'n a couple o' hour away.

CANDIDA: You'll be just as comfortable at the meeting. We'll sit on the platform and be great people.

EUGENE: [*Terrified*] Oh, please don't let us go on the platform. No—everyone will stare at us—I couldn't. I'll sit at the back of the room.

CANDIDA: Don't be afraid. They'll be too busy looking at James to notice you.

MORELL: [*Turning his head and looking meaningly at her over his shoulder*] Prossy's complaint, Candida! Eh?

CANDIDA: [*Gayly*] Yes.

BURGESS: [*Mystified*] Prossy's complaint. Wot are you talking about, James?

MORELL: [*Not heeding him, rises; goes to the door; and holds it open, shouting in a commanding voice*] Miss Garnett.

PROSERPINE: [*In the distance*] Yes, Mr. Morell. Coming.

[*They all wait, except* Burgess, *who goes stealthily to* Lexy *and draws him aside*]

BURGESS: Listen here, Mr. Mill. Wot's Prossy's complaint? Wot's wrong with 'er?

LEXY: [*Confidentially*] Well, I don't exactly know; but she spoke very strangely to me this morning. I'm afraid she's a little out of her mind sometimes.

BURGESS: [*Overwhelmed*] Why, it must be catchin'! Four in the same 'ouse! [*He goes back to the hearth, quite lost before the instability of the human intellect in a clergyman's house*]

PROSERPINE: [*Appearing on the threshold*] What is it, Mr. Morell?

MORELL: Telegraph to the Guild of St. Matthew that I am coming.

PROSERPINE: [*Surprised*] Don't they expect you?

MORELL: [*Peremptorily*] Do as I tell you.

[Proserpine, *frightened, sits down at her typewriter, and obeys.* Morell *goes across to* Burgess, Candida *watching his movements all the time with growing wonder and misgiving*]

MORELL: Burgess: you don't want to come?

BURGESS: [*In deprecation*] Oh, don't put it like that, James. It's only that it ain't Sunday, you know.

MORELL: I'm sorry, I thought you might like to be introduced to the chairman. He's on the Works Committee of the County Council and has some influence in the matter of contracts. [Burgess *wakes up at once.* Morell, *expecting as much, waits a moment, and says*] Will you come?

BURGESS: [*With enthusiasm*] Course I'll come, James. Ain' it always a pleasure to 'ear you.

MORELL: [*Turning from him*] I shall want you to take some notes at the meeting, Miss Garnett, if you have no other engagement. [*She nods, afraid to speak*] You are coming, Lexy, I suppose.

LEXY: Certainly.

CANDIDA: We are all coming, James.

MORELL: No: you are not coming; and Eugene is not coming. You will stay here and entertain him —to celebrate your return home. [Eugene *rises, breathless*]

CANDIDA: But James—

MORELL: [*Authoritatively*] I insist. You do not want to come, and he does not want to come. [Candida *is about to protest*] Oh, don't concern yourselves: I shall have plenty of people without you: your chairs will be wanted by unconverted people who have never heard me before.

CANDIDA: [*Troubled*] Eugene: wouldn't you like to come?

MORELL: I should be afraid to let myself go before Eugene: he is so critical of sermons. [*Looking at him*] He knows I am afraid of him: he told me as much this morning. Well, I shall show him how much afraid I am by leaving him here in your custody, Candida.

MARCHBANKS: [*To himself, with vivid feeling*] That's brave. That's beautiful. [*He sits down again listening with parted lips*]

CANDIDA: [*With anxious misgiving*] But—but— Is anything the matter, James? [*Greatly troubled*] I can't understand—

MORELL: Ah, I thought it was *I* who couldn't understand, dear. [*He takes her tenderly in his arms and kisses her on the forehead; then looks round quietly at* Marchbanks]

ACT III.

Late in the evening. Past ten. The curtains are drawn, and the lamps lighted. The typewriter is in its case; the large table has been cleared and tidied; everything indicates that the day's work is done.

Candida *and* Marchbanks *are seated at the fire. The reading lamp is on the mantel-shelf above* Marchbanks, *who is sitting on the small chair reading aloud from a manuscript. A little pile of manuscripts and a couple of volumes of poetry are on the carpet beside him.* Candida *is in the easy chair with the poker, a light brass one, upright in her hand. She is leaning back and looking at the point of it curiously, with her feet stretched towards the blaze and her heels resting on the fender, profoundly unconscious of her appearance and surroundings.*

MARCHBANKS: [*Breaking off in his recitation*] Every poet that ever lived has put that thought into a sonnet. He must: he can't help it. [*He looks to her for assent, and notices her absorption in the poker*] Haven't you been listening? [*No response*] Mrs. Morell!

CANDIDA: [*Starting*] Eh?

MARCHBANKS: Haven't you been listening?

CANDIDA: [*With a guilty excess of politeness*] Oh, yes. It's very nice. Go on, Eugene. I'm longing to hear what happens to the angel.

MARCHBANKS: [*Crushed—the manuscript dropping from his hand to the floor*] I beg your pardon for boring you.

CANDIDA: But you are not boring me, I assure you. Please go on. Do, Eugene.

MARCHBANKS: I finished the poem about the angel quarter of an hour ago. I've read you several things since.

CANDIDA: [*Remorsefully*] I'm so sorry, Eugene. I think the poker must have fascinated me. [*She puts it down*]

MARCHBANKS: It made me horribly uneasy.

CANDIDA: Why didn't you tell me? I'd have put it down at once.

MARCHBANKS: I was afraid of making you uneasy, too. It looked as if it were a weapon. If I were a hero of old, I should have laid my drawn sword between us. If Morell had come in he would have thought you had taken up the poker because there was no sword between us.

CANDIDA: [*Wondering*] What? [*With a puzzled glance at him*] I can't quite follow that. Those sonnets of yours have perfectly addled me. Why should there be a sword between us?

MARCHBANKS: [*Evasively*] Oh, never mind. [*He stoops to pick up the manuscript*]

CANDIDA: Put that down again, Eugene. There are limits to my appetite for poetry—even your poetry. You've been reading to me for more than two hours—ever since James went out. I want to talk.

MARCHBANKS: [*Rising, scared*] No: I mustn't talk. [*He looks round him in his lost way, and adds, suddenly*] I think I'll go out and take a walk in the park. [*Making for the door*]

CANDIDA: Nonsense: it's shut long ago. Come and sit down on the hearth-rug, and talk moonshine as you usually do. I want to be amused. Don't you want to?

MARCHBANKS: [*In half terror, half rapture*] Yes.

CANDIDA: Then come along. [*She moves her chair back a little to make room. He hesitates; then timidly stretches himself on the hearth-rug, face upwards, and throws back his head across her knees, looking up at her*]

MARCHBANKS: Oh, I've been so miserable all the evening, because I was doing right. Now I'm doing wrong; and I'm happy.

CANDIDA: [*Tenderly amused at him*] Yes: I'm sure you feel a great grown up wicked deceiver—quite proud of yourself, aren't you?

MARCHBANKS: [*Raising his head quickly and turning a little to look round at her*] Take care. I'm ever so much older than you, if you only knew. [*He turns quite over on his knees, with his hands clasped and his arms on her lap, and speaks with growing impulse, his blood beginning to stir*] May I say some wicked things to you?

CANDIDA: [*Without the least fear or coldness, quite nobly, and with perfect respect for his passion, but with a touch of her wise-hearted maternal humor*] No. But you may say anything you really and truly feel. Anything at all, no matter what it is. I am not afraid, so long as it is your real self that speaks, and not a mere attitude—a gallant attitude, or a wicked attitude, or even a poetic attitude. I put you on your honor and truth. Now say whatever you want to.

MARCHBANKS: [*The eager expression vanishing utterly from his lips and nostrils as his eyes light up with pathetic spirituality*] Oh, now I can't say anything: all the words I know belong to some attitude or other—all except one.

CANDIDA: What one is that?

MARCHBANKS: [*Softly, losing himself in the music of the name*] Candida, Candida, Candida, Candida, Candida. I must say that now, because you have put me on my honor and truth; and I never think or feel Mrs. Morell: it is always Candida.

CANDIDA: Of course. And what have you to say to Candida?

MARCHBANKS: Nothing, but to repeat your name a thousand times. Don't you feel that every time is a prayer to you?

CANDIDA: Doesn't it make you happy to be able to pray?

MARCHBANKS: Yes, very happy.

CANDIDA: Well, that happiness is the answer to your prayer. Do you want anything more?

MARCHBANKS: [*In beatitude*] No: I have come into heaven, where want is unknown.

[*Morell comes in. He halts on the threshold, and takes in the scene at a glance*]

MORELL: [*Grave and self-contained*] I hope I don't disturb you.

[*Candida starts up violently, but without the smallest embarrassment, laughing at herself. Eugene, still kneeling, saves himself from falling by putting his hands on the seat of the chair, and remains there, staring open mouthed at Morell*]

CANDIDA: [*As he rises*] Oh, James, how you startled me! I was so taken up with Eugene that I didn't hear your latchkey. How did the meeting go off? Did you speak well?

MORELL: I have never spoken better in my life.

CANDIDA: That was first rate! How much was the collection?

MORELL: I forgot to ask.

CANDIDA: [*To Eugene*] He must have spoken splendidly, or he would never have forgotten that. [*To Morell*] Where are all the others?

MORELL: They left long before I could get away: I thought I should never escape. I believe they are having supper somewhere.

CANDIDA: [*In her domestic business tone*] Oh; in that case, Maria may go to bed. I'll tell her. [*She goes out to the kitchen*]

MORELL: [*Looking sternly down at* Marchbanks] Well?

MARCHBANKS: [*Squatting cross-legged on the hearth-rug, and actually at ease with Morell—even impishly humorous*] Well?

MORELL: Have you anything to tell me?

MARCHBANKS: Only that I have been making a fool of myself here in private whilst you have been making a fool of yourself in public.

MORELL: Hardly in the same way, I think.

MARCHBANKS: [*Scrambling up—eagerly*] The very, very, very same way. I have been playing the good man just like you. When you began your heroics about leaving me here with Candida—

MORELL: [*Involuntarily*] Candida?

MARCHBANKS: Oh, yes: I've got that far. Heroics are infectious: I caught the disease from you. I swore not to say a word in your absence that I would not have said a month ago in your presence.

MORELL: Did you keep your oath?

MARCHBANKS: [*Suddenly perching himself grotesquely on the easy chair*] I was ass enough to keep it until about ten minutes ago. Up to that moment I went on desperately reading to her—reading my own poems—anybody's poems—to stave off a conversation. I was standing outside the gate of Heaven, and refusing to go in. Oh, you can't think how heroic it was, and how uncomfortable! Then—

MORELL: [*Steadily controlling his suspense*] Then?—

MARCHBANKS: [*Prosaically slipping down into a quite ordinary attitude in the chair*] Then she couldn't bear being read to any longer.

MORELL: And you approached the gate of Heaven at last?

MARCHBANKS: Yes.

MORELL: Well? [*Fiercely*] Speak, man: have you no feeling for me?

MARCHBANKS: [*Softly and musically*] Then she became an angel; and there was a flaming sword that turned every way, so that I couldn't go in; for I saw that that gate was really the gate of Hell.

MORELL: [*Triumphantly*] She repulsed you!

MARCHBANKS: [*Rising in wild scorn*] No, you fool: if she had done that I should never have seen that I was in Heaven already. Repulsed me! You think that would have saved me—virtuous indignation! Oh, you are not worthy to live in the same world with her. [*He turns away contemptuously to the other side of the room*]

MORELL: [*Who has watched him quietly without changing his place*] Do you think you make yourself more worthy by reviling me, Eugene?

MARCHBANKS: Here endeth the thousand and first

lesson. Morell: I don't think much of your preaching after all: I believe I could do it better myself. The man I want to meet is the man that Candida married.

MORELL: The man that—? Do you mean me?

MARCHBANKS: I don't mean the Reverend James Mavor Morell, moralist and windbag. I mean the real man that the Reverend James must have hidden somewhere inside his black coat—the man that Candida loved. You can't make a woman like Candida love you by merely buttoning your collar at the back instead of in front.

MORELL: [*Boldly and steadily*] When Candida promised to marry me, I was the same moralist and windbag that you now see. I wore my black coat; and my collar was buttoned behind instead of in front. Do you think she would have loved me any the better for being insincere in my profession?

MARCHBANKS: [*On the sofa hugging his ankles*] Oh, she forgave you, just as she forgives me for being a coward, and a weakling, and what you call a sniveling little whelp and all the rest of it. [*Dreamily*] A woman like that has divine insight: she loves our souls, and not our follies and vanities and illusions, or our collars and coats, or any other of the rags and tatters we are rolled up in. [*He reflects on this for an instant; then turns intently to question* Morell] What I want to know is how you got past the flaming sword that stopped me.

MORELL: [*Meaningly*] Perhaps because I was not interrupted at the end of ten minutes.

MARCHBANKS: [*Taken aback*] What!

MORELL: Man can climb to the highest summits; but he cannot dwell there long.

MARCHBANKS: It's false: there can he dwell for ever and there only. It's in the other moments that he can find no rest, no sense of the silent glory of life. Where would you have me spend my moments, if not on the summits?

MORELL: In the scullery, slicing onions and filling lamps.

MARCHBANKS: Or in the pulpit, scrubbing cheap earthenware souls?

MORELL: Yes, that, too. It was there that I earned my golden moment, and the right, in that moment, to ask her to love me. *I* did not take the moment on credit; nor did I use it to steal another man's happiness.

MARCHBANKS: [*Rather disgustedly, trotting back towards the fireplace*] I have no doubt you conducted the transaction as honestly as if you were buying a pound of cheese. [*He stops on the brink of the hearth-rug and adds, thoughtfully, to himself, with his back turned to* Morell] I could only go to her as a beggar.

MORELL: [*Starting*] A beggar dying of cold—asking for her shawl?

MARCHBANKS: [*Turning, surprised*] Thank you for touching up my poetry. Yes, if you like, a beggar dying of cold asking for her shawl.

MORELL: [*Excitedly*] And she refused. Shall I tell you why she refused? I can tell you, on her own authority. It was because of——

MARCHBANKS: She didn't refuse.

MORELL: Not!

MARCHBANKS: She offered me all I chose to ask for, her shawl, her wings, the wreath of stars on her head, the lilies in her hand, the crescent moon beneath her feet——

MORELL: [*Seizing him*] Out with the truth, man: my wife is my wife: I want no more of your poetic fripperies. I know well that if I have lost her love and you have gained it, no law will bind her.

MARCHBANKS: [*Quaintly, without fear or resistance*] Catch me by the shirt collar, Morell: she will arrange it for me afterwards as she did this morning. [*With quiet rapture*] I shall feel her hands touch me.

MORELL: You young imp, do you know how dangerous it is to say that to me? Or [*with a sudden misgiving*] has something made you brave?

MARCHBANKS: I'm not afraid now. I disliked you before: that was why I shrank from your touch. But I saw to-day—when she tortured you—that you love her. Since then I have been your friend: you may strangle me if you like.

MORELL: [*Releasing him*] Eugene: if that is not a heartless lie—if you have a spark of human feeling left in you—will you tell me what has happened during my absence?

MARCHBANKS: What happened! Why, the flaming sword— [Morell *stamps with impatience*] Well, in plain prose, I loved her so exquisitely that I wanted nothing more than the happiness of being in such love. And before I had time to come down from the highest summits, you came in.

MORELL: [*Suffering deeply*] So it is still unsettled —still the misery of doubt.

MARCHBANKS: Misery! I am the happiest of men. I desire nothing now but her happiness. [*With dreamy enthusiasm*] Oh, Morell, let us both give her up. Why should she have to choose between a wretched little nervous disease like me, and a pig-headed parson like you? Let us go on a pilgrimage, you to the east and I to the west, in search of a worthy lover for her—some beautiful archangel with purple wings——

MORELL: Some fiddlestick. Oh, if she is mad enough to leave me for you, who will protect her? Who will help her? who will work for her? who will be a father to her children? [*He sits down distractedly on the sofa, with his elbows on his knees and his head propped on his clenched fists*]

MARCHBANKS: [*Snapping his fingers wildly*] She does not ask those silly questions. It is she who wants somebody to protect, to help, to work for— somebody to give her children to protect, to help and to work for. Some grown up man who has become as a little child again. Oh, you fool, you fool, you triple fool! I am the man, Morell: I am the

man. [*He dances about excitedly, crying*] You don't understand what a woman is. Send for her, Morell: send for her and let her choose between—[*The door opens and* Candida *enters. He stops as if petrified*]

CANDIDA: [*Amazed, on the threshold*] What on earth are you at, Eugene?

MARCHBANKS: [*Oddly*] James and I are having a preaching match; and he is getting the worst of it. [Candida *looks quickly round at* Morell. *Seeing that he is distressed, she hurries down to him, greatly vexed, speaking with vigorous reproach to* Marchbanks]

CANDIDA: You have been annoying him. Now I won't have it, Eugene: do you hear? [*Putting her hand on* Morell's *shoulder, and quite forgetting her wifely tact in her annoyance*] My boy shall not be worried: I will protect him.

MORELL: [*Rising proudly*] Protect!

CANDIDA: [*Not heeding him—to* Eugene] What have you been saying?

MARCHBANKS: [*Appalled*] Nothing—I——

CANDIDA: Eugene! Nothing?

MARCHBANKS: [*Piteously*] I mean—I—I'm very sorry. I won't do it again: indeed I won't. I'll let him alone.

MORELL: [*Indignantly, with an aggressive movement towards* Eugene] Let me alone! You young——

CANDIDA: [*Stopping him*] Sh—no, let me deal with him, James.

MARCHBANKS: Oh, you're not angry with me, are you?

CANDIDA: [*Severely*] Yes, I am—very angry. I have a great mind to pack you out of the house.

MORELL: [*Taken aback by* Candida's *vigor, and by no means relishing the sense of being rescued by her from another man*] Gently, Candida, gently. I am able to take care of myself.

CANDIDA: [*Petting him*] Yes, dear: of course you are. But you mustn't be annoyed and made miserable.

MARCHBANKS: [*Almost in tears, turning to the door*] I'll go.

CANDIDA: Oh, you needn't go: I can't turn you out at this time of night. [*Vehemently*] Shame on you! For shame!

MARCHBANKS: [*Desperately*] But what have I done?

CANDIDA: I know what you have done—as well as if I had been here all the time. Oh, it was unworthy! You are like a child: you cannot hold your tongue.

MARCHBANKS: I would die ten times over sooner than give you a moment's pain.

CANDIDA: [*With infinite contempt for this puerility*] Much good your dying would do me!

MORELL: Candida, my dear: this altercation is hardly quite seeming. It is a matter between two men; and I am the right person to settle it.

CANDIDA: Two men! Do you call that a man? [*To* Eugene] *You bad boy!*

MARCHBANKS: [*Gathering a whimsically affectionate courage from the scolding*] If I am to be scolded like this, I must make a boy's excuse. He began it. And he's bigger than I am.

CANDIDA: [*Losing confidence a little as her concern for* Morell's *dignity takes the alarm*] That can't be true. [*To* Morell] You didn't begin it, James, did you?

MORELL: [*Contemptuously*] No.

MARCHBANKS: [*Indignant*] Oh!

MORELL: [*To* Eugene] You began it—this morning. [Candida, *instantly connecting this with his mysterious allusion in the afternoon to something told him by* Eugene *in the morning, looks quickly at him, wrestling with the enigma.* Morell *proceeds with the emphasis of offended superiority*] But your other point is true. I am certainly the bigger of the two, and, I hope, the stronger, Candida. So you had better leave the matter in my hands.

CANDIDA: [*Again soothing him*] Yes, dear; but— [*troubled*] I don't understand about this morning.

MORELL: [*Gently snubbing her*] You need not understand, my dear.

CANDIDA: But, James, I— [*The street bell rings*] Oh, bother! Here they all come. [*She goes out to let them in*]

MARCHBANKS: [*Running to* Morell] Oh, Morell, isn't it dreadful? She's angry with us: she hates me. What shall I do?

MORELL: [*With a quaint desperation, clutching himself by the hair*] Eugene: my head is spinning round. I shall begin to laugh presently. [*He walks up and down the middle of the room.*]

MARCHBANKS: [*Following him anxiously*] No, no: she'll think I've thrown you into hysterics. Don't laugh.

[*Boisterous voices and laughter are heard approaching.* Lexy Mill, *his eyes sparkling, and his bearing denoting unwonted elevation of spirit, enters with* Burgess, *who is greasy and self-complacent, but has all his wits about him.* Miss Garnett, *with her smartest hat and jacket on, follows them; but though her eyes are brighter than before, she is evidently a prey to misgiving. She places herself with her back to her typewriting table, with one hand on it to rest herself, passes the other across her forehead as if she were a little tired and giddy.* Marchbanks *relapses into shyness and edges away into the corner near the window, where* Morell's *books are*]

LEXY: [*Exhilaratedly*] Morell: I must congratulate you. [*Grasping his hand*] What a noble, splendid, inspired address you gave us! You surpassed yourself.

BURGESS: So you did, James. It fair kep' me awake to the last word. Didn't it, Miss Gornett?

PROSERPINE: [*Worriedly*] Oh, I wasn't minding you: I was trying to make notes. [*She takes out her note-book, and looks at her stenography, which nearly makes her cry*]

PROSERPINE: Much too fast. You know I can't do more than a hundred words a minute. [*She relieves her feelings by throwing her note-book angrily beside her machine, ready for use next morning*]

MORELL: [*Soothingly*] Oh, well, well, never mind, never mind, never mind. Have you all had supper?

LEXY: Mr. Burgess has been kind enough to give us a really splendid supper at the Belgrave.

BURGESS: [*With effusive magnanimity*] Don't mention it, Mr. Mill. [*Modestly*] You're 'arty welcome to my little treat.

PROSERPINE: We had champagne! I never tasted it before. I feel quite giddy.

MORELL: [*Surprised*] A champagne supper! That was very handsome. Was it my eloquence that produced all this extravagance?

LEXY: [*Rhetorically*] Your eloquence, and Mr. Burgess' goodness of heart. [*With a fresh burst of exhilaration*] And what a very fine fellow the chairman is, Morell! He came to supper with us.

MORELL: [*With long-drawn significance, looking at* Burgess] O-o-o-h, the chairman. Now I understand.

[Burgess, *covering a lively satisfaction in his diplomatic cunning with a deprecatory cough, retires to the hearth,* Lexy *folds his arms and leans against the cellaret in a high-spirited attitude.* Candida *comes in with glasses, lemons, and a jug of hot water on a tray*]

CANDIDA: Who will have some lemonade? You know our rules: total abstinence. [*She puts the tray on the table, and takes up the lemon squeezers, looking enquiringly around at them*]

MORELL: No use, dear. They've all had champagne. Pross has broken her pledge.

CANDIDA: [*To* Proserpine] You don't mean to say you've been drinking champagne!

PROSERPINE: [*Stubbornly*] Yes, I do. I'm only a beer teetotaler, not a champagne teetotaler. I don't like beer. Are there any letters for me to answer, Mr. Morell?

MORELL: No more to-night.

PROSERPINE: Very well. Good-night, everybody.

LEXY: [*Gallantly*] Had I not better see you home, Miss Garnett?

PROSERPINE: No, thank you. I shan't trust myself with anybody to-night. I wish I hadn't taken any of that stuff. [*She walks straight out*]

BURGESS: [*Indignantly*] Stuff, indeed! That gurl dunno wot champagne is! Pommery and Greeno at twelve and six a bottle. She took two glasses a'most straight hoff.

MORELL: [*A little anxious about her*] Go and look after her, Lexy.

LEXY: [*Alarmed*] But if she should really be— Suppose she began to sing in the street, or anything of that sort.

MORELL: Just so: she may. That's why you'd better see her safely home.

CANDIDA: Do, Lexy: there's a good fellow.

[She shakes his hand and pushes him gently to the door]

LEXY: It's evidently my duty to go. I hope it may not be necessary. Good-night, Mrs. Morell. *[To the rest]* Good-night. *[He goes. Candida shuts the door]*

BURGESS: He was gushin' with hextra piety hisself arter two sips. People carn't drink like they huseter. *[Dismissing the subject and bustling away from the hearth]* Well, James: it's time to lock up. Mr. Morchbanks: shall I 'ave the pleasure of your company for a bit of the way home?

MARCHBANKS: *[Affrightedly]* Yes: I'd better go. *[He hurries across to the door; but* Candida *places herself before it, barring his way]*

CANDIDA: *[With quiet authority]* You sit down. You're not going yet.

MARCHBANKS: *[Quailing]* No: I—I didn't mean to. *[He comes back into the room and sits down abjectly on the sofa]*

CANDIDA: Mr. Marchbanks will stay the night with us, papa.

BURGESS: Oh, well, I'll say good-night. So long, James. *[He shakes hands with* Morell *and goes on to* Eugene] Make 'em give you a night light by your bed, Mr. Morchbanks: it'll comfort you if you wake up in the night with a touch of that complaint of yores. Good-night.

MARCHBANKS: Thank you: I will. Good-night, Mr. Burgess. *[They shake hands and* Burgess *goes to the door]*

CANDIDA: *[Intercepting* Morell, *who is following* Burgess] Stay here, dear: I'll put on papa's coat for him. *[She goes out with* Burgess]

MARCHBANKS: Morell: there's going to be a terrible scene. Aren't you afraid?

MORELL: Not in the least.

MARCHBANKS: I never envied you your courage before. *[He rises timidly and puts his hand appealingly on* Morell's *forearm]* Stand by me, won't you?

MORELL: *[Casting him off gently, but resolutely]* Each for himself, Eugene. She must choose between us now. *[He goes to the other side of the room as* Candida *returns.* Eugene *sits down again on the sofa like a guilty schoolboy on his best behavior]*

CANDIDA: *[Between them, addressing* Eugene] Are you sorry?

MARCHBANKS: *[Earnestly]* Yes, heartbroken.

CANDIDA: Well, then, you are forgiven. Now go off to bed like a good little boy: I want to talk to James about you.

MARCHBANKS: *[Rising in great consternation]* Oh, I can't do that, Morell. I must be here. I'll not go away. Tell her.

CANDIDA: *[With quick suspicion]* Tell me what? *[His eyes avoid hers furtively. She turns and mutely transfers the question to* Morell]

MORELL: *[Bracing himself for the catastrophe]* I have nothing to tell her, except *[here his voice deepens to a measured and mournful tenderness]*

that she is my greatest treasure on earth—if she is really mine.

CANDIDA: *[Coldly, offended by his yielding to his orator's instinct and treating her as if she were the audience at the Guild of St. Matthew]* I am sure Eugene can say no less, if that is all.

MARCHBANKS: *[Discouraged]* Morell: she's laughing at us.

MORELL: *[With a quick touch of temper]* There is nothing to laugh at. Are you laughing at us, Candida?

CANDIDA: *[With quiet anger]* Eugene is very quick-witted, James. I hope I am going to laugh; but I am not sure that I am not going to be very angry. *[She goes to the fireplace, and stands there leaning with her arm on the mantelpiece, and her foot on the fender, whilst* Eugene *steals to* Morell *and plucks him by the sleeve]*

MARCHBANKS: *[Whispering]* Stop, Morell. Don't let us say anything.

MORELL: *[Pushing* Eugene *away without deigning to look at him]* I hope you don't mean that as a threat, Candida.

CANDIDA: *[With emphatic warning]* Take care, James. Eugene: I asked you to go. Are you going?

MORELL: *[Putting his foot down]* He shall not go. I wish him to remain.

MARCHBANKS: I'll go. I'll do whatever you want. *[He turns to the door]*

CANDIDA: Stop! *[He obeys]* Didn't you hear James say he wished you to stay? James is master here. Don't you know that?

MARCHBANKS: *[Flushing with a young poet's rage against tyranny]* By what right is he master?

CANDIDA: *[Quietly]* Tell him, James.

MORELL: *[Taken aback]* My dear: I don't know of any right that makes me master. I assert no such right.

CANDIDA: *[With infinite reproach]* You don't know! Oh, James, James! *[To* Eugene, *musingly]* I wonder do you understand, Eugene! No: you're too young. Well, I give you leave to stay—to stay and learn. *[She comes away from the hearth and places herself between them]* Now, James: what's the matter? Come: tell me.

MARCHBANKS: *[Whispering tremulously across to him]* Don't.

CANDIDA: Come. Out with it!

MORELL: *[Slowly]* I meant to prepare your mind carefully, Candida, so as to prevent misunderstanding.

CANDIDA: Yes, dear: I am sure you did. But never mind: I shan't misunderstand.

MORELL: Well—er—*[He hesitates, unable to find the long explanation which he supposed to be available]*

CANDIDA: Well?

MORELL: *[Baldly]* Eugene declares that you are in love with him.

MARCHBANKS: *[Frantically]* No, no, no, no, never.

I did not, Mrs. Morell: it's not true. I said I loved you, and that he didn't. I said that I understood you, and that he couldn't. And it was not after what passed there before the fire that I spoke: it was not, on my word. It was this morning.

CANDIDA: [*Enlightened*] This morning!

MARCHBANKS: Yes. [*He looks at her, pleading for credence, and then adds, simply*] That was what was the matter with my collar.

CANDIDA: [*After a pause; for she does not take in his meaning at once*] His collar! [*She turns to* Morell, *shocked*] Oh, James: did you?—[*She stops*]

MORELL: [*Ashamed*] You know, Candida, that I have a temper to struggle with. And he said [*shuddering*] that you despised me in your heart.

CANDIDA: [*Turning quickly on* Eugene] Did you say that?

MARCHBANKS: [*Terrified*] No!

CANDIDA: [*Severely*] Then James has just told me a falsehood. Is that what you mean?

MARCHBANKS: No, no: I—I—[*blurting out the explanation desperately*]—it was David's wife. And it wasn't at home: it was when she saw him dancing before all the people.

MORELL: [*Taking the cue with a debater's adroitness*] Dancing before all the people, Candida; and thinking he was moving their hearts by his mission when they were only suffering from—Prossy's complaint. [*She is about to protest: he raises his hand to silence her, exclaiming*] Don't try to look indignant, Candida:—

CANDIDA: [*Interjecting*] Try!

MORELL: [*Continuing*] Eugene was right. As you told me a few hours after, he is always right. He said nothing that you did not say far better yourself. He is the poet, who sees everything; and I am the poor parson, who understands nothing.

CANDIDA: [*Remorsefully*] Do you mind what is said by a foolish boy, because I said something like it again in jest?

MORELL: That foolish boy can speak with the inspiration of a child and the cunning of a serpent. He has claimed that you belong to him and not to me; and, rightly or wrongly, I have come to fear that it may be true. I will not go about tortured with doubts and suspicions. I will not live with you and keep a secret from you. I will not suffer the intolerable degradation of jealousy. We have agreed —he and I—that you shall choose between us now. I await your decision.

CANDIDA: [*Slowly recoiling a step, her heart hardened by his rhetoric in spite of the sincere feeling behind it*] Oh! I am to choose, am I? I suppose it is quite settled that I must belong to one or the other. Is that what you mean?

MORELL: [*Firmly*] Quite. You must choose definitely.

MARCHBANKS: [*Anxiously*] Morell: you don't understand. She means that she belongs to herself.

CANDIDA: [*Turning on him*] I mean that and a good deal more, Master Eugene, as you will both

find out presently. And pray, my lords and masters, what have you to offer for my choice? I am up for auction, it seems. What do you bid, James?

MORELL: [*Reproachfully*] Cand— [*He breaks down: his eyes and throat fill with tears: the orator becomes the wounded animal*] I can't speak—

CANDIDA: [*Impulsively going to him*] Ah, dearest—

MARCHBANKS: [*In wild alarm*] Stop: it's not fair. You mustn't show her that you suffer, Morell. I am on the rack, too; but I am not crying.

MORELL: [*Rallying all his forces*] Yes: you are right. It is not for pity that I am bidding. [*He disengages himself from* Candida]

CANDIDA: [*Retreating, chilled*] I beg your pardon, James; I did not mean to touch you. I am waiting to hear your bid.

MORELL: [*With proud humility*] I have nothing to offer you but my strength for your defence, my honesty of purpose for your surety, my ability and industry for your livelihood, and my authority and position for your dignity. That is all it becomes a man to offer to a woman.

CANDIDA: [*Quite quietly*] And you, Eugene? What do you offer?

MARCHBANKS: My weakness! my desolation! my heart's need!

CANDIDA: [*Impressed*] That's a good bid, Eugene. Now I know how to make my choice.

[*She pauses and looks curiously from one to the other, as if weighing them.* Morell, *whose lofty confidence has changed into heartbreaking dread at* Eugene's *bid, loses all power of concealing his anxiety.* Eugene, *strung to the highest tension, does not move a muscle*]

MORELL: [*In a suffocated voice—the appeal bursting from the depths of his anguish*] Candida!

MARCHBANKS: [*Aside, in a flash of contempt*] Coward!

CANDIDA: [*Significantly*] I give myself to the weaker of the two.

[Eugene *divines her meaning at once: his face whitens like steel in a furnace that cannot melt it*]

MORELL: [*Bowing his head with the calm of collapse*] I accept your sentence, Candida.

CANDIDA: Do you understand, Eugene?

MARCHBANKS: Oh, I feel I'm lost. He cannot bear the burden.

MORELL: [*Incredulously, raising his head with prosaic abruptness*] Do you mean me, Candida?

CANDIDA: [*Smiling a little*] Let us sit and talk comfortably over it like three friends. [*To* Morell] Sit down, dear. [Morell *takes the chair from the fireside—the children's chair*] Bring me that chair, Eugene. [*She indicates the easy chair. He fetches it silently, even with something like cold strength, and places it next* Morell, *a little behind him. She sits down. He goes to the sofa and sits there, still silent and inscrutable. When they are all settled she begins, throwing a spell of quietness on them by her calm, sane, tender tone*] You remember what you told me about yourself, Eugene: how nobody has cared for you since your old nurse died: how those clever, fashionable sisters and successful brothers of yours were your mother's and father's pets: how miserable you were at Eton: how your father is trying to starve you into returning to Oxford: how you have had to live without comfort or welcome or refuge, always lonely, and nearly always disliked and misunderstood, poor boy!

MARCHBANKS: [*Faithful to the nobility of his lot*] I had my books. I had Nature. And at last I met you.

CANDIDA: Never mind that just at present. Now I want you to look at this other boy here—my boy—spoiled from his cradle. We go once a fortnight to see his parents. You should come with us, Eugene, and see the pictures of the hero of that household. James as a baby! the most wonderful of all babies. James holding his first school prize, won at the ripe age of eight! James as the captain of his eleven! James in his first frock coat! James under all sorts of glorious circumstances! You know how strong he is (I hope he didn't hurt you)—how clever he is —how happy! [*With deepening gravity*] Ask James' mother and his three sisters what it cost to save James the trouble of doing anything but be strong and clever and happy. Ask me what it costs to be James' mother and three sisters and wife and mother to his children all in one. Ask Prossy and Maria how troublesome the house is even when we have no visitors to help us to slice the onions. Ask the tradesmen who want to worry James and spoil his beautiful sermons who it is that puts them off. When there is money to give, he gives it: when there is money to refuse, I refuse it. I build a castle of comfort and indulgence and love for him, and stand sentinel always to keep little vulgar cares out. I make him master here, though he does not know it, and could not tell you a moment ago how it came to be so. [*With sweet irony*] And when he thought I might go away with you, his only anxiety was what should become of me! And to tempt me to stay he offered me [*leaning forward to stroke his hair caressingly at each phrase*] his strength for my defence, his industry for my livelihood, his position for my dignity, his—[*relenting*] Ah, I am mixing up your beautiful sentences and spoiling them, am I not, darling? [*She lays her cheek fondly against his*]

MORELL: [*Quite overcome, kneeling beside her chair and embracing her with boyish ingenuousness*] It's all true, every word. What I am you have made me with the labor of your hands and the love of your heart! You are my wife, my mother, my sisters: you are the sum of all loving care to me.

CANDIDA: [*In his arms, smiling, to* Eugene] Am I your mother and sisters to you, Eugene?

MARCHBANKS: [*Rising with a fierce gesture of disgust*] Ah, never. Out, then, into the night with me!

CANDIDA: [*Rising quickly and intercepting him*] You are not going like that, Eugene?

MARCHBANKS: [*With the ring of a man's voice— no longer a boy's—in the words*] I know the hour when it strikes. I am impatient to do what must be done.

MORELL: [*Rising from his knee, alarmed*] Candida: don't let him do anything rash.

CANDIDA: [*Confident, smiling at* Eugene] Oh, there is no fear. He has learnt to live without happiness.

MARCHBANKS: I no longer desire happiness, life is nobler than that. Parson James: I give you my happiness with both hands: I love you because you have filled the heart of the woman I loved. Good-bye. [*He goes towards the door*]

CANDIDA: One last word. [*He stops, but without turning to her*] How old are you, Eugene?

MARCHBANKS: As old as the world now. This morning I was eighteen.

CANDIDA: [*Going to him, and standing behind him with one hand caressingly on his shoulder*] Eighteen! Will you, for my sake, make a little poem out of the two sentences I am going to say to you? And will you promise to repeat it to yourself whenever you think of me?

MARCHBANKS: [*Without moving*] Say the sentences.

CANDIDA: When I am thirty, she will be forty-five. When I am sixty, she will be seventy-five.

MARCHBANKS: [*Turning to her*] In a hundred years, we shall be the same age. But I have a better secret than that in my heart. Let me go now. The night outside grows impatient.

CANDIDA: Good-bye. [*She takes his face in her hands; and as he divines her intention and bends his knee, she kisses his forehead. Then he flies out into the night. She turns to Morell, holding out her arms to him*] Ah, James! [*They embrace. But they do not know the secret in the poet's heart*]

James M. Barrie

(1860–1937)

The novelist Graham Greene reminds us that "Barrie was as ill at ease in the world as Shaw was confident." Those who knew James Barrie are not apt to demur at this statement. "Favored from the very start of his career by Fortune," Greene continues, "he remained a misfit. He invented a dream world of sexless wives who mothered and understood their husbands, of children who never grew up because they had never really been born." But there were many good reasons why Barrie should have become England's best-loved modern playwright before 1920, quite apart from his exceptional understanding of the business of making a play move on the stage.

Barrie's life was a success story, though not of the aggressive kind celebrated in American fiction, since he was an extraordinarily shy and retiring person. Nor did he succeed with particularly rousing revelations. Rather, he owed his success to a lovable, volatile spirit and to extraordinary insight and ability for fantastication. The son of a displaced weaver from tiny Kirriemuir (Thrums), Scotland, he had the knack of making life seem endurable. He could be, it is true, a shrewd observer of reality, but he had an ingratiating way of leaving it for a whim or a fancy. If he was well aware of the world of cash and carry, he could always be counted on to have agreeable sentiments about such things as motherhood, childhood, and innocence.

The irreverent Bernard Shaw might laugh society out of countenance, but Barrie smiled it right back into countenance. According to many playgoers, England after 1890 was acquiring too many realists for comfort, but the deft magician from Thrums made the romantic spirit bloom again. And his romanticism was unlike that which had seethed with illicit passions and unfurled the banner of revolt in the days before respectability had mounted the throne of England with Victoria. In Barrie's enchanted gardens there were no flowers of evil. Always, it is true, he eluded definitions; always there was something in his temperament and outlook on life that perhaps he himself could never have defined, some disenchantment that made him seek and supply enchantment all the more eagerly. But his grateful public could easily overlook what it could not understand and would not have liked if it had understood. And Barrie, unlike the pertinacious Mr. Shaw, was not one to insist upon any special understanding, partly, perhaps, because his skepticism called reason itself into question.

Educated at Dumfries Academy and the University of Edinburgh, Barrie first practiced journalism in Nottingham, then in London, excelling in humorous little sketches of the Scottish life he knew so well. At the age of thirty-one he was acclaimed for his novel *The Little Minister,* and three years later he published another successful book, *Sentimental Tommy.* By 1892, after some trivial plays (including an anti-Ibsenite spoof *Ibsen's Ghost*) he also had a successful play, the farce *Walker, London,* to his credit. His next play, *The Professor's Love Story,* a sentimental comedy, may have been denounced by Ibsen's champion William Archer, as "a calculated disloyalty to art," but it ran for eighteen months at the Comedy Theatre, from midsummer of 1894 to Christmas 1895. (It also had a run of twenty-nine weeks in 1916, when it was revived in London, proving the steadfast attachment of the British public to Barriesque confections.) Next, he dramatized *The Little Minister,* in 1897, and both public response and encouragement from his manager Charles Frohman made him turn amost exclusively to playwriting. After five years, during which he produced only one play, *The Wedding Guest,* Barrie struck a stride which carried him into the hearts of Englishmen. He completed a play almost every year until 1920.

Although virtually everything he wrote between 1902 and 1920 won the affections of the playgoer, Barrie's reputation rests in the main on five full-length plays, four of them fantasies, and the perennial one-act comedy *The Twelve-Pound Look* (1910). Two of the full-length plays, *Peter Pan* (1904) and *Mary Rose* (1920), were triumphs of tender-hearted fancy. *Peter Pan* is likely to last as long as English is spoken on the stage. It has been produced every Christmas in London since 1904, and a statue of the young hero who believed in fairies will probably stand in London's Kensington Gardens as long as Nelson's monument. When, years after the first production of the play, Maeterlinck visited Barrie, he wrote on the whitewashed walls of the latter's study, "To the father of *Peter Pan* and the grandfather of *The Blue Bird,*" a handsome acknowledgment of indebtedness to this fantasy of the Never-Never Land. *Mary Rose,* a tenuous pathetic fantasy based on a Hebrides Islands legend, also succeeded mightily in its time, but was compounded of more perishable stuff. The other two fantasies, widely separated in time of composition, *The Admirable Crichton* (1902) and *Dear Brutus* (1917), belong to adult sophistication. The former, Barrie's contribution to the drama of ideas, presents an arch attitude toward class distinctions; the latter, his philosophical testament, takes a dim view of people's ability to lead better lives than they do: "The fault, dear Brutus, is not in our stars, But in ourselves, that we are underlings." The fifth important full-length play, *What Every Woman Knows* (1908), carries us somewhat beyond the limits of probability in the pursuit of a fiction—the pleasant one that there is always a woman behind the throne occupied by a seemingly self-sufficient male. But this play is an excursion into the realistic style of drama—Barrie's only satisfactory one.

In spite of the admiration of the public, controversy raged over Barrie's merits as a modern playwright. If the heat has dissipated, it is only because the taste for his work has diminished and he therefore furnishes less provocation. In America, Ludwig Lewisohn and George Jean Nathan were up in arms against Barrie's sentimentality, which was often unvarnished, if not downright shameless. "With great skill, he permits nothing to stand in the way of it," Nathan wrote, "—not life, not reality, none of the hard truths of the world. His characters are for the most part marionettes with human hearts, but with heads filled only with sawdust and good theatrical dialogue." And Nathan observed that the playwright succeeded so well because of his cunning in stating ordinary theatrical sentiment in a fresh theatrical manner: "He lays hold of ancient sugars and molds them into novel and pretty candies." In England, too, there were dissenting critics. Desmond MacCarthy, though granting him "inventiveness," even took exception to his depiction of youth and age "only in the light of the autumnal glow of elderly fancy," and objected to his stopping his ears to the jarring note of conflict in young lives.

Nevertheless, Barrie will be remembered as one of the four or five playwrights who gave the English theatre most of its vitality during the first two decades of the twentieth century, and the best of his work will continue to provide delight to those who do not look at it under the glare of merciless intellect. This delight is, moreover, enhanced for the reader by Barrie's ingratiating treatment of a playscript. For a long time, he refused to allow his plays to be published and when he finally did consent, he worked on the scripts with scrupulous attention to descriptions and stage directions irrelevant to stage production. As a result, he evolved a printed form that fuses the features of a play with those of a novel. Since the nondramatic embellishments were written in Barrie's best style of whimsy, the literary grace of the text is as gratifying as the dialogue.

The Admirable Crichton is unique among Barrie's plays because it represents a compromise between Barriesque fantasy and the drama of ideas that became current in England at the turn of the century largely under the inspiration of Ibsen. It is a Shavian fable with Barriesque sentiment—and without Shaw's dynamic philosophy of social change. In consequence of Barrie's immunity to both liberal and Marxist ideology, *The Admirable Crichton* ends as it begins. The structure of English society remains fundamentally unchallenged, and there is no suggestion that it is likely to undergo any drastic transformation. Yet within the limits of this premise, the comedy contains withering satire on the social order in addition to delightful spoofing of characters. Nor is the play devoid of a philosophical attitude toward such matters as the "law of nature" and the principle of "equality," both touted by old-time liberals with considerably more sentimentality than can be charged against Barrie himself. In London, where the British aristocracy is sustained by "civilization," it is natural for the lords to be lords and for the servants to be servants. In a state of nature, however, it is "natural" for the servants to become the masters. Environment and successful adaptation to it determine social status, both in Mayfair and in the South Sea Islands. On the island, as the critic Walkley noted, "Lord Loam sinks 'naturally' to the bottom, just as Crichton rises 'naturally' to the top."

Only in the last act does *The Admirable Crichton* falter in its logic, so that the play may be regarded as a vestige of the Victorian Compromise. Walkley, who was usually very well disposed toward Barrie's work, complained that it was not "natural" or credible for Crichton to dwindle into a servant again after having been master of the island. And Walkley would be entirely right if Barrie's concern had been with characterization. It is, however, in the parable on the relativity of social status that the playwright appears to have been interested, and it is the parable that comes full circle round in *The Admirable Crichton*. To which we may add that considerable bitterness lurks in the last act! Barrie is unfair to the hero, who is content to be a butler again once he returns to London, unfair, too, to the British social structure in assuming that a man of Crichton's ability will find no better use for his mind and spirit, and decidedly relentless toward Crichton's employers. As Walkley observed, "The aristocrats, who began by being merely fools, are driven in the end into being consummate liars." In view of Barrie's reputation for sentimentality, it is well to remember that the milk of human kindness, of which he had an excess, sometimes curdled with acid.

BIBLIOGRAPHY: Barrett H. Clark, *A Study of the Modern Drama* (pp. 310–320), 1938; William A. Darlington, *J. M. Barrie*, 1938; John Gassner, *Masters of the Drama* (pp. 622–624), 1940, 1945; Desmond MacCarthy, *Drama* (pp. 315–321), 1940; George Jean Nathan, *Art of the Night* (pp. 153–155), 1928; Ernest Short, *Theatrical Cavalcade* (pp. 82–90), 1942; A. B. Walkley, *Drama and Life* (pp. 194–213), 1908.

THE ADMIRABLE CRICHTON

By James M. Barrie

CHARACTERS

THE HON. ERNEST WOOLLEY	TREHERNE	TWEENY
CRICHTON	LORD BROCKLEHURST	OTHER SERVANTS AT LOAM HOUSE
LADY CATHERINE	THE EARL OF LOAM	NAVAL OFFICER
LADY AGATHA	FISHER	LADY BROCKLEHURST
LADY MARY		

ACT I. *Loam House, Mayfair, London.*
ACT II. *A desert isle in the Pacific. Two months later.*
ACT III. *Same as Act II. Two years later.*
ACT IV. *Loam House, London. Several months later.*

TIME—*About 1900.*

ACT I.

A moment before the curtain rises, the Hon. Ernest Woolley *drives up to the door of Loam House in Mayfair. There is a happy smile on his pleasant, insignificant face, and this presumably means that he is thinking of himself. He is too busy over nothing, this man about town, to be always thinking of himself, but, on the other hand, he almost never thinks of any other person. Probably Ernest's great moment is when he wakes of a morning and realizes that he really is Ernest, for we must all wish to be that which is our ideal. We can conceive of him springing out of bed light-heartedly and waiting for his man to do the rest. He is dressed in excellent taste, with just the little bit more which shows that he is not without a sense of humor: the dandiacal are often saved by carrying a smile at the whole thing in their spats, let us say. Ernest left Cambridge the other day, a member of the Athenaeum (which he would be sorry to have you confound with a club in London by the same name). He is a bachelor, but not of the arts, no mean epigrammatist (as you shall see), and a favorite of the ladies. He is almost a celebrity in restaurants, where he dines frequently, returning to sup; and during this last year he has probably paid as much in them for the privilege of handing his hat to an attendant as the rent of a working-man's flat. He complains brightly that he is hard up, and that if somebody or other at Westminster does not look out the country will go to the dogs. He is no fool. He has the shrewdness to float with the current because it is a labor-saving process, but he has sufficient pluck to fight, if fight he must (a brief contest, for he would soon be toppled over). He has a light nature, which would enable him to bob up cheerily in new conditions and return unal-*

tered to the old ones. His selfishness is his most endearing quality. If he has his way he will spend his life like a cat in pushing his betters out of the soft places, and until he is old he will be fondled in the process.

He gives his hat to one footman and his cane to another, and mounts the great staircase unassisted and undirected. As a nephew of the house he need show no credentials even to Crichton, *who is guarding a door above.*

It would not be good taste to describe Crichton, *who is only a servant; if to the scandal of all good houses he is to stand out as a figure in the play, he must do it on his own, as they say in the pantry and the boudoir. We are not going to help him. We have had misgivings ever since we found his name in the title, and we shall keep him out of his rights as long as we can. Even though we softened to him he would not be a hero in these clothes of servitude; and he loves his clothes. How to get him out of them? It would require a cataclysm. To be an indoor servant at all is to* Crichton *a badge of honor; to be a butler at thirty is the realization of his proudest ambitions. He is devotedly attached to his master, who, in his opinion, has but one fault, he is not sufficiently contemptuous of his inferiors. We are immediately to be introduced to this solitary failing of a great English peer.*

This perfect butler, then, opens a door, and ushers Ernest *into a certain room. At the same moment the curtain rises on this room, and the play begins.*

It is one of several reception-rooms in Loam House, not the most magnificent but quite the softest; and of a warm afternoon all that those who are anybody crave for is the softest. The larger rooms are magnificent and bare, carpetless, so that it is an accomplishment to keep one's feet on them; they are sometimes lent for charitable purposes; they are also all in use on the night of a dinner party, when you may find yourself alone in one, having taken a wrong turning; or alone, save for two others who are within hailing distance. This room, however, is comparatively small and very soft. There are so many cushions in it that you wonder why, if you are an outsider and don't know that it needs six cushions to make one fair head comfy. The couches themselves are cushions as large as beds, and there is an art of sinking into them and of waiting to be helped out of them. There are several famous paintings on the walls, of which you may say, "Jolly thing that," without losing caste as knowing too much; and in cases there are glorious miniatures, but the daughters of the house cannot tell you of whom; "there is a catalogue somewhere." There are a thousand or so of roses in basins, several library novels, and a row of weekly illustrated newspapers lying against each other like fallen soldiers. If any one disturbs this row Crichton *seems to know of it from afar and appears noiselessly and replaces the wanderer. One thing unexpected in such a room is a great array of tea things.* Ernest *spots them with a twinkle, and has his epigram at once unsheathed. He dallies, however, before delivering the thrust.*

ERNEST: I perceive, from the tea cups, Crichton, that the great function is to take place here.

CRICHTON: [*With a respectful sigh*] Yes, sir.

ERNEST: [*Chuckling heartlessly*] The servant's hall coming up to have tea in the drawing-room! [*With terrible sarcasm*] No wonder you look happy, Crichton.

CRICHTON: [*Under the knife*] No, sir.

ERNEST: Do you know, Crichton, I think that with an effort you might look even happier. [*Crichton smiles wanly*] You don't approve of his lordship's compelling his servants to be his equals—once a month?

CRICHTON: It is not for me, sir, to disapprove of his lordship's Radical views.

ERNEST: Certainly not. And, after all, it is only once a month that he is affable to you.

CRICHTON: On all other days of the month, sir, his lordship's treatment of us is everything that could be desired.

ERNEST: [*This is the epigram*] Tea cups! Life, Crichton, is like a cup of tea; the more heartily we drink, the sooner we reach the dregs.

CRICHTON: [*Obediently*] Thank you, sir.

ERNEST: [*Becoming confidential, as we do when we have need of an ally*] Crichton, in case I should be asked to say a few words to the servants, I have strung together a little speech. [*His hand strays to his pocket*] I was wondering where I should stand.

[*He tries various places and postures, and comes to rest leaning over a high chair, whence, in dumb show, he addresses a gathering.* Crichton, *with the best intentions, gives him a footstool to stand on, and departs, hap-*

pily unconscious that Ernest *in some dudgeon has kicked the footstool across the room*]

ERNEST: [*Addressing an imaginary audience, and desirous of startling them at once*] Suppose you were all little fishes at the bottom of the sea——

[*He is not quite satisfied with his position, though sure that the fault must lie with the chair for being too high, not with him for being too short.* Crichton's *suggestion was not perhaps a bad one after all. He lifts the stool, but hastily conceals it behind him on the entrance of the* Ladies Catherine *and* Agatha, *two daughters of the house.* Catherine *is twenty, and* Agatha *is two years younger. They are very fashionable young women indeed, who might wake up for a dance, but they are very lazy,* Catherine *being two years lazier than* Agatha]

ERNEST: [*Uneasily jocular, because he is concealing the footstool*] And how are my little friends to-day?

AGATHA: [*Contriving to reach a settee*] Don't be silly, Ernest. If you want to know how we are, we are dead. Even to think of entertaining the servants is so exhausting.

CATHERINE: [*Subsiding nearer the door*] Besides which, we have had to decide what frocks to take with us on the yacht, and that is such a mental strain.

ERNEST: You poor over-worked things. [*Evidently* Agatha *is his favorite, for he helps her to put her feet on the settee, while* Catherine *has to dispose of her own feet*] Rest your weary limbs.

CATHERINE: [*Perhaps in revenge*] But why have you a footstool in your hand?

AGATHA: Yes?

ERNEST: Why? [*Brilliantly; but to be sure he has had time to think it out*] You see, as the servants are to be the guests I must be butler. I was practising. This is a tray, observe. [*Holding the footstool as a tray, he minces across the room like an accomplished footman. The gods favor him, for just here* Lady Mary *enters and he holds out the footstool to her*] Tea, my lady?

[Lady Mary *is a beautiful creature of twenty-two, and is of a natural hauteur which is at once the fury and the envy of her sisters. If she chooses she can make you seem so insignificant that you feel you might be swept away with the crumb-brush. She seldom chooses, because of the trouble of preening herself as she does it; she is usually content to show that you merely tire her eyes. She often seems to be about to go to sleep in the middle of a remark: there is quite a long and anxious pause, and then she continues, like a clock that hesitates, bored in the middle of its strike*]

LADY MARY: [*Arching her brows*] It is only you, Ernest; I thought there was some one here. [*And she also bestows herself on cushions*]

ERNEST: [*A little piqued, and deserting the foot-stool*] Had a very tiring day also, Mary?

LADY MARY: [*Yawning*] Dreadfully. Been trying on engagement-rings all the morning.

ERNEST: [*Who is as fond of gossip as the oldest club member*] What's that? [*To* Agatha] Is it Brocklehurst? [*The energetic Agatha nods*] You have given your warm young heart to Brocky? [Lady Mary *is impervious to his humor, but he continues bravely*] I don't wish to fatigue you, Mary, by insisting on a verbal answer, but if, without straining yourself, you can signify Yes or No, won't you make the effort? [*She indolently flashes a ring on her most important finger, and he starts back melodramatically*] The ring! Then I am too late, too late! [*Fixing* Lady Mary *sternly, like a prosecuting counsel*] May I ask, Mary, does Brocky know? Of course it was that terrible mother of his who pulled this through. Mother does everything for Brocky. Still, in the eyes of the law you will be, not her wife, but his, and, therefore, I hold that Brocky ought to be informed. Now—— [*He discovers that their languorous eyes have closed*] If you girls are shamming sleep in the expectation that I shall awaken you in the manner beloved of ladies, abandon all such hopes.

[Catherine *and* Agatha *look up without speaking*]

LADY MARY: [*Speaking without looking up*] You impertinent boy.

ERNEST: [*Eagerly plucking another epigram from his quiver*] I knew that was it, though I don't know everything. Agatha, I'm not young enough to know everything.

[*He looks hopefully from one to another, but though they try to grasp this, his brilliance baffles them*]

AGATHA: [*His secret admirer*] Young enough?

ERNEST: [*Encouragingly*] Don't you see? I'm not young enough to know everything.

AGATHA: I'm sure it's awfully clever, but it's so puzzling.

[*Here* Crichton *ushers in an athletic, pleasant-faced young clergyman,* Mr. Treherne, *who greets the company*]

CATHERINE: Ernest, say it to Mr. Treherne.

ERNEST: Look here, Treherne, I'm not young enough to know everything.

TREHERNE: How do you mean, Ernest?

ERNEST: [*A little nettled*] I mean what I say.

LADY MARY: Say it again; say it more slowly.

ERNEST: I'm—not—young—enough—to—know—everything.

TREHERNE: *I* see. What you really mean, my boy, is that you are not old enough to know everything.

ERNEST: No, I don't.

TREHERNE: I assure you that's it.

LADY MARY: Of course it is.

CATHERINE: Yes, Ernest, that's it.

[Ernest, *in desperation, appeals to* Crichton]

ERNEST: I am not young enough, Crichton, to know everything.

[*It is an anxious moment, but a smile is at length extorted from* Crichton *as with a corkscrew*]

CRICHTON: Thank you, sir. [*He goes*]

ERNEST: [*Relieved*] Ah, if you had that fellow's head, Treherne, you would find something better to do with it than play cricket. I hear you bowl with your head.

TREHERNE: [*With proper humility*] I'm afraid cricket is all I'm good for, Ernest.

CATHERINE: [*Who thinks he has a heavenly nose*] Indeed, it isn't. You are sure to get on, Mr. Treherne.

TREHERNE: Thank you, Lady Catherine.

CATHERINE: But it was the bishop who told me so. He said a clergyman who breaks both ways is sure to get on in England.

TREHERNE: I'm jolly glad.

[*The master of the house comes in, accompanied by* Lord Brocklehurst. *The* Earl of Loam *is a widower, a philanthropist, and a peer of advanced ideas. As a widower he is at least able to interfere in the domestic concerns of his house—to rummage in the drawers, so to speak, for which he has felt an itching all his blameless life; his philanthropy has opened quite a number of other drawers to him; and his advanced ideas have blown out his figure. He takes in all the weightiest monthly reviews, and prefers those that are uncut, because he perhaps never looks better than when cutting them; but he does not read them, and save for the cutting, it would suit him as well merely to take in the covers. He writes letters to the papers, which are printed in a type to scale with himself, and he is very jealous of those other correspondents who get his type. Let laws and learning, art and commerce die, but leave the big type to an intellectual aristocracy. He is really the reformed House of Lords which will come some day.*

Young Lord Brocklehurst *is nothing, save for his rank. You could pick him up by the handful any day in Piccadilly or Holborn, buying socks—or selling them.*

LORD LOAM: [*Expansively*] You are here, Ernest. Feeling fit for the voyage, Treherne?

TREHERNE: Looking forward to it enormously.

LORD LOAM: That's right. [*He chases his children about as if they were chickens*] Now then, Mary, up and doing, up and doing. Time we had the servants in. They enjoy it so much.

LADY MARY: They hate it.

LORD LOAM: Mary, to your duties. [*And he points severely to the tea-table*]

ERNEST: [*Twinkling*] Congratulations, Brocky.

LORD BROCKLEHURST: [*Who detests humour*] Thanks.

ERNEST: Mother pleased?

LORD BROCKLEHURST: [*With dignity*] Mother is very pleased.

ERNEST: That's good. Do you go on the yacht with us?

LORD BROCKLEHURST: Sorry I can't. And look here, Ernest, I will *not* be called Brocky.

ERNEST: Mother don't like it?

LORD BROCKLEHURST: She does not. [*He leaves* Ernest, *who forgives him and begins to think about his speech.* Crichton *enters*]

LORD LOAM: [*Speaking as one man to another*] We are quite ready, Crichton.

[Crichton *is distressed*]

LADY MARY: [*Sarcastically*] How Crichton enjoys it!

LORD LOAM: [*Frowning*] He is the only one who doesn't; pitiful creature.

CRICHTON: [*Shuddering under his lord's displeasure*] I can't help being a Conservative, my lord.

LORD LOAM: Be a man, Crichton. You are the same flesh and blood as myself.

CRICHTON: [*In pain*] Oh, my lord!

LORD LOAM: [*Sharply*] Show them in; and, by the way, they were not all here last time.

CRICHTON: All, my lord, except the merest trifles.

LORD LOAM: It must be every one. [*Lowering*] And remember this, Crichton, for the time being you are my equal. [*Testily*] I shall soon show you whether you are not my equal. Do as you are told. [Crichton *departs to obey, and his lordship is now a general. He has no pity for his daughters, and uses a terrible threat*] And girls, remember, no condescension. The first who condescends recites. [*This sends them scurrying to their labors.*] By the way, Brocklehurst, can you do anything?

LORD BROCKLEHURST: How do you mean?

LORD LOAM: Can you do anything—with a penny or a handkerchief, make them disappear, for instance?

LORD BROCKLEHURST: Good heavens, no.

LORD LOAM: It's a pity. Every one in our position ought to be able to do something. Ernest, I shall probably ask you to say a few words; something bright and sparkling.

ERNEST: But, my dear uncle, I have prepared nothing.

LORD LOAM: Anything impromptu will do.

ERNEST: Oh—well—if anything strikes me on the spur of the moment. [*He unostentatiously gets the footstool into position behind the chair.* Crichton *reappears to announce the guests, of whom the first is the housekeeper*]

CRICHTON: [*Reluctantly*] Mrs. Perkins.

LORD LOAM: [*Shaking hands*] Very delighted, Mrs. Perkins. Mary, our friend, Mrs. Perkins.

LADY MARY: How do you do, Mrs. Perkins? Won't you sit here?

LORD LOAM: [*Threateningly*] Agatha!

AGATHA: [*Hastily*] How do you do? Won't you sit down?

LORD LOAM: [*Introducing*] Lord Brocklehurst— my valued friend Mrs. Perkins.

[Lord Brocklehurst *bows and escapes. He has to fall back on* Ernest]

LORD BROCKLEHURST: For heaven's sake, Ernest, don't leave me for a moment; this sort of thing is utterly opposed to all my principles.

ERNEST: [*Airily*] You stick to me, Brocky, and I'll pull you through.

CRICHTON: Monsieur Fleury.

ERNEST: The chef.

LORD LOAM: [*Shaking hands with the chef*] Very charmed to see you, Monsieur Fleury.

FLEURY: Thank you very much.

[Fleury *bows to Agatha, who is not effusive*]

LORD LOAM: [*Warningly*] Agatha—recitation!

[*She tosses her head, but immediately finds a seat and tea for* M. Fleury. Treherne *and* Ernest *move about, making themselves amiable.* Lady Mary *is presiding at the teatray*]

CRICHTON: Mr. Rolleston.

LORD LOAM: [*Shaking hands with his valet*] How do you do, Rolleston?

[Catherine *looks after the wants of* Rolleston]

CRICHTON: Mr. Tompsett.

[Tompsett, *the coachman, is received with honors, from which he shrinks*]

CRICHTON: Miss Fisher.

[*This superb creature is no less than* Lady Mary's *maid, and even* Lord Loam *is a little nervous*]

LORD LOAM: This is a pleasure, Miss Fisher.

ERNEST: [*Unabashed*] If I might venture, Miss Fisher. [*And he takes her unto himself*]

CRICHTON: Miss Simmons.

LORD LOAM: [*To* Catherine's *maid*] You are always welcome, Miss Simmons.

ERNEST: [*Perhaps to kindle jealousy in* Miss Fisher] At last we meet. Won't you sit down?

CRICHTON: Mademoiselle Jeanne.

LORD LOAM: Charmed to see you, Mademoiselle Jeanne.

[*A place is found for* Agatha's *maid, and the scene is now an animated one; but still our host thinks his girls are not sufficiently sociable. He frowns on* Lady Mary]

LADY MARY: [*In alarm*] Mr. Treherne, this is Fisher, my maid.

LORD LOAM: [*Sharply*] Your what, Mary?

LADY MARY: My friend.

CRICHTON: Thomas.

LORD LOAM: How do you do, Thomas?

[*The first footman gives him a reluctant hand*]

CRICHTON: John.

LORD LOAM: How do you do, John?

[Ernest *signs to* Lord Brocklehurst, *who hastens to him*]

ERNEST: [Introducing] Brocklehurst, this is John. I think you have already met on the door-step.

CRICHTON: Jane.

[She comes, wrapping her hands miserably in her apron]

LORD LOAM: [Doggedly] Give me your hand, Jane.

CRICHTON: Gladys.

ERNEST: How do you do, Gladys. You know my uncle?

LORD LOAM: Your hand, Gladys. [He bestows her on Agatha]

CRICHTON: Tweeny.

[She is a very humble and frightened kitchen-maid, of whom we are to see more]

LORD LOAM: So happy to see you.

FISHER: John, I saw you talking to Lord Brocklehurst just now; introduce me.

LORD BROCKLEHURST: [At the same moment to Ernest] That's an uncommon pretty girl; if I must feed one of them, Ernest, that's the one.

[But Ernest tries to part him and Fisher as they are about to shake hands]

ERNEST: No you don't, it won't do, Brocky. [To Miss Fisher] You are too pretty, my dear. Mother wouldn't like it. [Discovering Tweeny] Here's something safer. Charming girl, Brocky, dying to know you; let me introduce you. Tweeny, Lord Brocklehurst—Lord Brocklehurst, Tweeny.

[Brocklehurst accepts his fate; but he still has an eye for Fisher, and something may come of this]

LORD LOAM: [Severely] They are not all here, Crichton.

CRICHTON: [With a sigh] Odds and ends.

[A Stable-Boy and a Page are shown in, and for a moment no daughter of the house advances to them]

LORD LOAM: [With a roving eye on his children] Which is to recite?

[The last of the company are, so to say, embraced]

LORD LOAM: [To Tompsett, as they partake of tea together] And how are all at home?

TOMPSETT: Fairish, my lord, if 'tis the horses you are inquiring for?

LORD LOAM: No, no, the family. How's the baby?

TOMPSETT: Blooming, your lordship.

LORD LOAM: A very fine boy. I remember saying so when I saw him; nice little fellow.

TOMPSETT: [Not quite knowing whether to let it pass] Beg pardon, my lord, it's a girl.

LORD LOAM: A girl? Aha! ha! ha! exactly what I said. I distinctly remember saying, If it's spared it will be a girl.

[Crichton now comes down]

LORD LOAM: Very delighted to see you, Crichton. [Crichton has to shake hands] Mary, you know Mr. Crichton? [He wanders off in search of other prey]

LADY MARY: Milk and sugar, Crichton?

CRICHTON: I'm ashamed to be seen talking to you, my lady.

LADY MARY: To such a perfect servant as you all this must be most distasteful. [Crichton is too respectful to answer] Oh, please do speak, or I shall have to recite. You do hate it, don't you?

CRICHTON: It pains me, your ladyship. It disturbs the etiquette of the servants' hall. After last month's meeting the pageboy, in a burst of equality, called me Crichton. He was dismissed.

LADY MARY: I wonder—I really do—how you can remain with us.

CRICHTON: I should have felt compelled to give notice, my lady, if the master had not had a seat in the Upper House. I cling to that.

LADY MARY: Do go on speaking. Tell me, what did Mr. Ernest mean by saying that he was not young enough to know everything?

CRICHTON: I have no idea, my lady.

LADY MARY: But you laughed.

CRICHTON: My lady, he is the second son of a peer.

LADY MARY: Very proper sentiments. You are a good soul, Crichton.

LORD BROCKLEHURST: [Desperately to Tweeny] And now tell me, have you been to the Opera? What sort of weather have you been having in the kitchen? [Tweeny giggles] For heaven's sake, woman, be articulate.

CRICHTON: [Still talking to Lady Mary] No, my lady; his lordship may compel us to be equal upstairs, but there will never be equality in the servants' hall.

LORD LOAM: [Overhearing this] What's that? No equality? Can't you see, Crichton, that our divisions into classes are artificial, that if we were to return to Nature, which is the aspiration of my life, all would be equal?

CRICHTON: If I may make so bold as to contradict your lordship——

LORD LOAM: [With an effort] Go on.

CRICHTON: The divisions into classes, my lord, are not artificial. They are the natural outcome of a civilized society. [To Lady Mary] There must always be a master and servants in all civilized communities, my lady, for it is natural, and whatever is natural is right.

LORD LOAM: [Wincing] It is very unnatural for me to stand here and allow you to talk such nonsense.

CRICHTON: [Eagerly] Yes, my lord, it is. That is what I have been striving to point out to your lordship.

AGATHA: [To Catherine] What is the matter with Fisher? She is looking daggers.

CATHERINE: The tedious creature; some question of etiquette, I suppose. [She sails across to Fisher] How are you, Fisher?

FISHER: [With a toss of her head] I am nothing, my lady, I am nothing at all.

AGATHA: Oh dear, who says so?

FISHER: [Affronted] His lordship has asked that kitchen wench to have a second cup of tea.

CATHERINE: But why not?

FISHER: If it pleases his lordship to offer it to *her* before offering it to *me*——

AGATHA: So that is it. Do you want another cup of tea, Fisher?

FISHER: No, my lady—but my position—I should have been asked first.

AGATHA: Oh dear.

[*All this has taken some time, and by now the feeble appetites of the uncomfortable guests have been satiated. But they know there is still another ordeal to face—his lordship's monthly speech. Every one awaits it with misgiving— the servants lest they should applaud, as last time, in the wrong place, and the daughters because he may be personal about them, as the time before* Ernest *is annoyed that there should be this speech at all when there is such a much better one coming, and* Brocklehurst *foresees the degradation of the peerage. All are thinking of themselves alone save* Crichton, *who knows his master's weakness, and fears he may stick in the middle.* Lord Loam, *however, advances cheerfully to his doom. He sees* Ernest's *stool, and artfully stands on it, to his nephew's natural indignation. The three ladies knit their lips, the servants look down their noses, and the address begins*]

LORD LOAM: My friends, I am glad to see you all looking so happy. It used to be predicted by the scoffer that these meetings would prove distasteful to you. Are they distasteful? I hear you laughing at the question. [*He has not heard them, but he hears them now, the watchful* Crichton *giving them a lead*] No harm in saying that among us today is one who was formerly hostile to the movement, but who today has been won over. I refer to Lord Brocklehurst, who, I am sure, will presently say to me that if the charming lady now by his side has derived as much pleasure from his company as he has derived from hers, he will be more than satisfied. [*All look at* Tweeny, *who trembles*] For the time being the artificial and unnatural—I say unnatural [*Glaring at* Crichton, *who bows slightly*]— barriers of society are swept away. Would that they could be swept away for ever. [*The* Pageboy *cheers, and has the one moment of prominence in his life. He grows up, marries and has children, but is never really heard of again*] But that is entirely and utterly out of the question. And now for a few months we are to be separated. As you know, my daughters and Mr. Ernest and Mr. Treherne are to accompany me on my yacht, on a voyage to distant parts of the earth. In less than forty-eight hours we shall be under weigh. [*But for* Crichton's *eye the reckless* Pageboy *would repeat his success*] Do not think our life on the yacht is to be one long idle holiday. My

views on the excessive luxury of the day are well known, and what I preach I am resolved to practise. I have therefore decided that my daughters, instead of having one maid each as at present, shall on this voyage have but one maid between them.

[*Three maids rise; also three mistresses*]

CRICHTON: My lord!

LORD LOAM: My mind is made up.

ERNEST: I cordially agree.

LORD LOAM: And now, my friends, I should like to think that there is some piece of advice I might give you, some thought, some noble saying over which you might ponder in my absence. In this connection I remember a proverb, which has had a great effect on my own life. I first heard it many years ago. I have never forgotten it. It constantly cheers and guides me. That proverb is—that proverb was—the proverb I speak of——[*He grows pale and taps his forehead*]

LADY MARY: Oh dear, I believe he has forgotten it.

LORD LOAM: [*Desperately*] The proverb—that proverb to which I refer——[*Alas, it has gone. The distress is general. He has not even the sense to sit down. He gropes for the proverb in the air. They try applause, but it is no help*] I have it now—— [*not he*]

LADY MARY: [*With confidence*] Crichton.

[*He does not fail her. As quietly as if he were in goloshes, mind as well as feet, he dismisses the domestics; they go according to precedence as they entered yet, in a moment, they are gone. Then he signs to Mr.* Treherne, *and then they conduct* Lord Loam *with dignity from the room. His hands are still catching flies; he still mutters, "The proverb—that proverb"; but he continues, owing to* Crichton's *skilful treatment, to look every inch a peer. The ladies have now an opportunity to air their indignation*]

LADY MARY: One maid among three grown women!

LORD BROCKLEHURST: Mary, I think I had better go. That dreadful kitchenmaid——

LADY MARY: I can't blame you, George. [*He salutes her*]

LORD BROCKLEHURST: Your father's views are shocking to me, and I am glad I am not to be one of the party on the yacht. My respect for myself, Mary, my natural anxiety as to what mother will say. I shall see you, darling, before you sail. [*He bows to the others and goes*]

ERNEST: Selfish brute, only thinking of himself. What about my speech?

LADY MARY: One maid among three of us. What's to be done?

ERNEST: Pooh! You must do for yourselves, that's all.

LADY MARY: Do for ourselves. How can we know where our things are kept?

AGATHA: Are you aware that dresses button up the back?

CATHERINE: How are we to get into our shoes and be prepared for the carriage?

LADY MARY: Who is to put us to bed, and who is to get us up, and how shall we ever know it's morning if there is no one to pull up the blinds?

[Crichton *crosses on his way out*]

ERNEST: How is his lordship now?

CRICHTON: A little easier, sir.

LADY MARY: Crichton, send Fisher to me. [*He goes*]

ERNEST: I have no pity for you girls, I——

LADY MARY: Ernest, go away, and don't insult the broken-hearted.

ERNEST: And uncommon glad I am to go. Ta-ta, all of you. He asked me to say a few words. I came here to say a few words, and I'm not at all sure that I couldn't bring an action against him. [*He departs, feeling that he has left a dart behind him. The girls are alone with their tragic throughts*]

LADY MARY: [*Become a mother to the younger ones at last*] My poor sisters, come here. [*They go to her doubtfully*] We must make this draw us closer together. I shall do my best to help you in every way. Just now I cannot think of myself at all.

AGATHA: But how unlike you, Mary.

LADY MARY: It is my duty to protect my sisters.

CATHERINE: I never knew her so sweet before, Agatha. [*Cautiously*] What do you propose to do, Mary?

LADY MARY: I propose when we are on the yacht to lend Fisher to you when I don't need her myself.

AGATHA: Fisher?

LADY MARY: [*Who has the most character of the three*] Of course, as the eldest, I have decided that it is *my* maid we shall take with us.

CATHERINE: [*Speaking also for* Agatha] Mary, you toad.

AGATHA: Nothing on earth would induce Fisher to lift her hand for either me or Catherine.

LADY MARY: I was afraid of it, Agatha. That is why I am so sorry for you.

[*The further exchange of pleasantries is interrupted by the arrival of* Fisher]

LADY MARY: Fisher, you heard what his lordship said?

FISHER: Yes, my lady.

LADY MARY: [*Coldly, though the others would have tried blandishment*] You have given me some satisfaction of late, Fisher, and to mark my approval I have decided that you shall be the maid who accompanies us.

FISHER: [*Acidly*] I thank you, my lady.

LADY MARY: That is all; you may go.

FISHER: [*Rapping it out*] If you please, my lady, I wish to give notice.

[Catherine *and* Agatha *gleam, but* Lady Mary *is of sterner stuff*]

LADY MARY: [*Taking up a book*] Oh, certainly—you may go.

CATHERINE: But why, Fisher?

FISHER: I could not undertake, my lady, to wait upon three. *We* don't do it. [*In an indignant outburst to* Lady Mary] Oh, my lady, to think that this affront——

LADY MARY: [*Looking up*] I thought I told you to go, Fisher.

[Fisher *stands for a moment irresolute; then goes. As soon as she has gone* Lady Mary *puts down her book and weeps. She is a pretty woman, but this is the only pretty thing we have seen her do yet*]

AGATHA: [*Succinctly*] Serves you right.

[Crichton *comes*]

CATHERINE: It will be Simmons after all. Send Simmons to me.

CRICHTON: [*After hesitating*] My lady, might I venture to speak?

CATHERINE: What is it?

CRICHTON: I happen to know, your ladyship, that Simmons desires to give notice for the same reason as Fisher.

CATHERINE: Oh!

AGATHA: [*Triumphant*] Then, Catherine, we take Jeanne.

CRICHTON: And Jeanne also, my lady.

[Lady Mary *is reading, indifferent though the heavens fall, but her sisters are not ashamed to show their despair to* Crichton]

AGATHA: We can't blame them. Could any maid who respected herself be got to wait upon three?

LADY MARY: [*With languid interest*] I suppose there are such persons, Crichton?

CRICHTON: [*Guardedly*] I have heard, my lady, that there are such.

LADY MARY: [*A little desperate*] Crichton, what's to be done? We sail in two days; could one be discovered in the time?

AGATHA: [*Frankly a supplicant*] Surely you can think of some one?

CRICHTON: [*After hesitating*] There is in this establishment, your ladyship, a young woman——

LADY MARY: Yes?

CRICHTON: A young woman on whom I have for some time cast an eye.

CATHERINE: [*Eagerly*] Do you mean as a possible lady's-maid?

CRICHTON: I had thought of her, my lady, in another connection.

LADY MARY: Ah!

CRICHTON: But I believe she is quite the young person you require. Perhaps if you could see her, my lady——

LADY MARY: I shall certainly see her. Bring her to me. [*He goes*] You two needn't wait.

CATHERINE: Needn't we? We see your little game, Mary.

AGATHA: We shall certainly remain and have our two-thirds of her.

[*They sit there doggedly until* Crichton *returns with* Tweeny, *who looks scared*]

CRICHTON: This, my lady, is the young person.

CATHERINE: [*Frankly*] Oh dear!

[*It is evident that all three consider her quite unsuitable*]

LADY MARY: Come here, girl. Don't be afraid.

[Tweeny *looks imploringly at her idol*]

CRICHTON: Her appearance, my lady, is homely, and her manners, as you may have observed, deplorable, but she has a heart of gold.

LADY MARY: What is your position downstairs?

TWEENY: [*Bobbing*] I'm a tweeny, your ladyship.

CATHERINE: A what?

CRICHTON: A tweeny; that is to say, my lady, she is not at present, strictly speaking, anything; a *between* maid; she helps the vegetable maid. It is she, my lady, who conveys the dishes from the one end of the kitchen table where they are placed by the cook, to the other end, where they enter into the charge of Thomas and John.

LADY MARY: I see. And you and Crichton are—ah—keeping company?

[Crichton *draws himself up*]

TWEENY: [*Aghast*] A butler don't keep company, my lady.

LADY MARY: [*Indifferently*] Does he not?

CRICHTON: No, your ladyship, we butlers may—[*He makes a gesture with his arms*]—but we do not keep company.

AGATHA: I know what it is; you are engaged?

[Tweeny *looks longingly at* Crichton]

CRICHTON: Certainly not, my lady. The utmost I can say at present is that I have cast a favorable eye.

[*Even this is much to* Tweeny]

LADY MARY: As you choose. But I am afraid, Crichton, she will not suit us.

CRICHTON: My lady, beneath this simple exterior are concealed a very sweet nature and rare womanly gifts.

AGATHA: Unfortunately, that is not what we want.

CRICHTON: And it is she, my lady, who dresses the hair of the ladies'-maids for our evening meals.

[*The ladies are interested at last*]

LADY MARY: She dresses Fisher's hair?

TWEENY: Yes, my lady, and I does them up when they goes to parties.

CRICHTON: [*Pained, but not scolding*] Does!

TWEENY: Doos. And it's me what alters your gowns to fit them.

CRICHTON: *What* alters!

TWEENY: Which alters.

AGATHA: Mary?

LADY MARY: I shall certainly have her.

CATHERINE: *We* shall certainly have her. Tweeny, we have decided to make a lady's-maid of you.

TWEENY: Oh lawks!

AGATHA: We are doing this for you so that your position socially may be more nearly akin to that of Crichton.

CRICHTON: [*Gravely*] It will undoubtedly increase the young person's chances.

LADY MARY: Then if I get a good character for you from Mrs. Perkins, she will make the necessary arrangements. [*She resumes reading*]

TWEENY: [*Elated*] My lady!

LADY MARY: By the way, I hope you are a good sailor.

TWEENY: [*Startled*] You don't mean, my lady, that I'm to go on the ship?

LADY MARY: Certainly.

TWEENY: But—— [*To* Crichton] You ain't going, sir?

CRICHTON: No.

TWEENY: [*Firm at last*] Then neither ain't I.

AGATHA: You must.

TWEENY: Leave him! Not me.

LADY MARY: Girl, don't be silly. Crichton will be —considered in your wages.

TWEENY: I ain't going.

CRICHTON: I feared this, my lady.

TWEENY: Nothing will budge me.

LADY MARY: Leave the room.

[Crichton *shows* Tweeny *out with marked politeness*]

AGATHA: Crichton, I think you might have shown more displeasure with her.

CRICHTON: [*Contrite*] I was touched, my lady. I see, my lady, that to part from her would be a wrench to me, though I could not well say so in her presence, not having yet decided how far I shall go with her. [*He is about to go when* Lord Loam *returns, fuming*]

LORD LOAM: The ingrate! The smug! The fop!

CATHERINE: What is it now, father?

LORD LOAM: That man of mine, Rolleston, refuses to accompany us because you are to have but one maid.

AGATHA: Hurrah!

LADY MARY: [*In better taste*] Darling father, rather than you should lose Rolleston, we will consent to take all the three of them.

LORD LOAM: Pooh, nonsense! Crichton, find me a valet who can do without three maids.

CRICHTON: Yes, my lord. [*Troubled*] In the time —the more suitable the party, my lord, the less willing will he be to come without the—usual perquisites.

LORD LOAM: Any one will do.

CRICHTON: [*Shocked*] My lord!

LORD LOAM: The ingrate! The puppy!

[Agatha *has an idea, and whispers to* Lady Mary]

LADY MARY: I ask a favor of a servant?—never!

AGATHA: Then I will. Crichton, would it not be very distressing to you to let his lordship go, attended by a valet who might prove unworthy? It is only for three months; don't you think that you—you yourself—you—— [*As* Crichton *sees what she wants he pulls himself up with noble, offended dignity, and she is appalled*] I beg your pardon.

[*He bows stiffly*]

CATHERINE: [*To* Crichton] But think of the joy to Tweeny.

[Crichton *is moved, but he shakes his head*]

LADY MARY: [*So much the cleverest*] Crichton, do you think it safe to let the master you love go so far away without you while he has these dangerous views about equality?

[Crichton *is profoundly stirred. After a struggle he goes to his master, who has been pacing the room*]

CRICHTON: My lord, I have found a man.

LORD LOAM: Already? Who is he? [Crichton *presents himself with a gesture*] Yourself?

CATHERINE: Father, how good of him.

LORD LOAM: [*Pleased, but speaking of it as a small thing*] Uncommon good. Thank you, Crichton. This helps me nicely out of a hole; and how it will annoy Rolleston! Come with me, and we shall tell him. Not that I think you have lowered yourself in any way. Come along. [*He goes, and* Crichton *is to follow him, but is stopped by* Agatha *impulsively offering him her hand*]

CRICHTON: [*Who is much shaken*] My lady—a valet's hand!

AGATHA: I had no idea you would feel it so deeply; why did you do it?

[Crichton *is too respectful to reply*]

LADY MARY: [*Regarding him*] Crichton, I am curious. I insist upon an answer.

CRICHTON: My lady, I am the son of a butler and a lady's-maid—perhaps the happiest of all combinations, and to me the most beautiful thing in the world is a haughty, aristocratic English house, with every one kept in his place. Though I were equal to your ladyship, where would be the pleasure to me? It would be counterbalanced by the pain of feeling that Thomas and John were equal to me.

CATHERINE: But father says if we were to return to Nature——

CRICHTON: If we did, my lady, the first thing we should do would be to elect a head. Circumstances might alter cases; the same person might not be master; the same persons might not be servants. I can't say as to that, nor should we have the deciding of it. Nature would decide for us.

LADY MARY: You seem to have thought it all out carefully, Crichton.

CRICHTON: Yes, my lady.

CATHERINE: And you have done this for us, Crichton, because you thought that—that father needed to be kept in his place?

CRICHTON: I should prefer you to say, my lady, that I have done it for the house.

AGATHA: Thank you, Crichton. Mary, be nicer to him. [*But* Lady Mary *has begun to read again*] If

there was any way in which we could show our gratitude.

CRICHTON: If I might venture, my lady, would you kindly show it by becoming more like Lady Mary? That disdain is what we like from our superiors. Even so do we, the upper servants, disdain the lower servants, while they take it out of the odds and ends. [*He goes, and they bury themselves in cushions*]

AGATHA: Oh dear, what a tiring day.

CATHERINE: I feel dead. Tuck in your feet, you selfish thing.

[Lady Mary *is lying reading on another couch*]

LADY MARY: I wonder what he meant by circumstances might alter cases.

AGATHA: [*Yawning*] Don't talk, Mary, I was nearly asleep.

LADY MARY: I wonder what he meant by the same person might not be master, and the same persons might not be servants.

CATHERINE: Do be quiet, Mary, and leave it to Nature; he said Nature would decide.

LADY MARY: I wonder——

[*But she does not wonder very much. She would wonder more if she knew what was coming. Her book slips unregarded to the floor. The ladies are at rest until it is time to dress*]

END OF ACT I

ACT II.

Two months have elapsed, and the scene is a desert island in the Pacific, on which our adventurers have been wrecked.

The curtain rises on a sea of bamboo, which shuts out all view save the foliage of palm trees and some gaunt rocks. Occasionally Crichton *and* Treherne *come momentarily into sight, hacking and hewing the bamboo, through which they are making a clearing between the ladies and the shore; and by and by, owing to their efforts, we shall have an unrestricted outlook on to a sullen sea that is at present hidden. Then we shall also be able to note a mast standing out of the water—all that is left, saving floating wreckage, of the ill-fated yacht the* Bluebell. *The beginnings of a hut will also be seen, with* Crichton *driving its walls into the ground or astride its roof of saplings, for at present he is doing more than one thing at a time. In a red shirt, with the ends of his sailor's breeches thrust into wading-boots, he looks a man for the moment; we suddenly remember some one's saying—perhaps it was ourselves—that a cataclysm would be needed to get him out of his servant's clothes, and apparently it has been forthcoming. It is no longer beneath our dignity to cast an inquiring eye on his appearance. His features are not distinguished, but he has a strong jaw and green eyes, in which a yellow light burns that we have not seen before. His dark hair, hitherto so decorously sleek, has been ruffled this way and that by wind and weather, as if they were part of the cataclysm and wanted to help his chance. His muscles must be soft and flabby still, but though they shriek aloud to him to desist, he rains lusty blows with his axe, like one who has come upon the open for the first time in his life, and likes it. He is as yet far from being an expert woodsman—mark the blood on his hands at places where he has hit them instead of the tree; but note also that he does not waste time in bandaging them—he rubs them in the earth and goes on. His face is still of the discreet pallor that befits a butler, and he carries the smaller logs as if they were a salver; not in a day or a month will he shake off the badge of servitude, but without knowing it he has begun.*

But for the hatchets at work, and an occasional something horrible falling from a tree into the ladies' laps, they hear nothing save the mournful surf breaking on a coral shore.

They sit or recline huddled together against a rock, and they are farther from home, in every sense of the word, than ever before. Thirty-six hours ago, they were given three minutes in which to dress, without a maid, and reach the boats, and they have not made the best of that valuable time. None of them has boots, and had they known this prickly island they would have thought first of boots. They have a sufficiency of garments, but some of them were gifts dropped into the boat—Lady Mary's tarpaulin coat and hat, for instance, and Catherine's blue jersey and red cap, which certify that the two ladies were lately before the mast. Agatha is too gay in Ernest's dressing-gown, and clutches it to her person with both hands as if afraid that it may be claimed by its rightful owner. There are two pairs of bath slippers between the three of them, and their hair cries aloud and in vain for hairpins.

By their side, on an inverted bucket, sits Ernest, *clothed neatly in the garments of day and night, but, alas, barefooted. He is the only cheerful member of this company of four, but his brightness is due less to a manly desire to succour the helpless than to his having been lately in the throes of composition, and to his modest satisfaction with the result. He reads to the ladies, and they listen, each with one scared eye to the things that fall from trees.*

ERNEST: [*Who has written on the fly-leaf of the only book saved from the wreck*] This is what I have written. "Wrecked, wrecked, wrecked! on an island in the Tropics, the following: the Hon. Ernest Woolley, the Rev. John Treherne, the Ladies Mary, Catherine, and Agatha Lasenby, with two servants. We are the sole survivors of Lord Loam's steam yacht *Bluebell*, which encountered a fearful gale in these seas, and soon became a total wreck. The crew behaved gallantly, putting us all into the first boat.

What became of them I cannot tell, but we, after dreadful sufferings, and insufficiently clad, in whatever garments we could lay hold of in the dark——"

LADY MARY: Please don't describe our garments.

ERNEST: "succeeded in reaching this island, with the loss of only one of our party, namely, Lord Loam, who flung away his life in a gallant attempt to save a servant who had fallen overboard."

[*The ladies have wept long and sore for their father, but there is something in this last utterance that makes them look up*]

AGATHA: But, Ernest, it was Crichton who jumped overboard trying to save father.

ERNEST: [*With the candor that is one of his most engaging qualities*] Well, you know, it was rather silly of uncle to fling away his life by trying to get into the boat first; and as this document may be printed in the English papers, it struck me, an English peer, you know——

LADY MARY: [*Every inch an English peer's daughter*] Ernest, that is very thoughtful of you.

ERNEST: [*Continuing, well pleased*]—"By night the cries of wild cats and the hissing of snakes terrify us extremely"— [*This does not satisfy him so well, and he makes a correction*]—"terrify the ladies extremely. Against these we have no weapons except one cutlass and a hatchet. A bucket washed ashore is at present our only comfortable seat——"

LADY MARY: [*With some spirit*] And Ernest is sitting on it.

ERNEST: H'sh! Oh, do be quiet.—"To add to our horrors, night falls suddenly in these parts, and it is then that savage animals begin to prowl and roar."

LADY MARY: Have you said that vampire bats suck the blood from our toes as we sleep?

ERNEST: No, that's all. I end up, "Rescue us or we perish. Rich reward. Signed Ernest Woolley, in command of our little party." This is written on a leaf taken out of a book of poems that Crichton found in his pocket. Fancy Crichton being a reader of poetry. Now I shall put it into the bottle and fling it into the sea. [*He pushes the precious document into a soda-water bottle and rams the cork home. At the same moment, and without effort, he gives birth to one of his most characteristic epigrams*] The tide is going out, we mustn't miss the post.

[*They are so unhappy that they fail to grasp it, and a little petulantly he calls for* Crichton, *ever his stand-by in the hour of epigram.* Crichton *breaks through the undergrowth quickly, thinking the ladies are in danger*]

CRICHTON: Anything wrong, sir?

ERNEST: [*With fine confidence*] The tide, Crichton, is a postman who calls at our island twice a day for letters.

CRICHTON: [*After a pause*] Thank you, sir. [*He returns to his labors, however, without giving the smile which is the epigrammatist's right, and* Ernest *is a little disappointed in him*]

ERNEST: Poor Crichton! I sometimes think he is losing his sense of humor. Come along, Agatha. [*He helps his favorite up the rocks, and they disappear gingerly from view*]

CATHERINE: How horribly still it is.

LADY MARY: [*Remembering some recent sounds*] It is best when it is still.

CATHERINE: [*Drawing closer to her*] Mary, I have heard that they are always very still just before they jump.

LADY MARY: Don't.

[*A distinct chopping is heard, and they are startled*]

LADY MARY: [*Controlling herself*] It is only Crichton knocking down trees.

CATHERINE: [*Almost imploringly*] Mary, let us go and stand beside him.

LADY MARY: [*Coldly*] Let a servant see that I am afraid!

CATHERINE: Don't, then; but remember this, dear, they often drop on one from above.

[*She moves away, nearer to the friendly sound of the axe, and Lady Mary is left alone. She is the most courageous of them as well as the haughtiest, but when something she had thought to be a stick glides toward her, she forgets her dignity and screams*]

LADY MARY: [*Calling*] Crichton, Crichton!

[*It must have been* Treherne *who was tree-felling, for* Crichton *comes to her from the hut, drawing his cutlass*]

CRICHTON: [*Anxious*] Did you call, my lady?

LADY MARY: [*Herself again, now that he is there*] I! Why should I?

CRICHTON: I made a mistake, your ladyship. [*Hesitating*] If you are afraid of being alone, my lady——

LADY MARY: Afraid! Certainly not. [*Doggedly*] You may go. [*But she does not complain when he remains within eyesight cutting the bamboo. It is heavy work, and she watches him silently*]

LADY MARY: I wish, Crichton, you could work without getting so hot.

CRICHTON: [*Mopping his face*] I wish I could, my lady.

[*He continues his labors*]

LADY MARY: [*Taking off her oilskins*] It makes me hot to look at you.

CRICHTON: It almost makes me cool to look at your ladyship.

LADY MARY: [*Who perhaps thinks he is presuming*] Anything I can do for you in that way, Crichton, I shall do with pleasure.

CRICHTON: [*Quite humbly*] Thank you, my lady.

[*By this time most of the bamboo has been cut, and the shore and the sea are visible, except where they are hidden by the half-completed hut. The mast rising solitary from the water adds to the desolation of the scene, and at last tears run down* Lady Mary's *face*]

CRICHTON: Don't give way, my lady, things might be worse.

LADY MARY: My poor father.

CRICHTON: If I could have given my life for his.

LADY MARY: You did all a man could do. Indeed I thank you, Crichton. [*With some admiration and more wonder*] You are a man.

CRICHTON: Thank you, my lady.

LADY MARY: But it is all so awful. Crichton, is there any hope of a ship coming?

CRICHTON: [*After hesitation*] Of course there is, my lady.

LADY MARY: [*Facing him bravely*] Don't treat me as a child. I have got to know the worst, and to face it. Crichton, the truth.

CRICHTON: [*Reluctantly*] We were driven out of our course, my lady; I fear far from the track of commerce.

LADY MARY: Thank you; I understand. [*For a moment, however, she breaks down. Then she clenches her hands and stands erect*]

CRICHTON: [*Watching her, and forgetting perhaps for the moment that they are not just a man and woman*] You're a good plucky 'un, my lady.

LADY MARY: [*Falling into the same error*] I shall try to be. [*Extricating herself*] Crichton, how dare you?

CRICHTON: I beg your ladyship's pardon; but you are. [*She smiles, as if it were a comfort to be told this even by* Crichton] And until a ship comes we are three men who are going to do our best for you ladies.

LADY MARY: [*With a curl of the lip*] Mr. Ernest does no work.

CRICHTON: [*Cheerily*] But he will, my lady.

LADY MARY: I doubt it.

CRICHTON: [*Confidently, but perhaps thoughtlessly*] No work—no dinner—will make a great change in Mr. Ernest.

LADY MARY: No work—no dinner. When did you invent that rule, Crichton?

CRICHTON: [*Loaded with bamboo*] I didn't invent it, my lady. I seem to see it growing all over the island.

LADY MARY: [*Disquieted*] Crichton, your manner strikes me as curious.

CRICHTON: [*Pained*] I hope not, your ladyship.

LADY MARY: [*Determined to have it out with him*] You are not implying anything so unnatural, I presume, as that if I and my sisters don't work there will be no dinner for *us*?

CRICHTON: [*Brightly*] If it is unnatural, my lady, that is the end of it.

LADY MARY: If? Now I understand. The perfect servant at home holds that we are all equal now. I see.

CRICHTON: [*Wounded to the quick*] My lady, can you think me so inconsistent?

LADY MARY: That was it.

CRICHTON: [*Earnestly*] My lady, I disbelieved in equality at home because it was against nature, and for the same reason I as utterly disbelieve in it on an island.

LADY MARY: [*Relieved by his obvious sincerity*] I apologize.

CRICHTON: [*Continuing unfortunately*] There must always, my lady, be one to command and others to obey.

LADY MARY: [*Satisfied*] One to command, others to obey. Yes. [*Then suddenly she realizes that there may be a dire meaning in his confident words*] Crichton!

CRICHTON: [*Who has intended no dire meaning*] What is it, my lady?

[*But she only stares into his face and then hurries from him. Left alone he is puzzled, but being a practical man he busies himself gathering firewood, until* Tweeny *appears excitedly carrying cocoa-nuts in her skirt. She has made better use than the ladies of her three minutes' grace for dressing*]

TWEENY: [*Who can be happy even on an island if* Crichton *is with her*] Look what I found.

CRICHTON: Cocoa-nuts. Bravo!

TWEENY: They grow on trees.

CRICHTON: Where did you think they grew?

TWEENY: I thought as how they grew in rows on top of little sticks.

CRICHTON: [*Wrinkling his brows*] Oh Tweeny, Tweeny.

TWEENY: [*Anxiously*] Have I offended of your feelings again, sir?

CRICHTON: A little.

TWEENY: [*In a despairing outburst*] I'm full o' vulgar words and ways; and though I may keep them in their holes when you are by, as soon as I'm by myself out they comes in a rush like beetles when the house is dark. I says them gloatinglike, in my head—"Blooming" I says, and "All my eye," and "Ginger," and "Nothink"; and all the time we was being wrecked I was praying to myself, "Please the Lord it may be an island as it's natural to be vulgar on." [*A shudder passes through* Crichton, *and she is abject*] That's the kind I am, sir. I'm 'opeless. You'd better give me up. [*She is a pathetic forlorn creature, and his manhood is stirred*]

CRICHTON: [*Wondering a little at himself for saying it*] I won't give you up. It is strange that one so common should attract one so fastidious; but so it is. [*Thoughfully*] There is something about you, Tweeny, there is a *je ne sais quoi* about you.

TWEENY: [*Knowing only that he has found something in her to commend*] Is there, is there? Oh, I am glad.

CRICHTON: [*Putting his hand on her shoulder like a protector*] We shall fight your vulgarity together. [*All this time he has been arranging sticks for his fire*] Now get some dry grass.

[*She brings him grass, and he puts it under the sticks. He produces an old lens from his pocket, and tries to focus the sun's rays*]

TWEENY: Why, what is that?

CRICHTON: [*The ingenious creature*] That's the glass from my watch and one from Mr. Treherne's, with a little water between them. I am hoping to kindle a fire with it.

TWEENY: [*Properly impressed*] Oh sir!

[*After one failure the grass takes fire, and they are blowing on it when excited cries near by throw them sharply to their feet.* Agatha *runs to them, white of face, followed by* Ernest]

ERNEST: Danger! Crichton, a tiger-cat!

CRICHTON: [*Getting his cutlass*] Where?

AGATHA: It is at our heels.

ERNEST: Look out, Crichton.

CRICHTON: H'sh!

[Treherne *comes to his assistance, while* Lady Mary *and* Catherine *join* Agatha *in the hut*]

ERNEST: It will be on us in a moment. [*He seizes the hatchet and guards the hut. It is pleasing to see that* Ernest *is no coward*]

TREHERNE: Listen!

ERNEST: The grass is moving. It's coming.

[*It comes. But it is no tiger-cat; it is Lord Loam crawling on his hands and knees, a very exhausted and dishevelled peer, wondrously attired in rags. The girls see him, and with glad cries rush into his arms*]

LADY MARY: Father.

LORD LOAM: Mary—Catherine—Agatha. Oh dear, my dears, my dears, oh dear!

LADY MARY: Darling.

AGATHA: Sweetest.

CATHERINE: Love.

TREHERNE: Glad to see you, sir.

ERNEST: Uncle, uncle, dear old uncle.

[*For a time such happy cries fill the air, but presently* Treherne *is thoughtless*]

TREHERNE: Ernest thought you were a tiger-cat.

LORD LOAM: [*Stung somehow to the quick*] Oh, did you? I knew you at once, Ernest; I knew you by the way you ran.

[Ernest *smiles forgivingly*]

CRICHTON: [*Venturing forward at last*] My lord, I am glad.

ERNEST: [*With upraised finger*] But you are also idling, Crichton. [*Making himself comfortable on the ground*] We mustn't waste time. To work, to work.

CRICHTON: [*After contemplating him without rancor*] Yes, sir. [*He gets a pot from the hut and hangs it on a tripod over the fire, which is now burning brightly*]

TREHERNE: Ernest, you be a little more civil. Crichton, let me help.

[*He is soon busy helping* Crichton *to add to the strength of the hut*]

LORD LOAM: [*Gazing at the pot as ladies are said to gaze on precious stones*] Is that—but I suppose

I'm dreaming again. [*Timidly*] It isn't by any chance a pot on top of a fire, is it?

LADY MARY: Indeed, it is, dearest. It is our supper.

LORD LOAM: I have been dreaming of a pot on a fire for two days. [*Quivering*] There's nothing in it, is there?

ERNEST: Sniff, uncle.

[*Lord Loam sniffs*]

LORD LOAM: [*Reverently*] It smells of onions!

[*There is a sudden diversion*]

CATHERINE: Father, you have boots!

LADY MARY: So he has.

LORD LOAM: Of course I have.

ERNEST: [*With greedy cunning*] You are actually wearing boots, uncle. It's very unsafe, you know, in this climate.

LORD LOAM: Is it?

ERNEST: We have all abandoned them, you observe. The blood, the arteries, you know.

LORD LOAM: I hadn't a notion. [*He holds out his feet and* Ernest *kneels*]

ERNEST: O Lord yes.

[*In another moment those boots will be his*]

LADY MARY: [*Quickly*] Father, he is trying to get your boots from you. There is nothing in the world we would not give for boots.

ERNEST: [*Rising haughtily, a proud spirit misunderstood*] I only wanted the loan of them.

AGATHA: [*Running her fingers along them lovingly*] If you lend them to any one, it will be to us, won't it, father?

LORD LOAM: Certainly, my child.

ERNEST: Oh, very well. [*He is leaving these selfish ones*] I don't want your old boots. [*He gives his uncle a last chance*] You don't think you could spare me *one* boot?

LORD LOAM: [*Tartly*] I do not.

ERNEST: Quite so. Well, all I can say is I'm sorry for you. [*He departs to recline elsewhere*]

LADY MARY: Father, we thought we should never see you again.

LORD LOAM: I was washed ashore, my dear, clinging to a hencoop. How awful that first night was!

LADY MARY: Poor father.

LORD LOAM: When I woke, I wept. Then I began to feel extremely hungry. There was a large turtle on the beach. I remembered from the *Swiss Family Robinson* that if you turn a turtle over he is helpless. My dears, I crawled towards him, I flung myself upon him—[*Here he pauses to rub his leg*]—the nasty, spiteful brute.

LADY MARY: You didn't turn him over?

LORD LOAM: [*Vindictively, though he is a kindly man*] Mary, the senseless thing wouldn't wait; I found that none of them would wait.

CATHERINE: We should have been as badly off if Crichton hadn't——

LADY MARY: [*Quickly*] Don't praise Crichton.

LORD LOAM: And then those beastly monkeys. I always understood that if you flung stones at them they would retaliate by flinging cocoa-nuts at you. Would you believe it, I flung a hundred stones, and not one monkey had sufficient intelligence to grasp my meaning. How I longed for Crichton.

LADY MARY: [*Wincing*] For us also, father?

LORD LOAM: For you also. I tried for hours to make a fire. The authors say that when wrecked on an island you can obtain a light by rubbing two pieces of stick together. [*With feeling*] The liars!

LADY MARY: And all this time you thought there was no one on the island but yourself?

LORD LOAM: I thought so until this morning. I was searching the pools for little fishes, which I caught in my hat, when suddenly I saw before me—on the sand——

CATHERINE: What?

LORD LOAM: A hairpin.

LADY MARY: A hairpin! It must be one of ours. Give it me, father.

AGATHA: No, it's mine.

LORD LOAM: I didn't keep it.

LADY MARY: [*Speaking for all three*] Didn't keep it? Found a hairpin on an island and didn't keep it?

LORD LOAM: [*Humbly*] My dears.

AGATHA: [*Scarcely to be placated*] Oh father, we have returned to nature more than you bargained for.

LADY MARY: For shame, Agatha. [*She has something on her mind*] Father, there is something I want you to do at once—I mean assert your position as the chief person on the island.

[*They are all surprised*]

LORD LOAM: But who would presume to question it?

CATHERINE: She must mean Ernest.

LADY MARY: Must I?

AGATHA: It's cruel to say anything against Ernest.

LORD LOAM: [*Firmly*] If any one presumes to challenge my position, I shall make short work of him.

AGATHA: Here comes Ernest; now see if you can say these horrid things to his face.

LORD LOAM: I shall teach him his place at once.

LADY MARY: [*Anxiously*] But how?

LORD LOAM: [*Chuckling*] I have just thought of an extremely amusing way of doing it. [*As* Ernest *approaches*] Ernest.

ERNEST: [*Loftily*] Excuse me, uncle, I'm thinking. I'm planning out the building of this hut.

LORD LOAM: I also have been thinking.

ERNEST: That don't matter.

LORD LOAM: Eh?

ERNEST: Please, please, this is important.

LORD LOAM: I've been thinking that I ought to give you my boots.

ERNEST: What!

LADY MARY: Father.

LORD LOAM: [*Genially*] Take them, my boy. [*With a rapidity we had not thought him capable of,* Ernest *becomes the wearer of the boots*] And now I dare say you want to know why I give them to you, Ernest?

ERNEST: [*Moving up and down in them deliciously*] Not at all. The great thing is, "I've got 'em, I've got 'em."

LORD LOAM: [*Majestically, but with a knowing look at his daughters*] My reason is that, as head of our little party, you, Ernest, shall be our hunter, you shall clear the forests of those savage beasts that make them so dangerous. [*Pleasantly*] And now you know, my dear nephew, why I have given you my boots.

ERNEST: This is my answer. [*He kicks off the boots*]

LADY MARY: [*Still anxious*] Father, assert yourself.

LORD LOAM: I shall now assert myself. [*But how to do it? He has a happy thought*] Call Crichton.

LADY MARY: Oh father.

[Crichton *comes in answer to a summons and is followed by* Treherne]

ERNEST: [*Wondering a little at* Lady Mary's *grave face*] Crichton, look here.

LORD LOAM: [*Sturdily*] Silence! Crichton, I want your advice as to what I ought to do with Mr. Ernest. He has defied me.

ERNEST: Pooh!

CRICHTON: [*After considering*] May I speak openly, my lord?

LADY MARY: [*Keeping her eyes fixed on him*] That is what we desire.

CRICHTON: [*Quite humbly*] Then I may say, your lordship, that I have been considering Mr. Ernest's case at odd moments ever since we were wrecked.

ERNEST: My case?

LORD LOAM: [*Sternly*] Hush.

CRICHTON: Since we landed on the island, my lord, it seems to me that Mr. Ernest's epigrams have been particularly brilliant.

ERNEST: [*Gratified*] Thank you, Crichton.

CRICHTON: But I find—I seem to find it growing wild, my lord, in the woods, that sayings which would be justly admired in England are not much use on an island. I would therefore most respectfully propose that henceforth every time Mr. Ernest favors us with an epigram his head should be immersed in a bucket of cold spring water. [*There is a terrible silence*]

LORD LOAM: [*Uneasily*] Serve him right.

ERNEST: I should like to see you try to do it, uncle.

CRICHTON: [*Ever ready to come to the succour of his lordship*] My feeling, my lord, is that at the next offence I should convey him to a retired spot, where I shall carry out the undertaking in as respectful a manner as is consistent with thorough immersion. [*Though his manner is most respectful, he is firm; he evidently means what he says*]

LADY MARY: [*A ramrod*] Father, you must not permit this; Ernest is your nephew.

LORD LOAM: [*With his hand to his brow*] After all, he is my nephew, Crichton; and, as I am sure, he now sees that I am a strong man——

ERNEST: [*Foolishly in the circumstances*] A strong man. You mean a stout man. You are one of mind to two of matter. [*He looks round in the old way for approval. No one has smiled, and to his consternation he sees that* Crichton *is quietly turning up his sleeves.* Ernest *makes an appealing gesture to his uncle; then he turns defiantly to* Crichton]

CRICHTON: Is it to be before the ladies, Mr. Ernest, or in the privacy of the wood? [*He fixes* Ernest *with his eye.* Ernest *is cowed*] Come.

ERNEST: [*Affecting bravado*] Oh, all right.

CRICHTON: [*Succinctly*] Bring the bucket.

[Ernest *hesitates. He then lifts the bucket and follows* Crichton *to the nearest spring*]

LORD LOAM: [*Rather white*] I'm sorry for him, but I had to be firm.

LADY MARY: Oh, father, it wasn't you who was firm. Crichton did it himself.

LORD LOAM: Bless me, so he did.

LADY MARY: Father, be strong.

LORD LOAM: [*Bewildered*] You can't mean that my faithful Crichton——

LADY MARY: Yes, I do.

TREHERNE: Lady Mary, I stake my word that Crichton is incapable of acting dishonourably.

LADY MARY: I know that; I know it as well as you. Don't you see that that is what makes him so dangerous?

TREHERNE: By Jove, I—I believe I catch your meaning.

CATHERINE: He is coming back.

LORD LOAM: [*Who has always known himself to be a man of ideas*] Let us all go into the hut, just to show him at once that it is *our* hut.

LADY MARY: [*As they go*] Father, I implore you, assert yourself now and for ever.

LORD LOAM: I will.

LADY MARY: And, please, don't ask him how you are to do it.

[Crichton *returns with sticks to mend the fire*]

LORD LOAM: [*Loftily, from the door of the hut*] Have you carried out my instructions, Crichton?

CRICHTON: [*Deferentially*] Yes, my lord.

[Ernest *appears, mopping his hair, which has become very wet since we last saw him. He is not bearing malice, he is too busy drying, but* Agatha *is specially his champion*]

AGATHA: It's infamous, infamous.

LORD LOAM: [*Strongly*] My orders, Agatha.

LADY MARY: Now, father, please.

LORD LOAM: [*Striking an attitude*] Before I give you any further orders, Crichton——

CRICHTON: Yes, my lord.

LORD LOAM: [*Delighted*] Pooh! It's all right.

LADY MARY: No. Please go on.

LORD LOAM: Well, well. This question of leadership; what do you think now, Crichton?

CRICHTON: My Lord, I feel it is a matter with which *I* have nothing to do.

LORD LOAM: Excellent. Ha, Mary? That settles it, I think.

LADY MARY: It seems to, but—I'm not sure.

CRICHTON: It will settle itself naturally, my lord, without any interference from us. [*This reference to Nature gives general dissatisfaction*]

LADY MARY: Father.

LORD LOAM: [*A little severely*] It settled itself long ago, Crichton, when I was born a peer, and you, for instance, were born a servant.

CRICHTON: [*Acquiescing*] Yes, my lord, that was how it all came about quite naturally in England. We had nothing to do with it there, and we shall have as little to do with it here.

TREHERNE: [*Relieved*] That's all right.

LADY MARY: [*Determined to clinch the matter*] One moment. In short, Crichton, his lordship will continue to be our natural head.

CRICHTON: I dare say, my lady, I dare say.

CATHERINE: But you must *know.*

CRICHTON: Asking your pardon, my lady, one can't be sure—on an island.

[*They look at each other uneasily*]

LORD LOAM: [*Warningly*] Crichton, I don't like this.

CRICHTON: [*Harassed*] The more I think of it, your lordship, the more uneasy I become myself. When I heard, my lord, that you had left that hairpin behind——[*He is pained*]

LORD LOAM: [*Feebly*] One hairpin among so many would only have caused dissension.

CRICHTON: [*Very sorry to have to contradict him*] Not so, my lord. From that hairpin we could have made a needle; with that needle we could, out of skins, have sewn trousers—of which your lordship is in need; indeed, we are all in need of them.

LADY MARY: [*Suddenly self-conscious*] All?

CRICHTON: On an island, my lady.

LADY MARY: Father.

CRICHTON: [*Really more distressed by the prospect than she*] My lady, if Nature does not think them necessary, you may be sure she will not ask you to wear them. [*Shaking his head*] But among all this undergrowth——

LADY MARY: Now you see this man in his true colors.

LORD LOAM: [*Violently*] Crichton, you will either this moment say, "Down with Nature," or——

CRICHTON: [*Scandalized*] My lord!

LORD LOAM: [*Loftily*] Then this is my last word to you; take a month's notice.

[*If the hut had a door he would now shut it to indicate that the interview is closed*]

CRICHTON: [*In great distress*] Your lordship, the disgrace——

LORD LOAM: [*Swelling*] Not another word: you may go.

LADY MARY: [*Adamant*] And don't come to me, Crichton, for a character

ERNEST: [*Whose immersion has cleared his brain*] Aren't you all forgetting that this is an island?

[*This brings them to earth with a bump. Lord Loam looks to his eldest daughter for the fitting response*]

LADY MARY: [*Equal to the occasion*] It makes only this difference—that you may go at once, Crichton, to some other part of the island.

[*The faithful servant has been true to his superiors ever since he was created, and never more true than at this moment; but his fidelity is founded on trust in Nature, and to be untrue to it would be to be untrue to them. He lets the wood he has been gathering slip to the ground, and bows his sorrowful head. He turns to obey. Then affection for these great ones wells up in him*]

CRICHTON: My lady, let me work for you.

LADY MARY: Go.

CRICHTON: You need me sorely; I can't desert you; I won't.

LADY MARY: [*In alarm, lest the others may yield*] Then, father, there is but one alternative, *we* must leave him.

[Lord Loam *is looking yearningly at* Crichton]

TREHERNE: It seems a pity.

CATHERINE: [*Forlornly*] *You* will work for us?

TREHERNE: Most willingly. But I must warn you all that, so far, Crichton has done nine-tenths of the scoring.

LADY MARY: The question is, are we to leave this man?

LORD LOAM: [*Wrapping himself in his dignity*] Come, my dears.

CRICHTON: My lord!

LORD LOAM: Treherne—Ernest—get our things.

ERNEST: We don't have any, uncle. They all belong to Crichton.

TREHERNE: Everything we have he brought from the wreck—he went back to it before it sank. He risked his life.

CRICHTON: My lord, anything you would care to take is yours.

LADY MARY: [*Quickly*] Nothing.

ERNEST: Rot! If I could have your socks, Crichton——

LADY MARY: Come, father; we are ready.

[*Followed by the others, she and* Lord Loam *pick their way up the rocks. In their indignation they scarcely notice that daylight is coming to a sudden end*]

CRICHTON: My lord, I implore you—*I* am not desirous of being head. Do you have a try at it, my lord?

LORD LOAM: [*Outraged*] A try at it!

CRICHTON: [*Eagerly*] It may be that you will prove to be the best man.

LORD LOAM: *May* be! My children, come. [*They disappear proudly in single file*]

TREHERNE: Crichton, I'm sorry; but of course I must go with them.

CRICHTON: Certainly, sir. [*He calls to* Tweeny, *and she comes from behind the hut, where she has been watching breathlessly*] Will you be so kind, sir, as to take her to the others?

TREHERNE: Assuredly.

TWEENY: But what do it all mean?

CRICHTON: Does, Tweeny, does. [*He passes her up the rocks to* Treherne] We shall meet again soon, Tweeny. Good night, sir.

TREHERNE: Good night. I dare say they are not far away.

CRICHTON: [*Thoughtfully*] They went westward, sir, and the wind is blowing in that direction. That may mean, sir, that Nature is already taking the matter into her own hands. They are all hungry, sir, and the pot has come a-boil. [*He takes off the lid*] The smell will be borne westward. That pot is full of Nature, Mr. Treherne. Good night, sir.

TREHERNE: Good night.

[*He mounts the rocks with* Tweeny, *and they are heard for a little time after their figures are swallowed up in the fast growing darkness.* Crichton *stands motionless, the lid in his hand, though he has forgotten it, and his reason for taking it off the pot. He is deeply stirred, but presently is ashamed of his dejection, for it is as if he had doubted his principles. Bravely true to his faith that Nature will decide now as ever before, he proceeds manfully with his preparations for the night. He lights a ship's lantern, one of several treasures he has brought ashore, and is filling his pipe with crumbs of tobacco from various pockets, when the stealthy movements of some animal in the grass startles him. With the lantern in one hand and the cutlass in the other, he searches the ground around the hut. He returns, lights his pipe, and sits down by the fire, which casts weird moving shadows. There is a red gleam on his face; in the darkness he is a strong and perhaps rather sinister figure. In the great stillness that has fallen over the land, the wash of the surf seems to have increased in volume. The sound is indescribably mournful. Except where the fire is, desolation has fallen on the island like a pall.*

Once or twice, as Nature dictates, Crichton *leans forward to stir the pot, and the smell is borne westward. He then resumes his silent vigil.*

Shadows other than those cast by the fire begin to descend the rocks. They are the adventurers returning. One by one they steal nearer to the pot until they are squatted around it, with their hands out to the blaze. Lady Mary *only is absent. Presently she comes within sight of the others, then stands against a tree with her teeth clenched. One wonders, perhaps, what Nature is to make of her*]

END OF ACT II

ACT III.

The scene is the hall of their island home two years later. This sturdy log-house is no mere extension of the hut we have seen in process of erection, but has been built a mile or less to the west of it, on higher ground and near a stream. When the master chose this site, the others thought that all he expected from the stream was a sufficiency of drinking water. They know better now every time they go down to the mill or turn on the electric light.

This hall is the living-room of the house, and walls and roof are of stout logs. Across the joists supporting the roof are laid many home-made implements, such as spades, saws, fishing-rods, and from hooks in the joists are suspended cured foods, of which hams are specially in evidence. Deep recesses half way up the walls contain various provender in barrels and sacks. There are some skins, trophies of the chase, on the floor, which is otherwise bare. The chairs and tables are in some cases hewn out of solid wood, and in others the result of rough but efficient carpentering. Various pieces of wreckage from the yacht have been turned to novel uses; thus the steering wheel now hangs from the centre of the roof, with electric lights attached to it encased in bladders. A lifebuoy has become the back of a chair. Two barrels have been halved and turn coyly from each other as a settee.

The farther end of the room is more strictly the kitchen, and is a great recess, which can be shut off from the hall by folding doors. There is a large open fire in it. The chimney is half of one of the boats of the yacht. On the walls of the kitchen proper are many plate-racks, containing shells; there are rows of these of one size and shape, which mark them off as dinner plates or bowls; others are as obviously tureens. They are arranged primly as in a well-conducted kitchen; indeed, neatness and cleanliness are the note struck everywhere, yet the effect of the whole is romantic and barbaric.

The outer door into this hall is a little peculiar on an island. It is covered with skins and is in four leaves, like the swing doors of fashionable restaurants, which allow you to enter without allowing the hot air to escape. During the winter season our castaways have found the contrivance useful, but Crichton's *brain was perhaps a little lordly when he conceived it. Another door leads by a passage to the sleeping-rooms of the house, which are all on the ground-floor, and to* Crichton's *work-room, where he is at this moment, and whither we should like to follow him, but in a play we may not, as it is out of sight. There is a large window space without a window, which, however, can be shuttered, and through this we have a view of cattle-sheds, fowl-pens, and a field of grain. It is a fine summer evening.*

Tweeny *is sitting there, very busy plucking the feathers off a bird and dropping them on a sheet placed for that purpose on the floor. She is trilling to herself in the lightness of her heart. We may remember that* Tweeny, *alone among the women, had dressed wisely for an island when they fled the yacht, and her going-away gown still adheres to her, though in fragments. A score of pieces have been added here and there as necessity compelled, and these have been patched and repatched in incongruous colors; but, when all is said and done, it can still be maintained that* Tweeny *wears a skirt. She is deservedly proud of her skirt, and sometimes lends it on important occasions when approached in the proper spirit.*

Some one outside has been whistling to Tweeny; *the guarded whistle which, on a less savage island, is sometimes assumed to be an indication to cook that the constable is willing, if the coast be clear.* Tweeny, *however, is engrossed, or perhaps she is not in the mood for a follower, so he climbs in at the window undaunted, to take her willy-nilly. He is a jolly-looking laboring man, who answers to the name of* Daddy, *and—— But though that may be his island name, we recognize him at once. He is* Lord Loam, *settled down to the new conditions, and enjoying life heartily as handyman about the happy home. He is comfortably attired in skins. He is still stout, but all the flabbiness has dropped from him; gone, too, is his pomposity; his eye is clear, brown his skin; he could leap a gate.*

In his hands he carries an island-made concertina, and such is the exuberance of his spirits that, as he lights on the floor, he bursts into music and song, something about his being a chickety chickety chick chick, and will Tweeny *please to tell him whose chickety chick is she. Retribution follows sharp. We hear a whir, as if from insufficiently oiled machinery, and over the passage door appears a placard showing the one word "Silence." His lordship stops, and steals to* Tweeny *on his tiptoes.*

LORD LOAM: I thought the Gov. was out.
TWEENY: Well, you see he ain't. And if he were to catch you here idling——
  [Lord Loam *pales. He lays aside his musical instrument and hurriedly dons an apron.* Tweeny *gives him the bird to pluck, and busies herself laying the table for dinner*]
LORD LOAM: [*Softly*] What is he doing now?
TWEENY: I think he's working out that plan for laying on hot and cold.
LORD LOAM: [*Proud of his master*] And he'll manage it too. The man who could build a blacksmith's forge without tools——
TWEENY: [*Not less proud*] He made the tools.
LORD LOAM: Out of half a dozen rusty nails. The sawmill, Tweeny; the speaking-tube; the electric lighting; and look at the use he has made of the bits of the yacht that were washed ashore. And all in two years. He's a master I'm proud to pluck for.
  [*He chirps happily at his work, and she regards him curiously*]

TWEENY: Daddy, you're of little use, but you're a bright, cheerful creature to have about the house. [*He beams at this commendation*] Do you ever think of old times now? We was a bit different.
LORD LOAM: [*Pausing*] Circumstances alter cases.
  [*He resumes his plucking contentedly*]
TWEENY: But, Daddy, if the chance was to come of getting back?
LORD LOAM: I have given up bothering about it.
TWEENY: You bothered that day long ago when we saw a ship passing the island. How we all ran like crazy folk into the water, Daddy, and screamed and held out our arms. [*They are both a little agitated*] But it sailed away, and we've never seen another.
LORD LOAM: If we had had the electrical contrivance we have now we could have attracted that ship's notice. [*Their eyes rest on a mysterious apparatus that fills a corner of the hall*] A touch on that lever, Tweeny, and in a few moments bonfires would be blazing all round the shore.
TWEENY: [*Backing from the lever as if it might spring at her*] It's the most wonderful thing he has done.
LORD LOAM: [*In a reverie*] And then—England—home!
TWEENY: [*Also seeing visions*] London of a Saturday night!
LORD LOAM: My lords, in rising once more to address this historic chamber——
TWEENY: There was a little ham and beef shop off the Edgware Road——
  [*The visions fade; they return to the practical*]
LORD LOAM: Tweeny, do you think I could have an egg to my tea?
  [*At this moment a wiry, athletic figure in skins darkens the window. He is carrying two pails, which are suspended from a pole on his shoulder, and he is* Ernest. *We should say that he is* Ernest *completely changed if we were of those who hold that people change. As he enters by the window he has heard* Lord Loam's *appeal, and is perhaps justifiably indignant*]
ERNEST: What is that about an egg? Why should you have an egg?
LORD LOAM: [*With hauteur*] That is my affair, sir. [*With a Parthian shot as he withdraws stiffly from the room*] The Gov. has never put *my* head in a bucket.
ERNEST: [*Coming to rest on one of his buckets, and speaking with excusable pride. To* Tweeny] Nor mine for nearly three months. It was only last week, Tweeny, that he said to me, "Ernest, the water cure has worked marvels in you, and I question whether I shall require to dip you any more." [*Complacently*] Of course that sort of thing encourages a fellow.
TWEENY: [*Who has now arranged the dinner table to her satisfaction*] I will say, Erny, I never seen a young chap more improved.
ERNEST: [*Gratified*] Thank you, Tweeny; that's

very precious to me. [*She retires to the fire to work the great bellows with her foot, and* Ernest *turns to* Treherne, *who has come in looking more like a cowboy than a clergyman. He has a small box in his hand which he tries to conceal*] What have you got there, John?

TREHERNE: Don't tell anybody. It is a little present for the Gov.; a set of razors. One for each day in the week.

ERNEST: [*Opening the box and examining its contents*] Shells! He'll like that. He likes sets of things.

TREHERNE: [*In a guarded voice*] Have you noticed that?

ERNEST: Rather.

TREHERNE: He's becoming a bit magnificent in his ideas.

ERNEST: [*Huskily*] John, it sometimes gives me the creeps.

TREHERNE: [*Making sure that* Tweeny *is out of hearing*] What do you think of that brilliant robe he got the girls to make for him?

ERNEST: [*Uncomfortable*] I think he looks too regal in it.

TREHERNE: Regal! I sometimes fancy that that's why he's so fond of wearing it. [*Practically*] Well, I must take these down to the grindstone and put an edge on them.

ERNEST: [*Button-holing him*] I say, John, I want a word with you.

TREHERNE: Well?

ERNEST: [*Become suddenly diffident*] Dash it all, you know, you're a clergyman.

TREHERNE: One of the best things the Gov. has done is to insist that none of you forget it.

ERNEST: [*Taking his courage in his hands*] Then —would you, John?

TREHERNE: What?

ERNEST: [*Wistfully*] Officiate at a marriage ceremony, John?

TREHERNE: [*Slowly*] Now, that's really odd.

ERNEST: Odd? Seems to me it's natural. And whatever is natural, John, is right.

TREHERNE: I mean that same question has been put to me today already.

ERNEST: [*Eagerly*] By one of the women?

TREHERNE: Oh, no; they all put it to me long ago. This was by the Gov. himself.

ERNEST: By Jove! [*Admiringly*] I say, John, what an observant beggar he is.

TREHERNE: Ah! You fancy he was thinking of you?

ERNEST: I do not hesitate to affirm, John, that he has seen the love-light in my eyes. You answered——

TREHERNE: I said Yes, I thought it would be my duty to officiate if called upon.

ERNEST: You're a brick.

TREHERNE: [*Still pondering*] But I wonder whether he *was* thinking of you.

ERNEST: Make your mind easy about that.

TREHERNE: Well, my best wishes. Agatha is a very fine girl.

ERNEST: Agatha? What made you think it was Agatha?

TREHERNE: Man alive, you told me all about it soon after we were wrecked.

ERNEST: Pooh! Agatha's all very well in her way, John, but I'm flying after bigger game.

TREHERNE: Ernest, which is it?

ERNEST: Tweeny, of course.

TREHERNE: Tweeny? [*Reprovingly*] Ernest, I hope her cooking has nothing to do with this.

ERNEST: [*With dignity*] Her cooking has very little to do with it.

TREHERNE: But does she return your affection?

ERNEST: [*Simply*] Yes, John, I believe I may say so. I am unworthy of her, but I think I have touched her heart.

TREHERNE: [*With a sigh*] Some people seem to have all the luck. As you know, Catherine won't look at me.

ERNEST: I'm sorry, John.

TREHERNE: It's my deserts; I'm a second eleven sort of chap. Well, my heartiest good wishes, Ernest.

ERNEST: Thank you, John. How's the little black pig today?

TREHERNE: [*Departing*] He has begun to eat again.

[*After a moment's reflection* Ernest *calls to* Tweeny]

ERNEST: Are you very busy, Tweeny?

TWEENY: [*Coming to him good-naturedly*] There's always work to do; but if you want me, Ernest——

ERNEST: There's something I should like to say to you if you could spare me a moment.

TWEENY: Willingly. What is it?

ERNEST: What an ass I used to be, Tweeny.

TWEENY: [*Tolerantly*] Oh, let bygones be bygones.

ERNEST: [*Sincerely, and at his very best*] I'm no great shakes even now. But listen to this, Tweeny; I have known many women, but until I knew you I never knew any woman.

TWEENY: [*To whose uneducated ears this sounds dangerously like an epigram*] Take care—the bucket.

ERNEST: [*Hurriedly*] I didn't mean it in that way. [*He goes chivalrously on his knees*] Ah, Tweeny, I don't undervalue the bucket, but what I want to say now is that the sweet refinement of a dear girl has done more for me than any bucket could do.

TWEENY: [*With large eyes*] Are you offering to walk out with me, Erny?

ERNEST: [*Passionately*] More than that. I want to build a little house for you—in the sunny glade down by Porcupine Creek. I want to make chairs for you and tables; and knives and forks, and a sideboard for you.

TWEENY: [*Who is fond of language*] I like to hear you. [*Eyeing him*] Would there be any one in the house except myself, Ernest?

ERNEST: [*Humbly*] Not often; but just occasionally there would be your adoring husband.

TWEENY: [*Decisively*] It won't do, Ernest.

ERNEST: [*Pleading*] It isn't as if I should be much there.

TWEENY: I know, I know; but I don't love you, Ernest. I'm that sorry.

ERNEST: [*Putting his case clearly*] Twice a week I should be away altogether—at the dam. On the other days you would never see me from breakfast time to supper. [*With the self-abnegation of the true lover*] If you like I'll even go fishing on Sundays.

TWEENY: It's no use, Erny.

ERNEST: [*Rising manfully*] Thank you, Tweeny; it can't be helped. [*Then he remembers*] Tweeny, we shall be disappointing the Gov.

TWEENY: [*With a sinking*] What's that?

ERNEST: He wanted us to marry.

TWEENY: [*Blankly*] You and me? The Gov.! [*Her head droops woefully. From without is heard the whistling of a happier spirit, and* Tweeny *draws herself up fiercely*] That's her; that's the thing what has stolen his heart from me. [*A stalwart youth appears at the window, so handsome and tingling with vitality that, glad to depose* Crichton, *we cry thankfully, "The hero at last." But it is not the hero; it is the heroine. This splendid boy, clad in skins, is what Nature has done for* Lady Mary. *She carries bow and arrows and a blow-pipe, and over her shoulder is a fat buck, which she drops with a cry of triumph. Forgetting to enter demurely, she leaps through the window*] [*Sourly*] Drat you, Polly, why don't you wipe your feet?

LADY MARY: [*Good-naturedly*] Come, Tweeny, be nice to me. It's a splendid buck.

[*But* Tweeny *shakes her off, and retires to the kitchen fire*]

ERNEST: Where did you get it?

LADY MARY: [*Gaily*] I sighted a herd near Penguin's Creek, but had to creep round Silver Lake to get to windward of them. However, they spotted me and then the fun began. There was nothing for it but to try and run them down, so I singled out a fat buck and away we went down the shore of the lake, up the valley of rolling stones; he doubled into Brawling River and took to the water, but I swam after him; the river is only half a mile broad there, but it runs strong. He went spinning down the rapids, down I went in pursuit; he clambered ashore, I clambered ashore; away we tore helter-skelter up the hill and down again. I lost him in the marshes, got on his track again near Bread Fruit Wood, and brought him down with an arrow in Firefly Grove.

TWEENY: [*Staring at her*] Aren't you tired?

LADY MARY: Tired! It was gorgeous. [*She runs up a ladder and deposits her weapons on the joists. She is whistling again*]

TWEENY: [*Snapping*] I can't abide a woman whistling.

LADY MARY: [*Indifferently*] I like it.

TWEENY: [*Stamping her foot*] Drop it, Polly, I tell you.

LADY MARY: [*Stung*] I won't. I'm as good as you are. [*They are facing each other defiantly*]

ERNEST: [*Shocked*] Is this necessary? Think how it would pain *him.*

[*Lady Mary's eyes take a new expression. We see them soft for the first time*]

LADY MARY: [*Contritely*] Tweeny, I beg your pardon. If my whistling annoys you, I shall try to cure myself of it. [*Instead of calming* Tweeny, *this floods her face in tears*] Why, how can that hurt you, Tweeny, dear?

TWEENY: Because I can't make you lose your temper.

LADY MARY: [*Divinely*] Indeed, I often do. Would that I were nicer to everybody.

TWEENY: There you are again. [*Wistfully*] What makes you want to be so nice, Polly?

LADY MARY: [*With fervor*] Only thankfulness, Tweeny. [*She exults*] It is such fun to be alive.

[*So also seem to think* Catherine *and* Agatha, *who bounce in with fishing-rods and creel. They, too, are in manly attire*]

CATHERINE: We've got some ripping fish for the Gov.'s dinner. Are we in time? We ran all the way.

TWEENY: [*Tartly*] You'll please to cook them yourself, Kitty, and look sharp about it. [*She retires to her hearth, where* Agatha *follows her*]

AGATHA: [*Yearning*] Has the Gov. decided who is to wait upon him to-day?

CATHERINE: [*Who is cleaning her fish*] It's my turn.

AGATHA: [*Hotly*] I don't see that.

TWEENY: [*With bitterness*] It's to be neither of you, Aggy; he wants Polly again.

[*Lady Mary is unable to resist a joyous whistle*]

AGATHA: [*Jealously*] Polly, you toad.

[*But they cannot make* Lady Mary *angry*]

TWEENY: [*Storming*] How dare you look so happy?

LADY MARY: [*Willing to embrace her*] I wish, Tweeny, there was anything I could do to make you happy also.

TWEENY: Me! Oh, I'm happy. [*She remembers* Ernest, *whom it is easy to forget on an island*] I've just had a proposal, I tell you.

[*Lady Mary is shaken at last, and her sisters with her*]

AGATHA: A proposal?

CATHERINE: [*Going white*] Not—not—— [*She dare not say his name*]

ERNEST: [*With singular modesty*] You needn't be alarmed; it's only me.

LADY MARY: [*Relieved*] Oh, you!

AGATHA: [*Happy again*] Ernest, you dear, I got such a shock.

CATHERINE: It was only Ernest. [*Showing him her fish in thankfulness*] They are beautifully fresh; come and help me to cook them.

ERNEST: [*With simple dignity*] Do you mind if I don't cook fish to-night? [*She does not mind in the least. They have all forgotten him. A lark is singing in three hearts*] I think you might all be a little sorry for a chap. [*But they are not even sorry, and he addresses* Agatha *in these winged words:*] I'm particularly disappointed in you, Aggy; seeing that

I was half engaged to you, I think you might have had the good feeling to be a little more hurt.

AGATHA: Oh, bother.

ERNEST: [*Summing up the situation in so far as it affects himself*] I shall now go and lie down for a bit. [*He retires coldly but unregretted.* Lady Mary *approaches* Tweeny *with her most insinuating smile*]

LADY MARY: Tweeny, as the Gov. has chosen me to wait on him, please may I have the loan of it again?

[*The reference made with such charming delicacy is evidently to* Tweeny's *skirt*]

TWEENY: [*Doggedly*] No, you mayn't.

AGATHA: [*Supporting* Tweeny] Don't you give it to her.

LADY MARY: [*Still trying sweet persuasion*] You know quite well that he prefers to be waited on in a skirt.

TWEENY: I don't care. Get one for yourself.

LADY MARY: It is the only one on the island.

TWEENY: And it's mine.

LADY MARY: [*An aristocrat after all*] Tweeny, give me that skirt directly.

CATHERINE: Don't.

TWEENY: I won't.

LADY MARY: [*Clearing for action*] I shall make you.

TWEENY: I should like to see you try.

[*An unseemly fracas appears to be inevitable, but something happens. The whir is again heard, and the notice displayed "Dogs delight to bark and bite." Its effect is instantaneous and cheering. The ladies look at each other guiltily and immediately proceed on tiptoe to their duties. These are all concerned with the master's dinner.* Catherine *attends to his fish.* Agatha *fills a quaint toast-rack and brings the menu, which is written on a shell.* Lady Mary *twists a wreath of green leaves around her head, and places a flower beside the master's plate.* Tweeny *signs that all is ready, and she and the younger sisters retire into the kitchen, drawing the screen that separates it from the rest of the room.* Lady Mary *beats a tom-tom, which is the dinner bell. She then gently works a punkah, which we have not hitherto observed, and stands at attention. No doubt she is in hopes that the Gov. will enter into conversation with her, but she is too good a parlor-maid to let her hopes appear in her face. We may watch her manner with complete approval. There is not one of us who would not give her £26 a year.*

The master comes in quietly, a book in his hand, still the only book on the island, for he has not thought it worth while to build a printing-press. His dress is not noticeably different from that of the others, the skins are similar, but perhaps these are a trifle more carefully cut or he carries them better. One sees somehow that he has changed for his evening meal.

There is an odd suggestion of a dinner jacket about his doeskin coat. It is, perhaps, too grave a face for a man of thirty-two, as if he were over much immersed in affairs, yet there is a sunny smile left to lighten it at times and bring back its youth; perhaps too intellectual a face to pass as strictly handsome, not sufficiently suggestive of oats. His tall figure is very straight, slight rather than thickset, but nobly muscular. His big hands, firm and hard with labor though they be, are finely shaped— note the fingers so much more tapered, the nails better tended than those of his domestics; they are one of many indications that he is of a superior breed. Such signs, as has often been pointed out, are infallible. A romantic figure, too. One can easily see why the women-folks of this strong man's house both adore and fear him.

He does not seem to notice who is waiting on him tonight, but inclines his head slightly to whoever it is, as she takes her place at the back of his chair. Lady Mary *respectfully places the menu-shell before him, and he glances at it*]

CRICHTON: Clear, please.

[Lady Mary *knocks on the screen, and a serving hutch in it opens, through which* Tweeny *offers two soup plates.* Lady Mary *selects the clear and the aperture is closed. She works the punkah while the master partakes of his soup*]

CRICHTON: [*Who always gives praise where it is due*] An excellent soup, Polly, but still a trifle too rich.

LADY MARY: Thank you.

[*The next course is the fish, and while it is being passed through the hutch we have a glimpse of three jealous women.* Lady Mary's *movements are so deft and noiseless that any observant spectator can see that she was born to wait at table*]

CRICHTON: [*Unbending as he eats*] Polly, you are a very smart girl.

LADY MARY: [*Bridling, but naturally gratified*] La!

CRICHTON: [*Smiling*] And I'm not the first you've heard it from, I'll swear.

LADY MARY: [*Wriggling*] Oh Gov.!

CRICHTON: Got any followers on the island, Polly?

LADY MARY: [*Tossing her head*] Certainly not.

CRICHTON: I thought that perhaps John or Ernest——

LADY MARY: [*Tilting her nose*] I don't say that it's for want of asking.

CRICHTON: [*Emphatically*] I'm sure it isn't. [*Perhaps he thinks he has gone too far*] You may clear.

[*Flushed with pleasure, she puts before him a bird and vegetables, sees that his beaker is filled with wine, and returns to the punkah. She would love to continue their conversation, but it is for him to decide. For a time he seems to have forgotten her]*

CRICHTON: Did you lose any arrows to-day?

LADY MARY: Only one in Firefly Grove.

CRICHTON: You were as far as that? How did you get across the Black Gorge?

LADY MARY: I went across on the rope.

CRICHTON: Hand over hand?

LADY MARY: [*Swelling at the implied praise*] I wasn't in the least dizzy.

CRICHTON: [*Moved*] You brave girl! [*He sits back in his chair a little agitated*] But never do that again.

LADY MARY: [*Pouting*] It is such fun, Gov.

CRICHTON: [*Decisively*] I forbid it.

LADY MARY: [*The little rebel*] I shall.

CRICHTON: [*Surprised*] Polly! [*He signs to her sharply to step forward, but for a moment she holds back petulantly, and even when she comes it is less obediently than like a naughty, sulky child. Nevertheless, with the forbearance that is characteristic of the man, he addresses her with grave gentleness rather than severely*] You must do as I tell you, you know.

LADY MARY: [*Strangely passionate*] I shan't.

CRICHTON: [*Smiling at her fury*] We shall see. Frown at me, Polly; there you do it at once. Clench your little fists, stamp your feet, bite your ribbons —— [*A student of women, or at least of this woman, he knows that she is about to do these things, and thus she seems to do them to order*. Lady Mary *screws up her face like a baby and cries. He is immediately kind*] You child of nature; was it cruel of me to wish to save you from harm?

LADY MARY: [*Drying her eyes*] I'm an ungracious wretch. Oh Gov., I don't try half hard enough to please you. I'm even wearing—— [*She looks down sadly*]—when I know you prefer *it*.

CRICHTON: [*Thoughtfully*] I admit I do prefer *it*. Perhaps I am a little old-fashioned in these matters. [*Her tears again threaten*] Ah, don't, Polly; that's nothing.

LADY MARY: If I could only please you, Gov.

CRICHTON: [*Slowly*] You do please me, child, very much—— [*He half rises*]—very much indeed. [*If he meant to say more he checks himself. He looks at his plate*] No more, thank you.

[*The simple island meal is ended, save for the walnuts and the wine, and* Crichton *is too busy a man to linger long over them. But he is a stickler for etiquette, and the table is cleared charmingly, though with dispatch, before they are placed before him.* Lady Mary *is an artist with the crumb-brush, and there are few arts more delightful to watch. Dusk has come sharply, and she turns on the electric light. It awakens* Crichton *from a reverie in which he has been regarding her*]

CRICHTON: Polly, there is only one thing about you that I don't quite like. [*She looks up, making a moue, if that can be said of one who so well knows her place. He explains*] That action of the hands.

LADY MARY: What do I do?

CRICHTON: So—like one washing them. I have noticed that the others tend to do it also. It seems odd.

LADY MARY: [*Archly*] Oh Gov., have you forgotten?

CRICHTON: What?

LADY MARY: That once upon a time a certain other person did that.

CRICHTON: [*Groping*] You mean myself? [*She nods, and he shudders*] Horrible!

LADY MARY: [*Afraid she has hurt him*] You haven't for a very long time. Perhaps it is natural to servants.

CRICHTON: That must be it. [*He rises*] Polly!

[*She looks up expectantly, but he only sighs and turns away*]

LADY MARY: [*Gently*] You sighed, Gov.

CRICHTON: Did I? I was thinking. [*He paces the room and then turns to her agitatedly, yet with control over his agitation. There is some mournfulness in his voice*] I have always tried to do the right thing on this island. Above all, Polly, I want to do the right thing by you.

LADY MARY: [*With shining eyes*] How we all trust you. That is your reward, Gov.

CRICHTON: [*Who is having a fight with himself*] And now I want a greater reward. Is it fair to you? Am I playing the game? Bill Crichton would always like to play the game. If we were in England—— [*He pauses so long that she breaks in softly*]

LADY MARY: We know now that we shall never see England again.

CRICHTON: I am thinking of two people whom neither of us has seen for a long time—Lady Mary Lasenby, and one Crichton, a butler. [*He says the last word bravely, a word he once loved, though it is the most horrible of all words to him now*]

LADY MARY: That cold, haughty, insolent girl. Gov., look around you and forget them both.

CRICHTON: I had nigh forgotten them. He has had a chance, Polly,—that butler—in these two years of becoming a man, and he has tried to take it. There have been many failures, but there has been some success, and with it I have let the past drop off me, and turned my back on it. That butler seems a faraway figure to me now, and not myself. I hail him, but we scarcely know each other. If I am to bring him back it can only be done by force, for in my soul he is abhorrent to me. But if I thought it best for you I'd haul him back; I swear as an honest man, I would bring him back with all his obsequious ways and deferential airs, and let you see the man you call your Gov. melt forever into him who was your servant.

LADY MARY: [*Shivering*] You hurt me. You say these things, but you say them like a king. To me it is the past that was not real.

CRICHTON: [*Too grandly*] A king! I sometimes feel—— [*For a moment the yellow light gleams in his green eyes. We remember suddenly what Tre-*

herne *and* Ernest *said about his regal look. He checks himself*] I say it harshly, it is so hard to say, and all the time there is another voice within me crying—— [*He stops*]

LADY MARY: [*Trembling but not afraid*] If it is the voice of Nature——

CRICHTON: [*Strongly*] I know it to be the voice of Nature.

LADY MARY: [*In a whisper*] Then, if you want to say it very much, Gov., please say it to Polly Lasenby.

CRICHTON: [*Again in the grip of an idea*] A king! Polly, some people hold that the soul but leaves one human tenement for another, and so lives on through all the ages. I have occasionally thought of late that, in some past existence, I may have been a king. It has all come to me so naturally, not as if I had had to work it out, but—as—if—I—remembered.

> "Or ever the knightly years were gone,
> With the old world to the grave,
> I was a *king* in Babylon,
> And you were a Christian slave."

It may have been; you hear me, it may have been.

LADY MARY: [*Who is as one fascinated*] It may have been.

CRICHTON: I am lord over all. They are but hewers of wood and drawers of water for me. These shores are mine. Why should I hesitate; I have no longer any doubt. I do believe I am doing the right thing. Dear Polly, I have grown to love you; are you afraid to mate with me? [*She rocks her arms; no words will come from her*]

> "I was a king in Babylon,
> And you were a Christian slave."

LADY MARY: [*Bewitched*] You are the most wonderful man I have ever known, and I am not afraid. [*He takes her to him reverently. Presently he is seated, and she is at his feet looking up adoringly in his face. As the tension relaxes, she speaks with a smile*] I want you to tell me—every woman likes to know—when was the first time you thought me nicer than the others?

CRICHTON: [*Who like all big men is simple*] I think a year ago. We were chasing goats on the Big Slopes, and you out-distanced us all; you were the first of our party to run a goat down; I was proud of you that day.

LADY MARY: [*Blushing with pleasure*] Oh Gov., I only did it to please you. Everything I have done has been out of the desire to please you. [*Suddenly anxious*] If I thought that in taking a wife from among us you were imperilling your dignity——

CRICHTON: [*Perhaps a little masterful*] Have no fear of that, dear. I have thought it all out. The wife, Polly, always takes the same position as the husband.

LADY MARY: But I am so unworthy. It was sufficient to me that I should be allowed to wait on you at that table.

CRICHTON: You shall wait on me no longer. At whatever table I sit, Polly, you shall soon sit there,

also. [*Boyishly*] Come, let us try what it will be like.

LADY MARY: As your servant at your feet.

CRICHTON: No, as my consort by my side.

[*They are sitting thus when the hatch is again opened and coffee offered. But Lady Mary is no longer there to receive it. Her sisters peep through in consternation. In vain they rattle the cup and saucer. Agatha brings the coffee to* Crichton]

CRICHTON: [*Forgetting for the moment that it is not a month hence*] Help your mistress first, girl. [*Three women are bereft of speech, but he does not notice it. He addresses* Catherine *vaguely*] Are you a good girl, Kitty?

CATHERINE: [*When she finds her tongue*] I try to be, Gov.

CRICHTON: [*Still more vaguely*] That's right.

[*He takes command of himself again, and signs to them to sit down.* Ernest *comes in cheerily, but finding* Crichton *here is suddenly weak. He subsides on a chair, wondering what has happened*]

CRICHTON: [*Surveying him*] Ernest. [Ernest *rises*] You are becoming a little slovenly in your dress, Ernest; I don't like it.

ERNEST: [*Respectfully*] Thank you.

[Ernest *sits again.* Daddy *and* Treherne *arrive*]

CRICHTON: Daddy, I want you.

LORD LOAM: [*With a sinking*] Is it because I forgot to clean out the dam?

CRICHTON: [*Encouragingly*] No, no. [*He pours some wine into a goblet*] A glass of wine with you, Daddy.

LORD LOAM: [*Hastily*] Your health, Gov. [*He is about to drink, but the master checks him*]

CRICHTON: And hers. Daddy, this lady has done me the honor to promise to be my wife.

LORD LOAM: [*Astounded*] Polly!

CRICHTON: [*A little perturbed*] I ought first to have asked your consent. I deeply regret—but Nature; may I hope I have your approval?

LORD LOAM: May you, Gov.? [*Delighted*] Rather! Polly! [*He puts his proud arms around her*]

TREHERNE: We all congratulate you, Gov., most heartily.

ERNEST: Long life to you both, sir.

[*There is much shaking of hands, all of which is sincere*]

TREHERNE: When will it be, Gov.?

CRICHTON: [*After turning to* Lady Mary, *who whispers to him*] As soon as the bridal skirt can be prepared. [*His manner has been most indulgent, and without the slightest sign of patronage. But he knows it is best for all that he should keep his place, and that his presence hampers them*] My friends, I thank you for your good wishes, I thank you all. And now, perhaps you would like me to leave you to yourselves. Be joyous. Let there be song and dance tonight. Polly, I shall take my coffee in the Parlor—you understand.

[*He retires with pleasant dignity. Immediately there is a rush of two girls at* Lady Mary]

LADY MARY: Oh, oh! Father, they are pinching me.

LORD LOAM: [*Taking her under his protection*] Agatha, Catherine, never presume to pinch your sister again. On the other hand, she may pinch you henceforth as much as ever she chooses.

[*In the meantime* Tweeny *is weeping softly, and the two are not above using her as a weapon*]

CATHERINE: Poor Tweeny. It's a shame.

AGATHA: After he had almost promised *you*.

TWEENY: [*Loyally turning on them*] No, he never did. He was always honorable as could be. 'Twas me as was too vulgar. Don't you dare say a word agin that man.

ERNEST: [*To* Lord Loam] You'll get a lot of tid-bits out of this, Daddy.

LORD LOAM: That's what I was thinking.

ERNEST: [*Plunged in thought*] I dare say *I* shall have to clean out the dam now.

LORD LOAM: [*Heartlessly*] I dare say. [*His gay old heart makes him again proclaim that he is a chickety chick. He seizes the concertina*]

TREHERNE: [*Eagerly*] That's the proper spirit.

[*He puts his arm around* Catherine, *and in another moment they are all dancing to Daddy's music. Never were people happier on an island. A moment's pause is presently created by the return of* Crichton *wearing the wonderful robe of which we have already had dark mention. Never has he looked more regal, never perhaps felt so regal. We need not grudge him the one foible of his rule, for it is all coming to an end*]

CRICHTON: [*Graciously, seeing them hesitate*] No, no; I am delighted to see you all so happy. Go on.

TREHERNE: We don't like to before you, Gov.

CRICHTON: [*His last order*] It is my wish.

[*The merrymaking is resumed, and soon* Crichton *himself joins in the dance. It is when the fun is at its fastest and most furious that all stop abruptly as if turned to stone. They have heard the boom of a gun. Presently they are alive again.* Ernest *leaps to the window*]

TREHERNE: [*Huskily*] It was a ship's gun. [*They turn to* Crichton *for confirmation; even in that hour they turn to* Crichton] Gov.?

CRICHTON: Yes.

[*In another moment* Lady Mary *and* Lord Loam *are alone*]

LADY MARY: [*Seeing that her father is unconcerned*] Father, you heard.

LORD LOAM: [*Placidly*] Yes, my child.

LADY MARY: [*Alarmed by his unnatural calmness*] But it was a gun, father.

LORD LOAM: [*Looking an old man now, and shuddering a little*] Yes—a gun—I have often heard it. It's only a dream, you know; why don't we go on dancing?

[*She takes his hands, which have gone cold*]

LADY MARY: Father. Don't you see, they have all rushed down to the beach? Come.

LORD LOAM: Rushed down to the beach; yes, always that—I often dream it.

LADY MARY: Come, father, come.

LORD LOAM: Only a dream, my poor girl.

[Crichton *returns. He is pale but firm*]

CRICHTON: We can see lights within a mile of the shore—a great ship.

LORD LOAM: A ship—always a ship.

LADY MARY: Father, this is no dream.

LORD LOAM: [*Looking timidly at* Crichton] It's a dream, isn't it? There's no ship?

CRICHTON: [*Soothing him with a touch*] You are awake, Daddy, and there is a ship.

LORD LOAM: [*Clutching him*] You are not deceiving me?

CRICHTON: It is the truth.

LORD LOAM: [*Reeling*] True?—a ship—at last! [*He goes after the others pitifully*]

CRICHTON: [*Quietly*] There is a small boat between it and the island; they must have sent it ashore for water.

LADY MARY: Coming in?

CRICHTON: No. That gun must have been a signal to recall it. It is going back. They can't hear our cries.

LADY MARY: [*Pressing her temples*] Going away. So near—so near. [*Almost to herself*] I think I'm glad.

CRICHTON: [*Cheerily*] Have no fear. I shall bring them back. [*He goes towards the table on which is the electrical apparatus*]

LADY MARY: [*Standing on guard as it were between him and the table*] What are you going to do?

CRICHTON: To fire the beacons.

LADY MARY: Stop! [*She faces him*] Don't you see what it means?

CRICHTON: [*Firmly*] It means that our life on the island has come to a natural end.

LADY MARY: [*Huskily*] Gov., let the ship go.

CRICHTON: The old man—you saw what it means to him.

LADY MARY: But I am afraid.

CRICHTON: [*Adoringly*] Dear Polly.

LADY MARY: Gov., let the ship go.

CRICHTON: [*She clings to him, but though it is his death sentence he loosens her hold*] Bill Crichton has got to play the game. [*He pulls the levers. Soon through the window one of the beacons is seen flaring red. There is a long pause. Shouting is heard.* Ernest *is the first to arrive*]

ERNEST: Polly, Gov., the boat has turned back. They are English sailors; they have landed! We are rescued. I tell you, rescued!

LADY MARY: [*Wanly*] Is it anything to make so great a to-do about?

ERNEST: [*Staring*] Eh?

LADY MARY: Have we not been happy here?

ERNEST: Happy? lord, yes.

LADY MARY: [*Catching hold of his sleeve*] Ernest,

we must never forget all that the Gov. has done for us.

ERNEST: [*Stoutly*] Forget it? The man who could forget it would be a selfish wretch and a—— But I say, this makes a difference!

LADY MARY: [*Quickly*] No, it doesn't.

ERNEST: [*His mind tottering*] A mighty difference!

[*The others come running in, some weeping with joy, others boisterous. We see blue-jackets gazing through the window at the curious scene. Lord Loam comes accompanied by a naval officer, whom he is continually shaking by the hand*]

LORD LOAM: And here, sir, is our little home. Let me thank you again in the names of all of us, again and again and again.

OFFICER: Very proud, my lord. It is indeed an honor to have been able to assist so distinguished a gentleman as Lord Loam.

LORD LOAM: A glorious, glorious day. I shall show you our other room. Come, my pets. Come, Crichton. [*He has not meant to be cruel. He does not know he has said it. It is the old life that has come back to him. They all go. All leave* Crichton *except* Lady Mary]

LADY MARY: [*Stretching out her arms to him*] Dear Gov., I will never give you up.

[*There is a salt smile on his face as he shakes his head to her. He lets the cloak slip to the ground. She will not take this for an answer; again her arms go out to him. Then comes the great renunciation. By an effort of will he ceases to be an erect figure; he has the humble bearing of a servant. His hands come together as if he were washing them*]

CRICHTON: [*It is the speech of his life*] My lady.

[*She goes away. There is none to salute him now, unless we do it*]

END OF ACT III

ACT IV.

Some months has elapsed, and we have again the honor of waiting upon Lord Loam *in his London home. It is the room of the first act, but with a new scheme of decoration, for on the walls are exhibited many interesting trophies from the island, such as skins, stuffed birds, and weapons of the chase, labelled "Shot by* Lord Loam," "Hon. Ernest Woolley's *Blowpipe," etc. There are also two large glass cases containing other odds and ends, including, curiously enough, the bucket in which* Ernest *was first dipped, but there is no label calling attention to the incident.*

It is not yet time to dress for dinner, and his lordship is on a couch, hastily yet furtively cutting the pages of a new book. With him are his two younger daughters and his nephew, and they also are engaged in literary pursuits; that is to say, the ladies are eagerly but furtively reading the evening papers, of which Ernest *is sitting complacently but furtively on an endless number, and doling them out as called for. Note the frequent use of the word "furtive." It implies that they do not wish to be discovered by their butler, say, at their otherwise delightful task.*

AGATHA: [*Reading aloud, with emphasis on the wrong words*] "In conclusion, we must heartily congratulate the Hon. Ernest Woolley. This book of his, regarding the adventures of himself and his brave companions on a desert isle, stirs the heart like a trumpet."

[*Evidently the book referred to is the one in* Lord Loam's *hands*]

ERNEST: [*Handing her a pink paper*] Here is another.

CATHERINE: [*Reading*] "From the first to the last of Mr. Woolley's engrossing pages it is evident that he was an ideal man to be wrecked with, and a true hero." [*Large-eyed*] Ernest!

ERNEST: [*Calmly*] That's how it strikes *them*, you know. Here's another one.

AGATHA: [*Reading*] "There are many kindly references to the two servants who were wrecked with the family, and Mr. Woolley pays the butler a glowing tribute in a footnote."

[*Some one coughs uncomfortably*]

LORD LOAM: [*Who has been searching the index for the letter L*] Excellent, excellent. At the same time I must say, Ernest, that the whole book is about yourself.

ERNEST: [*Genially*] As the author——

LORD LOAM: Certainly, certainly. Still, you know, as a peer of the realm—— [*With dignity*] ——I think, Ernest, you might have given me one of your adventures.

ERNEST: I say it was you who taught us how to obtain a fire by rubbing two pieces of stick together.

LORD LOAM: [*Beaming*] Do you, do you? I call that very handsome. What page?

[*Here the door opens, and the well-bred Crichton enters with the evening papers as subscribed for by the house. Those we have already seen have perhaps been introduced by Ernest up his waistcoat. Every one except the intruder is immediately self-conscious, and when he withdraws there is a general sigh of relief. They pounce on the new papers. Ernest evidently gets a shock from one, which he casts contemptuously on the floor*]

AGATHA: [*More fortunate*] Father, see page 81. "It was a tiger-cat," says Mr. Woolley, "of the largest size. Death stared Lord Loam in the face, but he never flinched."

LORD LOAM: [*Searching his book eagerly*] Page 81.

AGATHA: "With presence of mind only equalled by his courage, he fixed an arrow in his bow."

LORD LOAM: Thank you, Ernest; thank you my boy.

AGATHA: "Unfortunately he missed."

LORD LOAM: Eh?

AGATHA: "But by great good luck I heard his cries——"

LORD LOAM: My cries?

AGATHA: "——and rushing forward with drawn knife, I stabbed the monster to the heart."

[Lord Loam *shuts his book with a pettish slam. There might be a scene here were it not that* Crichton *reappears and goes to one of the glass cases. All are at once on the alert, and his lordship is particularly sly*]

LORD LOAM: Anything in the papers, Catherine?

CATHERINE: No, father, nothing—nothing at all.

ERNEST: [*It pops out as of yore*] The papers! The papers are guides that tell us what we ought to do, and then we don't do it.

[Crichton *having opened the glass case has taken out the bucket, and* Ernest, *looking round for applause, sees him carrying it off and is undone. For a moment of time he forgets that he is no longer on the island, and with a sigh he is about to follow* Crichton *and the bucket to a retired spot. The door closes, and* Ernest *comes to himself*]

LORD LOAM: [*Uncomfortably*] I told him to take it away.

ERNEST: I thought—— [*He wipes his brow*] ——I shall go and dress. [*He goes*]

CATHERINE: Father, it's awful having Crichton here. It's like living on tiptoe.

LORD LOAM: [*Gloomily*] While he is here we are sitting on a volcano.

AGATHA: How mean of you! I am sure he has only stayed on with us to—to help us through. It would have looked so suspicious if he had gone at once.

CATHERINE: [*Revelling in the worst*] But suppose Lady Brocklehurst were to get at him and pump him. She's the most terrifying, suspicious old creature in England; and Crichton simply can't tell a lie.

LORD LOAM: My dear, that is the volcano to which I was referring. [*He has evidently something to communicate*] It's all Mary's fault. She said to me yesterday that she would break her engagement with Brocklehurst unless I told him about—you know what.

[*All conjure up the vision of* Crichton]

AGATHA: Is she mad?

LORD LOAM: She calls it common honesty.

CATHERINE: Father, have you told him?

LORD LOAM: [*Heavily*] She thinks I have, but I couldn't. She's sure to find out to-night.

[*Unconsciously he leans on the island concertina, which he has perhaps been lately showing to an interviewer as something he made for* Tweeny. *It squeaks, and they all jump*]

CATHERINE: It's like a bird of ill-omen.

LORD LOAM: [*Vindictively*] I must have it taken away; it has done that twice.

[Lady Mary *comes in. She is in evening dress.*

Undoubtedly she meant to sail in, but she forgets, and despite her garments it is a manly entrance. She is properly ashamed of herself. She tries again, and has an encouraging success. She indicates to her sisters that she wishes to be alone with papa]

AGATHA: All right, but we know what it's about. Come along, Kit.

[*They go.* Lady Mary *thoughtlessly sits like a boy, and again corrects herself. She addresses her father, but he is in a brown study, and she seeks to draw his attention by whistling. This troubles them both*]

LADY MARY: How horrid of me!

LORD LOAM: [*Depressed*] If you would try to remember——

LADY MARY: [*Sighing*] I do; but there are so many things to remember.

LORD LOAM: [*Sympathetically*] There are—— [*In a whisper*] Do you know, Mary, I constantly find myself secreting hairpins.

LADY MARY: I find it so difficult to go up steps one at a time.

LORD LOAM: I was dining with half dozen members of our party last Thursday, Mary, and they were so eloquent that I couldn't help wondering all the time how many of their heads *he* would have put in the bucket.

LADY MARY: I use so many of his phrases. And my appetite is so scandalous. Father, I usually have a chop before we sit down to dinner.

LORD LOAM: As for my clothes—[*Wriggling*] My dear, you can't think how irksome collars are to me nowadays.

LADY MARY: They can't be half such an annoyance, father, as——

[*She looks dolefully at her skirt*]

LORD LOAM: [*Hurriedly*] Quite so—quite so. You have dressed early to-night, Mary.

LADY MARY: That reminds me; I had a note from Brocklehurst saying he would come a few minutes before his mother as—as he wanted to have a talk with me. He didn't say what about, but of course we know. [*His lordship fidgets*] [*With feeling*] It was good of you to tell him, father. Oh, it is horrible to me—— [*Covering her face*] It seemed so natural at the time.

LORD LOAM: [*Petulantly*] Never again make use of that word in this house, Mary.

LADY MARY: [*With an effort*] Father, Brocklehurst has been so loyal to me for these two years that I should despise myself were I to keep my—my extraordinary lapse from him. Had Brocklehurst been a little less good, then you need not have told him my strange little secret.

LORD LOAM: [*Weakly*] Polly—I mean Mary—it was all Crichton's fault, he——

LADY MARY: [*With decision*] No, father, no; not a word against him though. I haven't the pluck to go on with it; I can't even understand how it ever was.

Father, do you not still hear the surf? Do you see the curve of the beach?

LORD LOAM: I have begun to forget—— [*In a low voice*] But they were happy days; there was something magical about them.

LADY MARY: It was glamour. Father, I have lived Arabian nights. I have sat out a dance with the evening star. But it was all in a past existence, in the days of Babylon, and I am myself again. But he has been chivalrous always. If the slothful, indolent creature I used to be has improved in any way, I owe it all to him. I am slipping back in many ways, but I am determined not to slip back altogether— in memory of him and his island. That is why I insisted on your telling Brocklehurst. He can break our engagement if he chooses. [*Proudly*] Mary Lasenby is going to play the game.

LORD LOAM: But my dear——

[*Lord Brocklehurst is announced*]

LADY MARY: [*Meaningly*] Father, dear, oughtn't you to be dressing?

LORD LOAM: [*Very unhappy*] The fact is—before I go—I want to say——

LORD BROCKLEHURST: Loam, if you don't mind, I wish very specially to have a word with Mary before dinner.

LORD LOAM: But——

LADY MARY: Yes, father. [*She induces him to go, and thus courageously faces* Lord Brocklehurst *to hear her fate*] I am ready, George.

LORD BROCKLEHURST: [*Who is so agitated that she ought to see he is thinking not of her but of himself*] It is a painful matter—I wish I could have spared you this, Mary.

LADY MARY: Please go on.

LORD BROCKLEHURST: In common fairness, of course, this should be remembered, that two years had elapsed. You and I had no reason to believe that we should ever meet again.

[*This is more considerate than she had expected*]

LADY MARY: [*Softening*] I was so lost to the world, George.

LORD BROCKLEHURST: [*With a groan*] At the same time, the thing is utterly and absolutely inexcusable.

LADY MARY: [*Recovering her hauteur*] Oh!

LORD BROCKLEHURST: And so I have already said to mother.

LADY MARY: [*Disdaining him*] You have told her?

LORD BROCKLEHURST: Certainly, Mary, certainly; I tell mother everything.

LADY MARY: [*Curling her lips*] And what did she say?

LORD BROCKLEHURST: To tell the truth, mother rather pooh-poohed the whole affair.

LADY MARY: [*Incredulous*] Lady Brocklehurst pooh-poohed the whole affair!

LORD BROCKLEHURST: She said, "Mary and I will have a good laugh over this."

LADY MARY: [*Outraged*] George, your mother is a hateful, depraved old woman.

LORD BROCKLEHURST: Mary!

LADY MARY: [*Turning away*] Laugh indeed, when it will always be such a pain to me.

LORD BROCKLEHURST: [*With strange humility*] If only you would let me bear all the pain, Mary.

LADY MARY: [*Who is taken aback*] George, I think you are the noblest man—— [*She is touched, and gives him both her hands. Unfortunately he simpers*]

LORD BROCKLEHURST: She was a pretty little thing. [*She stares, but he marches to his doom*] Ah, not beautiful like you. I assure you it was the merest flirtation; there were a few letters, but we have got them back. It was all owing to the boat being so late at Calais. You see she had such large, helpless eyes.

LADY MARY: [*Fixing him*] George, when you lunched with father to-day at the club——

LORD BROCKLEHURST: I didn't. He wired me that he couldn't come.

LADY MARY: [*With a tremor*] But he wrote you?

LORD BROCKLEHURST: No.

LADY MARY: [*A bird singing in her breast*] You haven't seen him since?

LORD BROCKLEHURST: No.

[*She is saved. Is he to be let off also? Not at all. She bears down on him like a ship of war*]

LADY MARY: George, who and what is this woman?

LORD BROCKLEHURST: [*Cowering*] She was—she is—the shame of it—a lady's-maid.

LADY MARY: [*Properly horrified*] A what?

LORD BROCKLEHURST: A lady's-maid. A mere servant, Mary. [Lady Mary *whirls round so that he shall not see her face*] I first met her at this house when you were entertaining the servants; so you see it was largely your father's fault.

LADY MARY: [*Looking him up and down*] A lady's-maid?

LORD BROCKLEHURST: [*Degraded*] Her name was Fisher.

LADY MARY: My maid!

LORD BROCKLEHURST: [*With open hands*] Can you forgive me, Mary?

LADY MARY: Oh George, George!

LORD BROCKLEHURST: Mother urged me not to tell you anything about it; but——

LADY MARY: [*From her heart*] I am so glad you told me.

LORD BROCKLEHURST: You see there was nothing wrong in it.

LADY MARY: [*Thinking perhaps of another incident*] No, indeed.

LORD BROCKLEHURST: [*Inclined to simper again*] And she behaved awfully well. She quite saw that it was because the boat was late. I suppose the glamor to a girl in service of a man in high position——

LADY MARY: Glamor!—yes, yes, that was it.

LORD BROCKLEHURST: Mother says that a girl in such circumstances is to be excused if she loses her head.

LADY MARY: [*Impulsively*] George, I am so sorry

if I said anything against your mother. I am sure she is the dearest old thing.

LORD BROCKLEHURST: [*In calm waters at last*] Of course for women of our class she has a very different standard.

LADY MARY: [*Grown tiny*] Of course.

LORD BROCKLEHURST: You see, knowing how good a woman she is herself, she was naturally anxious that I should marry some one like her. That is what has made her watch your conduct so jealously, Mary.

LADY MARY: [*Hurriedly thinking things out*] I know. I—I think, George, that before your mother comes I should like to say a word to father.

LORD BROCKLEHURST: [*Nervously*] About this?

LADY MARY: Oh no; I shan't tell him of this. About something else.

LORD BROCKLEHURST: And you do forgive me, Mary?

LADY MARY: [*Smiling on him*] Yes, yes. I—I am sure the boat was *very* late, George.

LORD BROCKLEHURST: [*Earnestly*] It really was.

LADY MARY: I am even relieved to know that you are not quite perfect, dear. [*She rests her hands on his shoulders. She has a moment of contrition*] George, when we are married, we shall try to be not an entirely frivolous couple, won't we? We must endeavour to be of some little use, dear.

LORD BROCKLEHURST: [*The ass*] Noblesse oblige.

LADY MARY: [*Haunted by the phrases of a better man*] Mary Lasenby is determined to play the game, George.

[*Perhaps she adds to herself, "Except just this once." A kiss closes this episode of the two lovers; and soon after the departure of* Lady Mary *the* Countess of Brocklehurst *is announced. She is a very formidable old lady*]

LADY BROCKLEHURST: Alone, George?

LORD BROCKLEHURST: Mother, I told her all; she has behaved magnificently.

LADY BROCKLEHURST: [*Who has not shared his fears*] Silly boy. [*She casts a supercilious eye on the island trophies*] So these are the wonders they brought back with them. Gone away to dry her eyes, I suppose?

LORD BROCKLEHURST: [*Proud of his mate*] She didn't cry, mother.

LADY BROCKLEHURST: No? [*She reflects*] You're quite right. I wouldn't have cried. Cold, icy. Yes, that was it.

LORD BROCKLEHURST: [*Who has not often contradicted her*] I assure you, mother, that wasn't it at all. She forgave me at once.

LADY BROCKLEHURST: [*Opening her eyes sharply to the full*] Oh!

LORD BROCKLEHURST: She was awfully nice about the boat being late; she even said she was relieved to find that I wasn't quite perfect.

LADY BROCKLEHURST: [*Pouncing*] She said that?

LORD BROCKLEHURST: She really did.

LADY BROCKLEHURST: I mean *I* wouldn't. Now if

I had said that, what would have made me say it? [*Suspiciously*] George, is Mary all we think her?

LORD BROCKLEHURST: [*With unexpected spirit*] If she wasn't, Mother, you would know it.

LADY BROCKLEHURST: Hold your tongue, boy. We don't really know what happened on that island.

LORD BROCKLEHURST: You were reading the book all the morning.

LADY BROCKLEHURST: How can I be sure that the book is true?

LORD BROCKLEHURST: They all talk of it as true.

LADY BROCKLEHURST: How do I know that they are not lying?

LORD BROCKLEHURST: Why should they lie?

LADY BROCKLEHURST: Why shouldn't they? [*She reflects again*] If I had been wrecked on an island, I think it highly probable that I should have lied when I came back. Weren't some of the servants with them?

LORD BROCKLEHURST: Crichton, the butler. [*He is surprised to see her ring the bell*] Why, Mother, you are not going to——

LADY BROCKLEHURST: Yes, I am. [*Pointedly*] George, watch whether Crichton begins any of his answers to my questions with "The fact is."

LORD BROCKLEHURST: Why?

LADY BROCKLEHURST: Because that is usually the beginning of a lie.

LORD BROCKLEHURST: [*As Crichton opens the door*] Mother, you can't do these things in other people's houses.

LADY BROCKLEHURST: [*Coolly, to* Crichton] It was I who rang. [*Surveying him through her eyeglass*] So you were one of the castaways, Crichton?

CRICHTON: Yes, my lady.

LADY BROCKLEHURST: Delightful book Mr. Woolley has written about your adventures. [Crichton *bows*] Don't you think so?

CRICHTON: I have not read it, my lady.

LADY BROCKLEHURST: Odd that they should not have presented you with a copy.

LORD BROCKLEHURST: Presumably Crichton is no reader.

LADY BROCKLEHURST: By the way, Crichton, were there any books on the island?

CRICHTON: I had one, my lady—Henley's poems.

LORD BROCKLEHURST: Never heard of him.

[Crichton *again bows*]

LADY BROCKLEHURST: [*Who has not heard of him either*] I think you were not the only servant wrecked?

CRICHTON: There was a young woman, my lady.

LADY BROCKLEHURST: I want to see her. [Crichton *bows, but remains*] Fetch her up. [*He goes*]

LORD BROCKLEHURST: [*Almost standing up to his mother*] This is scandalous.

LADY BROCKLEHURST: [*Defining her position*] I am a mother. [Catherine *and* Agatha *enter in dazzling confections and quake in secret to find themselves practically alone with* Lady Brocklehurst] [*Even as she greets them*] How d'you do, Catherine—Agatha?

You didn't dress like this on the island, I expect! By the way, how did you dress?

[*They have thought themselves prepared, but——*]

AGATHA: Not—so well, of course, but quite the same idea.

[*They are relieved by the arrival of* Treherne, *who is in clerical dress*]

LADY BROCKLEHURST: How do you do, Mr. Treherne? There is not so much of you in the book as I had hoped.

TREHERNE: [*Modestly*] There wasn't very much of me on the island, Lady Brocklehurst.

LADY BROCKLEHURST: How d'ye mean?

[*He shrugs his modest shoulders*]

LORD BROCKLEHURST: I hear you have got a living, Treherne. Congratulations.

TREHERNE: Thanks.

LORD BROCKLEHURST: Is it a good one?

TREHERNE: So-so. They are rather weak in bowling, but it's a good bit of turf.

[*Confidence is restored by the entrance of* Ernest, *who takes in the situation promptly, and, of course, knows he is a match for any old lady*]

ERNEST: [*With ease*] How do you do, Lady Brocklehurst.

LADY BROCKLEHURST: Our brilliant author!

ERNEST: [*Impervious to satire*] Oh, I don't know.

LADY BROCKLEHURST: It is as engrossing, Mr. Woolley, as if it were a work of fiction.

ERNEST: [*Suddenly uncomfortable*] Thanks, awfully. [*Recovering*] The fact is—— [*He is puzzled by seeing the Brocklehurst family exchange meaning looks*]

CATHERINE: [*To the rescue*] Lady Brocklehurst, Mr. Treherne and I—we are engaged.

AGATHA: And Ernest and I.

LADY BROCKLEHURST: [*Grimly*] I see, my dears; thought it wise to keep the island in the family.

[*An awkward moment this for the entrance of* Lord Loam *and* Lady Mary, *who, after a private talk upstairs, are feeling happy and secure*]

LORD LOAM: [*With two hands for his distinguished guest*] Aha! ha, ha! younger than any of them, Emily.

LADY BROCKLEHURST: Flatterer. [*To* Lady Mary] You seem in high spirits, Mary.

LADY MARY: [*Gaily*] I am.

LADY BROCKLEHURST: [*With a significant glance at* Lord Brocklehurst] After——

LADY MARY: I—I mean. The fact is——

[*Again that disconcerting glance between the countess and her son*]

LORD LOAM: [*Humorously*] She hears wedding bells, Emily, ha, ha!

LADY BROCKLEHURST: [*Coldly*] Do you, Mary? Can't say I do; but I'm hard of hearing.

LADY MARY: [*Instantly her match*] If you don't, Lady Brocklehurst, I'm sure I don't.

LORD LOAM: [*Nervously*] Tut, tut. Seen our curios from the island, Emily; I should like you to examine them.

LADY BROCKLEHURST: Thank you, Henry. I am glad you say that, for I have just taken the liberty of asking two of them to step upstairs.

[*There is an uncomfortable silence, which the entrance of* Crichton *and* Tweeny *does not seem to dissipate.* Crichton *is impenetrable, but* Tweeny *hangs back in fear*]

LORD BROCKLEHURST: [*Stoutly*] Loam, I have no hand in this.

LADY BROCKLEHURST: [*Undisturbed*] Pooh, what have I done? You always begged me to speak to the servants, Henry, and I merely wanted to discover whether the views you used to hold about equality were adopted on the island; it seemed a splendid opportunity, but Mr. Woolley has not a word on the subject.

[*All eyes turn on* Ernest]

ERNEST: [*With confidence*] The fact is—— [*The fatal words again*]

LORD LOAM: [*Not quite certain what he is to assure her of*] I assure you, Emily——

LADY MARY: [*Cold as steel*] Father, nothing whatever happened on the island of which I, for one, am ashamed, and I hope Crichton will be allowed to answer Lady Brocklehurst's questions.

LADY BROCKLEHURST: To be sure. There's nothing to make a fuss about, and we're a family party. [*To* Crichton] Now, truthfully, my man.

CRICHTON: [*Calmly*] I promise that, my lady.

[*Some hearts sink, the hearts that could never understand a* Crichton]

LADY BROCKLEHURST: [*Sharply*] Well, were you all equal on the island?

CRICHTON: No, my lady. I think I may say there was as little equality there as elsewhere.

LADY BROCKLEHURST: All the social distinctions were preserved?

CRICHTON: As at home, my lady.

LADY BROCKLEHURST: The servants?

CRICHTON: They had to keep their place.

LADY BROCKLEHURST: Wonderful. How was it managed? [*With an inspiration*] You, girl, tell me that?

[*Can there be a more critical moment?*]

TWEENY: [*In agony*] If you please, my lady, it was all the Gov.'s doing.

[*They give themselves up for lost.* Lord Loam *tries to sink out of sight*]

CRICHTON: In the regrettable slang of the servants' hall, my lady, the master is usually referred to as the Gov.

LADY BROCKLEHURST: I see. [*She turns to* Lord Loam] You——

LORD LOAM: [*Reappearing*] Yes, I understand that is what they call me.

LADY BROCKLEHURST: [*To* Crichton] You didn't even take your meals with the family?

CRICHTON: No, my lady, I dined apart.

[*Is all safe?*]

LADY BROCKLEHURST: [*Alas*] You, girl, also? Did you dine with Crichton?

TWEENY: [*Scared*] No, your ladyship.

LADY BROCKLEHURST: [*Fastening on her*] With whom?

TWEENY: I took my bit of supper with—with Daddy and Polly and the rest.

[*Væ victis*]

ERNEST: [*Leaping into the breach*] Dear old Daddy —he was our monkey. You remember our monkey, Agatha?

AGATHA: Rather! What a funny old darling he was.

CATHERINE: [*Thus encouraged*] And don't you think Polly was the sweetest little parrot, Mary?

LADY BROCKLEHURST: Ah! I understand; animals you had domesticated?

LORD LOAM: [*Heavily*] Quite so—quite so.

LADY BROCKLEHURST: The servants' teas that used to take place here once a month——

CRICHTON: They did not seem natural on the island, my lady, and were discontinued by the Gov.'s orders.

LORD BROCKLEHURST: A clear proof, Loam, that they were a mistake here.

LORD LOAM: [*Seeing the opportunity for a diversion*] I admit it frankly. I abandon them. Emily, as the result of our experiences on the island, I think of going over to the Tories.

LADY BROCKLEHURST: I am delighted to hear it.

LORD LOAM: [*Expanding*] Thank you, Crichton, thank you; that is all. [*He motions to them to go, but the time is not yet*]

LADY BROCKLEHURST: One moment. [*There is a universal but stifled groan*] Young people, Crichton, will be young people, even on an island; now, I suppose there was a certain amount of—shall we say sentimentalizing, going on?

CRICHTON: Yes, my lady, there was.

LORD BROCKLEHURST: [*Ashamed*] Mother!

LADY BROCKLEHURST: [*Disregarding him*] Which gentleman? [*To* Tweeny] You, girl, tell me.

TWEENY: [*Confused*] If you please, my lady——

ERNEST: [*Hurriedly*] The fact is—— [*He is checked as before, and probably says "D——n" to himself, but he has saved the situation*]

TWEENY: [*Gasping*] It was him—Mr. Ernest, your ladyship.

LADY BROCKLEHURST: [*Counsel for the prosecution*] With which lady?

AGATHA: I have already told you, Lady Brocklehurst, that Ernest and I——

LADY BROCKLEHURST: Yes, *now;* but you were two years on the island. [*Looking at* Lady Mary] Was it this lady?

TWEENY: No, your ladyship.

LADY BROCKLEHURST: Then I don't care which of the others it was. [Tweeny *gurgles*] Well, I suppose that will do.

LORD BROCKLEHURST: Do! I hope you are ashamed of yourself, mother. [*To* Crichton, *who is going*] You are an excellent fellow, Crichton; and if, after we are married, you ever wish to change your place, come to us.

LADY MARY: [*Losing her head for the only time*] Oh no, impossible.

LADY BROCKLEHURST: [*At once suspicious*] Why impossible? [Lady Mary *cannot answer, or perhaps she is too proud*] Do you see why it should be impossible, my man? [*He can make or mar his unworthy* Mary *now. Have you any doubt of him?*]

CRICHTON: Yes, my lady. I had not told you, my lord, but as soon as your lordship is suited I wish to leave service.

[*They are all immensely relieved, except poor* Tweeny]

TREHERNE: [*The only curious one*] What will you do, Crichton?

[Crichton *shrugs his shoulders "God knows," it may mean*]

CRICHTON: Shall I withdraw, my lord? [*He withdraws without a tremor,* Tweeny *accompanying him. They can all breathe again, the thunderstorm is over*]

LADY BROCKLEHURST: [*Thankful to have made herself unpleasant*] Horrid of me, wasn't it? But if one wasn't disagreeable now and again, it would be horribly tedious to be an old woman. He will soon be yours, Mary, and then—think of the opportunities you will have of being disagreeable to me. On that understanding, my dear, don't you think we might——?

[*Their cold lips meet*]

LORD LOAM: [*Vaguely*] Quite so—quite so.

[Crichton *announces dinner, and they file out. Lady Mary stays behind a moment and impulsively holds out her hand*]

LADY MARY: To wish you every dear happiness.

CRICHTON: [*An enigma to the last*] The same to you, my lady.

LADY MARY: Do you despise me, Crichton? [*The man who could never tell a lie makes no answer*] You are the best man among us.

CRICHTON: On an island, my lady, perhaps; but in England, no.

LADY MARY: Then there's something wrong with England.

CRICHTON: My lady, not even from you can I listen to a word against England.

LADY MARY: Tell me one thing; you have not lost your courage?

CRICHTON: No, my lady.

[*She goes. He turns out the lights*]

THE END

John Galsworthy

(1867–1933)

When realism gained a foothold in England, a number of dramatists turned to the writing of problem plays with resolution and talent. No one, however, practiced the objective social drama and the "naturalism" of Continental Europe with more scrupulousness than John Galsworthy.

To his self-imposed task Galsworthy brought a suitable education and temperament. Objectivity and balance were his by virtue of training at New College, Oxford, an honor degree in law in 1889, and extensive travel abroad from 1891 to 1893. A knowledge of the ponderable social realities, without which no dramatist could pretend to write problem drama, came inevitably to this levelheaded gentleman who interested himself for a time in the English socialist movement and generally championed the underdog. He was called to the bar in 1890, but instead of yielding to the legal profession began to write stories and novels, the first, *Jocelyn,* in 1899. Then, at the same time that his first Forsyte novel, *The Man of Property,* was published, he turned to the drama. His first play was *The Silver Box,* which Granville-Barker produced in 1906 at the venturesome Court Theatre.

The Silver Box presents a picture of unequal distribution of justice, leading to the conviction of a poor laborer and the acquittal of a rich man's son on the same charge. This play was followed year after year by other closely reasoned dramas concerned with the social scene. Thus, *Strife* (1909) was notable for its balanced treatment of the class struggle as an evil caused by obstinate leaders of both labor and capital. *Justice* (1910) was a deeply considered drama of a petty forger sucked into crime by his weak character and destroyed by the incomprehension of the law. The strong impression made by this play actually led to penal reforms, at the instigation of Winston Churchill, then Home Secretary of England.

Next, in 1912, Galsworthy fixed an inquiring and quizzical eye on the entire question of philanthropy, in *The Pigeon.* Subsequently, he again took account of social injustice, in *The Eldest Son* (1912) and *The Fugitive;* denounced war hysteria, in *The Mob* (1914); and attacked the caste system within a framework of racial prejudice, in *Loyalties* (1922). When Galsworthy died, in 1933, he left to posterity an impressive body of dramatic work, as well as some highly regarded fiction, most notably the group of novels published in 1922 under the collective title *The Forsyte Saga.*

All of Galsworthy's work bore the impress of an elevated spirit and of an inquiring, if not remarkably subtle, mind. The easily apparent limitations of the plays stem, as a rule, from the nature of the author's temperament and aims; the plays are so reasonable that they seem mild today and make one long for the excitement and transfiguration that passion might have brought to them. Their merits are, however, substantial, for Galsworthy was able to give his dramatic work much persuasiveness and authenticity. If the plays do not scintillate, they generally prove convincing; if they do not cut through all tissues of character and society, they manage to penetrate. Only occasionally obfuscated by sentimentality (most conspicuously in the least social of his plays, *Old English*), Galsworthy's work consists of lucid expositions in the form of spare and usually taut drama. Deliberately refraining from eloquence, Galsworthy wrote authentic dialogue and employed dialect where the social status required it. Above all, this scrupulous dramatist bore in mind the importance of presenting his thesis with credible characterization and without proffering ready-made solutions.

Galsworthy's complete consciousness of principle —largely naturalistic principle—was set forth in his essay *Some Platitudes Concerning Drama.* "A good plot," he wrote, "is that sure edifice which rises out of the interplay of circumstance on temperament, or of temperament on circumstance." Acting on this prescription in a species of playwriting that was antipodal to the well-made-play formula, he actually refrained from drafting scenarios, or outlines, for his plays. If the plays were, as a rule, extremely well organized and theatrically efficacious, Galsworthy preferred to believe that it was the result of his having allowed the characters to dictate their own line of conduct, character being, in his opinion, "the best plot" there is. As for dialogue, he insisted that it is "an austere art, denying itself all license, grudging every sentence devoted to the mere machinery of the play, suppressing all jokes and epigrams severed from character, relying for fun and pathos on the fun and tears of life."

It is not surprising, then, that Galsworthy should have formulated the best working definition of naturalism in England: "The aim of the dramatist employing it is evidently to create such an illusion of actual life passing on the stage as to compel the spectator to pass through an experience of his own, to think and talk and move with the people he sees thinking, talking, and moving." And Galsworthy did not allow himself to swerve from these critical principles except under the pressure of extreme compassion or indignation. He required self-discipline from his actors also, and so persistently in his early career that they sometimes protested against the rigor of his demands. In despair, during a rehearsal of *The Silver Box* at the Court Theatre, Dame Sybil Thorndike is reported to have cried out, "I can't do it. It's too hard. Do you want me to take away everything that is me?" Galsworthy replied, "Yes. If you would do that, I think it would be quite all right. Shall we try again?"

In exposing social wrong, Galsworthy tried to achieve a similar detachment, attacking not the individual but the institution or the human condition represented in the action. To a degree, like the European naturalists, he accepted the deterministic outlook. Ernest Short wrote in his *Theatrical Cavalcade*, "As Galsworthy saw the world of man, Society was the equivalent of the Greek Fate." Moreover, since Galsworthy was concerned with presenting life rather than with turning out machine-made stage pieces, he often suggested in his writing that there could be no resolution at the end of the play, that the life of the characters and the way of the world would continue past the segment he had exhibited on the stage. His curtains, it has been said, hesitated to come down. All these qualities made his work represent a new order in the English theatre during the first two decades of the century. It may be observed too that Winthrop Ames's New York productions of *Strife* and *The Pigeon*, between 1910 and 1912, gave Americans virtually their first experience of true naturalism, as opposed to the spectacular

variety offered by David Belasco and subsequently appropriated by the Hollywood movie industry.

Escape, written in 1926, was one of the last plays to come from Galsworthy's workshop. If, under some influence of the cinema, the play lacks the tightly knit structure of some of his best work, it nevertheless displays most of the playwright's characteristic virtues along with his faults. But for a trace of sentimentality, Galsworthy maintains an objective attitude toward both the fortunate and the unfortunate members of society. The characters are individualized, even if not deeply probed or fully rounded; the dialogue is unforced; and the vivid dialect bears the stamp of Galsworthian authenticity. Galsworthy wrote stronger plays than *Escape,* it is true, but none that appealed more widely to his growing public; the fact that this play should have done so provides an index of Britain's fondness for humane drama in preference to savage offensives. With Leslie Howard playing the hunted man who puts the charity and courage of others to the test, *Escape* became one of Galsworthy's most successful social dramas.

BIBLIOGRAPHY: Barrett H. Clark, *A Study of the Modern Drama* (pp. 272–280), 1938; John Galsworthy, "Some Platitudes Concerning Drama," in *The Inn of Tranquillity,* 1912, 1916; John Gassner, *Masters of the Drama* (pp. 616–618), 1940, 1945; H. W. Marrot, *John Galsworthy,* 1936; Herman Ould, *John Galsworthy,* 1934; Ernest Short, *Theatrical Cavalcade* (pp. 74–79), 1942.

ESCAPE

By John Galsworthy

CHARACTERS OF THE PLAY

MATT DENANT
THE GIRL OF THE TOWN
THE PLAIN CLOTHES MAN
THE TWO POLICEMEN
THE FELLOW CONVICT
THE TWO WARDERS
THE SHINGLED LADY

THE MAID
THE OLD GENTLEMAN
THE FOUR TRIPPERS
THE MAN IN PLUS FOURS AND HIS
    WIFE
THE VILLAGE CONSTABLE
THE TWO LABORERS

THE FARMER
THE LITTLE GIRL
THE TWO MAIDEN LADIES
THE PARSON
THE BELLRINGER
THE HUE AND CRY

PROLOGUE

Hyde Park at night. Summer. The Row with its iron railing, footwalk, seats, trees and bushes behind. A Woman, or Girl (you can't tell), is sitting alone, in dim radiance from lamps unseen to Right and Left. Her painted mask is not unattractive, her attitude slack and uneasy. A Plain Clothes Man passes Right to Left, glances at her inviting him and increases his pace. By the expression on her face as he approaches and recedes, it is easy for him to see what she is. Two People pass without glancing at her at all—they are talking of what "he said to me" and "I said to him." Then nobody passes, and, powdering her nose, she seems preparing to shift along, when from the Left Matt Denant appears strolling. He is a young man, tallish and athletic, dressed as if he has been racing in hot weather; he has a pair of race glasses and a cigar. The Girl shifts forward on her seat as he approaches. He is going by when she looks suddenly up and says in a low voice: "Good evening!" He halts, looks at her, gives a little shrug, carries his hand to his hat, and answering, "Good evening!" is moving on when she speaks again.

GIRL: Have you a match?
    [*She is holding out a cigarette; he stops and hands her his cigarette lighter*]
GIRL: [*Fingering the lighter*] Gold?
MATT: Brass.
GIRL: Have one?
    [*Offering her cigarette case*]
MATT: Thanks, I'm smoking.
    [*He shows her his cigar; resting his foot on the seat and dangling his race glasses*]
GIRL: Been racing?
MATT: Goodwood.
GIRL: I went to see the Jubilee this year.
MATT: And what did you back?
GIRL: Everything that didn't win. It's rotten when you don't back winners.
MATT: Don't you like the horses?

GIRL: They look pretty.
MATT: Prettiest things in the world.
GIRL: Pretty as women?
MATT: Saving your presence.
GIRL: Do you mean that?
MATT: Well, you get a woman once in a way that can arch her neck.
GIRL: You don't like women—that's clear.
MATT: Not too much.
GIRL: [*Smiling*] You speak your mind, anyway.
MATT: If you ask me, they've got such a lot of vice about 'em compared with horses.
GIRL: And who puts vice into them?
MATT: I know—you all say men, but d'you believe it?
GIRL: [*With a laugh*] Well, I don't know. Don't men put vice into horses?
MATT: [*Struck*] M'yes! [*Sitting down*] All the same, there's nothing wilder than a wild horse—I've seen 'em out West.
GIRL: There's nothing *so* wild as a wild woman.
    [*A momentary silence while they stare at each other*]
MATT: Women haven't the excuse of horses—they've been tame since Eve gave Adam his tea.
GIRL: Um! Garden of Eden! Must have been something like Hyde Park—there was a prize cop there, anyway.
MATT: D'you come here often?
GIRL: [*Nodding*] Where else *can* one go? They're so particular now.
MATT: They do seem to keep you on the run.
GIRL: What are you—soldier?
MATT: Once upon a time.
GIRL: What now?
MATT: Thinking of being a parson.
GIRL: [*Laughs*] You've got money of your own, then?
MATT: A little.
GIRL: [*With a sigh*] If I had money of my own, d'you know what I'd do?
MATT: Get rid of it.
GIRL: Just what I wouldn't. If ever I got myself

599

dependent on you men again, [*Very grimly*] shut my lights off.

MATT: Not like the lady under laughing gas.

GIRL: What was the matter with her?

MATT: Kept shouting, "I don't want to be a free, independent, economic agent! I want to be loved."

GIRL: She was wrong—No, *Sir!* Get my head under a second time? Not much! But we can't save —don't make enough. So there you are! It's a good bit worse than it used to be, they say——

MATT: The ordinary girl more free and easy now, you mean?

GIRL: [*Grimly*] The *ordinary* girl?

MATT: Well, you don't call yourself ordinary, do you?

[*The* Girl *sits quite still and doesn't answer*]

MATT: Sorry! Didn't mean to hurt you.

GIRL: Give me the fellow that does: he doesn't hurt half so much. But you're quite right. [*Bitterly*] There isn't much excuse for us, now.

MATT: Aren't we getting a bit solemn?

GIRL: The gay girl—eh? They say you get used to anything: but I'll tell you—you never get used to playing the canary when you don't feel like it.

MATT: Ah! I always sympathized with canaries— expected to sing, and so permanently yellow.

GIRL: It was nice of you to sit down and talk.

MATT: Thanks; it's all secondary education.

[*She slides her hand along to his, with a card*]

GIRL: Here's my address; you might come and see me now and then.

MATT: [*Twiddling the card—amused and embarrassed*] On verra!

GIRL: What's that?

MATT: It's an expression of hope.

GIRL: [*Mouth opening*] Ow! How about now?

MATT: Thanks—afraid not—due somewhere at ten.

GIRL: Another?

MATT: No.

GIRL: You don't like me, I believe.

MATT: [*With a shrug*] Oh! Don't say that. You're original.

GIRL: Original sin.

MATT: There are worse things, I guess.

GIRL: You bet! There's modest worth. If *that* isn't worse! Not that this is a pretty life. It's just about as rotten as it can be.

MATT: How did you get into it?

GIRL: Cut it out! You all ask that, and you can take it from me you never get told. Well! I belong to the oldest profession in the world! That isn't true, either—there's an older.

MATT: Not really.

GIRL: The cop's. Mine wouldn't ever have been a profession but for them.

MATT: Good for you!

GIRL: It isn't good for me. Look in at Bow Street on Monday morning.

MATT: To see 'em shoot the sitting pheasant?—no, thanks. The Law isn't exactly sporting. Can't be, I suppose, if it's got to keep the course clear.

GIRL: They might wait till one makes oneself a nuisance.

MATT: Ever been run in?

GIRL: [*With a look, and a decision*] Um! Not yet! [*Suddenly*] What can we do? If we don't make a sign, who's to know us?

MATT: That's delightful.

GIRL: Clean streets!—that's the cry. Clean men! That'd be better!

MATT: And then where'd you be?

GIRL: [*Passionately*] Not here!

MATT: [*After staring at her*] Um! The kettle and the pot. What! Give me horses and dogs, all the time.

GIRL: I've got a cat.

MATT: Persian?

GIRL: [*Nodding*] A real beauty. [*Suddenly*] Wouldn't you like to come and see him?

[*He shakes his head, rises, takes his glasses, and holds out his hand. She is going to take it— then draws her hand back sharply, frowning and biting her lips. He gives a shrug, salutes, and moves on. She catches at his sleeve, misses it, sits a second, then rises and follows. Unseen by her, the* Plain Clothes Man *has reappeared, Left. He moves swiftly and grasps her arm just as she is vanishing Right. The* Girl *gives a little squeal as he draws her back towards the seat. She resists*]

GIRL: Who are *you?*

PLAIN CLOTHES MAN: Plain clothes.

[*And, as she still resists, he tries to calm her by a slight twist of the arm*]

GIRL: You brute—you brute!

PLAIN CLOTHES MAN: Now then—quietly, and you won't get hurt.

GIRL: I wasn't doing anything.

PLAIN CLOTHES MAN: Oh! no, of course not.

GIRL: [*Looking after* Matt] I wasn't, I tell you; and he'll tell you so too!

[Matt *has reappeared, Right*]

Won't you? You talked to me of your own accord?

MATT: I did. Who may you be?

PLAIN CLOTHES MAN: [*Showing his card*] This woman accosted you. I've observed her carefully, and not for the first time.

MATT: Well, you've made a blooming error. We had a chat, that's all.

PLAIN CLOTHES MAN: I saw her accost you. I saw her try to detain you—and I've seen her do it before now.

MATT: I don't care what you've seen before now —you can't arrest her for that. You didn't see it this time.

PLAIN CLOTHES MAN: [*Still holding the* Girl *and looking at* Matt *steadily*] You know perfectly well the woman accosted you—and you'd better keep out of this.

MATT: Let the girl go, then. You're exceeding your duty.

PLAIN CLOTHES MAN: What do you know about my duty? It's my duty to keep the park decent, man or woman. Now then, are you going to clear off?

MATT: No, I'm going to stay on.

PLAIN CLOTHES MAN: All right then, you can follow us to the station.

MATT: Mayn't two people talk! I've made no complaint.

PLAIN CLOTHES MAN: I know this woman, I tell you. Don't interfere with me, or I shall want you too.

MATT: You can have me if you let the girl go.

PLAIN CLOTHES MAN: Now look here, I'm being very patient. But if you don't stop hindering me in the execution of my duty, I'll summon assistance and you'll *both* go to the station.

MATT: Don't lose your hair—I tell you, on my honor, this lady did not annoy me in the least. On the contrary——

PLAIN CLOTHES MAN: She was carrying on her profession here, as she's done before; my orders are to prevent that, and she's going to be charged. This is the third night I've watched her.

GIRL: I've never seen your face before.

PLAIN CLOTHES MAN: No, but I've seen yours— I've given you plenty of rope. That's enough, now—

[*He puts his whistle in his mouth*]

MATT: It's a rotten shame! Drop that girl's arm!

[*He lays his hand on the* Plain Clothes Man's *arm. The* Plain Clothes Man *blows his whistle, drops the* Girl's *arm and seizes* Matt]

MATT: [*Breaking from him; to the* Girl] Run for it!

GIRL: Oh! no—don't fight! The police have got it on you all the time. I'll go with him.

MATT: [*With fists up, keeping the* Plain Clothes Man *at arm's length*] Run, I tell you. He'll have his work cut out with me.

[*But the* Plain Clothes Man *is spryer than he thinks, runs in and catches him round the body*]

GIRL: Oh! Oh!

MATT: No, you don't!

[*In the violent struggle the* Plain Clothes Man's *bowler hat falls off.* Matt *emerges at arm's length again, squaring up*]

MATT: Come on, then, if you will have it!

[*The* Plain Clothes Man *rushes in. He gets* Matt's *right straight from the shoulder on the point of the jaw, topples back, and goes down like a log*]

GIRL: Oh! Oh!

MATT: Run, you little idiot; run!

GIRL: [*Aghast*] Oh! he hit his head—on the rail! I heard the crack. See, he don't move!

MATT: Well, of course. I knocked him out.

[*He goes a step nearer, looking down*]
The rail—did he——?

GIRL: [*Kneeling and feeling the* Plain Clothes Man's *head*] Feel!

MATT: My God! That was a wump. I say!

GIRL: I told you not to fight. What did you want to fight for?

MATT: [*Pulling open the* Plain Clothes Man's *coat, and diving for his heart*] I can't feel it. Curse! Now we can't leave him. [*Feeling for the heart*] Good God!

GIRL: [*Bending and snatching at his arm*] Quick! Before anybody comes. Across the grass back there. Who'd know?

MATT: [*Listening*] I can't leave the poor devil like this. [*Looking round*] Take his hat; go and get some water in it from the Serpentine.

[*The* Girl *picks up the hat and stands undecided*]

GIRL: [*Agonized*] No, no! Come away! It's awful, this! Suppose—suppose he's dead!

[*She pulls at him*]

MATT: [*Shaking her off*] Don't be a little fool! Go and get some water. Go on!

[*The* Girl *wrings her hands, then turns and runs off Left, with the hat.* Matt *continues to kneel, rubbing the* Plain Clothes Man's *temples, feeling his pulse, listening at his heart.*]

MATT: I don't see how it's possible!

[*With a gesture of despair he resumes his efforts to revive the body. Suddenly he looks up. Two* Policemen *have come from the Right*]

POLICEMAN: What's this?

MATT: I don't know. I'm a little afraid he——

POLICEMAN: What! Who is he? [*Looking at the face*] Phew! One of ours! [*Bending, kneeling, putting the back of his hand to the mouth*] Not a breath! How did this happen?

MATT: [*Pointing to the rail*] He knocked his head on that.

POLICEMAN: Where's his hat?

MATT: It fell off. Someone's gone to get water in it.

POLICEMAN: Who?

MATT: A girl——

POLICEMAN: He blew his whistle. Did you hit him?

MATT: There was a row. He seized me. I smote him on the jaw. He fell back and hit his head on the rail.

POLICEMAN: What was the row about?

MATT: [*Putting his hands to his head*] Oh! God knows! Original sin.

POLICEMAN: [*To the other* Policeman] Mate, stay with him. I'll get an ambulance. [*To Matt*] And you —come with me!

THE CURTAIN FALLS

EPISODE I.

More than a year has passed. On the prison farm, Dartmoor, in a heavy fog. The stone wall of the field runs along the back (on the back-cloth) and a stone wall joins it on the Left. Matt Denant *and a fellow convict are picking up the potatoes they have dug up earlier. They are but dimly seen in the fog, flinging the potatoes right and left into two baskets between them. They are speaking in low voices.*

MATT: The poor blighter was dead, and I got five years for manslaughter.

FELLOW CONVICT: Cripes! A cop! You were lucky not to swing, mate.

MATT: The girl stood by me like a brick. If she hadn't come forward——

FELLOW CONVICT: Lucky there, too. Most of 'em wouldn't. They're too mortal scared. 'Ow much you got left to do?

MATT: Three years, if I behave like a plaster saint. [*He stops and straightens himself*]

FELLOW CONVICT: I got four. I say, you're a torf, yn't you?

MATT: Toff! [*With a laugh*] Item, one Oxford accent; item, one objection to being spoken to like a dog.

FELLOW CONVICT: Hush! [*Jerking his thumb towards the wall, Right*] Fog don't prevent 'em hearin', blight 'em!

MATT: It's come up mighty sudden. Think it's going to last?

FELLOW CONVICT: After a wet spell—this time o' year, when the wind's gone—yus. They'll be roundin' us up in a minute, you'll see—and 'ome to Blighty. Makes 'em nervous—fog. That's when you get the escapes.

MATT: No one's ever got away from here, they say.

FELLOW CONVICT: There've been a good few tries, though.

MATT: Gosh! I'd like to have one.

FELLOW CONVICT: Don't you do it, mate. You want clothes, you want money, you want a car, to give you a dawg's chance. And then they'd get you. This moor's the 'ell of a place. I say, you must 'ave hit that cop a fair knock!

MATT: Just an ordinary knock-out on the jaw. It wasn't that. He landed the back of his head on the Row rail. [*He resumes potato picking*] Poor devil! He wasn't married, luckily.

FELLOW CONVICT: Luckily? Well, you never know about *that.* But get 'im off your chest, mate—'e wouldn't sit on mine—no more than an 'Un did in the War. That's a good fair potato. [*Holding one up*]

[*The figure of a* Warder *is dimly seen coming along from the Right under the wall. He stops*]

WARDER: No talking there! When you've finished that row, pick back the next and then stand by to fall in. [*No answer from the* Convicts] Hear me? Answer, can't you?

FELLOW CONVICT: Right, Sir! [*The* Warder's *figure is seen moving back*] Nice man, ain't he? Wot'd I tell you? Early 'ome to tea.

MATT: [*Very low*] Like a dog! Three more years—like a dog!

FELLOW CONVICT: 'E's all right, reely. It's the fog. Fog makes 'em nervous; an' when a man's nervous I've always noticed 'e speaks like that.

MATT: Yes; well, *I* can't get used to it.

FELLOW CONVICT: Too particular, you torfs—get too much corn when you're two-year-olds.

MATT: [*Sharp and low*] *You* know the moor—where's Two Bridges?

FELLOW CONVICT: There—a mile.

MATT: And Tavistock.

FELLOW CONVICT: [*Pointing right back*] Seven. Guv'nor—don't do it. There ain't a chance in a million. You'll only get pneumonium in this stinkin' wet, and they'll have you into the bargain, sure as eggs—bread and water, cells, and the rest of it.

MATT: I got out of Germany.

FELLOW CONVICT: Out of Germany? Cripes! That was none so dusty!

MATT: They've got no dogs here now, have they?

FELLOW CONVICT: Don't fancy they 'ave. But, Guv'nor, the whole countryside round 'ere's agynst you. They don't like convicts. Funny, yn't it?

[*They have reached the end of the row, Left, and stop, stooping, with their heads close together*]

MATT: Draw me a plan with this stick.

FELLOW CONVICT: Blimy! [*Marking the earth*] 'Ere's the main road, and 'ere's the cross road to Tavistock. 'Ere's the Inn at Two Bridges, and 'ere's Post Bridge. 'Ere's Bee Tor Cross, ten to twelve mile. Chagford up there, Moreton 'Ampstead 'ere.

MATT: What's across the main road from Two Bridges?

FELLOW CONVICT: Moor. A long bit o' wood about 'ere; then 'Ambledon; then you drops into fields to Widecombe; then up, and more moor to Heytor and Bovey. [*Pronounce* Buvvy] There's rail at Bovey or Lustleigh, or Moreton or Tavistock, and much good that'll do you with everybody as eager to see you as if you was the Prince of Wyles! Out this way you got Fox Tor Mire—ruddy bad bog, that!

[*A moment's silence while* Matt *studies the chart in the soil*]

WARDER'S VOICE: [*Off*] Hurry up with that last row—you two men!

[*The fog grows thicker*]

MATT: [*Smearing out the chart with his foot*] It's real thick now. Gosh! I'll have a shot!

[*They move back, Right, beginning the last row*]

FELLOW CONVICT: [*Jerking his thumb Left*] There's another blighter thirty yards out on the wall there. 'E'll shoot.

MATT: I know. I'm going over that wall in the corner, and then along under his nose on the near side. Ten to one he'll be looking out on the off side in this fog. If that chap there [*Jerking his head, Right*] doesn't spot me, I'll get by.

FELLOW CONVICT: You're mad, Guv'nor. They'll shoot at sight. And if they don' see you—in ten minutes I'll have finished this row, an' they're bound to know you're gone. You 'aven't the chance of a cock-louse.

MATT: All right, friend, don't worry! A bullet'd be a nice change for me. If I don't get one—I'll give 'em a run for their money.

FELLOW CONVICT: Well, if you must go, mate— Strike the main road and run that way. [*Pointing*] In this fog they'll 'ave to take us back before they dare start after you. You'll find a scrap of a wood a bit beyond the river on the left side. Get into it and cover yourself with leaves till it's dead dark. Then you'll still be close to the road and you can myke shift in a stack or something till the morning. If you go wandering about the moor all night in this fog, you won't get nowhere, and you'll be done in stiff before dawn.

MATT: Thanks. Sooner the better, now— Never stop to look at a fence. Next time the steam's full on. [*Puts some potatoes in his pocket*] Pommes crues— sauce Dartmoor. Can one eat these raw? I ate turnips in Germany.

FELLOW CONVICT: Never tried, Guv'nor. Tyke this. [*He holds out a slice of bread*]

MATT: Thanks awfully. You're a good chap.

FELLOW CONVICT: Wish you luck. Wish I was comin' too, but I 'aven't got the pluck, an' that's a fact.

MATT: Now! Turn your head the other way and keep it there. Remember me to Blighty. So long!

[*He moves three steps away from his fellow convict, pauses a few seconds, then suddenly, stooping low, runs to the wall, Left, and is over it like a cat. In the minute of silence that follows, one can see the* Convict *listening*]

FELLOW CONVICT: [*Counting the seconds to himself, up to twenty, in an excited murmur*] Gawd! 'E's past that blighter! [*Listens again*] Gawd! 'E's orf! [*With realization of his fellow's escape comes an itch to attempt it himself*] Shall I 'ave a shoot meself? Shall I? Gawd! I must!

[*He has just turned to sneak off, when the* Warder's *voice is heard off, Right*]

WARDER: You, man there! Where's your mate?

FELLOW CONVICT: 'Ad a call, Sir. [*He stands still*]

VOICE OF WARDER: [*Nearing*] What d'you mean?

FELLOW CONVICT: Went over to that wall, Sir.

WARDER: [*Appearing*] He's not there. Now then! Where is he?

FELLOW CONVICT: No use arstin' me. *I* don' know where he is.

WARDER: Come with me. [*He marches sharply along the wall back, towards the Left. Halting*] Convict! Out there! Answer! Warder! You, Williams! Anyone passed you? Lost a man here!

VOICE OF SECOND WARDER: No one's passed.

FIRST WARDER: Sharp, then! There's a man gone!

[*Second Warder appears on the top of the wall*]

SECOND WARDER: He must ha' got past *you,* then.

FIRST WARDER: Curse this fog! Fire a shot for warning. No, don't, or we'll have others running for it. Muster sharp and get off home and report— that's the only thing. [*To* Convict] Here, you! Keep your mouth shut. You know all about it, I bet.

FELLOW CONVICT: Not me, Sir. 'E just said 'e 'ad a call to 'ave tea with the Duchess; an' I went on pickin' up, knowin' you was in an 'urry.

FIRST WARDER: Mind your lip! Come on, Williams. March, you!

[*They are marching, Right, as*

THE CURTAIN FALLS]

EPISODE II.

Seven hours have passed. The moor in the dark and the fog, close to the main road. Nothing visible.

VOICE OF FIRST WARDER: What the hell's the use of picketing this blighted road—you can see nothing!

VOICE OF SECOND WARDER: I've seen two cops made just here. When a man's out on a night like this, it's human nature to cling to the road.

FIRST WARDER: But he may be anywhere.

SECOND WARDER: If he's traveling at all, he's on a road. You can't make it on the moor in fog as thick as this.

FIRST WARDER: He may have headed for Cornworthy.

SECOND WARDER: They never go that way—too afraid of Fox Tor Mire.

FIRST WARDER: Or Tavistock?

SECOND WARDER: Well, that road's picketed all right.

FIRST WARDER: I'd flog for escapes. They never think of us—out after these blighters nights like this. It's too bad, you know. Got a drain of the stuff?

SECOND WARDER: Here you are. Put it to your mouth by the smell.

FIRST WARDER: If I get this cove, I'll let him know it. 'Tisn't in nature not to feel murderous towards a chap that keeps you out all night in this sort o' muck!

[*He drinks*]

SECOND WARDER: Leave some for me, mate. [*In a whisper*] What was that? Hark!

[*They listen*]

FIRST WARDER: Don't 'ear nothing.

[*He is about to put the flask to his mouth again*]

SECOND WARDER: Thought I heard a scraping noise. Shall I show a glim?

FIRST WARDER: Better not!

[They listen]

SECOND WARDER: There's ponies round here.

FIRST WARDER: This fellow was a toff.

SECOND WARDER: Um! Captain in the War.

FIRST WARDER: Him that killed the 'tec in Hyde Park. He's a sporty beggar. Got blood in him. That's the worst sort when it comes to an escape—they run till they drop.

SECOND WARDER: Man of education—might have had more sense than to run for it. He must know he can't get off.

FIRST WARDER: There's a spirit in some of these higher-class chaps you can't break. D'you know that lawyer in the left wing—embezzlement? That chap gives me the creeps. He's got the self-possession of an image.

SECOND WARDER: I'm sorry for some of these fellows, but I'm damned if I'm ever sorry for a gentleman. They ought to know better than to get themselves here. And, as you say, they've got the devil's brass.

FIRST WARDER: Still—up on the ladder and down with a whump—it hits 'em harder than it does the others.

SECOND WARDER: [Yawning] Wish I was in bed! [Startlingly] There it is again! [They listen] It'll be a pony. A warder's life's about the limit. If it wasn't for the missus, I'd sooner sweep streets.

FIRST WARDER: I've got used to it, barring a circus like this. The devil himself couldn't get used to that. It's only fit for the movies.

SECOND WARDER: I believe you. Did you see that picture with Duggie in it? 'Ow'd you think 'e does that roof business? We got some pretty tidy cat burglars, but I don't believe there's one could do what he does.

FIRST WARDER: Well, I'll tell you. I think he has spring heels; and I notice his hands are very blurry in the picture. I believe he holds a rope, and they take that out afterwards, by some process.

SECOND WARDER: Never thought o' that! But when he falls and catches on that ledge?

FIRST WARDER: That's an optical deception. Some of those movie jossers ought to be in prison, the way they deceive the public.

SECOND WARDER: I never saw anything on the screen I liked better than "My Old Dutch"! That fair got me. I took the missus, and I tell you there wasn't a dry eye about the pair of us.

FIRST WARDER: Charlie knocks me. I feel a better man after I've seen 'im. Now, why is that?

SECOND WARDER: 'E's very 'uman. Must make a pot of money.

FIRST WARDER: I'm wet through—give me another drain. [Gurgling sounds] If I catch that chap, you'll 'ave to stop me quick, or I'll manhandle him for sure.

SECOND WARDER: Same here. We'd better toss up which stops the other. Call!

FIRST WARDER: 'Eads.

SECOND WARDER: Which is it? Throw a glim.

[The First Warder throws from an electric torch the first light of the scene. Their two faces, on the foot-light side of the road, are seen close together over the coin]

SECOND WARDER: Tails—You've lost. [The glim is dowsed] 'Ow do we stand, then? Do I stop you, or do you stop me?

FIRST WARDER: You stop me.

SECOND WARDER: No, I won. That means I get the go at him. Lawd Gawd! what a night! Just feel if that rope's all right across the road.

FIRST WARDER: It's taut. Bit too low, though—ought to catch him mid-thigh by rights.

SECOND WARDER: You trust me, old hoss; if it catches 'im as high as that, he stops and goes off sideways, or turns and runs back. It should catch him just below the knee. Then, ten to one he goes over, and we're on to him before he can get up. He'll be goin' a good bat, remember. You'll find me on 'is 'ead when you come to stoppin' me.

FIRST WARDER: To think we can't even smoke. D'you hold with givin' prisoners tobacco, Williams?

SECOND WARDER: On the whole, I do. It sweetens 'em, and that's better for us. I'd give 'em two pipes a week, and stop 'em if they gave a warder any trouble. I've got one or two fellers I'm quite fond of. I'd be glad for 'em to have a smoke every day. Listen! [They listen. In a whisper] Footsteps! They are!

FIRST WARDER: [Still in a whisper] Look here, mate! Just before he gets to the rope, I'll throw the light into his face, then dowse it sharp. He'll start to run forward and go head foremost. Stand by!

[They listen]

FIRST WARDER: He's comin' on! Suppose it isn't him?

SECOND WARDER: Must chance that. I'll throw the light as I say—[A moment of utter black tenseness, during which the footsteps are heard clearer and clearer] Now! Stand by! [He flashes the light on the figure of Matt advancing along the road. The light is dowsed, the Warders rush forward. Darkness and the sound of a scramble]

SECOND WARDER'S VOICE: I've got him!

FIRST WARDER'S VOICE: [Half strangled] No, you ruddy fool—you've got me!

THE CURTAIN FALLS

EPISODE III.

Thirty-two hours have passed. A bedroom at an Inn on the moor. Dark, with streaks of daylight coming in from two curtained windows, back, opening on to a long balcony. Between them a bed juts *into the room. Right, forward, a dressing-table with chair. Left, back, a washstand. Left, forward, a door opening inwards. At foot of the bed a chair with a woman's undergarments thrown on it. A dressing-gown over the footrail of the bed, some slippers on the left side of the bed. A Shingled Lady asleep in the bed. Knocking on the door, Left.*

LADY: [*Sleepily*] Come in!

[*A* Maid *enters with a can of hot water, which she places on the washstand, Left*]

MAID: 'Alf past seven, Madam.

LADY: [*Yawning*] What sort of day?

MAID: Foggy still. Taking a bath, Madam?

LADY: Yes. Oh! My husband's coming back this evening. I'm to be moved back to the double room.

MAID: Yes, Madam; they told me. [*She has drawn aside the curtains, Left, and now moves round and draws back the curtains, Right*] That escaped convict, Madam; they haven't got him yet.

LADY: No? How thrilling!

MAID: It's the fog. He's been out nearly two days. They say it's the young man who killed the detective in Hyde Park, that made such a fuss.

LADY: Oh? That Captain Denant! I remember. It might have been worse, then.

MAID: Of course they'll catch him—no one ever gets off.

LADY: Don't they?

MAID: Oh! no, Madam! It wouldn't never do.

LADY: I should have thought in fog like this——

MAID: You see, they got to eat and get clothes. That's where they're caught.

LADY: [*Yawning*] This horrible fog!—one can't ride or fish, or even walk. Shall I get up, or shall I——?

MAID: [*Rather coldly*] Just as you please, Madam.

LADY: [*With a laugh*] Well, I suppose I'd better.

MAID: I'll turn the bath on.

LADY: Thank you.

[*The* Maid *goes out, and the* Lady, *in her pajamas, emerges from bed, feels for her slippers, and puts on her dressing-gown. She goes to a window, and looks out. It is a French window, and slightly open on a short hook*]

LADY: Ugh! What a day!

[*Taking sponge and bath towel from the washstand, she goes to the door and out. As soon as the door is shut there is a commotion where the bed touches the wall, and from behind the window curtain* Matt Denant *cautiously emerges, glances quickly round, and stretches himself. He looks haggard, sodden, and crumpled, and has his boots in his hand*]

MATT: [*Muttering*] A lady! Dash it! I must get out!

[*He goes to the window and looks cautiously out, then recoils, drawing in his breath with a hiss. Then, after once more glancing round the room, he steps to the door*]

LADY'S VOICE: [*Off*] I simply can't take cold baths!

[Matt *flattens himself against the wall, so that he will be behind the door if it is opened. And suddenly it is*]

LADY'S VOICE: [*In doorway*] Let me know when the water's hot, please.

MAID'S VOICE: [*Off*] Yes, Madam.

[*The* Lady *re-enters, and passing the door knob from her right hand to her left behind her as she naturally would, closes it without seeing* Matt, *and crosses to the dressing-table, where she sits down and takes up a brush to brush her shingled hair.* Matt *moves quickly to the door, and has his hand on the handle, when his image passes into the mirror. The* Lady *drops the brush, and faces round with an exclamation on her open mouth.*]

MATT: Hush! It's quite O.K.

LADY: Who—how—what d'you mean by coming into my room?

[Matt *drops the door handle, turning the key in the lock*]

MATT: [*In a low voice*] Really, I'm most frightfully sorry.

[*Suddenly the fact that he is the escaped convict dawns on her*]

LADY: You're the escaped——

[*She starts up to go to the window and call for help; but stops at the gestures he makes*]

MATT: I wonder if you'd mind awfully speaking *pianissimo.*

LADY: [*Tersely*] What made you come in here? How did you get in?

MATT: I've been under the bed for hours. You see, I couldn't tell it was a lady.

LADY: D'you mean my hair?

MATT: Oh, no! I couldn't see that.

LADY: I didn't snore?

MATT: No; but that's not an infallible test of sex. I didn't either, or you'd have heard me.

LADY: D'you mean to say you went to sleep?

MATT: I'm afraid I did. Of course, if I'd known—

[*A pause*]

LADY: Well, as you're a gentleman, aren't you going?

MATT: I'd simply love to. But where?

LADY: Really, I can't tell you.

MATT: Look at me! What can one do in these togs?

LADY: D'you expect me to lend you some?

MATT: Hardly. But I'd be eternally grateful if you'd give me something to eat.

LADY: [*Opening a drawer and taking out some chocolate*] This is pretty cool, you know. I ought to ring and hand you over.

MATT: Yes. But—you look such a sport.

LADY: [*Subtly flattered*] I know who you are. Your name's in the paper. But do you realize my position?

MATT: Afraid I only realize my own.

LADY: If I don't hand you over, how on earth are you going to get out of here without being seen?

MATT: Might I have that chocolate?

LADY: [*Taking it from the dressing-table drawer*] It's only local.

MATT: That won't deter me. I've been forty hours on a piece of bread and two raw potatoes. [*He takes the chocolate, bites some off, and puts the rest in his pocket*] Would you mind frightfully if I drank some water?

LADY: Of course not.

> [Matt *goes over to the washstand. When his back is turned she springs to action, but instead of going to door or window, rapidly conceals underneath the bedclothes the corsets and underclothes flung on the chair at the foot of the bed, then returns to the dressing-table.* Matt *is drinking deeply.*]

MATT: [*Turning*] That's good. Ever had the hunted feeling? [*She shakes her head*] Well, don't! A coursed hare is nothing to it. Oh! I am so jolly stiff!

LADY: [*Thrilled in spite of herself*] Do you know you're only three miles from the Prison?

MATT: I do. The first night I meant to get near Exeter by morning, and where d'you think I was? A mile from where I started. I'd been ringing. That's what you do in fog. Is that a razor?

LADY: [*On stilts*] My husband's. Why? [*As* Matt *takes it up*] No! There's a limit, Captain Denant. You can't have a weapon.

MATT: No, of course! But would you mind awfully if I shaved? You see, like this [*Passes his hand over his chin*] I haven't an earthly, even if I could get clothes. There's nothing more attractive than a three days' beard. [*While speaking he has lathered himself without a brush*] I'm a very quick shaver. It takes me three minutes. I can do it in thirty-two and a half strokes.

LADY: [*Gasping*] Well, I never— It takes me [*Hand to her neck*] that is—I mean— Have you nearly been caught?

MATT: [*Between scraping motions of the razor*] Twice I've been within twenty feet of the hounds——

LADY: Hounds!

MATT: Human! Just out of their jaws. [*Groans*] D'you know anything so frightful as a shave like this?

LADY: Well, really——

MATT: I mean except, of course, not having it.

LADY: How did you get in here?

MATT: You see, I *did* so want a dry night, so I hid up and waited till every light was out. I tried to get in below, and couldn't; then I made a boss shot at the corner of the balcony and fell on my back—— Did you feel a sort of earthquake? No? I did. When I got over that, I had another shot at a pillar and made it that time. I chose your window because it

was open—hooked it up again and slid straight under the bed. I meant to sneak some clothes, and be off before daylight, but I only woke up when the maid came in. [*She indicates a towel; he steeps it in water and wipes his face*] D'you mind if I put on my boots? [*He stoops and puts them on*]

LADY: So you actually slept under there?

MATT: Alas! I did.

LADY: Well! It's about the limit.

MATT: Will be if I get clear—no one ever has.

LADY: Tell me, Captain Denant, weren't you at Harcheston with my brother—he used to talk of a Matt Denant, who was an awfully good runner.

MATT: Quite likely. I was at school with an awful lot of brothers. What was his name?

LADY: No. That won't do.

MATT: You're right. Never tell a convict anything he can tell anybody else.

LADY: I really don't see how I can help you.

MATT: Nor do I, worse luck!

LADY: I read your trial.

MATT: [*Standing up*] And you think me a bad lot, of course. [*Bitterly*] D'you know how I spend most of my time in prison? Holding imaginary conversations with the respectable.

LADY: [*With a smile*] Respectable! D'you think you're holding a real one now?

MATT: I certainly don't. . . . I . . . I beg your pardon. . . . You know what I mean. But I bet most people have put me down a rotter.

LADY: Was all you said true?

MATT: Gospel.

LADY: I suppose they do hunt those girls rather.

MATT: Yes, but you know, I didn't even really see red. I've been sorry enough for that poor chap.

LADY: Well, Captain Denant, what now?

MATT: You've been most awfully kind and I don't want to impose on you; but I shall never get out of here as I am.

LADY: Why not?

MATT: [*Jerking his head towards the window*] They're too thoughtful. There's a picket out there. [*The Lady turns to the window and looks out; then she turns to* Matt *and finds him smiling*] Oh! No, I wasn't scared. One doesn't give one's own kind away.

LADY: I don't know that. Go and try some of those other rooms. Try the couple next door to me.

> [*A knock on the door. Both stand alert*]

LADY: Yes?

VOICE OF MAID: [*Off*] The bath water's hot now, Madam.

LADY: All right. Thank you. [*Her finger is on her lips*] D'you think she could hear us?

MATT: Hope not. [*Going close*] Thanks most awfully. You don't know how decent it's been after a year in there, to talk to a lady. I won't leave any traces.

LADY: What are you going to do?

MATT: Wait till he's looking the other way, sneak

along the balcony, drop at the end, and bolt for it again.

LADY: Are you still a good runner?

MATT: Pretty fair, if I wasn't so stiff.

LADY: [After a long look at him] No! Look here! When I go to my bath I'll make sure there's no one. If I don't come back, slip down the stairs, they're almost opposite. In the hall, hanging, you'll find my husband's old Burberry and fishing basket, rod, and fishing hat; a long brown Burberry, with stains, and flies in the hat. Put them on and go out of the front door; the river's down to the left. Can you fish? [At his nod] You'd better, then. The bathroom's not that side, so I shan't see you. But— whistle "Lady, be good," if you know it.

MATT: Rather! It's the only tune that's got into prison. Well, I can't thank you—you're just a brick! [He holds out his hand]

LADY: [Taking it] Good luck! [She passes him to the door] Wait a second! [Getting a flask from drawer] Take this. If you see anyone looking at you—drink! Nothing gives one more confidence in a man than to see him drinking.

MATT: Splendid! What are you going to say to your husband?

LADY: Um! Yes! He comes to-night. Well, if he doesn't like it, he'll have to lump it. Oh! And these two pounds. It's all I've got here.

[She has taken two pounds out of her bag lying on the dressing-table]

MATT: [Moved] By George! I think you're sublime!

LADY: I'm afraid I doubt it.

MATT: If I'm caught, I shall say I pinched everything, of course; and if I get clear, I'll——

LADY: Oh! Don't bother about that. Get behind the door now.

[Matt gets behind the door, and she opens it and goes out. After a moment she returns]

LADY: All clear!

[Then closing the door behind her, she goes. Matt takes a look around the room to see that he has not left any trace, and moves softly to the door. His hand is on the handle, when it is opened by the Maid; he has just time to shrink behind it while she stands looking curiously round the room, as if for somebody or something]

LADY'S VOICE: [Off] Ellen! D'you mind going and getting me the suit I sent down to dry last night?

MAID: [Starting] Yes, Madam. [She goes, closing the door]

[Matt has just time for a breath of relief when it is opened again and the Lady reappears]

LADY: [Seeing him breathless] This is a bit hectic! [In a whisper] Now! Quick!

[Matt dives past her. She stands a moment, hustles out her underclothing from under the bedclothes, then drawing the door to, goes to the window, opens it a little wider, and stands

there listening. In half a minute the faint strains of "Lady, be good," whistled, are heard]

LADY: [Waving a stocking like a hat. Under her breath] Gone away!

[Whistling "Lady, be good," she crosses jauntily towards the door, meeting the Maid, who is coming in with the dried suit. Continuing to whistle, she passes her with a roll of the eyes, leaving the Maid in three minds as

THE CURTAIN FALLS]

EPISODE IV.

Seven hours have passed. Dartmeet. An open space of fern and grass, above the river and away from trippers.

Matt, who has been working along the river all the morning, is squatting with his catch beside him—some eight smallish trout. He is eating the last of his chocolate and drinking diligently from the already empty flask. The more so as an Old Gentleman in Lovat tweeds is straying towards him. Matt begins taking his rod to pieces.

OLD GENTLEMAN: [Approaching from Left] Afternoon! Cleared up too well for you, I'm afraid.

MATT: Yes, it's a bit bright now.

OLD GENTLEMAN: Best eating in the world, those little brown chaps. Except perhaps the blue trout in the Tirol. Blaue Forellen with butter and potatoes, and a bottle of Vöslauer Goldeck, eh?

MATT: My Golly, yes!

[He looks wolfishly at his trout]

OLD GENTLEMAN: [Eyeing him askance] Very foggy this morning. Worst point about the moor, these fogs. Only good for convicts—um?

MATT: [Subduing a start] Escapes, you mean? But they never get clear, I believe.

OLD GENTLEMAN: No, I'm told; but they try, you know—they try. I've often wondered what I should do if I blundered into an escaped convict.

MATT: Yes, sir; bit of a problem.

OLD GENTLEMAN: [Sitting down on his overcoat] Between the Law and one's gentlemanly instincts— if it's gentleman-like to dally with a felon—I wonder!

MATT: [Warming to the subject] A chap who tries to escape must be a sportsman, anyway. He takes a pretty long chance.

OLD GENTLEMAN: Yes, I don't envy a man in this country; we're a law-abiding people. I remember being very much struck with the difference in America last year—vital race, that—sublime disregard of the law themselves, and a strong sense of moral turpitude in others. Been in America?

MATT: I was out West ranching when the war broke out.

OLD GENTLEMAN: Indeed! Judging by the films, escaping justice is still fashionable there. I think I prefer a more settled country.

MATT: Personally, I've got rather a complex. Escaped from Germany in the war.

OLD GENTLEMAN: Did you? How very interesting!

MATT: If you want to get thin. It's a top-hole cure for adipose. An escape's no picnic.

OLD GENTLEMAN: I imagine not, indeed. Where did you get over the border?

MATT: Holland, after three days and nights on beets and turnips. Do you know the turnip in a state of nature, Sir? He's a homely fellow—only beaten by the beet. Beg your pardon, Sir, it slipped out. By the way, a convict got off the day before yesterday.

OLD GENTLEMAN: Yes, I saw that—a Captain Matt Denant. I read his case with interest at the time. How did it strike you?

MATT: [On guard] Don't believe I remember it.

OLD GENTLEMAN: What? The Hyde Park case!

MATT: Oh! Ah! yes. There was a girl. In those cases they might wait till you complain.

OLD GENTLEMAN: The detective was undoubtedly doing his duty. And yet, quite a question—Rather dangerous giving the police a discretion on morals. The police are very like ourselves; and—er—most of us haven't got discretion, and the rest haven't got morals. The young man didn't complain, I think. D'you happen to recollect?

MATT: [With an uneasy look] So far as I remember, he said she was an intellectual.

[The Old Gentleman has taken out a cigar-case and is offering it]

OLD GENTLEMAN: Smoke?

MATT: Thanks very much. I've got into a bad habit of coming out without tobacco.

[They bite and light cigars]

OLD GENTLEMAN: I suppose one might run across that convict fellow any moment. It would be a little like meeting an adder. The poor thing only wants to get away from you. And yet, if you don't break its back, ten to one it'll bite a dog. I had two dogs die of snakebite. It's a duty, perhaps—what do you say?

MATT: Probably. But I don't always do mine.

OLD GENTLEMAN: Oh! don't you? I'm so glad of that. Neither do I.

MATT: Do you know that Prison? It's a bad style of architecture.

OLD GENTLEMAN: No. The fact is, I've had the misfortune in my time to send a good many people to prison. And in those days I did make a point of seeing a prison now and then. I remember I used to give my Juries a pass to go and see where they sent their fellow-beings. Once I tested whether they went to look round or not, and out of three Juries—no, it was four—how many do you think had had the curiosity?

MATT: None.

OLD GENTLEMAN: Isn't that a little cynical? [With his sideway bird-like glance] No, it was—one. Ha!

MATT: Who'd want to go into a prison? I'd as soon visit the morgue. The bodies there aren't living, anyway.

OLD GENTLEMAN: They tell me prisons are much improved. They've introduced a human feeling.

MATT: Have they? Splendid! What was the date of that?

OLD GENTLEMAN: [His eyes busy] They've abolished the arrows, anyway. And I believe they don't shave their heads now. Do you know any convicts?

MATT: [With a wriggle] I? No. Only one.

OLD GENTLEMAN: Indeed? And is he interesting?

MATT: The most interesting chap I know.

OLD GENTLEMAN: Ha! Suppose this escaped convict suddenly turned up here? [Jerking his thumb towards Matt] What should you do?

MATT: Run like a hare.

OLD GENTLEMAN: Dear me, yes. I think it would depend on whether anyone was about. Human nature is very—er—sensitive. D'you find this climate bracing? Dartmoor has quite a reputation.

MATT: Overrated—I think.

OLD GENTLEMAN: You know it well?

MATT: No; this is my first visit.

OLD GENTLEMAN: And will you be here long?

MATT: Hope not.

OLD GENTLEMAN: Beautiful spot—Dartmeet!

MATT: I prefer Two Bridges.

[Putting up his rod and whistling "Lady, be good"]

OLD GENTLEMAN: I've not fished for years. [As Matt suddenly passes his hand over his brow under his hat] Anything the matter?

MATT: Afraid I shall have to abandon your excellent cigar. I've enjoyed it, but I'm smoking on a rather empty stomach.

[He looks ruefully at the unsmoked portion of his cigar, and pitches it away]

OLD GENTLEMAN: Dear me! Yes. I remember that feeling coming over me once at the Royal Academy banquet—just before I had to make a speech. [Another of his bird-like glances] Tobacco must be one of the great deprivations in prison, I always think. Didn't you find that so in—in—Germany?

MATT: [Breathing rather fast and completing the dismantlement of his fishing-rod] Oh! we got tobacco now and then.

OLD GENTLEMAN: And empty stomachs too, I'm afraid.

MATT: Yes.

OLD GENTLEMAN: One never ceases to be grateful to those who endured such things. [Offering his cigar-case] Will you try again after tea? These moor teas with cream and jam.

MATT: [Taking it] Well, thank you, Sir, I shall down him next time.

[Matt is now ready for departure, for he has been getting increasingly uneasy with this Old

Gentleman. *He takes up his basket and lays the fish within it*]

OLD GENTLEMAN: Well [*Getting up*] I must be getting on too. It's been very pleasant. I've enjoyed our little talk. At my time of life one doesn't often get new sensations.

MATT: [*Nonplussed*] Good Lord, Sir! Have I given you any?

OLD GENTLEMAN: Well, I don't remember ever having talked before to a prisoner who's escaped from—Germany.

MATT: Good-bye, Sir.

OLD GENTLEMAN: Good-bye, Captain Denant— [*Matt starts*] I hope you'll have a pleasant journey, especially as no one seems to have noticed our little chat.

MATT: [*Staring at him*] D'you mind frightfully telling me how you spotted me?

OLD GENTLEMAN: Not at all! First, the way you looked at your trout—shall I say—er—wolfishly? And then—forgive me—your legs.

MATT: [*Drawing up his Burberry and contemplating his legs*] Yes. I hoped you'd think I was a leader of fashion.

OLD GENTLEMAN: And there was another thing— your obvious sympathy with yourself.

MATT: That's a prison habit, Sir. You're not allowed to sympathize with other people, for fear of contaminating them. Before I got into quod I don't remember ever feeling sorry for myself. But I doubt if I shall ever again feel sorry for anyone else.

OLD GENTLEMAN: That must be very natural. Well, it's been most interesting, because now you see I know what I should do——

MATT: [*Intently*] Is it indiscreet to ask, Sir?

OLD GENTLEMAN: Well, Captain Denant, this time —I say *this* time—wink the other eye. Good-day to you!

MATT: Good-day, Sir. It's most frightfully sporting of you. For the moment I feel quite human.

OLD GENTLEMAN: Do you know, that's been rather the effect on me. Original sin, I suppose. Good-day!

[*He goes off, watching the smoke of his cigar and smiling faintly to himself. On* Matt, *affected by kindness*

THE CURTAIN FALLS]

EPISODE V.

An hour has passed. On the Moor; a high spot.

Four Trippers, *two men and two women, disgorged from a Ford car, are picnicking. One of the men, about fifty, in blue clothes, has a Merchant Service look and a concertina; the other looks more like a shopkeeper, and is perhaps fifty-five. His wife is a stout woman, about forty, of mellow appearance. The other woman is the shopkeeper's sister, dried-up*

and spinsterish. Their clothes are of a suitable nature —some feathers. They are all eating heavily.

WIFE: Captain, you're a prophet—considerin' what it was when we left Ashburton. I call this lovely!

[*Eats*]

CAPTAIN: Takes a bit o' weather to flummox a sailor, ma'am.

[*Drinks*]

WIFE: "You trust the Captain," I said to Pinkem this morning, didn't I, Father? *I* knew, you see; [*Archly*] my corns weren't shootin'.

SISTER: That's not very nice, Fanny.

WIFE: Why not? I'd like to see someone who 'asn't corns, if the truth was known. 'Ave another of these cut rounds, Dolly, and cheer up. Father, don't you eat any more cream—your eyes are yeller.

SHOPKEEPER: When I first came to Devonshire I could put away 'alf a pound o' cream at a meal.

WIFE: Yes, and it spoiled your temper for life.

SHOPKEEPER: Am I bad-tempered, Dolly?

SISTER: So-so, James.

SHOPKEEPER: What do you say, Captain?

CAPTAIN: You keep it for your wife, my boy. Outside the bosom of your family you're a perfect cherub.

WIFE: Captain, you're an 'opeless Benedict.

CAPTAIN: Bachelor born, Ma'am.

WIFE: With a wife in every port, eh?

SISTER: Oh! That reely isn't nice, Fanny; so old-fashioned, too.

CAPTAIN: Is it, Ma'am?

WIFE: Now, Captain, don't go shockin' Dolly. Oh! There's an insect on my skirt! I never seen one like it.

SHOPKEEPER: Kill it, then.

WIFE: Why?

SHOPKEEPER: Always kill what you don't know.

WIFE: [*Flipping it off*] It's only a biddle—poor thing! Give us a tune, Captain. [*The* Captain *draws a long blast from his concertina*] Hallo! 'Oo's this?

[Matt, *in Burberry, with rod and basket, has appeared Left, and stands lifting his hat*]

MATT: Afternoon! Wonder if you could put me right for Bovey?

SHOPKEEPER: Bovey! That's a goodish step— matter of twelve miles, I should say.

MATT: My Lord! Not really?

SHOPKEEPER: You go down the 'ill, through Ponsworthy to Widecombe, and up the 'ill turn to the left, and ask again.

MATT: I see. Will there be anyone to ask?

SHOPKEEPER: I shouldn't think so.

CAPTAIN: Had any sport, Sir?

MATT: [*Opening the basket*] Eight, rather small.

WIFE: My! Don't they look nice! Such good eatin', too.

MATT: Would you like them, Ma'am?

WIFE: [*With affected restraint*] I'm sure it's very good of you.

CAPTAIN: Don't you miss the chance, Mrs. Pinkem; nothing like moor trout, with a moor appetite.

SISTER: [*Distantly*] I'm sure it's most kind, from a stranger.

WIFE: [*Suddenly*] Well, I don't know, if you're so obliging. 'And me the *Daily Mail*, Father. I'll wrap 'em up; and thank you very much. I quite appreciate it.

MATT: That's splendid! [*He hands them*] Turned out quite nice, hasn't it? Have you come far?

SHOPKEEPER: From Ashburton—ten mile.

MATT: Heard anything there of the escaped convict?

SHOPKEEPER: What about it? Haven't looked at the paper last day or two.

WIFE: Another escape!—oh, my!

MATT: Rather! He got off in the fog, night before last.

SISTER: I always hate to think of one of those dreadful men at large. You can't sleep in your bed.

CAPTAIN: Don't you get too excited, Ma'am. Think of the choice 'e's got.

WIFE: [*Scanning the paper*] Why! It's the man that killed the poor detective in 'Yde Park! That villain! It says 'ere they nearly got him—twice.

[Matt, *who is eyeing them closely, eyes a loaf even more closely, and tries to maneuver into a position to annex it*]

SHOPKEEPER: I 'ope everybody's helping to catch him. He must be a regular desperado. That was a bad case. I never believed the girl.

SISTER: I should think not, indeed!

SHOPKEEPER: Nor the young man neither. They were up to no good there. They tell me those London parks are in a proper state.

CAPTAIN: They ain't a Sunday School, that's certain.

WIFE: Fie, Captain!

SISTER: [*Acidly*] I believe some people quite sympathized with him. Fancy!

MATT: Well, if you won't think it too eccentric, I did, for one.

SHOPKEEPER: You!—Why?

MATT: I thought he had devilish hard luck.

SHOPKEEPER: Ah! there's always a fuss made about the Law. You can't even 'ang a woman for murderin' her 'usband without a lot of 'ysterical nonsense. Look at that case not long ago—there was a petition as long as your arm.

CAPTAIN: I remember. The young chap was a steward. I don't recall this Hyde Park case.

WIFE: Why! the detective arrested one o' those women this young man had been sittin' with—a gentleman he was too—and if he didn't 'it him an' break 'is 'ead, an' kill 'im, poor man!

CAPTAIN: Then why didn't they string him up?

MATT: The jury found it was a quarrel, not an attempt to evade arrest. Besides, in falling the detective hit his head on the iron railing of the Row, and the doctors said he died of the concussion.

SHOPKEEPER: That didn't ought to have got 'im off. He hit the man. If 'e 'adn't 'it him, 'e wouldn't have fallen.

MATT: Exactly! Brilliant! But if the detective hadn't seized him, he wouldn't have hit him.

SHOPKEEPER: Well! *I'd* 'ave hung 'im.

WIFE: Don't be so bloodthirsty, Father!

SHOPKEEPER: Well, I would. Hitting an officer for doing his duty. Sitting with a woman in the Park, too! He only got off because he was quality.

MATT: Don't you think that's a superstition?

[*The* Shopkeeper *glares at him, but decides that he is a gentleman, and therefore prejudiced, and only snorts slightly*]

SISTER: Did they punish the woman?

MATT: What for, Ma'am?

SISTER: *I'd* keep them shut up; then they wouldn't tempt young men—the 'arpies!

MATT: [*Unexpectedly*] Oh! God!

[*They all stare at him. Then the* Shopkeeper *fatuously breaks the silence*]

SHOPKEEPER: Can't say I was ever tempted by a woman.

MATT: No, you've got a Ford car, I see. D'you find them good in this sort of country?

SHOPKEEPER: [*Distantly*] I do, Sir.

MATT: Do they get up these hills?

SHOPKEEPER: I should think so. I'd engage to catch any convict with my car.

MATT: Would you? [*A thought strikes him*] Splendid!

WIFE: Well, I think we ought to be gettin' 'ome. 'And me the teapot, Captain. Now, Dolly! Never mind those bits o' cake and bread—they're no good. Just leave the deebris. I'd like to be in before dark, with a convict loose like this. He might come prowlin' round, pickin' things up.

[Matt *with a secret movement pockets some scraps*]

MATT: Good afternoon! Hope you'll enjoy the trout.

[*He moves away out of the picture*]

WIFE AND CAPTAIN: Good afternoon—Good afternoon, Sir!

[*Matt* salutes and vanishes, Right]

SISTER: Here, Fanny! Did you see him pocket the scraps?

WIFE: No! Why, he's a gentleman—didn't you hear his sniffy way o' talkin'?

SISTER: I saw him with my own eyes—two bits of cake and a round.

[*Sound of a car being started*]

SHOPKEEPER: I say! [*Jumping up*] What's 'e doin' with the Ford?

CAPTAIN: Hi, there! You, Sir!

SHOPKEEPER: He's got in. Hi!

SISTER: The villain!

ALL: Hi! hi! hi!

[*Sounds of a levanting car, and a halloed "So long!"* The Two Men *run out of the picture*]

WIFE: Well, I——

SISTER: *You!* Taking his fish like that! You might ha' known he was a thief. Why—why—of course! He's the—oh! oh!

WIFE: Dry up, Dolly! 'Ow are we to get 'ome?

[*The* Two Men *run back into the picture, breathless*]

SHOPKEEPER: Well, of all the impudent villains!

CAPTAIN: I'm jiggered!

[*He sits down with his hands on his knees and goes off into wheezy laughter*]

SISTER: 'Ow *can* you? 'Ow *can* you, Captain? And we talking about him all the time!

CAPTAIN: [*Stopping*] What! Him!

SISTER: The escaped convict! He hadn't the leggins of a gentleman.

CAPTAIN: What! Did you look at his legs, Ma'am?

WIFE: It's all your fault, Pinkem; you and Dolly's —callin' 'im names. If you 'adn't called 'im names, he wouldn't 'a stole the car—talkin' of hanging 'im! I could see 'im gettin' heated.

SHOPKEEPER: You called 'im a villain yourself. Well—Bovey—we know where to look for him.

CAPTAIN: A blind, old bean.

SHOPKEEPER: I say 'e will go there.

CAPTAIN: I say 'e won't.

SHOPKEEPER: I say 'e'll see we'll think 'e won't, and put the double cross on us.

CAPTAIN: Well, I say, 'e'll see we'll think 'e's going to put the double cross on us.

WIFE: Oh! My corns!

SISTER: Impudence, givin' us 'is fish!

CAPTAIN: Well, there's nothin' for it but tote the things and walk till we get a lift.

WIFE: Oh! my corns are shootin'. I can't walk.

CAPTAIN: Cheerio, Ma'am! Be English.

SHOPKEEPER: English! 'Tisn't *your* car.

CAPTAIN: Don't worry, old sport. 'E'll leave that in a ditch when he gets there.

SHOPKEEPER: There—ye-es—John o' Groats?

CAPTAIN: Come along, Ma'am. Lift your corns well up. I'll give you a tune.

[*They have picked up the gear and are trailing off Right, leaving papers strewn about*]

WIFE: Oh! Look! We've left 'is fish.

SISTER: Fish! Infra dig, I call it. [*She sniffs*]

WIFE: Nonsense, Dolly! Dish of trout like that'll cost five shillings in Ashburton. May as well 'ave the worth of the petrol 'e'll use. Father, pick 'em up.

[*The* Shopkeeper *turns back, picks them up in the* Daily Mail, *puts the combination to his nose, finds it good and follows the others off as the* Captain *begins to play his concertina and*

THE CURTAIN FALLS]

EPISODE VI.

Half an hour has passed. An open space with the moor rising from it. A Man *in plus fours and his* Wife *are returning from a walk. The* Wife *has stopped and is moving her foot uneasily.*

WIFE: I've got something in my shoe, Philip.

MAN: What?

WIFE: I've got something in my shoe.

MAN: [*In front, stopping too*] Take it off, then. [*Goes back to her*] Hold on to me.

WIFE: [*Taking off shoe and shaking it*] It isn't in the shoe—it's inside the stocking.

MAN: You can't sit down here; the ground's still wet.

WIFE: There—feel!

MAN: Yes, I can feel it.

WIFE: [*Standing on one leg*] Well! Hold me.

[*He holds her and she has slipped her stocking off when there is the sound of an approaching car*]

MAN: Look out! Here's a car!

WIFE: [*Letting her skirt fall and standing on one leg*] Bother!

[*Sound of the car stopping*]

MAN: Hallo! He's coming to speak to us.

[*The* Wife *bends and slips the shoe on hurriedly, but the dress is short. She holds the stocking behind her*]

MATT: [*Appearing*] Beg your pardon, Sir, but can you direct me to Bovey?

MAN: Afraid we're strangers. Pity you didn't ask as you came through Widecombe.

MATT: Well, but it's up this hill, anyway, isn't it?

MAN: Must be, I think. That's the way to Heytor Rock.

MATT: Oh! Can you see the promised land from there?

WIFE: Yes. You go up the hill and turn to the right, then to the left through a gate.

MATT: And ask again, I suppose. [*Preparing to leave*] Thanks very much.

MAN: Fine place, the moor, Sir. Splendid air.

MATT: [*Drily*] Oh! Splendid. So dry and clear!

WIFE: [*With a giggle*] Yes, the fog *was* awful yesterday.

MAN: They say Bovey's pretty.

MATT: Yes, I've some Aunts there. Good place for Aunts.

WIFE: [*Laughing*] What makes a good place for Aunts?

MATT: Oh! not too stirring. Awfully good knitting there, I believe.

MAN: Ha! That's good. Ha!

MATT: I must get on, or I shall be late for tea. So I whizz past Heytor Rocks——?

WIFE: Yes, and come down on the church.

MATT: Thanks very much. My Aunts are close there, I know. Good afternoon.

[*He lifts his hat discreetly and goes, Right. The* Man *and* Wife *gaze after him*]

WIFE: What a nice young man!

MAN: That was good about Aunts. Ha!

[*Sound of car moving on*]

Now for your stocking!

WIFE: [*Bending down and taking off her shoe*] I should think he was County, wouldn't you?

MAN: [*Holding her from behind*] Um! Only "County" would drive such a shockin' bad car.

WIFE: He saw my leg and kept his eyes off it. I thought that was charming of him.

MAN: Fellow-feelin'; he had some shockin' leg gear on himself.

WIFE: [*Turning stocking inside out*] See, there it is—a beastly little three-cornered bit of grit. Extraordinary how they get in——

MAN: [*Suddenly*] Look out! Here's a constable on a bike.

[*The* Wife *drops her skirt and stands balancing again, the stocking in her hand. A very hot* Constable *appears, wheeling a bicycle*]

CONSTABLE: Zeen convict pass?

MAN: [*Astonished*] Convict? No.

CONSTABLE: Zeen anybody?

MAN: Only a car.

CONSTABLE: What zort of car?

MAN: Ford, I think.

CONSTABLE: Whu was in it?

MAN: A man.

CONSTABLE: What zort of man?

MAN: Oh!—er—a gentleman.

CONSTABLE: How d'yu know?

MAN: By his voice.

WIFE: He spoke to us.

CONSTABLE: What d'e zay?

MAN: Asked the way to Bovey.

CONSTABLE: Ha! What 'ad 'e on?

MAN: Long Burberry and a hat like mine; he was quite all right.

CONSTABLE: [*Mopping his face*] Was 'e? Bovey—yu zay?

WIFE: Yes, he had some Aunts there—he was going to tea with them.

CONSTABLE: [*Deeply*] Aunts in Bovey! Did yu direct 'im?

WIFE: We told him to go by Heytor Rocks. Wasn't that right?

CONSTABLE: Well, yu've directed the escaped convict.

MAN: [*Alarmed*] No, really! But I tell you——

WIFE: He was quite charming.

CONSTABLE: Was 'e? 'Ow much start's 'e got?

MAN: Oh! not five minutes. Of course, I didn't know—I should never have——

CONSTABLE: [*Muttering and mopping*] This plaguey 'ill!

MAN: Hadn't you better telephone to Bovey?

CONSTABLE: [*Smartly*] Bovey! Why d'yu suppose he spoke to 'ee? Because 'e idn' goin' to Bovey and wants me to think 'e is.

WIFE: But really he was a gentleman.

CONSTABLE: [*Drily*] Volk 'e stole that car from 'alf an hour gone, don't think so. [*He mops his face*]

WIFE: I can't believe——

MAN: There were his legs [*To* Constable, *whose eyes are on the lady's leg*] I noticed they looked like nothing at all.

CONSTABLE: Then why didn' yu stop 'im?

MAN: [*Flustered*] I would have, of course, if I'd suspected for a moment.

CONSTABLE: Stop first—suspect arterwards.

MAN: Well, I'm sorry. If I'd——

CONSTABLE: 'Tes done now. I must get down along sharp and telephone. [*He turns and wheels his bicycle off to the road*]

WIFE: [*On one leg*] I don't see why you need be sorry, Philip. He *was* a gentleman.

MAN: A convict's a convict; you can't play about with the Law.

WIFE: Well, we have, that's one comfort. That constable didn't keep *his* eyes off my leg.

MAN: I suppose you'd have had me get into a row with the police!

WIFE: Don't be silly, Philip! You needn't get angry because your nerves are rattled. No, don't hold me, I can put it on perfectly by myself. [*She stands wobbling on one leg, and pulls the stocking on*]

MAN: The brass of that chap—talking about his Aunts!

WIFE: You thought it very funny, when he did.

MAN: If I'd known——

WIFE: Oh! Yes, if you'd known—you haven't an ounce of original sin in you. Thank goodness, I have.

MAN: Where? *I've* never——

WIFE: No, I don't keep it for you.

MAN: Hallo! He's coming back.

WIFE: Who? The constable?

MAN: No—that chap—the convict.

[*Sounds of car*]

WIFE: Hooray!

MAN: What do you mean—hooray? What am I to do? This is infernal.

WIFE: [*Maliciously*] Run out and stop him, of course.

MAN: [*On one leg and the other*] He'd run over me. These chaps are desperate.

WIFE: Well, *I* will, then; and warn him of the constable.

MAN: You won't!—Hallo! He's stopping. That's worse. What the devil shall I do now?

[*The* Wife *laughs. Sounds of car stopping.* Matt *reappears*]

MATT: Awfully sorry, but my car jibbed. There's another way round, isn't there? Through Widecombe, to the right—I saw a road?

MAN: Um! Well—I—er——

WIFE: Yes, but I shouldn't advise you to take it.

MATT: Must, I'm afraid. My car started to back down the hill.

MAN: I'm afraid—er—that I—er—ought to——

WIFE: My husband means that there's a constable in Widecombe. [*Pointing*]

MATT: Yes. [*Looking back under his hand*] I see him.

WIFE: So you'd better go on up.

MATT: There are *two* up there, you see. My car's very sensitive.

WIFE: Oh, dear!

MAN: Joan! [*Resolutely*] Now, Sir, that constable's been talking to us. The game's up. If you don't mind, I'll take that car. He says it isn't yours.

MATT: [*Stepping back*] You know that's most frightfully true. But then—it isn't yours either.

MAN: Well, just let's argue it. I'm afraid you're helpless.

MATT: What do you take me for?

MAN: Why—er—the escaped convict, if you know what I mean.

MATT: Oh! Well—even so, I've still got a kick in me. I see your point of view, of course; but unfortunately I've got my own.

MAN: After that constable, I simply can't play about with it.

MATT: Look here! I've got a brain-wave. Let's all go into Widecombe in the car?

MAN: Ah! thanks very much; I thought you'd be sporting.

MATT: You see, if you're with me, I shall get through Widecombe all right, and I'll drop you just on the far side.

MAN: But—! What? No—that won't——

MATT: It's all right. You take me in custody into Widecombe—you can't help it if I whizz through and shoot you out. I want to make it easy for you, and I hope you want to make it easy for me.

MAN: Why should I? An escaped convict!

MATT: What do you call *yourself*?

MAN: What! Just an average man.

MATT: D'you mean to say the average man isn't a sportsman?

MAN: Yes. But I've had warning. I'm up against it.

WIFE: *I'll* come in the car. If you're with a lady, you'll get through without being spotted.

MATT: Splendid! Thanks ever so! Will you get in?

MAN: Joan!

MATT: Put yourself in my position, Sir——

MAN: Look here! I ought to be knocking you down and sitting on your head, if you know what I mean.

MATT: [*Squaring up*] Well, any little thing you've got to do, please do it quickly.

MAN: Well, I mean—that's very crude.

WIFE: [*Ironically*] Oh! no, Philip! Oh, no!

MAN: Well, suppose you let me drive.

MATT: Why should I? I stole the car. Now, Madam, shall we start?

WIFE: [*Winding her scarf round her face*] Righto!

MAN: This is monstrous! Look here, Sir, you seem to think——

MATT: I'll tell you what I think— [*Grimly*] I've

been in purgatory too long, and I'm going to get out, and you're not going to stop me, if you know what I mean.

MAN: I jolly well am!

WIFE: Philip!

MAN: I'm not going to have it. If you won't surrender, I shall tackle you.

MATT: [*Dangerously*] Oh! [*He takes a spanner out of his pocket*]

WIFE: [*Stepping between them—to* Matt] D'you know, I think you'd better go on.

MATT: I think so, too. Sorry to be a boor and bring out a thing like this. [*Tapping the spanner*] But I'm not playing, you see. [*Somberly*] The life we live spoils our sense of humor! Good-bye, Ma'am, I'm very grateful to *you*. [*He turns and vanishes*]

MAN: Look here! You're not going like that—I'm damned if you are! Stop!

WIFE: Masterly, Philip! Masterly! [*Sound of a car starting*] Run! My dear! Run! It's all right. You'll be too late.

MAN: You really *are*——

[*They stand looking at each other as the sound of the car fails slowly, and*

THE CURTAIN FALLS]

EPISODE VII.

An hour has passed.

In a gravel pit on the edge of the moor are a wheelbarrow, with a pick in it, and Matt *lying on his face, apparently asleep, waiting for dark.*

From Right comes the figure of a Laborer. *He is a burly great fellow with a shovel. Seeing the recumbent figure, he stands still, gazing. Then, turning, he goes back whence he came.* Matt, *who has been conscious of this visitor, gathers himself to spring up and rush away. Then he takes a resolution and lies down again in the same attitude, as if asleep. The* Laborer *returns, followed by another* Laborer *as big as himself. The* First Laborer *clears his throat.*

MATT: [*Sitting up with his feet under him*] Well, my men! What's the matter with you?

FIRST LABORER: Beg pardon, Zurr. We'm lukin' for th' escaped convict. We 'ad a zort of a thought as yu med be 'err.

MATT: Did you? That's pretty good! And now you see I'm not, suppose you apologize?

FIRST LABORER: [*Cautiously*] 'Course, ef we knu 'u'm yu werr——

MATT: Whom do you work for?

FIRST LABORER: Varmer Brownin'. 'Tes 'is grazin' yere.

MATT: I'll see Farmer Browning. It's funny, but I don't altogether like being taken for an escaped convict.

FIRST LABORER: Yas, I rackon as 'ow yu'd better

zee Maester Brownin'. George, goo and vind Maester. 'E'm in th' orchard long across.

[*The* Second Laborer *goes off, Left*]

FIRST LABORER: We'm 'ad nues o' this joker, yu zee. Zeemingly 'e pinched a car and we'm found it just back along in the ditch. 'Tes the zame old car, tu.

MATT: What on earth's the car to do with me?

FIRST LABORER: A don' zay nothin' 'bout that. Maester'll know when 'e comes.

MATT: I'll go and meet him. [*He makes as if to rise*]

FIRST LABORER: No, you zett therr.

MATT: Now, look here, my friend! Do I talk like a convict?

FIRST LABORER: Can't zay, never 'eerd none. They'm town folk, I rackon—mos'ly.

MATT: Well, I was bred in the country, like you. What wages do you get here?

[*He pulls the flask out of his pocket, whistling "Lady, be good"*]

FIRST LABORER: Wall, ef yu'm the convict, yu'm a cule customer arter that.

MATT: But why on earth should you *think* I'm the convict. I'm just a fisherman staying at Lustleigh. [*He takes a pull at the empty flask*] You're making a fool of yourself, you know.

FIRST LABORER: [*Scratching his head*] Ef so be as yu'm what yu zay yu be, wot d'you goo vur to 'ide yere?

MATT: Hide? I was having a nap out of the wind, before walking home.

FIRST LABORER: This joker 'ad a fishin'-rod wi' un, tu.

MATT: The convict? Bosh!

FIRST LABORER: Not zo much bosh, neither.

MATT: Look you, my man, I've had enough of this.

[*He stands up suddenly. The* Laborer *steps back and lifts his shovel. But at this moment the* Farmer *and* Second Laborer *step into the picture from Left, accompanied by a* Little Girl *of thirteen or so, who has been riding*]

FARMER: Now then, now then! That'll du, Jim. Yu there, on my land, kindly give me yure name, and account for yurself. There's a rough customer about, with a fishin'-rod, same as yu.

MATT: Mr. Browning?

FARMER: Ay! that's my name.

MATT: Mine's Matthew. Captain Matthew. I'm staying at the Inn at Lustleigh. There's some very absurd mistake. This good trusty dog thinks he's treed a convict.

FARMER: [*Impressed by* Matt's *accent and air, and the flask in his hand*] Well, Sir, when there's these escapes on the moor, we 'ave to be careful. Miss 'Lizabeth, yu run along. [*The* Little Girl *does not move, but remains spellbound*] Constable's just been in wi' nues from Widecombe of the car yonder, and the man that pinched it 'ad a long brown coat, a fishin'-rod, and an 'at like yurn.

MATT: If the constable's here still, you'd better take me to him.

FARMER: No, rackon I'll ask 'im to step over 'ere. George, run and fetch constable, he'm down along by thiccy car.

[*The* Second Laborer *departs, Right, the* First Laborer *retires a little to the Right, leaving the* Farmer *and* Matt *by themselves on the Left, the* Farmer *being on the outside. The* Little Girl *still lurks breathless*]

MATT: Now, Mr. Browning—dash it all!—you ought to know better than this!

FARMER: Oh! I daresay yu'm a gentleman, but so's this convict, seemin'ly. Leastways he'm a captain. Perhaps yu'll tell me the name o' the innkeeper where yu'm stayin' at Lustleigh?

MATT: Has he got a name? I hadn't noticed.

FARMER: No; nor the name of the Inn neither, maybe?

MATT: The Red Lion.

FARMER: Ha!

MATT: Well, it ought to be.

FARMER: And per'aps yu'll show me the clothes yu've got on.

MATT: [*Taking a resolution*] Well, I own up.

LITTLE GIRL: Oh!

FARMER: I thowt yu'd come to it.

MATT: [*Lowering his voice*] Be sporting. Give me a show!

FARMER: Now yu know I can't du that; what's the yuse of askin'?

MATT: Well, I've had forty-eight hours' freedom, and given them a good run. You haven't a cigarette?

FARMER: I don't smoke them things. Jim, got a fag for this gentleman?

[First Laborer *brings out a packet of cigarettes which he holds out.* Matt *takes one and lights it from a match sheltered in the horny hands of the* Laborer, *who then retires again, Right, with the shovel*]

MATT: Thanks very much! [*He sits on the wheelbarrow. There ensues a silence. The* Little Girl *steals up to* Matt]

LITTLE GIRL: [*Holding out a small book*] Would you mind giving me your autograph?

FARMER: Miss 'Lizabeth!

LITTLE GIRL: Well, I've only just begun—I *have* to ask anybody at all thrilling.

MATT: [*With a grin*] Ink or—blood?

LITTLE GIRL: Oh! that'd be splendid!

MATT: Mine or—yours?

LITTLE GIRL: Oh! I've got a fountain pen. [*Hands it.* Matt *writes his name*] Thank you so much.

MATT: [*Handing back the book*] Shake hands on it. [*The* Little Girl *and he shake hands*] When you're an old woman you'll be able to say you met Murderous Matt.—Mr. Browning you won't give me a chance?

FARMER: Aid and abet a convict? No, no, Captain!

MATT: Vermin, eh? [*Looking round him*] Well,

you see, I've gone to earth. D'you hold with digging foxes out?

FARMER: I du, the varmints!

MATT: Ah! Well, you may thank your stars you were never in prison.

FARMER: No, an' I 'ope I'll never du nothin' to putt me there.

MATT: Take care you don't have bad luck, that's all.

FARMER: Bad luck? I reckon a man as kills a man can think he's havin' *gude* luck if he don't swing for it.

MATT: [*Somberly*] I meant the poor beggar no harm.

LITTLE GIRL: Have you really killed a man?

MATT: Not yet.

FARMER: [*Removing the pick from the barrow*] Yu struck the blow, and he died of't. What's more, so far as I remember, he was duin' his duty, same as I'm duin' mine. [*He looks intently at* Matt, *as if warning him not to try another blow*]

MATT: You needn't be afraid; there's a child here. If there weren't! I hope you'll see that my friend here [*Pointing to the* Laborer] has the reward for my capture.

FARMER: 'E can 'ave it; I don' want no reward for duin' *my* duty.

MATT: [*Nodding gravely*] That's lucky! I appreciate your excellent intentions, Mr. Browning. Glad to have met you! Good-bye!

[*He leaps from the barrow, and with a twist like a footballer evading a tackle, is past him and away to the Left. The* Little Girl *claps her hands*]

FARMER: [*Astonished*] The varmint! Hi! Jim! Arter 'im!

[*The* Laborer *utters a sort of roar and starts running. The* Farmer *is about to follow*]

LITTLE GIRL: Oh! Mr. Browning!

FARMER: Well?

LITTLE GIRL: Oh! nothing.

FARMER: Darn!

[*He follows out, running, Left. The* Constable *and* Second Laborer *come hurrying from Right*]

CONSTABLE: Gone! Which way, Missy?

LITTLE GIRL: [*With distant blankness*] I don't know.

CONSTABLE: Come on, then! [*He and the* Laborer *go out, Left, running*]

LITTLE GIRL: Oh! I do hope he gets off! Oh!

[*On the hue and cry*

THE CURTAIN FALLS]

EPISODE VIII.

A few minutes have passed.
In the parlor of a cottage of gentility are two maiden ladies—Miss Grace, *about forty-seven, brew-ing tea at a little table before the fire, Right, and Miss* Dora, *much younger, still dressed in hunting togs, standing at the open French window, Back.*

MISS DORA: There's such a glow on the Cleave, Grace. Most lovely red. We killed. Everybody was looking out for that escaped convict.

MISS GRACE: Did you see him?

MISS DORA: No, thank goodness. Poor hunted wretch!

MISS GRACE: If you think hunted things are poor, why do you go hunting?

MISS DORA: Foxes hunt and expect to be hunted.

MISS GRACE: So do convicts. Sympathy's wasted on them. Tea, Dora.

MISS DORA: This isn't a common convict. It's that Captain Denant, you remember——

MISS GRACE: Oh!—not likely to forget the row we had about his case. Well! it served him right!

MISS DORA: [*Going to the table and sitting down. Looking steadily at her sister*] For a good woman, Grace, you know—you're awfully hard.

MISS GRACE: Tea-cake, please. I like consistency.

MISS DORA: [*Deeply*] I think you're right.

MISS GRACE: [*Surprised*] How?

MISS DORA: It *is* a shame to hunt a fox—much better to shoot it.

MISS GRACE: There'd soon be no foxes. Don't get *that* bee into your bonnet *here*. What with rabbits, and chained dogs, you've set the farmers by the ears as it is. Wait till we go to Bath. You can have as many bees as you like there.

MISS DORA: I shan't hunt any more.

MISS GRACE: Then you're very foolish, if you enjoy it. Will you come over to the Service with me this evening?

MISS DORA: D'you know what I wish *you'd* say, Grace? "I shan't go to church any more."

MISS GRACE: I wish to God, Dora, you'd give up free thought!

MISS DORA: I wish to God, Grace, you'd give up religion.

MISS GRACE: You only hurt the vicar by it.

MISS DORA: [*Shaking her head*] He's too good a sort to mind.

MISS GRACE: You're too perverse for anything. I've only to say something and you set your will to the opposite.

MISS DORA: My dear, my will is nothing to yours. I haven't the ego for it.

MISS GRACE: [*Coldly*] You mean I'm egoistic? Thank you.

MISS DORA: Sorry, Grace.

MISS GRACE: Will you have another cup?

MISS DORA: Please.

[*She is holding out her cup and Miss* Grace *has poured from the teapot, when a Figure comes rushing through the French window. They both drop their hands and stare. Matt, panting and distressed, makes a sudden reveal-ing gesture of appeal, and blots himself out be-*

hind a window curtain. The hue and cry is heard off. The two ladies are still staring in wild surprise, when the Farmer *appears at the French window*]

FARMER: Which way'd 'e go?

MISS DORA: Who?

FARMER: Convict. Mun cam' over your waal un' round the corner ther'.

MISS DORA: Oh! Yes. I thought I saw. Across the lawn, and over the wall at the far end, Mr. Browning. Quick!

[*Behind her the figure and face of* Miss Grace *are expressive*]

FARMER: Gude! Woi! Over the waal 'e went. To him, boys! Chop him before he'm into the spinney.

[*The hue and cry passes the window running— the* Two Laborers, *the* Constable, *and* Two Tourist Youths. *The cries die off and leave a charged silence—the* Two Ladies *on their feet*]

MATT: [*Emerging, still breathless, with his hat in his hand. Noting* Miss Dora's *riding kit, he turns to* Miss Grace] Thank you, Madam.

MISS GRACE: Not me.

MATT: [*Making a bow to* Miss Dora] That was great of you, great!

MISS DORA: Keep back—one of them might see. [*She draws the curtains as* Matt *shrinks back*]

MISS GRACE: Great! To tell such a lie! And for a convict!

MATT: [*Recovering his self-possession*] If you'll forgive my saying so, that makes it greater. To tell a lie for an archbishop wouldn't strain one a bit.

MISS GRACE: Please don't blaspheme.

MISS DORA: [*Pouring out tea*] Will you have a cup of tea, Sir?

MISS GRACE: [*In a low voice*] Really, Dora!

MATT: [*Dropping his hat and taking the cup from* Miss Dora] It's too good of you. [*He drinks it straight off and hands it back*] I'm most awfully sorry for butting in like this; but it was neck or nothing.

MISS GRACE: Then I think it should have been nothing, Sir, considering the position you've placed my poor sister in.

MISS DORA: [*Hotly*] *Poor* sister! Grace, you———!

MATT: When you're hunted all you think of is the next move.

MISS DORA: I'm afraid you're awfully done.

MATT: Thanks, I'm getting my wind back. I feel like kissing the hem of your garment.

MISS DORA: It hasn't got one. Wasn't it rather mad to escape?

MATT: I don't think so. It's shown me how decent people can be.

MISS DORA: Did they ill-treat you?

MATT: Oh! no, the treatment's all right—a trifle monotonous.

MISS DORA: Listen! [*They listen. Faint shouting*] Where are you making for?

MATT: No plan. They're no good. It's like a battle —you change 'em before you use 'em.

MISS DORA: I read who you were in the papers.

MATT: Oh! yes. I'm in big print? Thank you most awfully. I'll clear out now.

MISS DORA: No, wait! [*At the curtains*] I'll be back in a minute. [*She slips out*]

MISS GRACE: [*Turning round to him*] I suppose you call yourself a gentleman?

MATT: I really don't know. Depends on who I'm with. I might be contradicted.

MISS GRACE: You see the sort of woman my sister is—impulsive, humanitarian. I'm—I'm very fond of her.

MATT: Naturally. She's splendid.

MISS GRACE: If you don't want to involve her———

MISS DORA: [*Reappearing through the curtains*] I think I can hide you.

MISS GRACE: Dora!

MATT: No, no! It's not good enough. I can't let you———

MISS DORA: [*Turning on her sister*] I'm going to, Grace.

[*They speak together in rapid tones*]

MISS GRACE: Not in this house.

MISS DORA: It's as much my house as yours. You need have nothing to do with it.

MISS GRACE: [*Drawing her from the window*] At least you haven't broken the law yet. And you're not going to now.

MISS DORA: I can't bear to see a soldier and a gentleman chased by a lot of chawbacons.

MISS GRACE: [*With a glance at* Matt] Dora, you mustn't. It's wrong and it's absurd.

MISS DORA: [*Heated*] Go up-stairs. If I have to refer to you I'll say you've seen nothing. And so can you.

MISS GRACE: [*Her voice rising*] You expect *me* to tell lies!

[Matt, *unseen in the heat of this discussion, makes a motion of despair and slips out of the window*]

MISS DORA: I'm going to hide him, I tell you. Captain— [*Suddenly turning to* Matt, *she sees that he is no longer there*] Where is he? [*The* Two Sisters *stand silent, blankly gazing about them*]

MISS DORA: Did he go by the door or the window?

MISS GRACE: I don't know.

MISS DORA: Didn't you see him?

MISS GRACE: I did not. [*At the expression on her sister's face*] I say I did not.

[Miss Dora *looks behind the window curtain, then cautiously out of the window, then recoils before the* Constable, *who comes in heated and breathless, followed by the* Farmer *and the* First Laborer, *who stops outside*]

CONSTABLE: Beg pardon, Miss. We've lost un. He'm a fair twister. Maybe he doubled back. We'll 'ave a luke over, if an' in case he'm hidin' yere somewhere about. Can we go thru yere?

MISS DORA: He can't be in the house.

[Miss Grace *stands pursing her lips*]

FARMER: We med 'ave a luke, Miss, after that. 'E'm a proper varmint.

[*Without waiting for further permission, the two pass through the room and go out Left. The* Two Sisters *stand looking at each other*]

MISS DORA: I won't have him caught. [*She moves towards the door*]

MISS GRACE: [*Seizing her sister's skirt*] Stop! I tell you!

MISS DORA: Let go!

MISS GRACE: I shall not. You're crazy. What is it to you?

MISS DORA: Let go, Grace!

MISS GRACE: You can't help him without breaking the law.

MISS DORA: Will you let me go, Grace? I shall hit you.

MISS GRACE: Very well. Hit me, then!

[*The* Two Sisters *clinch and for a moment it looks as if there were to be a physical struggle between them. There are sounds of approach*]

MISS DORA: Let go!

[*They unclinch, and wait for the door to open. Re-enter the* Farmer *and* Constable]

FARMER: Well he'm not yere; that's certain for zure.

CONSTABLE: [*Between the two*] You're quite sure, Miss, yu saw 'im over that wall?

[*A tense moment*]

MISS DORA: Quite!

[*Miss Grace has drawn her breath in with a hiss*]

FARMER: And not seen un since?

MISS DORA: No.

FARMER: Nor yu, Miss?

[*Miss Dora stares at her sister*]

MISS GRACE: [*Throwing up her head, and with a face like a mask*] No.

FARMER: [*Picking up Matt's hat left by him as he fled*] 'Ere, what's this?

MISS DORA: [*Recovering*] That? An old hat of my brother's that I use sometimes.

FARMER: 'Tis uncommon like the one that varmint was wearin'.

MISS DORA: Is it? Those fishing hats are all the same. [*Taking the hat*] Have you tried the orchard, Mr. Browning?

FARMER: Ah! we mun try that, but 'tis gettin' powerful dimsy. Come boys, we mun 'ave a gude old luke. The varmint fuled me bravely. I mun get me own back.

MISS DORA: Try the vicarage!

CONSTABLE: Ah! we'll try that tu.

[*They pass out at the window. The* Two Sisters *are left silent. Miss Grace suddenly sits down at the table and covers her face with her hands*]

MISS DORA: You told it beautifully, Grace. Thank you!

MISS GRACE: [*Uncovering her face with a fierce gesture*] Thank me for telling a lie!

MISS DORA: I'm sorry.

MISS GRACE: Sorry? You'd make me do it again!

MISS DORA: [*Simply*] I would. [*Looking after the hunt*] Poor fellow!

[*On the look between them*

THE CURTAIN FALLS]

EPISODE IX.

No time has passed. In the vestry of a village church lighted by an oil lamp, where, at the back, surplices and cassocks are hanging on pegs, a door, Right, leads to the churchyard and an open door, Left, into the church. There is no furniture except a chair or two, and a small table with a jug on it against the wall "up" from the door, Left.

The stage is empty, but almost at once the Parson *enters from the church, carrying some overpast Harvest decorations, which he places on the table. He is a slim, grizzle-haired, brown, active, middle-aged man with a good, lined, clean-shaven face, and a black Norfolk jacket; obviously a little "High" in his doctrine. He pours water from a jug into two large vases, humming: "O for the wings—for the wings of a dove!" Then carrying the vases, one in each hand, he goes back into the church. The door on the Right is opened and the hunted, hatless Matt slips in, closing the door behind him. He stands taking in the situation, crosses to the open door opposite, spies the* Parson, *and, recoiling, blots himself out behind a cassock. His face, peeping out, is withdrawn as the* Parson *returns, this time literally singing: "O for the wings—for the wings of a dove!" Taking off his coat, he prepares to hang it on a peg and take a cassock, and as he reaches the highest note, he lifts the cassock from in front of* Matt *and starts back.*

PARSON: Hullo!

MATT: Sanctuary, Sir!

PARSON: What d'you mean? Who are you? [*Matt opens his Burberry*] Oh! [*That "Oh!" is something more than astonishment; it has in it an accent of dismay, as if the speaker were confronted by his own soul*] The escaped convict! You oughtn't to have come in here.

MATT: Then where, Sir? In old days the Church——

PARSON: In old days the Church was a thing apart; now it belongs to the State. [*Matt makes a move towards the door*] Wait a minute! [*He has hung up his coat and put on the cassock, as if to strengthen the priest within him*] I think I read that you were that Captain Denant who——

MATT: Yes.

PARSON: [*Almost to himself*] Poor fellow!

[*Matt stares at him and there is a silence*]

MATT: Death isn't as much to us who were in the war, as it is to you.

PARSON: I know; I was there.

MATT: Padre?

PARSON: [*Nodding*] Where have you come from?

MATT: House of the two ladies over there. Left them fighting over me. Couldn't stand that—not worth it.

PARSON: [*With a little smile*] Yes, Miss Dora wanted to keep you and Miss Grace to throw you out. H'm? And yet Miss Dora doesn't come to church, and Miss Grace does. Something wrong there; or it is something right? [*He stares at* Matt] Are they after you?

MATT: Full cry.

PARSON: Sanctuary? If I were a Roman. Sometimes wish I were.

MATT: More logical.

PARSON: More powerful. This is a situation I've never had to face, Captain Denant.

MATT: Well, Sir, I'm just about done. If you could let me rest a bit, that's all I ask.

PARSON: My dear fellow! Sit down! [*He pulls a chair forward*] I'll lock the door. [*He does so; then, as* Matt *looks up at the window, which is in the fourth wall*] No, they can't see in. I expect you're very hungry too.

MATT: [*Sitting*] No, thanks—beyond it. You know that feeling, I bet?

PARSON: [*Shaking his head*] I'm afraid we of the Church lead too regular lives.

MATT: Not at the Front? It was pretty rife *there*.

PARSON: No, I'm ashamed to say—not even there. [*While speaking, he is evidently pondering and torn*]

MATT: [*Suddenly*] Well, Padre, how does it look to you? Giving me up?

PARSON: [*Moved*] Padre! [*He takes a turn and comes to a sudden halt in front of* Matt's *chair*] As man to man—who am I to give you up? One poor fellow to another! [*Shaking his head*] I can't help you to escape, but if you want rest, take it.

MATT: [*Suddenly*] Wonder what Christ would have done!

PARSON: [*Gravely*] That, Captain Denant, is the hardest question in the world. Nobody ever knows. You may answer this or that, but nobody ever knows. The more you read those writings, the more you realize that He was incalculable. You see—He was a genius! It makes it hard for us who try to follow Him. [*Gazing at* Matt, *who is sitting forward with his elbows on his knees and his head on his hands*] Very tired?

MATT: Gosh! I didn't think one could feel so tired. My joints have gone on strike. I was a three-mile runner, too.

PARSON: Were you? Good man!

MATT: It's the strain here. [*Touching his head*] If they get me and I have to go back! Odd! I didn't feel it half as much when I was escaping from Germany.

PARSON: Did anyone see you come in here?

MATT: Can't have—they'd have been in on my heels.

PARSON: Who's after you?

MATT: Villagers—and a constable.

PARSON: My villagers—and here am I—

MATT: [*Standing up*] By George, yes, Padre! It's too bad. I'll clear out.

PARSON: [*Putting his hand on his shoulder and pressing him back into the chair*] No, no! Rest while you can. You've asked for sanctuary. I don't know that I've the right to turn you out of here. I don't know—anyway I can't. Take your time. I have a little brandy here. Sometimes we get a faint in church—[*He takes a bottle and a little glass from the corner cupboard*] Drink it down.

MATT: [*Drinking it off. Pulling out the flask*] I say—wonder if you'd return *this* for me; it's empty —to that name and address. [*He takes a tailor-sewn label out of his pocket*] I ripped it off this Burberry. You might say "with unending gratitude." But please don't give that name away.

PARSON: No, no; I'll see to it. [*Pockets it*] Tell me! What made you escape?

MATT: Stick a bob-cat in a cage and open the door by mistake; and see what happens [*Looking at the* Parson's *face*] Oh! Yes, I know what you mean— but I've paid my scot long ago.

PARSON: Didn't you have a fair trial?

MATT: You can't "try" bad luck.

PARSON: All bad luck?

MATT: Well, I oughtn't to have hit him, of course; original sin, you know; but for an ordinary knock-out six weeks is about all you'd get; and I got four years more for that Rotten Row rail. Yes, I think I was perfectly entitled to have a shot.

PARSON: If you're quiet in your own mind—that's the only thing.

MATT: Well, you needn't worry, Padre. I shall be caught all right.

PARSON: [*With a smile*] I'm not worying about that. Caesar can look after himself, he has the habit. What bothers me is my own peace of mind. I don't like the thoughts that keep rising in it. You led a company in the war. And I lead——

MATT: Your parishioners—um?

PARSON: Yes. [*Nodding*] When you're gone—shall I be entitled to have been silent about you without telling *them* that I have been silent? Am I entitled to refrain from helping the Law without letting them know it? If I let them know it, can I keep what little influence I now possess? And is it right for a parson to go on where he has no influence? That's my trouble, Captain Denant.

MATT: I see. [*With a start*] Some one's trying the door.

[*The* Parson *moves to the door, Right;* Matt *has started forward*]

PARSON: [*At the door*] Who is that?

VOICE OF BELLRINGER: Me, Zurr.

PARSON: No, Thomas, I'm busy; I can't let anyone into the church now till Service time. [*He stands listening, then returns, Center*] My bellringer.

MATT: [*In a low voice*] The hospitality of God—

I shan't forget, Padre. But I don't want to be on your conscience. I'll flit. Wish I had the wings of that dove, though!

PARSON: I have Service at half-past six. There will only be one or two gathered together, I'm afraid. Make a third. You can rest through the Service. No one comes in here.

MATT: You're a trump! But I'd rather go and take my chance again. It's dark now. I don't like to give in. I'll bolt, and be caught in the open. You might give me your blessing.

PARSON: [Shaking his head] Not certain enough of myself—not certain enough. It takes a bishop at least to give a blessing.

[A very loud knocking on the door]

MATT: Trapped, by George! [He springs towards the cassocks and blots himself out]

[The Parson has gone again to the door]

PARSON: [Rather sharply] What is that?

VOICE OF CONSTABLE: Open the door, Zurr, please!

PARSON: Who is it?

VOICE OF CONSTABLE: Constable, Zurr; open, please.

[The Parson, with a gesture of distress, opens the door. Enter the Constable, the Farmer, the Two Laborers, and the Bellringer]

PARSON: I told you, Thomas, I could see no one till after Service.

BELLRINGER: Yes, Zurr; but Constable 'e thought you ought to know as 'ow I zeed a man enter 'ere a while back. [He looks round]

PARSON: What's all this, Constable?

CONSTABLE: 'Tis th' escaped convict, Zurr. We'm after 'e. These tu men yere found 'e down to the old gravel-pit. 'E give 'em the slip, an' we chased un to the ladies' 'ouse yonder, wherr 'e gave us the goo-by again; and Tammas says 'e saw a man come in 'ere as sounds praaperly like the varmint. You ben 'ere long, Zurr?

PARSON: An hour, at least.

CONSTABLE: Front door's locked, but I got men in the porch. Be 'ee sure as there's no one in the church?

PARSON: [Moving towards the church door] I don't know whether you have the right to search a holy place; but look for yourselves, as quietly as you can, please. [He stands at the church door to let them pass. They go, with the exception of the Bellringer, who has remained by the vestry door. The Parson crosses to him] You can go too, Thomas. I'll stand here.

[The Bellringer, with uneasy eyes and motions, crosses under the compulsion of the Parson's glance]

PARSON: [Hardly moving his lips] Now, quick!

[But as he speaks, the Farmer reappears in the church doorway; the Parson has just time to make a warning gesture, Matt just time to blot himself out again]

PARSON: Well, Browning?

FARMER: 'Eem not therr; 'tes zo bare's me 'and 'Eem a proper twisty customer for sure, but we'll get 'e yet. [His eyes rest suspiciously on the Parson's face]

PARSON: [With a forced smile] He got away from you, then, did he?

FARMER: Aye! 'E can run an' twist like a rabbit. He'm a desperate foxy chap. What's behind they cassocks?

PARSON: [Still with that forced smile] I'll look, Browning.

[He moves to the cassocks, and, from the middle, takes a look behind them, but to the Left only. And at this moment they all return from the church and he turns to them]

CONSTABLE: Thank 'ee, Zurr; 'e'm not yere, Tammas. Yu made a fule of us zeemin'ly.

BELLRINGER: [Stammering] I zeed mun come in 'ere; I zeed mun wi' these eyes—I did zurely.

PARSON: [Looking at his watch] Service, Thomas. Go and ring the bell. [To the Constable] I'm afraid I must ask you to go too, please, unless you would all like to stay for Service.

[A certain length of face becomes apparent]

CONSTABLE: [Opening the door and beckoning the Men out] My juty, Zurr, ef yu'll excuse us.

PARSON: That's all right, Constable.

FARMER: [Suddenly] Jest a minute, Vicar. Yu'll pardon me askin', but are yo zartin zure as yu'm not zeen this joker?

PARSON: [Drawing himself up] What is it you are asking me?

FARMER: I'm askin' yu on yure honor as a Christian gentleman, whether or no yu've zeen the escaped convict?

[After a moment's intense silence]

PARSON: I——

MATT: [Stepping out without the Burberry] Certainly he's not. Sorry, Sir, I was hidden there. [Holding up his hands] I surrender, Constable.

FARMER: Woi! The varmint! Got un! Worry, worry, worry!

PARSON: Be quiet in this place; and go out— You shame God!

[Astonished at this outburst, they slink out, leaving Matt, Center, in the grip of the Constable. The Parson is on his Left]

MATT: [To the Parson] Forgive me, Sir! Oughtn't to have come in here. It wasn't playing cricket.

PARSON: No, no! That you have done—that you have done.

MATT: It's one's decent self one can't escape.

PARSON: Ah! that's it! [Very low] God keep you!

[He watches the Constable and Matt go out]

[The bell begins to ring, as

THE CURTAIN FALLS]

END

Lady Gregory

(1859–1932)

"During these first years," wrote Yeats, referring to the founding of the Irish theatre, "Lady Gregory was friend and hostess, a centre of peace, an adviser who never overestimated or underestimated trouble, but neither she nor we thought her a possible creator." There was no reason to expect her to undertake the labor of writing plays for the newly created Irish theatre in addition to fostering the new movement ever since her first decisive conversations with Yeats, in 1894. She was a great lady, beautiful and witty, and was married to a prominent figure in Irish life, the wealthy landowner and member of Parliament Sir William Gregory. She had evinced no great interest in politics and could not be regarded as a nationalist while Ireland was renewing the struggle for home rule after the lull that had followed the fall of Parnell. She was, besides, English by descent and a Protestant. Her efforts to draw closer to the peasantry because of her interest in folklore were actually regarded with suspicion, and malicious country people set her down as a "souper," or proselytizing Protestant.

It was sufficient that she had joined Yeats, George Moore, and Edward Martyn to form the Irish Literary Theatre in 1899, and that she had tided the little group over great difficulties until 1901, when it expired, largely from lack of funds. Two years later she also had helped to lay the foundations for the Irish National Theatre Society, and from then on she could be counted upon to leap into the breach whenever the Society's existence was in jeopardy, which happened to be always. The group was harassed from the beginning not only by lack of money but by defection in the ranks. It encountered attacks from the extremist Sinn Feiners, who saw no merit in a theatre not exclusively political. The patriots rioted at the *première* of Synge's first one-acter, *In the Shadow of the Glen*, because they felt it contained slurs on Irish womanhood, and rioting could be expected during every other important *première*. Lady Gregory had also undertaken the task of running the new Abbey Theatre efficiently and of giving numerous parties to promote public relations, especially strategic first-night suppers, for which she had become famous. In short, she was the social mainstay of the nascent Irish theatre; and if anything, she was, as George Moore noted, "a little too imposing, too suggestive of Corinne or Madame Sand."

It is true that she had written a few articles, but these could be dismissed as mere self-indulgence on the part of a gentlewoman. More recently she had edited her deceased husband's papers, but this could be set down as an act of matrimonial piety. As for her collecting Irish folklore, this could be regarded as a form of innocent dilettantism, although it ceased to be that soon enough and justified her favorite exhortation: "We work to add dignity to Ireland."

"And now," Yeats remarked in his *Dramatis Personae*, "all in a moment, as it seemed, she became the founder of modern Irish dialect literature." What Yeats may have overlooked, however, is that in Lady Gregory's opinion it had become absolutely imperative to create such a literature if the Irish theatre was to capture national interest instead of shrinking into a closed circle for esthetes. Yeats's own plays were beautifully spiritual and poetic, but they could not be expected to root the drama in Irish soil. After an initial effort in 1902, *Twenty-five*, Lady Gregory began to contribute a series of one-act folk plays so singularly adapted to the needs and talents of the Irish theatre that this great-hearted little stage organization continued to subsist largely on folk drama for many years, through many transformations and a shifting directorate.

Lady Gregory wrote a number of romantic dramas steeped in folk legend and one fairly incisive three-act satire on Irish weaknesses, *The Image*. She also translated four Molière pieces (*The Doctor in Spite of Himself, The Rogueries of Scapin, The Miser,* and *The Would-Be Gentleman*) into delectable Irish dialect, an inspired undertaking if there ever was one, especially for the Irish theatre, which did not favor foreign plays. But her major contribution to dramatic literature was a series of little tragedies and farces, flavorsomely colloquial and realistic, and abounding in peasant types and rural backgrounds.

Among the tragedies, *The Gaol Gate* (1906) was a masterpiece in miniature. It was calculated, moreover, to win the approbation of the patriots, since Ireland's struggle for independence had inspired this story of the hanging of a man who refuses to betray his comrades in spite of his neighbors' belief that he has turned informer. The poignancy of the hero's mother and wife, who have come to visit him in prison, made a deep impression, and the mother became one of the best character parts of the famous Sara Allgood's early career. Another political one-acter was the delightful *Rising of the Moon*, in which a police sergeant refrains from arresting a rebel who carries a tempting price on his head.

Even more successful were the folk farces. *Spreading the News,* in 1904, made turbulent fun out of country gossip which turns the simple accident of a man's dropping his hayfork into a hair-raising account of his chasing his neighbor with murderous intent. The long one-act folk farce *Hyacinth Halvey*, in 1906, turned cartwheels on the question of what constitutes a reputation and how much of a burden it can become to the bearer. Young Hyacinth's glowing letters of recommendation threaten to deprive him of all freedom and entertainment, and his efforts to blacken himself in the opinion of unwaveringly admiring neighbors grow increasingly frantic without bringing him nearer to coveted disgrace. Lady Gregory's comic masterpiece, however, is undoubtedly *The Workhouse Ward*, which she wrote in 1908. Here her preoccupation with peasant types was productive of several superbly realized characters.

John Millington Synge began to till the same soil about the time that Lady Gregory came to the aid of the national theatre. It was one of the marks of Synge's genius that he felt impelled to go beyond peasant drama, that he transfigured folk material into a highly personal creation. And since no one could follow Synge into his private world, he had no successors when he died in 1909. The lesson taught by Lady Gregory could, however, be easily absorbed, and to her influence may be traced much of the drama of the Irish stage, which manages to convey the realities of the countryside with colloquial salt and attractive local color. During the lean years when genius did not appear on the Abbey stage, it was good to have such plays. In any case, they were generally better than the artificial fluff that was so often favored in London. Of Synge, Yeats has said with perfect justice, "He had under charming and modest manners, in almost all things of life, a complete absorption in his own dream." Lady Gregory's dream was not her own but that of her fellow creators and of Ireland. Even the writing of comedies was a matter of serving the theatre she helped to create and preserve. Too few were being composed by her colleagues Yeats and Synge. Referring to her little comedy *Spreading the News,* she said, "The idea of this play first came to me as a tragedy. . . . But comedy and not tragedy was wanted at our theatre to put beside the high poetic work . . . and I let laughter have its way with the little play." It was in comedy, moreover, that her true talent lay, and *The Workhouse Ward* has had few rivals for the title of the best one-act comedy in the English language.

BIBLIOGRAPHY: Ernest Boyd, *Ireland's Literary Renaissance,* 1916; Dawson Byrne, *The Story of Ireland's National Theatre,* 1929; Barrett H. Clark, *A Study of the Modern Drama* (pp. 344–348), 1938; Lady Gregory, *Our Irish Theatre,* 1913; William Butler Yeats, *Dramatis Personae,* 1936.

THE WORKHOUSE WARD

By Lady Gregory

PERSONS

MICHAEL MISKELL }
MIKE MC INERNEY } *paupers*
MRS. DONOHOE, *a countrywoman*

SCENE: *A ward in Cloon Workhouse. The two old men in their beds.*

MICHAEL MISKELL: Isn't it a hard case, Mike McInerney, myself and yourself to be left here in the bed, and it the feast day of Saint Colman, and the rest of the ward attending on the Mass.

MIKE MC INERNEY: Is it sitting up by the hearth you are wishful to be, Michael Miskell, with cold in the shoulders and with speckled shins? Let you rise up so, and you well able to do it, not like myself that has pains the same as tin-tacks within in my inside.

MICHAEL MISKELL: If you have pains within in your inside there is no one can see it or know of it the way they can see my own knees that are swelled up with the rheumatism, and my hands that are twisted in ridges the same as an old cabbage stalk. It is easy to be talking about soreness and about pains, and they maybe not to be in it at all.

MIKE MC INERNEY: To open me and to analyze me you would know what sort of a pain and a soreness I have in my heart and in my chest. But I'm not one like yourself to be cursing and praying and tormenting the time the nuns are at hand, thinking to get a bigger share than myself of the nourishment and of the milk.

MICHAEL MISKELL: That's the way you do be picking at me and faulting me. I had a share and a good share in my early time, and it's well you know that, and the both of us reared in Skehanagh.

MIKE MC INERNEY: You may say that, indeed, we are both of us reared in Skehanagh. Little wonder you to have good nourishment the time we were both rising, and you bringing away my rabbits out of the snare.

MICHAEL MISKELL: And you didn't bring away my own eels, I suppose, I was after spearing in the Turlough? Selling them to the nuns in the convent you did, and letting on they to be your own. For you were always a cheater and a schemer, grabbing every earthly thing for your own profit.

MIKE MC INERNEY: And you were no grabber yourself, I suppose, till your land and all you had grabbed wore away from you!

MICHAEL MISKELL: If I lost it itself, it was through the crosses I met with and I going through the world. I never was a rambler and a card-player like yourself, Mike McInerney, that ran through all and lavished it unknown to your mother!

MIKE MC INERNEY: Lavished it, is it? And if I did was it you yourself led me to lavish it or some other one? It is on my own floor I would be to-day and in the face of my family, but for the misfortune I had to be put with a bad next door neighbor that was yourself. What way did my means go from me is it? Spending on fencing, spending on walls, making up gates, putting up doors, that would keep your hens and your ducks from coming in through starvation on my floor, and every four footed beast you had from preying and trespassing on my oats and my mangolds and my little lock of hay!

MICHAEL MISKELL: O to listen to you! And I striving to please you and to be kind to you and to close my ears to the abuse you would be calling and letting out of your mouth. To trespass on your crops is it? It's little temptation there was for my poor beasts to ask to cross the mering. My God Almighty! What had you but a little corner of a field!

MIKE MC INERNEY: And what do you say to my garden that your two pigs had destroyed on me the year of the big tree being knocked, and they making gaps in the wall.

MICHAEL MISKELL: Ah, there does be a great deal of gaps knocked in a twelve-month. Why wouldn't they be knocked by the thunder, the same as the tree, or some storm that came up from the west?

MIKE MC INERNEY: It was the west wind, I suppose, that devoured my green cabbage? And that rooted up my Champion potatoes? And that ate the gooseberries themselves from off the bush?

MICHAEL MISKELL: What are you saying? The two quietest pigs ever I had, no way wicked and well ringed. They were not ten minutes in it. It would be hard for them to eat strawberries in that time, let alone gooseberries that's full of thorns.

MIKE MC INERNEY: They were not quiet, but very ravenous pigs you had that time, as active as a fox they were, killing my young ducks. Once they had blood tasted you couldn't stop them.

MICHAEL MISKELL: And what happened myself the fair day of Esserkelly, the time I was passing your door? Two brazened dogs that rushed out and took a piece of me. I never was the better of it or of the start I got, but wasting from then till now!

MIKE MC INERNEY: Thinking you were a wild beast they did, that had made his escape out of the traveling show, with the red eyes of you and the ugly face of you, and the two crooked legs of you that wouldn't hardly stop a pig in a gap. Sure any dog that had any life in it at all would be roused and stirred seeing the like of you going the road!

MICHAEL MISKELL: I did well taking out a summons against you that time. It is a great wonder you not to have been bound over through your lifetime, but the laws of England is queer.

MIKE MC INERNEY: What ailed me that I did not summons yourself after you stealing away the clutch of eggs I had in the barrel, and I away in Ardrahan searching out a clocking hen.

MICHAEL MISKELL: To steal your eggs is it? Is that what you are saying now? [*Holds up his hands*] The Lord is in heaven, and Peter and the saints, and yourself that was in Ardrahan that day put a hand on them as soon as myself! Isn't it a bad story for me to be wearing out my days beside you the same as a spancelled goat. Chained I am and tethered I am to a man that is ram-shacking his mind for lies!

MIKE MC INERNEY: If it is a bad story for you, Michael Miskell, it is a worse story again for myself. A Miskell to be next and near me through the whole of the four quarters of the year. I never heard there to be any great name on the Miskells as there was on my own race and name.

MICHAEL MISKELL: You didn't, is it? Well, you could hear it if you had but ears to hear it. Go across to Lisheen Crannagh and down to the sea and to Newtown Lynch and the mills of Duras and you'll find a Miskell, and as far as Dublin!

MIKE MC INERNEY: What signifies Crannagh and the mills of Duras? Look at all my own generations that are buried at the Seven Churches. And how many generations of the Miskells are buried in it? Answer me that!

MICHAEL MISKELL: I tell you but for the wheat that was to be sowed there would be more side cars and more common cars at my father's funeral (God rest his soul!) than at any funeral ever left your own door. And as to my mother, she was a Cuffe from Claregalway, and it's she had the purer blood!

MIKE MC INERNEY: And what do you say to the banshee? Isn't she apt to have knowledge of the ancient race? Was ever she heard to screech or to cry for the Miskells? Or for the Cuffes from Claregalway? She was not, but for the six families, the Hyneses, the Foxes, the Faheys, the Dooleys, the McInerneys. It is of the nature of the McInerneys she is I am thinking, crying them the same as a king's children.

MICHAEL MISKELL: It is a pity the banshee not to be crying for yourself at this minute, and giving you a warning to quit your lies and your chat and your arguing and your contrary ways; for there is no one under the rising sun could stand you. I tell you you are not behaving as in the presence of the Lord.

MIKE MC INERNEY: Is it wishful for my death you are? Let it come and meet me now and welcome so long as it will part me from yourself! And I say, and I would kiss the book on it, I to have one request only to be granted, and I leaving it in my will, it is what I would request, nine furrows of the field, nine ridges of the hills, nine waves of the ocean to be put between your grave and my own grave the time we will be laid in the ground!

MICHAEL MISKELL: Amen to that! Nine ridges, is it? No, but let the whole ridge of the world separate us till the Day of Judgment! I would not be laid anear you at the Seven Churches, I to get Ireland without a divide!

MIKE MC INERNEY: And after that again! I'd sooner than ten pound in my hand, I to know that my shadow and my ghost will not be knocking about with your shadow and your ghost, and the both of us waiting our time. I'd sooner be delayed in Purgatory! Now, have you anything to say?

MICHAEL MISKELL: I have everything to say, if I had but the time to say it!

MIKE MC INERNEY: [*Sitting up*] Let me up out of this till I'll choke you!

MICHAEL MISKELL: You scolding pauper you!

MIKE MC INERNEY: [*Shaking his fist at him*] Wait a while!

MICHAEL MISKELL: [*Shaking his fist*] Wait a while yourself!

[Mrs. Donohoe *comes in with a parcel. She is a countrywoman with a frilled cap and a shawl. She stands still a minute. The two old men lie down and compose themselves*]

MRS. DONOHOE: They bade me come up here by the stair. I never was in this place at all. I don't know am I right. Which now of the two of ye is Mike McInerney?

MIKE MC INERNEY: Who is it is calling me by my name?

MRS. DONOHOE: Sure amn't I your sister, Honor McInerney that was, that is now Honor Donohoe.

MIKE MC INERNEY: So you are, I believe. I didn't know you till you pushed anear me. It is time indeed for you to come see me, and I in this place five year or more. Thinking me to be no credit to you, I suppose, among that tribe of the Donohoes. I wonder they to give you leave to come ask am I living yet or dead?

MRS. DONOHOE: Ah, sure, I buried the whole string of them. Himself was the last to go. [*Wipes her eyes*] The Lord be praised he got a fine natural death. Sure we must go through our crosses. And he got a lovely funeral; it would delight you to hear the priest reading the Mass. My poor John Donohoe! A nice clean man, you couldn't but be fond of him,

Very severe on the tobacco he was, but he wouldn't touch the drink.

MIKE MC INERNEY: And is it in Curranroe you are living yet?

MRS. DONOHOE: It is so. He left all to myself. But it is a lonesome thing the head of a house to have died!

MIKE MC INERNEY: I hope that he has left you a nice way of living?

MRS. DONOHOE: Fair enough, fair enough. A wide lovely house I have; a few acres of grass land . . . the grass does be very sweet that grows among the stones. And as to the sea, there is something from it every day of the year, a handful of periwinkles to make kitchen, or cockles maybe. There is many a thing in the sea is not decent, but cockles is fit to put before the Lord!

MIKE MC INERNEY: You have all that! And you without e'er a man in the house?

MRS. DONOHOE: It is what I am thinking, yourself might come and keep me company. It is no credit to me a brother of my own to be in this place at all.

MIKE MC INERNEY: I'll go with you! Let me out of this! It is the name of the McInerneys will be rising on every side!

MRS. DONOHOE: I don't know. I was ignorant of you being kept to the bed.

MIKE MC INERNEY: I am not kept to it, but maybe an odd time when there is a colic rises up within me. My stomach always gets better the time there is a change in the moon. I'd like well to draw anear you. My heavy blessing on you, Honor Donohoe, for the hand you have held out to me this day.

MRS. DONOHOE: Sure you could be keeping the fire in, and stirring the pot with the bit of Indian meal for the hens, and milking the goat and taking the tacklings off the donkey at the door; and maybe putting out the cabbage plants in their time. For when the old man died the garden died.

MIKE MC INERNEY: I could to be sure, and be cutting the potatoes for seed. What luck could there be in a place and a man not to be in it? Is that now a suit of clothes you have brought with you?

MRS. DONOHOE: It is so, the way you will be tasty coming in among the neighbors at Curranroe.

MIKE MC INERNEY: My joy you are! It is well you earned me! Let me up out of this! [He sits up and spreads out the clothes and tries on coat] That now is a good frieze coat . . . and a hat in the fashion. . . . [He puts on hat]

MICHAEL MISKELL: [Alarmed] And is it going out of this you are, Mike McInerney?

MIKE MC INERNEY: Don't you hear I am going? To Curranroe I am going. Going I am to a place where I will get every good thing!

MICHAEL MISKELL: And is it to leave me here after you you will?

MIKE MC INERNEY: [In a rising chant] Every good thing! The goat and the kid are there, the sheep and the lamb are there, the cow does be running and she coming to be milked! Plowing and seed sowing, blossom at Christmas time, the cuckoo speaking through the dark days of the year! Ah, what are you talking about? Wheat high in hedges, no talk about the rent! Salmon in the rivers as plenty as hurf! Spending and getting and nothing scarce! Sport and pleasure, and music on the strings! Age will go from me and I will be young again. Geese and turkeys for the hundreds and drink for the whole world!

MICHAEL MISKELL: Ah, Mike, is it truth you are saying, you to go from me and to leave me with rude people and townspeople, and with people of every parish in the union, and they having no respect for me or no wish for me at all!

MIKE MC INERNEY: Whist now and I'll leave you . . . my pipe [Hands it over]; and I'll engage it is Honor Donohoe won't refuse to be sending you a few ounces of tobacco an odd time, and neighbors coming to the fair in November or in the month of May.

MICHAEL MISKELL: Ah, what signifies tobacco? All that I am craving is the talk. There to be no one at all to say out to whatever thought might be rising in my innate mind! To be lying here and no conversible person in it would be the abomination of misery!

MIKE MC INERNEY: Look now, Honor. . . . It is what I often heard said, two to be better than one. . . . Sure if you had an old trouser was full of holes. . . . or a skirt. . . . wouldn't you put another in under it that might be as tattered as itself, and the two of them together would make some sort of a decent show?

MRS. DONOHOE: Ah, what are you saying? There is no holes in that suit I brought you now, but as sound it is as the day I spun it for himself.

MIKE MC INERNEY: It is what I am thinking, Honor. . . . I do be weak an odd time . . . Any load I would carry, it preys upon my side . . . and this man does be weak an odd time with the swelling in his knees . . . but the two of us together it's not likely it is at the one time we would fail. Bring the both of us with you, Honor, and the height of the castle of luck on you, and the both of us together will make one good hardy man!

MRS. DONOHOE: I'd like my job! Is it queer in the head you are grown asking me to bring in a stranger off the road?

MICHAEL MISKELL: I am not, ma'am, but an old neighbor I am. If I had forecasted this asking I would have asked it myself. Michael Miskell I am, that was in the next house to you in Skehanagh!

MRS. DONOHOE: For pity's sake! Michael Miskell is it? That's worse again. Yourself and Mike that never left fighting and scolding and attacking one another! Sparring at one another like two young pups you were, and threatening one another after like two grown dogs!

MIKE MC INERNEY: All the quarreling was ever in the place it was myself did it. Sure his anger rises fast and goes away like the wind. Bring him out with myself now, Honor Donohoe, and God bless you.

MRS. DONOHOE: Well, then, I will not bring him out, and I will not bring yourself out, and you not to learn better sense. Are you making yourself ready to come?

MIKE MC INERNEY: I am thinking, maybe . . . it is a mean thing for a man that is shivering into seventy years to go changing from place to place.

MRS. DONOHOE: Well, take your luck or leave it. All I asked was to save you from the hurt and the harm of the year.

MIKE MC INERNEY: Bring the both of us with you or I will not stir out of this.

MRS. DONOHOE: Give me back my fine suit so [Begins gathering up the clothes], till I go look for a man of my own!

MIKE MC INERNEY: Let you go so, as you are so unnatural and so disobliging, and look for some man of your own, God help him! For I will not go with you at all!

MRS. DONOHOE: It is too much time I lost with you, and dark night waiting to overtake me on the road. Let the two of you stop together, and the back of my hand to you. It is I will leave you there the same as God left the Jews!

[She goes out. The old men lie down and are silent for a moment]

MICHAEL MISKELL: Maybe the house is not so wide as what she says.

MIKE MC INERNEY: Why wouldn't it be wide?

MICHAEL MISKELL: Ah, there does be a good deal of middling poor houses down by the sea.

MIKE MC INERNEY: What would you know about wide houses? Whatever sort of a house you had yourself it was too wide for the provision you had into it.

MICHAEL MISKELL: Whatever provision I had in my house it was wholesome provision and natural provision. Herself and her periwinkles! Periwinkles is a hungry sort of food.

MIKE MC INERNEY: Stop your impudence and your chat or it will be the worse for you. I'd bear with my own father and mother as long as any man would, but if they'd vex me I would give them the length of a rope as soon as another!

MICHAEL MISKELL: I would never ask at all to go eating periwinkles.

MIKE MC INERNEY: [Sitting up] Have you any one to fight me?

MICHAEL MISKELL: [Whimpering] I have not, only the Lord!

MIKE MC INERNEY: Let you leave putting insults on me so, and death picking at you!

MICHAEL MISKELL: Sure I am saying nothing at all to displease you. It is why I wouldn't go eating periwinkles, I'm in dread I might swallow the pin.

MIKE MC INERNEY: Who in the world wide is asking you to eat them? You're as tricky as a fish in the full tide!

MICHAEL MISKELL: Tricky is it! Oh, my curse and the curse of the four and twenty men upon you!

MIKE MC INERNEY: That the worm may chew you from skin to marrow bone! [Seizes his pillow]

MICHAEL MISKELL: [Seizing his own pillow] I'll leave my death on you, you scheming vagabone!

MIKE MC INERNEY: By cripes! I'll pull out your pin feathers! [Throwing pillow]

MICHAEL MISKELL: [Throwing pillow] You tyrant! You big bully you!

MIKE MC INERNEY: [Throwing pillow and seizing mug] Take this so, you stobbing ruffian you!

[They throw all within their reach at one another, mugs, prayer books, pipes, etc.]

CURTAIN

John Millington Synge

(1871–1909)

As we have had occasion to observe, one of the most remarkable developments of the modern theatre was the meteoric rise of the Irish drama. Ireland made no contribution to the stage in modern times until the last decade of the nineteenth century. Then it roused itself in response to nationalistic promptings and in time gave the world not only that superb repertory company the Abbey Theatre, renowned for natural acting and musical speech, but a number of dramatic masterpieces. Ireland's contribution, moreover, was as timely as it was meritorious. Realism had achieved a well-deserved supremacy in Europe; but its frequently literal and uninspired dramaturgy had led to a romantic revolt under Maeterlinck and Rostand in the eighteen-nineties which was beginning to lose its vitality by the first decade of the new century. The playwrights of a still untamed, unstandardized country such as Ireland were in a position to revivify the drama by combining the best elements of romanticism and realism. One of the new writers, moreover, was a superb artist. John Millington Synge may have been theoretically in favor of romanticism, and his last tragedy, *Deirdre of the Sorrows,* is the greatest Irish romantic drama; but he acquired such a singular sensitivity to the nuances of common life that most of his work provided a perfect fusion of reality and imagination.

Born in the vicinity of Dublin in 1871, of Protestant, English-descended, and socially prominent parents, Synge received the customary upper-class education in art and letters. He became an ultrarefined young man, proficient in four languages and an admirer of Racine, on whom he wrote a study. Wanderlust and a talent for music drew him to the Continent after his graduation from Trinity College in 1892. Leading a somewhat Bohemian life, mostly in Paris, for six years and augmenting his slender means with book reviewing, he seemed headed for the rather futile career of an Irish emigrant and esthete. But at a critical moment in 1899, his neighbor at the Grand Hotel Corneille, William Butler Yeats, pointed out the meagerness of his prospects and persuaded him to return to Ireland. Synge, by then inclined to heed the good advice, returned to the Aran Islands, thirty miles off the west coast of Ireland, which he had visited the year before, and surrendered to the spell of the primitive ways and dialect of the islanders. Further travels in the western counties of Ireland steeped Synge in the life of the most colorful and eloquent countryfolk of the British Isles. The experience proved a greater boon to Irish literature than anything that had happened before, for it was the making of the first major playwright of Ireland. On the Aran Islands, as well as on the west coast of Ireland, he found people who were close to the plain realities of labor and struggle with the soil and sea. At the same time, however, the environment and the manners were romantically primitive and the speech was poetic.

Synge wrote of his good fortune in the preface to his greatest comedy, *The Playboy of the Western World* (1907). All art, he declared, was a collaboration, and he had found the best collaborators in his simple neighbors. The modern literature of the towns was unsatisfactory; on one hand, it produced exotic work such as that of Mallarmé and Huysmans, and on the other, Ibsen's and Zola's dealings with reality "in joyless and pallid words." Synge maintained that "on the stage one must have reality, and one must have joy"; only "what is superb and wild in reality" was capable of providing esthetic gratification; and a good play must contain speech that is "as fully flavored as a nut or apple." In Ireland he felt the presence of a popular imagination that was still "fiery and magnificent, and tender; so that those of us who wish to write start with a chance that is not given to writers in places where the springtime of local life has been forgotten, and the harvest is a memory only, and the straw has been turned into bricks."

A mild and retiring intellectual, who surprised John Masefield and others by the contrast between his appearance and his buoyant work, Synge nevertheless had the right dramatic temperament. Yeats described it well when he wrote of his friend that he favored "all that has edge, all that is salt in the mouth, all that is rough to the hand, all that heightens the emotions by contest, all that stings into life the sense of tragedy." He added sagely, "The food of the spiritual-minded is sweet, an Indian scripture says, but passionate minds love bitter food."

Everything that has "edge" prevails in Synge's plays, particularly in his comedies. "Bitter food" also appears in them. He may not have been as cynical as was charged by his enemies and, in fact, much compassion of an unsentimental nature will be found in his writing, but a trace of disillusionment and acerbity does run through most of his work. Although, in reacting against Ibsenism, he deplored the fact that "in these days the playhouse is too often stocked with the drugs of many seedy problems," life itself was a "problem" to him. He tried to flee from it, in a back-to-nature romantic spirit that is essentially a nineteenth-century phenomenon. But he could not free himself from the dour temperament with which he viewed life. His first one-acter, *In the Shadow of the Glen,* drew a sobering picture of an unhappily married young peasant woman who is driven out of her home by her crabbed husband; *Riders to the Sea* and *Deirdre of the Sorrows* are unmitigated tragedies; *The Well of Saints* is a commentary on mankind's need for protective self-delusion; and *The Playboy of the Western World* is tinged with disenchantment despite its brisk humor.

Nor was Synge, in spite of his Rousseauist love of nature, a naïve worshipper of the primitive. He took note of the common man's struggle with relentless nature in *Riders to the Sea,* of the misery of the poor in his thoughtful travel notes, of the shiftlessness and drunkenness of some of the Irish in *The Tinker's Wedding,* and of the instability of their affections in *The Playboy of the Western World.* He was a poet with the eye of a realist, or a realist with a poet's talent for transforming common ore into gold. Made oversensitive by their struggle for national independence, Irish patriots felt the sting of his irony so keenly, indeed, that they accused him of malicious intent to defame the Irish and their cause. They resented *In the Shadow of the Glen* as an insult to Irish womanhood and staged riots during the early performances of *The Playboy of the Western World,* alleging that it defamed the nation, in addition to being ribald, or, as the noble firebrand Arthur Griffith put it, "cloacine." More serious, however, than these aspersions on an artist endowed with singular integrity was the shadow that hovered over Synge's genius. He was productive only during the brief span of years between 1903 and 1909, for he died in his thirty-eighth year.

Although each of Synge's six plays is memorable, *Riders to the Sea* is generally considered his most perfect work. It gains intensity from its extreme simplicity and condensation, as well as from its vividly conveyed, fate-charged atmosphere. This little tragedy does not, of course, suggest its author's comic genius, but it is thoroughly representative of his mastery of plain yet impassioned utterance and of his feeling for common life.

To the studious historian, *Riders to the Sea* may represent the influence, by no means negligible in Ireland, of the Belgian symbolist Maeterlinck, and the piece is surely a triumphant vindication of Maeterlinck's theory of "static" drama. Since the catastrophe is not presented on the stage, the play represents a "stasis." But the expectation of disaster, the waiting for news, and its reception by the tragic old woman Maurya are supremely dramatic. The critic may also be prompted to point out that here we have drama without "plot," the possibility—and value—of which was first championed not by Maeterlinck but by the European naturalists about a quarter of a century before Synge began to write plays. For conflict—except for the struggle of men against the sea, only the effect of which is shown—the playwright successfully substituted "tension" as dramatic yeast. This does not prove, however, that the procedures of Synge guarantee comparable results of high drama for others. *Riders to the Sea* represents the triumph of a very personal sensibility and of a disciplined talent given to few who have served the theatre in any style or period. Although an artist of limited scope, Synge was touched with greatness; *Riders to the Sea* is pervaded with that greatness.

BIBLIOGRAPHY: Ernest Boyd, *Ireland's Literary Renaissance,* 1916; Dawson Byrne, *The Story of Ireland's National Theatre,* 1929; W. G. Fay and Catherine Carswell, *The Fays of the Abbey Theatre,* 1935; John Gassner, *Masters of the Drama* (pp. 553–562), 1940, 1945; Ronald Peacock, *The Poet in the Theatre* (pp. 105–116), 1946; William Butler Yeats, *Dramatis Personae,* 1936.

RIDERS TO THE SEA

By John Millington Synge

PERSONS

MAURYA, *an old woman*
BARTLEY, *her son*
CATHLEEN, *her daughter*
NORA, *a younger daughter*
MEN AND WOMEN

SCENE: *An Island off the west of Ireland.*

Cottage kitchen, with nets, oil-skins, spinning-wheel, some new boards standing by the wall, etc. Cathleen, a girl of about twenty, finishes kneading cake, and puts it down in the pot-oven by the fire; then wipes her hands, and begins to spin at the wheel. Nora, a young girl, puts her head in at the door.

NORA: [*In a low voice*] Where is she?

CATHLEEN: She's lying down, God help her, and may be sleeping, if she's able.

[*Nora comes in softly, and takes a bundle from under her shawl*]

CATHLEEN: [*Spinning the wheel rapidly*] What is it you have?

NORA: The young priest is after bringing them. It's a shirt and a plain stocking were got off a drowned man in Donegal.

[*Cathleen stops her wheel with a sudden movement, and leans out to listen*]

NORA: We're to find out if it's Michael's they are, some time herself will be down looking by the sea.

CATHLEEN: How would they be Michael's, Nora? How would he go the length of that way to the far north?

NORA: The young priest says he's known the like of it. "If it's Michael's they are," says he, "you can tell herself he's got a clean burial by the grace of God, and if they're not his, let no one say a word about them, for she'll be getting her death," says he, "with crying and lamenting."

[*The door which Nora half closed is blown open by a gust of wind*]

CATHLEEN: [*Looking out anxiously*] Did you ask him would he stop Bartley going this day with the horses to the Galway fair?

NORA: "I won't stop him," says he, "but let you not be afraid. Herself does be saying prayers half through the night, and the Almighty God won't leave her destitute," says he, "with no son living."

CATHLEEN: Is the sea bad by the white rocks, Nora?

NORA: Middling bad, God help us. There's a great roaring in the west, and it's worse it'll be getting when the tide's turned to the wind. [*She goes over to the table with the bundle*] Shall I open it now?

CATHLEEN: Maybe she'd wake up on us, and come in before we'd done. [*Coming to the table*] It's a long time we'll be, and the two of us crying.

NORA: [*Goes to the inner door and listens*] She's moving about on the bed. She'll be coming in a minute.

CATHLEEN: Give me the ladder, and I'll put them up in the turf-loft, the way she won't know of them at all, and maybe when the tide turns she'll be going down to see would he be floating from the east.

[*They put the ladder against the gable of the chimney; Cathleen goes up a few steps and hides the bundle in the turf-loft. Maurya comes from the inner room*]

MAURYA: [*Looking up at Cathleen and speaking querulously*] Isn't it turf enough you have for this day and evening?

CATHLEEN: There's a cake baking at the fire for a short space [*Throwing down the turf*] and Bartley will want it when the tide turns if he goes to Connemara.

[*Nora picks up the turf and puts it round the pot-oven*]

MAURYA: [*Sitting down on a stool at the fire*] He won't go this day with the wind rising from the south and west. He won't go this day, for the young priest will stop him surely.

NORA: He'll not stop him, mother, and I heard Eamon Simon and Stephen Pheety and Colum Shawn saying he would go.

MAURYA: Where is he itself?

NORA: He went down to see would there be another boat sailing in the week, and I'm thinking it won't be long till he's here now, for the tide's turning at the green head, and the hooker's tacking from the east.

CATHLEEN: I hear some one passing the big stones.

NORA: [*Looking out*] He's coming now, and he in a hurry.

BARTLEY: [*Comes in and looks round the room; speaking sadly and quietly*] Where is the bit of new rope, Cathleen, was bought in Connemara?

CATHLEEN: [*Coming down*] Give it to him, Nora; it's on a nail by the white boards. I hung it up this morning, for the pig with the black feet was eating it.

NORA: [*Giving him a rope*] Is that it, Bartley?

MAURYA: You'd do right to leave that rope, Bartley, hanging by the boards. [Bartley *takes the rope*] It will be wanting in this place. I'm telling you, if Michael is washed up to-morrow morning, or the next morning, or any morning in the week, for it's a deep grave we'll make him by the grace of God.

BARTLEY: [*Beginning to work with the rope*] I've no halter the way I can ride down on the mare, and I must go now quickly. This is the one boat going for two weeks or beyond it, and the fair will be a good fair for horses I heard them saying below.

MAURYA: It's a hard thing they'll be saying below if the body is washed up and there's no man in it to make the coffin, and I after giving a big price for the finest white boards you'd find in Connemara.

[*She looks round at the boards*]

BARTLEY: How would it be washed up, and we after looking each day for nine days, and a strong wind blowing a while back from the west and south?

MAURYA: If it wasn't found itself, that wind is raising the sea, and there was a star up against the moon, and it rising in the night. If it was a hundred horses, or a thousand horses you had itself, what is the price of a thousand horses against a son where there is one son only?

BARTLEY: [*Working at the halter, to* Cathleen] Let you go down each day, and see the sheep aren't jumping in on the rye, and if the jobber comes you can sell the pig with the black feet if there is a good price going.

MAURYA: How would the like of her get a good price for a pig?

BARTLEY: [*To* Cathleen] If the west wind holds with the last bit of the moon let you and Nora get up weed enough for another cock for the kelp. It's hard set we'll be from this day with no one in it but one man to work.

MAURYA: It's hard set we'll be surely the day you're drownd'd with the rest. What way will I live and the girls with me, and I an old woman looking for the grave?

[Bartley *lays down the halter, takes off his coat, and puts on a newer one of the same flannel*]

BARTLEY: [*To* Nora] Is she coming to the pier?

NORA: [*Looking out*] She's passing the green head and letting fall her sails.

BARTLEY: [*Getting his purse and tobacco*] I'll have half an hour to go down, and you'll see me coming again in two days, or in three days, or maybe in four days if the wind is bad.

MAURYA: [*Turning round to the fire, and putting her shawl over her head*] Isn't it a hard and cruel man won't hear a word from an old woman, and she holding him from the sea?

CATHLEEN: It's the life of a young man to be going on the sea, and who would listen to an old woman with one thing and she saying it over?

BARTLEY: [*Taking the halter*] I must go now quickly. I'll ride down on the red mare, and the gray pony'll run behind me. . . . The blessing of God on you.

[*He goes out*]

MAURYA: [*Crying out as he is in the door*] He's gone now, God spare us, and we'll not see him again. He's gone now, and when the black night is falling I'll have no son left me in the world.

CATHLEEN: Why wouldn't you give him your blessing and he looking round in the door? Isn't it sorrow enough is on every one in this house without your sending him out with an unlucky word behind him, and a hard word in his ear?

[Maurya *takes up the tongs and begins raking the fire aimlessly without looking round*]

NORA: [*Turning toward her*] You're taking away the turf from the cake.

CATHLEEN: [*Crying out*] The Son of God forgive us, Nora, we're after forgetting his bit of bread. [*She comes over to the fire*]

NORA: And it's destroyed he'll be going till dark night, and he after eating nothing since the sun went up.

CATHLEEN: [*Turning the cake out of the oven*] It's destroyed he'll be, surely. There's no sense left on any person in a house where an old woman will be talking forever. [Maurya *sways herself on her stool*]

CATHLEEN: [*Cutting off some of the bread and rolling it in a cloth; to* Maurya] Let you go down now to the spring well and give him this and he passing. You'll see him then and the dark word will be broken, and you can say "God speed you," the way he'll be easy in his mind.

MAURYA: [*Taking the bread*] Will I be in it as soon as himself?

CATHLEEN: If you go now quickly.

MAURYA: [*Standing up unsteadily*] It's hard set I am to walk.

CATHLEEN: [*Looking at her anxiously*] Give her the stick, Nora, or maybe she'll slip on the big stones.

NORA: What stick?

CATHLEEN: The stick Michael brought from Connemara.

MAURYA: [*Taking a stick* Nora *gives her*] In the big world the old people do be leaving things after them for their sons and children, but in this place it is the young men do be leaving things behind for them that do be old.

[*She goes out slowly*. Nora *goes over to the ladder*]

CATHLEEN: Wait, Nora, maybe she'd turn back quickly. She's that sorry, God help her, you wouldn't know the thing she'd do.

NORA: Is she gone round by the bush?

CATHLEEN: [*Looking out*] She's gone now. Throw it down quickly, for the Lord knows when she'll be out of it again.

NORA: [*Getting the bundle from the loft*] The young priest said he'd be passing to-morrow, and we might go down and speak to him below if it's Michael's they are surely.

CATHLEEN: [*Taking the bundle*] Did he say what way they were found?

NORA: [*Coming down*] "There were two men," says he, "and they rowing round with poteen before the cocks crowed, and the oar of one of them caught the body, and they passing the black cliffs of the north."

CATHLEEN: [*Trying to open the bundle*] Give me a knife, Nora, the string's perished with the salt water, and there's a black knot on it you wouldn't loosen in a week.

NORA: [*Giving her a knife*] I've heard tell it was a long way to Donegal.

CATHLEEN: [*Cutting the string*] It is surely. There was a man in here a while ago—the man sold us that knife—and he said if you set off walking from the rocks beyond, it would be seven days you'd be in Donegal.

NORA: And what time would a man take, and he floating?

[Cathleen *opens the bundle and takes out a bit of stocking. They look at them eagerly*]

CATHLEEN: [*In a low voice*] The Lord spare us, Nora! isn't it a queer hard thing to say if it's his they are surely?

NORA: I'll get his shirt off the hook the way we can put the one flannel on the other. [*She looks through some clothes hanging in the corner*] It's not with them, Cathleen, and where will it be?

CATHLEEN: I'm thinking Bartley put it on him in the morning, for his own shirt was heavy with the salt in it. [*Pointing to the corner*] There's a bit of a sleeve was of the same stuff. Give me that and it will do.

[Nora *brings it to her and they compare the flannel*]

CATHLEEN: It's the same stuff, Nora; but if it is itself aren't there great rolls of it in the shops of Galway, and isn't it many another man may have a shirt of it as well as Michael himself?

NORA: [*Who has taken up the stocking and counted the stitches, crying out*] It's Michael, Cathleen, it's Michael; God spare his soul, and what will herself say when she hears this story, and Bartley on the sea?

CATHLEEN: [*Taking the stocking*] It's a plain stocking.

NORA: It's the second one of the third pair I knitted, and I put up threescore stitches, and I dropped four of them.

CATHLEEN: [*Counts the stitches*] It's that number is in it. [*Crying out*] Ah, Nora, isn't it a bitter thing to think of him floating that way to the far north, and no one to keen him but the black hags that do be flying on the sea?

NORA: [*Swinging herself round, and throwing out her arms on the clothes*] And isn't it a pitiful thing when there is nothing left of a man who was a great rower and fisher, but a bit of an old shirt and a plain stocking?

CATHLEEN: [*After an instant*] Tell me is herself coming, Nora? I hear a little sound on the path.

NORA: [*Looking out*] She is, Cathleen. She's coming up to the door.

CATHLEEN: Put these things away before she'll come in. Maybe it's easier she'll be after giving her blessing to Bartley, and we won't let on we've heard anything the time he's on the sea.

NORA: [*Helping* Cathleen *to close the bundle*] We'll put them here in the corner.

[*They put them into a hole in the chimney corner.* Cathleen *goes back to the spinning-wheel*]

NORA: Will she see it was crying I was?

CATHLEEN: Keep your back to the door the way the light'll not be on you.

[Nora *sits down at the chimney corner, with her back to the door.* Maurya *comes in very slowly, without looking at the girls, and goes over to her stool at the other side of the fire. The cloth with the bread is still in her hand. The girls look at each other, and* Nora *points to the bundle of bread*]

CATHLEEN: [*After spinning for a moment*] You didn't give him his bit of bread?

[Maurya *begins to keen softly, without turning round*]

CATHLEEN: Did you see him riding down?

[Maurya *goes on keening*]

CATHLEEN: [*A little impatiently*] God forgive you; isn't it a better thing to raise your voice and tell what you seen, than to be making lamentation for a thing that's done? Did you see Bartley, I'm saying to you.

MAURYA: [*With a weak voice*] My heart's broken from this day.

CATHLEEN: [*As before*] Did you see Bartley?

MAURYA: I seen the fearfulest thing.

CATHLEEN: [*Leaves her wheel and looks out*] God forgive you; he's riding the mare now over the green head, and the gray pony behind him.

MAURYA: [*Starts, so that her shawl falls back from her head and shows her white tossed hair. With a frightened voice*] The gray pony behind him.

CATHLEEN: [*Coming to the fire*] What is it ails you, at all?

MAURYA: [*Speaking very slowly*] I've seen the fearfulest thing any person has seen, since the day Bride Dara seen the dead man with a child in his arms.

CATHLEEN AND NORA: Uah.

[*They crouch down in front of the old woman at the fire*]

NORA: Tell us what it is you seen.

MAURYA: I went down to the spring well, and I stood there saying a prayer to myself. Then Bartley came along, and he riding on the red mare with the gray pony behind him. [*She puts up her hands.*

as if to hide something from her eyes] The Son of God spare us, Nora!

CATHLEEN: What is it you seen?

MAURYA: I seen Michael himself.

CATHLEEN: [Speaking softly] You did not, mother; it wasn't Michael you seen, for his body is after being found in the Far North, and he's got a clean burial by the grace of God.

MAURYA: [A little defiantly] I'm after seeing him this day, and he riding and galloping. Bartley came first on the red mare; and I tried to say, "God speed you," but something choked the words in my throat. He went by quickly; and "the blessing of God on you," says he, and I could say nothing. I looked up then, and I crying, at the gray pony, and there was Michael upon it—with fine clothes on him, and new shoes on his feet.

CATHLEEN: [Begins to keen] It's destroyed we are from this day. It's destroyed, surely.

NORA: Didn't the young priest say the Almighty God wouldn't leave her destitute with no son living?

MAURYA: [In a low voice, but clearly] It's little the like of him knows of the sea. . . . Bartley will be lost now, and let you call in Eamon and make me a good coffin out of the white boards, for I won't live after them. I've had a husband, and a husband's father, and six sons in this house—six fine men, though it was a hard birth I had with every one of them and they coming to the world—and some of them were found and some of them were not found, but they're gone now the lot of them. . . . There were Stephen, and Shawn, were lost in the great wind, and found after in the Bay of Gregory of the Golden Mouth, and carried up the two of them on the one plank, and in by that door.

[She pauses for a moment, the girls start as if they heard something through the door that is half open behind them]

NORA: [In a whisper] Did you hear that, Cathleen? Did you hear a noise in the northeast?

CATHLEEN: [In a whisper] There's some one after crying out by the seashore.

MAURYA: [Continues without hearing anything] There was Sheamus and his father, and his own father again, were lost in a dark night, and not a stick or sign was seen of them when the sun went up. There was Patch after was drowned out of a curagh that turned over. I was sitting here with Bartley, and he a baby, lying on my two knees, and I seen two women, and three women, and four women coming in, and they crossing themselves, and not saying a word. I looked out then, and there were men coming after them, and they holding a thing in the half of a red sail, and water dripping out of it—it was a dry day, Nora—and leaving a track to the door.

[She pauses again with her hand stretched out toward the door. It opens softly and old women begin to come in, crossing themselves on the threshold, and kneeling down in front of the stage with red petticoats over their heads]

MAURYA: [Half in a dream, to Cathleen] Is it Patch, or Michael, or what is it at all?

CATHLEEN: Michael is after being found in the Far North, and when he is found there how could he be here in this place?

MAURYA: There does be a power of young men floating round in the sea, and what way would they know if it was Michael they had, or another man like him, for when a man is nine days in the sea, and the wind blowing, it's hard set his own mother would be to say what man was it.

CATHLEEN: It's Michael, God spare him, for they're after sending us a bit of his clothes from the Far North.

[She reaches out and hands Maurya the clothes that belonged to Michael. Maurya stands up slowly, and takes them in her hands. Nora looks out]

NORA: They're carrying a thing among them and there's water dripping out of it and leaving a track by the big stones.

CATHLEEN: [In a whisper to the women who have come in] Is it Bartley it is?

ONE OF THE WOMEN: It is surely, God rest his soul.

[Two younger women come in and pull out the table. Then men carry in the body of Bartley, laid on a plank, with a bit of sail over it, and lay it on the table]

CATHLEEN: [To the women, as they are doing so] What way was he drowned?

ONE OF THE WOMEN: The gray pony knocked him into the sea, and he was washed out where there is a great surf on the white rocks.

[Maurya has gone over and knelt down at the head of the table. The women are keening softly and swaying themselves with a slow movement. Cathleen and Nora kneel at the other end of the table. The men kneel near the door]

MAURYA: [Raising her head and speaking as if she did not see the people around her] They're all gone now, and there isn't anything more the sea can do to me. . . . I'll have no call now to be up crying and praying when the wind breaks from the south, and you can hear the surf is in the east, and the surf is in the west, making a great stir with the two noises, and they hitting one on the other. I'll have no call now to be going down and getting Holy Water in the dark nights after Samhain, and I won't care what way the sea is when the other women will be keening. [To Nora] Give me the Holy Water, Nora, there's a small sup still on the dresser. [Nora gives it to her]

MAURYA: [Drops Michael's clothes across Bartley's feet, and sprinkles the Holy Water over him] It isn't that I haven't prayed for you, Bartley, to the Almighty God. It isn't that I haven't said prayers in the dark night till you wouldn't know what I'd be saying; but it's a great rest I'll have now, and it's time surely. It's a great rest I'll have now, and great sleeping in the long nights after Samhain, if it's only a bit of wet flour we do have to eat, and maybe a fish that would be stinking.

[*She kneels down again, crossing herself, and saying prayers under her breath*]

CATHLEEN: [*To an old man*] Maybe yourself and Eamon would make a coffin when the sun rises. We have fine white boards herself bought, God help her, thinking Michael would be found, and I have a new cake you can eat while you'll be working.

THE OLD MAN: [*Looking at the boards*] Are there nails with them?

CATHLEEN: There are not, Colum; we didn't think of the nails.

ANOTHER MAN: It's a great wonder she wouldn't think of the nails, and all the coffins she's seen made already.

CATHLEEN: It's getting old she is, and broken.

[*Maurya stands up again very slowly and spreads out the pieces of* Michael's *clothes beside the body, sprinkling them with the last of the Holy Water*]

NORA: [*In a whisper to* Cathleen] She's quiet now and easy; but the day Michael was drowned you could hear her crying out from this to the spring well. It's fonder she was of Michael, and would any one have thought that?

CATHLEEN: [*Slowly and clearly*] An old woman will be soon tired with anything she will do, and isn't it nine days herself is after crying and keening, and making great sorrow in the house?

MAURYA: [*Puts the empty cup mouth downwards on the table, and lays her hands together on* Bartley's *feet*] They're all together this time, and the end is come. May the Almighty God have mercy on Bartley's soul, and on Michael's soul, and on the souls of Sheamus and Patch, and Stephen and Shawn [*bending her head*]; and may He have mercy on my soul, Nora, and on the soul of every one is left living in the world.

[*She pauses, and the keen rises a little more loudly from the women, then sinks away*]

MAURYA: [*Continuing*] Michael has a clean burial in the Far North, by the grace of the Almighty God. Bartley will have a fine coffin out of the white boards, and a deep grave surely. What more can we want than that? No man at all can be living forever, and we must be satisfied.

[*She kneels down again and the curtain falls slowly*]

Sean O'Casey

(1884– ——)

It must have been the dream of every trueborn Irish playwright that heaven would some day drop the mantle of Synge on his shoulders. When a new candidate for fame arrived in the shape of a gaunt, self-educated workingman, Sean O'Casey, the administrators of the Abbey must have rubbed their eyes. A man of rough ways and no graces, he was as unlikely an apparition as any of them could have expected.

O'Casey's progress was slow and painful. He was about forty when the Abbey produced his first play, *The Shadow of a Gunman,* a bitter exposé of the folly and tragedy associated with windy nationalist idealism. He was fourteen before he really learned to read and write. Having lost his father at the age of three, he was reared by a devoted but poverty-stricken mother. He was half starved as a child, living almost exclusively on a diet of hard bread and tea. His schooling, which started late and ended early, was made abhorrent to him by the tyranny and snobbery of schoolmasters. He was to remember this with bitterness in the first of his autobiographical books, *I Knock at the Door,* in which he recalls being introduced to learning by a clergyman, "lugged off along at the backside of this soft-hatted, stiff-collared, egg-headed oul' henchman of heaven, to be added to the swarm of urchins cowering and groping about in the rag-and-bone education provided by the church and state for the children of those who hadn't the wherewithal to do any better." Defective eyesight added to his difficulties, as did an extremely sensitive, rather irascible temperament. His rebelliousness led to his terminating his schooling abruptly. At thirteen he was already a workingman, earning four shillings a week in a Dublin chandlery.

The boy began to take on casual jobs, to which he could adjust no better than to the school and the chandlery. He became a dock worker, hod carrier, and stone breaker on road-building crews, working twelve hours a day with pick and shovel. His pride and temper cost him job after job. He scored his first dismissal for striking a senior clerk, but really earned his spurs at the age of fifteen, when he was fired from a news agency for which he folded papers at four in the morning for nine shillings a week; he had refused to remove his cap while receiving his pittance of pay. Later, his revolt became socially generalized rather than personal, but without any diminution of zeal or passion. He fought through the severe Dublin transport strike of 1913, and the Marxist idea of the class war, no theory but plain reality for O'Casey, was never to be far from his thoughts thereafter. It was to lead him later to denounce Irish nationalism as naïve, so long as it ignored the problem of poverty in the fever for national independence, and it was to bring him ultimately to radicalism and to a position on the editorial board of a radical publication in London in the nineteen-forties. He was not, indeed, impervious to the romanticism and rightness of the Irish cause, and he actually joined the Irish Citizen Army to fight British rule. If he did not participate in the Easter Rebellion, it was only because he was then an involuntary guest of the British military government. But the experiences of childhood and early manhood moved him to put common realities of poverty and daily living ahead of nationalist aspirations.

When O'Casey came to write his masterpieces *Juno and the Paycock* and *The Plough and the Stars,* he was not likely to forget his mother's painful efforts to keep her family alive, his hard-working brother's sickening and dying, his young sister's pauper burial, which was so shabby that the cabmen refused to follow her coffin for fear of losing their reputation. It is not difficult to discover the source of O'Casey's vast contempt for a windbag's revolutionary slogans, in *The Shadow of a Gunman;* of his picture of Captain Boyle's intoxication with nationalist oratory and liquor while his family is falling to pieces, in *Juno and the Paycock;* of his story of Clitheroe's death in the Easter uprising, in *The Plough and the Stars,* while the hero's wife goes mad with anxiety and a tubercular tenement child coughs out its lungs in the courtyard. Nor was O'Casey forgetful of what were to him first and fundamental truths, when, abandoning the realistic form, he wrote the half-realistic, half-expressionistic pacifist play *The Silver Tassie* in 1927; the symbolic *Within the Gates,* with its chorus of "Down and Outs," in 1933; and the later semipoetic revolutionary pieces *The Star Turns Red,* which divided Eire into fascist and antifascist camps, and *Red Roses for Me,* which lyrically turned a strike situation into an apocalyptic vision.

This review of O'Casey's proletarian and socialist conditioning is, nevertheless, only half the story. It accounts for his ideas and his realism, which is at once satiric and compassionate, Hogarthian and Tolstoyan. It does not account for O'Casey's music and poetry any more than it does for his wild humor. Steeping himself in books as soon as he could afford to buy them with pennies set aside from his earnings, intoxicating himself with Shakespeare ("Shakespeare was my education," he was to say later, recalling that he could recite whole passages from the plays), and responding to the magic of Irish speech and song in the old national literature as a member of the Gaelic League, the class-conscious workingman slowly transformed himself into an artist. From the same sources he was to acquire the grand manner that is an integral part of his style and thought; and somewhere along the line of his development he staked out a large area of humor, which is perhaps the greatest miracle for anyone carrying his burden of social anguish. Shakespeare and the visit of the Benson Company in Dublin introduced him to the mysteries of writing for the stage. He made his first stab at playwriting when he was seventeen, submitted a second play to the Abbey a year later, followed this with two other rejected pieces, absorbed criticism from the directors, and finally, in 1923, made his debut in Ireland's national theatre with *The Shadow of a Gunman.*

Concerning the metamorphosis of hod carrier into poet, there were soon no doubts. *Juno and the Paycock* (1924) is the first and, in the opinion of many, the best product of his fusion of realism and poetry, of somber tragedy and extravagant comedy. The very fact that it is an incomplete fusion may be more fortunate than regrettable. Perhaps the comedy and tragedy that jostle each other in the script detract from each other. But if this is so, it is not because each is not amply realized by itself; the contradictory aspects in *Juno and the Paycock* are cardinal facts of its author's observation of life. The play unsettles and whirls us about, leaving us no firmer foundation than the infirm world that is O'Casey's subject. "A state of chassis [chaos]" is his rueful commentary on the self-defeating humanity for which Mrs. Boyle requests Christ's compassion in one of the memorable speeches of modern drama.

O'Casey was never again to attain a comparable success except with the somewhat better integrated and even more bitter Easter Rebellion tragedy *The Plough and the Stars* (1926), an Irish masterpiece which was suitably baptized in another patriotic riot such as had greeted *The Playboy of the Western World.* Yeats, trying to howl down the mob, shouted with unfailing eloquence, "You have once more rocked the cradle of a reputation. The fame of O'Casey is born tonight. This is apotheosis." It was also the last time that the Abbey would unstintedly rejoice in a play by O'Casey.

The Silver Tassie was a divided play, although a turbulently powerful one, "bringing down all the Voodoo war poetry with an ironic crash," as Shaw wrote in a generous tribute. It was rejected by the Abbey, and was first produced by C. B. Cochran in London, with settings by the famous painter Augustus John. Since then, O'Casey has been living in England. *Within the Gates* subordinated the sense of immediate reality to the noble abstractions of morality drama. *The Star Turns Red,* an exalted antifascist vision, was likewise too generalized. *Oak Leaves and Lavender* was a riot of fantasy, as elusive as it was inspired. O'Casey started moving back to the style of his first masterpieces with the farcical comedy *The Purple Dust* (1940), in which blimpish Englishmen are worsted in an encounter with the Irish people, and with his strike drama *Red Roses for Me.* But the return was only partly successful, perhaps because it was only partly intended. O'Casey's random volume on the theatre, *The Flying Wasp* (1937), aired his differences with the Abbey directors and his dissatisfaction with the Irish and English stage; his criticism of his critics was no doubt justified but failed to consider his own part in his failures. He seemed temporarily more attuned to a medium that could give greater scope to his writing when he turned out a series of remarkable autobiographical volumes: *I Knock at the Door* (1939), *Pictures in the Hallway* (1942), *Drums Under the Windows* (1946), and *Inishfallen, Fare Thee Well* (1949).

Still, even in his most flawed plays, O'Casey remained a dramatist whose vitality was equaled by very few of his contemporaries, and whose power of language was approached by none of them. With at least two masterpieces, and with general superiority even in his alleged failures, O'Casey occupies a special niche in the English-speaking theatre. Should anyone who is impatient with the later plays ever be inclined to question their author's rank among playwrights, he can easily fortify his faith by returning to the quite inimitable pages of *Juno and the Paycock* and *The Plough and the Stars.* As for the latter, it may well be noted that O'Casey here wrote a triumphant example of the "mass drama" as first developed by the pioneering naturalists, and that it has not only that "spire of meaning" that Galsworthy recommended for modern naturalist plays but also poetry and a compassionate heart. It concerns elemental realities of social fact and private feeling and translates them through a number of tinglingly alive human beings. And if O'Casey was less than enthusiastic over the Easter Rebellion, it was not because he was indifferent to the cause of Irish freedom but because he was even more passionately devoted to the cause of all stricken humanity—a cause which transcends race and nationality.

BIBLIOGRAPHY: Brooks Atkinson, *Broadway Scrapbook* (pp. 13–16, 147–151), 1947; John Mason Brown, *Two on the Aisle* (pp. 126–130), 1938; John Gassner, *Masters of the Drama* (pp. 566–571), 1940, 1945; Desmond MacCarthy, *Drama* (pp. 349–355), 1940; Ernest Short, *Theatrical Cavalcade* (pp. 208–210), 1942; Sean O'Casey, *The Flying Wasp,* 1937, and the autobiographical volumes cited.

THE PLOUGH AND THE STARS

By Sean O'Casey

ACT I.

SCENE—*The home of the* Clitheroes. *It consists of the front and back drawing-rooms in a fine old Georgian house, struggling for its life against the assaults of time and the more savage assaults of the tenants. The room shown is the back drawing-room, wide, spacious and lofty. At back is the entrance to the front drawing-room. The space, originally occupied by folding doors, is now draped with casement cloth of a dark purple, decorated with a design in reddish-purple. One of the curtains is pulled aside, giving a glimpse of the front drawing-room, at the end of which can be seen the wide, lofty windows looking out into the street. The room directly in front of the audience is furnished in a way that suggests an attempt towards a finer expression of domestic life. The large fireplace on* L. *is of wood, painted to look like marble (the original has been taken away by the landlord). Below the fireplace, on the wall, is a small mirror. On the mantelshelf are two candlesticks of dark carved wood. Between them is a small clock. Over the clock, on wall, is a picture of "The Sleeping Venus." On the right of the entrance to the front drawing-room is a copy of "The Gleaners," on the opposite side a copy of "The Angelus." Underneath "The Gleaners" is a chest of drawers on which stands a green bowl filled with scarlet dahlias and white chrysanthemums. Near to the fireplace is a couch which at night forms a double bed for* Clitheroe *and* Nora. *Near the end of the room opposite to the fireplace is a gate-legged table, covered with a cloth. On top of the table a huge cavalry sword is lying. To the* L. *above fireplace is a door which leads to a lobby from which the staircase leads to the hall. The floor is covered with a dark green linoleum. The room is dim except where it is illuminated from the glow of the fire.* Fluther Good *is repairing the lock of door,* L. *A claw hammer is on a chair beside him, and he has a screwdriver in his hand. He is a man of 40 years of age, rarely surrendering to thoughts of anxiety, fond of his "oil" but determined to conquer the habit before he dies. He is square-jawed and harshly featured; under the left eye is a scar, and his nose is bent from a smashing blow received in a fistic battle long ago. He is bald, save for a few peeping tufts of reddish hair around his ears; and his upper lip is hidden by a scrubby red moustache, em-broidered here and there with a grey hair. He is dressed in a seedy black suit, cotton shirt with a soft collar, and wears a very respectable little black bow. On his head is a faded jerry hat, which, when he is excited, he has a habit of knocking farther back on his head, in a series of taps. In an argument he usually fills with sound and fury, generally signifying a row. He is in his shirt sleeves at present, and wears a soiled white apron, from a pocket in which sticks a carpenter's two-foot rule. He has just finished the job of putting on a new lock, and, filled with satisfaction, he is opening and shutting the door, enjoying the completion of a work well done. Sitting at the fire, airing a white shirt, is* Peter Flynn. *He is a little, thin bit of a man, with a face shaped like a lozenge; on his cheeks and under his chin is a straggling wiry beard of a dirty-white and lemon hue. His face invariably wears a look of animated anguish, mixed with irritated defiance, as if everybody was at war with him, and he at war with everybody. He is cocking his head in such a way that suggests resentment at the presence of* Fluther, *who pays no attention to him, apparently, but is really furtively watching him.* Peter *is clad in a singlet, white whipcord knee-breeches, and is in his stockinged feet. A voice is heard speaking outside of door* L. *(it is that of* Mrs. Gogan *talking to someone).*

MRS. GOGAN: [*Outside door* L.] Who are you lookin' for, sir? Who? Mrs. Clitheroe? . . . Oh, excuse me. Oh ay, up this way. She's out, I think: I seen her goin'. Oh, you've somethin' for her. Oh, excuse me. You're from Arnott's. . . . I see. . . . You've a parcel for her. . . . Righto. . . . I'll take it. . . . I'll give it to her the minute she comes in. . . . It'll be quite safe. . . . Oh, sign that. . . . Excuse me. . . . Where? . . . Here? . . . No, there; righto. Am I to put Maggie or Mrs.? What is it? You dunno? Oh, excuse me.

[Mrs. Gogan *opens the door and comes in. She is a doleful-looking little woman of 40, insinuating manner and sallow complexion. She is fidgety and nervous, terribly talkative, has a habit of taking up things that may be near her and fiddling with them while she is speaking. Her heart is aflame with curiosity, and a fly could not come into nor go out of the house without her knowing. She has a draper's parcel in her hand, the knot of the twine tying it is untied.* Mrs. Gogan *crosses in front of* Fluther,

635

behind the couch, to the table R., *where she puts the parcel, fingering it till she has the paper off, showing a cardboard box.* Peter, *more resentful of this intrusion than of* Fluther's *presence, gets up from the chair, and without looking around, his head carried at an angry cock, marches into the room at back. He leaves the shirt on the back of the chair*]

[*Removing the paper and opening the cardboard box it contains*] I wondher what's this now? A hat! [*She takes out a hat, black, with decorations in red and gold*] God, she's goin' to th' divil lately for style! That hat, now, cost more than a penny. Such notions of upperosity she's getting. [*Putting the hat on her head*] Swank! [*Turning to* Fluther] Eh, Fluther, swank, what! [Fluther *looks over at her, then goes on opening and shutting the door*]

FLUTHER: She's a pretty little Judy, all the same.

MRS. GOGAN: Ah, she is, an' she isn't. There's prettiness an' prettiness in it. I'm always sayin' that her skirts are a little too short for a married woman. An' to see her, sometimes of an evenin', in her glad-neck gown would make a body's blood run cold. I do be ashamed of me life before her husband. An' th' way she thries to be polite, with her "Good mornin', Mrs. Gogan," when she's goin' down, an' her "Good evenin', Mrs. Gogan," when she's comin' up. But there's politeness an' politeness in it.

FLUTHER: They seem to get on well together, all th' same.

MRS. GOGAN: Ah, they do, an' they don't. The pair o' them used to be like two turtle doves always billin' an' cooin'. You couldn't come into th' room but you'd feel, instinctive like, that they'd just been afther kissin' an' cuddlin' each other. . . . It often made me shiver, for, afther all, there's kissin' an' cuddlin' in it. But I'm thinkin' he's beginnin' to take things more quietly; the mysthery of havin' a woman's a mysthery no longer. . . . She dhresses herself to keep him with her, but it's no use—afther a month or two, th' wondher of a woman wears off. [Mrs. Gogan *takes off the hat, and puts it back in the box; going on to rearrange paper round box, and tie it up again*]

FLUTHER: I dunno, I dunno. Not wishin' to say anything derogatory, I think it's all a question of location: when a man find th' wondher of one woman beginnin' to die, it's usually beginnin' to live in another.

MRS. GOGAN: She's always grumblin' about havin' to live in a tenement house. "I wouldn't like to spend me last hour in one, let alone live me life in a tenement," says she. "Vaults," says she, "that are hidin' th' dead, instead of homes that are sheltherin' th' livin'." "Many a good one," says I, "was reared in a tenement house." Oh, you know, she's a well-up little lassie, too; able to make a shillin' go where another would have to spend a pound. She's wipin' th' eyes of th' Covey an' poor oul' Pether—everybody knows that—screwin' every penny she can out o' them, in ordher to turn th'

place into a babby-house. An' she has th' life frightened out o' them; washin' their face, combin' their hair, wipin' their feet, brushin' their clothes, thrimmin' their nails, cleanin' their teeth—God Almighty, you'd think th' poor men were undhergoin' penal servitude.

FLUTHER: [*With an exclamation of disgust*] A-a-ah, that's goin' beyond th' beyonds in a tenement house. That's a little bit too derogatory.

[Peter *enters from room, back, head elevated and resentful fire in his eyes; he is still in his singlet and trousers, but is now wearing a pair of unlaced boots—possibly to be decent in the presence of* Mrs. Gogan. Peter *comes down* C. *and crosses, front of settee, to chair in front of fire; he turns the shirt which he has left to air on the back of the chair, then goes, front of couch, to the chest of drawers, back* L., *opens drawer after drawer, looking for something; as he fails to find it, he closes each drawer with a snap. He jerks out things neatly folded, and shoves them back into the drawers any way*]

PETER: [*In anguish, snapping a drawer shut*] Well, God Almighty, give me patience. [Peter *returns, front of couch, to the fireplace, gives the shirt a vicious turn on the back of the chair, and goes back, front of couch, to room, back,* Fluther *and* Mrs. Gogan *watching him furtively all the time*]

MRS. GOGAN: [*Curiously*] I wonder what is he foostherin' for now?

FLUTHER: [*Coming* C.] He's adornin' himself for the meeting to-night. [*He pulls a handbill from one of his pockets, and reads*] "Great Demonsthration an' Torchlight Procession around places in the City sacred to th' memory of Irish Pathriots to be concluded be a meetin', at which will be taken an oath of fealty to th' Irish Republic. Formation in Parnell Square at eight o'clock." Well, they can hold it for Fluther. I'm up th' pole; no more dhrink for Fluther. It's three days now since I touched a dhrop, an' I feel a new man already. [*He goes back to door* L.]

MRS. GOGAN: Isn't oul' Peter a funny-lookin' little man? . . . Like somethin' you'd pick off a Christmas Tree. . . . When he's dhressed up in his canonicals, you'd wondher where he'd been got. God forgive me, when I see him in them, I always think he must ha' had a Mormon for a father! He an' th' Covey can't abide each other; th' pair o' them is always at it, thryin' to best each other. There'll be blood dhrawn one o' these days.

FLUTHER: How is it that Clitheroe himself, now, doesn't have anythin' to do with th' Citizen Army? A couple o' months ago, an' you'd hardly ever see him without his gun, an' th' Red Hand o' Liberty Hall in his hat.

MRS. GOGAN: Just because he wasn't made a Captain of. He wasn't goin' to be in anything where he couldn't be conspishuous. He was so cocksure o' being made one that he bought a Sam

Browne belt, an' was always puttin' it on an' standin' at th' door showing it off, till th' man came an' put out th' street lamps on him. God, I think he used to bring it to bed with him! But I'm tellin' you herself was delighted that that cock didn't crow, for she's like a clockin' hen if he leaves her sight for a minute. [*While she is talking she takes up a book from the table, looks into it in a near-sighted way, and then leaves it back. She now lifts up the sword, and proceeds to examine it*] Be th' look of it, this must ha' been a general's sword. . . . All th' gold lace an' th' fine figaries on it. . . . Sure it's twiced too big for him.

[Fluther *crosses from door* L. *behind couch, back of table, where* Mrs. Gogan *is examining the sword, and looks at it, standing to* L. *of* Mrs. Gogan]

FLUTHER: [*Contemptuously*] Ah, it's a baby's rattle he ought to have, an' he as he is, with thoughts tossin' in his head of what may happen to him on th' Day of Judgement.

[Peter *appears at the curtained door, back, sees* Mrs. Gogan *with the sword, and a look of vexation comes on to his face. He comes down* C. *to the table, snatches the sword out of* Mrs. Gogan's *hands, and bangs it back on the table. He then returns into room, back, without speaking*]

MRS. GOGAN: [*To* Peter, *as he snatches the sword*] Oh, excuse me. [*To* Fluther] Isn't he the surly oul' rascal, Fluther? [*She wanders from the table, back of the couch, to the chest of drawers, where she stops for a few moments, pulling out drawers and pushing them in again*]

FLUTHER: [*Leaning against left side of the table*] Take no notice of him. . . . You'd think he was dumb, but when you get his goat, or he has a few jars up, he's vice versa. [Fluther *coughs.* Mrs. Gogan, *who has wandered from the chest of drawers, down* L., *to the fireplace, where she is fingering* Peter's *shirt, turns to look at* Fluther, *as soon as she hears the cough*]

MRS. GOGAN: [*With an ominous note in her voice*] Oh, you've got a cold on you, Fluther.

FLUTHER: [*Carelessly*] Ah, it's only a little one.

MRS. GOGAN: You'd want to be careful, all th' same. I knew a woman, a big lump of a woman, red-faced an' round-bodied, a little awkard on her feet; you'd think, to look at her, she could put out her two arms an' lift a two-storied house on th' top of her head; got a ticklin' in her throat, an' a little cough, an' th' next mornin' she had a little catchin' in her chest, an' they had just time to wet her lips with a little rum, an' off she went. [*She begins to look at and handle the shirt*]

FLUTHER: [*A little nervously*] It's only a little cold I have; there's nothing derogatory wrong with me.

MRS. GOGAN: [*Warningly*] I dunno; there's many a man this minute lowerin' a pint, thinkin' of a woman, or pickin' out a winner, or doin' work as you're doin', while th' hearse dhrawn be th' horses with the black plumes is dhrivin' up to his own hall door, an' a voice that he doesn't hear is muttherin' in his ear, "Earth to earth, an' ashes t' ashes, an' dust to dust."

FLUTHER: [*Faintly, affected by her talk*] A man in th' pink o' health should have a holy horror of allowin' thoughts o' death to be festherin' in his mind, for [*With a frightened cough*] be God, I think I'm afther gettin' a little catch in me chest that time—it's a creepy thing to be thinkin' about. [Fluther *sits weakly in chair* L. *of table*]

MRS. GOGAN: It is, an' it isn't; it's both bad an' good. . . . It always gives meself a kind o' thresspassin' joy to feel meself movin' along in a mournin' couch, an' me thinkin' that, maybe, th' next funeral'll be me own, an' glad, in a quiet way, that this is somebody's else's.

FLUTHER: [*Very frightened*] An' a curious kind of a gaspin' for breath—I hope there's nothin' derogatory wrong with me.

MRS. GOGAN: [*Examining the shirt*] Frills on it, like a woman's petticoat.

FLUTHER: [*Panic-stricken*] Suddenly gettin' hot, an' then, just as suddenly, gettin' cold.

MRS. GOGAN: [*Holding out the shirt towards* Fluther] How would you like to be wearin' this Lord Mayor's nightdhress, Fluther?

FLUTHER: [*Vehemently*] Blast you an' your nightshirt! Is a man fermentin' with fear to stick th' showin' off to him of a thing that looks like a shinin' shroud?

MRS. GOGAN: [*Startled at* Fluther's *vehemence*] Oh, excuse me.

[Peter *appears at curtained door, back. Sees his shirt in* Mrs. Gogan's *hand, comes rapidly down* C., *goes front of couch to* Mrs. Gogan, *snatches shirt from her, and replaces it on the back of the chair; he returns the same way to room, back*]

PETER: [*Loudly, as he goes to room, back*] Well, God Almighty give me patience!

[*There is heard a cheer from the men working outside on the street, followed by the clang of tools being thrown down, then silence. Running into the back room to look out of the window*] What's the men repairin' the streets cheerin' for?

FLUTHER: [*Sitting down weakly on a chair*] You can't sneeze but that oul' one wants to know th' why an' th' wherefore. . . . I feel as dizzy as bedamned! I hope I didn't give up th' beer too suddenly.

[*The* Covey *comes in by door* L. *He is about 25, tall, thin, with lines on his face that form a perpetual protest against life as he conceives it to be. Heavy seams fall from each side of nose, down around his lips, as if they were suspenders keeping his mouth from falling. He speaks in a slow, wailing drawl; more rapidly when he is excited. He is dressed in dungarees, and is wearing a vividly red tie. He comes down* C. *and flings his cap with a gesture of disgust on the table, and begins to take off his overalls*]

MRS. GOGAN: [*To the* Covey, *as she runs back into the room*] What's after happenin', Covey?

THE COVEY: [*With contempt*] Th' job's stopped. They've been mobilized to march in th' demonstration to-night undher th' Plough an' th' Stars. Didn't you hear them cheerin', th' mugs. They have to renew their political baptismal vows to be faithful in *seculo seculorum*.

FLUTHER: [*Sitting on the chair* L. *of table, forgetting his fear in his indignation*] There's no reason to bring religion into it. I think we ought to have as great a regard for religion as we can, so as to keep it out of as many things as possible.

THE COVEY: [*Pausing in the taking off of his dungarees*] Oh, you're one o' the boys that climb into religion as high as a short Mass on Sunday mornin's? I suppose you'll be singin' songs o' Sion an' songs o' Tara at th' meetin', too.

FLUTHER: We're all Irishmen, anyhow; aren't we?

THE COVEY: [*With hand outstretched, and in a professional tone*] Look here, comrade, there's no such thing as an Irishman, or an Englishman, or a German or a Turk; we're all only human bein's. Scientifically speakin', it's all a question of the accidental gatherin' together of mollycewels an' atoms.

[Peter *comes in from room, back, with a stiff collar in his hand, comes down* C., *crosses, in front of couch, to the mirror on the wall* L., *below the fireplace. He stands before the mirror and tries to put on his collar.* Fluther *gets up from the chair, goes* C. *and stands to* R. *of the* Covey]

FLUTHER: Mollycewels an' atoms! D'ye think I'm goin' to listen to you thryin' to juggle Fluther's mind with complicated cunundhrums of mollycewels an' atoms?

THE COVEY: [*Rather loudly*] There's nothin' complicated in it. There's no fear o' th' Church tellin' you that mollycewels is a stickin' together of millions of atoms o' sodium, carbon, potassium o' iodide, etcetera, that, accordin' to th' way they're mixed, make a flower, a fish, a star that you see shinin' in th' sky, or a man with a big brain like me, or a man with a little brain like you!

FLUTHER: [*More loudly still*] There's no necessity to be raisin' your voice; shoutin's no manifestin' forth of a growin' mind.

[Fluther *and the* Covey *turn to look at* Peter]

PETER: [*Struggling with his collar*] God give me patience with this thing. . . . She makes these collars as stiff with starch as a shinin' band of solid steel! She does it purposely to thry an' twart me. If I can't get it on to the singlet, how in the name of God am I goin' to get it on the shirt!

[Fluther *and the* Covey *face each other again*]

THE COVEY: [*Loudly*] There's no use o' arguin' with you; it's education you want, comrade.

FLUTHER: [*Sarcastically*] The Covey an' God made th' world I suppose, wha'?

THE COVEY: [*Jeering*] When I hear some men talkin' I'm inclined to disbelieve that th' world's eight-hundhred million years old, for it's not long since th' fathers o' some o' them crawled out o' th' sheltherin' slime o' the sea.

MRS. GOGAN: [*From room at back*] There, they're afther formin' fours, an' now they're goin' to march away.

FLUTHER: [*Scornfully taking no notice of* Mrs. Gogan] Mollycewels! [*He begins to untie his apron*] What about Adam an' Eve?

THE COVEY: Well, what about them?

FLUTHER: [*Fiercely*] What about them, you?

THE COVEY: Adam an' Eve! Is that as far as you've got? Are you still thinkin' there was nobody in th' world before Adam an' Eve? [*Loudly*] Did you ever hear, man, of th' skeleton of th' man o' Java?

PETER: [*Casting the collar from him*] Blast it, blast it! [Peter *angrily picks up the collar he has thrown on the floor, goes up* C., *right of couch, to the chest of drawers, and begins to hunt again in the drawers*]

FLUTHER: [*To the* Covey, *as he viciously folds apron*] Ah, you're not goin' to be let tap your rubbidge o' thoughts into th' mind o' Fluther.

THE COVEY: You're afraid to listen to th' thruth!

FLUTHER: [*Pugnaciously*] Who's afraid?

THE COVEY: You are!

FLUTHER: [*With great contempt*] G'way, you wurum!

THE COVEY: Who's a worum?

FLUTHER: You are, or you wouldn't talk th' way you're talkin'.

[Mrs. Gogan *wanders in from room, back, turns* L., *sees* Peter *at the chest of drawers, turns back, comes down* C., *goes, front of couch, to the fireplace*]

THE COVEY: Th' oul', ignorant savage leppin' up in you, when science shows you that th' head of your god is an empty one. Well, I hope you're enjoyin' th' blessin' o' havin' to live be th' sweat of your brow.

FLUTHER: You'll be kickin' an' yellin' for th' priest yet, me boyo. I'm not goin' to stand silent an' simple listenin' to a thick like you makin' a maddenin' mockery o' God Almighty. It 'ud be a nice derogatory thing on me conscience, an' me dyin', to look back in rememberin' shame of talkin' to a word-weavin' little ignorant yahoo of a red flag Socialist!

MRS. GOGAN: [*At the fireplace, turning to look at the disputants*] For God's sake, Fluther, dhrop it; there's always th' makin's of a row in the mention of religion. [*She turns her head, and looks at the picture of "The Sleeping Venus," hanging over the mantelpiece. She looks at it intently and a look of astonishment comes on her face*] God bless us, it's the picture of a naked woman. [*With a titter*] Look, Fluther.

[Fluther *looks over at the fireplace; comes slowly to the fireplace; looks steadily at the picture. Peter, hearing what was said, leaves the chest of drawers, and comes down, standing a little behind* Fluther *and* Mrs. Gogan, *and looks at the picture. The* Covey *looks on from* C.]

FLUTHER: What's undher it? [*Reading slowly*] "Georgina: The Sleeping Vennis." Oh, that's a terrible picture. . . . Oh, that's a shockin' picture! [*Peering into it with evident pleasure*] Oh, the one that got that taken, she must ha' been a prime lassie!

PETER: [*Laughing in a silly way, with head tilted back*] Hee, hee, hee, hee, hee!

FLUTHER: [*Indignantly, to* Peter] What are you hee, hee-in' for? [*Pointing to the picture*] That's a nice thing to be hee, hee-in' at. Where's your morality, man?

MRS. GOGAN: [*Looking intently at it*] God forgive us, it's not right to be lookin' at it.

FLUTHER: It's nearly a derogatory thing to be in th' room where it is.

MRS. GOGAN: [*Giggling hysterically*] I couldn't stop any longer in th' same room with three men, afther lookin' at it! [Mrs. Gogan *goes upstage* L., *and out by door* L. *The* Covey, *who has taken off his dungarees, seeing* Peter's *shirt on the chair, throws dungarees over it with a contemptuous movement*]

PETER: [*Roused by the* Covey's *action*] Where are you throwin' your dungarees? Are you thryin' to twart an' torment me again?

THE COVEY: Who's thryin' to twart you?

[Peter *takes the dungarees from the back of the chair and flings them violently on floor*]

PETER: You're not goin' to make me lose me temper, me young covey!

[*The* Covey, *in retaliation, takes* Peter's *white shirt from the back of the chair, and flings it violently on the floor*]

THE COVEY: If you're Nora's pet aself, you're not goin' to get your own way in everything. [*The* Covey *moves to the back end of the table, enjoying* Peter's *anger*]

PETER: [*Plaintively, with his eyes looking up at the ceiling*] I'll say nothin'. . . . I'll leave you to th' day when th' all-pitiful, all-merciful, all-lovin' God'll be handin' you to th' angels to be rievin' an' roastin' you, tearin' an' tormentin' you, burnin' an' blastin' you!

THE COVEY: Aren't you th' little malignant oul' bastard, you lemon-whiskered oul' swine!

[Peter *rushes to the table, takes up the sword, draws it from its scabbard, and makes for the* Covey, *who runs round the table* R., *followed by* Peter]

THE COVEY: [*Dodging round the table—to* Fluther] Fluther, hold him, there. It's a nice thing

to have a lunatic, like this, lashing round with a lethal weapon! [*The* Covey, *after running round the table, rushes up* C., *and runs back of couch, out of door* L., *which he bangs to behind him in the face of* Peter. Fluther *remains near the fireplace, looking on*]

PETER: [*Hammering at the door—to the* Covey, *outside*] Lemme out, lemme out. Isn't it a poor thing for a man who wouldn't say a word against his greatest enemy to have to listen to that Covey's twartin' animosities, shovin' poor, patient people into a lashin' out of curses that darken his soul with th' shadow of th' wrath of th' last day!

FLUTHER: Why d'ye take notice of him? If he seen you didn't, he'd say nothin' derogatory.

PETER: I'll make him stop his laughin' an' leerin', jibin' an' jeerin' an' scarifyin' people with his cornerboy insinuations! . . . He's always thryin' to rouse me: if it's not a song, it's a whistle; if it isn't a whistle, it's a cough. But you can taunt an' taunt—I'm laughin' at you; he, hee, hee, hee, hee, heee!

THE COVEY: [*Jeering loudly through the keyhole*] Dear harp o' me counthry, in darkness I found thee, The dark chain of silence had hung o'er thee long—

PETER: [*Frantically to* Fluther] Jasus, d'ye hear that? D'ye hear him soundin' forth his divil-souled song o' provocation? [*Battering at door* L.] When I get out I'll do for you, I'll do for you, I'll do for you!

THE COVEY: [*Through the keyhole*] Cuckoo-oo!

[Nora *enters by door* L. *She is a young woman of 23, alert, swift, full of nervous energy, and a little anxious to get on in the world. The firm lines of her face are considerably opposed by a soft, amorous mouth, and gentle eyes. When her firmness fails her, she persuades with her feminine charm. She is dressed in a tailor-made costume, and wears around her neck a silver fox fur*]

NORA: [*Running in and pushing* Peter *away from the door*] Oh, can I not turn me back but th' two o' yous are at it like a pair o' fightin'-cocks! Uncle Peter . . . Uncle Peter . . . UNCLE PETER!

PETER: [*Vociferously*] Oh, Uncle Peter, Uncle Peter be damned! D'ye think I'm goin' to give a free pass to th' young Covey to turn me whole life into a Holy Manual o' penances an' martyrdoms?

THE COVEY: [*Angrily rushing into the room*] If you won't exercise some sort o' conthrol over that Uncle Peter o' yours, there'll be a funeral, an' it won't be me that'll be in th' hearse!

NORA: [C. *back, between* Peter *and the* Covey, *to the* Covey] Are yous always goin' to be tearin' down th' little bit of respectability that a body's thryin' to build up? Am I always goin' to be havin' to nurse yous into th' habit o' thryin' to keep up a little bit of appearance?

THE COVEY: Why weren't you here to see th' way he run at me with th' sword?

PETER: What did you call me a lemon-whiskered oul' swine for?

NORA: If th' two o' yous don't thry to make a generous altheration in your goin's on, an' keep on thryin' t' inaugurate th' customs o' th' rest o' th' house into this place, yous can flit into other lodgin's where your bowsey battlin' 'ill meet, maybe, with an encore.

[*The* Covey *comes down, back of couch to the fire, and sits down in the chair where* Peter's *shirt had hung; he takes a book from a pocket and begins to read*]

PETER: [*To* Nora] Would you like to be called a lemon-whiskered oul' swine?

[Nora *takes the sword from* Peter, *goes to the table, puts it back in the scabbard, goes to the chest of drawers, back* L., *and leaves it on the chest of drawers*]

NORA: [*To* Peter] If you attempt to wag that sword of yours at anybody again, it'll have to be taken off you, an' put in a safe place away from babies that don't know the danger of them things. [Nora *goes across back, taking off her hat and coat, which she leaves.* Peter *comes down* C., *takes up the shirt from the floor, and goes back* C. *towards room, back*]

PETER: [*At entrance to room, back*] Well, I'm not goin' to let anybody call me a lemon-whiskered oul' swine! [Peter *goes into room, back.* Fluther *moves from the fireplace,* L. *of couch, to door* L., *which he begins to open and shut, trying the movement*]

FLUTHER: [*Half to himself, half to* Nora] Openin' an' shuttin' now with a well-mannered motion, like a door of a select bar in a high-class pub.

[Nora *takes up the hat and coat from the table, carries them into the room, back, leaves them there, comes out, goes to the dresser, above table* R., *and puts a few tea things on the table*]

NORA: [*To the* Covey, *as she lays table for tea*] An', once for all, Willie, you'll have to thry to deliver yourself from th' desire to practice o' provokin' oul' Pether into a wild forgetfulness of what's proper an' allowable in a respectable home.

THE COVEY: Well, let him mind his own business, then. Yestherday, I caught him hee-hee-in' out of him an' he readin' bits out of Jenersky's *Thesis on th' Origin, Development an' Consolidation of th' Evolutionary Idea of th' Proletariat.*

NORA: Now, let it end at that, for God's sake; Jack'll be in any minute, an' I'm not goin' to have th' quiet of his evenin' tossed about in an everlastin' uproar between you an' Uncle Pether. [Nora *crosses back to* Fluther L., *and stands on his* R.]

NORA: [*To* Fluther] Well, did you manage to settle the lock yet, Mr. Good?

FLUTHER: [*Opening and shutting the door*] It's betther than a new one, now, Mrs. Clitheroe; it's almost ready to open and shut of its own accord.

NORA: [*Giving him a coin*] You're a whole man. How many pints will that get you?

FLUTHER: [*Seriously*] Ne'er a one at all, Mrs. Clitheroe, for Fluther's on th' wather waggon now. You could stan' where you're stannin' chantin', "Have a glass o' malt, Fluther; Fluther, have a glass o' malt," till th' bells would be ringin' th' ould year out an' th' New Year in, an' you'd have as much chance o' movin' Fluther as a tune on a tin whistle would move a deaf man a' he dead.

[*As* Nora *is opening and shutting the door,* Mrs. Bessie Burgess *appears at it. She is a woman of 40, vigorously built. Her face is a dogged one, hardened by toil, and a little coarsened by drink. She looks scornfully and viciously at* Nora *for a few moments before she speaks*]

BESSIE: Puttin' a new lock on her door . . . afraid her poor neighbours ud break through an' steal. . . . [*In a loud tone*] Maybe, now, they're a damn sight more honest than your ladyship . . . checkin' th' children playin' on th' stairs . . . gettin' on th' nerves of your ladyship. . . . Complainin' about Bessie Burgess singin' her hymns at night, when she has a few up. . . . [*She comes in half-way on the threshold, and screams*] Bessie Burgess 'll sing whenever she damn well likes!

[Nora *tries to shut the door, but* Bessie *violently shoves it in, and, gripping* Nora *by the shoulders, shakes her*]

BESSIE: [*Violently*] You little overdhressed throllope, you, for one pin, I'd paste th' white face o' you!

NORA: [*Frightened*] Fluther, Fluther!

FLUTHER: [*Breaking the hold of* Bessie *from* Nora] Now, now, Bessie, Bessie, leave poor Mrs. Clitheroe alone; she'd do no one any harm, an' minds no one's business but her own.

BESSIE: Why is she always thryin' to speak proud things, an' lookin' like a mighty one in th' congregation o' th' people!

[*The* Covey *looks up from his book, watches the encounter, but does not leave his seat by the fire.* Nora *sinks down on back of the couch.* Jack Clitheroe *enters by door,* L. *He is a tall, well-made fellow of 25. His face has none of the strength of* Nora's. *It is a face in which is the desire for authority, without the power to attain it*]

CLITHEROE: [*Excitedly*] What's up? What's afther happenin'?

FLUTHER: Nothin', Jack. Nothin'. It's all over now. Come on, Bessie, come on.

CLITHEROE: [*Coming to couch and bending over* Nora—*anxiously*] What's wrong, Nora? Did she say anything to you?

NORA: [*Agitatedly*] She was bargin' out of her, an' I only told her to go up ower that to her own place; an' before I knew where I was, she flew at me, like a tiger, an' tried to guzzle me.

[Clitheroe *goes close to* Bessie, *standing in*

*front of the chest of drawers, and takes hold
of her arm to get her away*]

CLITHEROE: Get up to your own place, Mrs.
Burgess, and don't you be interferin' with my wife,
or it'll be th' worse for you. . . . Go on, go on!

BESSIE: [*As* Clitheroe *is pushing her out*] Mind
who you're pushin', now. . . . I attend me place of
worship, anyhow. . . . Not like some of them that
go neither church, chapel or meetin' house. . . . If
me son was home from the threnches, he'd see me
righted.

[Fluther *takes* Bessie *by the arm, and brings
her out by the door L.* Clitheroe *closes the
door behind them, returns to* Nora, *and puts
his arm around her. The* Covey *resumes his
reading*]

CLITHEROE: [*His arm around her*] There, don't
mind that old bitch, Nora, darling; I'll soon put a
stop to her interferin'.

NORA: Some day or another, when I'm here be
meself, she'll come in an' do somethin' desperate.

CLITHEROE: [*Kissing her*] Oh, sorra fear of her
doin' anythin' desperate. I'll talk to her to-morrow
when she's sober. A taste o' me mind that'll shock
her into the sensibility of behavin' herself!

[Nora *gets up, crosses to the dresser R., and
finishes laying the table for tea. She catches
sight of the dungarees on the floor and speaks
indignantly to* Covey. Clitheroe *leaves his hat
on the chest of drawers, and sits, waiting for
tea, on the couch*]

NORA: [*To* Covey] Willie, is that the place for your
dungarees?

COVEY: [*Irritably rising, and taking them from the
floor*] Ah, they won't do the floor any harm, will
they? [*He carries them up C., into room back, comes
back again, down C., and sits by fire.* Nora *crosses
from the table to the fire, gets the teapot from the
hob, and returns to the table*]

NORA: [*To* Clitheroe *and* Covey] Tea's ready.

[Clitheroe *and* Covey *go to the table and sit
down L. of same,* Covey *nearest the audience.*
Nora *sits down on R. of table, leaving the
chair for* Peter *below, on same side*]

NORA: [*Calling towards room, back*] Uncle Peter,
Uncle Peter, tea's ready!

[Peter *comes in from room back.* Peter *is in the
full dress of the Irish National Foresters: bright
green, gold-braided coat, white breeches, black
top boots and frilled, white shirt. He carries a
large black slouch hat, from which waves a
long white ostrich plume, in his hand. He puts
the hat on the chest of drawers beside the
sword, he comes down C., goes round front
end of table, and sits on the vacant seat facing*
Covey *on opposite side of the table. They eat
for a few moments in silence, the* Covey
furtively watching Peter *with scorn in his eyes;*
Peter *knows this, and is fidgety*]

THE COVEY: [*Provokingly*] Another cut o' bread,
Uncle Peter? [Peter *maintains a dignified silence*]

CLITHEROE: It's sure to be a great meetin' to-night.
We ought to go, Nora.

NORA: [*Decisively*] I won't go, Jack; you can go
if you wish.

[*A pause*]

THE COVEY: [*With great politeness, to* Peter] D'ye
want th' sugar, Uncle Peter?

PETER: [*Explosively*] Now, are you goin' to start
your thryin' an' your twartin' again?

NORA: Now, Uncle Peter, you mustn't be so
touchy; Willie has only assed you if you wanted th'
sugar.

PETER: [*Angrily*] He doesn't care a damn whether
I want th' sugar or no. He's only thryin' to twart
me!

NORA: [*Angrily, to the* Covey] Can't you let him
alone, Willie? If he wants the sugar, let him stretch
his hand out an' get it himself!

THE COVEY: [*To* Peter] Now, if you want the
sugar, you can stretch out your hand and get it
yourself!

[*A pause*]

CLITHEROE: To-night is th' first chance that Brennan has got of showing himself off since they made
a Captain of him—why, God only knows. It'll be a
treat to see him swankin' it at th' head of the Citizen
Army carryin' th' flag of the Plough an' th' Stars.
. . . [*Looking roguishly at* Nora] He was sweet on
you, once, Nora?

NORA: He may have been. . . . I never liked him.
I always thought he was a bit of a thick.

THE COVEY: They're bringin' nice disgrace on that
banner now.

CLITHEROE: [*To* Covey, *remonstratively*] How are
they bringin' disgrace on it?

THE COVEY: [*Snappily*] Because it's a Labour flag,
an' was never meant for politics. . . . What does th'
design of th' field plough, bearin' on it th' stars of
th' heavenly plough, mean, if it's not Communism?
It's a flag that should only be used when we're
buildin' th' barricades to fight for a Workers' Republic!

PETER: [*With a puff of derision*] P-phuh.

THE COVEY: [*Angrily, to* Peter] What are you
phuhin' out o' you for? Your mind is th' mind of
a mummy. [*Rising*] I bebther go an' get a good place
to have a look at Ireland's warriors passin' by. [*He
goes into room L., and returns with his cap*]

NORA: [*To the* Covey] Oh, Willie, brush your
clothes before you go.

THE COVEY: [*Carelessly*] Oh, they'll do well
enough.

NORA: Go an' brush them; th' brush is in th'
drawer there.

[*The* Covey *goes to the drawer, muttering, gets
the brush, and starts to brush his clothes*]

THE COVEY: [*Reciting at* Peter, *as he does so*]
  Oh, where's the slave so lowly,

Condemn'd to chains unholy,
Who, could he burst his bonds at first,
Would pine beneath them slowly?
We tread th' land that . . . bore us,
Th' green flag glitters . . . o'er us,
Th' friends we've tried are by our side,
An' th' foe we hate . . . before us!

PETER: [*Leaping to his feet in a whirl of rage*] Now, I'm tellin' you, me young Covey, once for all, that I'll not stick any longer these tittherin' taunts of yours, rovin' around to sing your slights an' slandhers, reddenin' th' mind of a man to th' thinkin' an' sayin' of things that sicken his soul with sin! [*Hysterically; lifting up a cup to fling at the* Covey] Be God, I'll—

CLITHEROE: [*Catching his arm*] Now then, none o' that, none o' that!

NORA: [*Loudly*] Uncle Pether, Uncle Pether, UNCLE PETHER!

THE COVEY: [*At the door* L., *about to go out*] Isn't that th' malignant oul' varmint! Lookin' like th' illegitimate son of an illegitimate child of a corporal in th' Mexican army! [*He goes out door* L.]

PETER: [*Plaintively*] He's afther leavin' me now in such a state of agitation that I won't be able to do meself justice when I'm marchin' to th' meetin'.

[Nora *jumps up from the table, crosses back end of table to the chest of drawers, back, and takes up* Peter's *sword*]

NORA: Oh, for God's sake, here, buckle your sword on, an' go to your meetin', so that we'll have at least one hour of peace.

[Peter *gets up from the chair, goes over to* Nora, *and she helps him to put on his sword*]

CLITHEROE: For God's sake, hurry him up out o' this, Nora.

PETER: Are yous all goin' to thry to start to twart me now?

NORA: [*Putting on his plumed hat*] S-s-sh. Now, your hat's on, your house is thatched; off you pop! [*She gently pushes him from her, towards door* L.]

PETER: [*Going and turning as he reaches the door* L.] Now, if that young Covey—

NORA: Go on, go on. [*He goes out door* L.]

[Clitheroe *goes from the table to the couch and sits down on end nearest the fire, lights a cigarette, and looks thoughtfully into the fire.* Nora *takes things from the table, and puts them on the dresser. She goes into room, back, and comes back with a lighted shaded lamp, which she puts on the table. She then goes on tidying things on the dresser. Softly speaking over from the dresser, to* Clitheroe]

A penny for them, Jack.

CLITHEROE: Me? Oh, I was thinkin' of nothing.

NORA: You were thinkin' of th' . . . meetin' . . . Jack. When we were courtin' an' I wanted you to go, you'd say, "Oh, to hell with meetin's," an' that you felt lonely in cheerin' crowds when I was absent.

An' we weren't a month married when you began that you couldn't keep away from them.

CLITHEROE: [*Crossly*] Oh, that's enough about th' meetin'. It looks as if you wanted me to go th' way you're talkin'. You were always at me to give up the Citizen Army, an' I gave it up: surely that ought to satisfy you.

NORA: [*From dresser*] Aye, you gave it up, because you got the sulks when they didn't make a captain of you. [*She crosses over to* Clitheroe, *and sits on the couch to his* R.]

NORA: [*Softly*] It wasn't for my sake, Jack.

CLITHEROE: For your sake or no, you're benefitin' by it, aren't you? I didn't forget this was your birthday, did I? [*He puts his arms around her*] And you liked your new hat; didn't you, didn't you? [*He kisses her rapidly several times*]

NORA: [*Panting*] Jack, Jack; please, Jack! I thought you were tired of that sort of thing long ago.

CLITHEROE: Well, you're finding out now that I amn't tired of it yet, anyhow. Mrs. Clitheroe doesn't want to be kissed, sure she doesn't? [*He kisses her again*] Little, little red-lipped Nora!

NORA: [*Coquettishly removing his arm from around her*] Oh, yes, your little, little red-lipped Nora's a sweet little girl when th' fit seizes you; but your little, little red-lipped Nora has to clean your boots every mornin', all the same.

CLITHEROE: [*With a movement of irritation*] Oh, well, if we're goin' to be snotty! [*A pause*]

NORA: It's lookin' like as if it was you that was goin' to be . . . snotty! Bridlin' up with bitherness, th' minute a body attempts t'open her mouth.

CLITHEROE: Is it any wondher, turnin' a tendher sayin' into a meanin' o' malice an' spite!

NORA: It's hard for a body to be always keepin' her mind bent on makin' thoughts that'll be no longer than th' length of your own satisfaction.

[*A pause*]

NORA: [*Standing up*] If we're goin' to dhribble th' time away sittin' here like a pair o' cranky mummies, I'd be as well sewin' or doin' something about th' place.

[*She looks appealingly at him for a few moments; he doesn't speak. She swiftly sits down beside him, and puts her arms around his neck*]

NORA: [*Imploringly*] Ah, Jack, don't be so cross!

CLITHEROE: [*Doggedly*] Cross? I'm not cross; I'm not a bit cross. It was yourself started it.

NORA: [*Coaxingly*] I didn't mean to say anything out o' th' way. You take a body up too quickly, Jack. [*In an ordinary tone as if nothing of an angry nature had been said*] You didn't offer me evenin' allowance yet.

[Clitheroe *silently takes out a cigarette for her and himself and lights both. Trying to make conversation*] How quiet th' house is now; they must be all out.

CLITHEROE: [*Rather shortly*] I suppose so.

NORA: [*Rising from the seat*] I'm longin' to show

you me new hat, to see what you think of it. Would you like to see it?

CLITHEROE: Ah, I don't mind.

[Nora *hesitates a moment, then goes up* C. *to the chest of drawers, takes the hat out of the box, comes down* C., *stands front of the couch, looks into the mirror on the wall below the fireplace, and fixes hat on her head. She then turns to face* Clitheroe]

NORA: Well, how does Mr. Clitheroe like me new hat?

CLITHEROE: It suits you, Nora, it does right enough. [*He stands up, puts his hand beneath her chin, and tilts her head up. She looks at him roguishly. He bends down and kisses her*]

NORA: Here, sit down, an' don't let me hear another cross word out of you for th' rest o' the night. [*The two sit on the couch again,* Clitheroe *nearest the fire*]

CLITHEROE: [*His arms round* Nora] Little red-lipped Nora.

NORA: [*With a coaxing movement of her body towards him*] Jack!

CLITHEROE: [*Tightening his arms around her*] Well?

NORA: You haven't sung me a song since our honeymoon. Sing me one now, do . . . please, Jack!

CLITHEROE: What song? "Since Maggie Went Away"?

NORA: Ah, no, Jack, not that; it's too sad. "When You Said You Loved Me."

[*Clearing his throat,* Clitheroe *thinks for a moment, and then begins to sing.* Nora, *putting an arm around him, nestles her head on his breast and listens delightedly*]

CLITHEROE: [*Singing verses following to the air of "When You and I Were Young, Maggie"*]

Th' violets were scenting th' woods, Nora,
    Displaying their charm to th' bee,
When I first said I lov'd only you, Nora,
    An' you said you lov'd only me!

Th' chestnut blooms gleam'd through th' glade, Nora,
    A robin sang loud from a tree,
When I first said I lov'd only you, Nora
    An' you said you lov'd only me!

Th' golden-rob'd daffodils shone, Nora,
    An' danc'd in th' breeze on th' lea;
When I first said I lov'd only you, Nora,
    An' you said you lov'd only me!

Th' trees, birds an' bees sang a song, Nora,
    Of happier transports to be,
When I first said I lov'd only you, Nora,
    An' you said you lov'd only me!

[Nora *kisses him. A knock is heard at the door,* R.; *a pause as they listen.* Nora *clings closely to* Clitheroe. *Another knock, more imperative than the first*] I wonder who can that be, now?

NORA: [*A little nervous*] Take no notice of it, Jack; they'll go away in a minute.

[*Another knock, followed by the voice of Captain Brennan*]

THE VOICE OF CAPT. BRENNAN: Commandant Clitheroe, Commandant Clitheroe, are you there? A message from General Jim Connolly.

CLITHEROE: [*Taking her arms from round him*] Damn it, it's Captain Brennan.

NORA: [*Anxiously*] Don't mind him, don't mind, Jack. Don't break our happiness. . . . Pretend we're not in. . . . Let us forget everything to-night but our two selves!

CLITHEROE: [*Reassuringly*] Don't be alarmed, darling; I'll just see what he wants, an' send him about his business.

NORA: [*Tremulously—putting her arms around him*] No, no. Please, Jack; don't open it. Please, for your own little Nora's sake!

CLITHEROE: [*Taking her arms away and rising to open the door*] Now don't be silly, Nora. [Clitheroe *opens door, and admits a young man in the full uniform of the Irish Citizen Army—green suit; slouch green hat caught up at one side by a small Red Hand badge; Sam Browne belt, with a revolver in the holster. He carries a letter in his hand. When he comes in he smartly salutes* Clitheroe. *The young man is* Captain Brennan. *He stands in front of the chest of drawers*]

CAPT. BRENNAN: [*Giving the letter to* Clitheroe] A dispatch from General Connolly.

CLITHEROE: [*Reading. While he is doing so,* Brennan's *eyes are fixed on* Nora, *who droops as she sits on the lounge*] "Commandant Clitheroe is to take command of the eighth battalion of the I.C.A. which will assemble to proceed to the meeting at nine o'clock. He is to see that all units are provided with full equipment: two day's rations and fifty rounds of ammunition. At two o'clock A.M. the army will leave Liberty Hall for a reconnaissance attack on Dublin Castle.—Com.-Gen. Connolly."

CLITHEROE: [*In surprise, to* Capt. Brennan] I don't understand this. Why does General Connolly call me Commandant?

CAPT. BRENNAN: Th' Staff appointed you Commandant, and th' General agreed with their selection.

CLITHEROE: When did this happen?

CAPT. BRENNAN: A fortnight ago.

CLITHEROE: How is it word was never sent to me?

CAPT. BRENNAN: Word was sent to you. . . . I meself brought it.

CLITHEROE: Who did you give it to, then?

CAPT. BRENNAN: [*After a pause*] I think I gave it to Mrs. Clitheroe, there.

CLITHEROE: Nora, d'ye hear that? [Nora *makes no answer. Standing* C.—*there is a note of hardness in his voice*] Nora . . . Captain Brennan says he brought a letter to me from General Connolly, and that he gave it to you. . . . Where is it? What did you do with it?

[*Capt. Brennan stands in front of the chest of drawers, and softly whistles "The Soldiers' Song"*]

NORA: [*Running over to him, and pleadingly putting her arms around him*] Jack, please Jack, don't go out to-night an' I'll tell you; I'll explain everything. . . . Send him away, an' stay with your own little red-lipp'd Nora.

CLITHEROE: [*Removing her arms from around him*] None o' this nonsense, now; I want to know what you did with th' letter? [*Nora goes slowly to the couch and sits down again. Angrily*] Why didn't you give me th' letter? What did you do with it? . . . [*Goes over and shakes her by the shoulder*] What did you do with th' letter?

NORA: [*Flaming up and standing on her feet*] I burned it, I burned it! That's what I did with it! Is General Connolly an' th' Citizen Army goin' to be your only care? Is your home goin' to be only a place to rest in? Am I goin' to be only somethin' to provide merrymakin' at night for you? Your vanity 'll be th' ruin of you an' me yet. . . . That's what's movin' you: because they've made an officer of you, you'll make a glorious cause of what you're doin', while your little red-lipp'd Nora can go on sittin' here, makin' a companion of th' loneliness of th' night!

CLITHEROE: [*Fiercely*] You burned it, did you? [*He grips her arm*] Well, me good lady—

NORA: Let go—you're hurtin' me!

CLITHEROE: You deserve to be hurt. . . . Any letther that comes to me for th' future, take care that I get it. . . . D'ye hear—take care that I get it! [*He lets her go, and she sinks down, crying on the couch. He goes to the chest of drawers and takes out a Sam Browne belt, which he puts on, and then puts a revolver in the holster. He puts on his hat, and looks towards Nora. At door L., about to go out*] You needn't wait up for me; if I'm in at all, it won't be before six in th' morning.

NORA: [*Bitterly*] I don't care if you never came back!

CLITHEROE: [*To Capt. Brennan*] Come along, Ned. [*They go out; there is a pause. Nora pulls the new hat from her head and with a bitter movement flings it to the other end of the room. There is a gentle knock at door L., which opens, and Mollser comes into the room. She is about 15, but looks to be only about 10, for the ravages of consumption have shrivelled her up. She is pitifully worn, walks feebly, and frequently coughs. She goes over and sits down L. of Nora*]

MOLLSER: [*To Nora*] Mother's gone to th' meetin', an' I was feelin' terrible lonely, so I come down to see if you'd let me sit with you, thinkin' you mightn't be goin' yourself. . . . I do be terrible afraid I'll die sometime when I'm be meself. . . . I

often envy you, Mrs. Clitheroe, seein' th' health you have, an' th' lovely place you have here, an' wonderin' if I'll ever be sthrong enough to be keepin' a home together for a man.

[*The faint sound of a band playing is heard in the distance outside in the street*]

MOLLSER: Oh this must be some more of the Dublin Fusiliers flyin' off to the front.

[*The band, passing in the street outside, is now heard loudly playing as they pass the house. It is the music of a brass band playing a regiment to the boat on the way to the front. The tune that is being played is "It's a Long Way to Tipperary"; as the band comes to the chorus, the regiment is swinging into the street by Nora's house, and the voices of the soldiers can be heard lustily singing the chorus of the song*]

It's a long way to Tipperary, it's a long
    way to go;
It's a long way to Tipperary, to th'
    sweetest girl I know!
Good-bye, Piccadilly, farewell Leicester
    Square.
It's a long way to Tipperary, but my
    heart's right there!

[*Nora and Mollser remain silently listening. As the chorus ends, and the music is faint in the distance again, Bessie Burgess appears at door L., which Mollser has left open*]

BESSIE: [*Speaking in towards the room*] There's th' men marchin' out into th' dhread dimness o' danger, while th' lice is crawlin' about feedin' on th' fatness o' the land! But yous'll not escape from th' arrow that flieth be night, or th' sickness that wasteth be day. . . . An' ladyship an' all, as some o' them may be, they'll be scaththered abroad, like th' dust in th' darkness! [*Bessie goes away; Nora steals over and quietly shuts the door. She comes back to the lounge and wearily throws herself on it beside Mollser*]

MOLLSER: [*After a pause and a cough*] Is there anybody goin', Mrs. Clitheroe, with a titther o' sense?

ACT II.

SCENE—*A public-house at the corner of the street in which the meeting is being addressed from Platform No. 1. One end of the house is visible to the audience. Part of the counter at the back, L., extending out towards L., occupies one-third of the width of the scene from R. to L. On the counter are glasses, beer-pulls, and a carafe filled with water. Behind the counter, on the back wall, are shelves containing bottles of wine, whisky and beer. At back C. is a wide, high, plate-glass window. Under the window is a seat to hold three or four persons seated.* L. *are the wide swing-doors. At wall,* R., *is a seat to hold two persons. A few gaudy-coloured show-cards on the walls. A band is heard outside playing "The Soldiers' Song," before the* Curtain *rises, and for a few moments afterwards, accompanied by the sounds of marching men. The* Barman *is seen wiping the part of the counter which is in view.* Rosie Redmond *is standing at the counter toying with what remains of a half of whisky in a wine-glass. She is a sturdy well-shaped girl of 20; pretty and pert in manner. She is wearing a cream blouse, with an obviously suggestive glad neck; a grey tweed dress, brown stockings and shoes. The blouse and most of the dress are hidden by a black shawl. She has no hat, and in her hair is jauntily set a cheap, glittering, jewelled ornament. It is an hour later.*

BARMAN: [*Wiping counter*] Nothin' much doin' in your line to-night, Rosie?

ROSIE: Curse o' God on th' haporth, hardly, Tom. There isn't much notice taken of a pretty petticoat of a night like this. . . . They're all in a holy mood. Th' solemn-lookin' dials on th' whole o' them an' they marchin' to th' meetin'. You'd think they were th' glorious company of th' saints, an' th' noble army of martyrs thrampin' through th' streets of Paradise. They're all thinkin' of higher things than a girl's garthers. . . . It's a tremendous meetin'; four platforms they have—there's one o' them just outside opposite th' window.

BARMAN: Oh, ay; sure when th' speaker comes [*Motioning with his hand*] to th' near end, here, you can see him plain, an' hear nearly everythin' he's spoutin' out of him.

ROSIE: It's no joke thryin' to make up fifty-five shillin's a week for your keep an' laundhry, an' then taxin' you a quid for your own room if you bring home a friend for th' night. . . . If I could only put by a couple of quid for a swankier outfit, everythin' in th' garden ud look lovely—

[*In the window, back, appears the figure of a tall man, who, standing on a platform, is addressing a crowd outside. The figure is almost like a silhouette. The* Barman *comes to* L. *end of counter to listen, and* Rosie *moves* C. *to see and listen too*]

BARMAN: [*To* Rosie] Whisht, till we hear what he's sayin'.

THE VOICE OF THE MAN: It is a glorious thing to see arms in the hands of Irishmen. We must accustom ourselves to the thought of arms, we must accustom ourselves to the sight of arms, we must accustom ourselves to the use of arms. . . . Bloodshed is a cleansing and sanctifying thing, and the nation that regards it as the final horror has lost its manhood. . . . There are many things more horrible than bloodshed, and slavery is one of them!

[*The figure, moving towards* L., *passes the window, and is lost to sight and hearing. The* Bar-

man *goes back to wiping of the counter.* Rosie *remains looking out of the window*]

ROSIE: It's th' sacred thruth, mind you, what that man's afther sayin'.

BARMAN: If I was only a little younger, I'd be plungin' mad into th' middle of it!

ROSIE: [*Who is still looking out of the window*] Oh, here's th' two gems runnin' over again for their oil!

[*The doors* L. *swing open, and* Fluther *and* Peter *enter tumultuously. They are hot and hasty with the things they have seen and heard. They hurry across to the counter,* Peter *leading the way.* Rosie, *after looking at them listlessly for a moment, retires to the seat under the window, sits down, takes a cigarette from her pocket, lights it and smokes*]

PETER: [*Splutteringly to the* Barman] Two halves . . . [*To* Fluther] A meetin' like this always makes me feel as if I could dhrink Loch Erinn dhry!

FLUTHER: You couldn't feel anyway else at a time like this when th' spirit of a man is pulsin' to be out fightin' for th' thruth with his feet thremblin' on th' way, maybe to th' gallows, an' his ears tinglin' with th' faint, far-away sound of burstin' rifle-shots that'll maybe whip th' last little shock o' life out of him that's left lingerin' in his body!

PETER: I felt a burnin' lump in me throat when I heard th' band playin' "The Soldiers' Song," rememberin' last hearin' it marchin' in military formation, with th' people starin' on both sides at us, carrin' with us th' pride an' resolution o' Dublin to th' grave of Wolfe Tone.

FLUTHER: Get th' Dublin men goin' an' they'll go on full force for anything that's thryin' to bar them away from what they're wantin', where th' slim thinkin' counthry boyo ud limp away from th' first faintest touch of compromization!

PETER: [*Hurriedly to the* Barman] Two more, Tom! . . . [*To* Fluther] Th' memory of all th' things that was done, an' all th' things that was suffered be th' people, was boomin' in me brain. . . . Every nerve in me body was quiverin' to do somethin' desperate!

FLUTHER: Jammed as I was in th' crowd, I listened to th' speeches pattherin' on th' people's head, like rain fallin' on th' corn; every derogatory thought went out o' me mind, an' I said to meself, "You can die now, Fluther, for you've seen th' shadow-dhreams of th' last leppin' to life in th' bodies of livin' men that show, if we were without a tither o' courage for centuries, we're vice versa now!" Looka here. [*He stretches out his arm under* Peter's *face and rolls up his sleeve*] The blood was *boilin'* in me veins!

[*The silhouette of the tall figure again moves into the frame of the window, speaking to the people*]

PETER: [*Unaware, in his enthusiasm, of the*

speaker's appearance, to Fluther] I was burnin' to dhraw me sword, an' wave it over me—

FLUTHER: [*Overwhelming* Peter] Will you stop your blatherin' for a minute, man, an' let us hear what he's sayin'!

[*The* Barman *comes to* L. *end of the counter to look at the figure in the window; Rosie rises from the seat, stands and looks.* Fluther *and* Peter *move towards* C. *to see and listen*]

THE VOICE OF THE MAN: Comrade soldiers of the Irish Volunteers and of the Citizen Army, we rejoice in this terrible war. The old heart of the earth needed to be warmed with the red wine of the battlefields. . . . Such august homage was never offered to God as this: the homage of millions of lives given gladly for love of country. And we must be ready to pour out the same red wine in the same glorious sacrifice, for without shedding of blood there is no redemption!

[*The figure moves out of sight and hearing. Fluther runs back to the counter and gulps down the drink remaining in his glass; Peter does the same, less rapidly; the Barman leaves the end of the counter; Rosie sits on the seat again*]

FLUTHER: [*Finishing drink, to* Peter] Come on, man; this is too good to be missed! [*Fluther rushes across the stage and out by doors* L. Peter *wipes his mouth and hurries after* Fluther. *The doors swing open, and the* Covey *enters. He collides with* Peter C. Peter *stiffens his body, like a cock, and, with a look of hatred on his face, marches stiffly out by doors* L. *The* Covey *looks scornfully after* Peter, *and then crosses to the counter.* Rosie *sees possibilities in the* Covey, *gets up and comes to the counter, a little to the* L. *of the* Covey]

THE COVEY: [*To* Barman] Give us a glass o' malt, for God's sake, till I stimulate meself from the shock of seeing the sight that's afther goin' out.

ROSIE: [*Slyly, to the* Barman] Another one for me, Tommy; the young gentleman's ordherin' it in the corner of his eye.

[*The* Barman *gets a drink for the* Covey, *leaves it on the counter;* Rosie *whips it up. The Barman catches* Rosie's *arm, and takes glass from her, putting it down beside the* Covey]

BARMAN: [*Taking the glass from* Rosie] Eh, houl' on there, houl' on there, Rosie.

ROSIE: [*Angrily, to the* Barman] What are you houldin' on out o' you for? Didn't you hear th' young gentleman say that he couldn't refuse anything to a nice little bird? [*To the* Covey] Isn't that right, Jiggs? [*The* Covey *says nothing*] Didn't I know, Tommy, it would be all right? It takes Rosie to size a young man up, an' tell th' thoughts that are thremblin' in his mind. Isn't that right, Jiggs? [*The* Covey *stirs uneasily, moves a little farther away, and pulls his cap over his eyes. Moving after him*] Great meetin' that's gettin' held outside. Well, it's up to us all, anyway, to fight for our freedom.

THE COVEY: [*To the* Barman] Two more, please. [*To* Rosie] Freedom! What's th' use o' freedom, if it's not economic freedom?

ROSIE: [*Emphasizing with extended arm and moving finger*] I used them very words just before you come in. "A lot o' thricksters," says I, "that wouldn't know what freedom was if they got it from their mother." . . . [*To the* Barman] Didn't I, Tommy?

BARMAN: I disremember.

ROSIE: [*To the* Barman] No, you don't disremember. Remember you said, yourself, it was all "only a flash in th' pan." Well, "flash in th' pan, or no flash in th' pan," says I, "they're not goin' to get Rosie Redmond," says I, "to fight for freedom that wouldn't be worth winnin' in a raffle!"

THE COVEY: [*Contemptuously*] There's only one freedom for th' workin' man: conthrol o' th' means o' production, rates of exchange an' th' means of disthribution. [*Tapping* Rosie *on the shoulder*] Look here, comrade, I'll leave here to-morrow night for you a copy of Jenersky's *Thesis on the Origin, Development an' Consolidation of the Evolutionary Idea of th' Proletariat.*

ROSIE: [*Throwing off her shawl on to the counter, and showing an exemplified glad neck, which reveals a good deal of a white bosom*] If y'ass Rosie, it's heartbreakin' to see a young fella thinkin' of anything, or admirin' anything, but silk thransparent stockin's showin' off the shape of a little lassie's legs! [*The* Covey *is frightened, and moves away from* Rosie *along the counter, towards* R. Rosie *follows, gliding after him in a seductive way. Following him*] Out in th' park in th' shade of a warm summery evenin', with your little darlin' bridie to be, kissin' an' cuddlin' [*She tries to put her arm around his neck*] kissin' an' cuddlin', ay?

THE COVEY: [*Frightened*] Ay, what are you doin'? None o' that, now; none o' that. I've something else to do besides shinannickin' after Judies! [*The* Covey *turns to* L. *and moves slowly to* L., *away from* Rosie; *she turns with him, keeping him facing her, holding his arm. They move this way to* C.]

ROSIE: Oh, little duckey, oh, shy little duckey! Never held a mot's hand, an' wouldn't know how to tittle a little Judy! [*She clips him under the chin*] Tittle him undher th' chin, tittle him undher th' chin!

THE COVEY: [*Breaking away and running out by doors* L.] Aye, go on, now; I don't want to have any meddlin' with a lassie like you!

ROSIE: [*Enraged—returning to the seat at the window*] Jasus, it's in a monasthery some of us ought to be, spendin' our holidays kneelin' on our adorers, tellin' our beads an' knockin' hell out of our buzzums!

[*The voice of the* Covey *is heard outside doors* L. *calling in a scale of notes, "Cuckoo-ooooo." Then the swing-doors open, and* Peter *and* Fluther, *followed by* Mrs. Gogan, *come in.* Mrs. Gogan *carries a baby in her arms*]

PETER: [*In plaintive anger, looking towards the door* L.] It's terrible that young Covey can't let me pass without proddin' at me! Did you hear him murmurin' "cuckoo" when he were passin'?

FLUTHER: [*Irritably—to* Peter] I wouldn't be everlastin' cockin' me ear to hear every little whisper that was floatin' around about me! It's my rule never to lose me temper till it would be dethrimental to keep it. There's nothin' derogatory in th' use o' th' word "cuckoo," is there?

[Mrs. Gogan, *followed by* Peter, *go up to the seat under the window and sit down,* Peter *to the* R. *of* Mrs. Gogan. Rosie, *after a look at those who've come in, goes out by doors* L.]

PETER: [*Tearfully*] It's not the word, it's the way he says it! He never says it straight, but murmurs it with curious quiverin' ripples, like variations on a flute.

FLUTHER: [*Standing in front of the seat*] A' what odds if he gave it with variations on a thrombone? [*To* Mrs. Gogan] What's yours goin' to be, maam?

MRS. GOGAN: Ah, half a malt, Fluther.

[Fluther *goes from the seat over to the counter*]

FLUTHER: [*To the* Barman] Three halves, Tommy. [*The* Barman *gets the drinks, leaves them on the counter.* Fluther *pays the* Barman; *takes drinks to the seat under the window; gives one to* Mrs. Gogan, *one to* Peter, *and keeps the third for himself. He then sits on the seat to the* L. *of* Mrs. Gogan]

MRS. GOGAN: [*Drinking, and looking admiringly at* Peter's *costume*] The Foresthers' is a gorgeous dhress! I don't think I've seen nicer, mind you, in a pantomine. . . . Th' loveliest part of th' dhress, I think, is th' osthrichess plume. . . . When yous are goin' along, an' I see them wavin' an' noddin' an' waggin', I seem to be lookin' at each of yous hangin' at th' end of a rope, your eyes bulgin' an' your legs twistin' an' jerkin', gaspin' an' gaspin' for breath while yous are thryin' to die for Ireland!

FLUTHER: [*Scornfully*] If any o' them is ever hangin' at the end of a rope, it won't be for Ireland!

PETER: Are you goin' to start th' young Covey's game o' proddin' an' twartin' a man? There's not many that's talkin' can say that for twenty-five years he never missed a pilgrimage to Bodenstown!

FLUTHER: [*Looking angrily at* Peter] You're always blowin' about goin' to Bodenstown. D'ye think no one but yourself ever went to *Bodenstown?* [Fluther *emphasizes the word* "Bodenstown"]

PETER: [*Plaintively*] I'm not blowin' about it; but there's not a year that I go there but I pluck a leaf off Tone's grave, an' this very day me prayer-book is nearly full of them.

FLUTHER: [*Scornfully*] Then Fluther has a vice-versa opinion of them that put ivy leaves into their prayer-books, scabbin' it on th' clergy, an' thryin' to out-do th' haloes o' th' saints be lookin' as if he was wearin' around his head a glitherin' aroree boree allis! [*Fiercely*] Sure, I don't care a damn if

you slep' in *Bodenstown!* You can take your breakfast, dinner an' tea on th' grave, in Bodenstown, if you like, for Fluther!

MRS. GOGAN: Oh, don't start a fight, boys, for God's sake; I was only sayin' what a nice costume it is—nicer than th' kilts, for, God forgive me, I always think th' kilts is hardly decent.

FLUTHER: [*Laughing scornfully*] Ah, sure when you'd look at him, you'd wondher whether th' man was makin' fun o' th' costume, or th' costume was makin' fun o' th' man!

BARMAN: [*Over to them*] Now, then, thry to speak asy, will yous? We don't want no shoutin' here.

[*The swing-doors open and the* Covey, *followed by* Bessie Burgess, *come in. They go over and stand at the counter. Passing,* Bessie *gives a scornful look at those seated near the window.* Bessie *and the* Covey *talk together, but frequently eye the group at the window*]

COVEY: [*To the* Barman] Two glasses o' malt.

[*The* Barman *gets the drinks; leaves them on the counter. The* Covey *puts one beside* Bessie *and keeps the other. He pays the* Barman]

PETER: [*Plaintively*] There he is now—I knew he wouldn't be long till he folleyed me in.

BESSIE: [*Speaking to the* Covey, *but really at the other party*] I can't for th' life o' me undherstand how they can call themselves Catholics when they won't lift a finger to help poor little Catholic Belgium.

MRS. GOGAN: [*Raising her voice*] What about poor little Catholic Ireland?

BESSIE: [*Over to* Mrs. Gogan] You mind your own business, maam, an' stupify your foolishness be gettin' dhrunk.

PETER: [*Anxiously—to* Mrs. Gogan] Take no notice of her; pay no attention to her. She's just tormentin' herself towards havin' a row with somebody.

BESSIE: [*In a quiet anger*] There's a storm of anger tossin' in me heart, thinkin' of all th' poor Tommies, an' with them me own son, dhrenched in water an' soaked in blood, gropin' their way to a shatherin' death, in a shower o' shells! Young men with th' sunny lust o' life beamin' in them, layin' down their white bodies, shredded into torn an' bloody pieces, on th' altar that God Himself has built for th' sacrifice of heroes!

MRS. GOGAN: [*Indignantly*] Isn't it a nice thing to have to be listenin' to a lassie an' hangin' our heads in a dead silence, knowin' that some persons think more of a ball of malt than they do of th' blessed saints.

FLUTHER: [*Deprecatingly*] Whisht; she's always dangerous an' derogatory when she's well oiled. Th' safest way to hindher her from havin' any enjoyment out of her spite, is to dip our thoughts into the fact of her bein' a female person that has moved out of th' sight of ordinary sensible people.

BESSIE: [*Over to* Mrs. Gogan, *viciously*] To look

at some o' th' women that's knockin' about, now, is a thing to make a body sigh. . . . A woman on her own, dhrinkin' with a bevy o' men is hardly an example to her sex. . . . A woman dhrinkin' with a woman is one thing, an' a woman dhrinkin' with herself is still a woman—flappers may be put in another category altogether—but a middle-aged married woman makin' herself th' centre of a circle of men is as a woman that is loud an' stubborn, whose feet abideth not in her own house.

THE COVEY: [*To* Bessie—*with a scornful look at* Peter] When I think of all th' problems in front o' th' workers, it makes me sick to be lookin' at oul' codgers goin' about dhressed up like green-accoutered figures gone asthray out of a toyshop!

PETER: [*Angrily*] Gracious God, give me patience to be listenin' to that blasted young Covey proddin' at me from over at th' other end of th' shop!

MRS. GOGAN: [*Dipping her finger in the whisky, and moistening with it the lips of her baby*] Cissie Gogan's a woman livin' for nigh on twenty-five years in her own room, an' beyond biddin' th' time o' day to her neighbours, never yet as much as nodded her head in th' direction of other people's business, while she knows some [*With a look at* Bessie] as are never content unless they're standin' senthry over other people's doin's!

[*Again the figure appears, like a silhouette, in the window, back, and all hear the voice of the speaker declaiming passionately to the gathering outside.* Fluther, Peter *and* Mrs. Gogan *stand up, turn, and look towards the window. The* Barman *comes to the end of the counter;* Bessie *and the* Covey *stop talking, and look towards the window*]

THE VOICE OF THE SPEAKER: The last sixteen months have been the most glorious in the history of Europe. Heroism has come back to the earth. War is a terrible thing, but war is not an evil thing. People in Ireland dread war because they do not know it. Ireland has not known the exhilaration of war for over a hundred years. When war comes to Ireland she must welcome it as she would welcome the Angel of God!

[*The figure passes out of sight and hearing,* L.]

THE COVEY: [*Towards all present*] Dope, dope. There's only one war worth havin': th' war for th' economic emancipation of th' proletariat.

BESSIE: [*Referring to* Mrs. Gogan] They may crow away out o' them; but it ud be fitther for some o' them to mend their ways an' cease from havin' scouts out watchin' for th' comin' of th' Saint Vincent de Paul man, for fear they'd be nailed lowerin' a pint of beer, mockin' th' man with an angel face, shinin' with th' glamour of deceit an' lies!

MRS. GOGAN: [*Over to* Bessie] An' a certain lassie standin' stiff behind her own door with her ears cocked listenin' to what's being said, stuffed till she's sthrained with envy of a neighbour thryin' for a few little things that may be got be hard sthrivin' to keep up to th' letther an' th' law, an' th' practices of th' Church!

PETER: [*To* Mrs. Gogan] If I was you, Mrs. Gogan, I'd parry her jabbin' remarks be a powerful silence that'll keep her tantalizin' words from penethratin' into your feelin's. It's always betther to leave these people to th' vengeance o' God!

BESSIE: [*At the counter*] Bessie Burgess doesn't put up to know much, never havin' a swaggerin' mind, thanks be to God, but goin' on packin' up knowledge accordin' to her conscience: precept upon precept, line upon line; here a little, an' there a little. [Bessie, *with a vigorous swing of her shawl, turns, and with a quick movement goes* C., *facing* Mrs. Gogan. *Furiously*] But, thanks be to Christ, she knows when she was got, where she was got, an' how she was got; while there's some she knows, decoratin' their finger with a well-polished weddin' ring, would be hard put to it if they were assed to show their weddin' lines!

[Mrs. Gogan *springs up from the seat and bounces to* C., *facing* Bessie Burgess. Mrs. Gogan *is wild with anger*]

MRS. GOGAN: [*With hysterical rage*] Y' oul' rip of a blasted liar, me weddin' ring's been well earned be twenty years be th' side o' me husband, now takin' his rest in heaven, married to me be Father Dempsey, in th' Chapel o' Saint Jude's, in th' Christmas Week of eighteen hundred an' ninety-five; an' any kid, livin' or dead, that Jinnie Gogan's had since, was got between th' bordhers of th' Ten Commandments! . . .

BESSIE: [*Bringing the palms of her hands together in sharp claps to emphasize her remarks*] Liar to you, too, maam, y' oul' hardened thresspasser on other people's good nature, wizenin' up your soul in th' arts o' dodgeries, till every dhrop of respectability in a female is dhried up in her, lookin' at your ready-made manœuverin' with th' menkind!

BARMAN: [*Anxiously leaning over the counter*] Here, there; here, there; speak asy there. No rowin' here, no rowin' here, now.

[Fluther *comes from the seat, gets in front of* Mrs. Gogan, *and tries to pacify her;* Peter *leaves the seat, and tries to do the same with* Bessie, *holding her back from* Mrs. Gogan. *The positions are:* Barman *behind the counter, leaning forward;* Bessie R., *next* Peter; *next* Fluther; *next* Mrs. Gogan, *with baby in her arms. The* Covey *remains leaning on the counter, looking on*]

FLUTHER: [*Trying to calm* Mrs. Gogan] Now, Jinnie, Jinnie, it's a derogatory thing to be smirchin' a night like this with a row; it's rompin' with th' feelin's of hope we ought to be, instead o' bein' vice versa!

PETER: [*Trying to quiet* Bessie] I'm terrible dawny, Mrs. Burgess, an' a fight leaves me weak for a long time afterwards. . . . Please, Mrs. Burgess, before there's damage done, thry to have a little respect for yourself.

BESSIE: [*With a push of her hand that sends* Peter *tottering to the end of the counter*] G'way, you little sermonizing, little yella-faced, little consequential, little pudgy, little bum, you!

MRS. GOGAN: [*Screaming and struggling*] Fluther, leggo! I'm not goin' to keep an unresistin' silence, an' her scatherin' her festherin' words in me face, stirrin' up every dhrop of decency in a respectable female, with her restless rally o' lies that would make a saint say his prayer backwards!

BESSIE: [*Shouting*] Ah, everybody knows well that th' best charity that can be shown to you is to hide th' thruth as much as our thrue worship of God Almighty will allow us!

MRS. GOGAN: [*Frantically*] Here, houl' th' kid, one o' yous; houl' th' kid for a minute! There's nothin' for it but to show this lassie a lesson or two. . . . [*To* Peter] Here, houl' th' kid, you. [Mrs. Gogan *suddenly rushes over to* Peter, *standing, trembling with fear, between the end of the counter and the seat under the window. Bewildered, and before he's aware of it,* Mrs. Gogan *has put the baby in his arms.* Mrs. Gogan *rushes back* C. *and puts herself in a fighting attitude in front of* Bessie. *To* Bessie, *standing before her in a fighting attitude*] Come on, now, me loyal lassie, dyin' with grief for little Catholic Belgium! When Jinnie Gogan's done with you, you'll have a little leisure lyin' down to think an' pray for your king an' counthry!

BARMAN: [*Coming from behind the counter, getting between the women, and proceeding to push* Bessie *towards the door*] Here, now, since yous can't have a little friendly argument quietly, yous'll get out o' this place in quick time. Go on, an' settle your differences somewhere else—I don't want to have another endorsement on me licence. [*The* Barman *pushes* Bessie *towards the doors* L., Mrs. Gogan *following*]

PETER: [*Anxiously calling to* Mrs. Gogan] Here, take your kid back ower this. How nicely I was picked now for it to be plumped into my arms!

THE COVEY: [*Meaningly*] She knew who she was givin' it to, maybe.

[Peter *goes over near to the* Covey *at the counter to retort indignantly, as the* Barman *pushes* Bessie *out of the doors* L. *and gets hold of* Mrs. Gogan *to put her out too*]

PETER: [*Hotly to the* Covey] Now, I'm givin' you fair warnin', me young Covey, to quit firin' your jibes an' jeers at me. . . . For one o' these days, I'll run out in front o' God Almighty an' take your sacred life!

BARMAN: [*Pushing* Mrs. Gogan *out after* Bessie] Go on, now; out you go.

PETER: [*Leaving the baby down on the floor* C.] Ay, be Jasus, wait there, till I give her back her youngster! [Peter *runs to the door* L., *opens it, and calls out after* Mrs. Gogan]

PETER: [*Calling at the door* L.] Eh, there, eh! What about the kid? [*He runs back in,* C., *and looks at* Fluther *and the* Covey] There, she's afther goin' without her kid—what are we goin' to do with it now?

THE COVEY: [*Jeering*] What are *you* goin' to do with it? Bring it outside an' show everybody what you're afther findin'.

PETER: [*In a panic—to* Fluther] Pick it up, you, Fluther, an' run afther her with it, will you?

FLUTHER: [*With a long look at* Peter] What d'ye take Fluther for? You must think Fluther's a right gom. D'ye think Fluther's like yourself, destitute of a titther of undherstandin'?

BARMAN: [*Imperatively to* Peter] Take it up, man, an' run out afther her with it before she's gone too far. You're not goin' to leave th' bloody thing there, are you?

PETER: [*Plaintively, as he lifts up the baby*] Well, God Almighty, give me patience with all th' scorners, tormentors, an' twarters that are always an' ever thryin' to goad me into prayin' for their blindin' an' blastin' an' burnin' in th' world to come! [Peter, *with the baby, goes out of the door* L. Fluther *comes from the front of the window to the counter and stands there, beside the* Covey]

FLUTHER: [*With an air of relief*] God, it's a relief to get rid o' that crowd. Women is terrible when they start to fight. There's no holdin' them back. [*To the* Covey] Are you goin' to have anything?

THE COVEY: Ah, I don't mind if I have another half.

FLUTHER: [*To the* Barman] Two more, Tommy, me son. [*The* Barman *gets the drinks,* Fluther *pays*]

FLUTHER: [*To the* Covey] You know there's no conthrollin' a woman when she loses her head.

[Rosie *appears at the doors* L. *She looks over at the counter, sees the two men, then crosses over to the* L. *end of the counter, where she stands, with a suggestive look towards* Fluther]

ROSIE: [*To the* Barman] Divil a use o' havin' a thrim little leg on a night like this; things was never worse. . . . Give us a half till to-morrow, Tom, duckey.

BARMAN: [*Coldly*] No more to-night, Rosie; you owe me for three already.

ROSIE: [*Combatively*] You'll be paid, won't you?

BARMAN: I hope so.

ROSIE: You hope so! Is that th' way with you, now?

FLUTHER: [*With a long glance at* Rosie, *to the* Barman] Give her one—it'll be all right.

[*The* Barman *gets a drink, and puts it on the counter before* Rosie; Fluther *pays for it*]

ROSIE: [*Clapping* Fluther *on the back*] Oul' sport!

FLUTHER: [*To* Covey] Th' meetin' should be soon over, now.

THE COVEY: [*In a superior way*] Th' sooner th' betther. It's alla lot o' blasted nonsense, comrade.

FLUTHER: Oh, I wouldn't say it was all nonsense.

After all, Fluther can remember th' time, an' him only a dawny chiselur, bein' taught at his mother's knee to be faithful to th' Shan Vok Vok!

THE COVEY: That's all dope, comrade; th' sort o' thing that workers are fed on be th' Boorzwawzee.

FLUTHER: [*A little sharply*] What's all dope? Though I'm sayin' it that shouldn't: [*Catching his cheek with his hand, and pulling down the flesh from the eye*] d'ye see that mark there, undher me eye? . . . A sabre slice from a dragoon in O'Connell Street! [*Thrusting his head forward towards* Rosie] Feel that dint in th' middle o' me nut!

ROSIE: [*Rubbing* Fluther's *head, and winking at the* Covey] My God, there's a holla!

FLUTHER: [*Putting on his hat with quiet pride*] A skelp from a bobby's baton at a Labour meetin' in th' Phœnix Park!

THE COVEY: [*Sarcastically*] He must ha' hitten you in mistake. I don't know what you ever done for th' Labour movement.

FLUTHER: [*Loudly*] D'ye not? Maybe, then, I done as much, an' know as much about th' Labour movement as th' chancers that are blowin' about it!

BARMAN: [*Over the counter*] Speak easy, Fluther, thry to speak easy.

THE COVEY: [*Quietly*] There's no necessity to get excited about it, comrade.

FLUTHER: [*More loudly*] Excited? Who's gettin' excited? There's no one gettin' excited! It would take something more than a thing like you to flutther a feather o' Fluther. Blatherin', an', when all is said, you know as much as th' rest in th' wind up!

THE COVEY: [*Emphatically*] Well, let us put it to th' test, then, an' see what you know about th' Labour movement: what's the mechanism of exchange?

FLUTHER: [*Roaring, because he feels he is beaten*] How th' hell do I know what it is? There's nothin' about that in th' rules of our Thrades Union!

BARMAN: [*Protesting*] For God's sake, thry to speak easy, Fluther.

THE COVEY: What does Karl Marx say about th' Relation of Value to th' Cost o' Production?

FLUTHER: [*Angrily*] What th' hell do I care what he says? I'm Irishman enough not to lose me head be folloyin' foreigners!

BARMAN: Speak easy, Fluther.

THE COVEY: [*Contemptuously*] It's only waste o' time talkin' to you, comrade.

FLUTHER: Don't be comradin' me, mate. I'd be on me last legs if I wanted you for a comrade.

ROSIE: [*To the* Covey, *taking* Fluther's *part*] It seems a highly rediculous thing to hear a thing that's only an inch or two away from a kid, swingin' heavy words about he doesn't know th' meanin' of, an' uppishly thryin' to down a man like Misther Fluther here, that's well flavoured in th' knowledge of th' world he's livin' in.

THE COVEY: [*Bending over the counter—savagely to* Rosie] Nobody's askin' you to be buttin' in with

your prate. . . . I have you well taped, me lassie. . . . Just you keep your opinions for your own place. . . . It'll be a long time before th' Covey takes any insthructions or reprimandin' from a prostitute!

[Rosie, *wild with humiliation, bounds from the end of the counter to* C. *and with eyes blazing, faces towards the* Covey]

ROSIE: You louse, you louse, you! . . . You're no man. . . . You're no man . . . I'm a woman, anyhow, an' if I'm a prostitute aself, I have me feelin's. . . . Thryin' to put his arm around me a minute ago, an' givin' me th' glad eye, th' little wrigglin' lump o' desolation turns on me now, because he saw there was nothin' doin'. . . . You louse, you! If I was a man, or you were a woman, I'd bate th' puss o' you!

BARMAN: Ay, Rosie, ay! You'll have to shut your mouth altogether, if you can't learn to speak easy!

[Fluther, *with a dignified walk, goes over to* Rosie C. *and puts a hand on her shoulder*]

FLUTHER: [*To* Rosie] Houl' on there, Rosie; houl' on, there. There's no necessity to flutther yourself when you're with Fluther. . . . Any lady that's in th' company of Fluther is goin' to get a fair hunt. . . . This is outside your province. . . . I'm not goin' to let you demean yourself be talkin' to a tittherin' chancer. . . . Leave this to Fluther—this is a man's job. . . . [*He turns from* Rosie, *comes back, crosses the* Covey, *then turns and faces him. To the* Covey] Now, if you've anything to say, say it to Fluther; an' let me tell you, you're not goin' to be pass-remarkable to any lady in my company.

THE COVEY: Sure I don't care if you were runnin' all night afther your Mary o' th' Curlin' Hair, but, when you start tellin' luscious lies about what you done for th' Labour movement, it's nearly time to show y'up!

FLUTHER: [*Fiercely*] Is it you show Fluther up? G'way, man, I'd beat two o' you before me breakfast!

THE COVEY: [*Contemptuously*] Tell us where you bury your dead, will you?

FLUTHER: [*With his face stuck into the face of the* Covey] Sing a little less on th' high note, or, when I'm done with you, you'll put a Christianable consthruction on things, I'm tellin' you!

THE COVEY: You're a big fella, you are.

FLUTHER: [*Tapping the* Covey *threateningly on the shoulder*] Now, you're temptin' Providence when you're temptin' Fluther!

THE COVEY: [*Losing his temper, knocking* Fluther's *hands away, and bawling*] Easy with them hands, there, easy with them hands! You're startin' to take a little risk when you commence to paw the Covey!

[Fluther *suddenly springs into the* C. *of the shop, flings his hat into the corner, whips off his coat, and begins to paw the air like a pugilist*]

FLUTHER: [*Roaring*] Come on, come on, you

lowser; put your mitts up now, if there's a man's blood in you! Be God, in a few minutes you'll see some snots flyin' around, I'm tellin' you. . . . When Fluther's done with you, you'll have a vice-versa opinion of him! Come on, now, come on!

[*The* Covey *squares up to* Fluther]

BARMAN: [*Running from behind the counter and catching hold of the* Covey] Here, out you go, me little bowsey. Because you got a couple o' halves you think you can act as you like. [*He pushes the* Covey *to the doors* L] Fluther's a friend o' mine, an' I'll not have him insulted.

THE COVEY: [*Struggling with the* Barman] Ay, leggo, leggo there; fair hunt, give a man a fair hunt! One minute with him is all I ask; one minute alone with him, while you're runnin' for th' priest an' th' doctor!

FLUTHER: [*To the* Barman] Let him go, let him go, Tom: let him open th' door to sudden death if he wants to!

BARMAN: [*Grappling with the* Covey] Go on, out you go an' do th' bowsey somewhere else. [*The* Barman *pushes the* Covey *out by doors* L., *and goes back behind the counter.* Fluther *assumes a proud air of victory.* Rosie *gets his coat, and helps him to put it on; she then gets his hat and puts it on his head*]

ROSIE: [*Helping* Fluther *with his coat*] Be God, you put th' fear o' God in his heart that time! I thought you'd have to be dug out of him. . . . Th' way you lepped out without any of your fancy side-steppin'! "Men like Fluther," says I to myself, "is gettin' scarce nowadays."

FLUTHER: [*With proud complacency*, C.] I wasn't goin' to let meself be malignified by a chancer. . . . He got a little bit too derogatory for Fluther. . . . Be God, to think of a cur like that comin' to talk to a man like me!

ROSIE: [*Fixing on his hat*] Did j'ever!

FLUTHER: He's lucky he got off safe. I hit a man last week, Rosie, an' he's fallin' yet!

ROSIE: Sure, you'd ha' broken him in two if you'd ha' hitten him one clatther!

FLUTHER: [*Amorously, putting his arm around* Rosie] Come on into th' snug, me little darlin', an' we'll have a few dhrinks before I see you home.

ROSIE: Oh, Fluther, I'm afraid you're a terrible man for th' women.

[Fluther *leads* Rosie *to the seat with the round table in front,* R. *She sits down on the seat. He goes to the counter*]

FLUTHER: [*To the* Barman] Two, full ones, Tommy.

[Barman *gets the drinks.* Fluther *brings them over to seat* R., *leaves them on the table, and sits down beside* Rosie. *The swing-doors* L. *open and* Captain Brennan, Commandant Clitheroe, *and* Lieutenant Langon *enter, and cross quickly to the counter.* Capt. Brennan *carries the banner of* The Plough and the Stars, *and* Lieut. Langon *a green, white and*

orange Tricolour. *They are in a state of emotional excitement. Their faces are flushed and their eyes sparkle; they speak rapidly, as if unaware of the meaning of what they say. They have been mesmerized by the fervency of the speeches*]

CLITHEROE: [*Almost pantingly to the* Barman] Three glasses o' port!

[*The* Barman *brings the drinks,* Clitheroe *pays*]

CAPT. BRENNAN: We won't have long to wait now.

LIEUT. LANGON: Th' time is rotten ripe for revolution.

CLITHEROE: [*To* Lieut. Langon] You have a mother, Langon.

LIEUT. LANGON: Ireland is greater than a mother.

CAPT. BRENNAN: [*To* Clitheroe] You have a wife, Clitheroe.

CLITHEROE: Ireland is greater than a wife.

LIEUT. LANGON: Th' time for Ireland's battle is now—th' place for Ireland's battle is here.

[*The tall, dark figure again appears in the window. The three men stiffen to attention. They stand out from the* L. *of the counter,* Brennan *nearest counter, then* Clitheroe, *then* Lieut. Langon. Fluther *and* Rosie, *busy with each other, take no notice*]

THE VOICE OF THE MAN: Our foes are strong, but strong as they are, they cannot undo the miracles of God, who ripens in the heart of young men the seeds sown by the young men of a former generation. They think they have pacified Ireland; think they have foreseen everything; think they have provided against everything; but the fools, the fools, the fools!—they have left us our Fenian dead, and, while Ireland holds these graves, Ireland, unfree, shall never be at peace!

CAPT. BRENNAN: [*Lifting up the* Plough and the Stars] Imprisonment for th' Independence of Ireland!

LIEUT. LANGON: [*Lifting up the* Tri-colour] Wounds for th' Independence of Ireland!

CLITHEROE: Death for th' Independence of Ireland!

THE THREE: [*Together*] So help us God!

[*They lift their glasses and drink together. The "Assembly" is heard on a bugle outside. They leave their glasses on the counter, and hurry out by doors* L. *A pause. Then* Fluther *and* Rosie *rise from the seat, and start to go* L. Rosie *is linking* Fluther, *who is a little drunk. Both are in a merry mood*]

ROSIE: Are you afraid or what? Are you goin' to come home, or are you not?

FLUTHER: Of course I'm goin' home. What ud ail me that I wouldn't go?

ROSIE: [*Lovingly*] Come on, then, oul' sport.

OFFICER'S VOICE: [*Giving command outside*] Irish Volunteers, by th' right, quick march!

ROSIE: [*Putting her arm round* Fluther *and singing to the air "Twenty-four Strings to My Bow"*]

I once had a lover, a tailor, but he could do nothin'
    for me,

An' then I fell in with a sailor as strong an' as wild
as th' sea.
We cuddled an' kissed with devotion, till th' night
from th' mornin' had fled;
An' there, to our joy, a bright bouncin' boy
Was dancin' a jig in th' bed!
Dancin' a jig in th' bed, an' bawlin' for butther an'
bread.
An' there, to our joy, a bright bouncin' boy
Was dancin' a jig in th' bed!

[*They go out with their arms round each other*]

CLITHEROE'S VOICE: [*In command outside*] Dublin
Battalion of the Irish Citizen Army, by th' right,
quick march!

ACT III.

SCENE—*A corner house of a street of tenements;
exterior of house in which the Clitheroes live. It is a
tall, gaunt five-storey tenement. Its brick front is
dull from weather and age. It juts out from* L. *more
than half-way across stage, showing part of the front
elevation, with wide, heavy door, having windows
above and on both sides. The windows on* L., *looking
into the rooms of the Clitheroes, are hung with
good casement cloth. The others are draped with
grimy lace curtains. Stone steps lead from the door
to the path on the street. From these steps, on each
side of the door are railings to prevent anyone from
falling down the area. To the extreme* R. *the front
of another house is merely indicated by the side
aspect of a wall with steps leading from the door,
on which the wounded* Langon *rests later on in the
scene. Between the two runs a lane which, upstage,
turns to the* R. *At the corner of the lane, nearest the
house shown almost full front, is a street lamp.
As the house is revealed,* Mrs. Gogan *is seen helping* Mollser *to a chair, which stands on the path
beside the railings, at the* L. *side of the steps. She
then wraps a shawl around* Mollser's *shoulders. It is
some months later.*

MRS. GOGAN: [*Arranging shawl around* Mollser] Th'
sun'll do you all th' good in th' world. A few more
weeks o' this weather, an' there's no knowin' how
well you'll be. . . . Are you comfy, now?

MOLLSER: [*Weakly and wearily*] Yis, ma; I'm all
right.

MRS. GOGAN: [*Bending over her*] How are you
feelin'?

MOLLSER: Betther, ma, betther. If th' horrible
sinkin' feelin' ud go, I'd be all right.

MRS. GOGAN: Ah, I wouldn't put much pass on
that. Your stomach maybe's out of ordher. . . . Is
th' poor breathin' any betther, d'ye think?

MOLLSER: Yis, yis, ma; a lot betther.

MRS. GOGAN: Well, that's somethin' anyhow. . . .
With th' help o' God, you'll be on th' mend from
this out. . . . D'your legs feel any sthronger undher
you, d'ye think?

MOLLSER: [*Irritably*] I can't tell, ma. I think so.
. . . A little.

MRS. GOGAN: Well, a little aself is somethin'.
I thought I heard you coughin' a little more than
usual last night. . . . D'you think you were?

MOLLSER: I wasn't, ma, I wasn't.

MRS. GOGAN: I thought I heard you, for I was
kep' awake all night with th' shootin'. An' thinkin'
o' that madman, Fluther, runnin' about through th'
night lookin' for Nora Clitheroe to bring her back
when he heard she'd gone to folly her husband, an'
in dhread any minute he might come staggerin' in
covered with bandages, splashed all over with th'
red of his own blood, an' givin' us barely time to
bring th' priest to hear th' last whisper of his final
confession, as his soul was passin' through th' dark
doorway o' death into th' way o' th' wondherin'
dead. . . . You don't feel cold, do you?

MOLLSER: No, ma; I'm all right.

MRS. GOGAN: Keep your chest well covered, for
that's th' delicate spot in you . . . if there's any
danger, I'll whip you in again. . . . [Mrs. Gogan
crosses to R., *goes up the lane, turns and looks* R.,
as if looking down the street] Oh, here's the Covey
an' oul' Peter hurryin' along. [*She comes down the
lane, and crosses to* Mollser] God Almighty, sthrange
things is happenin' when them two is pullin' together. [*The* Covey *and* Peter *come into the lane* R.,
come down, and stand R.C. Mrs. Gogan *stands* C.,
*near the steps. The two men are breathless and ex-
cited. To the two men*] Were yous far up th' town?
Did yous see any sign o' Fluther or Nora? How is
things lookin'? I hear they're blazin' away out o' th'
G.P.O. That th' Tommies is sthretched in heaps
around Nelson's Pillar an' th' Parnell Statue, an'
that th' pavin' sets in O'Connell Street is nearly
covered be pools o' blood.

PETER: We seen no sign o' Nora or Fluther anywhere.

MRS. GOGAN: We should ha' held her back be
main force from goin' to look for her husband.
. . . God knows what's happened to her—I'm always seein' her sthretched on her back in some
hospital, moanin' with th' pain of a bullet in her
vitals, an' nuns thryin' to get her to take a last look
at th' crucifix!

THE COVEY: We can do nothin'. You can't stick
your nose into O'Connell Street, an' Tyler's is on fire.

PETER: An' we seen th' Lancers—

THE COVEY: [*Interrupting*] Throttin' along, heads
in th' air; spurs an' sabres jinglin', an' lances quiverin', an' lookin' as if they were assin' themselves,
"Where's these blighters, till we get a prod at them,"
when there was a volley from th' Post Office that
stretched half o' them, an' sent th' rest gallopin'
away wondherin' how far they'd have to go before
they'd feel safe.

PETER: [*Rubbing his hands*] "Damn it," says I to
meself, "this looks like business!"

THE COVEY: An' then out comes General Pearse

an' his staff, an', standin' in th' middle o' th' street, he reads th' Proclamation.

MRS. GOGAN: What proclamation?

PETER: Declarin' an Irish Republic.

MRS. GOGAN: [*With amazement*] Go to God!

PETER: The gunboat *Helga's* shellin' Liberty Hall, an' I hear that people livin' on th' quays had to crawl on their bellies to Mass with th' bullets that were flyin' around from Boland's Mills.

MRS. GOGAN: God bless us, what's goin' to be th' end of it all!

BESSIE: [*Opening and looking out of a window*] Maybe yous are satisfied now; maybe yous are satisfied now! Go on an' get guns if yous are men— Johnny get your gun, get your gun, get your gun! Yous are all nicely shanghaied now; th' boyo hasn't a sword on his thigh, now! Oh, yous are all nicely shanghaied now! [*She shuts down the window viciously*]

MRS. GOGAN: [*Warningly to* Peter *and the* Covey] S-s-sh, don't answer her. She's th' right oul' Orange bitch! She's been chantin' "Rule, Britannia" all th' mornin'.

PETER: I hope Fluther hasn't met with any accident, he's such a wild card.

THE COVEY: Fluther's well able to take care of himself.

MRS. GOGAN: [*Dolefully*] God grant it; but last night I dreamt I seen gettin' carried into th' house a sthretcher with a figure lyin' on it, stiff an' still, dhressed in th' habit of Saint Francis. An' then, I heard th' murmurs of a crowd no one could see sayin' th' litany for th' dead; an' then it got so dark that nothin' was seen but th' white face of th' corpse, gleamin' like a white wather lily floatin' on th' top of a dark lake. Then a tiny whisper thrickled into me ear, sayin', "Isn't the face very like th' face o' Fluther," an' then, with a thremblin' flutther, th' dead lips opened, an', although I couldn't hear, I knew they were sayin', "Poor oul' Fluther, afther havin' handin' in his gun at last, his shakin' soul moored in th' place where th' wicked are at rest an' th' weary cease from throublin'."

[*While* Mrs. Gogan *is speaking,* Peter *wanders up the lane, looks* R., *then stares; then puts on spectacles and looks again. He turns and shouts at* Mrs. Gogan *and the* Covey]

PETER: [*Shouting*] Here they are, be God, here they are; just afther turnin' the corner—Nora an' Fluther!

[*The* Covey *runs up the lane and looks* R. *with* Peter]

COVEY: She must be wounded or something— Fluther seems to be carryin' her.

[Fluther, *half carrying* Nora, *comes in* R.; Nora's *eyes are dim and hollow; her face pale and strained-looking; her hair is tossed and her clothes are dusty. They pass by* Covey *and* Peter, *come down the lane, and cross over to the door of the house* C. Peter *and the* Covey *follow, and stand* R. Mrs. Gogan *goes over*

solicitously to Nora. Nora *wears a brown mackintosh*]

MRS. GOGAN: [*Running over to them*] God bless us, is it wounded y'are, Mrs. Clitheroe, or what?

FLUTHER: [*Confidently*] Ah, she's all right, Mrs. Gogan; only worn out from thravellin' an' want o' sleep. A night's rest, now, an' she'll be as fit as a fiddle. Bring her in, an' make her lie down.

MRS. GOGAN: [*To* Nora] Did you hear e'er a whisper o' Mr. Clitheroe?

NORA: [*Wearily*] I could find him nowhere, Mrs. Gogan. None o' them would tell me where he was. They told me I shamed my husband an' th' women of Ireland be carryin' on as I was. . . . They said th' women must learn to be brave an' cease to be cowardly. . . . Me who risked more for love than they would risk for hate. . . . [*Raising her voice in hysterical protest*] My Jack will be killed, my Jack will be killed! . . . He is to be butchered as a sacrifice to th' dead! [Nora *sinks down on the steps at the door.* Bessie Burgess *opens the window, and shouts at them. They do not look at her*]

BESSIE: Yous are all nicely shanghaied now! Sorra mend the lassies who have been kissin' an' cuddlin' their boys into th' sheddin' of blood. Fillin' their minds with fairy tales that had no beginnin', but, please God, 'll have a bloody quick endin'! [*She shuts the window with a bang*]

FLUTHER: [*Losing control*] Y' ignorant oul' throllope, you!

MRS. GOGAN: [*Coaxingly, to* Nora] You'll find he'll come home safe enough to you, Mrs. Clitheroe. Afther all, there's a power o' women that's handed over sons an' husbands, to take a runnin' risk in th' fight they're wagin'.

NORA: I can't help thinkin' every shot fired 'll be fired at Jack, an' every shot fired at Jack 'll be fired at me. What do I care for th' others? I can think only of me own self. . . . An' there's no woman gives a son or a husband to be killed—if they say it, they're lyin', lyin', against God, Nature, an' against themselves! . . . One blasted hussy at a barricade told me to go home an' not be thryin' to dishearten th' men . . .

PETER: [*Unctuously*] You'll have to have patience, Nora. We all have to put up with twarthers an' tormentors in this world.

THE COVEY: If they were fightin' for anything worth while, I wouldn't mind.

FLUTHER: [*To* Nora] Nothin' derogatory 'll happen to Mr. Clitheroe. You'll find, now, in th' finish up, it'll be vice versa.

NORA: Oh, I know that wherever he is, he's thinkin' of wantin' to be with me. I know he's longin' to be passin' his hand through me hair, to be caressin' me neck, to fondle me hand an' to feel me kisses clingin' to his mouth. . . . An' he stands wherever he is because he's brave? [*Vehemently*] No, but because he's a coward, a coward, a coward!

MRS. GOGAN: Oh, they're not cowards anyway.

NORA: [*With denunciatory anger*] I tell you they're

afraid to say they're afraid! . . . Oh, I saw it, I saw it, Mrs. Gogan. . . . At th' barricade in North King Street I saw fear glowin' in all their eyes. . . . An' in th' middle o' th' sthreet was somethin' huddled up in a horrible tangled heap. . . . An' I saw that they were afraid to look at it. . . . I tell you they were afraid to look at it. . . . I tell you they were afraid, afraid, afraid!

MRS. GOGAN: [*Lifting her up from the steps*] Come on in, dear. If you'd been a little longer together the wrench asundher wouldn't have been so sharp.

NORA: [*Painfully ascending the steps, helped by* Mrs. Gogan] Th' agony I'm in since he left me has thrust away every rough thing he done, an' every unkind word he spoke; only th' blossoms that grew out of our lives are before me now; shakin' their colours before me face, an' breathin' their sweet scent on every thought springin' up in me mind, till, sometimes, Mrs. Gogan, sometimes I think I'm goin' mad!

MRS. GOGAN: You'll be a lot betther when you have a little lie down.

NORA: [*Turning toward* Fluther *as she is going in*] I don't know what I'd have done, only for Fluther. I'd have been lyin' in th' sthreets, only for him. . . . [*As she goes in*] They have dhriven away th' little happiness life had to spare for me. He has gone from me for ever, for ever. . . . Oh, Jack, Jack, Jack!

[*As* Nora *is led in,* Bessie *comes out. She passes down the steps with her head in the air; at the bottom she stops to look back. When they have gone in, she takes a mug of milk from under a shawl she is wearing and gives it to* Mollser *silently.* Mollser *takes it from her*]

FLUTHER: [*Going from* C. *to the* Covey *and* Peter, R.] Which of yous has the tossers?

THE COVEY: I have.

[Bessie *crosses from* Mollser *to* R. *She pauses at the corner of the lane,* R., *to speak to the two men*]

BESSIE: [*Scornfully, to* Fluther *and the* Covey] You an' your Leadhers, and their sham-battle soldiers has landed a body in a nice way, havin' to go an' ferret out a bit o' bread, God knows where. . . . Why aren't yous in the G.P.O., if yous are men? It's paler an paler yous are gettin'. . . . A lot of vipers—that's what the Irish people is! [Bessie *goes up the lane, turns* R., *and goes out*]

FLUTHER: [*Warningly*] Never mind her. [*To the* Covey] Make a start, an' keep us from th' sin of idleness. [*He crosses from* R. *to* Mollser *and speaks to her*] Well, how are you to-day, Mollser, oul' son? What are you dhrinkin'? Milk?

MOLLSER: Grand, Fluther, grand, thanks—yes, milk.

FLUTHER: [*To* Mollser] You couldn't get a betther thing down you. . . . This turnup has done one good thing, anyhow; you can't get dhrink anywhere, an' if it lasts a week I'll be so used to it that I won't

think of a pint. [Fluther *returns and joins the two men* R. *The* Covey *takes from his pocket two worn coins and a thin strip of wood (or tin) about four inches long. He puts the coins on the strip of wood and holds the strip out from him*]

THE COVEY: What's the bettin'?

PETER: Heads, a juice.

FLUTHER: Harps, a tanner.

[*The* Covey *flips the coins from the wood into the air. As they jingle on the ground the distant boom of a big gun is heard. They leave the coins where they are and listen intently*]

FLUTHER: [*Awed*] What th' hell's that?

THE COVEY: [*Awed*] It's like the boom of a big gun!

FLUTHER: Surely to God, they're not goin' to use artillery on us!

THE COVEY: [*Scornfully*] Not goin'! [*Vehemently*] Wouldn't they use anything on us, man?

FLUTHER: Aw, holy Christ, that's not playin' th' game!

PETER: [*Plaintively*] What would happen if a shell landed here now?

THE COVEY: [*Ironically*] You'd be off to heaven in a fiery chariot.

PETER: In spite of all th' warnin's that's ringin' around us, are you goin' to start your pickin' at me again?

FLUTHER: Go on, toss them again, toss them again. . . . Harps, a tanner.

PETER: Heads, a juice.

[*The* Covey *tosses the coins as before; they fall on the ground and roll a little.* Fluther *waves the other two back as they bend over the rolling coins*]

FLUTHER: Let them roll, let them roll—heads be God!

[Bessie *runs in* R., *runs downs the lane towards the three men. She is breathless with excitement. She has a new fox fur round her neck over her shawl, a number of new umbrellas under one arm, a box of biscuits under the other, and she wears a gaudily trimmed hat on her head. She speaks rapidly and breathlessly*]

BESSIE: They're breakin' into th' shops, they're breakin' into th' shops! Smashin' th' windows, batterin' in th' doors an' whippin' away everything! An' th' Volunteers is firin' on them. I seen two men an' a lassie pushin' a piano down th' street, an' th' sweat rollin' off them thryin' to get it up on th' pavement; an' an oul' wan that must ha' been seventy lookin' as if she'd dhrop every minute with th' dint o' heart beatin', thryin' to pull a big double bed out of a broken shop window! I was goin' to wait till I dhressed meself from th' skin out.

MOLLSER: [*To* Bessie, *as she is going into the house* C.] Help me in, Bessie; I'm feelin' curious.

[Bessie *leaves the looted things in the house, and, rapidly returning, helps* Mollser *in*]

THE COVEY: [*To* Fluther] Th' selfishness of that one—she waited till she got all she could carry before she'd come to tell anyone!

FLUTHER: [*Running over to the door of the house and shouting in to* Bessie] Ay, Bessie, did you hear of e'er a pub gettin' a shake up?

BESSIE: [*Inside*] I didn't hear o' none.

FLUTHER: [*In a burst of enthusiasm*] Well, you're goin' to hear of one soon!

THE COVEY: [*To* Fluther, *excitedly*] Come on, man, an' don't be wastin' time.

PETER: [*Calling to them as they run up the lane*] E, eh, are yous goin' to leave me here, alone?

[Fluther *and* Covey *halt in middle of lane, and turn to look and reply to* Peter]

FLUTHER: Are you goin' to leave yourself here?

PETER: [*Anxiously*] Didn't yous hear her sayin' they were firin' on them?

THE COVEY AND FLUTHER: [*Together*] Well?

PETER: Supposin' I happened to be potted?

FLUTHER: We'd give you a Christian burial, anyhow.

THE COVEY: [*Ironically*] Dhressed up in your regimentals.

PETER: [*To the* Covey, *passionately*] May th' alllovin' God give you a hot knock one o' these days, me young Covey, tuthorin' Fluther up now to be tiltin' at me, an' crossin' me with his mockeries an' jibin'!

[Fluther *and* Covey *run up the lane, and go off* R. Peter *looks after them and then goes slowly into the house,* C. *After a slight pause,* Mrs. Gogan *appears at the door of the house* C., *pushing a pram in front of her. As she gets the pram over the threshold* Bessie *appears, catches the pram, and stops* Mrs. Gogan's *progress*]

BESSIE: [*Angrily*] Here, where are you goin' with that? How quick you were, me lady, to clap your eyes on th' pram. . . . Maybe you don't know that Mrs. Sullivan, before she went to spend Easther with her people in Dunboyne, gave me sthrict injunctions to give an occasional look to see if it was still standin' where it was left in th' corner of th' lobby.

MRS. GOGAN: [*Indignantly*] That remark of yours, Mrs. Bessie Burgess, requires a little considheration, seein' that th' pram was left on our lobby, an' not on yours; a foot or two a little to th' left of th' jamb of me own room door; nor is it needful to mention th' name of th' person that gave a squint to see if it was there th' first thing in th' mornin', an' th' last thing in th' stillness o' th' night; never failin' to realize that her eyes couldn't be goin' wrong, be sthretchin' out her arm an' runnin' her hand over th' pram, to make sure that th' sight was no deception! Moreover, somethin' tellin' me that th' runnin' hurry of an inthrest you're takin' in it now is a sudden ambition to use th' pram for a purpose, that a loyal woman of law an' ordher would stagger away from! [Mrs. Gogan *pushes the pram violently down the steps, pulling* Bessie *with her, who holds her up again when they reach the street*]

BESSIE: [*Still holding the pram*] There's not as much as one body in th' house that doesn't know that it wasn't Bessie Burgess that was always shakin' her voice complainin' about people leavin' bassinettes in th' way of them that, week in an' week out, had to pay their rent, an' always had to find a regular accommodation for her own furniture in her own room. . . . An' as for law an' ordher, puttin' aside th' harp an' shamrock, Bessie Burgess 'll have as much respect as she wants for th' lion an' unicorn!

PETER: [*Appearing at the door of the house,* C.] I think I'll go with th' pair of yous an' see th' fun, A fella might as well chance it, anyhow.

MRS. GOGAN: [*Taking no notice of* Peter, *and pushing the pram on towards the lane*] Take your rovin' lumps o' hands from pattin' th' bassinette, if you please, ma'am; an', steppin' from th' threshold of good manners, let me tell you, Mrs. Burgess, that it's a fat wondher to Jennie Gogan that a lady-like singer o' hymns like yourself would lower her thoughts from sky-thinkin' to sthretch out her arm in a sly-seekin' way to pinch anything dhriven asthray in th' confusion of th' battle our boys is makin' for th' freedom of their counthry!

PETER: [*Laughing and rubbing his hands together*] Hee, hee, hee, hee, hee! I'll go with th' pair o' yous an' give yous a hand.

MRS. GOGAN: [*With a rapid turn of her head as she shoves the pram forward*] Get up in th' prambulator an' we'll wheel you down.

BESSIE: [*To* Mrs. Gogan *as she halts the pram again*] Poverty an' hardship has sent Bessie Burgess to abide with sthrange company, but she always knew them she had to live with from backside to breakfast time; an' she can tell them, always havin' had a Christian kinch on her conscience, that a passion for thievin' an' pinchin' would find her soul a foreign place to live in, an' that her present intention is quite th' lofty-hearted one of pickin' up anything shaken up an' scatthered about in th' loose confusion of a general plundher!

[Mrs. Gogan, Bessie *and the pram run up the lane and go off* R. Peter *follows, but as he reaches the corner of the lane the boom of the big guns brings him to a sudden halt*]

PETER: [*Frightened into staying behind by the sound of the gun*] God Almighty, that's th' big gun again! God forbid any harm would happen to them, but sorra mind I'd mind if they met with a dhrop in their mad endeyvours to plundher an' desthroy. [*He looks down the street from the lane for a moment, then runs to the hall door of the house,* C., *which is open, and shuts it with a vicious pull; he then goes to the chair in which* Mollser *had sat, sits down, takes out his pipe, lights it and begins to smoke with his head carried at a haughty angle. The* Covey *comes in* R. *and down the lane, staggering with a tenstone sack of flour on his back. He goes over to the door, pushes it with his head, and finds he can't open it; he turns slightly in the direction of* Peter]

THE COVEY: [*To* Peter] Who shut th' door? . . . [*He kicks at it*] Here, come on an' open it, will you? This isn't a mot's hand-bag I've got on me back.

PETER: Now, me young Covey, d'ye think I'm goin' to be your lackey?

THE COVEY: [*Angrily*] Will you open th' door, y'oul'—

PETER: [*Shouting*] Don't be assin' me to open any door, don't be assin' me to open any door for you. . . . Makin' a shame an' a sin o' th' cause that good men are fightin' for. . . . Oh, God forgive th' people that, instead o' burnishin' th' work th' boys is doin' to-day, with quiet honesty an' patience, is revilin' their sacrifices with a riot of lootin' an' roguery!

THE COVEY: [*Sarcastically*] Isn't your own eyes leppin' out o' your head with envy that you haven't th' guts to ketch a few o' th' things that God is givin' to His chosen people? . . . Y'oul' hypocrite, if every one was blind you'd steal a cross off an ass's back!

PETER: [*Very calmly*] You're not goin' to make me lose me temper; you can go on with your proddin' as long as you like; goad an' goad an' goad away; hee hee, heee! I'll not lose me temper.

[*Somebody opens door and the* Covey *goes in*]

COVEY: [*Inside house, to mock* Peter] Cuckoo-oo!

[*Peter gets up from chair in a blaze of passion, and follows the* Covey *in, shouting*]

PETER: [*Shouting*] You lean, long, lanky lath of a lowsey bastard. [*Going in door of house,* C.] Lowsey bastard, lowsey bastard!

[Mrs. Gogan *and* Bessie, *pushing the pram, come in* R., *come down lane to front of the house,* C. Bessie *is pushing the pram, which is filled with loot.* Mrs. Gogan *carries a tall standard lamp, topped with a wide and bright-coloured shade. The pram is filled with fancy-coloured dresses, and boots and shoes. They are talking as they appear* R.]

MRS. GOGAN: [*Appearing* R.] I don't remember ever havin' seen such lovely pairs as them with the pointed toes an' the cuban heels.

BESSIE: [*They are now* C., *lifting one of the evening dresses from the pram, holding it up admiringly*] They'll go grand with th' dhresses we're afther liftin', when we've stitched a sthray bit o' silk to lift th' bodices up a little bit higher, so as to shake th' shame out o' them, an' make them fit for women that hasn't lost themselves in th' nakedness o' th' times.

PETER: [*At door, sourly to* Mrs. Gogan] Ay, you. Mollser looks as if she was goin' to faint, an' your youngster is roarin' in convulsions in her lap.

MRS. GOGAN: [*Snappily*] She's never any other way but faintin'! [Mrs Gogan *runs into the house with her arm full of things. She comes back, takes up the lamp and is about to go in, when a rifleshot very near is heard.* Mrs. Gogan, *with lamp, and* Bessie, *with pram, rush to the door which* Peter, *in a panic, has shut*]

MRS. GOGAN: [*Banging at the door*] Eh, eh, you cowardly oul' fool, what are you thryin' to shut the door on us for? [Mrs. Gogan *pushes the door open and runs in, followed by* Bessie *dragging in the pram. They shut the door. A pause. Then* Capt. Brennan, *supporting* Lieut. Langon, *comes in* L., *along the street in front of the house,* C. *As* Brennan *and* Langon *reach* C. *going* R., Clitheroe, *pale and in a state of calm nervousness, appears at* L., *walking backwards or looking back in the direction from which they've come; he has a rifle held at the ready in his hands.* Langon *is ghastly white and now and again his face is twisted in agony*]

CAPT. BRENNAN: [*Back to* Clitheroe] Why did you fire over their heads? Why didn't you fire to kill?

CLITHEROE: No, no, Bill; bad as they are, they're Irish men an' women.

[Brennan *gently lets* Langon *recline on the steps of the house indicated to the extreme* R., *holding him by an arm.* Clitheroe *is* C., *watching* Langon]

CAPT. BRENNAN: [*Savagely*] Irish be damned! Attackin' an' mobbin' th' men that are riskin' their lives for them. If these slum lice gather at our heels again, plug one o' them, or I'll soon shock them with a shot or two meself!

LIEUT. LANGON: [*Moaningly*] My God, is there ne'er an ambulance knockin' around anywhere? . . . Th' stomach is ripped out o' me; I feel it—o-o-oh, Christ!

CAPT. BRENNAN: Keep th' heart up, Jim; we'll soon get help, now.

[*Door of house* C. *opens and* Nora *rushes out, dashes down steps into* Clitheroe's *arms at bottom. She flings her arms around his neck. Her hair is down, her face haggard, but her eyes are agleam with happy relief*]

NORA: [*To* Clitheroe] Jack, Jack, oh, God be thanked. Kiss me, kiss me, Jack; kiss your own Nora.

CLITHEROE: [*Kissing her, and speaking brokenly*] My Nora; my little, beautiful Nora, I wish to God I'd never left you.

NORA: It doesn't matter—not now, not now, Jack. It will make us dearer than ever to each other. . . . Kiss me, kiss me again.

CLITHEROE: Now, for God's sake, Nora, don't make a scene.

NORA: [*Fervently*] I won't, I won't; I promise, Jack—honest to God.

[Bessie *opens window of house to the* R., *puts out her head, and shouts at* Clitheroe *and* Brennan]

BESSIE: [*At window*] Has th' big guns knocked all th' harps out of your hands? General Clitheroe'd rather be unlacin' his wife's bodice now than standin' at a barricade. [*To* Brennan] An' the professor of chicken butcherin', there, finds he's up against something a little tougher than his own chickens, an' that's sayin' a lot!

CAPT. BRENNAN: [*Over to* Bessie] Shut up, y'oul' hag!

BESSIE: [*Down to* Brennan] Choke th' chicken, choke th' chicken, choke th' chicken!

LIEUT. LANGON: For God's sake, Bill, bring me some place where me wound 'll be looked afther. . . . Am I to die before anything is done to save me?

CAPT. BRENNAN: [*To* Clitheroe] Come on, Jack. We've got to get help for Jim, here—have you no thought for his pain an' danger?

BESSIE: Choke th' chicken, choke th' chicken, choke th' chicken!

CLITHEROE: [*To* Nora] Loosen me, darling, let me go.

NORA: [*Clinging to him*] No, no, no, I'll not let you go! Come on, come up to our home, Jack, my sweetheart, my lover, my husband, an' we'll forget th' last few terrible days! . . .

LIEUT. LANGON: [*Appealingly*] Oh, if I'd kep' down only a little longer, I mightn't ha' been hit! Every one else escapin', an' me gettin' me belly ripped asundher! . . . I couldn't scream, couldn't even scream. . . . D'ye think I'm really badly wounded, Bill? Me clothes seem to be all soakin' wet. . . . It's blood . . . My God, it must be me own blood!

CAPT. BRENNAN: [*To* Clitheroe] Go on, Jack, bid her good-bye with another kiss, an' be done with it! D'ye want Langon to die in me arms while you're dallyin' with your Nora?

CLITHEROE: [*To* Nora] I must go, I must go, Nora. I'm sorry we met at all. . . . It couldn't be helped —all other ways were blocked be th' British. . . . Let me go, can't you, Nora? D'ye want me to be unthrue to me comrades?

NORA: No, I won't let you go. . . . I want you to be thrue to me, Jack. . . . I'm your dearest comrade; I'm your thruest comrade. [*Tightening her arms round* Clitheroe] Oh, Jack, I can't let you go!

CLITHEROE: [*With anger, mixed with affection*] You must, Nora, you must.

NORA: All last night at the barricades I sought you, Jack. I asked for you everywhere. I didn't think of the danger—I could only think of you. They dhrove me away, but I came back again.

CLITHEROE: [*Ashamed of her action*] What possessed you to make a show of yourself, like that! What are you more than any other woman?

NORA: No more, maybe; but you are more to me than any other man, Jack. . . . I couldn't help it. I shouldn't have told you. . . . My love for you made me mad with terror.

CLITHEROE: [*Angrily*] They'll say now that I sent you out th' way I'd have an excuse to bring you home. . . . Are you goin' to turn all th' risks I'm takin' into a laugh?

LIEUT. LANGON: Let me lie down, let me lie down, Bill; th' pain would be easier, maybe, lyin' down. Oh, God, have mercy on me!

CAPT. BRENNAN: [*Encouragingly to* Langon] A few steps more, Jim, a few steps more; thry to stick it for a few steps more.

LIEUT. LANGON: Oh, I can't, I can't, I can't!

CAPT. BRENNAN: [*To* Clitheroe] Are you comin', man, or are you goin' to make an arrangement for another honeymoon? . . . If you want to act th' renegade, say so, an' we'll be off!

BESSIE: [*From window*] Runnin' from th' Tommies—choke th' chicken. Runnin' from th' Tommies —choke th' chicken!

CLITHEROE: [*Savagely to* Brennan] Damn you, man, who wants to act th' renegade? [*To* Nora] Here, let go your hold; let go, I say!

NORA: [*Clinging to* Clitheroe, *and indicating* Brennan] Look, Jack, look at th' anger in his face; look at th' fear glintin' in his eyes. . . . He, himself's afraid, afraid, afraid! . . . He wants you to go th' way he'll have th' chance of death sthrikin' you an' missin' him! . . .

CLITHEROE: [*Struggling to release himself from* Nora] Damn you, woman, will you let me go!

CAPT. BRENNAN: [*Fiercely, to* Clitheroe] Break her hold on you, man; or go up an' sit on her lap!

[Clitheroe *tries to break her hold with his right hand (he's holding rifle in the other), but* Nora *clings to him*]

NORA: [*Imploringly*] Jack, Jack, Jack!

LIEUT. LANGON: [*Agonizingly*] Brennan, a priest; I'm dyin', I think. I'm dyin'.

CLITHEROE: [*To* Nora] If you won't do it quietly, I'll have to make you! [*To* Brennan] Here, hold this gun, you, for a minute. [*He hands the gun to* Brennan]

NORA: [*Pitifully*] Please, Jack. . . . You're hurting me, Jack. . . . Honestly. . . . Oh, you're hurting . . . me! . . . I won't, I won't, I won't! . . . Oh, Jack, I gave you everything you asked of me. . . . Don't fling me from you, now! [*He roughly loosens her grip, and pushes her away from him.* Nora *sinks to the steps at the door, and lies there*]

NORA: [*Weakly*] Ah, Jack. . . . Jack. . . . Jack!

CLITHEROE: [*Taking the gun back from* Brennan] Come on, come on. [Clitheroe *hurries over to* Brennan, *catches hold of* Langon's *other arm; they both lift him up from steps, and supporting him, turn into the lane and go off* R. Bessie *looks at* Nora *lying on the street, for a few moments, then, leaving the window, she comes out, runs over to* Nora, *lifts her up in her arms, and carries her swiftly into the house. A short pause, then down the street is heard a wild, drunken yell; it comes nearer, and* Fluther *enters, frenzied, wild-eyed, mad, roaring drunk. In his arms is an earthen half-gallon jar of whisky; streaming from one of the pockets of his coat is the arm of a new tunic shirt; on his head is a woman's vivid blue hat with gold lacing, all of which he has looted. The evening begins to darken*]

FLUTHER: [*Singing in a frenzy, as he comes down the lane*]

Fluther's a jolly good fella . . .
Fluther's a jolly good fella . . . up th' rebels!
. . . that nobody can deny!

[*He reels across to* L., *staggers up the steps of the house,* C., *and hammers at the door*] Get us a mug, or a jug, or somethin', some o' yous, one o' yous, will yous, before I lay one o' yous out! [*Rifle firing is heard some distance away and the boom of the big gun.* Fluther *turns from the door, and looks off* R.] Bang an' fire away for all Fluther cares. [*He beats at the door*] Come down an' open th' door, some o' yous, one o' yous, will yous, before I lay some o' yous out! . . . Th' whole city can topple home to hell, for Fluther. [*Inside the house,* C., *is heard a scream from* Nora, *followed by a moan. Singing frantically*] That nobody can deny, that nobody can deny.

For Fluther's a jolly good fella,
Fluther's a jolly good fella,
Fluther's a jolly good fella . . . up th' rebels!
. . . that nobody can deny!

[*His frantic movements cause him to spill some of the whisky out of the jar. Looking down at jar*] Blast you, Fluther, don't be spillin' th' precious liquor! [*He kicks at the door*] Give us a mug, or a jug, or somethin', one o' yous, some o' yous, will yous, before I lay one o' yous out!

[*The door suddenly opens, and* Bessie, *coming out, grips him by the collar*]

BESSIE: [*Indignantly*] You bowsey, come in ower o' that. . . , I'll thrim your thricks o' dhrunken dancin' for you, an' none of us knowin' how soon we'll bump into a world we were never in before!

FLUTHER: [*As she is pulling him in*] Ay, th' jar, th' jar, th' jar. *Mind th' jar!*

[*A short pause, then again is heard a scream of pain from* Nora. *The door opens and* Mrs. Gogan *and* Bessie *are seen standing at it. The light gets dim*]

BESSIE: Fluther would go, only he's too dhrunk. . . . Oh, God, isn't it a pity he's so dhrunk! We'll have to thry to get a docthor somewhere.

MRS. GOGAN: I'd be afraid to go. . . . Besides, Mollser's terrible bad. I don't think you'll get a docthor to come. It's hardly any use goin'.

BESSIE: [*Determinedly*] I'll risk it, . . . Give her a little of Fluther's whisky. . . . It's th' fright that's brought it on her so soon. . . . Go on back to her, you. [Mrs. Gogan *goes into the house, and* Bessie *softly closes the door. She comes down steps, and is half-way across to* R., *when rifle-firing and the tok-tok-tok of a machine gun bring her to a sudden halt. She hesitates for a moment, then tightens her shawl round her, as if it were a shield. Softly*] O God, be Thou my help in time o' throuble; an' shelther me safely in th' shadow of Thy wings. [*She goes forward, goes up the lane, and goes off* R.]

CURTAIN

ACT IV.

SCENE—*The living-room of* Bessie Burgess. *It is one of two small attic rooms (the other, used as a bedroom, is on the* L.), *the low ceiling slopes down towards the back. There is an unmistakable air of poverty about the room. The paper on the walls is torn and soiled. On the* R., *downstage is a door. A small window* C. *back. To* L. *of window, a well-worn dresser, with a small quantity of Delft. On the* L. *wall, upstage is a door leading to a bedroom. The door on* R. *leads to the rest of the house and street. Below door on* L. *wall, the fireplace. Inside fender is a kettle and saucepan. On the hob a teapot. In front of fire a well-worn armchair. In front of window, back, a little to* R., *an oak coffin stands on two kitchen chairs. On floor, front of coffin, is a wooden box, on which are two lighted candles in candlesticks. In front of coffin, a little to* L., *a small kitchen table. At* R. *end of table, a kitchen chair. In corner where* R. *and back walls meet, the standard lamp, with coloured shade, looted in Third Act, stands; beside the lamp, hanging from nail in wall, back, hangs one of the evening dresses. There is no light in the room but that given from the two candles and the fire. The dusk has well fallen, and the glare of the burning buildings in the town can be seen through the windows in the distant sky. The* Covey, Fluther *and* Peter *have been playing cards, sitting on the floor by the light of the candles on the box near the coffin. When the Curtain rises the* Covey *is shuffling the cards,* Peter *is sitting in a stiff, dignified way opposite him, and* Fluther *is kneeling beside the window, back, cautiously looking out into street. It is a few days later.*

FLUTHER: [*Furtively peeping out of the window*] Give them a good shuffling. . . . Th' sky's gettin' reddher an' reddher. . . . You'd think it was afire. . . . Half o' th' city must be burnin'.

THE COVEY: [*Warningly*] If I was you, Fluther, I'd keep away from that window. . . . It's dangerous, an', besides, if they see you, you'll only bring a nose on th' house.

PETER: [*Anxiously*] Yes; an' he knows we had to leave our own place th' way they were riddlin' it with machine-gun fire. . . . He'll keep on pimpin' an' pimpin' there, till we have to fly out o' this place too.

FLUTHER: [*Ironically to* Peter] If they make any attack here, we'll send you out in your green an' glory uniform, shakin' your sword over your head, an' they'll fly before you as th' Danes flew before Brian Boru!

THE COVEY: [*Placing the cards on the floor, after shuffling them*] Come on, an' cut. [Fluther *creeps* L. *end of table, over to where* Covey *and* Peter *are seated, and squats down on floor between them. Having dealt the cards*] Spuds up again.

[Nora *moans feebly in room on* L. *They listen for a moment*]

FLUTHER: There, she's at it again. She's been quiet for a good long time, all th' same.

THE COVEY: She was quiet before, sure, an' she broke out again worse than ever. . . . What was led that time?

PETER: [*Impatiently*] Thray o' Hearts, Thray o' Hearts, Thray o' Hearts.

FLUTHER: It's damned hard lines to think of her dead-born kiddie lyin' there in th' arms o' poor little Mollser. Mollser snuffed it, sudden too, afther all.

THE COVEY: Sure she never got any care. How could she get it, an' th' mother out day and night lookin' for work, an' her consumptive husband leavin' her with a baby to be born before he died.

VOICES: [*In a lilting chant to the* L. *in an outside street*] Red Cr . . . oss, Red Cr . . . oss! . . . Ambu . . . lance, Ambu . . . lance!

THE COVEY: [*To Fluther*] Your deal, Fluther.

FLUTHER: [*Shuffling and dealing the cards*] It'll take a lot out o' Nora—if she'll ever be th' same.

THE COVEY: Th' docthor thinks she'll never be th' same; thinks she'll be a little touched here. [*He touches his forehead*] She's ramblin' a lot; thinkin' she's out in th' counthry with Jack; or, gettin' his dinner ready for him before he comes home; or, yellin' for her kiddie. All that, though, might be th' chloroform she got. . . . I don't know what we'd have done only for oul' Bessie: up with her for th' past three nights, hand runnin'.

FLUTHER: [*Approvingly*] I always knew there was never anything really derogatory wrong with poor Bessie. [*Suddenly catching* Peter's *arm as he is taking a trick*] Eh, houl' on there, don't be so damn quick —that's my thrick!

PETER: [*Resentfully*] What's your thrick? It's my thrick, man.

FLUTHER: [*Loudly*] How is it your thrick?

PETER: [*Answering as loudly*] Didn't I lead th' deuce!

FLUTHER: You must be gettin' blind, man; don't you see th' ace?

BESSIE: [*Appearing at door of room,* L.; *in a tense whisper*] D'ye want to waken her again on me, when she's just gone asleep? If she wakes will yous come an' mind her? If I hear a whisper out o' one o' yous again, I'll . . . gut yous!

THE COVEY: [*In a whisper*] S-s-s-h. She can hear anything above a whisper.

PETER: [*Looking up at the ceiling*] Th' gentle an' merciful God 'll give th' pair o' yous a scawldin' an' a scarifyin' one o' these days!

[Fluther *takes a bottle of whisky from his pocket, and takes a drink*]

THE COVEY: [*To* Fluther] Why don't you spread that out, man, an' thry to keep a sup for to-morrow?

FLUTHER: Spread it out? Keep a sup for to-morrow? How th' hell does a fella know there'll be any to-morrow? If I'm goin' to be whipped away, let me be whipped away when it's empty, an' not when it's half-full! [Bessie *comes in a tired way from door of room* L., *down to armchair by fire, and sits down. Over to* Bessie] Well, how is she now, Bessie?

BESSIE: I left her sleeping quietly. When I'm listenin' to her babblin' I think she'll never be much betther than she is. Her eyes have a hauntin' way of lookin' in instead of lookin' out, as if her mind had been lost alive in madly minglin' memories of th' past. . . . [*Sleepily*] Crushin' her thoughts . . . together . . . in a fierce . . . an' fanciful . . . [*She nods her head and starts wakefully*] idea that dead things are livin', an' livin' things are dead. . . . [*With a start*] Was that a scream I heard her give? [*Reassured*] Blessed God, I think I hear her screamin' every minute! An' it's only there with me that I'm able to keep awake.

THE COVEY: She'll sleep, maybe, for a long time, now. Ten here.

FLUTHER: [*Gathering up cards*] Ten here. If she gets a long sleep, she might be all right. Peter's th' lone five.

THE COVEY: [*Suddenly*] Whisht! I think I hear somebody movin' below. Whoever it is, he's comin' up.

[*A pause. Then the door,* R. *opens, and* Capt. Brennan *comes timidly in. He has changed his uniform for a suit of civies. His eyes droop with the heaviness of exhaustion; his face is pallid and drawn. His clothes are dusty and stained here and there with mud. He leans heavily on the back of a chair* R. *end of table*]

CAPT. BRENNAN: Mrs. Clitheroe; where's Mrs. Clitheroe? I was told I'd find her here.

BESSIE: What d'ye want with Mrs. Clitheroe?

CAPT. BRENNAN: I've a message, a last message for her from her husband.

BESSIE: Killed! He's not killed, is he!

CAPT. BRENNAN: [*Sinking stiffly and painfully on to a chair*] In th' Imperial Hotel; we fought till th' place was in flames. He was shot through th' arm, an' then through th' lung. . . . I could do nothin' for him—only watch his breath comin' an' goin' in quick, jerky gasps, an' a tiny sthream o' blood thricklin' out of his mouth down over his lower lip. I said a prayer for th' dyin', an' twined his Rosary beads around his fingers. . . . Then I had to leave him to save meself. . . . [*He shows some holes in his coat*] Look at th' way a machine-gun tore at me coat, as I belted out o' th' buildin' an' darted across th' sthreet for shelter. . . . An' then, I seen The Plough an' th' Stars fallin' like a shot as th' roof crashed in, an' where I'd left poor Jack was nothin' but a leppin' spout o' flame!

BESSIE: [*With partly repressed vehemence*] Ay, you left him! You twined his Rosary beads round his fingers, an' then, you run like a hare to get out o' danger!

CAPT. BRENNAN: [*Defensively*] I took me chance as well as him. . . . He took it like a man. His last whisper was to "Tell Nora to be brave; that I'm ready to meet my God, an' that I'm proud to die for Ireland." An' when our General heard it he said that "Commandant Clitheroe's end was a gleam of glory." Mrs. Clitheroe's grief will be a joy when she realizes that she has had a hero for a husband.

BESSIE: If you only seen her, you'd know to th' differ.

[Nora *appears at door,* L. *She is clad only in her nightdress and slippers; her hair, uncared for some days, is hanging in disorder over her shoulders. Her pale face looks paler still because of a vivid red spot on the tip of each cheek. Her eyes are glimmering with the light of incipient insanity; her hands are nervously fiddling with her nightgown. She halts at the door for a moment, looks vacantly around the room, and then comes slowly in. The rest do not notice her till she speaks.* Bessie *has fallen asleep in chair.* Peter, Covey *and* Fluther *stop their card-playing and watch her*]

NORA: [*Roaming slowly towards* R. *to back of table*] No . . . not there, Jack . . . I feel very, very tired . . . [*Passing her hand across her eyes*] Curious mist on my eyes. Why don't you hold my hand, Jack. . . . [*Excitedly*] No, no, Jack, it's not: can't you see it's a goldfinch? Look at the black satiny wings, with the gold bars, an' th' splash of crimson on its head. . . . [*Wearily*] Something ails me, something ails me. . . . [*Frightened*] You're goin' away, an' I can't follow you! [*She wanders back to* L. *end of table*] I can't follow you. [*Crying out*] Jack, Jack, Jack!

[Bessie *wakes with a start, sees* Nora, *gets up and runs to her*]

BESSIE: [*Putting arm round* Nora] Mrs. Clitheroe, aren't you a terrible woman to get out o' bed. . . . You'll get cold if you stay here in them clothes.

NORA: [*Monotonously*] Cold? I'm feelin' very cold . . . it's chilly out here in the counthry. [*Looking around, frightened*] What place is this? Where am I?

BESSIE: [*Coaxingly*] You're all right, Nora; you're with friends, an' in a safe place. Don't you know your uncle an' your cousin, an' poor oul' Fluther?

PETER: [*Rising to go over to* Nora] Nora, darlin', now—

FLUTHER: [*Pulling him back*] Now, leave her to Bessie, man. A crowd 'll only make her worse.

NORA: [*Thoughtfully*] There is something I want to remember, an' I can't. [*With agony*] I can't, I can't, I can't! My head, my head! [*Suddenly breaking from* Bessie, *and running over to the men, and gripping* Fluther *by the shoulders*] Where is it? Where's my baby? Tell me where you've put it, where've you hidden it? My baby, my baby; I want my baby! My head, my poor head. . . . Oh, I can't tell what is wrong with me. [*Screaming*] Give him to me, give me my husband!

BESSIE: Blessin' o' God on us, isn't this pitiful!

NORA: [*Struggling with* Bessie] I won't go away for you; I won't. Not till you give me back my husband. [*Screaming*] Murderers, that's what yous are; murderers, murderers!

[Bessie *gently, but firmly, pulls her from* Fluther, *and tries to lead her to room,* L.]

BESSIE: [*Tenderly*] Ss-s-sh. We'll bring Mr. Clitheroe back to you, if you'll only lie down an' stop quiet. . . . [*Trying to lead her in*] Come on, now, Nora, an' I'll sing something to you.

NORA: I feel as if my life was thryin' to force its way out of my body. . . . I can hardly breathe . . . I'm frightened, I'm frightened, I'm frightened! For God's sake, don't leave me, Bessie. Hold my hand, put your arms around me!

FLUTHER: [*To* Brennan] Now you can see th' way she is, man.

PETER: An' what way would she be if she heard Jack had gone west?

THE COVEY: [*To* Peter, *warningly*] Shut up, you, man!

BESSIE: [*To* Nora] We'll have to be brave, an' let patience clip away th' heaviness of th' slow-movin' hours, rememberin' that sorrow may endure for th' night, but joy cometh in th' mornin'. . . . Come on in, an' I'll sing to you, an' you'll rest quietly.

NORA: [*Stopping suddenly on her way to the room*] Jack an' me are goin' out somewhere this evenin'. Where I can't tell. Isn't it curious I can't remember. . . . [*Screaming, and pointing* R.] He's there, he's there, an' they won't give him back to me!

BESSIE: Sh-s-sh, darlin', s-ssh. I won't sing to you, if you're not quiet.

NORA: [*Nervously holding* Bessie] Hold my hand, hold my hand, an' sing to me, sing to me!

BESSIE: Come in an' lie down, an' I'll sing to you.

NORA: [*Vehemently*] Sing to me, sing to me; sing, sing!

BESSIE: [*Singing as she leads* Nora *into room,* L.]
Lead, kindly light, amid th' encircling gloom,
    Lead Thou me on.
Th' night is dark an' I am far from home,
    Lead Thou me on.

[*Leading* Nora, Bessie *goes into room* L. *Singing softly inside room,* L.]
Keep thou my feet, I do not ask to see
The distant scene—one step enough for me.

THE COVEY: [*To* Brennan] Now that you've seen how bad she is, an' that we daren't tell her what has happened till she's betther, you'd best be slippin' back to where you come from.

CAPT. BRENNAN: There's no chance o' slippin' back now, for th' military are everywhere: a fly couldn't get through. I'd never have got here, only I managed to change me uniform for what I'm wearin'. . . . I'll have to take me chance, an' thry to lie low here for a while.

THE COVEY: [*Frightened*] There's no place here to lie low. Th' Tommies 'll be hoppin' in here, any minute!

PETER: [*Aghast*] An' then we'd all be shanghaied!

THE COVEY: Be God, there's enough afther happenin' to us!

FLUTHER: [*Warningly, as he listens*] Whisht, whisht, th' whole o' yous. I think I heard th' clang of a rifle butt on th' floor of th' hall below. [*All alertness*] Here, come on with th' cards again. I'll deal. [*He shuffles and deals the cards to all*] Clubs up. [*To Brennan*] Thry to keep your hands from shakin', man. You lead, Peter. [*As Peter throws out a card*] Four o' Hearts led. [*Heavy steps are heard coming up stairs, outside door R. The door opens and Corporal Stoddart of the Wiltshires enters in full war kit—steel helmet, rifle, bayonet and trench tools. He stands near door R., looks around the room, and at the men who go on silently playing cards. A pause. Gathering up cards, and breaking the silence*] Two tens an' a five.

CORPORAL STODDART: 'Ello. [*Indicating the coffin*] This the stiff?

THE COVEY: Yis.

CORPORAL STODDART: Who's gowing with it? Ownly one allowed to gow with it, you knaow.

THE COVEY: I dunno.

CORPORAL STODDART: You dunnow?

THE COVEY: I dunno.

BESSIE: [*Coming into the room*] She's afther slippin' off to sleep again, thanks be to God. I'm hardly able to keep me own eyes open. [*To the soldier*] Oh, are yous goin' to take away poor little Mollser?

CORPORAL STODDART: Ay; 'oo's agowing with 'er?

BESSIE: Oh, th' poor mother, o' course. God help her, it's a terrible blow to her!

FLUTHER: A terrible blow? Sure, she's in her element now, woman, mixin' earth to earth, an' ashes t'ashes, an' dust to dust, an' revellin' in plumes an' hearses, last days an' judgements!

BESSIE: [*Falling into chair by the fire*] God bless us! I'm jaded!

CORPORAL STODDART: Was she plugged?

COVEY: [*Shortly*] No; died of consumption.

CORPORAL STODDART: [*Carelessly*] Ow, is that all—thought she might 'ave been plugged.

COVEY: [*Indignantly*] Is that all! Isn't it enough? D'ye know, comrade, that more die o' consumption than are killed in the war? An' it's all because of th' system we're livin' undher.

CORPORAL STODDART: Ow, I know. I'm a Socialist, myself, but I 'as to do my dooty.

COVEY: [*Ironically*] Dooty! Th' only dooty of a Socialist is th' emancipation of th' workers.

CORPORAL STODDART: Ow, a man's a man, an' 'e 'as to fight for 'is country, 'asn't 'e?

FLUTHER: [*Aggressively*] You're not fightin' for your counthry here, are you?

PETER: [*Anxiously, to Fluther*] Ay, ay, Fluther, none o' that, none o' that!

THE COVEY: Fight for your counthry! Did y'ever read, comrade, Jenersky's *Thesis on the Origin, Development an' Consolidation of th' Evolutionary Idea of the Proletariat?*

CORPORAL STODDART: [*Good-humouredly*] Ow, cheese it, Paddy, cheese it!

BESSIE: [*Sleepily*] How is things in th' town, Tommy?

CORPORAL STODDART: Ow, I think it's nearly over. We've got 'em surrounded, an' we're closing in on the blighters. It was only a bit of a dorg-fight.

[*Outside in the street is heard the sharp ping of a sniper's rifle, followed by a squeal of pain*]

VOICES: [*To the L. in a chant, outside in street*] Red Cr . . . oss, Red Cr . . . oss! Ambu . . . lance, Ambu . . . lance!

CORPORAL STODDART: [*Going up R. and looking out of window, back*] Christ, there's another of our men 'it by the blarsted sniper! 'E's knocking abaht 'ere somewheres. [*Venomously*] Gord, wen we gets the blighter, we'll give 'im the cold steel, we will. We'll jab the belly aht of 'im, we will!

[*Mrs. Gogan enters tearfully by door R.; she is a little proud of the importance of being connected with death*]

MRS. GOGAN: [*To Fluther*] I'll never forget what you done for me, Fluther, goin' around at th' risk of your life settlin' everything with th' undhertaker an' th' cemetery people. When all me own were afraid to put their noses out, you plunged like a good one through hummin' bullets, an' they knockin' fire out o' th' road, tinklin' through th' frightened windows, an' splashin' themselves to pieces on th' walls! An' you'll find, that Mollser in th' happy place she's gone to, won't forget to whisper, now an' again, th' name o' Fluther.

[*Corporal Stoddart comes from window down R. to door R., and stands near the door*]

CORPORAL STODDART: [*To Mrs. Gogan*] Git it aht, mother, git it aht.

BESSIE: [*From the chair*] It's excusin' me you'll be, Mrs. Gogan, for not stannin' up, seein' I'm shaky on me feet for want of a little sleep, an' not desirin' to show any disrespect to poor little Mollser.

FLUTHER: Sure, we all know, Bessie, that it's vice versa with you.

MRS. GOGAN: [*To Bessie*] Indeed, it's meself that has well chronicled, Mrs. Burgess, all your gentle hurryin' to me little Mollser, when she was alive, bringin' her somethin' to dhrink, or somethin' t'eat, an' never passin' her without lifting up her heart with a delicate word o' kindness.

CORPORAL STODDART: [*Impatiently, but kindly*] Git it aht, git it aht, mother. [*The men rise from their card-playing; Fluther and Brennan go R. to R. end of coffin; Peter and Covey go L. of table to L. end of coffin. One of them takes box and candles out of way. They carry coffin down R. and out by door R., Corporal Stoddart watching them. Mrs. Gogan follows the coffin out. A pause. Corporal Stoddart, at door R., turns towards Bessie. To Bessie, who is almost asleep*] 'Ow many men is in this 'ere 'ouse? [*No answer. Loudly*] 'Ow many men is in this 'ere 'ouse?

BESSIE: [*Waking with a start*] God, I was nearly asleep! . . . How many men? Didn't you see them?

CORPORAL STODDART: Are they all that are in the 'ouse?

BESSIE: [*Sleepily*] Oh, there's none higher up, but there may be more lower down. Why?

CORPORAL STODDART: All men in the district 'as to be rounded up. Somebody's giving 'elp to the snipers, an' we 'as to tike precautions. If I 'ad my wy I'd mike 'em all join up an' do their bit! But I suppose they an' you are all Shinners.

BESSIE: [*Who has been sinking into sleep, waking up to a sleepy vehemence*] Bessie Burgess is no Shinner, an' never had no thruck with anything spotted be th' fingers o' th' Fenians. But always made it her business to harness herself for Church whenever she knew that God Save The King was goin' to be sung at t'end of th' service; whose only son went to th' front in th' first contingent of the Dublin Fusiliers, an' that's on his way home carryin' a shathered arm that he got fightin' for his King an' counthry!

[*Bessie's head sinks slowly forward again. Door, R., opens and Peter comes in, his body stiff, and his face contorted with anger. He goes up R., to back, and paces angrily from side to side. Covey, with a sly grin on his face, and Fluther follow Peter. Fluther goes to L. and Covey goes to R. end of table. Brennan follows in and slinks to back of table to L. corner between dresser and door, L. Corporal Stoddart remains standing a little in from door R.*]

FLUTHER: [*After an embarrassing pause*] Th' air in th' sthreet outside's shakin' with the firin' o' rifles, an' machine-guns. It must be a hot shop in th' middle o' th' scrap.

CORPORAL STODDART: We're pumping lead in on 'em from every side, now; they'll soon be shoving up th' white flag.

PETER: [*With a shout at Fluther and Covey*] I'm tellin' you either o' yous two lowsers 'ud make a betther hearseman than Peter! proddin' an' pokin' at me an' I helpin' to carry out a corpse!

FLUTHER: [*Provokingly*] It wasn't a very derogatory thing for th' Covey to say that you'd make a fancy hearseman, was it?

PETER: [*Furiously*] A pair o' redjesthered, bowseys pondherin' from mornin' till night on how they'll get a chance to break a gap through th' quiet nature of a man that's always endeavourin' to chase out of him any sthray thought of venom against his fellaman!

THE COVEY: Oh, shut it, shut it, shut it!

PETER: [*Furiously*] As long as I'm a livin' man, responsible for me thoughts, words an' deeds to th' Man above, I'll feel meself instituted to fight again' th' sliddherin' ways of a pair o' picaroons, whisperin', concurrin', concoctin' an' conspirin' together to rendher me unconscious of th' life I'm thryin' to live!

CORPORAL STODDART: [*Dumbfounded*] What's wrong, Paddy; wot 'ave they done to you?

PETER: [*Savagely to the Corporal*] You mind your own business! What's it got to do with you, what's wrong with me?

BESSIE: [*In a sleepy murmur*] Will yous thry to conthrol yourselves into quietness? Yous'll waken her . . . up . . . on . . . me . . . again. [*She sleeps*]

FLUTHER: [*Coming C.*] Come on, boys, to th' cards again, an' never mind him.

CORPORAL STODDART: No use of you going to start cards; you'll be going aht of 'ere, soon as Sergeant comes.

FLUTHER: [*In surprise*] Goin' out o' here? An' why're we goin' out o' here?

CORPORAL STODDART: All men in district 'as to be rounded up, an' 'eld in till the scrap is over.

FLUTHER: [*Concerned*] An' where're we goin' to be held in?

CORPORAL STODDART: They're puttin' them in a church.

COVEY: [*Astounded*] A church?

FLUTHER: What sort of a church? Is it a Protestan' church?

CORPORAL STODDART: I dunno; I suppose so.

FLUTHER: [*In dismay*] Be God, it'll be a nice thing to be stuck all night in a Protestan' church!

CORPORAL STODDART: If I was you, I'd bring the cards—you might get a chance of a gime.

FLUTHER: [*Hesitant*] Ah, no, that wouldn't do. . . . I wondher. . . . [*After a moment's thought*] Ah, I don't think we'd be doin' anything derogatory be playin' cards in a Protestan' church.

CORPORAL STODDART: If I was you I'd bring a little snack with me; you might be glad of it before the morning [*Lilting*]

Oh, I do like a snice mince pie,
Oh, I do like a snice mince pie.

[*Again the snap of the sniper's rifle rings out, followed by a scream of pain. Corporal Stoddart goes pale, runs up R. to near window, C., with his rifle at the ready*]

VOICES: [*In street to R., chanting*] Red Cr . . . oss . . . Red Cr . . . oss! Ambu . . . lance . . . Ambu . . . lance!

[*The door R. is dashed open, and Sergeant Tinley, pale, agitated, and angry, comes rapidly in. He stands inside the door, glaring at men in the room. Corporal Stoddart swings round at the ready as Tinley enters and lets his rifle drop when he sees the Sergeant*]

CORPORAL STODDART: [*To Sergeant*] One of our men 'it again, Sergeant?

SERGEANT TINLEY: [*Angrily*] Private Taylor: got it right through the chest, 'e did; an 'ole in front as ow you could put your 'and through, an' arf 'is back blown away! Dum-dum bullets they're using. Gang of assassins potting at us from behind roofs. That's not plying the gime: why don't they come into the open and fight fair?

FLUTHER: [*Unable to stand the slight, facing*

Sergeant] Fight fair! A few hundhred scrawls o'
chaps with a couple o' guns an' Rosary beads, again'
a hundhred thousand thrained men with horse, fut
an' artillery. . . . [To others in room] An' he wants
us to fight fair! [To Sergeant] D'ye want us to come
out in our skins an' throw stones?

SERGEANT TINLEY: [To Corporal] Are these four
all that are 'ere?

CORPORAL STODDART: Four; that's hall, Sergeant.

SERGEANT TINLEY: [Roughly] Come on, then, get
the blighters aht. [To the men] 'Ere, 'op it aht! Aht
into the street with you, an' if another of our men
goes west, you go with 'im. [He catches Fluther by
the arm] Go on, git aht!

FLUTHER: [Pulling himself free] Eh, who are you
chuckin', eh?

SERGEANT TINLEY: [Roughly] Go on, git aht, you
blighter.

FLUTHER: [Truculently] Who're you callin' a
blighter to, eh? I'm a Dublin man, born an' bred
in th' City, see?

SERGEANT TINLEY: Oh, I don't care if you were
Bryan Buroo; git aht, git aht.

FLUTHER: [Pausing as he reaches door R., to face
the Sergeant defiantly] Jasus, you an' your guns!
Leave them down, an' I'd beat th' two of yous without sweatin'!

[Shepherded by the two soldiers, who follow
them out, Peter, Covey, Fluther and Brennan
go out by door R. Bessie is sleeping heavily on
the chair by the fire. After a pause Nora appears at door L., in her nightdress. Remaining
at door for a few moments she looks vaguely
around the room. She then comes in quietly,
goes over to the fire, pokes it and puts the
kettle on. She thinks for a few moments,
pressing her hand to her forehead. She looks
questioningly at the fire, and then at the press
at back. She goes to the dresser L., back, opens
drawer, takes out a soiled cloth and spreads
it on the table. She then places things for tea
on the table]

NORA: I imagine th' room looks very odd, some-
how. . . . I was nearly forgetting Jack's tea. . . . Ah,
I think I'll have everything done before he gets in.
. . . [She lilts gently, as she arranges the table]

Th' violets were scenting th' woods,
    Nora,
Displaying their charms to th' bee,
When I first said I lov'd only you, Nora,
An' you said you lov'd only me.
Th' chestnut blooms gleam'd through
    th' glade, Nora,
A robin sang loud from a tree,
When I first said I lov'd only you, Nora,
An' you said you lov'd only me.

[She pauses suddenly, and glances round the room.
Doubtfully] I can't help feelin' this room very
strange. . . . What is it? . . . What is it? . . . I must
think. . . . I must thry to remember. . . .

VOICES: [Chanting in a distant street] Ambu . . .
lance, Ambu . . . lance! Red Cro . . . ss, Red Cro
. . . ss!

NORA: [Startled and listening for a moment, then
resuming the arrangement of the table]

Trees, birds an' bees sang a song, Nora,
    Of happier transports to be,
When I first said I lov'd only you, Nora,
An' you said you lov'd only me.

[A burst of rifle-fire is heard in a street near by,
followed by the rapid tok-tok-tok of a machine-gun.
Staring in front of her and screaming] Jack, Jack,
Jack! My baby, my baby, my baby!

BESSIE: [Waking with a start] You divil, are you
afther gettin' out o' bed again! [She rises and runs
towards Nora, who rushes to the window, back L.,
which she frantically opens]

NORA: [At the window, screaming] Jack, Jack,
for God's sake, come to me!

SOLDIERS: [Outside, shouting] Git awoy, git awoy
from that window, there!

BESSIE: [Seizing hold of Nora] Come away, come
away, woman, from that window!

NORA: [Struggling with Bessie] Where is it; where
have you hidden it? Oh, Jack, Jack, where are you?

BESSIE: [Imploringly] Mrs. Clitheroe, for God's
sake, come away!

NORA: [Fiercely] I won't; he's below. Let . . . me
. . . go! You're thryin' to keep me from me husband.
I'll follow him. Jack, Jack, come to your Nora!

BESSIE: Hus-s-sh, Nora, Nora! He'll be here in
a minute. I'll bring him to you, if you'll only be
quiet—honest to God, I will. [With a great effort
Bessie pushes Nora away from the window, the
force used causing her to stagger against it herself.
Two rifle-shots ring out in quick succession. Bessie
jerks her body convulsively; stands stiffly upright for
a moment, a look of agonized astonishment on her
face, then she staggers forward, leaning heavily on
the table with her hands. With an arrested scream
of fear and pain] Merciful God, I'm shot, I'm shot,
I'm shot! . . . Th' life's pourin' out o' me! [To
Nora] I've got this through . . . through you . . .
through you, you bitch, you! . . . O God, have
mercy on me! . . . [To Nora] You wouldn't stop
quiet, no you wouldn't, you wouldn't, blast you!
Look at what I'm afther gettin', look at what I'm
afther gettin' . . . I'm bleedin' to death, an' no
one's here to stop th' flowin' blood! [Calling] Mrs.
Gogan, Mrs. Gogan! Fluther, Fluther, for God's
sake, somebody, a doctor, a doctor!

[Bessie, leaving R. end of table, staggers down
towards door R., but, weakening, she sinks
down on her knees, R.C., then reclining, she
supports herself by her right hand resting on
floor. Nora is rigid with her back to wall, L.,
her trembling hands held out a little from her
sides; her lips quivering, her breast heaving,
staring wildly at the figure of Bessie]

NORA: [In a breathless whisper] Jack, I'm frightened. . . . I'm frightened, Jack. . . . Oh, Jack, where are you?

BESSIE: [*Moaningly*] This is what's afther comin' on me for nursin' you day an' night. . . . I was a fool, a fool, a fool! Get me a dhrink o' wather, you jade, will you? There's a fire burnin' in me blood! [*Pleadingly*] Nora, Nora, dear, for God's sake, run out an' get Mrs. Gogan, or Fluther, or somebody to bring a doctor, quick, quick, quick! [*As* Nora *does not stir*] Blast you, stir yourself, before I'm gone!

NORA: Oh, Jack, Jack, where are you?

BESSIE: [*In a whispered moan*] Jesus Christ, me sight's goin'! It's all dark, dark! Nora, hold me hand! [Bessie's *body lists over and she sinks into a prostrate position on the floor*] I'm dyin', I'm dyin' . . . I feel it. . . . Oh God, oh God! [*She feebly sings*]

I do believe . . . I will believe
That . . . Jesus . . . died . . . for . . . me,
That . . . on . . . the . . . cross He . . .
    shed . . . His . . . blood
From . . . sin . . . to . . . set . . . free.

[*She ceases singing, and lies stretched out, still and rigid. A pause; then* Mrs. Gogan *runs hastily in by door* R. *She halts at door and looks round with a frightened air*]

MRS. GOGAN: [*Quivering with fear*] Blessed be God, what's afther happenin'! [*To* Nora] What's wrong, child, what's wrong? [*She sees* Bessie, *runs to her and bends over the body*] Bessie, Bessie! [*She shakes the body*] Mrs. Burgess, Mrs. Burgess! [*She feels* Bessie's *forehead*] My God, she's as cold as death. They're afther murdherin' th' poor inoffensive woman!

[Sergeant Tinley *and* Corporal Stoddart, *in agitation, enter by door* R., *their rifles at the ready*]

SERGEANT TINLEY: [*Excitedly*] This is the 'ouse! [*They go rapidly to window, back,* C.] That's the window!

NORA: [*Pressing back against the wall*] Hide it, hide it; cover it up, cover it up!

[Sergeant Tinley, *looking round room, sees body. He comes from window to* Bessie, *and bends over her*]

SERGEANT TINLEY: [*Bending over body*] 'Ere, wot's this? Oo's this? Oh, God, we've plugged one of the women of the 'ouse!

CORPORAL STODDART: [*At window*] W'y the 'ell did she go to the window? Is she dead?

SERGEANT TINLEY: Dead as bedamned. Well, we couldn't afford to tike any chances.

[Sergeant Tinley *goes back to window, and looks out*]

NORA: [*Screaming, and putting her hands before her face*] Hide it, hide it; don't let me see it! Take me away, take me away, Mrs. Gogan!

[Mrs. Gogan, *who has been weeping softly over* Bessie, *rises, and crosses by front of table to room,* L., *goes in and comes out with a sheet in her hands. She crosses over and spreads the sheet over* Bessie's *body*]

MRS. GOGAN: [*As she spreads the sheet*] Oh, God help her, th' poor woman, she's stiffenin' out as hard as she can! Her face has written on it th' shock o' sudden agony, an' her hands is whitenin' into th' smooth shininess of wax.

NORA: [*Whimperingly*] Take me away, take me away; don't leave me here to be lookin' an' lookin' at it!

MRS. GOGAN: [*Going over to* Nora *and putting her arm round her*] Come on with me, dear, an' you can doss in poor Mollser's bed, till we gather some neighbours to come an' give th' last friendly touches to Bessie in th' lonely layin' of her out. [Mrs. Gogan *puts her arms round* Nora, *leads her across from* L. *to* R., *and they both go slowly out by door* R. Corporal Stoddart *comes from window to table, looks at tea-things on table; goes to fireplace, takes the teapot up in his hand*]

CORPORAL STODDART: [*Over to* Tinley, *at window*] Tea here, Sergeant; wot abaht a cup of scald?

SERGEANT TINLEY: Pour it aht, pour it aht, Stoddart—I could scoff anything just now.

[Corporal Stoddart *pours out two cups of tea.* Sergeant Tinley *comes from window to table, and sits on* R. *end;* Corporal Stoddart *sits on opposite end of table, and they drink the tea. In the distance is heard a bitter burst of rifle and machine-gun fire, interspersed with the boom, boom of artillery. The glare in the sky seen through the window* C., *back, flares into a fuller and a deeper red*]

SERGEANT TINLEY: There gows the general attack on the Powst Office.

VOICES: [*In a distant street*] Ambu . . . lance, Ambu . . . lance! Red Cro . . . ss, Red Cro . . . ss!

[*The voices of soldiers at a barricade outside the house are heard singing*]

They were summoned from the 'illside,
They were called in from the glen,
And the country found 'em ready
At the stirring call for men.
Let not tears add to their 'ardship,
As the soldiers pass along,
And although our 'eart is breaking
Make it sing this cheery song.

[Sergeant Tinley *and* Corporal Stoddart *join in the chorus as they sip the tea.* Sergeant Tinley *and* Corporal Stoddart *singing*]

Keep the 'ome fires burning,
While your 'earts are yearning.
Though your lads are far away,
They dream of 'ome;
There's a silver lining
Through the dark cloud shining,
Turn the dark cloud inside out,
Till the boys come 'ome!

THE END

W. Somerset Maugham

(1874————)

Novelist, essayist, and playwright, W. Somerset Maugham was one of the most successful of English writers during the first half of the century. Readers of fiction will remember him longest for his autobiographical novel *Of Human Bondage* (1915); for the book based on the story of Gauguin, *The Moon and Sixpence* (1919), and for the controversial but incisive tale *Cakes and Ale* (1930). Two of his long short stories are also likely to wear rather well, *The Letter* and *Miss Thompson* (1921), which furnished the basis of one of the most successful American plays, John Colton and Clemence Randolph's *Rain*. And there will always be much pleasure awaiting the reader in *The Summing Up* (1937), in which the writer collected sage observations on life and letters. Playwriting was only one of Maugham's interests—and the one that he professed to esteem least. Yet even in this hazardous occupation Maugham was extraordinarily successful, in particular when he concentrated mainly on entertainment.

For a dramatist's career, as well as for a novelist's, this fortunate author was well qualified from the start. He was cosmopolitan by background and education, trained in science and well read in literature, polished in manners and speech, extraordinarily well traveled, and altogether experienced in the ways of the world. Born in Paris of a father who served as Solicitor in the British embassy, Maugham spoke French more fluently than English in early childhood. After studying at King's School in Canterbury, he became a medical student at the University of Heidelberg. From there he went to St. Thomas's Hospital in London and in due time became a member of both the Royal College of Physicians and the Royal College of Surgeons. But, although he profited from this training, acquiring or refining the scientific detachment and power of observation notable in his writing, he evaded the exacting practice of medicine. During his period of internship, in 1897, he wrote the novel *Liza of Lambeth,* and henceforth it was literature that claimed his allegiance. It gave him leisure and occasion for travel. Once he had amassed the financial means to enjoy liberty and satisfy curiosity, he led the life of a man of the world with a relish that he never tried to conceal. His travels took him to most of the countries in Europe, to North and South America, and to the East, and he made his home in the congenial South of France. "Without an adequate income half the possibilities of the world are cut off," he wrote in *The Summing Up,* and he was resolved not to be cut off from anything pleasurable or stimulating within the bounds of reason.

The drama was an early interest with Maugham, and he first expressed it with a play written in German in 1902, *Schiffbrüchig,* translated as *Marriages Are Made in Heaven.* He followed it in 1903 with a serious drama in English, *The Man of Honour,* produced experimentally by the Stage Society of London but frowned upon by the commercial managements as too depressing for the popular taste. Four years later, however, he corrected this error by writing *Lady Frederick,* a light comedy of a spendthrift adventuress, which ran for a year after its *première* on October 26, 1907. While waiting for *Lady Frederick* to interest a management, he wrote two other plays, *Mrs. Dot* and *Jack Straw.* With still another play, *The Explorer,* on the boards, Maugham had four pieces running in London during the year 1908. He completed two plays in 1909 and two more the following year, his productivity tapering off only after 1911. During the First World War he was occupied with the ambulance service and, more importantly, with British Intelligence Service. In 1917, however, he started another spurt of playwriting, turning out his most important work, which falls into the two categories of serious drama and high comedy.

Perhaps because he found scant encouragement for his most earnest efforts, he grew cynical about them. He concluded in *The Summing Up* that "the aim of the drama is not to instruct but to please," adding that "art is indifferent to morals" and that "a lofty purpose will not serve you so well as a competent technique." He learned this from the failure of a number of plays: *The Unknown* (1920), the drama of a returning soldier who can no longer believe in the existence of God; *The Sacred Flame* (1929), a grim melodrama of the "whodunit" variety in which a mother gives her maimed son an overdose of sleeping tablets to prevent his learning that his wife has betrayed him; *For Services Rendered* (1932), a picture of the postwar dislocation of British life; and, finally, *Sheppey,* a morality drama in the form of a sardonic comedy about the fate of a humble sweepstakes winner who tries to pattern his life after Christ's teachings. The serious plays did not conspicuously depart from Maugham's characteristic vein of detached observation and urbane disenchantment. Sheppey, the sweepstakes winner, for instance, is adjudged mad because he distributes his gains among the poor. The world and Christ are plainly not on speaking terms. "It's obvious," declares Sheppey's psychiatrist, "that a sane man is not going to give all his money away to the poor. A sane man *takes* from the poor. . . ." But Maugham was not at top form when he grew somber, perhaps because there was too great a discrepancy between his contempt for humanity and his desire to be sympathetic. His public was left ill at ease rather than stirred. After the failure of *Sheppey*, in 1933, Maugham resolved to write no more for the theatre, declaring, "I am conscious that I am no longer in touch with the public that patronizes the theatre. This happens in the end to most dramatists and they are wise to accept the warning."

This would hardly have been Maugham's decision had he continued to write the kind of comedies he began to turn out with *Our Betters* (1917). They represented the ripe fruit of his way of life and observation, and they proved eminently satisfying. *Our Betters* was a devastating satire on the snobbery and selfish emptiness of the fashionable set. The American girl Bessie Saunders is so aghast at the society into which she is introduced by her titled sister that she takes the boat home. It is a society in which noblemen such as Lord Bleane lay ancient coronets at the feet of every *nouveau riche* American woman, spurious noblewomen such as the Duchess de Surennes (her maiden name in Chicago was Hodgson) bestow their favor on idle boys half their age, and expatriated dandies such as Clay speak condescendingly of "you Americans in America." *Our Betters* was one of the most brilliant high comedies since the time of Congreve and Wycherley. In 1921 Maugham wrote *The Circle* and six years later, *The Constant Wife*, in which amoral Restoration comedy fused with modern thesis drama and Shavian comedy of ideas. When Constance learns that her distinguished husband has been unfaithful to her, she refuses to create a scandal, convinced that she has no grievance after fifteen years of marriage during which she has led a parasitical existence. Once she has ceased to please, she has no right to demand loyalty from her husband, since she is of no use to him. Only by earning her own livelihood can she recover her dignity. She goes into business and makes herself economically independent of him. In consequence, the double standard of morality for the sexes vanishes and she pays her husband in his own coin by being openly unfaithful to him. Returning to the theme of marriage in 1930 and using a middle-class setting, Maugham wrote the less lively comedy *The Breadwinner*, in which a husband leaves his tiresomely parasitical household.

It is *The Circle*, however, that displays the best features of the art of high comedy. *The Circle* is comedy of manners, with its many recognizable details of upper-class life and its telling commentary on the social climate. But to this comparatively perishable stuff, Maugham added substantial comedy of character with portraits, such as those of Lady Kitty and Lord Porteous, which have human as well as comic dimension within the framework of a clever plot. The idea of the play—the cycle of romantic passion and the inability of one generation to learn from the experience of another —is so interfused with the importance of character in any situation that Porteous is made to say to Lady Kitty, "If we made rather a hash of things perhaps it was because we are rather trivial people. You can do anything in this world if you're prepared to take the consequences, and consequences depend upon character."

Worldly wisdom in *The Circle* results in a perceptive and tolerant work. It shatters no precedents, but neither does it accept them. There is an organized intellect at work in the play, for which there are evidences in the style and technique. Dialogue suits character and situation instead of being displayed for its own sake, though we may be sure that Maugham would have been at no loss if he had wanted to scintillate. Structurally, too, the play shows Maugham in full command of his medium. With *The Circle*, he brought drawing-room comedy to perfection. It is a "well-made play" in which intrigue is kept within the bounds of naturalness. Surprises, as when Lady Kitty and Lord Porteous make their first entrance and when Elizabeth elopes, were no doubt calculated by the clever showman, who kept a notebook and worked at his craft methodically; but he refrained from trying to startle the playgoer with the ingenuity of his invention. Maugham had the cleverness here not to be too clever. Indeed, it is cleverness that comes a cropper in the play when Arnold, taking his father's advice, offers his wife her freedom on the theory that when the bars and bolts are removed "the prisoner won't escape"—and yet the prisoner does.

BIBLIOGRAPHY: Richard Aldington, *W. Somerset Maugham*, 1939; John Mason Brown, *Two on the Aisle* (pp. 108–113), 1938; Barrett H. Clark, *A Study of the Modern Drama* (pp. 320–327), 1938; Desmond MacCarthy, *Drama* (pp. 343–348), 1940; W. Somerset Maugham, *The Summing Up*, (especially ch. 30–43, 1938; Ernest Short, *Theatrical Cavalcade* (pp. 165–170), 1942.

THE CIRCLE

By W. Somerset Maugham

PERSONS OF THE PLAY

CLIVE CHAMPION-CHENEY   EDWARD LUTON   ELIZABETH
ARNOLD CHAMPION-CHENEY, M.P.   LADY CATHERINE CHAMPION-CHENEY   MRS. SHENSTONE
LORD PORTEOUS

The action takes place at Aston-Adey, Arnold Champion-Cheney's house in Dorset.

ACT I.

The Scene is a stately drawing-room at Aston-Adey, with fine pictures on the walls and Georgian furniture. Aston-Adey has been described, with many illustrations, in Country Life. *It is not a house, but a place. Its owner takes a great pride in it, and there is nothing in the room which is not of the period. Through the French windows at the back can be seen the beautiful gardens which are one of the features. It is a fine summer morning.*

Arnold comes in. He is a man of about thirty-five, tall and good-looking, fair, with a clean-cut, sensitive face. He has a look that is intellectual, but somewhat bloodless. He is very well dressed.

ARNOLD: [*Calling*] Elizabeth. [*He goes to the window and calls again*] Elizabeth! [*He rings the bell. While he is waiting he gives a look round the room. He slightly alters the position of one of the chairs. He takes an ornament from the chimney-piece and blows the dust from it. A* Footman *comes in*] Oh, George! See if you can find Mrs. Cheney, and ask her if she'd be good enough to come here.

FOOTMAN: Very good, sir.

[*The* Footman *turns to go*]

ARNOLD: Who is supposed to look after this room?

FOOTMAN: I don't know, sir.

ARNOLD: I wish when they dust they'd take care to replace the things exactly as they were before.

FOOTMAN: Yes, sir.

ARNOLD: [*Dismissing him*] All right.

[*The* Footman *goes out. Arnold goes again to the window and calls*]

ARNOLD: Elizabeth! [*He sees* Mrs. Shenstone] Oh, Anna, do you know where Elizabeth is?

[Mrs. Shenstone *comes in from the garden. She is a woman of forty, pleasant, and of elegant appearance*]

ANNA: Isn't she playing tennis?

ARNOLD: No, I've been down to the tennis court. Something very tiresome has happened.

ANNA: Oh?

ARNOLD: I wonder where the deuce she is.

ANNA: When do you expect Lord Porteous and Lady Kitty?

ARNOLD: They're motoring down in time for luncheon.

ANNA: Are you sure you want me to be here? It's not too late yet, you know. I can have my things packed and catch a train for somewhere or other.

ARNOLD: No, of course we want you. It'll make it so much easier if there are people here. It was exceedingly kind of you to come.

ANNA: Oh, nonsense!

ARNOLD: And I think it was a good thing to have Teddie Luton down.

ANNA: He is so breezy, isn't he?

ARNOLD: Yes, that's his great asset. I don't know that he's very intelligent, but, you know, there are occasions when you want a bull in a china shop. I sent one of the servants to find Elizabeth.

ANNA: I daresay she's putting on her shoes. She and Teddie were going to have a single.

ARNOLD: It can't take all this time to change one's shoes.

ANNA: [*With a smile*] One can't change one's shoes without powdering one's nose, you know.

[Elizabeth *comes in. She is a very pretty creature in the early twenties. She wears a light summer frock*]

ARNOLD: My dear, I've been hunting for you everywhere. What *have* you been doing?

ELIZABETH: Nothing! I've been standing on my head.

ARNOLD: My father's here.

ELIZABETH: [*Startled*] Where?

ARNOLD: At the cottage. He arrived last night.

ELIZABETH: Damn!

ARNOLD: [*Good-humoredly*] I wish you wouldn't say that, Elizabeth.

ELIZABETH: If you're not going to say "Damn" when a thing's damnable, when are you going to say "Damn"?

ARNOLD: I should have thought you could say, "Oh, bother!" or something like that.

ELIZABETH: But that wouldn't express my sentiments. Besides, at that speech day when you were giving away the prizes you said there were no synonyms in the English language.

ANNA: [*Smiling*] Oh, Elizabeth! It's very unfair to expect a politician to live in private up to the statements he makes in public.

ARNOLD: I'm always willing to stand by anything I've said. There *are* no synonyms in the English language.

ELIZABETH: In that case, I shall be regretfully forced to continue to say "Damn" whenever I feel like it.

[Edward Luton *shows himself at the window. He is an attractive youth in flannels*]

TEDDIE: I say, what about this tennis?

ELIZABETH: Come in. We're having a scene.

TEDDIE: [*Entering*] How splendid! What about?

ELIZABETH: The English language.

TEDDIE: Don't tell me you've been splitting your infinitives.

ARNOLD: [*With the shadow of a frown*] I wish you'd be serious, Elizabeth. The situation is none too pleasant.

ANNA: I think Teddie and I had better make ourselves scarce.

ELIZABETH: Nonsense! You're both in it. If there's going to be any unpleasantness we want your moral support. That's why we asked you to come.

TEDDIE: And I thought I'd been asked for my blue eyes.

ELIZABETH: Vain beast! And they happen to be brown.

TEDDIE: Is anything up?

ELIZABETH: Arnold's father arrived last night.

TEDDIE: Did he, by Jove! I thought he was in Paris.

ARNOLD: So did we all. He told me he'd be there for the next month.

ANNA: Have you seen him?

ARNOLD: No! He rang me up. It's a mercy he had a telephone put in the cottage. It would have been a pretty kettle of fish if he'd just walked in.

ELIZABETH: Did you tell him Lady Catherine was coming?

ARNOLD: Of course not. I was flabbergasted to know he was here. And then I thought we'd better talk it over first.

ELIZABETH: Is he coming along here?

ARNOLD: Yes. He suggested it, and I couldn't think of any excuse to prevent him.

TEDDIE: Couldn't you put the other people off?

ARNOLD: They're coming by car. They may be here any minute. It's too late to do that.

ELIZABETH: Besides, it would be beastly.

ARNOLD: I knew it was silly to have them here. Elizabeth insisted.

ELIZABETH: After all, she *is* your mother, Arnold.

ARNOLD: That meant precious little to her when she—went away. You can't imagine it means very much to me now.

ELIZABETH: It's thirty years ago. It seems so absurd to bear malice after all that time.

ARNOLD: I don't bear malice, but the fact remains that she did me the most irreparable harm. I can find no excuse for her.

ELIZABETH: Have you ever tried to?

ARNOLD: My dear Elizabeth, it's no good going over all that again. The facts are lamentably simple. She had a husband who adored her, a wonderful position, all the money she could want, and a child of five. And she ran away with a married man.

ELIZABETH: Lady Porteous is not a very attractive woman, Arnold. [*To* Anna] Do you know her?

ANNA: [*Smiling*] "Forbidding" is the word, I think.

ARNOLD: If you're going to make little jokes about it, I have nothing more to say.

ANNA: I'm sorry, Arnold.

ELIZABETH: Perhaps your mother couldn't help herself—if she was in love?

ARNOLD: And had no sense of honor, duty, or decency? Oh, yes, under those circumstances you can explain a great deal.

ELIZABETH: That's not a very pretty way to speak of your mother.

ARNOLD: I can't look on her as my mother.

ELIZABETH: What you can't get over is that she didn't think of you. Some of us are more mother and some of us more woman. It gives me a little thrill when I think that she loved that man so much. She sacrificed her name, her position, and her child to him.

ARNOLD: You really can't expect the said child to have any great affection for the mother who treated him like that.

ELIZABETH: No, I don't think I do. But I think it's a pity after all these years that you shouldn't be friends.

ARNOLD: I wonder if you realize what it was to grow up under the shadow of that horrible scandal. Everywhere, at school, and at Oxford, and afterward in London, I was always the son of Lady Kitty Cheney. Oh, it was cruel, cruel!

ELIZABETH: Yes, I know, Arnold. It was beastly for you.

ARNOLD: It would have been bad enough if it had been an ordinary case, but the position of the people made it ten times worse. My father was in the House then, and Porteous—he hadn't succeeded to the title—was in the House too; he was Under-Secretary for Foreign Affairs, and he was very much in the public eye.

ANNA: My father always used to say he was the ablest man in the party. Everyone was expecting him to be Prime Minister.

ARNOLD: You can imagine what a boon it was to the British public. They hadn't had such a treat for a generation. The most popular song of the day was about my mother. Did you ever hear it? "Naughty Lady Kitty. Thought it such a pity . . ."

ELIZABETH: [*Interrupting*] Oh, Arnold, don't!

ARNOLD: And then they never let people forget them. If they'd lived quietly in Florence and not made a fuss the scandal would have died down. But those constant actions between Lord and Lady Porteous kept on reminding everyone.

TEDDIE: What were they having actions about?

ARNOLD: Of course my father divorced his wife, but Lady Porteous refused to divorce Porteous. He tried to force her by refusing to support her and turning her out of her house, and heaven knows what. They were constantly wrangling in the law courts.

ANNA: I think it was monstrous of Lady Porteous.

ARNOLD: She knew he wanted to marry my mother, and she hated my mother. You can't blame her.

ANNA: It must have been very difficult for them.

ARNOLD: That's why they've lived in Florence. Porteous has money. They found people there who were willing to accept the situation.

ELIZABETH: This is the first time they've ever come to England.

ARNOLD: My father will have to be told, Elizabeth.

ELIZABETH: Yes.

ANNA: [To Elizabeth] Has he ever spoken to you about Lady Kitty?

ELIZABETH: Never.

ARNOLD: I don't think her name has passed his lips since she ran away from this house thirty years ago.

TEDDIE: Oh, they lived here?

ARNOLD: Naturally. There was a houseparty, and one evening neither Porteous nor my mother came down to dinner. The rest of them waited. They couldn't make it out. My father sent up to my mother's room, and a note was found on the pincushion.

ELIZABETH: [With a faint smile] That's what they did in the Dark Ages.

ARNOLD: I think he took a dislike to this house from that horrible night. He never lived here again, and when I married he handed the place over to me. He just has a cottage now on the estate that he comes to when he feels inclined.

ELIZABETH: It's been very nice for us.

ARNOLD: I owe everything to my father. I don't think he'll ever forgive me for asking these people to come here.

ELIZABETH: I'm going to take all the blame on myself, Arnold.

ARNOLD: [Irritably] The situation was embarrassing enough anyhow. I don't know how I ought to treat them.

ELIZABETH: Don't you think that'll settle itself when you see them?

ARNOLD: After all, they're my guests. I shall try and behave like a gentleman.

ELIZABETH: I wouldn't. We haven't got central heating.

ARNOLD: [Taking no notice] Will she expect me to kiss her?

ELIZABETH: [With a smile] Surely.

ARNOLD: It always makes me uncomfortable when people are effusive.

ANNA: But I can't understand why you never saw her before.

ARNOLD: I believe she tried to see me when I was little, but my father thought it better she shouldn't.

ANNA: Yes, but when you were grown up?

ARNOLD: She was always in Italy. I never went to Italy.

ELIZABETH: It seems to me so pathetic that if you saw one another in the street you wouldn't recognize each other.

ARNOLD: Is it my fault?

ELIZABETH: You've promised to be very gentle with her and very kind.

ARNOLD: The mistake was asking Porteous to come too. It looks as though we condoned the whole thing. And how am I to treat him? Am I to shake him by the hand and slap him on the back? He absolutely ruined my father's life.

ELIZABETH: [Smiling] How much would you give for a nice motor accident that prevented them from coming?

ARNOLD: I let you persuade me against my better judgment, and I've regretted it ever since.

ELIZABETH: [Good-humoredly] I think it's very lucky that Anna and Teddie are here. I don't foresee a very successful party.

ARNOLD: I'm going to do my best. I gave you my promise and I shall keep it. But I can't answer for my father.

ANNA: Here is your father.

[Mr. Champion-Cheney shows himself at one of the French windows]

C.-C.: May I come in through the window, or shall I have myself announced by a supercilious flunkey?

ELIZABETH: Come in. We've been expecting you.

C.-C.: Impatiently, I hope, my dear child.

[Mr. Champion-Cheney is a tall man in the early sixties, spare, with a fine head of gray hair and an intelligent, somewhat ascetic face. He is very carefully dressed. He is a man who makes the most of himself. He bears his years jauntily. He kisses Elizabeth and then holds out his hand to Arnold]

ELIZABETH: We thought you'd be in Paris for another month.

C.-C.: How are you, Arnold? I always reserve to myself the privilege of changing my mind. It's the only one elderly gentlemen share with pretty women.

ELIZABETH: You know Anna.

C.-C.: [Shaking hands with her] Of course I do. How very nice to see you here! Are you staying long?

ANNA: As long as I'm welcome.

ELIZABETH: And this is Mr. Luton.

C.-C.: How do you do? Do you play bridge?

LUTON: I do.

C.-C.: Capital. Do you declare without top honors?

LUTON: Never.

C.-C.: Of such is the kingdom of heaven. I see that you are a good young man.

LUTON: But, like the good in general, I am poor.

C.-C.: Never mind; if your principles are right, you can play ten shillings a hundred without danger. I never play less, and I never play more.

ARNOLD: And you—are going to stay long, Father?

C.-C.: To luncheon, if you'll have me.

[Arnold *gives* Elizabeth *a harassed look*]

ELIZABETH: That'll be jolly.

ARNOLD: I didn't mean that. Of course you're going to stay for luncheon. I meant, how long are you going to stay down here?

C.-C.: A week.

[*There is a moment's pause. Everyone but* Champion-Cheney *is slightly embarrassed*]

TEDDIE: I think we'd better chuck our tennis.

ELIZABETH: Yes. I want my father-in-law to tell me what they're wearing in Paris this week.

TEDDIE: I'll go and put the rackets away.

[Teddie *goes out*]

ARNOLD: It's nearly one o'clock, Elizabeth.

ELIZABETH: I didn't know it was so late.

ANNA: [*To* Arnold] I wonder if I can persuade you to take a turn in the garden before luncheon.

ARNOLD: [*Jumping at the idea*] I'd love it. [Anna *goes out of the windows, and as he follows her he stops irresolutely*] I want you to look at this chair I've just got. I think it's rather good.

C.-C.: Charming.

ARNOLD: About 1750, I should say. Good design, isn't it? It hasn't been restored or anything.

C.-C.: Very pretty.

ARNOLD: I think it was a good buy, don't you?

C.-C.: Oh, my dear boy! You know I'm entirely ignorant about these things.

ARNOLD: It's exactly my period . . . I shall see you at luncheon, then. [*He follows* Anna *through the window*]

C.-C.: Who is that young man?

ELIZABETH: Mr. Luton. He's only just been demobilized. He's the manager of a rubber estate in the F. M. S.

C.-C.: And what are the F. M. S. when they're at home?

ELIZABETH: The Federated Malay States. He joined up at the beginning of the war. He's just going back there.

C.-C.: And why have we been left alone in this very marked manner?

ELIZABETH: Have we? I didn't notice it.

C.-C.: I suppose it's difficult for the young to realize that one may be old without being a fool.

ELIZABETH: I never thought you that. Everyone knows you're very intelligent.

C.-C.: They certainly ought to by now. I've told them often enough. Are you a little nervous?

ELIZABETH: Let me feel my pulse. [*She puts her finger on her wrist*] It's perfectly regular.

C.-C.: When I suggested staying to luncheon Arnold looked exactly like a dose of castor oil.

ELIZABETH: I wish you'd sit down.

C.-C.: Will it make it easier for you? [*He takes a chair*] You have evidently something very disagreeable to say to me.

ELIZABETH: You won't be cross with me?

C.-C.: How old are you?

ELIZABETH: Twenty-five.

C.-C.: I'm never cross with a woman under thirty.

ELIZABETH: Oh, then I've got ten years.

C.-C.: Mathematics?

ELIZABETH: No. Paint.

C.-C.: Well?

ELIZABETH: [*Reflectively*] I think it would be easier if I sat on your knees.

C.-C.: That is a pleasing taste of yours, but you must take care not to put on weight.

[*She sits down on his knees*]

ELIZABETH: Am I bony?

C.-C.: On the contrary. . . . I'm listening.

ELIZABETH: Lady Catherine's coming here.

C.-C.: Who's Lady Catherine?

ELIZABETH: Your—Arnold's mother.

C.-C.: Is she?

[*He withdraws himself a little and* Elizabeth *gets up*]

ELIZABETH: You mustn't blame Arnold. It's my fault. I insisted. He was against it. I nagged till he gave way. And then I wrote and asked her to come.

C.-C.: I didn't know you knew her.

ELIZABETH: I don't. But I heard she was in London. She's staying at Claridge's. It seemed so heartless not to take the smallest notice of her.

C.-C.: When is she coming?

ELIZABETH: We're expecting her in time for luncheon.

C.-C.: As soon as that? I understand the embarrassment.

ELIZABETH: You see, we never expected you to be here. You said you'd be in Paris for another month.

C.-C.: My dear child, this is your house. There's no reason why you shouldn't ask whom you please to stay with you.

ELIZABETH: After all, whatever her faults, she's Arnold's mother. It seemed so unnatural that they should never see one another. My heart ached for that poor lonely woman.

C.-C.: I never heard that she was lonely, and she certainly isn't poor.

ELIZABETH: And there's something else. I couldn't ask her by herself. It would have been so—so insulting. I asked Lord Porteous, too.

C.-C.: I see.

ELIZABETH: I daresay you'd rather not meet them.

C.-C.: I daresay they'd rather not meet me. I shall get a capital luncheon at the cottage. I've noticed you always get the best food if you come in unexpectedly and have the same as they're having in the servants' hall.

ELIZABETH: No one's ever talked to me about Lady Kitty. It's always been a subject that everyone has avoided. I've never even seen a photograph of her.

C.-C.: The house was full of them when she left. I think I told the butler to throw them in the dustbin. She was very much photographed.

ELIZABETH: Won't you tell me what she was like?

C.-C.: She was very like you, Elizabeth, only she had dark hair instead of red.

ELIZABETH: Poor dear! It must be quite white now.

C.-C.: I daresay. She was a pretty little thing.

ELIZABETH: But she was one of the great beauties of her day. They say she was lovely.

C.-C.: She had the most adorable little nose, like yours. . . .

ELIZABETH: D'you like my nose?

C.-C.: And she was very dainty, with a beautiful little figure; very light on her feet. She was like a *marquise* in an old French comedy. Yes, she was lovely.

ELIZABETH: And I'm sure she's lovely still.

C.-C.: She's no chicken, you know.

ELIZABETH: You can't expect me to look at it as you and Arnold do. When you've loved as she's loved you may grow old, but you grow old beautifully.

C.-C.: You're very romantic.

ELIZABETH: If everyone hadn't made such a mystery of it I daresay I shouldn't feel as I do. I know she did a great wrong to you and a great wrong to Arnold. I'm willing to acknowledge that.

C.-C.: I'm sure it's very kind of you.

ELIZABETH: But she loved and she dared. Romance is such an elusive thing. You read of it in books, but it's seldom you see it face to face. I can't help it if it thrills me.

C.-C.: I am painfully aware that the husband in these cases is not a romantic object.

ELIZABETH: She had the world at her feet. You were rich. She was a figure in society. And she gave up everything for love.

C.-C.: [*Dryly*] I'm beginning to suspect it wasn't only for her sake and for Arnold's that you asked her to come here.

ELIZABETH: I seem to know her already. I think her face is a little sad, for a love like that doesn't leave you gay, it leaves you grave, but I think her pale face is unlined. It's like a child's.

C.-C.: My dear, how you let your imagination run away with you!

ELIZABETH: I imagine her slight and frail.

C.-C.: Frail, certainly.

ELIZABETH: With beautiful thin hands and white hair. I've pictured her so often in that Renaissance Palace that they live in, with old Masters on the walls and lovely carved things all round, sitting in a black silk dress with old lace round her neck and old-fashioned diamonds. You see, I never knew my mother; she died when I was a baby. You can't confide in aunts with huge families of their own. I want Arnold's mother to be a mother to me. I've got so much to say to her.

C.-C.: Are you happy with Arnold?

ELIZABETH: Why shouldn't I be?

C.-C.: Why haven't you got any babies?

ELIZABETH: Give us a little time. We've only been married three years.

C.-C.: I wonder what Hughie is like now!

ELIZABETH: Lord Porteous?

C.-C.: He wore his clothes better than any man in London. You know he'd have been Prime Minister if he'd remained in politics.

ELIZABETH: What was he like then?

C.-C.: He was a nice-looking fellow. Fine horseman. I suppose there was something very fascinating about him. Yellow hair and blue eyes, you know. He had a very good figure. I liked him. I was his parliamentary secretary. He was Arnold's god-father.

ELIZABETH: I know.

C.-C.: I wonder if he ever regrets!

ELIZABETH: I wouldn't.

C.-C.: Well, I must be strolling back to my cottage.

ELIZABETH: You're not angry with me?

C.-C.: Not a bit.

[*She puts up her face for him to kiss. He kisses her on both cheeks and then goes out. In a moment* Teddie *is seen at the window*]

TEDDIE: I saw the old blighter go.

ELIZABETH: Come in.

TEDDIE: Everything all right?

ELIZABETH: Oh, quite, as far as he's concerned. He's going to keep out of the way.

TEDDIE: Was it beastly?

ELIZABETH: No, he made it very easy for me. He's a nice old thing.

TEDDIE: You were rather scared.

ELIZABETH: A little. I am still. I don't know why.

TEDDIE: I guessed you were. I thought I'd come and give you a little moral support. It's ripping here, isn't it?

ELIZABETH: It is rather nice.

TEDDIE: It'll be jolly to think of it when I'm back in the F. M. S.

ELIZABETH: Aren't you homesick sometimes?

TEDDIE: Oh, everyone is now and then, you know.

ELIZABETH: You could have got a job in England if you'd wanted to, couldn't you?

TEDDIE: Oh, but I love it out there. England's ripping to come back to, but I couldn't live here now. It's like a woman you're desperately in love with as long as you don't see her, but when you're with her she maddens you so that you can't bear her.

ELIZABETH: [Smiling] What's wrong with England?

TEDDIE: I don't think anything's wrong with England. I expect something's wrong with me. I've been away too long. England seems to me full of people doing things they don't want to because other people expect it of them.

ELIZABETH: Isn't that what you call a high degree of civilization?

TEDDIE: People seem to me so insincere. When you go to parties in London they're all babbling about art, and you feel that in their hearts they don't care two-pence about it. They read the books that everybody is talking about because they don't want to be out of it. In the F. M. S. we don't get very many books, and we read those we have over and over again. They mean so much to us. I don't think the people over there are half so clever as the people at home, but one gets to know them better. You see, there are so few of us that we have to make the best of one another.

ELIZABETH: I imagine that frills are not much worn in the F. M. S. It must be a comfort.

TEDDIE: It's not much good being pretentious where everyone knows exactly who you are and what your income is.

ELIZABETH: I don't think you want too much sincerity in society. It would be like an iron girder in a house of cards.

TEDDIE: And then, you know, the place is ripping. You get used to a blue sky and you miss it in England.

ELIZABETH: What do you do with yourself all the time?

TEDDIE: Oh, one works like blazes. You have to be a pretty hefty fellow to be a planter. And then there's ripping bathing. You know, it's lovely, with palm trees all along the beach. And there's shooting. And now and then we have a little dance to a gramophone.

ELIZABETH: [Pretending to tease him] I think you've got a young woman out there, Teddie.

TEDDIE: [Vehemently] Oh, no!

[She is a little taken aback by the earnestness of his disclaimer. There is a moment's silence, then she recovers herself]

ELIZABETH: But you'll have to marry and settle down one of these days, you know.

TEDDIE: I want to, but it's not a thing you can do lightly.

ELIZABETH: I don't know why there more than elsewhere.

TEDDIE: In England if people don't get on they go their own ways and jog along after a fashion. In a place like that you're thrown a great deal on your own resources.

ELIZABETH: Of course.

TEDDIE: Lots of girls come out because they think they're going to have a good time. But if they're empty-headed, then they're just faced with their own emptiness and they're done. If their husbands can afford it they go home and settle down as grass-widows.

ELIZABETH: I've met them. They seem to find it a very pleasant occupation.

TEDDIE: It's rotten for their husbands, though.

ELIZABETH: And if the husbands can't afford it?

TEDDIE: Oh, then they tipple.

ELIZABETH: It's not a very alluring prospect.

TEDDIE: But if the woman's the right sort she wouldn't exchange it for any life in the world. When all's said and done it's we who've made the Empire.

ELIZABETH: What sort is the right sort?

TEDDIE: A woman of courage and endurance and sincerity. Of course, it's hopeless unless she's in love with her husband.

[He is looking at her earnestly and she, raising her eyes, gives him a long look. There is silence between them]

TEDDIE: My house stands on the side of a hill, and the coconut trees wind down to the shore. Azaleas grow in my garden, and camellias, and all sorts of ripping flowers. And in front of me is the winding coast line, and then the blue sea. [A pause] Do you know that I'm awfully in love with you?

ELIZABETH: [Gravely] I wasn't quite sure. I wondered.

TEDDIE: And you? [She nods slowly] I've never kissed you.

ELIZABETH: I don't want you to.

[They look at one another steadily. They are both grave. Arnold comes in hurriedly]

ARNOLD: They're coming, Elizabeth.

ELIZABETH: [As though returning from a distant world] Who?

ARNOLD: [Impatiently] My dear! My mother, of course. The car is just coming up the drive.

TEDDIE: Would you like me to clear out?

ARNOLD: No, no! For goodness' sake stay.

ELIZABETH: We'd better go and meet them, Arnold.

ARNOLD: No, no; I think they'd much better be shown in. I feel simply sick with nervousness.

[Anna comes in from the garden]

ANNA: Your guests have arrived.

ELIZABETH: Yes, I know.

ARNOLD: I've given orders that luncheon should be served at once.

ELIZABETH: Why? It's not half-past one already, is it?

ARNOLD: I thought it would help. When you don't know exactly what to say you can always eat.

[The Butler comes in and announces]

BUTLER: Lady Catherine Champion-Cheney! Lord Porteous!

[Lady Kitty comes in followed by Porteous, and the Butler goes out. Lady Kitty is a gay little lady, with dyed red hair and painted cheeks. She is somewhat outrageously dressed. She never forgets that she has been a *pretty woman and she still behaves as if she were twenty-five.* Lord Porteous *is a very bald, elderly gentleman in loose, rather eccentric clothes. He is snappy and gruff. This is not at all the couple that* Elizabeth *expected, and for a moment she stares at them with round, startled eyes.* Lady Kitty *goes up to her with outstretched hands*]

LADY KITTY: Elizabeth! Elizabeth! [*She kisses her effusively*] What an adorable creature. [*Turning to* Porteous] Hughie, isn't she adorable?

PORTEOUS: [*With a grunt*] Ugh!

[Elizabeth, *smiling now, turns to him and gives him her hand*]

ELIZABETH: How d'you do?

PORTEOUS: Damnable road you've got down here. How d'you do, my dear? Why d'you have such damnable roads in England?

[Lady Kitty's *eyes fall on* Teddie *and she goes up to him with her arms thrown back, prepared to throw them round him*]

LADY KITTY: My boy, my boy! I should have known you anywhere!

ELIZABETH: [*Hastily*] That's Arnold.

LADY KITTY: [*Without a moment's hesitation*] The image of his father! I should have known him anywhere! [*She throws her arms round his neck*] My boy, my boy!

PORTEOUS: [*With a grunt*] Ugh!

LADY KITTY: Tell me, would you have known me again? Have I changed?

ARNOLD: I was only five, you know, when—when you . . .

LADY KITTY: [*Emotionally*] I remember as if it was yesterday. I went up into your room. [*With a sudden change of manner*] By the way, I always thought that nurse drank. Did you ever find out if she really did?

PORTEOUS: How the devil can you expect him to know that, Kitty?

LADY KITTY: You've never had a child, Hughie; how can you tell what they know and what they don't?

ELIZABETH: [*Coming to the rescue*] This is Arnold, Lord Porteous.

PORTEOUS: [*Shaking hands with him*] How d'you do? I knew your father.

ARNOLD: Yes.

PORTEOUS: Alive still?

ARNOLD: Yes.

PORTEOUS: He must be getting on. Is he well?

ARNOLD: Very.

PORTEOUS: Ugh! Takes care of himself, I suppose. I'm not at all well. This damned climate doesn't agree with me.

ELIZABETH: [*To* Lady Kitty] This is Mrs. Shenstone. And this is Mr. Luton. I hope you don't mind a very small party.

LADY KITTY: [*Shaking hands with* Anna *and* Teddie] Oh, no, I shall enjoy it. I used to give enormous parties here. Political, you know. How nice you've made this room!

ELIZABETH: Oh, that's Arnold.

ARNOLD: [*Nervously*] D'you like this chair? I've just bought it. It's exactly my period.

PORTEOUS: [*Bluntly*] It's a fake.

ARNOLD: [*Indignantly*] I don't think it is for a minute.

PORTEOUS: The legs are not right.

ARNOLD: I don't know how you can say that. If there is anything right about it, it's the legs.

LADY KITTY: I'm sure they're right.

PORTEOUS: You know nothing whatever about it, Kitty.

LADY KITTY: That's what you think. *I* think it's a beautiful chair. Hepplewhite?

ARNOLD: No, Sheraton.

LADY KITTY: Oh, I know. "The School for Scandal."

PORTEOUS: Sheraton, my dear. Sheraton.

LADY KITTY: Yes, that's what I say. I acted the screen scene at some amateur theatricals in Florence, and Ermeto Novelli, the great Italian tragedian, told me he'd never seen a Lady Teazle like me.

PORTEOUS: Ugh!

LADY KITTY: [*To* Elizabeth] Do you act?

ELIZABETH: Oh, I couldn't. I should be too nervous.

LADY KITTY: I'm never nervous. I'm a born actress. Of course, if I had my time over again I'd go on the stage. You know, it's extraordinary how they keep young. Actresses, I mean. I think it's because they're always playing different parts. Hughie, do you think Arnold takes after me or after his father? Of course I think he's the very image of me. Arnold, I think I ought to tell you that I was received into the Catholic Church last winter. I've been thinking about it for years, and the last time we were at Monte Carlo I met such a nice monsignore. I told him what my difficulties were and he was too wonderful. I knew Hughie wouldn't approve, so I kept it a secret. [*To* Elizabeth] Are you interested in religion? I think it's too wonderful. We must have a long talk about it one of these days. [*Pointing to her frock*] Callot?

ELIZABETH: No, Worth.

LADY KITTY: I knew it was either Worth or Callot. Of course, it's line that's the important thing. I go to Worth myself, and I always say to him, "Line, my dear Worth, line." What *is* the matter, Hughie?

PORTEOUS: These new teeth of mine are so damned uncomfortable.

LADY KITTY: Men are extraordinary. They can't stand the smallest discomfort. Why, a woman's life is uncomfortable from the moment she gets up in the morning till the moment she goes to bed at night. And d'you think it's comfortable to sleep with a mask on your face?

PORTEOUS: They don't seem to hold up properly.

LADY KITTY: Well, that's not the fault of your teeth. That's the fault of your gums.

PORTEOUS: Damned rotten dentist. That's what's the matter.

LADY KITTY: I thought he was a very nice dentist. He told me *my* teeth would last till I was fifty. He has a Chinese room. It's so interesting; while he scrapes your teeth he tells you all about the dear Empress Dowager. Are you interested in China? I think it's too wonderful. You know they've cut off their pigtails. I think it's such a pity. They were so picturesque.

[*The* Butler *comes in*]

BUTLER: Luncheon is served, sir.

ELIZABETH: Would you like to see your rooms?

PORTEOUS: We can see our rooms after luncheon.

LADY KITTY: I must powder my nose, Hughie.

PORTEOUS: Powder it down here.

LADY KITTY: I never saw anyone so inconsiderate.

PORTEOUS: You'll keep us waiting half an hour. I know you.

LADY KITTY: [*Fumbling in her bag*] Oh, well, peace at any price, as Lord Beaconsfield said.

PORTEOUS: He said a lot of damned silly things, Kitty, but he never said that.

[Lady Kitty's *face changes. Perplexity is followed by dismay, and dismay by consternation*]

LADY KITTY: Oh!

ELIZABETH: What is the matter?

LADY KITTY: [*With anguish*] My lip-stick!

ELIZABETH: Can't you find it?

LADY KITTY: I had it in the car. Hughie, you remember that I had it in the car.

PORTEOUS: I don't remember anything about it.

LADY KITTY: Don't be so stupid, Hughie. Why, when we came through the gates I said: "My home, my home!" and I took it out and put some on my lips.

ELIZABETH: Perhaps you dropped it in the car.

LADY KITTY: For heaven's sake send some one to look for it.

ARNOLD: I'll ring.

LADY KITTY: I'm absolutely lost without my lip-stick. Lend me yours, darling, will you?

ELIZABETH: I'm awfully sorry. I'm afraid I haven't got one.

LADY KITTY: Do you mean to say you don't use a lip-stick?

ELIZABETH: Never.

PORTEOUS: Look at her lips. What the devil d'you think she wants muck like that for?

LADY KITTY: Oh, my dear, what a mistake you make! You *must* use a lip-stick. It's so good for the lips. Men like it, you know. I couldn't *live* without a lip-stick.

[Champion-Cheney *appears at the window holding in his upstretched hand a little gold case*]

C.-C.: [*As he comes in*] Has anyone here lost a diminutive utensil containing, unless I am mistaken, a favorite preparation for the toilet?

[Arnold *and* Elizabeth *are thunderstruck at his appearance and even* Teddie *and* Anna *are taken aback. But* Lady Kitty *is overjoyed*]

LADY KITTY: My lip-stick!

C.-C.: I found it in the drive and I ventured to bring it in.

LADY KITTY: It's Saint Antony. I said a little prayer to him when I was hunting in my bag.

PORTEOUS: Saint Antony be blowed! It's Clive, by God!

LADY KITTY: [*Startled, her attention suddenly turning from the lip-stick*] Clive!

C.-C.: You didn't recognize me. It's many years since we met.

LADY KITTY: My poor Clive, your hair has gone quite white!

C.-C.: [*Holding out his hand*] I hope you had a pleasant journey down from London.

LADY KITTY: [*Offering him her cheek*] You may kiss me, Clive.

C.-C.: [*Kissing her*] You don't mind, Hughie?

PORTEOUS: [*With a grunt*] Ugh!

C.-C.: [*Going up to him cordially*] And how are you, my dear Hughie?

PORTEOUS: Damned rheumatic if you want to know. Filthy climate you have in this country.

C.-C.: Aren't you going to shake hands with me, Hughie?

PORTEOUS: I have no objection to shaking hands with you.

C.-C.: You've aged, my poor Hughie.

PORTEOUS: Some one was asking me how old you were the other day.

C.-C.: Were they surprised when you told them?

PORTEOUS: Surprised! They wondered you weren't dead. [*The* Butler *comes in*]

BUTLER: Did you ring, sir?

ARNOLD: No. Oh, yes, I did. It doesn't matter now.

C.-C.: [*As the* Butler *is going*] One moment. My dear Elizabeth, I've come to throw myself on your mercy. My servants are busy with their own affairs. There's not a thing for me to eat in my cottage.

ELIZABETH: Oh, but we shall be delighted if you'll lunch with us.

C.-C.: It either means that or my immediate death from starvation. You don't mind, Arnold?

ARNOLD: My dear father!

ELIZABETH: [*To the* Butler] Mr. Cheney will lunch here.

BUTLER: Very good, ma'am.

C.-C.: [*To* Lady Kitty] And what do you think of Arnold?

LADY KITTY: I adore him.

C.-C.: He's grown, hasn't he? But then you'd expect him to do that in thirty years.

ARNOLD: For God's sake let's go in to lunch, Elizabeth!

CURTAIN

ACT II.

The Scene is the same as in the preceding act. It is afternoon. When the curtain rises Porteous *and* Lady Kitty, Anna *and* Teddie *are playing bridge.* Elizabeth *and* Champion-Cheney *are watching.* Porteous *and* Lady Kitty *are partners.*

C.-C.: When will Arnold be back, Elizabeth?

ELIZABETH: Soon, I think.

C.-C.: Is he addressing a meeting?

ELIZABETH: No, it's only a conference with his agent and one or two constituents.

PORTEOUS: [*Irritably*] How anyone can be expected to play bridge when people are shouting at the top of their voices all round them, I for one cannot understand.

ELIZABETH: [*Smiling*] I'm so sorry.

ANNA: I can see your hand, Lord Porteous.

PORTEOUS: It may help you.

LADY KITTY: I've told you over and over again to hold your cards up. It ruins one's game when one can't help seeing one's opponent's hand.

PORTEOUS: One isn't obliged to look.

LADY KITTY: What was Arnold's majority at the last election?

ELIZABETH: Seven hundred and something.

C.-C.: He'll have to fight for it if he wants to keep his seat next time.

PORTEOUS: Are we playing bridge, or talking politics?

LADY KITTY: I never find that conversation interferes with my game.

PORTEOUS: You certainly play no worse when you talk than when you hold your tongue.

LADY KITTY: I think that's a very offensive thing to say, Hughie. Just because I don't play the same game as you do you think I can't play.

PORTEOUS: I'm glad you acknowledge it's not the same game as I play. But why in God's name do you call it bridge?

C.-C.: I agree with Kitty. I hate people who play bridge as though they were at a funeral and knew their feet were getting wet.

PORTEOUS: Of course you take Kitty's part.

LADY KITTY: That's the least he can do.

C.-C.: I have a naturally cheerful disposition.

PORTEOUS: You've never had anything to sour it.

LADY KITTY: I don't know what you mean by that, Hughie.

PORTEOUS: [*Trying to contain himself*] Must you trump my ace?

LADY KITTY: [*Innocently*] Oh, was that your ace, darling?

PORTEOUS: [*Furiously*] Yes, it was my ace.

LADY KITTY: Oh, well, it was the only trump I had. I shouldn't have made it anyway.

PORTEOUS: You needn't have told them that. Now she knows exactly what I've got.

LADY KITTY: She knew before.

PORTEOUS: How could she know?

LADY KITTY: She said she'd seen your hand.

ANNA: Oh, I didn't. I said I could see it.

LADY KITTY: Well, I naturally supposed that if she could see it she did.

PORTEOUS: Really, Kitty, you have the most extraordinary ideas.

C.-C.: Not at all. If anyone is such a fool as to show me his hand, of course I look at it.

PORTEOUS: [*Fuming*] If you study the etiquette of bridge, you'll discover that onlookers are expected not to interfere with the game.

C.-C.: My dear Hughie, this is a matter of ethics, not of bridge.

ANNA: Anyhow, I get the game. And rubber.

TEDDIE: I claim a revoke.

PORTEOUS: Who revoked?

TEDDIE: You did.

PORTEOUS: Nonsense. I've never revoked in my life.

TEDDIE: I'll show you. [*He turns over the tricks to show the faces of the cards*] You threw away a club on the third heart trick and you had another heart.

PORTEOUS: I never had more than two hearts.

TEDDIE: Oh, yes, you had. Look here. That's the card you played on the last trick but one.

LADY KITTY: [*Delighted to catch him out*] There's no doubt about it, Hughie. You revoked.

PORTEOUS: I tell you I did not revoke. I never revoke.

C.-C.: You did, Hughie. I wondered what on earth you were doing.

PORTEOUS: I don't know how anyone can be expected not to revoke when there's this confounded chatter going on all the time.

TEDDIE: Well, that's another hundred to us.

PORTEOUS: [*To* Champion-Cheney] I wish you wouldn't breathe down my neck. I never can play bridge when there's somebody breathing down my neck.

[*The party have risen from the bridge-table, and they scatter about the room*]

ANNA: Well, I'm going to take a book and lie down in the hammock till it's time to dress.

TEDDIE: [*Who has been adding up*] I'll put it down in the book, shall I?

PORTEOUS: [*Who has not moved, setting out the cards for a patience*] Yes, yes, put it down. I never revoke. [Anna *goes out*]

LADY KITTY: Would you like to come for a little stroll, Hughie?

PORTEOUS: What for?

LADY KITTY: Exercise.

PORTEOUS: I hate exercise.

C.-C.: [*Looking at the patience*] The seven goes on the eight.

[Porteous *takes no notice*]

LADY KITTY: The seven goes on the eight, Hughie.

PORTEOUS: I don't choose to put the seven on the eight.

C.-C.: That knave goes on the queen.

PORTEOUS: I'm not blind, thank you.

LADY KITTY: The three goes on the four.

C.-C.: All these go over.

PORTEOUS: [*Furiously*] Am I playing this patience, or are you playing it?

LADY KITTY: But you're missing everything.

PORTEOUS: That's my business.

C.-C.: It's no good losing your temper over it, Hughie.

PORTEOUS: Go away, both of you. You irritate me.

LADY KITTY: We were only trying to help you, Hughie.

PORTEOUS: I don't want to be helped. I want to do it by myself.

LADY KITTY: I think your manners are perfectly deplorable, Hughie.

PORTEOUS: It's simply maddening when you're playing patience and people won't leave you alone.

C.-C.: We won't say another word.

PORTEOUS: That three goes. I believe it's coming out. If I'd been such a fool as to put that seven up I shouldn't have been able to bring these down. [*He puts down several cards while they watch him silently*]

LADY KITTY AND C.-C.: [*Together*] The four goes on the five.

PORTEOUS: [*Throwing down the cards violently*] Damn you! Why don't you leave me alone? It's intolerable.

C.-C.: It was coming out, my dear fellow.

PORTEOUS: I know it was coming out. Confound you!

LADY KITTY: How petty you are, Hughie!

PORTEOUS: Petty, be damned! I've told you over and over again that I will not be interfered with when I'm playing patience.

LADY KITTY: Don't talk to me like that, Hughie.

PORTEOUS: I shall talk to you as I please.

LADY KITTY: [*Beginning to cry*] Oh, you brute! You brute! [*She flings out of the room*]

PORTEOUS: Oh, damn! Now she's going to cry.

[*He stumbles out into the garden,* Champion-Cheney, Elizabeth *and* Teddie *are left alone. There is a moment's pause.* Champion-Cheney *looks from* Teddie *to* Elizabeth, *with an ironical smile*]

C.-C.: Upon my soul, they might be married. They frip so much.

ELIZABETH: [*Frigidly*] It's been nice of you to come here so often since they arrived. It's helped to make things easy.

C.-C.: Irony? It's a rhetorical form not much favored in this blessed plot, this earth, this realm, this England.

ELIZABETH: What exactly are you getting at?

C.-C.: How slangy the young women of the present day are! I suppose the fact that Arnold is a purist leads you to the contrary extravagance.

ELIZABETH: Anyhow you know what I mean.

C.-C.: [*With a smile*] I have a dim, groping suspicion.

ELIZABETH: You promised to keep away. Why did you come back the moment they arrived?

C.-C.: Curiosity, my dear child. A surely pardonable curiosity.

ELIZABETH: And since then you've been here all the time. You don't generally favor us with so much of your company when you're down at your cottage.

C.-C.: I've been excessively amused.

ELIZABETH: It has struck me that whenever they started fripping you took a malicious pleasure in goading them on.

C.-C.: I don't think there's much love lost between them now, do you?

[Teddie *is making as though to leave the room*]

ELIZABETH: Don't go, Teddie.

C.-C.: No, please don't. I'm only staying a minute. We were talking about Lady Kitty just before she arrived. [*To* Elizabeth] Do you remember? The pale, frail lady in black satin and old lace.

ELIZABETH: [*With a chuckle*] You are a devil, you know.

C.-C.: Ah, well, he's always had the reputation of being a humorist and a gentleman.

ELIZABETH: Did you expect her to be like that, poor dear?

C.-C.: My dear child, I hadn't the vaguest idea. You were asking me the other day what she was like when she ran away. I didn't tell you half. She was so gay and so natural. Who would have thought that animation would turn into such frivolity, and that charming impulsiveness lead to such a ridiculous affectation?

ELIZABETH: It rather sets my nerves on edge to hear the way you talk of her.

C.-C.: It's the truth that sets your nerves on edge, not I.

ELIZABETH: You loved her once. Have you no feeling for her at all?

C.-C.: None. Why should I?

ELIZABETH: She's the mother of your son.

C.-C.: My dear child, you have a charming nature, as simple, frank, and artless as hers was. Don't let pure humbug obscure your common sense.

ELIZABETH: We have no right to judge. She's only been here two days. We know nothing about her.

C.-C.: My dear, her soul is as thickly rouged as her face. She hasn't an emotion that's sincere. She's tinsel. You think I'm a cruel, cynical old man. Why, when I think of what she was, if I didn't laugh at what she has become I should cry.

ELIZABETH: How do you know she wouldn't be just the same now if she'd remained your wife? Do you think your influence would have had such a salutary effect on her?

c.-c.: [*Good-humoredly*] I like you when you're bitter and rather insolent.

ELIZABETH: D'you like me enough to answer my question?

c.-c.: She was only twenty-seven when she went away. She might have become anything. She might have become the woman you expected her to be. There are very few of us who are strong enough to make circumstances serve us. We are the creatures of our environment. She's a silly, worthless woman because she's led a silly, worthless life.

ELIZABETH: [*Disturbed*] You're horrible today.

c.-c.: I don't say it's I who could have prevented her from becoming this ridiculous caricature of a pretty woman grown old. But life could. Here she would have had the friends fit to her station, and a decent activity, and worthy interests. Ask her what her life has been all these years among divorced women and kept women and the men who consort with them. There is no more lamentable pursuit than a life of pleasure.

ELIZABETH: At all events she loved and she loved greatly. I have only pity and affection for her.

c.-c.: And if she loved what d'you think she felt when she saw that she had ruined Hughie? Look at him. He was tight last night after dinner and tight the night before.

ELIZABETH: I know.

c.-c.: And she took it as a matter of course. How long do you suppose he's been getting tight every night? Do you think he was like that thirty years ago? Can you imagine that that was a brilliant young man, whom everyone expected to be Prime Minister? Look at him now. A grumpy sodden old fellow with false teeth.

ELIZABETH: You have false teeth, too.

c.-c.: Yes, but damn it all, they fit. She's ruined him and she knows she's ruined him.

ELIZABETH: [*Looking at him suspiciously*] Why are you saying all this to me?

c.-c.: Am I hurting your feelings?

ELIZABETH: I think I've had enough for the present.

c.-c.: I'll go and have a look at the goldfish. I want to see Arnold when he comes in. [*Politely*] I'm afraid we've been boring Mr. Luton.

TEDDIE: Not at all.

c.-c.: When are you going back to the F. M. S.?

TEDDIE: In about a month.

c.-c.: I see. [*He goes out*]

ELIZABETH: I wonder what he has at the back of his head.

TEDDIE: D'you think he was talking at you?

ELIZABETH: He's as clever as a bagful of monkeys.

[*There is a moment's pause. Teddie hesitates a little and when he speaks it is in a different tone. He is grave and somewhat nervous*]

TEDDIE: It seems very difficult to get a few minutes alone with you. I wonder if you've been making it difficult?

ELIZABETH: I wanted to think.

TEDDIE: I've made up my mind to go away to-morrow.

ELIZABETH: Why?

TEDDIE: I want you altogether or not at all.

ELIZABETH: You're so arbitrary.

TEDDIE: You said so—you said you cared for me.

ELIZABETH: I do.

TEDDIE: Do you mind if we talk it over now?

ELIZABETH: No.

TEDDIE: [*Frowning*] It makes me feel rather shy and awkward. I've repeated to myself over and over again exactly what I want to say to you, and now all I'd prepared seems rather footling.

ELIZABETH: I'm so afraid I'm going to cry.

TEDDIE: I feel it's all so tremendously serious and I think we ought to keep emotion out of it. You're rather emotional, aren't you?

ELIZABETH: [*Half smiling and half in tears*] So are you for the matter of that.

TEDDIE: That's why I wanted to have everything I meant to say to you cut and dried. I think it would be awfully unfair if I made love to you and all that sort of thing, and you were carried away. I wrote it all down and thought I'd send it you as a letter.

ELIZABETH: Why didn't you?

TEDDIE: I got the wind up. A letter seems so—so cold. You see, I love you so awfully.

ELIZABETH: For goodness' sake don't say that.

TEDDIE: You mustn't cry. Please don't, or I shall go all to pieces.

ELIZABETH: [*Trying to smile*] I'm sorry. It doesn't mean anything really. It's only tears running out of my eyes.

TEDDIE: Our only chance is to be awfully matter-of-fact. [*He stops for a moment. He finds it quite difficult to control himself. He clears his throat. He frowns with annoyance at himself*]

ELIZABETH: What's the matter?

TEDDIE: I've got a sort of lump in my throat. It is idiotic. I think I'll have a cigarette. [*She watches him in silence while he lights a cigarette*] You see, I've never been in love with anyone before, not really. It's knocked me endways. I don't know how I can live without you now. . . . Does that old fool know I'm in love with you?

ELIZABETH: I think so.

TEDDIE: When he was talking about Lady Kitty smashing up Lord Porteous' career I thought there was something at the back of it.

ELIZABETH: I think he was trying to persuade me not to smash up yours.

TEDDIE: I'm sure that's very considerate of him, but I don't happen to have one to smash. I wish I had. It's the only time in my life I've wished I were a hell of a swell so I could chuck it all and show you how much more you are to me than anything else in the world.

ELIZABETH: [*Affectionately*] You're a dear old thing, Teddie.

TEDDIE: You know, I don't really know how to make love, but if I did I couldn't do it now because I just want to be absolutely practical.

ELIZABETH: [*Chaffing him*] I'm glad you don't know how to make love. It would be almost more than I could bear.

TEDDIE: You see, I'm not at all romantic and that sort of thing. I'm just a common or garden business man. All this is so dreadfully serious and I think we ought to be sensible.

ELIZABETH: [*With a break in her voice*] You owl!

TEDDIE: No, Elizabeth, don't say things like that to me. I want you to consider all the *pros* and *cons*, and my heart's thumping against my chest, and you know I love you, I love you, I love you.

ELIZABETH: [*In a sigh of passion*] Oh, my precious!

TEDDIE: [*Impatiently, but with himself, rather than with* Elizabeth] Don't be idiotic, Elizabeth. I'm not going to tell you that I can't live without you and a lot of muck like that. You know that you mean everything in the world to me. [*Almost giving it up as a bad job*] Oh, my God!

ELIZABETH: [*Her voice faltering*] D'you think there's anything you can say to me that I don't know already?

TEDDIE: [*Desperately*] But I haven't said a single thing I wanted to. I'm a business man. I want to put it all in a business way, if you understand what I mean.

ELIZABETH: [*Smiling*] I don't believe you're a very good business man.

TEDDIE: [*Sharply*] You don't know what you're talking about. I'm a first rate business man, but somehow this is different. [*Hopelessly*] I don't know why it won't go right.

ELIZABETH: What are we going to do about it?

TEDDIE: You see, it's not just because you're awfully pretty that I love you. I'd love you just as much if you were old and ugly. It's you I love, not what you look like. And it's not only love; love be blowed! It's that I *like* you so tremendously. I think you're such a ripping good sort. I just want to be with you. I feel so jolly and happy just to think you're there. I'm so awfully *fond* of you.

ELIZABETH: [*Laughing through her tears*] I don't know if this is your idea of introducing a business proposition.

TEDDIE: Damn you, you won't let me.

ELIZABETH: You said "Damn you."

TEDDIE: I meant it.

ELIZABETH: Your voice sounded as if you meant it, you perfect duck!

TEDDIE: Really, Elizabeth, you're intolerable.

ELIZABETH: I'm doing nothing.

TEDDIE: Yes, you are, you're putting me off my blow. What I want to say is perfectly simple. I'm a very ordinary business man.

ELIZABETH: You've said that before.

TEDDIE: [*Angrily*] Shut up. I haven't got a bob besides what I earn. I've got no position. I'm nothing.

You're rich and you're a big pot and you've got everything that anyone can want. It's awful cheek my saying anything to you at all. But after all there's only one thing that really matters in the world, and that's love. I love you. Chuck all this, Elizabeth, and come to me.

ELIZABETH: Are you cross with me?

TEDDIE: Furious.

ELIZABETH: Darling!

TEDDIE: If you don't want me tell me so at once and let me get out quickly.

ELIZABETH: Teddie, nothing in the world matters anything to me but you. I'll go wherever you take me. I love you.

TEDDIE: [*All to pieces*] Oh, my God!

ELIZABETH: Does it mean as much to you as that? Oh, Teddie!

TEDDIE: [*Trying to control himself*] Don't be a fool, Elizabeth.

ELIZABETH: It's you're the fool. You're making me cry.

TEDDIE: You're so damned emotional.

ELIZABETH: Damned emotional yourself. I'm sure you're a rotten business man.

TEDDIE: I don't care what you think. You've made me so awfully happy. I say, what a lark life's going to be!

ELIZABETH: Teddie, you are an angel.

TEDDIE: Let's get out quick. It's no good wasting time. Elizabeth.

ELIZABETH: What?

TEDDIE: Nothing. I just like to say Elizabeth.

ELIZABETH: You fool!

TEDDIE: I say, can you shoot?

ELIZABETH: No.

TEDDIE: I'll teach you. You don't know how ripping it is to start out from your camp at dawn and travel through the jungle. And you're so tired at night and the sky's all starry. It's a fair treat. Of course I didn't want to say anything about all that till you'd decided. I'd made up my mind to be absolutely practical.

ELIZABETH: [*Chaffing him*] The only practical thing you said was that love is the only thing that really matters.

TEDDIE: [*Happily*] Pull the other leg next time, will you? I should hate to have one longer than the other.

ELIZABETH: Isn't it fun being in love with some one who's in love with you?

TEDDIE: I say, I think I'd better clear out at once, don't you? It seems rather rotten to stay on in—in this house.

ELIZABETH: You can't go tonight. There's no train.

TEDDIE: I'll go tomorrow. I'll wait in London till you're ready to join me.

ELIZABETH: I'm not going to leave a note on the pincushion like Lady Kitty, you know. I'm going to tell Arnold.

TEDDIE: Are you? Don't you think there'll be an awful bother?

ELIZABETH: I must face it. I should hate to be sly and deceitful.

TEDDIE: Well, then, let's face it together.

ELIZABETH: No, I'll talk to Arnold by myself.

TEDDIE: You won't let anyone influence you?

ELIZABETH: No.

[*He holds out his hand and she takes it. They look into one another's eyes with grave, almost solemn affection. There is the sound outside of a car driving up*]

ELIZABETH: There's the car. Arnold's come back. I must go and bathe my eyes. I don't want them to see I've been crying.

TEDDIE: All right. [*As she is going*] Elizabeth.

ELIZABETH: [*Stopping*] What?

TEDDIE: Bless you.

ELIZABETH: [*Affectionately*] Idiot!

[*She goes out of the door and* Teddie *through the French window into the garden. For an instant the room is empty.* Arnold *comes in. He sits down and takes some papers out of his despatch-case.* Lady Kitty *enters. He gets up*]

LADY KITTY: I saw you come in. Oh, my dear, don't get up. There's no reason why you should be so dreadfully polite to me.

ARNOLD: I've just rung for a cup of tea.

LADY KITTY: Perhaps we shall have the chance of a little talk. We don't seem to have had five minutes by ourselves. I want to make your acquaintance, you know.

ARNOLD: I should like you to know that it's not by my wish that my father is here.

LADY KITTY: But I'm so interested to see him.

ARNOLD: I was afraid that you and Lord Porteous must find it embarrassing.

LADY KITTY: Oh, no. Hughie was his greatest friend. They were at Eton and Oxford together. I think your father has improved so much since I saw him last. He wasn't good-looking as a young man, but now he's quite handsome.

[*The* Footman *brings in a tray on which are tea-things*]

LADY KITTY: Shall I pour it out for you?

ARNOLD: Thank you very much.

LADY KITTY: Do you take sugar?

ARNOLD: No. I gave it up during the war.

LADY KITTY: So wise of you. It's so bad for the figure. Besides being patriotic, of course. Isn't it absurd that I should ask my son if he takes sugar or not? Life is really very quaint. Sad, of course, but oh, so quaint! Often I lie in bed at night and have a good laugh to myself as I think how quaint life is.

ARNOLD: I'm afraid I'm a very serious person.

LADY KITTY: How old are you now, Arnold?

ARNOLD: Thirty-five.

LADY KITTY: Are you really? Of course, I was a child when I married your father.

ARNOLD: Really. He always told me you were twenty-two.

LADY KITTY: Oh, what nonsense! Why, I was married out of the nursery. I put my hair up for the first time on my wedding-day.

ARNOLD: Where is Lord Porteous?

LADY KITTY: My dear, it sounds too absurd to hear you call him Lord Porteous. Why don't you call him —Uncle Hughie?

ARNOLD: He doesn't happen to be my uncle.

LADY KITTY: No, but he's your godfather. You know, I'm sure you'll like him when you know him better. I'm so hoping that you and Elizabeth will come and stay with us in Florence. I simply adore Elizabeth. She's too beautiful.

ARNOLD: Her hair is very pretty.

LADY KITTY: It's not touched up, is it?

ARNOLD: Oh, no.

LADY KITTY: I just wondered. It's rather a coincidence that her hair should be the same color as mine. I suppose it shows that your father and you are attracted by just the same thing. So interesting, heredity, isn't it?

ARNOLD: Very.

LADY KITTY: Of course, since I joined the Catholic Church I don't believe in it any more. Darwin and all that sort of thing. Too dreadful. Wicked, you know. Besides, it's not very good form, is it?

[Champion-Cheney *comes in from the garden*]

C.-C.: Do I intrude?

LADY KITTY: Come in, Clive. Arnold and I have been having such a wonderful heart-to-heart talk.

C.-C.: Very nice.

ARNOLD: Father, I stepped in for a moment at the Harveys' on my way back. It's simply criminal what they're doing with that house.

C.-C.: What are they doing?

ARNOLD: It's an almost perfect Georgian house and they've got a lot of dreadful Victorian furniture. I gave them my ideas on the subject, but it's quite hopeless. They said they were attached to their furniture.

C.-C.: Arnold should have been an interior decorator.

LADY KITTY: He has wonderful taste. He gets that from me.

ARNOLD: I suppose I have a certain *flair*. I have a passion for decorating houses.

LADY KITTY: You've made this one charming.

C.-C.: D'you remember, we just had chintzes and comfortable chairs when we lived here, Kitty.

LADY KITTY: Perfectly hideous, wasn't it?

C.-C.: In those days gentlemen and ladies were not expected to have taste.

ARNOLD: You know, I've been looking at this chair again. Since Lord Porteous said the legs weren't right I've been very uneasy.

LADY KITTY: He only said that because he was in a bad temper.

C.-C.: His temper seems to me very short these days, Kitty.

LADY KITTY: Oh, it is.

ARNOLD: You feel he knows what he's talking about. I gave seventy-five pounds for that chair. I'm very seldom taken in. I always think if a thing's right you feel it.

C.-C.: Well, don't let it disturb your night's rest.

ARNOLD: But, my dear father, that's just what it does. I had a most horrible dream about it last night.

LADY KITTY: Here is Hughie.

ARNOLD: I'm going to fetch a book I have on Old English furniture. There's an illustration of a chair which is almost identical with this one.

[Porteous comes in]

PORTEOUS: Quite a family gathering, by George!

C.-C.: I was thinking just now we'd make a very pleasing picture of a typical English home.

ARNOLD: I'll be back in five minutes. There's something I want to show you, Lord Porteous. [He goes out]

C.-C.: Would you like to play piquet with me, Hughie?

PORTEOUS: Not particularly.

C.-C.: You were never much of a piquet player, were you?

PORTEOUS: My dear Clive, you people don't know what piquet is in England.

C.-C.: Let's have a game then. You may make money.

PORTEOUS: I don't want to play with you.

LADY KITTY: I don't know why not, Hughie.

PORTEOUS: Let me tell you that I don't like your manner.

C.-C.: I'm sorry for that. I'm afraid I can't offer to change it at my age.

PORTEOUS: I don't know what you want to be hanging around here for.

C.-C.: A natural attachment to my home.

PORTEOUS: If you'd had any tact you'd have kept out of the way while we were here.

C.-C.: My dear Hughie. I don't understand your attitude at all. If I'm willing to let bygones be bygones why should you object?

PORTEOUS: Damn it all, they're not bygones.

C.-C.: After all, I am the injured party.

PORTEOUS: How the devil are you the injured party?

C.-C.: Well, you did run away with my wife, didn't you?

LADY KITTY: Now, don't let's go into ancient history. I can't see why we shouldn't all be friends.

PORTEOUS: I beg you not to interfere, Kitty.

LADY KITTY: I'm very fond of Clive.

PORTEOUS: You never cared two straws for Clive. You only say that to irritate me.

LADY KITTY: Not at all. I don't see why he shouldn't come and stay with us.

C.-C.: I'd love to. I think Florence in spring-time is delightful. Have you central heating?

PORTEOUS: I never liked you, I don't like you now, and I never shall like you.

C.-C.: How very unfortunate! Because I liked you, I like you now, and I shall continue to like you.

LADY KITTY: There's something very nice about you, Clive.

PORTEOUS: If you think that, why the devil did you leave him?

LADY KITTY: Are you going to reproach me because I loved you? How utterly, utterly, utterly detestable you are!

C.-C.: Now, now, don't quarrel with one another.

LADY KITTY: It's all his fault. I'm the easiest person in the world to live with. But really he'd try the patience of a saint.

C.-C.: Come, come, don't get upset, Kitty. When two people live together there must be a certain amount of give and take.

PORTEOUS: I don't know what the devil you're talking about.

C.-C.: It hasn't escaped my observation that you are a little inclined to frip. Many couples are. I think it's a pity.

PORTEOUS: Would you have the very great kindness to mind your own business?

LADY KITTY: It is his business. He naturally wants me to be happy.

C.-C.: I have the very greatest affection for Kitty.

PORTEOUS: Then why the devil didn't you look after her properly?

C.-C.: My dear Hughie, you were my greatest friend. I trusted you. It may have been rash.

PORTEOUS: It was inexcusable.

LADY KITTY: I don't know what you mean by that, Hughie.

PORTEOUS: Don't, don't, don't try and bully me, Kitty.

LADY KITTY: Oh, I know what you mean.

PORTEOUS: Then why the devil did you say you didn't?

LADY KITTY: When I think that I sacrificed everything for that man! And for thirty years I've had to live in a filthy marble palace with no sanitary conveniences.

C.-C.: D'you mean to say you haven't got a bathroom?

LADY KITTY: I've had to wash in a tub.

C.-C.: My poor Kitty, how you've suffered!

PORTEOUS: Really, Kitty, I'm sick of hearing of the sacrifices you made. I suppose you think I sacrificed nothing. I should have been Prime Minister by now if it hadn't been for you.

LADY KITTY: Nonsense!

PORTEOUS: What do you mean by that? Everyone said I should be Prime Minister. Shouldn't I have been Prime Minister, Clive?

C.-C.: It was certainly the general expectation.

PORTEOUS: I was the most promising young man of my day. I was bound to get a seat in the Cabinet at the next election.

LADY KITTY: They'd have found you out just as I've found you out. I'm sick of hearing that I ruined your career. You never had a career to ruin. Prime Minister! You haven't the brain. You haven't the character.

C.-C.: Cheek, push, and a gift of the gab will serve very well instead, you know.

LADY KITTY: Besides, in politics it's not the men that matter. It's the women at the back of them. I could have made Clive a Cabinet Minister if I'd wanted to.

PORTEOUS: Clive?

LADY KITTY: With my beauty, my charm, my force of character, my wit, I could have done anything.

PORTEOUS: Clive was nothing but my political secretary. When I was Prime Minister I might have made him Governor of some Colony or other. Western Australia, say. Out of pure kindness.

LADY KITTY: [With flashing eyes] D'you think I would have buried myself in Western Australia? With my beauty? My charm?

PORTEOUS: Or Barbadoes, perhaps.

LADY KITTY: [Furiously] Barbadoes! Barbadoes can go to——Barbadoes.

PORTEOUS: That's all you'd have got.

LADY KITTY: Nonsense! I'd have India.

PORTEOUS: I would never have given you India.

LADY KITTY: You would have given me India.

PORTEOUS: I tell you I wouldn't.

LADY KITTY: The King would have given me India. The nation would have insisted on my having India. I would have been a vice-reine or nothing.

PORTEOUS: I tell you that as long as the interests of the British Empire——damn it all, my teeth are coming out! [He hurries from the room]

LADY KITTY: It's too much. I can't bear it any more. I've put up with him for thirty years and now I'm at the end of my tether.

C.-C.: Calm yourself, my dear Kitty.

LADY KITTY: I won't listen to a word. I've quite made up my mind. It's finished, finished, finished. [With a change of tone] I was so touched when I heard that you never lived in this house again after I left it.

C.-C.: The cuckoos have always been very plentiful. Their note has a personal application which, I must say, I have found extremely offensive.

LADY KITTY: When I saw that you didn't marry again I couldn't help thinking that you still loved me.

C.-C.: I am one of the few men I know who is able to profit by experience.

LADY KITTY: In the eyes of the Church I am still your wife. The Church is so wise. It knows that in the end a woman always comes back to her first love. Clive, I am willing to return to you.

C.-C.: My dear Kitty, I couldn't take advantage of your momentary vexation with Hughie to let you take a step which I know you would bitterly regret.

LADY KITTY: You've waited for me a long time. For Arnold's sake.

C.-C.: Do you think we really need bother about Arnold? In the last thirty years he's had time to grow used to the situation.

LADY KITTY: [With a little smile] I think I've sown my wild oats, Clive.

C.-C.: I haven't. I was a good young man, Kitty.

LADY KITTY: I know.

C.-C.: And I'm very glad, because it has enabled me to be a wicked old one.

LADY KITTY: I beg your pardon.

[Arnold comes in with a large book in his hand]

ARNOLD: I say, I've found the book I was hunting for. Oh! Isn't Lord Porteous here?

LADY KITTY: One moment, Arnold. Your father and I are busy.

ARNOLD: I'm so sorry. [He goes out into the garden]

LADY KITTY: Explain yourself, Clive.

C.-C.: When you ran away from me, Kitty, I was sore and angry and miserable. But above all I felt a fool.

LADY KITTY: Men are so vain.

C.-C.: But I was a student of history, and presently I reflected that I shared my misfortune with very nearly all the greatest men.

LADY KITTY: I'm a great reader myself. It has always struck me as peculiar.

C.-C.: The explanation is very simple. Women dislike intelligence, and when they find it in their husbands they revenge themselves on them in the only way they can, by making them——well, what you made me.

LADY KITTY: It's ingenious. It may be true.

C.-C.: I felt I had done my duty by society and I determined to devote the rest of my life to my own entertainment. The House of Commons had always bored me excessively and the scandal of our divorce gave me an opportunity to resign my seat. I have been relieved to find that the country got on perfectly well without me.

LADY KITTY: But has love never entered your life?

C.-C.: Tell me frankly, Kitty, don't you think people make a lot of unnecessary fuss about love?

LADY KITTY: It's the most wonderful thing in the world.

C.-C.: You're incorrigible. Do you really think it was worth sacrificing so much for?

LADY KITTY: My dear Clive, I don't mind telling you that if I had my time over again I should be unfaithful to you, but I should not leave you.

C.-C.: For some years I was notoriously the prey of a secret sorrow. But I found so many charming creatures who were anxious to console that in the end it grew rather fatiguing. Out of regard to my health I ceased to frequent the drawing-rooms of Mayfair.

LADY KITTY: And since then?

c.-c.: Since then I have allowed myself the luxury of assisting financially a succession of dear little things, in a somewhat humble sphere, between the ages of twenty and twenty-five.

LADY KITTY: I cannot understand the infatuation of men for young girls. I think they're so dull.

c.-c.: It's a matter of taste. I love old wine, old friends, and old books, but I like young women. On their twenty-fifth birthday I give them a diamond ring and tell them they must no longer waste their youth and beauty on an old fogey like me. We have a most affecting scene, my technique on these occasions is perfect, and then I start all over again.

LADY KITTY: You're a wicked old man, Clive.

c.-c.: That's what I told you. But, by George! I'm a happy one.

LADY KITTY: There's only one course open to me now.

c.-c.: What is that?

LADY KITTY: [With a flashing smile] To go and dress for dinner.

c.-c.: Capital. I will follow your example.

[As Lady Kitty goes out Elizabeth comes in]

ELIZABETH: Where is Arnold?

c.-c.: He's on the terrace. I'll call him.

ELIZABETH: Don't bother.

c.-c.: I was just strolling along to my cottage to put on a dinner jacket. [As he goes out] Arnold.

[Exit C.-C.]

ARNOLD: Hulloa! [He comes in] Oh, Elizabeth, I've found an illustration here of a chair which is almost identical with mine. It's dated 1750. Look!

ELIZABETH: That's very interesting.

ARNOLD: I want to show it to Porteous. [Moving a chair which has been misplaced] You know, it does exasperate me the way people will not leave things alone. I no sooner put a thing in its place than somebody moves it.

ELIZABETH: It must be maddening for you.

ARNOLD: It is. You are the worst offender. I can't think why you don't take the pride that I do in the house. After all, it's one of the show places in the country.

ELIZABETH: I'm afraid you find me very unsatisfactory.

ARNOLD: [Good-humoredly] I don't know about that. But my two subjects are politics and decoration. I should be a perfect fool if I didn't see that you don't care two straws about either.

ELIZABETH: We haven't very much in common, Arnold, have we?

ARNOLD: I don't think you can blame me for that.

ELIZABETH: I don't. I blame you for nothing. I have no fault to find with you.

ARNOLD: [Surprised at her significant tone] Good gracious me! What's the meaning of all this?

ELIZABETH: Well, I don't think there's any object in beating about the bush. I want you to let me go.

ARNOLD: Go where?

ELIZABETH: Away. For always.

ARNOLD: My dear child, what are you talking about?

ELIZABETH: I want to be free.

ARNOLD: [Amused rather than disconcerted] Don't be ridiculous, darling. I daresay you're run down and want a change. I'll take you over to Paris for a fortnight if you like.

ELIZABETH: I shouldn't have spoken to you if I hadn't quite made up my mind. We've been married for three years and I don't think it's been a great success. I'm frankly bored by the life you want me to lead.

ARNOLD: Well, if you'll allow me to say so, the fault is yours. We lead a very distinguished, useful life. We know a lot of extremely nice people.

ELIZABETH: I'm quite willing to allow that the fault is mine. But how does that make it any better? I'm only twenty-five. If I've made a mistake I have time to correct it.

ARNOLD: I can't bring myself to take you very seriously.

ELIZABETH: You see, I don't love you.

ARNOLD: Well, I'm awfully sorry. But you weren't obliged to marry me. You've made your bed and I'm afraid you must lie on it.

ELIZABETH: That's one of the falsest proverbs in the English language. Why should you lie on the bed you've made if you don't want to? There's always the floor.

ARNOLD: For goodness' sake, don't be funny, Elizabeth.

ELIZABETH: I've quite made up my mind to leave you, Arnold.

ARNOLD: Come, come, Elizabeth, you must be sensible. You haven't any reason to leave me.

ELIZABETH: Why should you wish to keep a woman tied to you who wants to be free?

ARNOLD: I happen to be in love with you.

ELIZABETH: You might have said that before.

ARNOLD: I thought you'd take it for granted. You can't expect a man to go on making love to his wife after three years. I'm very busy. I'm awfully keen on politics and I've worked like a dog to make this house a thing of beauty. After all, a man marries to have a home, but also because he doesn't want to be bothered with sex and all that sort of thing. I fell in love with you the first time I saw you and I've been in love ever since.

ELIZABETH: I'm sorry, but if you're not in love with a man his love doesn't mean very much to you.

ARNOLD: It's so ungrateful. I've done everything in the world for you.

ELIZABETH: You've been very kind to me. But you've asked me to lead a life I don't like and that I'm not suited for. I'm awfully sorry to cause you pain, but now you must let me go.

ARNOLD: Nonsense! I'm a good deal older than you are and I think I have a little more sense. In your interests as well as in mine I'm not going to do anything of the sort.

ELIZABETH: [*With a smile*] How can you prevent me? You can't keep me under lock and key.

ARNOLD: Please don't talk to me as if I were a foolish child. You're my wife and you're going to remain my wife.

ELIZABETH: What sort of a life do you think we should lead? Do you think there'd be any more happiness for you than for me?

ARNOLD: But what is it precisely that you suggest?

ELIZABETH: Well, I want you to let me divorce you.

ARNOLD: [*Astounded*] Me? Thank you very much. Are you under the impression I'm going to sacrifice my career for a whim of yours?

ELIZABETH: How will it do that?

ARNOLD: My seat's wobbly enough as it is. Do you think I'd be able to hold it if I were in a divorce case? Even if it were a put-up job, as most divorces are nowadays, it would damn me.

ELIZABETH: It's rather hard on a woman to be divorced.

ARNOLD: [*With sudden suspicion*] What do you mean by that? Are you in love with some one?

ELIZABETH: Yes.

ARNOLD: Who?

ELIZABETH: Teddie Luton.

[*He is astonished for a moment, then bursts into a laugh*]

ARNOLD: My poor child, how can you be so ridiculous? Why, he hasn't a bob. He's a perfectly commonplace young man. It's so absurd I can't even be angry with you.

ELIZABETH: I've fallen desperately in love with him, Arnold.

ARNOLD: Well, you'd better fall desperately out.

ELIZABETH: He wants to marry me.

ARNOLD: I daresay he does. He can go to hell.

ELIZABETH: It's no good talking like that.

ARNOLD: Is he your lover?

ELIZABETH: No, certainly not.

ARNOLD: It shows that he's a mean skunk to take advantage of my hospitality to make love to you.

ELIZABETH: He's never even kissed me.

ARNOLD: I'd try telling that to the horse marines if I were you.

ELIZABETH: It's because I wanted to do nothing shabby that I told you straight out how things were.

ARNOLD: How long have you been thinking of this?

ELIZABETH: I've been in love with Teddie ever since I knew him.

ARNOLD: And you never thought of me at all, I suppose.

ELIZABETH: Oh, yes, I did. I was miserable. But I can't help myself. I wish I loved you, but I don't.

ARNOLD: I recommend you to think very carefully before you do anything foolish.

ELIZABETH: I have thought very carefully.

ARNOLD: By God! I don't know why I don't give you a sound hiding. I'm not sure if that wouldn't be the best thing to bring you to your senses.

ELIZABETH: Oh, Arnold, don't take it like that.

ARNOLD: How do you expect me to take it? You come to me quite calmly and say: "I've had enough of you. We've been married three years and I think I'd like to marry somebody else now. Shall I break up your home? What a bore for you! Do you mind my divorcing you? It'll smash up your career, will it? What a pity!" Oh, no, my girl, I may be a fool, but I'm not a damned fool.

ELIZABETH: Teddie is leaving here by the first train tomorrow. I warn you that I mean to join him as soon as he can make the necessary arrangements.

ARNOLD: Where is he?

ELIZABETH: I don't know. I suppose he's in his room.

[Arnold *goes to the door and calls*]

ARNOLD: George!

[*For a moment he walks up and down the room impatiently.* Elizabeth *watches him. The* Footman *comes in*]

FOOTMAN: Yes, sir.

ARNOLD: Tell Mr. Luton to come here at once.

ELIZABETH: Ask Mr. Luton if he wouldn't mind coming here for a moment.

FOOTMAN: Very good, madam.

[*Exit* Footman]

ELIZABETH: What are you going to say to him?

ARNOLD: That's my business.

ELIZABETH: I wouldn't make a scene if I were you.

ARNOLD: I'm not going to make a scene. [*They wait in silence*] Why did you insist on my mother coming here?

ELIZABETH: It seemed to me rather absurd to take up the attitude that I should be contaminated by her when . . .

ARNOLD: [*Interrupting*] When you were proposing to do exactly the same thing. Well, now you've seen her what do you think of her? Do you think it's been a success? Is that the sort of woman a man would like his mother to be?

ELIZABETH: I've been ashamed. I've been so sorry. It all seemed dreadful and horrible. This morning I happened to notice a rose in the garden. It was all over-blown and bedraggled. It looked like a painted old woman. And I remembered that I'd looked at it a day or two ago. It was lovely then, fresh and blooming and fragrant. It may be hideous now, but that doesn't take away from the beauty it had once. That was real.

ARNOLD: Poetry, by God! As if this were the moment for poetry!

[Teddie *comes in. He has changed into a dinner jacket*]

TEDDIE: [*To* Elizabeth] Did you want me?

ARNOLD: *I* sent for you. [Teddie *looks from* Arnold *to* Elizabeth. *He sees that something has happened*] When would it be convenient for you to leave this house?

TEDDIE: I was proposing to go tomorrow morning. But I can very well go at once if you like.

ARNOLD: I do like.

TEDDIE: Very well. Is there anything else you wish to say to me?

ARNOLD: Do you think it was a very honorable thing to come down here and make love to my wife?

TEDDIE: No, I don't. I haven't been very happy about it. That's why I wanted to go away.

ARNOLD: Upon my word, you're cool.

TEDDIE: I'm afraid it's no good saying I'm sorry and that sort of thing. You know what the situation is.

ARNOLD: Is it true that you want to marry Elizabeth?

TEDDIE: Yes. I should like to marry her as soon as ever I can.

ARNOLD: Have you thought of me at all? Has it struck you that you're destroying my home and breaking up my happiness?

TEDDIE: I don't see how there could be much happiness for you if Elizabeth doesn't care for you.

ARNOLD: Let me tell you that I refuse to have my home broken up by a twopenny-halfpenny adventurer who takes advantage of a foolish woman. I refuse to allow myself to be divorced. I can't prevent my wife from going off with you if she's determined to make a damned fool of herself, but this I tell you: nothing will induce me to divorce her.

ELIZABETH: Arnold, that would be monstrous.

TEDDIE: We could force you.

ARNOLD: How?

TEDDIE: If we went away together openly you'd have to bring an action.

ARNOLD: Twenty-four hours after you leave this house I shall go down to Brighton with a chorus-girl. And neither you nor I will be able to get a divorce. We've had enough divorces in our family. And now get out, get out, get out!

[Teddie *looks uncertainly at* Elizabeth]

ELIZABETH: [*With a little smile*] Don't bother about me. I shall be all right.

ARNOLD: Get out! Get out!

CURTAIN

ACT III.

The Scene is the same as in the preceding acts. It is the night of the same day as that on which takes place the action of the second act.

Champion-Cheney *and* Arnold, *both in dinner jackets, are discovered.* Champion-Cheney *is seated.* Arnold *walks restlessly up and down the room.*

c.-c.: I think, if you'll follow my advice to the letter, you'll probably work the trick.

ARNOLD: I don't like it, you know. It's against all my principles.

c.-c.: My dear Arnold, we all hope that you have before you a distinguished political career. You can't learn too soon that the most useful thing about a principle is that it can always be sacrificed to expediency.

ARNOLD: But supposing it doesn't come off? Women are incalculable.

c.-c.: Nonsense! Men are romantic. A woman will always sacrifice herself if you give her the opportunity. It is her favorite form of self-indulgence.

ARNOLD: I never know whether you're a humorist or a cynic, Father.

c.-c.: I'm neither, my dear boy; I'm merely a very truthful man. But people are so unused to the truth that they're apt to mistake it for a joke or a sneer.

ARNOLD: [*Irritably*] It seems so unfair that this should happen to me.

c.-c.: Keep your head, my boy, and do what I tell you.

[Lady Kitty *and* Elizabeth *come in.* Lady Kitty *is in a gorgeous evening gown*]

ELIZABETH: Where is Lord Porteous?

c.-c.: He's on the terrace. He's smoking a cigar. [*Going to window*] Hughie!

[Porteous *comes in*]

PORTEOUS: [*With a grunt*] Yes? Where's Mrs. Shenstone?

ELIZABETH: Oh, she had a headache. She's gone to bed.

[*When* Porteous *comes in* Lady Kitty *with a very haughty air purses her lips and takes up an illustrated paper.* Porteous *gives her an irritated look, takes another illustrated paper and sits himself down at the other end of the room. They are not on speaking terms*]

c.-c.: Arnold and I have just been down to my cottage.

ELIZABETH: I wondered where you'd gone.

c.-c.: I came across an old photograph album this afternoon. I meant to bring it along before dinner, but I forgot, so we went and fetched it.

ELIZABETH: Oh, do let me see it! I love old photographs.

[*He gives her the album, and she, sitting down, puts it on her knees and begins to turn over the pages. He stands over her.* Lady Kitty *and* Porteous *take surreptitious glances at one another*]

c.-c.: I thought it might amuse you to see what pretty women looked like five-and-thirty years ago. That was the day of beautiful women.

ELIZABETH: Do you think they were more beautiful then than they are now?

c.-c.: Oh, much. Now you see lots of pretty little things, but very few beautiful women.

ELIZABETH: Aren't their clothes funny?

C.-C.: [*Pointing to a photograph*] That's Mrs. Langtry.

ELIZABETH: She has a lovely nose.

C.-C.: She was the most wonderful thing you ever saw. Dowagers used to jump on chairs in order to get a good look at her when she came into a drawing-room. I was riding with her once, and we had to have the gates of the livery-stable closed when she was getting on her horse because the crowd was so great.

ELIZABETH: And who's that?

C.-C.: Lady Lonsdale. That's Lady Dudley.

ELIZABETH: This is an actress, isn't it?

C.-C.: It is, indeed. Ellen Terry. By George! How I loved that woman!

ELIZABETH: [*With a smile*] Dear Ellen Terry!

C.-C.: That's Bwabs. I never saw a smarter man in my life. And Oliver Montagu. Henry Manners with his eye-glass.

ELIZABETH: Nice-looking, isn't he? And this?

C.-C.: That's Mary Anderson. I wish you could have seen her in "A Winter's Tale." Her beauty just took your breath away. And look! There's Lady Randolph. Bernal Osborne—the wittiest man I ever knew.

ELIZABETH: I think it's too sweet. I love their absurd bustles and those tight sleeves.

C.-C.: What figures they had! In those days a woman wasn't supposed to be as thin as a rail and as flat as a pancake.

ELIZABETH: Oh, but aren't they laced in? How could they bear it?

C.-C.: They didn't play golf then, and nonsense like that, you know. They hunted, in a tall hat and a long black habit, and they were very gracious and charitable to the poor in the village.

ELIZABETH: Did the poor like it?

C.-C.: They had a very thin time if they didn't. When they were in London they drove in the Park every afternoon, and they went to ten-course dinners, where they never met anybody they didn't know. And they had their box at the opera when Patti was singing or Madam Albani.

ELIZABETH: Oh, what a lovely little thing! Who on earth is that?

C.-C.: That?

ELIZABETH: She looks so fragile, like a piece of exquisite china, with all those furs on and her face up against her muff, and the snow falling.

C.-C.: Yes, there was quite a rage at that time for being taken in an artificial snowstorm.

ELIZABETH: What a sweet smile, so roguish and frank, and debonair! Oh, I wish I looked like that! Do tell me who it is!

C.-C.: Don't you know?

ELIZABETH: No.

C.-C.: Why—it's Kitty.

ELIZABETH: Lady Kitty. [*To* Lady Kitty] Oh, my dear, do look! It's too ravishing. [*She takes the album over to her impulsively*] Why didn't you tell me you looked like that? Everybody must have been in love with you.

[Lady Kitty *takes the album and looks at it. Then she lets it slip from her hands and covers her face with her hands. She is crying*]

[*In consternation*] My dear, what's the matter? Oh, what have I done? I'm so sorry.

LADY KITTY: Don't, don't talk to me. Leave me alone. It's stupid of me.

[Elizabeth *looks at her for a moment perplexed, then, turning round, slips her arm in* Champion-Cheney's *and leads him out on to the terrace*]

ELIZABETH: [*As they are going, in a whisper*] Did you do that on purpose?

[Porteous *gets up and goes over to* Lady Kitty. *He puts his hand on her shoulder. They remain thus for a little while*]

PORTEOUS: I'm afraid I was very rude to you before dinner, Kitty.

LADY KITTY: [*Taking his hand which is on her shoulder*] It doesn't matter. I'm sure I was very exasperating.

PORTEOUS: I didn't mean what I said, you know.

LADY KITTY: Neither did I.

PORTEOUS: Of course I know that I'd never have been Prime Minister.

LADY KITTY: How can you talk such nonsense, Hughie? No one would have had a chance if you'd remained in politics.

PORTEOUS: I haven't the character.

LADY KITTY: You have more character than anyone I've ever met.

PORTEOUS: Besides, I don't know that I much wanted to be Prime Minister.

LADY KITTY: Oh, but I should have been so proud of you. Of course you'd have been Prime Minister.

PORTEOUS: I'd have given you India, you know. I think it would have been a very popular appointment.

LADY KITTY: I don't care twopence about India. I'd have been quite content with Western Australia.

PORTEOUS: My dear, you don't think I'd have let you bury yourself in Western Australia?

LADY KITTY: Or Barbadoes.

PORTEOUS: Never. It sounds like a cure for flat feet. I'd have kept you in London.

[*He picks up the album and is about to look at the photograph of* Lady Kitty. *She puts her hands over it*]

LADY KITTY: No, don't look.

[*He takes her hand away*]

PORTEOUS: Don't be so silly.

LADY KITTY: Isn't it hateful to grow old?

PORTEOUS: You know, you haven't changed much.

LADY KITTY: [*Enchanted*] Oh, Hughie, how can you talk such nonsense?

PORTEOUS: Of course you're a little more mature,

but that's all. A woman's all the better for being rather mature.

LADY KITTY: Do you really think that?

PORTEOUS: Upon my soul I do.

LADY KITTY: You're not saying it just to please me?

PORTEOUS: No, no.

LADY KITTY: Let me look at the photograph again. [*She takes the album and looks at the photograph complacently*] The fact is, if your bones are good, age doesn't really matter. You'll always be beautiful.

PORTEOUS: [*With a little smile, almost as if he were talking to a child*] It was silly of you to cry.

LADY KITTY: It hasn't made my eyelashes run, has it?

PORTEOUS: Not a bit.

LADY KITTY: It's very good stuff I use now. They don't stick together either.

PORTEOUS: Look here, Kitty, how much longer do you want to stay here?

LADY KITTY: Oh, I'm quite ready to go whenever you like.

PORTEOUS: Clive gets on my nerves. I don't like the way he keeps hanging about you.

LADY KITTY: [*Surprised, rather amused, and delighted*] Hughie, you don't mean to say you're jealous of poor Clive?

PORTEOUS: Of course I'm not jealous of him, but he does look at you in a way that I can't help thinking rather objectionable.

LADY KITTY: Hughie, you may throw me downstairs like Amy Robsart; you may drag me about the floor by the hair of my head; I don't care, you're jealous. I shall never grow old.

PORTEOUS: Damn it all, the man was your husband.

LADY KITTY: My dear Hughie, he never had your style. Why, the moment you come into a room everyone looks and says: "Who the devil is that?"

PORTEOUS: What? You think that, do you? Well, I daresay there's something in what you say. These damned Radicals can say what they like, but, by God, Kitty! When a man's a gentleman—well, damn it all, you know what I mean.

LADY KITTY: I think Clive has degenerated dreadfully since we left him.

PORTEOUS: What do you say to making a bee-line for Italy and going to San Michele?

LADY KITTY: Oh, Hughie! It's years since we were there.

PORTEOUS: Wouldn't you like to see it again—just once more?

LADY KITTY: Do you remember the first time we went? It was the most heavenly place I'd ever seen. We'd only left England a month, and I said I'd like to spend all my life there.

PORTEOUS: Of course I remember. And in a fortnight it was yours, lock, stock, and barrel.

LADY KITTY: We were very happy there, Hughie.

PORTEOUS: Let's go back once more.

LADY KITTY: I daren't. It must be all peopled with the ghosts of our past. One should never go again to a place where one has been happy. It would break my heart.

PORTEOUS: Do you remember how we used to sit on the terrace of the old castle and look at the Adriatic? We might have been the only people in the world, you and I, Kitty.

LADY KITTY: [*Tragically*] And we thought our love would last forever.

[*Enter* Champion-Cheney]

PORTEOUS: Is there any chance of bridge this evening?

C.-C.: I don't think we can make up a four.

PORTEOUS: What a nuisance that boy went away like that! He wasn't a bad player.

C.-C.: Teddie Luton?

LADY KITTY: I think it was very funny his going without saying good-by to anyone.

C.-C.: The young men of the present day are very casual.

PORTEOUS: I thought there was no train in the evening.

C.-C.: There isn't. The last train leaves at 5.45.

PORTEOUS: How did he go then?

C.-C.: He went.

PORTEOUS: Damned selfish I call it.

LADY KITTY: [*Intrigued*] Why did he go, Clive?

[Champion-Cheney *looks at her for a moment reflectively*]

C.-C.: I have something very grave to say to you. Elizabeth wants to leave Arnold.

LADY KITTY: Clive! What on earth for?

C.-C.: She's in love with Teddie Luton. That's why he went. The men of my family are really very unfortunate.

PORTEOUS: Does she want to run away with him?

LADY KITTY: [*With consternation*] My dear, what's to be done?

C.-C.: I think you can do a great deal.

LADY KITTY: I? What?

C.-C.: Tell her, tell her what it means.

[*He looks at her fixedly. She stares at him*]

LADY KITTY: Oh, no, no!

C.-C.: She's a child. Not for Arnold's sake. For her sake. You must.

LADY KITTY: You don't know what you're asking.

C.-C.: Yes, I do.

LADY KITTY: Hughie, what shall I do?

PORTEOUS: Do what you like. I shall never blame you for anything.

[*The* Footman *comes in with a letter on a salver. He hesitates on seeing that* Elizabeth *is not in the room*]

C.-C.: What is it?

FOOTMAN: I was looking for Mrs. Champion-Cheney, sir.

C.-C.: She's not here. Is that a letter?

FOOTMAN: Yes, sir. It's just been sent up from the "Champion Arms."

c.-c.: Leave it. I'll give it to Mrs. Cheney.

FOOTMAN: Very good, sir. [*He brings the tray to* Clive, *who takes the letter. The* Footman *goes out*]

PORTEOUS: Is the "Champion Arms" the local pub?

c.-c.: [*Looking at the letter*] It's by way of being a hotel, but I never heard of anyone staying there.

LADY KITTY: If there was no train I suppose he has to go there.

c.-c.: Great minds. I wonder what he has to write about! [*He goes to the door leading on to the garden*] Elizabeth!

ELIZABETH: [*Outside*] Yes.

c.-c.: Here's a note for you.

[*There is silence. They wait for* Elizabeth *to come. She enters*]

ELIZABETH: It's lovely in the garden tonight.

c.-c.: They've just sent this up from the "Champion Arms."

ELIZABETH: Thank you.

[*Without embarrassment she opens the letter. They watch her while she reads it. It covers three pages. She puts it away in her bag*]

LADY KITTY: Hughie, I wish you'd fetch me a cloak. I'd like to take a little stroll in the garden, but after thirty years in Italy I find these English summers rather chilly. [*Without a word* Porteous *goes out.* Elizabeth *is lost in thought*] I want to talk to Elizabeth, Clive.

c.-c.: I'll leave you. [*He goes out*]

LADY KITTY: What does he say?

ELIZABETH: Who?

LADY KITTY: Mr. Luton.

ELIZABETH: [*Gives a little start. Then she looks at* Lady Kitty] They've told you?

LADY KITTY: Yes. And now they have, I think I knew it all along.

ELIZABETH: I don't expect you to have much sympathy for me. Arnold is your son.

LADY KITTY: So pitifully little.

ELIZABETH: I'm not suited for this sort of existence. Arnold wants me to take what he calls my place in Society. Oh, I get so bored with those parties in London. All those middle-aged painted women, in beautiful clothes, lolloping round ballrooms with rather old young men. And the endless luncheons where they gossip about so-and-so's love affairs.

LADY KITTY: Are you very much in love with Mr. Luton?

ELIZABETH: I love him with all my heart.

LADY KITTY: And he?

ELIZABETH: He's never cared for anyone but me. He never will.

LADY KITTY: Will Arnold let you divorce him?

ELIZABETH: No, he won't hear of it. He refuses even to divorce me.

LADY KITTY: Why?

ELIZABETH: He thinks a scandal will revive all the old gossip.

LADY KITTY: Oh, my poor child!

ELIZABETH: It can't be helped. I'm quite willing to accept the consequences.

LADY KITTY: You don't know what it is to have a man tied to you only by his honor. When married people don't get on they can separate, but if they're not married it's impossible. It's a tie that only death can sever.

ELIZABETH: If Teddie stopped caring for me I shouldn't want him to stay with me for five minutes.

LADY KITTY: One says that when one's sure of a man's love, but when one isn't any more—oh, it's so different. In those circumstances one's got to keep a man's love. It's the only thing one has.

ELIZABETH: I'm a human being. I can stand on my own feet.

LADY KITTY: Have you any money of your own?

ELIZABETH: None.

LADY KITTY: Then how can you stand on your own feet? You think I'm a silly, frivolous woman, but I've learned something in a bitter school. They can make what laws they like, they can give us the suffrage, but when you come down to bedrock it's the man who pays the piper who calls the tune. Woman will only be the equal of man when she earns her living in the same way that he does.

ELIZABETH: [*Smiling*] It sounds rather funny to hear you talk like that.

LADY KITTY: A cook who marries a butler can snap her fingers in his face because she can earn just as much as he can. But a woman in your position and a woman in mine will always be dependent on the men who keep them.

ELIZABETH: I don't want luxury. You don't know how sick I am of all this beautiful furniture. These over-decorated houses are like a prison in which I can't breathe. When I drive about in a Callot frock and a Rolls-Royce I envy the shop-girl in a coat and skirt whom I see jumping on the tailboard of a bus.

LADY KITTY: You mean that if need be you could earn your own living?

ELIZABETH: Yes.

LADY KITTY: What could you be? A nurse or a typist. It's nonsense. Luxury saps a woman's nerve. And when she's known it once it becomes a necessity.

ELIZABETH: That depends on the woman.

LADY KITTY: When we're young we think we're different from everyone else, but when we grow a little older we discover we're all very much of a muchness.

ELIZABETH: You're very kind to take so much trouble about me.

LADY KITTY: It breaks my heart to think that you're going to make the same pitiful mistake that I made.

ELIZABETH: Oh, don't say it was that, don't, don't.

LADY KITTY: Look at me, Elizabeth, and look at Hughie. Do you think it's been a success? If I had my time over again do you think I'd do it again? Do you think he would?

ELIZABETH: You see, you don't know how much I love Teddie.

LADY KITTY: And do you think I didn't love Hughie? Do you think he didn't love me?

ELIZABETH: I'm sure he did.

LADY KITTY: Oh, of course in the beginning it was heavenly. We felt so brave and adventurous and we were so much in love. The first two years were wonderful. People cut me, you know, but I didn't mind. I thought love was everything. It *is* a little uncomfortable when you come upon an old friend and go towards her eagerly, so glad to see her, and are met with an icy stare.

ELIZABETH: Do you think friends like that are worth having?

LADY KITTY: Perhaps they're not very sure of themselves. Perhaps they're honestly shocked. It's a test one had better not put one's friends to if one can help it. It's rather bitter to find how few one has.

ELIZABETH: But one has some.

LADY KITTY: Yes, they ask you to come and see them when they're quite certain no one will be there who might object to meeting you. Or else they say to you: "My dear, you know I'm devoted to you, and I wouldn't mind at all, but my girl's growing up—I'm sure you understand; you won't think it unkind of me if I don't ask you to the house?"

ELIZABETH: [*Smiling*] That doesn't seem to me very serious.

LADY KITTY: At first I thought it rather a relief, because it threw Hughie and me together more. But you know, men are very funny. Even when they are in love they're not in love all day long. They want change and recreation.

ELIZABETH: I'm not inclined to blame them for that, poor dears.

LADY KITTY: Then we settled in Florence. And because we couldn't get the society we'd been used to we became used to the society we could get. Loose women and vicious men. Snobs who liked to patronize people with a handle to their names. Vague Italian Princes who were glad to borrow a few francs from Hughie and seedy countesses who liked to drive with me in the Cascine. And then Hughie began to hanker after his old life. He wanted to go big game shooting, but I dared not let him go. I was afraid he'd never come back.

ELIZABETH: But you knew he loved you.

LADY KITTY: Oh, my dear, what a blessed institution marriage is—for women, and what fools they are to meddle with it! The Church is so wise to take its stand on the indi—indi——

ELIZABETH: Solu——

LADY KITTY: Bility of marriage. Believe me, it's no joke when you have to rely only on yourself to keep a man. I could never afford to grow old. My dear, I'll tell you a secret that I've never told a living soul.

ELIZABETH: What is that?

LADY KITTY: My hair is not naturally this color.

ELIZABETH: Really.

LADY KITTY: I touch it up. You would never have guessed, would you?

ELIZABETH: Never.

LADY KITTY: Nobody does. My dear, it's white, premature of course, but white. I always think it's a symbol of my life. Are you interested in symbolism? I think it's too wonderful.

ELIZABETH: I don't think I know very much about it.

LADY KITTY: However tired I've been I've had to be brilliant and gay. I've never let Hughie see the aching heart behind my smiling eyes.

ELIZABETH: [*Amused and touched*] You poor dear.

LADY KITTY: And when I saw he was attracted by some one else the fear and the jealousy that seized me! You see, I didn't dare make a scene as I should have done if I'd been married—I had to pretend not to notice.

ELIZABETH: [*Taken aback*] But do you mean to say he fell in love with anyone else?

LADY KITTY: Of course he did eventually.

ELIZABETH: [*Hardly knowing what to say*] You must have been very unhappy.

LADY KITTY: Oh, I was dreadfully. Night after night I sobbed my heart out when Hughie told me he was going to play cards at the club and I knew he was with that odious woman. Of course, it wasn't as if there weren't plenty of men who were only too anxious to console me. Men have always been attracted by me, you know.

ELIZABETH: Oh, of course, I can quite understand it.

LADY KITTY: But I had my self-respect to think of. I felt that whatever Hughie did I would do nothing that I should regret.

ELIZABETH: You must be very glad now.

LADY KITTY: Oh, yes. Notwithstanding all my temptations I've been absolutely faithful to Hughie in spirit.

ELIZABETH: I don't think I quite understand what you mean.

LADY KITTY: Well, there was a poor Italian boy, young Count Castel Giovanni, who was so desperately in love with me that his mother begged me not to be too cruel. She was afraid he'd go into a consumption. What could I do? And then, oh, years later, there was Antonio Melita. He said he'd shoot himself unless I—well, you understand I couldn't let the poor boy shoot himself.

ELIZABETH: D'you think he really would have shot himself?

LADY KITTY: Oh, one never knows, you know. Those Italians are so passionate. He was really rather a lamb. He had such beautiful eyes.

[Elizabeth *looks at her for a long time and a certain horror seizes her of this dissolute, painted old woman*]

ELIZABETH: [*Hoarsely*] Oh, but I think that's—dreadful.

LADY KITTY: Are you shocked? One sacrifices one's life for love and then one finds that love doesn't last. The tragedy of love isn't death or separation. One gets over them. The tragedy of love is indifference.

[Arnold *comes in*]

ARNOLD: Can I have a little talk with you, Elizabeth?

ELIZABETH: Of course.

ARNOLD: Shall we go for a stroll in the garden?

ELIZABETH: If you like.

LADY KITTY: No, stay here. I'm going out anyway. [*Exit* Lady Kitty]

ARNOLD: I want you to listen to me for a few minutes, Elizabeth. I was so taken aback by what you told me just now that I lost my head. I was rather absurd and I beg your pardon. I said things I regret.

ELIZABETH: Oh, don't blame yourself. I'm sorry that I should have given you occasion to say them.

ARNOLD: I want to ask you if you've quite made up your mind to go.

ELIZABETH: Quite.

ARNOLD: Just now I seem to have said all that I didn't want to say and nothing that I did. I'm stupid and tongue-tied. I never told you how deeply I loved you.

ELIZABETH: Oh, Arnold!

ARNOLD: Please let me speak now. It's so very difficult. If I seemed absorbed in politics and the house, and so on, to the exclusion of my interest in you, I'm dreadfully sorry. I suppose it was absurd of me to think you would take my great love for granted.

ELIZABETH: But, Arnold, I'm not reproaching you.

ARNOLD: I'm reproaching myself. I've been tactless and neglectful. But I do ask you to believe that it hasn't been because I didn't love you. Can you forgive me?

ELIZABETH: I don't think that there's anything to forgive.

ARNOLD: It wasn't till today when you talked of leaving me that I realized how desperately in love with you I was.

ELIZABETH: After three years?

ARNOLD: I'm so proud of you. I admire you so much. When I see you at a party, so fresh and lovely, and everybody wondering at you, I have a sort of little thrill because you're mine, and afterwards I shall take you home.

ELIZABETH: Oh, Arnold, you're exaggerating.

ARNOLD: I can't imagine this house without you. Life seems on a sudden all empty and meaningless. Oh, Elizabeth, don't you love me at all?

ELIZABETH: It's much better to be honest. No.

ARNOLD: Doesn't my love mean anything to you?

ELIZABETH: I'm very grateful to you. I'm sorry to cause you pain. What would be the good of my staying with you when I should be wretched all the time?

ARNOLD: Do you love that man as much as all that? Does my unhappiness mean nothing to you?

ELIZABETH: Of course it does. It breaks my heart. You see, I never knew I meant so much to you. I'm so touched. And I'm so sorry, Arnold, really sorry. But I can't help myself.

ARNOLD: Poor child, it's cruel of me to torture you.

ELIZABETH: Oh, Arnold, believe me, I have tried to make the best of it. I've tried to love you, but I can't. After all, one either loves or one doesn't. Trying is no help. And now I'm at the end of my tether. I can't help the consequences—I must do what my whole self yearns for.

ARNOLD: My poor child, I'm so afraid you'll be unhappy. I'm so afraid you'll regret.

ELIZABETH: You must leave me to my fate. I hope you'll forget me and all the unhappiness I've caused you.

ARNOLD: [*There is a pause. Arnold walks up and down the room reflectively. He stops and faces her*] If you love this man and want to go to him I'll do nothing to prevent you. My only wish is to do what is best for you.

ELIZABETH: Arnold, that's awfully kind of you. If I'm treating you badly at least I want you to know that I'm grateful for all your kindness to me.

ARNOLD: But there's one favor I should like you to do me. Will you?

ELIZABETH: Oh, Arnold, of course I'll do anything I can.

ARNOLD: Teddie hasn't very much money. You've been used to a certain amount of luxury, and I can't bear to think that you should do without anything you've had. It would kill me to think that you were suffering any hardship or privation.

ELIZABETH: Oh, but Teddie can earn enough for our needs. After all, we don't want much money.

ARNOLD: I'm afraid my mother's life hasn't been easy, but it's obvious that the only thing that's made it possible is that Porteous was rich. I want you to let me make you an allowance of two thousand a year.

ELIZABETH: Oh, no, I couldn't think of it. It's absurd.

ARNOLD: I beg you to accept it. You don't know what a difference it will make.

ELIZABETH: It's awfully kind of you, Arnold. It humiliates me to speak about it. Nothing would induce me to take a penny from you.

ARNOLD: Well, you can't prevent me from opening an account at my bank in your name. The money shall be paid in every quarter whether you touch it or not, and if you happen to want it, it will be there waiting for you.

ELIZABETH: You overwhelm me, Arnold. There's

only one thing I want you to do for me. I should be very grateful if you would divorce me as soon as you possibly can.

ARNOLD: No, I won't do that. But I'll give you cause to divorce me.

ELIZABETH: You!

ARNOLD: Yes. But of course you'll have to be very careful for a bit. I'll put it through as quickly as possible, but I'm afraid you can't hope to be free for over six months.

ELIZABETH: But, Arnold, your seat and your political career!

ARNOLD: Oh, well, my father gave up his seat under very similar circumstances. He's got along very comfortably without politics.

ELIZABETH: But they're your whole life.

ARNOLD: After all one can't have it both ways. You can't serve God and Mammon. If you want to do the decent thing you have to be prepared to suffer for it.

ELIZABETH: But I don't want you to suffer for it.

ARNOLD: At first I rather hesitated at the scandal. But I daresay that was only weakness on my part. Under the circumstances I should have liked to keep out of the Divorce Court if I could.

ELIZABETH: Arnold, you're making me absolutely miserable.

ARNOLD: What you said before dinner was quite right. It's nothing for a man, but it makes so much difference to a woman. Naturally I must think of you first.

ELIZABETH: That's absurd. It's out of the question. Whatever there's to pay I must pay it.

ARNOLD: It's not very much I'm asking you, Elizabeth.

ELIZABETH: I'm taking everything from you.

ARNOLD: It's the only condition I make. My mind is absolutely made up. I will never divorce you, but I will enable you to divorce me.

ELIZABETH: Oh, Arnold, it's cruel to be so generous.

ARNOLD: It's not generous at all. It's the only way I have of showing you how deep and passionate and sincere my love is for you. [*There is a silence. He holds out his hand*] Good night. I have a great deal of work to do before I go to bed.

ELIZABETH: Good night.

ARNOLD: Do you mind if I kiss you?

ELIZABETH: [*With agony*] Oh, Arnold!

[*He gravely kisses her on the forehead and then goes out. Elizabeth stands lost in thought. She is shattered. Lady Kitty and Porteous come in. Lady Kitty wears a cloak*]

LADY KITTY: You're alone, Elizabeth?

ELIZABETH: That note you asked me about, Lady Kitty, from Teddie . . .

LADY KITTIE: Yes?

ELIZABETH: He wanted to have a talk with me before he went away. He's waiting for me in the summer house by the tennis court. Would Lord Porteous mind going down and asking him to come here?

PORTEOUS: Certainly. Certainly.

ELIZABETH: Forgive me for troubling you. But it's very important.

PORTEOUS: No trouble at all. [*He goes out*]

LADY KITTY: Hughie and I will leave you alone.

ELIZABETH: But I don't want to be left alone. I want you to stay.

LADY KITTY: What are you going to say to him?

ELIZABETH: [*Desperately*] Please don't ask me questions. I'm so frightfully unhappy.

LADY KITTY: My poor child!

ELIZABETH: Oh, isn't life rotten? Why can't one be happy without making other people unhappy?

LADY KITTY: I wish I knew how to help you. I'm simply devoted to you. [*She hunts about in her mind for something to do or say*] Would you like my lipstick?

ELIZABETH: [*Smiling through her tears*] Thanks. I never use one.

LADY KITTY: Oh, but just try. It's such a comfort when you're in trouble.

[*Enter Porteous and Teddie*]

PORTEOUS: I brought him. He said he'd be damned if he'd come.

LADY KITTY: When a lady sent for him? Are these the manners of the young men of today?

TEDDIE: When you've been solemnly kicked out of a house once I think it seems rather pushing to come back again as though nothing had happened.

ELIZABETH: Teddie, I want you to be serious.

TEDDIE: Darling, I had such a rotten dinner at that pub. If you ask me to be serious on the top of that I shall cry.

ELIZABETH: Don't be idiotic, Teddie. [*Her voice faltering*] I'm so utterly wretched.

[*He looks at her for a moment gravely*]

TEDDIE: What is it?

ELIZABETH: I can't come away with you, Teddie.

TEDDIE: Why not?

ELIZABETH: [*Looking away in embarrassment*] I don't love you enough.

TEDDIE: Fiddle!

ELIZABETH: [*With a flash of anger*] Don't say "Fiddle" to me.

TEDDIE: I shall say exactly what I like to you.

ELIZABETH: I won't be bullied.

TEDDIE: Now look here, Elizabeth, you know perfectly well that I'm in love with you, and I know perfectly well that you're in love with me. So what are you talking nonsense for?

ELIZABETH: [*Her voice breaking*] I can't say it if you're cross with me.

TEDDIE: [*Smiling very tenderly*] I'm not cross with with you, silly.

ELIZABETH: It's harder still when you're being rather an owl.

TEDDIE: [*With a chuckle*] Am I mistaken in thinking you're not very easy to please?

ELIZABETH: Oh, it's monstrous. I was all wrought up and ready to do anything, and now you've thoroughly put me out. I feel like a great big fat balloon that some one has put a long pin into. [*With a sudden look at him*] Have you done it on purpose?

TEDDIE: Upon my soul I don't know what you're talking about.

ELIZABETH: I wonder if you're really much cleverer than I think you are.

TEDDIE: [*Taking her hands and making her sit down*] Now tell me exactly what you want to say. By the way, do you want Lady Kitty and Lord Porteous to be here?

ELIZABETH: Yes.

LADY KITTY: Elizabeth asked us to stay.

TEDDIE: Oh, I don't mind, bless you. I only thought you might feel rather in the way.

LADY KITTY: [*Frigidly*] A gentlewoman never feels in the way, Mr. Luton.

TEDDIE: Won't you call me Teddie? Everybody does, you know.

[Lady Kitty *tries to give him a withering look, but she finds it very difficult to prevent herself from smiling.* Teddie *strokes* Elizabeth's *hands. She draws them away*]

ELIZABETH: No, don't do that. Teddie, it wasn't true when I said I didn't love you. Of course I love you. But Arnold loves me, too. I didn't know how much.

TEDDIE: What has he been saying to you?

ELIZABETH: He's been very good to me, and so kind. I didn't know he could be so kind. He offered to let me divorce him.

TEDDIE: That's very decent of him.

ELIZABETH: But don't you see, it ties my hands. How can I accept such a sacrifice? I should never forgive myself if I profited by his generosity.

TEDDIE: If another man and I were devilish hungry and there was only one mutton chop between us, and he said, "You eat it," I wouldn't waste a lot of time arguing. I'd wolf it before he changed his mind.

ELIZABETH: Don't talk like that. It maddens me. I'm trying to do the right thing.

TEDDIE: You're not in love with Arnold; you're in love with me. It's idiotic to sacrifice your life for a slushy sentiment.

ELIZABETH: After all, I did marry him.

TEDDIE: Well, you made a mistake. A marriage without love is no marriage at all.

ELIZABETH: *I* made the mistake. Why should he suffer for it? If anyone has to suffer it's only right that I should.

TEDDIE: What sort of a life do you think it would be with him? When two people are married it's very difficult for one of them to be unhappy without making the other unhappy too.

ELIZABETH: I can't take advantage of his generosity.

TEDDIE: I daresay he'll get a lot of satisfaction out of it.

ELIZABETH: You're being beastly, Teddie. He was simply wonderful. I never knew he had it in him. He was really noble.

TEDDIE: You are talking rot, Elizabeth.

ELIZABETH: I wonder if you'd be capable of acting like that.

TEDDIE: Acting like what?

ELIZABETH: What would you do if I were married to you and came and told you I loved somebody else and wanted to leave you?

TEDDIE: You have very pretty blue eyes, Elizabeth. I'd black first one and then the other. And after that we'd see.

ELIZABETH: You damned brute!

TEDDIE: I've often thought I wasn't quite a gentleman. Had it ever struck you?

[*They look at one another for a while*]

ELIZABETH: You know, you are taking an unfair advantage of me. I feel as if I came to you quite unsuspectingly and when I wasn't looking you kicked me on the shins.

TEDDIE: Don't you think we'd get on rather well together?

PORTEOUS: Elizabeth's a fool if she don't stick to her husband. It's bad enough for the man, but for the woman—it's damnable. I hold no brief for Arnold. He plays bridge like a foot. Saving your presence, Kitty, I think he's a prig.

LADY KITTY: Poor dear, his father was at his age. I daresay he'll grow out of it.

PORTEOUS: But you stick to him, Elizabeth, stick to him. Man is a gregarious animal. We're members of a herd. If we break the herd's laws we suffer for it. And we suffer damnably.

LADY KITTY: Oh, Elizabeth, my dear child, don't go. It's not worth it. It's not worth it. I tell you that, and I've sacrificed everything to love.

[*A pause*]

ELIZABETH: I'm afraid.

TEDDIE: [*In a whisper*] Elizabeth.

ELIZABETH: I can't face it. It's asking too much of me. Let's say good-by to one another, Teddie. It's the only thing to do. And have pity on me. I'm giving up all my hope of happiness.

[*He goes up to her and looks into her eyes*]

TEDDIE: But I wasn't offering you happiness. I don't think my sort of love tends to happiness. I'm jealous. I'm not a very easy man to get on with. I'm often out of temper and irritable. I should be fed to the teeth with you sometimes, and so would you be with me. I daresay we'd fight like cat and dog, and sometimes we'd hate each other. Often you'd be wretched and bored stiff and lonely, and often you'd be frightfully homesick, and then you'd regret all you'd lost. Stupid women would be rude to you because we'd run away together. And some of them would cut you. I don't offer you peace and quietness. I offer you unrest and anxiety. I don't offer you happiness. I offer you love.

ELIZABETH: [*Stretching out her arms*] You hateful creature. I absolutely adore you!

[*He throws his arms round her and kisses her passionately on the lips*]

LADY KITTY: Of course the moment he said he'd give her a black eye I knew it was finished.

PORTEOUS: [*Good-humoredly*] You are a fool, Kitty.

LADY KITTY: I know I am, but I can't help it.

TEDDIE: Let's make a bolt for it now.

ELIZABETH: Shall we?

TEDDIE: This minute.

PORTEOUS: You're damned fools, both of you, damned fools! If you like you can have my car.

TEDDIE: That's awfully kind of you. As a matter of fact I got it out of the garage. It's just along the drive.

PORTEOUS: [*Indignantly*] How do you mean, you got it out of the garage?

TEDDIE: Well, I thought there'd be a lot of bother, and it seemed to me the best thing would be for Elizabeth and me not to stand upon the order of our going, you know. Do it now. An excellent motto for a business man.

PORTEOUS: Do you mean to say you were going to steal my car?

TEDDIE: Not exactly. I was only going to bolshevize it, so to speak.

PORTEOUS: I'm speechless. I'm absolutely speechless.

TEDDIE: Hang it all, I couldn't carry Elizabeth all the way to London. She's so damned plump.

ELIZABETH: You dirty dog!

PORTEOUS: [*Spluttering*] Well, well, well! . . . [*Helplessly*] I like him, Kitty, it's no good pretending I don't. I like him.

TEDDIE: The moon's shining, Elizabeth. We'll drive all through the night.

PORTEOUS: They'd better go to San Michele. I'll wire to have it got ready for them.

LADY KITTY: That's where we went when Hughie and I . . . [*Faltering*] Oh, you dear things, how I envy you!

PORTEOUS: [*Mopping his eyes*] Now don't cry, Kitty. Confound you, don't cry.

TEDDIE: Come, darling.

ELIZABETH: But I can't go like this.

TEDDIE: Nonsense! Lady Kitty will lend you her cloak. Won't you?

LADY KITTY: [*Taking it off*] You're capable of tearing it off my back if I don't.

TEDDIE: [*Putting the cloak on* Elizabeth] And

we'll buy you a tooth-brush in London in the morning.

LADY KITTY: She must write a note for Arnold. I'll put it on her pin-cushion.

TEDDIE: Pin-cushion be blowed! Come, darling. We'll drive through the dawn and through the sunrise.

ELIZABETH: [*Kissing* Lady Kitty *and* Porteous] Good-by. Good-by.

[Teddie *stretches out his hand and she takes it. Hand in hand they go out into the night*]

LADY KITTY: Oh, Hughie, how it all comes back to me! Will they suffer all we suffered? And have we suffered all in vain?

PORTEOUS: My dear, I don't know that in life it matters so much what you do as what you are. No one can learn by the experience of another because no circumstances are quite the same. If we made rather a hash of things perhaps it was because we were rather trivial people. You can do anything in this world if you're prepared to take the consequences, and consequences depend on character.

[*Enter* Champion-Cheney, *rubbing his hands. He is as pleased as Punch*]

C.-C.: Well, I think I've settled the hash of that young man.

LADY KITTY: Oh!

C.-C.: You have to get up very early in the morning to get the better of your humble servant.

[*There is the sound of a car starting*]

LADY KITTY: What is that?

C.-C.: It sounds like a car. I expect it's your chauffeur taking one of the maids for a joy-ride.

PORTEOUS: Whose hash are you talking about?

C.-C.: Mr. Edward Luton's, my dear Hughie. I told Arnold exactly what to do and he's done it. What makes a prison? Why, bars and bolts. Remove them and a prisoner won't want to escape. Clever, I flatter myself.

PORTEOUS: You were always that, Clive, but at the moment you're obscure.

C.-C.: I told Arnold to go to Elizabeth and tell her she could have her freedom. I told him to sacrifice himself all along the line. I know what women are. The moment every obstacle was removed to her marriage with Teddie Luton, half the allurement was gone.

LADY KITTY: Arnold did that?

C.-C.: He followed my instructions to the letter. I've just seen him. She's shaken. I'm willing to bet five hundred pounds to a penny that she won't bolt. A downy old bird, eh? Downy's the word. Downy.

[*He begins to laugh. They laugh, too. Presently they are all three in fits of laughter*]

CURTAIN

R. C. Sherriff

(1896– ——)

England, proverbially the land where people move slowly if steadily, first had its big season of antiwar drama in 1929—eleven years after the end of the First World War and only four years before Adolf Hitler began preparing a second holocaust. And even that season is memorable largely for one play by a hitherto inconspicuous young man: *Journey's End*.

Robert Cedric Sherriff was to all appearances a typical member of the World War generation. Born in 1896, he had hardly completed his education at New College, Oxford, and joined the Sun Insurance Company, when he was called to take up arms in his country's service. Like his Stanhope in *Journey's End*, he became a captain in the British forces at the green age of twenty-one. Then, upon being discharged, he became just another young man in pursuit of a livelihood. He returned to his commonplace profession of junior insurance clerk, relieving the tedium with week-end sports and amateur playwriting for schools and clubs. His memories of Armageddon were not, however, eradicated by civilian life but merely submerged. When it became necessary for him to compose a play for his boat club, which required an all-male cast, he drew readily enough upon his recollections. The result was the war play *Journey's End*.

From 1914 to 1919, England's commercial West End theatres subsisted on musical fluff and saccharine. *Chu Chin Chow* delighted the multitude; *Romance* rolled up over a thousand performances; *Peg o' My Heart* enjoyed a three years' run; *Daddy Long Legs* was a great favorite; and James M. Barrie's *A Kiss for Cinderella* and *The Old Lady Shows Her Medals* tugged at the heartstrings. Then the First World War gradually found expression. Not unexpectedly, the quickest and profoundest response came from Shaw, whose *Heartbreak House* announced a general collapse of the old order. Many of Shaw's later blasts on the sad state of affairs in Europe and on the ruinous folly of mankind are also traceable to the war's effects. Galsworthy's reaction, in *The Skin-Game*, was typically that of a gentleman, moralist, and moderator. Among the younger playwrights, Somerset Maugham, who had served in the medical corps and eased his convalescence in a Swiss sanatorium with the farcical amenities of *Home and Beauty,* delivered himself in 1933 of a long-suppressed bitterness in the drama of postwar doldrums *For Services Rendered*. The still younger playwright Noel Coward reflected the cynicism and instability of the postwar generation in his comedies and farces. (It is perhaps significant that he wrote one of the most successful of these, *Private Lives*, while performing in *Journey's End* with a theatrical company in Shanghai.) Direct attacks on imperialism or militarism, such as C. K. Munro's *The Rumour* and Allan Monkhouse's *The Conquering Hero,* also appeared on the stage, and Robert Nichols and Maurice Browne, in *Wings Over Europe*, envisioned the possibility of war-making statesmen being checkmated by resolute men of science who have split the atom.

It is true, nevertheless, that the keenest effects of the war, as well as of its aftermath, were not felt in the British theatre. It was in Central Europe, which had been defeated and was most thoroughly shaken by the postwar upheaval, that the drama of protest reached the highest pitch, with Toller's *Man and the Masses,* Werfel's *Goat Song,* Chlumberg's *Miracle at Verdun,* Piscator's *The Good Soldier Schweik,* and Friedrich Wolf's revolutionary *Sailors of Cattaro*. In England, only Sherriff's *Journey's End,* presented in the same year as Munro's *The Rumour* and O'Casey's *The Silver Tassie* (produced in London because the Dublin Abbey Theatre had rejected it), gave complete testimony of the trenches and the shellfire, the terror and the fortitude of the men at the front, and the dreadful waste of young blood. "For ten years," writes the English chronicler Ernest Short in his *Theatrical Cavalcade,* "the topic had seemed too painful for public discussion."

Journey's End was typically British in its refinement of taste, its emphasis on courtesy, its strict division of the characters into gentlemen and comic plebeians, and its tribute to hero-worship and gallantry, which almost suggested a glorification of war not intended by the author. ("There were those," Ernest Short recalls, "who welcomed *Journey's End* as excellent anti-war propaganda, but its stark picture of life in the trenches stirred many more to a sense of nobility which underlies even the ugliest battle when it is waged for something other than self.") But the quiet truthfulness of the play, its picture of shattered nerves and summary annihilation, proved overwhelming. After vain attempts to place the seemingly unpromising play with commercial managements and a single Sunday-evening performance by the Stage Society of London, Sherriff won the interest of the enterprising Arts Theatre Club producer Maurice Browne. The West End production, which opened in January 1929, won immediate acclaim; it became, in fact, one of the most memorable successes of the postwar theatre. As a result, Browne was sufficiently supplied with funds to give London eleven unconventional productions within a year, including an *Othello* with Paul Robeson playing the Moor, more than a dozen years before he played this role in New York for the Theatre Guild. And Sherriff became the young writer of whom the English theatre expected most in serious drama.

Nothing that Sherriff created after this war drama added materially to his reputation as a playwright. He wrote a successful novel, *A Fortnight in September,* and the scenario of the postwar film *The Road Back* (1932). But his comedy *Badger's Green* failed to interest London; and although his *St. Helena,* a collaboration with Jeanne de Casalis, was a considered antiheroic treatment of Napoleon in exile and enjoyed the services of Maurice Evans, it proved too static for the stage. Its author may have defined his limitations when he wrote, "If I had not been a quite ordinary man, I should have got *Journey's End* all wrong." But *Journey's End* was not an ordinary play, and at least for one brief period Sherriff was no ordinary man.

Burns Mantle wrote of Sherriff's play: "If his drama lacks something of the vitality of the Stallings-Anderson study [*What Price Glory?*] of the American doughboy cursing his way through the grime and muck of the trenches, or playing at hearts with the wenches back of the line, it added something a little finer in the way of character analyses and psychological problems and never failed to give its human soldier men something interesting to say or do at entrance and exit and in between. It is an ambling play, in a physical sense, but one that weaves a spell of reality about its players and stimulates the imagination of its auditors quite as much by the art of understatement as by the crash of exciting scenes. The big dramatic moment in *Journey's End* is a daylight raid conducted by twelve men of whom five come back. But a scene of quiet intensity in which a former headmaster of a boy's school talks of hollyhocks and *Alice in Wonderland* to keep the young lieutenant's mind off the approach of the zero hour is one that many *Journey's End* enthusiasts boast of remembering most vividly."

This description can hardly be improved upon, and will be questioned only by Americans who resented traces of British snobbery after seeing the New York performance. Such criticism may be considered inconsequential, however, beside the quality that Stark Young has called its "poetry of human concern," its "tenderness toward all life," its "shyness and passion." That Sherriff sometimes tended to be romantic or sentimental does not invalidate his genuineness. The play, with its objective note-taking, is essentially British in its restraint. Stark Young expressed this well when, reporting on the March 1929 Broadway production, in which Colin Keith-Johnston distinguished himself as Stanhope, he wrote, "The best things in *Journey's End* are not so much written there as they are felt by the author."

BIBLIOGRAPHY: Ernest Short, *Theatrical Cavalcade* (pp. 152–154), 1942; Stark Young, *Immortal Shadows* (pp. 110–113), 1948.

JOURNEY'S END

By R. C. Sherriff

CHARACTERS

CAPTAIN HARDY
LIEUTENANT OSBORNE
PRIVATE MASON

SECOND LIEUTENANT RALEIGH
CAPTAIN STANHOPE
SECOND LIEUTENANT HIBBERT
COMPANY SERGEANT-MAJOR

THE COLONEL
SECOND LIEUTENANT TROTTER
GERMAN SOLDIER

THE SCENE.—*A dug-out in the British trenches before St. Quentin.*

A few rough steps lead into the trench above, through a low doorway. A table occupies a good space of the dug-out floor. A wooden frame, covered with wire netting, stands against the left wall and serves the double purpose of a bed and a seat for the table. A wooden bench against the back wall makes another seat, and two boxes serve for the other sides.

Another wire-covered bed is fixed in the right corner beyond the doorway.

Gloomy tunnels lead out of the dug-out to left and right.

Except for the table, beds, and seats, there is no furniture save the bottles holding the candles, and a few tattered magazine pictures pinned to the wall of girls in flimsy costumes.

The earth walls deaden the sounds of war, making them faint and far away, although the front line is only fifty yards ahead. The flames of the candles that burn day and night are steady in the still, damp air.

ACT ONE: Evening on Monday, March 18, 1918
ACT TWO:
  Scene I: Tuesday morning
  Scene II: Tuesday afternoon
ACT THREE:
  Scene I: Wednesday afternoon
  Scene II: Wednesday night
  Scene III: Thursday, towards dawn

ACT I.

The evening of a March day. A pale glimmer of moonlight shines down the narrow steps into one corner of the dug-out. Warm yellow candle-flames light the other corner from the necks of two bottles on the table. Through the doorway can be seen the misty gray parapet of a trench and a narrow strip of starlit sky. A bottle of whisky, a jar of water, and a mug stand on the table among a litter of papers and magazines. An officer's equipment hangs in a jumbled mass from a nail in the wall.

Captain Hardy, *a red-faced, cheerful-looking man, is sitting on a box by the table, intently drying a sock over a candle-flame. He wears a heavy trench-boot on his left leg, and his right foot, which is naked, is held above the damp floor by resting it on his left knee. His right boot stands on the floor beside him. As he carefully turns the sock this way and that—feeling it against his face to see if it is dry—he half sings, half hums a song—humming when he is not quite sure of the words, and marking time with the toes of his right foot.*

HARDY: "One and Two it's with Maud and Lou;
Three and Four, two girls more;
Five and Six it's with—hm—hm—hm—
Seven, Eight, Clara and Caroline——"
  [*He lapses into an indefinite humming, and finishes with a lively burst*]
"Tick!—Tock!—wind up the clock,
And we'll start the day over again."
  [*A man's legs appear in the moonlit trench above, and a tall, thin man comes slowly down the dug-out steps, stooping low to avoid the roof. He takes his helmet off and reveals a fine head, with close-cropped, iron-gray hair. He looks about forty-five—physically as hard as nails*]
HARDY: [*Looking round*] Hullo, Osborne! Your fellows arriving?
OSBORNE: [*Hitching off his pack and dropping it in a corner*] Yes. They're just coming in.
HARDY: Splendid! Have a drink.
OSBORNE: Thanks.
  [*He crosses and sits on the left-hand bed*]
HARDY: [*Passing the whisky and a mug*] Don't have too much water. It's rather strong to-day.
OSBORNE: [*Slowly mixing a drink*] I wonder what it *is* they put in the water.
HARDY: Some sort of disinfectant, I suppose.
OSBORNE: I'd rather have the microbes, wouldn't you?
HARDY: *I* would—yes—
OSBORNE: Well, cheero.

HARDY: Cheero. Excuse my sock, won't you?

OSBORNE: Certainly. It's a nice-looking sock.

HARDY: It is rather, isn't it? Guaranteed to keep the feet dry. Trouble is, it gets so wet doing it.

OSBORNE: Stanhope asked me to come and take over. He's looking after the men coming in.

HARDY: Splendid! You know, I'm awfully glad you've come.

OSBORNE: I heard it was a quiet bit of line up here.

HARDY: Well, yes—in a way. But you never know. Sometimes nothing happens for hours on end; then —all of a sudden—"over she comes!"—rifle grenades —Minnies—and those horrid little things like pine-apples—you know.

OSBORNE: I know.

HARDY: Swish—swish—swish—swish—*bang!*

OSBORNE: All right—all right—I know.

HARDY: They simply blew us to bits yesterday. Minnies—enormous ones; about twenty. Three bang in the trench. I really *am* glad you've come; I'm not simply being polite.

OSBORNE: Do much damage?

HARDY: Awful. A dug-out got blown up and came down in the men's tea. They were frightfully annoyed.

OSBORNE: I know. There's nothing worse than dirt in your tea.

HARDY: By the way, you know the big German attack's expected any day now?

OSBORNE: It's been expected for the last month.

HARDY: Yes, but it's very near now; there's funny things happening over in the Boche country. I've been out listening at night when it's quiet. There's more transport than usual coming up—you can hear it rattling over the *pavé* all night; more trains in the distance—puffing up and going away again, one after another, bringing up loads and loads of men——

OSBORNE: Yes. It's coming—pretty soon now.

HARDY: Are you here for six days?

OSBORNE: Yes.

HARDY: Then I should think you'll get it—right in the neck.

OSBORNE: Well, you won't be far away. Come along, let's do this handing over. Where's the map?

HARDY: Here we are. [*He gropes among the papers on the table and finds a tattered map*] We hold about two hundred yards of front line. We've got a Lewis gun just here—and one here, in this little sap. Sentry posts where the crosses are——

OSBORNE: Where do the men sleep?

HARDY: *I* don't know. The sergeant-major sees to that. [*He points off to the left*] The servants and signalers sleep in there. Two officers in here, and three in there. [*He points to the right-hand tunnel*] That is, if you've *got* five officers.

OSBORNE: We've only got four at present, but a new man's coming up to-night. He arrived at trans-port lines a day or two ago.

HARDY: I hope you get better luck than I did with

my last officer. He got lumbago the first night and went home. Now he's got a job lecturing young officers on "Life in the Front Line."

OSBORNE: Yes. They do send some funny people over here nowadays. I hope we're lucky and get a youngster straight from school. They're the kind that do best.

HARDY: I suppose they are, really.

OSBORNE: Five beds, you say? [*He examines the one he is sitting on*] Is this the best one?

HARDY: Oh, no. [*He points to the bed in the right corner*] That's mine. The ones in the other dug-out haven't got any bottoms to them. You keep yourself in by hanging your arms and legs over the sides. Mustn't hang your legs too low, or the rats gnaw your boots.

OSBORNE: You got many rats here?

HARDY: I should say—roughly—about two million; but then, of course, I don't see them all. [*He begins to put on his sock and draw on his boot*] Well, there's nothing else you want to know, is there?

OSBORNE: You haven't told me anything yet.

HARDY: What else do you *want* to know?

OSBORNE: Well, what about trench stores?

HARDY: You *are* a fussy old man. Anybody'd think you were in the army. [*He finds a tattered piece of paper*] Here you are: 115 rifle grenades— I shouldn't use them if I were you; they upset Jerry and make him offensive. Besides, they are rusty, in any case. Then there's 500 Mills bombs, 34 gum boots—

OSBORNE: That's seventeen pairs——

HARDY: Oh, no; twenty-five right leg, and nine left leg. But everything's down here. [*He hands the list to* Osborne]

OSBORNE: Did you check it when you took over?

HARDY: No. I think the sergeant-major did. It's quite all right.

OSBORNE: I expect Stanhope would like to see you before you go. He always likes a word with the com-pany commander he's relieving.

HARDY: How *is* the dear young boy? Drinking like a fish, as usual?

OSBORNE: Why do you say that?

HARDY: Well, damn it, it's just the natural thing to ask about Stanhope. [*He pauses, and looks curi-ously at* Osborne] Poor old man. It must be pretty rotten for you, being his second in command, and you such a quiet, sober old thing.

OSBORNE: He's a long way the best company com-mander we've got.

HARDY: Oh, he's a good chap, I know. But I never *did* see a youngster put away the whisky he does. D'you know, the last time we were out resting at Valennes he came to supper with us and drank a whole bottle in one hour fourteen minutes—we timed him.

OSBORNE: I suppose it amused everybody; I sup-pose everybody cheered him on, and said what a splendid achievement it was.

HARDY: He didn't want any "cheering" on——

OSBORNE: No, but everybody thought it was a big thing to do. [*There is a pause*] Didn't they?

HARDY: Well, you can't help, somehow, *admiring* a fellow who can do that—and then pick out his own hat all by himself and walk home——

OSBORNE: When a boy like Stanhope gets a reputation out here for drinking, he turns into a kind of freak show exhibit. People pay with a bottle of whisky for the morbid curiosity of seeing him drink it.

HARDY: Well, naturally, you're biased. You have to put him to bed when he gets home.

OSBORNE: It rather reminds you of bear-baiting—or cock-fighting—to sit and watch a boy drink himself unconscious.

HARDY: Well, damn it, it's pretty dull without *something* to liven people up. I mean, after all—Stanhope really *is* a sort of freak; I mean it *is* jolly fascinating to see a fellow drink like he does—glass after glass. He didn't go home on his last leave, did he?

OSBORNE: No.

HARDY: I suppose he didn't think he was fit to meet Papa. [*A pause*] You know his father's vicar of a country village?

OSBORNE: I know.

HARDY: [*Laughing*] Imagine Stanhope spending his leave in a country vicarage sipping tea! He spent his last leave in Paris, didn't he?

OSBORNE: Yes.

HARDY: I bet it was *some* leave!

OSBORNE: Do you know how long he's been out here?

HARDY: A good time, I know.

OSBORNE: Nearly three years. He came out straight from school—when he was eighteen. He's commanded this company for a year—in and out of the front line. He's never had a rest. Other men come over here and go home ill, and young Stanhope goes on sticking it, month in and month out.

HARDY: Oh, I know he's a jolly good fellow——

OSBORNE: I've seen him on his back all day with trench fever—then on duty all night——

HARDY: Oh, I know; he's a splendid chap!

OSBORNE: And because he's stuck it till his nerves have got battered to bits, he's called a drunkard.

HARDY: Not a drunkard; just a—just a hard drinker; but you're quite right about his nerves. They *are* all to blazes. Last time out resting we were playing bridge and something happened—I don't remember what it was; some silly little argument—and all of a sudden he jumped up and knocked all the glasses off the table! Lost control of himself; and then he—sort of—came to—and cried——

OSBORNE: Yes, I know.

HARDY: You heard about it?

OSBORNE: He told me.

HARDY: Did he? We tried to hush it up. It just shows the state he's in. [*He rises and puts on his pack. There is a pause*] You know, Osborne, you ought to be commanding this company.

OSBORNE: Rubbish!

HARDY: Of course you ought. It sticks out a mile. I know he's got pluck and all that, but, damn it, man, you're twice his age—and think what a dear, level-headed old thing you are.

OSBORNE: Don't be an ass. He was out here before I joined up. His experience alone makes him worth a dozen people like me.

HARDY: You know as well as I do, you ought to be in command.

OSBORNE: There isn't a man to touch him as a commander of men. He'll command the battalion one day if——

HARDY: Yes, if! [*He laughs*]

OSBORNE: You don't know him as I do; I love that fellow. I'd go to hell with him.

HARDY: Oh, you sweet, sentimental old darling!

OSBORNE: Come along. Finish handing over and stop blithering.

HARDY: There's nothing else to do.

OSBORNE: What about the log-book?

HARDY: God! you are a worker. Oh, well. Here we are. [*He finds a tattered little book among the papers on the table*] Written right up to date; here's my last entry: "5 p.m. to 8 p.m. All quiet. German airman flew over trenches. Shot a rat."

OSBORNE: Did he?

HARDY: No. I shot the rat, you ass. Well, finish up your whisky. I want to pack my mug. I'll leave you that drop in the bottle.

OSBORNE: Thanks.

[*He drinks up his whisky and hands* Hardy *the mug*]

HARDY: [*Tucking the mug into his pack*] I'll be off.

OSBORNE: Aren't you going to wait and see Stanhope?

HARDY: Well, no, I don't specially want to see him. He's so fussy about the trenches. I expect they *are* rather dirty. He'll talk for hours if he catches me. [*He hitches his pack over his shoulders, hangs on his gas satchel, map-case, binoculars, compass-case, until he looks like a traveling peddler. As he dresses:*] Well, I hope you have a nice six days. Don't forget to change your clothes if you get wet.

OSBORNE: No, Papa.

HARDY: And don't forget about the big attack.

OSBORNE: Oh, Lord, no, I mustn't miss that; I'll make a note in my diary.

HARDY: [*Fully dressed*] There we are! Do I look every inch a soldier?

OSBORNE: Yes. I should get quite a fright if I were a German and met you coming round a corner.

HARDY: I should bloody well hope you would.

OSBORNE: Shouldn't be able to run away for laughing.

HARDY: Now, don't be rude. [*He leans over to*

light a cigarette from a candle, and looks down on the table] Well, I'm damned. Still at it!

OSBORNE: What is?

HARDY: Why, that little cockroach. It's been running round and round that candle since tea-time; must have done a mile.

OSBORNE: I shouldn't hang about here if I were a cockroach.

HARDY: Nor should I. I'd go home. Ever had cockroach races?

OSBORNE: No.

HARDY: Great fun. We've had 'em every evening.

OSBORNE: What are the rules?

HARDY: Oh, you each have a cockroach, and start 'em in a line. On the word "Go" you dig your cockroach in the ribs and steer him with a match across the table. I won ten francs last night—had a *splendid* cockroach. I'll give you a tip.

OSBORNE: Yes?

HARDY: Promise not to let it go any farther?

OSBORNE: Yes.

HARDY: Well, if you want to get the best pace out of a cockroach, dip it in whisky—makes 'em go like hell!

OSBORNE: Right. Thanks awfully.

HARDY: Well, I must be off. Cheero!

OSBORNE: Cheero!

HARDY: [*Goes up the narrow steps into the trench above, singing softly and happily to himself*]
    "One and Two, it's with Maud and Lou;
    Three and Four, two girls more———"
[*The words trail away into the night. Osborne rises and takes his pack from the floor to the bed by the table. While he undoes it a* Soldier Servant *comes out of the tunnel from the left with a tablecloth over his arm and a plate with half a loaf of bread on it*]

MASON: Excuse me, sir. Can I lay supper?

OSBORNE: Yes, do.
[*He shuffles up the papers from the table and puts them on the bed*]

MASON: Thank you, sir.
[*He lays the table*]

OSBORNE: What are you going to tempt us with to-night, Mason?

MASON: Soup, sir—cutlets—and pineapple.

OSBORNE: [*Suspiciously*] Cutlets?

MASON: Well, sir—well, yes, sir!—cutlets.

OSBORNE: What sort of cutlets?

MASON: Now, sir, you've got me. I shouldn't like to commit meself too deep, sir.

OSBORNE: Ordinary ration meat?

MASON: Yes, sir. Ordinary ration meat, but a noo shape, sir. Smells like liver, sir, but it 'asn't got that smooth, wet look that liver's got. [Mason *leaves the dug-out. Osborne* sits up to the table and examines the map. *Voices come from trench above; a gruff voice says:*] "This is 'C' Company 'Eadquarters, sir."
[*A boyish voice replies*] "Oh, thanks." [*There is a*

pause, then the gruff voice says*] "Better go down, sir." [*The boyish voice replies*] "Yes. Righto."
[*An* Officer *comes groping down the steps and stands in the candle-light. He looks round, a little bewildered. He is a well-built, healthy-looking boy of about eighteen, with the very new uniform of a second lieutenant. Osborne looks up from the trench map, surprised and interested to see a stranger*]

OSBORNE: Hullo!

RALEIGH: Good evening [*He notices Osborne's gray hair and adds*] sir.

OSBORNE: You the new officer?

RALEIGH: Er—yes. I've been to Battalion Headquarters. They told me to report here.

OSBORNE: Good. We've been expecting you. Sit down, won't you?

RALEIGH: Thanks.
[*He sits gingerly on the box opposite* Osborne]

OSBORNE: I should take your pack off.

RALEIGH: Oh, right.
[*He slips his pack from his shoulders*]

OSBORNE: Will you have a drink?

RALEIGH: Er—well———

OSBORNE: You don't drink whisky?

RALEIGH: [*Hastily*] Oh, yes—er—just a small one, sir.

OSBORNE: [*Pouring out a small whisky and adding water*] Whisky takes away the taste of the water———

RALEIGH: Oh, yes?
[*He pauses, and laughs nervously*]

OSBORNE: —and the water takes away the taste of the whisky. [*He hands* Raleigh *the drink*] Just out from England?

RALEIGH: Yes, I landed a week ago.

OSBORNE: Boulogne?

RALEIGH: Yes. [*A pause, then he self-consciously holds up his drink*] Well, here's luck, sir.

OSBORNE: [*Taking a drink himself*] Good luck.
[*He takes out a cigarette case*] Cigarette?

RALEIGH: Thanks.

OSBORNE: [*Holding a bottle across so that* Raleigh *can light his cigarette from the candle in it*] Ever been up in the line before?

RALEIGH: Oh, no. You see, I only left school at the end of last summer term.

OSBORNE: I expect you find it a bit strange.

RALEIGH: [*Laughing*] Yes—I do—a bit———

OSBORNE: My name's Osborne. I'm second in command of the company. You only call me "sir" in front of the men.

RALEIGH: I see. Thanks.

OSBORNE: You'll find the other officers call me "Uncle."

RALEIGH: Oh, yes? [*He smiles*]

OSBORNE: What's *your* name?

RALEIGH: Raleigh.

OSBORNE: I knew a Raleigh. A master at Rugby.

RALEIGH: Oh? He may be a relation. I don't

know. I've got lots of uncles and—and things like that.

OSBORNE: We've only just moved into these trenches. Captain Stanhope commands the company.

RALEIGH: [*Suddenly brightening up*] I know. It's a frightful bit of luck.

OSBORNE: Why? D'you know him?

RALEIGH: Yes, rather! We were at school together—at least—of course—I was only a kid and he was one of the big fellows; he's three years older than I am.

[*There is a pause; Osborne seems to be waiting for Raleigh to go on, then suddenly he says:*]

OSBORNE: He's up in the front line at present, looking after the relief. [*Another pause*] He's a splendid chap.

RALEIGH: Isn't he? He was skipper of football at Barford, and kept wicket for the eleven. A jolly good bat, too.

OSBORNE: Did you play football—and cricket?

RALEIGH: Oh, yes. Of course, I wasn't in the same class as Dennis—I say, I suppose I ought to call him Captain Stanhope?

OSBORNE: Just "Stanhope."

RALEIGH: I see. Thanks.

OSBORNE: Did you get your colors?

RALEIGH: I did for football. Not cricket.

OSBORNE: Football and cricket seem a long way from here.

RALEIGH: [*Laughing*] They do, rather.

OSBORNE: We play a bit when we're out of the line.

RALEIGH: Good!

OSBORNE: [*Thoughtfully*] So you were at school with Stanhope. [*Pause*] I wonder if he'll remember you? I expect you've grown in the last three years.

RALEIGH: Oh, I think he'll remember me. [*He stops, and goes on rather awkwardly*] You see, it wasn't only that we were just at school together; our fathers were friends, and Dennis used to come and stay with us in the holidays. Of course, at school I didn't see much of him, but in the holidays we were terrific pals.

OSBORNE: He's a fine company commander.

RALEIGH: I bet he is. Last time he was on leave he came down to school; he'd just got his M.C. and been made a captain. He looked splendid! It sort of—made me feel——

OSBORNE: —keen?

RALEIGH: Yes. Keen to get out here. I was frightfully keen to get into Dennis' regiment. I thought, perhaps, with a bit of luck I might get to the same battalion.

OSBORNE: It's a big fluke to have got to the same company.

RALEIGH: I know. It's an amazing bit of luck. When I was at the base I did an awful thing. You see, my uncle's at the base—he has to detail officers to regiments——

OSBORNE: General Raleigh?

RALEIGH: Yes. I went to see him on the quiet and asked him if he could get me into this battalion. He bit my head off, and said I'd got to be treated like everybody else——

OSBORNE: Yes?

RALEIGH: —and the next day I was told I *was* coming to this battalion. Funny, wasn't it?

OSBORNE: Extraordinary coincidence!

RALEIGH: And when I got to Battalion Headquarters, and the colonel told me to report to "C" Company, I could have cheered. I expect Dennis'll be frightfully surprised to see me. I've got a message for him.

OSBORNE: From the colonel?

RALEIGH: No. From my sister.

OSBORNE: Your sister?

RALEIGH: Yes. You see, Dennis used to stay with us, and naturally my sister [*He hesitates*]—well—perhaps I ought not—

OSBORNE: That's all right. I didn't actually know that Stanhope——

RALEIGH: They're not—er—officially engaged——

OSBORNE: No?

RALEIGH: She'll be awfully glad I'm with him here; I can write and tell her about him. He doesn't say much in his letters; can we write often?

OSBORNE: Oh, yes. Letters are collected every day. [*There is a pause*]

RALEIGH: You don't think Dennis'll mind my—sort of—forcing myself into his company? I never thought of that; I was so keen.

OSBORNE: No, of course he won't. [*Pause*] You say it's—it's a good time since you last saw him?

RALEIGH: Let's see. It was in the summer last year—nearly a year ago.

OSBORNE: You know, Raleigh, you mustn't expect to find him—quite the same.

RALEIGH: Oh?

OSBORNE: You see, he's been out here a long time. It—it tells on a man—rather badly ——

RALEIGH: [*Thinking*] Yes, of course, I suppose it does.

OSBORNE: You may find he's—he's a little bit quick-tempered.

RALEIGH: [*Laughing*] Oh, I know old Dennis' temper! I remember once at school he caught some chaps in a study with a bottle of whisky. Lord! the roof nearly blew off. He gave them a dozen each with a cricket stump. [*Osborne laughs*] He was so keen on the fellows in the house keeping fit. He was frightfully down on smoking—and that sort of thing.

OSBORNE: You must remember he's commanded this company for a long time—through all sorts of rotten times. It's—it's a big strain on a man.

RALEIGH: Oh, it must be.

OSBORNE: If you notice a—difference in Stanhope—you'll know it's only the strain——

RALEIGH: Oh, yes.

[Osborne *rouses himself and speaks briskly*]

OSBORNE: Now, let's see. We've got five beds here —one each. Two in here and three in that dug-out there. I'm afraid you'll have to wait until the others come and pick the beds they want.

RALEIGH: Righto!

OSBORNE: Have you got a blanket?

RALEIGH: Yes, in my pack.

[*He rises to get it*]

OSBORNE: Better wait and unpack when you know where you're sleeping.

RALEIGH: Righto!

[*He sits down again*]

OSBORNE: We never undress when we're in the line. You can take your boots off now and then in the daytime, but it's better to keep pretty well dressed always.

RALEIGH: I see. Thanks.

OSBORNE: I expect we shall each do about three hours on duty at a time and then six off. We all go on duty at stand-to. That's at dawn and dusk.

RALEIGH: Yes.

OSBORNE: I expect Stanhope'll send you on duty with one of us at first—till you get used to it.

[*There is a pause*. Raleigh *turns, and looks curiously up the steps into the night*]

RALEIGH: Are we in the front line here?

OSBORNE: No. That's the support line outside. The front line's about fifty yards farther on.

RALEIGH: How frightfully quiet it is!

OSBORNE: It's often quiet—like this.

RALEIGH: I thought there would be an awful row here—all the time.

OSBORNE: Most people think that.

[*Pause*]

RALEIGH: I've never known anything so quiet as those trenches we came by; just now and then I heard a rifle firing, like the range at Bisley, and a sort of rumble in the distance.

OSBORNE: Those are the guns up north—up Wipers way. The guns are always going up there; it's never quiet like this. [*Pause*] I expect it's all very strange to you?

RALEIGH: It's—it's not exactly what I thought. It's just this—this quiet that seems so funny.

OSBORNE: A hundred yards from here the Germans are sitting in *their* dug-outs, thinking how quiet it is.

RALEIGH: Are they as near as that?

OSBORNE: About a hundred yards.

RALEIGH: It seems—uncanny. It makes me feel we're—we're all just waiting for something.

OSBORNE: We are, generally, just waiting for something. When anything happens, it happens quickly. Then we just start waiting again.

RALEIGH: I never thought it was like that.

OSBORNE: You thought it was fighting all the time?

RALEIGH: [*Laughing*] Well, yes, in a way.

OSBORNE: [*After puffing at his pipe in silence for a while*] Did you come up by trench to-night—or over the top?

RALEIGH: By trench. An amazing trench—turning and twisting for miles, over a sort of plain.

OSBORNE: Lancer's Alley it's called.

RALEIGH: Is it? It's funny the way it begins—in that ruined village, a few steps down into the cellar of a house—then right under the house and through a little garden—and then under the garden wall— then alongside an enormous ruined factory place— then miles and miles of plains, with those green lights bobbing up and down ahead—all along the front as far as you can see.

OSBORNE: Those are the Very lights. Both sides fire them over No Man's Land—to watch for raids and patrols.

RALEIGH: I knew they fired lights. [*Pause*] I didn't expect so many—and to see them so far away.

OSBORNE: I know. [*He puffs at his pipe*] There's something rather romantic about it all.

RALEIGH: [*Eagerly*] Yes, I thought that, too.

OSBORNE: You must always think of it like that if you can. Think of it all as—as romantic. It helps.

[Mason *comes in with more dinner utensils*]

MASON: D'you expect the captain soon, sir? The soup's 'ot.

OSBORNE: He ought to be here very soon now. This is Mr. Raleigh, Mason.

MASON: Good evening, sir.

RALEIGH: Good evening.

MASON: [*To* Osborne] I've 'ad rather a unpleasant surprise, sir.

OSBORNE: What's happened?

MASON: You know that tin o' pineapple chunks I got, sir?

OSBORNE: Yes?

MASON: Well, sir, I'm sorry to say it's apricots.

OSBORNE: Good heavens! It must have given you a turn.

MASON: I distinctly said "pineapple chunks" at the canteen.

OSBORNE: Wasn't there a label on the tin?

MASON: No, sir. I pointed that out to the man. I said was 'e *certain* it was pineapple chunks?

OSBORNE: I suppose he said he was.

MASON: Yes, sir. 'E said a leopard can't change its spots, sir.

OSBORNE: What have leopards got to do with pine-apple?

MASON: That's just what *I* thought, sir. Made me *think* there was something fishy about it. You see, sir, I know the captain can't stand the sight of apricots. 'E said next time we 'ad them 'e'd wring my neck.

OSBORNE: Haven't you anything else?

MASON: There's a pink blancmange I've made, sir. But it ain't anywhere near stiff yet.

OSBORNE: Never mind. We must have the apricots and chance it.

MASON: Only I thought I'd tell you, sir, so as the captain wouldn't blame me.

OSBORNE: All right, Mason. [*Voices are heard in the trench above*] That sounds like the captain coming now.

MASON [*Hastening away*] I'll go and dish out the soup, sir.

[*The voices grow nearer; two figures appear in the trench above and grope down the steps—the leading figure tall and thin, the other short and fat. The tall figure is* Captain Stanhope. *At the bottom of the steps he straightens himself, pulls off his pack and drops it on the floor. Then he takes off his helmet and throws it on the right-hand bed. Despite his stars of rank he is no more than a boy; tall, slimly built, but broad-shouldered. His dark hair is carefully brushed; his uniform, though old and war-stained, is well cut and cared for. He is good-looking, rather from attractive features than the healthy good looks of* Raleigh. *Although tanned by months in the open air, there is a pallor under his skin and dark shadows under his eyes. His short and fat companion—Second Lieutenant Trotter—is middle-aged and homely-looking. His face is red, fat, and round; apparently he has put on weight during his war service, for his tunic appears to be on the verge of bursting at the waist. He carries an extra pack belonging to the officer left on duty in the line*]

STANHOPE: [*As he takes off his pack, gas satchel, and belt*] Has Hardy gone?

OSBORNE: Yes. He cleared off a few minutes ago.

STANHOPE: Lucky for him he did. I had a few words to say to Master Hardy. You never saw the blasted mess those fellows left the trenches in. Dug-outs smell like cess-pits; rusty bombs; damp rifle grenades; it's perfectly foul. Where are the servants?

OSBORNE: In there.

STANHOPE: [*Calling into* Mason's *dug-out*] Hi! Mason!

MASON: [*Outside*] Coming, sir! Just bringing the soup, sir.

STANHOPE: [*Taking a cigarette from his case and lighting it*] Damn the soup! Bring some whisky!

OSBORNE: Here's a new officer, Stanhope—just arrived.

STANHOPE: Oh, sorry. [*He turns and peers into the dim corner where* Raleigh *stands smiling awkwardly*] I didn't see you in this miserable light.

[*He stops short at the sight of* Raleigh. *There is silence*]

RALEIGH: Hullo, Stanhope!

[Stanhope *stares at* Raleigh *as though dazed.* Raleigh *takes a step forward, half raises his hand, then lets it drop to his side*]

STANHOPE: [*In a low voice*] How did you—get here?

RALEIGH: I was told to report to your company, Stanhope.

STANHOPE: Oh. I see. Rather a coincidence.

RALEIGH: [*With a nervous laugh*] Yes.

[*There is a silence for a moment, broken by* Osborne *in a matter-of-fact voice*]

OSBORNE: I say, Stanhope, it's a terrible business. We thought we'd got a tin of pineapple chunks; it turns out to be apricots.

TROTTER: Ha! Give me apricots every time! I 'ate pineapple chunks; too bloomin' sickly for me!

RALEIGH: I'm awfully glad I got to your company, Stanhope.

STANHOPE: When did you get here?

RALEIGH: Well, I've only just come.

OSBORNE: He came up with the transport while you were taking over.

STANHOPE: I see.

[Mason *brings in a bottle of whisky, a mug, and two plates of soup—so precariously that* Osborne *has to help with the soup plates onto the table*]

STANHOPE: [*With sudden forced gaiety*] Come along, Uncle! Come and sit here. [*He waves towards the box on the right of the table*] You better sit there, Raleigh.

RALEIGH: Right!

TROTTER: [*Taking a pair of pince-nez from his tunic pocket, putting them on, and looking curiously at* Raleigh] You Raleigh?

RALEIGH: Yes. [*Pause*]

TROTTER: I'm Trotter.

RALEIGH: Oh, yes? [*Pause*]

TROTTER: How *are* you?

RALEIGH: Oh, all right, thanks.

TROTTER: Been out 'ere before?

RALEIGH: No.

TROTTER: Feel a bit odd, I s'pose?

RALEIGH: Yes. A bit.

TROTTER: [*Getting a box to sit on*] Oh, well, you'll get used to it; you'll feel you've been 'ere a year in about an hour's time.

[*He puts the box on its side and sits on it. It is too low for the table, and he puts it on its end. It is then too high. He tries the other side, which is too low; he finally contrives to make himself comfortable by sitting on his pack, placed on the side of the box.* Mason *arrives with two more plates of soup*]

OSBORNE: What kind of soup is this, Mason?

MASON: It's yellow soup, sir.

OSBORNE: It's got a very deep yellow flavor.

TROTTER: [*Taking a melodious sip*] It wants some pepper; bring some pepper, Mason.

MASON: [*Anxiously*] I'm very sorry, sir. When the mess box was packed the pepper was omitted, sir.

TROTTER: [*Throwing his spoon with a clatter into the plate*] Oh, I say, but damn it!

OSBORNE: We must have pepper. It's a disinfectant.

TROTTER: You must have pepper in soup!

STANHOPE: [*Quietly*] Why wasn't it packed, Mason?

MASON: It—it was missed, sir.

STANHOPE: Why?

MASON: [*Miserably*] Well, sir, I left it to——

STANHOPE: Then I advise you never to leave it to anyone else again—unless you want to rejoin your platoon out there.

[*He points into the moonlit trench*]

MASON: I'm—I'm very sorry, sir.

STANHOPE: Send one of the signalers.

MASON: Yes, sir. [*He hastens to the tunnel entrance and calls*] Bert, you're wanted!

[*A* Soldier *appears, with a rifle slung over his shoulder. He stands stiffly to attention*]

STANHOPE: Do you know "A" Company Headquarters?

SOLDIER: Yes, sir.

STANHOPE: Go there at once and ask Captain Willis, with my compliments, if he can lend me a little pepper.

SOLDIER: Very good, sir.

[*He turns smartly and goes up the steps,* Mason *stopping him for a moment to say confidentially:* "A *screw* of pepper you ask for."]

OSBORNE: We must have pepper.

TROTTER: I mean—after all—war's bad enough with pepper—[*noisy sip*]—but war without pepper—it's—it's bloody awful!

OSBORNE: What's it like outside?

TROTTER: Quiet as an empty 'ouse. There's a nasty noise going on up north.

OSBORNE: Wipers, I expect. I believe there's trouble up there. I wish we knew more of what's going on.

TROTTER: So do I. Still, my wife reads the papers every morning and writes and tells me.

OSBORNE: Hardy says they had a lively time here yesterday. Three big Minnies right in the trench.

TROTTER: I know. And they left the bloomin' 'oles for us to fill in. [Mason *arrives with cutlets on enamel plates*] What's this?

MASON: Meat, sir.

TROTTER: I know that. What sort?

MASON: Sort of cutlet, sir.

TROTTER: Sort of cutlet, is it? You know, Mason, there's cutlets and cutlets.

MASON: I know, sir; that one's a cutlet.

TROTTER: Well, it won't let me cut it.

MASON: No, sir?

TROTTER: That's a joke.

MASON: Oh. Right, sir. [*He goes out*]

OSBORNE: [*Studying the map*] There's a sort of ruin marked on this map—just in front of here, in No Man's Land—called Beauvais Farm.

TROTTER: That's what we saw sticking up, skipper. I wondered what it was.

STANHOPE: Better go out and look at it to-night.

TROTTER: I 'ate ruins in No Man's Land; too bloomin' creepy for me.

OSBORNE: There's only about sixty yards of No Man's Land, according to this map—narrower on the left, from the head of this sap; only about fifty.

TROTTER: [*Who has been looking curiously at* Stanhope, *eating his meal with lowered head*] Cheer up, skipper. You *do* look glum!

STANHOPE: I'm tired.

OSBORNE: I should turn in and get some sleep after supper.

STANHOPE: I've got hours of work before I sleep.

OSBORNE: I'll do the duty roll and see the sergeant-major—and all that.

STANHOPE: That's all right, Uncle. I'll see to it. [*He turns to* Raleigh *for the first time*] Trotter goes on duty directly he's had supper. You better go on with him—to learn.

RALEIGH: Oh, right.

TROTTER: Look 'ere, skipper, it's nearly eight now; couldn't we make it 'alf-past?

STANHOPE: No, I told Hibbert he'd be relieved at eight. Will you take from eleven till two, Uncle?

OSBORNE: Right.

STANHOPE: Hibbert can do from two till four, and I'll go on from then till standto. That'll be at six.

TROTTER: Well, boys! 'Ere we are for six days again. Six bloomin' eternal days. [*He makes a calculation on the table*] That's a hundred and forty-four hours; eight thousand six 'undred and forty minutes. *That* doesn't sound so bad; we've done twenty of 'em already. I've got an idea! I'm going to draw a hundred and forty-four little circles on a bit o' paper, and every hour I'm going to black one in; that'll make the time go all right.

STANHOPE: It's five to eight now. You better go and relieve Hibbert. Then you can come back at eleven o'clock and black in three of your bloody little circles.

TROTTER: I 'aven't 'ad my apricots yet!

STANHOPE: We'll keep your apricots till you come back.

TROTTER: I never knew anything like a war for upsetting meals. I'm always down for dooty in the middle of one.

STANHOPE: That's because you never stop eating.

TROTTER: Any'ow, let's 'ave some coffee. Hi! Mason! Coffee!

MASON: Coming, sir!

TROTTER: [*Getting up*] Well, I'll get dressed. Come on, Raleigh.

TROTTER: Just wear your belt with revolver case on it. Must have your revolver to shoot rats. And your gas mask—come here—I'll show you. [*He helps* Raleigh] You wear it sort of tucked up under your chin like a serviette.

RALEIGH: Yes. I was shown the way at home.

TROTTER: Now your hat. That's right. You don't

want a walking-stick. It gets in your way if you have to run fast.

RALEIGH: Why—er—do you have to run fast?

TROTTER: Oh, Lord, yes, often! If you see a Minnie coming—that's a big trench-mortar shell, you know—short for *Minnywerfer*—you see 'em coming right out of the Boche trenches, right up in the air, then down, down, down; and you have to judge it and run like stink sometimes.

[Mason *comes in with two cups of coffee*]

MASON: Coffee, sir?

TROTTER: Thanks.

[*He takes the cup and drinks standing up*]

RALEIGH: Thanks.

TROTTER: You might leave my apricots out, Mason. Put 'em on a separate plate and keep 'em in there.

[*He points to* Mason's *dug-out*]

MASON: Very good, sir.

TROTTER: If you bring 'em in 'ere you never know *what* might 'appen to 'em.

MASON: No, sir.

TROTTER: "B" Company on our right, aren't they, skipper?

STANHOPE: Yes. There's fifty yards of undefended area in between. You better patrol that a good deal.

TROTTER: Aye, aye, sir.

STANHOPE: Have a look at that Lewis gun position on the left. See what field of fire they've got.

TROTTER: Aye, aye, sir. You don't want me to go out and look at that blinkin' ruin?

STANHOPE: I'll see to that.

TROTTER: Good. I don't fancy crawling about on my belly after that cutlet. [*To* Raleigh] Well, come on, my lad, let's go and see about this 'ere war.

[*The two go up the steps, leaving* Stanhope *and* Osborne *alone.* Mason *appears at his dug-out door*]

MASON: Will you take apricots, sir?

STANHOPE: No, thanks.

MASON: Mr. Osborne?

OSBORNE: No, thanks.

MASON: I'm sorry about them being apricots, sir. I explained to Mr. Osborne——

STANHOPE: [*Curtly*] That's all right, Mason—thank you.

MASON: Very good, sir. [*He goes out*]

OSBORNE: [*Over by the right-hand bed*] Will you sleep here? This was Hardy's bed.

STANHOPE: No. You sleep there. I'd rather sleep by the table here. I can get up and work without disturbing you.

OSBORNE: This is a better one.

STANHOPE: You take it. Must have a little comfort in your old age, Uncle.

OSBORNE: I wish you'd turn in and sleep for a bit.

STANHOPE: Sleep?—I can't sleep. [*He takes a whisky and water. A man appears in the trench and comes down the steps—a small, slightly built man*

in the early twenties, with a little mustache and a pallid face. Looking hard at the newcomer] Well, Hibbert?

HIBBERT: Everything's fairly quiet. Bit of sniping somewhere to our left; some rifle grenades coming over just on our right.

STANHOPE: I see. Mason's got your supper.

HIBBERT: [*Gently rubbing his forehead*] I don't think I can manage any supper to-night, Stanhope. It's this beastly neuralgia. It seems to be right inside this eye. The beastly pain gets worse every day.

STANHOPE: Some hot soup and a good tough chop'll put that right.

HIBBERT: I'm afraid the pain rather takes my appetite away. I'm damn sorry to keep on talking about it, Stanhope, only I thought you'd wonder why I don't eat anything much.

STANHOPE: Try and forget about it.

HIBBERT: [*With a little laugh*] Well— I wish I could.

STANHOPE: Get tight.

HIBBERT: I think I'll turn straight in for a rest—and try and get some sleep.

STANHOPE: All right. Turn in. You're in that dug-out there. Here's your pack. [*He picks up the pack that* Trotter *brought down*] You go on duty at two. I take over from you at four. I'll tell Mason to call you.

HIBBERT: [*Faintly*] Oh, right—thanks, Stanhope—cheero.

STANHOPE: Cheero.

[*He watches* Hibbert *go down the tunnel into the dark*]

HIBBERT: [*Returning*] Can I have a candle?

STANHOPE: [*Taking one from the table*] Here you are.

HIBBERT: Thanks.

[*He goes out again. There is silence.* Stanhope *turns to* Osborne]

STANHOPE: Another little worm trying to wriggle home.

OSBORNE: [*Filling his pipe*] I wonder if he really is bad. He looks rotten.

STANHOPE: Pure bloody funk, that's all. He could eat if he wanted to; he's starving himself purposely. Artful little swine! Neuralgia's a splendid idea. No proof as far as I can see.

OSBORNE: You can't help feeling sorry for him. I think he's tried hard.

STANHOPE: How long's he been out here? Three months, I suppose. Now he's decided he's done his bit. He's decided to go home and spend the rest of the war in comfortable nerve hospitals. Well, he's mistaken. I let Warren get away like that, but no more.

OSBORNE: I don't see how you can prevent a fellow going sick.

STANHOPE: I'll have a quiet word with the doctor before *he* does. He thinks he's going to wriggle off before the attack. We'll just see about that. No man of mine's going sick before the attack. They're going to take an equal chance—together.

OSBORNE: Raleigh looks a nice chap.

STANHOPE: [Looking hard at Osborne before replying] Yes.

OSBORNE: Good-looking youngster. At school with you, wasn't he?

STANHOPE: Has he been talking already?

OSBORNE: He just mentioned it. It was a natural thing to tell me when he knew you were in command [Stanhope is lounging at the table with his back to the wall. Osborne, sitting on the right-hand bed, begins to puff clouds of smoke into the air as he lights his pipe] He's awfully pleased to get into your company. [Stanhope makes no reply. He picks up a pencil and scribbles on the back of a magazine] He seems to think a lot of you.

STANHOPE: [Looking up quickly at Osborne and laughing] Yes, I'm his hero.

OSBORNE: It's quite natural.

STANHOPE: You think so?

OSBORNE: Small boys at school generally have their heroes.

STANHOPE: Yes. Small boys at school do.

OSBORNE: Often it goes on as long as——

STANHOPE: —as long as the hero's a hero.

OSBORNE: It often goes on all through life.

STANHOPE: I wonder. How many battalions are there in France?

OSBORNE: Why?

STANHOPE: We'll say fifty divisions. That's a hundred and fifty brigades—four hundred and fifty battalions. That's one thousand eight hundred companies [He looks up at Osborne from his calculations on the magazine cover] There are one thousand eight hundred companies in France, Uncle. Raleigh might have been sent to any one of those, and, my God! he comes to mine.

OSBORNE: You ought to be glad. He's a good-looking youngster. I like him.

STANHOPE: I knew you'd like him. Personality, isn't it? [He takes a worn leather case from his breast pocket and hands a small photograph to Osborne] I've never shown you that, have I?

OSBORNE: [Looking at the photograph] No. [Pause] Raleigh's sister, isn't it?

STANHOPE: How did you know?

OSBORNE: There's a strong likeness.

STANHOPE: I suppose there is.

OSBORNE: [Intent on the picture] She's an awfully nice-looking girl.

STANHOPE: A photo doesn't show much, really. Just a face.

OSBORNE: She looks awfully nice. [There is silence. Stanhope lights a cigarette. Osborne hands the photo back] You're a lucky chap.

STANHOPE: [Putting the photo back into his case] I don't know why I keep it, really.

OSBORNE: Why? Isn't she—I thought——

STANHOPE: What did you think?

OSBORNE: Well, I thought that perhaps she was waiting for you.

STANHOPE: Yes. She is waiting for me—and she doesn't know. She thinks I'm a wonderful chap—commanding a company. [He turns to Osborne and points up the steps into the line] She doesn't know that if I went up those steps into the front line—without being doped with whisky—I'd go mad with fright.

[There is a pause. Osborne stirs himself to speak]

OSBORNE: Look here, old man. I've meant to say it for a long time, but it sounds like damned impudence. You've done longer out here than any man in the battalion. It's time you went away for a rest. It's due to you.

STANHOPE: You suggest that I go sick, like that little worm in there—neuralgia in the eye?

[He laughs and takes a drink]

OSBORNE: No. Not that. The colonel would have sent you down long ago, only——

STANHOPE: Only—what?

OSBORNE: Only he can't spare you.

STANHOPE: [Laughing] Oh, rot!

OSBORNE: He told me.

STANHOPE: He thinks I'm in such a state I want a rest, is that it?

OSBORNE: No. He thinks it's due to you.

STANHOPE: It's all right, Uncle. I'll stick it out now. It may not be much longer now. I've had my share of luck—more than my share. There's not a man left who was here when I came. But it's rather damnable for that boy—of all the boys in the world—to have come to me. I might at least have been spared that.

OSBORNE: You're looking at things in rather a black sort of way.

STANHOPE: I've just told you. That boy's a hero-worshiper. I'm three years older than he is. You know what that means at school. I was skipper of football and all that sort of thing. It doesn't sound much to a man out here—but it does at school with a kid of fourteen. Damn it, Uncle, you're a schoolmaster; you know.

OSBORNE: I've just told you what I think of hero-worship.

STANHOPE: Raleigh's father knew mine, and I was told to keep an eye on the kid. I rather liked the idea of looking after him. I made him keen on the right things—and all that. His people asked me to stay with them one summer. I met his sister then——

OSBORNE: Yes?

STANHOPE: At first I thought of her as another kid like Raleigh. It was just before I came out here for the first time that I realized what a topping girl she was. Funny how you realize it suddenly. I just prayed to come through the war—and—and do things—and keep absolutely fit for her.

OSBORNE: You've done pretty well. An M.C. and a company.

STANHOPE: [*Taking another whisky*] It was all right at first. When I went home on leave after the first six months it was jolly fine to feel I'd done a little to make her pleased. [*He takes a gulp of his drink*] It was after I came back here—in that awful affair on Vimy Ridge. I knew I'd go mad if I didn't break the strain. I couldn't bear being fully conscious all the time—you've felt that, Uncle, haven't you?

OSBORNE: Yes, often.

STANHOPE: There were only two ways of breaking the strain. One was pretending I was ill—and going home; the other was this. [*He holds up his glass*] Which would you pick, Uncle?

OSBORNE: I haven't been through as much as you. I don't know yet.

STANHOPE: I thought it all out. It's a slimy thing to go home if you're not really ill, isn't it?

OSBORNE: I think it is.

STANHOPE: Well, then [*He holds his glass up to Osborne*] Cheero, and long live the men who go home with neuralgia. [*He puts his glass down*] I didn't go home on my last leave. I couldn't bear to meet her, in case she realized——

OSBORNE: When the war's over—and the strain's gone—you'll soon be as fit as ever, at your age.

STANHOPE: I've hoped that all the time. I'd go away for months and live in the open air—and get fit—and then go back to her.

OSBORNE: And so you can.

STANHOPE: If Raleigh had gone to one of those other one thousand eight hundred companies.

OSBORNE: I don't see why you should think——

STANHOPE: Oh, for Lord's sake, don't be a damn fool. *You* know! You know he'll write and tell her I reek of whisky all day.

OSBORNE: Why should he? He's not a——

STANHOPE: Exactly. He's not a damned little swine who'd deceive his sister.

OSBORNE: He's very young; he's got hundreds of strange things to learn; he'll realize that men are—different—out here.

STANHOPE: It's no good, Uncle. Didn't you see him sitting there at supper?—staring at me?—and wondering? He's up in those trenches now—still wondering—and beginning to understand. All these months he's wanted to be with me out here. Poor little devil!

OSBORNE: I believe Raleigh'll go on liking you—and looking up to you—through everything. There's something very deep and rather fine about hero-worship.

STANHOPE: Hero-worship be damned! [*He pauses, then goes on, in a strange, high-pitched voice*] You know, Uncle, I'm an *awful* fool. I'm *captain* of this company. What's that bloody little prig of a boy matter? D'you see? He's a little prig. Wants to write home and tell Madge all about *me*. Well, he

won't; d'you see, Uncle? He *won't* write. Censorship! I censor his letters—cross out all he says about me.

OSBORNE: You can't read his letters!

STANHOPE: [*Dreamily*] Cross out all he says about me. Then we all go west in the big attack—and she goes on thinking I'm a fine fellow forever—and ever—and ever.

[*He pours out a drink, murmuring "Ever—and ever—and ever"*]

OSBORNE: [*Rising from his bed*] It's not as bad as all that. Turn in and have a sleep.

STANHOPE: Sleep! Catch *me* wasting my time with sleep.

OSBORNE: [*Picking up* Stanhope's *pack and pulling out the blanket*] Come along, old chap. You come and lie down here.

[*He puts the pack as a pillow on* Stanhope's *bed, and spreads out the blanket*]

STANHOPE: [*With his chin in his hands*] Little prig —that's what he is. Did *I* ask him to force his way into my company? No! I didn't. Very well, he'll pay for his damn cheek. [Osborne *lays his hand gently on* Stanhope's *shoulder to persuade him to lie down*] Go away! [*He shakes* Osborne's *hand off*] What the hell are you trying to do?

OSBORNE: Come and lie down and go to sleep.

STANHOPE: Go sleep y'self. I censor his letters, d'you see, Uncle? You watch and see he doesn't smuggle any letters away.

OSBORNE: Righto. Now come and lie down. You've had a hard day of it.

STANHOPE: [*Looking up suddenly*] Where's Hardy? D'you say he's gone?

OSBORNE: Yes. He's gone.

STANHOPE: Gone, has he? Y'know, I had a word to say to Master Hardy. He *would* go, the swine! Dirty trenches—everything dirty—I wanner tell him to keep his trenches clean.

OSBORNE: [*Standing beside* Stanhope *and putting his hand gently on his shoulder again*] We'll clean them up to-morrow.

[Stanhope *looks up at* Osborne *and laughs gaily*]

STANHOPE: Dear old Uncle! Clean trenches up—with little dust pan and brush. [*He laughs*] Make you a little apron—with lace on it.

OSBORNE: That'll be fine. Now then, come along, old chap. I'll see you get called at two o'clock. [*He firmly takes* Stanhope *by the arm and draws him over to the bed*] You *must* be tired.

STANHOPE: [*In a dull voice*] God, I'm bloody tired; ache—all over—feel sick——

[Osborne *helps him on to the bed, takes the blanket and puts it over him*]

OSBORNE: You'll feel all right in a minute. How's that? Comfortable?

STANHOPE: Yes. Comfortable. [*He looks up into* Osborne's *face and laughs again*] Dear old Uncle. Tuck me up.

[Osborne *fumbles the blankets round* Stanhope]

OSBORNE: There we are.

STANHOPE: Kiss me, Uncle.

OSBORNE: Kiss you be blowed! You go to sleep.

STANHOPE: [*Closing his eyes*] Yes—I go sleep.

[*He turns slowly on to his side with his face to the earth wall. Osborne stands watching for a while, then blows out the candle by* Stanhope's *bed.* Stanhope *gives a deep sigh, and begins to breathe heavily.* Osborne *crosses to the servant's dug-out and calls softly*]

OSBORNE: Mason!

MASON: [*Appearing with unbuttoned tunic at the tunnel entrance*] Yessir?

OSBORNE: Will you call me at ten minutes to eleven—and Mr. Hibbert at ten minutes to two? I'm going to turn in for a little while.

MASON: Very good, sir. [*Pause*] The pepper's come, sir.

OSBORNE: Oh, good.

MASON: I'm very sorry about the pepper, sir.

OSBORNE: That's all right, Mason.

MASON: Good night, sir.

OSBORNE: Good night.

[Mason *leaves the dug-out.* Osborne *turns, and looks up the narrow steps into the night, where the Very lights rise and fade against the starlit sky. He glances once more at* Stanhope, *then crosses to his own bed, takes out from his tunic a large, old-fashioned watch, and quietly winds it up. Through the stillness comes the low rumble of distant guns*]

THE CURTAIN FALLS

ACT II. SCENE I.

Early next morning.

A pale shaft of sunlight shines down the steps, but candles still burn in the dark corner where Osborne *and* Raleigh *are at breakfast.* Mason *has put a large plate of bacon before each, and turns to go as* Trotter *comes down the steps, whistling gaily and rubbing his hands.*

TROTTER: What a lovely smell of bacon!

MASON: Yes, sir. I reckon there's enough smell of bacon in 'ere to last for dinner.

TROTTER: Well, there's nothing like a good fat bacon rasher when you're as empty as I am.

MASON: I'm glad you like it fat, sir.

TROTTER: Well, I like a bit o' lean, too.

MASON: There *was* a bit of lean in the middle of yours, sir, but it's kind of shrunk up in the cooking.

TROTTER: Bad cooking, that's all. Any porridge?

MASON: Oh, yes, sir. There's porridge.

TROTTER: Lumpy, I s'pose?

MASON: Yes, sir. Quite nice and lumpy.

TROTTER: Well, take all the lumps out o' mine.

MASON: And just bring you the gravy, sir? Very good, sir.

[Mason *goes out.* Trotter *looks after him suspiciously*]

TROTTER: You know, that man's getting familiar.

OSBORNE: He's not a bad cook.

[Trotter *has picked up his coffee mug, and is smelling it*]

TROTTER: I say, d'you realize he's washed out his dish-cloth?

OSBORNE: I know. I told him about it.

TROTTER: Did you really? You've got some pluck. 'Ow did you go about it?

OSBORNE: I wrote and asked my wife for a packet of Lux. Then I gave it to Mason and suggested he try it on something.

TROTTER: Good man. No, he's not a bad cook. Might be a lot worse. When I was in the ranks we 'ad a prize cook—used to be a plumber before the war. Ought to 'ave seen the stew 'e made. Thin! Thin wasn't the word. Put a bucketful of 'is stew in a bath and pull the plug, and the whole lot would go down in a couple of gurgles.

[Mason *brings* Trotter's *porridge*]

MASON: I've took the lumps out.

TROTTER: Good. Keep 'em and use 'em for dumplings next time we 'ave boiled beef.

MASON: Very good, sir. [*He goes out*]

TROTTER: Yes. That plumber was a prize cook, 'e was. Lucky for us one day 'e set 'imself on fire making the tea. 'E went 'ome pretty well fried. Did Mason get that pepper?

OSBORNE: Yes.

TROTTER: Good. Must 'ave pepper.

OSBORNE: I thought you were on duty now.

TROTTER. I'm supposed to be. Stanhope sent me down to get my breakfast. He's looking after things till I finish.

OSBORNE: He's got a long job then.

TROTTER: Oh, no. I'm a quick eater. Hi! Mason! Bacon!

MASON: [*Outside*] Coming, sir!

OSBORNE: It's a wonderful morning.

TROTTER: Isn't it lovely? Makes you feel sort of young and 'opeful. I was up in that old trench under the brick wall just now, and damned if a bloomin' little bird didn't start singing! Didn't 'arf sound funny. Sign of spring, I s'pose. [Mason *arrives with* Trotter's *bacon*] That looks all right.

MASON: If you look down straight on it from above, you can see a bit o' lean quite clear.

TROTTER: Good Lord, yes! That's it, isn't it?

MASON: No, sir, that's a bit o' rust off the pan.

TROTTER: Ah! *That's* it, then!

MASON: You've got it, sir. [*He goes out*]

TROTTER: Cut us a chunk of bread, Uncle.

[Osborne *cuts him off a chunk*]

OSBORNE: How are things going up there?

TROTTER: I don't like the look of things a bit.

OSBORNE: You mean—the quiet?

TROTTER: Yes. Standing up there in the dark last night there didn't seem a thing in the world alive—except the rats squeaking and my stomach grumbling about that cutlet.

OSBORNE: It's quiet even now.

TROTTER: Too damn quiet. You can bet your boots the Boche is up to something. The big attack soon, I reckon. I don't like it, Uncle. Pass the jam.

OSBORNE: It's strawberry.

TROTTER: Is it? I'm glad we got rid o' that raspberry jam. Can't stand raspberry jam. Pips get be'ind your plate.

OSBORNE: Did Stanhope tell you he wants two wiring parties out to-night?

TROTTER: Yes. He's fixing it up now. [*He pauses, and goes on in a low voice*] My goodness, Uncle, doesn't he look ill!

OSBORNE: I'm afraid he's not well.

TROTTER: Nobody'd be well who went on like he does. [*There is another pause*] You know when you came up to relieve me last night?

OSBORNE: Yes?

TROTTER: Well, Raleigh and me came back here, and there was Stanhope sitting on that bed drinking a whisky. He looked as white as a sheet. God, he looked awful; he'd drunk a bottle since dinner. I said "Ullo!" and he didn't seem to know who I was. Uncanny, wasn't it, Raleigh?

RALEIGH: [*With lowered head*] Yes.

TROTTER: He just said, "Better go to bed, Raleigh"—just as if Raleigh'd been a school kid.

OSBORNE: Did he? [*There is a pause*] Look at the sun. It'll be quite warm soon.

[*They look at the pale square sunlight on the floor*]

TROTTER: It's warm now. You can feel it on your face outside if you stand in it. First time this year. Ope we 'ave an 'ot summer.

OSBORNE: So do I.

TROTTER: Funny about that bird. Made me feel quite braced up. Sort of made me think about my garden of an evening—walking round in me slippers after supper, smoking me pipe.

OSBORNE: You keen on gardening?

TROTTER: Oh, I used to do a bit of an evening. I 'ad a decent little grass plot in front, with flower-borders—geraniums, lobelia, and calsularia—you know, red, white, and blue. Looked rather nice in the summer.

OSBORNE: Yes.

TROTTER: 'Ad some fine 'olly'ocks out the back. One year I'd one eight feet 'igh. Took a photer of it. [*He fumbles in his pocket case*] Like to look at it?

OSBORNE: I would. [*He looks at the photo*] By Jove, it's a beauty.

TROTTER: [*Looking over* Osborne's *shoulder*] You see that, just there?

OSBORNE: Yes?

TROTTER: That's the roof of the summer-'ouse.

OSBORNE: Is it really!

TROTTER: Just shows the 'ite of the 'olly-'ock.

OSBORNE: It does. [*He shows the photo to* Raleigh] A beauty, isn't it?

RALEIGH: Rather!

TROTTER: It never wanted no stick to keep it straight, neether. [*There is a pause*] You keen on gardening?

OSBORNE: Yes. A bit. I made a rockery when I was home on leave. I used to cycle out to the woods and get primroses and things like that, and try and get 'em to grow in my garden.

TROTTER: I don't suppose they would!

OSBORNE: They would if you pressed a bit of moss round them——

TROTTER: —to make 'em feel at 'ome, eh? [*He laughs*]

OSBORNE: They'll be coming out again soon if they've got this sun at home.

TROTTER: I reckon they will. I remember one morning last spring—we was coming out of the salient. Just when it was getting light in the morning—it was at the time when the Boche was sending over a lot of that gas that smells like pear-drops, you know?

OSBORNE: I know. Phosgene.

TROTTER: That's it. We were scared to hell of it. All of a sudden we smelt that funny sweet smell, and a fellow shouted "Gas!"—and we put on our masks; and then I spotted what it was.

OSBORNE: What was it?

TROTTER: Why, a blinkin' may-tree! All out in bloom, growing beside the path! We did feel a lot of silly poops—putting on gas masks because of a damn may-tree! [*He stretches himself and tries to button his tunic*] Lord! I *must* get my fat down. [*He gets up*] Well, I better go and relieve Stanhope. He'll curse like hell if I don't. I bet he's got a red-hot liver this morning.

OSBORNE: I relieve you at eleven.

TROTTER: That's right. I don't like this time of day in the line. The old Boche 'as just 'ad 'is breakfast, and sends over a few whizz-bangs and rifle grenades to show 'e ain't forgotten us. Still, I'd rather 'ave a bang or two than this damn quiet. [*He puts on his helmet and gas mask satchel and goes up the steps*] Cheero!

OSBORNE: Cheero!

RALEIGH: Cheero!

OSBORNE: [*to* Raleigh] I expect Stanhope'll let you go on duty alone now.

RALEIGH: Will he? About what time?

OSBORNE: Well, after me, I expect. From about two till four.

RALEIGH: I see.

[*There is a pause. Then* Osborne *looks at* Raleigh *and laughs*]

OSBORNE: What do you think about it all?

RALEIGH: Oh, all right, thanks. [*He laughs*] I feel I've been here ages.

OSBORNE: [*Filling his pipe*] I expect you do. The time passes, though.

RALEIGH: Are we here for six days?

OSBORNE: Yes. Seems a long time, doesn't it?

RALEIGH: [*Laughing shortly*] It does rather. I can't imagine—the end of six days here——

OSBORNE: Anyhow, we've done twelve hours already. It's fine when you are relieved and go down the line to billets, and have a good hot bath, and sit and read under trees.

RALEIGH: Good Lord, I feel I haven't seen a tree for ages—not a real tree with leaves and branches—and yet I've only been here twelve hours.

OSBORNE: How did you feel—in front line?

RALEIGH: Oh, all right. It seemed so frightfully quiet and uncanny—everybody creeping about and talking in low voices. I suppose you've *got* to talk quietly when you're so near the German front line—only about seventy yards, isn't it?

OSBORNE: Yes. About the breadth of a football field.

RALEIGH: It's funny to think of it like that.

OSBORNE: I always measure distances like that out here. Keeps them in proportion.

RALEIGH: Did you play football?

OSBORNE: Yes. But mostly reffing at school in the last few years.

RALEIGH: Are you a schoolmaster, then?

OSBORNE: Yes. I must apologize.

RALEIGH: Oh, I don't mind schoolmasters. [*Hastily*] I—I mean, I never met one outside a school.

OSBORNE: They do get out sometimes.

RALEIGH: [*Laughing*] Who did you play for?

OSBORNE: The Harlequins.

RALEIGH: I say, really!

OSBORNE: I played for the English team on one great occasion.

RALEIGH: What! For *England*!

OSBORNE: I was awfully lucky to get the chance. It's a long time ago now.

RALEIGH: [*With awe*] Oh, but, good Lord! that must have been simply topping. Where did you play?

OSBORNE: Wing three.

RALEIGH: I say, I—I never realized—you'd played for England.

OSBORNE: Tuppence to talk to me now! Anyhow, don't breeze it about.

RALEIGH: Don't the others know?

OSBORNE: We never talk about football.

RALEIGH: They ought to know. It'd make them feel jolly bucked.

OSBORNE: [*Laughing*] It doesn't make much difference out here!

RALEIGH: It must be awfully thrilling, playing in front of a huge crowd—all shouting and cheering—

OSBORNE: You don't notice it when the game begins.

RALEIGH: You're too taken up with the game?

OSBORNE: Yes.

RALEIGH: I used to get wind up playing at school with only a few kids looking on.

OSBORNE: You feel it more when there are only a few. [*He has picked up a slip of paper from the table; suddenly he laughs*] Look at this!

RALEIGH: [*Looking curiously at it*] What is it?

OSBORNE: Trotter's plan to make the time pass quickly. One hundred and forty-four little circles—one for each hour of six days. He's blacked in six already. He's six hours behind.

RALEIGH: It's rather a good idea. I like Trotter.

OSBORNE: He's a good chap.

RALEIGH: He makes things feel—natural.

OSBORNE: He's a genuine sort of chap.

RALEIGH: That's it. He's genuine. [*There is a pause. He has been filling a new pipe. Osborne is puffing at his old one*] How topping—to have played for England!

OSBORNE: It was rather fun. [*There is a pause*]

RALEIGH: The Germans are really quite decent, aren't they? I mean, outside the newspapers?

OSBORNE: Yes. [*Pause*] I remember up at Wipers we had a man shot when he was out on patrol. Just at dawn. We couldn't get him in that night. He lay out there groaning all day. Next night three of our men crawled out to get him. It was so near the German trenches that they could have shot our fellows one by one. But, when our men began dragging the wounded man back over the rough ground, a big German officer stood up in their trenches and called out: "Carry him!"—and our fellows stood up and carried the man back, and the German officer fired some lights for them to see by.

RALEIGH: How topping!

OSBORNE: Next day we blew each other's trenches to blazes.

RALEIGH: It all seems rather—*silly*, doesn't it?

OSBORNE: It does, rather. [*There is silence for a while*]

RALEIGH: I started a letter when I came off duty last night. How do we send letters?

OSBORNE: The quartermaster-sergeant takes them down after he brings rations up in the evenings.

[Stanhope *is coming slowly down the steps. Raleigh rises*]

RALEIGH: I think I'll go and finish it now—if I go on duty soon.

OSBORNE: Come and write in here. It's more cheery.

RALEIGH: It's all right, thanks; I'm quite comfortable in there. I've rigged up a sort of little table beside my bed.

OSBORNE: Righto.

[Raleigh *goes into his dug-out. Stanhope is slowly taking off his equipment*]

STANHOPE: What a foul smell of bacon.

OSBORNE: Yes. We've got bacon for breakfast.

STANHOPE: So I gather. Have you told Raleigh about rifle inspection?

OSBORNE: No.

STANHOPE: [*At the entrance to* Raleigh's *dug-out*] Raleigh!

RALEIGH: [*Appearing*] Yes?

STANHOPE: You inspect your platoon's rifles at nine o'clock.

RALEIGH: Oh, righto, Stanhope. [*He goes again*]

STANHOPE: [*Sitting at the table*] I've arranged two wiring parties to begin at eight o'clock to-night—Corporal Burt with two men and Sergeant Smith with two. I want them to strengthen the wire all along the front.

OSBORNE: It's very weak at present.

STANHOPE: Every company leaves it for the next one to do. There're great holes blown out weeks ago.

OSBORNE: I know.

STANHOPE: Next night we'll start putting a belt of wire down both sides of us.

OSBORNE: Down the sides?

STANHOPE: Yes. We'll wire ourselves right in. If this attack comes, I'm not going to trust the companies on our sides to hold their ground.

[*Mason has come in, and stands diffidently in the background*]

MASON: Would you like a nice bit o' bacon, sir?

STANHOPE: No, thanks. I'll have a cup of tea.

MASON: Right, sir. [*He goes out*]

STANHOPE: I've been having a good look round. We've got a strong position here—if we wire ourselves right in. The colonel's been talking to me up there.

OSBORNE: Oh. Has he been round?

STANHOPE: Yes. He says a German prisoner gave the day of attack as the 21st.

OSBORNE: That's Thursday?

STANHOPE: Yes. To-day's Tuesday.

OSBORNE: That means about dawn the day after to-morrow.

STANHOPE: The second dawn from now. [*There is a pause*]

OSBORNE: Then it'll come while we're here.

STANHOPE: Yes. It'll come while we're here. And we shall be in the front seats.

OSBORNE: Oh, well——

[*In the silence that follows,* Mason *enters with a cup of tea*]

MASON: Would you like a nice plate of sardines, sir?

STANHOPE: I should loathe it.

MASON: Very good, sir. [*He goes out*]

OSBORNE: Did the colonel have much to say?

STANHOPE: Only that when the attack comes we can't expect any help from behind. We're not to move from here. We've got to stick it.

OSBORNE: I see.

STANHOPE: We'll wire ourselves in as strongly as possible. I've got to arrange battle positions for each platoon and section this afternoon.

OSBORNE: Well, I'm glad it's coming at last. I'm sick of waiting.

STANHOPE: [*Looking at* Trotter's *chart*] What's this extraordinary affair?

OSBORNE: Trotter's plan to make the time pass by. A hundred and forty-four circles—one for each hour of the six days.

STANHOPE: How many hours are there till dawn on the 21st?

OSBORNE: Goodness knows. Not many, I hope.

STANHOPE: Nearly nine o'clock now. Twenty-four till nine to-morrow; twelve till nine at night—that's thirty-six; nine till six next morning; that's forty-five altogether.

[*He begins to count off forty-five circles on* Trotter's *chart*]

OSBORNE: What are you going to do?

STANHOPE: At the end of the forty-fifth circle I'm going to draw a picture of Trotter being blown up in four pieces.

OSBORNE: Don't spoil his chart. It took him an hour to make that.

STANHOPE: He won't see the point. He's no imagination.

OSBORNE: I don't suppose he has.

STANHOPE: Funny not to have any imagination. Must be rather nice.

OSBORNE: A bit dull, I should think.

STANHOPE: It must be, rather. I suppose all his life Trotter feels like you and I do when we're drowsily drunk.

OSBORNE: Poor chap!

STANHOPE: I suppose if Trotter looks at that wall he just sees a brown surface. He doesn't see into the earth beyond—the worms wandering about round the stones and roots of trees. I wonder how a worm knows when it's going up or down.

OSBORNE: When it's going down I suppose the blood runs into its head and makes it throb.

STANHOPE: Worms haven't got any blood.

OSBORNE: Then I don't suppose it ever does know.

STANHOPE: Rotten if it didn't—and went on going down when it thought it was coming up.

OSBORNE: Yes, I expect that's the one thing worms dread.

STANHOPE: D'you think this life sharpens the imagination?

OSBORNE: It must.

STANHOPE: Whenever I look at anything nowadays I see right through it. Looking at you now there's your uniform—your jersey—shirt—vest—then beyond that——

OSBORNE: Let's talk about something else—croquet, or the war.

STANHOPE: [*Laughing*] Sorry! It's a habit that's grown on me lately—to look right through things, and on and on—till I get frightened and stop.

OSBORNE: I suppose everybody out here—*feels* more keenly.

STANHOPE: I hope so. I wondered if there was anything wrong with me. D'you ever get a sudden feeling that everything's going farther and farther away—till you're the only thing in the world—and then the world begins going away—until you're the only thing in—in the universe—and you struggle to get back—and can't?

OSBORNE: Bit of nerve strain, that's all.

STANHOPE: You don't think I'm going potty?

OSBORNE: Oh, Lord, no!

STANHOPE: [*Throwing back his head and laughing*] Dear old Uncle! you don't really know, do you? You just pretend you do, to make me feel all right.

OSBORNE: When people are going potty they never talk about it; they keep it to themselves.

STANHOPE: Oh, well, that's all right, then. [*There is silence for a while*] I had that feeling this morning, standing out there in the line while the sun was rising. By the way, did you see the sunrise? Wasn't it gorgeous?

OSBORNE: Splendid—this morning.

STANHOPE: I was looking across at the Boche trenches and right beyond—not a sound or a soul; just an enormous plain, all churned up like a sea that's got muddier and muddier till it's so stiff that it can't move. You could have heard a pin drop in the quiet; yet you knew thousands of guns were hidden there, all ready, cleaned and oiled—millions of bullets lying in pouches—thousands of Germans, waiting and thinking. Then, gradually, that feeling came—

OSBORNE: I never knew the sun could rise in so many ways till I came out here. Green, and pink, and red, and blue, and gray. Extraordinary, isn't it?

STANHOPE: Yes. Hi! Mason!

MASON: [*Outside*] Yessir!

STANHOPE: Bring some mugs and a bottle of whisky.

MASON: Yessir.

OSBORNE: [*Smiling*] So early in the morning?

STANHOPE: Just a spot. It's damned cold in here.

OSBORNE: [*Turning over the pages of a magazine*] This show at the Hippodrome has been running a long time.

STANHOPE: What? *Zig-zag?*

OSBORNE: Yes. George Robey's in it.

STANHOPE: Harper saw it on leave. Says it's damn good. Robey's pricelessly funny.

[Mason *brings whisky and mugs and water*]

OSBORNE: Wish I'd seen a show on leave.

STANHOPE: D'you mean to say you didn't go to any shows?

OSBORNE: [*Laughing*] No. I spent all the time in the garden, making a rockery. In the evenings I used to sit and smoke and read—and my wife used to knit socks and play the piano a bit. We pretended there wasn't any war at all—till my two youngsters made me help in a tin-soldier battle on the floor.

STANHOPE: Poor old Uncle! You can't get away from it, can you?

OSBORNE: I wish I knew how to fight a battle like those boys of mine. You ought to have seen the way they lured my men under the sofa and mowed them down.

STANHOPE: [*Laughing and helping himself to a drink*] You going to have one?

OSBORNE: Not now, thanks.

STANHOPE: You go on duty at eleven, don't you?

OSBORNE: Yes. I relieve Trotter.

STANHOPE: Raleigh better go on at one o'clock and stay with you for an hour. Then he can stay on alone till four. Hibbert relieves him at four.

OSBORNE: Righto.

STANHOPE: What's Raleigh doing now?

OSBORNE: Finishing a letter.

STANHOPE: Did you tell him?

OSBORNE: About what?

STANHOPE: Censorship.

OSBORNE: You don't mean that seriously?

STANHOPE: Mean it? Of course I mean it.

OSBORNE: You can't do that.

STANHOPE: Officially I'm supposed to read all your letters. Damn it all, Uncle! Imagine yourself in my place—a letter going away from here—from that boy——

OSBORNE: He'll say nothing—rotten—about you.

STANHOPE: You think so? [*There is a pause*] I heard you go on duty last night. After you'd gone, I got up. I was feeling bad. I forgot Raleigh was out there with Trotter. I'd forgotten all about him. I was sleepy. I just knew something beastly had happened. Then he came in with Trotter—and looked at me. After coming in out of the night air, this place must have reeked of candle-grease, and rats—and whisky. One thing a boy like that can't stand is a smell that isn't fresh. He looked at me as if I'd hit him between the eyes—as if I'd spat on him——

OSBORNE: You imagine things.

STANHOPE: [*Laughing*] Imagine things! No need to imagine!

OSBORNE: Why can't you treat him like any other youngster?

[Raleigh *comes in from his dug-out with a letter in his hand. He stops short as he notices the abrupt silence that follows his entry*]

RALEIGH: I'm sorry.

OSBORNE: It's all right, Raleigh. Going to inspect rifles?

RALEIGH: Yes.

OSBORNE: You needn't bother if the wood's a bit dirty—just the barrels and magazines and all the metal parts.

RALEIGH: Righto.

OSBORNE: See there's plenty of oil on it. And look at the ammunition in the men's pouches.

RALEIGH: Right. [*He crosses towards the door and turns*] Where do we put the letters to be collected?

OSBORNE: Oh, just on the table.

RALEIGH: Thanks.

[*He begins to lick the flap of the envelope*]

STANHOPE: [*In a quiet voice*] You leave it open.

RALEIGH: [*Surprised*] Open?

STANHOPE: Yes. I have to censor all letters.

RALEIGH: [Stammering] Oh, but—I haven't said anything about—where we are——

STANHOPE: It's the rule that letters must be read.

RALEIGH: [Nervously] Oh, I—I didn't realize that. [He stands embarrassed; then gives a short laugh] I —I think—I'll just leave it, then.

[He unbuttons his tunic pocket to put the letter away. Stanhope rises, crosses slowly and faces Raleigh]

STANHOPE: Give me that letter!

RALEIGH: [Astonished] But—Dennis——

STANHOPE: [Trembling] Give me that letter!

RALEIGH: But it's—it's private. I didn't know——

STANHOPE: D'you understand an order? Give me that letter!

RALEIGH: But I tell you—there's nothing— [Stanhope clutches Raleigh's wrist and tears the letter from his hand] Dennis—I'm——

STANHOPE: Don't "Dennis" me! Stanhope's my name! You're not at school! Go and inspect your rifles.

[Raleigh stands in amazement at the foot of the steps]

STANHOPE: [Shouting] D'you understand an order? [For a moment Raleigh stares wide-eyed at Stanhope, who is trembling and breathing heavily, then almost in a whisper he says: "Right," and goes quietly up the narrow steps. Stanhope turns toward the table]

OSBORNE: Good heavens, Stanhope!

STANHOPE: [Wheeling furiously on Osborne] Look here, Osborne, I'm commanding this company. I ask for advice when I want it!

OSBORNE: Very well.

[Stanhope sinks down at the table with the letter in his hand. There is silence for a moment. Then he throws the letter on the table and rests his head between his hands]

STANHOPE: Oh, God! I don't want to read the blasted thing!

OSBORNE: You'll let it go then?

STANHOPE: I don't care. [There is a pause]

OSBORNE: Shall I glance through it—for you?

STANHOPE: If you like.

OSBORNE: I don't want to.

STANHOPE: You better, I can't.

[Osborne takes the letter from the table and opens it. Stanhope sits with his head in his hand, digging a magazine with a pencil. After a while, Osborne glances up at Stanhope]

OSBORNE: D'you want to hear?

STANHOPE: I suppose I better know.

OSBORNE: He begins with a description of his getting here—he doesn't mention the names of any places.

STANHOPE: What does he say then?

OSBORNE: The last piece is about you.

STANHOPE: Go on.

OSBORNE: [Reading] He says: "And now I come to

the great news. I reported at Battalion Headquarters, and the colonel looked in a little book, and said, 'You report to "C" Company—Captain Stanhope.' Can't you imagine what I felt? I was taken along some trenches and shown a dug-out. There was an awfully nice officer there—quite old—with gray hair"— [Osborne clears his throat]—"and then later Dennis came in. He looked tired, but that's because he works so frightfully hard, and because of the responsibility. Then I went on duty in the front line, and a sergeant told me all about Dennis. He said that Dennis is the finest officer in the battalion, and the men simply love him. He hardly ever sleeps in the dug-out; he's always up in the front line with the men, cheering them on with jokes, and making them keen about things, like he did the kids at school. I'm awfully proud to think he's my friend." [There is silence. Stanhope has not moved while Osborne has read] That's all. [Pause] Shall I stick it down?

[Stanhope sits with lowered head. He murmurs something that sounds like "Yes, please." He rises heavily and crosses to the shadows by Osborne's bed. The sun is shining quite brightly in the trench outside]

THE CURTAIN FALLS

SCENE II.

Afternoon on the same day. The sunlight has gone from the dug-out floor, but still shines brightly in the trench.

Stanhope is lying on his bed reading by the light of a candle on the table beside him. A burly Figure comes groping down the steps and stands blinking in the shadows of the dug-out. A huge man, with a heavy black mustache, a fat red face, and massive chin.

Stanhope puts the magazine down, rises and sits up to the table.

STANHOPE: I want to talk with you, sergeant-major.

S.-M.: [Standing stolidly by the steps] Yes, sir?

STANHOPE: Sit down. Have a whisky?

S.-M.: [A suspicion of brightness in his voice] Thank you, sir.

[The Sergeant-Major diffidently takes a small tot]

STANHOPE: I say. You won't taste that. Take a proper one.

S.-M.: Well—sir [Stanhope reaches over, helps the Sergeant-Major to a large tot, and takes one himself] Turning chilly again, sir. Quite warm this morning.

STANHOPE: Yes.

S.-M.: Well, here's your very good health, sir. [He raises his glass and drinks]

STANHOPE: Cheero. [*He puts down his glass and abruptly changes his tone*] Now, look here, sergeant-major. We must expect this attack on Thursday morning at dawn. That's the second dawn from now.

[*The* Sergeant-Major *takes a very dirty little notebook from his pocket and jots down notes with a very small stub of a pencil*]

S.-M.: Thursday morning. Very good, sir.

STANHOPE: We're to hold these trenches, and no man's to move from here.

S.-M.: Very good, sir.

STANHOPE: It may happen that companies on our sides will give way, leaving our flanks exposed; so I want a screen of wire in the support line.

S.-M.: [*Writing hurriedly*] Both flanks—yes, sir.

STANHOPE: When the attack begins, I shall take charge of the left, and Mr. Osborne the right. You will be with Mr. Osborne, and Sergeant Baker with me; 9 and 10 Platoons will move over here. [*He points out the position on the trench map*] 11 and 12 Platoons to the left.

S.-M.: I see, sir.

STANHOPE: Is there anything you're not clear about?

S.-M.: [*Looking at his notes*] Seems all clear, sir.

STANHOPE: Anything you want to know?

S.-M.: Well, sir [*Clears his throat*]—when the attack comes, of course, we beat 'em off—but what if they keep on attacking?

STANHOPE: Then we keep on beating them off.

S.-M.: Yes, sir. But what I mean is—they're bound to make a big thing of it.

STANHOPE: [*Cheerily*] Oh, I think they will!

S.-M.: Well, then, sir. If they don't get through the first day they'll attack the next day and the next——

STANHOPE: They're bound to.

S.-M.: Then oughtn't we to fix up something about, well [*He gropes for the right words*]—er—falling back?

STANHOPE: There's no need to—you see, this company's a lot better than "A" and "B" Companies on either side of us.

S.-M.: Quite, sir.

STANHOPE: Well, then, if anyone breaks, "A" and "B" will break before we do. As long as we stick here when the other companies have given way, we can fire into the Boche as they try and get through the gaps on our sides—we'll make a hell of a mess of them. We might delay the advance a whole day.

S.-M.: [*Diffidently*] Yes, sir, but what 'appens when the Boche 'as all got round the back of us?

STANHOPE: Then we advance and win the war.

S.-M.: [*Pretending to make a note*] Win the war. Very good, sir.

STANHOPE: But you understand exactly what I mean, sergeant-major. Our orders are to stick here. If you're told to stick where you are you don't make plans to retire.

S.-M.: Quite, sir.

[*Osborne's voice is calling down the steps.* Sergeant-Major *rises*]

OSBORNE: Are you there, Stanhope?

STANHOPE: [*Rising quickly*] Yes. What's the matter?

OSBORNE: The colonel's up here. Wants to see you——

STANHOPE: Oh, right, I'll come up.

COLONEL: [*From above*] All right, Stanhope—I'll come down.

S.-M.: [*Who has risen*] Anything more, sir?

STANHOPE: I don't think so. I'll see you at stand-to this evening.

S.-M.: Very good, sir.

[*He stands back a pace and salutes* Stanhope *smartly.* Stanhope's *eye falls on the* Sergeant-Major's *nearly finished drink on the table. He points to it*]

STANHOPE: Hoy! What about that?

S.-M.: Thank you, sir.

[*He finishes the drink. The* Colonel *comes down the steps.*]

COLONEL: Good morning, sergeant-major.

S.-M.: Good morning, sir.

[*The* Sergeant-Major *goes up the steps*]

STANHOPE: Hullo, sir!

COLONEL: Hullo, Stanhope! [*He sniffs*] Strong smell of bacon.

STANHOPE: Yes, sir. We had some bacon for breakfast.

COLONEL: Hangs about, doesn't it?

STANHOPE: Yes, sir. Clings to the walls.

COLONEL: Lovely day.

STANHOPE: Splendid, sir.

COLONEL: Spring's coming. [*There is a pause*] I'm glad you're alone. I've got some rather serious news.

STANHOPE: I'm sorry to hear that, sir. Will you have a drink?

COLONEL: Well, thanks—just a spot. [Stanhope *mixes a drink for the* Colonel *and himself*] Here's luck.

STANHOPE: Cheero, sir. [*Bringing forward a box*] Sit down, sir.

COLONEL: Thanks.

STANHOPE: What's the news, sir?

COLONEL: The brigadier came to see me this morning. [*He pauses*] It seems almost certain the attack's to come on Thursday morning. They've got information from more than one source—but they don't know where it's going to fall the hardest. The Boche began relieving his front-line troops yesterday. They're bound to put in certain regiments where they intend to make the hardest push——

STANHOPE: Naturally——

COLONEL: And the general wants us to make a raid to find out who's come into the line opposite here. [*There is a pause*]

STANHOPE: I see. When?

COLONEL: As soon as possible. He said to-night.

STANHOPE: Oh, but that's absurd!

COLONEL: I told him so. I said the earliest would be to-morrow afternoon. A surprise daylight raid under a smoke screen from the trench-mortar people. I think daylight best. There's not much moon now, and it's vitally important to get hold of a Boche or two.

STANHOPE: Quite.

COLONEL: I suggest sending two officers and ten men. Quite enough for the purpose. Just opposite here there's only seventy yards of No Man's Land. To-night the trench-mortars can blow a hole in the Boche wire and you can cut a hole in yours. Harrison of the trench-mortars is coming in to dinner with me this evening to discuss everything. I'd like you to come too. Eight o'clock suit you?

STANHOPE: Very good, sir.

COLONEL: I'll leave you to select the men.

STANHOPE: You want me to go with them, sir?

COLONEL: Oh, no, Stanhope. I—I can't let you go. No. I want one officer to direct the raid and one to make the dash in and collar some Boche.

STANHOPE: Who do you suggest, sir?

COLONEL: Well, I suggest Osborne, for one. He's a very level-headed chap. He can direct it.

STANHOPE: And who else?

COLONEL: Well, there's Trotter—but he's a bit fat, isn't he? Not much good at dashing in?

STANHOPE: No. D'you suggest Hibbert?

COLONEL: Well, what do *you* think of Hibbert?

STANHOPE: I don't think so.

COLONEL: No. [*There is a pause*]

STANHOPE: Why not send a good sergeant, sir?

COLONEL: No. I don't think a sergeant. The men expect officers to lead a raid.

STANHOPE: Yes. There is that.

COLONEL: As a matter of fact, Stanhope, I'm thinking of that youngster I sent up to you last night.

STANHOPE: Raleigh?

COLONEL: Yes. Just the type. Plenty of guts——

STANHOPE: He's awfully new to it all——

COLONEL: All to the good. His nerves are sound.

STANHOPE: It's rotten to send a fellow who's only just arrived.

COLONEL: Well, who else is there? I could send an officer from another company——

STANHOPE: [*Quickly*] Oh, Lord, no. We'll do it.

COLONEL: Then I suggest Osborne to lead the raid and Raleigh to make the dash—with ten good men. We'll meet Harrison at supper and arrange the smoke bombs—and blowing a hole in the wire. You select the men and talk to Osborne and Raleigh about it in the meantime.

STANHOPE: Very well, sir.

COLONEL: Better send Osborne and Raleigh down to me in the morning to talk things over. Or, better still—I'll come up here first thing to-morrow morning.

STANHOPE: Right, sir.

COLONEL: It's all a damn nuisance; but, after all—it's necessary.

STANHOPE: I suppose it is.

COLONEL: Well, so long, Stanhope. I'll see you at eight o'clock. Do you like fish?

STANHOPE: Fish, sir?

COLONEL: Yes. We've had some fresh fish sent up from railhead for supper to-night.

STANHOPE: Splendid, sir!

COLONEL: Whiting, I think it is.

STANHOPE: Good!

COLONEL: Well, bye-bye.

[*The* Colonel *goes up the steps.* Stanhope *stands watching for a moment, then turns and walks slowly to the table.* Hibbert *comes quietly into the dug-out from the tunnel leading from his sleeping quarters*]

STANHOPE: Hullo! I thought you were asleep.

HIBBERT: I just wanted a word with you, Stanhope.

STANHOPE: Fire away.

HIBBERT: This neuralgia of mine. I'm awfully sorry. I'm afraid I can't stick it any longer——

STANHOPE: I know. It's rotten, isn't it? I've got it like hell——

HIBBERT: [*Taken aback*] You have?

STANHOPE: Had it for weeks.

HIBBERT: Well, I'm sorry, Stanhope. It's no good. I've tried damned hard; but I must go down——

STANHOPE: Go down—where?

HIBBERT: Why, go sick—go down the line. I must go into hospital and have some kind of treatment. [*There is a silence for a moment.* Stanhope *is looking at* Hibbert—*till* Hibbert *turns away and walks towards his dug-out*] I'll go right along now, I think.

STANHOPE: [*Quietly*] You're going to stay here.

HIBBERT: I'm going down to see the doctor. He'll send me to hospital when he understands——

STANHOPE: I've seen the doctor. I saw him this morning. He won't send you to hospital, Hibbert; he'll send you back here. He promised me he would. [*There is silence*] So you can save yourself a walk.

HIBBERT: [*Fiercely*] What the hell——!

STANHOPE: Stop that!

HIBBERT: I've a perfect right to go sick if I want to. The men can—why can't an officer?

STANHOPE: No man's sent down unless he's very ill. There's nothing wrong with you, Hibbert. The German attack's on Thursday; almost for certain. You're going to stay here and see it through with the rest of us.

HIBBERT: [*Hysterically*] I tell you, I can't—the pain's nearly sending me mad. I'm going! I've got all my stuff packed. I'm going now—you can't stop me!

[*He goes excitedly into the dug-out.* Stanhope *walks slowly towards the steps, turns, and undoes the flap of his revolver holster. He takes out his revolver, and stands casually examining it.* Hibbert *returns with his pack slung on his back and a walking-stick in his hand. He pauses at the sight of* Stanhope *by the steps*]

HIBBERT: Let's get by, Stanhope.

STANHOPE: You're going to stay here and do your job.

HIBBERT: Haven't I *told* you? I *can't!* Don't you understand? Let—let me get by.

STANHOPE: Now look here, Hibbert. I've got a lot of work to do and no time to waste. Once and for all, you're going to stay here and see it through with the rest of us.

HIBBERT: I shall die of this pain if I don't go!

STANHOPE: Better die of pain than be shot for deserting.

HIBBERT: [*In a low voice*] What do you mean?

STANHOPE: You know what I mean——

HIBBERT: I've a right to see the doctor!

STANHOPE: Good God! Don't you understand!—he'll send you back here. Doctor Preston's never let a shirker pass him yet—and he's not going to start now—two days before the attack——

HIBBERT: [*Pleadingly*] Stanhope—if you only *knew* how awful I feel—Please do let me go by——

[*He walks slowly round behind* Stanhope. Stanhope *turns and thrusts him roughly back. With a lightning movement* Hibbert *raises his stick and strikes blindly at* Stanhope, *who catches the stick, tears it from* Hibbert's *hands, smashes it across his knee, and throws it on the ground*]

STANHOPE: God!—you little swine. You know what that means—don't you? Striking a superior officer! [*There is silence.* Stanhope *takes hold of his revolver as it swings from its lanyard.* Hibbert *stands quivering in front of* Stanhope] Never mind, though. I won't have you shot for that——

HIBBERT: Let me go——

STANHOPE: If you went, I'd have you shot—for deserting. It's a hell of a disgrace—to die like that. I'd rather spare you the disgrace. I give you half a minute to think. You either stay here and try and be a man—or you try to get out of that door—to desert. If you do that, there's going to be an accident. D'you understand? I'm fiddling with my revolver, d'you see?—cleaning it—and it's going off by accident. It often happens out here. It's going off, and it's going to shoot you between the eyes.

HIBBERT: [*In a whisper*] You daren't——

STANHOPE: You don't deserve to be shot by accident—but I'd save you the disgrace of the other way—I give you half a minute to decide. [*He holds up his wrist to look at his watch*] Half a minute from now——

[*There is silence; a few seconds go by. Suddenly* Hibbert *bursts into a high-pitched laugh*]

HIBBERT: Go on, then, shoot! You won't let me go to the hospital. I swear I'll never go into those trenches again. Shoot!—and thank God——

STANHOPE: [*With his eyes on his watch*] Fifteen more seconds——

HIBBERT: Go on! I'm ready——

STANHOPE: Ten [*He looks up at* Hibbert *who has closed his eyes*] Five.

[*Again* Stanhope *looks up. After a moment he quietly drops his revolver into its holster and steps towards* Hibbert, *who stands with lowered head and eyes tightly screwed up, his arms stretched stiffly by his sides, his hands tightly clutching the edges of his tunic. Gently* Stanhope *places his hands on* Hibbert's *shoulders.* Hibbert *starts violently and gives a little cry. He opens his eyes and stares vacantly into* Stanhope's *face.* Stanhope *is smiling*]

STANHOPE: Good man, Hibbert. I liked the way you stuck that.

HIBBERT: [*Hoarsely*] Why didn't you shoot?

STANHOPE: Stay here, old chap—and see it through——

[Hibbert *stands trembling, trying to speak. Suddenly he breaks down and cries.* Stanhope *takes his hands from his shoulders and turns away*]

HIBBERT: Stanhope! I've tried like hell—I swear I have. Ever since I came out here I've hated and loathed it. Every sound up there makes me all—cold and sick. I'm different to—to the others—you don't understand. It's got worse and worse, and now I can't bear it any longer. I'll never go up those steps again—into the line—with the men looking at me—and knowing—I'd rather die here.

[*He is sitting on* Stanhope's *bed, crying without an effort to restrain himself*]

STANHOPE: [*Pouring out a whisky*] Try a drop of this, old chap——

HIBBERT. No, thanks.

STANHOPE: Go on. Drink it. [Hibbert *takes the mug and drinks.* Stanhope *sits down beside* Hibbert *and puts an arm round his shoulder*] I know what you feel, Hibbert. I've known all along——

HIBBERT: How *can* you know?

STANHOPE: Because I feel the same—exactly the same! Every little noise up there makes me feel—just as you feel. Why didn't you tell me instead of talking about neuralgia? We *all* feel like you do sometimes, if you only knew. I hate and loathe it all. Sometimes I feel I could just lie down on this bed and pretend I was paralyzed or something—and couldn't move—and just lie there till I died—or was dragged away.

HIBBERT: I can't bear to go up into those awful trenches again.

STANHOPE: When are you due to go on?

HIBBERT: Quite soon. At four.

STANHOPE: Shall we go on together? We know how we both feel now. Shall we see if we can stick it together?

HIBBERT: I can't——

STANHOPE: Supposing I said *I* can't—supposing we *all* say we can't—what would happen then?

HIBBERT: I don't care. What does it matter? It's all so—so beastly—nothing matters——

STANHOPE: Supposing the worst happened—supposing we were knocked right out. Think of all the chaps who've gone already. It can't be very lonely there—with all those fellows. Sometimes I think it's lonelier here. [*He pauses. Hibbert is sitting quietly now, his eyes roving vacantly in front of him*] Just go and have a quiet rest. Then we'll go out together.

HIBBERT: Do please let me go, Stanhope——

STANHOPE: If you went—and left Osborne and Trotter and Raleigh and all those men up there to do your work—could you ever look a man straight in the face again—in all your life? [*There is silence again*] You may be wounded. Then you can go home and feel proud—and if you're killed, you—you won't have to stand this hell any more. I might have fired just now. If I had you would have been dead now. But you're still alive—with a straight fighting chance of coming through. Take the chance, old chap, and stand in with Osborne and Trotter and Raleigh. Don't you think it worth standing in with men like that?—when you know they all feel like you do—in their hearts—and just go on sticking it because they know it's—it's the only thing a decent man can do. [*Again there is silence*] What about it?

HIBBERT: I'll—I'll try——

STANHOPE: Good man!

HIBBERT: You—you won't say anything, Stanhope—about this?

STANHOPE: If you promise not to tell any one what a blasted funk *I* am.

HIBBERT: [*With a little laugh*] No.

STANHOPE: Splendid! Now go and have ten minutes' rest and a smoke—then we'll go up together and hold each other's hands—and jump every time a rat squeaks. [*Hibbert rises and blows his nose*] We've all got a good fighting chance. I mean to come through—don't you think?

HIBBERT: Yes. Rather. [*He goes timidly towards his dug-out, and turns at the doorway*] It's awfully decent of you, Stanhope—— [*Stanhope is pouring himself out a whisky*] And thanks most awfully for——

STANHOPE: That's all right.

[*Hibbert goes away. Stanhope takes a drink and sits down at the table to write. Mason comes in*]

MASON: Will you have a nice cup of tea, sir?

STANHOPE: Can you guarantee it's nice?

MASON: Well, sir—it's a bit oniony, but that's only because of the saucepan.

STANHOPE: In other words, it's onion soup with tea-leaves in it?

MASON: Not till dinner-time, sir.

STANHOPE: All right, Mason. Bring two cups of onion tea. One for Mr. Hibbert.

MASON: Very good, sir. [*Going towards the door, he meets Osborne coming in*] Will you have a nice cup of tea, sir?

OSBORNE: Please, Mason—and plenty of bread and butter and strawberry jam.

MASON: Very good, sir.

STANHOPE: Well, Uncle—how are things going on up there?

OSBORNE: Two lonely rifle grenades came over just now.

STANHOPE: I heard them. Where did they pitch?

OSBORNE: Just over the front line on the left. Otherwise nothing doing. [*Pause*]

STANHOPE: The colonel's been talking to me.

OSBORNE: About the attack?

STANHOPE: Partly. We've got to make a raid, Uncle.

OSBORNE: Oh? When?

STANHOPE: To-morrow afternoon. Under a smoke screen. Two officers and ten men.

OSBORNE: Who's going?

STANHOPE: You and Raleigh.

[*Pause*]

OSBORNE: Oh! [*There is another pause*] Why Raleigh?

STANHOPE: The colonel picked you to direct and Raleigh to dash in.

OSBORNE: I see.

STANHOPE: The brigade wants to know who's opposite here.

OSBORNE: To-morrow? What time?

STANHOPE: I suggest about five o'clock. A little before dusk——

OSBORNE: I see.

STANHOPE: I'm damn sorry.

OSBORNE: That's all right, old chap.

STANHOPE: I'm dining with the colonel to arrange everything. Then I'll come back and go through it with you.

OSBORNE: Where do we raid from?

STANHOPE: Out of the sap on our left. Straight across.

OSBORNE: Where's the map?

STANHOPE: Here we are. Look. Straight across to this sentry post of the Boche. Sixty yards. To-night we'll lay out a guiding tape as far as possible. After dark the toch-emmas are going to break the Boche wire and we'll cut a passage in ours.

OSBORNE: Will you fix up the men who are to go?

STANHOPE: Are you keen on any special men?

OSBORNE: Can I take a corporal?

STANHOPE: Sure.

OSBORNE: May I have young Crooks?

STANHOPE: Righto.

OSBORNE: You'll ask for volunteers, I suppose?

STANHOPE: Yes. I'll see the sergeant-major and get him to go round for names.

[*He crosses to the doorway as Mason comes in with the tea*]

MASON: Your tea, sir!

STANHOPE: Keep it hot, Mason.

MASON: Will you take this cup, Mr. Osborne?

STANHOPE: Take the other in to Mr. Hibbert, in there.

MASON: Very good, sir.

[*He goes in to* Hibbert's *dug-out*]

STANHOPE: Shan't be long, Uncle.

[*He goes up the steps*]

OSBORNE: Righto.

[Mason *returns*]

MASON: Will you have cut bread and butter—or shall I bring the loaf, sir?

OSBORNE: Cut it, Mason, please.

MASON: Just bringing the jam separately?

OSBORNE: Yes.

MASON: Very good, sir.

[Mason *goes out.* Osborne *takes a small leather-bound book from his pocket, opens it at a marker, and begins to read.* Trotter *appears from the sleeping dug-out looking very sleepy*]

TROTTER: Tea ready?

OSBORNE: Yes.

TROTTER: Why's Hibbert got his tea in there?

OSBORNE: I don't know.

TROTTER: [*Rubbing his eyes*] Oh, Lord, I do feel frowsy. 'Ad a fine sleep, though.

[Mason *brings more tea and a pot of jam*]

MASON: Bread just coming, sir. 'Ere's the strawberry jam, sir.

TROTTER: [*Reciting*] " 'Tell me, Mother, what is that

That looks like strawberry jam?'

'Hush, hush, my dear; 'tis only Pa

Run over by a tram——' "

OSBORNE: The colonel came here while you were asleep.

TROTTER: Oh?

OSBORNE: We've got to make a raid to-morrow afternoon.

TROTTER: Oh, Lord! What—all of us?

OSBORNE: Two officers and ten men.

TROTTER: Who's got to do it?

OSBORNE: Raleigh and I.

TROTTER: Raleigh!

OSBORNE: Yes.

TROTTER: But 'e's only just come!

OSBORNE: Apparently that's the reason.

TROTTER: And you're going too?

OSBORNE: Yes.

TROTTER: Let's 'ear all about it.

OSBORNE: I know nothing yet. Except that it's got to be done.

TROTTER: What a damn nuisance!

OSBORNE: It is, rather.

TROTTER: I reckon the Boche are all ready waiting for it. Did you 'ear about the raid just south of 'ere the other night?

OSBORNE: Nothing much.

TROTTER: The trench-mortars go and knock an 'ole in the Boche wire to let our fellers through— and in the night the Boche went out and tied bits o' red rag on each side of the 'ole.

OSBORNE: Yes. I heard about that.

TROTTER: And even then our fellers 'ad to make the raid. It was murder. Doesn't this tea taste of onions?

OSBORNE: It does a bit.

TROTTER: Pity Mason don't clean 'is pots better. [Mason *brings some bread on a plate*] This tea tastes of onions.

MASON: I'm sorry, sir. Onions do 'ave such a way of cropping up again.

TROTTER: Yes, but we 'aven't 'ad onions for days!

MASON: I know, sir. That's what makes it so funny.

TROTTER: Well, you better do something about it.

MASON: I'll look into it, sir.

[*He goes out*]

[Osborne *and* Trotter *prepare themselves slices of bread and jam*]

TROTTER: Joking apart. It's damn ridiculous making a raid when the Boche are expecting it.

OSBORNE: We're not doing it for fun.

TROTTER: I know.

OSBORNE: You might avoid talking to Raleigh about it.

TROTTER: Why? How do you mean?

OSBORNE: There's no need to tell him it's murder——

TROTTER: Oh! Lord! no. [*He pauses*] I'm sorry 'e's got to go. 'E's a nice young feller— [Osborne *turns to his book. There is silence*] What are you reading?

OSBORNE: [*Wearily*] Oh, just a book.

TROTTER: What's the title?

OSBORNE: [*Showing him the cover*] Ever read it?

TROTTER: [*Leaning over and reading the cover*] *Alice's Adventures in Wonderland*—Why, that's a kid's book!

OSBORNE: Yes.

TROTTER: You aren't *reading* it?

OSBORNE: Yes.

TROTTER: What—a *kid's* book?

OSBORNE: Haven't you read it?

TROTTER: [*Scornfully*] No!

OSBORNE: You ought to. [*Reads*]

"How doth the little crocodile
    Improve his shining tail,
And pour the waters of the Nile
    On every golden scale?

"How cheerfully he seems to grin
    And neatly spread his claws,
And welcomes little fishes in
    With gently smiling jaws!"

TROTTER: [*After a moment's thought*] I don't see no point in that.

OSBORNE: [*Wearily*] Exactly. That's just the point.

TROTTER: [*Looking curiously at* Osborne] You are a funny chap!

[Stanhope *returns*]

STANHOPE: The sergeant-major's getting volunteers

OSBORNE: Good!

TROTTER: Sorry to 'ear about the raid, skipper.

STANHOPE: [*Shortly*] So am I. What do you make the time?

TROTTER: Just on four.

[Mason *brings in more tea*]

STANHOPE: [*Taking the mug of tea*] Was Hibbert asleep when you came out of there?

TROTTER: No. 'E was just lying on 'is bed, smoking.

STANHOPE: [*Going to the sleeping dug-out*] Hibbert!

HIBBERT: [*Coming out*] I'm ready, Stanhope.

STANHOPE: Had some tea?

HIBBERT: Yes, thanks.

TROTTER: I reckon Raleigh'll be glad to be relieved. Rotten being on dooty for the first time alone.

OSBORNE: I don't think he minds.

STANHOPE: I shall be up there some time, Uncle.

OSBORNE: I say, why don't you have a rest—you've been on the go all day.

STANHOPE: There's too much to do. This raid's going to upset the arrangements of the wiring party to-night. Can't have men out there while the toch-emmas are blowing' holes in the Boche wire. [*He drinks up his tea*] Ready, Hibbert? Come on, my lad.

[Stanhope *and* Hibbert *leave the dug-out together.* Trotter *looks after them curiously, and turns to* Osborne]

TROTTER: Can't understand that little feller, can you?

OSBORNE: Who?

TROTTER: Why, 'Ibbert. D'you see 's eyes? All red. 'E told me in there 'e'd got 'ay-fever.

OSBORNE: Rotten thing, hay-fever.

TROTTER: If you ask me, 'e's been crying——

[Osborne *is writing at the table*]

OSBORNE: Maybe.

TROTTER: Funny little bloke, isn't 'e?

OSBORNE: Yes. I say—d'you mind? I just want to get a letter off.

TROTTER: Oh, sorry. They 'aven't collected the letters yet, then?

OSBORNE: Not yet.

TROTTER: I'll get one off to my old lady. [*He goes towards his dug-out*] She's wrote and asked if I've got fleas.

OSBORNE: Have you?

TROTTER: [*Gently rotating his shoulders*] I wish it *was* fleas.

[Trotter *goes into his dug-out*; Osborne *continues his letter*. Raleigh *comes down the steps from the trench*]

RALEIGH: [*Excitedly*] I say, Stanhope's told me about the raid.

OSBORNE: Has he?

RALEIGH: Just you and me, isn't it—and ten men?

OSBORNE: Yes, to-morrow. Just before dusk. Under a smoke cloud.

RALEIGH: I say—it's most frightfully exciting!

OSBORNE: We shall know more about it after Stanhope sees the colonel to-night.

RALEIGH: Were you and I picked—specially?

OSBORNE: Yes.

RALEIGH: I—say!

THE CURTAIN FALLS

ACT III. SCENE I.

The following day, towards sunset. The earth wall of the trench outside glows with a light that slowly fades with the sinking sun.

Stanhope *is alone, wandering to and fro across the dug-out. He looks up the steps for a moment, crosses to the table, and glances down at the map. He looks anxiously at his watch, and, going to the servants' dug-out, calls:*

STANHOPE: Mason!

MASON: [*Outside*] Yessir!

STANHOPE: Are you making the coffee?

MASON: Yessir!

STANHOPE: Make it hot and strong. Ready in five minutes. I'll call when it's wanted.

MASON: Very good, sir.

[*Again* Stanhope *wanders restlessly to and fro. The* Colonel *comes down the steps*]

COLONEL: Everything ready?

STANHOPE: Yes, sir. [*There is silence*] You've no news, then?

COLONEL: I'm afraid not. It's got to be done.

STANHOPE: [*After a pause*] I see.

COLONEL: The brigadier says the Boche did the same thing just south of here the other day.

STANHOPE: I know, but didn't you suggest we alter our plans and make a surprise raid farther up the line after dark?

COLONEL: Yes. I suggested that.

STANHOPE: What did he say?

COLONEL: He said the present arrangements have got to stand.

STANHOPE: But surely he must realize——

COLONEL: [*Impatiently breaking in*] Look here, Stanhope, I've done all I can, but my report's got to be at headquarters by seven this evening. If we wait till it's dark we shall be too late.

STANHOPE: Why seven?

COLONEL: They've got some conference to arrange the placing of reserves.

STANHOPE: They can't have it later because of dinner, I suppose.

COLONEL: Lots of raids have taken place along the line to-day. With the attack to-morrow morning, headquarters naturally want all the information they can get as early as possible.

STANHOPE: Meanwhile the Boche are sitting over there with a dozen machine-guns trained on that hole—waiting for our fellows to come.

COLONEL: Well, I can't disobey orders.

STANHOPE: Why didn't the trench-mortars blow a dozen holes in different places—so the Boche wouldn't know which we were going to use?

COLONEL: It took three hours to blow that one. How could they blow a dozen in the time? It's no good worrying about that now. It's too late. Where's Osborne and Raleigh?

STANHOPE: They're up in the sap, having a last look around. What d'you make the time, sir?

COLONEL: Exactly nineteen minutes to.

STANHOPE: I'm thirty seconds behind you.

COLONEL: Funny. We checked this morning.

STANHOPE: Still, it's near enough. We shan't go till the smoke blows across.

COLONEL: The smoke ought to blow across nicely. The wind's just right. I called on the trench-mortars on the way up. Everything's ready. They'll drop the bombs thirty yards to the right.

STANHOPE: Are you going to stay here?

COLONEL: I'll watch from the trench just above, I think. Bring the prisoners straight back here. We'll question them right away.

STANHOPE: Why not take them straight down to your quarters?

COLONEL: Well, the Boche are bound to shell pretty heavily. I don't want the risk of the prisoners being knocked out before we've talked to them.

STANHOPE: All right. I'll have them brought back here.

[There is a pause. The Colonel sucks hard at his pipe. Stanhope roves restlessly about, smoking a cigarette]

COLONEL: It's no good getting depressed. After all, it's only sixty yards. The Boche'll be firing into a blank fog. Osborne's a cool, level-headed chap, and Raleigh's the very man to dash in. You've picked good men to follow them?

STANHOPE: The best. All youngsters. Strong, keen chaps.

COLONEL: Good. [Another pause] You know quite well I'd give anything to cancel the beastly affair.

STANHOPE: I know you would, sir.

COLONEL: Have these red rags on the wire upset the men at all?

STANHOPE: It's hard to tell. They naturally take it as a joke. They say the rags are just what they want to show them the way through the gap.

COLONEL: That's the spirit, Stanhope. [Osborne and Raleigh come down the steps] Well, Osborne. Everything ready?

OSBORNE: Yes, I think we're all ready, sir. I make it just a quarter to.

COLONEL: That's right.

OSBORNE: The men are going to stand by at three minutes to.

COLONEL: The smoke bombs drop exactly on the hour. You'll give the word to go when the smoke's thick enough?

OSBORNE: That's right, sir.

STANHOPE: [At the servants' dug-out] Mason!

MASON: Coming, sir!

STANHOPE: Were the men having their rum, Uncle?

OSBORNE: Yes. Just as we left. It gives it a quarter of an hour to soak in.

COLONEL: That's right. Are they cheerful?

OSBORNE: Yes. Quite.

[Mason brings in two cups of coffee and puts them on the table]

STANHOPE: Would you like to go up and speak to them, sir?

COLONEL: Well, don't you think they'd rather be left alone?

STANHOPE: I think they would appreciate a word or two.

COLONEL: All right. If you think they would.

OSBORNE: They're all in the center dug-out, sir.

COLONEL: Right. You coming, Stanhope?

STANHOPE: Yes. I'll come, sir.

[The Colonel lingers a moment. There is an awkward pause. Then the Colonel clears his throat and speaks]

COLONEL: Well, good luck, Osborne. I'm certain you'll put up a good show.

OSBORNE: [Taking the Colonel's hand] Thank you, sir.

COLONEL: And, Raleigh, just go in like blazes. Grab hold of the first Boche you see and bundle him across here. One'll do, but bring more if you see any handy.

RALEIGH: [Taking the Colonel's offered hand] Right, sir.

COLONEL: And, if you succeed, I'll recommend you both for the M.C. [Osborne and Raleigh murmur their thanks] Remember, a great deal may depend on bringing in a German. It may mean the winning of the whole war. You never know. [Another pause] Well, good luck to you both.

[Again Osborne and Raleigh murmur their thanks. The Colonel and Stanhope go towards the door]

COLONEL: [Over his shoulder] Don't forget to empty your pockets of papers and things.

RALEIGH: Oh, no.

[He goes into his dug-out, taking letters and papers from his pockets. Stanhope is about to follow the Colonel up the steps when Osborne calls him back]

OSBORNE: Er—Stanhope—just a moment.

STANHOPE: [Returning] Hullo!

OSBORNE: I say, don't think I'm being morbid, or anything like that, but would you mind taking these?

STANHOPE: Sure. Until you come back, old man.

OSBORNE: It's only just in case—[He takes his watch and a letter from his tunic pocket and puts them on the table. Then he pulls off his ring] If anything should happen, would you send these along to my wife?

[He pauses, and gives an awkward little laugh]

STANHOPE: [*Putting the articles together on the table*] You're coming back, old man. Damn it! what on earth should I do without you?

OSBORNE: [*Laughing*] Goodness knows!

STANHOPE: Must have somebody to tuck me up in bed. [*There is a pause*] Well, I'll see you up in the sap, before you go. Just have a spot of rum in that coffee.

OSBORNE: Righto.

[Stanhope *goes to the steps and lingers for a moment*]

STANHOPE: Cheero!

[*For a second their eyes meet; they laugh. Stanhope goes slowly up the steps. There is a silence in the dug-out. Osborne has been filling his pipe, and stands lighting it as* Raleigh *returns*]

OSBORNE: Just time for a small pipe.

RALEIGH: Good. I'll have a cigarette, I think.

[*He feels in his pocket*]

OSBORNE: Here you are.

[*He offers his case to* Raleigh]

RALEIGH: I say, I'm always smoking yours.

OSBORNE: That's all right. [*Pause*] What about this coffee?

RALEIGH: Sure.

[*They sit at the table*]

OSBORNE: Are you going to have a drop of rum in it?

RALEIGH: Don't you think it might make us a— a bit muzzy?

OSBORNE: I'm just having the coffee as it is.

RALEIGH: I think I will, too.

OSBORNE: We'll have the rum afterwards—to celebrate.

RALEIGH: That's a much better idea.

[*They stir their coffee in silence. Osborne's eyes meet* Raleigh's. *He smiles*]

OSBORNE: How d'you feel?

RALEIGH: All right.

OSBORNE: I've got a sort of empty feeling inside.

RALEIGH: That's just what I've got!

OSBORNE: Wind up!

RALEIGH: I keep wanting to yawn.

OSBORNE: That's it. Wind up. I keep wanting to yawn too. It'll pass off directly we start.

RALEIGH: [*Taking a deep breath*] I wish we could go now.

OSBORNE: [*Looking at his watch on the table*] We've got eight minutes yet.

RALEIGH: Oh, Lord!

OSBORNE: Let's just have a last look at the map. [*He picks up the map and spreads it out*] Directly the smoke's thick enough, I'll give the word. You run straight for this point here——

RALEIGH: When I get to the Boche wire I lie down and wait for you.

OSBORNE: Don't forget to throw your bombs.

RALEIGH: [*Patting his pocket*] No. I've got them here.

OSBORNE: When I shout "Righto!"—in you go with your eight men. I shall lie on the Boche parapet, and blow my whistle now and then to show you where I am. Pounce on the first Boche you see and bundle him out to me.

RALEIGH: Righto.

OSBORNE: Then we come back like blazes.

RALEIGH: The whole thing'll be over quite quickly?

OSBORNE: I reckon with luck we shall be back in three minutes.

RALEIGH: As quick as that?

OSBORNE: I think so. [*He folds up the map*] And now let's forget all about it for—[*He looks at his watch*]—for six minutes.

RALEIGH: Oh, Lord, I can't!

OSBORNE: You must.

RALEIGH: How topping if we both get the M.C.!

OSBORNE: Yes. [*Pause*] Your coffee sweet enough?

RALEIGH: Yes, thanks. It's jolly good coffee. [*Pause*] I wonder what the Boche are doing over there now?

OSBORNE: I don't know. D'you like coffee better than tea?

RALEIGH: I do for breakfast. [*Pause*] Do these smoke bombs make much row when they burst?

OSBORNE: Not much. [*Pause*] Personally, I like cocoa for breakfast.

RALEIGH: [*Laughing*] I'm sorry!

OSBORNE: Why sorry? Why shouldn't I have cocoa for breakfast?

RALEIGH: I don't mean that. I—mean—I'm sorry to keep talking about the raid. It's so difficult to— to talk about anything else. I was just wondering— will the Boche retaliate in any way after the raid?

OSBORNE: Bound to—a bit.

RALEIGH: Shelling?

OSBORNE: " 'The time has come,' the Walrus said, 'To talk of many things: Of shoes—and ships—and sealing-wax— Of cabbages—and kings.' "

RALEIGH: " 'And why the sea is boiling hot— And whether pigs have wings.' "

OSBORNE: Now we're off! Quick, let's talk about pigs! Black pigs or white pigs?

RALEIGH: Black pigs. In the New Forest you find them, quite wild.

OSBORNE: You know the New Forest?

RALEIGH: Rather! My home's down there. A little place called Allum Green just outside Lyndhurst.

OSBORNE: I know Lyndhurst well.

RALEIGH: It's rather nice down there.

OSBORNE: I like it more than any place I know.

RALEIGH: I think I do, too. Of course, it's different when you've always lived in a place.

OSBORNE: You like it in a different way.

RALEIGH: Yes. Just behind our house there's a stream called the Highland; it runs for miles—right through the middle of the forest. Dennis and I followed it once as far as we could.

OSBORNE: I used to walk a lot round Lyndhurst.

RALEIGH: I wish we'd known each other then. You could have come with Dennis and me.

OSBORNE: I wish I had. I used to walk alone.

RALEIGH: You must come and stay with us one day.

OSBORNE: I should like to—awfully.

RALEIGH: I can show you places in the forest that nobody knows about except Dennis and me. It gets thicker and darker and cooler, and you stir up all kinds of funny wild animals.

OSBORNE: They say there are ruins, somewhere in the forest, of villages that William the Conqueror pulled down to let the forest grow.

RALEIGH: I know. We often used to look for them, but we haven't found them yet. [Pause] You must come and help look one day.

OSBORNE: I'll find them, all right!

RALEIGH: Then you can write to the papers. "Dramatic Discovery of Professor Osborne!"

[Osborne laughs]

OSBORNE: I did go exploring once—digging up Roman remains.

RALEIGH: Where was that?

OSBORNE: Near my home in Sussex there's a Roman road called Stane Street; it runs as straight as a line from the coast to London.

RALEIGH: I know it.

OSBORNE: Near where I live the road runs over Bignor Hill, but in recent times a new road's been cut round the foot of the hill, meeting the old road again farther on. The old road over the hill hasn't been used for years and years—and it's all grown over with grass, and bushes and trees grow in the middle of it.

RALEIGH: Can you still see where it runs?

OSBORNE: Quite easily, in places.

RALEIGH: Did you dig a bit of it up, then?

OSBORNE: Yes. We got permission to dig out a section. It was in wonderful condition.

RALEIGH: Did you find anything?

OSBORNE: We found a horseshoe—and a Roman penny.

RALEIGH: [Laughing] Splendid!

OSBORNE: It's awfully fascinating, digging like that.

RALEIGH: It must be. [Osborne glances at his watch] It is time yet?

OSBORNE: Two minutes. Then we must go up. I wish we had a good hot bath waiting for us when we get back.

RALEIGH: So do I. [Pause] We're having something special for dinner, aren't we?

OSBORNE: How did you know? It's supposed to be a secret.

RALEIGH: Mason dropped a hint.

OSBORNE: Well, we've a fresh chicken sent up from Noyelle Farm.

RALEIGH: I say!

OSBORNE: And a most awful luxury—two bottles of champagne and a half-dozen cigars! One each, and one spare one in case one explodes!

RALEIGH: I've never smoked a cigar.

[Raleigh notices Osborne's ring on the table; he picks it up]

RALEIGH: I say, here's your ring.

OSBORNE: Yes. I'm—I'm leaving it here. I don't want to risk losing it.

RALEIGH: Oh!

[There is silence. He puts the ring slowly down]

OSBORNE: [Rising] Well, I think perhaps we ought to get ready.

RALEIGH: Yes. Righto.

[He also rises]

OSBORNE: I'm not going to wear a belt—just my revolver, with the lanyard round my neck.

RALEIGH: I see. [He puts his lanyard round his neck and grips his revolver] I feel better with this in my hand, don't you?

OSBORNE: Yes, something to hold. Loaded all right?

RALEIGH: Yes.

[They put on their helmets. Osborne takes his pipe from his mouth and lays it carefully on the table]

OSBORNE: I do hate leaving a pipe when it's got a nice glow on the top like that.

RALEIGH: [With a short laugh] What a pity!

[There is another pause. Osborne glances at his watch as it lies on the table]

OSBORNE: Three minutes to. I think we'd better go.

RALEIGH: Righto.

[Their eyes meet as Osborne turns from the table]

OSBORNE: I'm glad it's you and I—together, Raleigh.

RALEIGH: [Eagerly] Are you—really?

OSBORNE: Yes.

RALEIGH: So am I—awfully.

OSBORNE: We must put up a good show.

RALEIGH: Yes. Rather!

[There is a short pause]

OSBORNE: Let's go along, shall we?

RALEIGH: Righto.

[They go towards the steps. Mason comes to the entrance of his dug-out as they pass]

MASON: Good luck, sir.

OSBORNE: Thanks, Mason.

MASON: It's a lovely chicken for dinner, sir.

OSBORNE: [Slowly going up the steps] Splendid!

MASON: Good luck, Mr. Raleigh.

RALEIGH: Thanks.

[Osborne and Raleigh go up together into the pale evening sun. Mason tidies the papers on the table, picks up the two coffee mugs, and goes away. There is silence in the trenches above the deserted dug-out. Then, suddenly, there comes the dull "crush" of bursting smoke bombs, followed in a second by the vicious *rattle of machine-guns. The red and green glow of German alarm rockets comes faintly through the dug-out door. Then comes the thin whistle and crash of falling shells; first one by itself, then two, almost together. Quicker and quicker they come, till the noise mingles together in confused turmoil. Yet the noise is deadened by the earth walls of the tiny dug-out, and comes quite softly till the whine of one shell rises above the others to a shriek and a crash. A dark funnel of earth leaps up beyond the parapet of the trench outside; earth falls and rattles down the steps, and a black cloud of smoke rises slowly out of sight. Gradually the noise dies away—there is a longer pause between the crash of each bursting shell. The machine-guns stop—rattle again and stop—rattle for the last time—and stop. Voices are calling in the trench outside; Stanhope's voice is heard]*

STANHOPE: All right, sir. Come down quickly!

COLONEL: How many?

STANHOPE: Only one. *[Another shell whines and shrieks and crashes near by. There is silence for a moment, then Stanhope speaks again]* Hurt, sir?

COLONEL: No. It's all right.

[Stanhope, pale and haggard, comes down the steps, followed by the Colonel]

STANHOPE: *[Calling up the steps]* Bring him down, sergeant-major.

S.-M.: *[Above]* Coming, sir.

STANHOPE: *[To the Colonel]* You won't want me, will you?

COLONEL: Well—er—

STANHOPE: I want to go and see those men.

COLONEL: Oh, all right.

[Stanhope goes to the door, making way for the Sergeant-Major to come down, followed by a bare-headed German Boy, in field gray, sobbing bitterly. Behind come two Soldiers with fixed bayonets. Stanhope goes up the steps. The Sergeant-Major takes the German Boy by the arm and draws him into the center of the dug-out to face the Colonel, who has seated himself at the table. The two Soldiers stand behind]

S.-M.: *[Soothingly to the German Boy]* All right, sonny, we ain't going to 'urt you.

[Suddenly the Boy falls on his knees and sobs out some words in broken English]

GERMAN: Mercy—mister—mercy!

S.-M.: Come on, lad, get up.

[With a huge fist he takes the Boy by the collar and draws him to his feet. The Boy sobs hysterically. The Colonel clears his throat and begins in somewhat poor German]

COLONEL: *Was ist sein Regiment?*

GERMAN: *Würtembergisches.*

COLONEL: *Was ist der Nummer von sein Regiment?*

GERMAN: *Zwanzig.*

COLONEL: *[Making a note]* Twentieth Würtembergers. *[He looks up again]* *Wann kommen Sie hier?*

GERMAN: *Gestern abend.*

COLONEL: *[Making a note and looking up again]* *Wo kommen Sie hier?*

GERMAN: *[After a moment's thought]* *Mein Gerburtsort?*

COLONEL: *[Forgetting himself for a moment]* What's that?

GERMAN: *[In halting English]* You—wish—to know—where I was—born?

COLONEL: No! What town did you come up to the line from?

GERMAN: *[After a little hesitation]* I—do not tell you.

COLONEL: Oh, well, that's all right. *[To the Sergeant-Major]* Search him.

[The Sergeant-Major's big fists grope over the Boy's pockets. He produces a small book]

S.-M.: *[Giving it to the Colonel]* Looks like 'is pay-book, sir.

COLONEL: *[Looking eagerly into the book]* Good.

[The Sergeant-Major has found a pocket-book; the German Boy clutches at it impulsively]

S.-M.: 'Ere, stop that!

GERMAN: *Lass mich!* *[He pauses]* Let—me—please keep—that.

S.-M.: *[Very embarrassed]* You let go.

[He wrenches the case away and gives it to the Colonel]

COLONEL: *[Glancing at the papers in the case]* Look like letters. May be useful. Is that all, sergeant-major?

S.-M.: *[Looking at a few articles in his hands]* 'Ere's a few oddments, sir—bit o' string, sir; little box o' fruit drops; pocket-knife; bit o' cedar pencil—and a stick o' chocolate, sir.

COLONEL: Let him have those back, except the pocket-knife.

S.-M.: Very good, sir. *[He turns to the German Boy with a smile]* 'Ere you are, sonny.

[The German Boy takes back the oddments]

COLONEL: All right, sergeant-major. Send him straight back to my headquarters. I'll question him again there.

S.-M.: Very good, sir. *[He turns to the German]* Come on, sonny, up you go.

[He points up the steps]

[The German Boy, calm now, bows stiffly to the Colonel, and goes away, followed by the two Soldiers and the Sergeant-Major. The Colonel is deeply absorbed in the German's pay-book. He mutters "Splendid!" to himself, then looks at his watch and rises quickly. Stanhope comes slowly down the steps]

COLONEL: *[Excitedly]* Splendid, Stanhope! We've got all we wanted—20th Würtembergers! His regiment came into the line last night. I must go right away and phone the brigadier. He'll be very pleased about it. It's a feather in our cap, Stanhope.

[Stanhope *has given one look of astonishment at the* Colonel *and strolled past him. He turns at the table and speaks in a dead voice*]

STANHOPE: How awfully nice—if the brigadier's pleased.

[*The* Colonel *stares at* Stanhope *and suddenly collects himself*]

COLONEL: Oh—er—what about the raiding-party—are they all safely back?

STANHOPE: Did you expect them to be all safely back, sir?

COLONEL: Oh—er—what—er——

STANHOPE: Four men and Raleigh came safely back, sir.

COLONEL: Oh, I say, I'm sorry! That's—er—six men and—er—Osborne?

STANHOPE: Yes, sir.

COLONEL: I'm very sorry. Poor Osborne!

STANHOPE: Still it'll be awfully nice if the brigadier's pleased.

COLONEL: Don't be silly, Stanhope. Do you know —er—what happened to Osborne?

STANHOPE: A hand grenade—while he was waiting for Raleigh.

COLONEL: I'm very sorry. And the six men?

STANHOPE: Machine-gun bullets, I suppose.

COLONEL: Yes. I was afraid—er— [*His words trail away; he fidgets uneasily as* Stanhope *looks at him with a pale, expressionless face.* Raleigh *comes slowly down the steps, walking as though he were asleep; his hands are bleeding. The* Colonel *turns to the boy with enthusiasm*] Very well done, Raleigh. Well done, my boy. I'll get you a Military Cross for this! Splendid! [Raleigh *looks at the* Colonel *and tries to speak. He raises his hand to his forehead and sways. The* Colonel *takes him by the arm*] Sit down here, my boy. [Raleigh *sits on the edge of Osborne's bed*] Have a good rest. Well, I must be off. [*He moves towards the steps, and turns once more to* Raleigh *as he leaves*] Very well done.

[*With a quick glance at* Stanhope, *the* Colonel *goes away. There is silence now in the trenches outside; the last shell has whistled over and crashed. Dusk is beginning to fall over the German lines. The glow of Very lights begins to rise and fade against the evening sky.* Stanhope *is staring dumbly at the table—at Osborne's watch and ring. Presently he turns his haggard face towards* Raleigh, *who sits with lowered head, looking at the palms of his hands.* Stanhope *moves slowly across towards the doorway, and pauses to look down at* Raleigh. Raleigh *looks up into* Stanhope's *face, and their eyes meet. When* Stanhope *speaks, his voice is still expressionless and dead*]

STANHOPE: Must you sit on Osborne's bed?

[*He turns and goes slowly up the steps.* Raleigh *rises unsteadily, murmurs "sorry"—and stands with lowered head. Heavy guns are booming miles away*]

THE CURTAIN FALLS

SCENE II.

Late evening on the same day. The dug-out is lit quite festively by an unusual number of candles. Two champagne bottles stand prominently on the table. Dinner is over.

Stanhope, *with a cigar between his teeth, lounges across the table, one elbow among the plates and mugs. His hair is ruffled; there is a bright red flush on his cheeks. He has just made a remark which has sent* Hibbert *and* Trotter *into uproarious laughter; he listens with a smile.* Trotter *is sitting on the box to the right of the table, leaning back against the wall. A cigar is embedded in his podgy fingers; his face is a shiny scarlet, with deep red patches below the ears. The three bottom buttons of his tunic are undone, and now and then his hands steal gently over his distended stomach.* Hibbert *sits on the bed to the left, his thin white fingers nervously twitching the ash from his cigar. His pale face is shiny with sweat from the heat of the candles; his laugh is high-pitched and excited.* Trotter *speaks in a husky voice as the laughter dies away.*

TROTTER: And what did she say to that?

STANHOPE: She said, "Not in these trousers"—in French.

[Trotter *and* Hibbert *burst into laughter again*]

TROTTER: [*Coughing and wheezing*] Oh—dear-o-dear!

STANHOPE: I simply drew myself up and said, "Very well, mam'sel, have it your own way."

TROTTER: And she did?

STANHOPE: No. She didn't.

[*Again the others laugh.* Trotter *wipes a tear from his eye*]

TROTTER: Oh, skipper, you *are* a scream—and no mistake!

HIBBERT: I never forget picking up a couple of tarts one night and taking 'em out to dinner.

TROTTER: [*Winking at* Stanhope] 'E's orf again.

HIBBERT: We drank enough bubbly to sink a battleship——

STANHOPE: To *float* a battleship.

HIBBERT: Well—to float a battleship. Then I took 'em for a joy-ride out to Maidenhead—did sixty all the way. We danced a bit at Skindles, and drank a lot of port and muck. Then damned if I didn't lose the way coming back—got landed miles from any-where. And those tarts began cursing me like hell— said I'd done it on purpose. I said if they didn't damn well shut up I'd chuck 'em both out in the road and leave 'em.

STANHOPE: [*Ironically*] Hurrah! That's the idea! Treat 'em rough!

HIBBERT: [*Giggling*] That shut 'em up all right! Then I started doing about sixty down all sorts of roads—I went round a corner on two wheels with those girls' hair on end—didn't have any more trouble from *them*!

[*He chuckles at the memory, and takes an unsteady gulp of champagne*]

STANHOPE: You're the sort of fellow who makes girls hard to please.

TROTTER: [*Heavily*] Well, I never 'ad no motorcar, my old lady and me used to walk; legs is good enough for me.

STANHOPE: You satisfied with legs?

TROTTER: *I* am—yes!

STANHOPE: Much cheaper.

HIBBERT: [*Laughing delightedly*] That's damn good!

STANHOPE: [*Raising his mug*] Well, here's to a toast to legs—God bless 'em!

HIBBERT: [*Raising his mug*] Good old legs!

TROTTER: [*Raising his mug*] Shank's mare.

STANHOPE: Shank's *what?*

TROTTER: Shank's mare, they call 'em.

STANHOPE: Call what?

TROTTER: Why—legs.

HIBBERT: [*Almost screaming with delight*] Oh, Trotter! you're a dream!

TROTTER: [*Turning a baleful eye on* Hibbert] You've 'ad too much champagne, you 'ave.

[Hibbert *takes a leather case from his pocket and produces some picture post-cards*]

HIBBERT: I say, I've never shown you these, have I?

[*He hands them one by one to* Stanhope, *smiling up into* Stanhope's *face for approval*]

STANHOPE: Where did you get these from?

HIBBERT: In Béthune. [*He hands up a card*] She's all right, isn't she?

STANHOPE: Too fat.

HIBBERT: [*Looking over* Stanhope's *shoulder*] Oh, I don't know.

STANHOPE: Much too fat. [*He hands the card to* Trotter] What do you think, Trotter?

[Trotter *takes a pair of pince-nez from his pocket, balances them on his fat nose, and looks at the picture*]

HIBBERT: All right, isn't she?

TROTTER: Well, I don't know. If you ask me I'd rather 'ave a decent picture of Margate Pier.

HIBBERT: [*Impatiently*] Oh, you don't understand art. [*He hands another card to* Stanhope] There's a nice pair of legs for you.

STANHOPE: Too thin—aren't they, Trotter?

[*He hands* Trotter *the card*]

TROTTER: [*After some thought*] Scraggy, I call 'em.

HIBBERT: [*Handing* Stanhope *another card*] That's the one I like best.

STANHOPE: Not bad.

HIBBERT: Glorious bedroom eyes.

STANHOPE: She's all right.

HIBBERT: Ever seen that show *Zip* at the Hippodrome? Couple of damn fine girls in that—twins. Did you see 'em, skipper?

STANHOPE: [*Wearily*] I don't know—seen stacks of shows—can't remember them all. [*He brightens up*]

Now then, swallow up that bubbly! Hi! Mason!

MASON: Yessir!

[Mason *appears*]

STANHOPE: Bring some whisky.

MASON: Yessir.

[*He disappears*]

TROTTER: What? Whisky on top of champagne?

STANHOPE: Why not? It's all right.

TROTTER: Well, I don't know; doesn't sound right to me. I feel as if somebody's blown me up with a bicycle pump.

STANHOPE: You look it, too.

TROTTER: [*Blowing a stream of cigar smoke up to the dark ceiling*] Any'ow, it was a jolly bit o' chicken —and I'd go a mile any day for a chunk o' that jam pudding.

[Mason *brings a bottle of whisky*]

STANHOPE: Your pudding's made Mr. Trotter feel all blown out, Mason.

MASON: I'm sorry, sir; it wasn't meant, sir.

TROTTER: It was all right, Mason, take it from me I know a decent bit o' pudden when I see it.

MASON: It was only boiled ration biscuits and jam, sir. [*He turns to* Stanhope] I thought I better tell you, sir—this is the last bottle.

STANHOPE: The last bottle! Why, damn it, we bought six!

MASON: I know, sir. But five's gone.

STANHOPE: Where the devil's it gone to?

MASON: Well, sir, you remember there was one on the first night—and then one——

STANHOPE: Oh, for Lord's sake don't go through them one by one; this'll last till sunrise. [*He turns to* Trotter *and* Hibbert] Sunrise to-morrow, my lads!

TROTTER: Oh, forget that.

STANHOPE: You bet we will! Now then! Who's for a spot of whisky?

TROTTER: I reckon I'm about full up. I'd like a nice cup o' tea, Mason.

MASON: Very good, sir. [*He goes out*]

STANHOPE: Tea!

TROTTER: Yes. That's what I want. Decent cup o' tea. Still, I'll just have about a spoonful o' whisky— got a touch of pulpitations.

STANHOPE: Here you are—say when!

TROTTER: Wo! That's enough!

STANHOPE: You'll have a decent spot, won't you, Hibbert?

HIBBERT: Yes. I'm game!

TROTTER: [*Stifling a hiccup*] Just a cup o' tea— then I'll go and relieve young Raleigh. Pity 'e didn't come down to supper.

STANHOPE: I told him to. I told him to come down for an hour and let the sergeant-major take over.

TROTTER: I wonder why 'e didn't come.

HIBBERT: That lad's too keen on his "duty." He told me he liked being up there with the men better than down here with us.

STANHOPE: [*Quietly*] He *said* that?

HIBBERT: Yes, I told him about the chicken and champagne and cigars and he stared at me and said,

"You're not having that, are you?"—just as if he thought we were going to chuck it away!

TROTTER: I reckon that raid shook 'im up more'n we thought. I like that youngster. 'E's got pluck. Strong lad, too—the way he came back through the smoke after that raid, carrying that Boche under 'is arm like a baby.

HIBBERT: Did you see him afterwards, though? He came into that dugout and never said a word—didn't seem to know where he was.

TROTTER: Well, 'e's only a lad.

STANHOPE: [To Hibbert] He actually told you he preferred being up with the men better than down here?

HIBBERT: That's what he said.

TROTTER: Well, I 'ope 'e gets the M.C., that's all; 'e's just the kid I'd like if I ever 'ave a kid—strong and plucky.

STANHOPE: Oh, for God's sake forget that bloody raid! Think I want to talk about it?

TROTTER: [Surprised] No—but, after all——

STANHOPE: Well—shut up!

TROTTER: [Uneasily] All right—all right.

STANHOPE: We were having a jolly decent evening till you started blabbing about the war.

TROTTER: I didn't start it.

STANHOPE: You did.

TROTTER: You began it about——

STANHOPE: Well, for God's sake stop it, then!

TROTTER: All right—all right.

HIBBERT: Did I ever tell you the story about the girl I met in Soho?

STANHOPE: I don't know—I expect you did.

HIBBERT: [Undismayed] It'll amuse you. I'd been to a dance, and I was coming home quite late——

STANHOPE: Yes, and it's late now. You go on duty at eleven. You better go and get some sleep.

HIBBERT: It's all right. I'm as fresh as a daisy.

STANHOPE: You may be. But go to bed.

HIBBERT: What?

STANHOPE: [Louder] I said, "Go to bed!"

HIBBERT: I say, that's a nice end to a jolly evening!

STANHOPE: I'm sorry. I'm tired.

HIBBERT: [Perkily] Well, you better go to bed!

[There is silence. Stanhope looks at Hibbert, who sniggers]

STANHOPE: What was that you said?

HIBBERT: I was only joking.

STANHOPE: I asked what you said.

HIBBERT: I said, "You better go to bed."

[Stanhope's flushed face is looking full into Hibbert's. Hibbert gives the ghost of a snigger]

STANHOPE: Clear out of here!

HIBBERT: [Rising unsteadily] What—d'you mean?

STANHOPE: Get out of here, for God's sake!

HIBBERT: [Blustering] I say—look here——

STANHOPE: Get out of my sight! [With a frightened glance at Stanhope, Hibbert sneaks quietly away into his dug-out. There is silence, and the guns can be heard—deep and ominous] Little worm gets on my nerves.

TROTTER: Poor little bloke. Never seen 'im so cheerful before out 'ere.

STANHOPE: Doesn't he nearly drive you mad?

TROTTER: I reckon 'e only wanted to keep cheerful.

STANHOPE: Doesn't his repulsive little mind make you sick? [Mason brings Trotter's mug of tea and goes away] I envy you, Trotter. Nothing upsets you, does it? You're always the same.

TROTTER: Always the same, am I? [He sighs] Little you know——

STANHOPE: You never get sick to death of everything, or so happy you want to sing.

TROTTER: I don't know—I whistle sometimes.

STANHOPE: But you always feel the same.

TROTTER: I feel all blown out now. [There is a pause. Trotter sips his tea and Stanhope takes a whisky] 'Ere's 'Ibbert's post-cards. Funny a bloke carrying pictures like this about. Satisfies 'is lust, I s'pose—poor little feller. [He rises] Well, I'll go and relieve young Raleigh. Pity 'e didn't come down to supper.

[He tries to button his tunic, without success. He buckles his webbing belt over his unbuttoned tunic, puts on his helmet, and slings his respirator over his shoulder] Well, cheero!

STANHOPE: You realize you're my second-in-command now, don't you?

TROTTER: Well, you 'adn't said nothing about it, but——

STANHOPE: Well, you are.

TROTTER: Righto, skipper. [He pauses] Thanks. [He goes towards the door] I won't let you down.

STANHOPE: After your duty, have a decent sleep. We must be ready at half-past five.

TROTTER: Righto, skipper. Well, I'll be going up. Give me a chance to cool off up there. It's as 'ot as 'ell in 'ere, with all them damn candles burning.

STANHOPE: I suppose it is. My head's nearly splitting.

[He blows out three of the candles, leaving the dim light of one]

TROTTER: [Half up the steps] There's a bit of a mist rising.

STANHOPE: [Dully] Is there? [Trotter disappears into the night. Stanhope broods over the table] Mason!

MASON: [Outside] Yessir!

STANHOPE: You can bring Mr. Raleigh's dinner.

MASON: Very good, sir.

[Mason brings a plate of steaming food, gathering up and taking away some of the used crockery. Presently Raleigh comes slowly down the steps. He pauses at the bottom, takes off his helmet and hesitates. Stanhope is sitting at the table puffing at the remains of his cigar. There is silence except for the rumble of the guns]

STANHOPE: I thought I told you to come down to dinner at eight o'clock?

RALEIGH: Oh, I'm sorry. I didn't think you—er——

STANHOPE: Well? You didn't think I—er—what?

RALEIGH: I didn't think you'd—you'd mind—if I didn't.

STANHOPE: I see. And why do you think I asked you—if I didn't mind?

RALEIGH: I'm sorry.

STANHOPE: Well, we've kept your dinner. It's ready for you here.

RALEIGH: Oh, it's awfully good of you to have kept it for me, but I—I had something to eat up there.

STANHOPE: You—had something to eat up there? What do you mean, exactly?

RALEIGH: They brought the tea around while I was on duty. I had a cup, and some bread and cheese.

STANHOPE: Are you telling me—you've been feeding with the men?

RALEIGH: Well, Sergeant Baker suggested——

STANHOPE: So you take your orders from Sergeant Baker, do you?

RALEIGH: No, but——

STANHOPE: You eat the men's rations when there's barely enough for each man?

RALEIGH: They asked me to share.

STANHOPE: Now, look here. I know you're new to this, but I thought you'd have the common sense to leave the men alone to their meals. Do you think they want an officer prowling round eating their rations, and sucking up to them like that? My officers are here to be respected—not laughed at.

RALEIGH: Why did they ask me—if they didn't mean it?

STANHOPE: Don't you realize they were making a fool of you?

RALEIGH: Why should they?

STANHOPE: So you know more about my men than I do?

[There is silence, Raleigh is facing Stanhope squarely]

RALEIGH: I'm sorry then—if I was wrong.

STANHOPE: Sit down.

RALEIGH: It's all right, thanks.

STANHOPE: [Suddenly shouting] Sit down! [Raleigh sits on the box to the right of the table. Stanhope speaks quietly again] I understand you prefer being up there with the men than being down here with us?

RALEIGH: I don't see what you mean.

STANHOPE: What did you tell Hibbert?

RALEIGH: Hibbert? I—I didn't say——

STANHOPE: Don't lie.

RALEIGH: [Rising] I'm not lying! Why should I—lie?

STANHOPE: Then why didn't you come down to supper when I told you to?

RALEIGH: I—I wasn't hungry. I had rather a headache. It's cooler up there.

STANHOPE: You insulted Trotter and Hibbert by not coming. You realize that, I suppose?

RALEIGH: I didn't mean to do anything like that.

STANHOPE: Well, you did. You know now—don't you? [Raleigh makes no reply. He is trying to understand why Stanhope's temper has risen to a trembling fury. Stanhope can scarcely control his voice. Loudly] I say—you know now, don't you?

RALEIGH: Yes. I'm sorry.

STANHOPE: My officers work together. I'll have no damn prigs.

RALEIGH: I'll speak to Trotter and Hibbert. I didn't realize——

[Stanhope raises his cigar. His hand trembles so violently that he can scarcely take the cigar between his teeth. Raleigh looks at Stanhope, fascinated and horrified]

STANHOPE: What are you looking at?

RALEIGH: [Lowering his head] Nothing.

STANHOPE: Anything—funny about me?

RALEIGH: No. [After a moment's silence Raleigh speaks in a low, halting voice] I'm awfully sorry, Dennis, if—if I annoyed you by coming to your company.

STANHOPE: What on earth are you talking about? What do you mean?

RALEIGH: You resent my being here.

STANHOPE: Resent you being here?

RALEIGH: Ever since I came——

STANHOPE: I don't know what you mean. I resent you being a damn fool, that's all. [There is a pause] Better eat your dinner before it's cold.

RALEIGH: I'm not hungry, thanks.

STANHOPE: Oh, for God's sake, sit down and eat it like a man!

RALEIGH: I can't eat it, thanks.

STANHOPE: [Shouting] Are you going to eat your dinner?

RALEIGH: Oh! Good God! Don't you understand? How can I sit down and eat that—when—[His voice is nearly breaking]—when Osborne's—lying—out there——

[Stanhope rises slowly. His eyes are wide and staring; he is fighting for breath, and his words come brokenly]

STANHOPE: My God! You bloody little swine! You think I don't care—you think you're the only soul that cares!

RALEIGH: And yet you can sit there and drink champagne—and smoke cigars—

STANHOPE: The one man I could trust—my best friend—the one man I could talk to as man to man —who understood everything—and you think I don't care——

RALEIGH: But how can you when——?

STANHOPE: To forget, you little fool—to forget! D'you understand? To forget! You think there's no limit to what a man can bear?

[He turns quickly from Raleigh and goes to the dark corner by Osborne's bed. He stands with his face towards the wall, his shoulders heaving as he fights for breath]

RALEIGH: I'm awfully sorry, Dennis. I—I didn't understand. [Stanhope *makes no reply*] You don't know how—I—

STANHOPE: Go away, please—leave me alone.

RALEIGH: Can't I——

[Stanhope *turns wildly upon* Raleigh]

STANHOPE: Oh, get out! For God's sake, get out! [Raleigh *goes away into his dug-out, and* Stanhope *is alone. The Very lights rise and fall outside, softly breaking the darkness with their glow—sometimes steel-blue, sometimes gray. Through the night there comes the impatient grumble of gun fire that never dies away*]

THE CURTAIN FALLS

SCENE III.

Towards dawn. The candles are no longer burning. The intense darkness of the dug-out is softened by the glow of the Very lights in the sky beyond the doorway. There is no sound except the distant mutter of the guns.

A Man comes from the servants' dug-out; for a moment his head and shoulders stand out black against the glowing sky, then he passes on into the darkness by the table. There comes the rasp of a striking match—a tiny flame—and a candle gleams. Mason blinks in the light and turns to Stanhope's bed. Stanhope lies huddled with his blanket drawn tightly round him.

MASON: [*Softly*] Sir—— [Stanhope *does not move;* Mason *shakes him gently by the knee. A little louder*] Sir——

STANHOPE: Yes? [*There is a pause*] That you, Mason?

MASON: 'Arf-past five, sir.

STANHOPE: Oh, right. [*He raises himself on his elbow*] I was only half-asleep. I keep on waking up. It's so frightfully cold in here.

MASON: It's a cold dug-out, this one, sir. I've made some 'ot tea.

STANHOPE: Good. You might bring me some.

MASON: Right you are, sir.

STANHOPE: And take some to the officers in there —and wake them up.

MASON: Very good, sir.

[Mason *goes to his dug-out.* Stanhope *rises stiffly from his bed, shudders from the cold, and slowly begins putting his equipment on.* Trotter *wanders in from his dug-out vigorously lathering his face. He is dressed, except for his collar*]

TROTTER: Wash and brush-up, tuppence!

STANHOPE: [*Looking up, surprised*] Hullo! I thought you were asleep.

TROTTER: I 'ad a decent sleep when I came off dooty. What's the time?

STANHOPE: Half-past five. It'll be getting light soon. You better buck up.

TROTTER: All right. I shan't be long. Sounds quiet enough out there.

STANHOPE: Yes.

[Mason *brings four mugs of tea*]

TROTTER: Ah! that's what I want. A decent cup of tea.

MASON: [*Putting a mug on the table for* Stanhope] Nice and 'ot, sir. I've cut a packet of sambridge for each gentleman, sir.

STANHOPE: Good.

[Mason *takes the other mugs of tea into the right-hand dug-out.* Trotter *follows, lathering with gusto*]

STANHOPE: You might give Hibbert and Raleigh a call.

TROTTER: I woke 'em up, skipper. They're getting their things on.

[Mason *returns*]

STANHOPE: When you've cleared up your kitchen, you must dress and join your platoon in the line.

MASON: Very good, sir.

STANHOPE: If things are going well at eleven o'clock, come down here and do your best to get some lunch for us. We shall come down in turn as we can.

MASON: Very good, sir.

[Stanhope *sits at the table and begins to write a short report. The first sign of dawn is beginning to gleam in the dark sky.* Stanhope *calls "Runner!" as he writes. A Soldier comes from the servants' dug-out*]

STANHOPE: [*Folding the note*] Take this to Battalion Headquarters. There's no reply.

SOLDIER: Yessir.

[*The* Soldier *salutes and goes up the steps. A plaintive noise comes from the other dug-out.* Trotter *is singing "There's a long, long trail a-winding."* Stanhope *listens for a moment, then rises, takes a few small coins from his pocket, and throws them into* Trotter's *dug-out. The singing stops abruptly. After a moment* Trotter's *voice comes*]

TROTTER: Thank you kindly, gov'nor!

[*The* Sergeant-Major *comes down the steps*]

STANHOPE: Morning, sergeant-major.

S.-M.: Morning, sir. Wiring parties are just in, sir. Made a decent job of it—right down to the support line.

STANHOPE: Good. Everything quiet?

S.-M.: It's all right opposite 'ere, sir, but the guns are goin' 'ard down south. 'Eavy bombardment. Not sure if it ain't spreading up this way, sir.

STANHOPE: Very likely it is. The officers are coming up in a minute. They'll stand by with their platoons. I must stay here awhile in case of messages. I shall come up directly things begin to happen.

S.-M.: Very good, sir.

STANHOPE: Are the men having their tea?

S.-M.: Yessir.

STANHOPE: Let 'em have a decent drop of rum.

S.-M.: About 'arf again, sir?

STANHOPE: Yes.

S.-M.: If the attack don't come, sir, 'ow long are we to stand-to?

STANHOPE: We must expect the attack any time up till mid-day. After then I don't think it'll come till to-morrow.

S.-M.: Very good, sir.

STANHOPE: We must naturally make our plans to meet things as they happen.

S.-M.: Quite, sir.

STANHOPE: All right, sergeant-major. I'll see you up there soon.

S.-M.: Yes, sir.

[*He salutes and goes away.* Mason *brings in four little packets of sandwiches, and puts one packet on the table for* Stanhope]

MASON: Your sambridges, sir. 'Arf bully beef and 'arf sardine. Sardine on top, sir.

STANHOPE: How delicious. No *pâté de foie gras?*

MASON: No what, sir?

STANHOPE: No *pâté de fois gras?*

MASON: No, sir. The milkman 'asn't been yet.

[Mason *takes the other parcels to the left-hand dug-out.* Stanhope *pours a little whisky into his tea and the remainder of the contents of the bottle into his flask.* Mason *returns*]

STANHOPE: Get dressed as soon as you can.

MASON: Yessir.

[Mason *goes out.* Trotter *comes in, fully dressed for the line*]

TROTTER: All ready, skipper. Want me to go up?

STANHOPE: Yes. I think so. Go right round the line and see everything's all right. I'll be up soon.

[*Suddenly there comes the faint whistle and thud of falling shells—a few seconds between each.* Stanhope *and* Trotter *listen intently, four shells fall, then silence*]

TROTTER: 'Ullo, 'ullo.

[Stanhope *strides to the doorway, goes up a few steps, and looks out into the night. He comes slowly back*]

STANHOPE: Over on Lancer's Alley—somewhere by the reserve line.

[*There comes the louder thud of three more shells*]

TROTTER: That's nearer.

STANHOPE: Better go up, Trotter. Call the others.

TROTTER: [*At the left-hand dug-out*] 'Ibbert! Raleigh! come on! [*He lights a cigarette over the candle—lingers a moment, and slowly goes up the steps*] Cheero, skipper. See you later.

STANHOPE: Send your runner down to tell me how things are going.

TROTTER: Righto.

[Trotter *disappears into the dark. A vague white line of dawn is broadening above the dark trench wall outside.* Stanhope *sits at the table and sips his tea. He takes a cigarette and lights it with a quivering hand.* Raleigh *comes from his dug-out.* Stanhope *lowers his head and writes in his note-book*]

RALEIGH: Do you want me to go up?

STANHOPE: [*Without looking up*] Yes. Trotter's gone.

RALEIGH: Right. [*He goes to the steps and turns shyly*] Cheero—Stanhope.

STANHOPE: [*Still writing with lowered head*] Cheero, Raleigh. I shall be coming up soon. [Raleigh *goes up the steps.* Stanhope *stops writing, raises his head, and listens. The shells are falling steadily now. He glances towards the left-hand dug-out and calls*] Hibbert! [*There is no reply. He slowly rises and goes to the left-hand dug-out doorway. He calls again—louder*] Hibbert!! [*He looks into the doorway and says:*] What are you doing? [Hibbert *appears. He is very pale; he moves as if half asleep*] Come along, man!

HIBBERT: You want me to go up now?

STANHOPE: Of course I do. The others have gone.

HIBBERT: Got a drop of water?

STANHOPE: What d'you want water for?

HIBBERT: I'm so frightfully thirsty. All that champagne and stuff—dried my mouth up.

[Stanhope *pours a drop of water into a mug and gives it to* Hibbert]

STANHOPE: Here you are. Didn't you have tea?

HIBBERT: Yes. It was a bit sweet, though.

[*The shelling is steadily increasing, and now, above the lighter "crush" of the smaller shells, there comes the deep, resounding "boom" of Minenwerfer.* Hibbert *sips his water very slowly, rinsing his mouth deliberately with each sip.* Stanhope *is by the doorway, looking up into the trench. He has just turned away as a sonorous drawn-out call comes floating through the dawn: "Stretcher-bear—ers!"* Stanhope *half turns, then faces* Hibbert]

STANHOPE: Come on. Buck up.

HIBBERT: There's no appalling hurry, is there?

STANHOPE: No hurry! Why d'you think the others have gone up?

HIBBERT: [*Slowly*] What? Trotter and Raleigh?

STANHOPE: [*Sharply*] Wake up, man! What the devil's the matter with you?

HIBBERT: [*Slowly putting down his mug*] Champagne dries the mouth up so. Makes the tongue feel like a bit of paper.

[*There is a slight pause*]

STANHOPE: The longer you stay here, the harder it'll be to go up.

HIBBERT: Good Lord! You don't think I'm——

STANHOPE: You're just wasting as much time as you can.

HIBBERT: Well, damn it, it's no good going up till I feel fit. Let's just have another spot of water.

[Hibbert *takes the jug and pours out a little more water. He is the picture of misery.* Stanhope *stands impatiently beside him.* Mason *appears from his dug-out, fully dressed for the line, his rifle slung over his shoulder*]

MASON: I'll go right along, sir. I've made up the fire to last a good three hours—if you don't mind me popping down about nine o'clock to 'ave a look at it.

STANHOPE: All right, Mason. Mr. Hibbert's coming up now. You can go along with him.

MASON: [To Hibbert] I'd like to come along of you if you don't mind, sir. I ain't bin up in this part of the front line. Don't want to get lorst.

STANHOPE: Mr. Hibbert'll show you the way up. [He turns to Hibbert] Keep your men against the back wall of the trench as long as the shells are dropping behind. Cheero! [Hibbert looks at Stanhope for a moment, then with a slight smile, he goes slowly up the steps and into the trench, Mason following behind. A dark figure stands out against the pale sky; comes hurrying down the steps—a Private Soldier, out of breath and excited] Yes?

SOLDIER: Message from Mr. Trotter, sir. Shells falling mostly behind support line. Minnies along front line.

STANHOPE: Who's just been hit?

SOLDIER: Corporal Ross, I think it was, sir. Minnie dropped in the trench at the corner—just as I come away.

[The Sergeant-Major comes down the steps very much out of breath]

STANHOPE: [To the Soldier] All right, thanks.

[The Soldier salutes, and goes up the steps slower than he came down]

S.-M.: Beginning to get 'ot, sir.

STANHOPE: Corporal Ross hit?

S.-M.: Yessir.

STANHOPE: Badly?

S.-M.: Pretty badly, sir.

STANHOPE: Most of the shelling's going over, isn't it?

S.-M.: Most of the shells is be'ind, sir, but there's Minnies and rifle grenades along the front line. Pretty 'ot it's getting, sir. They're attacking down south—there's rifle fire.

STANHOPE: All right, sergeant-major; thanks.

S.-M.: What I come to ask, sir—what about the wounded—getting 'em down, sir? The shelling's pretty thick over Lancer's Alley.

STANHOPE: What about Fosse Way?

S.-M.: Pretty bad there, too, sir.

STANHOPE: Don't try then. Take any one badly hit down into the big dug-out on the right. Let the stretcher-bearers do what they can there.

S.-M.: Very good, sir.

STANHOPE: Only Corporal Ross hit?

S.-M.: That's all, sir——

[Again there comes the drawn-out call—several times as it passes from man to man: "Stretcher-bear—ers!" The Sergeant-Major's eyes meet Stanhope's. He turns and goes up the steps. Stanhope is alone. Flying fragments of shell whistle and hiss and moan overhead. The sharp "crack" of the rifle grenades, the thud of the shells, and the boom of the Minenwerfer mingle together in a muffled roar. Stanhope takes his belt from the table and buckles it on, puts his revolver lanyard round his neck, and drops his flask and sandwiches into his pocket. The Sergeant-Major reappears and comes hurrying down the steps]

STANHOPE: [Turning quickly] What is it, sergeant-major?

S.-M.: Mr. Raleigh, sir——

STANHOPE: What!

S.-M.: Mr. Raleigh's been 'it, sir. Bit of shell's got 'im in the back.

STANHOPE: Badly?

S.-M.: 'Fraid it's broke 'is spine, sir; can't move 'is legs.

STANHOPE: Bring him down here.

S.-M.: Down 'ere, sir?

STANHOPE: [Shouting] Yes! Down here—quickly!

[The Sergeant-Major hurries up the steps. A shell screams and bursts very near. The Sergeant-Major shrinks back and throws his hand across his face, as though a human hand could ward off the hot flying pieces. He stumbles on again into the trench, and hurriedly away. Stanhope is by Osborne's bed, fumbling a blanket over it. He takes a trench coat off the wall and rolls it for a pillow. He goes to his own bed, takes up his blanket, and turns as the Sergeant-Major comes carefully down the steps carrying Raleigh like a child in his huge arms]

STANHOPE: [With blanket ready] Lay him down there.

S.-M.: 'E's fainted, sir. 'E was conscious when I picked 'im up.

[The Sergeant-Major lays the boy gently on the bed; he draws away his hands, looks furtively at the palms, and wipes the blood on the sides of his trousers. Stanhope covers Raleigh with his blanket, looks intently at the boy, and turns to the Sergeant-Major]

STANHOPE: Have they dressed the wound?

S.-M.: They've just put a pad on it, sir. Can't do no more.

STANHOPE: Go at once and bring two men with a stretcher.

S.-M.: We'll never get 'im down, sir, with them shells falling on Lancer's Alley.

STANHOPE: Did you hear what I said? Go and get two men with a stretcher.

S.-M.: [After a moment's hesitation] Very good, sir.

[The Sergeant-Major goes slowly away. Stanhope turns to Raleigh once more, then goes to the table, pushes his handkerchief into the water-jug, and brings it, wringing wet, to Raleigh's bed. He bathes the boy's face. Presently Raleigh gives a little moan opens his eyes, and turns his head]

RALEIGH: Hullo—Dennis——

STANHOPE: Well, Jimmy—[He smiles]—you got one quickly.

[*There is silence for a while.* Stanhope *is sitting on a box beside* Raleigh. *Presently* Raleigh *speaks again—in a wondering voice*]

RALEIGH: Why—how did I get down here?

STANHOPE: Sergeant-major brought you down.

[Raleigh *speaks again, vaguely, trying to recollect*]

RALEIGH: Something—hit me in the back—knocked me clean over—sort of—winded me—I'm all right now.

[*He tries to rise*]

STANHOPE: Steady, old boy. Just lie there quietly for a bit.

RALEIGH: I'll be better if I get up and walk about. It happened once before—I got kicked in just the same place at football; it—it soon wore off. It—it just numbs you a bit. [*There is a pause*] What's that rumbling noise?

STANHOPE: The guns are making a bit of a row.

RALEIGH: Our guns?

STANHOPE: No. Mostly theirs.

[*Again there is silence in the dug-out. A very faint rose light is beginning to glow in the dawn sky.* Raleigh *speaks again—uneasily*]

RALEIGH: I say—Dennis——

STANHOPE: Yes, old boy?

RALEIGH: It—it hasn't gone through, has it? It only just hit me?—and knocked me down?

STANHOPE: It's just gone through a bit, Jimmy.

RALEIGH: I won't have to—go on lying here?

STANHOPE: I'm going to have you taken away.

RALEIGH: Away? Where?

STANHOPE: Down to the dressing-station—then hospital—then home. [*He smiles*] You've got a Blighty one, Jimmy.

RALEIGH: But I—I can't go home just for—for a knock in the back. [*He stirs restlessly*] I'm certain I'll be better if—if I get up. [*He tries to raise himself, and gives a sudden cry*] Oh—God! It does hurt!

STANHOPE: It's bound to hurt, Jimmy.

RALEIGH: What's—on my legs? Something holding them down——

STANHOPE: It's all right, old chap; it's just the shock—numbed them.

[*Again there is a pause. When* Raleigh *speaks there is a different note in his voice*]

RALEIGH: It's awfully decent of you to bother, Dennis. I feel rotten lying here—everybody else—up there.

STANHOPE: It's not your fault, Jimmy.

RALEIGH: So—damn—silly—getting hit. [*Pause*] Is there—just a drop of water?

STANHOPE: [*Rising quickly*] Sure. I've got some here. [*He pours some water into the mug and brings it to* Raleigh. *Cheerfully*] Got some tea-leaves in it. D'you mind?

RALEIGH: No. That's all right—thanks—[Stanhope *holds the mug to* Raleigh's *lips, and the boy drinks*] I say, Dennis, don't you wait—if—if you want to be getting on.

STANHOPE: It's quite all right, Jimmy.

RALEIGH: Can you stay for a bit?

STANHOPE: Of course I can.

RALEIGH: [*Faintly*] Thanks awfully. [*There is quiet in the dug-out for a long time.* Stanhope *sits with one hand on* Raleigh's *arm, and* Raleigh *lies very still. Presently he speaks again—hardly above a whisper*] Dennis——

STANHOPE: Yes, old boy?

RALEIGH: Could we have a light? It's—it's so frightfully dark and cold.

STANHOPE: [*Rising*] Sure! I'll bring a candle and get another blanket. [Stanhope *goes to the left-hand dug-out, and* Raleigh *is alone, very still and quiet, on* Osborne's *bed. The faint rosy glow of the dawn is deepening to an angry red. The gray night is dissolving, and the stars begin to go. A tiny sound comes from where* Raleigh *is lying—something between a sob and a moan.* Stanhope *comes back with a blanket. He takes a candle from the table and carries it to* Raleigh's *bed. He puts it on the box beside* Raleigh *and speaks cheerfully*] Is that better, Jimmy? [Raleigh *makes no sign*] Jimmy——

[*Still* Raleigh *is quiet.* Stanhope *gently takes his hand. There is a long silence.* Stanhope *lowers* Raleigh's *hand to the bed, rises and takes the candle back to the table. He sits on the bench behind the table with his back to the wall, and stares listlessly across at the boy on* Osborne's *bed. The solitary candle-flame throws up the lines of his pale, drawn face, and the dark shadows under his tired eyes. The thudding of the shells rises and falls like an angry sea. A* Private Soldier *comes scrambling down the steps, his round, red face wet with perspiration, his chest heaving for breath*]

SOLDIER: Message from Mr. Trotter, sir—will you come at once? [Stanhope *gazes round at the* Soldier *—and makes no other sign*] Mr. Trotter, sir—says will you come at once!

[Stanhope *rises stiffly and takes his helmet from the table*]

STANHOPE: All right, Broughton, I'm coming.

[*The* Soldier *turns and goes away.* Stanhope *pauses for a moment by* Osborne's *bed and lightly runs his fingers over* Raleigh's *tousled hair. He goes stiffly up the steps, his tall figure black against the dawn sky. The shelling has risen to a great fury. The solitary candle burns with a steady flame, and* Raleigh *lies in the shadows. The whine of a shell rises to a shriek and bursts on the dug-out roof. The shock stabs out the candle-flame; the timber props of the door cave slowly in, sandbags fall and block the passage to the open air. There is darkness in the dug-out. Here and there the red dawn glows through the jagged holes of the broken doorway. Very faintly there come the dull rattle of machine-guns and the fevered spatter of rifle fire*]

THE PLAY ENDS

Noel Coward

(1899– ———)

"Past master of the inconsequential," as Brooks Atkinson called him, and able to "transform old hat into harlequinade," Noel Coward descended upon London in the early nineteen-twenties as the representative of the cynical postwar generation and the *enfant terrible* of the klieg lights. The word "sophistication" which was applied by a twist of meaning to the generation's outlook or lack of one was appropriated by him as the slogan under which he fought for a reputation.

In the process Coward drew upon his head the opprobrium of some who called his art "decadent," which it was, in the broad sense of reflecting the deterioration of a once stable society. He also invited a sniff from those who lifted an eyebrow at an emptiness that somehow escaped seeming fatuous and that was elegantly and extravagantly successful. George Jean Nathan put the case against him particularly well when he accused him of "blowing soap bubbles through an upturned nose." He noted that it was a feat unimpressive to anyone "who is not likely to mistake an upturned nose for an upturned mind and a studiously acquired attitude for a natural superior air." But Nathan had the sagacity to observe that the enjoyment of the trick is not necessarily confined to those who can't see through it. And whether one saw through it or not, Coward prevailed upon audiences on both sides of the Atlantic with remarkable ease. Most of his plays were good for at least one successful turn on the stage. For winding up a contrivance so that it would make what Atkinson has called "spinning entertainment," there was no one in Britain to equal Noel Coward. Had he not also tried for seriousness on the stage, he might never have been found out except by the astutest critics. And even so, it is only on the stage that his seriousness betrayed him; on the screen, to judge from such exhibits as *Brief Encounter* and *In Which We Serve,* his gravity won a deserved respect—a fact that may serve someone as the basis for an essay on the differences between the screen and the stage.

Born in Teddington, Middlesex, to a father who worked for music publishers and later sold pianos and to a mother who encouraged musical and dramatic talent, Noel Coward dispensed with formal schooling at an early age and made his debut on the stage when he was eleven. He continued to exercise his acting ability until 1918, when he was called up for military service in the First World War. But an injury contracted during his training in the Artists' Rifles O. T. C. kept him hospitalized up to the Armistice. In 1920 he saw his first play, *I'll Leave It to You,* staged in London. Written when he was only eighteen years old, it was, not surprisingly, a failure, and he had to serve an apprenticeship of three years before playwriting became his forte to the same degree that acting already was.

He tasted success first, in 1923, with a serious drama of postwar decadence, *The Vortex.* It concerned a woman who resigns herself to age only when deserted by her gigolo, and her son, who clings to her and is psychologically disqualified for marriage. Since the background was "society" and the characters were "sophisticated," Coward was able to display some sharp observation in the play.

Coward's success became fabulous. In 1925, for example, he had five plays on the boards in London, and thereafter he was never to fear again the poverty that had been his greatest dread. His facility was so extraordinary that before he was thirty-five he already had twenty-four plays, revues, and musical comedies to his credit—and discredit. He wrote with great speed and was a perfect reflector of the manners practiced by the upper classes and admired by all but the most class-conscious of their social inferiors. He gave scrupulous attention to all theatrical details. He may have made a profitable specialty of frivolity, but he was able to do so only because he was anything but frivolous about his occupation. To it he brought not only craftsmanship but facility in virtually all other branches of theatre. He had an expert knowledge of directing, musical talent as both a composer and a pianist, and an acting style so sure in its timing and movement and speech that John Gielgud, after playing Coward parts, declared that it was impossible to speak lines after Coward had spoken them without giving a poor imitation. And he had a way of interesting the cleverest actors in his roles. Tallulah Bankhead was supremely at ease in the parts he wrote, and so was Gertrude Lawrence. With the latter, indeed, he made an acting team of unusual attractiveness, their partnership having had an auspicious beginning when she was fourteen and he fifteen and both appeared for the Liverpool Repertory Company in Hauptmann's *Hannele.*

It was by virtue of wit and airy charm that Coward captivated London and New York with numerous comedies such as *Hay Fever* (1925), *Private Lives* (1930), *Design for Living* (1933), and *Blithe Spirit* (1941), as well as with musicals such as *Bittersweet* (1929) and *Conversation Piece.* His activity was ceaseless. He also wrote a series of nine one-acters, *Tonight at 8:30,* a number of short and full-length melodramas and pseudo tragedies, and patriotic chronicles such as *Cavalcade* and *This Happy Breed.* He made a number of motion pictures: *Cavalcade, This Happy Breed, In Which We Serve* (a tribute to the British navy during the Second World War), *The Astonished Heart,* and *Brief Encounter,* a noteworthy treatment of his long one-act play *Still Life.* With these multiple activities and with his superb acting style and his production activities (as a partner of John C. Wilson and the Lunts), Noel Coward made himself the wonder of the British theatre.

The three full-length comedies which most advanced Coward's reputation are *Design for Living, Private Lives,* and *Blithe Spirit. Design for Living* was a breezy variant of the *ménage à trois* type of boulevard comedy; *Private Lives* made farcical entertainment out of a double marriage; and *Blithe Spirit* enlivened the theatre with the reasoned opinion that ghosts of first wives are an embarrassing superfluity in a household.

For Coward, as for Wilde, "the Book of Life begins with a man and woman in a garden" and ends "with Revelations"—in a drawing room. *Blithe Spirit* is less strenuously entertaining than *Design for Living* and *Private Lives.* Its plot is also less ingeniously galvanized into a semblance of liveliness on every occasion than *Private Lives.* But *Blithe Spirit* is somewhat more mature in humor and is written with greater taste. It has less smartness won at any cost. And it is less indicative of a high-strung personality than the earlier comedies.

If one had to select a play among the domestic comedies that proliferated in England for half a century, comedies of manners notable for their verve rather than their ideas, one could do worse than choose *Blithe Spirit.* It is the most original of these plays, a tour de force of fancy in which Coward also displays the cutting edge of his wit. He takes human beings as they are, and society as it is, in this sophisticated lark, but rates neither person nor milieu very highly. His, as Shaw might have said, is essentially "mindless" writing, but it would be difficult to match its cleverness. Many writers who pride themselves on the higher order of their cerebration might well envy Noel Coward's technical skill and showmanship. His showmanship is, indeed, so facile that it is arrogant. In *Blithe Spirit,* however, this is patently a virtue, not a defect. Coward carries off his trickery with a jaunty air, which is more than half the fun. If there are unappeasable souls who will persist in calling the play, along with other comedies by Coward, hollow, it is difficult to understand how they could fail to concede that it has very pleasant reverberations.

In England, engaged in the life-and-death struggle with Hitler's war machine, there could be only gratitude for the kind of relief offered by *Blithe Spirit.* London took Coward's ghost story for what it really was—another variant of drawing-room comedy, with which England and its writers feel particularly at ease. It is perhaps significant that when that Englishman by adoption T. S. Eliot resolved to woo the British playgoer in 1949 with *The Cocktail Party,* he, too, found it expedient to adopt the style of drawing-room comedy. At the mid-point of the century in which nothing stood fast, the urbane art of the British stage remained steadfast. It was still capable of supporting a faith or a frolic. There might also be a skeptic here and there who would rather take a frolic from Coward than a faith from Eliot.

BIBLIOGRAPHY: Brooks Atkinson, *Broadway Scrapbook* (pp. 200–203), 1947; John Mason Brown, *Two on the Aisle* (pp. 108–120), 1938; Brown, *Seeing More Things* (pp. 200–208, 301–304), 1948; Noel Coward, *Present Indicative,* 1937, 1947; W. Somerset Maugham, Prefaces to Coward, *Bitter Sweet and Other Plays,* 1929; George Jean Nathan, *The Theatre Book of the Year 1946–1947* (pp. 142–145), 1947; Ernest Short, *Theatrical Cavalcade* (pp. 188–193), 1942.

BLITHE SPIRIT[1]

By Noel Coward

CHARACTERS

EDITH, *a maid*   DR. BRADMAN   MADAME ARCATI
RUTH   MRS. BRADMAN   ELVIRA
CHARLES

The action of the play takes place in the living room of Charles Condomine's house in Kent.

ACT ONE.
Scene 1. Before dinner on a summer evening.
Scene 2. After dinner.

ACT TWO.
Scene 1. The next morning.
Scene 2. Late the following afternoon.
Scene 3. Early evening. A few days later.

ACT THREE.
Scene 1. After dinner. A few days later.
Scene 2. Several hours later.

ACT I. SCENE I.

The scene is the living-room of the Condomines' house in Kent. The room is light, attractive and comfortably furnished. The arrangement of it may be left to the discretion of the producer. On the right there are French windows opening on to the garden. On the left there is an open fireplace. At the back, on the left, there are double doors leading into the dining-room. Up left, on an angle, there are double doors leading to the hall, the stairs, and the servants' quarters. When the curtain rises it is about eight o'clock on a summer evening. There is a wood fire burning because it is an English summer evening. Edith comes to table with tray of drinks. Ruth comes in. She is a smart-looking woman in the middle thirties. She is dressed for dinner but not elaborately.

RUTH: That's right, Edith.
EDITH: Yes'm.
RUTH: Now you'd better fetch me the ice bucket.
EDITH: Yes'm.

[1] This is the complete text for *Blithe Spirit* as Mr. Coward wrote it. The playgoer, having seen a performance and turning now to the book, may discover that in the acting version some lines, and in certain cases short scenes, are missing. The explanation is simple: those lines were eliminated on the stage because the play ran far beyond the usual time allotted to a Broadway production and because the necessity of bringing the curtain down at a reasonable and convenient hour seemed essential to the producer.

RUTH: Did you manage to get the ice out of those little tin trays?
EDITH: Yes'm—I 'ad a bit of a struggle though—but it's all right.
RUTH: And you filled the little trays up again with water?
EDITH: Yes'm.
RUTH: Very good, Edith—you're making giant strides.
EDITH: Yes'm.
RUTH: Madame Arcati, Mrs. Bradman and I will have our coffee in here after dinner and Mr. Condomine and Dr. Bradman will have theirs in the dining-room—is that quite clear?
EDITH: Yes'm.
RUTH: And when you're serving dinner, Edith, try to remember to do it calmly and methodically.
EDITH: Yes'm.
RUTH: As you are not in the Navy it is unnecessary to do everything at the double.
EDITH: Very good, 'M.
RUTH: Now go and get the ice.
EDITH: [*Straining at the leash*] Yes'm. [*She starts off at full speed*]
RUTH: *Not* at a run, Edith.
EDITH: [*Slowing down*] Yes'm. [Edith *goes*]
    [Charles *comes in. He is a nice-looking man of about forty wearing a loose-fitting velvet smoking jacket*]
CHARLES: No sign of the advancing hordes?
RUTH: Not yet.
CHARLES: [*Going to the cocktail tray*] No ice.

RUTH: It's coming. I've been trying to discourage Edith from being quite so fleet of foot. You mustn't mind if everything is a little slow motion tonight.

CHARLES: I shall welcome it. The last few days have been extremely agitating. What do you suppose induced Agnes to leave us and go and get married?

RUTH: The reason was becoming increasingly obvious, dear.

CHARLES: Yes, but in these days nobody thinks anything of that sort of thing—she could have popped into the cottage hospital, had it, and popped out again.

RUTH: Her social life would have been seriously undermined.

CHARLES: We must keep Edith in the house more. [Edith *comes in slowly with the ice bucket*]

RUTH: That's right, Edith—put it down on the table.

EDITH: Yes'm. [*She does so*]

CHARLES: I left my cigarette case on my dressing table, Edith—would you get it for me?

EDITH: Yes, sir. [*She runs out of the room*]

CHARLES: There now!

RUTH: You took her by surprise.

CHARLES: [*At the cocktail table*] A dry Martini I think, don't you?

RUTH: Yes, darling—I expect Madame Arcati will want something sweeter.

CHARLES: We'll have this one for ourselves anyhow.

RUTH: [*Taking a cigarette and sitting down*] Oh dear!

CHARLES: What's the matter?

RUTH: I have a feeling that this evening's going to be awful.

CHARLES: It'll probably be funny, but not awful.

RUTH: You must promise not to catch my eye—if I giggle—and I'm very likely to—it will ruin everything.

CHARLES: You mustn't—you must be dead serious and if possible a little intense. We can't hurt the old girl's feelings however funny she is.

RUTH: But why the Bradmans, darling? He's as skeptical as we are—he'll probably say the most dreadful things.

CHARLES: I've warned him. There must be more than three people and we couldn't have the Vicar and his wife because (a) they're dreary, and (b) they probably wouldn't have approved at all. It had to be the Bradmans. [Edith *rushes into the room with* Charles' *cigarette case. Taking it*] Thank you, Edith. Steady does it.

EDITH: [*Breathlessly*] Yes, sir. [Edith, *with an obvious effort, goes out slowly*]

CHARLES: We might make her walk about with a book on her head like they do in deportment lessons. [Charles *gives* Ruth *cocktail*] Here, try this.

RUTH: [*Sipping it*] Lovely—dry as a bone.

CHARLES: [*Raising his glass to her*] To *The Unseen!*

RUTH: I must say that's a wonderful title.

CHARLES: If this evening's a success I shall start on the first draft tomorrow.

RUTH: How extraordinary it is.

CHARLES: What?

RUTH: Oh, I don't know—being in right at the beginning of something—it gives one an odd feeling.

CHARLES: Do you remember how I got the idea for "The Light Goes Out"?

RUTH: Suddenly seeing that haggard, raddled woman in the hotel at Biarritz—of course I remember—we sat up half the night talking about it—

CHARLES: She certainly came in very handy—I wonder who she was.

RUTH: And if she ever knew, I mean ever recognized, that description of herself—poor thing . . . here's to her, anyhow . . . [*She finishes her drink*]

CHARLES: [*Takes her glass and goes to drinks table*] Have another.

RUTH: Darling—it's most awfully strong.

CHARLES: [*Pouring it*] Never mind.

RUTH: Used Elvira to be a help to you—when you were thinking something out, I mean?

CHARLES: [*Pouring out another cocktail for himself*] Every now and then—when she concentrated—but she didn't concentrate very often.

RUTH: I do wish I'd known her.

CHARLES: I wonder if you'd have liked her.

RUTH: I'm sure I should—as you talk of her she sounds enchanting—yes, I'm sure I should have liked her because you know I have never for an instant felt in the least jealous of her—that's a good sign.

CHARLES: Poor Elvira.

RUTH: Does it still hurt—when you think of her?

CHARLES: No, not really—sometimes I almost wish it did— I feel rather guilty—

RUTH: I wonder if I died before you'd grown tired of me if you'd forget me so soon?

CHARLES: What a horrible thing to say . . .

RUTH: No—I think it's interesting.

CHARLES: Well to begin with I *haven't* forgotten Elvira— I *remember* her very distinctly indeed—I remember how fascinating she was, and how maddening—[*Sits*] I remember how badly she played all games and how cross she got when she didn't win—I remember her gay charm when she had achieved her own way over something and her extreme acidity when she didn't—I remember her physical attractiveness, which was tremendous—and her spiritual integrity which was nil . . .

RUTH: You can't remember something that was nil.

CHARLES: I remember how morally untidy she was . . .

RUTH: Was she more physically attractive than I am?

CHARLES: That was a very tiresome question, dear, and fully deserves the wrong answer.

RUTH: You really are very sweet.

CHARLES: Thank you.

RUTH: And a little naïve, too.

CHARLES: Why?

RUTH: Because you imagine that I mind about Elvira being more physically attractive than I am.

CHARLES: I should have thought any woman would mind—if it were true. Or perhaps I'm old-fashioned in my views of female psychology. . . .

RUTH: Not exactly old-fashioned, darling, just a bit didactic.

CHARLES: How do you mean?

RUTH: It's didactic to attribute to one type the defects of another type—for instance, because you know perfectly well that Elvira would mind terribly if you found another woman more attractive physically than she was, it doesn't necessarily follow that I should. Elvira was a more physical person than I—I'm certain of that—it's all a question of degree.

CHARLES: [Smiling] I love you, my love.

RUTH: I know you do—but not the wildest stretch of imagination could describe it as the first fine careless rapture.

CHARLES: Would you like it to be?

RUTH: Good God, no!

CHARLES: Wasn't that a shade too vehement?

RUTH: We're neither of us adolescent, Charles, we've neither of us led exactly prim lives, have we? And we've both been married before—careless rapture at this stage would be incongruous and embarrassing.

CHARLES: I hope I haven't been in any way a disappointment, dear.

RUTH: Don't be so idiotic.

CHARLES: After all your first husband was a great deal older than you, wasn't he? I shouldn't like to think that you'd missed out all along the line.

RUTH: There are moments, Charles, when you go too far.

CHARLES: Sorry, darling.

RUTH: As far as waspish female psychology goes, there's a strong vein of it in you.

CHARLES: I've heard that said about Julius Caesar.

RUTH: Julius Caesar is neither here nor there.

CHARLES: He may be for all we know—we'll ask Madame Arcati.

RUTH: You're awfully irritating when you're determined to be witty at all costs—almost supercilious.

CHARLES: That's exactly what Elvira used to say.

RUTH: I'm not at all surprised—I never imagined —physically triumphant as she was—that she was entirely lacking in perception.

CHARLES: Darling Ruth!

RUTH: There you go again . . .

CHARLES: [Kissing her lightly] As I think I mentioned before—I love you, my love.

RUTH: Poor Elvira.

CHARLES: Didn't that light, comradely kiss mollify you at all?

RUTH: You're very annoying, you know you are—

when I said "Poor Elvira" it came from the heart— you must have bewildered her so horribly.

CHARLES: Don't I ever bewilder you at all?

RUTH: Never for an instant—I know every trick.

CHARLES: Well, all I can say is that we'd better get a divorce immediately . . .

RUTH: Put my glass down, there's a darling.

CHARLES: [Taking it] She certainly had a great talent for living—it was a pity that she died so young.

RUTH: Poor Elvira.

CHARLES: That remark is getting monotonous.

RUTH: Poor Charles, then.

CHARLES: That's better.

RUTH: And later on, poor Ruth, I expect.

CHARLES: You have no faith, Ruth. I really do think you should try to have a little faith.

RUTH: I shall strain every nerve.

CHARLES: Life without faith is an arid business.

RUTH: How beautifully you put things, dear.

CHARLES: I aim to please.

RUTH: If I died, I wonder how long it would be before you married again?

CHARLES: You won't die—you're not the dying sort.

RUTH: Neither was Elvira.

CHARLES: Oh yes, she was, now that I look back on it—she had a certain ethereal, not quite of this world quality—nobody could call you even remotely ethereal.

RUTH: Nonsense—she was of the earth earthy.

CHARLES: Well, she is now, anyhow.

RUTH: You know that's the kind of observation that shocks people.

CHARLES: It's discouraging to think how many people are shocked by honesty and how few by deceit.

RUTH: Write that down, you might forget it.

CHARLES: You underrate me.

RUTH: Anyhow it was a question of bad taste more than honesty.

CHARLES: I was devoted to Elvira. We were married for five years. She died. I missed her very much. That was seven years ago. I have now, with your help, my love, risen above the whole thing.

RUTH: Admirable. But if tragedy should darken our lives, I still say—with prophetic foreboding— poor Ruth! [Bell]

CHARLES: That's probably the Bradmans.

RUTH: It might be Madame Arcati.

CHARLES: No, she'll come on her bicycle—she always goes everywhere on her bicycle.

RUTH: It really is very spirited of the old girl.

CHARLES: Shall I go, or shall we let Edith have her fling?

RUTH: Wait a minute and see what happens. [There is a slight pause]

CHARLES: Perhaps she didn't hear.

RUTH: She's probably on one knee in a pre-sprint-ing position waiting for cook to open the kitchen door.

[*There is the sound of a door banging and* Edith *is seen scampering across the hall*]

CHARLES: Steady, Edith.

EDITH: [*Dropping to a walk*] Yes, sir.

[Mrs. Bradman *comes to* Ruth—*shakes hands.* Dr. Bradman *shakes hands with* Charles. Dr. Bradman *is a pleasant-looking middle-aged man.* Mrs. Bradman *is fair and rather faded*]

EDITH: Dr. and Mrs. Bradman.

DR. BRADMAN: We're not late, are we? I only got back from the hospital about half an hour ago.

CHARLES: Of course not—Madame Arcati isn't here yet.

MRS. BRADMAN: That must have been her we passed coming down the hill—I said I thought it was.

RUTH: Then she won't be long. I'm so glad you were able to come.

MRS. BRADMAN: We've been looking forward to it—I feel really quite excited . . .

DR. BRADMAN: [*Shaking hands with* Ruth] I guarantee that Violet will be good—I made her promise.

MRS. BRADMAN: There wasn't any need—I'm absolutely thrilled. I've only seen Madame Arcati two or three times in the village—I mean I've never seen her do anything at all peculiar, if you know what I mean.

CHARLES: Dry Martini?

DR. BRADMAN: By all means.

CHARLES: She certainly is a strange woman. It was only a chance remark of the Vicar's about seeing her up on the Knoll on Midsummer Eve dressed in sort of Indian robes that made me realize that she was psychic at all. Then I began to make inquiries—apparently she's been a professional in London for years.

MRS. BRADMAN: It is funny, isn't it? I mean anybody doing it as a profession.

DR. BRADMAN: I believe it's very lucrative.

MRS. BRADMAN: Do you believe in it, Mrs. Condomine—do you think there's anything really genuine about it at all?

RUTH: I'm afraid not—but I do think it's interesting how easily people allow themselves to be deceived . . .

MRS. BRADMAN: But she must believe in herself, mustn't she—or is the whole business a fake?

CHARLES: I suspect the worst. A real professional charlatan. That's what I am hoping for anyhow—the character I am planning for my book must be a complete impostor, that's one of the most important factors of the whole story.

DR. BRADMAN: What exactly are you hoping to get from her?

CHARLES: [*Handing* Dr. *and* Mrs. Bradman *cocktails*] Jargon, principally—a few of the tricks of the trade—it's many years since I went to a séance. I want to refresh my memory.

DR. BRADMAN: Then it's not entirely new to you?

CHARLES: Oh no—when I was a little boy an aunt of mine used to come and stay with us—she imagined that she was a medium and used to go off into the most elaborate trances after dinner. My mother was fascinated by it.

MRS. BRADMAN: Was she convinced?

CHARLES: [*Gets cocktail for himself*] Good heavens, no—she just naturally disliked my aunt and loved making a fool of her.

DR. BRADMAN: [*Laughing*] I gather that there were never any tangible results?

CHARLES: Oh sometimes she didn't do so badly. On one occasion when we were all sitting round in the pitch dark with my mother groping her way through Chaminade at the piano, my aunt suddenly gave a shrill scream and said that she saw a small black dog by my chair, then someone switched on the lights and sure enough there was.

MRS. BRADMAN: But how extraordinary.

CHARLES: It was obviously a stray that had come in from the street. But I must say I took off my hat to Auntie for producing it, or rather for utilizing—even Mother was a bit shaken.

MRS. BRADMAN: What happened to it?

CHARLES: It lived with us for years.

RUTH: I sincerely hope Madame Arcati won't produce any livestock—we have so very little room in this house.

MRS. BRADMAN: Do you think she tells fortunes? I love having my fortune told.

CHARLES: I expect so—

RUTH: I was told once on the pier at Southsea that I was surrounded by lilies and a golden seven—it worried me for days.

[*All laugh*]

CHARLES: We really must all be serious, you know, and pretend that we believe implicitly, otherwise she won't play.

RUTH: Also, she might really mind—it would be cruel to upset her.

DR. BRADMAN: I shall be as good as gold.

RUTH: Have you ever attended her, Doctor—professionally, I mean?

DR. BRADMAN: Yes—she had influenza in January—she's only been here just over a year, you know. I must say she was singularly unpsychic then—I always understood that she was an authoress.

CHARLES: Oh yes, we originally met as colleagues at one of Mrs. Wilmot's Sunday evenings in Sandgate . . .

MRS. BRADMAN: What sort of books does she write?

CHARLES: Two sorts. Rather whimsical children's stories about enchanted woods filled with highly conversational flora and fauna, and enthusiastic biographies of minor royalties. Very sentimental, reverent and extremely funny.

[*There is the sound of the front door bell*]

RUTH: Here she is.

DR. BRADMAN: She knows, doesn't she, about to-night? You're not going to spring it on her.

CHARLES: Of course—it was all arranged last week—I told her how profoundly interested I was in anything to do with the occult, and she blossomed like a rose.

RUTH: I really feel quite nervous—as though I were going to make a speech.

[Edith *is seen sedately going towards the door*]

CHARLES: You go and meet her, darling.

[Edith *has opened the door, and* Madame Arcati's *voice very high and clear, is heard*]

MADAME ARCATI: I've leant my bike up against that little bush, it will be *perfectly* all right if no one touches it.

EDITH: Madame Arcati.

RUTH: How nice of you to have come all this way.

[Ruth *and* Charles *greet her simultaneously.* Madame Arcati *enters. She is a striking woman, dressed not too extravagantly but with a decided bias towards the barbaric. She might be any age between forty-five and sixty-five.* Ruth *ushers her in*]

CHARLES: [*Advancing*] My dear Madame Arcati!

MADAME ARCATI: I'm afraid I'm rather late, but I had a sudden presentiment that I was going to have a puncture so I went back to fetch my pump, and then of course I didn't have a puncture at all.

[Madame Arcati *takes off cloak and hands it to* Ruth]

CHARLES: Perhaps you will on the way home.

MADAME ARCATI: Doctor Bradman—the man with the gentle hands!

DR. BRADMAN: I'm delighted to see you looking so well. This is my wife.

MADAME ARCATI: We are old friends— [*Shakes hands with* Mrs. Bradman] We meet coming out of shops.

CHARLES: Would you like a cocktail?

MADAME ARCATI: [*Peeling off some rather strange-looking gloves*] If it's a dry Martini, yes—if it's a concoction, no. Experience has taught me to be wary of concoctions.

CHARLES: It is a dry Martini.

MADAME ARCATI: How delicious. It was wonderful cycling through the woods this evening—I was deafened with bird-song.

RUTH: It's been lovely all day.

MADAME ARCATI: But the evening's the time—mark my words. [*She takes the cocktail* Charles *gives her. To others*] Thank you. Cheers! Cheers!

RUTH: Don't you find it very tiring bicycling everywhere?

MADAME ARCATI: On the contrary—it stimulates me—I was getting far too sedentary in London, that horrid little flat with the dim lights—they had to be dim, you know, the clients expect it.

MRS. BRADMAN: I must say I find bicycling very exhausting.

MADAME ARCATI: Steady rhythm—that's what counts. Once you get the knack of it you need never look back—on you get and away you go.

MRS. BRADMAN: But the hills, Madame Arcati—pushing up those awful hills—

MADAME ARCATI: Just knack again—down with your head, up with your heart, and you're over the top like a flash and skimming down the other side like a dragon-fly. This is the best dry Martini I've had for years.

CHARLES: Will you have another?

MADAME ARCATI: [*Holding out her glass*] Certainly. [Charles *takes her glass and refills it at drinks table*] You're a very clever man. Anybody can write books, but it takes an artist to make a dry Martini that's dry enough.

RUTH: Are you writing anything nowadays, Madame Arcati?

MADAME ARCATI: Every morning regular as clockwork, seven till one.

CHARLES: [*Gives* Madame Arcati *cocktail*] Is it a novel or a memoir?

MADAME ARCATI: It's a children's book—I have to finish it by the end of October to catch the Christmas sales. It's mostly about very small animals, the hero is a moss beetle. [Mrs. Bradman *laughs nervously*] I had to give up my memoir of Princess Palliatini because she died in April—I talked to her about it the other day and she implored me to go on with it, but I really hadn't the heart.

MRS. BRADMAN: [*Incredulously*] You *talked* to her about it the other day?

MADAME ARCATI: Yes, through my control, of course. She sounded very irritable.

MRS. BRADMAN: It's funny to think of people in the spirit world being irritable, isn't it? I mean, one can hardly imagine it, can one?

CHARLES: We have no reliable guarantee that the after life will be any less exasperating than this one, have we?

MRS. BRADMAN: [*Laughing*] Oh, Mr. Condomine, how *can* you!

RUTH: I expect it's dreadfully ignorant of me not to know—but who was Princess Palliatini?

MADAME ARCATI: She was originally a Jewess from Odessa of quite remarkable beauty. It was an accepted fact that people used to stand on the seats of railway stations to watch her whizz by.

CHARLES: She was a keen traveler?

MADAME ARCATI: In her younger days, yes—later on she married a Mr. Clarke in the Consular Service and settled down for a while . . .

RUTH: How did she become Princess Palliatini?

MADAME ARCATI: That was years later. Mr. Clarke passed over and left her penniless with two strapping girls—

RUTH: How unpleasant.

MADAME ARCATI: And so there was nothing for

it but to obey the beckoning finger of adventure and take to the road again—so off she went, bag and baggage, to Vladivostok.

CHARLES: What an extraordinary place to go!

MADAME ARCATI: She had cousins there. Some years later she met old Palliatini who was returning from a secret mission in Japan. He was immediately staggered by her beauty and very shortly afterwards married her. From then on her life became really interesting.

DR. BRADMAN: I should hardly have described it as dull before.

RUTH: What happened to the girls?

MADAME ARCATI: She neither saw them nor spoke to them for twenty-three years.

MRS. BRADMAN: How extraordinary.

MADAME ARCATI: Not at all. She was always very erratic emotionally.

[*The double doors of the dining-room open and* Edith *comes in*]

EDITH: [*Nervously*] Dinner is served, Mum.

RUTH: Thank you, Edith. Shall we?

[Edith *retires backwards into the dining-room*]

MADAME ARCATI: No red meat, I hope?

RUTH: There's meat, but I don't think it will be very red—would you rather have an egg or something?

MADAME ARCATI: [*She and* Ruth *rise*] No, thank you—it's just that I make it a rule never to eat red meat before I work—it sometimes has an odd effect . . .

CHARLES: What sort of effect?

MADAME ARCATI: Oh, nothing of the least importance—if it isn't very red it won't matter much—anyhow, we'll risk it.

RUTH: [Mrs. Bradman *rises*. Madame Arcati *goes out first with* Ruth *followed by* Mrs. Bradman, Dr. Bradman *and* Charles] Come along, then—Mrs. Bradman—Madame Arcati—you're on Charles's right . . .

[*They all move into the dining-room as the lights fade on the scene*]

SCENE II.

When the lights go up again, dinner is over, and Ruth, Mrs. Bradman *and* Madame Arcati *are sitting having their coffee.*

MADAME ARCATI: . . . on her mother's side she went right back to the Borgias which I think accounted for a lot one way and another—even as a child she was given to the most violent destructive tempers—very inbred, you know.

MRS. BRADMAN: Yes, she must have been.

MADAME ARCATI: My control was quite scared the other day when we were talking—I could hear it in her voice—after all, she's only a child . . .

RUTH: Do you always have a child as a control?

MADAME ARCATI: Yes, they're generally the best—some mediums prefer Indians, of course, but personally I've always found them unreliable.

RUTH: In what way unreliable?

MADAME ARCATI: Well, for one thing they're frightfully lazy and also, when faced with any sort of difficulty, they're rather apt to go off into their own tribal language which is naturally unintelligible—that generally spoils everything and wastes a great deal of time. No, children are undoubtedly more satisfactory, particularly when they get to know you and understand your ways. Daphne has worked for me for years.

MRS. BRADMAN: And she still goes on being a child—I mean, she doesn't show signs of growing any older?

MADAME ARCATI: [*Patiently*] Time values on the "Other Side" are utterly different from ours.

MRS. BRADMAN: Do you feel funny when you go off into a trance?

MADAME ARCATI: In what way funny?

RUTH: [*Hastily*] Mrs. Bradman doesn't mean funny in its comic implication, I think she meant odd or strange—

MADAME ARCATI: The word was an unfortunate choice.

MRS. BRADMAN: I'm sure I'm very sorry.

MADAME ARCATI: It doesn't matter in the least—please don't apologize.

RUTH: When did you first discover that you had these extraordinary powers?

MADAME ARCATI: When I was quite tiny. My mother was a medium before me, you know, and so I had every opportunity of starting on the ground floor as you might say. I had my first trance when I was four years old and my first protoplasmic manifestation when I was five and a half—what an exciting day that was, I shall never forget it—of course the manifestation itself was quite small and of very short duration, but, for a child of my tender years, it was most gratifying.

MRS. BRADMAN: Your mother must have been so pleased.

MADAME ARCATI: [*Modestly*] She was.

MRS. BRADMAN: Can you foretell the future?

MADAME ARCATI: Certainly not. I disapprove of fortune tellers most strongly.

MRS. BRADMAN: [*Disappointed*] Oh really—why?

MADAME ARCATI: Too much guesswork and fake mixed up with it—even when the gift is genuine—and it only very occasionally is—you can't count on it.

RUTH: Why not?

MADAME ARCATI: Time again—time is the reef upon which all our frail mystic ships are wrecked.

RUTH: You mean because it has never yet been proved that the past and the present and the future are not one and the same thing.

MADAME ARCATI: I long ago came to the conclusion that nothing has ever been definitely proved about anything.

RUTH: How very wise.

[Edith *comes in with a tray of drinks. This she brings over to the table by* Ruth. Ruth *moves a coffee cup and a vase to make room for it.*]

RUTH: Edith, we don't want to be disturbed for the next hour or so for any reason whatsoever—is that clear?

EDITH: Yes'm.

RUTH: And if anyone should telephone, just say we are out and take a message.

MRS BRADMAN: Unless it's an urgent call for George.

RUTH: Unless it's an urgent call for Dr. Bradman.

EDITH: Yes'm. [Edith *goes out swiftly*]

RUTH: There's not likely to be one, is there?

MRS. BRADMAN: No, I don't think so.

MADAME ARCATI: Once I am off it won't matter, but an interruption during the preliminary stages might be disastrous.

MRS. BRADMAN: I wish the men would hurry up—I'm terribly excited.

MADAME ARCATI: Please don't be—it makes everything very much more difficult.

[Charles *and* Dr. Bradman *come out of the dining-room. They are smoking cigars*]

CHARLES: [*Cheerfully*] Well, Madame Arcati—the time is drawing near.

MADAME ARCATI: Who knows? It may be receding!

CHARLES: How very true.

DR. BRADMAN: I hope you feel in the mood, Madame Arcati.

MADAME ARCATI: It isn't a question of mood—it's a question of concentration.

RUTH: You must forgive us being impatient. We can perfectly easily wait though, if you're not quite ready to start . . .

MADAME ARCATI: Nonsense, my dear, I'm absolutely ready— [*She rises*] Heigho, heigho, to work we go!

CHARLES: Is there anything you'd like us to do?

MADAME ARCATI: Do?

CHARLES: Yes—hold hands or anything?

MADAME ARCATI: All that will come later— [*She goes to the window*] First a few deep, deep breaths of fresh air— [*Over her shoulder*] You may talk if you wish, it will not disturb me in the least. [*She flings open the windows wide and inhales deeply and a trifle noisily*]

RUTH: [*With a quizzical glance at* Charles] Oh dear!

CHARLES: [*Putting his finger to his lips warningly*] An excellent dinner, darling—I congratulate you.

RUTH: The mousse wasn't quite right.

CHARLES: It looked a bit hysterical but it tasted delicious.

MADAME ARCATI: That cuckoo is very angry.

CHARLES: I beg your pardon?

MADAME ARCATI: I said that cuckoo is very angry . . . listen . . .

[*They all listen obediently*]

CHARLES: How can you tell?

MADAME ARCATI: Timbre . . . No moon—that's as well, I think—there's mist rising from the marshes— [*A thought strikes her*] There's no need for me to light my bicycle lamp, is there? I mean, nobody is likely to fall over it?

RUTH: No, we're not expecting anybody else.

MADAME ARCATI: Good-night, you foolish bird. You have a table?

CHARLES: Yes. We thought that one would do.

MADAME ARCATI: [*Closing the window, she comes over to the table and touches it lightly with her finger*] I think the one that has the drinks on it would be better.

DR. BRADMAN: [*Lifting off the tray*] Change over.

CHARLES: [*To* Ruth] You told Edith we didn't want to be disturbed?

RUTH: Yes, darling.

MADAME ARCATI: [*Walking about the room—twisting and untwisting her hands*] This is a moment I always hate.

RUTH: Are you nervous?

MADAME ARCATI: Yes. When I was a girl I always used to be sick.

DR. BRADMAN: How fortunate that you grew out of it.

RUTH: [*Hurriedly*] Children are always much more prone to be sick than grown-ups, though, aren't they? I know I could never travel in a train with any degree of safety until I was fourteen.

MADAME ARCATI: [*Still walking*] Little Tommy Tucker sings for his supper, what shall he have but brown bread and butter? I despise that because it doesn't rhyme at all—but Daphne loves it.

DR. BRADMAN: Who's Daphne?

RUTH: Daphne is Madame Arcati's control—she's a little girl.

DR. BRADMAN: Oh, I see—yes, of course.

CHARLES: How old is she?

MADAME ARCATI: Rising seven when she died.

MRS. BRADMAN: And when was that?

MADAME ARCATI: February the sixth, 1884.

MRS. BRADMAN: Poor little thing.

DR. BRADMAN: She must be a bit long in the tooth by now, I should think.

MADAME ARCATI: You should think, Dr. Bradman, but I fear you don't—at least, not profoundly enough.

MRS. BRADMAN: Do be quiet, George—you'll put Madame Arcati off.

MADAME ARCATI: [Charles *brings piano chair down to table*] Don't worry, my dear—I am quite used to skeptics—they generally turn out to be the most vulnerable and receptive in the long run.

RUTH: You'd better take that warning to heart, Dr. Bradman.

DR. BRADMAN: Please forgive me, Madame Arcati—I assure you I am most deeply interested.

MADAME ARCATI: It is of no consequence—will you all sit round the table please and place your hands downwards on it?

[Ruth, Mrs. Bradman and Dr. Bradman are seated at table]

CHARLES: What about the lights?

MADAME ARCATI: All in good time, Mr. Condomine. [The four of them sit down at each side of a small square table. Madame Arcati surveys them critically, her head on one side. She is whistling a little tune] The fingers should be touching . . . that's right . . . I presume that that is the gramophone, Mr. Condomine?

CHARLES: Yes—would you like me to start it? It's an electric one.

MADAME ARCATI: Please stay where you are—I can manage— [She goes over to the gramophone and looks over the records] Now let me see—what have we here—Brahms—oh dear me, no—Rachmaninoff—too florid—where is the dance music?

RUTH: They're the loose ones on the left.

MADAME ARCATI: I see. [She stoops down and produces a pile of dance records—these she sorts rapidly on the piano]

CHARLES: I'm afraid they're none of them very new.

MADAME ARCATI: Daphne is really more attached to Irving Berlin than anybody else—she likes a tune she can hum—ah, here's one—"Always"—

CHARLES: [Half jumping up again] "Always"!

RUTH: Do sit down, Charles—what is the matter?

CHARLES: [Subsiding] Nothing—nothing at all.

MADAME ARCATI: The light switch is by the door?

RUTH: Yes, all except the small one on the desk, and the gramophone.

MADAME ARCATI: Very well—I understand.

RUTH: Charles, do keep still.

MRS. BRADMAN: Fingers touching, George—remember what Madame Arcati said.

MADAME ARCATI: Now there are one or two things I should like to explain, so will you all listen attentively?

RUTH: Of course.

MADAME ARCATI: Presently, when the music begins, I am going to switch out the lights. I may then either walk about the room for a little or lie down flat—in due course I shall draw up this dear little stool and join you at the table—I shall place myself between you and your wife, Mr. Condomine, and rest my hands lightly upon yours—I must ask you not to address me or move or do anything in the least distracting—is that quite, quite clear?

CHARLES: Perfectly.

MADAME ARCATI: Of course I cannot guarantee that anything will happen at all—Daphne may be unavailable—she had a head cold very recently, and was rather under the weather, poor child. On the other hand, a great many things might occur—one

of you might have an emanation, for instance, or we might contact a poltergeist which would be extremely destructive and noisy . . .

RUTH: [Anxiously] In what way destructive?

MADAME ARCATI: They throw things, you know.

RUTH: No—I didn't know.

MADAME ARCATI: But we must cross that bridge when we come to it, mustn't we?

CHARLES: Certainly—by all means.

MADAME ARCATI: Fortunately an Elemental at this time of the year is most unlikely . . .

RUTH: What do Elementals do?

MADAME ARCATI: Oh, my dear, one can never tell—they're dreadfully unpredictable—usually they take the form of a very cold wind . . .

MRS. BRADMAN: I don't think I shall like that—

MADAME ARCATI: Occasionally reaching almost hurricane velocity—

RUTH: You don't think it would be a good idea to take the more breakable ornaments off the mantelpiece before we start?

MADAME ARCATI: [Indulgently] That really is not necessary, Mrs. Condomine—I assure you I have my own methods of dealing with Elementals.

RUTH: I'm so glad.

MADAME ARCATI: Now then—are you ready to empty your minds?

DR. BRADMAN: Do you mean we're to try to think of nothing?

MADAME ARCATI: Absolutely nothing, Dr. Bradman. Concentrate on a space or a nondescript colour, that's really the best way . . .

DR. BRADMAN: I'll do my damnedest.

MADAME ARCATI: Good work!—I will now start the music. [She goes to the gramophone, puts on the record of "Always," and begins to walk about the room; occasionally she moves into an abortive little dance step, and once, on passing a mirror on the mantelpiece, she surveys herself critically for a moment and adjusts her hair. Then, with sudden speed, she runs across the room and switches off the lights]

MRS. BRADMAN: Oh dear!

MADAME ARCATI: Quiet—please . . . [Presently in the gloom Madame Arcati, after wandering about a little, draws up a stool and sits at the table between Charles and Ruth. The gramophone record comes to an end. There is dead silence] Is there anyone there? . . . [A long pause] Is there anyone there? [Another long pause] One rap for yes—two raps for no—now then—is there anyone there? . . .

[After a shorter pause the table gives a little bump]

MRS. BRADMAN: [Involuntarily] Oh!

MADAME ARCATI: Shhhh! . . . Is that you, Daphne? [The table gives a louder bump] Is your cold better, dear? [The table gives two loud bumps very quickly] Oh, I'm so sorry—are you doing anything for it? [The table bumps several times] I'm afraid she's rather fretful . . . [There is a silence] Is there anyone there who wishes to speak to anyone here? [*After a pause the table gives one bump*] Ah! Now we're getting somewhere. No. Daphne, don't do that, dear, you're hurting me . . . Daphne, dear, please . . . Oh, oh, oh! . . . be good, there's a dear child . . . You say there is someone there who wishes to speak to someone here? [*One bump*] Is it I? [*Two bumps*] Is it Dr. Bradman? [*Two bumps*] Is it Mrs. Bradman? [*Two bumps*] Is it Mrs. Condomine? [*Several very loud bumps, which continue until* Madame Arcati *shouts it down*] Stop it! Behave yourself! Is it Mr. Condomine? [*There is a dead silence for a moment, and then a very loud single bump*] There's someone who wishes to speak to you, Mr. Condomine . . .

CHARLES: Tell them to leave a message.

[*The table bangs about loudly*]

MADAME ARCATI: I really must ask you not to be flippant, Mr. Condomine . . .

RUTH: Charles, how can you be so idiotic? You'll spoil everything.

CHARLES: I'm sorry—it slipped out.

MADAME ARCATI: Do you know anybody who has passed over recently?

CHARLES: Not recently, except my cousin in the Civil Service, and he wouldn't be likely to want to communicate with me—we haven't spoken for years.

MADAME ARCATI: [*Mystically*] Are you Mr. Condomine's cousin in the Civil Service? [*The table bumps violently several times*] I'm afraid we've drawn a blank . . . Can't you think of anyone else? Rack your brains . . .

RUTH: [*Helpfully*] It might be old Mrs. Plummet, you know—she died on Whit Monday . . .

CHARLES: I can't imagine why old Mrs. Plummet should wish to talk to me—we had very little in common.

RUTH: It's worth trying, anyhow.

MADAME ARCATI: Are you old Mrs. Plummet? [*The table remains still*]

RUTH: She was very deaf—perhaps you'd better shout—

MADAME ARCATI: [*Shouting*] Are you old Mrs. Plummet? [*Nothing happens*] There's nobody there at all.

MRS. BRADMAN: How disappointing—just as we were getting on so nicely.

DR. BRADMAN: Violet, be quiet.

MADAME ARCATI: [*Rising*] Well, I'm afraid there's nothing for it but for me to go into a trance. I had hoped to avoid it because it's so exhausting—however, what must be must be. Excuse me a moment while I start the gramophone again.

CHARLES: [*In a strained voice*] Not "Always"—don't play "Always"—

RUTH: Why ever not, Charles? Don't be absurd.

MADAME ARCATI: [*Gently*] I'm afraid I must—it would be unwise to change horses in midstream if you know what I mean . . . [*She restarts the gramophone*]

CHARLES: Have it your own way.

[Madame Arcati *comes slowly back toward the table and sits down again. After a few moments she begins to moan—then in the darkness a child's voice is heard reciting rather breathily "Little Tommy Tucker"*]

DR. BRADMAN: That would be Daphne—she ought to have had her adenoids out.

MRS. BRADMAN: George—please— [Madame Arcati *suddenly gives a loud scream and falls off the stool on to the floor*]

CHARLES: Good God!

RUTH: Keep still, Charles . . . [Charles *subsides. Everyone sits in silence for a moment, then the table starts bouncing about*]

MRS. BRADMAN: It's trying to get away . . . I can't hold it . . .

RUTH: Press down hard. [*The table falls over with a crash*]

RUTH: There now!

MRS. BRADMAN: Ought we to pick it up or leave it where it is?

DR. BRADMAN: How the hell do I know?

MRS. BRADMAN: There's no need to snap at me. [*A perfectly strange and very charming voice says, "Leave it where it is!"*]

CHARLES: Who said that?

RUTH: Who said what?

CHARLES: Somebody said, "Leave it where it is."

RUTH: Nonsense, dear.

CHARLES: I heard it distinctly.

RUTH: Well, nobody else did—did they?

MRS. BRADMAN: I never heard a sound.

CHARLES: It was you, Ruth—you're playing tricks.

RUTH: I'm not doing anything of the sort. I haven't uttered. [*There is another pause, and then the voice says, "Good evening, Charles"*]

CHARLES: [*Very agitated*] Ventriloquism—that's what it is—ventriloquism . . .

RUTH: [*Irritably*] What is the matter with you?

CHARLES: You must have heard *that*—one of you must have heard *that!*

RUTH: Heard *what?*

CHARLES: You mean to sit there solemnly and tell me that none of you heard anything at all?

DR. BRADMAN: I certainly didn't.

MRS. BRADMAN: Neither did I—I wish I had. I should love to hear something.

RUTH: It's you who are playing the tricks, Charles —you're acting to try to frighten us . . .

CHARLES: [*Breathlessly*] I'm not—I swear I'm not. [*The voice speaks again. It says, "It's difficult to think of what to say after seven years, but I suppose good evening is as good as anything else"*]

CHARLES: [*Intensely*] Who are you? [*The voice says, "Elvira, of course—don't be so silly"*] I can't bear this for another minute . . . [*He rises violently*] Get up, everybody—the entertainment's over . . .

RUTH: Oh, Charles, how tiresome you are—just

as we were beginning to enjoy ourselves. What on earth is the matter with you?

CHARLES: Nothing's the matter with me—I'm just sick of the whole business, that's all.

DR. BRADMAN: Did you hear anything that we didn't hear really?

CHARLES: [With a forced laugh] Of course not—I was only pretending . . .

RUTH: I knew you were . . .

MRS. BRADMAN: Oh dear . . . look at Madame Arcati!

[Madame Arcati is lying on the floor with her feet up on the stool from which she fell. She is obviously quite unconscious]

RUTH: What are we to do with her?

CHARLES: Bring her round—bring her round as soon as possible.

DR. BRADMAN: [Going over and kneeling down beside her] I think we'd better leave her alone.

RUTH: But she might stay like that for hours.

DR. BRADMAN: [After feeling her pulse and examining her eye] She's out all right.

CHARLES: [Almost hysterically] Bring her around! It's dangerous to leave her like that . . .

RUTH: Really, Charles, you are behaving most peculiarly.

CHARLES: [Going to Madame Arcati and shaking her violently] Wake up, Madame Arcati—wake up—it's time to go home!

DR. BRADMAN: Here—go easy, old man . . .

CHARLES: Get some brandy—give her some brandy—lift her into the chair—help me, Bradman . . . [Ruth pours out some brandy while Charles and Dr. Bradman lift Madame Arcati laboriously into an armchair. Leaning over her] Wake up, Madame Arcati—Little Tommy Tucker, Madame Arcati!

RUTH: Here's the brandy. [Madame Arcati gives a slight moan and a shiver]

CHARLES: [Forcing some brandy between her lips] Wake up!— [Madame Arcati gives a prolonged shiver and chokes slightly over the brandy]

MRS. BRADMAN: She's coming round.

RUTH: Be careful, Charles—you're spilling it all down her dress.

MADAME ARCATI: [Opening her eyes] Well, that's that.

RUTH: [Solicitously] Are you all right?

MADAME ARCATI: Certainly I am—never felt better in my life.

CHARLES: Would you like some more brandy?

MADAME ARCATI: So that's the funny taste in my mouth—well, really! Fancy allowing them to give me brandy! Doctor Bradman, you ought to have known better—brandy on top of trance might have been catastrophic. Take it away, please—I probably shan't sleep a wink tonight as it is.

CHARLES: I know I shan't.

RUTH: Why on earth not?

CHARLES: The whole experience has unhinged me.

MADAME ARCATI: Well, what happened—was it satisfactory?

RUTH: Nothing much happened, Madame Arcati, after you went off.

MADAME ARCATI: Something happened all right. I can feel it. [She rises and sniffs] No poltergeist, at any rate—that's a good thing. Any apparitions?

DR. BRADMAN: Not a thing.

MADAME ARCATI: No protoplasm?

RUTH: I'm not quite sure what it is, but I don't think so.

MADAME ARCATI: Very curious. I feel as though something tremendous had taken place.

RUTH: Charles pretended he heard a voice, in order to frighten us.

CHARLES: It was only a joke.

MADAME ARCATI: A very poor one, if I may say so—[She walks about a little more] Nevertheless, I am prepared to swear that there is someone else psychic in this room apart from myself.

RUTH: I don't see how there can be really, Madame Arcati.

MADAME ARCATI: I do hope I haven't gone and released something—however, we are bound to find out within a day or two—if any manifestation should occur or you hear any unexpected noises —you might let me know at once.

RUTH: Of course we will—we'll telephone immediately.

MADAME ARCATI: I think I really must be on my way now.

RUTH: Wouldn't you like anything before you go?

MADAME ARCATI: No, thank you—I have some Ovaltine all ready in a saucepan at home—it only needs hotting up.

DR. BRADMAN: Wouldn't you like to leave your bicycle here and let us drive you?

MRS. BRADMAN: I honestly do think you should, Madame Arcati, after that trance and everything— you can't be feeling quite yourself.

MADAME ARCATI: Nonsense, my dear, I'm as fit as a fiddle—always feel capital after a trance—rejuvenates me. Good night, Mrs. Condomine.

RUTH: It was awfully sweet of you to take so much trouble.

MADAME ARCATI: I'm sorry so little occurred—it's that cold of Daphne's, I expect—you know what children are when they have anything wrong with them. We must try again some other evening.

RUTH: That would be lovely.

MADAME ARCATI: Good night, Mrs. Bradman—

MRS. BRADMAN: It was thrilling, it really was— I felt the table absolutely shaking under my hands.

MADAME ARCATI: Good night, Doctor.

DR. BRADMAN: Congratulations, Madame Arcati.

MADAME ARCATI: I am fully aware of the irony in your voice, Doctor Bradman. As a matter of fact you'd be an admirable subject for telepathic hypnosis—a great chum of mine is an expert—I should like her to look you over.

DR. BRADMAN: I'm sure I should be charmed.

MADAME ARCATI: Good night, everyone—next time we must really put our backs into it!

[*With a comprehensive smile and a wave of the hand, she goes out followed by* Charles. Ruth *sinks down into a chair, laughing helplessly*]

RUTH: Oh dear! . . . Oh dear! . . .

MRS. BRADMAN: [*Beginning to laugh too*] Be careful, Mrs. Condomine—she might hear you.

RUTH: I can't help it—I really can't—I've been holding this in for ages.

MRS. BRADMAN: She certainly put you in your place, George, and serves you right.

RUTH: She's raving mad, of course—mad as a hatter.

MRS. BRADMAN: But do you really think she *believes?*

DR. BRADMAN: Of course not—the whole thing's a put-up job—I must say, though, she shoots a more original line than they generally do.

RUTH: I should think that she's probably half convinced herself by now.

DR. BRADMAN: Possibly—the trance was genuine enough—but that, of course, is easily accounted for.

RUTH: Hysteria?

DR. BRADMAN: Yes—a form of hysteria, I should imagine.

MRS. BRADMAN: I do hope Mr. Condomine got all the atmosphere he wanted for his book.

RUTH: He might have got a great deal more if he hadn't spoiled everything by showing off . . . I'm really very cross with him. [*At this moment* Elvira *comes in through the closed French windows. She is charmingly dressed in a sort of negligee. Everything about her is grey: hair, skin, dress, hands, so we must accept the fact that she is not quite of this world. She passes between* Dr. *and* Mrs. Bradman *and* Ruth *while they are talking. None of them sees her. She goes usptage and sits soundlessly on a chair. She regards them with interest, a slight smile on her face*] I suddenly felt a draught—there must be a window open.

DR. BRADMAN: [*Looking*] No—they're shut.

MRS. BRADMAN: [*Laughing*] Perhaps it was one of those what you may call 'ems that Madame Arcati was talking about.

DR. BRADMAN: Elementals.

RUTH: [*Also laughing again*] Oh no, it couldn't be—she distinctly said that it was the wrong time of the year for Elementals.

[Charles *comes in again*]

CHARLES: Well, the old girl's gone pedalling off down the drive at the hell of a speed—we had a bit of trouble lighting her lamp.

MRS. BRADMAN: Poor thing.

CHARLES: I've got a theory about her, you know—I believe she is completely sincere.

RUTH: Charles! How could she be?

CHARLES: Wouldn't it be possible, Doctor? Some form of self-hypnotism?

DR. BRADMAN: It might be . . . as I was explaining to your wife just now, there are certain types of hysterical subjects . . .

MRS. BRADMAN: George dear—it's getting terribly late, we really must go home—you have to get up so early in the morning.

DR. BRADMAN: You see? The moment I begin to talk about anything that really interests me, my wife interrupts me . . .

MRS. BRADMAN: You know I'm right, darling—it's past eleven.

DR. BRADMAN: [*To* Charles] I'll do a little reading up on the whole business—just for the fun of it.

CHARLES: You must have a drink before you go.

DR. BRADMAN: No, really, thank you—Violet's quite right, I'm afraid. I have got to get up abominably early tomorrow—I have a patient being operated on in Canterbury.

MRS. BRADMAN: [*To* Ruth] It has been a thrilling evening—I shall never forget—it was sweet of you to include us.

DR. BRADMAN: Good night, Mrs. Condomine—thank you so much.

CHARLES: You're sure about the drink!

DR. BRADMAN: Quite sure, thanks.

RUTH: We'll let you know if we find any poltergeists whirling about.

DR. BRADMAN: I should never forgive you if you didn't.

MRS. BRADMAN: Come along, darling . . .

[Charles *leads the* Bradmans *out into the hall.* Ruth, *passing close to* Elvira, *goes over to the fire and turns over a log with her foot. Then she takes a cigarette and is lighting it as* Charles *comes back into the room*]

RUTH: Well, darling?

CHARLES: [*Absently*] Well?

RUTH: Would you say the evening had been profitable?

CHARLES: Yes—I suppose so.

RUTH: I must say it was extremely funny at moments.

CHARLES: Yes—it certainly was.

RUTH: What's the matter?

CHARLES: The matter?

RUTH: Yes—you seem odd somehow—do you feel quite well?

CHARLES: Perfectly. I think I'll have a drink. Do you want one?

RUTH: No, thank you, dear.

CHARLES: [*Pouring himself out a drink*] It's rather chilly in this room.

RUTH: Come over by the fire.

CHARLES: I don't think I'll make any notes tonight—I'll start fresh in the morning. [*He is bringing his drink over to the fire when he sees* Elvira]

My God! [*He drops the drink on the floor.* Ruth *jumps up*]

RUTH: Charles!

ELVIRA: That was very clumsy, Charles dear.

CHARLES: Elvira!—then it's true—it was you!

ELVIRA: Of course it was.

RUTH: [*Coming to him*] Charles—darling Charles —what are you talking about?

CHARLES: [*To* Elvira] Are you a ghost?

ELVIRA: I suppose I must be—it's all very confusing.

RUTH: [*Becoming agitated*] Charles—what do you keep looking over there for? Look at me—what's happened?

CHARLES: Don't you see?

RUTH: See what?

CHARLES: Elvira.

RUTH: [*Staring at him incredulously*] Elvira!!

CHARLES: [*With an effort at social grace*] Yes— Elvira dear, this is Ruth—Ruth, this is Elvira.

RUTH: [*With forced calmness*] Come and sit down, darling.

CHARLES: Do you mean to say you can't see her?

RUTH: Listen, Charles—you just sit down quietly by the fire and I'll mix you another drink. Don't worry about the mess on the carpet—Edith can clean it up in the morning. [*She takes him by the arm*]

CHARLES: [*Breaking away*] But you must be able to see her—she's there—look—right in front of you —there—

RUTH: Are you mad? What's happened to you?

CHARLES: You can't see her?

RUTH: If this is a joke, dear, it's gone quite far enough. Sit down for God's sake and don't be idiotic.

CHARLES: [*Clutching his head*] What am I to do—what the hell am I to do!

ELVIRA: I think you might at least be a little more pleased to see me—after all, you conjured me up.

CHARLES: I didn't do any such thing. I did nothing of the sort.

ELVIRA: Nonsense, of course you did. That awful child with the cold came and told me you wanted to see me urgently.

CHARLES: It was all a mistake—a horrible mistake.

RUTH: Stop talking like that, Charles—as I told you before, the *joke's* gone far enough.

CHARLES: [*Aside*] I've gone mad, that's what it is —I've just gone raving mad.

RUTH: [*Going to the table and quickly pouring him out some neat brandy*] Here—let me get you a drink.

CHARLES: [*Mechanically—taking it*] This is appalling!

RUTH: Relax.

CHARLES: How can I relax? I shall never be able to relax again as long as I live.

RUTH: Drink some brandy.

CHARLES: [*Drinking it at a gulp*] There now—are you satisfied?

RUTH: Now sit down.

CHARLES: Why are you so anxious for me to sit down—what good will that do?

RUTH: I want you to relax—you can't relax standing up.

ELVIRA: African natives can—they can stand on one leg for hours.

CHARLES: I don't happen to be an African native.

RUTH: You don't happen to be a *what?*

CHARLES: [*Savagely*] An African native!

RUTH: What's that got to do with it?

CHARLES: It doesn't matter, Ruth—really it doesn't matter—we'll say no more about it. [*He sits down*] See, I've sat down.

RUTH: Would you like some more brandy?

CHARLES: Yes, please.

ELVIRA: Very unwise—you always had a weak head.

CHARLES: I could drink you under the table.

RUTH: There's no need to be aggressive, Charles— I'm doing my best to help you.

CHARLES: I'm sorry.

RUTH: [*Bringing him some more brandy*] Here— drink this—and then we'll go to bed.

ELVIRA: Get rid of her, Charles—then we can talk in peace.

CHARLES: That's a thoroughly immoral suggestion, you ought to be ashamed of yourself.

RUTH: What is there immoral in that?

CHARLES: I wasn't talking to you.

RUTH: Who were you talking to, then?

CHARLES: Elvira, of course.

RUTH: To hell with Elvira!

ELVIRA: There now—she's getting cross.

CHARLES: I don't blame her.

RUTH: What don't you blame her for?

CHARLES: Oh, God!

RUTH: Now look here, Charles— I gather you've got some sort of plan behind all this. I'm not quite a fool. I suspected you when we were doing that idiotic séance.

CHARLES: Don't be so silly—what plan could I have?

RUTH: I don't know—it's probably something to do with the characters in your book—how they, or one of them would react to a certain situation—I refuse to be used as a guinea pig unless I'm warned beforehand what it's all about.

CHARLES: [*Patiently*] Ruth, Elvira is here—she's standing a few yards away from you.

RUTH: [*Sarcastically*] Yes, dear, I can see her distinctly—under the piano with a horse.

CHARLES: But, Ruth . . .

RUTH: I am not going to stay here arguing any longer . . .

ELVIRA: Hurray!

CHARLES: Shut up.

RUTH: [*Incensed*] How dare you speak to me like that!

CHARLES: Listen, Ruth—please listen—

RUTH: I will not listen to any more of this nonsense—I am going up to bed now. I'll leave you to turn out the lights. I shan't be asleep—I'm too upset so you can come in and say good night to me if you feel like it.

ELVIRA: That's big of her, I must say.

CHARLES: Be quiet—you're behaving like a guttersnipe.

RUTH: [*Icily—at door*] That is all I have to say. Good night, Charles. [Ruth *walks swiftly out of the room without looking at him again*]

CHARLES: Ruth . . .

ELVIRA: That was one of the most enjoyable half-hours I have ever spent.

CHARLES: Oh, Elvira—how could you!

ELVIRA: Poor Ruth.

CHARLES: [*Staring at her*] This is obviously an hallucination, isn't it?

ELVIRA: I'm afraid I don't know the technical term for it.

CHARLES: [*Rising and walking about the room*] What am I to do?

ELVIRA: What Ruth suggested—relax.

CHARLES: Where have you come from?

ELVIRA: Do you know, it's very peculiar, but I've sort of forgotten.

CHARLES: Are you here to stay indefinitely?

ELVIRA: I don't know that either.

CHARLES: Oh, my God!

ELVIRA: Why, would you hate it so much if I did?

CHARLES: Well, you must admit it would be embarrassing.

ELVIRA: I don't see why, really—it's all a question of adjusting yourself—anyhow I think it's horrid of you to be so unwelcoming and disagreeable.

CHARLES: Now look here, Elvira . . .

ELVIRA: [*Near tears*] I do—I think you're mean.

CHARLES: Try to see my point, dear—I've been married to Ruth for five years, and you've been dead for seven . . .

ELVIRA: Not dead, Charles—"passed over." It's considered vulgar to say "dead" where I come from.

CHARLES: Passed over, then.

ELVIRA: At any rate, now that I'm here, the least you can do is to make a pretense of being amiable about it . . .

CHARLES: Of course, my dear, I'm delighted in one way . . .

ELVIRA: I don't believe you love me any more.

CHARLES: I shall always love the memory of you.

ELVIRA: [*Rising and walking about*] You mustn't think me unreasonable, but I really am a little hurt. You called me back—and at great inconvenience I came—and you've been thoroughly churlish ever since I arrived.

CHARLES: [*Gently*] Believe me, Elvira, I most emphatically did not send for you—there's been some mistake.

ELVIRA: [*Irritably*] Well, somebody did—and that child said it was you—I remember I was playing backgammon with a very sweet old Oriental gentleman—I think his name was Genghis Khan—and I'd just thrown double sixes, and then that child paged me and the next thing I knew I was in this room . . . perhaps it was your subconscious.

CHARLES: Well, you must find out whether you are going to stay or not, and we can make arrangements accordingly.

ELVIRA: I don't see how I can.

CHARLES: Well, try to think—isn't there anyone that you know, that you can get in touch with over there—on the other side, or whatever it's called—who could advise you?

ELVIRA: I can't think—it seems so far away—as though I'd dreamed it . . .

CHARLES: You must know somebody else beside Genghis Khan.

ELVIRA: Oh, Charles . . .

CHARLES: What is it?

ELVIRA: I want to cry, but I don't think I'm able to . . .

CHARLES: What do you want to cry for?

ELVIRA: It's seeing you again—and you being so irascible like you always used to be . . .

CHARLES: I don't mean to be irascible, Elvira . . .

ELVIRA: Darling—I don't mind really—I never did.

CHARLES: Is it cold—being a ghost?

ELVIRA: No—I don't think so.

CHARLES: What happens if I touch you?

ELVIRA: I doubt if you can. Do you want to?

CHARLES: Oh, Elvira . . . [*He buries his face in his hands*]

ELVIRA: What is it, darling?

CHARLES: I really do feel strange, seeing you again . . .

ELVIRA: That's better.

CHARLES: [*Looking up*] What's better?

ELVIRA: Your voice was kinder.

CHARLES: Was I ever unkind to you when you were alive?

ELVIRA: Often . . .

CHARLES: Oh, how can you! I'm sure that's an exaggeration.

ELVIRA: Not at all—you were an absolute pig that time we went to Cornwall and stayed in that awful hotel—you hit me with a billiard cue.

CHARLES: Only very, very gently . . .

ELVIRA: I loved you very much.

CHARLES: I loved you too . . . [*He puts out his hand to her and then draws it away*] No, I can't touch you—isn't that horrible?

ELVIRA: Perhaps it's as well if I'm going to stay for any length of time . . .

CHARLES: I feel strangely peaceful—I suppose I shall wake up eventually . . .

ELVIRA: Put your head back.

CHARLES: [*Doing so*] Like that?

ELVIRA: [*Stroking his hair*] Can you feel anything . . . ?

CHARLES: Only a very little breeze through my hair. . . .

ELVIRA: Well, that's better than nothing.

CHARLES: [*Drowsily*] I suppose if I'm really out of my mind they'll put me in an asylum.

ELVIRA: Don't worry about that—just relax—

CHARLES: [*Very drowsily indeed*] Poor Ruth . . .

ELVIRA: [*Gently and sweetly*] To hell with Ruth.

THE CURTAIN FALLS

ACT II. SCENE I.

It is about nine-thirty the next morning. The sun is pouring in through the open French windows. Ruth *is sitting at the breakfast table, drinking coffee and reading the* Times. *After a few moments* Charles *comes in. He kisses her.*

CHARLES: Good morning, darling.

RUTH: [*With a certain stiffness*] Good morning, Charles.

CHARLES: [*Going to the open window and taking a deep breath*] It certainly is.

RUTH: What certainly is what?

CHARLES: A good morning—a tremendously good morning—there isn't a cloud in the sky and everything looks newly washed.

RUTH: [*Turning a page of the* Times] Edith's keeping your breakfast hot—you'd better ring.

CHARLES: [*Pressing the bell by the fireplace*] Anything interesting in the *Times*?

RUTH: Don't be silly, Charles.

CHARLES: [*Coming to the table*] I intend to work all day.

RUTH: Good.

CHARLES: It's extraordinary about daylight, isn't it?

RUTH: How do you mean?

CHARLES: The way it reduces everything to normal.

RUTH: Does it?

CHARLES: [*Sits. Firmly*] Yes—it does.

RUTH: I'm sure I'm very glad to hear it.

CHARLES: You're very glacial this morning.

RUTH: Are you surprised?

CHARLES: Frankly—yes. I expected more of *you*.

RUTH: Well, really!

CHARLES: I've always looked upon you as a woman of perception and understanding.

RUTH: Perhaps this is one of my off days. [Edith *comes in with some bacon and eggs and toast*]

CHARLES: [*Cheerfully*] Good morning, Edith.

EDITH: Good morning, sir.

CHARLES: Feeling fit?

EDITH: Yes, sir—thank you, sir.

CHARLES: How's cook?

EDITH: I don't know, sir—I haven't asked her.

CHARLES: You should. You should begin every day by asking everyone how they are—it oils the wheels.

EDITH: Yes, sir.

CHARLES: Greet her for me, will you?

EDITH: Yes, sir.

RUTH: That will be all for the moment, Edith.

EDITH: Yes'm. [Edith *goes out*]

RUTH: I wish you wouldn't be facetious with the servants, Charles—it confuses them and undermines their morale.

CHARLES: I consider that point of view retrogressive, if not downright feudal.

RUTH: I don't care what you consider it, I have to run the house and you don't.

CHARLES: Are you implying that I couldn't?

RUTH: You're at liberty to try.

CHARLES: I take back what I said about it being a good morning—it's a dreadful morning.

RUTH: You'd better eat your breakfast while it's hot.

CHARLES: It isn't.

RUTH: [*Putting down the* Times] Now look here, Charles—in your younger days this display of roguish flippancy might have been alluring—in a middle-aged novelist it's nauseating.

CHARLES: Would you like me to writhe at your feet in a frenzy of self-abasement?

RUTH: That would be equally nauseating but certainly more appropriate.

CHARLES: I really don't see what I've done that's so awful.

RUTH: You behaved abominably last night. You wounded me and insulted me.

CHARLES: I was the victim of an aberration.

RUTH: Nonsense—you were drunk.

CHARLES: Drunk?

RUTH: You had four strong dry Martinis before dinner—a great deal too much burgundy at dinner—heaven knows how much port and kümmel with Doctor Bradman while I was doing my best to entertain that madwoman—and then two double brandies later—I gave them to you myself—of course you were drunk.

CHARLES: So that's your story, is it?

RUTH: You refused to come to bed and finally when I came down at three in the morning to see what had happened to you I found you in an alcoholic coma on the sofa with the fire out and your hair all over your face.

CHARLES: I was not in the least drunk, Ruth. Something happened to me—you really must believe that—something very peculiar happened to me.

RUTH: Nonsense.

CHARLES: It isn't nonsense—I know it looks like nonsense now in the clear, remorseless light of day, but last night it was far from being nonsense—I honestly had some sort of hallucination—

RUTH: I would really rather not discuss it any further.

CHARLES: But you must discuss it—it's very disturbing.

RUTH: There I agree with you. It showed you up in a most unpleasant light—I find that extremely disturbing.

CHARLES: I swear to you that during the séance I was convinced that I heard Elvira's voice—

RUTH: Nobody else did.

CHARLES: I can't help that—I did.

RUTH: You couldn't have.

CHARLES: And later on I was equally convinced that she was in this room—I saw her distinctly and talked to her. After you'd gone up to bed we had quite a cosy little chat.

RUTH: And you seriously expect me to believe that you weren't drunk?

CHARLES: I *know* I wasn't drunk. If I'd been all that drunk I should have a dreadful hangover now, shouldn't I?

RUTH: I'm not at all sure that you haven't.

CHARLES: I haven't got a trace of a headache—my tongue's not coated—look at it. [*He puts out his tongue*]

RUTH: I've not the least desire to look at your tongue; kindly put it in again.

CHARLES: I know what it is—you're frightened.

RUTH: Frightened? Rubbish! What is there to be frightened of?

CHARLES: Elvira. You wouldn't have minded all that much even if I had been drunk—it's only because it was all mixed up with Elvira.

RUTH: I seem to remember last night before dinner telling you that your views of female psychology were rather didactic. I was right. I should have added that they were puerile.

CHARLES: That was when it all began.

RUTH: When what all began?

CHARLES: We were talking too much about Elvira—it's dangerous to have somebody very strongly in your mind when you start dabbling with the occult.

RUTH: She certainly wasn't strongly in my mind.

CHARLES: She was in mine.

RUTH: Oh, she was, was she?

CHARLES: You tried to make me say that she was more physically attractive than you, so that you could hold it over me.

RUTH: I did not. I don't give a hoot how physically attractive she was.

CHARLES: Oh yes, you do—your whole being is devoured with jealousy.

RUTH: [*Rises and starts to clear table*] This is *too* much!

CHARLES: Women! My God, what I think of women!

RUTH: Your view of women is academic to say the least of it—just because you've always been

dominated by them it doesn't necessarily follow that you know anything about them.

CHARLES: I've never been dominated by anyone.

RUTH: You were hag-ridden by your mother until you were twenty-three—then you got into the clutches of that awful Mrs. Whatever-her-name-was—

CHARLES: Mrs. Winthrop-Lewellyn.

RUTH: I'm not interested. Then there was Elvira—she ruled you with a rod of iron.

CHARLES: Elvira never ruled anyone, she was much too elusive—that was one of her greatest charms. [*Sits*]

RUTH: Then there was Maud Charteris—

CHARLES: My affair with Maud Charteris lasted exactly seven and a half weeks and she cried all the time.

RUTH: The tyranny of tears! Then there was—

CHARLES: If you wish to make an inventory of my sex life, dear, I think it only fair to tell you that you've missed out several episodes—I'll consult my diary and give you the complete list after lunch.

RUTH: It's no use trying to impress me with your routine amorous exploits—

CHARLES: The only woman in my whole life who's ever attempted to dominate me is you—you've been at it for years.

RUTH: That is completely untrue.

CHARLES: Oh, no, it isn't. You boss me and bully me and order me about—you won't even allow me to have an hallucination if I want to.

RUTH: Alcohol will ruin your whole life if you allow it to get a hold on you, you know.

CHARLES: Once and for all, Ruth, I would like you to understand that what happened last night has nothing whatever to do with alcohol. You've very adroitly rationalized the whole affair to your own satisfaction, but your deductions are based on complete fallacy. I am willing to grant you that it was an aberration, some sort of odd psychic delusion brought on by suggestion or hypnosis. I was stone cold sober from first to last and extremely upset into the bargain.

RUTH: *You* were upset indeed! What about me?

CHARLES: You behaved with a stolid, obtuse lack of comprehension that frankly shocked me!

RUTH: I consider that I was remarkably patient. I shall know better next time.

CHARLES: Instead of putting out a gentle, comradely hand to guide me you shouted staccato orders at me like a sergeant-major.

RUTH: You seem to forget that you gratuitously insulted me.

CHARLES: I did not.

RUTH: You called me a guttersnipe—you told me to shut up—and when I quietly suggested that we should go up to bed you said, with the most disgusting leer, that it was an immoral suggestion.

CHARLES: [*Exasperated*] I was talking to Elvira!

RUTH: If you were I can only say that it conjures up a fragrant picture of your first marriage.

CHARLES: My first marriage was perfectly charming and I think it's in the worst possible taste for you to sneer at it.

RUTH: I am not nearly so interested in your first marriage as you think I am. It's your second marriage that is absorbing me at the moment—it seems to me to be on the rocks.

CHARLES: Only because you persist in taking up this ridiculous attitude.

RUTH: My attitude is that of any normal woman whose husband gets drunk and hurls abuse at her.

CHARLES: [Shouting] I was not drunk!

RUTH: Be quiet, they'll hear you in the kitchen.

CHARLES: I don't care if they hear me in the Folkestone Town Hall—I was not drunk!

RUTH: Control yourself, Charles.

CHARLES: How can I control myself in the face of your idiotic damned stubbornness? It's giving me claustrophobia.

RUTH: [Quietly] You'd better ring up Doctor Bradman. [Edith comes in with a tray to clear away the breakfast things]

EDITH: Can I clear, please'm?

RUTH: Yes, Edith.

EDITH: Cook wants to know about lunch, mum.

RUTH: [Coldly] Will you be in to lunch, Charles?

CHARLES: Please don't worry about me—I shall be perfectly happy with a bottle of gin in my bedroom.

RUTH: Don't be silly, dear. [To Edith] Tell cook we shall both be in.

EDITH: Yes'm.

RUTH: [Conversationally—after a long pause] I'm going into Hythe this morning—is there anything you want?

CHARLES: Yes—a great deal—but I doubt if you could get it in Hythe.

RUTH: Tell cook to put Alka-Seltzer down on my list, will you, Edith?

EDITH: Yes'm.

RUTH: [At the window—after another long pause] It's clouding over.

CHARLES: You have a genius for understatement. [In silence, but breathing heavily, Edith staggers out with the tray]

RUTH: [As she goes] Don't worry about the table, Edith—I'll put it away.

EDITH: Yes'm. [When Edith has gone Charles goes over to Ruth]

CHARLES: Please, Ruth—be reasonable.

RUTH: I'm perfectly reasonable.

CHARLES: I wasn't pretending—I really did believe that I saw Elvira and when I heard her voice I was appalled.

RUTH: You put up with it for five years. [Puts chair by gramophone]

CHARLES: [Puts table in hall] Naturally when I saw her I had the shock of my life—that's why I dropped the glass.

RUTH: But you couldn't have seen her.

CHARLES: I know I couldn't have but I did!

RUTH: I'm willing to concede then that you imagined you did.

CHARLES: That's what I've been trying to explain to you for hours.

RUTH: Well, then, there's obviously something wrong with you.

CHARLES: Exactly—there is something wrong with me—something fundamentally wrong with me—that's why I've been imploring your sympathy and all I got was a sterile temperance lecture.

RUTH: You had been drinking, Charles—there's no denying that.

CHARLES: No more than usual.

RUTH: Well, how do you account for it then?

CHARLES: [Frantically] I can't account for it—that's what's so awful.

RUTH: [Practically] Did you feel quite well yesterday—during the day, I mean?

CHARLES: Of course I did.

RUTH: What did you have for lunch?

CHARLES: You ought to know, you had it with me.

RUTH: [Thinking] Let me see now, there was lemon sole and that cheese thing—

CHARLES: Why should having a cheese thing for lunch make me see my deceased wife after dinner?

RUTH: You never know—it was rather rich.

CHARLES: Why didn't you see your dead husband then? You had just as much of it as I did.

RUTH: This is not getting us anywhere at all.

CHARLES: Of course it isn't, and it won't as long as you insist on ascribing supernatural phenomena to colonic irritation.

RUTH: Supernatural grandmother!

CHARLES: I admit she'd have been much less agitating.

RUTH: [Sits] Perhaps you ought to see a nerve specialist.

CHARLES: I am not in the least neurotic and never have been.

RUTH: A psychoanalyst then.

CHARLES: I refuse to endure months of expensive humiliation only to be told at the end of it that at the age of four I was in love with my rocking horse.

RUTH: What do you suggest then?

CHARLES: I don't suggest anything—I'm profoundly uneasy.

RUTH: Perhaps there's something pressing on your brain.

CHARLES: If there were something pressing on my brain I should have violent headaches, shouldn't I?

RUTH: Not necessarily. An uncle of mine had a lump the size of a cricket ball pressing on his brain for years and he never felt a thing.

CHARLES: [Rises] I know I should know if I had anything like that.

RUTH: He didn't.

CHARLES: What happened to him?

RUTH: He had it taken out and he's been as bright as a button ever since.

CHARLES: Did he have any sort of delusions—did he think he saw things that weren't there?

RUTH: No, I don't think so.

CHARLES: Well, what the hell are we talking about him for then? It's sheer waste of valuable time.

RUTH: I only brought him up as an example.

CHARLES: I think I'm going mad.

RUTH: How do you feel now?

CHARLES: Physically do you mean?

RUTH: Altogether.

CHARLES: [After due reflection] Apart from being worried I feel quite normal.

RUTH: Good. You're not hearing or seeing anything in the least unusual?

CHARLES: Not a thing.

[At this moment Elvira comes in from the garden, carrying an armful of roses. The roses are as grey as the rest of her]

ELVIRA: You've absolutely ruined that border by the sundial—it looks like a mixed salad.

CHARLES: O my God!

RUTH: What's the matter now?

CHARLES: She's here again!

RUTH: What do you mean? Who's here again?

CHARLES: Elvira.

RUTH: Pull yourself together and don't be absurd.

ELVIRA: It's all those nasturtiums—they're so vulgar.

CHARLES: I like nasturtiums.

RUTH: You like what?

ELVIRA: [Putting her grey roses into a vase] They're all right in moderation but in a mass like that they look beastly.

CHARLES: Help me, Ruth—you've got to help me—

RUTH: [Rises] What did you mean about nasturtiums?

CHARLES: Never mind about that now—I tell you she's here again.

ELVIRA: You have been having a nice scene, haven't you? I could hear you right down the garden.

CHARLES: Please mind your own business.

RUTH: If your behaving like a lunatic isn't my business nothing is.

ELVIRA: I expect it was about me, wasn't it? I know I ought to feel sorry but I'm not—I'm delighted.

CHARLES: How can you be so inconsiderate?

RUTH: [Shrilly] Inconsiderate!—I like that, I must say—

CHARLES: Ruth—darling—please . . .

RUTH: I've done everything I can to help—I've controlled myself admirably—and I should like to say here and now that I don't believe a word about your damned hallucinations—you're up to something, Charles—there's been a certain furtiveness in your manner for weeks— Why don't you be honest and tell me what it is?

CHARLES: You're wrong—you're dead wrong—I haven't been in the least furtive—I—

RUTH: You're trying to upset me—for some obscure reason you're trying to goad me into doing something that I might regret—I won't stand for it any more— You're making me utterly miserable— [She bursts into tears and collapses on sofa]

CHARLES: Ruth—please— [Sits on sofa beside Ruth]

RUTH: Don't come near me——

ELVIRA: Let her have a nice cry—it'll do her good.

CHARLES: You're utterly heartless!

RUTH: Heartless!

CHARLES: [Wildly] I was not talking to you—I was talking to Elvira.

RUTH: Go on talking to her then, talk to her until you're blue in the face but don't talk to me—

CHARLES: Help me, Elvira—

ELVIRA: How?

CHARLES: Make her see you or something.

ELVIRA: I'm afraid I couldn't manage that—it's technically the most difficult business—frightfully complicated, you know—it takes years of study—

CHARLES: You are here, aren't you? You're not an illusion?

ELVIRA: I may be an illusion but I'm most definitely here.

CHARLES: How did you get here?

ELVIRA: I told you last night—I don't exactly know—

CHARLES: Well, you must make me a promise that in future you only come and talk to me when I'm alone—

ELVIRA: [Pouting] How unkind you are—making me feel so unwanted—I've never been treated so rudely—

CHARLES: I don't mean to be rude, but you must see—

ELVIRA: It's all your own fault for having married a woman who is incapable of seeing beyond the nose on her face—if she had a grain of real sympathy or affection for you she'd believe what you tell her.

CHARLES: How could you expect anybody to believe this?

ELVIRA: You'd be surprised how gullible people are—we often laugh about it on the other side.

[Ruth, who has stopped crying and been staring at Charles in horror, suddenly gets up]

RUTH: [Gently] Charles—

CHARLES: [Surprised at her tone] Yes, dear—

RUTH: I'm awfully sorry I was cross—

CHARLES: But, my dear—

RUTH: I understand everything now, I do really—

CHARLES: You do?

RUTH: [Patting his arm reassuringly] Of course I do.

ELVIRA: Look out—she's up to something—

CHARLES: Will you please be quiet?

RUTH: Of course, darling—we'll all be quiet, won't we? We'll be as quiet as little mice.

CHARLES: Ruth dear, listen—

RUTH: I want you to come upstairs with me and go to bed—

ELVIRA: The way that woman harps on bed is nothing short of erotic.

CHARLES: I'll deal with you later—

RUTH: Whenever you like, darling. Come along.

CHARLES: Ruth dear—I'd really rather not go to bed in the middle of the morning—

ELVIRA: How you've changed, darling!

CHARLES: Don't be disgusting.

RUTH: [Sweetly] I'm sorry, dear—I didn't mean to be.

CHARLES: What are you up to?

RUTH: I'm not up to anything—I just want you to go quietly to bed and wait there until Doctor Bradman comes—

CHARLES: No, Ruth—you're wrong—

RUTH: [Firmly] Come, dear—

ELVIRA: She'll have you in a strait jacket before you know where you are.

CHARLES: [Frantically] Help me—you must help me—

ELVIRA: [Enjoying herself] My dear, I would with pleasure, but I can't think how—

CHARLES: I can—listen, Ruth—

RUTH: Yes, dear?

CHARLES: If I promise to go to bed will you let me stay here for five minutes longer?

RUTH: I really think it would be better—

CHARLES: Bear with me—however mad it may seem—bear with me for just five minutes longer—

RUTH: [Letting go of him] Very well—what is it?

CHARLES: Sit down then.

RUTH: [Sitting down] All right—there.

CHARLES: Now listen—listen carefully—

ELVIRA: Have a cigarette, it will soothe your nerves.

CHARLES: I don't want a cigarette.

RUTH: [Indulgently] Then you shan't have one, darling.

CHARLES: Ruth, I want to explain to you clearly and without emotion that beyond any shadow of doubt the ghost or shade or whatever you like to call it of my first wife Elvira is in this room now.

RUTH: Yes, dear.

CHARLES: I know you don't believe it and are trying valiantly to humour me but I intend to prove it to you.

RUTH: Why not lie down and have a nice rest and you can prove anything you want to later on?

CHARLES: She may not be here later on.

ELVIRA: Don't worry—she will!

CHARLES: O God!

RUTH: Hush, dear.

CHARLES: [To Elvira] Promise you'll do what I ask?

ELVIRA: That all depends what it is.

CHARLES: Ruth—you see that bowl of flowers on the piano?

RUTH: Yes, dear—I did it myself this morning.

ELVIRA: Very untidily if I may say so.

CHARLES: You may not.

RUTH: Very well—I never will again—I promise.

CHARLES: Elvira will now carry that bowl of flowers to the mantelpiece and back again. You will, Elvira, won't you—just to please me?

ELVIRA: I don't really see why I should—you've been quite insufferable to me ever since I materialized.

CHARLES: Please.

ELVIRA: All right, I will just this once—not that I approve of all these Herman The Great carryings on. [She goes over to the piano]

CHARLES: Now, Ruth—watch carefully.

RUTH: [Patiently] Very well, dear.

CHARLES: Go on, Elvira—bring it to the mantelpiece and back again.

[Elvira does so, taking obvious pleasure in doing it in a very roundabout way. At one moment she brings it up to within an inch of Ruth's face. Ruth shrinks back with a scream and then jumps to her feet]

RUTH: [Furiously] How dare you, Charles! You ought to be ashamed of yourself!

CHARLES: What on earth for?

RUTH: [Hysterically] It's a trick—I know perfectly well it's a trick—you've been working up to this—it's all part of some horrible plan—

CHARLES: It isn't—I swear it isn't—Elvira—do something else for God's sake—

ELVIRA: Certainly—anything to oblige.

RUTH: [Becoming really frightened] You want to get rid of me—you're trying to drive me out of my mind—

CHARLES: Don't be so silly.

RUTH: You're cruel and sadistic and I'll never forgive you—[Elvira lifts up a light chair and waltzes solemnly round the room with it, then she puts it down with a bang. Making a dive for the door] I'm not going to put up with this any more.

CHARLES: [Holding her] You must believe it—you must—

RUTH: Let me go immediately—

CHARLES: That was Elvira—I swear it was—

RUTH: [Struggling] Let me go—

CHARLES: Ruth—please—

[Ruth breaks away from him and runs towards the windows. Elvira gets there just before her and shuts them in her face. Ruth starts back, appalled]

RUTH: [Looking at Charles with eyes of horror] Charles—this is madness—sheer madness! It's some sort of auto-suggestion, isn't it—some form of hypnotism, swear to me it's only that? Swear to me it's only that.

ELVIRA: [*Taking an expensive vase from the man-telpiece and crashing it into the grate*] Hypnotism my foot!

[*Ruth gives a scream and goes into violent hysterics as the curtain falls*]

SCENE II.

The time is late on the following afternoon. When the curtain rises Ruth is sitting alone at the tea table, which is set in front of the fire. After a moment or two she gets up and, frowning thoughtfully, goes over to the piano and takes a cigarette out of a box. As she returns to the table the front door bell rings. She hears it and straightens herself as though preparing for a difficult interview. Edith enters.

EDITH: Madame Arcati. [*Edith steps aside and Madame Arcati comes in. Edith goes out. Madame Arcati is wearing a tweed coat and skirt and a great many amber beads and, possibly, a beret*]

MADAME ARCATI: My dear Mrs. Condomine, I came directly I got your message.

RUTH: That was very kind of you.

MADAME ARCATI: [*Briskly*] Kind? Nonsense! Nothing kind about it—I look upon it as an outing.

RUTH: I'm so glad—will you have some tea?

MADAME ARCATI: China or Indian?

RUTH: China.

MADAME ARCATI: Good. I never touch Indian, it upsets my vibrations.

RUTH: Do sit down.

MADAME ARCATI: [*Turning her head and sniffing*] I find this room very interesting—very interesting indeed. I noticed it the other night.

RUTH: I'm not entirely surprised. [*She proceeds to pour out tea*]

MADAME ARCATI: [*Sitting down and pulling off her gloves*] Have you ever been to Cowden Manor?

RUTH: No, I'm afraid I haven't.

MADAME ARCATI: That's very interesting too—strikes you like a blow between the eyes the moment you walk into the drawing-room. Two lumps of sugar, please, and no milk at all.

RUTH: I am profoundly disturbed, Madame Arcati, and I want your help.

MADAME ARCATI: Aha! I thought as much. What's in these sandwiches?

RUTH: Cucumber.

MADAME ARCATI: Couldn't be better. [*She takes one*] Fire away.

RUTH: It's most awfully difficult to explain.

MADAME ARCATI: Facts first—explanations afterwards.

RUTH: It's the facts that are difficult to explain—they're so fantastic.

MADAME ARCATI: Facts very often are. Take creative talent for instance, how do you account for

that? Look at Shakespeare and Michael Angelo! Try to explain Mozart snatching sounds out of the air and putting them down on paper when he was practically a baby—facts—plain facts. I know it's the fashion nowadays to ascribe it all to glands but my reply to that is fiddlededee.

RUTH: Yes, I'm sure you're quite right.

MADAME ARCATI: There are more things in heaven and earth than are dreamt of in your philosophy, Mrs. Condomine.

RUTH: There certainly are.

MADAME ARCATI: Come now—take the plunge—out with it. You've heard strange noises in the night no doubt—boards creaking—doors slamming—subdued moaning in the passages—is that it?

RUTH: No—I'm afraid it isn't.

MADAME ARCATI: No sudden gusts of cold wind, I hope.

RUTH: No, it's worse than that.

MADAME ARCATI: I'm all attention.

RUTH: [*With an effort*] I know it sounds idiotic but the other night—during the séance—something happened—

MADAME ARCATI: I knew it! Probably a poltergeist, they're enormously cunning, you know, they sometimes lie doggo for days—

RUTH: You know that my husband was married before?

MADAME ARCATI: Yes—I have heard it mentioned.

RUTH: His first wife, Elvira, died comparatively young—

MADAME ARCATI: [*Sharply*] Where?

RUTH: Here—in this house—in this very room.

MADAME ARCATI: [*Whistling*] Whew! I'm beginning to see daylight!

RUTH: She was convalescing after pneumonia and one evening she started to laugh helplessly at one of the B.B.C. musical programmes and died of a heart attack.

MADAME ARCATI: And she materialized the other evening—after I had gone?

RUTH: Not to me, but to my husband.

MADAME ARCATI: [*Rising impulsively*] Capital—capital! Oh, but that's splendid!

RUTH: [*Coldly*] From your own professional standpoint I can see that it might be regarded as a major achievement!

MADAME ARCATI: [*Delighted*] A triumph, my dear! Nothing more nor less than a triumph!

RUTH: But from my own personal point of view you must see that, to say the least of it, it's embarrassing.

MADAME ARCATI: [*Walking about the room*] At last—at last—a genuine materialization!

RUTH: Please sit down again, Madame Arcati.

MADAME ARCATI: How could anyone sit down at a moment like this? It's tremendous! I haven't had such a success since the Sudbury case.

RUTH: [*Sharply*] Nevertheless I must insist upon you sitting down and controlling your natural exuberance. I appreciate fully your pride in your achievement but I would like to point out that it has made my position in this house untenable and that I hold you entirely responsible.

MADAME ARCATI: [Contrite] Forgive me, Mrs. Condomine—I am being abominably selfish—[She sits down] How can I help you?

RUTH: How? By sending her back immediately to where she came from, of course.

MADAME ARCATI: I'm afraid that that is easier said than done.

RUTH: Do you mean to tell me that she is liable to stay here indefinitely?

MADAME ARCATI: It's difficult to say—I fear it depends largely on her.

RUTH: But my dear Madame Arcati—

MADAME ARCATI: Where is she now?

RUTH: My husband has driven her into Folkestone—apparently she was anxious to see an old friend of hers who is staying at the Grand.

MADAME ARCATI: [Producing a notebook] Forgive this formality, but I shall have to make a report to the Psychical Research people—

RUTH: I would be very much obliged if there were no names mentioned.

MADAME ARCATI: The report will be confidential.

RUTH: This is a small village you know and gossip would be most undesirable.

MADAME ARCATI: I quite understand. You say she is visible only to your husband?

RUTH: Yes.

MADAME ARCATI: "Visible only to husband." Audible too I presume?

RUTH: Extremely audible.

MADAME ARCATI: "Extremely audible." Your husband was devoted to her?

RUTH: [With slight irritation] I believe so—

MADAME ARCATI: "Husband devoted."

RUTH: It was apparently a reasonably happy marriage—

MADAME ARCATI: Tut, tut, Mrs. Condomine.

RUTH: I beg your pardon?

MADAME ARCATI: When did she pass over?

RUTH: Seven years ago.

MADAME ARCATI: Aha! That means she must have been on the waiting list.

RUTH: Waiting list?

MADAME ARCATI: Yes, otherwise she would have got beyond the materialization stage by now. She must have marked herself down for a return visit and she'd never have been able to manage it unless there were a strong influence at work.

RUTH: Do you mean that Charles—my husband—wanted her back all that much?

MADAME ARCATI: Possibly, or it might have been her own determination—

RUTH: That sounds much more likely.

MADAME ARCATI: Would you say that she was a woman of strong character?

RUTH: [With rising annoyance] I really don't know, Madame Arcati. I never met her. Nor am I particularly interested in how and why she got here. I am solely concerned with the question of how to get her away again as soon as possible.

MADAME ARCATI: I fully sympathize with you, Mrs. Condomine, and I assure you I will do anything in my power to help—but at the moment I fear I cannot offer any great hopes.

RUTH: But I always understood that there was a way of exorcising ghosts—some sort of ritual?

MADAME ARCATI: You mean the old Bell and Book method?

RUTH: Yes—I suppose I do.

MADAME ARCATI: Poppycock, Mrs. Condomine. It was quite effective in the days of genuine religious belief but that's all changed now. I believe the decline of faith in the Spirit World has been causing grave concern.

RUTH: [Impatiently] Has it indeed?

MADAME ARCATI: There was a time of course when a drop of holy water could send even a poltergeist scampering for cover, but not any more—"Où sont les neiges d'antan?"

RUTH: Be that as it may, Madame Arcati, I must beg of you to do your utmost to dematerialize my husband's first wife as soon as possible.

MADAME ARCATI: The time has come for me to admit to you frankly, Mrs. Condomine, that I haven't the faintest idea how to set about it.

RUTH: [Rises] Do you mean to sit there and tell me that having mischievously conjured up this ghost or spirit or whatever she is and placed me in a hideous position you are unable to do anything about it at all?

MADAME ARCATI: Honesty is the best policy.

RUTH: But it's outrageous! I ought to hand you over to the police.

MADAME ARCATI: [Rising] You go too far, Mrs. Condomine.

RUTH: [Furiously] I go too far indeed? Do you realize what your insane amateur muddling has done?

MADAME ARCATI: I have been a professional since I was a child, Mrs. Condomine—"Amateur" is a word I cannot tolerate.

RUTH: It seems to me to be the height of amateurishness to evoke malignant spirits and not be able to get rid of them again.

MADAME ARCATI: [With dignity] I was in a trance. Anything might happen when I am in a trance.

RUTH: Well, all I can suggest is that you go into another one immediately and get this damned woman out of my house.

MADAME ARCATI: I can't go into trances at a moment's notice—it takes hours of preparation—in addition to which I have to be extremely careful of my diet for days beforehand. Today, for instance, I happened to lunch with friends and had pigeon pie which, plus these cucumber sandwiches, would make a trance out of the question.

RUTH: Well, you'll have to do something.

MADAME ARCATI: I will report the whole matter to the Society for Psychical Research at the earliest possible moment.

RUTH: Will they be able to do anything?

MADAME ARCATI: I doubt it. They'd send an investigating committee, I expect, and do a lot of questioning and wall tapping and mumbo jumbo and then they'd have a conference and you would probably have to go up to London to testify—

RUTH: [Near tears] It's too humiliating—it really is.

MADAME ARCATI: Please try not to upset yourself—nothing can be achieved by upsetting yourself.

RUTH: It's all very fine for you to talk like that, Madame Arcati—you don't seem to have the faintest realization of my position.

MADAME ARCATI: Try to look on the bright side.

RUTH: Bright side indeed! If your husband's first wife suddenly appeared from the grave and came to live in the house with you, do you suppose you'd be able to look on the bright side?

MADAME ARCATI: I resent your tone, Mrs. Condomine, I really do.

RUTH: You most decidedly have no right to—you are entirely to blame for the whole horrible situation.

MADAME ARCATI: Kindly remember that I came here the other night on your own invitation.

RUTH: On my husband's invitation.

MADAME ARCATI: I did what I was requested to do, which was to give a séance and establish contact with the other side—I had no idea that there was any ulterior motive mixed up with it.

RUTH: Ulterior motive?

MADAME ARCATI: Your husband was obviously eager to get in touch with his former wife. If I had been aware of that at the time I should naturally have consulted you beforehand—after all "Noblesse oblige"!

RUTH: He had no intention of trying to get in touch with anyone—the whole thing was planned in order for him to get material for a mystery story he is writing about a homicidal medium.

MADAME ARCATI: [Drawing herself up] Am I to understand that I was only invited in a spirit of mockery?

RUTH: Not at all—he merely wanted to make notes of some of the tricks of the trade.

MADAME ARCATI: [Incensed] Tricks of the trade! Insufferable! I've never been so insulted in my life. I feel we have nothing more to say to one another, Mrs. Condomine. Good-bye—[She goes towards the door]

RUTH: Please don't go—please—

MADAME ARCATI: Your attitude from the outset has been most unpleasant, Mrs. Condomine. Some of your remarks have been discourteous in the extreme and I should like to say without umbrage that

if you and your husband were foolish enough to tamper with the unseen for paltry motives and in a spirit of ribaldry, whatever has happened to you is your own fault, and, to coin a phrase, as far as I'm concerned you can stew in your own juice! [Madame Arcati goes majestically from the room]

RUTH: [Left alone, walks about the room] Damn—damn—damn!

[After a moment or two Charles comes in with Elvira]

CHARLES: What on earth was Madame Arcati doing here?

RUTH: She came to tea.

CHARLES: Did you ask her?

RUTH: Of course I did.

CHARLES: You never told me you were going to.

RUTH: You never told me you were going to ask Elvira to live with us.

CHARLES: I didn't.

ELVIRA: [Sauntering over to the tea table] Oh, yes, you did, darling—it was your subconscious.

CHARLES: What was the old girl so cross about?—she practically cut me dead.

RUTH: I told her the truth about why we invited her the other night.

CHARLES: That was quite unnecessary and most unkind.

RUTH: She needed taking down a bit, she was blowing herself out like a pouter pigeon.

CHARLES: Why did you ask her to tea?

ELVIRA: To get me exorcised, of course. Oh dear, I wish I could have a cucumber sandwich—I did love them so.

CHARLES: Is that true, Ruth?

RUTH: Is what true?

CHARLES: What Elvira said.

RUTH: You know perfectly well I can't hear what Elvira says.

CHARLES: She said that you got Madame Arcati here to try to get her exorcised. Is that true?

RUTH: We discussed the possibilities.

ELVIRA: There's a snake in the grass for you.

CHARLES: You had no right to do such a thing without consulting me.

RUTH: I have every right—this situation is absolutely impossible and you know it.

CHARLES: If only you'd make an effort and try to be a little more friendly to Elvira we might all have quite a jolly time.

RUTH: I have no wish to have a jolly time with Elvira.

ELVIRA: She's certainly very bad tempered, isn't she? I can't think why you married her.

CHARLES: She's naturally a bit upset—we must make allowances.

ELVIRA: I was never bad tempered though, was I, darling? Not even when you were beastly to me—

CHARLES: I was never beastly to you.

RUTH: [Exasperated] Where is Elvira at the moment?

CHARLES: In the chair, by the table.

RUTH: Now look here, Elvira—I shall have to call you Elvira, shan't I? I can't very well go on saying Mrs. Condomine all the time, it would sound too silly—

ELVIRA: I don't see why not.

RUTH: Did she say anything?

CHARLES: She said she'd like nothing better.

ELVIRA: [Giggling] You really are sweet, Charles darling—I worship you.

RUTH: I wish to be absolutely honest with you, Elvira—

ELVIRA: Hold on to your hats, boys!

RUTH: I admit I did ask Madame Arcati here with a view to getting you exorcised and I think that if you were in my position you'd have done exactly the same thing—wouldn't you?

ELVIRA: I shouldn't have done it so obviously.

RUTH: What did she say?

CHARLES: Nothing—she just nodded and smiled.

RUTH: [With a forced smile] Thank you, Elvira—that's generous of you. I really would so much rather that there were no misunderstandings between us—

CHARLES: That's very sensible, Ruth—I agree entirely.

RUTH: [To Elvira] I want, before we go any further, to ask you a frank question. Why did you really come here? I don't see that you could have hoped to have achieved anything by it beyond the immediate joke of making Charles into a sort of astral bigamist.

ELVIRA: I came because the power of Charles's love tugged and tugged and tugged at me. Didn't it, my sweet?

RUTH: What did she say?

CHARLES: She said that she came because she wanted to see me again.

RUTH: Well, she's done that now, hasn't she?

CHARLES: We can't be inhospitable, Ruth.

RUTH: I have no wish to be inhospitable, but I should like to have just an idea of how long you intend to stay, Elvira?

ELVIRA: I don't know—I really don't know! [She giggles] Isn't it awful?

CHARLES: She says she doesn't know.

RUTH: Surely that's a little inconsiderate?

ELVIRA: Didn't the old spiritualist have any constructive ideas about getting rid of me?

CHARLES: What did Madame Arcati say?

RUTH: She said she couldn't do a thing.

ELVIRA: [Moving gaily over to the window] Hurray!

CHARLES: Don't be upset, Ruth dear—we shall soon adjust ourselves, you know—you must admit it's a unique experience—I can see no valid reason why we shouldn't get a great deal of fun out of it.

RUTH: Fun? Charles, how can you—you must be out of your mind!

CHARLES: Not at all—I thought I was at first—but now I must say I'm beginning to enjoy myself.

RUTH: [Bursting into tears] Oh, Charles—Charles—

ELVIRA: She's off again.

CHARLES: You really must not be so callous, Elvira—try to see her point a little—

RUTH: I suppose she said something insulting—

CHARLES: No, dear, she didn't do anything of the sort.

RUTH: Now look here, Elvira—

CHARLES: She's over by the window now.

RUTH: Why the hell can't she stay in the same place!

ELVIRA: Temper again—my poor Charles, what a terrible life you must lead.

CHARLES: Do shut up, darling, you'll only make everything worse.

RUTH: Who was that "darling" addressed to—her or me?

CHARLES: Both of you.

RUTH: [Rises. Stamping her foot] This is intolerable!

CHARLES: For heaven's sake don't get into another state—

RUTH: [Furiously] I've been doing my level best to control myself ever since yesterday morning and I'm damned if I'm going to try any more, the strain is too much. She has the advantage of being able to say whatever she pleases without me being able to hear her, but she can hear me all right, can't she, without any modified interpreting?

CHARLES: Modified interpreting? I don't know what you mean.

RUTH: Oh yes, you do—you haven't told me once what she really said—you wouldn't dare. Judging from her photograph she's the type who would use most unpleasant language—

CHARLES: Ruth—you're not to talk like that.

RUTH: I've been making polite conversation all through dinner last night and breakfast and lunch today—and it's been a nightmare—and I am not going to do it any more. I don't like Elvira any more than she likes me and what's more I'm certain that I never could have, dead or alive. If, since her untimely arrival here the other evening, she had shown the slightest sign of good manners, the slightest sign of breeding, I might have felt differently towards her, but all she has done is try to make mischief between us and have private jokes with you against me. I am now going up to my room and I shall have my dinner on a tray. You and she can have the house to yourselves and joke and gossip with each other to your heart's content. The first thing in the morning I am going up to London to interview the Psychical Research Society and if they fail me I shall go straight to the Archbishop of Canterbury—[She goes out]

CHARLES: [Making a movement to follow her] Ruth—

ELVIRA: Let her go—she'll calm down later on.

CHARLES: It's unlike her to behave like this—she's generally so equable.

ELVIRA: No, she isn't, not really, her mouth gives her away—it's a hard mouth, Charles.

CHARLES: Her mouth's got nothing to do with it—I resent you discussing Ruth as though she were a horse.

ELVIRA: Do you love her?

CHARLES: Of course I do.

ELVIRA: As much as you loved me?

CHARLES: Don't be silly—it's all entirely different.

ELVIRA: I'm so glad. Nothing could ever have been quite the same, could it?

CHARLES: You always behaved very badly.

ELVIRA: Oh, Charles!

CHARLES: I'm grieved to see that your sojourn in the other world hasn't improved you in the least.

ELVIRA: [Curling up in sofa] Go on, darling—I love it when you pretend to be cross with me—

CHARLES: I'm now going up to talk to Ruth.

ELVIRA: Cowardy custard.

CHARLES: Don't be so idiotic. I can't let her go like that—I must be a little nice and sympathetic to her.

ELVIRA: I don't see why! If she's set on being disagreeable I should just let her get on with it.

CHARLES: The whole business is very difficult for her—we must be fair.

ELVIRA: She should learn to be more adaptable.

CHARLES: She probably will in time—it's been a shock—

ELVIRA: Has it been a shock for you too, darling?

CHARLES: Of course—what did you expect?

ELVIRA: A nice shock?

CHARLES: What do you want, Elvira?

ELVIRA: Want? I don't know what you mean.

CHARLES: I remember that whenever you were overpoweringly demure like that it usually meant that you wanted something.

ELVIRA: It's horrid of you to be so suspicious. All I want is to be with you.

CHARLES: Well, you are.

ELVIRA: I mean alone, darling. If you go and pamper Ruth and smalm her over, she'll probably come flouncing down again and our lovely quiet evening together will be spoilt.

CHARLES: You're incorrigibly selfish.

ELVIRA: Well, I haven't seen you for seven years—it's only natural that I should want a little time alone with you—to talk over old times. I'll let you go up just for a little while if you really think it's your duty.

CHARLES: Of course it is.

ELVIRA: [Smiling] Then I don't mind.

CHARLES: [Rises] You're disgraceful, Elvira.

ELVIRA: You won't be long, will you? You'll come down again very soon?

CHARLES: I shall most likely dress for dinner while I'm upstairs—you can read the Tatler or something.

ELVIRA: Darling, you don't have to dress—for me.

CHARLES: I always dress for dinner.

ELVIRA: What are you going to have? I should like to watch you eat something really delicious—

CHARLES: [Smiling and kissing his hand to her] Be a good girl now—you can play the gramophone if you like.

ELVIRA: [Demurely] Thank you, Charles.

[Charles goes out. Elvira gets up, looks in the gramophone cupboard, finds the record of "Always" and puts it on. She starts to waltz lightly round the room to it. Edith comes in to fetch the tea tray. She sees the gramophone playing by itself so she turns it off and puts the record back in the cupboard. While she is picking up the tray Elvira takes the record out and puts it on again. Edith gives a shriek, drops the tray and rushes out of the room. Elvira continues to waltz gaily]

CURTAIN

SCENE III.

The time is evening several days later. When the curtain rises Mrs. Bradman is sitting in an armchair. Ruth is standing by the window drumming on the pane with her fingers.

MRS. BRADMAN: [In armchair] Does it show any signs of clearing?

RUTH: [At window—looking out] No, it's still pouring.

MRS. BRADMAN: I do sympathize with you, really I do—it's really been quite a chapter of accidents, hasn't it?

RUTH: It certainly has.

MRS. BRADMAN: That happens sometimes, you know—everything seems to go wrong at once—exactly as though there were some evil forces at work. I remember once when George and I went away for a fortnight's holiday not long after we were married—we were dogged by bad luck from beginning to end—the weather was vile—George sprained his ankle—I caught a terrible cold and had to stay in bed for two days—and to crown everything the lamp fell over in the sitting-room and set fire to the treatise George had written on hyperplasia of the abdominal glands.

RUTH: [Absently] How dreadful.

MRS. BRADMAN: He had to write it all over again—every single word.

RUTH: You're sure you wouldn't like a cocktail or some sherry or anything?

MRS. BRADMAN: No, thank you—really not—George will be down in a minute and we've got to go like lightning—we were supposed to be at the Wilmots' at seven and it's nearly that now.

RUTH: I think I'll have a little sherry—I feel I need it. [*She goes to the side table and pours herself some sherry*]

MRS. BRADMAN: Don't worry about your husband's arm, Mrs. Condomine—I'm sure it's only a sprain.

RUTH: It's not his arm I'm worried about.

MRS. BRADMAN: And I'm sure Edith will be up and about again in a few days—

RUTH: My cook gave notice this morning.

MRS. BRADMAN: Well, really! Servants are awful, aren't they? Not a shred of gratitude—at the first sign of trouble they run out on you—like rats leaving a sinking ship.

RUTH: I can't feel that your simile was entirely fortunate, Mrs. Bradman.

MRS. BRADMAN: [*Flustered*] Oh, I didn't mean that, really I didn't!

[*Dr. Bradman comes in*]

DR. BRADMAN: Nothing to worry about, Mrs. Condomine—it's only a slight sprain—

RUTH: I'm so relieved.

DR. BRADMAN: He made a good deal of fuss when I examined it—men are much worse patients than women, you know—particularly highly strung men like your husband.

RUTH: Is he so highly strung, do you think?

DR. BRADMAN: Yes, as a matter of fact I wanted to talk to you about that. I'm afraid he's been overworking lately.

RUTH: [*Frowning*] Overworking?

DR. BRADMAN: He's in rather a nervous condition —nothing serious, you understand—

RUTH: What makes you think so?

DR. BRADMAN: I know the symptoms. Of course the shock of his fall might have something to do with it, but I certainly should advise a complete rest for a couple of weeks—

RUTH: You mean he ought to go away?

DR. BRADMAN: I do. In cases like that a change of atmosphere can work wonders.

RUTH: What symptoms did you notice?

DR. BRADMAN: Oh, nothing to be unduly alarmed about—a certain air of strain—an inability to focus his eyes on the person he is talking to—a few rather marked irrelevancies in his conversation.

RUTH: I see. Can you remember any specific example?

DR. BRADMAN: Oh, he suddenly shouted "What are you doing in the bathroom?" and then, a little later, while I was writing him a prescription, he suddenly said "For God's sake behave yourself!"

MRS. BRADMAN: How extraordinary.

RUTH: [*Nervously*] He often goes on like that— particularly when he's immersed in writing a book—

DR. BRADMAN: Oh, I am not in the least perturbed about it really—but I do think a rest and a change would be a good idea.

RUTH: Thank you so much, Doctor. Would you like some sherry?

DR. BRADMAN: No, thank you—we really must be off.

RUTH: How is poor Edith?

DR. BRADMAN: She'll be all right in a few days— she's still recovering from the concussion.

MRS. BRADMAN: It's funny, isn't it, that both your housemaid and your husband should fall down on the same day, isn't it?

RUTH: Yes, if that sort of thing amuses you.

MRS. BRADMAN: [*Giggling nervously*] Of course I didn't mean it like that, Mrs. Condomine—

DR. BRADMAN: Come along, my dear—you're talking too much as usual.

MRS. BRADMAN: You are horrid, George. Goodbye, Mrs. Condomine—[*Rises*]

RUTH: [*Shaking hands*] Good-bye.

DR. BRADMAN: [*Also shaking hands*] I'll pop in and have a look at both patients sometime tomorrow morning.

RUTH: Thank you so much.

[*Charles comes in. His left arm is in a sling. Elvira follows him and sits down by the fire*]

DR. BRADMAN: Well—how does it feel?

CHARLES: All right.

DR. BRADMAN: It's only a slight sprain, you know.

CHARLES: Is this damned sling really essential?

DR. BRADMAN: It's a wise precaution—it will prevent you using your left hand except when it's really necessary.

CHARLES: I had intended to drive into Folkestone this evening—

DR. BRADMAN: It would be much better if you didn't.

CHARLES: It's extremely inconvenient—

RUTH: You can easily wait and go tomorrow, Charles—

ELVIRA: I can't stand another of those dreary evenings at home. Charles—it'll drive me dotty—and I haven't seen a movie for seven years—

CHARLES: Let me be the first to congratulate you.

DR. BRADMAN: [*Kindly*] What's that, old man?

RUTH: [*With intense meaning*] Charles dear—try to be sensible, I implore you.

CHARLES: Sorry—I forgot.

DR. BRADMAN: You can drive the car if you promise to go very slowly and carefully. Your gear shift is on the right, isn't it?

CHARLES: Yes.

DR. BRADMAN: Well, use your left hand as little as possible.

CHARLES: All right.

RUTH: You'd much better stay at home.

DR. BRADMAN: Couldn't you drive him in?

RUTH: [*Stiffly*] I'm afraid not—I have lots to do in the house and there's Edith to be attended to.

DR. BRADMAN: Well, I'll leave you to fight it out among yourselves—[*To* Charles] But remember if you do insist on going—carefully does it—the roads are very slippery anyhow. Come along, Violet.

MRS. BRADMAN: Good-bye again— Good-bye, Mr. Condomine.

CHARLES: Good-bye. [*He goes into the hall with the* Bradmans. Ruth, *left alone, puts her sherry glass down on the table irritably*]

RUTH: You really are infuriating, Elvira—surely you could wait and go to the movies another night— [Elvira *gives a little laugh and, taking a rose out of a vase, throws it at* Ruth *and vanishes through the French windows. Picking up the rose and putting it back in the vase*] And stop behaving like a school-girl—you're old enough to know better.

CHARLES: [*Coming in*] What?

RUTH: I was talking to Elvira.

CHARLES: She isn't here.

RUTH: She was a moment ago—she threw a rose at me.

CHARLES: She's been very high-spirited all day. I know this mood of old. It usually meant that she was up to something.

RUTH: You're sure she isn't here?

CHARLES: Quite sure.

RUTH: I want to talk with you.

CHARLES: O God!

RUTH: I must—it's important.

CHARLES: You've behaved very well for the last few days, Ruth—you're not going to start making scenes again, are you?

RUTH: I resent that air of patronage, Charles. I have behaved well, as you call it, because there was nothing else to do, but I think it only fair to warn you that I offer no guarantee for the future. My patience is being stretched to its uttermost.

CHARLES: As far as I can see the position is just as difficult for Elvira as it is for you—if not more so. The poor little thing comes back trustingly after all those years in the other world and what is she faced with? Nothing but brawling and hostility?

RUTH: What did she expect?

CHARLES: Surely even a protoplasmic manifestation has the right to expect a little of the milk of human kindness?

RUTH: Milk of human fiddlesticks.

CHARLES: That just doesn't make sense, dear.

RUTH: Elvira is about as trusting as a puff adder.

CHARLES: You're granite, Ruth—sheer, unyielding granite.

RUTH: And a good deal more dangerous into the bargain.

CHARLES: Dangerous? I never heard anything so ridiculous. How could a poor lonely, wistful little spirit like Elvira be dangerous?

RUTH: Quite easily—and she is. She's beginning to show her hand.

CHARLES: How do you mean—in what way?

RUTH: [*Sits on sofa*] This is a fight, Charles—a bloody battle—a duel to the death between Elvira and me. Don't you realize that?

CHARLES: Melodramatic hysteria.

RUTH: It isn't melodramatic hysteria—it's true. Can't you see?

CHARLES: No, I can't. You're imagining things—jealousy causes people to have the most curious delusions.

RUTH: I am making every effort not to lose my temper with you, Charles, but I must say you are making it increasingly difficult for me.

CHARLES: All this talk of battles and duels—

RUTH: She came here with one purpose and one purpose only—and if you can't see it you're a bigger fool than I thought you.

CHARLES: What purpose could she have had beyond a natural desire to see me again? After all, you must remember that she was extremely attached to me, poor child.

RUTH: Her purpose is perfectly obvious. It is to get you to herself forever.

CHARLES: That's absurd—how could she?

RUTH: By killing you off of course.

CHARLES: Killing me off? You're mad!

RUTH: Why do you suppose Edith fell down the stairs and nearly cracked her skull?

CHARLES: What's Edith got to do with it?

RUTH: Because the whole of the top stair was covered with axle grease. Cook discovered it afterwards.

CHARLES: You're making this up, Ruth—

RUTH: I'm not. I swear I'm not. Why do you suppose when you were lopping that dead branch off the pear tree that the ladder broke? Because it had been practically sawn through on both sides.

CHARLES: But why should she want to kill me? I could understand her wanting to kill you, but why me?

RUTH: If you were dead it would be her final triumph over me. She'd have you with her forever on her damned astral plane and I'd be left high and dry. She's probably planning a sort of spiritual remarriage. I wouldn't put anything past her.

CHARLES: [*Rises. Really shocked*] Ruth!

RUTH: Don't you see now?

CHARLES: [*Walking about the room*] She couldn't be so sly, so wicked—she couldn't.

RUTH: Couldn't she just!

CHARLES: I grant you that as a character she was always rather light and irresponsible but I would never have believed her capable of low cunning—

RUTH: Perhaps the spirit world has deteriorated her.

CHARLES: Oh, Ruth!

RUTH: For heaven's sake stop looking like a wounded spaniel and concentrate—this is serious.

CHARLES: What are we to do?

RUTH: You're not to let her know that we suspect a thing—behave perfectly ordinarily—as though nothing had happened. I'm going to Madame Arcati immediately—I don't care how cross she is she's got to help us—even if she can't get rid of Elvira she must know some technical method of rendering her harmless. If a trance is necessary she shall go into a trance if I have to beat her into it. I'll be back in a half an hour—tell Elvira I've gone to see the Vicar—

CHARLES: This is appalling—

RUTH: Never mind about that—remember now, don't give yourself away by so much as a flick of an eyelid—

[Elvira *comes in from the garden*]

CHARLES: Look out—

RUTH: What?

CHARLES: I merely said it's a nice lookout.

ELVIRA: What's a nice lookout?

CHARLES: The weather, Elvira—the glass is going down and down and down—it's positively macabre.

ELVIRA: I find it difficult to believe that you and Ruth, at this particular moment, can't think of anything more interesting to talk about than the weather.

RUTH: [*Rises*] I can't stand this any more. I really can't.

CHARLES: Ruth dear—please—

ELVIRA: Has she broken out again?

RUTH: What did she say?

CHARLES: She asked if you had broken out again.

RUTH: How dare you talk like that, Elvira!

CHARLES: Now then, Ruth—

RUTH: [*With dignity*] Charles and I were not talking about the weather, Elvira, as you so very shrewdly suspected. I should loathe you to think *that we had any secrets from you* and so I will explain exactly what we were talking about. I was trying to persuade him *not* to drive you into Folkestone this evening. It will be bad for his arm and you can perfectly easily wait until tomorrow. However, as he seems to be determined to place your wishes before mine in everything, I have nothing further to say. I'm sure I hope you both enjoy yourselves. [*She goes out and slams the door*]

CHARLES: There now.

ELVIRA: Oh, Charles—have you been beastly to her?

CHARLES: No—Ruth doesn't like being thwarted any more than you do.

ELVIRA: She's a woman of sterling character. It's a pity she's so unforgiving.

CHARLES: As I told you before—I would rather not discuss Ruth with you—it makes me uncomfortable.

ELVIRA: I won't mention her again. Are you ready?

CHARLES: What for?

ELVIRA: To go to Folkestone of course.

CHARLES: [*Rises from pouffe*] I want a glass of sherry first.

ELVIRA: I don't believe you want to take me at all.

CHARLES: Of course I want to take you, but I still think it would be more sensible to wait until tomorrow—it's a filthy night.

ELVIRA: [*Crossly*] How familiar this is.

CHARLES: In what way familiar?

ELVIRA: All through our married life I only had to suggest something for you immediately to start hedging me off—

CHARLES: I'm not hedging you off, I merely said—

ELVIRA: All right—all right—we'll spend another cosy, intimate evening at home with Ruth sewing away at that hideous table centre and snapping at us like a terrier.

CHARLES: Ruth is perfectly aware that the table centre is hideous. It happens to be a birthday present for her mother—

ELVIRA: It's no use trying to defend Ruth's taste to me—it's thoroughly artsy craftsy and you know it.

CHARLES: It is not artsy craftsy.

ELVIRA: She's ruined this room—look at those curtains and that awful shawl on the piano—

CHARLES: Lady Mackinley sent it to us from Burma.

ELVIRA: Obviously because it had been sent to her from Birmingham.

CHARLES: If you don't behave yourself I shan't take you into Folkestone ever.

ELVIRA: [*Coaxingly*] Please, Charles—don't be elderly and grand with me! Please let's go now.

CHARLES: Not until I've had my sherry.

ELVIRA: You are tiresome, darling—I've been waiting about for hours—

CHARLES: A few more minutes won't make any difference then. [*He pours himself out some sherry*]

ELVIRA: [*Petulantly, flinging herself into a chair*] Oh, very well.

CHARLES: Besides, the car won't be back for a half an hour at least.

ELVIRA: [*Sharply*] What do you mean?

CHARLES: [*Sipping his sherry nonchalantly*] Ruth's taken it—she had to go and see the Vicar—

ELVIRA: [*Jumping up—in extreme agitation*] What!!

CHARLES: What on earth's the matter?

ELVIRA: You say *Ruth's* taken the car?

CHARLES: Yes—to go and see the vicar—but she won't be long.

ELVIRA: [*Wildly*] O, my God! O, my God!

CHARLES: Elvira!—

ELVIRA: Stop her! You must stop her at once—

CHARLES: Why—what for?—

ELVIRA: [*Jumping up and down*] Stop her—go out and stop her immediately!

CHARLES: It's too late now—she's gone already.

ELVIRA: [*Backs away towards window*] Oh! Oh! Oh! Oh!!!

CHARLES: What are you going on like this for? What have you done?

ELVIRA: [*Frightened*] Done?—I haven't done anything—

CHARLES: Elvira—you're lying—

ELVIRA: [*Backing away from him*] I'm not lying. What is there to lie about?

CHARLES: What are you in such a state for?

ELVIRA: [Almost hysterical] I'm not in a state—I don't know what you mean—

CHARLES: You've done something dreadful—

ELVIRA: [Backs away] Don't look at me like that, Charles—I haven't—I swear I haven't—

CHARLES: [Striking his forehead] My God, the car!

ELVIRA: No, Charles—no—

CHARLES: Ruth was right—you did want to kill me—you've done something to the car—

ELVIRA: [Howling like a banshee] Oh—oh—oh—oh!—

CHARLES: What did you do—answer me?

[At this moment the telephone rings. Charles stops dead; then with slow steps goes to it]

CHARLES: [At telephone] Hallo—hallo—yes, speaking—I see—the bridge at the bottom of the hill—thank you. No, I'll come at once— [He slowly puts back the receiver. As he does so the door bursts open]

ELVIRA: [Obviously retreating from someone] Well, of all the filthy, low-down tricks— [She shields her head with her hands and screams] Ow—stop it —Ruth—let go—

[She runs out of the room and slams the door. It opens again immediately and slams again. Charles stares, aghast]

CURTAIN

ACT III. SCENE I.

The time is evening a few days later. Charles is standing before the fire drinking his after-dinner coffee. He is in deep mourning. He finishes his coffee, puts the cup down on the mantelpiece, lights a cigarette and settles himself comfortably in an armchair. He adjusts a reading lamp and with a sigh of well-being opens a novel and begins to read it. There is a ring at the front doorbell. With an exclamation of annoyance he puts down the book, gets up and goes out into the hall. After a moment or so Madame Arcati comes in. Charles follows her and shuts the door. Madame Arcati is wearing the strange, rather barbaric evening clothes that she wore in Act One.

MADAME ARCATI: I hope you will not consider this an intrusion, Mr. Condomine.

CHARLES: Not at all—please sit down, won't you?

MADAME ARCATI: Thank you. [She does so]

CHARLES: Would you like some coffee—or a liqueur?

MADAME ARCATI: No, thank you. I had to come, Mr. Condomine.

CHARLES: [Politely] Yes?

MADAME ARCATI: I felt a tremendous urge—like a rushing wind, and so I hopped on my bike and here I am.

CHARLES: It was very kind of you.

MADAME ARCATI: No, no, no—not kind at all—it was my duty—I know it strongly.

CHARLES: Duty?

MADAME ARCATI: I reproach myself bitterly, you know.

CHARLES: Please don't—there is no necessity for that. [Sits in armchair]

MADAME ARCATI: I allowed myself to get into a huff the other day with your late wife. I rode all the way home in the grip of temper, Mr. Condomine.—I have regretted it ever since.

CHARLES: My dear Madame Arcati . . .

MADAME ARCATI: [Holding up her hand] Please let me go on. Mine is the shame, mine is the blame —I shall never forgive myself. Had I not been so impetuous—had I listened to the cool voice of reason—much might have been averted. . . .

CHARLES: You told my wife distinctly that you were unable to help her—you were perfectly honest. Over and above the original unfortunate mistake I see no reason for you to reproach yourself.

MADAME ARCATI: I threw up the sponge—in a moment of crisis I threw up the sponge instead of throwing down the gauntlet . . .

CHARLES: Whatever you threw, Madame Arcati, I very much fear nothing could have been done—it seems that circumstances have been a little too strong for all of us.

MADAME ARCATI: I cannot bring myself to admit defeat so easily—it is gall and wormwood to me— I could have at least concentrated—made an effort.

CHARLES: Never mind.

MADAME ARCATI: I do mind. I cannot help it. I mind with every fibre of my being. I have been thinking very carefully, I have also been reading up a good deal during the last few dreadful days . . . I gather that we are alone?

CHARLES: [Looking round] My first wife is not in the room, she is upstairs lying down, the funeral exhausted her. I imagine that my second wife is with her but of course I have no way of knowing for certain.

MADAME ARCATI: You have remarked no difference in the texture of your first wife since the accident?

CHARLES: No, she seems much as usual, a little under the weather perhaps, a trifle low-spirited, but that's all.

MADAME ARCATI: Well, that washes that out.

CHARLES: I'm afraid I don't understand.

MADAME ARCATI: Just a little theory I had. In the nineteenth century there was a pretty widespread belief that a ghost who participated in the death of a human being disintegrated automatically—

CHARLES: How do you know that Elvira was in any way responsible for Ruth's death?

MADAME ARCATI: Elvira—such a pretty name—it has a definite lilt to it, hasn't it? [She hums for a moment singing the Elvi-i-ira] Elvira—Elvi-ira . . .

CHARLES: [*Rather agitated*] You haven't answered my question. How did you know?

MADAME ARCATI: It came to me last night, Mr. Condomine—it came to me in a blinding flash—I had just finished my Ovaltine and turned the light out when I suddenly started up in bed with a loud cry—"Great Scott. I've got it!" I said—after that I began to put two and two together. At three in the morning—with my brain fairly seething—I went to work on my crystal for a little but it wasn't very satisfactory—cloudy, you know—

CHARLES: [*Moving about uneasily*] I would be very much obliged if you would keep any theories you have regarding my wife's death to yourself, Madame Arcati . . .

MADAME ARCATI: My one desire is to help you. I feel I have been dreadfully remiss over the whole affair—not only remiss but untidy.

CHARLES: I am afraid there is nothing whatever to be done.

MADAME ARCATI: [*Triumphantly*] But there is—there is! [*She produces a piece of paper from her bag and brandishes it*] I have found a formula—here it is! I copied it out of Edmondson's *Witchcraft and Its Byways.*

CHARLES: [*Irritably*] What the hell are you talking about?

MADAME ARCATI: [*Rises*] Pluck up your heart, Mr. Condomine . . . all is not lost!

CHARLES: [*Rises*] Now look here, Madame Arcati—

MADAME ARCATI: You are still anxious to dematerialize your first wife, I suppose?

CHARLES: [*In a lower voice, with a cautious look towards the door*] Of course I am—I'm perfectly furious with her, but—

MADAME ARCATI: But what?

CHARLES: Well—she's been very upset for the last few days—you see apart from me being angry with her which she always hated even when she was alive, Ruth, my second wife, has hardly left her side for a moment—you must see that she's been having a pretty bad time what with one thing and another . . .

MADAME ARCATI: Your delicacy of feeling does you credit but I must say, if you will forgive my bluntness, that you are a damned fool, Mr. Condomine.

CHARLES: [*Stiffly*] You are at liberty to think whatever you please.

MADAME ARCATI: Now, now, now—don't get on your high horse—there's no sense in that, is there? I have a formula here that I think will be able to get rid of her without hurting her feelings in the least. It's extremely simple and requires nothing more than complete concentration from you and minor trance from me—I may even be able to manage it without lying down.

CHARLES: Honestly I would rather—

[*At this moment the door opens and* Elvira *enters, coming quickly into the room. She is obviously very upset*]

ELVIRA: Charles—

CHARLES: What on earth's the matter?

ELVIRA: [*Seeing* Madame Arcati] Oh! What's she doing here?

CHARLES: She came to offer me her condolences.

ELVIRA: They should have been congratulations.

CHARLES: Please don't say things like that, Elvira—it is in the worst possible taste. Madame Arcati—allow me to introduce my first wife Elvira—

MADAME ARCATI: How do you do?

ELVIRA: What does she want, Charles? Send her away—[*She walks about the room*]

MADAME ARCATI: In what part of the room is she at the moment?

CHARLES: She's moving about rather rapidly. I'll tell you when and where she settles.

ELVIRA: She's the one who got me here in the first place, isn't she?

CHARLES: Yes.

ELVIRA: Well, please tell her to get me away again as soon as possible—I can't stand this house another minute.

CHARLES: Really, Elvira—I'm surprised at you.

ELVIRA: [*Nearly in tears*] I don't care how surprised you are—I want to go home—I'm sick of the whole thing.

CHARLES: Don't be childish, Elvira.

ELVIRA: I'm not being childish—I mean it.

MADAME ARCATI: [*Sniffling*] Very interesting—very interesting—I smell protoplasm strongly!

ELVIRA: What a disgusting thing to say.

MADAME ARCATI: [*Very excited*] Where is she now?

CHARLES: Here—close to me.

MADAME ARCATI: [*Mystically—stretching out her hands*] Are you happy, my dear—?

ELVIRA: [*Stamping her foot*] Tell the silly old bitch to mind her own business.

MADAME ARCATI: [*In a sing-song voice*] Was the journey difficult? Are you weary?

ELVIRA: She's dotty.

CHARLES: Just a moment, Madame Arcati . . .

MADAME ARCATI: [*With her eyes shut*] This is wonderful—wonderful—

ELVIRA: For God's sake tell her to go into the other room, Charles. I've got to talk to you.

CHARLES: Madame Arcati . . .

MADAME ARCATI: Just a moment. I almost have contact—I can sense the vibrations—this is magnificent . . .

CHARLES: Go on, Elvira—don't be a spoilsport—give her a bit of encouragement.

ELVIRA: If you'll promise to get her into the other room.

CHARLES: All right. [Elvira *goes up to* Madame Arcati *and blows gently into her ear*]

MADAME ARCATI: [*Jumping*] Yes, yes—again—again—

ELVIRA: [*Blowing in the other ear behind* Madame Arcati] How's that?

MADAME ARCATI: [*Clasping and unclasping her hands in a frenzy of excitement*] This is first rate—it really is first rate. Absolutely stunning!

CHARLES: I'm so glad you're pleased.

ELVIRA: Please get rid of her. Ruth will be in in a minute.

CHARLES: Madame Arcati, would you think it most frightfully rude if I asked you to go into the dining room for a moment? My first wife wishes to speak to me alone.

MADAME ARCATI: Oh, must I? It's so lovely being actually in the room with her.

CHARLES: Only for a few minutes—I promise she'll be here when you come back.

MADAME ARCATI: Very well. Hand me my bag, will you?—it's on the sofa.

ELVIRA: [*Picking it up and handing it to her*] Here you are.

MADAME ARCATI: [*Taking it and blowing her a kiss*] Oh, you darling—you little darling. [Madame Arcati, *humming ecstatically, goes into the dining-room and shuts the door*]

ELVIRA: How good is she really?

CHARLES: I don't know.

ELVIRA: Do you think she really could get me back again?

CHARLES: But my dear child . . .

ELVIRA: And don't call me your dear child—it's smug and supercilious.

CHARLES: There's no need to be rude.

ELVIRA: [*Turning away*] The whole thing's been a failure—a miserable, dreary failure—and oh! what *high hopes* I started out with.

CHARLES: You can't expect much sympathy from me, you know. I am perfectly aware that your highest hope was to murder me.

ELVIRA: Don't put it like that, it sounds so beastly.

CHARLES: It is beastly. It's one of the beastliest ideas I've ever heard.

ELVIRA: There was a time when you'd have welcomed the chance of being with me forever.

CHARLES: Your behaviour has shocked me immeasurably, Elvira, I had no idea you were so unscrupulous.

ELVIRA: [*Bursting into tears*] Oh, Charles.

CHARLES: Stop crying.

ELVIRA: They're only ghost tears—they don't mean anything really—but they're very painful.

CHARLES: You've brought all this on yourself, you know. [*Sits on sofa*]

ELVIRA: That's right—rub it in. Anyhow, it was only because I loved you—the silliest thing I ever did in my whole life was to love you—you were always unworthy of me.

CHARLES: That remark comes perilously near impertinence, Elvira.

ELVIRA: I sat there, on the other side, just longing for you day after day. I did really—all through your affair with that brassy-looking woman in the South of France I went on loving you and thinking truly of you—then you married Ruth and even then I forgave you and tried to understand because all the time I believed deep inside that you really loved me best . . . that's why I put myself down for a return visit and had to fill in all those forms and wait about in draughty passages for hours—if only you'd died before you met Ruth everything might have been all right—she's absolutely ruined you—I hadn't been in the house a day before I realized that. Your books aren't a quarter as good as they used to be either.

CHARLES: [*Incensed. Rises*] That is entirely untrue . . . Ruth helped me and encouraged me with my work which is a damned sight more than you ever did.

ELVIRA: That's probably what's wrong with it.

CHARLES: All you ever thought of was going to parties and enjoying yourself.

ELVIRA: Why shouldn't I have fun? I died young, didn't I?

CHARLES: You needn't have died at all if you hadn't been idiotic enough to go out on the river with Guy Henderson and get soaked to the skin—

ELVIRA: So we're back at Guy Henderson again, are we?

CHARLES: You behaved abominably over Guy Henderson and it's no use pretending that you didn't.

ELVIRA: [*Sits on arm of chair*] Guy adored me—and anyhow he was very attractive.

CHARLES: You told me distinctly that he didn't attract you in the least.

ELVIRA: You'd have gone through the roof if I'd told you that he did.

CHARLES: Did you have an affair with Guy Henderson?

ELVIRA: I would rather not discuss it if you don't mind.

CHARLES: Answer me—did you or didn't you?

ELVIRA: Of course I didn't.

CHARLES: You let him kiss you though, didn't you?

ELVIRA: How could I stop him? He was bigger than I was.

CHARLES: [*Furiously*] And you swore to me—

ELVIRA: Of course I did. You were always making scenes over nothing at all.

CHARLES: Nothing at all.

ELVIRA: You never loved me a bit really—it was only your beastly vanity.

CHARLES: You seriously believe that it was only vanity that upset me when you went out in the punt with Guy Henderson?

ELVIRA: It was not a punt—it was a little launch.

CHARLES: I don't care if it was a three-masted schooner you had no right to go!

ELVIRA: You seem to forget *why* I went! You seem to forget that you had spent the entire evening making sheep's eyes at that overblown looking harridan with the false pearls.

CHARLES: A woman in Cynthia Cheviot's position would hardly wear false pearls.

ELVIRA: They were practically all she was wearing.

CHARLES: I am pained to observe that seven years in the echoing vaults of eternity have in no way impaired your native vulgarity.

ELVIRA: That was the remark of a pompous ass.

CHARLES: There is nothing to be gained by continuing this discussion.

ELVIRA: You always used to say that when you were thoroughly worsted.

CHARLES: On looking back on our married years, Elvira, I see now, with horrid clarity, that they were nothing but a mockery.

ELVIRA: You invite mockery, Charles—it's something to do with your personality, I think, a certain seedy grandeur.

CHARLES: Once and for all, Elvira—

ELVIRA: You never suspected it but I laughed at you steadily from the altar to the grave—all your ridiculous petty jealousies and your fussings and fumings—

CHARLES: You were feckless and irresponsible and morally unstable—I realized that before we left Budleigh Salterton.

ELVIRA: Nobody but a monumental bore would have thought of having a honeymoon at Budleigh Salterton.

CHARLES: What's the matter with Budleigh Salterton?

ELVIRA: I was an eager young bride, Charles—I wanted glamour and music and romance—all I got was potted palms, seven hours of every day on a damp golf course and a three-piece orchestra playing "Merrie England."

CHARLES: It's a pity you didn't tell me so at the time.

ELVIRA: I did—but you wouldn't listen—that's why I went out on the moors that day with Captain Bracegirdle. I was desperate.

CHARLES: You swore to me that you'd gone over to see your aunt in Exmouth!

ELVIRA: It was the moors.

CHARLES: With Captain Bracegirdle?

ELVIRA: With Captain Bracegirdle.

CHARLES: [Furiously] I might have known it—what a fool I was—what a blind fool! Did he make love to you?

ELVIRA: [Sucking her finger and regarding it thoughtfully] Of course.

CHARLES: Oh, Elvira!

ELVIRA: Only very discreetly—he was in the cavalry, you know—

CHARLES: Well, all I can say is that I'm well rid of you.

ELVIRA: Unfortunately you're not.

CHARLES: Oh yes, I am—you're dead and Ruth's dead—I shall sell this house lock, stock and barrel and go away.

ELVIRA: I shall follow you.

CHARLES: I shall go a long way away—I shall go to South America—you'll hate that, you were always a bad traveller.

ELVIRA: [At piano] That can't be helped—I shall have to follow you—you called me back.

CHARLES: I did not call you back!

ELVIRA: Well somebody did—and it's hardly likely to have been Ruth.

CHARLES: Nothing in the world was further from my thoughts.

ELVIRA: You were talking about me before dinner that evening.

CHARLES: I might just as easily have been talking about Joan of Arc but that wouldn't necessarily mean that I wanted her to come and live with me.

ELVIRA: As a matter of fact she's rather fun.

CHARLES: Stick to the point.

ELVIRA: When I think of what might have happened if I'd succeeded in getting you to the other world after all—it makes me shudder, it does honestly . . . it would be nothing but bickering and squabbling forever and ever and ever . . . I swear I'll be better off with Ruth—at least she'll find her own set and not get in my way.

CHARLES: So I get in your way, do I?

ELVIRA: Only because I was idiotic enough to imagine that you loved me, and I sort of felt sorry for you.

CHARLES: I'm sick of these insults—please go away.

ELVIRA: There's nothing I should like better—I've always believed in cutting my losses. That's why I died.

CHARLES: [Rises] Of all the brazen sophistry—

ELVIRA: Call that old girl in again—set her to work—I won't tolerate this any longer—I want to go home. [She starts to cry]

CHARLES: For heaven's sake don't snivel.

ELVIRA: [Stamping her foot] Call her in—she's got to get me out of this.

CHARLES: [Going to the dining-room door] I quite agree—and the sooner the better. [He opens the door] Madame Arcati—would you please come in now?

[Madame Arcati comes in eagerly]

MADAME ARCATI: Is the darling still here?

CHARLES: [Grimly] Yes, she is.

MADAME ARCATI: Where—tell me where?

CHARLES: Over by the piano—blowing her nose.

MADAME ARCATI: [Approaching the piano] My dear—oh, my dear—

ELVIRA: Stop her fawning on me, Charles, or I shall break something.

CHARLES: Elvira and I have discussed the whole situation, Madame Arcati, and she wishes to go home immediately.

MADAME ARCATI: Home?

CHARLES: Wherever she came from.

MADAME ARCATI: You don't think she would like to stay a few days longer—while I try to get things a little more organized?

ELVIRA: No—no—I want to go now.

MADAME ARCATI: I could come and be here with her—I could bring my crystal—

ELVIRA: God forbid!

CHARLES: We are both agreed that she must go as soon as possible. Please strain every nerve, Madame Arcati—make every effort—you said something about a formula—what is it?

MADAME ARCATI: [Reluctantly] Well—if you insist.

CHARLES: I most emphatically do insist.

ELVIRA: [Wailing] Oh, Charles. . . .

CHARLES: Shut up.

MADAME ARCATI: I can't guarantee anything, you know—I'll do my best but it may not work.

CHARLES: What is the formula?

MADAME ARCATI: Nothing more than a little verse really—it fell into disuse after the seventeenth century—I shall need some pepper and salt—

CHARLES: There's pepper and salt in the dining-room—I'll get it. [He goes]

MADAME ARCATI: We ought of course to have some Shepherd's Wort and a frog or two but I think I can manage without. You won't be frightened, dear, will you? It's absolutely painless.

CHARLES: [Coming back with the cruet] Will this be enough?

MADAME ARCATI: Oh yes—I only need a little—put it on the table please. Now then, let me see—[She fumbles in her bag for the paper and her glasses] Ah yes—[To Charles] Sprinkle it, will you—just a soupçon—there, right in the middle—[Charles does so]

ELVIRA: This is going to be a flop—I can tell you that here and now.

MADAME ARCATI: Now a few snapdragons out of that vase, there's a good chap.

ELVIRA: [Contemptuously] Merlin does all this sort of thing at parties and bores us all stiff with it, only he always uses blackthorn and a great deal of whimsy!

CHARLES: Here you are.

MADAME ARCATI: Now then—the gramophone—in the old days of course they used a zither or reed pipes—[She goes to the gramophone] We'd better have the same record we had before, I think.

ELVIRA: I'll get it. [She takes out the record and puts it on the gramophone]

MADAME ARCATI: [Watching, fascinated] Oh, if only that Mr. Emsworth of the Psychical Research Society could see this—he'd have a fit, he would really! Don't start it yet, dear. Now then—[Charles gets piano chair and brings it down to table] Sit down, please, Mr. Condomine, rest your hands on the table but don't put your fingers in the pepper —I shall turn out the lights myself. Oh, shucks, I'd

nearly forgotten—[She goes to the table and makes designs in the sprinkled pepper and salt with her forefinger] One triangle—[She consults the paper] One half circle and one little dot—there!

ELVIRA: This is waste of time—she's a complete fake.

CHARLES: Anything's worth trying.

ELVIRA: I'm as eager for it to succeed as you are —don't make any mistake about that. But I'll lay you ten to one it's a dead failure.

MADAME ARCATI: Now, if your wife would be kind enough to lie down on the sofa—

CHARLES: Go on, Elvira.

ELVIRA: [Lies down on sofa] This is sheer nonsense—don't blame me if I get the giggles.

CHARLES: Concentrate—think of nothing.

MADAME ARCATI: That's right—quite right—hands at the sides—legs extended—breathe steadily—one two—one two—one two—is she comfortable?

CHARLES: Are you comfortable, Elvira?

ELVIRA: No.

CHARLES: She's quite comfortable.

MADAME ARCATI: I shall join you in a moment, Mr. Condomine—I may have to go into a slight trance but if I do pay no attention—Now first the music and away we go! [Madame Arcati turns on the gramophone and stands quite still by the side of it with her hands behind her head for a little— then suddenly, with great swiftness, she runs to the door and switches out the lights. Her form can dimly be discerned moving about in the darkness. Charles gives a loud sneeze]

ELVIRA: [Giggling] Oh, dear—it's the pepper.

CHARLES: Damn!

MADAME ARCATI: Hold on to yourself—concentrate—[Madame Arcati recites in a sing-song voice]
"Ghostly spectre—ghoul or fiend
Never more be thou convened
Shepherd's Wort and Holy Rite
Banish thee into the night."

ELVIRA: What a disagreeable little verse.

CHARLES: Be quiet, Elvira.

MADAME ARCATI: Shhh! [There is silence] Is there anyone there? . . . Is there anyone there?—one rap for yes—two raps for no. Is there anyone there? . . . [The table gives a loud bump] Aha! Good stuff! Is it Daphne? . . . [The table gives another bump] I'm sorry to bother you, dear, but Mrs. Condomine wants to return. [The table bumps several times very quickly] Now then, Daphne . . . Did you hear what I said? [After a pause the table gives one bump] Can you help us? . . . [There is another pause, then the table begins to bump violently without stopping] Hold tight, Mr. Condomine —it's trying to break away. Oh! Oh! Oh— [The table falls over with a crash]

CHARLES: What's the matter, Madame Arcati? Are you hurt?

MADAME ARCATI: [Wailing] Oh! Oh! Oh—

CHARLES: [Turns on lights] What on earth's happening? [*Madame Arcati is lying on the floor with the table upside down on her back.* Charles *hurriedly lifts it off. Shaking her*] Are you hurt, Madame Arcati?

ELVIRA: She's in one of her damned trances again and I'm here as much as ever I was.

CHARLES: [*Shaking* Madame Arcati] For God's sake wake up.

MADAME ARCATI: [*Moaning*] Oh! Oh! Oh—

ELVIRA: Leave her alone—she's having a whale of a time. If I ever do get back I'll strangle that bloody little Daphne. . . .

CHARLES: Wake up!

MADAME ARCATI: [*Sitting up suddenly*] What happened?

CHARLES: Nothing—nothing at all.

MADAME ARCATI: [*Rising and dusting herself*] Oh yes, it did—I know something happened.

CHARLES: You fell over—that's all that happened.

MADAME ARCATI: Is she still here?

CHARLES: Of course she is.

MADAME ARCATI: Something must have gone wrong.

ELVIRA: Make her do it properly. I'm sick of being messed about like this.

CHARLES: She's doing her best. Be quiet, Elvira.

MADAME ARCATI: Something happened—I sensed it in my trance—I felt it—it shivered through me.

[*Suddenly the window curtains blow out almost straight and* Ruth *walks into the room. She is still wearing the brightly colored clothes in which we last saw her but now they are entirely grey. So is her hair and her skin*]

RUTH: Once and for all, Charles, what the hell does this mean?

THE LIGHTS FADE

SCENE II.

When the lights go up again several hours have elapsed. The whole room is in slight disarray. There are birch branches and evergreens laid on the floor in front of the doors and crossed birch branches pinned rather untidily onto the curtains. The furniture has been moved about a bit. On the bridge table there is a pile of playing cards, Madame Arcati's *crystal and a Ouija board. Also a plate of sandwiches and two empty beer mugs.* Madame Arcati *is stretched out on the sofa with her eyes shut.* Elvira *is seated at the bridge table looking despondently at the debris.* Ruth *is by the fireplace.* Charles *is walking irritably about the room.*

RUTH: Well—we've done all we can—I must say I couldn't be more exhausted.

ELVIRA: It will be daylight soon. [*The clock strikes five, very slowly*]

RUTH: That clock's always irritated me—it strikes far too slowly.

CHARLES: It was a wedding present from Uncle Walter.

RUTH: Whose Uncle Walter?

CHARLES: Elvira's.

RUTH: Well, all I can say is he might have chosen something a little more decorative.

ELVIRA: If that really were all you could say, Ruth, I'm sure it would be a great comfort to us all.

RUTH: [*Grandly*] You can be as rude as you like, Elvira, I don't mind a bit—as a matter of fact I should be extremely surprised if you weren't.

ELVIRA: [*Truculently*] Why?

RUTH: The reply to that is really too obvious.

CHARLES: I wish you two would stop bickering for one minute.

RUTH: This is quite definitely one of the most frustrating nights I have ever spent.

ELVIRA: The reply to that is pretty obvious too.

RUTH: I'm sure I don't know what you mean.

ELVIRA: Skip it.

RUTH: Now listen to me, Elvira. If you and I have got to stay together indefinitely in this house—and it looks unpleasantly—[*Turns to* Madame Arcati] —likely—we had better come to some sort of an arrangement.

ELVIRA: What sort of an arrangement?

CHARLES: You're *not* going to stay indefinitely in this house.

RUTH: With you then—we shall have to be with you.

CHARLES: I don't see why—why don't you take a cottage somewhere?

RUTH: You called us back.

CHARLES: I've already explained until I'm black in the face that I did nothing of the sort.

RUTH: Madame Arcati said you did.

CHARLES: Madame Arcati's a muddling old fool.

ELVIRA: I could have told you that in the first place.

RUTH: I think you're behaving very shabbily, Charles.

CHARLES: I don't see what I've done.

RUTH: We have all agreed that as Elvira and I are dead that it would be both right and proper for us to dematerialize again as soon as possible. That, I admit. We have allowed ourselves to be subjected to the most humiliating hocus-pocus for hours and hours without complaining—

CHARLES: Without complaining?

RUTH: We've stood up—we've lain down—we've concentrated. We've sat interminably while that tiresome old woman recited extremely unflattering verses at us. We've endured five séances—we've watched her fling herself in and out of trances until we're dizzy and at the end of it all we find ourselves exactly where we were at the beginning. . . .

CHARLES: Well, it's not my fault.

RUTH: Be that as it may, the least you could do is

to admit failure gracefully and try to make the best of it—your manners are boorish to a degree.

CHARLES: I'm just as exhausted as you are. I've had to do all the damned table tapping, remember.

RUTH: If she can't get us back, she can't and that's that. We shall have to think of something else.

CHARLES: She *must* get you back—anything else is unthinkable.

ELVIRA: There's gratitude for you!

CHARLES: Gratitude?

ELVIRA: Yes, for all the years we've both devoted to you—you ought to be ashamed.

CHARLES: What about all the years I've devoted to you?

ELVIRA: Nonsense—we've waited on you hand and foot—haven't we, Ruth? You're exceedingly selfish and always were.

CHARLES: In that case I fail to see why you were both so anxious to get back to me.

RUTH: You called us back. And you've done nothing but try to get rid of us ever since we came —hasn't he, Elvira?

ELVIRA: He certainly has.

RUTH: And now, owing to your idiotic ineffi- ciency, we find ourselves in the most mortifying position—we're neither fish, flesh nor fowl nor what- ever it is.

ELVIRA: Good red herring.

RUTH: It can't be.

CHARLES: Well, why don't you do something about it? Why don't you go back on your own?

RUTH: We can't—you know perfectly well we can't.

CHARLES: Isn't there anybody on the other side who can help?

RUTH: How do I know? I've only been there a few days . . . ask Elvira.

ELVIRA: I've already told you, that's no good— if we got Cagliostro, Mesmer, Merlin, Gil de Retz and the Black Douglas in a row they couldn't do a thing—the impetus has got to come from here. . . . Perhaps darling Charles doesn't want us to go quite enough.

CHARLES: I certainly do.

ELVIRA: Well, you must have a very weak will then. I always suspected it.

RUTH: It's no use arguing any more—wake up Madame Arcati.

ELVIRA: Oh, not another séance—please, not an- other séance!

CHARLES: [Loudly—bending over Madame Arcati] Please wake up, Madame Arcati . . .

RUTH: Shake her.

CHARLES: It might upset her.

RUTH: I don't care if it kills her.

CHARLES: Please wake up, Madame Arcati. . . .

MADAME ARCATI: [Waking] What time is it?

CHARLES: Ten past five!

MADAME ARCATI: What time did I go off? [She sits up]

CHARLES: Over an hour ago.

MADAME ARCATI: [Reaching for her bag] Curious . . . very curious. Forgive me for a moment, I must just make a note of that for my diary. [She takes a book out of her bag and scribbles in it] Are they still here?

CHARLES: Yes.

MADAME ARCATI: How disappointing.

CHARLES: Have you any suggestions?

MADAME ARCATI: [Rising briskly] We mustn't give up hope. Chin up—never give in—that's my motto.

RUTH: This schoolgirl phraseology's driving me mad.

MADAME ARCATI: Now then . . .

CHARLES: Now then what?

MADAME ARCATI: What do you say we have an- other séance and really put our shoulders to the wheel?—Make it a real rouser!

ELVIRA: For God's sake not another séance.

MADAME ARCATI: I might be able to materialize a trumpet if I tried hard enough—better than nothing, you know—I feel as fit as a fiddle after my rest.

ELVIRA: I don't care if she materializes a whole symphony orchestra—I implore you not to let her have another séance.

CHARLES: Don't you think, Madame Arcati, that perhaps we've had enough séances? After all they haven't achieved much, have they?

MADAME ARCATI: Rome wasn't built in a day, you know.

CHARLES: I know it wasn't, but. . . .

MADAME ARCATI: Well then—cheer up—away with melancholy.

CHARLES: Now listen, Madame Arcati . . . be- fore you go off into any further trances I really think we ought to discuss the situation a little.

MADAME ARCATI: Good—an excellent idea—and while we're doing it I shall have another of these delicious sandwiches—I'm as hungry as a hunter.

CHARLES: Would you like some more beer?

MADAME ARCATI: No, thank you—better not.

CHARLES: Very well—I think I'll have a small whisky and soda.

MADAME ARCATI: Make it a double and enjoy yourself.

[Charles goes to the drinks table and mixes himself a whisky and soda]

RUTH: One day I intend to give myself the pleas- ure of telling Madame Arcati exactly what I think of her.

CHARLES: She's been doing her best.

MADAME ARCATI: Are the girls getting despondent?

CHARLES: I'm afraid they are *rather*.

MADAME ARCATI: We'll win through yet—don't be downhearted.

RUTH: If we're not very careful she'll materialize a hockey team.

MADAME ARCATI: Now then, Mr. Condomine— the discussion—fire away.

CHARLES: Well, my wives and I have been talking

it over and they are both absolutely convinced that I somehow or other called them back.

MADAME ARCATI: Very natural.

CHARLES: I am equally convinced that I did not.

MADAME ARCATI: Love is a strong psychic force, Mr. Condomine—it can work untold miracles. A true love call can encompass the universe—

CHARLES: [Hastily] I'm sure it can, but I must confess to you frankly that although my affection for both Elvira and Ruth is of the warmest I cannot truthfully feel that it would come under the heading that you describe.

ELVIRA: I should just think not indeed.

MADAME ARCATI: You may not know your own strength, Mr. Condomine.

CHARLES: [Firmly] I did not call them back—either consciously or subconsciously.

MADAME ARCATI: But, Mr. Condomine . . .

CHARLES: That is my final word on the subject.

MADAME ARCATI: Neither of them could have appeared unless there had been somebody—a psychic subject—in the house, who wished for them . . .

CHARLES: Well, it wasn't me.

ELVIRA: Perhaps it was Doctor Bradman—I never knew he cared.

MADAME ARCATI: Are you sure?—Are you really sure?

CHARLES: Absolutely positive.

MADAME ARCATI: [Snapping her fingers] Great Scott, I believe we've been barking up the wrong tree!

CHARLES: How do you mean?

MADAME ARCATI: The Sudbury case!

CHARLES: I don't understand.

MADAME ARCATI: There's no reason why you should—it was before your day—I wonder—oh, I wonder. . . .

CHARLES: What was the Sudbury case? I wish you'd explain.

MADAME ARCATI: It was the case that made me famous, Mr. Condomine—it was what you might describe in theatrical parlance as my first smash hit! I had letters from all over the world about it—especially India.

CHARLES: What did you do?

MADAME ARCATI: I dematerialized old Lady Sudbury after she'd been firmly entrenched in the private chapel for over seventeen years.

CHARLES: [Rises] How?—Can't you remember how?

MADAME ARCATI: Chance—a fluke—I happened on it by the merest coincidence.

CHARLES: What fluke—what was it?

MADAME ARCATI: Wait—all in good time. [She begins to walk about the room] Now let me see—who was in the house during our first séance?

CHARLES: Only the Bradmans, Ruth and me and yourself.

MADAME ARCATI: Ah, yes—yes—to be sure—but the Bradmans weren't here last night, were they?

CHARLES: No.

MADAME ARCATI: Quickly . . . my crystal—

CHARLES: [Handing it to her] Here. . . .

MADAME ARCATI: [Shaking it crossly] Damn the thing, it's cloudy again—[She looks again] Ah!—that's better—it's there again—it's there again—I'm beginning to understand.

CHARLES: I wish I was. What's there again?

MADAME ARCATI: A bandage—a white bandage—hold on to a white bandage. . . .

CHARLES: I haven't got a white bandage.

MADAME ARCATI: Shhh! [She puts the crystal down and stands silent for a moment]

ELVIRA: She's too good, you know—she ought to be in a circus.

[Madame Arcati advances to the middle of the room and raises her arms slowly—she begins to intone]

MADAME ARCATI:
Be you in nook or cranny answer me
Do you in Still-room or closet answer me
Do you behind the panel, above the stairs
Beneath the eaves—waking or sleeping
Answer me!

That ought to do it or I'm a Dutchman.

CHARLES: Do what?

MADAME ARCATI: Hush—wait— [She picks up one of the birch branches and waves it solemnly to and fro]

RUTH: For God's sake don't let her throw any more of that garlic about. It nearly made me sick last time.

CHARLES: Would you like the gramophone on or the lights out or anything?

MADAME ARCATI: No, no—it's near—it's very near—

ELVIRA: If it's a ghost I shall scream.

RUTH: I hope it's nobody we know—I shall feel so silly.

[Suddenly the door opens and Edith comes into the room. She is wearing a pink flannel dressing gown and bedroom slippers. Her head is bandaged]

EDITH: Did you ring, sir?

MADAME ARCATI: The bandage! The white bandage!

CHARLES: No, Edith.

EDITH: I'm sorry, sir—I could have sworn I heard the bell—or somebody calling—I was asleep—I don't rightly know which it was. . . .

MADAME ARCATI: Come here, child.

EDITH: Oh! [She looks anxiously at Charles]

CHARLES: Go on—go to Madame Arcati—it's quite all right.

MADAME ARCATI: Who do you see in this room, child?

EDITH: Oh, dear. . . .

MADAME ARCATI: Answer please.

EDITH: [Falteringly] You; madame—[She stops]

MADAME ARCATI: Go on.

EDITH: The Master.

MADAME ARCATI: Anyone else?

EDITH: Oh no, madame. . . .

MADAME ARCATI: [*Inflexibly*] Look again.

EDITH: [*Imploringly, to* Charles] I don't understand, sir—I—

MADAME ARCATI: Come, child—don't beat about the bush—look again.

    [Elvira *begins to move about the room almost as though she were being pulled.* Edith *follows with her eyes*]

RUTH: Do concentrate, Elvira, and keep still.

ELVIRA: I can't.

MADAME ARCATI: Do you see anyone else now?

EDITH: [*Slyly*] Oh no, madame.

MADAME ARCATI: She's lying.

EDITH: Oh, madame!

MADAME ARCATI: They always do.

CHARLES: They? .

MADAME ARCATI: [*Sharply*] Where are they now?

EDITH: By the fireplace. Oh!

CHARLES: She can see them—do you mean she can see them?

MADAME ARCATI: Probably not very clearly—but enough—

EDITH: [*Bursting into tears*] Let me go—I haven't done nothing nor seen nobody—let me go back to bed.

MADAME ARCATI: Give her a sandwich.

EDITH: [*Drawing away*] I don't want a sandwich. I want to go back to bed. . . .

CHARLES: [*Handing* Edith *the plate*] Here, Edith.

MADAME ARCATI: Nonsense—a big healthy girl like you saying no to a delicious sandwich—I never heard of such a thing—sit down.

EDITH: [*To* Charles] Please, sir, I . . .

CHARLES: Please do as Madame Arcati says, Edith.

EDITH: [*Sitting down and sniffing*] I haven't done nothing wrong.

CHARLES: It's all right—nobody said you had.

RUTH: If she's been the cause of all this unpleasantness I'll give her a week's notice tomorrow.

ELVIRA: You may not be here tomorrow—

MADAME ARCATI: Look at me, Edith. [Edith *obediently does so*] Cuckoo—cuckoo—cuckoo—

EDITH: [*Jumping*] Oh, dear—what's the matter with her? Is she barmy?

MADAME ARCATI: Here, Edith—this is my finger—look—[*She waggles it*] Have you ever seen such a long, long, long finger? Look now it's on the right—now it's on the left—backwards and forwards it goes—see—very quietly backwards and forwards—tic-toc—tic—toc—tic-toc.

ELVIRA: The mouse ran up the clock.

RUTH: Be quiet—*you'll* ruin everything.

    [Madame Arcati *whistles a little tune close to* Edith's *face—then she snaps her fingers.* Edith *looks stolidly in front of her without flinching.* Madame Arcati *stands back*]

MADAME ARCATI: Well—so far so good—she's off all right.

CHARLES: Off?

MADAME ARCATI: She's a Natural—just the same as the Sudbury case—it really is the most amusing coincidence. Now then—would you ask your wives to stand close together please?

CHARLES: Where?

MADAME ARCATI: Over there by you.

CHARLES: Elvira—Ruth—

RUTH: I resent being ordered about like this.

ELVIRA: I don't like this at all—I don't like any of it—I feel peculiar.

CHARLES: I'm afraid I must insist.

ELVIRA: It would serve you right if we flatly refused to do anything at all.

MADAME ARCATI: Are you sorry for having been so mischievous, Edith?

EDITH: [*Cheerfully*] Oh yes, madame.

MADAME ARCATI: You know what you have to do now, don't you, Edith?

EDITH: Oh yes, madame.

RUTH: I believe it's going to work whatever it is. Oh, Charles.

CHARLES: Shhh!

RUTH: This is good-bye, Charles.

ELVIRA: Tell her to stop for a minute—there's something I want to say before I go.

CHARLES: You should have thought of that before—it's too late now.

ELVIRA: Of all the mean, ungracious—

RUTH: Charles, listen a moment . . .

MADAME ARCATI: [*In a shrill voice*] Lights! [Madame Arcati *rushes to the door and switches off the lights. In the dark* Edith *is singing "Always" in a very high cockney voice*]

ELVIRA: [*In the dark*] I saw Captain Bracegirdle again, Charles—several times—I went to the Four Hundred with him twice when you were in Nottingham. And I must say I couldn't have enjoyed it more.

RUTH: Don't think you're getting rid of us quite so easily, my dear—you may not be able to see us but we shall be here all right—I consider that you have behaved atrociously over the whole miserable business. And I should like to say here and now—[*Her voice fades into a whisper and then disappears altogether*]

MADAME ARCATI: [*Exultantly*] Splendid! Hurrah! We've done it! That's quite enough singing for the moment, Edith.

CHARLES: [*After a pause*] Shall I put on the lights?

MADAME ARCATI: No—I will.

    [Charles *pulls the curtains and daylight floods into the room.* Ruth *and* Elvira *have disappeared.* Edith *is still sitting on the chair*]

CHARLES: They've gone—they've really gone.

MADAME ARCATI: Yes—I think we've really pulled it off this time.

CHARLES: You'd better wake her up, hadn't you? She might bring them back again.

MADAME ARCATI: [Clapping her hands in Edith's face] Wake up, child!

EDITH: [Nearly jumping out of the chair] Good 'eavens! Where am I?

CHARLES: It's all right, Edith—you can go back to bed now.

EDITH: Why, it's morning.

CHARLES: Yes—I know it is.

EDITH: But I was in bed—how did I get down 'ere?

CHARLES: I rang, Edith—I rang the bell and you answered it—didn't I, Madame Arcati?

EDITH: Did I drop off? Do you think it's my concussion again? Oh, dear!

CHARLES: Off you go, Edith, and thank you very much. [He presses a pound note into her hand] Thank you very much indeed.

EDITH: Oh, sir, whatever for? [She looks at him in sudden horror] Oh, sir!! [She bolts from the room]

CHARLES: [Surprised] What on earth did she mean by that?

MADAME ARCATI: Golly, what a night! I'm ready to drop in my tracks.

CHARLES: Would you like to stay here?—there's the spare room, you know.

MADAME ARCATI: No, thank you—each to his own nest—I'll pedal home in a jiffy—it's only seven miles.

CHARLES: I'm deeply grateful to you, Madame Arcati. I don't know what arrangements you generally make but I trust you will send in your account in due course.

MADAME ARCATI: Good heavens, Mr. Condomine —it was a pleasure—I wouldn't dream of such a thing.

CHARLES: But really I feel that all those trances. . . .

MADAME ARCATI: I enjoy them, Mr. Condomine, thoroughly. I always have since a child.

CHARLES: Perhaps you'd give me the pleasure of lunching with me one day soon?

MADAME ARCATI: When you come back—I should be delighted.

CHARLES: Come back?

MADAME ARCATI: [Lowering her voice] Take my advice, Mr. Condomine, and go away immediately.

CHARLES: But, Madame Arcati! You don't mean that . . . ?

MADAME ARCATI: [Clearing her stuff from table] This must be an unhappy house for you—there must be memories both grave and gay in every corner of it—also—[She pauses]

CHARLES: Also what?

MADAME ARCATI: [Thinking better of it] There are more things in heaven and earth, Mr. Condomine. [She places her finger to her lips] Just go—pack your traps and go as soon as possible.

CHARLES: [Also in lowered tones] Do you mean that they may still be here?

MADAME ARCATI: [She nods and then nonchalantly whistles a little tune] Quien sabe, as the Spanish say. [She collects her bag and her crystal]

CHARLES: [Looking furtively round the room] I wonder—I wonder. I'll follow your advice, Madame Arcati. Thank you again.

MADAME ARCATI: Well, good-bye, Mr. Condomine —it's been fascinating—from first to last—fascinating. Do you mind if I take just one more sandwich to munch on my way home? [Comes down to table for sandwich]

CHARLES: By all means.

[Madame Arcati goes to the door. Charles follows her to see her safely out]

MADAME ARCATI: [As they go] Don't trouble—I can find my way. Cheerio once more and good hunting!

[Charles watches her into the hall and then comes back into the room. He prowls about for a moment as though he were not sure that he was alone]

CHARLES: [Softly] Ruth—Elvira—are you there? [A pause] Ruth—Elvira—I know damn well you're there—[Another pause] I just want to tell you that I'm going away so there's no point in your hanging about any longer—I'm going a long way away— somewhere where I don't believe you'll be able to follow me. In spite of what Elvira said I don't think spirits can travel over water. Is that quite clear, my darlings? You said in one of your more acid moments, Ruth, that I had been hag-ridden all my life! How right you were—but now I'm free, Ruth dear, not only of Mother and Elvira and Mrs. Winthrop-Lewellyn, but free of you too, and I should like to take this farewell opportunity of saying I'm enjoying it immensely—[A vase crashes into the fireplace] Aha—I thought so—you were very silly, Elvira, to imagine that I didn't know all about you and Captain Bracegirdle—I did. But what you didn't know was that I was extremely attached to Paula Westlake at the time! [The clock strikes sixteen viciously and very quickly] I was reasonably faithful to you, Ruth, but I doubt if it would have lasted much longer—you were becoming increasingly domineering, you know, and there's nothing more off putting than that, is there? [A large picture falls down with a crash] Good-bye for the moment, my dears. I expect we are bound to meet again one day, but until we do I'm going to enjoy myself as I've never enjoyed myself before. You can break up the house as much as you like—I'm leaving it anyhow. Think kindly of me and send out good thoughts —[The overmantel begins to shake and tremble as though someone were tugging at it] Nice work, Elvira—persevere. Good-bye again—parting is such sweet sorrow! [He goes out of the room just as the overmantel crashes to the floor and the curtain pole comes tumbling down]

CURTAIN

Modern American Drama

Modern American Drama

The American theatre was the last theatre of major proportions to come of age. *A Doll's House* was nearly forty years old when O'Neill's first short plays were written. Ibsen, Strindberg, Becque, and Chekhov were dead. Shaw had been writing plays for nearly three decades. Realism and naturalism had already triumphed in Europe and in England, and the symbolists had established the claims of imagination and poetry in the theatre. When, after the conclusion of the First World War, the American drama attained its maturity, Europe had already taken the major steps in the modern theatre. As a matter of fact, across the Atlantic new theatrical movements in the drama were again beginning to teem, and one of these, using the name "expressionism," was exciting interest with its turbulent writing and esoteric explosions; the latest modernists were now the German dramatists Georg Kaiser and Ernst Toller and the Czech Karel Capek.

When playwriting and stagecraft in America became permeated with the modern spirit, the result was a fusion of dramatic elements. Writers and stage directors helped themselves to anything that happened to suit their interests. In some of his work, Eugene O'Neill, for example, was a realist or naturalist, but with poetic overtones. In *The Emperor Jones* and *The Hairy Ape* he could be designated an expressionist. In still other plays, such as *Strange Interlude* and *Mourning Becomes Electra,* he worked out forms for which no particular school could claim paternity. Actually, modern American drama, instead of serving a single principle or style, telescoped the experiments and strivings of several decades of theatrical pioneering.

Our twentieth-century playwrights and their associates did not have to fight the desperate battles that Ibsen and his champions had waged. Yet their advent was quite revolutionary in the hitherto retarded American theatre, and it was not unproductive of plays considered worthy of the modern spirit. America fell short, it is true, of ideal aims, failing to develop a subsidized national theatre (except for a brief period of federal relief between 1935 and 1939) and never quite developing a successful repertory system. Production methods on Broadway were often haphazard and superficial. Brashness was mistaken for vitality. We credited originality to plays which were actually derivative, and we mistook significant subject matter for significant art. Our drama became attuned, nevertheless, to modern ideas and acquired literary value. We even began to contribute to the European stage instead of merely borrowing from it. O'Neill's plays were produced throughout Europe, and productions of more and more works by Elmer Rice, Clifford Odets, Lillian Hellman, Robert Sherwood, Arthur Miller, and Tennessee

Williams traveled as far as Australia. It is not too much to say, indeed, that our theatre was more vital than England's during the nineteen-thirties, and that between 1930 and 1950 we were well ahead of Germany, Italy, and Russia in the production of plays expressive of individual feeling and independent thought. After 1920, except for the appearance of so remarkable a drama as *Saint Joan* or *The Plough and the Stars* across the Atlantic, American playwriting was at least on a par with that of any other nation.

A historical survey and critical overview of modern American drama must differ in some respects from an examination of modern European drama. When we deal with the latter, we are able to trace well-defined movements and to single out conspicuously important playwrights, each of whom deserves attention for his substantial contribution and for his individual mode of expression and point of view. In discussing American drama, we have no such clear-cut pattern to follow. Although experimental groups arose in America after 1915, they developed no distinctive styles important to the history of dramatic form.

A review of the American drama cannot be written around a ruling concept, a succession of influential ideas or dramatic principles, or an evolution of special types of drama. We did not change or subvert the nature of tragedy, as the European naturalists did; we did not modify the approach of comedy; we did not invent some major mode of social, historical, or biographical drama. Nor did we give rise to important modifications of realism, naturalism, symbolism, expressionism, or theatricalism that may be called peculiarly American. Much as the critic, historian, or teacher may want to illuminate our modern drama by means of some philosophical or esthetic concept, he is bound to be contradicted by the eclectic character of our theatre. He cannot even hope to elaborate the kind of synthesis that scholars of the major European cultures are apt to favor. The modern drama of France can be viewed as part of a tradition that includes not only the neoclassic tragedy of Corneille and Racine and the comedy of Molière but certain influential early-nineteenth-century movements as well. Spanish drama can be related to the dramatic literature of the late sixteenth and the seventeenth centuries. England's modern drama can be considered as part of a theatre that produced Congreve and Sheridan long before it gave rise to Wilde and Shaw, Maugham and Coward; and insofar as there has been a poetic drama in Britain, it can be studied in relation to the great poetic theatre of Shakespeare and his contemporaries or to the closet drama of later poet-playwrights. But the modern drama of the United States has no significant national tradition to provide a perspective.

At most, we can trace some continuity of robust vaudeville-like entertainment from the nonliterary farces of Harrigan and Hart (the Mulligan Guard series) to later "fast" comedies. The story of our modern theatre consists largely of efforts to cut adrift from the earlier trends of the American stage.

We can go no further than this in an effort to find distinctive attributes in our drama: We can say that our humor tended to be broader and more robust than European humor. We used bludgeons more frequently than rapiers in attacking absurdities in private and public behavior. We were far less deft at writing high comedy and did so less frequently than the British. We were less brittle and pointed than the French, less airy than the Viennese, less sentimental than the Hungarians, less metaphysical than the modern Italians. We also favored a speedier type of playwriting than prevailed in Europe; our writing was more nervous and, in the main, less intellectual. It may also be noted that we were moderate in experimentation, except in the case of O'Neill's work; we avoided the extreme stridency that characterized the German expressionist stage after the First World War, the overemphasis on utilitarian theatre that the Russians favored after their Revolution, and the odd surrealism that the French made fashionable in Paris. By comparison with the European stage, our theatre after 1918 possessed vigor without fanaticism, speed without turbulence, skepticism without bitterness, interest in ideas without metaphysical complexity, and, except for a brief period during the depression, awareness of social reality without marked propagandistic bias.

These differences between ourselves and Europe were, however, unremarkable. We cannot erect a system of significant "American" drama on this basis. If we are inclined to credit some of our playwrights with greater stature than they actually possess, it is because we inevitably think of them in terms of American rather than of world drama. Their plays receive emphasis in the present volume primarily as American productions, whereas the works of Ibsen, Strindberg, Chekhov, or Shaw concern us less because they represent Scandinavian, Russian, or British drama than because they affected the course of the theatre throughout the Western world. The American drama is of interest as a result of the great many plays of merit contributed by a variety of playwrights, most of whom have individually created neither an extensive nor a distinguished dramatic literature.

The work of America's modern dramatists is part of a single cultural stream to which novelists, poets, and even painters and composers contributed. The drama of the 1919–1929 decade was one manifestation of our maturing creative expression and of our rebellion against the values dominant during the early years of the century. Similarly, the plays of the next twenty years reflected the shifting concerns of dramatists, as well as of other writers and artists, as they faced the depression years and the onset of the Second World War. We may therefore concern ourselves with over-all directions in the theatre, bearing in mind always that a "trend" is not the same thing as a work of art and is never a substitute for it. A chronicle which follows developments in our cultural history and traces the changing sociocultural context of our drama may help to create some order out of our vital and disorderly theatre.

THE EARLY CURRENTS

Before we discover how far we came, we must, of course, know where we started. Our progress is measurable, at least partly, by the limitations with which we began and the efforts we made to overcome them. America has a theatrical past, and it is a mistake to assume that a modern American theatre was suddenly born on a certain date, when, for instance, the Provincetown Players produced O'Neill's first one-act play or when the infant Theatre Guild was saved by the success of St. John Ervine's *John Ferguson*. The fact is that the theatre moved into the modern world, gradually, in a stream of mingled currents, some of them faintly observable in America decades before 1920.

The American theatre started fumbling toward maturity during the eighteen-eighties and 'nineties, having produced little during the earlier part of the century but adaptations of European plays, a few sentimental comedies, the most endurable being Anna Cora Mowatt's *Fashion* (1845), and a great number of melodramas. After 1880, we began to create glossy comedy of manners with some evidence of wit and intelligence, problem plays, and realistic studies of character and situation. Clyde Fitch turned out comedies of manners which had less moss on them than the older, sentimental plays. Bronson Howard considered capital and labor in *Baron Rudolph* and Wall Street speculation in *The Henrietta*, and Steele MacKaye took note of radical movements in *Paul Kauvar, or Anarchy*. Augustus Thomas painted pictures of the American hinterland in such set pieces as *In Mizzoura* and *Arizona*. And quite remarkably for an American playwright in 1890, the actor-manager James A. Herne wrote the first native realistic drama, *Margaret Fleming*, in which human weakness and adultery were for once treated with understanding rather than horror.

The first decade of the new century brought only slight improvement. Clyde Fitch worked himself up to glimmerings of social satire in *The Climbers* (1901) and in *The Truth* (1907). He also arrived at some comedy of character in *The Girl with the Green Eyes* (1901) and at some social realism in *The City* (1910), with its story of a corrupt public career. Human relations began to be treated with more candor. William Vaughn Moody contrasted the free West with puritanical New England in *The Great Divide* (1906), going so far as vaguely to imply that a woman might fall in love with the man who had violated her. Eugene Walter supplied a slice of life in *The Easiest Way* (1908) by presenting a woman's vacillations between the man who had been keeping her and the man who offered her respectability but also poverty. Some interest in psychology thrust itself into the theatre with such pieces as Augustus Thomas' *The Witching Hour* and Moody's *The Faith Healer* (1909). Awareness of social problems grew with the rise of muckraking journalism, especially after Theodore Roosevelt began waving his "big stick" at big business. Even such a purveyor of popular entertainment as Charles Klein concerned himself with malefactors of great wealth, in *The Lion and the Mouse*. Edward Sheldon discussed a racial problem in *The Nigger* (1910) and municipal corruption in *The Boss* (1911). Domestic relations, too, came to be treated with more sharpness: there is still some vitality in Langdon Mitchell's witty divorce comedy *The New York Idea*, produced in 1906. By 1914, the "new woman" had become a topic rather than a monster.

It cannot be said that the commercial theatre before 1920 produced vigorous drama of ideas, penetrating studies of reality, plays transfigured by deeply personal expression—or even particularly bright comedy of manners. New York had already seen a number of Shaw's plays without greatly benefiting from the example. It had familiarized itself with Ibsen's work without being stirred to produce any powerful protest or character analysis. And it had acquired some knowledge of the new romantic plays of Maeterlinck and Rostand without creating better poetic drama than Josephine Preston Peabody's *The Piper* and Percy MacKaye's *The Scarecrow*. Clyde Fitch called for modern plays "reflecting absolutely and truthfully the life and environment about us; every class, every kind, every emotion, every motive, every occupation, every business, every idleness." It was a good program, even if Fitch himself did not follow it. It had yet to be followed when the First World War broke out.

Even during the war years, American plays were about as modern, for the most part, as the horse-drawn wagon is today. By comparison with the novels already written by Henry James, Stephen Crane, Frank Norris, and Theodore Dreiser, even our best dramas were monumentally inconsequential. It is true that in Jesse Lynch Williams' *Why Marry?* (the first Pulitzer Prize play), produced in 1914, the "new woman" proposed to live with a gentleman without benefit of the law. The times having changed somewhat, no one rose up in arms against this comedy. But we must remember that the heroine was duly married at the end by an uncle who happened to be a magistrate. It is also true that Clare Kummer contributed several sophisticated comedies—the frivolous antic *Good Gra-*cious, Annabelle* (1916) and the mildly Shavian piece *A Successful Calamity* (1917). How modern these and similar pieces really were, however, can be determined by comparing them to plays long familiar abroad. Melodrama continued to proliferate, with some farcical deviations from the old "unhand her, villain" type of contrivance (our classic example of farce melodrama, George M. Cohan's *Seven Keys to Baldpate,* is of 1913 vintage) and with some modernity, especially in plays by Bayard Veiller and Elmer Rice. (The latter even introduced the "flashback" method of the cinema into his 1914 melodrama *On Trial;* being a man of conviction, he tried also to write thesis plays, to which the wartime theatre was unfavorable.) Inevitably, the war also spawned a number of flag-waving exercises and spy melodramas. And the public gave enthusiastic reception to a succession of such sentimental pieces as the perennial *Peg o' My Heart* and that apotheosis of the "Glad Girl" *Pollyanna.* (Laurette Taylor, later the Amanda of *The Glass Menagerie,* was the adorable Peg; Patricia Collinge, later the Birdie of *The Little Foxes,* was the Glad Girl.)

A minor revolution in the theatre, brewing since 1910, had to make itself felt before the tentative forays into modern drama could became distinctive and before the time-honored genteel comedies and vacuous melodramas would cease to be honored. This revolution came to a head after the First World War, and the result was the drama that made its first appearance with O'Neill and moved toward the middle of the century with Tennessee Williams and Arthur Miller.

A word of caution is needed at this point. Only a part of the American theatre has been modern since 1918; the rest has merely seemed modern because it shaved off its whiskers and talked fast. Progress in the theatre is generally uneven, and the common denominator of taste on the part of a nation's playgoing public is rarely very high. (It will be remembered that *Abie's Irish Rose* came as late as 1922 and rolled up 2,327 performances—in a strenuously sophisticated decade—and that Broadway could bring itself to the point of producing *Grandma's Diary* hopefully as late as 1948.) The general tenor was evident in the years immediately following the First World War, when the commercial theatre fluttered about and proffered more sentimental wares of the *Smilin' Through* and *The Charm School* variety. Affectionate writing also was still in vogue. But the flavor was sometimes new and salty, as in the best product of this genial style, Winchell Smith and Frank Bacon's *Lightnin'* (1918). The Pinero standard was well maintained by Zoë Akins in *Déclassée* (1919), the drama of an impetuous woman's descent from high society. Ethel Barrymore covered herself with glory in the role, and Miss Akins' play was regarded as a very modern drama. Frank Craven was alleged to be a singularly acute dramatist when he described the difficulties of the first year of marriage in the contrived comedy *The First Year.*

THE MODERNIZATION OF THE AMERICAN THEATRE

The real modernization of the American theatre was the work of a few insurgent individuals and groups. Modern American drama as a whole may be described as a brew concocted of domesticated naturalism and expressionism, sophisticated comedy, drama of ideas, cheeky treatment of American manners, protest against puritanical morals, and revolt against the middle-class values of the postwar period. Offered first in pure form by resolute rebels, our modernism began to be purveyed in adulterated versions. The combination of the genuine article with imitations in the form of watered-down realism and protest has constituted the American drama since 1920. But in order to understand what happened to give the American theatre a more or less new dispensation, we must retrace our steps a little.

After 1916, the commercial theatre lost much of its hold outside New York City. The vast touring-company system, on which the managers had thrived for many decades, dwindled as a result of the high cost of railroad transportation and the competition of the motion-picture industry. The theatre lost its mass public which had exhibited very little discrimination. The audience that remained was more cosmopolitan and demanding. It consisted of people with European background, people living in or near New York and a few other cities, and fairly well-educated leaders of the hinterland who had some interest in art and ideas; often their focal institution in the smaller communities was a university or club. Faced with a new audience, the commercial managements in time found it expedient to present plays and production styles that would have seemed altogether too esoteric in 1890, 1900, or 1910. Moreover, among the new managers were men of taste and discrimination, such as Winthrop Ames and Arthur Hopkins, who were eager to associate themselves with modern drama and modern scenic art.

In consequence, the commercial theatre began to include productions that reflected an interest in the stage as an art rather than exclusively as a business; in some instances the managers were also gratified to discover that the gulf between art and business could be narrowed. Thus, in 1912, Winthrop Ames imported the Max Reinhardt Japanese-styled pantomime *Sumurûn;* and Hazelton and Benrimo's fantasy in the Chinese manner, *The Yellow Jacket,* was presented by the practical management of Harris and Selwyn in the same year. Ames also produced the Granville-Barker and Laurence Housman imaginative play *Prunella,* and Arthur Hopkins began an association with the scene designer Robert Edmond Jones which resulted in memorable John Barrymore

productions of *Richard III, Hamlet,* and *The Jest.* John D. Williams, who later presented O'Neill's *Beyond the Horizon,* produced Galsworthy's *Justice* in 1916. (With John Barrymore in the leading role, *Justice* won great popularity; as a result, the play became required reading for schoolboys, whose induction into modern drama at school had hitherto not carried them beyond Charles Rann Kennedy's sermon *The Servant in the House.*) Granville-Barker was invited to stage plays in New York, and in 1915 Robert Edmond Jones gave New Yorkers a famous example of scenic design in one of Granville-Barker's productions, Anatole France's *The Man Who Married a Dumb Wife.*

Between 1911 and 1919, moreover, a "little theatre" movement developed momentum with a notable mushrooming of community and university productions. George Pierce Baker's 47 Workshop Theatre at Harvard produced the first efforts of young playwrights. E. C. Mabie, at the University of Iowa, encouraged native playwriting, and so did a number of other teachers: Thomas H. Dickinson, at the University of Wisconsin; Glenn Hughes, at the University of Washington; A. M. Drummond, at Cornell; and Frederick H. Koch, at the University of North Dakota and later at the University of North Carolina, where Thomas Wolfe, Paul Green, and Dorothy and Du Bose Heyward's dramatic talents germinated. A Chicago Little Theatre was founded in 1912; the Toy Theatre in Boston served as a laboratory for modern art between 1912 and 1916; the Arts and Crafts Theatre arose in Detroit under Sam Hume, a disciple of Gordon Craig; the Cleveland Playhouse became active in 1916. Such groups as these were resolved to create the kind of theatre the commercial managers, with the few exceptions already noted, were not yet willing to supply.

In New York, moreover, there arose three important organizations fired with enthusiasm for modern art and with animus against the old-fashioned drama that George Jean Nathan was then blasting from the pages of the magazine *The Smart Set.* One of these experimental groups, the Neighborhood Playhouse, was established on the East Side in 1915 by the daughters of the philanthropist Adolph Lewisohn. It served the theatre best with stylized productions of such esoteric classics as the Jewish folk fantasy *The Dybbuk* and the Hindu romance *The Little Clay Cart.* The other two groups were started in Greenwich Village, then the Mecca—and inexpensive residence—of rebellious young artists. One was the Washington Square Players; the other, the Provincetown Players. The one-act play, requiring as a rule a small cast and a simple set suitable for tiny stages, served the rebels as a wedge with which to force their way into the theatre.

The Washington Square unit was founded in 1914 by the Welsh-born patent lawyer Lawrence Langner, the clever playwright (later a brilliant stage director) Philip Moeller, the actress Helen Westley, and others. Soon joined by the scene designer Lee Simonson and by such promising young actors as Katherine Cornell and Roland Young, the founders announced a program: they would produce plays of all kinds that were usually ignored by the commercial managements. For this purpose they rented a little theatre, the Bandbox, uptown. In addition to staging European one-acters—Maeterlinck's *Interior* and Chekhov's *The Bear,* for example—they produced such irreverent little American pieces as Moeller's spoof on Helen of Troy, *Helena's Husband,* and Alice Gerstenberg's *Overtones,* a comedy of alter egos, typical of experimental sophistication. Later, the Washington Square Players presented such realistic one-acters as Zona Gale's farm play *Neighbors,* Susan Glaspell's stark drama *Trifles,* and Eugene O'Neill's early sea piece *In the Zone.* The Players also began producing modernistic full-length plays: Andreyev's symbolic *Life of Man,* Ibsen's perennial realistic drama *Ghosts,* Shaw's *Mrs. Warren's Profession,* and others. America's entry into the war dispersed the group in May 1918, after it had enjoyed four years of flamboyant activity. By then it had brought to production sixty-two one-act and six full-length plays.

In 1919, upon returning from war service, a number of the Washington Square amateurs founded America's first professional art theatre, the Theatre Guild, on a subscription-audience basis. The Guild gave its first two performances (Benavente's *The Bonds of Interest* and Ervine's *John Ferguson*) in the spring of 1919. During the next thirty years, this extraordinarily successful theatre was to bring to the fore many of our best-known actors, introduce or revive extreme experiments as well as masterpieces of the modern European drama, and give successful productions of many of the best plays of O'Neill, Sidney Howard, S. N. Behrman, Maxwell Anderson, Philip Barry, Robert Sherwood, and William Saroyan. By reviving many of Shaw's plays and by producing a number of them for the first time in the English language, the Guild also made itself Shaw's official theatre in America.

A more modest, yet in one respect even more important, destiny—namely, the discovery of O'Neill—was in store for the Theatre Guild's sister organization, the Provincetown Players. Among the stalwarts who created this group, in 1915, were the novelist and man of many parts George Cram Cook; his wife, Susan Glaspell (the novelist and playwright, who was to win a Pulitzer Prize in 1930 for the Emily Dickinson drama *Alison's House*); Robert Edmond Jones; and Eugene O'Neill. Before long, they were joined by the veteran of American naturalism Theodore Dreiser, the Harvard firebrand John Reed, the short-story writer Wilbur Daniel Steele, the novelist and writer on labor problems Mary Heaton Vorse, and the then Bohemian poets Harry Kemp, Maxwell Bodenheim, Alfred Kreymborg, and Edna St. Vincent Millay. It seemed that a large part of the vanguard of American letters was rallying to the experimental theatre.

The first theatre of the Provincetown Players stood on an abandoned wharf in the summer colony of Provincetown, Massachusetts. Here, in 1915, they produced their first playlets, the best known being the Freudian one-acter *Suppressed Desires* by Susan Glaspell and George Cram Cook. The next summer, the group made theatrical history by giving O'Neill his first production: *Bound East for Cardiff.* After staging plays at their Wharf Theatre for three summers, they took city quarters in New York's Greenwich Village. Remodeling an abandoned stable on Macdougal Street and hopefully calling it the Playwrights' Theatre, the experimentalists made this unattractive building their temple of the arts from 1918 to 1929.

Here (and for brief periods in a larger Village theatre and on Broadway) the Provincetown Players presented not only unique examples of European modernism but a great many one-act and full-length plays by new American writers. Among the pioneering playwrights were Susan Glaspell, Edmund Wilson and Stark Young (who became better known as novelists and critics), Edna St. Vincent Millay (whose short, poetic *Aria da Capo* is still being played), Hatcher Hughes and Paul Green, both of whom won Pulitzer Prizes, and Eugene O'Neill. Playgoers with long memories may remember the ingratiating style of such revivals as *Patience* and *Fashion,* the electrifying performance of Charles Gilpin in *The Emperor Jones,* and the original staging of some of the experimental plays. But this theatre is less important for its experiments in stagecraft than for its discovery of new American drama. The Provincetown became a playwrights' theatre in fact as well as in name.

It is to the credit of Broadway managements that O'Neill's *Beyond the Horizon* was produced by John D. Williams in 1920 and that *Anna Christie* was presented by Arthur Hopkins a year later. It is also true that the Theatre Guild inherited O'Neill after 1928, when the Provincetown died, and that the Guild gave noteworthy first productions to *Marco Millions, Strange Interlude, Mourning Becomes Electra, Ah, Wilderness!,* and *The Iceman Cometh* over a period of twenty years. But the "revolution" in the American theatre was effected largely by the Provincetown Players' productions of O'Neill's early sea-pieces and of his longer dramatic experiments—the plays in which he passed beyond realism or naturalism and at the same time incorporated modern life. Most notable among these were *The Emperor Jones, The Hairy Ape, All God's Chillun Got Wings, Desire Under the Elms* (all produced between 1920 and 1924), and *The Great God Brown* (produced in 1926 by the directorate of the Provincetown, then consisting of the critic Kenneth MacGowan, Robert Edmond Jones, and O'Neill himself).

It was in these plays that O'Neill gave uniquely

personal expression to modern man's conflicts and experimented with methods of symbolizing them. It was in this body of work that he gave dimension to the themes of race, labor, the artist's struggle in a materialistic society, the duality of love and hate, and the quest for meaning in a world devoid of faith. He exposed a turbulent and turbid mind as a spectacle for playgoers hitherto accustomed to being entertained rather than troubled. He dredged up for them the weird shapes of desire and anxiety, hitherto discreetly ignored by American playwrights. He gave dramatic expression to the "unconscious," which Freudian psychologists were making a household word among educated and semieducated people. Squeamish citizens might rage and ask the government to intervene, but O'Neill, flanked by the Provincetown faithful and by a growing number of admirers, stood his ground. America had a major modern playwright at last.

In the early nineteen-twenties, O'Neill was, however, no longer alone in forging a new drama, and the Provincetown was no longer alone in providing the suitable setting. The Washington Square Players was now the powerful Theatre Guild. The commercial managements were ready to produce the plays of the rebellious young dramatists—Maxwell Anderson, Laurence Stallings, Elmer Rice, Philip Barry, Sidney Howard, and others too numerous to name here. The new stage directors and the scene designers, led by Robert Edmond Jones and Lee Simonson, were able to translate the work of these writers into expressive theatre. A magazine, *Theatre Arts*, served as an organ for progressive thinkers in the field of the dramatic arts, and such critics as Alexander Woollcott and Heywood Broun greeted the new American plays with a contagious enthusiasm. Writers of fiction and poetry helped educate the theatre public with books that presented a modern outlook. The playwrights now had an audience that was ready for any revelations they cared to make.

THE FIRST DECADE: 1919–1929

The ferment at work in the theatre in the nineteen-twenties can be variously described, for it was compounded of many elements. Its large measure of passion for an art theatre could be seen in the continuing work of the little theatres, in the refinement of stagecraft, in the rise of the stage director to eminence, and in the work of the scenic designer as a creative artist. Unity of design in the stage production and the interpenetration of all aspects of the performance by the meaning and mood of the play were now the ideals of both the experimental and commercial theatres. Attempts were made to establish repertory companies, most notably by Eva Le Gallienne at her Civic Repertory Theatre on New York's Fourteenth Street and by the Theatre Guild, which founded an acting studio also. Actors created their own theatre, the Actors' Company. Playwrights banded together, with financial support from the philanthropist Otto Kahn, to form a New Playwrights Company, which presented works of an extremely stylized nature.

The progressive playwright who made himself heard during the decade was bent upon expressing his emotions and conveying his convictions. He was, or conceived himself to be, a rebel, although we must remember, as Joseph Wood Krutch has pointed out in *The American Drama Since 1918*, that "the radical who got a hearing was the radical whose criticism was directed rather at the culture than the political organization of America." He belonged to the literary movement that included such iconoclasts as H. L. Mencken, Theodore Dreiser, Sherwood Anderson, Sinclair Lewis, Edna St. Vincent Millay, T. S. Eliot, F. Scott Fitzgerald, and Ernest Hemingway.

The object of attack was not the social structure of America but its external manifestations, which were regarded as offensive and crude—that is, esthetically repellent and unfavorable to the development of a freely creative personality. Insofar as political criticism existed, it was leveled at such illiberal manifestations as vigilantism of the Ku Klux Klan variety, attacks on labor organizations, and restriction of civil liberties. The main assault was directed at the excrescences of an economy bloated with war profits, and at mechanization and commercialization. The revolt was spearheaded by vigorous literary critics. Mencken flailed at middle-class complacency and narrow-mindedness with many a jibe but also with valiant support of every genuinely realistic or critical writer. The critic Vernon L. Parrington (1871–1929) studied our literary history in *Main Currents in American Thought* (1927–1930) and showed that it had always involved a struggle against illiberal forces. Van Wyck Brooks examined the failure of our literary past (which he himself was later loudest in praising in *The Flowering of New England*). Between 1915 and 1930, he viewed our literature and the careers of our writers as a tragedy of frustration. Brooks maintained, in such books as *The Ordeal of Mark Twain* (1920) and *The Pilgrimage of Henry James* (1925), that our Puritan tradition and our materialism had prevented the full flowering of the creative life in America. It was the intention of an entire generation of young writers after 1915 not to allow its spiritual and artistic growth to be stunted. Writers left their home towns and gathered their forces in literary circles in Chicago, where Harriet Monroe published her *Poetry* magazine, and in New York, where Greenwich Village was the haven of the rebel. If they were sufficiently provoked, they left America altogether and lived abroad, usually on the Bohemian left bank of Paris.

A vivid example of the writer's rejection of his milieu was Sherwood Anderson's *Winesburg, Ohio*

(1919). Its stories of small-town life pictured the frustrations and gropings for self-realization in a community deprived of ruling vision and purpose. In his subsequent books Anderson explored related materials, treating of a town's spiritual impoverishment through industrialization, of a businessman's effort to break the stalemate of his existence, of the spiritual richness of the uninhibited Negroes as contrasted with the emptiness of the whites. No less concerned with maladjustments in American life were the novels of Sinclair Lewis. *Main Street,* the most widely read book in 1920, described a young woman's rebellion against a narrow, middle-class society and her search for cosmopolitan culture. For the next eight years, Lewis continued to criticize American life through fictional portraits that have become well-known types: the businessman Babbitt submerged in a humdrum, materialistic life; the scientist Arrowsmith striving to effectuate his ideals in an unfavorable social climate; the hypocrite Elmer Gantry, commercializing religion. During the 'twenties, in short, the rebellious playwright was by no means an isolated phenomenon. His work was part of the critical cultural awakening of the United States, which produced no literary giants but gave rise to a great many artists who placed self-expression above conformity and regarded the prevailing manners and values of their environment with skepticism and distaste.

The new playwrights and their fellow artists abominated the high-pressure salesmanship, the cheap entertainment, the complacency, and the esthetic anesthesia of the Harding-Coolidge-Hoover period. In this age of revivalism of the Billy Sunday tent-show variety, they lashed at religious hypocrisy. As the smaller communities from which they came still imposed taboos on love, sex, and the freer kind of social relations, the playwrights flailed at "puritanism." And they found a special provocation in Prohibition and in the "blue laws" of the period—that is, the regulations imposed by reformers bent upon stifling the "joy of life" and making the natural man feel "blue." All in all, the vanguard in the theatre was dead set against the middle classes, the bourgeoisie known to readers of Mencken's magazine, *The American Mercury,* as the "booboisie."

To flout the herd that followed the golden calf of prosperity—the "go-getters," the "Babbitts," and the "boosters"—became a favorite sport of the theatre. To scorn the mass production of commonplace minds was considered an obligation. To expose, or, in popular parlance, "debunk," inflated reputations was, in addition, a reliable way of providing entertainment. Ever since the rise of muckraking journalism, favored by Joseph Pulitzer of the *New York World* and practiced by such experts as Ida M. Tarbell and Lincoln Steffens, the art of revealing sordid or questionable business practices was highly prized, and playwrights became as experienced in muckraking as the journalists.

Consequently, a great deal of the playwriting of the nineteen-twenties was devoted to the ungentle art of "spoofing." Many writers who came up for notice at this time practiced it with a vigor and ingenuity hitherto absent from the American stage. George S. Kaufman was the master of ceremonies at this burlesque, and he had many assistants. Marc Connelly, Edna Ferber, Ring Lardner, and Moss Hart were his actual collaborators; Charles MacArthur, George Abbott, Preston Sturges, and others practiced nose-thumbing independently. But it is far from certain that they were not also rather fond of the life they travestied. A breezy type of comedy and farce, studded with the irreverent "wisecrack" and briskly satiric, came into vogue. Kaufman and his collaborators, for example, "ribbed" the muddleheaded middle-class woman in *Dulcy* and the motion pictures and tin-pan alley in *Merton of the Movies, Once in a Lifetime,* and *June Moon.* Ben Hecht and Charles MacArthur extracted rowdy fun from the yellow press in *The Front Page,* and George Kelly hilariously satirized the current high-pressure ideal of salesmanship in *The Show-Off.* If it is too much to say that most of these low comedies have more than historical interest for us by now, it must be conceded that they were bright and tart and that they still possess more liveliness than the polite high comedies of Clyde Fitch.

Practitioners of a more polished or penetrating kind of "debunking" comedy also arose. Philip Barry cross-examined the conservative upper classes in such plays as *Paris Bound* and *Holiday,* and George Kelly flayed a grasping middle-class wife in *Craig's Wife.* The generally morose O'Neill joined the Babbitt-baiting game with the romantic satire *Marco Millions;* its insensitive Florentine hero, Marco Polo, was the Main Street businessman in medieval robes.

Imagination was impressed into the service of the critical assault: expressionism, it was found, enabled the playwright to distort the scene and exaggerate its features for purposes of satire. O'Neill used this technique in *The Hairy Ape* with much dramatic effect when he showed that his stoker, Yank, could not even make a physical impression upon the well-dressed gentlemen leaving Sunday service on Fifth Avenue. Whenever he collided with them, Yank rebounded while they walked on, undisturbed and unruffled. George S. Kaufman and Marc Connelly employed the expressionist dream technique in *Beggar on Horseback* (1924) to express the anxiety of a young artist on the verge of marrying a rich heiress and being absorbed in her father's business. The artist has a nightmare in which one of his strange experiences is finding himself employed in a "Consolidated Art Factory," where he has to fill out endless requisitions for pencils.

John Howard Lawson traced a young Iowan's social and sexual maladjustment in *Roger Bloomer* (1923), the story of a youth who, in the opinion of a prospective employer, lacks the "money-making manner"; he experiences a variety of weird frustrations that bring him to prison after the suicide of his equally baffled girl friend. A little later in the same year, Elmer Rice presented his most original play, *The Adding Machine,* on the subject of man's depersonalization in a humdrum life. Rice's hero, the bookkeeper Mr. Zero, has lost all traces of individuality in the course of twenty-five years of service in a department store. He lives contentedly with a dull and nagging wife with whom he has no conversation whatsoever, and he barely notices the fellow employee Daisy, who is secretly in love with him. He is displaced from his job by the installation of an adding machine. In a fury, Zero kills his employer. He is tried in a courtroom in which all the walls seem to cave in on him. After his execution, he finds himself in the Elysian fields, but its happy and uninhibited life so offends his conventional morality that he insists on leaving. He is to be reborn as a baby who, after the usual education in the machine age, will come to run "a super-hyper-adding machine" with a toe of his left foot. It is for this destiny that the universe came into being, the earth cooled sufficiently to support life, and the evolutionary process began to shape the creature called man! In 1925, John Howard Lawson took a kaleidoscopic view of society in *Processional,* interpreting the vulgarity, the mindlessness, and the struggle between labor and local vigilantism in terms of an utterly mad "jazz symphony." And in 1928, Sophie Treadwell projected a well-publicized murder case, in *Machinal,* as a series of automatic responses on the part of a woman frustrated and emotionally numbed at the office and in the home.

The subjects of military heroism and war naturally presented an excellent target for the assault on accepted values in a period of disillusionment with President Wilson's "war for democracy" and with his failure to create effective machinery for maintaining peace. Among the antiwar plays, one could find a comedy as brightly skeptical as Robert Sherwood's *The Road to Rome* (1926) or as slashing as *What Price Glory?,* written by the then pacifistic Maxwell Anderson and the former marine captain Laurence Stalling. The innuendo in *The Road to Rome* was that a military conqueror, such as the great Hannibal, would lose his taste for war if he could find a natural outlet for his libido. A Roman lady turns Hannibal away from the gates of Rome when no army could effectively oppose his entry. The authors' disenchantment in *What Price Glory?* led them to present war as a sorry occupation and professional soldiering as a callous affair. The Anderson-Stallings play may be used, indeed (as it is in this anthology), to represent the entire antiheroic, cynical school of playwriting. It reduced the war to a rough and foulmouthed competition between a marine sergeant and a captain for the favors of a French tart.

Other dramas of the period were equally animated by the critical spirit, which did not always have to assume the mask of mockery to be penetrating or challenging. Paul Green and other writers of folk drama, for example, were not always content to derive gratification from local color; instead, they took note of frustrations in country life. Green painted a picture of racial struggle in his Negro play *In Abraham's Bosom* that departed drastically from glorifications of the Southern landscape. Sidney Howard's *They Knew What They Wanted* (1924) presented a tolerant view of adultery that would have been considered outrageous ten or fifteen years earlier; Howard's *The Silver Cord* (1926) took a skeptical view of American mother-worship and indicated the dangers of overpossessive motherhood. Elmer Rice's *Street Scene* (1929), a panorama of life in the slums, was full of matter that would have been regarded as repellently seedy and crude in an age of genteel sentiment. The play showed, among other things, how a drab existence poisoned human relationships. Maxwell Anderson and Harold Hickerson delivered themselves of a singularly bitter play about the Sacco-Vanzetti case, *Gods of the Lightning.* Mingling furious melodrama with even more furious rhetoric, the authors indicted our system of law and presented an anarchist's case against organized society. And glowering over the entire human scene stood Eugene O'Neill, for whom life was at once a tragedy of alienation and a grim jest.

In O'Neill's *The Hairy Ape,* man still had not achieved humanity and hung suspended between the ape and the human being. In *Beyond the Horizon, All God's Chillun Got Wings* (in which man-made racial prejudice added a major complication), and *Desire Under the Elms,* an ironic fate snared and defeated those who strove for happiness and love. In *The Great God Brown,* man was hopelessly divided between his craving for freedom and creativeness and his subservience to restrictive moral codes. In *Strange Interlude* and *Mourning Becomes Electra,* man and woman were whirled about in a storm of passions. Nowhere in O'Neill's picture of life was there any peace for the divided spirit of humanity. All the complacencies were shattered by this playwright who rejected easy consolations and refused to be distracted from man's tragedy by the material gratifications and optimism of a prosperous nation.

It is true that time can whittle down the stature of the playwrights of the 'twenties and has indeed already done so in a number of instances. They did not join, with the much-debated exception of O'Neill, the first echelon of the master dramatists; but they unquestionably deserve a place in the history of American letters and culture. As they took their place in the theatre of modern ideas, they developed effectiveness. A number of them achieved sincere expression and made our drama worthy of regard as a form of literature. They wrote with force and point; they developed a sense of form; and they found expressive techniques that carried playwriting beyond mild manifestations of realism and sentiment. A generation of dramatists started its ascent in this decade, and we may list a number of them with the assurance that they have claims upon our attention.

Foremost, of course, was Eugene O'Neill, memorable for his wrestlings with life's enigmas and ironies, for his concern with the private demons of obsessed and inwardly tormented individuals, and for his sympathy with men's alienation in a world bereft of spiritual ideals and of the certainties of religious faith. O'Neill started with a natural flair for dramatic fireworks that made him translate his themes into exciting melodrama and impassioned psychological conflict. He steeped his plays in moods of longing, anxiety, and doom, thus creating a poetic drama in spite of an inability to supply a language equal to the dramatic turbulence of his plays. And he had the theatrical imagination necessary to visualize psychological and even mystical experience in scenes memorable on the stage even when they were less than memorable on the printed page.

Relentless in his demands upon an audience, O'Neill departed from the neat conventions in plays that required not only intense concentration but patience with dramas twice as long as the usual three-act piece. *Strange Interlude* had nine acts; *Mourning Becomes Electra* (1931) was a trilogy. Drama was for O'Neill a rite rather than an entertainment. It was also a mode of expressing a seething temperament and a spiritual quest. O'Neill approached playwriting with the high seriousness of the masters. He honored the drama as an art that had been practiced by the giants of humane letters—the Greek tragedians, Shakespeare, and Goethe. Although he lacked their transcendent talent for poetic expression, he was touched with their grandeur and their sense of man's capacity to desire, seek, and suffer greatly. He possessed some of their ability to present man as a creature who casts a long shadow on the earth, which is his throne and his prison.

The theatre of the 'twenties contained a number of other well-endowed mortals. Maxwell Anderson sent roots into the American soil with his collaborations, *What Price Glory?* and *Gods of the Lightning*, with *Saturday's Children* (1927), his rueful comedy of marriage destroyed by the disenchanting humdrum realities, and with less effective studies of the American scene. In the midst of his success, he was pondering the possibilities of restoring tragic grandeur to the theatre's characters and investing them with the eloquence of verse. After 1929, he was to write the best romantic verse plays of the American theatre, *Elizabeth the Queen, Mary of Scotland, Anne of the Thousand Days;* to create poetic fantasy, in *High Tor;* and to wrestle at least half successfully with the difficult problem of writing tragedy in verse about contemporary characters, in *Winterset.* He had high expectations for the American drama, which he tried to effectuate in the ensuing decades of depression and war.

Elmer Rice, who had written successful melodrama before 1918, devoted himself to American life with some talent for expressively fantastic commentary, in *The Adding Machine,* and with a strongly developed aptitude for painting vivid pictures of men and their world, in *Street Scene.* Later, even in unsuccessful or only half-successful ventures, he maintained high standards of observation and thought and displayed sound, if not always exciting, craftsmanship.

Splendid in craftsmanship and rich in human sympathy was Sidney Howard, who, although he rarely soared as high as Rice, created an understanding kind of native drama. From such plays as *They Knew What They Wanted, Ned McCobb's Daughter, Lucky Sam McCarver,* and *Dodsworth* (a dramatization of Sinclair Lewis' novel) one derived the feeling that Howard not only knew people and their environment but envisioned for them broad horizons; later, in his treatment of the struggle against yellow fever, *Yellow Jack* (1933), his view widened into a conception of a life dedicated to serving humanity.

Also among the emerging realists was the Southerner Paul Green, whose short plays of life in the South are among the most moving one-acters in the language and whose longer studies, *In Abraham's Bosom* and *The House of Connelly* (1932), a drama of the decay of the Southern gentry, revealed deep sympathy. At about the same time that Paul Green made his first impression in the theatre, there arose other sympathetic regional writers. Dorothy and Du Bose Heyward contributed *Porgy* (1927)—which later formed the basis of our first important folk opera, Gershwin's *Porgy and Bess*—and *Mamba's Daughters.* E. P. Conkle may have attracted little notice on Broadway, but some of his one-acters of Midwestern life, collected under the title of *Crick Bottom Plays* (1928), are surely masterpieces of their kind. Lynn Riggs proved himself a poet with his Oklahoma and Southwestern plays *Roadside* and *Green Grow the Lilacs*—which provided the basis for the musical comedy *Oklahoma,* in 1943—although the regional quality of his work often limited its effectiveness on Broadway.

Nor, finally, may we overlook the writers of literary comedy. Marc Connelly was surely among these, and he later won a place in the theatre as the author of the biblical fantasia *The Green Pastures* (1930). Robert Sherwood first came to the attention of playgoers as the author of *The Road to Rome* and of the brilliant romantic comedy *Reunion in Vienna* (1931). Capable of considerably greater seriousness than his early plays revealed, Sherwood was to prove himself one of the most probing and earnest dramatists of the depression and war periods.

Philip Barry brought a divided talent to the theatre. While he hankered for success as the author of philosophical drama (chiefly with *Hotel Universe* and *Here Come the Clowns,* written in the nineteen-thirties), he displayed a well-rewarded capacity for polished comedy of manners that expressed modern discontents and confusions. Such plays as *Paris Bound* and *Holiday* in the 'twenties and *The Animal Kingdom* and *The Philadelphia Story* in the 'thirties possessed grace and point. They were superior to the drawing-room plays of the American past in that they questioned convention and investigated traditional values. Thus, in *Paris Bound* Barry urbanely doubted that adultery was a sufficient reason for divorce; in *Holiday* he showed the younger generation rejecting its upper-class traditions; and in *The Animal Kingdom* he posited the notion that an understanding mistress was the true wife of the man she led to spiritual freedom, whereas the legal wife became morally the mistress when she proved to be a parasite.

In the late 'twenties, too, arose America's most brilliant writer of high comedy, S. N. Behrman. His gifts were fully developed when, in 1927, the Theatre Guild produced *The Second Man*. Behrman was a stylist. He was also a man endowed with a probing intelligence, which he was to exercise with particular acuity in *Meteor* (1929), a satire on the conceit of a Napoleon of the business world, and later, when he responded to the tensions of the 'thirties, in such plays as *Biography, Rain from Heaven,* and *End of Summer*.

With assistance from authors of single plays of distinction, these writers forged an American drama which its champions were proud to call "adult." The adjective is significant; it indicates that the dream of the American theatre was for its playwrights to achieve a mature outlook upon the world.

THE DECADE OF THE DEPRESSION: 1929–1939

On October 29, 1929, the bubble of American prosperity burst amid a flurry of ticker tape and a rain of suicides from office windows. For the theatre, as for the nation as a whole, the nineteen-thirties comprised a trying period. The economics of the stage took a turn for the worse, and writers found themselves working for an impoverished medium. As artists and men of their times, they were assailed, besides, by two major anxieties—fear of the collapse of American society and fear of the triumph of fascism, foreign and native. They faced a world to which sophistication and Bohemianism were no longer acceptable responses. Although it was still possible to concern oneself with matters of artistry, it became impossible to deal seriously with the world without considering economic facts and political issues and, in the case of young writers, without considering the possibility of reorganizing the social system. If playwrights could still amuse themselves and their public with familiar antics, it is nevertheless to be noted that even "entertainment" felt a pinch of anxiety or rebellion. In general, the mood of the 'thirties was often somber, if not indeed desperate; often rebellious, if not indeed downright revolutionary.

When we glance at the economic situation of the theatre we find that it became increasingly difficult to finance productions, that fewer plays were presented on Broadway, and that the "road" beyond New York City became closed to all but a few greatly publicized successes. It became virtually impossible to tour a play unless the cast included a big Broadway or Hollywood "name." Meanwhile, the motion-picture industry, which now produced "talkies," had won the allegiance of all but a small portion of the public. Hollywood offered extremely inexpensive entertainment; and, indeed, there was now available an even less expensive form of amusement in the form of radio shows. The Broadway theatre began to rely upon a very small public. Worse still, it began to lose the writers, directors, and actors it could not afford to support. Artists went to Hollywood to repair their damaged fortunes or to sustain body and soul. They often set forth with noble resolutions to come back to the theatre as soon as they could afford to do so. But many of them never returned; and of those who did, many found their craftsmanship and their creative spirit lamed by years of servitude to celluloid. And one must add to this dreary history the fact that an evil fate had befallen and continued to haunt the institutional theatres that had played an important role in advancing modern drama in America. When the thirties began, the Neighborhood Playhouse and the Provincetown Players had already disappeared. Even the powerful Theatre Guild felt the pinch of poverty for a number of years during the decade, while the noncommercial community-theatre movement outside New York found itself seriously hampered by lack of subsidies.

The story of the 'thirties is, nevertheless, by no means a record of stalemate. A wave of idealism and protest lifted the drama and the theatre from despondency. New forces gathered strength in the theatre, as in the cultural life of the nation as a whole. New theatrical groups came to the fore, even when their resources consisted of little more than a determination to produce art or to raise an outcry. They created new audiences with low-priced productions or helped themselves to Broadway audiences by offering challenging plays. They gave birth to new playwrights, and they even attracted the playwrights who had won standing in the previous decade and were regarded by the younger rebels as middle aged and a trifle stuffy. The new theatrical movement appears to have influenced in one way or another even some of the writers whose plays continued to be produced by the commercial managements. Besides, quite a number of these managements were themselves inclined to accept a grim and protesting kind of drama which they would have rejected summarily in the past.

First to emerge was a company of young actors and directors who had been loosely associated with the Theatre Guild as a studio acting company. Led by Cheryl Crawford, Lee Strasberg, and Harold Clurman, and calling themselves the Group Theatre, they dedicated themselves to perfecting their ensemble. It did not take them long to make themselves the best modern acting company America had ever had. Sympathetic with the underdog and hopeful of a more or less socialistic dispensation to replace the system of "free enterprise" that then seemed bankrupt, they favored plays critical of the social order and descriptive of the common man's struggles. Somehow they uncovered—they did not "discover" —a few new playwrights and introduced them to the public with sensitive, sometimes powerful productions. Among these writers were Clifford Odets and Sidney Kingsley, who proceeded to write such effective plays as *Awake and Sing!*, *Golden Boy*, *Men in White*, and *Dead End*. (The last-mentioned play was not produced by the Group.) Toward the very end of the decade, in the spring of 1939, the Group also brought William Saroyan to the playgoing public, with *My Heart's in the Highlands*.

Another organization, the nonprofit Theatre Union, was founded in December 1932 for the purpose of producing plays of social significance at popular prices. Leasing Eva Le Gallienne's now abandoned Civic Repertory Theatre for its quarters, the Theatre Union drew a working-class and middle-class audience that lacked either the means or the incentive to patronize Broadway regularly. The new company produced, on the whole, the period's most radical plays (by Albert Maltz, later an able novelist, George Sklar, Paul Peters, John Howard Lawson, Bertolt Brecht, Friedrich Wolf, and others). But it is significant of the extent to which the spirit of protest had seized the literary world that the Theatre Union's sponsors should have included Sherwood Anderson, the poet Stephen Vincent Benét, Elmer Rice, and Sidney Howard. Characteristic of the kind of plays favored was Paul Peters and George Sklar's *Stevedore* (1934), a powerful melodrama in which black and white workers in the South unite to prevent a lynching. The authors expressed the conviction that racial conflict was artificially fomented by the exploiters of the common people and that the interests of the working class transcended color, race, and religion.

The influence of the Theatre Union and the mushrooming of theatre groups among workers and discontented intellectuals resulted in the formation of a New Theatre League, which correlated the efforts of a new, socially conscious little-theatre movement. The New Theatre League's numerous branches provided theatrical experience for an entire generation of young actors, directors, and writers. Like the little art theatres of the 1915–1920 period, the new groups relied almost entirely on one-act plays which could be staged with little scenery and

slight preparation. In the one-act form, new playwrights could gain experience and reveal their aptitude for dramatic art. Since, moreover, the one-acters now contained a great deal of social material instead of local color, they required a talent for something more than dramatic sketches. It was the New Theatre League that discovered Clifford Odets by giving him a prize and a first production for the best one-act play about a social issue. One of the last contests sponsored by the New Theatre League discovered Marc Blitzstein, with his original music drama about social discontent and vigilantism, *The Cradle Will Rock*. The League also gave encouragement to the young writer Irwin Shaw, by staging his long one-act antiwar fantasy, *Bury the Dead*, previously produced by another new theatrical group, the American Repertory Theatre. Later, Shaw's parable on the revolt of the little people against their bullies, *The Gentle People*, proved to be one of the successful plays of the Group Theatre, and he won even greater distinction with numerous short stories and a Second World War novel, *The Young Lions*.

Mention may also be made of the Mercury Theatre, founded by Orson Welles and John Houseman, which gave memorable productions of *Julius Caesar* and of Thomas Dekker's Elizabethan comedy *The Shoemaker's Holiday*, as well as interesting treatments of George Bernard Shaw's *Heartbreak House* and Büchner's nineteenth-century classic *Danton's Death*. The Mercury Theatre closed its brief career with *The Cradle Will Rock*. The strikingly theatrical style of the productions directed by Orson Welles made him the boy wonder of the American theatre and launched him on a generally successful motion-picture career. The Labor Stage, founded by New York's ladies'-garment-workers' union, aroused enthusiasm and unfulfilled hopes by producing two incisive editions of a topical musical revue, *Pins and Needles*.

The most extensive theatrical venture of the nineteen-thirties was, however, an outgrowth of President Roosevelt's work-relief program. Between 1935 and 1939, the Federal Theatre, as it was called, not only absorbed some ten thousand unemployed actors, directors, designers, writers, and vaudevillians, at a gross cost of forty-six million dollars, but provided theatre for over thirty million people in twenty-nine states, giving approximately twelve hundred productions at popular prices. Led by a great-spirited woman, Hallie Flanagan Davis, who left her Vassar Experimental Theatre to take charge of this far-flung and always tumultuous project, the Federal Theatre presented numerous classics and seventy-seven new plays. It came closest to constituting a "national theatre" for the United States and might have become just that if it had not been abolished by an act of Congress on June 30, 1939. This New Deal institution also gave rise to the one original form of drama developed in the United States. This was a collectively written documentary dealing with such subjects of social interest as public utilities, housing, and venereal disease (*Power, One-Third of a Nation,* and *Spirochete*). In dramatic construction and production style, these "living newspapers" were imaginative and frankly theatrical, being compounded of all kinds of visual aids to knowledge, symbolization, folk humor, and improvisation. Although no particular literary distinction could be claimed for the "living newspaper," it generally constituted provocative and informative theatre. This type of drama had no future on the commercial stage because it required too many collaborators and was generally expensive, but it proved to be of great value in the documentary and war-training films of the Second World War and in educational radio. It could have been adopted with profit by university theatres; it was used once with considerable effect after the war, when Hallie Flanagan Davis created a "living newspaper" on the atom bomb, $E = MC^2$, at Smith College and brought it to Columbia University's Brander Matthews Theatre with a cast of professional and college actors.

All told, the reaction against the economic dislocation of the United States and the concern with the imminence of a new world war produced a large and vigorous theatrical movement. It was augmented by the Broadway theatre when, for example, the Theatre Guild produced such plays as John Wexley's race-prejudice drama *They Shall Not Die* and a variety of other social-problem dramas, when the independent manager Herman Shumlin introduced Lillian Hellman with her first important work, and when the older playwrights (Howard, Anderson, Rice, Sherwood, and Behrman) formed their own producing organization, the Playwrights Company, and triumphed with a series of provocative plays, the best of which was Sherwood's *Abe Lincoln in Illinois.*

Most important to our purpose, however, is the continued force and the extension of dramatic talent among American playwrights. To understand this development we must understand the temper of the country during the decade of unemployment and the literary stream as a whole. The country's writers were, in the main, no longer content to jibe at the vulgarity of Main Street, to exalt art as an escape from the humdrum world, to glorify sophistication, to exploit the discoveries of Freud, to fulminate against puritanical morality, and to call for sexual freedom. Nor did they, with the notable exception of Maxwell Anderson in *High Tor,* air their contempt for the machine as an enemy of individual self-realization. Except for Eugene O'Neill, who continued to deal with man's private devils (in *Mourning Becomes Electra* and in the religious drama *Days Without End*) and who recalled his youth nostalgically with the charming comedy *Ah, Wilderness!,* the playwrights concerned themselves more and more with the social and political organization of the country and with the threat of fascism

from abroad. They were interested less in private difficulties of the ego than in the difficulties that individuals faced together—unemployment, lack of means of subsistence, and racial prejudice. Instead of deploring the introduction of mass production and machinery into the world, they were troubled by the fact that the economic system had broken down. The stress frequently fell on the conflict between employers and the working class and on the disappearance of the hard-pressed middle class, which lost its businesses, homes, and farms. Thus a literature of social protest, variously described as "leftist" or "proletarian," made its appearance. And some of the writers even looked forward to an overthrow of our economic and political system, to its replacement by a socialist society, and to a thoroughgoing defeat of capitalism by an irate, Marxist-directed working class and its intellectual sympathizers. If the theatre of the nineteen-twenties could be described as rebellious, a portion of the theatre of the nineteen-thirties could be called revolutionary.

The playwrights of the period formed only one wing of a movement that included artists, poets, writers of fiction and nonfiction, stage actors, and even Hollywood stars. The dramatist moved along the same road of protest traveled by many poets and novelists. Even authors who in the previous decade had concerned themselves with individual self-realization and sexual frustration (Sherwood Anderson), with objective naturalism (Theodore Dreiser), or with private despair (Ernest Hemingway) joined the literary movement of protest, which was simultaneously anticapitalist and antifascist.

Out of this social and cultural ferment arose the new playwrights. The most widely acclaimed of these was Clifford Odets, the Group Theatre actor who became known as a playwright after the writing of his long one-act strike drama, *Waiting for Lefty.* With the production of *Awake and Sing!,* he came to be considered the most promising playwright to have been discovered in our theatre after the advent of O'Neill. Odets specialized in dramas of middle-class failure, such as *Awake and Sing!, Paradise Lost,* and *Rocket to the Moon,* and in plays which analyzed the social situation generally. He expressed the restiveness of the younger generation and the sense of failure of the older generation, and he supplied his characters with colloquial speech, highly seasoned with the argot of the city streets and with poetic variations based on it. Since his concern was with people collectively, he dealt not with a single central figure but with a group, such as a family and its friends, or members of some profession or business. His dramatic writing was therefore fluid, and his technique recalled Chekhov's. His dialogue frequently got out of hand, his sympathies sometimes resulted in sentimentality, his anger occasionally produced anarchic writing of questionable logic. But there was much human feeling in his work, and his plays contained memorable moments of veracious

observation and of explosive self-revelation or protest on the part of the characters. If Odets had
developed his artistry, he might have become a remarkable playwright. His accomplishment in the
nineteen-thirties was a major source of gratification
to the champions of social drama.

Impressive, too, was the arrival of Lillian Hellman,
with her psychological drama *The Children's Hour*
and her picture of the industrialization of the South
by a breed of robber barons, *The Little Foxes* (1938).
A clearminded grasp of dramatic essentials ruled
her playwriting: her characterization was invariably
sure and skillful, and her plots were always tautly
drawn out. She was relentless in her exposition and
resolution, and once she was on the track of anti-
social behavior, she never lost sight of the objective
of stripping it bare. Although she gave even her villains some interesting characteristics or some human
dimension, she always caught them red-handed. The
poetic spirit was absent from Miss Hellman's work,
and the force of her writing was often gained at the
cost of very heavy plots. But relaxed playwriting
was not natural during the period of tension and
protest; nor was Miss Hellman by nature a relaxed
playwright.

Another effective newcomer was Sidney Kingsley,
introduced by the Group Theatre with a brilliant
production, *Men in White* (1931), a hospital drama
dealing with the conflicting claims of a life of ease
and a life dedicated to medical service. In 1934,
Kingsley aroused much attention with *Dead End*, a
compassionate picture of poverty and slum-bred
crime. Later, his psychological drama *The World
We Make* (1939), a dramatization of Millen Brand's
The Outward Room, revealed a glowing appreciation
of the common man's courage and human warmth,
which save him from desperation and neurotic complications. Kingsley proved himself a painstaking
observer who documented his realism and gave much
of his writing sociological significance. His creativeness did not, as a rule, rise above the mundane scene,
but it was generally convincing and compelling.

Along with such writers as George Sklar and
John Wexley, who knew how to make a fact ring
with drama, the aforementioned social dramatists
brought to the American theatre renewed vigor. It
seemed for a time, indeed, as if no new playwright
worthy of attention could arise without giving his
allegiance to social realism.

The only important member of the group of new
playwrights who could not be classified with the
sociological or revolutionary school was Thornton
Wilder. Having written short plays and such notable
novels as *The Cabala* and *The Bridge of San Luis
Rey* in the previous decade, he emerged in 1938 as
a dramatist of singular talent, with one of the most
original modern plays, *Our Town*. On the surface
his theme was a nostalgic recollection of life in New
England at the beginning of the century, and the
play was therefore removed in time from the tensions then being reflected in the theatre. More
essentially, Wilder addressed himself to the universal
problems of living and dying, so that topical considerations were, in the main, irrelevant to his
purpose. He wrote an originally constructed, beautifully styled drama that could not be subsumed in
any category other than that of imaginative art. At
the most, it could be said that *Our Town* was the
sort of play that could not have arisen quite so
naturally in any large Western European nation
and that its earnest concern with the common way
of life had an American ring. *Our Town*, however,
would always have been an exception to the general
run of playwriting, whether it had appeared in the
'twenties or in any other period.

The playwrights of the generation of the nineteen-
twenties, moreover, added their response to the
social situation in the new decade of social realism.
Philip Barry symbolized the confusions of the times
in such plays as *Hotel Universe* (1930) and *Here
Come the Clowns* (1938) with much magic, if also
with some confusion, and S. N. Behrman turned
to comedy of ideas, dramatizing social and political
conflict. In *Biography*, he presented the irreconcila-
ble attitudes of an embattled reformer and of a woman too good-natured to join his crusade; in *Rain
from Heaven*, the impossibility of leading a detached
intellectual life in the contemporary world of lust for
power, race hatred, and totalitarian ambition; in
End of Summer, the emotional bankruptcy of the
idle rich. Throughout his work, Behrman retained
an intelligent detachment such as we expect from a
writer of high comedies with a style distinguished
by lucidity and wit.

Still another member of the old guard, Sidney
Howard, wrote two antiwar plays and a drama of
scientific idealism, *Yellow Jack*. Elmer Rice offered
impassioned works of protest, such as *We, the
People*, as well as character comedy, such as *Counsellor-at-Law*, in which he flayed snobbery and
hypocrisy. And Paul Green joined the protesting
dramatists with his antiwar drama *Johnny Johnson*
and with a powerful one-act chain-gang drama,
Hymn to the Rising Sun. Kaufman and his collaborators satirized politics in the bright musical
comedy *Of Thee I Sing*, reviewed the failure of the
intelligentsia in a rueful, if also sentimental, chronicle, *Merrily We Roll Along*, and reflected the depression with a madcap comedy, *You Can't Take It
With You*.

It was during the 'thirties, too, that Robert Sherwood reached the peak of his powers and importance. His ascent after *Reunion in Vienna* was entirely a response to the spirit of the times: a concern
with the loss of nerve in our civilization and the
triumph of international gangsterism (*The Petrified
Forest*), with the inevitability of a second world war
(*Idiot's Delight*), and with an affirmation of ideals
of social justice in another era of stress (*Abe
Lincoln in Illinois*). The age of anxiety produced in

Sherwood's work first a sense of acute distress and then a positive stand that turned him into an ardent supporter of Franklin Delano Roosevelt and his New Deal philosophy of government. Since Sherwood was an expert showman, he was able to give theatrical effectiveness to his concerns and convictions.

Seemingly, Maxwell Anderson strove to stand above the contemporary scene, convinced as he was that greatness in the drama lay in the universality of its meaning, in the heroic stature of its characters, and in the distinction of its language. Beginning with *Elizabeth the Queen* (1930), he wrote his most ambitious plays mostly in verse and achieved in them some largeness of spirit. In his chronicles of Elizabeth and Mary Stuart, followed in the nineteen-forties by his drama of Anne Boleyn and Henry VIII, *Anne of the Thousand Days,* he inevitably also achieved an independence of the times. But in a number of other plays, Anderson was stirred to comment on the concerns of the decade. Contempt for self-seeking politicians was mingled with affirmations of the common man's passion for liberty in *Valley Forge*. Detestation of corrupt politicians animated the prose satire on Congress *Both Your Houses,* and hatred for social injustice flared magnificently in the powerful second act of *Winterset*. Scorn for modern materialism gave a sharp edge to the verse fantasy *High Tor*. Anderson's concern with the question of revolution and his disenchantment with its results lifted portions of *The Masque of Kings* out of the Graustark category of political romance. The realization that one could not escape a conflict with fascism or equivalent evils motivated the writing of *Key Largo*.

That even such a writer as Anderson, bent upon universalizing the drama, could not remain disengaged from the struggles of the decade may indicate the intensity of the claims of contemporary problems upon the dramatists who tried to create significant art. To be sure, not all playwrights became embattled or somber. Comedy and farce removed from social issues continued to be written and enjoyed. One may cite such examples as Rachel Crothers' *Susan and God* (the best play of an old hand at comedy), *The Philadelphia Story* (one of Philip Barry's best works), Clare Boothe's vitriolic comedy *The Women,* the Sam and Bella Spewack broad Hollywood satire *Boy Meets Girl,* the brisk farces *Three Men on a Horse* and *Room Service,* and the immensely successful *Life With Father*. But the dominant note of social concern continued throughout the decade, now also concerned with the imminence of armed conflict. Even the related arts responded to the turmoil. Dance drama and pantomime acquired social connotations; for a brief time, radio offered antifascist poetic dramas, such as Archibald MacLeish's *The Fall of the City* and *Air Raid;* Hollywood turned out such films as *Mr. Smith Goes to Washington* and *The Grapes of Wrath*. When the decade ended, Europe was already engaged in the Second World War and new challenges were arising to bedevil the playwright and his audience.

THE WAR AND ITS AFTERMATH

As a result of the wartime industrial boom, the economic situation of the theatre in the nineteen-forties seemed greatly relieved. The demand for entertainment increased rapidly; theatres filled quickly despite fantastic admission prices. Nonetheless, the theatre was in an unhealthy condition and its ailments became visible the moment wartime spending ceased. Production costs mounted and remained stabilized on an inflationary basis even after the playgoing public became more economical in its spending for entertainment. For the state of the drama, however, two factors were of the most serious consequence: First, the number of productions decreased and new playwrights found too little opportunity to serve an apprenticeship; secondly, it became increasingly uneconomic to undertake or keep on the boards plays that did not gross huge weekly sums.

Little room was left in the professional theatre for the "in-between" play—that is, the play that could command only moderately large audiences. Such plays were, as a rule, closed by the producer within two days or at the most three weeks (on which basis the producer could share in the sale of motion-picture rights). The alternatives for the drama were superfluity or starvation. Since most of the important plays of the modern theatre were not "smash hits" when first produced, the inability to put on in-between drama became a deterrent to experiment. This situation became even more grave when Hollywood began to suffer sharp reverses as a result of both falling box-office receipts and discriminatory taxation in Britain. Hollywood had invested huge sums of money in Broadway productions and paid even larger sums for rights to Broadway successes. After 1948, the motion-picture industry ceased to finance Broadway productions and severely limited its purchases of even successfully produced plays.

Another and incalculable difficulty that a number of dramatists had to overcome during the decade of the 'forties was the disappearance to a great extent of the social enthusiasm of the 'thirties and of the groups that it had sustained. The Theatre Union disbanded in 1937; the American Repertory Company disappeared at about the same time; the Mercury Theatre collapsed after three exciting seasons; the Federal Theatre was abolished in 1939; the New Theatre League disintegrated; and even the important Group Theatre succumbed in 1941. The few new organizations that arose to take the place of the old proved feeble, although the Group Theatre's influence continued to be felt on Broadway and in such experimental theatres as the Actor's Laboratory Theatre in Los Angeles and New Stages in Greenwich Village. An effort was made shortly after the war by ANTA (the American National Theatre and Academy) to revitalize the theatre in communities outside New York and to establish an Experimental Theatre in New York. But the results were still uncertain in 1950.

The old social drama lost standing after 1940, and the fervor of the playwrights, along with those of the novelists and poets, cooled considerably. Many writers who in the 'thirties had been or had thought they were radicals, or even communists, lost their revolutionary faith. They were deeply troubled by events in Soviet Russia and, after a brief renewal of faith during the years when Russia resisted and crushed the Germans, their dismay even increased as the Stalin government turned its neighboring nations into satellites. One of the conspicuous tendencies of the decade, especially after 1945, was the rise of literature of disillusionment with communism, socialism, and even New Deal philosophy. To a large degree, the social-protest movement of the previous decade fell apart. A vacuum developed in the theatre, as in other forms of recreation. To what extent it was filled is a question to which the following pages propose an answer.

For one thing, the period's theatre was enriched by a succession of musical comedies and music dramas which represented considerable progress in this form of imaginative drama. Judged solely by the printed text, their theatrical charm and power seem, as a rule, nonexistent but for an occasionally felicitous expression and effective lyric. As theatre, however, the fusion of text, music, dance, and scenery can be vastly attractive. Playgoers in a period of anxiety and wartime prosperity welcomed such entertainment, and able teams of writers, composers, and theatre artists collaborated to provide it. The classic of the period was, of course, *Oklahoma* (1943), the folk musical by Richard Rodgers and Oscar Hammerstein II.

The war naturally provided a stimulus to the writing of war plays, antifascist drama, and works of liberal sentiment. Immediately after the war, a certain degree of democratic enthusiasm also made itself felt, taking the form of attacks on racial discrimination. Even Hollywood responded to this desire to combat the racism that had been defeated on the battle fronts of Europe but was not yet eradicated at home, as may be seen from such films as *Gentleman's Agreement* and *Home of the Brave*.

But the advent of the atom bomb, followed by a struggle for power—this time between the West and Russia—proved by 1950 beyond the capacity of the theatre to absorb. No great American war literature arose during this period—in poetry, fiction, or drama. Our satisfaction with the theatre could be only moderate; we could take pride chiefly in the reflection that our war-inspired drama was rarely objectionable and often considerably intelligent.

Our one noteworthy antifascist melodrama, Lillian Hellman's *Watch on the Rhine*, was written so intelligently that "melodrama" is actually a misnomer. A lean kind of writing characterized pictures of the fighting or of the Resistance movement in Europe, as in the work of such newcomers as the poet Harry Brown (*A Sound of Hunting*) and Dan James (*Winter Soldiers*). Among several efforts by Maxwell Anderson, *The Eve of St. Mark* was honestly poignant until its conclusion—one of sentimental fantasy. Elmer Rice wrote a closely reasoned treatment of the conflict between democratic and fascist ideals in *Flight to the West*. Robert Sherwood contributed a thoughtful treatment of men of peace resisting tyranny, *There Shall Be No Night*. It is to be noted, too, that plays stimulated by the war crisis but not directly concerned with it occasionally possessed impressive features. Among these plays were such historical dramas as Sidney Kingsley's early-American chronicle *The Patriots* and Howard Koch and John Huston's story of Woodrow Wilson's struggle for a League of Nations, *In Time to Come*. Thornton Wilder, moreover, interpreted the crisis in one original, imaginative drama that telescoped the history of man's struggle for survival through the ages, *The Skin of Our Teeth*.

It was, in fact, a distinguishing feature of the theatre that its awareness of humanity and of principle overshadowed the details of battle and strategy usually unmanageable on the stage. This was true even when, as in William Wister Haines's *Command Decision*, the actual plot concerned strategic bombing, or when the war was used with a flair for Broadway showmanship, as in Thomas Heggen and Joshua Logan's *Mister Roberts*. The human being was not often lost even in the pursuit of principle, as could be seen in Paul Osborn's dramatization of *A Bell for Adano*, in John Patrick's back-of-the-lines hospital drama, *The Hasty Heart*, and in Arthur Laurents' psychological drama of racial prejudice, *Home of the Brave*. A play about the conditioning of German youth under Hitler, James Gow and Arnaud d'Usseau's *Tomorrow the World*, was written not only with sympathetic understanding but with clinical objectivity. When Emmet Lavery wanted to uphold American ideals, he drew a warm portrait of Oliver Wendell Holmes, *The Magnificent Yankee*. Elsewhere, across the Atlantic Ocean (especially in Central Europe and in Italy), destructive forces were at work in the theatre. In America, the difficulty was chiefly the absence of constructive forces, except, possibly, for a trend toward the composition of comedies of liberal persuasion, such as Garson Kanin's *Born Yesterday* and Howard Lindsay and Russel Crouse's *State of the Union*.

However, when nothing in the social or cultural matrix proves to be particularly provocative, we can always look to personal endowment, as we must do in any case. In the final reckoning, the decade exhibits some distinction because Wilder wrote *The Skin of Our Teeth*, because O'Neill finally released for production his "lower depths" drama *The Iceman Cometh,* and because William Saroyan, Tennessee Williams, and Arthur Miller unfolded their talent.

Saroyan, already known as a story writer, was the most promising early discovery of the theatre of the nineteen-forties. After *My Heart's in the Highlands,* produced in 1939, his star blazed for a while when he wrote *The Time of Your Life* and was still luminous when he added *Love's Old Sweet Song, The Beautiful People,* and the powerful one-acter *Hello, Out There.* These plays came at the beginning of the decade, before an undisciplined talent removed him from the theatrical firmament. He brought to the stage a highly individual poetry—a bizarre improvisation and, at times, an oddly touching lyricism. Because his sentimentality was gritty, it escaped the usual American objections to sentiment. Saroyan was aggressively in love with the common man, the failure, and the outcast. Such enthusiasm was appealing at a time when the economic depression was just beginning to lift; a few years later, when the memory of seedy times had been banished, the public might have been less grateful for the balm offered in his plays. Saroyan was also a rhapsodist of freedom and of the brotherhood of man, and he expressed his enthusiasm for these ideals with much verve just when they were being driven from large segments of the globe by the advance of totalitarianism.

Explanations of Tennessee Williams' success are less dependent upon the spirit of the times. Although he had been introduced to Boston by the Theatre Guild at the beginning of the decade, he first arrived on Broadway, with *The Glass Menagerie,* in 1945, when anxiety over the outcome of the war was receding and we were less in need of such reassurances as Saroyan had offered. With Williams, we could settle down again to the enjoyment of sober artistry and the study of character. His specialty was an acute dramatic sensibility, delicately presented in his first Broadway success, forcefully—if also somewhat sensationally—thrust forth in his most popular play, *A Streetcar Named Desire,* and less successfully but still impressively revealed in *Summer and Smoke.* He managed, up to a point, to universalize the drama of failure and to give his plays a poetic texture.

Arthur Miller was the third important newcomer. His was the latest arrival on Broadway (an early play had failed), but it became the most heralded as the nineteen-forties ended. His first well-received drama, *All My Sons,* recalled the realistic Ibsen in technique and Sardou in its contrived, last-minute revelation; it also recalled the Group Theatre style of realistic social indictment or lesson. Its moral fervor was strong, its characterization firm, its dramaturgy tightly packed. Miller's remarkably successful next effort, *Death of a Salesman,* was also rooted in familiar middle-class realism and it contained overtones of social criticism. But the strength of this extraordinary play came, in part, from its moving presentation of a little man's failure and, in part, from the author's use of the discontinuous fantasy technique made familiar by the expressionists of the 'twenties but rarely applied so cogently. Miller succeeded in pulling together the past and the present and in giving his work psychological and dramatic force. In *Death of a Salesman* he carried the long familiar trend toward middle-class tragedy to a triumphant climax. He managed, moreover, to convey a poetry of the commonplace, partly in his writing and largely in his imaginative use of the stage. Miller proved himself one of the most successful exponents of the school of playwriting that blends modern realism with a poetry of the theatre.

The foundations for an important American drama have been firmly laid since 1918, and the past three decades have brought a variety of achievements. Realism has been used with vividness; social drama has acquired vigor and fire. Naturalism has not only dealt with tabooed subjects but has become permeated with poetry and feeling. Since the early 'twenties our playwrights have shown an adeptness at folk drama and a promise in the direction of fantasy. It has been no small achievement to have developed two kinds of comedy: a "low," unliterary type that has the virtue of being briskly shrewd and a high comedy that has glittered, now and then, with keen edge, whether dealing with manners or with ideas in conflict. Moreover, American dramatists have not bound themselves to any particular technique; they have not hesitated to move from a play written in a realistic mode to one conceived in imaginative theatrical form.

The interpenetration of the truth of everyday life with the truth of the imagination (especially theatrical imagination) has appeared, in differing degrees, in the plays of O'Neill, Wilder, Maxwell Anderson, Connelly, Saroyan, Williams, Miller, and even Odets. Indeed, if any important tendency emerges from the entire course of our drama since the advent of O'Neill, it is this effort on the part of our most significant playwrights to mediate the requirements of realistic description and of the creative imagination. This is a singular tendency in a nation regarded as the exemplar of down-to-earth practicality. When our theatre arrived at maturity, it absorbed two originally divergent aims of the modern European theatre—that of the realists and naturalists and that of the symbolists and expressionists. This circumstance is surely significant, though it may prove to be merely a contributory factor. In the end, of course, to account for this characteristic of much of our best drama we must look to the intentions and to the temperaments of the individual playwrights. We shall give some discussion to these elements in the introductions that precede our eleven examples of modern American drama.

Eugene O'Neill

(1888– ——)

Although the American theatre gave rise to a number of able playwrights after 1920 and great claims were made for some of them, no one in a responsible mood has ever disputed Eugene O'Neill's pre-eminence among our dramatists. He is the only American playwright whose international reputation has been firmly established, a fact that was formally acknowledged with a Nobel Prize in 1936. Since he experimented in many forms and explored a variety of themes, it is not easy to describe O'Neill's efforts comprehensively without examining them in detail. But they all had the same intention: the promotion of a theatre that would illuminate the inner man and would possess as much human significance as the drama could hold. This significance was for O'Neill, moreover, almost always a fundamentally spiritual one.

As the son of the successful actor James O'Neill, who toured extensively with his wife, Eugene O'Neill had a childhood that was not blessed with much stability. He was born in a Broadway hotel and educated intermittently at various Catholic schools while his parents roved across the country. Later, his stay at Princeton was of brief duration; he was suspended for a freshman prank and did not bother to return. He married early and entered business. But he felt the call of the sea almost immediately and ultimately dissolved his marriage. In 1909, he went prospecting for gold in Honduras with a mining engineer. Returning without gold after contracting malaria, he joined his father's company as assistant manager for a time but grew restless again and signed on a Norwegian vessel for a voyage from Boston to Buenos Aires. In Argentina, he worked at various occupations—in the Westinghouse Electric Company, in a packing plant, and in the office of the Singer Sewing Machine Company. Tiring of the sedentary life of a clerk, he embarked on a cattle steamer from Buenos Aires to South Africa and tended mules on the ship. He experienced a period of destitution on his return to Argentina, finally found a berth on a British tramp steamer bound for New York, and once in New York lived "on the beach" in a water-front bar. He became an able seaman on the American Line, made a trip that took him to Southampton, and then decided to settle down. After playing a small part for his father in the popular melodrama *The Count of Monte Cristo,* he found a position in Connecticut on the *New London Telegraph,* and began contributing a humorous column. But his strenuous life had undermined his health. He developed tuberculosis and spent six months in a sanatorium.

During his convalescence, O'Neill gave special attention to the drama, particularly to the works of the Greeks and of Strindberg, and began to write short plays of his own. Desiring some formal training, he enrolled in Professor George Pierce Baker's "47 Workshop" course at Harvard during 1914–1915. Next, he associated himself with the Greenwich Village writers who formed the Provincetown Players in 1915, and acted and wrote plays for them at their Wharf Theatre in Provincetown, Massachusetts. In the summer of 1916, they gave O'Neill his first production, *Bound East for Cardiff,* a short sea piece notable for its brooding and somber mood. When the group settled in its Greenwich Village playhouse, O'Neill became one of its most active members, as well as an associate of the equally young and experimental Washington Square Players. All of O'Neill's early short plays were produced by these two organizations.

Between 1915 and 1919, a radical transformation took place in the American theatre largely as a result of the activity of "little theatres" devoted to art instead of to the prevailing commercialism of the stage. O'Neill became the major discovery of the little-theatre movement. The Provincetown Players produced most of his early work, and the Theatre Guild, an outgrowth of the Washington Square Players, became his official theatre afer the financial collapse of the Provincetown.

But after 1919 the commercial managers also began to show interest in O'Neill's writing. John D. Williams produced two of his early plays: his first full-length tragedy of fate, *Beyond the Horizon* (1920), and his romantic drama *Gold* (1921). George C. Tyler presented the first version of *Anna Christie* under the title *Chris Christopherson* (1920) and the psychological drama *The Straw* (1921). Arthur Hopkins staged *Anna Christie* in November 1921.

O'Neill was never a neglected artist. He found a champion in the critic and man of the world George Jean Nathan. He won the Pulitzer Prize in 1920, 1922, and 1928, made many friends who valued him highly, and found such able associates in the theatre as Robert Edmond Jones, Kenneth MacGowan, and the brilliant Theatre Guild stage director Philip Moeller. If a number of O'Neill's plays did not reach a very large public, it was largely because he experimented with dramatic forms and psychological complications that at first required a select audience. When he broadened the interest of his plays and they were given good productions, he found, more often than not, a large public, willing and eager to follow as far as he wished to lead. O'Neill won signal honors for the modern American theatre and, since he was an uncompromising artist, he always won them on his own terms. In England, a number of critics felt uncomfortable in the presence of his uninhibited playwriting and his passionate creativeness. But he commanded, and still commands, great respect in America and on the Continent.

O'Neill's search for dramatic expression took him into every conceivable field except the militant social drama of the nineteen-thirties, and even this genre owes much to his pioneering in realism. His vigorously descriptive and colloquial one-act plays, assembled in the "S.S. Glencairn cycle," presented the loneliness and bedevilment of common sailors. Despite a romantically charged atmosphere, these dramatic pictures, often fatalistic in philosophy and concerned with human failure and desperation, constituted a triumph for the realistic or, more accurately, naturalistic theatre. His first full-length work, *Beyond the Horizon,* a tragedy of frustration on a farm, extended this victory; and *Anna Christie* confirmed it by setting forth the life of the water front and the fate of a fallen woman. Such minor and unsuccessful efforts as *The First Man* (1922) and *Welded* (1924) revealed Strindbergian influences in the psychological tensions of the characters. A bleak naturalistic background was presented in the slum environment of *All God's Chillun Got Wings* (1924), an original work that went far beyond its ostensible problem of miscegenation. *Desire Under the Elms* (1924) was psychologically centered—in a tense father-son conflict.

O'Neill did not confine himself, however, to any single style; nor was he ever content with photographic representations of reality. His realistic plays had poetic and symbolic qualities. As early as 1920, moreover, he wrote one of the first expressionistic plays in America, *The Emperor Jones,* turning it into a tour de force. It dramatized a self-confident Negro dictator's growing fears and mental breakdown in short, rapidly shifting, subjective scenes intensified by the incessant beat of native tom-toms. Two years later, in *The Hairy Ape,* O'Neill added symbolism to the expressionistic presentation of a brutish stoker's search for a place in society, converting the play into an allegory of modern man's torment. In *All God's Chillun Got Wings,* he used expressionistic emphases and symbolism. In 1925, after *The Fountain,* a mild, romantic play about Ponce de León's search for eternal youth, O'Neill went even further in the direction of subjective drama, with *The Great God Brown.* This remarkable, if somewhat puzzling, tragedy of dual personality expressed the anguish of divided souls by means of masks worn and exchanged by two complementary characters. Three

other symbolic plays followed this tantalizing exploration of the inner self: *Lazarus Laughed* (1927), a poetic, but repetitiously static and rather fulsome, defiance of death; *Dynamo* (1929), a strained quest for a satisfying faith, which materialism fails to supply; and *Days Without End* (1934), another study of "split personality," here concluded with a reconciliation between self-tortured intellectuality and religious faith. These and other works gave effective testimony to their author's conviction that "it is only by means of some form of 'super-naturalism' that we may express in the theatre what we comprehend intuitively of that self-obsession which is the particular discount we moderns have to pay for the loan of life."

After composing the romantic satire on materialism *Marco Millions,* O'Neill climaxed his efforts with his novelistic nine-act drama *Strange Interlude* (1928), one of the most ambitious works written for the modern theatre. Striving to present the complex inner life of a woman from girlhood to middle age (that is, the "strange interlude" of her sexual awakening and maturity), he invented the device of the "interior monologue," a bold and elaborate variant of the old-fashioned "aside." Each character spoke both his conscious and unconscious thoughts, thus revealing himself more completely than ordinary dialogue permits. The procedure of presenting the story on two complementary levels amplified modern dramatic technique and gave *Strange Interlude* the same status in the history of the modern drama that James Joyce's stream-of-consciousness narrative *Ulysses* occupies in the history of the modern novel. But O'Neill did not expend this technical virtuosity and psychological method on humdrum material. Nothing less than the substance of an extensive life history involving other life histories went into *Strange Interlude.* If the technique was complex, so was the life of O'Neill's heroine, Nina Leeds. Frustrated by the jealousy of her father and the death of the lover who might have fulfilled her, she is driven to complete herself through simultaneous attachments to three men, who are for her, respectively, father image, husband, and lover.

For his other large venture, *Mourning Becomes Electra* (1931), O'Neill needed no new methods of representation; he told the story of his New England aristocrats, the Mannons, without marked deviation from realism or much formal embellishment. The play could be accepted on the level of psychological melodrama as the story of hereditary evil and hate, adultery, murder, incestuous drives, and suicide. Nevertheless, this drama possessed greater tragic depth and scope than any American play written before or after it. This Freudian transcription of the Oresteian trilogy of Aeschylus and of the other Greek Electra plays was a trilogy in thirteen acts. Although the treatment took into consideration the influence of puritanical religion and possessiveness in a New England mercantile family, its chief accomplishment was the unearthing of the complexes that psychoanalysis had brought to the attention of the age. The effect of the play was that of tragic catharsis on an almost epic scale. O'Neill defined his masterpiece perhaps better than any of his critics when he framed this question in his first note on *Mourning Becomes Electra,* five years before the play's completion: "Is it possible to get modern psychological approximation of the Greek sense of fate into such a play which an intelligent audience of today, possessed by no belief in gods or supernatural retribution, could accept and be moved by?" This play appears to have provided purgation even for its author, since it was followed, in 1933, by a genial comedy of adolescence and small-town life, *Ah, Wilderness!* If O'Neill felt any relief in 1933, however, it was a temporary one, for the exceptionally long and painful play he wrote in 1939, *The Iceman Cometh* (produced in 1946) is perhaps the most relentlessly depressing drama written by any modern playwright. *The Iceman Cometh* refuted a belief that its author had become reconciled with the Catholic faith of his childhood—a belief which had gained some currency after the presentation of his earlier play *Days Without End* (1933).

In 1940, O'Neill completed a play which he resolved not to have produced during his lifetime: *Long Day's Journey into Night.* In 1947, he exposed to public view *A Moon for the Misbegotten,* written four years earlier; he withdrew it after a brief Midwestern tryout because of a difficult casting problem. In addition, from 1934 to 1947, years of virtual seclusion and ill health spent on Sea Island, Georgia, and in California's Valley of the Moon, he was engaged on a long cycle of eleven plays carrying the working title *A Tale of Possessors Self-Dispossessed.* One of these, *A Touch of the Poet,* intended to start the cycle, was ready for production by 1947. In 1949, however, O'Neill, whose condition had taken a turn for the worse, let it be known that no more plays were to be expected from him.

A complete estimate of this dedicated artist must await publication, or at least perusal, of what has surely been the most Cyclopean dramatic enterprise in the English language. Even without the cycle, however, O'Neill's work is a challenge to dramatic criticism and has evoked a sharp division of opinion. His claims to respect as our most important playwright are nevertheless beyond questioning.

If O'Neill tended to be anything but sparing in his complexities, it is nonetheless true that he was able to hold American audiences, the most restless in the world, with his theatrical force and earnestness. If he often schematized and overexplained psychological complications, his insistence on their presence and force was impressive. If his ideas often seemed borrowed and too baldly expressed, they were maintained with sufficient passion to appear to be discoveries in the American theatre, even though they were discoveries nowhere else. If his plots were

frequently melodramatic and if he seemed to pile one violent effect on top of another, one could always be certain that O'Neill was oppressed, as the Elizabethans John Webster and Cyril Tourneur were, with the terror of man's passions and with the baleful machinery of evil in the world. And if his language often lagged woefully behind the vaulting quality of his action, in the theatre the great sweep of drama in his plays created a tide of emotion difficult to resist. The well-trained and discriminating reader may have been appalled at some of the writing when he saw it on the printed page, but the playgoer was generally awed. Other playwrights might have been cleverer and more graceful than O'Neill, and it is certain that he was no Olympian artist; yet no one matched his sultry turbulence, in which there was considerable splendor. In his early work, moreover, he often displayed his dramatic effects with comparative freedom from prolixity and excess.

Anna Christie, which follows, by no means reveals the greatest depth and furthest range of O'Neill's powers and ambitions. But if it lacks the scope of several of its author's later works, it has the merit of comparative compactness; and if it does not probe as deeply into human nature, it is also free from their more troublesome obscurities, their schematization of psychological forces, and their tragic straining. A fairly simple human drama, it provides emotions more or less readily accessible to the reader. Its pungently colloquial speech and its seedy heroine represent the early portion of O'Neill's career, when he rooted the American theatre in naturalism. The play also suggests some of the characteristics of his later writing—namely, his poetic vein, present here in his feeling for the sea, his concern with obsessed characters, and his saturnine sense of fatality in human experience.

Anna Christie grew out of an earlier written play, *Chris* or *Chris Christopherson,* produced unsuccessfully and withdrawn during its tryout tour. As Barrett H. Clark, O'Neill's biographer, explains, "In its final version *Anna Christie* is a play about a woman. It was in the beginning a play about the woman's father." One objection that has been raised is that the play suffers from this shift in emphasis. Another is that Anna's story bears too much resemblance to the fallen-woman drama we associate with old-fashioned sentimental plays. Critics have also questioned the "happy ending" and suspected O'Neill of compromising the integrity of his play in the manner of Henry Arthur Jones and other pseudo modernists. O'Neill was particularly troubled by the last charge and wrote George Jean Nathan expressing regret that the conclusion, in which Anna and the sailor are reunited, gave a "happy-ever-after" impression that he never intended. "And the sea outside—life—waits," he wrote. "The happy ending is merely the comma at the end of a gaudy introductory clause, with the body of the sentence still unwritten." He added that he had once thought of calling the play

Comma, and complained that it was impossible to project clearly the "sincerity of life pent up in the trappings of theatre." That is, he feared he had not pointed up sufficiently the tentativeness of the happy reunion, in spite of Anna's father's foreboding last speech, the Irish sailor's doubts about the non-Catholic Anna's oath, and the implication that although the characters "have had their moment, the decision still rests with the sea. . . ."

Whether there is any way of reconciling different and seemingly unfused aspects of the play is open to question. So friendly a critic as Barrett H. Clark does not think there is. More than a quarter of a century after the production of the play, however, George Jean Nathan, who had been the first to raise points of criticism, could write: "1920 . . . *Anna Christie* is a new and forceful handling of a familiar theme, deep in its characterizations, driving in its firm composition, and etched with real observation and understanding." Since this is the considered opinion of a critic who was as eagle-eyed in 1947 as he was in 1920, it bears thinking about. As Eleanor Flexner has suggested in her *American Playwrights 1918–1938,* O'Neill is at his best when, as in *Anna Christie,* his creative instinct is emotional rather than intellectual in origin. *Anna Christie* did not deal primarily with "ideas"—at which O'Neill was no master—but with living people trapped by their circumstances. They are shown trying desperately to wriggle out of a net of fate partly of their own making, partly woven by the environment to which they succumbed, and partly knotted by a destiny undefined but poetically sensed by O'Neill. We may add the possibility that the crudity of the play—that is, a certain incomplete fusion of emphases—makes *Anna Christie* all the more genuine by giving it a feeling of "life observed" rather than of "play plotted."

BIBLIOGRAPHY: Brooks Atkinson, *Broadway Scrapbook* (pp. 52–55, 241–246), 1947; Eric Bentley, *The Playwright as Thinker* (pp. 67–69, 223–285, 318–322), 1946; Anita Block, *The Changing World in Plays and Theatre* (pp. 137–193), 1939; John Mason Brown, *Letters from the Greenroom* (pp. 71–116), 1934; Brown, *Two on the Aisle* (pp. 136–142), 1938; Brown, *Seeing More Things,* (pp. 257–265), 1948; Barrett H. Clark, *Eugene O'Neill: The Man and His Work,* 1947; Eleanor Flexner, *American Playwrights 1918–1938* (pp. 130–197), 1938; John Gassner, *Masters of the Drama* (pp. 641–661), 1940, 1945; Joseph Wood Krutch, Introduction to *Nine Plays by Eugene O'Neill,* 1932; Krutch, *The American Drama Since 1918* (pp. 23–29, 73–133, 288–291), 1939; George Jean Nathan, *The Theatre Book of the Year 1946–1947* (pp. 93–111), 1947; Richard Dana Skinner, *Eugene O'Neill, a Poet's Quest,* 1935; Sophus Keith Winther, *Eugene O'Neill: A Critical Study,* 1934; Stark Young, *Immortal Shadows,* (pp. 61–66, 132–139, 271–274), 1948.

For additional commentary, see pages 817–818.

ANNA CHRISTIE

By Eugene O'Neill

CHARACTERS

"JOHNNY-THE-PRIEST"
TWO LONGSHOREMEN
A POSTMAN
LARRY, *bartender*

CHRIS CHRISTOPHERSON, *captain of the barge* Simeon Winthrop
MARTHY OWEN
ANNA CHRISTOPHERSON, *Chris' daughter*

THREE MEN OF A STEAMER'S CREW
MAT BURKE, *a stoker*
JOHNSON, *deckhand on the barge*

ACT I.

SCENE. "Johnny-the-Priest's" *saloon near South Street, New York City. The stage is divided into two sections, showing a small back room on the right. On the left, forward, of the barroom, a large window looking out on the street. Beyond it, the main entrance—a double swinging door. Farther back, another window. The bar runs from left to right nearly the whole length of the rear wall. In back of the bar, a small show-case displaying a few bottles of case goods, for which there is evidently little call. The remainder of the rear space in front of the large mirrors is occupied by half-barrels of cheap whisky of the "nickel-a-shot" variety, from which the liquor is drawn by means of spigots. On the right is an open doorway leading to the back room. In the back room are four round wooden tables with five chairs grouped about each. In the rear, a family entrance opening on a side street.*

It is late afternoon of a day in fall.

As the curtain rises, Johnny *is discovered.* "Johnny-the-Priest" *deserves his nickname. With his pale, thin, clean-shaven face, mild blue eyes and white hair, a cassock would seem more suited to him than the apron he wears. Neither his voice nor his general manner dispel this illusion which has made him a personage of the water front. They are soft and bland. But beneath all his mildness one senses the man behind the mask—cynical, callous, hard as nails. He is lounging at ease behind the bar, a pair of spectacles on his nose, reading an evening paper.*

Two longshoremen enter from the street, wearing their working aprons, the button of the union pinned conspicuously on the caps pulled sideways on their heads at an aggressive angle.

FIRST LONGSHOREMAN: [*As they range themselves at the bar*] Gimme a shock. Number Two.

[*He tosses a coin on the bar*]

SECOND LONGSHOREMAN: Same here.

[Johnny *sets two glasses of barrel whisky before them*]

FIRST LONGSHOREMAN: Here's luck!

[*The other nods. They gulp down their whisky*]

SECOND LONGSHOREMAN: [*Putting money on the bar*] Give us another.

FIRST LONGSHOREMAN: Gimme a scoop this time —lager and porter. I'm dry.

SECOND LONGSHOREMAN: Same here.

[Johnny *draws the lager and porter and sets the big, foaming schooners before them. They drink down half the contents and start to talk together hurriedly in low tones. The door on the left is swung open and* Larry *enters. He is a boyish, red-cheeked, rather good-looking young fellow of twenty or so*]

LARRY: [*Nodding to* Johnny—*cheerily*] Hello, boss.

JOHNNY: Hello, Larry. [*With a glance at his watch*] Just on time.

[Larry *goes to the right behind the bar, takes off his coat, and puts on an apron*]

FIRST LONGSHOREMAN: [*Abruptly*] Let's drink up and get back to it.

[*They finish their drinks and go out left. The* Postman *enters as they leave. He exchanges nods with* Johnny *and throws a letter on the bar*]

THE POSTMAN: Addressed care of you, Johnny. Know him?

JOHNNY: [*Picks up the letter, adjusting his spectacles.* Larry *comes and peers over his shoulders.* Johnny *reads very slowly*] Christopher Christopherson.

THE POSTMAN: [*Helpfully*] Square-head name.

LARRY: Old Chris—that's who.

JOHNNY: Oh, sure. I was forgetting Chris carried a hell of a name like that. Letters come here for him sometimes before, I remember now. Long time ago, though.

THE POSTMAN: It'll get him all right then?

JOHNNY: Sure thing. He comes here whenever he's in port.

THE POSTMAN: [*Turning to go*] Sailor, eh?

JOHNNY: [*With a grin*] Captain of a coal barge.

THE POSTMAN: [*Laughing*] Some job! Well, s'long.

JOHNNY: S'long. I'll see he gets it.

[*The Postman goes out. Johnny scrutinizes the*

letter] You got good eyes, Larry. Where's it from?

LARRY: [*After a glance*] St. Paul. That'll be in Minnesota, I'm thinkin'. Looks like a woman's writing, too, the old divil!

JOHNNY: He's got a daughter somewhere's out West, I think he told me once. [*He puts the letter on the cash register*] Come to think of it, I ain't seen old Chris in a dog's age. [*Putting his overcoat on, he comes around the end of the bar*] Guess I'll be gettin' home. See you tomorrow.

LARRY: Good night to ye, boss.

[*As Johnny goes toward the street door, it is pushed open and* Christopher Christopherson *enters. He is a short, squat, broad-shouldered man of about fifty, with a round, weather-beaten, red face from which his light blue eyes peer short-sightedly, twinkling with a simple good humor. His large mouth, overhung by a thick, drooping, yellow mustache, is childishly self-willed and weak, of an obstinate kindliness. A thick neck is jammed like a post into the heavy trunk of his body. His arms with their big, hairy, freckled hands, and his stumpy legs terminating in large flat feet, are awkwardly short and muscular. He walks with a clumsy, rolling gait. His voice, when not raised in a hollow boom, is toned down to a sly, confidential half-whisper with something vaguely plaintive in its quality. He is dressed in a wrinkled, ill-fitting dark suit of shore clothes, and wears a faded cap of gray cloth over his mop of grizzled, blond hair. Just now his face beams with a too-blissful happiness, and he has evidently been drinking. He reaches his hand out to* Johnny]

CHRIS: Hello, Johnny! Have drink on me. Come on, Larry. Give us drink. Have one yourself. [*Putting his hand in his pocket*] Ay gat money—plenty money.

JOHNNY: [*Shakes* Chris *by the hand*] Speak of the devil. We was just talkin' about you.

LARRY: [*Coming to the end of the bar*] Hello, Chris. Put it there.

[*They shake hands*]

CHRIS: [*Beaming*] Give us drink.

JOHNNY: [*With a grin*] You got a half-snootful now. Where'd you get it?

CHRIS: [*Grinning*] Oder fallar on oder barge—Irish fallar—he gat bottle vhisky and we drank it, yust us two. Dot vhisky gat kick, by yingo! Ay yust come ashore. Give us drink, Larry. Ay vas little drunk, not much. Yust feel good. [*He laughs and commences to sing in a nasal, high-pitched quaver*] "My Yosephine, come board de ship. Long time Ay vait for you.
De moon, she shi-i-i-ine. She looka yust like you.
Tchee-tchee, tchee-tchee, tchee-tchee, tchee-tchee."
[*To the accompaniment of this last he waves*

his hand as if he were conducting an orchestra]

JOHNNY: [*With a laugh*] Same old Yosie, eh, Chris?

CHRIS: You don't know good song when you hear him. Italian fallar on oder barge, he learn me dat. Give us drink.

[*He throws change on the bar*]

LARRY: [*With a professional air*] What's your pleasure, gentlemen?

JOHNNY: Small beer, Larry.

CHRIS: Vhisky—Number Two.

LARRY: [*As he gets their drinks*] I'll take a cigar on you.

CHRIS: [*Lifting his glass*] Skoal!

[*He drinks*]

JOHNNY: Drink hearty.

CHRIS: [*Immediately*] Have oder drink.

JOHNNY: No. Some other time. Got to go home now. So you've just landed? Where are you in from this time?

CHRIS: Norfolk. Ve make slow voyage—dirty vedder—yust fog, fog, fog, all bloody time! [*There is an insistent ring from the doorbell at the family entrance in the back room. Chris gives a start—hurriedly*] Ay go open, Larry. Ay forgat. It vas Marthy. She come with me.

[*He goes into the back room*]

LARRY: [*With a chuckle*] He's still got that same cow livin' with him, the old fool!

JOHNNY: [*With a grin*] A sport, Chris is. Well, I'll beat it home. S'long.

[*He goes to the street door*]

LARRY: So long, boss.

JOHNNY: Oh—don't forget to give him his letter.

LARRY: I won't.

[*Johnny goes out. In the meantime, Chris has opened the family entrance door, admitting Marthy. She might be forty or fifty. Her jowly, mottled face, with its thick red nose, is streaked with interlacing purple veins. Her thick, gray hair is piled anyhow in a greasy mop on top of her round head. Her figure is flabby and fat; her breath comes in wheezy gasps; she speaks in a loud, mannish voice, punctuated by explosions of hoarse laughter. But there still twinkles in her blood-shot blue eyes a youthful lust for life which hard usage has failed to stifle, a sense of humor mocking, but good-tempered. She wears a man's cap, double-breasted man's jacket, and a grimy, calico skirt. Her bare feet are encased in a man's brogans several sizes too large for her, which gives her a shuffling gait*]

MARTHY: [*Grumblingly*] What yuh tryin' to do, Dutchy—keep me standin' out there all day?

[*She comes forward and sits at the table in the right corner, front*]

CHRIS: [*Mollifyingly*] Ay'm sorry, Marthy. Ay talk to Yohnny. Ay forgat. What you goin' take for drink?

MARTHY: [*Appeased*] Gimme a scoop of lager an' ale.

CHRIS: Ay go bring him back. [*He returns to the bar*] Lager and ale for Marthy, Larry. Vhisky for me.

[*He throws change on the bar*]

LARRY: Right you are. [*Then remembering, he takes the letter from in back of the bar*] Here's a letter for you—from St. Paul, Minnesota—and a lady's writin'.

[*He grins*]

CHRIS: [*Quickly—taking it*] Oh, den it come from my daughter, Anna. She live dere. [*He turns the letter over in his hands uncertainly*] Ay don't gat letter from Anna—must be a year.

LARRY: [*Jokingly*] That's a fine fairy tale to be tellin'—your daughter! Sure I'll bet it's some bum.

CHRIS: [*Soberly*] No. Dis come from Anna. *Engrossed by the letter in his hand—uncertainly*] By golly, Ay tank Ay'm too drunk for read dis letter from Anna. Ay tank Ay sat down for a minute. You bring drinks in back room, Larry.

[*He goes into the room on right*]

MARTHY: [*Angrily*] Where's my lager an' ale, yuh big stiff?

CHRIS: [*Preoccupied*] Larry bring him.

[*He sits down opposite her. Larry brings in the drinks and sets them on the table. He and Marthy exchange nods of recognition. Larry stands looking at Chris curiously. Marthy takes a long draught of her schooner and heaves a huge sigh of satisfaction, wiping her mouth with the back of her hand. Chris stares at the letter for a moment—slowly opens it, and, squinting his eyes, commences to read laboriously, his lips moving as he spells out the words. As he reads his face lights up with an expression of mingled joy and bewilderment*]

LARRY: Good news?

MARTHY: [*Her curiosity also aroused*] What's that yuh got—a letter, fur Gawd's sake?

CHRIS: [*Pauses for a moment, after finishing the letter, as if to let the news sink in—then suddenly pounds his fist on the table with happy excitement*] Py yiminy! Yust tank, Anna say she's comin' here right avay! She gat sick on yob in St. Paul, she say. It's short letter, don't tal me much more'n dat. [*Beaming*] Py golly, dat's good news all at one time for ole fallar! [*Then turning to Marthy, rather shamefacedly*] You know, Marthy, Ay've tole you Ay don't see my Anna since she vas little gel in Sweden five year ole.

MARTHY: How old'll she be now?

CHRIS: She must be—lat me see—she must be twenty year ole, py Yo!

LARRY: [*Surprised*] You've not seen her in fifteen years?

CHRIS: [*Suddenly growing somber—in a low tone*] No. Ven she vas little gel, Ay vas bo'sun on vindjammer. Ay never gat home only few time dem

year. Ay'm fool sailor fallar. My voman—Anna's mo'der—she gat tired vait all time Sweden for me ven Ay don't never come. She come dis country, bring Anna, dey go out Minnesota, live with her cousins on farm. Den ven her mo'der died ven Ay vas on voyage, Ay tank it's better dem cousins keep Anna. Ay tank it's better Anna live on farm, den she don't know dat ole davil, sea, she don't know fa'der like me.

LARRY: [*With a wink at* Marthy] This girl, now, 'll be marryin' a sailor herself, likely. It's in the blood.

CHRIS: [*Suddenly springing to his feet and smashing his fist on the table in a rage*] No, py God! She don't do dat!

MARTHY: [*Grasping her schooner hastily—angrily*] Hey, look out, yuh nut! Wanta spill my suds for me?

LARRY: [*Amazed*] Oho, what's up with you? Ain't you a sailor yourself now, and always been?

CHRIS: [*Slowly*] Dat's yust vhy Ay say it. [*Forcing a smile*] Sailor vas all right fallar, but not for marry gel. No. Ay know dat. Anna's mo'der, she know it, too.

LARRY: [*As* Chris *remains sunk in gloomy reflection*] When is your daughter comin'? Soon?

CHRIS: [*Roused*] Py yiminy, Ay forgat. [*Reads through the letter hurriedly*] She say she come right avay, dat's all.

LARRY: She'll maybe be comin' here to look for you, I s'pose.

[*He returns to the bar, whistling. Left alone with* Marthy, *who stares at him with a twinkle of malicious humor in her eyes,* Chris *suddenly becomes desperately ill-at-ease. He fidgets, then gets up hurriedly*]

CHRIS: Ay gat speak with Larry. Ay be right back. [*Mollifyingly*] Ay bring you oder drink.

MARTHY: [*Emptying her glass*] Sure. That's me.

[*As he retreats with the glass she guffaws after him derisively*]

CHRIS: [*To* Larry *in an alarmed whisper*] Py yingo, Ay gat gat Marthy shore off barge before Anna come! Anna raise hell if she find dat out. Marthy raise hell, too, for go, py golly!

LARRY: [*With a chuckle*] Serve ye right, ye old divil—havin' a woman at your age!

CHRIS: [*Scratching his head in a quandary*] You tal me lie for tal Marthy, Larry, so's she gat off barge quick.

LARRY: She knows your daughter's comin'. Tell her to get the hell out of it.

CHRIS: No. Ay don't like make her feel bad.

LARRY: You're an old mush! Keep your girl away from the barge, then. She'll likely want to stay ashore anyway. [*Curiously*] What does she work at, your Anna?

CHRIS: She stay on dem cousins' farm till two year ago. Dan she gat yob nurse gel in St. Paul. [*Then shaking his head resolutely*] But Ay don't vant for her gat yob now. Ay vant for her stay with me.

LARRY: [*Scornfully*] On a coal barge! She'll not like that, I'm thinkin'.

MARTHY: [*Shouts from the next room*] Don't I get that bucket o' suds, Dutchy?

CHRIS: [*Startled—in apprehensive confusion*] Yes, Ay come, Marthy.

LARRY: [*Drawing the lager and ale, hands it to* Chris—*laughing*] Now you're in for it! You'd better tell her straight to get out!

CHRIS: [*Shaking in his boots*] Py golly. [*He takes her drink in to* Marthy *and sits down at the table. She sips it in silence.* Larry *moves quietly close to the partition to listen, grinning with expectation.* Chris *seems on the verge of speaking, hesitates, gulps down his whisky desperately as if seeking for courage. He attempts to whistle a few bars of "Yosephine" with careless bravado, but the whistle peters out futilely.* Marthy *stares at him keenly, taking in his embarrassment with a malicious twinkle of amusement in her eye.* Chris *clears his throat*] Marthy—

MARTHY: [*Aggressively*] Wha's that? [*Then, pretending to fly into a rage, her eyes enjoying* Chris' *misery*] I'm wise to what's in back of your nut, Dutchy. Yuh want to git rid o' me, huh?—now she's comin'. Gimme the bum's rush ashore, huh? Lemme tell yuh, Dutchy, there ain't a square-head workin' on a boat man enough to git away with that. Don't start nothin' yuh can't finish!

CHRIS: [*Miserably*] Ay don't start nutting, Marthy.

MARTHY: [*Glares at him for a second—then cannot control a burst of laughter*] Ho-ho! Yuh're a scream, Square-head—an honest-ter-Gawd knockout! Ho-ho!

[*She wheezes, panting for breath*]

CHRIS: [*With childish pique*] Ay don't see nutting for laugh at.

MARTHY: Take a slant in the mirror and yuh'll see. Ho-ho! [*Recovering from her mirth—chuckling, scornfully*] A square-head tryin' to kid Marthy Owen at this late day!—after me campin' with barge men the last twenty years. I'm wise to the game, up, down, and sideways. I ain't been born and dragged up on the water front for nothin'. Think I'd make trouble, huh? Not me! I'll pack up me duds an' beat it. I'm quittin' yuh, get me? I'm tellin' yuh I'm sick of stickin' with yuh, and I'm leavin' yuh flat, see? There's plenty of other guys on other barges waitin' for me. Always was, I always found. [*She claps the astonished* Chris *on the back*] So cheer up, Dutchy! I'll be offen the barge before she comes. You'll be rid o' me for good—and me o' you— good riddance for both of us. Ho-ho!

CHRIS: [*Seriously*] Ay don' tank dat. You vas good gel, Marthy.

MARTHY: [*Grinning*] Good girl? Aw, can the bull! Well, yuh treated me square, yuhself. So it's fifty-fifty. Nobody's sore at nobody. We're still good frien's, huh?

[Larry *returns to bar*]

CHRIS: [*Beaming now that he sees his troubles disappearing*] Yes, py golly.

MARTHY: That's the talkin'! In all my time I tried never to split with a guy with no hard feelin's. But what was yuh so scared about—that I'd kick up a row? That ain't Marthy's way. [*Scornfully*] Think I'd break my heart to lose yuh? Commit suicide, huh? Ho-ho. Gawd! The world's full o' men if that's all I'd worry about! [*Then with a grin, after emptying her glass*] Blow me to another scoop, huh? I'll drink your kid's health for yuh.

CHRIS: [*Eagerly*] Sure tang. Ay go gat him. [*He takes the two glasses into the bar*] Oder drink. Same for both.

LARRY: [*Getting the drinks and putting them on the bar*] She's not such a bad lot, that one.

CHRIS: [*Jovially*] She's good gel, Ay tal you! Py golly, Ay calabrate now! Give me vhisky here at bar, too. [*He puts down money.* Larry *serves him*] You have drink, Larry.

LARRY: [*Virtuously*] You know I never touch it.

CHRIS: You don't know what you miss. Skoal! [*He drinks—then begins to sing loudly*]
"My Yosephine, come board de ship——"

[*He picks up the drinks for* Marthy *and himself and walks unsteadily into the back room, singing*]

"De moon, she shi-i-ine. She looks yust like you.
Tchee-tchee, tchee-tchee, tchee-tchee tchee-tchee."

MARTHY: [*Grinning, hands to ears*] Gawd!

CHRIS: [*Sitting down*] Ay'm good singer, yes? Ve drink, eh? Skoal! Ay calabrate! [*He drinks*] Ay calabrate 'cause Anna's coming home. You know, Marthy, Ay never write for her to come, 'cause Ay tank Ay'm no good for her. But all time Ay hope like hell some day she vant for see me and den she come. And dat's vay it happen now, py yiminy! [*His face beaming*] What you tank she look like, Marthy? Ay bet you she's fine, good, strong gel, pooty like hell! Living on farm made her like dat. And Ay bet you some day she marry good, steady land fallar here in East, have home all her own, have kits—and dan Ay'm ole grandfa'der, py golly! And Ay go visit dem every time Ay gat in port near! [*Bursting with joy*] By yiminy crickens, Ay calabrate dat! [*Shouts*] Bring oder drink, Larry! [*He smashes his fist on the table with a bang*]

LARRY: [*Coming in from bar—irritably*] Easy there! Don't be breakin' the table, you old goat!

CHRIS: [*By way of reply, grins foolishly and begins to sing*] "My Yosephine, come board de ship——"

MARTHY: [*Touching* Chris' *arm persuasively*] You're soused to the ears, Dutchy. Go out and put a feed into you. It'll sober you up. [*Then as* Chris *shakes his head obstinately*] Listen, yuh old nut! Yuh don't know what time your kid's liable to show up. Yuh want to be sober when she comes, don't yuh?

CHRIS: [*Aroused—gets unsteadily to his feet*] **Py golly, yes.**

LARRY: That's good sense for you. A good beef stew'll fix you. Go round the corner.

CHRIS: All right. Ay be back soon, Marthy.

[Chris *goes through the bar and out the street door*]

LARRY: He'll come round all right with some grub in him.

MARTHY: Sure.

[Larry *goes back to the bar and resumes his newspaper. Marthy sips what is left of her schooner reflectively. There is the ring of the family entrance bell. Larry comes to the door and opens it a trifle—then, with a puzzled expression, pulls it wide. Anna Christopherson enters. She is a tall, blond, fully-developed girl of twenty, handsome after a large, Viking-daughter fashion but now run down in health and plainly showing all the outward evidences of belonging to the world's oldest profession. Her youthful face is already hard and cynical beneath its layer of make-up. Her clothes are the tawdry finery of peasant stock turned prostitute. She comes and sinks wearily in a chair by the table, left front*]

ANNA: Gimme a whisky—ginger ale on the side. [*Then, as Larry turns to go, forcing a winning smile at him*] And don't be stingy, baby.

LARRY: [*Sarcastically*] Shall I serve it in a pail?

ANNA: [*With a hard laugh*] That suits me down to the ground. [Larry *goes into the bar. The two women size each other up with frank stares. Larry comes back with the drink which he sets before* Anna *and returns to the bar again.* Anna *downs her drink at a gulp. Then, after a moment, as the alcohol begins to rouse her, she turns to* Marthy *with a friendly smile*] Gee, I needed that bad, all right, all right!

MARTHY: [*Nodding her head sympathetically*] Sure—yuh look all in. Been on a bat?

ANNA: No—traveling—day and a half on the train. Had to sit up all night in the dirty coach, too. Gawd, I thought I'd never get here!

MARTHY: [*With a start—looking at her intently*] Where'd yuh come from, huh?

ANNA: St. Paul—out in Minnesota.

MARTHY: [*Staring at her in amazement—slowly*] So—yuh're— [*She suddenly bursts out into hoarse, ironical laughter*] Gawd!

ANNA: All the way from Minnesota, sure. [*Flaring up*] What you laughing at? Me?

MARTHY: [*Hastily*] No, honest, kid. I was thinkin' of somethin' else.

ANNA: [*Mollified—with a smile*] Well, I wouldn't blame you, at that. Guess I do look rotten—yust out of the hospital two weeks. I'm going to have another 'ski. What d'you say? Have something on me?

MARTHY: Sure I will. T'anks. [*She calls*] Hey, Larry! Little service!

[*He comes in*]

ANNA: Same for me.

MARTHY: Same here.

[Larry *takes their glasses and goes out*]

ANNA: Why don't you come sit over here, be sociable. I'm a dead stranger in this burg—and I ain't spoke a word with no one since day before yesterday.

MARTHY: Sure thing.

[*She shuffles over to* Anna's *table and sits down opposite her.* Larry *brings the drinks and* Anna *pays him*]

ANNA: Skoal! Here's how! [*She drinks*]

MARTHY: Here's luck! [*She takes a gulp from her schooner*]

ANNA: [*Taking a package of Sweet Caporal cigarettes from her bag*] Let you smoke in here, won't they?

MARTHY: [*Doubtfully*] Sure. [*Then with evident anxiety*] On'y trow it away if yuh hear someone comin'.

ANNA: [*Lighting one and taking a deep inhale*] Gee, they're fussy in this dump, ain't they? [*She puffs, staring at the table top.* Marthy *looks her over with a new penetrating interest, taking in every detail of her face.* Anna *suddenly becomes conscious of this appraising stare—resentfully*] Ain't nothing wrong with me, is there? You're looking hard enough.

MARTHY: [*Irritated by the other's tone—scornfully*] Ain't got to look much. I got your number the minute you stepped in the door.

ANNA: [*Her eyes narrowing*] Ain't you smart! Well, I got yours, too, without no trouble. You're me forty years from now. That's you! [*She gives a hard little laugh*]

MARTHY: [*Angrily*] Is that so? Well, I'll tell you straight, kiddo, that Marthy Owen never—— [*She catches herself up short—with a grin*] What are you and me scrappin' over? Let's cut it out, huh? Me, I don't want no hard feelin's with no one. [*Extending her hand*] Shake and forget it, huh?

ANNA: [*Shakes her hand gladly*] Only too glad to. I ain't looking for trouble. Let's have 'nother. What d'you say?

MARTHY: [*Shaking her head*] Not for mine. I'm full up. And you—— Had anythin' to eat lately?

ANNA: Not since this morning on the train.

MARTHY: Then yuh better go easy on it, hadn't yuh?

ANNA: [*After a moment's hesitation*] Guess you're right. I got to meet someone, too. But my nerves is on edge after that rotten trip.

MARTHY: Yuh said yuh was just outa the hospital?

ANNA: Two weeks ago. [*Leaning over to* Marthy *confidentially*] The joint I was in out in St. Paul got raided. That was the start. The judge give all us girls thirty days. The others didn't seem to mind being in the cooler much. Some of 'em was used to it. But me, I couldn't stand it. It got my goat right—

couldn't eat or sleep or nothing. I never could stand being caged up nowheres. I got good and sick and they had to send me to the hospital. It was nice there. I was sorry to leave it, honest!

MARTHY: [*After a slight pause*] Did yuh say yuh got to meet someone here?

ANNA: Yes. Oh, not what you mean. It's my Old Man I got to meet. Honest! It's funny, too. I ain't seen him since I was a kid—don't even know what he looks like—yust had a letter every now and then. This was always the only address he gave me to write him back. He's yanitor of some building here now—used to be a sailor.

MARTHY: [*Astonished*] Janitor!

ANNA: Sure. And I was thinking maybe, seeing he ain't never done a thing for me in my life, he might be willing to stake me to a room and eats till I get rested up. [*Wearily*] Gee, I sure need that rest! I'm knocked out. [*Then resignedly*] But I ain't expecting much from him. Give you a kick when you're down, that's what all men do. [*With sudden passion*] Men, I hate 'em—all of 'em! And I don't expect he'll turn out no better than the rest. [*Then with sudden interest*] Say, do you hang out around this dump much?

MARTHY: Oh, off and on.

ANNA: Then maybe you know him—my Old Man —or at least seen him?

MARTHY: It ain't old Chris, is it?

ANNA: Old Chris?

MARTHY: Chris Christopherson, his full name is.

ANNA: [*Excitedly*] Yes, that's him! Anna Christopherson—that's my real name—only out there I called myself Anna Christie. So you know him, eh?

MARTHY: [*Evasively*] Seen him about for years.

ANNA: Say, what's he like, tell me, honest?

MARTHY: Oh, he's short and——

ANNA: [*Impatiently*] I don't care what he looks like. What kind is he?

MARTHY: [*Earnestly*] Well, yuh can bet your life, kid, he's as good an old guy as ever walked on two feet. That goes!

ANNA: [*Pleased*] I'm glad to hear it. Then you think he'll stake me to that rest cure I'm after?

MARTHY: [*Emphatically*] Surest thing you know. [*Disgustedly*] But where'd yuh get the idea he was a janitor?

ANNA: He wrote me he was himself.

MARTHY: Well, he was lyin'. He ain't. He's captain of a barge—five men under him.

ANNA: [*Disgusted in her turn*] A barge? What kind of a barge?

MARTHY: Coal, mostly.

ANNA: A coal barge! [*With a harsh laugh*] If that ain't a swell job to find your long lost Old Man working at! Gee, I knew something'd be bound to turn out wrong—always does with me. That puts my idea of his giving me a rest on the bum.

MARTHY: What d'yuh mean?

ANNA: I s'pose he lives on the boat, don't he?

MARTHY: Sure. What about it? Can't you live on it, too?

ANNA: [*Scornfully*] Me? On a dirty coal barge! What d'you think I am?

MARTHY: [*Resentfully*] What d'yuh know about barges, huh? Bet yuh ain't never seen one. That's what comes of his bringing yuh up inland—away from the old devil sea—where yuh'd be safe—Gawd! [*The irony of it strikes her sense of humor and she laughs hoarsely*]

ANNA: [*Angrily*] His bringing me up! Is that what he tells people! I like his nerve! He let them cousins of my Old Woman's keep me on their farm and work me to death like a dog.

MARTHY: Well, he's got queer notions on some things. I've heard him say a farm was the best place for a kid.

ANNA: Sure. That's what he'd always answer back —and a lot of crazy stuff about staying away from the sea—stuff I couldn't make head or tail to. I thought he must be nutty.

MARTHY: He is on that one point. [*Casually*] So yuh didn't fall for life on the farm, huh?

ANNA: I should say not! The old man of the family, his wife, and four sons—I had to slave for all of 'em. I was only a poor relation, and they treated me worse than they dare treat a hired girl. [*After a moment's hesitation—somberly*] It was one of the sons—the youngest—started me—when I was sixteen. After that, I hated 'em so I'd killed 'em all if I'd stayed. So I run away—to St. Paul.

MARTHY: [*Who has been listening sympathetically*] I've heard Old Chris talkin' about your bein' a nurse girl out there. Was that all a bluff yuh put up when yuh wrote him?

ANNA: Not on your life, it wasn't. It was true for two years. I didn't go wrong all at one jump. Being a nurse girl was yust what finished me. Taking care of other people's kids, always listening to their bawling and crying, caged in, when you're only a kid yourself and want to go out and see things. At last I got the chance—to get into that house. And you bet your life I took it! [*Defiantly*] And I ain't sorry neither. [*After a pause—with bitter hatred*] It was all men's fault—the whole business. It was men on the farm ordering and beating me—and giving me the wrong start. Then when I was a nurse, it was men again hanging around, bothering me, trying to see what they could get. [*She gives a hard laugh*] And now it's men all the time. Gawd, I hate 'em all, every mother's son of 'em! Don't you?

MARTHY: Oh, I dunno. There's good ones and bad ones, kid. You've just had a run of bad luck with 'em, that's all. Your Old Man, now—Old Chris— he's a good one.

ANNA: [*Skeptically*] He'll have to show me.

MARTHY: Yuh kept right on writing him yuh was a nurse girl still, even after yuh was in the house, didn't yuh?

ANNA: Sure. [*Cynically*] Not that I think he'd care a darn.

MARTHY: Yuh're all wrong about him, kid. [*Earnestly*] I know Old Chris well for a long time. He's talked to me 'bout you lots o' times. He thinks the world o' you, honest he does.

ANNA: Aw, quit the kiddin'!

MARTHY: Honest! Only, he's a simple old guy, see? He's got nutty notions. But he means well, honest. Listen to me, kid—— [*She is interrupted by the opening and shutting of the street door in the bar and by hearing* Chris' *voice*] Ssshh!

ANNA: What's up?

CHRIS: [*Who has entered the bar. He seems considerably sobered up*] Py golly, Larry, dat grub taste good. Marthy in back?

LARRY: Sure—and another tramp with her.

[Chris *starts for the entrance to the back room*]

MARTHY: [*To* Anna *in a hurried, nervous whisper*] That's him now. He's comin' in here. Brace up!

ANNA: Who?

[Chris *opens the door*]

MARTHY: [*As if she were greeting him for the first time*] Why, hello, Old Chris. [*Then before he can speak, she shuffles hurriedly past him into the bar, beckoning him to follow her*] Come here. I wanta tell yuh somethin'. [*He goes out to her. She speaks hurriedly in a low voice*] Listen! I'm goin' to beat it down to the barge—pack up me duds and blow. That's her in there—your Anna—just come—waitin' for yuh. Treat her right, see? She's been sick. Well, s'long! [*She goes into the back room—to* Anna] S'long kid. I gotta beat it now. See yuh later.

ANNA: [*Nervously*] So long.

[Marthy *goes quickly out of the family entrance*]

LARRY: [*Looking at the stupefied* Chris *curiously*] Well, what's up now?

CHRIS: [*Vaguely*] Nutting—nutting. [*He stands before the door to the back room in an agony of embarrassed emotion—then he forces himself to a bold decision, pushes open the door and walks in. He stands there, casts a shy glance at* Anna, *whose brilliant clothes, and, to him, high-toned appearance, awe him terribly. He looks about him with pitiful nervousness as if to avoid the appraising look with which she takes in his face, his clothes, etc.—his voice seeming to plead for her forbearance*] Anna!

ANNA: [*Acutely embarrassed in her turn*] Hello—father. She told me it was you. I yust got here a little while ago.

CHRIS: [*Goes slowly over to her chair*] It's good—for see you—after all dem years, Anna.

[*He bends down over her. After an embarrassed struggle they manage to kiss each other*]

ANNA: [*A trace of genuine feeling in her voice*] It's good to see you, too.

CHRIS: [*Grasps her arms and looks into her face—then overcome by a wave of fierce tenderness*] Anna lilla! Anna lilla!

[*Takes her in his arms*]

ANNA: [*Shrinks away from him, half-frightened*] What's that—Swedish? I don't know it. [*Then as if seeking relief from the tension in a voluble chatter*] Gee, I had an awful trip coming here. I'm all in. I had to sit up in the dirty coach all night—couldn't get no sleep, hardly—and then I had a hard job finding this place. I never been in New York before, you know, and——

CHRIS: [*Who has been staring down at her face admiringly, not hearing what she says—impulsively*] You know you vas awful pooty gel, Anna? Ay bet all men see you fall in love with you, py yiminy!

ANNA: [*Repelled—harshly*] Cut it! You talk same as they all do.

CHRIS: [*Hurt—humbly*] Ain't no harm for your fa'der talk dat vay, Anna.

ANNA: [*Forcing a short laugh*] No—course not. Only—it's funny to see you and not remember nothing. You're like—a stranger.

CHRIS: [*Sadly*] Ay s'pose. Ay never come home only few times ven you vas kit in Sveden. You don't remember dat?

ANNA: No. [*Resentfully*] But why didn't you never come home them days? Why didn't you never come out West to see me?

CHRIS: [*Slowly*] Ay tank, after your mo'der die, ven Ay vas avay on voyage, it's better for you you don't never see me! [*He sinks down in the chair opposite her dejectedly—then turns to her—sadly*] Ay don't know, Anna, vhy Ay never come home Sveden in ole year. Ay vant come home end of every voyage. Ay vant see your mo'der, your two bro'der before dey vas drowned, you ven you vas born—but—Ay—don't go. Ay sign on oder ships— go South America, go Australia, go China, go every port all over world many times—but Ay never go aboard ship sail for Sveden. Ven Ay gat money for pay passage home as passenger den—— [*He bows his head guiltily*] Ay forgat and Ay spend all money. Ven Ay tank again, it's too late. [*He sighs*] Ay don't know why but dat's vay with most sailor fallar, Anna. Dat ole davil sea make dem crazy fools with her dirty tricks. It's so.

ANNA: [*Who has watched him keenly while he has been speaking—with a trace of scorn in her voice*] Then you think the sea's to blame for everything, eh? Well, you're still workin' on it, ain't you, spite of all you used to write me about hating it. That dame was here told me you was captain of a coal barge—and you wrote me you was yanitor of a building!

CHRIS: [*Embarrassed but lying glibly*] Oh, Ay vork on land long time as yanitor. Yust short time ago Ay got dis yob cause Ay vas sick, need open air.

ANNA: [*Skeptically*] Sick? You? You'd never think it.

CHRIS: And Anna, dis ain't real sailor yob. Dis

ain't real boat on sea. She's yust ole tub—like piece of land with house on it dat float. Yob on her ain't sea yob. No. Ay don't gat yob on sea, Anna, if Ay die first. Ay swear dat ven your mo'der die. Ay keep my word, py yingo!

ANNA: [*Perplexed*] Well, I can't see no difference. [*Dismissing the subject*] Speaking of being sick, I been there myself—yust out of the hospital two weeks ago.

CHRIS: [*Immediately all concern*] You, Anna? Py golly! [*Anxiously*] You feel better now, dough, don't you? You look little tired, dat's all!

ANNA: [*Wearily*] I am. Tired to death. I need a long rest and I don't see much chance of getting it.

CHRIS: What you mean, Anna?

ANNA: Well, when I made up my mind to come to see you, I thought you was a yanitor—that you'd have a place where, maybe if you didn't mind having me, I could visit a while and rest up—till I felt able to get back on the yob again.

CHRIS: [*Eagerly*] But Ay gat place, Anna—nice place. You rest all you want, py yiminy! You don't never have to vork as nurse gel no more. You stay with me, py golly!

ANNA: [*Surprised and pleased by his eagerness—with a smile*] Then you're really glad to see me—honest?

CHRIS: [*Pressing one of her hands in both of his*] Anna, Ay like see you like hell, Ay tal you! And don't you talk no more about gatting yob. You stay with me. Ay don't see you for long time, you don't forgat dat. [*His voice trembles*] Ay'm gatting ole. Ay gat no one in world but you.

ANNA: [*Touched—embarrassed by this unfamiliar emotion*] Thanks. It sounds good to hear someone —talk to me that way. Say, though—if you're so lonely—it's funny—why ain't you ever married again?

CHRIS: [*Shaking his head emphatically—after a pause*] Ay love your mo'der too much for ever do dat, Anna.

ANNA: [*Impressed—slowly*] I don't remember nothing about her. What was she like? Tell me.

CHRIS: Ay tal you all about everytang—and you tal me all tangs happen to you. But not here now. Dis ain't good place for young gel, anyway. Only no good sailor fallar come here for gat drunk. [*He gets to his feet quickly and picks up her bag*] You come with me, Anna. You need lie down, gat rest.

ANNA: [*Half rises to her feet, then sits down again*] Where're you going?

CHRIS: Come. Ve gat on board.

ANNA: [*Disappointedly*] On board your barge, you mean? [*Dryly*] Nix for mine! [*Then seeing his crestfallen look—forcing a smile*] Do you think that's a good place for a young girl like me—a coal barge?

CHRIS: [*Dully*] Yes, Ay tank. [*He hesitates—then continues more and more pleadingly*] You don't know how nice it's on barge, Anna. Tug come and ve gat towed out on voyage—yust water all round,

and sun, and fresh air, and good grub for make you strong, healthy gel. You see many tangs you don't see before. You gat moonlight at night, maybe; see steamer pass; see schooner make sail—see everytang dat's pooty. You need take rest like dat. You work too hard for young gel already. You need vacation, yes!

ANNA: [*Who has listened to him with a growing interest—with an uncertain laugh*] It sounds good to hear you tell it. I'd sure like a trip on the water, all right. It's the barge idea has me stopped. Well, I'll go down with you and have a look—and maybe I'll take a chance. Gee, I'd do anything once.

CHRIS: [*Picks up her bag again*] Ve go, eh?

ANNA: What's the rush? Wait a second. [*Forgetting the situation for a moment, she relapses into the familiar form and flashes one of her winning trade smiles at him*] Gee, I'm thirsty.

CHRIS: [*Sets down her bag immediately—hastily*] Ay'm sorry, Anna. What you tank you like for drink, eh?

ANNA: [*Promptly*] I'll take a—— [*Then suddenly reminded—confusedly*] I don't know. What'a they got here?

CHRIS: [*With a grin*] Ay don't tank dey got much fancy drink for young gel in dis place, Anna. Yinger ale—sas'prilla, maybe.

ANNA: [*Forcing a laugh herself*] Make it sas, then.

CHRIS: [*Coming up to her—with a wink*] Ay tal you, Anna, ve calabrate, yes—dis one time because ve meet after many year. [*In a half whisper, embarrassedly*] Dey gat good port vine, Anna. It's good for you, Ay tank—little bit—for give you appetite. It ain't strong, neider. One glass don't go to your head, Ay promise.

ANNA: [*With a half-hysterical laugh*] All right. I'll take port.

CHRIS: Ay go gat him.

[*He goes out to the bar. As soon as the door closes, Anna starts to her feet*]

ANNA: [*Picking up her bag—half-aloud—stammeringly*] Gawd, I can't stand this! I better beat it.

[*Then she lets her bag drop, stumbles over to her chair again, and covering her face with her hands, begins to sob*]

LARRY: [*Putting down his paper as* Chris *comes up—with a grin*] Well, who's the blond?

CHRIS: [*Proudly*] Dat vas Anna, Larry.

LARRY: [*In amazement*] Your daughter, Anna?

[Chris *nods.* Larry *lets a long, low whistle escape him and turns away embarrassedly*]

CHRIS: Don't you tank she vas pooty gel, Larry?

LARRY: [*Rising to the occasion*] Sure! A peach!

CHRIS: You bet you! Give me drink for take back —one port vine for Anna—she calabrate dis one time with me—and small beer for me.

LARRY: [*As he gets the drinks*] Small beer for you, eh? She's reformin' you already.

CHRIS: [*Pleased*] You bet! [*He takes the drinks. As she hears him coming, Anna hastily dries her eyes, tries to smile.* Chris *comes in and sets the drinks down on the table—stares at her for a second anxiously—patting her hand*] You look tired, Anna. Vell, Ay make you take good long rest now. [*Picking up his beer*] Come, you drink vine. It put new life in you. [*She lifts her glass—he grins*] Skoal, Anna! You know dat Svedish word?

ANNA: Skoal! [*Downing her port at a gulp like a drink of whisky—her lips trembling*] Skoal? Guess I know that word, all right, all right!

[THE CURTAIN FALLS]

ACT II.

SCENE: *Ten days later. The stern of the deeply laden barge,* Simeon Winthrop, *at anchor in the outer harbor of Provincetown, Mass. It is ten o'clock at night. Dense fog shrouds the barge on all sides, and she floats motionless on a calm. A lantern set up on an immense coil of thick hawser sheds a dull, filtering light on objects near it—the heavy steel bits for making fast the tow lines, etc. In the rear is the cabin, its misty windows glowing wanly with the light of a lamp inside. The chimney of the cabin stove rises a few feet above the roof. The doleful tolling of bells, on Long Point, on ships at anchor, breaks the silence at regular intervals.*

As the curtain rises, Anna *is discovered standing near the coil of rope on which the lantern is placed. She looks healthy, transformed, the natural color has come back to her face. She has on a black oilskin coat, but wears no hat. She is staring out into the fog astern with an expression of awed wonder. The cabin door is pushed open and* Chris *appears. He is dressed in yellow oilskins—coat, pants, sou'-wester—and wears high seaboots.*

CHRIS: [*The glare from the cabin still in his eyes, peers blinkingly astern*] Anna! [*Receiving no reply, he calls again, this time with apparent apprehension*] Anna!

ANNA: [*With a start—making a gesture with her hand as if to impose silence—in a hushed whisper*] Yes, here I am. What d'you want?

CHRIS: [*Walks over to her—solicitously*] Don't you come turn in, Anna? It's late—after four bells. It ain't good for you stay out here in fog, Ay tank.

ANNA: Why not? [*With a trace of strange exultation*] I love this fog! Honest! It's so—— [*She hesitates, groping for a word*] funny and still. I feel as if I was—out of things altogether.

CHRIS: [*Spitting disgustedly*] Fog's vorst one of her dirty tricks, py yingo!

ANNA: [*With a short laugh*] Beefing about the sea again? I'm getting so's I love it, the little I've seen.

CHRIS: [*Glancing at her moodily*] Dat's foolish talk, Anna. You see her more, you don't talk dat vay. [*Then seeing her irritation, he hastily adopts a more*

cheerful tone] But Ay'm glad you like it on barge. Ay'm glad it makes you feel good again. [*With a placating grin*] You like live like dis alone with ole fa'der, eh?

ANNA: Sure I do. Everything's been so different from anything I ever come across before. And now —this fog—Gee, I wouldn't have missed it for nothing. I never thought living on ships was so different from land. Gee, I'd yust love to work on it, honest I would, if I was a man. I don't wonder you always been a sailor.

CHRIS: [*Vehemently*] Ay ain't sailor, Anna. And dis ain't real sea. You only see nice part. [*Then as she doesn't answer, he continues hopefully*] Vell, fog lift in morning, Ay tank.

ANNA: [*The exultation again in her voice*] I love it! I don't give a rap if it never lifts! [Chris *fidgets from one foot to the other worriedly.* Anna *continues slowly, after a pause*] It makes me feel clean—out here—'s if I'd taken a bath.

CHRIS: [*After a pause*] You better go in cabin read book. Dat put you to sleep.

ANNA: I don't want to sleep. I want to stay out here—and think about things.

CHRIS: [*Walks away from her toward the cabin—then comes back*] You act funny tonight, Anna.

ANNA: [*Her voice rising angrily*] Say, what're you trying to do—make things rotten? You been kind as kind can be to me and I certainly appreciate it—only don't spoil it all now. [*Then, seeing the hurt expression on her father's face, she forces a smile*] Let's talk of something else. Come. Sit down here. [*She points to the coil of rope*]

CHRIS: [*Sits down beside her with a sigh*] It's gatting pooty late in night, Anna. Must be near five bells.

ANNA: [*Interestedly*] Five bells? What time is that?

CHRIS: Half past ten.

ANNA: Funny I don't know nothing about sea talk —but those cousins was always talking crops and that stuff. Gee, wasn't I sick of it—and of them!

CHRIS: You don't like live on farm, Anna?

ANNA: I've told you a hundred times I hated it. [*Decidedly*] I'd rather have one drop of ocean than all the farms in the world! Honest! And you wouldn't like a farm, neither. Here's where you belong. [*She makes a sweeping gesture seaward*] But not on a coal barge. You belong on a real ship, sailing all over the world.

CHRIS: [*Moodily*] Ay've done dat many year, Anna, when Ay was damn fool.

ANNA: [*Disgustedly*] Oh, rats! [*After a pause she speaks musingly*] Was the men in our family always sailors—as far back as you know about?

CHRIS: [*Shortly*] Yes. Damn fools! All men in our village on coast, Sveden, go to sea. Ain't nutting else for dem to do. My fa'der die on board ship in Indian Ocean. He's buried at sea. Ay don't never know him only little bit. Den my tree bro'der, older'n me, dey go on ships. Den Ay go, too. Den my mo'der she's left all 'lone. She die pooty quick after dat all 'lone. Ve vas all avay on voyage when she die. [*He pauses sadly*] Two my bro'der dey gat lost on fishing boat same like your bro'ders vas drowned. My oder bro'der, he save money, give up sea, den he die home in bed. He's only one dat ole davil don't kill. [*Defiantly*] But me, Ay bet you Ay die ashore in bed, too!

ANNA: Were all of 'em yust plain sailors?

CHRIS: Able body seaman, most of dem. [*With a certain pride*] Dey vas all smart seaman, too—A one. [*Then after hesitating a moment—shyly*] Ay vas bo'sun.

ANNA: Bo'sun?

CHRIS: Dat's kind of officer.

ANNA: Gee, that was fine. What does he do?

CHRIS: [*After a second's hesitation, plunged into gloom again by his fear of her enthusiasm*] Hard vork all time. It's rotten, Ay tal you, for go to sea. [*Determined to disgust her with sea life—volubly*] Dey're all fool fallar, dem fallar in our family. Dey all vork rotten yob on sea for nutting, don't care nutting but yust gat big pay day in pocket, gat drunk, gat robbed, ship avay again on oder voyage. Dey don't come home. Dey don't do anytang like good man do. And dat ole davil, sea, sooner, later she swallow dem up.

ANNA: [*With an excited laugh*] Good sports, I'd call 'em. [*Then hastily*] But say—listen—did all the women of the family marry sailors?

CHRIS: [*Eagerly—seeing a chance to drive home his point*] Yes—and it's bad on dem like hell vorst of all. Dey don't see deir men only once in long while. Dey set and vait all 'lone. And vhen deir boys grows up, go to sea, dey sit and vait some more. [*Vehemently*] Any gel marry sailor, she's crazy fool! Your mo'der she tal you same tang if she vas alive. [*He relapses into an attitude of somber brooding*]

ANNA: [*After a pause—dreamily*] Funny! I do feel sort of—nutty, tonight. I feel old.

CHRIS: [*Mystified*] Ole?

ANNA: Sure—like I'd been living a long, long time —out here in the fog. [*Frowning perplexedly*] I don't know how to tell you yust what I mean. It's like I'd come home after a long visit away some place. It all seems like I'd been here before lots of times— on boats—in this same fog. [*With a short laugh*] You must think I'm off my base.

CHRIS: [*Gruffly*] Anybody feel funny dat vay in fog.

ANNA: [*Persistently*] But why d'you s'pose I feel so —so—like I'd found something I'd missed and been looking for—'s if this was the right place for me to fit in? And I seem to have forgot—everything that's happened—like it didn't matter no more. And I feel clean, somehow—like you feel yust after you've took a bath. And I feel happy for once—yes, honest!—happier than I ever been anywhere before! [*As* Chris *makes no comment but a heavy sigh, she*

continues wonderingly] It's nutty for me to feel that way, don't you think?

CHRIS: [*A grim foreboding in his voice*] Ay tank Ay'm damn fool for bring you on voyage, Anna.

ANNA: [*Impressed by his tone*] You talk—nutty tonight yourself. You act 's if you was scared something was going to happen.

CHRIS: Only God know dat, Anna.

ANNA: [*Half-mockingly*] Then it'll be Gawd's will. like the preachers say—what does happen.

CHRIS: [*Starts to his feet with fierce protest*] No! Dat ole davil, sea, she ain't God! [*In the pause of silence that comes after his defiance a hail in a man's husky, exhausted voice comes faintly out of the fog to port*] "Ahoy!" [*Chris gives a startled exclamation*]

ANNA: [*Jumping to her feet*] What's that?

CHRIS: [*Who has regained his composure—sheepishly*] Py golly, dat scare me for minute. It's only some fallar hail, Anna—loose his course in fog. Must be fisherman's power boat. His engine break down, Ay guess. [*The "ahoy" comes again through the wall of fog, sounding much nearer this time. Chris goes over to the port bulwark*] Sound from dis side. She come in from open sea. [*He holds his hands to his mouth, megaphone-fashion, and shouts back*] Ahoy, dere! Vat's trouble?

THE VOICE: [*This time sounding nearer but up forward toward the bow*] Heave a rope when we come alongside [*Then irritably*] Where are ye, ye scut?

CHRIS: Ay hear dem rowing. Dey come up by bow, Ay tank. [*Then shouting out again*] Dis vay!

THE VOICE: Right ye are!

[*There is a muffled sound of oars in oar-locks*]

ANNA: [*Half to herself—resentfully*] Why don't that guy stay where he belongs?

CHRIS: [*Hurriedly*] Ay go up bow. All hands asleep 'cepting fallar on vatch. Ay gat heave line to dat fallar. [*He picks up a coil of rope and hurries off toward the bow. Anna walks back toward the extreme stern as if she wanted to remain as much isolated as possible. She turns her back on the proceedings and stares out into the fog. The Voice is heard again shouting "Ahoy" and Chris answering "Dis vay." Then there is a pause—the murmur of excited voices —then the scuffling of feet. Chris appears from around the cabin to port. He is supporting the limp form of a man dressed in dungarees, holding one of the man's arms around his neck. The deckhand, Johnson, a young blond Swede, follows him, helping along another exhausted man similar fashion. Anna turns to look at them. Chris stops for a second— volubly*] Anna! You come help, vill you? You find vhisky in cabin. Dese fallars need drink for fix them. Dey vas near dead.

ANNA: [*Hurrying to him*] Sure—but who are they? What's the trouble?

CHRIS: Sailor fallars. Deir steamer gat wrecked. Dey been five days in open boat—four fallars—only one left able stand up. Come, Anna. [*She precedes*

*him into the cabin, holding the door open while he
and* Johnson *carry in their burdens. The door is shut,
then opened again as* Johnson *comes out.* Chris'
voice shouts after him] Go gat oder fallar, Yohnson.

JOHNSON: Yes, sir.

[*He goes. The door is closed again.* Mat Burke
*stumbles in around the port side of the cabin.
He moves slowly, feeling his way uncertainly,
keeping hold of the port bulwark with his right
hand to steady himself. He is stripped to the
waist, has on nothing but a pair of dirty dungaree pants. He is a powerful, broad-chested
six-footer, his face handsome in a hard, rough,
bold, defiant way. He is about thirty, in the full
power of his heavy-muscled, immense strength.
His dark eyes are bloodshot and wild from
sleeplessness. The muscles of his arms and
shoulders are lumped in knots and bunches,
the veins of his fore-arms stand out like blue
cords. He finds his way to the coil of hawser
and sits down on it facing the cabin, his back
bowed, head in his hands, in an attitude of
spent weariness*]

BURKE: [*Talking aloud to himself*] Row, ye divil!
Row! [*Then lifting his head and looking about him*]
What's this tub? Well, we're safe anyway—with the
help of God. [*He makes the sign of the cross mechanically.* Johnson *comes along the deck to port,
supporting the fourth man, who is babbling to himself incoherently.* Burke *glances at him disdainfully*]
Is it losing the small wits ye iver had, ye are? Deck-
scrubbing scut! [*They pass him and go into the cabin,
leaving the door open.* Burke *sags forward wearily*]
I'm bate out—bate out entirely.

ANNA: [*Comes out of the cabin with a tumbler
quarter-full of whisky in her hand. She gives a start
when she sees* Burke *so near her, the light from the
open door falling full on him. Then, overcoming
what is evidently a feeling of repulsion, she comes
up beside him*] Here you are. Here's a drink for you.
You need it, I guess.

BURKE: [*Lifting his head slowly—confusedly*] Is
it dreaming I am?

ANNA: [*Half smiling*] Drink it and you'll find it
ain't no dream.

BURKE: To hell with the drink—but I'll take it
just the same. [*He tosses it down*] Ahah! I'm needin'
that—and 'tis fine stuff. [*Looking up at her with
frank, grinning admiration*] But 'twasn't the booze
I meant when I said, was I dreaming. I thought you
was some mermaid out of the sea come to torment
me. [*He reaches out to feel of her arm*] Aye, rale
flesh and blood, divil a less.

ANNA: [*Coldly. Stepping back from him*] Cut that.

BURKE: But tell me, isn't this a barge I'm on—or
isn't it?

ANNA: Sure.

BURKE: And what is a fine handsome woman the
like of you doing on this scow?

ANNA: [*Coldly*] Never you mind. [*Then half*

amused in spite of herself] Say, you're a great one,
honest—starting right in kidding after what you been
through.

BURKE: [*Delighted—proudly*] Ah, it was nothing—
aisy for a rale man with guts to him, the like of me.
[*He laughs*] All in the day's work, darlin'. [*Then,
more seriously but still in a boastful tone, confidentially*] But I won't be denying 'twas a damn narrow
squeak. We'd all ought to be with Davy Jones at
the bottom of the sea, be rights. And only for me,
I'm telling you, and the great strength and guts is
in me, we'd be being scoffed by the fishes this
minute!

ANNA: [*Contemptuously*] Gee, you hate yourself,
don't you? [*Then turning away from him indifferently*] Well, you'd better come in and lie down.
You must want to sleep.

BURKE: [*Stung—rising unsteadily to his feet with
chest out and head thrown back—resentfully*] Lie
down and sleep, is it? Divil a wink I'm after having
for two days and nights and divil a bit I'm needing
now. Let you not be thinking I'm the like of them
three weak scuts come in the boat with me. I could
lick the three of them sitting down with one hand
tied behind me. They may be bate out, but I'm
not—and I've been rowing the boat with them lying
in the bottom not able to raise a hand for the last
two days we was in it. [*Furiously, as he sees this is
making no impression on her*] And I can lick all
hands on this tub, wan by wan, tired as I am!

ANNA: [*Sarcastically*] Gee, ain't you a hard guy!
[*Then, with a trace of sympathy, as she notices him
swaying from weakness*] But never mind that fight
talk. I'll take your word for all you've said. Go on
and sit down out here, anyway, if I can't get you
to come inside. [*He sits down weakly*] You're all in,
you might as well own up to it.

BURKE: [*Fiercely*] The hell I am!

ANNA: [*Coldly*] Well, be stubborn then for all I
care. And I must say I don't care for your language.
The men I know don't pull that rough stuff when
ladies are around.

BURKE: [*Getting unsteadily to his feet again—in
a rage*] Ladies! Ho-ho! Divil mend you! Let you not
be making game of me. What would ladies be doing
on this bloody hulk? [*As* Anna *attempts to go to the
cabin, he lurches into her path*] Aisy, now! You're
not the old Square-head's woman, I suppose you'll
be telling me next—living in his cabin with him no
less! [*Seeing the cold, hostile expression on* Anna's
*face, he suddenly changes his tone to one of bois-
terous joviality*] But I do be thinking, iver since the
first look my eyes took at you, that it's a fool you
are to be wasting yourself—a fine, handsome girl—
on a stumpy runt of a man like that old Swede.
There's too many strapping great lads on the sea
would give their heart's blood for one kiss of you!

ANNA: [*Scornfully*] Lads like you, eh?

BURKE: [*Grinning*] Ye take the words out o' my
mouth. I'm the proper lad for you, if it's meself

do be saying it. [*With a quick movement he puts his arms about her waist*] Whist, now, me daisy! Himself's in the cabin. It's wan of your kisses I'm needing to take the tiredness from me bones. Wan kiss, now! [*He presses her to him and attempts to kiss her*]

ANNA: [*Struggling fiercely*] Leggo of me, you big mutt!

[*She pushes him away with all her might. Burke, weak and tottering, is caught off his guard. He is thrown down backward and, in falling, hits his head a hard thump against the bulwark. He lies there still, knocked out for the moment. Anna stands for a second, looking down at him frightenedly. Then she kneels down beside him and raises his head to her knee, staring into his face anxiously for some sign of life*]

BURKE: [*Stirring a bit—mutteringly*] God stiffen it! [*He opens his eyes and blinks up at her with vague wonder*]

ANNA: [*Letting his head sink back on the deck, rising to her feet with a sigh of relief*] You're coming to all right, eh? Gee, I was scared for a moment I'd killed you.

BURKE: [*With difficulty rising to a sitting position—scornfully*] Killed, is it? It'd take more than a bit of a blow to crack my thick skull. [*Then looking at her with the most intense admiration*] But, glory be, it's a power of strength is in them two fine arms of yours. There's not a man in the world can say the same as you, that he seen Mat Burke lying at his feet and him dead to the world.

ANNA: [*Rather remorsefully*] Forget it. I'm sorry it happened, see? [*Burke rises and sits on bench. Then severely*] Only you had no right to be getting fresh with me. Listen, now, and don't go getting any more wrong notions. I'm on this barge because I'm making a trip with my father. The captain's my father. Now you know.

BURKE: The old square—the old Swede, I mean?

ANNA: Yes.

BURKE: [*Rising—peering at her face*] Sure I might have known it, if I wasn't a bloody fool from birth. Where else'd you get that fine yellow hair is like a golden crown on your head.

ANNA: [*With an amused laugh*] Say, nothing stops you, does it? [*Then attempting a severe tone again*] But don't you think you ought to be apologizing for what you said and done yust a minute ago, instead of trying to kid me with that mush?

BURKE: [*Indignantly*] Mush! [*Then bending forward toward her with very intense earnestness*] Indade and I will ask your pardon a thousand times —and on my knees, if ye like. I didn't mean a word of what I said or did. [*Resentful again for a second*] But divil a woman in all the ports of the world has iver made a great fool of me that way before!

ANNA: [*With amused sarcasm*] I see. You mean you're a lady-killer and they all fall for you.

BURKE: [*Offended. Passionately*] Leave off your fooling! 'Tis that is after getting my back up at you. [*Earnestly*] 'Tis no lie I'm telling you about the women. [*Ruefully*] Though it's a great jackass I am to be mistaking you, even in anger, for the like of them cows on the waterfront is the only women I've met up with since I was growed to a man. [*As Anna shrinks away from him at this, he hurries on pleadingly*] I'm a hard, rough man and I'm not fit, I'm thinking, to be kissing the shoe-soles of a fine, dacent girl the like of yourself. 'Tis only the ignorance of your kind made me see you wrong. So you'll forgive me, for the love of God, and let us be friends from this out. [*Passionately*] I'm thinking I'd rather be friends with you than have my wish for anything else in the world. [*He holds out his hand to her shyly*]

ANNA: [*Looking queerly at him, perplexed and worried, but moved and pleased in spite of herself —takes his hand uncertainly*] Sure.

BURKE: [*With boyish delight*] God bless you! [*In his excitement he squeezes her hand tight*]

ANNA: Ouch!

BURKE: [*Hastily dropping her hand—ruefully*] Your pardon, Miss. 'Tis a clumsy ape I am. [*Then simply—glancing down his arm proudly*] It's great power I have in my hand and arm, and I do be forgetting it at times.

ANNA: [*Nursing her crushed hand and glancing at his arm, not without a trace of his own admiration*] Gee, you're some strong, all right.

BURKE: [*Delighted*] It's no lie, and why shouldn't I be, with me shoveling a million tons of coal in the stokeholes of ships since I was a lad only. [*He pats the coil of hawser invitingly*] Let you sit down, now, Miss, and I'll be telling you a bit of myself, and you'll be telling me a bit of yourself, and in an hour we'll be as old friends as if we was born in the same house. [*He pulls at her sleeve shyly*] Sit down now, if you plaze.

ANNA: [*With a half laugh*] Well—— [*She sits down*] But we won't talk about me, see? You tell me about yourself and about the wreck.

BURKE: [*Flattered*] I'll tell you, surely. But can I be asking you one question, Miss, has my head in a puzzle?

ANNA: [*Guardedly*] Well—I dunno—what is it?

BURKE: What is it you do when you're not taking a trip with the Old Man? For I'm thinking a fine girl the like of you ain't living always on this tub.

ANNA: [*Uneasily*] No—of course I ain't. [*She searches his face suspiciously, afraid there may be some hidden insinuation in his words. Seeing his simple frankness, she goes on confidently*] Well, I'll tell you. I'm a governess, see? I take care of kids for people and learn them things.

BURKE: [*Impressed*] A governess, is it? You must be smart, surely.

ANNA: But let's not talk about me. Tell me about the wreck, like you promised me you would.

BURKE: [*Importantly*] 'Twas this way, Miss. Two weeks out we ran into the divil's own storm, and she sprang wan hell of a leak up for'ard. The skipper was hoping to make Boston before another blow would finish her, but ten days back we met up with another storm the like of the first, only worse. Four days we was in it with green seas raking over her from bow to stern. That was a terrible time, God help us. [*Proudly*] And if 'twasn't for me and my great strength, I'm telling you—and it's God's truth —there'd been mutiny itself in the stokehole. 'Twas me held them to it, with a kick to wan and a clout to another, and they not caring a damn for the engineers any more, but fearing a clout of my right arm more than they'd fear the sea itself. [*He glances at her anxiously, eager for her approval*]

ANNA: [*Concealing a smile—amused by this boyish boasting of his*] You did some hard work, didn't you?

BURKE: [*Promptly*] I did that! I'm a divil for sticking it out when them that's weak give up. But much good it did anyone! 'Twas a mad, fightin' scramble in the last seconds with each man for himself I disremember how it come about, but there was the four of us in wan boat and when we was raised high on a great wave I took a look about and divil a sight there was of ship or men on top of the sea.

ANNA: [*In a subdued voice*] Then all the others was drowned?

BURKE: They was, surely.

ANNA: [*With a shudder*] What a terrible end!

BURKE: [*Turns to her*] A terrible end for the like of them swabs does live on land, maybe. But for the like of us does be roaming the seas, a good end, I'm telling you—quick and clane.

ANNA: [*Struck by the word*] Yes, clean. That's yust the word for—all of it—the way it makes me feel.

BURKE: The sea, you mean? [*Interestedly*] I'm thinking you have a bit of it in your blood, too. Your Old Man wasn't only a barge rat—begging your pardon—all his life, by the cut of him.

ANNA: No, he was bo'sun on sailing ships for years. And all the men on both sides of the family have gone to sea as far back as he remembers, he says. All the women have married sailors, too.

BURKE: [*With intense satisfaction*] Did they, now? They had spirit in them. It's only on the sea you'd find rale men with guts is fit to wed with fine, high-tempered girls [*Then he adds half-boldly*] the like of yourself.

ANNA: [*With a laugh*] There you go kiddin' again. [*Then seeing his hurt expression—quickly*] But you was going to tell me about yourself. You're Irish, of course I can tell that.

BURKE: [*Stoutly*] Yes, thank God, though I've not seen a sight of it in fifteen years or more.

ANNA: [*Thoughtfully*] Sailors never do go home hardly, do they? That's what my father was saying.

BURKE: He wasn't telling no lie. [*With sudden melancholy*] It's a hard and lonesome life, the sea is.

The only women you'd meet in the ports of the world who'd be willing to speak you a kind word isn't woman at all. You know the kind I mane, and they're a poor, wicked lot, God forgive them. They're looking to steal the money from you only.

ANNA: [*Her face averted—rising to her feet— agitatedly*] I think—I guess I'd better see what's doing inside.

BURKE: [*Afraid he has offended her—beseechingly*] Don't go, I'm saying! Is it I've given you offense with my talk of the like of them? Don't heed it at all! I'm clumsy in my wits when it comes to talking proper with a girl the like of you. And why wouldn't I be? Since the day I left home for to go to sea punching coal, this is the first time I've had a word with a rale, dacent woman. So don't turn your back on me now, and we beginning to be friends.

ANNA: [*Turning to him again—forcing a smile*] I'm not sore at you, honest.

BURKE: [*Gratefully*] God bless you!

ANNA: [*Changing the subject abruptly*] But if you honestly think the sea's such a rotten life, why don't you get out of it?

BURKE: [*Surprised*] Work on land, is it? [*She nods. He spits scornfully*] Digging spuds in the muck from dawn to dark, I suppose? [*Vehemently*] I wasn't made for it, Miss.

ANNA: [*With a laugh*] I thought you'd say that.

BURKE: [*Argumentatively*] But there's good jobs and bad jobs at sea, like there'd be on land. I'm thinking if it's in the stokehole of a proper liner I was, I'd be able to have a little house and be home to it wan week out of four. And I'm thinking that maybe then I'd have the luck to find a fine dacent girl—the like of yourself, now—would be willing to wed with me.

ANNA: [*Turning away from him with a short laugh —uneasily*] Why, sure. Why not?

BURKE: [*Edging up close to her—exultantly*] Then you think a girl the like of yourself might maybe not mind the past at all but only be seeing the good herself put in me?

ANNA: [*In the same tone*] Why, sure.

BURKE: [*Passionately*] She'd not be sorry for it, I'd take my oath! 'Tis no more drinking and roving about I'd be doing then, but giving my pay day into her hand and staying at home with her as meek as a lamb each night of the week I'd be in port.

ANNA: [*Moved in spite of herself and troubled by this half-concealed proposal—with a forced laugh*] All you got to do is find the girl.

BURKE: I have found her!

ANNA: [*Half-frightenedly—trying to laugh it off*] You have? When? I thought you was saying——

BURKE: [*Boldly and forcefully*] This night. [*Hanging his head—humbly*] If she'll be having me. [*Then raising his eyes to hers—simply*] 'Tis you I mean.

ANNA: [*Is held by his eyes for a moment—then shrinks back from him with a strange, broken laugh*] Say—are you—going crazy? Are you trying to kid me? Proposing—to me!—for Gawd's sake!—on such short acquaintance?

[Chris *comes out of the cabin and stands staring blinkingly astern. When he makes out* Anna *in such intimate proximity to this strange sailor, an angry expression comes over his face*]

BURKE: [*Following her—with fierce, pleading insistence*] I'm telling you there's the will of God in it that brought me safe through the storm and fog to the wan spot in the world where you was! Think of that now, and isn't it queer——

CHRIS: Anna! [*He comes toward them, raging, his fists clenched*] Anna, you gat in cabin, you hear!

ANNA: [*All her emotions immediately transformed into resentment at his bullying tone*] Who d'you think you're talking to—a slave?

CHRIS: [*Hurt—his voice breaking—pleading*] You need gat rest, Anna. You gat sleep. [*She does not move. He turns on* Burke *furiously*] What you doing here, you sailor fallar? You ain't sick like oders. You gat in fo'c's'tle. Dey give you bunk. [*Threateningly*] You hurry, Ay tal you!

ANNA: [*Impulsively*] But he is sick. Look at him. He can hardly stand up.

BURKE: [*Straightening and throwing out his chest—with a bold laugh*] Is it giving me orders ye are, me bucko? Let you look out, then! With wan hand, weak as I am, I can break ye in two and fling the pieces over the side—and your crew after you. [*Stopping abruptly*] I was forgetting. You're her Old Man and I'd not raise a fist to you for the world.

[*His knees sag, he wavers and seems about to fall.* Anna *utters an exclamation of alarm and hurries to his side*]

ANNA: [*Taking one of his arms over her shoulder*] Come on in the cabin. You can have my bed if there ain't no other place.

BURKE: [*With jubilant happiness—as they proceed toward the cabin*] Glory be to God, is it holding my arm about your neck you are! Anna! Anna! Sure it's a sweet name is suited to you.

ANNA: [*Guiding him carefully*] Sssh! Sssh!

BURKE: Whisht, is it? Indade, and I'll not. I'll be roaring it out like a fog horn over the sea! You're the girl of the world and we'll be marrying soon and I don't care who knows it!

ANNA: [*As she guides him through the cabin door*] Ssshh! Never mind that talk. You go to sleep.

[*They go out of sight in the cabin.* Chris, *who has been listening to* Burke's *last words with open-mouthed amazement, stands looking after them desperately*]

CHRIS: [*Turns suddenly and shakes his fist out at the sea—with bitter hatred*] Dat's your dirty trick, damn ole davil, you! [*Then in a frenzy of rage*] But, py God, you don't do dat! Not while Ay'm living! No, py God, you don't!

[THE CURTAIN FALLS]

ACT III.

SCENE: *The interior of the cabin on the barge* Simeon Winthrop [*at dock in Boston*]—*a narrow, low-ceilinged compartment the walls of which are painted a light brown with white trimmings. In the rear on the left, a door leading to the sleeping quarters. In the far left corner, a large locker-closet, painted white, on the door of which a mirror hangs on a nail. In the rear wall, two small square windows and a door opening out on the deck toward the stern. In the right wall, two more windows looking out on the port deck. White curtains, clean and stiff, are at the windows. A table with two cane-bottomed chairs stands in the center of the cabin. A dilapidated, wicker rocker, painted brown, is also by the table.*

It is afternoon of a sunny day about a week later. From the harbor and docks outside, muffled by the closed door and windows, comes the sound of steamers' whistles and the puffing snort of the donkey engines of some ship unloading nearby.

As the curtain rises, Chris *and* Anna *are discovered.* Anna *is seated in the rocking-chair by the table, with a newspaper in her hands. She is not reading but staring straight in front of her. She looks unhappy, troubled, frowningly concentrated on her thoughts.* Chris *wanders about the room, casting quick, uneasy side glances at her face, then stopping to peer absent-mindedly out of the window. His attitude betrays an overwhelming, gloomy anxiety which has him on tenterhooks. He pretends to be engaged in setting things ship-shape, but this occupation is confined to picking up some object, staring at it stupidly for a second, then aimlessly putting it down again. He clears his throat and starts to sing to himself in a low, doleful voice:* "My Yosephine, come board de ship. Long time Ay vait for you."

ANNA: [*Turning on him, sarcastically*] I'm glad someone's feeling good. [*Wearily*] Gee, I sure wish we was out of this dump and back in New York.

CHRIS: [*With a sigh*] Ay'm glad vhen ve sail again, too. [*Then, as she makes no comment, he goes on with a ponderous attempt at sarcasm*] Ay don't see vhy you don't like Boston, dough. You have good time here, Ay tank. You go ashore all time, every day and night veek ve've been here. You go to movies, see show, gat all kinds fun—— [*His eyes hard with hatred*] All with that damn Irish fallar!

ANNA: [*With weary scorn*] Oh, for heaven's sake, are you off on that again? Where's the harm in his taking me around? D'you want me to sit all day and night in this cabin with you—and knit? Ain't I got a right to have as good a time as I can?

CHRIS: It ain't right kind of fun—not with that fallar, no.

ANNA: I been back on board every night by eleven, ain't I? [*Then struck by some thought—looks at him with keen suspicion—with rising anger*] Say, look here, what d'you mean by what you yust said?

CHRIS: [*Hastily*] Nutting but what Ay say, Anna.

ANNA: You said "ain't right" and you said it funny. Say, listen here, you ain't trying to insinuate that there's something wrong between us, are you?

CHRIS: [*Horrified*] No, Anna! No, Ay svear to God, Ay never tank dat!

ANNA: [*Mollified by his very evident sincerity—sitting down again*] Well, don't you never think it neither if you want me ever to speak to you again. [*Angrily again*] If I ever dreamt you thought that, I'd get the hell out of this barge so quick you couldn't see me for dust.

CHRIS: [*Soothingly*] Ay wouldn't never dream—— [*Then after a second's pause, reprovingly*] You vas gatting learn to swear. Dat ain't nice for young gel, you tank?

ANNA: [*With a faint trace of a smile*] Excuse me. You ain't used to such language, I know. [*Mockingly*] That's what your taking me to sea has done for me.

CHRIS: [*Indignantly*] No, it ain't me. It's dat damn sailor fallar learn you bad tangs.

ANNA: He ain't a sailor. He's a stoker.

CHRIS: [*Forcibly*] Dat vas million times vorse, Ay tal you! Dem fallars dat vork below shoveling coal vas de dirtiest, rough gang of no-good fallars in vorld!

ANNA: I'd hate to hear you say that to Mat.

CHRIS: Oh, Ay tal him same tang. You don't gat it in head Ay'm scared of him yust 'cause he vas stronger'n Ay vas. [*Menacingly*] You don't gat for fight with fists with dem fallars. Dere's oder vay for fix him.

ANNA: [*Glancing at him with sudden alarm*] What d'you mean?

CHRIS: [*Sullenly*] Nutting.

ANNA: You'd better not. I wouldn't start no trouble with him if I was you. He might forget some time that you was old and my father—and then you'd be out of luck.

CHRIS: [*With smoldering hatred*] Vell, yust let him! Ay'm ole bird maybe, but Ay bet Ay show him trick or two.

ANNA: [*Suddenly changing her tone—persuasively*] Aw come on, be good. What's eating you, anyway? Don't you want no one to be nice to me except yourself?

CHRIS: [*Placated—coming to her—eagerly*] Yes, Ay do, Anna—only not fallar on sea. Ay like for you marry steady fallar got good yob on land. You have little home in country all your own——

ANNA: [*Rising to her feet—brusquely*] Oh, cut it out! [*Scornfully*] Little home in the country! I wish you could have seen the little home in the country where you had me in jail till I was sixteen! [*With rising irritation*] Some day you're going to get me

so mad with that talk, I'm going to turn loose on you and tell you—a lot of things that'll open your eyes.

CHRIS: [*Alarmed*] Ay don't vant——

ANNA: I know you don't; but you keep on talking yust the same.

CHRIS: Ay don't talk no more den, Anna.

ANNA: Then promise me you'll cut out saying nasty things about Mat Burke every chance you get.

CHRIS: [*Evasive and suspicious*] Vhy? You like dat fallar—very much, Anna?

ANNA: Yes, I certainly do! He's a regular man, no matter what faults he's got. One of his fingers is worth all the hundreds of men I met out there—inland.

CHRIS: [*His face darkening*] Maybe you tank you love him, den?

ANNA: [*Defiantly*] What of it if I do?

CHRIS: [*Scowling and forcing out the words*] Maybe—you tank you—marry him?

ANNA: [*Shaking her head*] No! [Chris' *face lights up with relief.* Anna *continues slowly, a trace of sadness in her voice*] I'd met him four years ago—or even two years ago—I'd have jumped at the chance, I tell you that straight. And I would now—only he's such a simple guy—a big kid—and I ain't got the heart to fool him. [*She breaks off suddenly*] But don't never say again he ain't good enough for me. It's me ain't good enough for him.

CHRIS: [*Snorts scornfully*] Py yiminy, you go crazy, Ay tank!

ANNA: [*With a mournful laugh*] Well, I been thinking I was myself the last few days. [*She goes and takes a shawl from the hook near the door and throws it over her shoulders*] Guess I'll take a walk down to the end of the dock for a minute and see what's doing. I love to watch the ships passing. Mat'll be along before long, I guess. Tell him where I am, will you?

CHRIS: [*Despondently*] All right, Ay tal him.

[Anna *goes out the doorway on rear.* Chris *follows her out and stands on the deck outside for a moment looking after her. Then he comes back inside and shuts the door. He stands looking out of the window—mutters—"Dirty ole davil, you." Then he goes to the table, sets the cloth straight mechanically, picks up the newspaper* Anna *has let fall to the floor and sits down in the rocking-chair. He stares at the paper for a while, then puts it on table, holds his head in his hands and sighs drearily. The noise of a man's heavy footsteps comes from the deck outside and there is a loud knock on the door.* Chris *starts, makes a move as if to get up and go to the door, then thinks better of it and sits still. The knock is repeated—then as no answer comes, the door is flung open and* Mat Burke *appears.* Chris *scowls at the intruder and his hand instinctively goes back to the sheath knife on his hip.* Burke* *is dressed up—wears a cheap blue suit, a striped cotton shirt with a black tie, and black shoes newly shined. His face is beaming with good humor]*

BURKE: [*As he sees* Chris—*in a jovial tone of mockery*] Well, God bless who's here! [*He bends down and squeezes his huge form through the narrow doorway*] And how is the world treating you this afternoon, Anna's father?

CHRIS: [*Sullenly*] Pooty goot—if it ain't for some fallars.

BURKE: [*With a grin*] Meaning me, do you? [*He laughs*] Well, if you ain't the funny old crank of a man! [*Then soberly*] Where's herself? [Chris *sits dumb, scowling, his eyes averted.* Burke *is irritated by this silence*] Where's Anna, I'm asking you?

CHRIS: [*Hesitating—then grouchily*] She go down end of dock.

BURKE: I'll be going down to her, then. But first I'm thinking I'll take this chance when we're alone to have a word with you. [*He sits down opposite* Chris *at the table and leans over toward him*] And that word is soon said. I'm marrying your Anna before this day is out, and you might as well make up your mind to it whether you like it or no.

CHRIS: [*Glaring at him with hatred and forcing a scornful laugh*] Ho-ho! Dat's easy for say!

BURKE: You mean I won't? [*Scornfully*] Is it the like of yourself will stop me, are you thinking?

CHRIS: Yes, Ay stop it, if it come to vorst.

BURKE: [*With a scornful pity*] God help you!

CHRIS: But ain't no need for me do dat. Anna——

BURKE: [*Smiling confidently*] Is it Anna you think will prevent me?

CHRIS: Yes.

BURKE: And I'm telling you she'll not. She knows I'm loving her, and she loves me the same, and I know it.

CHRIS: Ho-ho! She only have fun. She make big fool of you, dat's all!

BURKE: [*Unshaken—pleasantly*] That's a lie in your throat, divil mend you!

CHRIS: No, it ain't lie. She tal me yust before she go out she never marry fallar like you.

BURKE: I'll not believe it. 'Tis a great old liar you are, and a divil to be making a power of trouble if you had your way. But 'tis not trouble I'm looking for, and me sitting down here. [*Earnestly*] Let us be talking it out now as man to man. You're her father, and wouldn't it be a shame for us to be at each other's throats like a pair of dogs, and I married with Anna. So out with the truth, man alive. What is it you're holding against me at all?

CHRIS: [*A bit placated, in spite of himself, by* Burke's *evident sincerity—but puzzled and suspicious*] Vell—Ay don't vant for Anna gat married. Listen, you fallar. Ay'm a ole man. Ay don't see Anna for fifteen year. She vas all Ay gat in vorld. And now ven she come on first trip—you tank Ay vant her leave me 'lone again?

BURKE: [*Heartily*] Let you not be thinking I have no heart at all for the way you'd be feeling.

CHRIS: [*Astonished and encouraged—trying to plead persuasively*] Den you do right tang, eh? You ship avay again, leave Anna alone. [*Cajolingly*] Big fallar like you dat's on sea, he don't need vife. He gat new gel in every port, you know dat.

BURKE: [*Angrily for a second*] God stiffen you! [*Then controlling himself—calmly*] I'll not be giving you the lie on that. But divil take you, there's a time comes to every man, on sea or land, that isn't a born fool, when he's sick of the lot of them cows, and wearing his heart out to meet up with a fine dacent girl, and have a home to call his own and be rearing up children in it. 'Tis small use you're asking me to leave Anna. She's the wan woman of the world for me, and I can't live without her now, I'm thinking.

CHRIS: You forgat all about her in one veek out of port, Ay bet you!

BURKE: You don't know the like I am. Death itself wouldn't make me forget her. So let you not be making talk to me about leaving her. I'll not, and be damned to you! It won't be so bad for you as you'd make out at all. She'll be living here in the States, and her married to me. And you'd be seeing her often so—a sight more often than ever you saw her the fifteen years she was growing up in the West. It's quare you'd be the one to be making great trouble about her leaving you when you never laid eyes on her once in all them years.

CHRIS: [*Guiltily*] Ay t'ought it vas better Anna stay away, grow up inland where she don't ever know ole davil, sea.

BURKE: [*Scornfully*] Is it blaming the sea for your troubles ye are again, God help you? Well, Anna knows it now. 'Twas in her blood, anyway.

CHRIS: And Ay don't vant she ever know no-good fallar on sea——

BURKE: She knows one now.

CHRIS: [*Banging the table with his fist—furiously*] Dat's yust it! Dat's yust what you are—no-good, sailor fallar! You tank Ay lat her life be made sorry by you like her mo'der's vas by me! No, Ay svear! She don't marry you if Ay gat kill you first!

BURKE: [*Looks at him a moment, in astonishment—then laughing uproariously*] Ho-ho! Glory be to God, it's bold talk you have for a stumpy runt of a man!

CHRIS: [*Threateningly*] Vell—you see!

BURKE: [*With grinning defiance*] I'll see, surely! I'll see myself and Anna married this day, I'm telling you. [*Then with contemptuous exasperation*] It's quare fool's blather you have about the sea done this and the sea done that. You'd ought to be 'shamed to be saying the like, and you an old sailor yourself. I'm after hearing a lot of it from you and a lot more that Anna's told me you do be saying to her, and I'm thinking it's a poor weak thing you are, and not a man at all!

CHRIS: [*Darkly*] You see if Ay'm man—maybe quicker'n you tank.

BURKE: [*Contemptuously*] Yerra, don't be boasting. I'm thinking 'tis out of your wits you've got with fright of the sea. You'd be wishing Anna married to a farmer, she told me. That'd be a swate match, surely! Would you have a fine girl the like of Anna lying down at nights with a muddy scut stinking of pigs and dung? Or would you have her tied for life to the like of them skinny, shriveled swabs does be working in cities?

CHRIS: Dat's lie, you fool!

BURKE: 'Tis not. 'Tis your own mad notions I'm after telling. But you know the truth in your heart, if great fear of the sea has made you a liar and coward itself. [*Pounding the table*] The sea's the only life for a man with guts in him isn't afraid of his own shadow! 'Tis only on the sea he's free, and him roving the face of the world, seeing all things, and not giving a damn for saving up money, or stealing from his friends, or any of the black tricks that a landlubber'd waste his life on. 'Twas yourself knew it once, and you a bo'sun for years.

CHRIS: [*Sputtering with rage*] You vas crazy fool, Ay tal you!

BURKE: You've swallowed the anchor. The sea give you a clout once, knocked you down, and you're not man enough to get up for another, but lie there for the rest of your life howling bloody murder. [*Proudly*] Isn't it myself the sea has nearly drowned, and me battered and bate till I was that close to hell I could hear the flames roaring, and never a groan out of me till the sea gave up and it seeing the great strength and guts of a man was in me?

CHRIS: [*Scornfully*] Yes, you vas hell of fallar, hear you tal it!

BURKE: [*Angrily*] You'll be calling me a liar once too often, me old bucko! Wasn't the whole story of it and my picture itself in the newspapers of Boston a week back? [*Looking* Chris *up and down belittlingly*] Sure I'd like to see you in the best of your youth do the like of what I done in the storm and after. 'Tis a mad lunatic, screeching with fear, you'd be this minute!

CHRIS: Ho-ho! You vas young fool! In ole years when Ay vas on windyammer, Ay vas through hundred storms vorse'n dat! Ships vas ships den—and men dat sail on dem vas real men. And now what you gat on steamers? You gat fallars on deck don't know ship from mudscow. [*With a meaning glance at* Burke] And below deck you gat fallars yust know how for shovel coal—might yust as vell vork on coal vagon ashore!

BURKE: [*Stung—angrily*] Is it casting insults at the men in the stokehole ye are, ye old ape? God stiffen you! Wan of them is worth any ten stock-fish-swilling Square-heads ever shipped on a windbag!

CHRIS: [*His face working with rage, his hand going back to the sheath-knife on his hip*] Irish svine, you!

BURKE: [*Tauntingly*] Don't ye like the Irish, ye old baboon? 'Tis that you're needing in your family, I'm telling you—an Irishman and a man of the stokehole—to put guts in it so that you'll not be having grandchildren would be fearful cowards and jackasses the like of yourself!

CHRIS: [*Half rising from his chair—in a voice choked with rage*] You look out!

BURKE: [*Watching him intently—a mocking smile on his lips*] And it's that you'll be having, no matter what you'll do to prevent; for Anna and me'll be married this day, and no old fool the like of you will stop us when I've made up my mind.

CHRIS: [*With a hoarse cry*] You don't!

[*He throws himself at* Burke, *knife in hand, knocking his chair over backwards.* Burke *springs to his feet quickly in time to meet the attack. He laughs with the pure love of battle. The old Swede is like a child in his hands.* Burke *does not strike or mistreat him in any way, but simply twists his right hand behind his back and forces the knife from his fingers. He throws the knife into a far corner of the room—tauntingly*]

BURKE: Old men is getting childish shouldn't play with knives. [*Holding the struggling* Chris *at arm's length—with a sudden rush of anger, drawing back his fist*] I've half a mind to hit you a great clout will put sense in your square head. Kape off me now, I'm warning you!

[*He gives* Chris *a push with the flat of his hand which sends the old Swede staggering back against the cabin wall, where he remains standing, panting heavily, his eyes fixed on* Burke *with hatred, as if he were only collecting his strength to rush at him again*]

BURKE: [*Warningly*] Now don't be coming at me again, I'm saying, or I'll flatten you on the floor with a blow, if 'tis Anna's father you are itself! I've no patience left for you. [*Then with an amused laugh*] Well, 'tis a bold old man you are just the same, and I'd never think it was in you to come tackling me alone.

[*A shadow crosses the cabin windows. Both men start.* Anna *appears in the doorway*]

ANNA: [*With pleased surprise as she sees* Burke] Hello, Mat. Are you here already? I was down—— [*She stops, looking from one to the other, sensing immediately that something has happened*] What's up? [*Then noticing the overturned chair—in alarm*] How'd that chair get knocked over? [*Turning on* Burke *reproachfully*] You ain't been fighting with him, Mat—after you promised?

BURKE: [*His old self again*] I've not laid a hand on him, Anna. [*He goes and picks up the chair, then turning on the still questioning* Anna—*with a reassuring smile*] Let you not be worried at all. 'Twas only a bit of an argument we was having to pass the time till you'd come.

ANNA: It must have been some argument when you got to throwing chairs. [*She turns on* Chris] Why don't you say something? What was it about?

CHRIS: [*Relaxing at last—avoiding her eyes—sheepishly*] Ve vas talking about ships and fallars on sea.

ANNA: [*With a relieved smile*] Oh—the old stuff, eh?

BURKE: [*Suddenly seeming to come to a bold decision—with a defiant grin at* Chris] He's not after telling you the whole of it. We was arguing about you mostly.

ANNA: [*With a frown*] About me?

BURKE: And we'll be finishing it out right here and now in your presence if you're willing.

[*He sits down at the left of table*]

ANNA: [*Uncertainly—looking from him to her father*] Sure. Tell me what it's all about.

CHRIS: [*Advancing toward the table—protesting to* Burke] No! You don't do dat, you! You tal him you don't vant for hear him talk, Anna.

ANNA: But I do. I want this cleared up.

CHRIS: [*Miserably afraid now*] Vell, not now, anyvay. You vas going ashore, yes? You ain't got time——

ANNA: [*Firmly*] Yes, right here and now. [*She turns to* Burke] You tell me, Mat, since he don't want to.

BURKE: [*Draws a deep breath—then plunges in boldly*] The whole of it's in a few words only. So's he'd make no mistake, and him hating the sight of me, I told him in his teeth I loved you. [*Passionately*] And that's God truth, Anna, and well you know it!

CHRIS: [*Scornfully—forcing a laugh*] Ho-ho! He tal same tang to gel every port he go!

ANNA: [*Shrinking from her father with repulsion —resentfully*] Shut up, can't you? [*Then to* Burke— *feelingly*] I know it's true, Mat. I don't mind what he says.

BURKE: [*Humbly grateful*] God bless you!

ANNA: And then what?

BURKE: And then—— [*Hesitatingly*] And then I said—— [*He looks at her pleadingly*] I said I was sure—I told him I thought you have a bit of love for me, too. [*Passionately*] Say you do, Anna! Let you not destroy me entirely, for the love of God!

[*He grasps both her hands in his two*]

ANNA: [*Deeply moved and troubled—forcing a trembling laugh*] So you told him that, Mat? No wonder he was mad. [*Forcing out the words*] Well, maybe it's true, Mat. Maybe I do. I been thinking and thinking—I didn't want to, Mat, I'll own up to that—I tried to cut it out—but—— [*She laughs helplessly*] I guess I can't help it anyhow. So I guess I do, Mat. [*Then with a sudden joyous defiance*] Sure I do! What's the use of kidding myself different? Sure I love you, Mat!

CHRIS: [*With a cry of pain*] Anna!

[*He sits crushed*]

BURKE: [*With a great depth of sincerity in his humble gratitude*] God be praised!

ANNA: [*Assertively*] And I ain't never loved a man in my life before, you can always believe that —no matter what happens.

BURKE: [*Goes over to her and puts his arms around her*] Sure I do be believing ivery word you iver said or iver will say. And 'tis you and me will be having a grand, beautiful life together to the end of our days!

[*He tries to kiss her. At first she turns away her head—then, overcome by a fierce impulse of passionate love, she takes his head in both her hands and holds his face close to hers, staring into his eyes. Then she kisses him full on the lips*]

ANNA: [*Pushing him away from her—forcing a broken laugh*] Good-by.

[*She walks to the doorway in rear—stands with her back toward them, looking out. Her shoulders quiver once or twice as if she were fighting back her sobs*]

BURKE: [*Too in the seventh heaven of bliss to get any correct interpretation of her word—with a laugh*] Good-by, is it? The divil you say! I'll be coming back at you in a second for more of the same! [*To* Chris, *who has quickened to instant attention at his daughter's good-by, and has looked back at her with a stirring of foolish hope in his eyes*] Now, me old bucko, what'll you be saying? You heard the words from her own lips. Confess I've bate you. Own up like a man when you're bate fair and square. And here's my hand to you—— [*Holds out his hand*] And let you take it and we'll shake and forget what's over and done, and be friends from this out.

CHRIS: [*With implacable hatred*] Ay don't shake hands with you fallar—not vile Ay live!

BURKE: [*Offended*] The back of my hand to you then, if that suits you better. [*Growling*] 'Tis a rotten bad loser you are, divil mend you!

CHRIS: Ay don't lose. [*Trying to be scornful and self-convincing*] Anna say she like you little bit but you don't hear her say she marry you, Ay bet.

[*At the sound of her name* Anna *has turned round to them. Her face is composed and calm again, but it is the dead calm of despair*]

BURKE: [*Scornfully*] No, and I wasn't hearing her say the sun is shining either.

CHRIS: [*Doggedly*] Dat's all right. She don't say it, yust same.

ANNA: [*Quietly—coming forward to them*] No, I didn't say it, Mat.

CHRIS: [*Eagerly*] Dere! You hear!

BURKE: [*Misunderstanding her—with a grin*] You're waiting till you do be asked, you mane? Well, I'm asking you now. And we'll be married this day, with the help of God!

ANNA: [*Gently*] You heard what I said, Mat—after I kissed you?

BURKE: [*Alarmed by something in her manner*] No—I disremember.

ANNA: I said good-by. [*Her voice trembling*] That kiss was for good-by, Mat.

BURKE: [*Terrified*] What d'you mane?

ANNA: I can't marry you, Mat—and we've said good-by. That's all.

CHRIS: [*Unable to hold back his exultation*] Ay know it! Ay know dat vas so!

BURKE: [*Jumping to his feet—unable to believe his ears*] Anna! Is it making game of me you'd be? 'Tis a quare time to joke with me, and don't be doing it, for the love of God.

ANNA: [*Looking him in the eyes—steadily*] D'you think I'd kid you? No, I'm not joking, Mat. I mean what I said.

BURKE: Ye don't! Ye can't! 'Tis mad you are, I'm telling you!

ANNA: [*Fixedly*] No, I'm not.

BURKE: [*Desperately*] But what's come over you so sudden? You was saying you loved me——

ANNA: I'll say that as often as you want me to. It's true.

BURKE: [*Bewilderedly*] Then why—what, in the divil's name—— Oh, God help me, I can't make head or tail to it at all!

ANNA: Because it's the best way out I can figure, Mat. [*Her voice catching*] I been thinking it over and thinking it over day and night all week. Don't think it ain't hard on me, too, Mat.

BURKE: For the love of God, tell me then, what is it that's preventing you wedding me when the two of us has love? [*Suddenly getting an idea and pointing at* Chris—*exasperatedly*] Is it giving heed to the like of that old fool ye are, and him hating me and filling your ears full of bloody lies against me?

CHRIS: [*Getting to his feet—raging triumphantly before* Anna *has a chance to get in a word*] Yes, Anna believe me, not you! She know her old fa'der don't lie like you.

ANNA: [*Turning on her father angrily*] You sit down, d'you hear? Where do you come in butting in and making things worse? You're like a devil, you are! [*Harshly*] Good Lord, and I was beginning to like you, beginning to forget all I've got held up against you!

CHRIS: [*Crushed feebly*] You ain't got nutting for hold against me, Anna.

ANNA: Ain't I yust! Well, lemme tell you—— [*She glances at* Burke *and stops abruptly*] Say, Mat, I'm s'prised at you. You didn't think anything he'd said——

BURKE: [*Glumly*] Sure, what else would it be?

ANNA: Think I've ever paid any attention to all his crazy bull? Gee, you must take me for a five-year-old kid.

BURKE: [*Puzzled and beginning to be irritated at her too*] I don't know how to take you, with your saying this one minute and that the next.

ANNA: Well, he has nothing to do with it.

BURKE: Then what is it has? Tell me, and don't keep me waiting and sweating blood.

ANNA: [*Resolutely*] I can't tell you—and I won't. I got a good reason—and that's all you need to know. I can't marry you, that's all there is to it. [*Distractedly*] So, for Gawd's sake, let's talk of something else.

BURKE: I'll not! [*Then fearfully*] Is it married to someone else you are—in the West maybe?

ANNA: [*Vehemently*] I should say not.

BURKE: [*Regaining his courage*] To the divil with all other reasons then. They don't matter with me at all. [*He gets to his feet confidently, assuming a masterful tone*] I'm thinking you're the like of them women can't make up their mind till they're drove to it. Well, then, I'll make up your mind for you bloody quick. [*He takes her by the arms, grinning to soften his serious bullying*] We've had enough of talk! Let you be going into your room now and be dressing in your best and we'll be going ashore.

CHRIS: [*Aroused—angrily*] No, py God, she don't do that!

[*Takes hold of her arm*]

ANNA: [*Who has listened to* Burke *in astonishment. She draws away from him, instinctively repelled by his tone, but not exactly sure if he is serious or not—a trace of resentment in her voice*] Say, where do you get that stuff?

BURKE: [*Imperiously*] Never mind, now! Let you go get dressed, I'm saying. [*Then turning to* Chris] We'll be seeing who'll win in the end—me or you.

CHRIS: [*To* Anna—*also in an authoritative tone*] You stay right here, Anna, you hear!

[Anna *stands looking from one to the other of them as if she thought they had both gone crazy. Then the expression of her face freezes into the hardened sneer of her experience*]

BURKE: [*Violently*] She'll not! She'll do what I say! You've had your hold on her long enough. It's my turn now.

ANNA: [*With a hard laugh*] Your turn? Say, what am I, anyway?

BURKE: 'Tis not what you are, 'tis what you're going to be this day—and that's wedded to me before night comes. Hurry up now with your dressing.

CHRIS: [*Commandingly*] You don't do one tang he say, Anna!

[Anna *laughs mockingly*]

BURKE: She will, so!

CHRIS: Ay tal you she don't! Ay'm her fa'der.

BURKE: She will in spite of you. She's taking my orders from this out, not yours.

ANNA: [*Laughing again*] Orders is good!

BURKE: [*Turning to her impatiently*] Hurry up now, and shake a leg. We've no time to be wasting.

[*Irritated as she doesn't move*] Do you hear what I'm telling you?

CHRIS: You stay dere, Anna!

ANNA: [*At the end of her patience—blazing out at them passionately*] You can go to hell, both of you! [*There is something in her tone that makes them forget their quarrel and turn to her in a stunned amazement. Anna laughs wildly*] You're just like all the rest of them—you two! Gawd, you'd think I was a piece of furniture! I'll show you! Sit down now! [*As they hesitate—furiously*] Sit down and let me talk for a minute. You're all wrong, see? Listen to me! I'm going to tell you something—and then I'm going to beat it. [*To Burke—with a harsh laugh*] I'm going to tell you a funny story, so pay attention. [*Pointing to* Chris] I've been meaning to turn it loose on him every time he'd get my goat with his bull about keeping me safe inland. I wasn't going to tell you, but you've forced me into it. What's the dif? It's all wrong anyway, and you might as well get cured that way as any other. [*With hard mocking*] Only don't forget what you said a minute ago about it not mattering to you what other reason I got so long as I wasn't married to no one else.

BURKE: [*Manfully*] That's my word, and I'll stick to it!

ANNA: [*Laughing bitterly*] What a chance! You make me laugh, honest! Want to bet you will? Wait 'n' see! [*She stands at the table rear, looking from one to the other of the two men with her hard, mocking smile. Then she begins, fighting to control her emotion and speak calmly*] First thing is, I want to tell you two guys something. You was going on 's if one of you had got to own me. But nobody owns me, see?—'cepting myself. I'll do what I please and no man, I don't give a hoot who he is, can tell me what to do! I ain't asking either of you for a living. I can make it myself—one way or other. I'm my own boss. So put that in your pipe and smoke it! You and your orders!

BURKE: [*Protestingly*] I wasn't meaning it that way at all and well you know it. You've no call to be raising this rumpus with me. [*Pointing to* Chris] 'Tis him you've a right——

ANNA: I'm coming to him. But you—you did mean it that way, too. You sounded—yust like all the rest. [*Hysterically*] But, damn it, shut up! Let me talk for a change!

BURKE: 'Tis square, rough talk, that—for a dacent girl the like of you!

ANNA: [*With a hard laugh*] Decent? Who told you I was? [Chris *is sitting with bowed shoulders, his head in his hands. She leans over in exasperation and shakes him violently by the shoulder*] Don't go to sleep, Old Man! Listen here, I'm talking to you now!

CHRIS: [*Straightening up and looking about as if he were seeking a way to escape—with frightened foreboding in his voice*] Ay don't vant for hear it. You vas going out of head, Ay tank, Anna.

ANNA: [*Violently*] Well, living with you is enough to drive anyone off their nut. Your bunk about the farm being so fine! Didn't I write you year after year how rotten it was and what a dirty slave them cousins made of me? What'd you care? Nothing! Not even enough to come out and see me! That crazy bull about wanting to keep me away from the sea don't go down with me! You yust didn't want to be bothered with me! You're like all the rest of 'em!

CHRIS: [*Feebly*] Anna! It ain't so——

ANNA: [*Not heeding his interruption—revengefully*] But one thing I never wrote you. It was one of them cousins that you think is such nice people—the youngest son—Paul—that started me wrong. [*Loudly*] It wasn't none of my fault. I hated him worse'n hell and he knew it. But he was big and strong—[*Pointing to* Burke]—like you!

BURKE: [*Half springing to his feet—his fists clenched*] God blarst it!

[*He sinks slowly back in his chair again, the knuckles showing white on his clenched hands, his face tense with the effort to suppress his grief and rage*]

CHRIS: [*In a cry of horrified pain*] Anna!

ANNA: [*To him—seeming not to have heard their interruptions*] That was why I run away from the farm. That was what made me get a yob as nurse girl in St. Paul. [*With a hard, mocking laugh*] And you think that was a nice yob for a girl, too, don't you? [*Sarcastically*] With all them nice inland fellers yust looking for a chance to marry me, I s'pose. Marry me? What a chance! They wasn't looking for marrying. [*As* Burke *lets a groan of fury escape him—desperately*] I'm owning up to everything fair and square. I was caged in, I tell you—yust like in yail—taking care of other people's kids—listening to 'em bawling and crying day and night—when I wanted to be out—and I was lonesome—lonesome as hell! [*With a sudden weariness in her voice*] So I give up finally. What was the use? [*She stops and looks at the two men. Both are motionless and silent. Chris *seems in a stupor of despair, his house of cards fallen about him.* Burke's *face is livid with the rage that is eating him up, but he is too stunned and bewildered yet to find a vent for it. The condemnation she feels in their silence goads* Anna *into a harsh, strident defiance*] You don't say nothing—either of you—but I know what you're thinking. You're like all the rest! [*To* Chris—*furiously*] And who's to blame for it, me or you? If you'd even acted like a man—if you even had been a regular father and had me with you—maybe things would be different!

CHRIS: [*In agony*] Don't talk dat vay, Anna! Ay go crazy! Ay von't listen!

[*Puts his hands over his ears*]

ANNA: [*Infuriated by his action—stridently*] You

will too listen! [*She leans over and pulls his hands from his ears—with hysterical rage*] You—keeping me safe inland—I wasn't no nurse girl the last two years—I lied when I wrote you—I was in a house, that's what!—yes, that kind of a house—the kind sailors like you and Mat goes to in port—and your nice inland men, too—and all men, God damn 'em! I hate 'em! Hate 'em!

[*She breaks into hysterical sobbing, throwing herself into the chair and hiding her face in her hands on the table. The two men have sprung to their feet*]

CHRIS: [*Whimpering like a child*] Anna! Anna! It's lie. It's lie!

[*He stands wringing his hands together and begins to weep*]

BURKE: [*His whole great body tense like a spring —dully and gropingly*] So that's what's in it!

ANNA: [*Raising her head at the sound of his voice —with extreme mocking bitterness*] I s'pose you remember your promise, Mat? No other reason was to count with you so long as I wasn't married already. So I s'pose you want me to get dressed and go ashore, don't you? [*She laughs*] Yes, you do!

BURKE: [*On the verge of his outbreak—stammeringly*] God stiffen you!

ANNA: [*Trying to keep up her hard, bitter tone, but gradually letting a note of pitiful pleading creep in*] I s'pose if I tried to tell you I wasn't—that—no more you'd believe me, wouldn't you? Yes, you would! And if I told you that yust getting out in this barge, and being on the sea had changed me and made me feel different about things, 's if all I'd been through wasn't me and didn't count and yust like it never happened—you'd laugh, wouldn't you? And you'd die laughing sure if I said that meeting you that funny way that night in the fog, and afterwards seeing that you was straight goods stuck on me, had got me thinking for the first time, and I sized you up as a different kind of man—a sea man as different from the ones on land as water is from mud—and that was why I got stuck on you, too. I wanted to marry you and fool you, but I couldn't. Don't you see how I've changed? I couldn't marry you with you believing a lie—and I was shamed to tell you the truth—till the both of you forced my hand, and I seen you was the same as all the rest. And now, give me a bawling out and beat it, like I can tell you're going to. [*She stops, looking at Burke. He is silent, his face averted, his features beginning to work with fury. She pleads passionately*] Will you believe it if I tell you that loving you has made me—clean? It's the straight goods, honest! [*Then as he doesn't reply—bitterly*] Like hell you will! You're like all the rest!

BURKE: [*Blazing out—turning on her in a perfect frenzy of rage—his voice trembling with passion*] The rest, is it? God's curse on you! Clane, is it? You slut, you, I'll be killing you now!

[*He picks up the chair on which he has been sitting and, swinging it high over his shoulder, springs toward her. Chris rushes forward with a cry of alarm, trying to ward off the blow from his daughter. Anna looks up into Burke's eyes with the fearlessness of despair. Burke checks himself, the chair held in the air*]

CHRIS: [*Wildly*] Stop, you crazy fool! You vant for murder her!

ANNA: [*Pushing her father away brusquely, her eyes still holding Burke's*] Keep out of this, you! [*To Burke—dully*] Well, ain't you got the nerve to do it? Go ahead! I'll be thankful to you, honest. I'm sick of the whole game.

BURKE: [*Throwing the chair away into a corner of the room—helplessly*] I can't do it, God help me, and your two eyes looking at me. [*Furiously*] Though I do be thinking I'd have a good right to smash your skull like a rotten egg. Was there iver a woman in the world had the rottenness in her that you have, and was there iver a man the like of me was made the fool of the world, and me thinking thoughts about you, and having great love for you, and dreaming dreams of the fine life we'd have when we'd be wedded! [*His voice high pitched in a lamentation that is like a keen*] Yerra, God help me! I'm destroyed entirely and my heart is broken in bits! I'm asking God Himself, was it for this He'd have me roaming the earth since I was a lad only, to come to black shame in the end, where I'd be giving a power of love to a woman is the same as others you'd meet in any hookershanty in port, with red gowns on them and paint on their grinning mugs, would be sleeping with any man for a dollar or two!

ANNA: [*In a scream*] Don't, Mat! For Gawd's sake! [*Then raging and pounding on the table with her hands*] Get out of here! Leave me alone! Get out of here!

BURKE: [*His anger rushing back on him*] I'll be going, surely! And I'll be drinking sloos of whisky will wash that black kiss of yours off my lips; and I'll be getting dead rotten drunk so I'll not remember if 'twas iver born you was at all; and I'll be shipping away on some boat will take me to the other end of the world where I'll never see your face again!

[*He turns toward the door*]

CHRIS: [*Who has been standing in a stupor—suddenly grasping Burke by the arm—stupidly*] No, you don't go. Ay tank maybe it's better Anna marry you now.

BURKE: [*Shaking Chris off—furiously*] Lave go of me, ye old ape! Marry her, is it? I'd see her roasting in hell first! I'm shipping away out of this, I'm telling you! [*Pointing to Anna—passionately*] And my curse on you and the curse of Almighty God and all the Saints! You've destroyed me this day and may you lie awake in the long nights, tormented with thoughts of Mat Burke and the great wrong you've done him!

ANNA: [*In anguish*] Mat!

[*But he turns without another word and strides out of the doorway. Anna looks after him*] *wildly, starts to run after him, then hides her face in her outstretched arms, sobbing.* Chris *stands in a stupor, staring at the floor*]

CHRIS: [*After a pause, dully*] Ay tank Ay go ashore, too.

ANNA: [*Looking up, wildly*] Not after him! Let him go! Don't you dare——

CHRIS: [*Somberly*] Ay go for gat drink.

ANNA: [*With a harsh laugh*] So I'm driving you to drink, too, eh? I s'pose you want to get drunk so's you can forget—like him?

CHRIS: [*Bursting out angrily*] Yes, Ay vant! You tank Ay like to hear dem tangs. [*Breaking down—weeping*] Ay tank you vasn't dat kind of gel, Anna.

ANNA: [*Mockingly*] And I s'pose you want me to beat it, don't you? You don't want me here disgracing you, I s'pose?

CHRIS: No, you stay here! [*Goes over and pats her on the shoulder, the tears running down his face*] Ain't your fault, Anna, Ay know dat. [*She looks up at him, softened. He bursts into rage*] It's dat ole davil, sea, do this to me! [*He shakes his fist at the door*] It's her dirty tricks! It vas all right on barge with yust you and me. Den she bring dat Irish fallar in fog, she make you like him, she make you fight with me all time! If dat Irish fallar don't never come, you don't never tal me dem tangs, Ay don't never know, and everytang's all right. [*He shakes his fist again*] Dirty ole davil!

ANNA: [*With spent weariness*] Oh, what's the use? Go on ashore and get drunk.

CHRIS: [*Goes into room on left and gets his cap. He goes to the door, silent and stupid—then turns*] You vait here, Anna?

ANNA: [*Dully*] Maybe—and maybe not. Maybe I'll get drunk, too. Maybe I'll—— But what the hell do you care what I do? Go on and beat it.

[Chris *turns stupidly and goes out.* Anna *sits at the table, staring straight in front of her*]

[THE CURTAIN FALLS]

ACT IV.

SCENE. *Same as Act Three, about nine o'clock of a foggy night two days later. The whistles of steamers in the harbor can be heard. The cabin is lighted by a small lamp on the table. A suitcase stands in the middle of the floor.* Anna *is sitting in the rocking-chair. She wears a hat, is all dressed up as in Act One. Her face is pale, looks terribly tired and worn, as if the two days just past had been ones of suffering and sleepless nights. She stares before her despondently, her chin in her hands. There is a timid knock on the door in rear.* Anna *jumps to her feet with a startled exclamation and looks toward the door with an expression of mingled fear and hope.*

ANNA: [*Faintly*] Come in. [*Then summoning her courage—more resolutely*] Come in. [*The door is opened and* Chris *appears in the doorway. He is in a very bleary, bedraggled condition, suffering from the after effects of his drunk. A tin pail full of foaming beer is in his hand. He comes forward, his eyes avoiding Anna's. He mutters stupidly*] It's foggy.

ANNA: [*Looking him over with contempt*] So you come back at last, did you? You're a fine-looking sight! [*Then jeeringly*] I thought you'd beaten it for good on account of the disgrace I'd brought on you.

CHRIS: [*Wincing—faintly*] Don't say dat, Anna, please!

[*He sits in a chair by the table, setting down the can of beer, holding his head in his hands*]

ANNA: [*Looks at him with a certain sympathy*] What's the trouble? Feeling sick?

CHRIS: [*Dully*] Inside my head feel sick.

ANNA: Well, what d'you expect after being soused for two days? [*Resentfully*] It serves you right. A fine thing—you leaving me alone on this barge all that time!

CHRIS: [*Humbly*] Ay'm sorry, Anna.

ANNA: [*Scornfully*] Sorry!

CHRIS: But Ay'm not sick inside head vay you mean. Ay'm sick from tank too much about you, about me.

ANNA: And how about me? D'you suppose I ain't been thinking, too?

CHRIS: Ay'm sorry, Anna. [*He sees her bag and gives a start*] You pack your bag, Anna? You vas going——?

ANNA: [*Forcibly*] Yes, I was going right back to what you think.

CHRIS: Anna!

ANNA: I went ashore to get a train for New York. I'd been waiting and waiting till I was sick of it. Then I changed my mind and decided not to go today. But I'm going first thing tomorrow, so it'll all be the same in the end.

CHRIS: [*Raising his head—pleadingly*] No, you never do dat, Anna!

ANNA: [*With a sneer*] Why not, I'd like to know?

CHRIS: You don't never gat to do—dat vay—no more, Ay tal you. Ay fix dat up all right.

ANNA: [*Suspiciously*] Fix what up?

CHRIS: [*Not seeming to have heard her question—sadly*] You vas vaiting, you say? You vasn't vaiting for me, Ay bet.

ANNA: [*Callously*] You'd win.

CHRIS: For dat Irish fallar?

ANNA: [*Defiantly*] Yes—if you want to know! [*Then with a forlorn laugh*] If he did come back it'd only be 'cause he wanted to beat me up or kill me, I suppose. But even if he did, I'd rather have him come than not show up at all. I wouldn't care what he did.

CHRIS: Ay guess it's true you vas in love with him all right.

ANNA: You guess!

CHRIS: [*Turning to her earnestly*] And Ay'm sorry for you like hell he don't come, Anna!

ANNA: [*Softened*] Seems to me you've changed your tune a lot.

CHRIS: Ay've been tanking, and Ay guess it vas all my fault—all bad tangs dat happen to you. [*Pleadingly*] You try for not hate me, Anna. Ay'm crazy ole fool, dat's all.

ANNA: Who said I hated you?

CHRIS: Ay'm sorry for everytank Ay do wrong for you, Anna. Ay vant for you be happy all rest of your life for make up! It make you happy marry dat Irish fallar, Ay vant it, too.

ANNA: [*Dully*] Well, there ain't no chance. But I'm glad you think different about it, anyway.

CHRIS: [*Supplicatingly*] And you tank—maybe—you forgive me sometime?

ANNA: [*With a wan smile*] I'll forgive you right now.

CHRIS: [*Seizing her hand and kissing it—brokenly*] Anna lilla! Anna lilla!

ANNA: [*Touched but a bit embarrassed*] Don't bawl about it. There ain't nothing to forgive, anyway. It ain't your fault, and it ain't mine, and it ain't his neither. We're all poor nuts, and things happen, and we yust get mixed in wrong, that's all.

CHRIS: [*Eagerly*] You say right tang, Anna, py golly! It ain't nobody's fault! [*Shaking his fist*] It's dat ole davil, sea!

ANNA: [*With an exasperated laugh*] Gee, won't you ever can that stuff? [Chris *relapses into injured silence. After a pause* Anna *continues curiously*] You said a minute ago you'd fixed something up—about me. What was it?

CHRIS: [*After a hesitating pause*] Ay'm shipping avay on sea again, Anna.

ANNA: [*Astounded*] You're—what?

CHRIS: Ay sign on steamer sail tomorrow. Ay gat my ole yob—bo'sun. [Anna *stares at him. As he goes on, a bitter smile comes over her face*] Ay tank dat's best tang for you. Ay only bring you bad luck, Ay tank. Ay make your mo'der's life sorry. Ay don't vant make yours dat vay, but Ay do yust same. Dat ole davil, sea, she make me Yonah man ain't no good for nobody. And Ay tank now it ain't no use fight with sea. No man dat live going to beat her, py yingo!

ANNA: [*With a laugh of helpless bitterness*] So that's how you've fixed me, is it?

CHRIS: Yes, Ay tank if dat ole davil gat me back she leave you alone den.

ANNA: [*Bitterly*] But, for Gawd's sake, don't you see you're doing the same thing you've always done? Don't you see——? [*But she sees the look of obsessed stubbornness on her father's face and gives it up helplessly*] But what's the use of talking? You ain't right, that's what. I'll never blame you for nothing no more. But how could you figure out that was fixing me——!

CHRIS: Dat ain't all. Ay gat dem fallars in steamship office to pay you all money coming to me every month vhile Ay'm avay.

ANNA: [*With a hard laugh*] Thanks. But I guess I won't be hard up for no small change.

CHRIS: [*Hurt—humbly*] It ain't much, Ay know, but it's plenty for keep you so you never gat go back——

ANNA: [*Shortly*] Shut up, will you? We'll talk about it later, see?

CHRIS: [*After a pause—ingratiatingly*] You like Ay go ashore look for dat Irish fallar, Anna?

ANNA: [*Angrily*] Not much! Think I want to drag him back?

CHRIS: [*After a pause—uncomfortably*] Py golly, dat booze don't go vell. Give me fever, Ay tank. Ay feel hot like hell.

[*He takes off his coat and lets it drop on the floor. There is a loud thud*]

ANNA: [*With a start*] What you got in your pocket, for Pete's sake—a ton of lead? [*She reaches down, takes the coat and pulls out a revolver—looks from it to him in amazement*] A gun? What were you doing with this?

CHRIS: [*Sheepishly*] Ay forget. Ain't nothing. Ain't loaded, anyvay.

ANNA: [*Breaking it open to make sure—then closing it again—looking at him suspiciously*] That ain't telling me why you got it.

CHRIS: Ay'm ole fool. Ay got it when Ay go ashore first. Ay tank den it's all fault of dat Irish fallar.

ANNA: [*With a shudder*] Say, you're crazier than I thought. I never dreamt you'd go that far.

CHRIS: [*Quickly*] Ay don't. Ay gat better sense right avay. Ay don't never buy bullets even. It ain't his fault, Ay know.

ANNA: [*Still suspicious of him*] Well, I'll take care of this for a while, loaded or not.

[*She puts it in the drawer of table and closes the drawer*]

CHRIS: [*Placatingly*] Throw it overboard if you vant. Ay don't care. [*Then after a pause*] Py golly, Ay tank Ay go lie down. Ay feel sick. [Anna *takes a magazine from the table.* Chris *hesitates by her chair*] Ve talk again before Ay go, yes?

ANNA: [*Dully*] Where's this ship going to?

CHRIS: Cape Town. Dat's in South Africa. She's British steamer called Londonderry. [*He stands hesitatingly—finally blurts out*] Anna—you forgive me sure?

ANNA: [*Wearily*] Sure I do. You ain't to blame. You're yust—what you are—like me.

CHRIS: [*Pleadingly*] Den—you lat me kiss you again once?

ANNA: [*Raising her face—forcing a wan smile*] Sure. No hard feelings.

CHRIS: [*Kisses her brokenly*] Anna lilla! Ay—— [*He fights for words to express himself, but finds none—miserably—with a sob*] Ay can't say it. Good night, Anna.

ANNA: Good night. [*He picks up the can of beer and goes slowly into the room on left, his shoulders bowed, his head sunk forward dejectedly. He closes the door after him.* Anna *turns over the pages of the magazine, trying desperately to banish her thoughts by looking at the pictures. This fails to distract her, and flinging the magazine back on the table, she springs to her feet and walks about the cabin distractedly, clenching and unclenching her hands. She speaks aloud to herself in a tense, trembling voice*] Gawd, I can't stand this much longer! What am I waiting for anyway?—like a damn fool! [*She laughs helplessly, then checks herself abruptly, as she hears the sound of heavy footsteps on the deck outside. She appears to recognize these and her face lights up with joy. She gasps*] Mat! [*A strange terror seems suddenly to seize her. She rushes to the table, takes the revolver out of drawer and crouches down in the corner, left, behind the cupboard. A moment later the door is flung open and Mat Burke appears in the doorway. He is in bad shape—his clothes torn and dirty, covered with sawdust as if he had been groveling or sleeping on barroom floors. There is a red bruise on his forehead over one of his eyes, another over one cheekbone, his knuckles are skinned and raw—plain evidence of the fighting he has been through on his "bat." His eyes are bloodshot and heavy-lidded, his face has a bloated look. But beyond these appearances—the results of heavy drinking—there is an expression in his eyes of wild mental turmoil, of impotent animal rage baffled by its own abject misery*]

BURKE: [*Peers blinkingly about the cabin—hoarsely*] Let you not be hiding from me, whoever's here—though 'tis well you know I'd have a right to come back and murder you. [*He stops to listen. Hearing no sound, he closes the door behind him and comes forward to the table. He throws himself into the rocking-chair—despondently*] There's no one here, I'm thinking, and 'tis a great fool I am to be coming. [*With a sort of dumb, uncomprehending anguish*] Yerra, Mat Burke, 'tis a great jackass you've become and what's got into you at all, at all? She's gone out of this long ago, I'm telling you, and you'll never see her face again [Anna *stands up, hesitating, struggling between joy and fear. Burke's eyes fall on Anna's bag. He leans over to examine it*] What's this? [*Joyfully*] It's hers. She's not gone! But where is she? Ashore? [*Darkly*] What would she be doing ashore on this rotten night? [*His face suddenly convulsed with grief and rage*] 'Tis that, is it? Oh, God's curse on her! [*Raging*] I'll wait 'till she comes and choke her dirty life out.

[Anna *starts, her face grows hard. She steps into the room, the revolver in her right hand by her side*]

ANNA: [*In a cold, hard tone*] What are you doing here?

BURKE: [*Wheeling about with a terrified gasp*] Glory be to God!

[*They remain motionless and silent for a moment, holding each other's eyes*]

ANNA: [*In the same hard voice*] Well, can't you talk?

BURKE: [*Trying to fall into an easy, careless tone*] You've a year's growth scared out of me, coming at me so sudden and me thinking I was alone.

ANNA: You've got your nerve butting in here without knocking or nothing. What d'you want?

BURKE: [*Airily*] Oh, nothing much. I was wanting to have a last word with you, that's all.

[*He moves a step toward her*]

ANNA: [*Sharply—raising the revolver in her hand*] Careful now! Don't try getting too close. I heard what you said you'd do to me.

BURKE: [*Noticing the revolver for the first time*] Is it murdering me you'd be now, God forgive you? [*Then with a contemptuous laugh*] Or is it thinking I'd be frightened by that old tin whistle?

[*He walks straight for her*]

ANNA: [*Wildly*] Look out, I tell you!

BURKE: [*Who has come so close that the revolver is almost touching his chest*] Let you shoot, then! [*Then with sudden wild grief*] Let you shoot, I'm saying, and be done with it! Let you end me with a shot and I'll be thanking you, for it's a rotten dog's life I've lived the past two days since I've known what you are, 'til I'm after wishing I was never born at all!

ANNA: [*Overcome—letting the revolver drop to the floor, as if her fingers had no strength to hold it—hysterically*] What d'you want coming here? Why don't you beat it? Go on!

[*She passes him and sinks down in the rocking-chair*]

BURKE: [*Following her—mournfully*] 'Tis right you'd be asking why did I come [*Then angrily*] 'Tis because 'tis a great weak fool of the world I am, and me tormented with the wickedness you'd told of yourself, and drinking oceans of booze that'd make me forget. Forget? Divil a word I'd forget, and your face grinning always in front of my eyes, awake or asleep, 'til I do be thinking a madhouse is the proper place for me.

ANNA: [*Glancing at his hands and face—scornfully*] You look like you ought to be put away some place. Wonder you wasn't pulled in. You been scrapping, too, ain't you?

BURKE: I have—with every scut would take off his coat to me! [*Fiercely*] And each time I'd be hitting one a clout in the mug, it wasn't his face I'd be seeing at all, but yours, and me wanting to drive you a blow would knock you out of this world where I wouldn't be seeing or thinking more of you.

ANNA: [*Her lips trembling pitifully*] Thanks!

BURKE: [*Walking up and down—distractedly*] That's right, make game of me! Oh, I'm a great coward surely, to be coming back to speak with you at all. You've a right to laugh at me.

ANNA: I ain't laughing at you, Mat.

BURKE: [*Unheeding*] You to be what you are, and

me to be Mat Burke, and me to be drove back to look at you again! 'Tis black shame is on me!

ANNA: [*Resentfully*] Then get out. No one's holding you!

BURKE: [*Bewilderedly*] And me to listen to that talk from a woman like you and be frightened to close her mouth with a slap! Oh, God help me, I'm a yellow coward for all men to spit at! [*Then furiously*] But I'll not be getting out of this 'til I've had me word. [*Raising his fist threateningly*] And let you look out how you'd drive me! [*Letting his fist fall helplessly*] Don't be angry now! I'm raving like a real lunatic, I'm thinking, and the sorrow you put on me has my brains drownded in grief. [*Suddenly bending down to her and grasping her arm intensely*] Tell me it's a lie, I'm saying! That's what I'm after coming to hear you say.

ANNA: [*Dully*] A lie? What?

BURKE: [*With passionate entreaty*] All the badness you told me two days back. Sure it must be a lie! You was only making game of me, wasn't you? Tell me 'twas a lie, Anna, and I'll be saying prayers of thanks on my two knees to the Almighty God!

ANNA: [*Terribly shaken—faintly*] I can't, Mat. [*As he turns away—imploringly*] Oh, Mat, won't you see that no matter what I was I ain't that any more? Why, listen! I packed up my bag this afternoon and went ashore. I'd been waiting here all alone for two days, thinking maybe you'd come back—thinking maybe you'd think over all I'd said—and maybe—oh, I don't know what I was hoping! But I was afraid to even go out of the cabin for a second, honest—afraid you might come and not find me here. Then I gave up hope when you didn't show up and I went to the railroad station. I was going to New York. I was going back——

BURKE: [*Hoarsely*] God's curse on you!

ANNA: Listen, Mat! You hadn't come, and I gave up hope. But—in the station—I couldn't go. I'd bought my ticket and everything. [*She takes the ticket from her dress and tries to hold it before his eyes*] But I got to thinking about you—and I couldn't take the train—I couldn't! So I come back here—to wait some more. Oh, Mat, don't you see I've changed? Can't you forgive what's dead and gone—and forget it?

BURKE: [*Turning on her—overcome by rage again*] Forget, is it? I'll not forget 'til my dying day, I'm telling you, and me tormented with thoughts. [*In a frenzy*] Oh, I'm wishing I had wan of them fornenst me this minute and I'd beat him with my fists 'til he'd be a bloody corpse! I'm wishing the whole lot of them will roast in hell 'til the Judgment Day—and yourself along with them, for you're as bad as they are.

ANNA: [*Shuddering*] Mat! [*Then after a pause—in a voice of dead, stony calm*] Well, you've had your say. Now you better beat it.

BURKE: [*Starts slowly for the door—hesitates—then after a pause*] And what'll you be doing?

ANNA: What difference does it make to you?

BURKE: I'm asking you!

ANNA: [*In the same tone*] My bag's packed and I got my ticket. I'll go to New York tomorrow.

BURKE: [*Helplessly*] You mean—you'll be doing the same again?

ANNA: [*Stonily*] Yes.

BURKE: [*In anguish*] You'll not! Don't torment me with that talk! 'Tis a she-divil you are sent to drive me mad entirely!

ANNA: [*Her voice breaking*] Oh, for Gawd's sake, Mat, leave me alone! Go away! Don't you see I'm licked? Why d'you want to keep on kicking me?

BURKE: [*Indignantly*] And don't you deserve the worst I'd say, God forgive you?

ANNA: All right. Maybe I do. But don't rub it in. Why ain't you done what you said you was going to? Why ain't you got that ship was going to take you to the other side of the earth where you'd never see me again?

BURKE: I have.

ANNA: [*Startled*] What—then you're going—honest?

BURKE: I signed on today at noon, drunk as I was—and she's sailing tomorrow.

ANNA: And where's she going to?

BURKE: Cape Town.

ANNA: [*The memory of having heard that name a little while before coming to her—with a start, confusedly*] Cape Town? Where's that? Far away?

BURKE: 'Tis at the end of Africa. That's far for you.

ANNA: [*Forcing a laugh*] You're keeping your word all right, ain't you? [*After a slight pause—curiously*] What's the boat's name?

BURKE: The Londonderry.

ANNA: [*It suddenly comes to her that this is the same ship her father is sailing on*] The Londonderry! It's the same—Oh, this is too much! [*With wild, ironical laughter*] Ha-ha-ha!

BURKE: What's up with you now?

ANNA: Ha-ha-ha! It's funny, funny! I'll die laughing!

BURKE: [*Irritated*] Laughing at what?

ANNA: It's a secret. You'll know soon enough. It's funny. [*Controlling herself—after a pause—cynically*] What kind of a place is this Cape Town? Plenty of dames there, I suppose?

BURKE: To hell with them! That I may never see another woman to my dying hour!

ANNA: That's what you say now, but I'll bet by the time you get there you'll have forgot all about me and start in talking the same old bull you talked to me to the first one you meet.

BURKE: [*Offended*] I'll not, then! God mend you, is it making me out to be the like of yourself you are, and you taking up with this one and that all the years of your life?

ANNA: [*Angrily assertive*] Yes, that's yust what I do mean! You been doing the same thing all your life, picking up a new girl in every port. How're you any better than I was?

BURKE: [*Thoroughly exasperated*] Is it no shame you have at all? I'm a fool to be wasting talk on you and you hardened in badness. I'll go out of this and lave you alone forever. [*He starts for the door—then stops to turn on her furiously*] And I suppose 'tis the same lies you told them all before that you told to me?

ANNA: [*Indignantly*] That's a lie! I never did!

BURKE: [*Miserably*] You'd be saying that, anyway.

ANNA: [*Forcibly, with growing intensity*] Are you trying to accuse me—of being in love—really in love—with them?

BURKE: I'm thinking you were, surely.

ANNA: [*Furiously, as if this were the last insult—advancing on him threateningly*] You mutt, you! I've stood enough from you. Don't you dare. [*With scornful bitterness*] Love 'em! Oh, my Gawd! You damn thick-head! Love 'em? [*Savagely*] I hated 'em, I tell you! Hated 'em, hated 'em, hated 'em! And may Gawd strike me dead this minute and my mother, too, if she was alive, if I ain't telling you the honest truth!

BURKE: [*Immensely pleased by her vehemence—a light beginning to break over his face—but still uncertain, torn between doubt and the desire to believe—helplessly*] If I could only be believing you now!

ANNA: [*Distractedly*] Oh, what's the use? What's the use of me talking? What's the use of anything? [*Pleadingly*] Oh, Mat, you mustn't think that for a second! You mustn't! Think all the other bad about me you want to, and I won't kick, 'cause you've a right to. But don't think that! [*On the point of tears*] I couldn't bear it! It'd be yust too much to know you was going away where I'd never see you again—thinking that about me!

BURKE: [*After an inward struggle—tensely—forcing out the words with difficulty*] If I was believing—that you'd never had love for any other man in the world but me—I could be forgetting the rest, maybe.

ANNA: [*With a cry of joy*] Mat!

BURKE: [*Slowly*] If 'tis truth you're after telling, I'd have a right, maybe, to believe you'd changed—and that I'd changed you myself 'til the thing you'd been all your life wouldn't be you any more at all.

ANNA: [*Hanging on his words—breathlessly*] Oh, Mat! That's what I been trying to tell you all along!

BURKE: [*Simply*] For I've a power of strength in me to lead men the way I want, and women, too, maybe, and I'm thinking I'd change you to a new woman entirely, so I'd never know, or you either, what kind of woman you'd been in the past at all.

ANNA: Yes, you could, Mat! I know you could!

BURKE: And I'm thinking 'twasn't your fault, maybe, but having that old ape for a father that left you to grow up alone, made you what you was. And if I could be believing 'tis only me you—

ANNA: [*Distractedly*] You got to believe it, Mat! What can I do? I'll do anything, anything you want to prove I'm not lying!

BURKE: [*Suddenly seems to have a solution. He feels in the pocket of his coat and grasps something—solemnly*] Would you be willing to swear an oath, now—a terrible, fearful oath would send your soul to the divils in hell if you was lying?

ANNA: [*Eagerly*] Sure, I'll swear, Mat—on anything!

BURKE: [*Takes a small, cheap old crucifix from his pocket and holds it up for her to see*] Will you swear on this?

ANNA: [*Reaching out for it*] Yes. Sure I will. Give it to me.

BURKE: [*Holding it away*] 'Tis a cross was given me by my mother, God rest her soul. [*He makes the sign of the cross mechanically*] I was a lad only, and she told me to keep it by me if I'd be waking or sleeping and never lose it, and it'd bring me luck. She died soon after. But I'm after keeping it with me from that day to this, and I'm telling you there's great power in it, and 'tis great bad luck it's saved me from and me roaming the seas, and I having it tied round my neck when my last ship sunk, and it bringing me safe to land when the others went to their death. [*Very earnestly*] And I'm warning you now, if you'd swear an oath on this, 'tis my old woman herself will be looking down from Hivin above, and praying Almighty God and the Saints to put a great curse on you if she'd hear you swearing a lie!

ANNA: [*Awed by his manner—superstitiously*] I wouldn't have the nerve—honest—if it was a lie. But it's the truth and I ain't scared to swear. Give it to me.

BURKE: [*Handing it to her—almost frightenedly, as if he feared for her safety*] Be careful what you'd swear, I'm saying.

ANNA: [*Holding the cross gingerly*] Well—what do you want me to swear? You say it.

BURKE: Swear I'm the only man in the world ivir you felt love for.

ANNA: [*Looking into his eyes steadily*] I swear it.

BURKE: And that you'll be forgetting from this day all the badness you've done and never do the like of it again.

ANNA: [*Forcibly*] I swear it! I swear it by God!

BURKE: And may the blackest curse of God strike you if you're lying. Say it now!

ANNA: And may the blackest curse of God strike me if I'm lying!

BURKE: [*With a stupendous sigh*] Oh, glory be to God, I'm after believing you now!

[*He takes the cross from her hand, his face beaming with joy, and puts it back in his pocket. He puts his arm about her waist and is about to kiss her when he stops, appalled by some terrible doubt*]

ANNA: [*Alarmed*] What's the matter with you?

BURKE: [*With sudden fierce questioning*] Is it Catholic ye are?

ANNA: [*Confused*] No. Why?

BURKE: [*Filled with a sort of bewildered fore-*

boding] Oh, God, help me! [*With a dark glance of suspicion at her*] There's some divil's trickery in it, to be swearing an oath on a Catholic cross and you wan of the others.

ANNA: [*Distractedly*] Oh, Mat, don't you believe me?

BURKE: [*Miserably*] If it isn't a Catholic you are——

ANNA: I ain't nothing. What's the difference? Didn't you hear me swear?

BURKE: [*Passionately*] Oh, I'd a right to stay away from you—but I couldn't! I was loving you in spite of it all and wanting to be with you, God forgive me, no matter what you are. I'd go mad if I'd not have you! I'd be killing the world——

[*He seizes her in his arms and kisses her fiercely*]

ANNA: [*With a gasp of joy*] Mat!

BURKE: [*Suddenly holding her away from him and staring into her eyes as if to probe into her soul —slowly*] If your oath is no proper oath at all, I'll have to be taking your naked word for it and have you anyway, I'm thinking—I'm needing you that bad!

ANNA: [*Hurt—reproachfully*] Mat! I swore, didn't I?

BURKE: [*Defiantly, as if challenging fate*] Oath or no oath, 'tis no matter. We'll be wedded in the morning, with the help of God. [*Still more defiantly*] We'll be happy now, the two of us, in spite of the divil!

[*He crushes her to him and kisses her again. The door on the left is pushed open and Chris appears in the doorway. He stands blinking at them. At first the old expression of hatred of Burke comes into his eyes instinctively. Then a look of resignation and relief takes its place. His face lights up with a sudden happy thought. He turns back into the bedroom—reappears immediately with the tin can of beer in his hand—grinning*]

CHRIS: Ve have drink on this, py golly! [*They break away from each other with startled exclamations*]

BURKE: [*Explosively*] God stiffen it!

[*He takes a step toward Chris threateningly*]

ANNA: [*Happily—to her father*] That's the way to talk [*With a laugh*] And say, it's about time for you and Mat to kiss and make up. You're going to be shipmates on the Londonderry, did you know it?

BURKE: [*Astounded*] Shipmates—— Has himself——

CHRIS: [*Equally astounded*] Ay vas bo'sun on her.

BURKE: The divil! [*Then angrily*] You'd be going back to sea and leaving her alone, wouldn't you?

ANNA: [*Quickly*] It's all right, Mat. That's where he belongs, and I want him to go. You got to go, too; we'll need the money. [*With a laugh, as she gets the glasses*] And as for me being alone, that runs in the family, and I'll get used to it. [*Pouring out their glasses*] I'll get a little house somewhere and I'll make a regular place for you two to come back to

—wait and see. And now you drink up and be friends.

BURKE: [*Happily—but still a bit resentful against the old man*] Sure! [*Clinking his glass against* Chris'] Here's luck to you!

[*He drinks*]

CHRIS: [*Subdued—his face melancholy*] Skoal.

[*He drinks*]

BURKE: [*To Anna, with a wink*] You'll not be lonesome long. I'll see to that, with the help of God. 'Tis himself here will be having a grandchild to ride on his foot, I'm telling you!

ANNA: [*Turning away in embarrassment*] Quit the kidding now.

[*She picks up her bag and goes into the room on left. As soon as she is gone Burke relapses into an attitude of gloomy thought. Chris stares at his beer absent-mindedly. Finally Burke turns on him*]

BURKE: Is it any religion at all you have, you and your Anna?

CHRIS: [*Surprised*] Why, yes. Ve vas Lutheran in ole country.

BURKE: [*Horrified*] Luthers, is it? [*Then with a grim resignation, slowly, aloud to himself*] Well, I'm damned then surely. Yerra, what's the difference? 'Tis the will of God, anyway.

CHRIS: [*Moodily preoccupied with his own thoughts—speaks with somber premonition as Anna re-enters from the left*] It's funny. It's queer, yes—you and me shipping on same boat dat vay. It ain't right. Ay don't know—it's dat funny vay ole davil sea do her vorst dirty tricks, yes. It's so.

[*He gets up and goes back and, opening the door, stares out into the darkness*]

BURKE: [*Nodding his head in gloomy acquiescence—with a great sigh*] I'm fearing maybe you have the right of it for once, divil take you.

ANNA: [*Forcing a laugh*] Gee, Mat, you ain't agreeing with him, are you? [*She comes forward and puts her arm about his shoulder—with a determined gaiety*] Aw, say, what's the matter? Cut out the gloom. We're all fixed now, ain't we, me and you? [*Pours out more beer into his glass and fills one for herself—slaps him on the back*] Come on! Here's to the sea, no matter what! Be a game sport and drink to that! Come on!

[*She gulps down her glass. Burke banishes his superstitious premonitions with a defiant jerk of his head, grins up at her, and drinks to her toast*]

CHRIS: [*Looking out into the night—lost in his somber preoccupation—shakes his head and mutters*] Fog, fog, fog, all bloody time. You can't see vhere you vas going, no. Only dat ole davil, sea—she knows!

[*The two stare at him. From the harbor comes the muffled, mournful wail of steamers' whistles*]

[THE CURTAIN FALLS]

Eugene O'Neill

(1888– ——)

Perhaps nothing in Eugene O'Neill's career drew so much attention to him as his incessant experimentation. After seeing, at the beginning of the 'twenties, such plays as *The Emperor Jones* and *The Hairy Ape*, American playgoers came to expect almost anything from him. They even complied when he required them to change lifetime habits of playgoing. Thus, to see the nine-act stream-of-consciousness drama *Strange Interlude*, they arrived for the performance at 5:30 in the afternoon, had dinner during an intermission, and then dutifully returned to their seats to await the conclusion of the longest interlude they had ever known.

Virtually every play O'Neill wrote after 1920 presented itself to him as a very special problem in structure and style. Unlike the average playwright, he could not accept a conventional dramatic mold. Plainly, too, he preferred a "theatrical" kind of theatre as opposed to one that called itself realistic or naturalistic and pretended to be an unassuming facsimile of life.

Theatricality, indeed, was ingrained in the son of the romantic actor-manager James O'Neill. But there were more important reasons for O'Neill's experimentation than his virtuosity and the pleasure he found in displaying it. In a program note on Strindberg written for the Provincetown Players, O'Neill bade farewell to naturalism as an outmoded style, describing it as "our fathers' daring aspirations toward self-recognition by holding the family kodak up to ill-nature." He complained that "we have taken too many snapshots of each other in every graceless position." Dissatisfied with "the banality of surfaces," O'Neill was, indeed, a symbol-using poet from the very start of his career. Symbol and reality were fused even in the short sea plays, in *Beyond the Horizon,* and in *Anna Christie.* In these plays, however, situations were never deliberately distorted and scenes never "stylized," as they were in *The Emperor Jones* and *The Hairy Ape.* Distortion, for purposes of heightening reality and rendering dream experience, is a method introduced into the modern drama by Strindberg, whose work left a strong impression on O'Neill and who was the father of the expressionism in O'Neill's work. After 1918, moreover, the vogue of expressionistic theatre in Central Europe attracted the American theatrical vanguard, to which O'Neill belonged. Both *The Emperor Jones* (1920) and *The Hairy Ape* (1922) contain expressionistic features; they are the best serious American plays written partly or wholly in that style. In both

plays, O'Neill placed much reliance on pantomime and on a pattern of delirious fantastication. Once the Negro hero, "Emperor" Jones, escapes into the jungle, he becomes the victim of one nightmare after another. *The Emperor Jones* is a drama of atavism and it is told chiefly by visual means. The greater part of the play is little more than a monologue by Jones interrupted by vignettes of fantasy. The effect is one of sheer theatre. But *The Hairy Ape* is the story of a quest, and it is drama as well as theatre. It contains much more text than *The Emperor Jones* because it is more than a mere procession of fear images.

O'Neill believed he had an important idea to propound in *The Hairy Ape,* and the idea was charged with his very personal sense of man's alienation in the modern world. In this play he experimented with dramatic style and form not for the sake of theatrical virtuosity, at which no man was to prove more adept, but for the sake of self-expression. "Self-expression" is, of course, a big word, but it is not too big for a playwright who always tried to find theatrical projection for his inner tensions and spiritual quests. O'Neill was even willing to exhibit these in the inchoate or half-crystallized form in which they appeared to him, thus exposing himself to the charges of excessive emotionalism and callow thinking. Such criticism was inevitable, once he began to do more and more of his groping in public.

In *The Hairy Ape,* fortunately, O'Neill's metaphysics has the advantage of a loamy substratum of reality. The person of the heroic stoker, Yank, is ultimately transformed into the abstraction Man as the play moves on. But before Yank is thus abstracted by O'Neill, the two-fisted stoker possesses a lyric vitality. He is half man, half symbol, like Carl Sandburg's Chicago—"Hog Butcher for the World, Tool Maker, Stacker of Wheat. . . ." O'Neill, as he explained to the press, regarded the play as "a symbol of man, who has lost his old harmony with nature, the harmony which he used to have as an animal and has not yet acquired in a spiritual way. . . . Yank can't go forward, and so he tries to go back. This is what his shaking hands with the gorilla meant. But he can't go back to 'belonging' either. The gorilla kills him. The subject here is the ancient one that always was and always will be the one subject for drama, and that is man and his struggle with his own fate. The struggle used to be with the gods, but is now with himself, his own past, his attempt to 'belong.' " How far *The Hairy Ape* actually sustains this interpretation and benefits from it can prove a subject for lively debate.

O'Neill himself insisted on the value of his interpretation, writing in the *New York Tribune*, "The public saw just the stoker, not the symbol, and the symbol makes the play either important or just another play." He was quite correct, although his explanation does not necessarily indicate the only level on which the play can be followed. The theme is "not belonging." Yank is not just the abstraction Man, but the abstraction Worker or Proletariat. Yank discovers that he doesn't "belong," and this is his situation whether he is conceived as Man in the world of nature or as Worker in the world of modern industrial society. Even the early, seemingly ultra-realistic scenes in the hold of the ship, scenes which were strikingly new in 1922 to a public only recently weaned from the genteel tradition, are poetically evocative; they are an example of realism theatrically displayed to create an emotional and symbolic effect.

Because O'Neill used realistic material and vigorous colloquial dialogue in *The Hairy Ape*, it is one of his most satisfactory early experimental plays. For all its allegorical implication, it has a rich texture virtually throughout; even the distorted, expressionistic part beginning with Scene V, on Fifth Avenue, is anything but abstrusely presented. This may explain the play's power and the fascination it holds for persons who are not prepared to say that they understand or accept the author's argument. Poetically, however, they do of course understand—and probably also accept. That is, they experience the play as a metaphor of modern experience—of alienation in the universe and in society. It is not as a system of ideas that we can approach *The Hairy Ape* but as a felt distress for which O'Neill's ideas form nothing more than a sort of algebraic notation. O'Neill's mood here is saturnine and uncompromisingly pessimistic. It is a mood that rarely left him when he contemplated the world at large and man's chances in it.

Writing about *The Hairy Ape* in 1947, George Jean Nathan remembered its "theme of despairing humanity gazing blinded at the stars." It is, indeed, the large measure of frustration that playgoers were most apt to recall. But they were able to remember it, fortunately, in the context of driving drama and in an atmosphere of angry, broken light. The play radiated a febrile magnificence that made many an intellectually sounder play seem inconsequential. When, in later years, O'Neill's boiler-room explosions began to take longer, they also tended to become tamer, and O'Neill was to lose, at times, one of his most attractive early qualities—his unreconciled fierceness in negation.

For additional commentary and bibliography, see pages 786–789.

THE HAIRY APE

By Eugene O'Neill

CHARACTERS

ROBERT SMITH, "YANK"	SECOND ENGINEER
PADDY	A GUARD
LONG	A SECRETARY OF AN ORGANIZATION
MILDRED DOUGLAS	STOKERS, LADIES, GENTLEMEN, ETC.
HER AUNT	

SCENES

I. *The firemen's forecastle of an ocean liner—an hour after sailing from New York.*

II. *Section of promenade deck, two days out—morning.*

III. *The stockade. A few minutes later.*

IV. *Same as Scene I. Half an hour later.*

V. *Fifth Avenue, New York. Three weeks later.*

VI. *An island near the city. The next night.*

VII. *In the city. About a month later.*

VIII. *In the city. Twilight of the next day.*

TIME—*The Modern.*

SCENE I.

The firemen's forecastle of a transatlantic liner an hour after sailing from New York for the voyage across. Tiers of narrow, steel bunks, three deep, on all sides. An entrance in rear. Benches on the floor before the bunks. The room is crowded with men, shouting, cursing, laughing, singing—a confused, inchoate uproar swelling into a sort of unity, a meaning—the bewildered, furious, baffled defiance of a beast in a cage. Nearly all the men are drunk. Many bottles are passed from hand to hand. All are dressed in dungaree pants, heavy ugly shoes. Some wear singlets, but the majority are stripped to the waist.

The treatment of this scene, or of any other scene in the play, should by no means be naturalistic. The effect sought after is a cramped space in the bowels of a ship, imprisoned by white steel. The lines of bunks, the uprights supporting them, cross each other like the steel framework of a cage. The ceiling crushes down upon the men's heads. They cannot stand upright. This accentuates the natural stooping posture which shoveling coal and the resultant over-development of back and shoulder muscles have given them. The men themselves should resemble those pictures in which the appearance of Neanderthal Man is guessed at. All are hairy-chested, with long arms of tremendous power, and low, receding brows above their small, fierce, resentful eyes. All the civilized white races are represented, but except for the slight differentiation in color of hair, skin, eyes, all these men are alike.

The curtain rises on a tumult of sound. Yank is seated in the foreground. He seems broader, fiercer, more truculent, more powerful, more sure of himself than the rest. They respect his superior strength—the grudging respect of fear. Then, too, he represents to them a self-expression, the very last word in what they are, their most highly developed individual.

VOICES: Gif me trink dere, you!

'Ave a wet!

Salute!

Gesundheit!

Skoal!

Drunk as a lord, God stiffen you!

Here's how!

Luck!

Pass back that bottle, damn you!

Pourin' it down his neck!

Ho, Groggy! Where the devil have you been?

La Touraine.

I hit him smash in yaw, py Gott!

Jenkins—the First—he's a rotten swine——

And the coppers nabbed him—and I run——

I like peer better. It don't pig head gif you.

A slut, I'm sayin'! She robbed me aslape——

To hell with 'em all!

You're a bloody liar!

Say dot again! [*Commotion. Two men about to fight are pulled apart*]

No scrappin' now!

Tonight——

See who's the best man!

Bloody Dutchman!

Tonight on the for'ard square.

I'll bet on Dutchy.

He packa da wallop, I tella you!

Shut up, Wop!

No fightin', maties. We're all chums, ain't we?

[*A voice starts bawling a song*]

"Beer, beer, glorious beer!

Fill yourselves right up to here."

YANK: [*For the first time seeming to take notice of the uproar about him, turns around threateningly—in a tone of contemptuous authority*] Choke off dat noise! Where d'yuh get dat beer stuff? Beer, hell! Beer's for goils—and Dutchmen. Me for somep'n wit a kick to it! Gimme a drink, one of youse guys. [*Several bottles are eagerly offered. He takes a tremendous gulp at one of them; then, keeping the bottle in his hand, glares belligerently at the* Owner, *who hastens to acquiesce in this robbery by saying:*] All righto, Yank. Keep it and have another.

[Yank *contemptuously turns his back on the crowd again. For a second there is an embarrassed silence. Then:*]

VOICES: We must be passing the Hook.

She's beginning to roll to it.

Six days in hell—and then Southampton.

Py Yesus, I vish somepody take my first vatch for me!

Gittin' seasick, Square-head?

Drink up and forget it!

What's in your bottle?

Gin.

Dot's nigger trink.

Absinthe? It's doped. You'll go off your chump, Froggy!

Cochon!

Whiskey, that's the ticket!

Where's Paddy?

Going asleep.

Sing us that whiskey song, Paddy.

[*They all turn to an old, wizened* Irishman *who is dozing, very drunk, on the benches forward. His face is extremely monkey-like with all the sad, patient pathos of that animal in his small eyes*]

Singa da song, Caruso Pat!

He's getting old. The drink is too much for him.

He's too drunk.

PADDY: [*Blinking about him, starts to his feet resentfully, swaying, holding on to the edge of a bunk*] I'm never too drunk to sing. 'Tis only when I'm dead to the world I'd be wishful to sing at all. [*With a sort of sad contempt*] "Whiskey Johnny," ye want? A chanty, ye want? Now that's a queer wish from the ugly like of you, God help you. But no matther. [*He starts to sing in a thin, nasal, doleful tone*]

Oh, whiskey is the life of man!

Whiskey! O Johnny! [*They all join in on this*]

Oh, whiskey is the life of man!

Whiskey for my Johnny! [*Again chorus*]

Oh, whiskey drove my old man mad!

Whiskey! O Johnny!

Oh, whiskey drove my old man mad!

Whiskey for my Johnny!

YANK: [*Again turning around scornfully*] Aw hell! Nix on dat old sailing ship stuff! All dat bull's dead, see? And you're dead, too, yuh damned old Harp, on'y yuh don't know it. Take it easy, see? Give us a rest. Nix on de loud noise. [*With a cynical grin*] Can't youse see I'm tryin' to t'ink?

ALL: [*Repeating the word after him, as one, with the same cynical amused mockery*] Think!

[*The chorused word has a brazen metallic quality as if their throats were phonograph horns. It is followed by a general uproar of hard, barking laughter*]

VOICES: Don't be cracking your head wit ut, Yank.

You gat headache, py yingo!

One thing about it—it rhymes with drink!

Ha, ha, ha!

Drink, don't think!

Drink, don't think!

Drink, don't think!

[*A whole chorus of voices has taken up this refrain, stamping on the floor, pounding on the benches with fists*]

YANK: [*Taking a gulp from his bottle—good-naturedly:*] Aw right. Can de noise. I got yuh de foist time.

[*The uproar subsides. A very drunken sentimental* Tenor *begins to sing*]

"Far away in Canada,

Far across the sea,

There's a lass who fondly waits

Making a home for me——"

YANK: [*Fiercely contemptuous*] Shut up, yuh lousy boob! Where d'yuh get dat tripe? Home? Home, hell! I'll make a home for yuh! I'll knock yuh dead. Home! T'hell wit home! Where d'yuh get dat tripe? Dis is home, see? What d'yuh want wit home? [*Proudly*] I runned away from mine when I was a kid. On'y too glad to beat it, dat was me. Home was lickings for me, dat's all. But yuh can bet your shoit no one ain't never licked me since! Wanter try it, any of youse? Huh! I guess not. [*In a more placated but still contemptuous tone*] Goils waitin' for yuh, huh? Aw, hell! Dat's all tripe. Dey don't wait for no one. Dey'd double-cross yuh for a nickel. Dey're all tarts, get me? Treat 'em rough, dat's me. To hell wit 'em. Tarts, dat's what, de whole bunch of 'em.

LONG: [*Very drunk, jumps on a bench excitedly, gesticulating with a bottle in his hand*] Listen 'ere, Comrades! Yank 'ere is right. 'E says this 'ere stinkin' ship is our 'ome. And 'e says as 'ome is 'ell. And 'e's right! This is 'ell. We lives in 'ell, Comrades—and right enough we'll die in it. [*Raging*] And who's ter blame, I arsks yer. We ain't. We wasn't born this rotten way. All men is born free and ekal. That's in the bleedin' Bible, maties. But what d'they care for the Bible—them lazy, bloated swine what travels first cabin? Them's the ones. They dragged us down 'til we're on'y wage slaves in the bowels of a bloody ship, sweatin', burnin' up, eatin' coal dust! Hit's them's ter blame—the damned Capitalist clarss!

[*There had been a gradual murmur of contemptuous resentment rising among the* Men *until now he is interrupted by a storm of catcalls, hisses, boos, hard laughter*]

VOICES: Turn it off!
Shut up!
Sit down!
Closa da face!
Tamn fool! [*Etc.*]

YANK: [*Standing up and glaring at* Long] Sit down before I knock yuh down! [Long *makes haste to efface himself.* Yank *goes on contemptuously*] De Bible, huh? De Cap'tlist class, huh? Aw, nix on dat Salvation Army-Socialist bull. Git a soapbox! Hire a hall! Come and be saved, huh? Jerk us to Jesus, huh? Aw g'wan! I've listened to lots of guys like you, see? Yuh're all wrong. Wanter know what I t'ink? Yuh ain't no good for no one. Yuh're de bunk. Yuh ain't got no noive, get me? Yuh're yellow, dat's what. Yellow, dat's you. Say! What's dem slobs in de foist cabin got to do wit us? We're better men dan dey are, ain't we? Sure! One of us guys could clean up de whole mob wit one mit. Put one of 'em down here for one watch in de stokehole, what'd happen? Dey'd carry him off on a stretcher. Dem boids don't amount to nothin'. Dey're just baggage. Who makes dis old tub run? Ain't it us guys? Well den, we belong, don't we? We belong and dey don't. Dat's all. [*A loud chorus of approval.* Yank *goes on*] As for dis bein' hell—aw, nuts! Yuh lost your noive, dat's what. Dis is a man's job, get me? It belongs. It runs dis tub. No stiffs need apply. But yuh're a stiff, see? Yuh're yellow, dat's you.

VOICES: [*With a great hard pride in them*] Righto!
A man's job!
Talk is cheap, Long.
He never could hold up his end.
Divil take him!
Yank's right. We make it go.
Py Gott, Yank say right ting!
We don't need no one cryin' over us.
Makin' speeches.
Throw him out!
Yellow!
Chuck him overboard!
I'll break his jaw for him!

[*They crowd around* Long *threateningly*]

YANK: [*Half good-natured again—contemptuously*] Aw, take it easy. Leave him alone. He ain't woith a punch. Drink up. Here's how, whoever owns dis.

[*He takes a long swallow from his bottle. All drink with him. In a flash all is hilarious amiability again, back-slapping, loud talk, etc.*]

PADDY: [*Who has been sitting in a blinking, melancholy daze—suddenly cries out in a voice full of old sorrow*] We belong to this, you're saying? We make the ship to go, you're saying? Yerra then, that Almighty God have pity on us! [*His voice runs into the wail of a keen; he rocks back and forth on his bench. The men stare at him, startled and impressed in spite of themselves*] Oh, to be back in the fine days of my youth, ochone! Oh, there was fine beautiful ships them days—clippers wid tall masts touching the sky—fine strong men in them—men that was sons of the sea as if 'twas the mother that bore them. Oh, the clean skins of them, and the clear eyes, the straight backs and full chests of them! Brave men they was, and bold men surely! We'd be sailing out, bound down round the Horn maybe. We'd be making sail in the dawn, with a fair breeze, singing a chanty song wid no care to it. And astern the land would be sinking low and dying out, but we'd give it no heed but a laugh, and never a look behind. For the day that was, was enough, for we was free men—and I'm thinking 'tis only slaves do be giving heed to the day that's gone or the day to come—until they're old like me. [*With a sort of religious exaltation*] Oh, to be scudding south again wid the power of the Trade Wind driving her on steady through the nights and the days! Full sail on her! Nights and days! Nights when the foam of the wake would be flaming wid fire, when the sky'd be blazing and winking wid stars. Or the full of the moon maybe. Then you'd see her driving through the gray night, her sails stretching aloft all silver and white, not a sound on the deck, the lot of us dreaming dreams, till you'd believe 'twas no real ship at all you was on but a ghost ship like the *Flying Dutchman* they says does be roaming the seas forevermore widout touching a port. And there was the days, too. A warm sun on the clean decks. Sun warming the blood of you, and wind over the miles of shiny green ocean like strong drink to your lungs. Work—aye, hard work—but who'd mind that at all? Sure, you worked under the sky and 'twas work wid skill and daring to it. And wid the day done, in the dog watch, smoking me pipe at ease, the lookout would be raising land maybe, and we'd see the mountains of South Americy wid the red fire of the setting sun painting their white tops and the clouds floating by them! [*His tone of exaltation ceases. He goes on mournfully*] Yerra, what's the use of talking? 'Tis a dead man's whisper. [*To Yank resentfully*] 'Twas them days a ship was part of the sea, and a man was part of a ship, and the sea joined all together and made it one. [*Scornfully*] Is it one wid this you'd be, Yank—black smoke from the funnels smudging the sea, smudging the decks—the bloody engines pounding and throbbing and shaking—wid divil a sight of sun or a breath of clean air—choking our lungs wid coal dust—breaking our backs and hearts in the hell of the stokehole—feeding the bloody furnace—feeding our lives along wid the coal, I'm thinking—caged in by steel from a sight of the sky like bloody apes in the zoo! [*With a harsh laugh*] Ho-ho, divil mend you! Is it to belong to that you're wishing? Is it a flesh and blood wheel of the engines you'd be?

YANK: [*Who has been listening with a contemptuous sneer, barks out the answer*] Sure ting! Dat's me. What about it?

PADDY: [*As if to himself—with great sorrow:*] Me time is past due. That a great wave wid sun in the heart of it may sweep me over the side sometime I'd be dreaming of the days that's gone!

YANK: Aw, yuh crazy Mick! [*He springs to his feet and advances on* Paddy *threateningly—then stops, fighting some queer struggle within himself— lets his hands fall to his sides—contemptuously:*] Aw, take it easy. Yuh're aw right, at dat. Yuh're bugs, dat's all—nutty as a cuckoo. All dat tripe yuh been pullin'—Aw, dat's all right. On'y it's dead, get me? Yuh don't belong no more, see. Yuh don't get de stuff. Yuh're too old. [*Disgustedly*] But aw say, come up for air onct in a while, can't yuh? See what's happened since yuh croaked. [*He suddenly bursts forth vehemently, growing more and more excited*] Say! Sure! Sure I meant it! What de hell— Say, lemme talk! Hey! Hey, you old Harp! Hey, youse guys! Say, listen to me—wait a moment—I gotter talk, see? I belong and he don't. He's dead but I'm livin'. Listen to me! Sure I'm part of de engines! Why de hell not! Dey move, don't they? Dey're speed, ain't dey? Dey smash trou, don't dey? Twenty-five knots a hour! Dat's goin' some! Dat's new stuff! Dat belongs! But him, he's too old. He gets dizzy. Say, listen. All dat crazy tripe about nights and days; all dat crazy tripe about stars and moons; all dat crazy tripe about suns and winds, fresh air and de rest of it—Aw hell, dat's all a dope dream! Hittin' de pipe of de past, dat's what he's doin'. He's old and don't belong no more. But me, I'm young! I'm in de pink! I move wit it! It, get me! I mean de ting dat's de guts of all dis. It ploughs trou all de tripe he's been sayin'. It blows dat up! It knocks dat dead! It slams dat offen de face of de oith! It, get me! De engines and de coal and de smoke and all de rest of it! He can't breathe and swallow coal dust, but I kin, see? Dat's fresh air for me! Dat's food for me! I'm new, get me? Hell in de stokehole? Sure! It takes a man to work in hell. Hell, sure, dat's my fav'rite climate. I eat it up! I git fat on it! It's me makes it hot! It's me makes it roar! It's me makes it move! Sure, on'y for me everything stops. It all goes dead, get me? De noise and smoke and all de engines movin' de woild, dey stop. Dere ain't nothin' no more! Dat's what I'm sayin'. Everyting else dat makes de woild move, somep'n makes it move. It can't move witout somep'n else, see? Den yuh get down to me. I'm at de bottom, get me! Dere ain't nothin' foither. I'm de end! I'm de start! I start somep'n and de woild moves! It—dat's me!—de new dat's moiderin' de old! I'm de ting in coal dat makes it boin; I'm steam and oil for de engines; I'm de ting in noise dat makes yuh hear it; I'm smoke and express trains and steamers and factory whistles; I'm de ting in gold dat makes it money! And I'm what makes iron into steel! Steel, dat stands for de whole ting! And I'm steel—steel—steel! I'm de muscles in steel, de punch behind it! [*As he says this he pounds with his fist against the steel bunks. All the* Men, *roused to a pitch of frenzied self-glorification by his speech, do likewise. There is a deafening metallic roar, through which* Yank's *voice can be heard bellowing:*] Slaves, hell! We run de whole woiks. All de rich guys dat tink dey're somep'n, dey ain't nothin'! Dey don't belong. But us guys, we're in de move, we're at de bottom, de whole ting is us! [Paddy *from the start of* Yank's *speech has been taking one gulp after another from his bottle, at first frightenedly, as if he were afraid to listen, then desperately, as if to drown his senses, but finally has achieved complete indifferent, even amused, drunkeness.* Yank *sees his lips moving. He quells the uproar with a shout*] Hey, youse guys, take it easy! Wait a moment! De nutty Harp is sayin' somep'n.

PADDY: [*Is heard now—throws his head back with a mocking burst of laughter*] Ho-ho-ho-ho-ho——

YANK: [*Drawing back his fist, with a snarl*] Aw! Look out who yuh're givin' the bark!

PADDY: [*Begins to sing the "Miller of Dee" with enormous good nature*]

"I care for nobody, no, not I,
        And nobody cares for me."

YANK: [*Good-natured himself in a flash, interrupts* Paddy *with a slap on the bare back like a report*] Dat's de stuff! Now yuh're gettin' wise to somep'n. Care for nobody, dat's de dope! To hell wit 'em all! And nix on nobody else carin'. I kin care for myself, get me! [*Eight bells sound, muffled, vibrating through the steel walls as if some enormous brazen gong were imbedded in the heart of the ship. All the men jump up mechanically, file through the door silently, close upon each other's neels in what is very like a prisoners' lock-step.* Yank *slaps* Paddy *on the back*] Our watch, yuh old Harp! [*Mockingly*] Come on down in hell. Eat up de coal dust. Drink in de heat. It's it, see! Act like yuh liked it, yuh better—or croak yuhself.

PADDY: [*With jovial defiance*] To the divil wid it! I'll not report this watch. Let thim log me and be damned. I'm no slave the like of you. I'll be settin' here at me ease, and drinking, and thinking, and dreaming dreams.

YANK: [*Contemptuously*] Tinkin' and dreamin', what'll that get yuh? What's tinkin' got to do wit it? We move, don't we? Speed, ain't it? Fog, dat's all you stand for. But we drive trou dat, don't we? We split dat up and smash trou—twenty-five knots a hour! [*Turns his back on* Paddy *scornfully*] Aw, yuh make me sick! Yuh don't belong!

[*He strides out the door in rear.* Paddy *hums to himself, blinking drowsily*]

CURTAIN

SCENE II.

Two days out. A section of the promenade deck.
Mildred Douglas *and her* Aunt *are discovered reclining in deck chairs. The former is a girl of twenty, slender, delicate, with a pale, pretty face marred by a self-conscious expression of disdainful superiority. She looks fretful, nervous, and discontented, bored by her own anemia. Her* Aunt *is a pompous and proud—and fat—old lady. She is a type even to the point of a double chin and lorgnettes. She is dressed pretentiously, as if afraid her face alone would never indicate her position in life.* Mildred *is dressed all in white.*

The impression to be conveyed by this scene is one of the beautiful, vivid life of the sea all about—sunshine on the deck in a great flood, the fresh sea wind blowing across it. In the midst of this, these two incongruous, artificial figures, inert and disharmonious, the elder like a gray lump of dough touched up with rouge, the younger looking as if the vitality of her stock had been sapped before she was conceived, so that she is the expression not of its life energy but merely of the artificialities that energy had won for itself in the spending.

MILDRED: [*Looking up with affected dreaminess*]
How the black smoke swirls back against the sky!
Is it not beautiful?

AUNT: [*Without looking up*] I dislike smoke of
any kind.

MILDRED: My great-grandmother smoked a pipe—
a clay pipe.

AUNT: [*Ruffling*] Vulgar!

MILDRED: She was too distant a relative to be
vulgar. Time mellows pipes.

AUNT: [*Pretending boredom but irritated*] Did the
sociology you took up at college teach you that—
to play the ghoul on every possible occasion, excavating old bones? Why not let your great-grandmother rest in her grave?

MILDRED: [*Dreamily*] With her pipe beside her—
puffing in Paradise.

AUNT: [*With spite*] Yes, you are a natural born
ghoul. You are even getting to look like one, my
dear.

MILDRED: [*In a passionless tone*] I detest you,
Aunt. [*Looking at her critically*] Do you know what
you remind me of? Of a cold pork pudding against
a background of linoleum tablecloth in the kitchen
of a—but the possibilities are wearisome. [*She closes
her eyes*]

AUNT: [*With a bitter laugh*] Merci for your candor. But since I am and must be your chaperon—
in appearance, at least—let us patch up some sort
of armed truce. For my part you are quite free to
indulge any pose of eccentricity that beguiles you—
as long as you observe the amenities——

MILDRED: [*Drawling*] The inanities?

AUNT: [*Going on as if she hadn't heard*] After

exhausting the morbid thrills of social service work
on New York's East Side—how they must have
hated you, by the way, the poor that you made so
much poorer in their own eyes!—you are now bent
on making your slumming international. Well, I
hope Whitechapel will provide the needed nerve
tonic. Do not ask me to chaperon you there, however. I told your father I would not. I loathe deformity. We will hire an army of detectives and you
may investigate everything—they allow you to see.

MILDRED: [*Protesting with a trace of genuine
earnestness*] Please do not mock at my attempts to
discover how the other half lives. Give me credit
for some sort of groping sincerity in that at least.
I would like to help them. I would like to be some
use in the world. Is it my fault I don't know how?
I would like to be sincere, to touch life somewhere.
[*With weary bitterness*] But I'm afraid I have neither
the vitality nor integrity. All that was burnt out in
our stock before I was born. Grandfather's blast
furnaces, flaming to the sky, melting steel, making
millions—then father keeping those home fires burning, making more millions—and little me at the
tail-end of it all. I'm a waste product in the Bessemer process—like the millions. Or rather, I inherit the acquired trait of the by-product, wealth,
but none of the energy, none of the strength of the
steel that made it. I am sired by gold and dammed
by it, as they say at the race track—damned in
more ways than one. [*She laughs mirthlessly*]

AUNT: [*Unimpressed—superciliously*] You seem
to be going in for sincerity today. It isn't becoming
to you, really—except as an obvious pose. Be as
artificial as you are, I advise. There's a sort of sincerity in that, you know. And, after all, you must
confess you like that better.

MILDRED: [*Again affected and bored*] Yes, I suppose I do. Pardon me for my outburst. When a
leopard complains of its spots, it must sound rather
grotesque. [*In a mocking tone*] Purr, little leopard.
Purr, scratch, tear, kill, gorge yourself and be happy
—only stay in the jungle where your spots are camouflage. In a cage they make you conspicuous.

AUNT: I don't know what you are talking about.

MILDRED: It would be rude to talk about anything to you. Let's just talk. [*She looks at her wrist
watch*] Well, thank goodness, it's about time for
them to come for me. That ought to give me a new
thrill, Aunt.

AUNT: [*Affectedly troubled*] You don't mean to
say you're really going? The dirt—the heat must be
frightful——

MILDRED: Grandfather started as a puddler. I
should have inherited an immunity to heat that
would make a salamander shiver. It will be fun to
put it to the test.

AUNT: But don't you have to have the captain's—
or someone's—permission to visit the stokehole?

MILDRED: [*With a triumphant smile*] I have it—
both his and the chief engineer's. Oh, they didn't

want to at first, in spite of my social service credentials. They didn't seem a bit anxious that I should investigate how the other half lives and works on a ship. So I had to tell them that my father, the president of Nazareth Steel, chairman of the board of directors of this line, had told me it would be all right.

AUNT: He didn't.

MILDRED: How naïve age makes one! But I said he did, Aunt. I even said he had given me a letter to them—which I had lost. And they were afraid to take the chance that I might be lying. [*Excitedly*] So it's ho! for the stokehole. The second engineer is to escort me. [*Looking at her watch again*] It's time. And here he comes, I think.

> [*The* Second Engineer *enters. He is a husky, fine-looking man of thirty-five or so. He stops before the two and tips his cap, visibly embarrassed and ill-at-ease*]

SECOND ENGINEER: Miss Douglas?

MILDRED: Yes. [*Throwing off her rugs and getting to her feet*] Are we all ready to start?

SECOND ENGINEER: In just a second, ma'am. I'm waiting for the Fourth. He's coming along.

MILDRED: [*With a scornful smile*] You don't care to shoulder this responsibility alone, is that it?

SECOND ENGINEER: [*Forcing a smile*] Two are better than one. [*Disturbed by her eyes, glances out to sea—blurts out:*] A fine day we're having.

MILDRED: Is it?

SECOND ENGINEER: A nice warm breeze——

MILDRED: It feels cold to me.

SECOND ENGINEER: But it's hot enough in the sun——

MILDRED: Not hot enough for me. I don't like Nature. I was never athletic.

SECOND ENGINEER: [*Forcing a smile*] Well, you'll find it hot enough where you're going.

MILDRED: Do you mean hell?

SECOND ENGINEER: [*Flabbergasted, decides to laugh*] Ho-ho! No, I mean the stokehole.

MILDRED: My grandfather was a puddler. He played with boiling steel.

SECOND ENGINEER: [*All at sea—uneasily*] Is that so? Hum, you'll excuse me, ma'am, but are you intending to wear that dress?

MILDRED: Why not?

SECOND ENGINEER: You'll likely rub against oil and dirt. It can't be helped.

MILDRED: It doesn't matter. I have lots of white dresses.

SECOND ENGINEER: I have an old coat you might throw over——

MILDRED: I have fifty dresses like this. I will throw this one into the sea when I come back. That ought to wash it clean, don't you think?

SECOND ENGINEER: [*Doggedly*] There's ladders to climb down that are none too clean—and dark alleyways——

MILDRED: I will wear this very dress and none other.

SECOND ENGINEER: No offense meant. It's none of my business. I was only warning you——

MILDRED: Warning? That sounds thrilling.

SECOND ENGINEER: [*Looking down the deck—with a sigh of relief*] There's the Fourth now. He's waiting for us. If you'll come——

MILDRED: Go on. I'll follow you. [*He goes.* Mildred *turns a mocking smile on her* Aunt] An oaf—but a handsome, virile oaf.

AUNT: [*Scornfully*] Poser!

MILDRED: Take care. He said there were dark alleyways——

AUNT: [*In the same tone*] Poser!

MILDRED: [*Biting her lips angrily*] You are right. But would that my millions were not so anemically chaste!

AUNT: Yes, for a fresh pose I have no doubt you would drag the name of Douglas in the gutter!

MILDRED: From which it sprang. Good-by, Aunt. Don't pray too hard that I may fall into the fiery furnace.

AUNT: Poser!

MILDRED: [*Viciously*] Old hag!

> [*She slaps her* Aunt *insultingly across the face and walks off, laughing gaily*]

AUNT: [*Screams after her:*] I said poser!

CURTAIN

SCENE III.

The stokehole. In the rear, the dimly outlined bulks of the furnaces and boilers. High overhead one hanging electric bulb sheds just enough light through the murky air laden with coal dust to pile up masses of shadows everywhere. A line of men, stripped to the waist, is before the furnace doors. They bend over, looking neither to right nor left, handling their shovels as if they were part of their bodies, with a strange, awkward, swinging rhythm. They use the shovels to throw open the furnace doors. Then from these fiery round holes in the black a flood of terrific light and heat pours full upon the men who are outlined in silhouette in the crouching, inhuman attitudes of chained gorillas. The men shovel with a rhythmic motion, swinging as on a pivot from the coal which lies in heaps on the floor behind to hurl it into the flaming mouths before them. There is a tumult of noise—the brazen clang of the furnace doors as they are flung open or slammed shut, the grating, teeth-gritting grind of steel against steel, and of crunching coal. This clash of sounds stuns one's ears with its rending dissonance. But there is order in it, rhythm, a mechanical, regulated recurrence, a tempo. And rising above all, making the air hum with the quiver of liberated energy, the roar of leaping flames in the furnaces, the monotonous throbbing beat of the engines.

As the curtain rises, the furnace doors are shut. The Men *are taking a breathing spell. One or two are arranging the coal behind them, pulling it into more accessible heaps. The others can be dimly made out leaning on their shovels in relaxed attitudes of exhaustion.*

PADDY: [*From somewhere in the line—plaintively*] Yerra, will this divil's own watch nivir end? Me back is broke. I'm destroyed entirely.

YANK: [*From the center of the line—with exuberant scorn*] Aw, yuh make me sick! Lie down and croak, why don't yuh? Always beefin', dat's you! Say, dis is a cinch! Dis was made for me! It's my meat, get me! [*A whistle is blown—a thin, shrill note from somewhere overhead in the darkness.* Yank *curses without resentment*] Dere's de damn engineer crackin' de whip. He tinks we're loafin'.

PADDY: [*Vindictively*] God stiffen him!

YANK: [*In an exultant tone of command*] Come on, youse guys! Git into de game! She's gittin' hungry! Pile some grub in her. Trow it into her belly! Come on now, all of youse! Open her up!

[*At this last all the* Men, *who have followed his movements of getting into position, throw open their furnace doors with a deafening clang. The fiery light floods over their shoulders as they bend round for the coal. Rivulets of sooty sweat have traced maps on their backs. The enlarged muscles form bunches of high light and shadow*]

YANK: [*Chanting a count as he shovels without seeming effort*] One-two-three——[*His voice rising exultantly in the joy of battle*] Dat's de stuff! Let her have it! All togedder now! Sling it into her! Let her ride! Shoot de piece now! Call de toin on her! Drive her into it! Feel her move! Watch her smoke! Speed, dat's her middle name! Give her coal, youse guys! Coal, dat's her booze! Drink it up, baby! Let's see yuh sprint! Dig in and gain a lap! Dere she go-o-es.

[*This last in the chanting formula of the gallery gods at the six-day bike race. He slams his furnace door shut. The others do likewise with as much unison as their wearied bodies will permit. The effect is of one fiery eye after another being blotted out with a series of accompanying bangs*]

PADDY: [*Groaning*] Me back is broke. I'm bate out—bate——

[*There is a pause. Then the inexorable whistle sounds again from the dim regions above the electric light. There is a growl of cursing rage from all sides*]

YANK: [*Shaking his fist upward—contemptuously*] Take it easy dere, you! Who d'yuh tink's runnin' dis game, me or you? When I git ready, we move. Not before! When I git ready, get me!

VOICES: [*Approvingly*] That's the stuff! Yank tal him, py golly!
Yank ain't affeerd.
Goot poy, Yank!
Give him hell!
Tell 'im 'e's a bloody swine!
Bloody slave-driver!

YANK: [*Contemptuously*] He ain't got no noive. He's yellow, get me? All de engineers is yellow. Dey got streaks a mile wide. Aw, to hell wit him! Let's move, youse guys. We had a rest. Come on, she needs it! Give her pep! It ain't for him. Him and his whistle, dey don't belong. But we belong, see! We gotter feed de baby! Come on!

[*He turns and flings his furnace door open. They all follow his lead. At this instant the* Second *and* Fourth Engineers *enter from the darkness on the left with* Mildred *between them. She starts, turns paler, her pose is crumbling, she shivers with fright in spite of the blazing heat, but forces herself to leave the* Engineers *and take a few steps nearer the men. She is right behind* Yank. *All this happens quickly while the men have their backs turned*]

YANK: Come on, youse guys!

[*He is turning to get coal when the whistle sounds again in a peremptory, irritating note. This drives* Yank *into a sudden fury. While the other* Men *have turned full around and stopped dumbfounded by the spectacle of* Mildred *standing there in her white dress,* Yank *does not turn far enough to see her. Besides, his head is thrown back, he blinks upward through the murk trying to find the owner of the whistle, he brandishes his shovel murderously over his head in one hand, pounding on his chest, gorilla-like, with the other, shouting*]

YANK: Toin off dat whistle! Come down outa dere, yuh yellow, brass-buttoned, Belfast bum, yuh! Come down and I'll knock yer brains out! Yuh lousy, stinkin', yellow mut of a Catholic-moiderin' bastard! Come down and I'll moider yuh! Pullin' dat whistle on me, huh? I'll show yuh! I'll crash yer skull in! I'll drive yer teet' down yer troat! I'll slam yer nose trou de back of yer head! I'll cut yer guts out for a nickel, yuh lousy boob, yuh dirty, crummy, muck-eatin' son of a——

[*Suddenly he becomes conscious of all the other* Men *staring at something directly behind his back. He whirls defensively with a snarling, murderous growl, crouching to spring, his lips drawn back over his teeth, his small eyes gleaming ferociously. He sees* Mildred, *like a white apparition in the full light from the open furnace doors. He glares into her eyes, turned to stone. As for her, during his speech she has listened, paralyzed with horror, terror, her whole personality crushed, beaten in, collapsed, by the terrific impact of this unknown, abys-*

mal brutality, naked and shameless. As she looks at his gorilla face, as his eyes bore into hers, she utters a low, choking cry and shrinks away from him, putting both hands up before her eyes to shut out the sight of his face, to protect her own. This startles Yank to a reaction. His mouth falls open, his eyes grow bewildered]

MILDRED: [About to faint—to the Engineers, who now have her one by each arm—whimperingly] Take me away! Oh, the filthy beast!

[She faints. They carry her quickly back, disappearing in the darkness at the left, rear. An iron door clangs shut. Rage and bewildered fury rush back on Yank. He feels himself insulted in some unknown fashion in the very heart of his pride. He roars]

YANK: God damn yuh!

[And hurls his shovel after them at the door which has just closed. It hits the steel bulkhead with a clang and falls clattering on the steel floor. From overhead the whistle sounds again in a long, angry, insistent command]

CURTAIN

SCENE IV.

The firemen's forecastle. Yank's watch has just come off duty and had dinner. Their faces and bodies shine from a soap and water scrubbing but around their eyes, where a hasty dousing does not touch, the coal dust sticks like black make-up, giving them a queer, sinister expression.

Yank has not washed either face or body. He stands out in contrast to them, a blackened, brooding figure. He is seated forward on a bench in the exact attitude of Rodin's "The Thinker." The others, most of them smoking pipes, are staring at Yank half-apprehensively, as if fearing an outburst; half-amusedly, as if they saw a joke somewhere that tickled them.

VOICES: He ain't ate nothin'.
Py golly, a fallar gat to gat grub in him.
Divil a lie.
Yank feeda da fire, no feeda da face.
Ha-ha.
He ain't even washed hisself.
He's forgot.
Hey, Yank, you forgot to wash.

YANK: [Sullenly] Forgot nothin'! To hell wit washin'.

VOICES: It'll stick to you.
It'll get under your skin.
Give yer the bleedin' itch, that's wot.
It makes spots on you—like a leopard.
Like a piebald nigger, you mean.

Better wash up, Yank.
You sleep better.
Wash up, Yank.
Wash up! Wash up!

YANK: [Resentfully] Aw say, youse guys. Lemme alone. Can't youse see I'm tryin' to tink?

ALL: [Repeating the word after him, as one, with cynical mockery] Think!

[The word has a brazen, metallic quality as if their throats were phonograph horns. It is followed by a chorus of hard, barking laughter]

YANK: [Springing to his feet and glaring at them belligerently] Yes, tink! Tink, dat's what I said! What about it?

[They are silent, puzzled by his sudden resentment at what used to be one of his jokes. Yank sits down again in the same attitude of "The Thinker"]

VOICES: Leave him alone.
He's got a grouch on.
Why wouldn't he?

PADDY: [With a wink at the others] Sure I know what's the matther. 'Tis aisy to see. He's fallen in love, I'm telling you.

ALL: [Repeating the word after him, as one, with cynical mockery] Love!

[The word has a brazen metallic quality as if their throats were phonograph horns. It is followed by a chorus of hard, barking laughter]

YANK: [With a contemptuous snort] Love, hell! Hate, dat's what. I've fallen in hate, get me?

PADDY: [Philosophically] 'Twould take a wise man to tell one from the other. [With a bitter, ironical scorn, increasing as he goes on] But I'm telling you it's love that's in it. Sure what else but love for us poor bastes in the stokehole would be bringing a fine lady, dressed like a white quane, down a mile of ladders and steps to be havin' a look at us?

[A growl of anger goes up from all sides]

LONG: [Jumping on a bench—hecticly] Hinsultin' us! Hinsultin' us, the bloody cow! And them bloody engineers! What right 'as they got to be exhibitin' us 's if we was bleedin' monkeys in a menagerie? Did we sign for hinsults to our dignity as 'onest workers? Is that in the ship's articles? You kin bloody well bet it ain't! But I knows why they done it. I arsked a deck steward 'oo she was and 'e told me. 'Er old man's a bleedin' millionaire, a bloody Capitalist! 'E's got enuf bloody gold to sink this bleedin' ship! 'E makes arf the bloody steel in the world! 'E owns this bloody boat! And you and me, Comrades, we're 'is slaves! And the skipper and mates and engineers, they're 'is slaves! And she's 'is bloody daughter and we're all 'er slaves, too! And she gives 'er orders as 'ow she wants to see the bloody animals below decks and down they takes 'er!

[There is a roar of rage from all sides]

YANK: [Blinking at him bewilderedly] Say! Wait a moment! Is all dat straight goods?

LONG: Straight as string! The bleedin' steward as

waits on 'em, 'e told me about 'er. And what're we goin' ter do, I arsks yer? 'Ave we got ter swaller 'er hinsults like dogs? It ain't in the ship's articles. I tell yer we got a case. We kin go to law——

YANK: [*With abysmal contempt*] Hell! Law!

ALL: [*Repeating the word after him, as one, with cynical mockery*] Law!

[*The word has a brazen metallic quality as if their throats were phonograph horns. It is followed by a chorus of hard, barking laughter*]

LONG: [*Feeling the ground slipping from under his feet—desperately*] As voters and citizens we kin force the bloody governments——

YANK: [*With abysmal contempt*] Hell! Governments!

ALL: [*Repeating the word after him, as one, with cynical mockery*] Governments!

[*The word has a brazen metallic quality as if their throats were phonograph horns. It is followed by a chorus of hard, barking laughter*]

LONG: [*Hysterically*] We're free and equal in the sight of God——

YANK: [*With abysmal contempt*] Hell! God!

ALL: [*Repeating the word after him, as one, with cynical mockery*] God!

[*The word has a brazen metallic quality as if their throats were phonograph horns. It is followed by a chorus of hard, barking laughter*]

YANK: [*Witheringly*] Aw, join de Salvation Army!

ALL: Sit down! Shut up! Damn fool! Sea-lawyer!

[Long *slinks back out of sight*]

PADDY: [*Continuing the trend of his thoughts as if he had never been interrupted—bitterly*] And there she was standing behind us, and the Second pointing at us like a man you'd hear in a circus would be saying: In this cage is a queerer kind of baboon than ever you'd find in darkest Africy. We roast them in their own sweat—and be damned if you won't hear some of thim saying they like it! [*He glances scornfully at* Yank]

YANK: [*With a bewildered uncertain growl*] Aw!

PADDY: And there was Yank roarin' curses and turning round wid his shovel to brain her—and she looked at him, and him at her——

YANK: [*Slowly*] She was all white. I tought she was a ghost. Sure.

PADDY: [*With heavy, biting sarcasm*] 'Twas love at first sight, divil a doubt of it! If you'd seen the endearin' look on her pale mug when she shriveled away with her hands over her eyes to shut out the sight of him! Sure, 'twas as if she'd seen a great hairy ape escaped from the Zoo!

YANK: [*Stung—with a growl of rage*] Aw!

PADDY: And the loving way Yank heaved his shovel at the skull of her, only she was out the door! [*A grin breaking over his face*] 'Twas touching, I'm telling you! It put the touch of home, swate home in the stokehole.

[*There is a roar of laughter from all*]

YANK: [*Glaring at* Paddy *menacingly*] Aw, choke dat off, see!

PADDY: [*Not heeding him—to the others*] And her grabbin' at the Second's arm for protection. [*With a grotesque imitation of a woman's voice*] Kiss me, Engineer dear, for it's dark down here and me old man's in Wall Street making money; Hug me tight, darlin', for I'm afeerd in the dark and me mother's on deck makin' eyes at the skipper!

[*Another roar of laughter*]

YANK: [*Threateningly*] Say! What yuh tryin' to do, kid me, yuh old Harp?

PADDY: Divil a bit! Ain't I wishin' myself you'd brained her?

YANK: [*Fiercely*] I'll brain her! I'll brain her yet, wait 'n' see! [*Coming over to* Paddy—*slowly*] Say, is dat what she called me—a hairy ape?

PADDY: She looked it at you if she didn't say the word itself.

YANK: [*Grinning horribly*] Hairy ape, huh? Sure! Dat's de way she looked at me, aw right. Hairy ape! So dat's me, huh? [*Bursting into rage—as if she were still in front of him*] Yuh skinny tart! Yuh white-faced bum, yuh! I'll show yuh who's a ape! [*Turning to the others, bewilderment seizing him again*] Say, youse guys. I was bawlin' him out for pullin' de whistle on us. You heard me. And den I seen youse lookin' at somep'n and I tought he'd sneaked down to come up in back of me, and I hopped round to knock him dead wit de shovel. And dere she was wit de light on her! Christ, yuh coulda pushed me over wit a finger! I was scared, get me? Sure! I tought she was a ghost, see? She was all in white like dey wrap around stiffs. You seen her. Kin yuh blame me? She didn't belong, dat's what. And den when I come to and seen it was a real skoit and seen de way she was lookin' at me—like Paddy said—Christ, I was sore, get me? I don't stand for dat stuff from nobody. And I flung de shovel—on'y she'd beat it. [*Furiously*] I wished it'd banged her! I wished it'd knocked her block off!

LONG: And be 'anged for murder or 'lectrocuted? She ain't bleedin' well worth it.

YANK: I don't give a damn what! I'd be square wit her, wouldn't I? Tink I wanter let her put somep'n over on me? Tink I'm goin' to let her git away wit dat stuff? Yuh don't know me! No one ain't never put nothin' over on me and got away wit it, see!—not dat kind of stuff—no guy and no skoit neither! I'll fix her! Maybe she'll come down again——

VOICE: No chance, Yank. You scared her out of a year's growth.

YANK: I scared her? Why de hell should I scare her? Who de hell is she? Ain't she de same as me? Hairy ape, huh? [*With his old confident bravado*] I'll show her I'm better'n her, if she on'y knew it. I belong and she don't, see! I move and she's dead! Twenty-five knots a hour, dat's me! Dat carries her but I make dat. She's on'y baggage. Sure! [*Again*

bewilderedly] But, Christ, she was funny lookin'!
Did yuh pipe her hands? White and skinny. Yuh
could see de bones through 'em. And her mush, dat
was dead white, too. And her eyes, dey was like
dey'd seen a ghost. Me, dat was! Sure! Hairy ape!
Ghost, huh? Look at dat arm! [*He extends his right
arm, swelling out the great muscles*] I coulda took
her wit dat, wit just my little finger even, and broke
her in two. [*Again bewilderedly*] Say, who is dat
skoit, huh? What is she? What's she come from?
Who made her? Who give her de noive to look at
me like dat? Dis ting's got my goat right. I don't get
her. She's new to me. What does a skoit like her
mean, huh? She don't belong, get me! I can't see
her. [*With growing anger*] But one ting I'm wise to,
aw right, aw right! Youse all kin bet your shoits I'll
git even wit her. I'll show her if she tinks she— She
grinds de organ and I'm on de string, huh? I'll fix
her! Let her come down again and I'll fling her in de
furnace! She'll move den! She won't shiver at nothin',
den! Speed, dat'll be her! She'll belong den! [*He
grins horribly*]

PADDY: She'll never come. She's had her belly-
full, I'm telling you. She'll be in bed now, I'm thinking, wid ten doctors and nurses feedin' her salts to
clean the fear out of her.

YANK: [*Enraged*] Yuh tink I made her sick too,
do yuh? Just lookin' at me, huh? Hairy ape, huh?
[*In a frenzy of rage*] I'll fix her! I'll tell her where
to git off! She'll git down on her knees and take it
back or I'll bust de face offen her! [*Shaking one fist
upward and beating on his chest with the other*] I'll
find yuh! I'm comin', d'yuh hear? I'll fix yuh, God
damn yuh! [*He makes a rush for the door*]

VOICES: Stop him!
He'll get shot!
He'll murder her!
Trip him up!
Hold him!
He's gone crazy!
Gott, he's strong!
Hold him down!
Look out for a kick!
Pin his arms!

　　[*They have all piled on him and, after a fierce
　　struggle, by sheer weight of numbers have
　　borne him to the floor just inside the door*]

PADDY: [*Who has remained detached*] Kape him
down till he's cooled off. [*Scornfully*] Yerra, Yank,
you're a great fool. Is it payin' attention at all you
are to the like of that skinny sow widout one drop
of rale blood in her?

YANK: [*Frenziedly, from the bottom of the heap*]
She done me doit! She done me doit, didn't she?
I'll git square wit her! I'll get her some way! Git
offen me, youse guys! Lemme up! I'll show her who's
a ape!

　　　　CURTAIN

SCENE V.

*Three weeks later. A corner of Fifth Avenue in
the Fifties on a fine Sunday morning. A general atmosphere of clean, well-tidied, wide street; a flood
of mellow, tempered sunshine; gentle, genteel
breezes. In the rear, the show windows of two shops,
a jewelry establishment on the corner, a furrier's
next to it. Here the adornments of extreme wealth
are tantalizingly displayed. The jeweler's window is
gaudy with glittering diamonds, emeralds, rubies,
pearls, etc., fashioned in ornate tiaras, crowns, neck-
laces, collars, etc. From each piece hangs an enormous tag from which a dollar sign and numerals in
intermittent electric lights wink out the incredible
prices. The same in the furrier's. Rich furs of all
varieties hang there bathed in a downpour of artificial light. The general effect is of a background of
magnificence cheapened and made grotesque by
commercialism, a background in tawdry disharmony
with the clear light and sunshine on the street itself.*

*Up the side street Yank and Long come swagger-
ing. Long is dressed in shore clothes, wears a black
Windsor tie, cloth cap. Yank is in his dirty dungarees. A fireman's cap with black peak is cocked defiantly on the side of his head. He has not shaved
for days and around his fierce, resentful eyes—as
around those of Long to a lesser degree—the black
smudge of coal dust still sticks like make-up. They
hesitate and stand together at the corner, swaggering, looking about them with a forced, defiant contempt.*

LONG: [*Indicating it all with an oratorical gesture*]
Well, 'ere we are. Fif' Avenoo. This 'ere's their
bleedin' private lane, as yer might say. [*Bitterly*]
We're trespassers 'ere. Proletarians keep orf the
grass!

YANK: [*Dully*] I don't see no grass, yuh boob.
[*Staring at the sidewalk*] Clean, ain't it? Yuh could
eat a fried egg offen it. The white wings got some
job sweepin' dis up. [*Looking up and down the avenue—surlily*] Where's all de white-collar stiffs yuh
said was here—and de skoits—*her* kind?

LONG: In church, blarst 'em! Arskin' Jesus to give
'em more money.

YANK: Choich, huh? I useter go to choich onct—
sure—when I was a kid. Me old man and woman,
dey made me. Dey never went demselves, dough.
Always got too big a head on Sunday mornin', dat
was dem. [*With a grin*] Dey was scrappers for fair,
bot' of dem. On Satiday nights when dey bot' got
a skinful dey could put up a bout oughter been
staged at de Garden. When dey got trough dere
wasn't a chair or table wit a leg under it. Or else
dey bot' jumped on me for somep'n. Dat was where
I loined to take punishment. [*With a grin and a
swagger*] I'm a chip offen de old block, get me?

LONG: Did yer old man follow the sea?

YANK: Naw. Worked along shore. I runned away when me old lady croaked wit de tremens. I helped at truckin' and in de market. Den I shipped in de stokehole. Sure. Dat belongs. De rest was nothin'. [*Looking around him*] I ain't never seen dis before. De Brooklyn waterfront, dat was where I was dragged up. [*Taking a deep breath*] Dis ain't so bad at dat, huh?

LONG: Not bad? Well, we pays for it wiv our bloody sweat, if yer wants to know!

YANK: [*With sudden angry disgust*] Aw, hell! I don't see no one, see—like her. All dis gives me a pain. It don't belong. Say, ain't dere a back room around dis dump? Let's go shoot a ball. All dis is too clean and quiet and dolled-up, get me? It gives me a pain.

LONG: Wait and yer'll bloody well see——

YANK: I don't wait for no one. I keep on de move. Say, what yuh drag me up here for, anyway? Tryin' to kid me, yuh simp, yuh?

LONG: Yer wants to get back at 'er, don't yer? That's what yer been sayin' every bloomin' hour since she hinsulted yer.

YANK: [*Vehemently*] Sure ting I do! Didn't I try to get even wit her in Southampton? Didn't I sneak on de deck and wait for her by de gangplank? I was goin' to spit in her pale mug, see! Sure, right in her pop-eyes! Dat woulda made me even, see? But no chanct. Dere was a whole army of plainclothes bulls around. Dey spotted me and gimme de bum's rush. I never seen her. But I'll git square wit her yet, you watch! [*Furiously*] De lousy tart! She tinks she kin get away wit moider—but not wit me! I'll fix her! I'll tink of a way!

LONG: [*As disgusted as he dares to be*] Ain't that why I brought yer up 'ere—to show yer? Yer been lookin' at this 'ere 'ole affair wrong. Yer been actin' an' talkin' 's if it was all a bleedin' personal matter between yer and that bloody cow. I wants to convince yer she was on'y a representative of 'er clarss. I wants to awaken yer bloody clarss consciousness. Then yer'll see it's 'er clarss ye've got to fight, not 'er alone. There's a 'ole mob of 'em like 'er, Gawd blind 'em!

YANK: [*Spitting on his hands—belligerently*] De more de merrier when I gits started. Bring on de gang!

LONG: Yer'll see 'em in arf a mo', when that church lets out. [*He turns and sees the window display in the two stores for the first time*] Blimey! Look at that, will yer? [*They both walk back and stand looking in the jeweler's. Long flies into a fury*] Just look at this 'ere bloomin' mess! Just look at it! Look at the bleedin' prices on 'em—more'n our 'ole bloody stokehole makes in ten voyages sweatin' in 'ell! And they—'er and 'er bloody clarss—buys 'em for toys to dangle on 'em! One of these 'ere would buy scoff for a starvin' family for a year!

YANK: Aw, cut de sob stuff! T' hell wit de starvin' family! Yuh'll be passin' de hat to me next. [*With naïve admiration*] Say, dem tings is pretty, huh? Bet yuh dey'd hock for a piece of change aw right. [*Then turning away, bored*] But, aw hell, what good are dey? Let her have 'em. Dey don't belong no more'n she does. [*With a gesture of sweeping the jeweler's into oblivion*] All dat don't count, get me?

LONG: [*Who has moved to the furrier's—indignantly*] And I s'pose this 'ere don't count neither—skins of poor, 'armless animals slaughtered so as 'er and 'ers can keep their bleedin' noses warm!

YANK: [*Who has been staring at something inside—with queer excitement*] Take a slant at dat! Give it de once-over! Monkey fur—two t'ousand bucks! [*Bewilderedly*] Is dat straight goods—monkey fur? What de hell——?

LONG: [*Bitterly*] It's straight enuf. [*With grim humor*] They wouldn't bloody well pay that for a 'airy ape's skin—no, nor for the 'ole livin' ape with all 'is 'ead, and body, and soul thrown in!

YANK: [*Clenching his fists, his face growing pale with rage as if the skin in the window were a personal insult*] Trowin' it up in my face! Christ! I'll fix her!

LONG: [*Excitedly*] Church is out. 'Ere they come, the bleedin' swine. [*After a glance at Yank's lowering face—uneasily*] Easy goes, Comrade. Keep yer bloomin' temper. Remember force defeats itself. It ain't our weapon. We must impress our demands through peaceful means—the votes of the on-marching proletarians of the bloody world!

YANK: [*With abysmal contempt*] Votes, hell! Votes is a joke, see? Votes for women! Let dem do it!

LONG: [*Still more uneasily*] Calm, now. Treat 'em wiv the proper contempt. Observe the bleedin' parasites but 'old yer 'orses.

YANK: [*Angrily*] Git away from me! Yuh're yellow, dat's what. Force, dat's me! De punch, dat's me every time, see!

[*The* Crowd *from church enter from the right, sauntering slowly and affectedly, their heads held stiffly up, looking neither to right nor left, talking in toneless, simpering voices. The* Women *are rouged, calcimined, dyed, overdressed to the nth degree. The* Men *are in Prince Alberts, high hats, spats, canes, etc. A procession of gaudy marionettes, yet with something of the relentless horror of Frankensteins in their detached, mechanical unawareness*]

VOICES: Dear Doctor Caiaphas! He is so sincere! What was the sermon? I dozed off.

About the radicals, my dear—and the false doctrines that are being preached.

We must organize a hundred per cent American bazaar.

And let everyone contribute one one-hundredth per cent of their income tax.

What an original idea!

We can devote the proceeds to rehabilitating the veil of the temple.

But that has been done so many times.

YANK: [*Glaring from one to the other of them—with an insulting snort of scorn*] Huh! Huh!

[*Without seeming to see him, they make wide detours to avoid the spot where he stands in the middle of the sidewalk*]

LONG: [*Frightenedly*] Keep yer bloomin' mouth shut, I tells yer.

YANK: [*Viciously*] G'wan! Tell it to Sweeney! [*He swaggers away and deliberately lurches into a top-hatted* Gentleman, *then glares at him pugnaciously*] Say, who d'yuh tink yuh're bumpin'? Tink yuh own de oith?

GENTLEMAN: [*Coldly and affectedly*] I beg your pardon. [*He has not looked at* Yank *and passes on without a glance, leaving him bewildered*]

LONG: [*Rushing up and grabbing* Yank's *arm*] 'Ere! Come away! This wasn't what I meant. Yer'll 'ave the bloody coppers down on us.

YANK: [*Savagely—giving him a push that sends him sprawling*] G'wan!

LONG: [*Picks himself up—hysterically*] I'll pop orf then. This ain't what I meant. And whatever 'appens, yer can't blame me. [*He slinks off left*]

YANK: T' hell wit youse! [*He approaches a* Lady —*with a vicious grin and a smirking wink*] Hello, Kiddo. How's every little ting? Got anything on for tonight? I know an old boiler down to de docks we kin crawl into. [*The* Lady *stalks by without a look, without a change of pace.* Yank *turns to others— insultingly*] Holy smokes, what a mug! Go hide yuhself before de horses shy at yuh. Gee, pipe de heinie on dat one! Say, youse, yuh look like de stoin of a ferryboat. Paint and powder! All dolled up to kill! Yuh look like stiffs laid out for de boneyard! Aw, g'wan, de lot of youse! Yuh give me de eye-ache. Yuh don't belong, get me! Look at me, why don't youse dare? I belong, dat's me! [*Pointing to a sky-scraper across the street which is in process of construction—with bravado*] See dat building goin' up dere? See de steel work? Steel, dat's me! Youse guys live on it and tink yuh're somep'n. But I'm *in* it, see! I'm de hoistin' engine dat makes it go up! I'm it—de inside and bottom of it! Sure! I'm steel and steam and smoke and de rest of it! It moves—speed—twenty-five stories up—and me at de top and bottom—movin'! Youse simps don't move. Yuh're on'y dolls I winds up to see 'm spin. Yuh're de garbage, get me—de leavins—de ashes we dump over de side! Now, what 'a' yuh gotta say? [*But as they seem neither to see nor hear him, he flies into a fury*] Bums! Pigs! Tarts! Bitches! [*He turns in a rage on the* Men, *bumping viciously into them but not jarring them the least bit. Rather it is he who recoils after each collision. He keeps growling*] Git off de oith! G'wan, yuh bum! Look where yuh're goin', can't yuh? Git outa here! Fight, why don't yuh? Put up yer mits! Don't be a dog! Fight or I'll knock yuh dead! [*But, without seeming to see him, they all answer with mechanical affected politeness:*] I beg your pardon.

[*Then, at a cry from one of the* Women, *they all scurry to the furrier's window*]

THE WOMAN: [*Ecstatically, with a gasp of delight*] Monkey fur! [*The whole crowd of* Men *and* Women *chorus after her in the same tone of affected delight*] Monkey fur!

YANK: [*With a jerk of his head back on his shoulders, as if he had received a punch full in the face —raging*] I see yuh, all in white! I see yuh, yuh white-faced tart, yuh! Hairy ape, huh? I'll hairy ape yuh!

[*He bends down and grips at the street curbing as if to pluck it out and hurl it. Foiled in this, snarling with passion, he leaps to the lamp-post on the corner and tries to pull it up for a club. Just at that moment a bus is heard rumbling up. A fat, high-hatted, spatted* Gentleman *runs out from the side street. He calls out plaintively:*]

GENTLEMAN: Bus! Bus! Stop there! [*And runs full tilt into the bending, straining* Yank, *who is bowled off his balance*]

YANK: [*Seeing a fight—with a roar of joy as he springs to his feet*] At last! Bus, huh? I'll bust yuh! [*He lets drive a terrific swing, his fist landing full on the fat* Gentleman's *face. But the* Gentleman *stands unmoved as if nothing had happened*]

GENTLEMAN: I beg your pardon. [*Then irritably*] You have made me lose my bus. [*He claps his hands and begins to scream:*] Officer! Officer!

[*Many police whistles shrill out on the instant and a whole platoon of* Policemen *rush in on* Yank *from all sides. He tries to fight but is clubbed to the pavement and fallen upon. The* Crowd *at the window have not moved or noticed this disturbance. The clanging gong of the patrol wagon approaches with a clamoring din*]

CURTAIN

SCENE VI.

Night of the following day. A row of cells in the prison on Blackwell's Island. The cells extend back diagonally from right front to left rear. They do not stop, but disappear in the dark background as if they ran on, numberless, into infinity. One electric bulb from the low ceiling of the narrow corridor sheds its light through the heavy steel bars of the cell at the extreme front and reveals part of the interior.

Yank *can be seen within, crouched on the edge of his cot in the attitude of Rodin's "The Thinker." His face is spotted with black and blue bruises. A blood-stained bandage is wrapped around his head.*

YANK: [*Suddenly starting as if awakening from a dream, reaches out and shakes the bars—aloud to himself, wonderingly*] Steel. Dis is de Zoo, huh?

> [*A burst of hard, barking laughter comes from the unseen* Occupants *of the cells, runs back down the tier, and abruptly ceases*]

VOICES: [*Mockingly*] The Zoo? That's a new name for this coop—a damn good name!

Steel, eh? You said a mouthful. This is the old iron house.

Who is that boob talkin'?

He's the bloke they brung in out of his head. The bulls had beat him up fierce.

YANK: [*Dully*] I musta been dreamin'. I tought I was in a cage at de Zoo—but de apes don't talk, do dey?

VOICES: [*With mocking laughter*] You're in a cage aw right.

A coop!

A pen!

A sty!

A kennel!

> [*Hard laughter—a pause*]

Say, guy! Who are you? No, never mind lying. What are you?

Yes, tell us your sad story. What's your game?

What did they jug yuh for?

YANK: [*Dully*] I was a fireman—stokin' on de liners. [*Then with sudden rage, rattling his cell bars*] I'm a hairy ape, get me? And I'll bust youse all in de jaw if yuh don't lay off kiddin' me.

VOICES: Huh! You're a hard boiled duck, ain't youse!

When you spit, it bounces!

> [*Laughter*]

Aw, can it. He's a regular guy. Ain't you?

What did he say he was—a ape?

YANK: [*Defiantly*] Sure ting! Ain't dat what youse all are—apes?

> [*A silence. Then a furious rattling of bars from down the corridor*]

A VOICE: [*Thick with rage*] I'll show yuh who's a ape, yuh bum!

VOICES: Ssshh! Nix!

Can de noise!

Piano!

You'll have the guard down on us!

YANK: [*Scornfully*] De guard? Yuh mean de keeper, don't yuh?

> [*Angry exclamations from all the cells*]

VOICE: [*Placatingly*] Aw, don't pay no attention to him. He's off his nut from the beatin'-up he got. Say, you guy! We're waitin' to hear what they landed you for—or ain't yuh tellin'?

YANK: Sure, I'll tell youse. Sure! Why de hell not? On'y—youse won't get me. Nobody gets me but me, see? I started to tell de Judge and all he says was: "Toity days to tink it over." Tink it over! Christ, dat's all I been doin' for weeks! [*After a pause*] I was tryin' to git even wit someone, see?—someone dat done me doit.

VOICES: [*Cynically*] De old stuff, I bet. Your goil, huh?

Give yuh the double-cross, huh?

That's them every time!

Did yuh beat up de odder guy?

YANK: [*Disgustedly*] Aw, yuh're all wrong! Sure dere was a skoit in it—but not what youse mean, not dat old tripe. Dis was a new kind of skoit. She was dolled up all in white—in de stokehole. I tought she was a ghost. Sure.

> [*A pause*]

VOICES: [*Whispering*] Gee, he's still nutty.

Let him rave. It's fun listenin'.

YANK: [*Unheeding—groping in his thoughts*] Her hands—dey was skinny and white like dey wasn't real but painted on somep'n. Dere was a million miles from me to her—twenty-five knots a hour. She was like some dead ting de cat brung in. Sure, dat's what. She didn't belong. She belonged in de window of a toy store, or on de top of a garbage can, see! Sure! [*He breaks out angrily*] But would yuh believe it, she had de noive to do me doit. She lamped me like she was seein' somep'n broke loose from de menagerie. Christ, yuh'd oughter seen her eyes! [*He rattles the bars of his cell furiously*] But I'll get back at her yet, you watch! And if I can't find her I'll take it out on de gang she runs wit. I'm wise to where dey hangs out now. I'll show her who belongs! I'll show her who's in de move and who ain't. You watch my smoke!

VOICES: [*Serious and joking*] Dat's de talkin'!

Take her for all she's got!

What was this dame, anyway? Who was she, eh?

YANK: I dunno. First cabin stiff. Her old man's a millionaire, dey says—name of Douglas.

VOICES: Douglas? That's the president of the Steel Trust, I bet.

Sure. I seen his mug in de papers.

He's filthy with dough.

VOICE: Hey, feller, take a tip from me. If you want to get back at that dame, you better join the Wobblies. You'll get some action then.

YANK: Wobblies? What de hell's dat?

VOICE: Ain't you ever heard of the I. W. W.?

YANK: Naw. What is it?

VOICE: A gang of blokes—a tough gang. I been readin' about 'em today in the paper. The guard give me the *Sunday Times*. There's a long spiel about 'em. It's from a speech made in the Senate by a guy named Senator Queen. [*He is in the cell next to* Yank's. *There is a rustling of paper*] Wait'll I see if I got light enough and I'll read you. Listen. [*He reads:*] "There is a menace existing in this country today which threatens the vitals of our fair Republic—as foul a menace against the very life-blood of the American Eagle as was the foul conspiracy of Catiline against the eagles of ancient Rome!"

VOICE: [*Disgustedly*] Aw, hell! Tell him to salt de tail of dat eagle!

VOICE: [*Reading:*] "I refer to that devil's brew of rascals, jailbirds, murderers and cutthroats who libel all honest working men by calling themselves the Industrial Workers of the World; but in the light of their nefarious plots, I call them the Industrious *Wreckers* of the World!"

YANK: [*With vengeful satisfaction*] Wreckers, dat's de right dope! Dat belongs! Me for dem!

VOICE: Ssshh! [*Reading:*] "This fiendish organization is a foul ulcer on the fair body of our Democracy——"

VOICE: Democracy, hell! Give him the boid, fellers—the raspberry! [*They do*]

VOICE: Ssshh! [*Reading:*] "Like Cato I say to this Senate, the I. W. W. must be destroyed! For they represent an ever-present dagger pointed at the heart of the greatest nation the world has ever known, where all men are born free and equal, with equal opportunities to all, where the Founding Fathers have guaranteed to each one happiness, where Truth, Honor, Liberty, Justice, and the Brotherhood of Man are a religion absorbed with one's mother milk, taught at our father's knee, sealed, signed, and stamped in the glorious Constitution of these United States!"

[*A perfect storm of hisses, catcalls, boos, and hard laughter*]

VOICES: [*Scornfully*] Hurrah for de Fort' of July! Pass de hat!
Liberty!
Justice!
Honor!
Opportunity!
Brotherhood!

ALL: [*With abysmal scorn*] Aw, hell!

VOICE: Give the Queen Senator guy the bark! All togedder now—one—two—three——

[*A terrific chorus of barking and yapping*]

GUARD: [*From a distance*] Quiet there, youse—or I'll git the hose.

[*The noise subsides*]

YANK: [*With growling rage*] I'd like to catch dat senator guy alone for a second. I'd loin him some trute!

VOICE: Ssshh! Here's where he gits down to cases on the Wobblies. [*Reads:*] "They plot with fire in one hand and dynamite in the other. They stop not before murder to gain their ends, nor at the outraging of defenseless womanhood. They would tear down society, put the lowest scum in the seats of the mighty, turn Almighty God's revealed plan for the world topsy-turvy, and make of our sweet and lovely civilization a shambles, a desolation where man, God's masterpiece, would soon degenerate back to the ape!"

VOICE: [*To Yank*] Hey, you guy. There's your ape stuff again.

YANK: [*With a growl of fury*] I got him. So dey blow up tings, do they? Dey turn tings round, do dey? Hey, lend me dat paper, will yuh?

VOICE: Sure. Give it to him. On'y keep it to yourself, see? We don't wanter listen to no more of that slop.

VOICE: Here you are. Hide it under your mattress.

YANK: [*Reaching out*] Tanks. I can't read much but I kin manage. [*He sits, the paper in the hand at his side, in the attitude of Rodin's "The Thinker." A pause. Several snores from down the corridor. Suddenly* Yank *jumps to his feet with a furious groan as if some appalling thought had crashed on him—bewilderedly*] Sure—her old man—president of de Steel Trust—makes half de steel in de world —steel—where I thought I belonged—drivin' trou —movin'—in dat—to make *her*—and cage me in for her to spit on! Christ! [*He shakes the bars of his cell door till the whole tier trembles. Irritated, protesting exclamations from those awakened or trying to get to sleep*] He made dis—dis cage! Steel! *It* don't belong, dat's what! Cages, cells, locks, bolts, bars—dat's what it means!—holdin' me down with him at de top! But I'll drive trou! Fire, dat melts it! I'll be fire—under de heap—fire dat never goes out —hot as hell—breakin' out in de night——

[*While he has been saying this last he has shaken his cell door to a clanging accompaniment. As he comes to the "breakin' out" he seizes one bar with both hands and, putting his two feet up against the others so that his position is parallel to the floor like a monkey's, he gives a great wrench backwards. The bar bends like a licorice stick under his tremendous strength. Just at this moment the* Prison Guard *rushes in, dragging a hose behind him*]

GUARD: [*Angrily*] I'll loin youse bums to wake me up! [*Sees* Yank] Hello, it's you, huh? Got the D. Ts., hey? Well, I'll cure 'em. I'll drown your snakes for yuh! [*Noticing the bar*] Hell, look at dat bar bended! On'y a bug is strong enough for dat!

YANK: [*Glaring at him*] Or a hairy ape, yuh big yellow bum! Look out! Here I come! [*He grabs another bar*]

GUARD: [*Scared now—yelling off left*] Toin de hose on, Ben!—full pressure! And call de others— and a straitjacket!

[*The curtain is falling. As it hides* Yank *from view, there is a splattering smash as the stream of water hits the steel of* Yank's *cell*]

CURTAIN

SCENE VII.

Nearly a month later. An I. W. W. local near the waterfront, showing the interior of a front room on the ground floor, and the street outside. Moonlight on the narrow street, buildings massed in black shadow. The interior of the room, which is general assembly room, office, and reading room, resembles some dingy settlement boys' club. A desk and high stool are in one corner. A table with paper, stacks of pamphlets, chairs about it, is at center. The whole is decidedly cheap, banal, commonplace, and un-mysterious as a room could well be.

The Secretary *is perched on the stool making entries in a large ledger. An eye shade casts his face into shadows. Eight or ten* Men, Longshoremen, Iron Workers, *and the like, are grouped about the table. Two are playing checkers. One is writing a letter. Most of them are smoking pipes. A big sign-board is on the wall at the rear, "Industrial Workers of the World—Local No. 57."* Yank *comes down the street outside. He is dressed as in Scene Five. He moves cautiously, mysteriously. He comes to a point opposite the door; tiptoes softly up to it, listens, is impressed by the silence within, knocks carefully, as if he were guessing at the password to some secret rite. Listens. No answer. Knocks again a bit louder. No answer. Knocks impatiently, much louder.*

SECRETARY: [*Turning around on his stool*] What the hell is that—someone knocking? [*Shouts:*] Come in, why don't you?

    [*All the* Men *in the room look up.* Yank *opens the door slowly, gingerly, as if afraid of an ambush. He looks around for the secret doors, mystery, is taken aback by the commonplace-ness of the room and the* Men *in it, thinks he may have gotten in the wrong place, then sees the signboard on the wall and is reassured*]

YANK: [*Blurts out:*] Hello.

MEN: [*Reservedly*] Hello.

YANK: [*More easily*] I thought I'd bumped into de wrong dump.

SECRETARY: [*Scrutinizing him carefully*] Maybe you have. Are you a member?

YANK: Naw, not yet. Dat's what I come for—to join.

SECRETARY: That's easy. What's your job—long-shore?

YANK: Naw. Fireman—stoker on de liners.

SECRETARY: [*With satisfaction*] Welcome to our city. Glad to know you people are waking up at last. We haven't got many members in your line.

YANK: Naw. Dey're all dead to de woild.

SECRETARY: Well, you can help to wake 'em. What's your name? I'll make out your card.

YANK: [*Confused*] Name? Lemme tink.

SECRETARY: [*Sharply*] Don't you know your own name?

YANK: Sure; but I been just Yank for so long—Bob, dat's it—Bob Smith.

SECRETARY: [*Writing*] Robert Smith. [*Fills out the rest of card*] Here you are. Cost you half a dollar.

YANK: Is dat all—four bits? Dat's easy.

    [*Gives the* Secretary *the money*]

SECRETARY: [*Throwing it in drawer*] Thanks. Well, make yourself at home. No introductions needed. There's literature on the table. Take some of those pamphlets with you to distribute aboard ship. They may bring results. Sow the seed, only go about it right. Don't get caught and fired. We got plenty out of work. What we need is men who can hold their jobs—and work for us at the same time.

YANK: Sure. [*But he still stands, embarrassed and uneasy*]

SECRETARY: [*Looking at him—curiously*] What did you knock for? Think we had a coon in uniform to open doors?

YANK: Naw. I tought it was locked—and dat yuh'd wanter give me the once-over trou a peep-hole or somep'n to see if I was right.

SECRETARY: [*Alert and suspicious but with an easy laugh*] Think we were running a crap game? That door is never locked. What put that in your nut?

YANK: [*With a knowing grin, convinced that this is all camouflage, a part of the secrecy*] Dis burg is full of bulls, ain't it?

SECRETARY: [*Sharply*] What have the cops got to do with us? We're breaking no laws.

YANK: [*With a knowing wink*] Sure. Youse wouldn't for woilds. Sure. I'm wise to dat.

SECRETARY: You seem to be wise to a lot of stuff none of us knows about.

YANK: [*With another wink*] Aw, dat's aw right, see? [*Then made a bit resentful by the suspicious glances from all sides*] Aw, can it! Youse needn't put me trou de toid degree. Can't youse see I be-long? Sure! I'm reg'lar. I'll stick, get me? I'll shoot de woiks for youse. Dat's why I wanted to join in.

SECRETARY: [*Breezily, feeling him out*] That's the right spirit. Only are you sure you understand what you've joined? It's all plain and above board; still, some guys get a wrong slant on us. [*Sharply*] What's your notion of the purpose of the I. W. W.?

YANK: Aw, I know all about it.

SECRETARY: [*Sarcastically*] Well, give us some of your valuable information.

YANK: [*Cunningly*] I know enough not to speak outa my toin. [*Then resentfully again*] Aw, say! I'm reg'lar. I'm wise to de game. I know yuh got to watch your step wit a stranger. For all youse know, I might be a plain-clothes dick, or somep'n, dat's what yuh're thinkin', huh? Aw, forget it! I belong, see? Ask any guy down to de docks if I don't.

SECRETARY: Who said you didn't?

YANK: After I'm 'nitiated, I'll show yuh.

SECRETARY: [*Astounded*] Initiated? There's no in-itiation.

YANK: [*Disappointed*] Ain't there no password—no grip nor nothin'?

SECRETARY: What'd you think this is—the Elks—or the Black Hand?

YANK: De Elks, hell! De Black Hand, dey're a lot of yellow backstickin' Ginees. Naw. Dis is a man's gang, ain't it?

SECRETARY: You said it! That's why we stand on two feet in the open. We got no secrets.

YANK: [*Surprised but admiringly*] Yuh mean to say yuh always run wide open—like dis?

SECRETARY: Exactly.

YANK: Den yuh sure got your noive wit youse!

SECRETARY: [*Sharply*] Just what was it made you want to join us? Come out with that straight.

YANK: Yuh call me? Well, I got noive, too! Here's my hand. Yuh wanter blow tings up, don't yuh? Well, dat's me! I belong!

SECRETARY: [*With pretended carelessness*] You mean change the unequal conditions of society by legitimate direct action—or with dynamite?

YANK: *Dynamite!* Blow it offen de oith—steel—all de cages—all de factories, steamers, buildings, jails—de Steel Trust and all dat makes it go.

SECRETARY: So—that's your idea, eh? And did you have any special job in that line you wanted to propose to us? [*He makes a sign to the* Men, *who get up cautiously one by one and group behind* Yank]

YANK: [*Boldly*] Sure, I'll come out wit it. I'll show youse I'm one of de gang. Dere's dat millionaire guy, Douglas——

SECRETARY: President of the Steel Trust, you mean? Do you want to assassinate him?

YANK: Naw, dat don't get yuh nothin'. I mean blow up de factory, de woiks, where he makes de steel. Dat's what I'm after—to blow up de steel, knock all de steel in de woild up to de moon. Dat'll fix tings! [*Eagerly, with a touch of bravado*] I'll do it by me lonesome! I'll show yuh! Tell me where his woiks is, how to git there, all de dope. Gimme de stuff, de old butter—and watch me do de rest! Watch de smoke and see it move! I don't give a damn if dey nab me—long as it's done! I'll soive life for it—and give 'em de laugh! [*Half to himself*] And I'll write her a letter and tell her de hairy ape done it. Dat'll square tings.

SECRETARY: [*Stepping away from* Yank] Very interesting.

[*He gives a signal. The* Men, *huskies all, throw themselves on* Yank *and before he knows it they have his legs and arms pinioned. But he is too flabbergasted to make a struggle, anyway. They feel him over for weapons*]

MAN: No gat, no knife. Shall we give him what's what and put the boots to him?

SECRETARY: No. He isn't worth the trouble we'd get into. He's too stupid. [*He comes closer and laughs mockingly in* Yank's *face*] Ho-ho! By God, this is the biggest joke they've put up on us yet. Hey, you Joke! Who sent you—Burns or Pinkerton? No, by God, you're such a bonehead I'll bet you're in the Secret Service! Well, you dirty spy, you rotten agent provocator, you can go back and tell whatever skunk is paying you blood-money for betraying your brothers that he's wasting his coin. You couldn't catch a cold. And tell him that all he'll ever get on us, or ever has got, is just his own sneaking plots that he's framed up to put us in jail. We are what our manifesto says we are, neither more nor less—and we'll give him a copy of that any time he calls. And as for you—— [*He glares scornfully at* Yank, *who is sunk in an oblivious stupor*] Oh, hell, what's the use of talking? You're a brainless ape.

YANK: [*Aroused by the word to fierce but futile struggles*] What's dat, yuh Sheeny bum, yuh!

SECRETARY: Throw him out, boys.

[*In spite of his struggles, this is done with gusto and éclat. Propelled by several parting kicks,* Yank *lands sprawling in the middle of the narrow cobbled street. With a growl he starts to get up and storm the closed door, but stops bewildered by the confusion in his brain, pathetically impotent. He sits there, brooding, in as near to the attitude of Rodin's "Thinker" as he can get in his position*]

YANK: [*Bitterly*] So dem boids don't tink I belong, neider. Aw, to hell wit 'em! Dey're in de wrong pew—de same old bull—soapboxes and Salvation Army—no guts! Cut out an hour offen de job a day and make me happy! Gimme a dollar more a day and make me happy! Tree squares a day, and cauliflowers in de front yard—ekal rights—a woman and kids—a lousy vote—and I'm all fixed for Jesus, huh? Aw, hell! What does dat get yuh? Dis ting's in your inside, but it ain't your belly. Feedin' your face—sinkers and coffee—dat don't touch it. It's way down—at de bottom. Yuh can't grab it, and yuh can't stop it. It moves, and everything moves. It stops and de whole woild stops. Dat's me now—I don't tick, see?—I'm a busted Ingersoll, dat's what. Steel was me, and I owned de woild. Now I ain't steel, and de woild owns me. Aw, hell! I can't see—it's all dark, get me? It's all wrong! [*He turns a bitter mocking face up like a ape gibbering at the moon*] Say, youse up dere, Man in de Moon, yuh look so wise, gimme de answer, huh? Slip me de inside dope, de information right from de stable—where do I get off at, huh?

A POLICEMAN: [*Who has come up the street in time to hear this last—with grim humor*] You'll get off at the station, you boob, if you don't get up out of that and keep movin'.

YANK: [*Looking up at him—with a hard, bitter laugh*] Sure! Lock me up! Put me in a cage! Dat's de on'y answer yuh know. G'wan, lock me up!

POLICEMAN: What you been doin'?

YANK: Enuf to gimme life for! I was born, see? Sure, dat's de charge. Write it in de blotter. I was born, get me?

POLICEMAN: [*Jocosely*] God pity your old woman! [*Then matter-of-fact*] But I've no time for kidding. You're soused. I'd run you in but it's too long a walk to the station. Come on now, get up, or I'll fan your ears with this club. Beat it now! [*He hauls* Yank *to his feet*]

YANK: [*In a vague mocking tone*] Say, where do I go from here?

POLICEMAN: [*Giving him a push—with a grin, indifferently*] Go to hell.

CURTAIN

SCENE VIII.

Twilight of the next day. The monkey house at the Zoo. One spot of clear gray light falls on the front of one cage so that the interior can be seen. The other cages are vague, shrouded in shadow from which chatterings pitched in a conversational tone can be heard. On the one cage a sign from which the word "gorilla" stands out. The gigantic Animal *himself is seen squatting on his haunches on a bench in much the same attitute as Rodin's "Thinker."*

Yank *enters from the left. Immediately a chorus of angry chattering and screeching breaks out. The* Gorilla *turns his eyes but makes no sound or move.*

YANK: [*With a hard, bitter laugh*] Welcome to your city, huh? Hail, hail, de gang's all here! [*At the sound of his voice the chattering dies away into an attentive silence.* Yank *walks up to the* Gorilla's *cage and, leaning over the railing, stares in at its occupant, who stares back at him, silent and motionless. There is a pause of dead stillness. Then* Yank *begins to talk in a friendly confidential tone, half-mockingly, but with a deep undercurrent of sympathy*] Say, yuh're some hard-lookin' guy, ain't yuh? I seen lots of tough nuts dat de gang called gorillas, but yuh're de foist real one I ever seen. Some chest yuh got, and shoulders, and dem arms and mits! I bet yuh got a punch in eider fist dat'd knock 'em all silly! [*This with genuine admiration. The* Gorilla, *as if he understood, stands upright, swelling out his chest and pounding on it with his fist.* Yank *grins sympathetically*] Sure, I get yuh. Yuh challenge de whole woild, huh? Yuh got what I was sayin' even if yuh muffed de woids. [*Then bitterness creeping in*] And why wouldn't yuh get me? Ain't we both members of de same club—de Hairy Apes? [*They stare at each other—a pause—then* Yank *goes on slowly and bitterly*] So yuh're what she seen when she looked at me, de white-faced tart! I was you to her, get me? On'y outa de cage—broke out—free to moider her, see? Sure! Dat's what she tought. She wasn't wise dat I was in a cage, too—worser'n yours —sure—a damn sight—'cause you got some chanct to bust loose—but me—— [*He grows confused*] Aw, hell! It's wrong, ain't it? [*A pause*] I s'pose yuh wanter know what I'm doin' here, huh? I been warmin' a bench down to de Battery—ever since last night. Sure. I seen de sun come up. Dat was pretty, too—all red and pink and green. I was lookin' at de skyscrapers—steel—and all de ships comin'

in, sailin' out, all over de oith—and dey was steel, too. De sun was warm, dey wasn't no clouds, and dere was a breeze blowin'. Sure, it was great stuff. I got it aw right—what Paddy said about dat bein' de right dope—on'y I couldn't get *in* it, see? I couldn't belong in dat. It was over my head. And I kept tinkin'—and den I beat it up here to see what youse was like. And I waited till dey was all gone to git yuh alone. Say, how d'yuh feel sittin' in dat pen all de time, havin' to stand for 'em comin' and starin' at yuh—de white-faced, skinny tarts and de boobs what marry 'em—makin' fun of yuh, laughin' at yuh, gittin' scared of yuh—damn 'em! [*He pounds on the rail with his fist. The* Gorilla *rattles the bars of his cage and snarls. All the other monkeys set up an angry chattering in the darkness.* Yank *goes on excitedly*] Sure! Dat's de way it hits me, too. On'y yuh're lucky, see? Yuh don't belong wit 'em and yuh know it. But me, I belong wit 'em—but I don't, see? Dey don't belong wit me, dat's what. Get me? Tinkin' is hard—— [*He passes one hand across his forehead with a painful gesture. The* Gorilla *growls impatiently.* Yank *goes on gropingly*] It's dis way, what I'm drivin' at. Youse can sit and dope dream in de past, green woods, de jungle, and de rest of it. Den yuh belong and dey don't. Den yuh kin laugh at 'em, see? Yuh're de champ of de woild. But me—I ain't got no past to tink in, nor nothin' dat's comin', on'y what's now—and dat don't belong. Sure, you're de best off! Yuh can't tink, can yuh? Yuh can't talk neider. But I kin make a bluff at talkin' and tinkin'—a'most git away wit it—a'most! —and dat's where de joker comes in. [*He laughs*] I ain't on oith and I ain't in heaven, get me? I'm in de middle tryin' to separate 'em, takin' all de woist punches from bot' of 'em. Maybe dat's what dey call hell, huh? But you, yuh're at de bottom. You belong! Sure! Yuh're de on'y one in de woild dat does, yuh lucky stiff! [*The* Gorilla *growls proudly*] And dat's why dey gotter put yuh in a cage, see? [*The* Gorilla *roars angrily*] Sure! Yuh get me. It beats it when you try to tink it or talk it—it's way down—deep—behind—you 'n' me we feel it. Sure! Bot' members of dis club! [*He laughs—then in a savage tone*] What de hell! T'hell wit it! A little action, dat's our meat! Dat belongs! Knock 'em down and keep bustin' 'em till dey croaks yuh wit a gat— wit steel! Sure! Are yuh game? Dey've looked at youse, ain't dey—in a cage? Wanter git even? Wanter wind up like a sport 'stead of croakin' slow in dere? [*The* Gorilla *roars an emphatic affirmative.* Yank *goes on with a sort of furious exaltation*] Sure! Yuh're reg'lar. Yuh'll stick to de finish! Me 'n' you, huh?—bot' members of this club! We'll put up one last star bout dat'll knock 'em offen deir seats! Dey'll have to make de cages stronger after we're trou! [*The* Gorilla *is straining at his bars, growling, hopping from one foot to the other.* Yank *takes a jimmy from under his coat and forces the lock on the cage door. He throws this open*] Pardon from de governor! Step out and shake hands! I'll take yuh for a walk down Fif' Avenoo. We'll knock 'em offen de oith and croak wit de band playin'. Come on, Brother. [*The* Gorilla *scrambles gingerly out of his cage. Goes to* Yank *and stands looking at him.* Yank *keeps his mocking tone—holds out his hand*] Shake—de secret grip of our order. [*Something, the tone of mockery, perhaps, suddenly enrages the* Animal. *With a spring he wraps his huge arms around* Yank *in a murderous hug. There is a crackling snap of crushed ribs—a gasping cry, still mocking, from* Yank] Hey, I didn't say kiss me! [*The* Gorilla *lets the crushed body slip to the floor; stands over it uncertainly, considering; then picks it up, throws it in the cage, shuts the door, and shuffles off menacingly into the darkness at left. A great uproar of frightened chattering and whimpering comes from the other cages. Then* Yank *moves, groaning, opening his eyes, and there is silence. He mutters painfully:*] Say—dey ougher match him—wit Zybszko. He got me, aw right. I'm trou. Even him didn't tink I belonged. [*Then, with sudden passionate despair*] Christ, where do I get off at? Where do I fit in? [*Checking himself as suddenly*] Aw, what de hell! No squawkin', see! No quittin', get me! Croak wit your boots on! [*He grabs hold of the bars of the cage and hauls himself painfully to his feet—looks around him bewilderedly—forces a mocking laugh*] In de cage, huh? [*In the strident tones of a circus barker*] Ladies and gents, step forward and take a slant at de one and only—[*His voice weakening*]—one and original—Hairy Ape from de wilds of——

[*He slips in a heap on the floor and dies. The monkeys set up a chattering, whimpering wail. And, perhaps, the Hairy Ape at last belongs*]

CURTAIN

Laurence Stallings · Maxwell Anderson

(1894–——) (1888–——)

Laurence Stallings will be remembered in the theatre chiefly for *What Price Glory?*, the best modern war play in the English language. The rest of his work in the field of playwriting was not notably successful. After writing *What Price Glory?* with Maxwell Anderson, in 1924, he collaborated with him on two historical romances. The earlier of these, *First Flight* (1925), was a mild treatment of an adventurous episode in Andrew Jackson's romantic life; the other, *The Buccaneer,* revived the career of the swashbuckling pirate Henry Morgan. Next, Stallings turned his attention to musical drama, contributing texts to the opera *Deep River* (1926) and to the musical melodrama *Rainbow* (1928). He also dramatized Hemingway's war novel *A Farewell to Arms,* which was, however, more successful on the screen than on the stage; and he wrote the libretto for a lavish musical spectacle, *Virginia,* in 1937. A tribute to the United States Marines, *The Streets Are Guarded* (1944) proved too mystical and confusing. It was only as the scenarist of two important Hollywood films, *The Big Parade* and *Old Ironsides,* that Stallings won prominence comparable to that which *What Price Glory?* earned for him.

Stallings was born in Macon, Georgia, and attended Wake Forest College in North Carolina. He became a reporter in Atlanta, and one of his assignments, an interview intended to promote enlistments to the United States Marines, in 1917, proved decisive in his career. After writing his piece on the Marines, he himself decided to join. When America came to the rescue of the Allies, he saw heavy action in France and earned a captaincy. He lost a leg in battle at Château-Thierry and spent many months in a military hospital. Returning to civilian life, he resumed his journalistic career but contemplated entering the teaching profession. Instead, he found a job with the *New York World*—first as second-string drama critic and then as book reviewer—and published a novel, *Plumes,* about his war experiences.

Maxwell Anderson was then an editorial writer on the *World,* and the two men decided to collaborate on plays. When the question of a subject was discussed, Stallings remembered his war experiences, and the result was *What Price Glory?* (1924). The First World War was still a topic of considerable interest to the public, and the play was only one of several trenchant reminiscences, among which were such notable novels as John Dos Passos' *Three Soldiers* and Stallings' own *Plumes.* But the popularity of the subject alone could not have assured *What Price Glory?* its extraordinary success.

By judiciously combining robust comedy with the muck and grime of modern warfare, Stallings and Anderson created pungent theatre. The comic matter was accentuated with colloquial speech that bristled with the "high-astounding" oaths of native warriors. The broadly conceived characters bore the stamp of reality; the soldiers were no Galahads fighting for glory, although they were courageous and had a rough-hewn nobility. Although the authors indulged in some romantic, masculine swagger and contented themselves with only random commentary, they drew an unflattering picture of military life such as had never before been seen on an American stage. Most playgoers agreed that Alexander Woollcott, reviewing the play in the *New York Evening Sun,* did not greatly exaggerate when he wrote that "in the tremendous irony of the comedy and in the sardonic laughter which fills its every scene, there is more said about the war than in all the editorials on the subject which, if placed end to end, would reach nowhere."

What Price Glory? became one of the most successful productions of the American stage. The performances of Louis Wolheim and William Boyd as rivals for the favors of the eternal woman and French camp follower Charmaine provided the breeziest entertainment the American public had yet seen; the language was the freest it had yet heard. The mood of cynicism was in vogue at the time, and playgoers were delighted by the satire on brass hats, "thirty-day-wonder lieutenants," and "the band of Gideons from Headquarters bringing more of that world safe for democracy slush." The cry of Lieutenant Moore, "What price glory now?" echoed through the period of postwar disillusionment. The play banished the romantic treatment of fighting that had prevailed in the American theatre after every previous war. Recalling the eventful Arthur Hopkins production on September 3, 1924, after a decade of playgoing, Burns Mantle wrote in the first edition of this *Treasury of the Theatre:* "One of the famous first nights in the theatre going history of New York is that on which *What Price Glory?* was introduced to a slightly startled audience. For the first time in theatre history a war play was presented with something resembling literal realism, and spoken with more regard for a reasonable verisimilitude than for the sensibilities of convention-protected auditors. The shock was a little severe, particularly to the ladies, but it gave way in the end to such cheering as the theatre does not often hear. That night a new blow was struck for freedom of speech in the drama."

Since war is hardly a novel experience for the human race, the subject has been familiar in the theatre ever since Aeschylus wrote *The Persians,* in 472 B.C., eight years after the battle of Salamis. In the opinion of many, the greatest antiwar play is still Euripides' *The Trojan Women,* written in 415 B.C., a year after the civilized Athenians destroyed a neutral island and exterminated the entire male population. These and other classic plays belong to a high tragic tradition that would have seemed remote to the American public. Even the example of Shakespeare, who brought comic, as well as antiheroic, matter into his chronicles but invested war with majesty, could not have satisfied the "debunkers" of the nineteen-twenties. At the same time, however, they could not count upon much public response to the unrelieved bitterness of the plays engendered by the First World War in Continental Europe, especially in Germany. America had not experienced war on its own soil, nor had it tasted defeat. The mood of the American playgoer favored a play of intermediate quality, neither majestic, on the one hand, nor notably embittered, on the other. Stallings and Anderson wrote *What Price Glory?* with an instinctive awareness of the mood of the nation that disavowed Woodrow Wilson's wartime ideals and regarded our embroilment in the European war as an error.

It was only a decade later that American antiwar plays became less "sophisticated" than impassioned, less cynical than rebellious; and this was because war was no longer viewed as something experienced in the past but as an imminent possibility. The altered mood was reflected in Irwin Shaw's *Bury the Dead* (1936), in which a number of soldiers killed in a new war refuse to be buried and are joined by living soldiers in their protest against a society that breeds both poverty and armed conflict. In the same year appeared Paul Green's *Johnny Johnson,* whose pacifist hero is confined to an asylum after an at-

tempt to make the nations lay down their arms, and Robert Sherwood's *Idiot's Delight,* which whipped up much comic complication but without losing sight of its bitter point that the only genuine internationalists in the world were the munitions manufacturers. When the protests went out of fashion with the start of the Second World War, they were replaced by rueful yet heroic plays— Robert Sherwood's *There Shall Be No Night* (1940) and Maxwell Anderson's *The Eve of St. Mark* (1942). Anderson, it is true, tried to combine heroic and antiheroic moods in his next play, *Storm Operation,* but without success. The first war play he wrote remained the best, and it probably would not have been written with such zest at any other time than the early 'twenties.

What Price Glory? has often been discussed as an "antiwar" play. It was so regarded by most of its admirers in the nineteen-twenties. It was criticized in the nineteen-thirties for lacking the qualities of an antiwar play—that is, for failing to present an analysis of war and for making the life of the fighting man seem too attractive. And, indeed, it would be too much to maintain that *What Price Glory?* is a profound study or protest. What the authors accomplished was something else: a picture of war which provides its deepest commentary not in any argument but in its matter-of-fact description of how soldiers live and think "on the spot." It showed, as Joseph Wood Krutch wrote in *The Nation,* "a way of life"; it indicated that actual warfare develops a civilization or "anti-civilization" of its own, "with a language, a philosophy, and a whole *kultur* as different from normal life as the *kultur* and philosophy of the Stone Age were different. . . ." It is as a naturalistic comedy with implicit commentary that *What Price Glory?* retains vitality.

BIBLIOGRAPHY: Anita Block, *The Changing World in Plays and Theatre* (pp. 306–310), 1939; Eleanor Flexner, *American Playwrights 1918–1938* (pp. 80–81), 1938; Joseph Wood Krutch, *The American Drama Since 1918* (pp. 30–43), 1939; Burns Mantle, *Contemporary American Playwrights* (pp. 41–43), 1938.

WHAT PRICE GLORY?

By Laurence Stallings and Maxwell Anderson

CHARACTERS

CORPORAL GOWDY	GUNNERY SERGEANT SOCKEL	A COLONEL
CORPORAL KIPER	PRIVATE MULCAHY	A CAPTAIN
CORPORAL LIPINSKY	SERGEANT FERGUSON	A LIEUTENANT
SERGEANT QUIRT	A BRIGADE RUNNER	ANOTHER LIEUTENANT
CAPTAIN FLAGG	MONSIEUR PETE DE LA COGNAC	A CHAPLAIN
CHARMAINE DE LA COGNAC	ANOTHER BRIGADE RUNNER	TOWN MAYOR
PRIVATE LEWISOHN	BRIGADIER GENERAL COKELEY	SPIKE
LIEUTENANT ALDRICH		PHARMACIST'S MATE
LIEUTENANT MOORE		LIEUTENANT CUNNINGHAM
LIEUTENANT SCHMIDT		LIEUTENANT LUNDSTROM

Headquarters Staff — (A COLONEL, A CAPTAIN, A LIEUTENANT, ANOTHER LIEUTENANT)

AUTHOR'S NOTE

What Price Glory? is a play of war as it is, not as it has been presented theatrically for thousands of years. The soldiers talk and act much as soldiers the world over. The speech of men under arms is universally and consistently interlarded with profanity. Oaths mean nothing to a soldier save a means to obtain emphasis. He uses them in place of more polite adjectives.

The authors of *What Price Glory?* have attempted to reproduce this mannerism along with other general atmosphere they believe to be true. In a theater where war has been lied about, romantically, effectively—and in a city where the war play has usually meant sugary dissimulation—*What Price Glory?* may seem bold. The audience is asked to bear with certain expletives which, under other circumstances, might be used for melodramatic effect, but herein are employed because the mood and truth of the play demand their employment.

ACT I. SCENE I.

A room in a French farmhouse—now a U. S. Marine company headquarters. A couple of desks covered with maps and papers. Several scattered chairs. Three runners sit talking and smoking, very much at ease. Lipinsky is seated at one end of bench, Kiper at the other; Gowdy is sitting on a stool near Kiper.

GOWDY: Well, where the hell did you come from?

KIPER: Who, me? I come from every place I've been to.

GOWDY: Yeah, well, where you been to?

KIPER: Me? I've been to China, Cuba, the Philippines, San Francisco, Buenos Aires, Cape Town, Madagascar . . . wait a minute—Indiana, San Domingo, Tripoli, and Blackwell's Island.

LIPINSKY: Ever going home?

KIPER: Who, me? I can't go anywhere without going home.

GOWDY: By the time this war's over you ought to be pretty near ready to marry and settle down.

KIPER: There ain't going to be any after-this-war. Anyway, I got married after the last two wars and when I get through paying my debt to Lafayette, I'm through settling down. I never have settled down in so many hick towns in my life.

LIPINSKY: What became of them two broads?

KIPER: My wives?

LIPINSKY: Yeah.

KIPER: The first one never knew my last name, and when I left town she was out of luck.

GOWDY: And the next one?

KIPER: Ain't I signing the payroll for her every month? A twenty-dollar allotment, and she gives it to a fireman in Buffalo. Here I am saving democracy, and he's turning in a twenty-bell alarm the first of every month.

GOWDY: That's a waste of cash, the way I look at it. It stands to reason when a girl gets rid of one bozo she's looking for another. Now why does the late unlamented finance that little game? There's no justice in that.

KIPER: Who said it was justice? It ain't justice; it's alimony.

GOWDY: Well, alimony's all right if you're well fixed; hell, a girl ought to have some fun! I don't want a girl to quit living just because she ain't living with me, but the guy that's getting his ought to pay for it. What do you want to pay alimony for?

KIPER: What did you want to come to France for? It's the same reason why I pay alimony. So's to see the rest of the girls. Join the Marines and see the girls—from a porthole.

GOWDY: God! I came to France because I had a brain-storm one day and signed on the dotted line.

LIPINSKY: There ain't but one man in the world that came to France to see the mam'selles, and that's the skipper. When there's women around the skipper's got trick eyes like a horsefly.

KIPER: The old man? Say, he can't look at a mam'selle without blushing. Compared to me he's an amateur. He don't know the difference between a

Hong-Kong honky-tonk and a Santo Domingo smoongy.

LIPINSKY: No, oh, no! I suppose women is an open book to you. You're damn well right—a code book.

KIPER: Yeah, you're damn well right. When I was in Turkey with that landing party the Sultan had to hunt through his harem with a flashlight to find a decent-looking girl, and when I left China the Yangtse was full of the bodies of virgins that drowned their beautiful selves because I was shipping over. And when I was in Spain the king of Spain put an ad in the paper offering a reward for the return of the queen.

GOWDY: What did you do?

KIPER: Took her back for the reward.

LIPINSKY: Huh! I notice you've got Cognac Pete's daughter, too.

KIPER: If I had the skipper's uniform and his Sam Browne belt, I could take that little wench away from him before you could say squads right! You ain't never seen it done. The skip's full of wind.

GOWDY: Anyway, Flagg's got Pete's kid sewed up —and she's as pretty a little frog as ever made a dish of frog's legs.

KIPER: Pete's kid! The poor little tart! What could she do? Ain't the skipper billeted there? God! I guess even Lippy could make a kid if she slept on the other side of a paper wall.

LIPINSKY: God! I don't know. Ain't it the truth some guys just naturally walk away with women? Damned if I could ever do it!

KIPER: Take one good long look at yourself and you'll see why. There ain't many as unfortunate as you are. I guess there ain't anybody handicapped with features like them there.

LIPINSKY: Sometimes I think it's features, and sometimes I think it's luck. Once I spent three hundred dollars on a dame at Asbury Park in two days, and she keeping her damn chum with her all the time. Finally I got the extra one so drunk she couldn't tell her own name, and I ditched her. Then this broad I was trying to make insisted on riding on the merry-go-round. . . . God! the merry-go-round. Nothing else would satisfy her. She'd rung ducks till it rained ducks. She'd shot up more powder in shooting galleries than's been shot in this war, and she wanted to ride on the merry-go-round! So we got on the merry-go-round, and I threw her into a chariot and I piled on a horse. She hollers, "Whoopee, whoopee, let's do it again!" Jeez, I had spent three hundred bucks and I said, "Now, honey, let's not ride any more. Come on, let's do what you promised." She said she would after one more turn on the merry-go-round. So I, like a bloody fool, tries to save twenty cents by catching a brass ring. Son-of-a-bitch! I fall off and break my leg!

KIPER: My God!

LIPINSKY: Yes, sir. I broke my leg.

GOWDY: You certainly have had your share of tough luck.

LIPINSKY: So when the captain walks off with the top soldier's girl I say to myself, maybe there's luck in it. Maybe the breaks favored him. They never did favor me.

GOWDY: Any skipper can walk off with any top soldier's girl in my opinion. Say, maybe that's the lowdown on why the sergeant left.

KIPER: Naw—he was too damn good. Regimental took him. We'll probably get a lousy replacement. Probably get a corporal with ten years' experience chasing prisoners at Portsmouth. Soon's the new sergeant gets here the skip's going on ten days' leave.

LIPINSKY: Yeah? Where?

KIPER: Paris.

LIPINSKY: You going with him?

KIPER: Yep.

LIPINSKY: Some guys have all the luck.

[*The door opens. Sergeant Quirt, the very picture of an old-timer, enters and looks quickly around. All rise*]

QUIRT: L Company?

KIPER: Company Headquarters.

QUIRT: Where's the company commander?

KIPER: Just stepped down the street. Will be back soon.

QUIRT: He's going on leave?

KIPER: Right.

QUIRT: What's his name?

KIPER: Captain Flagg.

QUIRT: Whew!

KIPER: You know him?

QUIRT: Do you?

KIPER: Yes, sir!

QUIRT: Company Headquarters. Looks like a God-damn reception room to me.

KIPER: We aim to please.

QUIRT: Yeah, to please yourself. Well, listen, I'm the new top soldier here. Who's the company clerk?

LIPINSKY: I am, sir.

QUIRT: Clear this jam out of here and let's have a look at what you're doing.

LIPINSKY: Will you get the hell out? And don't come back till you're sent for.

[*Kiper and Gowdy go out*]

QUIRT: I've been ten kilometers west of you. Took the wrong turn.

LIPINSKY: Here's the map. That's the only road there is, and we can't use it. The damn thing is one long shell-hole from last May.

QUIRT: Jeez!

LIPINSKY: That's what they all say.

QUIRT: Don't you ever clean these galleys?

LIPINSKY: We don't do anything else.

QUIRT: You haven't got a police sergeant, I suppose?

LIPINSKY: We've got an acting corporal. Old Hennessey was bumped off last time up.

QUIRT: Spud Hennessey?

LIPINSKY: That's the soldier.

QUIRT: Tough for Spud to go. A grand soldier. Too damn finicky, though.

LIPINSKY: We've gone to hell for chow since he left.

QUIRT: That's queer. I never knew Flagg to let his men go to hell.

LIPINSKY: Not his fault. These cooks are no good. Hennessey was acting mess sergeant, too.

QUIRT: That's like old times.

LIPINSKY: Yeah?

QUIRT: Say, if the skipper's going ashore they'd better get him out of here before he gets too drunk to navigate. I've seen him shove off with a liberty party and spend a forty-eight-hour leave sleeping it off on the beach.

LIPINSKY: It's the same skip, all right. You know him.

QUIRT: I'll say I do . . . I think I'll look him up. Where's he likely to be?

LIPINSKY: Damned if I know. He might be at Pete's place. Anybody can tell you where that is— just this side of the river.

QUIRT: All right. I'll find it.

[*Goes out briskly. After he has gone* Lipinsky *goes to the door and whistles.* Kiper *and* Gowdy *come in*]

LIPINSKY: Did you take a slant at the amphibian?

GOWDY: Yeah.

KIPER: What of it?

LIPINSKY: He's our new papa.

KIPER: So he says.

LIPINSKY: He's soldiered with the skipper before. Says he never saw the chief sober.

KIPER: Is he hard-boiled?

LIPINSKY: There's only one place in the world they boil them as hard as that, and that's the Tropic of Cancer.

KIPER: What does he know?

LIPINSKY: This God-damn army's going to run right from now on or get off on its ear.

GOWDY: He must have used some language on you?

LIPINSKY: Not a word, and I'm not going to give him a chance, either.

KIPER: Scared, huh?

LIPINSKY: You meet a top with two glass eyes, a slit across his face for a mouth and a piece out of his ear, and you might just as well heave out and lash up. That bird could curse the hide off a whole Senegalese regiment.

[Captain Flagg *enters and comes to chair above table. He is a fine, magnificently endowed man*]

FLAGG: 'Tenshun! [*Reading report which he picks up from table*] Where's that first sergeant?

KIPER: Went out looking for you, sir.

FLAGG: Scatter and find him, a couple of you. [Lipinsky, Gowdy, *and* Kiper *start out*] Stay here, Kiper. [Kiper *comes back*] Damn him, why couldn't he sit still? [Lipinsky *and* Gowdy *go out*] What's he like?

KIPER: Tough.

FLAGG: Yeah? I hope he damn well hangs the whole damn company up by the thumbs. About time we had a little discipline around here.

KIPER: Yes, sir.

FLAGG: "Yes, sir!" "Yes, sir!" Shut your trap, will you?

KIPER: Oh, yes, sir.

FLAGG: Go to hell! Everything packed?

KIPER: Absolutely.

FLAGG: Bike working? Side-care trimmed?

KIPER: Tuned it up this morning.

FLAGG: Well, we're going ashore as soon as I see the new top soldier, you understand? And we don't stop for anything smaller than shell-holes!

KIPER: Ay, ay, sir!

FLAGG: Go sit down! Go read a book! You make me nervous. [Kiper *sits*. Charmaine *slips in. She is a drab.* Flagg, *who is busy at the desk, does not see her at first. He looks up impatiently*] Well, hello! Hello! What are you doing here? You better run along back to your papa. Listen, *mon amie,* you better beat it back to *le père,* understand?

CHARMAINE: Why?

[*She comes nearer*]

FLAGG: Well, I'm busy.

CHARMAINE: You are going away.

FLAGG: So that's it. Kiper, did you tell the kid I was going away?

KIPER: No, sir, she saw me with your *musette* bag.

CHARMAINE: The sergeant went away. He is not coming back. Now you go away. You are not coming back.

FLAGG: As far as the sergeant's concerned, you're quite right, dearie; but as far as I'm concerned, you're dead wrong. The sergeant isn't coming back. We have a new sergeant, see? But I am coming back.

CHARMAINE: *Oui?*

FLAGG: *Oui, oui, oui!*

CHARMAINE: No. You are such a lovely liar. You don't want to make me cry. So you lie a little— *n'est-ce pas?*

FLAGG: [*Takes her by shoulders*] I'm not lying, Charmaine. I don't know how I can prove it to you, but I'm telling the solemn truth. [*A knock on the door*] See who that is, and keep him out, whoever it is.

KIPER: [*Opens the door, goes out, and returns*] It's Lewisohn, third platoon replacement. He wants permission to speak with you, sir.

FLAGG: What about?

KIPER: Lost something, sir.

FLAGG: Let him in. [Lewisohn *enters. He is a pale little boy*] Let's have it quick, soldier.

LEWISOHN: [*Saluting*] Beg pardon, sir.

[*Very much scared*]

FLAGG: What do you want?

LEWISOHN: The truth is, sir, I've lost my identification tag.

FLAGG: What? What? Lost what?

LEWISOHN: My identification tag.

FLAGG: Well, I thought I'd been around a good deal, and I've had 'em ask me to show 'em where they live and button up their pants for them and put on their little night-drawers, but I'm a son-of-a-gun if this isn't the first time anybody has ever asked me to help him find his identification tag!

LEWISOHN: Sorry, sir. I—I thought it was—I. . . .

FLAGG: What did you think?

LEWISOHN: I thought it was important, sir.

FLAGG: And what, may I ask, made you think it was important?

LEWISOHN: In case I was—ah—hit, sir. They wouldn't know who I was. I thought maybe it would matter.

FLAGG: Matter? To whom?

LEWISOHN: Well—to keep the records—or to my folks.

FLAGG: Listen, boy, why did you ever leave your home and come over here?

LEWISOHN: Why, to fight, sir.

FLAGG: Yeah. Well, you'll get a chance, don't you worry, and for God's sake learn to act like a man. Never mind your identification tag. If you want to know what your name is look in your hat.

LEWISOHN: Yes, sir.

FLAGG: By the way, what is your name?

LEWISOHN: Louis Lewisohn.

FLAGG: [To Kiper] Make a note of that, Kiper. [Kiper makes a note in the book he carries in his pocket] Now, anything else? Hope you got a good room with a view and running water and everything.

LEWISOHN: No, sir.

[Swallowing a lump in his throat]

FLAGG: No? I'm surprised. Well, go on outside and swear at me a while. It'll do you good, and that's what I'm here for. I'm here to keep you in hot water till you're hard-boiled. See? You can go.

LEWISOHN: Yes, sir.

[He salutes and goes]

FLAGG: Make a note of that, Kiper, and get him a new tag if they have to build a new factory in Hoboken to turn it out. The God-forsaken fool's dying of grief away from mother. Got it?

KIPER: Yes, Captain Flagg.

FLAGG: Then step outside and guard the door a minute. [Kiper salutes and goes out, closing the door carefully. Flagg then turns to Charmaine] Now, you little she-woman, what do you want?

CHARMAINE: You are going away.

FLAGG: Damn it, I'm not going away. I'm going to Paris—coming back in eight days. Eight days in Paris, see, then I come back.

CHARMAINE: The sergeant did not come back.

FLAGG: My God, child, get this! The sergeant is not coming back. I am coming back. We have a new sergeant, see?

CHARMAINE: Oui?

FLAGG: Oui, oui.

CHARMAINE: No. I think the captain does not love me, not any more?

FLAGG: Girlie, I love you fit to kill. I love you no end, same as always. Come here. [She puts her arms around his neck. Flagg takes her in his arms] You're as sweet as Burgundy, and you've got a kick like triple sec. Sure I love you. Everybody loves you. I love you, dearie girl, but I don't trust you.

CHARMAINE: You take me to Paris? Yes? Take me to Paris?

FLAGG: No. I guess not.

CHARMAINE: But I'm so unhappy when you go away.

FLAGG: Yes, you are! I wish you were. Why, you little geisha [Chucking her under the chin], if I didn't wear captain's stripes you wouldn't know me from the K.P.'s.

CHARMAINE: No, dear Captain Flagg. [Her arms on his shoulders. She runs a hand through his hair] It is true, I shall be so lonesome. I shall be all alone at the inn, crying every day to break your heart.

FLAGG: You'll be dancing all night and flirting all day with the Y.M.C.A. boys, you mean. Ain't it so?

CHARMAINE: Oui. But you could take me. I can't be good—unless you take me. I want to be good for you. We could have so good time—in Paris.

FLAGG: No, I can't take you. But listen. [Takes hold of her shoulders] While I'm gone you wait for me. Remember, you're my girl, see? Just my girl, and you wait for me, see?

CHARMAINE: Oui, I will.

FLAGG: And listen to this. [Putting her away] If I find out you've been running with someone else, I'll break you in two, see? [He makes the motion of breaking something] Now, will you be good while I'm gone?

CHARMAINE: [Coming into his arms] Oui, monsieur.

FLAGG: That's better. You know what I mean?

CHARMAINE: Oui.

FLAGG: That's right, little kitten, purr. . . . And remember, I don't trust you any further than I can see you. Now run along. [Flagg turns to table, but Charmaine follows him]

CHARMAINE: But you will take me to Paris?

FLAGG: [Seating himself on edge of table, he beckons her with his finger and takes her on his knee, between his legs] You ever been to Paris?

CHARMAINE: Non . . .

FLAGG: Well, there's a river in Paris.

CHARMAINE: La Seine.

FLAGG: Yeah, the Seine. That's where they drown little girls like you. Every time the police catch a little girl in Paris, they drown her in the Seine. You can't go there. They'd drown you.

CHARMAINE: It is not true.

FLAGG: It is true. I'll tell you another thing. There's nothing to eat in Paris, no food but horses; no wine, only water. No young girls, only old women. Some of the girls they drown in the Seine; some they make into sausages for the generals. Paris is full of generals that won't eat anything but young girls. You can't go to Paris.

CHARMAINE: You are full of lovely lies. Oh, it is not true.

FLAGG: Uh, you don't know Paris.

CHARMAINE: Oh, but I know these captains and sergeants! They do not ever put anything, what you say, past me. But, oh, I love you for a lovely liar! [*Embraces him*] And I will be good; I will, *vraiment!*

FLAGG: That's a good girl. Now you go back to Papa Pete's. Stay home nights. Wait for Captain Flagg. Kiss me good-bye. [*She kisses him*] Now run along. [*She goes*] Kiper!

KIPER: [*Coming in*] Yes, sir.

FLAGG: Have you found that sergeant yet?

KIPER: He's coming with Lipinsky, sir.

FLAGG: Tell him to damn well get a wiggle on.

KIPER: [*To* Quirt, *outside*] He's waiting for you, sir.

[Lipinsky *enters with* Quirt]

QUIRT: [*Saluting*] Captain Flagg?

FLAGG: [*Returns salute and remains seated, not even glancing at* Quirt] Hello, Sergeant. Where've you been all day?

QUIRT: Ten kilometers west by mistake.

FLAGG: Do you know our lay-out?

QUIRT: I've got a general idea.

FLAGG: What kind of a hole were you in over there?

QUIRT: Much the same as yours, only we had a road.

FLAGG: Do you think you can handle this company? It's a rough crowd of old men and little baa-lamb recruits.

[*He still does not look up*]

QUIRT: It's an army, ain't it? Sure.

FLAGG: I damn well hope you can. We're in a devilish sector here, and it's going to be worse when we move up again. We just hold half a town; the Heinies hold the other half. It rains grenades most of the time. About half our men are green replacements. They damned near ruined us in that last tour of duty. You'll have to whip some of 'em into shape before we go up. Close order drill is best.

QUIRT: Half of 'em raw?

FLAGG: Over half.

QUIRT: Well, I've seen worse.

FLAGG: Now, I'm going on leave, you see. Eight days. While I'm gone you feed 'em up and give 'em hell. Teach 'em where they are. Make 'em so bad they'll eat steel rather than get another dressing from you. Make 'em hard, but don't break 'em. Give 'em eats and about eight hours of drill and guns a day. They're mostly Bible Class boys, and God knows most of 'em haven't got long to live.

QUIRT: [*Takes step toward table*] Cut the comedy, Captain. You must know me.

FLAGG: [*Rising, looks at* Quirt *for the first time*]

Yeah? I'm a cuckoo if it ain't the old Hoppergrass!

QUIRT: Thought you didn't know me. Well, I'm glad to meet you again, Captain Flagg.

FLAGG: Kiper——

KIPER: Yes, sir.

FLAGG: Step out and tell all platoon commanders to report here at once.

KIPER: Ay, ay, sir.

[*Exits*]

FLAGG: Well, Quirt, I'm glad to see you, because if there was ever a good soldier needed I need one here, and you're as good as there is; but I'm damned if I take any particular joy in meeting you again. You've been poison to me everywhere I've served with you.

QUIRT: [*At right of table*] Same to you, I'm sure, and many of 'em. Personally I'd as soon meet a skunk in a dugout, and officially I don't think much of your crew. I broke you the first time in China, and you broke me in Cuba. You're in a position to break me now, and if you didn't need me worse than the wildcat needed what he didn't have, you'd break me again.

FLAGG: I'd see you in hell before I'd break you, and you know it. I'll give you exactly what you deserve, and as long as you're straight we'll get along, always providing we don't have to shake hands. If that's understood, why, take hold. The company's yours.

QUIRT: Well, before I take hold, let me get one more remark in the record. I wish to God I could jump your damn gang. I've heard of it all along the line. You've got a rabble, and I know it. I saw it coming into Is-sur-Tille once when you didn't see me. A shambling bunch of hams that wouldn't salute anything under a general.

FLAGG: All right, and what's my outfit's rating at regimental?

QUIRT: Oh, I got to hand it to you. You can hypnotize 'em. They'd start out to cut their way to Berlin if you gave the word. But, my God, they ain't much to look at, Captain Flagg.

FLAGG: Well, teach 'em to salute if it'll make you feel any happier, Hoppergrass. And before the platoon commanders get here, there's one thing I'd like to ask you. What did you do with the little girl?

QUIRT: What little girl?

FLAGG: You damn well know what little girl.

QUIRT: It's a small world, Captain Flagg, but the number of soldiers' sluts is numerous.

FLAGG: I was a corporal under you in China. You broke me to get her.

QUIRT: You were a damn fool. You'd have married her if it hadn't been for me, and be running a laundry now with the seat of your pants hanging down between your knees.

FLAGG: What happened to her?

QUIRT: What happened to the battleship *Maine*?

FLAGG: My God. . . .

QUIRT: I broke you in China. I admit I broke

you for that little Chink. And when I served under you in Cuba you got even. That's why I'm still a sergeant. [*A knock at the door from* Kiper] Let it go at that.

FLAGG: Kiper?

KIPER: [*Outside*] Ay, ay, sir!

FLAGG: Bring 'em in. [Kiper *opens the door and follows into the room* Lieutenants Aldrich, Moore, and Schmidt, *and Gunnery Sergeant Sockel. They salute. They line up*] Gentlemen, this is First Sergeant Quirt, who is in charge. This is Lieutenant Aldrich; this is Lieutenant Moore, and this is Lieutenant Schmidt, and you'll remember Sockel from Cuba. He's commanding the fourth platoon.

QUIRT: [*Turns to* Sockel] Hello, Joe. How's tricks?

SOCKEL: Pretty good. How's yourself?

[*They smile broadly, two old-timers among green lieutenants*]

QUIRT: Ticking like a clock.

FLAGG: Aldrich, you're senior here, aren't you?

ALDRICH: Yes, sir. Two days ahead of the others.

FLAGG: You'll be in command here. Ask Quirt for any advice you need. I'll be back Wednesday week. . . . Now, men, Sergeant Quirt here is one of the best God-damn soldiers that ever destroyed a memorandum receipt. I've soldiered with him around the world, and there isn't a finer, cleaner, smarter Marine afloat than Quirt—when he's sober. As long as he's sober, he'll run this outfit—whether I'm here or absent; but Quirt loves the bottle; and when he's drunk he's the lousiest, filthiest bum that ever wore a uniform. When drunk, he's worse than I am, and you know damn well I don't allow anybody to get as bad as that. If he tanks up I'll break him. I've broken him once, and he knows I'll do it again. The first raw crack he makes will find him drilling in the rear rank of Sockel's platoon, drilling like a tramp with a broom for a rifle. Get that, Aldrich; the first time you find him down in the square with a face in the dirt in front of all these young nipple-nursers, you lock him up and keep him locked up till I return.

ALDRICH: Yes, sir.

FLAGG: Give him his head, and let him have anything he wants, and don't forget he's forgotten more about being a soldier than any of you college boys will ever know. But if you're wise you won't play cards with him, and before you lend him any money you'd better kiss it a last long farewell. That's all. Kiper, have you got the waterproofs in that side-car?

KIPER: Ay, ay, sir.

FLAGG: Give her a spin, and we'll shove off.

[*Picks up cap and stick from table and goes out, followed by all save* Quirt. *Off stage, the motorcycle clatters. The* Lieutenants *shout farewell.* Quirt *goes up to right window, looks out, and then sits at table, takes out dice, and practices a few turns. He holds the dice up to his eyes and then spins.* Quirt *whistles "Pretty Baby"*]

QUIRT: Seven, baby. [*He smiles with satisfaction*]

Look at those acrobats act. You got to treat the old man right, now. [*There is a light tap on the door to left.* Quirt *puts dice in pocket and looks at map*] Come in.

[Charmaine *enters*]

CHARMAINE: *Le capitaine—il est parti?*

QUIRT: Just left. Don't cry, little one.

CHARMAINE: *Le nouveau sergeant. N'est-ce pas?*

QUIRT: *N'est-ce pas* is right.

CHARMAINE: I wanted to see the captain.

QUIRT: Just too late, sorry to say. [*Looks at her for first time*] You one piecie captain's fella boy? You captain's fella?

CHARMAINE: *Le capitaine? Mais non!*

QUIRT: I'll bet it's *mais mon.* Say, ain't you Cognac Pete's daughter?

CHARMAINE: *Oui.* You stay at Pete's?

QUIRT: Sure. [*Pause*] *Et vous?*

CHARMAINE: *C'est mon père.*

QUIRT: Uh-huh. I thought so. [*Rises; crosses to her*] Well, baby, you better stick to me, and you'll have another papa.

[*A terrific commotion begins outside. A vociferous Irish voice is heard shouting over and over again, "I'll get that lousy German son-of-a-bitch, I'll get the German bastard," while* Lipinsky *and* Gowdy *yell, "Cut it out, you loafer. Dry up, dry up or you'll get yours."* Lipinsky *opens the door.* Charmaine *steps back. The shouting is audible only when door is open*]

LIPINSKY: Sergeant, there's a drunken Mick named Mulcahy raising hell outside. Can't do a thing with him. Got blood in his eyes for a guy from Cincinnati.

QUIRT: [*Sternly, out of the corner of his mouth, not looking at him*] Tell him to pipe down. [Lipinsky *goes out. Door closes; shouting stops.* Charmaine *goes toward door*] Better not go out there now, honey. Some rough language is taking place out there.

[Lipinsky *re-enters. Shouting is started again*]

LIPINSKY: Sergeant, the Mick's sitting on Gowdy, and I can't pull him off.

QUIRT: [*Quietly, as before*] Tell him to pipe down. [Lipinsky *goes out. Shouting stops.* Quirt *crosses to* Charmaine] You going to promenade *avec moi* tonight? Down by the canal? Under the lime trees?

CHARMAINE: No. [*She is trembling*]

QUIRT: No? Captain's own private darling, huh? Say, you're a damned pretty frog. For a frog, I don't know as I ever saw a prettier.

[*The hullabaloo redoubles outside.* Lipinsky *comes in again*]

LIPINSKY: Shall we lock him up, Sergeant?

QUIRT: Drag him in.

[Lipinsky *and* Gowdy *drag in a huge, red-faced Irishman and stand him groggily on his feet below* Quirt]

MULCAHY: That damn Nussbaum from Cincinnati is a German spy, and I'll have his guts out of him before I'm through.

QUIRT: [*Quietly*] Mulcahy, pipe down.

MULCAHY: I tell you that Nussbaum is a German spy! I'll get the lousy German and every German out of Cincinnati. . . .

[*The* Sergeant *plants one squarely on* Mulcahy's *jaw. He goes down like a log*]

QUIRT: [*Still out of the corner of his mouth*] Drag him out.

[Lipinsky *and* Gowdy *take him by arms, turn him around, and drag him out.* Quirt, *rubbing his knuckles, crosses back of table to* Charmaine, *who is smiling at her wonderful hero with the powerful punch*]

QUIRT: Why, hello, Pittsburgh, you love me?

[*They embrace and hold a long kiss*]

CURTAIN

SCENE II.

Late afternoon, eight days later. The scene is unchanged. Lipinsky *is lying along bench, smoking a cigarette and trying to sleep at the same time.* Kiper *enters, singing at the top of his voice.* Lipinsky's *cap is down over his eyes. Police Sergeant* Ferguson *is at table toward back, working over papers; he is smoking a pipe.*

KIPER: "Mademoiselle from Armentiere, parlez-vous?
Mademoiselle from Armentiere, parlez vous?
Mademoiselle from Armentiere——"
Hullo, hullo—Jeezus.

[*Puts musette bags in corner*]

LIPINSKY: Knock off that chat.

[*On bench; doesn't move*]

KIPER: Say, are you running this God-damn army?

LIPINSKY: You're damn well right, I'm running this army.

KIPER: Well, you had better God-damn well snap out of it. You're relieved.

LIPINSKY: [*Sitting up*] Skipper come back?

KIPER: Almost. He's at the Last Chance.

LIPINSKY: Still soaked?

KIPER: He ain't soaked. He's just the drunkest bum you ever saw in your life.

LIPINSKY: Trying to whip the world?

KIPER: Naw, just quiet drunk. Looks out of those eyes of his like two red holes in the snow.

LIPINSKY: How's Paris?

KIPER: Never got that far. Washed ashore at Bar-le-Duc.

LIPINSKY: Yeah? Good time?

KIPER: Pretty good the first day.

LIPINSKY: What'd you do the rest?

KIPER: You see, it was this way. The skip and me was promenading, and he was swinging that damn little Pekin swagger-stick of his when up comes an M.P. "Sorry, sir," says the M.P. "Corps commander's regulations, sir, no swagger-sticks." The skip says, "Well, and who, may I ask, is the corps commander? Tell him he can take his lousy army and sell it for cheese." "Sorry, sir," says the M.P. "Corps commander's regulations, sir, and I'll have to take that stick away from you." "All right," says the skip, whirling the stick around his head, "pitch in, soldier, pitch in!"

LIPINSKY: Did he take it away?

KIPER: Aw, take it away! Listen to the poor nut. I spent the next six days of my leave detained as a material witness for attempted manslaughter.

LIPINSKY: I guess the skip didn't draw much?

KIPER: Draw hell! Didn't I swear this yellow-bellied M.P. came up and knocked him into the road?

LIPINSKY: Yeah?

KIPER: And the court looks at this M.P. and says, "Right face! Take him away and give him ten days, bread and water."

LIPINSKY: Serve him right, the Boy Scout! They ought to take away those guys' whistles before they blow themselves to death. And speaking of whistles, this new top of ours don't do nothing else at all besides blow a whistle. It's been one bloody formation after another ever since you left.

KIPER: Is that the kind of hombre he is?

LIPINSKY: He's a sea-going son-of-a-bitch. He ain't sit down since he was here. He's got the first platoon down in the village now taking up the dirt from the courtyard with teaspoons. You can't get in the chow line until you catch twenty horseflies. He seen Cooper pulling a fag at reveille this morning. What's Cooper doing now? Boy, following the ponies, following the ponies. *He's* out collecting apples.

KIPER: Well, the skip will make him cut that stuff. Me and the skip ain't going to see the little boys bullied.

LIPINSKY: You and the skip, yeah. But say, the skip and this top soldier are going to tangle pant-legs over another little matter before they have been together one day.

KIPER: What t'hell!

LIPINSKY: This horny pelican is going aboard the skip's old hooker every night.

KIPER: Down at Cognac Pete's house?

LIPINSKY: Parking his dogs in Pete's kitchen every night with that little black-eyed frog sitting in his lap lighting his pipe.

KIPER: If the skip finds that out there'll be a noise like you'd throw a tomcat in a dog-pound.

[*Enter Sergeant Quirt*]

QUIRT: [*To Kiper*] Where's Captain Flagg?

KIPER: Last Chance.

QUIRT: What the hell do you mean, coming in

here without him? What do you think you're paid for?

KIPER: I tried to argue with him, Sergeant, and he picked me up and threw me out the window. Lucky for me it was open.

QUIRT: Go get him. Don't argue. Get him. Take Lippy along.

[Lipinsky *and* Kiper *start, hesitate, and talk.* Quirt *starts toward chair above table.* Lieutenant Aldrich *enters*]

ALDRICH: Heard the skipper was aboard.

QUIRT: [*Turning to* Aldrich] Grounded on the last bar.

ALDRICH: Yeah?

QUIRT: [*To* Kiper *and* Lipinsky, *who hurry off*] Cast off, will you? Travel! Hit the deck! [*To* Aldrich] Sending out a salvage party. He's full to the scuppers.

ALDRICH: All I hope is he comes in mild and goes to sleep. He's got too damn much talent for raising hell to suit me.

QUIRT: You ought to see him in China. Straight as a mast, muscled like a gorilla, Christian as hell. Good deal of liquor has flowed under his belt since then.

ALDRICH: Expect any trouble?

QUIRT: What do you mean?

ALDRICH: This here now little wild woman.

QUIRT: I don't know what's your game.

ALDRICH: Oh, all right! Just the same, you'd be a damn sight wiser to lay off, in my opinion.

QUIRT: Lay off what?

ALDRICH: Charmaine.

QUIRT: [*Turning to* Aldrich] Are you thinking of making this a three-handed game?

ALDRICH: I am not.

QUIRT: Because if you are, all I got to say is, help yourself to whatever you can get. It's love in a manner of speaking, and it's certainly war. Everything dirty goes.

ALDRICH: Suit yourself. You've known him longer than I have.

QUIRT: He's got a grudge against me, I don't mind telling you. And I ain't wasting any ardent affection on him. If it hadn't been for him, I'd had a company of my own. I didn't know she was his meat when I first saw her. But when I found out, d'you think I'd apologize and back out the door out of deference to him? I says, Kippy-dope, you're mine!

ALDRICH: Yeah—but do you know what I heard at mess to-day?

QUIRT: Nope.

ALDRICH: Well, now listen. I didn't intend to mix into this unless it was necessary, but Schmidt got it straight yesterday that old Cognac Pete was going to prosecute some soldier or other for corrupting Charmaine's morals.

QUIRT: Charmaine's what? Jeez, that's good!

ALDRICH: Maybe so. Just the same, he's got a case.

QUIRT: He has not.

ALDRICH: No? Suppose he gets you before a court martial? It's a hanging matter if he wants to push it. You know the regulations.

QUIRT: You mean he's after me?

ALDRICH: I don't know who he's after. You—or Flagg. Has Cognac anything on you?

QUIRT: Well, they might hang me once as a sort of lesson to me.

[*Motorcycle clatters outside*]

ALDRICH: Well, there you are. Suppose he takes it to headquarters. Where's Quirt then? Sitting pretty?

QUIRT: Well, I just resign all rights and interests in the mam'selle and avoid possible complications.

ALDRICH: Fine. There's Kiper already. If Flagg's with him, for God's sake use a little diplomacy.

[*Outside,* Flagg *in drunken voice says, "Get out of my way, Kiper." Noise of* Kiper *being pushed*]

QUIRT: Diplomacy, with that?

[Flagg *enters, coat in hand and hair mussed. He still carries stick.* Lipinsky *and* Kiper *follow. All stand at attention until the* Captain *is seated*]

ALDRICH: [*Saluting*] How are you, Captain Flagg?

FLAGG: I'm a wreck, that's what I am! I'm an epoch-making disaster! You see before you, Mr. Aldrich, one of the seven great calamities of the world!

QUIRT: Hope you had a pleasant leave, sir.

FLAGG: Well, I didn't. Held for carrying a stick. Picked up the second day by one of Pershing's Sunday-school teachers. By God, he must think he's running a day nursery! . . . What's happened?

QUIRT: Not a thing.

FLAGG: Boys in shape?

QUIRT: They'll do. Three more days, and I'd risk them on the line.

FLAGG: Try and get three days. If we aren't digging in somewhere before then, I'll pay the Russian national debt out of my salary. How much do you think I spent in Bar-le-Duc?

QUIRT: How much did you have?

FLAGG: Eight hundred francs, and I got a chance to get rid of thirty. Here's the whole roll. Does anybody want it? Just my luck to have to move in again with seven hundred and seventy francs on me and get bumped off. [*A knock at the door by* Brigade Runner] Come in.

[*A* Brigade Runner *enters*]

THE RUNNER: Captain Flagg?

FLAGG: Right here.

THE RUNNER: From Captain Simpson, sir. He wanted you to know the "G One" crowd is on the way over.

FLAGG: Tell him I'm much obliged. Anything else?

THE RUNNER: That's all. How do I get to the Twelfth?

FLAGG: Show him, Kiper. [Kiper *and the* Runner

salute and go out. Flagg *starts to button his coat*]
Damn headquarters! It's some more of that world-
safe-for-democracy slush! Every time they come
around here I've got to ask myself is this an army
or is it a stinking theosophical society for ethical
culture and the Bible-backing uplift! I don't want
that band of Gideons from headquarters. Now you
watch that door. Watch it! In ten minutes we're
going to have another of these round-headed gentlemen of the old school here giving us a prepared
lecture on what we're fighting the war for and how
we're to do it—one of these bill-poster chocolate
soldiers with decorations running clear around to his
backbone and a thrilling speech on army morale and
the last drop of fighting blood that puts your drive
over to glorious victory! . . . The side-whiskered
butter-eaters! I'd like to rub their noses in a few of
the latrines I've slept in, keeping up army morale and
losing men because some screaming fool back in the
New Jersey sector thinks he's playing with paper
dolls. [*A knock*] Well, come in, come in. [Lieutenant
Moore *enters*] Hello.

MOORE: How are you, Captain Flagg? Hope you
liked Bar-le-Duc?

FLAGG: Ever been there?

MOORE: Once.

FLAGG: Ever put in much time in the redecorated
chicken stable where they detain the A.W.O.L.'s?

MOORE: Afraid I never saw it, sir.

FLAGG: Well, you haven't missed a great deal.
They whitewashed the damn shanty right over the
hen manure. Phew! I can smell it yet. If I stayed
there another day I'd have laid an egg.

MOORE: Tough luck! But what I really wanted to
say, sir, was there's an old fellow outside here who
wants to see you about his daughter. He seems to
think somebody's taken advantage of her.

FLAGG: Somebody in this outfit?

MOORE: Yes, sir.

FLAGG: Took advantage of the girl, huh?

MOORE: That's what he says.

FLAGG: He means she took advantage of her opportunities and now he's taking advantage of his.
What's the old boy's name?

MOORE: Can't quite make it out, but it seems to
be Pete something or other. Are there any Petes in
France? Sounded like Cognac Pete.

FLAGG: Yeah?

MOORE: Sounded like it.

FLAGG: [*Rising, perturbed*] Well, wait a minute.
Cognac Pete's, huh? Is the girl with him?

MOORE: No.

FLAGG: Hell!

QUIRT: Think fast, Captain. Think fast.

FLAGG: Quirt, do you know anything about this?

QUIRT: [*Starting to leave*] Not a thing.

FLAGG: You leaving us?

QUIRT: [*Unembarrassed*] A few orders to make
out, sir. [*He grins*] Can't very well work here, you
see.

FLAGG: I'm damned if I see. Sit down and spill
your ink. And if you've put a game on me, you
crawling crab. . . .

QUIRT: Me? What have I got to do with it? Think
fast, Captain, think fast.

FLAGG: Damn it, send him in, and we'll see.
[Moore *goes out*] Hell!

QUIRT: [*Laughing*] Think fast, Captain. Don't forget to think fast.

FLAGG: You sit where you are, you hyena; and
laugh, damn you, laugh. [*Enter* Cognac Pete, *an
ancient nut-brown Frenchman, very polite and humble, followed by* Moore *and* Kiper. Moore *and* Pete
stand by the table. Kiper *sits on bench*] Pete, what's
this I hear about a complaint? What's the matter,
huh? One of my men, huh?

PETE: *Oui, mon capitaine.*

FLAGG: I'm damned if I can leave this damn army
half a day without hell breaking loose somewhere.
Come on, let's have it; spit it out.

MOORE: Allay, Pete.

PETE: [*Speaking in an unintelligible rush of
French*] Ah, monsieur le capitaine, je suis un vieil-
lard; mais j'ai vécu heureusement, et mes enfants ont
été toujours honnêtes, mais hélas, mon capitaine,
quelque chose de terrible vient de passer, une cala-
mité monstrueuse. . . .

FLAGG: [*To* Moore] What's on the menu? Do you
get anything out of that?

MOORE: He says something has happened.

FLAGG: [*Distressed*] Does it take all that vocabu-
lary to say something has happened in French? Well,
keep going, keep going.

MOORE: Allay, Pete.

PETE: *Mais, mon capitaine, voilà que les Américains arrivent. Ils sont grands et forts, et ils de-
mandent toujours ce qu'ils veulent. Ils ne s'accoutu-
ment pas à nos mœurs ni à nos habitudes, mais—
nom de Dieu!—pourquoi choisissent-ils la seule
fleur de ma vie, quand ils peuvent trouver n'importe
où qu'ils vont des poules qui les désirent? Ma seule
fleur, ma fleur Charmaine, ma fleur délicate!*

FLAGG: What language is he talking now?

MOORE: He says the soldiers take what they want,
and they have trampled the one flower of his life.

FLAGG: Is that all he said?

MOORE: The rest is poetry.

FLAGG: [*Impatiently*] Well, tell him to omit
flowers, see, omit flowers.

MOORE: [*To* Pete] *Brièvement.*

PETE: *Ma fille. Ma fille bien-aimée. Elle est défleurée. Elle est dans la boue, elle est déshonorée.*

FLAGG: [*To* Moore] More flowers?

MOORE: No, sir. He says his daughter's been—ah
—ruined [*Pause*] . . . so to speak.

FLAGG: Ruined, huh? Rape or seduction?

MOORE: [*To* Pete] *S'est-elle soumise, ou l'a-t-on
forcée?*

PETE: *Les Américains sont si forts. Ils se forcent
sur elle, ils ferment sa bouche de façon qu'elle ne*

peut donner l'alarme. Que peut faire la petite fille?
L'Américaine est forte, elle peut se défendre, mais
la Française, elle est gentille et modeste et craintive
et ne sait se défendre.

FLAGG: [*To* Moore] Now what's all that?

MOORE: Rape, sir.

FLAGG: Does he allude to any specific girl, or is he
speaking of French wenches in general?

MOORE: [*To* Pete] *Comment s'appelle ta fille?*

PETE: Charmaine.

MOORE: Charmaine, sir.

FLAGG: [*Very seriously*] Look here, Moore. You
know as well as I do, this same little baggage has
been pretty free with me. What's the old boy's
game? And for God's sake, what do you think
you're up to, bringing him in here?

MOORE: You mean you're . . . God, I didn't
know that!

FLAGG: You didn't! You must go around here
wearing blinders. You see the fix you've got me in?

QUIRT: Think fast, Captain, think fast.

MOORE: To tell the truth, I got the impression it
was somebody else. Honest to God, I thought he said
it was a soldier. . . . [Flagg *hesitates and then gives*
Moore *a quick look.* Moore *is embarrassed*] I wasn't
sure, but I got that impression.

FLAGG: Did he name anybody?

MOORE: No.

FLAGG: [*Turning away*] Well, damn her little soul.
No, I know damn well it wasn't anybody else. [*Turns
to* Moore] Ask him how much he wants.

MOORE: How much what?

FLAGG: Money, you highbrow, money! What do
you think he wants?

MOORE: I don't know, but if I thought he wanted
money I certainly would not have listened to him.

FLAGG: You're just a bleating babe in the woods,
you are. That's what they all want.

MOORE: He told me he wanted the man to marry
the girl.

FLAGG: Marry her!

PETE: *Elle était une petite enfant innocente, une*
fleur à demi ouverte.

FLAGG: What's that? Flowers again?

MOORE: He says she was an innocent child.

FLAGG: Listen. You tell him I'm sure she's still an
innocent girl. Tell him Charmaine is one of the
most virtuous and respectable ladies I've ever had
the pleasure of meeting.

MOORE: [*To* Pete] *Monsieur le capitaine dit que*
c'est impossible et que vous vous trompez, monsieur,
parce que Charmaine est tout à fait honnête et
vertueuse.

PETE: [*Shaking his head*] *Non! non! non!—je ne*
me trompe pas—malheureusement c'est bien la
vérité.

MOORE: He's sure of it.

FLAGG: Ask him if he wants to bring charges.

MOORE: *Désirez-vous le faire passer au conseil de*
guerre?

PETE: *Conseil de guerre? Ça se peut.*

MOORE: He says perhaps.

FLAGG: What does he mean, "perhaps"? Ask him
how much he wants.

MOORE: *Il demande ce que vous voulez.*

PETE: *Mais la petite qui est défleurée—il faut*
qu'on la fasse honnête, et moi—est-ce donc que
l'honneur de ma famille ne vaut rien? Il faut qu'ils
se marient, et quant à moi—il faut me payer si je
ne le fais pas passer devant le conseil de guerre. Il
me faut cinq cent francs.

FLAGG: Flowers?

MOORE: No, he wants the fellow to marry the girl
—and he wants five hundred francs.

FLAGG: I see. That's better. Tell him he can have
three hundred. Tell him he can pick any son-in-
law he wants out of the whole damn army.

MOORE: [*To* Pete] *Elle peut choisir n'importe qui*
qu'il soit de toute la compagnie—et vous—vous
aurez trois cent francs.

PETE: [*Suddenly wildly angry*] *Ça ne va pas!*
Vous vous moquez de moi, vous officiers américains.
Je connais le truc—moi—de vous voir m'insulter
quand il s'agit de la rapace. Alors, messieurs, j'irai
au G.H.Q. et vous verrez. C'est la mort, et gare à
votre peau! Me voilà qui vient vous voir ici, mal-
heureux mais amical, et je ne reçois que des insultes.
Cinq cent francs! Rien de moins, et il la marie.

[*He starts for door*]

FLAGG: Wait a minute. [Aldrich *bars the door*]
What's wrong?

MOORE: He's insulted. Going to headquarters.
Five hundred, he wants; and it's a certain man, he
says.

FLAGG: What man?

MOORE: *Quel homme?*

PETE: [*Turning, crosses in front of table; to* Quirt,
dramatically] *Le voilà! Alors je m'en vais. Vous*
vous moquez de moi! Laissez-moi partir.

[Quirt *rises, knocking over chair*]

FLAGG: [*Taking a step toward* Quirt] Quirt, what's
the meaning of this?

QUIRT: Sorry, sir, I don't quite catch the drift
myself.

FLAGG: Have you been around with Charmaine?

QUIRT: Charmaine? I don't think so, Captain. But
I've got a poor memory for names.

FLAGG: You're a liar. You knew Charmaine was
mine, and you couldn't keep your hands off her.

QUIRT: Yeah? It's getting to be a habit of mine,
huh? Whaddye going to do about it, Captain Flagg?

FLAGG: Oh? What [*Walks to table*] am I going to
do about it?—I'm going to marry you to Charmaine
and let you make an honest woman out of her!
Quirt, you've taken the detail right off my shoulders,
and it's your turn to think fast! [*Turns to* Moore]
Mr. Moore, now tell the old man that the sergeant
was making honest proposals and desperate love!
Ask what church he belongs to, or whether he
wants 'em married by the cashier of the bank.

[*Turns to* Quirt. Moore *turns to* Pete; *they start toward the door*] Sergeant, you arrived in the nick of time with replacements! You saved the day! The Marines have landed and have the situation well in hand! We're going to decorate you! We're going to let you hold the bag!

QUIRT: All very interesting, Captain. But how are you going to do it? I may have landed, but I don't remember seeing any article in what I signed saying you could pick my woman for me. Seems to me you'd learned that I pick my women for myself.

FLAGG: Quirt, you've signed on for a cruise with this woman, and you can't jump ship. I can tell Aldrich to stand out of the way and let this old man go to headquarters with his story about you . . . and what chance has a lousy Marine sergeant got before an army court-martial when ten majors start the iron ball rolling? Ten army majors back in Paris, who ain't going to let anybody do any seducing but themselves. Don't be a hayshaker, Quirt. You can't play guardhouse lawyer in this country. You're in the army now, with a lot of western shysters sitting in the judge advocate general's room.

QUIRT: And who's going to be witness against me? You couldn't get that little frog to swear anything. I'm too damned handsome a soldier. I'm strong with this little French broad. Told me last night, just before you come back, she never loved a soldier who loved like me. Said she wished the whole damned outfit would move away and leave us in peace. Why, she's jealous every time I have to go to formation.

FLAGG: Sergeant, in about five minutes you're going to be married; in about eight you're going to please this old man by leaving an allotment here for about two-thirds of your pay in regular army style. The more you talk, the more you hang yourself up by the thumbs.

QUIRT: This ain't talk. What do you say I go get this little baby and ask her if she'll say anything about me that ain't praise and admiration? What do you say I go get her? What do I care a whoop in hell what this old bozo says about me? I ain't seduced *him!* He's after money. Well, I ain't got money. I don't have to carry money around in my love affairs. What do you say I go get her?

FLAGG: Of course, you'll go get her. And propose marriage to her on the way, because you'll meet the wedding detail when you get here. Gowdy, go to the Y tent and get the chaplain. [Gowdy *goes out*] Aldrich, accompany Sergeant Quirt to the tavern and tell Charmaine that I'm giving away in marriage the handsomest sergeant in the corps. Tell her she's a woman in a thousand, because Quirt has already run away from a thousand; and if it weren't for my seeing justice done him, he'd run away from that many more. All right, Quirt, we'll be waiting for you. [Quirt *and* Aldrich *go out.* Ferguson *fixes chair, returns to seat, and turns to* Moore] Mr. Moore, tell papa the wedding bells are going to ring, and there's money in it for him, money in it!

[Moore *seats* Pete *on stool at window; then whispers. A knock at the door.* Lipinsky *opens it*]

LIPINSKY: Brigade runner, Captain Flagg.

FLAGG: Send him in.

[*The* Runner *enters*]

RUNNER: Company commander?

FLAGG: What is it—shoving off?

RUNNER: Moving in an hour, sir.

FLAGG: In an hour?

RUNNER: Please initial.

[*Offers pencil and paper*]

FLAGG: [*Signing*] You hear that, Moore?

MOORE: Yes, sir.

FLAGG: [*Up and business-like*] Going in an hour. You know what that means.

MOORE: Yes, sir.

FLAGG: Pass the word to our platoon commanders to stand in heavy packs in thirty minutes. The *camions* are waiting at the crossroad with ammunition. [Moore *goes out*] Kiper, tell Quirt to salvage all rations in the square. [Kiper *starts for door but stops as Flagg says, "Wait a minute"*] Don't let on to Quirt we're going in. We'll marry him to Charmaine and march the blushing bridegroom off to war.

[*Walks up and down*]

FERGUSON: Afraid you can't marry them this evening, Captain Flagg. Chaplain very sticky on that point. Have to be married in the morning.

FLAGG: Well, then, the mayor could marry them, couldn't he? Lipinsky, go get the mayor. Who's seen the mayor to-day?

KIPER: Just saw him down by the bridge on a load of manure.

FLAGG: There you are, Lipinsky—load of manure, near the bridge. Get the mayor, dust him off, and bring him here toot pronto. If the chaplain can't do it, the mayor can.

[Lipinsky *starts to go out but halts and calls* " 'Tenshun." Pete *still sits on stool. In walk a* Brigadier-General, *one* Colonel, *one* Captain, *and two* Lieutenants]

THE GENERAL: Hello, Flagg. Haven't you received that order yet? Not a soul stirring on your damned street. [*All salute*] Flagg, you run the most disreputable outfit of the brigade. I come into town to hold a staff conference and find the whole shebang asleep. What kind of platoon commanders have you got, anyway, sitting round here like a nest of hobos when you're moving in forty-five minutes?

[*The staff remains standing at attention*]

FLAGG: Just got the order, General. We'll get off in time. Never missed a train in my life.

THE GENERAL: Well, I don't see how you do it. *Camions* back two miles at the crossroads. Your men will have ammunition there, and I want every man to carry two extra bandoliers.

FLAGG: If you don't mind my saying so, General,

we're the refuse of the brigade back of the line and we carry extra bandoliers into it.

THE GENERAL: Well, I'll tell you why. Division wants a line straightened that we're going to take over. Isn't straight enough for him. Where's the map? Map, Davis!

THE COLONEL: [Turns] Map, Tolbert!

THE LIEUTENANT: Map, Price!

THE CAPTAIN: Where's that map? [Looks wildly around. The last Lieutenant to enter hands map to Price] Here's the map, sir.

[Hands map to General]

THE GENERAL: Good boy, good boy. A map, after all, among you soldiers. Now, see here, Flagg. [Pointing to map, which he spreads out on table] There she is, and here's the line. The corps wants it straightened out. It will take the steel, the cold steel. But they've got to have it straightened out. Give them the steel and you can do it. You'll hold the town—our half of it—and you'll get these fellows out if it takes a week. Your men are a bunch of tramps, but they can do this sort of thing.

FLAGG: Individualists, General, individualists.

THE GENERAL: Well, it's the penalty you pay for laxity. I admit it has its compensations. But you've got to give 'em the steel. You've got to run 'em down like rats. You give them the old cowering point. We've got to get them out. We want to go in there and run 'em out. We want to give 'em steel.

FLAGG: We? Staff going in there too, General?

THE GENERAL: [Disconsolately] No—they won't risk us fellows, curse the luck.

FLAGG: That's too bad, General.

THE GENERAL: But we'll be behind you, Flagg.

FLAGG: How far, General?

THE GENERAL: We'll probably be at Cemetery Farm. We haven't studied the indirect fire properly yet, but we'll be behind you.

THE COLONEL: [Handing bundle of posters to General] Beg pardon, sir; these posters.

THE GENERAL: And, Flagg, some Yankee Doodle back in Hoboken sends you some posters with his compliments.

FLAGG: Posters? What for?

THE GENERAL: To post behind the German lines—sent to all companies of this brigade.

FLAGG: My God! What are we advertising? Camels?

THE GENERAL: Oh, no! It's intelligence work. Explaining our mission over here to the German soldier. There are three hundred posters. Send a small detail through the German lines some night and tack 'em up all over the place.

FLAGG: How many men am I supposed to lose on that job?

THE GENERAL: Not one. We don't want to lose a man. But tack 'em up.

FLAGG: Yeah, that's easy to say. I'd like to tack up a few in Hoboken containing my sentiments on two-starred idiots who waste men on that kind of monkey-business.

THE GENERAL: Well, here is another thing, Flagg, the big G. one wants a prisoner out of that town of yours. Wants an officer from one of those Alsatian regiments where the deserters are filtering through. And I've got to get him.

FLAGG: Oh, don't say that, General, don't break our hearts. I've got to get him. I knew damn well you had a bolt of black crepe up your sleeve when you came in the door.

THE GENERAL: Hold down the losses, Flagg . . . and listen. If you send me one of those Alsatian officers in good condition I'll send your whole company back for a month's rest.

FLAGG: You mean it?

THE GENERAL: Mean it! You know me, Flagg. I'll do more if you get me an officer without a scratch. I'll give you eight days in any hotel in France. If you weren't such a bum, Flagg, I'd put you on staff.

FLAGG: I've been a bum, General, but I'm damned if I'd go on staff.

THE GENERAL: [At the door] Hold down the losses, Flagg, and give 'em the steel—and don't forget those posters, for they're damned important—and if you fetch me that prisoner you get a month's rest and eight days' leave. [The door opens. In walk the Chaplain, Charmaine and Quirt, Mayor, Kiper, and Lipinsky] Hullo! My God, what's this? A wedding party?

FLAGG: Why, yes, General. I don't suppose we ought to wait for it, but it's a sort of special case and won't take long.

THE GENERAL: You aren't getting married, are you, Flagg?

FLAGG: Not this trip; no sir. It's Sergeant Quirt.

THE GENERAL: [Turning to Quirt] Oh, yes, I remember Sergeant Quirt very well.

FLAGG: I didn't like to intrude company matters when you were in haste, General, but the truth is, Sergeant Quirt has expressed a wish to marry the inn-keeper's daughter here, and her father was waiting to press charges; so, you see—

THE GENERAL: Oh! Charges? . . .

FLAGG: Personally, I'm opposed to Quirt's marrying at all, but he insists his intentions were honorable, and he's such a fine soldier I should hate to carry this old man to H.Q. with a complaint.

THE GENERAL: What's this, Sergeant?

QUIRT: A courtship, General; a love match from the start. Honorable intentions on both sides.

THE GENERAL: Sounds a little fishy to me, I must say, but go right ahead. Don't waste time.

[Ferguson comes forward]

PETE: Monsieur le général, les Américains sont si forts—ils m'ont déshonoré—ma petite fille—ma fleur charmante—ma fleur délicate . . .

FERGUSON: In case of a marriage, Captain Flagg, a little allotment is regulation.

FLAGG: Thanks, Fergy; I almost forgot the allotment.

QUIRT: Hell, we don't need no allotment. This is a love match.

FLAGG: Of course, it holds us up a bit, but if the General doesn't mind?

FERGUSON: A little allotment is regulation, sir.

THE GENERAL: Go ahead, go ahead.

FLAGG: Ferguson, where are those allotment blanks?

FERGUSON: Right here, sir.

THE GENERAL: [*To* Ferguson] Make it out for two-thirds of the sergeant's pay, Ferguson.

FERGUSON: [*Sits and fills papers*] Yes, sir.

QUIRT: [*Standing, with* Charmaine] I don't know about this, General.

THE GENERAL: It's for your own good, Quirt. How do you plan to get out of it, otherwise?

QUIRT: Get out of it? Didn't I tell you it was a love match?

THE GENERAL: No more talk, Sergeant; sign up or stand trial.

FLAGG: For your own good, Quirt.

QUIRT: For whose good, Captain Flagg?

THE GENERAL: Sign up, Quirt.

[Ferguson *gives paper to* Flagg. Quirt *reluctantly signs*]

FLAGG: All in order. [*Looks over paper*] Shipshape, Sergeant Quirt. Beautiful hand you write, sir. And now, Chaplain, Sergeant Quirt is next.

THE GENERAL: Let's get it over with. And here's her father ready to give her away.

PETE: *Merci, mon général.*

THE GENERAL: A regular church wedding, and Captain Flagg can be best man.

FLAGG: Get that, Sergeant Quirt? Charmaine [*He crosses and hands her allotment papers with a bow*], keep this in a good safe place. It means money to you the first of every month.

CHARMAINE: *Merci.*

THE GENERAL: Turn on the ceremony.

CHAPLAIN: Run it through. Sorry we can't wait to kiss the bride, Quirt. You have about twenty minutes, Flagg.

FLAGG: Right, sir.

THE GENERAL: One word, Quirt. You're going in to-night. You're going in twenty minutes. If you take your men into the line in first-rate condition, looking like soldiers, you'll square yourself with me. Keep that in mind.

QUIRT: We're going in in twenty minutes?

THE GENERAL: Yes. We're off, men. So long, Flagg. Twenty minutes.

FLAGG: Good-bye, General.

[*All salute. The* General *and his retinue file out at door*]

CHAPLAIN: Do you, Charmaine, take this man for your husband, to love, honor—

QUIRT: She does not, I do not, we do not. So we're going in in twenty minutes, eh—and you were going to tie me up before I knew anything about it? And I suppose if I don't marry her you'll lock me up. If you think you can take your men in to-night without a first sergeant, you lock me up. I would like to see you take this gang of tiny tots across that last two miles without a sergeant. Well, if this sergeant goes in, he goes in single; so you God-damn well better make up your mind what you're going to do.

FLAGG: Well, skunk, you've got me. You win. Hit the deck.

QUIRT: Sorry, Charmaine, but I've got work to do. I can't marry you to-night, I can't marry you any God-damn time at all, and if I never see you again— why, then I never see you again, understand? What's more, don't you try cashing that allotment, or by God I'll pull something that'll stop my pay for good. Get out of my way.

[*He goes out. Instantly a whistle blows*]

FLAGG: Sorry, Charmaine, but I need that sergeant. Shake a leg, you hayshakers. Pass the word for inspection in five minutes, and they'd better be ship-shape. *Camions* at the crossroad. Extra bandoliers and V.B. grenades for the outside ranks. Don't let Quirt do all the work.

THE RUNNERS: Ay ay, sir.

[*They go out hastily*]

PETE: [*Angry*] *Sont-ils mariés? Ou votre sergeant, se moque-t-il de moi?*

FLAGG: Sure, they're married.

PETE: [*Beats on table*] *Prenez garde! Je viendrai!*

FLAGG: [*Turns—speaks ominously*] Don't bother me. Don't get in my way, see? We're fighting a war with Germany. I don't give a damn whether he's married or not. Run along outside. [*Turns* Pete *around; spanks him*] I'm busy. [Pete *goes out, stops near* Charmaine *and says, "Sale vache"; then goes out.* Flagg *goes to table, gets his hat, turns toward the door*] So long, Fergy. Take care of the stuff.

FERGUSON: Yes, sir.

[*Turns to desk.* Flagg *starts out.* Charmaine *crosses to him*]

CHARMAINE: [*Her hand on his arm*] I'm so sorry. You should have taken me to Paris. I told you to take me to Paris. I could not be good all alone.

FLAGG: [*Takes her by shoulders*] That's all right, Charmaine. You're a damn fine little animal. Go right on having a good time. It's a great life, and you've got a genius for it.

CHARMAINE: But you do not love me, not any more?

FLAGG: Sure I love you! Everybody loves you.

CHARMAINE: You think I am *pas bonne?*

FLAGG: Listen, Charmaine. Don't you worry any more about Quirt and me. It's a thousand to one you'll never see either of us again. I'm damned sorry I have to take your sergeant away, but this war's lousy with sergeants. There'll be thirty along in thirty days. Anyway you'll probably never see us again. Kiss me good-bye. [*They kiss*] Now you forget me!

CHARMAINE: I never forget you.

[*A whistle blows outside*]

FLAGG: You won't forget me? Well, if I get leave, Charmaine . . . you never can tell. [*The whistle blows twice*] It's a hell of a war, but it's the only one we've got.

[*He goes out. She stands staring after him*]

FERGUSON: [*From his table; turning*] Well, little missy. You're a single woman *with* an allotment. There ain't many as fortunate as that.

CHARMAINE: He will come back?

FERGUSON: Which one?

CHARMAINE: The captain.

FERGUSON: Not likely. Not likely either of them will. A soldier hardly ever doubles on his trail in this war.

CHARMAINE: No?

FERGUSON: Hardly ever. And you're just as fortunate you didn't marry a soldier, darling. They're a bad lot to keep house for. I know. I've been keeping house for one regiment or another since I was as young as you are.

CHARMAINE: Oh, but they are beautiful.

FERGUSON: The girls always like them. I don't know why.

CHARMAINE: They go into hell to die—and they are not old enough to die.

FERGUSON: I shouldn't think it would matter much to you, dear. Some get killed, but plenty more come in to relieve them. Never any shortage of soldiers.

CHARMAINE: It's terrible!

FERGUSON: It's their business. Some of 'em get killed at it, same as in any trade.

CHARMAINE: [*Crosses to back of* Ferguson's *chair; leans over him*] Can I help you?

FERGUSON: No.

CHARMAINE: To-morrow?

FERGUSON: No.

CHARMAINE: You are unkind.

FERGUSON: Just because I'm the only man around here do you think I'm going to let you bother me? You run along home and pray God to keep you out of mischief a few days. It won't do you any harm.

[*He bends over his work*]

CHARMAINE: *Bon soir.* [*He does not hear her*] *Bon soir!*

FERGUSON: What?

CHARMAINE: *Bon soir.*

FERGUSON: Oh, yes, good night. [*She slowly crosses to door, looking back at him all the way. She quietly closes door, and just as she does so,* Ferguson *very loudly says,* "Good night." *He bends over his desk, alone, writing and sings*]

"The French they are a funny race, parlez-vous,
The French they are a funny race, parlez-vous . . ."

CURTAIN

ACT II.

A cellar in a disputed town, a typical deep wine cellar of a prosperous farmhouse on the edge of a village in France. It resembles half of a culvert thirty feet in diameter, with a corresponding curved roof and walls. One end is open, and the other is walled up, admitting a narrow and rather low door in the center, through which a flight of stairs extends to the ground floor above. This cellar is lit dimly by two candles placed at either side of the front stage and held in bottle on small bully-beef boxes. The rear wall can only barely be discerned. Along the sides of this culvert are dirty white ticks stuffed with straw for sleeping quarters, the sort of ticks headquarters detachment men carry about with them. There are four on each side, arranged with all the litter of miscellany a soldier carries about tucked at their heads, and with the foot of these pallets extending into the center of the culvert. The effect is not unlike in design that of a hospital ward, with feet toward the center aisle. Back of Flagg's *bunk all manner of stuff—first-aid kits, bandages, chocolates, sticks, pistols and rifles, notes, books of memoranda, etc.*

Two men are asleep, snoring gently—gas masks at alert on chests, tin hats on back of heads, and heads on floor. They are indescribably dirty, and with six or eight days' beard.

The two men are Spike *and* Kiper. Kiper *is on second bunk at left,* Spike *on third bunk at right.* Gowdy *enters. Stirs* Spike *with his foot.*

GOWDY: All right. Heave out and lash up. Lively now. Rations are in. Go draw for ten. At the gray stable to-night. Take that sack there.

[*Points to a muddy sack on the floor near by*]

SPIKE: What time is it? Rations in?

GOWDY: You heard me, Spike. Shake a leg and go draw rations for ten men, at the gray stable near the square. It's after two o'clock.

SPIKE: Where's Captain Flagg?

GOWDY: Down tying up Mr. Aldrich.

SPIKE: So they got him. Bad?

GOWDY: I'll say they did. A ticket home. Right arm torn all to hell.

SPIKE: A damned dirty shame. He's lucky, though, to get out with an arm. I'd sell 'em mine, and at the same price. What was it—that one-pounder again?

GOWDY: No. Fuse cap from a grenade. Made a hell of a mess on Mr. Aldrich. He was crawling on the embankment near the railway station, and somebody inside threw him a present.

SPIKE: [*Now up and re-winding a spiral legging*] A damned swell officer, if you ask me. Taking him out to-night?

GOWDY: No. The skipper is bringing him here. Send him out to-morrow night. He's lost too much blood to walk it before dawn. God, it's getting on my nerves.

KIPER: [*Who has been awakened*] Who? Mr. Aldrich hit bad?

GOWDY: Pretty bad. Arm. Make a bunk for him, willya? Shake it down and pile another in the back. He'll want to sit up with it. Make up Harry's bunk.

SPIKE: [*At door, about to go upstairs, turns at this*] Harry's bunk? Why, Harry?

GOWDY: Harry's through with bunks.

SPIKE: Bumped off?

GOWDY: Worse. In the belly crossing the square.

[Spike *goes out*]

KIPER: Where is he?

GOWDY: The skipper rushed him back an hour ago. No use, though; Harry was unconscious—halfway—holding half his guts in his bare hands and hollering for somebody to turn him loose so he could shoot himself.

KIPER: Captain Flagg want me?

GOWDY: He said not to wake you. Might need you later on.

KIPER: A good job for me, I suppose. Jeez, with this daylight saving I ain't going to live forever, that's sure. I think I'll go crazy and get the doc to gimme a ticket.

GOWDY: Flagg's crazy now. Raving crazy, Hasn't slept for five nights. We'll be sitting on him in another night like he's had to-night.

KIPER: The whole damned universe is crazy now.

[Kiper *has come forward to* Flagg's *bunk, smoking. Enter* Pharmacist's Mate, *with a large clothing roll trussed up in leather straps with a portmanteau handle. He is young, pink-faced, but horribly callous, probably some kid from a medical school of 1917*]

MATE: [*Looking about in the dark as he approaches* Kiper] Flagg's company P.C.?

KIPER: [*Hostile;* Gowdy *sits up*] Yeah.

MATE: Where'd I better set up shop, soldier?

[*He looks about the cellar*]

KIPER: [*Worried*] What do you want to set up shop for, sailor?

MATE: [*Sitting down on bunk; starts unpacking, takes off helmet*] How'd I know? This ain't my party. Flagg wants it here.

KIPER: What's he want it for to-night?

MATE: He's going to put on a little party before morning. [*He uncovers a litter of blue-rolled bandages on bunk; absorbent cotton, a jar of iodine which he unscrews, and some wooden sticks around which he begins to twist wisps of cotton for daubs*] A little party.

KIPER: The whole damn company, I suppose, and all the engineers he can find to boot.

MATE: [*Professionally*] Oh, no. He ain't got arrangements here for that many. I'd say a small party, according to the stuff they gave me at the dressing station.

KIPER: [*Incredulous*] How small?

MATE: [*With immense indifference, busy about his detail*] Oh, I'd say about two operating tables . . . [*A pause as he enjoys the effect on* Kiper] A small party. About four couples for bridge.

KIPER: Yeah. [*Rather miserable*] Low bridge around that lousy railroad station.

MATE: I guess so. They were passing out V.B. grenades down the street to the station when I came through.

KIPER: [*Immensely friendly all of a sudden*] Look here, sailor. You are smarter than me. . . .

MATE: [*Interrupting*] Oh, no!

KIPER: [*Insistently*] Oh, hell, yes! Any man smart enough not to join in them four couples is smarter than I am. Even you're smarter. Now that being the case, tell me why the hell we want the Heinies out of that God-damn railway station. Leave 'em there, I say. Let 'em sit where they damned well are. They ain't going anywheres.

MATE: I can't tell you.

KIPER: Nobody can. Like as not General Pershing himself couldn't tell you about it . . . and . . . oh, sweet baby, but last night down there I swore to God so long as I lived I'd never let another German in that railroad station throw a potato masher at me.

MATE: You can throw a grenade at him.

KIPER: Sure I can. But I don't want to no more. I pitched yesterday, and my arm is sore. I know I can do it, and it ain't fun any more. I know all about Flagg's invitations to parties. I know why they all got R.S.V.P. on 'em. Right smart of V.B. grenades provided. . . .

[*Enter* Lipinsky, *who comes down; looks first at* Kiper]

LIPINSKY: [*Immediately perceiving the litter*] Jeez, Kiper, I wish you'd keep the undertakers out of here. What's all this, Jack?

[*He waves to the mate's stuff*]

MATE: [*Selecting a small bandage*] Well, this one is yours, and the rest is for your friends.

LIPINSKY: [*Cheerily*] Don't try to put the bug on me. I ain't no queen bee. They ain't made one that could burst alongside of me. If they'd made it, I'd be down with the daisies long ago. I'm proof now. It's down in the cards that I'll live to see the navy at Mare Island again. [*He lights a cigarette which he has taken from* Flagg's *bunk*] Yes, sir, I'll live to beat the pants off that bird that sold me the wrist watch down by the main gate.

KIPER: How do you know you're going to live? Said your prayers, I suppose, and got an answer.

LIPINSKY: And who'd send me an answer?

KIPER: The great cosmic top sergeant who runs this world.

LIPINSKY: Well, I don't want any answer from that bird. He'd send the answer collect, and it would say, "Fall in and get the manure outa the French angels' backyards. Clean up heaven, you lowdown Marine.

so's the National Guard won't get typhoid when they all die and come here."

KIPER: There ain't any heaven. Paris is heaven enough. If I ever get outa hell, I'm certainly going to stay in heaven until I die.

LIPINSKY: Of course, there's a heaven.

MATE: On the level, now. You birds know your souls go somewheres. You've seen too many men die. A fellow is walking along, blood in his face and breath in his lungs, and whizz - eeee - zzzz, boommmmm . . . he's down on the ground and something's gone. Something's gone, I tell you. Something that was in that bird a minute before has left, and all you've got is a pack of bloody rags and a lot of dirt. Well, for the want of a better name, you call that something a soul . . . and you can't kid me . . . the soul's gone somewheres.

KIPER: What of it? That soul ain't any of my business. It ain't got to eat, it ain't got to run; it ain't got to stand in line ten days a week to sign the pay-roll. I should get on my ear about where this doodle-bug in my chest is going after I die. It ain't never helped me none. It can go to hell for all I care.

LIPINSKY: Jeez, Kiper, don't talk that way around me. [Raises eyes] It wasn't me, God; it wasn't your little Vladysek Lipinsky. Not him. He knows too damn well if he was to talk that way you would certainly make him cover up and yell for mercy before morning.

KIPER: And you were the one wasn't going to be hit a while ago.

LIPINSKY: That's why I ain't going to be hit. My little soul's all ready to turn out for every formation, boots blacked and buttons shined. A little sea-going soul that knows its top sergeant can give it a kick in the pants any time he gets ready.

KIPER: Well, if there is a God, he ain't got medicine big enough to worry me. Why the hell doesn't he win the war for one side or the other and get this mess over? I know plenty of men could win it. Flagg probably could, if you gave him the army and a barrel of whiskey.

LIPINSKY: But you like the chaplain, Kiper. You said he was a swell bird the other day.

KIPER: Sure I like the chaplain. Gimme two packs of Camels two nights ago. If God was to show himself, now——come down with a bunch of angels driving a wagon-load of cigarettes, that would be something like it. The chaplain said my folks was all praying for me to come through, and for God to spare me after hearing their prayers. God, I ain't that dirty a coward! That's a case of saying, "Oh, God, don't kill our child. Kill every kid in the neighborhood, but bring the one marked Kiper safe back home. . . ." No, I don't want none of that for mine. . . . And you can take all your New Testaments with the khaki backs and throw 'em in the incinerator so far as I want anything out of 'em. I'd rather have a book of cigarette papers any time. . . . I ain't asking anybody for a damned thing in this war. And you can take all your Bible backers and psalm singers and hitch 'em to the ration wagons, if you ask me.

MATE: Well, this is all very pleasant, but I got business over in the next company now. Bad curve in the position there, and 'long toward daybreak they start hollering "First Aid" as regular as a clock. If I was you fellows I'd go out and sleep in different shell-holes to-night . . . see which one of you is right. . . . Tell your skipper I'll be back around three-thirty.

[He steps on his cigarette and prepares to go out after Quirt enters, which he does. Quirt enters. Sergeant Quirt is tired]

QUIRT: Captain Flagg here?

GOWDY: Still in the orchard . . . digging those new rifle pits. We've got nine captured Maxims there. Those birds can't change the belts, but they can tap a thousand rounds apiece by pressing the buttons in the dark. Fifteen men could hold this half of the town, the way he's got the positions staked out.

QUIRT: There'll be about fifteen holding it if this business of reconnoitering patrols keeps up. I'd like to have that divisional staff in this town one night. Still bad in the square?

GOWDY: Pretty bad. Rifles in box rest in the railway stations . . . light automatics.

QUIRT: I thought Flagg got 'em out last night.

GOWDY: They filtered back in at dusk to-night. Our cross-fire couldn't stop 'em. The skipper says they are working them from pulleys from the first floor, and the railroad embankment covers them from us.

QUIRT: [Stretching out and sighing as he takes off his tin hat and mops his forehead] Running rations down that ravine every night is the toughest job I've ever soldiered.

GOWDY: Lucky to-night?

QUIRT: Pretty lucky. Six out of ten come back. Them two Jameson boys got it from the same shell going down. Dutchy and the little Jew were hit right at the dump. Easy ones, though. They'll be back in ten days.

[A commotion at head of stairs. Enter Captain Flagg supporting Aldrich by gripping Aldrich's uninjured wrist over his shoulder and easing him gently down steps. Aldrich is not groaning. After all, it won't hurt for fifteen minutes or so. But he is weak from loss of blood and soaked through, and is in an indescribable mess of dried blood and dirt, which appears black. Flagg, who is unkempt, has no leggings or laces in his breeches, these flapping in the most disillusioning fashion about his bare legs. His blouse, an old army blouse many sizes too big and without a sign of any insignia, is tied with a piece of twine. He is bareheaded—no tin hat and no accoutrements of any sort. He is a very weary-looking man. He wears belt and *holster with automatic bound to leg. As* Flagg *enters, followed by* Mate, Gowdy *jumps up and spreads blanket on bunk*]

FLAGG: Right here, Aldrich. [*Lowers him down on bunk. The* Pharmacist's Mate *follows him.* Flagg *kneels above* Aldrich. *The* Mate *stands*] Gimme a stick of that dope, Holsen.

MATE: They are quarter grains, Captain.

FLAGG: [*To* Aldrich, *lying down*] Take these two now. [*He puts two tablets from a tiny vial in the wounded officer's mouth*] I'm putting these in your blouse. Get somebody to give you one every three hours until you are carried out.

ALDRICH: What are they?

FLAGG: Morphine—quarter grains——

ALDRICH: [*Not dramatic, just casual*] What if I take them all when your back is turned?

FLAGG: [*Turning his back and crossing to his own bunk down left; sits on bunk*] Go ahead. It's your affair.

[*After* Flagg *is seated on his bunk a strange sob is heard at the head of the stairs.* Lieutenant Moore, *last seen in company headquarters, rushes in and goes straight over to* Aldrich, *where he stands and looks down at his arm, and not his face*]

MOORE: Oh, God, Dave, but they got you. God, but they got you a beauty, the dirty swine. God DAMN them for keeping us up in this hellish town. Why can't they send in some of the million men they've got back there and give us a chance? Men in my platoons are so hysterical every time I get a message from Flagg, they want to know if they're being relieved. What can I tell them? They look at me like whipped dogs—as if I had just beaten them —and I've had enough of them this time. I've got to get them out, I tell you. They've had enough. Every night the same way. [*He turns to* Flagg] And since six o'clock there's been a wounded sniper in the tree by that orchard angel crying *"Kamerad! Kamerad!"* Just like a big crippled whippoorwill. What price glory now? Why in God's name can't we all go home? Who gives a damn for this lousy, stinking little town but the poor French bastards who live here? God damn it! You talk about courage, and all night long you hear a man who's bleeding to death on a tree calling you *"Kamerad"* and asking you to save him. God damn every son of a bitch in the world, who isn't here! I won't stand for it. I won't stand for it! I won't have the platoon asking me every minute of the livelong night when they are going to be relieved. . . . Flagg, I tell you you can shoot me, but I won't stand for it. . . . I'll take 'em out to-night and kill you if you get in my way. . . .

[*Starts sobbing again.* Gowdy *and* Kiper *sit up*]

FLAGG: [*Rising quickly as though he might kill the man, and then putting his arm around the chap, who has clearly gone smash for a few minutes. He speaks in a quiet, chastening tone, with a gentility*

never before revealed] Here, boy, you can't do this before all these men. [*Walks him*] They are rubbed up, too. You are all tuckered out with your side of the line. Don't worry about your platoon. We'll get them out. You turn in here. [*Walks him to bunk on the left side of the room.* Kiper *crosses and throws blanket on him; stops at bunk nearest entrance*] And dope off for a little while . . . that's it, give him a blanket, Kiper . . . and now take it easy a while, and you can go back to your platoon in time to stand to. Sleep it off, boy, sleep it off. . . . You're in a deep wide hole, and shells can't get you. Sleep it off.

[Flagg *crosses to his own bunk, lights cigarette at candle, seats himself on bunk.* Gowdy *rests head on arm.* Quirt *kneels on floor, gets a piece of chocolate out of his pocket; rises, as though his legs were asleep. He carries his helmet. He crosses and tosses candy to* Moore]

QUIRT: Just a little chocolate I bought off a Y.M.C.A. wagon down at the base. [Quirt *is sympathetic and begins to talk nervously*] I got hit myself once. In Nicaragua. We were washed up before we made a landing. I was a corporal, and when we were scrubbing down and putting on clean uniforms —doctors' orders, you know, so they wouldn't have to wash us when we were hit—[*Turns to* Gowdy]— a bird said to me—it was old Smoke Plangetch, who was killed in 1913 in a chippie joint in Yokohama —Smoke said to me: "You'd better swab down, you son of a sea-bitch, because I dreamed last night they wrote your name on a bullet." I said to him, "The bullet ain't been cast that can shoot Micky Quirt." He said, "If your name is on one, it will turn the corner and go upstairs to find you." Jeez! That afternoon when we made a landing and hit the beach, the spigs was on a hill five hundred yards off shore. We started up the hill—they weren't many of us dropping—and I came to a log I had to jump [Quirt *illustrates this*] and I lost my balance and threw my hand up in the air. [Quirt *extends his wrist*] Look, right through the God-damn fin, as pretty as a pinwheel . . . Smoke saw it. "Oh, yeah, you wisenheimer son of a Chinese tart," he says to me, "your name was on that one and you had to reach up for it." [Gowdy *laughs.* Quirt *is obviously embarrassed by having spoken of himself so much. He turns and recollects his business and goes over to* Flagg. *Crosses to the foot of* Flagg's *bunk*] Rations detail in, sir. Lost the two Jameson boys in the ravine going down. Both badly hit. Lost Fleischman and Rosenthal in the dump. Both slight. Brought back all the ammunition and two sacks of bread, one of canned willie, French; I carried a sack of beet sugar on my back. Got a piece of shrapnel in it where they are shelling the crossroads—stopped it square. In the next war, I'm going to wear a suit of beet sugar and stand forest fire watch in the Rocky Mountains. [*He turns, and then remembers and comes back*] Oh, I brought up two of these thirty-day-wonder lieutenants from a training camp. Sent up by divisional for instruction.

FLAGG: By God, I won't stand for it. They wipe their damned dirty feet on this company. They can give my men all their damned good jobs. They can keep us in the line all during the whole damned war. But I'll be damned if my sergeants have got time to teach army lieutenants how to button their pants in the dark.

QUIRT: They are in my hole now, sir. Pretty badly shaken up by the ravine. First time up, you know. Shall I send them to you, sir?

FLAGG: Send them to me, and for God's sake, don't call me sir any more to-night.

QUIRT: [To Gowdy] All right. You heard him. Hit the deck. You'll find 'em in my hole. [Gowdy goes] Those Huns in the railway station again?

FLAGG: Try to cross the town square when there's a flare up, and you'll see.

QUIRT: You get a visit from brigade headquarters to-night. I saw their party in the ravine as we were going down to the dump.

FLAGG: The old man says we've got to drive them off the embankment. Huh! He can give me five general courts and I'll not waste another man at that business. It will take a brigade action to get them out for good.

QUIRT: Do you mind if I take a look around there now? I'd like to see this damned war some. For six days I've been a lousy bakery wagon— haven't seen a spiggoty yet, except stinking dead ones —I never see soldiers stink like these Heinies.

FLAGG: All right. Go get your blooming can blown off. But bury yourself, while you're about it. The burying detail is in for the night.

QUIRT: Gosh, I wish to hell I was home.

FLAGG: Go get one of those Alsatian lootnants then, and you'll get a leave.

QUIRT: I don't want to die yet, thanking you just the same. Well, here goes.

[Exit]

FLAGG: Well, keep your head down. I can't waste any grave-diggers on sergeants. [Flagg shrugs his shoulders and walks over to above Aldrich] Sorry Moore blew up that way, Aldrich . . . you are a damned sight luckier than he is, but he doesn't know it. I'll have you out to-morrow night with the ration detail, and you'll be parking your body in a big white bed in another two days. Good luck . . . You've been a damned good man. I wish you could get a ribbon for this town.

[As Flagg leaves, Gowdy enters with two lieutenants. They are just like tailor's dummies of a Burberry outfit, slicked to the notch and perky and eager. As they enter, Flagg steps on his cigarette and stands facing them. The Lieutenants come down and stand side by side]

FLAGG: [Starts back in mock admiration and salaams deeply as they come forward] So this is the last of the old guard, eh? In the name of the holy sweet Jumping, are you gentlemen bound for a masked ball, that you come disguised as officers? Or do you wish to save the snipers the trouble of picking you off with a glass, that you wear sign-boards? [He goes nearer them, inspecting their clothes] Can't you go without those trench coats even to the trenches? How long will you last in those boots? Take 'em off before you even part your hair in the morning. . . . [He changes to a thundering staccato] My name is Flagg, gentlemen, and I'm the sinkhole and cesspool of this regiment, frowned on in the Y.M.C.A. huts and sneered at by the divisional Beau Brummells. I am a lousy, good-for-nothing company commander. I corrupt youth and lead little boys astray into the black shadows between the lines of hell, killing more men than any other company commander in the regiment, and drawing all the dirty jobs in the world. I take chocolate soldiers and make dead heroes out of them. I did not send for you, Mister . . . [He leans forward, and the first officer salutes and speaks: "Cunningham, sir"] nor for you . . . ["Lundstrom, sir," also salutes]; and I confess I am in a quandary. Four days ago I should have been more hospitable, for I had four gunnery sergeants then. Now I have two, and can't spare them to teach little boys how to adjust their diapers. I've no doubt that one of you was an all-American half-back and the other the editor of the college paper, but we neither follow the ball nor the news here. We are all dirt, and we propose to die in order that corps headquarters may be decorated. I should be happy to receive suggestions as to what should be done with you. Ah, I have it! There are two German gunners over in the enemy railway station. Two bright young men might get them out and cut their throats before dawn; then no more could get in the station all day. Two bright young men, who know very little of anything just yet. I have two bright ones, but they are far too valuable. They are corporals with ten years' experience.

[The Lieutenants are speechless. There is not a smile in the cellar. Cunningham, who is the bigger of the two, finally answers, in a slow Southern drawl]

CUNNINGHAM: I'll do anything you will. Where is the railway station and the two bucks that have got you buffaloed?

FLAGG: Why, it's Frank Merriwell! All right, Frank. You and me will be playing ball in hell by three o'clock this morning.

LUNDSTROM: Put me in too, sir.

FLAGG: Oh, no, no, no! We must have officers left. Rule of the game. Must have officers. Men would get right up and go home, and then there wouldn't be any war at all. Besides, three would be a crowd, and I hate crowds early in the morning around the railway station. They are so noisy, and they die so fast. [He turns to Gowdy] Gowdy! Take Mr. Lundstrom to the fourth platoon sergeant, and tell him that here's his new officer. [Runner *and* Lundstrom *move to door.* Flagg *is all business now*] And by the way, Mr. Lundstrom, they filter through and bomb twice a week, small parties slipping down that ravine you'll find on your left. Watch it closely, or you'll all have your throats cut before you know it. And let that sergeant sleep for the next two days. Remember, he'll do no details until he's rested. Of course you can wake him for advice. That's all. Shove off. [Runner *and* Lundstrom *salute, and go out.* Cunningham *sits down.* Quirt *enters with his helmet on, limping; steals forward quietly, and sits down on his bunk. There is a nice bloody mess on his right calf.* Flagg *happens to turn, sees what's going on, sits up, watches* Quirt. Quirt *looks back, finally grins, then tries to open a first-aid pack*]

FLAGG: What's the matter with you?

QUIRT: Got a can opener?

FLAGG: You crook!

QUIRT: I say, Captain, got a can opener?

FLAGG: Those things are supposed to be opened with the teeth.

QUIRT: You don't say! Well, this'n' wasn't. This here can was evidently made for the Red Cross by the Columbia Red Salmon Company. Like as not instead of bandages I'll find the God-damnedest mess of goldfish in it.

FLAGG: [*Rises, crosses to* Quirt, *takes can away from him*] Where were you? [*He comes over, strains at the tin. He is looking daggers*] Where were you?

QUIRT: Just looking around.

FLAGG: Here.

[*Hands him tin, opened*]

QUIRT: Thanks.

FLAGG: Where were you, I said.

QUIRT: [*Takes out bandage*] In the vegetable garden, pulling turnips.

[*Starts wiping leg*]

FLAGG: God-damn you, Quirt, I believe you stuck your leg out.

[*Goes back and sits on bunk*]

QUIRT: Like hell I did. If I'd wanted to stick my leg out don't you think I've had plenty of chances to do it before? No, sir, I stuck my head out and some bird in the church tower took a shot at me. There she is. In and out without touching the bone. Just let me squeeze the juice out and she'll be all right. Ain't she the prettiest little damn puncture you ever saw, Captain? Ain't she a beauty?

FLAGG: I suppose you think you're going back to Cognac Pete's, huh?

QUIRT: How'd you guess it? Yes, sir, back to my little skookum lady you tried to make me a present of. Am I happy? Am I happy? Oh, boy! Ask me, Captain, am I happy?

FLAGG: You mean to say you aren't cured of Charmaine yet?

QUIRT: Cured of Charmaine? No, sir, I ain't even getting better. Oh, Captain Flagg, ain't you proud of yourself, ain't you a wizard? God, ain't I sorry to leave you all alone here in this mess? Think of her sitting on my lap, lighting my pipe in the kitchen, and you dodging machine guns. I wonder I don't bust out crying. You know, I wouldn't wonder if you got bumped off and never came back. As a matter of fact, I hope you damn well get your head blown off.

FLAGG: Yeah, you always did have a charming disposition.

QUIRT: [*Squeezing his wound*] Oh, pretty baby, papa doesn't mean to hurt you. Lookit, Captain. By God, I wouldn't take a hundred dollars Mex. for that little bumble-bee that flew in there.

FLAGG: Feel pretty cocky, don't you? Well, you can't go out to-night. I guess you can work all right with that. You'll wait here till Cunningham and I get back with that Alsatian shavetail from the railroad embankment. Then I get leave, the company gets a rest, and we go back together, see?

QUIRT: Not much, I don't see. I've got a very important engagement back to Pete's place. Can't be postponed, not even for the pleasure of your enjoyable company, such as it is. I don't wait for nothing in the world but a medical tag.

[*Enter* Pharmacist's Mate; *stands on steps, leans head in door*]

MATE: Heard your first sergeant was hit in that turnip patch. [Flagg *indicates* Quirt. Mate *crosses to* Quirt; *kneels*] Let's have a look. Um. Night soil in that patch, and you, like a damned fool, crawl after they hit you, and now you're full of that muck. Can you walk, Sergeant?

QUIRT: [*Lying back*] Well, depends on what I see.

MATE: [*Helps up* Quirt, *who carries helmet*] Go to the sick bay at once for a shot of tetanus, and then get out of here. [*Takes his arm, and both cross*] You can reach a collecting station before you're done.

QUIRT: Ain't this heart-breaking, Flagg? Well, duty calls. But my eyes fill with tears at the thought of leaving my old company commander. I don't know as I can go through with it.

FLAGG: Make it snappy, Quirt, or you'll find the door locked.

QUIRT: Yeah? What door?

FLAGG: Charmaine's.

QUIRT: Are you wounded, too, Mr. Flagg?

FLAGG: No, but inside ten minutes I'm going to be wounded or bumped off or have that God-damned prisoner for the Brig.

QUIRT: Try to get killed, will you? To please me— just this once?

[Quirt *and the* Mate *go out*]

FLAGG: Mr. Cunningham . . . I guess you thought I was joking when I proposed that little expedition to the railroad embankments?

CUNNINGHAM: I did not. When do we start?

[*Coming to* Flagg]

FLAGG: Well, I was. I was kidding hell out of you. I'd no more let you go in there, boy, than I'd knife you in the back. The air is full of steel this side of that embankment, and a green man has about as much chance as a cootie on Fifth Avenue.

CUNNINGHAM: You going?

FLAGG: I've got official reasons for going, see? The Brig. wants a prisoner, and he also wants that nest wiped out. Also, I got private and personal reasons for wanting to catch up with that baboon that got the little present through his leg.

CUNNINGHAM: If you're going, that suits me. I ain't no green man. I can crawl on my belly.

FLAGG: Yeah?

CUNNINGHAM: I'm a locomotive engineer and I've been crawling under trains for fifteen years. Had several engines shot out from under me likewise. You think you can scare me with this here war? Christ! You ought to see a few railroad wrecks!

FLAGG: Well, Mr. Cunningham, I'm inclined to think you'll do.

CUNNINGHAM: You're God-damn right, I'll do.

FLAGG: What do you say we black our faces and give a little party, now the guests will be asleep?

CUNNINGHAM: Sure. I like the cut of your jib, and you can lead me to it. Show me which one is the lootenant, so I won't hurt him.

FLAGG: You from Texas?

CUNNINGHAM: You hit it.

FLAGG: Now I get you. So we've got another damned Texan in this outfit, wanting to fight anybody that ain't from Texas.

CUNNINGHAM: Yep, and I ain't no God-damn college boy, either.

FLAGG: Good stuff! Now throw away them fancy-dress clothes of yours and dip in here.

[He offers a can of lamp-black]

CUNNINGHAM: Sure. [Takes off overcoat] I was a locomotive engineer on the Louisiana Midland. Three wrecks in my division last year. Christ, but this war shore is a great relief to me. [Both black their faces] I'm an engineer officer attached to infantry. My brother's still driving an engine back home. Had a letter last month from him. He says, "You dirty yellow sapsucker, quitting your job on the Louisiana Midland. I knew you always were a yellow dog, but I didn't think you'd go back on the road thataway."

FLAGG: Now if I only had a pretty little engine. [Suddenly there is a scream upstairs, a shout in a burly strange tongue. "Heraus!" and three bombs explode. Flagg, the Runners, and all save Aldrich dash for the door] Marines! Marines! Marines! [The lieutenant who had been put to sleep stirs uneasily. After a brief tumult, the people of the cellar descend stairs, Flagg holding a German officer by the collar. He takes him straight to the candle] Let me have a look at you, sweetheart, let me have a look! Boys, he's an Alsatian lieutenant! He couldn't wait for us to go after him, so he came over. [He embraces his captive] Oh, sweetheart—you're the sweetest sight I've seen since Charmaine! Here, Kiper [Pushes him to Kiper]—take care of him for me, and for God's sake don't scare him to death, because he's our ticket of leave!

LEWISOHN: [Screams, outside] Captain Flagg . . .

FLAGG: Who's that?

LIPINSKY: It's little Lewisohn, sir.

[Lewisohn is carried in by Gowdy followed by Pharmacist's Mate, and he is crying monotonously for Captain Flagg]

LEWISOHN: Captain Flagg. Captain Flagg. Stop the blood. Stop the blood.

FLAGG: [Takes him from Gowdy and puts him on floor] I can't stop it, Lewisohn, I'm sorry.

[He examines wound in left side]

LEWISOHN: Oh, Captain Flagg, stop the blood.

FLAGG: Fix him with your needle, Mate.

[Mate gives him needle in arm]

LEWISOHN: Oh, Captain Flagg, can't you please, sir, stop the blood?

FLAGG: [Puts hand behind Lewisohn's head and gently lowers him to floor] You'll be all right, boy. You'll be all right. You'll be all right.

[Lewisohn sighs and relaxes his body]

CURTAIN

ACT III.

A tavern known colloquially as Cognac Pete's. Evening, two days later. The outside door is in the rear, small bar at the right, stairway left, an inside door at right. Windows rear. Ferguson sits at long table smoking and playing solitaire, a bottle of Martell and a brandy pony at his elbow. Charmaine is in front of the table by the candles, sewing. Ferguson is enjoying the luxury of talking to himself, for it is apparent that Charmaine is not following all he says.

FERGUSON: I'm glad they're coming back here. [He sips, between sentences] It's a good, quiet town . . . quiet . . . last time we were in a town where the M.P.'s and the mule skinners fought every night . . . glad they sent 'em back here. . . . You ought to be. . . . Your father'll do a land office business when the outfit gets here. He better knock the bung in every barrel of red ink he's got. God, how they'll eat . . . what's left of 'em. When two hundred leave me behind with the stuff, I always get ready to mess two hundred when they return. Of course a hundred may not return . . . but they'll eat right through to the bottom of the kettle just the same. Now you take that big oakum-haired Swede named Swenson. I never see a Marine eat more than he did . . . I damn well hope Swenson gets back . . . I like to see him eat. There was a little Jew named Lewisohn that could out-eat him, weight for weight; but the Swede weighed twice as much. That Swede could eat anything but a horse collar. [*He chuckles and* Charmaine *smiles*] Well, I'll say we've kept each other company. We sure have, even if you can't speak a white man's lingo; that is, not to say *speak* it. Now if you'd been a Spanish girl we could have got together a little better . . . I lived with a Spanish girl at Cavite back in '99 . . . in those days I was salty as hell, a sea-going buckaroo.

CHARMAINE: *Est-ce que* . . . you are lonely?

FERGUSON: It ain't so bad, staying behind this way. It ain't so bad. Twenty years now I've had 'em leave me. When I was younger I believed some of the liars who said they liked to fight . . . liked being under fire . . . but it always bored me to sit around and be sniped at. Somehow I never did get angry. And you've got to get angry when a bird's shooting at you if you're going to enjoy it. So I didn't have a good time . . . Now you take Flagg there . . . there's the sort likes it. Flagg gets mad as hell if you don't even like him, let alone shoot at him. Flagg and me are different. Now Flagg——

CHARMAINE: Where is *le capitaine?*

FERGUSON: Pretty near here, I suppose.

CHARMAINE: Near here?

FERGUSON: He'll be here presently, General.

CHARMAINE: *Le Capitaine Flagg*—he has been wounded ever?

FERGUSON: Naw! Flagg ain't never been wounded. Never will, neither, if you ask me. You can't hurt his kind. When you see a man like Flagg, it's curious, but they always have the pleasure of drinking themselves to death . . . funny thing . . . I never knew a man who could float a load of liquor, didn't hold all the cards besides. Now you take Flagg . . . he'll be here in fifteen minutes mebbe—mebbe two hours —but just the same as ever . . . thirsty as hell, wishing he had forty geisha girls to play with.

CHARMAINE: Fifteen minutes. . . .

FERGUSON: [*With elaborate gestures*] Le Capitany . . . ici . . . sank . . . min-use ici, sank min-use . . . Compree?

CHARMAINE: *Oui, oui, oui! Merci bien.*

[*She runs upstairs.* Ferguson *continues smoking, pouring a pony of brandy. Presently the door at rear opens slowly. Enter* Sergeant Quirt *in a major's army overcoat, with black braids and a leather-visored garrison cap. He is shaven, crafty-faced. Below the overcoat, which is bursting on his chest, may be seen rough army shoes, gray woolen socks pulled over the bottoms of striped outing-flannel pajamas. He looks exactly what he is, a slightly wounded soldier escaped from hospital in borrowed clothes.* Ferguson *turns, and seeing him, comes to attention.* Quirt *also has a bottle with about half a drink in it*]

FERGUSON: [*Rising courteously*] Good evening, Major.

QUIRT: [*Pours what remains in the bottle he carries into* Ferguson's *glass; then, taking the full bottle,*

sets his empty one in its place] Sit down, Fergy, and use your eyes. Help me to get out of this rigging.

FERGUSON: [*Sitting; irritated*] What are you doing in those gadgets, Quirt? Where's the outfit? Where you been to?

QUIRT: Listen. I ain't writing my memoirs of this war till it's over. All you need to know is, I got two M.P.'s on my trail, and I don't want to meet 'em in these.

[*He removes his coat and is found to be in striped pajamas. A small red cross on the jumper pocket*]

FERGUSON: You come from the lines in that outfit, Quirt? In night-drawers?

QUIRT: I suppose you think I go 'round this way because I like it. [*He stows the overcoat and cap under the bench*] Major, you're relieved. [*Takes slicker from peg on stair rail*] Lend me your slicker, Fergy. I'll give it back if it thunders.

[*He goes to chair at table, seizes the cognac, pours out two ponies and swallows them, looks at* Ferguson, *then pours a third drink; drinks it*]

FERGUSON: Of course you're paying for those, Quirt, even if you have gone cuckoo.

QUIRT: All right, all right! Don't get on your ear about it . . . and now you want to know where I've been.

FERGUSON: Oh, no, if a soldier wants to campaign in a pair of night-drawers, it ain't none of my parade. It takes all kinds of sergeants to make an army.

QUIRT: [*Drinking his third*] You're too hardhearted, Fergy. I ain't in my right mind. I was wounded, and now I've got aspasia. [*Mysteriously*] My name is Field Marshal von Hindenburg, and I'm looking for a wagonload of pants that got lost in shipment.

FERGUSON: Yeah?

QUIRT: Yeah, sure. I wandered outta a hospital about five miles over at a place called Noisy. It was damned well named too, Fergy. Noisy was no name for it when I came outta the ether after I'd shipped in there with a piece of pants driven through a bullet hole in my leg.

FERGUSON: Have to give you ether to take off your pants?

QUIRT: No. They gave me ether so the stretcher bearers could steal a gold watch and eight hundred bucks off me. I certainly put up a squawk when I woke up and found 'em missing. But a hell of a lot of good it did me. I went looking for the bird that got them and ran into a guy in a bartender's coat in the operating room. He tried to pipe me down and I hung a shanty on the bimbo's eye [*Enjoying the picture himself*] and when they washed him off he was a captain. So they locked me up, wound and all. And then I got aspasia, and here I am. You ain't seen me.

FERGUSON: No, I ain't seen you [*Distant voices shouting "Fergy!" "When do we eat?" "Chow," etc.*

At this sound, very faint, Quirt *rises quickly, starting for the stairs with a skip and jump*] Keep your drawers on, Quirt. They ain't no M.P.'s. That's the outfit. I've got old Pete and his brother down at the bridge, keeping coffee and slum hot for 'em. Better go and give yourself up to Flagg as soon as he drives in. You'll be safe then. I'd like to see a set of doctors take Flagg's first sergeant off him when he's just out of the lines. It surely would be a pretty sight afterwards, them doctors working on each other like monkeys. [*The voices come nearer. The cry, long drawn out like a wolf's, comes from many throats: "Ch-o-o-o-w-w!"*] That's me. They're calling for me. Well, old Fergy's got their chow, and hot too.

> [*He goes.* Quirt *limps quickly to door after* Ferguson *goes.* Charmaine *comes down the stairs at the same time*]

QUIRT: [*Turning to find* Charmaine] Hello, Pittsburgh.

CHARMAINE: [*With a small cry, comes toward him*] You are wounded.

QUIRT: Sure I'm wounded. Ain't that enough to put me nine miles ahead of Flagg with you? I certainly beat him here.

CHARMAINE: [*Trying to put arms around his neck*] Mais, mais . . . you are . . .

QUIRT: [*Restraining her*] Don't embarrass me, darling, because I ain't clothed and in my right mind. I just been waiting for Fergy to leave so I could steal a uniform from him. Where's his room? [Charmaine *points to door*] Wait a minute, dearie, until I salvage a pair of breeches. [*He goes out.* Charmaine *goes to the outside door, where voices are now heard.* Quirt *reappears*] Damn it, he's locked his chest! Gimme a ice pick.

> [Quirt *takes bottle from bar. There are steps and voices at the door, and* Quirt *withdraws hastily to the right,* Charmaine *following. Enter* Kiper, Gowdy, *and* Lipinsky. Kiper *spies the cognac bottle and holds it over his open gullet. The other two rush him. There is a tough scuffle*]

KIPER: Lay off my bottle.

GOWDY: Say, don't drink it all! [*All then sit behind the table and deliberately begin a tremendous racket*]

KIPER: Hey! *Vin rouge! Vin blanc!* You, Pete! *Venez ici.* Toot sweet!

LIPINSKY: Toot sweet—toot sweet—toot God-damn sweet—*jambon? Des œufs! Fromages! Vin! Vin!*

GOWDY: *Bière, bière, bière!*

> [Flagg *enters. The three jump up and push back their chairs. When he yells "Clear out," the tumult instantly ceases.* Flagg *is cold sober, still in his old clothes and dusty, but recently shaven, and possessed of rolled leggings and an old brown shirt*]

FLAGG: Clear out, you yapping hounds, and tell the new platoon commander to billet every man down the moment he finishes mess. Tell him I don't want to see one of 'em around this tavern till that's done. [*Turns; crosses to bar*] Tell them not to rag a man to-night. [*Takes bottle; turns to them*] As soon as they know their billets, let 'em out. Let 'em drink. Let 'em fight. Get out.

THE RUNNERS: [*Gently; somewhat discouraged*] Ay, ay, sir.

> [*They disappear.* Charmaine *enters quietly and stands leaning in the doorway.* Flagg *pours a beaker and drinks it pleasantly, enjoyingly. Then he pours a second and walks around to chair at table and sits down.* Charmaine *has watched this from the doorway. He sees her at last*]

FLAGG: [*Arising and bowing grandiosely, holding aloft the drink*] Madame la comtesse de la Cognac!

CHARMAINE: [*Embarrassed*] Le grand capitaine de ma cœur.

FLAGG: Yes, I'm the captain of your heart! Like hell I am. Why don't you come and kiss me? None but the brave, you know . . .

CHARMAINE: *Je ne comprends pas.*

FLAGG: Oh, no. You don't understand me. Well, I'm a weary man, and I don't want any finagling from you.

CHARMAINE: [*At door*] You want me to kiss you?

FLAGG: Sure I want you to kiss me. Even though you played the dirtiest sort of trick on me. [*The liquor is beginning to deaden him*] A dirty trick on your poor old Captain Flagg. [*Turns to her*] If I weren't so kind and gentle I'd go out in the orchard, cut a cherry switch, and give you a tanning.

> [*She crosses over, kisses him quickly, and draws back, a charmed bird before a snake*]

CHARMAINE: You're a terrible man, *monsieur.*

FLAGG: I ain't terrible to you, honey. Come sit by your old man. [*She sits on the table and looks down into his eyes*] Ain't I tired? Jeez, but I'm off war for life. It's all right with thirty or forty men in the hills who know their business. But there's so many little boys along with me ain't got any business here at all. [*He sighs and drinks the rest of the brandy*] Ah! There ain't no strength in this stuff any more. [*Hands her his glass, which she places on table. He gets up unsteadily*] Le's go walk by the canal. I wanna get away from these new lieutenants. Le's walk along that bicycle path.

CHARMAINE: *Non, non, non. Demain soir. Demain soir.*

FLAGG: To-morrow? All right. I'm tired anyhow. Never been so tired before. Liquor just takes the pins out of my knees. Gimme a bottle to drink in bed. I don't want to think to-night.

CHARMAINE: [*Bringing him a bottle from the bar, smiling*] Ah, monsieur, vous êtes un grand soldat.

FLAGG: [*Wandering to the door, suddenly apathetic*] Nighty, sweetie. See you tomorrow.

> [*He goes out at rear*]

QUIRT: [*Entering stealthily, in a farmer's smock*

which comes to his waist] So he's gone away. . . . What's the matter with the old boy?

[*He attempts to kiss her. She shudders*]

CHARMAINE: [*Drawing away from him*] Non, non, non! Merci.

QUIRT: Why, what's the matter, Pittsburgh? Don't you love me no more?

CHARMAINE: *Oui—mais——*

QUIRT: Of course I understand. Seeing him that way sort of cut you up, especially when I was wearing such a lousy outfit, you liking them all in uniforms. Just wait, baby. When I git that brass lock off Fergie's box and turn out in his blues on sick leave, you'll forget this Flagg person. I understand. Sure. I been with soldiers' girls a lot, myself.

CHARMAINE: When you are beautiful, *mon sergeant*, then I love you——

[*She runs up steps*]

QUIRT: Come back here!

[*She disappears, laughing. Kiper and Lipinsky enter*]

KIPER: Jeez, Sergeant, but you picked a funny outfit to be buried in.

QUIRT: [*At foot of stairs—hostile*] Who's thinking of burying me?

KIPER: I expect Flagg'll make me bury you. But he's going to lay you out himself.

QUIRT: Is he looking for me? How did he know I'm here.

LIPINSKY: We just heard Ferguson telling him. I ain't never heard him swear so much since I been with him. We came to ask you to run away some more.

QUIRT: You did, eh? Well, you can go down to the bridge and head him off. You can tell him he passed up visiting this place just before the outfit shoved last time. You can tell him if he comes up here I'll cut his gizzard out for him. You can tell him I'm engaged to be married, and I ain't got no duty for him around here.

[*Flagg enters, drunk and swaggering*]

FLAGG: Who's the hay-shaker? Well, if it ain't Sergeant Quirt! A regular family reunion. Quirt, how are you? When you coming back to the factory?

QUIRT: Flagg, you're out of this here detail. You're hands off my business after that dirty trick you put over on me. If I kill you there isn't a court can touch me for it in this man's army.

FLAGG: Quirt, you're drunk.

QUIRT: Both of us.

FLAGG: Yeah, both of us.

QUIRT: Well, then, Flagg, you're drunk. What are you going to do about it?

FLAGG: I'm gonna have a drink.

[*Turns to bar and takes bottle; pours two drinks*]

QUIRT: Both of us.

FLAGG: Yeah, both of us. [*They drink, first bowing to each other*] Quirt, I got something I want to tell you.

QUIRT: The hell!

FLAGG: You want to hear it?

QUIRT: I ain't particular.

FLAGG: Well, this is it, Sergeant. You can go jump in the canal. I knew you'd head for Charmaine as soon as you got that bullet under your hide. You had half a day's start of me and you didn't beat me more than five minutes. You might just as well 'a' stayed on the bakery route. You ain't no more needed here than a third leg on a kangaroo. Have one on me.

[*Flagg pours for both*]

QUIRT: [*They bow*] Delighted, I'm sure. [*They drink and replace glasses*] You're a hell of an officer, Flagg [*Quirt wipes right hand on smock*], and your views on me probably ain't worth a damn. On the other hand, it's only fair to warn you that I'm the sole survivor of seven catastrophes, any one of which was calculated to carry off every man-jack in the immediate neighborhood as was adjacent, and if there was to be a catastrophe of any dimensions in this here vicinity in the near future, I have expectations of survival exceeding your own. Have one on me.

[*Quirt pours drinks*]

FLAGG: Thank you, Quirt, I will. [*They drink, and Flagg drunkenly points finger at Quirt until he can get his mind to working*] Your method of expressing yourself, Quirt, is complicated by your tongue being as thick as your God-damn head. But if you mean trouble, let me point out to you that among other things, you forgot to bring your gun along. [*Quirt feels for his absent weapon; Flagg laughs heartily*] Ain't you a neat little fool, Hoppergrass, and will you drink?

QUIRT: I will.

[*Flagg pours. Both bow, then drink again; but Quirt has taken a sip before he realizes he hasn't bowed*]

FLAGG: Do you give up?

QUIRT: No.

FLAGG: [*Turns to bar and starts pouring*] Have another.

[*As Flagg starts to pour, Quirt leaps like a flash on his back. Kiper catches Quirt's wrists from behind. Lipinsky drags Flagg away. When Quirt jumps Flagg, he takes the gun out of Flagg's holster with his right hand; his left is in stranglehold around Flagg's neck. Flagg reaches back and holds Quirt by back of neck. They scuffle until separated*]

KIPER: [*Holding Quirt*] What do you want done with him, sir?

FLAGG: [*To Lipinsky, who is holding him*] Let me go or I'll knock you for a row of G.I. cans. Take the gun away from him. [*Quirt throws the automatic on the floor. Flagg puts his foot on it*] Let go, all. [*Quirt is turned loose*] Well, bo, had enough?

QUIRT: I'll tell you what I'll do with you. I'll go

outside with you and try two of them little toys at fifty yards.

FLAGG: And you, the best pistol shot in the corps, would put one through my carburetor as easy as pitching a penny in a well. Come again.

QUIRT: I'll take you on any way you can think of, you baboon. I can out-shoot you and out-think you and out-drink you. There ain't nothing I can't do better than you.

FLAGG: You're a liar, Quirt, and you know it. I could break you in two. You got my gun because you jumped me without warning. No soldier you ever soldiered with could head me when I got started . . . and by the way, Quirt, if you can out-drink me you ain't leading out very well to-night. You're talking thick and wild, Quirt, thick and wild. You'd better turn in somewhere and sleep it off.

QUIRT: Me? Sleep off a couple of drinks? I was living on cognac when all your buttons was safety pins.

FLAGG: Yeah, well, you can't carry it the way you used to, then. You're getting old, Quirt. Old and feeble. Yeah, you're getting old.

QUIRT: Not me, *You* may be an old man, Flagg. Or an old woman if it suits you better, but not me. Captains and generals, they pass along. I've seen hundreds of 'em. Better men than you, Flagg. They passed along. But top sergeants is eternal. They don't never die.

FLAGG: Well, if you don't want to die, you top sergeant, don't fool with me. I've seen top sergeants go damn fast—Now, listen, Quirt, are you going to jump in that canal or are you going to need six pall-bearers to take you there?

QUIRT: It'll take more than six pall-bearers to put me in one of these French canals. I don't like the taste of them.

[Charmaine *re-enters*]

FLAGG: Charmaine! Cognac!

[Charmaine *crosses behind table; gets bottle; pours drink for* Quirt, *also for* Flagg]

CHARMAINE: [*Laying a hand on the* Captain's *shoulder*] Is it now—friends again?

FLAGG: [*Putting an arm about her*] Best you ever saw, Charmaine. We'll drink to it, Quirt. Flagg and Quirt forever—till you get bumped off. Flagg and Quirt, the tropical twins! There ain't room for both of 'em in the whole world!

[Flagg *pats* Charmaine *on hip*]

QUIRT: [*Sets down his glass, hard*] Damn you, Flagg!

FLAGG: [*Setting down his glass*] What's the matter, Hoppergrass? Aren't you drinking?

QUIRT: I got here first, Flagg.

FLAGG: I know it. Nobody said you didn't.

QUIRT: [*Rising*] You take your hands off Charmaine.

FLAGG: Any time you want my hands off Charmaine, you come and take 'em off.

CHARMAINE: No. No! You must be friends.

FLAGG: With you around!

QUIRT: It strikes me there's only room for one of us in this shanty to-night. Do you plan on going somewhere, or not?

FLAGG: Did you ever see me leaving any place I didn't feel like leaving?

CHARMAINE: [*Touching the* Captain's *sleeve*] Don't fight—please.

FLAGG: [*Not looking at her—pushing her back*] The hell you say! First time in six months I've had a good reason for fighting. The Germans don't want my woman. I been fighting them for eight dollars a day. . . . Go on back of the counter.

CHARMAINE: I—I love you both.

QUIRT: You get to hell outta here, Flagg. Dig up a broad of your own.

FLAGG: Sorry. Rejected.

QUIRT: You ain't man enough to shoot me for her. Well, here's what I'll do. I'll shoot you dice for her. [*Tosses out dice on table*] High dice, aces low. [Kiper *and* Lipinsky *take steps forward, interested*]

FLAGG: Boys, is Quirt crooked with the bones?

[Lipinsky *goes back to lean on platform*]

KIPER: He's got a pair out to be in a circus. [Quirt *gives* Kiper *a bad look*]

FLAGG: Then we'll deal a hand at blackjack.

QUIRT: [*Picks up dice; puts them back in pocket, while* Kiper *goes back with* Lipinsky] And the guy that loses beats it for somewhere else.

FLAGG: What do you mean, beats it? We'll shoot, but my way. The man that wins gets a gun, and the man that loses gets a head start. Everybody wins, see? One gets the girl and the other gets a chance to stay in bed the rest of this war.

KIPER: Captain Flagg, I don't think you ought to do this.

FLAGG: Close your hatch. I'll try anything once, soldier. [*Briskly*] Now for a game of blackjack for one automatic.

QUIRT: That's all right with me.

FLAGG: And the gun on the table between us.

[*He picks it up*]

KIPER: [*As he and* Lipinsky *seize* Quirt's *arms*] Come quiet now, before he notices.

QUIRT: [*Writhing loose*] Keep off me, you swine!

[Kiper *and* Lipinsky *fall back*]

FLAGG: [*Having recovered gun, starts to straighten up*] March out that door, both of you, and if you stick a neck in here before the game's over, I promise to wreck you for life. Are you going, or do I demonstrate? [*They go out quickly*] Charmaine! Upstairs!

[*She goes.* Flagg *sits at table;* Quirt *on table.* Flagg *shuffles cards, and offering them to* Quirt, *says* "Cut." Quirt *fondles cards; says* "Be good to me, babies, and I'll let moonlight into a captain." *He cuts.* Flagg *deals one to* Quirt, *then one to himself; then one to* Quirt, *and looks at the next one for himself*]

QUIRT: What's that, a king?

FLAGG: How many you want? Make it snappy and knock off that guff. Here's looking down your grave. May you have many worms, Quirt.

QUIRT: Crawling, right out of your teeth, Flagg. Hit me.

FLAGG: [*Deals a card face up*] A two-spot. Well, any more?

QUIRT: Hit me again.

FLAGG: [*Dealing one*] Well, you got a king that time. Remember, if you hold six cards without going bust you can empty the automatic at me.

QUIRT: Hit me again.

FLAGG: A king, by God! [Quirt, *with one sweep turns over the table, with candles and chairs, and dives through the door; runs off*] You double-dealing Chinaman! [Flagg *finds the gun in the darkness and fires shot just outside the door. He is heard reentering*] Show a light, somebody, Charmaine!

[Flagg *sets up the table*]

CHARMAINE: [*At the head of the stairs with a lamp*] What is it? You have killed him?

[*Goes up to door*]

FLAGG: Killed hell! He knocked out the light and ran, the dirty hound! [Charmaine *looks out the door, shielding the lamp from the wind*] Oh, he's gone.

CHARMAINE: Maybe you hit him.

[*Puts lamp on table; then crosses to* Flagg]

FLAGG: Don't you worry. He was halfway to the river, the rate he was going, before I found the door. Don't you weep, sweetheart [*Puts her on his left knee*]; you're weeping for a skunk that'd run out on a game of cards. It's you and me to-night, lady. Listen, Charmaine [*Putting his arm around her*]; I love you like the devil. I always did. You love me, Charmaine?

CHARMAINE: Only you.

FLAGG: God, I'm dead—I'm going to sleep for three days.

[Flagg *rests head on her breast and sighs. Then* Lipinsky *and* Gowdy *walk in*]

LIPINSKY: Sorry to disturb you, sir.

FLAGG: My God, did you hear what I told you?

LIPINSKY: Got bad news, Captain Flagg.

FLAGG: Spit it out.

LIPINSKY: The outfit's going back. Battalion moving at once.

FLAGG: What? What?

LIPINSKY: We're ordered back. Ordered back in. Everybody's going back in. General movement.

FLAGG: Dammit, I'm on leave.

GOWDY: All leaves revoked, Captain Flagg.

FLAGG: Well, why couldn't you stay away from here? You knew where I was. Why in hell did you have to come and tell me?

GOWDY: Well, headquarters sent out, looking for you.

LIPINSKY: Kiper wouldn't come, Captain Flagg. He was for leaving you alone.

FLAGG: He was, was he? Well, Kiper's got sense. Look here, you never found me to give me the message, and I'm not going. Can you remember, or have I got to bury you to keep your mouth shut? What right have they got to offer a man leave and then revoke it? I gave them their prisoner! I've got their damn papers!

LIPINSKY: Well, you see, the company's going to shove off. What could we do?

FLAGG: You could have an attack of something, damn it to hell! You could fall and break your neck on the way here.

LIPINSKY: I was afraid not to let you know. You always wanted to know.

FLAGG: Well, you've got to do some tall lying to make up for it, because I'm not going. Tell them any story you think of, only I never got the news. I earned my leave, and it's signed, sealed, and delivered. That crowd at headquarters has got to live up to its end of the bargain. They can't take these men back in. I won't stand for it. [*Turns to* Charmaine] Shall we stay here, Charmaine?

CHARMAINE: *Oui, ici.*

[*They embrace.* Flagg *rests head on her breast*]

FLAGG: [*After a pause, shakes himself a bit*] No, I'll go. I may be drunk, but I know I'll go. There's something rotten about this profession of arms, some kind of damned religion connected with it that you can't shake. When they tell you to die, you have to do it, even if you're a better man than they are. Good-bye, Charmaine, put your money in real estate, and marry that cuckoo if you can. You'll never see me again. This town is a jinx for me. [*Again rests head on* Charmaine] God Almighty, but I'm tired. [*He rises and crosses to where* Ferguson *has entered.* Charmaine *sits in chair watching*] Hello, Fergy. We're shoving off. Follow us, because we don't know where we're going. Nobody knows.

[*He goes out, staggering, tired.* Ferguson *follows him out.* Gowdy *and* Lipinsky *follow* Ferguson. Charmaine *buries her head in arms on table*]

QUIRT: [*Comes in upper floor stairway*] Hello, Pittsburgh!

CHARMAINE: You are not *killed?*

QUIRT: [*Coming downstairs to bottom step*] No. It's me all right. Everybody gone?

CHARMAINE: Everybody.

QUIRT: Outfit's going in again, huh?

CHARMAINE: *Oui.*

QUIRT: Well, well! I been upstairs. Climbed up the kitchen roof. Do you love your papa?

CHARMAINE: *Mais oui.*

QUIRT: Then you better kiss him good-bye. [*Pats her face; then kisses her. Staggers up to door*] What a lot of God-damn fools it takes to make a war! Hey, Flagg, wait for baby!

[Charmaine *watches from the table*]

CURTAIN

Maxwell Anderson

(1888– ——)

After Eugene O'Neill, no one envisioned higher standards for the American theatre than Maxwell Anderson. Although quite at home in prose, he set up precepts for verse drama; and although adept at writing salty humor, he decided that nothing less than the composition of poetic tragedy could be a proper aim for American dramatists. Whether his approach to poetic drama was not somewhat more academic than necessary, and whether he did not often say less than he seemed to be saying in his purple patches—these and other matters concerning his playwriting could be widely debated. But it was surely an accomplishment for Maxwell Anderson to be the only American (except for the American-born naturalized Englishman T. S. Eliot) to make the Broadway playgoer accept verse drama, and this not merely once but on some half-dozen occasions between 1930 and 1950.

Anderson was the son of a Baptist preacher who occupied various pastorates in Pennsylvania and the Middle West. Having developed a love of literature at an early age, Anderson took a Bachelor of Arts degree at the University of North Dakota and a Master of Arts at Stanford University and in 1914 began to teach English. Soon, however, his ideals began to exercise a disturbing influence on his career. He was dismissed from a post at Whittier College, in California, for advocating pacifism during the First World War, and then found himself in difficulties in the field of journalism, to which he had turned for a living. He lost his job on the *San Francisco Bulletin* in 1918 for his unorthodox editorials and was discharged from other positions quickly and with fateful regularity. He found a refuge at last on Pulitzer's liberal morning newspaper, the *New York World,* then the haven of many men who later achieved literary distinction. When he left the *World,* in 1924, it was not as an unwanted editorial writer but as coauthor of one of the most successful plays of his time, *What Price Glory?*

Anderson's first victories in the field of playwriting were in the service of prose realism. After collaborating with Laurence Stallings on *What Price Glory?,* he adapted Jim Tully's novel about hobos, *Beggars of Life,* under the title *Outside Looking In* (1925); he then wrote a highly successful comedy of marriage, *Saturday's Children* (1927), in which economics destroys domestic happiness; and he collaborated with the journalist Harold Hickerson on a treatment of the Sacco-Vanzetti case, *Gods of the Lightning* (1928), which crackled with indignation at evidences of social injustice. Later, in 1933, he produced a stinging satire on Congressional logrolling, *Both Your Houses,* which won a Pulitzer Prize, and he continued to write plays in prose whenever he felt that prose dialogue suited his theme. But he had had romantic and poetic aspirations from the very start of his career. He wrote a youthful volume of lyrics, *You Who Have Dreams,* and his very first play to be produced, *White Desert* (1923), was a poetic tragedy. It failed, and he bided his time until 1930 before venturing into poetry again.

When Anderson wrote *Elizabeth the Queen,* he was already an experienced playwright and showman. He reflected that successful verse drama had never been written about contemporary life and decided upon a historical subject: the fatal love affair of Elizabeth and Lord Essex. Superbly produced by the Theatre Guild, with Lynn Fontanne playing Elizabeth and Alfred Lunt as Essex, this tragedy proved highly successful. It was, in fact, the first successful drama of the modern American theatre to be written in verse. Encouraged by his success, Anderson wrote a number of other historical plays, the best being *Mary of Scotland* (1933) and *Anne of the Thousand Days* (1948). The three plays form a Tudor trilogy, although they were not written in chronological order. Anderson turned to American history in *Night over Taos* (1932) and *Valley Forge* (1934), to Austrian history in *The Masque of Kings* (1937), and to the Middle Ages in *Joan of Lorraine* (1946).

In these and other histories, Anderson was more than a chronicler of romantic events. He employed the past to illuminate the present in his story of Joan of Arc, in an effort to dramatize the problem of heroism. He used the story of the ill-starred Rudolph of Hapsburg, in *The Masque of Kings,* to ask whether a true idealist could align himself with any revolutionary movement: that is, whether one was not apt to overthrow a tyrannical government only to become saddled with a new and possibly worse tyranny. Anderson's libretto for the Kurt Weill musical comedy *Knickerbocker Holiday* (1938) revived early New York history with a view to denouncing authoritarian tendencies in American life; the play was even prefaced with an attack on the New Deal. And in the Tudor romances, Anderson never veered far from his customary suspicions of government as a magnet for power lust.

But Anderson did not confine himself to historical drama. In *Winterset* (1935), he returned to the Sacco-Vanzetti case and wrote a contemporary poetic tragedy filled with indignation and pity. He satirized the modern materialistic world in the poetic fantasy *High Tor* (1937). And he turned to the question of fascism in *Key Largo* (1938), dramatizing his conviction that one could not evade the challenge of the times. Anderson's chief interest, however, lay not in asserting political beliefs so much as in demonstrating his tragic view of life. He saw man as a creature of high passion, who is raised to tragic stature by the intensity of his nature. Anderson created characters whose wills clash mightily and send sparks into the night of human error and evil. It is the wonder of man's spiritual resources that has fascinated him most, and his ultimate objective has always been the writing of universal drama. Even in dealing with such topical matters as the Second World War—in *Candle in the Wind* (1941) and *The Eve of St. Mark* (1942)—or the problem of racial prejudice—in *Lost in the Stars* (1949), his dramatization of the novel *Cry, the Beloved Country* —he tried to universalize the immediate issues. In fact, he conscientiously differentiated between universal and topical plays, writing the latter in prose. He came to be most at home in the romantic past and in the drama of "universals" and was least successful when he was most journalistic.

An estimate of Anderson's work as a poetic dramatist cannot be made without examining each of the plays in some detail. It can be said, however, that he became to the American theatre what Schiller was to the German and Rostand to the French. If he was by no means so true a poet as Schiller or so fine an ironist as Rostand, he too gave the stage a romantic drama high in spirit and vaguely idealistic in aim. In *High Tor* he wrote the best romantic comedy and fantasy of the American theatre. In *Winterset* he came closer than any other American playwright to writing a poetic tragedy in verse about modern life. Although he did not quite create an integrated and completely satisfying play in *Winterset,* the second act of this tragedy, in which the quest for justice flares into passionate drama, is one of the memorable pieces of modern playwriting. And the Tudor plays are filled with spirited writing and with rousing conflict. Even the derivativeness of much of his verse in these plays was no great impediment to effectiveness except when he became too prolix; and the questionable profundity of his statement here, as in other plays, was no serious hindrance to dramatic exaltation. A good deal of vigor and vivacity, as well as elevation, came into our theatre when Anderson began reacquainting us with Elizabethan heroes and scoundrels. The question uppermost in the minds of his severest critics was simply whether Anderson was on the right track in trying to make the drama literary in conventional terms, and this is a question that apparently troubled the author himself from time to time. But every writer works within the limits of his endowment, and Anderson's was rich if not remarkably original.

Elizabeth the Queen is unquestionably the cornerstone of Anderson's achievement in verse drama. This play holds in solution the points of view that ruled most of his later work—namely, his distrust of government and of power politics, his conviction that men of good will are apt to be destroyed while "the rats inherit the earth," and his belief that the pageant of human desire and suffering is nevertheless awe-inspiring and magnificent. *Elizabeth the Queen* fulfills the Aristotelian principles which Anderson accepted as right and necessary. The tragedy revolves around strong personalities who are fired by high passion and who dignify the human spirit in the very act of destroying themselves through their failings; they are, in other words, heroic characters destroyed by a "tragic flaw" but capable of asserting the splendor of the soul even in error and defeat.

Anderson believed that the audience of the theatre, which he celebrated as the "phoenix of the arts," wants to be convinced "that men have a desire to break the molds of earth which encase them." This could be accomplished by "the spiritual awakening, or regeneration" of the hero, and Anderson gave much thought to the nature of tragic art in the prefaces he wrote to several of his plays. These prefaces, collected in a volume entitled *Off Broadway* (1947), contain a good deal of considered, if also somewhat "inspirational," writing. But all his thoughts led him to one unavoidable conclusion: high matter required a heightened style of writing, and the American drama needed "the touch of a great poet." Without ever claiming to be that poet, Anderson decided that he had to write his tragedies in verse. *Elizabeth the Queen* represents his first mature attempt to develop a workmanlike poetic style. The over-all pattern is Elizabethan blank verse, although a good deal of the writing is more Tennysonian than Elizabethan in quality. The metrical form does not, however, impose any restraints upon the dramatic flow of the dialogue, and Anderson takes as many liberties with the blank-verse line as he feels it necessary or expedient to take in the modern theatre. The general effect of the writing is one of passionateness and elevated expression.

BIBLIOGRAPHY: Maxwell Anderson, *Off Broadway: Essays about the Theatre,* 1947; Brooks Atkinson, *Broadway Scrapbook* (pp. 251–254), 1947; John Mason Brown, *Two on the Aisle* (pp. 148–159, 208–211), 1938; Eleanor Flexner, *American Playwrights 1918–1938* (pp. 78–129), 1938; John Gassner, *Masters of the Drama* (pp. 678–693, 696), 1945; Joseph Wood Krutch, *The American Drama Since 1918* (pp. 286–318), 1939; Burns Mantle, *Contemporary American Playwrights* (pp. 37–46), 1938; George Jean Nathan, *The Theatre Book of the Year 1946–1947* (pp. 189–196), 1947; Stark Young, *Immortal Shadows* (pp. 165–168, 185–188), 1948.

ELIZABETH THE QUEEN

By Maxwell Anderson

CHARACTERS

SIR WALTER RALEIGH	THE FOOL	HEMMINGS
PENELOPE GRAY	CAPTAIN ARMIN	FALSTAFF
A CAPTAIN	MARY	PRINCE HENRY
SIR ROBERT CECIL	ELLEN	GADSHILL
LORD ESSEX	TRESSA	PETO
FRANCIS BACON	MARVEL	POINS
QUEEN ELIZABETH	A COURIER	ALSO GUARDS, MEN-AT-ARMS,
LORD BURGHLEY	A HERALD	MAIDS-IN-WAITING, AND
LORD HOWARD	BURBAGE	OTHERS

Players in the scene from Henry IV (bracketed with HEMMINGS, FALSTAFF, PRINCE HENRY, GADSHILL, PETO, POINS)

ACT I. SCENE I.

An entrance hall before a council chamber in the palace at Whitehall. The entrance to the council room is closed and four Guards *with halberds stand at either side. A small door at the left of the entrance is also shut. It is early morning. The* Guards *stand immobile.*

FIRST GUARD: The sun's out again, and it's guineas to pounds the earl comes back this morning.

SECOND GUARD: I'll be glad of it, for one. You get nothing but black looks about the court when he's away.

FIRST GUARD: You'll get little else now he's back, my bully. They quarreled too far for mending, this time.

THIRD GUARD: Tut! They quarrel no more than the cock with the hen. The earl's been sick.

FIRST GUARD: Sick of the queen's displeasure. It's a disease a favorite can die of, and many have.

FOURTH GUARD: He's no sicker of her displeasure than she of his, if a man may judge. Once the earl's gone there's no dancing, no plays, no feasting . . . nothing to do nights but sleep. The very scullery-maids grow cold, and go to bed alone—like the queen.

FIRST GUARD: There are some even a scullery-maid would seldom kiss, save in moments of great excitement. Poor Wat looks forward to feast nights.

FOURTH GUARD: I've had my luck.

FIRST GUARD: You've had what was coming to you. Mucklemouth Jean, of the back kitchen.

FOURTH GUARD: You'd have been glad of her yourself if you could have had her.

FIRST GUARD: Consider, man. She may not have been true. When she wouldn't play with you, may-hap she was playing with somebody else. And if the queen could live without her Earl of Essex, it may

have been because Sir Walter had a new suit of silver armor.

THIRD GUARD: And there's a handsome man.

FOURTH GUARD: God defend me from speaking lightly of the queen!

FIRST GUARD: Eh? God defend you? Let no man accuse me of speaking lightly of the queen, nor of any other woman . . . unless she be a light woman, in which case, God defend me, I will speak lightly of her if I choose.

THIRD GUARD: What say you of the queen?

FIRST GUARD: Of the queen? I say she is well-known to be the virgin queen; I say no more.

SECOND GUARD: But do you think she is a virgin?

FIRST GUARD: She has doubtless been a virgin, bully, for all women have been virgins, but the question is: First, when . . . and, second, where?

SECOND GUARD: Where?

FIRST GUARD: Where, bully, where?

THIRD GUARD: Would you not say, in the proper place?

FIRST GUARD: No. I would not say in the proper place. Because it is hard to say if there is a proper place wherein to be a virgin . . . unless it be in church, and, God defend me, I do not go to church.

SECOND GUARD: You do not go to church?

FIRST GUARD: No, for my sins, I do not go to church . . . or, if you like, I do not go to church for my sins.

SECOND GUARD: Does it follow that the church is a proper place for virgins?

FIRST GUARD: It does. Did I not tell you I do not go there for my sins?

FOURTH GUARD: They say the queen's getting to be an old woman; but I swear she looks younger than my wife, whom I married a young thing, six years come Easter.

THIRD GUARD: It would age a girl fast, just the look of you.

FIRST GUARD: As for the queen, powder and paint

, i

account for some of it. To say nothing of the earl.
A young lover will do much for a lady's face.

FOURTH GUARD: Now God defend me . . .

FIRST GUARD: Aye, aye . . . God defend poor
Nat.

[A Nobleman *enters in silver armor. It is* Sir
Walter Raleigh, *no other*]

RALEIGH: Has the queen come forth yet?

FIRST GUARD: No, Sir Walter.

RALEIGH: The Earl of Essex . . . is he here?

FIRST GUARD: No, my lord.

RALEIGH: When he comes send me word. I shall
be in the north corridor. [*He turns*]

FIRST GUARD: Good, my lord.

[Penelope Gray *comes in from the right, passing through*]

RALEIGH: [*Meeting her*] Greetings, lady, from my
heart.

PENELOPE: Good-morrow, lord, from my soul.

RALEIGH: I take my oath in your face that you are
rushing to the window to witness the arrival of my
lord of Essex.

PENELOPE: And in your teeth I swear I am on no
such errand . . . but only to see the sunrise.

RALEIGH: The sun has been up this hour, my dear.

PENELOPE: The more reason to hurry, gracious
night.

RALEIGH: Do you think to pull the bag over my
head so easily, Penelope? On a day when the earl
returns every petticoat in the palace is hung with an
eye to pleasing him. Yours not the least.

PENELOPE: I deny him thrice.

RALEIGH: I relinquish you, lady. Run, run to the
window! He will be here and you will miss him!

PENELOPE: Is there a lady would run from Sir
Walter in his silver suiting? Since the sun is up . . .
I have no errand.

RALEIGH: Is there no limit to a woman's deception,
wench? Would you go so far as to appear pleased
if I kissed you?

PENELOPE: And no deception. [*He kisses her*] I
call the Gods to witness . . . did I not blush
prettily?

RALEIGH: And meant it not at all. Tell me, did the
queen send you to look out the casement for news
of her Essex, or did you come at the prompting of
your heart?

PENELOPE: Shall I tell you the truth?

RALEIGH: Verily.

PENELOPE: The truth is I cannot answer.

RALEIGH: Both, then?

PENELOPE: Both or one or neither.

RALEIGH: Fie on the baggage.

PENELOPE: Is it not a virtue to be close-mouthed
in the queen's service?

RALEIGH: If you kept the rest of your person as
close as your mouth what a paragon of virtue you
would be!

PENELOPE: Indeed, my lord, I am.

RALEIGH: Indeed, my lady? Have there not been
certain deeds on dark nights?

PENELOPE: Sh! Under the rose.

RALEIGH: Meaning under covers . . .

PENELOPE: Fie on my lord, to make me out a
strumpet!

RALEIGH: It is my manner of wooing, fair maid!
I woo by suggestion of images . . .

PENELOPE: Like small boys on the closet wall . . .

RALEIGH: Like a soldier . . .

PENELOPE: Aye, a veteran . . . of encounters . . .

RALEIGH: I will have you yet, my love; I will take
lessons from this earl . . .

PENELOPE: Take this lesson from me, my lord:
You must learn to desire what you would have.
Much wanting makes many a maid a wanton. You
want me not . . . nor I you. You wear your silver
for a queen.

[A Captain *enters from the left*]

CAPTAIN: Good-morrow, Sir Walter. Is the queen
still under canopy?

RALEIGH: I know not.

CAPTAIN: The earl is here and would see her.

RALEIGH: Bid him hurry if he wishes to find her
abed as usual.

PENELOPE: She is dressed and stirring, captain,
and awaits my lord.

RALEIGH: And many another fair maid awaits him
likewise, captain. Take him that message from me.
Run, girl, run. Tell the queen.

[*The* Captain *goes out left*]

PENELOPE: [*Going*] You make yourself so easily
disliked.

[*She goes right.* Cecil *enters, passing her*]

CECIL: He is here?

RALEIGH: So. The heavenly boy, clad in the
regalia of the sun, even now extracts his gallant foot
from his golden stirrup and makes shift to descend
from his heaving charger. Acclamation lifts in every
voice, tears well to every eye . . . with the exception
of mine, perhaps, and yours, I hope . . .

CECIL: I am at a pass to welcome him, myself.
This Elizabeth of ours can be difficult on her good
days . . . and there have been no good ones lately.

[*Two* Men-at-Arms *enter with silver armor in
their arms*]

RALEIGH: And what is all this, sirrah?

FIRST MAN: Armor, my lord.

RALEIGH: For whom?

FIRST MAN: We know not.

RALEIGH: Now by the ten thousand holy names!
Am I mistaken, Robert, or is this armor much like
my own?

CECIL: Very like, I should say. Is it sterling?

RALEIGH: And the self-same pattern. Has the earl
gone lunatic?

CECIL: He means to outshine you, perhaps.

RALEIGH: Has it come to this? Do I set the style
for Essex?

That would be a mad trick, to dress himself like me!

[Bacon *appears in the doorway at right*]
What do you know of this, Sir Francis?
  BACON: Greeks, my lord, bearing gifts.
  RALEIGH: To hell with your Greeks! The devil
    damn him!
This is some blackguardry!
    [*Two more* Men-at-Arms *enter, carrying armor*]
There's more of it! Good God, it comes in bales!
I say, who's to wear this, sirrah? Who is it for?
    [Essex *enters from corridor between the two
    files of soldiers, pushing them aside as he does
    so, and crosses to right of* Raleigh, *speaking
    as he enters*]
  ESSEX: Their name is legion, Sir Walter. Happily
    met!
Felicitations on your effulgence, sir!
You're more splendid than I had imagined. News
    came of your silver
Even in my retreat! I was ill, and I swear it cured
    me!
You should have heard the compliments I've heard
Passed on you! Sir Walter's in silver! The world's
    outdone,
They said—the moon out-mooned. He gleams down
    every corridor
And every head's turned after him. The queen
Herself has admired it—the design—the workman-
    ship!
There's nothing like it this side of Heaven's streets.
And I said to myself—the great man—this is what
    we have needed——
More silver everywhere—oceans of silver!
Sir Walter has set the style, the world will follow.
So I sent for the silver-smiths, and by their sweat
Here's for you lads, tailored to every man's meas-
    ure——
Shall Raleigh wear silver alone? Why, no,
The whole court shall go argent!
  RALEIGH: Take care, my lord.
I bear insults badly.
  ESSEX: And where are you insulted?
For the queen's service you buy you a silver armor.
In the queen's service I buy you a dozen more.
A gift, my friends, each man to own his own,
As you own yours. What insult?
  RALEIGH: Have your laugh,
Let the queen and court laugh with you! Since you
    are envious
You may have my suit. I had not thought even
    Essex
Bore so petty a mind.
  ESSEX: I misunderstood you
Perhaps, Sir Walter. I had supposed you donned
Silver for our queen, but I was mistaken . . .
Keep these all for yourself. The men shall have
    others . . .
Some duller color.
  RALEIGH: I have borne much from you
Out of regard for the queen, my lord of Essex.

  ESSEX: And I from you.
By God . . .
  CECIL: You have forgotten, Sir Walter,
A certain appointment . . .
  RALEIGH: And you will bear more, by Heaven! . .
  CECIL: He is going to the queen,
Remember. And we have an errand.
  ESSEX: You presume to protect me,
Master Secretary?
  CECIL: I protect you both, and our mistress.
There can be no quarreling here.
  RALEIGH: That's very true. Let us go.
    [Cecil *and* Raleigh *go out right*]
  BACON: And this armor? What becomes of it?
  ESSEX: I have given it.
Would you have me take it back?
  BACON: There has seldom been
A man so little wise, so headstrong, but he
Could sometimes see how necessary it is
To keep friends and not make enemies at court.
But you . . . God knows.
  ESSEX: Let him make friends with me.
He may need friends himself.
[*To the* Guards] These are your armors.
Keep them, wear them, sell them, whatever you
    like . . .
Or your captain directs you.
  FIRST GUARD: We thank you.
    [*They retire to examine the armor*]
  BACON: You are going to the queen?
  ESSEX: Yes. God help us both!
  BACON: Then hear me a moment. . . .
  ESSEX: Speak, schoolmaster,
I knew it was coming. You've been quiet too long.
  BACON: Listen to me this once, and listen this once
To purpose, my lord, or it may hardly be worth
My while ever to give you advice again
Or for you to take it. You have enough on your
    hands
Without quarrelling with Raleigh. You have quar-
    relled with the queen
Against my judgment. . . .
  ESSEX: God and the devil! Can a man
Quarrel on order or avoid a quarrel at will?
  BACON: Why certainly, if he knows his way.
  ESSEX: Not I.
  BACON: You quarrelled with her, because she
    wished to keep peace.
And you wanted war. . . .
  ESSEX: We are at war with Spain!
But such a silly, frightened, womanish war
As only a woman would fight. . . .
  BACON: She is a woman and fights a womanish
    war;
But ask yourself one question and answer it
Honestly, dear Essex, and perhaps you will see then
Why I speak sharply. You are my friend and patron
Where you gain I gain . . . where you lose I lose . .
And I see you riding straight to a fall today . . .
And I'd rather your neck weren't broken.

ESSEX: Ask myself
What question?

BACON: Ask yourself what you want:
To retain the favor of the queen, remain
Her favorite, keep all that goes with this;
Or set yourself against her and trust your fortune
To popular favor?

ESSEX: I'll not answer that.

BACON: Then . . . I have done.

ESSEX: Forgive me, dear friend, forgive me,
I have been ill, and this silly jackanapes
Of a Raleigh angers me with his silver mountings
Till I forget who's my friend. You know my answer
In regard to the queen. I must keep her favor.
Only it makes me mad to see all this . . .
This utter mismanagement, when a man's hand and
    brain
Are needed and cannot be used.

BACON: Let me answer for you;
You are not forthright with yourself. The queen
Fights wars with tergiversation and ambiguities . . .
You wish to complete your record as general,
Crush Spain, subdue Ireland, make a name like
    Cæsar's,
Climb to the pinnacle of fame. Take care.
You are too popular already. You have
Won at Cadiz, caught the people's hearts,
Caught their voices till the streets ring your name
Whenever you pass. You are loved better than
The queen. That is your danger. She will not suffer
A subject to eclipse her; she cannot suffer it.
Make no mistake. She will not.

ESSEX: And I must wait,
Bite my nails in a corner, let her lose to Spain,
Keep myself back for policy?

BACON: Even so.

ESSEX: I come of better blood than Elizabeth.
My name was among the earls around King John
Under the oak. What the nobles have taught a king
A noble may teach a queen.

BACON: You talk treason and death.
The old order is dead, and you and your house will
    die
With it if you cannot learn.

ESSEX: So said King John
Under the oak, or wherever he was standing,
And little he got by it, as you may recall.
What the devil's a king but a man, or a queen but
    a woman?

BACON: King John is dead; this is Elizabeth,
Queen in her own right, daughter of a haughty line.
There is one man in all her kingdom she fears
And that man's yourself, and she has good reason to
    fear you.
You're a man not easily governed, a natural rebel,
Moreover, a general, popular and acclaimed,
And, last, she loves you, which makes you the more
    to be feared,
Whether you love her or not.

ESSEX: I do love her! I do!

BACON: My lord, a man as young as you——

ESSEX: If she were my mother's kitchen hag,
Toothless and wooden-legged, she'd make all others
Colorless.

BACON: You play dangerously there, my lord.

ESSEX: I've never yet loved or hated
For policy nor a purpose. I tell you she's a witch——
And has a witch's brain. I love her, I fear her,
I hate her, I adore her——

BACON: That side of it you must know
For yourself.

ESSEX: I will walk softly—here is my hand.
Distress yourself no more—I can carry myself.

BACON: Only count not too much on the loves of
queens.

ESSEX: I'll remember.
    [Cecil and Raleigh reappear in the doorway at
    the right. Raleigh is wearing ordinary armor
    and carries his silver suit. Essex looks at him,
    biting his lip]
Sir Walter, take care of your health!

RALEIGH: My health, sir?

ESSEX: [Going out] Wearing no silver, in this
chilly weather.

RALEIGH: [Tossing his silver armor into the pile]
Put that with the others.

FIRST GUARD: Are we to wear them, sir?

RALEIGH: No. Melt them down and sell the silver.
And thus see for yourself how soon a fool is parted
from his money. Take station in the outer hall and
carry this trash with you.

FIRST GUARD: Yes, sir.
    [The Guards go out right]

RALEIGH: [To Bacon] And you, sir, you are his
friend. . . .

BACON: And yours, Sir Walter. . . .

RALEIGH: It's the first I've heard of it, but if you're
mine too, so much the better. Carry this news to
him: his suits go to the melting-pot.

BACON: Willingly, my lord, if I see him. You have
done quite properly.

RALEIGH: I do not ask your commendation!

BACON: No, but you have it.
    [He bows low and goes out to left]

RALEIGH: There's the viper under our flower, this
    Francis.
He should be on the winning side.

CECIL: He will be yet . . .
Like all wise men. For myself, I no longer
Stomach Lord Essex. Every word he speaks
Makes me feel queasy.

RALEIGH: Then why put up with him?

CECIL: The queen, my friend, the queen. What
    she wants she will have,
And she must have her earl.

RALEIGH: Which does she love more,
Her earl or her kingdom?

CECIL: Yes, which? I have wondered.

RALEIGH: Then you're less sapient

Than I've always thought you, Cecil. She loves her
    kingdom
More than all men, and always will. If he could
Be made to look like a rebel, which he's close to
    being . . .
And she could be made to believe it, which is harder,
You'd be first man in the council.
    CECIL: And you would be? . . .
    RALEIGH: Wherever I turn he's stood
Square in my way! My life long here at court
He's snatched honor and favor from before my eyes
Till his voice and walk and aspect make me
    writhe . . .
There's a fatality in it!
    CECIL: If he could be sent from England . . . we
      might have a chance
To come between them.
    RALEIGH: Would she let him go?
    CECIL: No . . . but if he could be teased
And stung about his generalship till he was
Too angry to reflect. . . . Suppose you were pro-
    posed
As general for the next Spanish raid?
    RALEIGH: He would see it,
And so would she.
    CECIL: Then if you were named
For the expedition to Ireland?
    RALEIGH: No, I thank you.
He'd let me go, and I'd be sunk in a bog
This next three hundred years. I've seen enough
Good men try to conquer Ireland.
    CECIL: Then how would this be?
We name three men for Ireland of his own sup-
    porters;
He will oppose them, not wishing his party weak-
    ened
At the court. Then we ask what he suggests
And hint at his name for leader. . . .
    RALEIGH: Good so far.
    CECIL: He will be angry and hint at your name;
      you will offer
To go if he will.
    RALEIGH: No. Not to Ireland.
    CECIL: Yes!
Do you think he'd let you go with him and share
The military glory? It will go hard,
Having once brought up his name, if we do not
    manage
To ship him alone to Dublin.
    RALEIGH: We can try it, then,
Always remembering that no matter what
Is said . . . no matter what I say or you . . .
I do not go. You must get me out of that,
By Christ, for I know Ireland.
    CECIL: I will. Be easy.
    RALEIGH: When is the council?
    CECIL: At nine.
    RALEIGH: You'll make these suggestions?
    CECIL: If you'll play up to them.
    RALEIGH: Count on me. I must look after

These silver soldiers.
    CECIL: At nine then.
    RALEIGH: Count on me.
    [*They go out in opposite directions*]

CURTAIN

SCENE II.

*The queen's study, which adjoins her bed-cham-
bers and the council hall. It is a severe little room
with chairs, a desk, and a few books, huge and
leather-bound. Penelope comes in from the bed-
chamber and looks out through a curtain opposite.
She returns to the chamber, then re-enters to wait.
Essex enters.*

    PENELOPE: [*Rising*] Good-morrow, my lord.
    ESSEX: Good-morrow, Penelope. Have I kept the
queen?
    PENELOPE: If so, would I acknowledge it?
    ESSEX: I commend me to your discretion.
    PENELOPE: Only to my discretion?
    ESSEX: Take her what message you will . . . only
let it be that I am here.
    PENELOPE: May I have one moment, my lord?
She is not quite ready.
    ESSEX: As many as you like. What is it, my dear?
    PENELOPE: Do you love the queen?
    ESSEX: Is that a fair question, as between man
and man?
    PENELOPE: An honest question.
    ESSEX: Then I will answer honestly. Yes, my dear.
    PENELOPE: Dearly?
    ESSEX: Yes.
    PENELOPE: I would you loved someone who loved
you better.
    ESSEX: Meaning . . . whom?
    PENELOPE: Meaning . . . no one. Myself, perhaps.
That's no one. Or . . . anyone who loved you better.
    ESSEX: Does she not love me, sweet?
    PENELOPE: She loves you, loves you not, loves
you, loves you not. . . .
    ESSEX: And why do you tell me this?
    PENELOPE: Because I am afraid.
    ESSEX: For me?
    PENELOPE: I have heard her when she thought
she was alone, walk up and down her room soundlessly, night long, cursing you . . . cursing you because she must love you and could not help herself
. . . swearing to be even with you for this love she
scorns to bear you. My lord, you anger her too
much.
    ESSEX: But is this not common to lovers?
    PENELOPE: No, I have never cursed you. And I
have good cause.
    ESSEX: But if I were your lover, you would, sweet.
So thank God I am not.

PENELOPE: I must go and tell her you are here. [*She lifts her face to be kissed*] Good-bye.

ESSEX: Good-bye, my dear. [*He kisses her*] And thank you.

PENELOPE: Will you beware of her?

ESSEX: Lover, beware your lover, might well be an old maxim: I will beware.

PENELOPE: For I am afraid.

[*A Maid-in-Waiting appears in the doorway*]

MAID: Her Majesty is ready.

PENELOPE: I will tell her my lord is here.

[*She runs out hastily.* Elizabeth *enters, signing imperiously to the* Maid, *who disappears. There is a moment's silence*]

ELIZABETH: When we met last it was, as I remember,
Ill-met by moonlight, sir.

ESSEX: Well-met by day,
My queen.

ELIZABETH: I had hardly hoped to see you again,
My lord of Essex, after what was vowed
Forever when you left.

ESSEX: You are unkind
To remind me.

ELIZABETH: I think I also used
The word forever, and meant it as much, at least . . .
Therefore, no apology. Only my Penelope
Passed me just now in the door with eyes and lips
That looked the softer for kissing. I'm not sure
But I'm inopportune.

ESSEX: She's a crazy child.

ELIZABETH: A child! That's for me, too, no doubt!
These children
Have their little ways with each other!

ESSEX: Must we begin
With charges and counter-charges, when you know. . . .

ELIZABETH: Do I indeed? . . .
You have been gone a week, at this Wanstock of yours . . .
And a week's a long time at court. You forget that I
Must live and draw breath whether I see you or not . . .
And there are other men and women, oh yes, all fully
Equipped for loving and being loved! Penelope . . .
You find Penelope charming. And as for me
There's always Mountjoy . . . or Sir Walter . . . the handsome,
Sir Walter, the silver-plated . . .

ESSEX: He'll wear no more
Silver at your door.

ELIZABETH: What have you done . . . come, tell me.
I knew this silver would draw fire. What happened?

ESSEX: Nothing . . . but the fashion's gone out.

ELIZABETH: No, but tell me!

ESSEX: He happened to be in the way
When the upstairs pot was emptied.
He's gone to change his clothes.

ELIZABETH: You shall not be allowed
To do this to him . . .

ESSEX: [*Moving toward her*] You shall not be allowed
To mock me, my queen. [*He kisses her*]

ELIZABETH: Isn't it strange how one man's kiss can grow
To be like any other's . . . or a woman's
To be like any woman's?

ESSEX: Not yours for me,
No, and not mine for you, you lying villain,
You villain and queen, you double-tongued seductress,
You bitch of brass!

ELIZABETH: Silver, my dear. Let me be
A bitch of silver. It reminds me of Raleigh.

ESSEX: Damn you!

ELIZABETH: Damn you and double-damn you for a damner!
Come some day when I'm in the mood. What day's this? . . .
Thursday? Try next Wednesday . . . or any Wednesday
Later on in the summer . . . Any summer
Will do. Why are you still here?

ESSEX: Oh, God, if I could but walk out that door
And stay away!

ELIZABETH: It's not locked.

ESSEX: But I'd come back!
Where do you think I've been this last week? Trying,
Trying not to be here! But you see, I am here.

ELIZABETH: Yes, I see.

ESSEX: Why did you plague me without a word?

ELIZABETH: Why did you not come?

ESSEX: You are a queen, my queen. You had proscribed me.
Sent formal word I'd not be admitted if I came.

ELIZABETH: I may have meant it at the time.

ESSEX: I think I have a demon, and you are it!

ELIZABETH: If ever a mocking devil tortured a woman
You're my devil and torture me! Let us part and quickly,
Or there'll be worse to come. Go.

ESSEX: I tell you I will not.

ELIZABETH: Come to me, my Essex. Let us be kind
For a moment. I will be kind. You need not be.
You are young and strangely winning and strangely sweet.
My heart goes out to you wherever you are.
And something in me has drawn you. But this same thing
That draws us together hurts and blinds us until
We strike at one another. This has gone on
A long while. It grows worse with the years. It will end badly.
Go, my dear, and do not see me again.

ESSEX: All this
Is what I said when last I went away.

Yet here I am.

ELIZABETH: Love someone else, my dear.
I will forgive you.

ESSEX: You mean you would try to forgive me.

ELIZABETH: Aye, but I would.

ESSEX: What would you have to forgive? I have
tried to love others. It's empty as ashes.

ELIZABETH: What others?

ESSEX: No one.

ELIZABETH: What others?

ESSEX: Everyone.

ELIZABETH: Everyone?

ESSEX: That too has been your triumph! What is
a cry
Of love in the night, when I am sick and angry
And care not? I would rather hear your mocking
laughter——
Your laughter—mocking at me—defying me
Ever to be happy—with another.

ELIZABETH: You have done this to me?

ESSEX: You have done this to me! You've made
it all empty
Away from you! And with you too!

ELIZABETH: And me—what of me while you were
gone?

ESSEX: If we
Must quarrel when we meet, why then, for God's
sake,
Let us quarrel. At least we can quarrel together.

ELIZABETH: I think if we are to love we must love
and be silent——
For when we speak——

ESSEX: I'll be silent then.
And you shall speak——

ELIZABETH: [Her finger to her lips] Hush!

ESSEX: If you would sometimes heed me——

ELIZABETH: Hush!

ESSEX: Only sometimes—only when I'm right.
If you would
Say to yourself that even your lover might be
Right sometimes, instead of flying instantly
Into opposition as soon as I propose
A shift in policy!

ELIZABETH: But you were wrong! You were
wrong!
A campaign into Spain's pure madness, and to
strike at Flanders
At the same moment . . . think of the drain in men
And the drain on the treasury, and the risks we'd
run
Of being unable to follow success or failure
For lack of troops and money . . . !

ESSEX: [Letting his arms fall] But why lack
money . . .
And why lack men? There's no richer country in
Europe
In men or money than England! It's this same
ancient
Unprofitable niggardliness that pinches pennies

And wastes a world of treasure! You could have all
Spain,
And Spain's dominions in the new world, an empire
Of untold wealth . . . and you forgo them because
You fear to lay new taxes!

ELIZABETH: I have tried that . . .
And never yet has a warlike expedition
Brought me back what it cost!

ESSEX: You've tried half-measures . . .
Raids on the Spanish coast, a few horsemen sent
Into Flanders and out again, always defeating
Yourself by trying too little! What I plead for
Is to be bold once, just once, give the gods a chance
To be kind to us . . . walk through this cobweb
Philip
And take his lazy cities with a storm
Of troops and ships!
If we are to trifle we might better sit
At home forever, and rot!

ELIZABETH: Here we sit then,
And rot, as you put it.

ESSEX: I'm sorry. . . .

ELIZABETH: It seems to me
We rot to some purpose here. I have kept the peace
And kept my people happy and prosperous.

ESSEX: And at what a price . . .
What a cowardly price!

ELIZABETH: I am no coward, either.
It requires more courage not to fight than to fight
When one is surrounded by hasty hot-heads, urging
Campaigns in all directions.

ESSEX: Think of the name
You will leave. . . . They will set you down in
histories
As the weasel queen who fought and ran away,
Who struck one stroke, preferably in the back,
And then turned and ran. . . .

ELIZABETH: Is it my fame you think of,
Or your own, my lord? Have you not built your
name
High enough? I gave you your chance at Cadiz,
And you took it, and now there's no name in all
England
Like yours to the common people. When we ride
in the streets
Together, it's Essex they cheer and not their queen.
What more would you have?

ESSEX: Is it for fear of me
And this hollow cheering you hold me back from
Spain?

ELIZABETH: It's because I believe in peace, and
have no faith
In wars or what wars win.

ESSEX: You do not fear me?

ELIZABETH: Yes, and I fear you, too! You believe
yourself
Fitter to be king than I to be queen! You are
flattered
By this crying of your name by fools! You trust me
no more

Than you'd trust . . . Penelope . . . or any other
    woman
To be in power! You believe you'd rule England
    better
Because you're a man!
    ESSEX: That last is true. I would.
And that doesn't mean I don't love you . . . remem-
    ber that.
I love you, my queen, madly, beyond all measure,
But that's not to say I cannot see where you fail
As sovereign here, and see that why you fail
When you do is merely because a woman cannot
Act and think like a man.
    ELIZABETH: Act and think like a man . . . !
Why should I
Think like a man when a woman's thinking's wiser?
What do you plan? To depose me, take over the
    kingdom?
    ESSEX: [Smiling] You are a touchy queen.
    ELIZABETH: I had bad bringing up.
I was never sure who my mother was going to be
Next day, and it shook my nerves.
    ESSEX: You're your father's daughter,
I'll swear to that. I can tell by your inconstancy.
    ELIZABETH: I wish you had need
To fear for me . . . or at any rate that I'd never
Let you see how much I'm yours.
    ESSEX: But why?
    ELIZABETH: Tell me, my dear,
Do you tire of me . . . do I wear upon you a little?
    ESSEX: Never.
    ELIZABETH: But you'd have to say that, you can
    see . . .
You'd have to say it, because you wouldn't hurt me,
And because I'm your queen. And so I'll never
    know
Until everyone else has known and is laughing at
    me,
When I've lost you. Wait, let me say this, please . . .
    When the time
Does come, and I seem old to you, and you love
Someone else, tell me, tell me the first . . .
    ESSEX: You are not old! I will not have you old!
    ELIZABETH: Will you do that, in all kindness, in
    memory
Of great love past? No. You could not, could not.
It's not in a man to be kind that way, nor in
A woman to take it kindly. I think I'd kill you,
In a first blind rage.
    ESSEX: Kill me when I can say it.
    ELIZABETH: Love, will you let me
Say one more thing that will hurt you?
    ESSEX: Anything.
    ELIZABETH: Your blood's on fire to lead a new
    command
Now that you've won so handsomely in Spain,
And when I need a general anywhere
You'll ask to go. Don't ask it . . . and don't go.
You're better here in London.

    ESSEX: Was this all you wanted?
    [Stepping back]
To make me promise this?
    ELIZABETH: [Softly] Not for myself,
I swear it, not because I think you reckless
With men and money, though I do think that,
Not because you might return in too much triumph
And take my kingdom from me, which I can im-
    agine,
And not because I want to keep you here
And hate to risk you, though that's also true . . .
But rather . . . and for this you must forgive
    me . . .
Because you're more a poet than general . . .
And I fear you might fail, and lose what you have
    gained,
If you went again.
    ESSEX: God's death! Whom would you send?
    ELIZABETH: I asked you not to be angry.
    ESSEX: Not to be angry!
How do you judge a leader except by whether
He wins or loses? Was it by chance, do you think,
That I took Cadiz?
    ELIZABETH: Very well. You shall go.
Go if you will. Only I love you, and I say
What would be wiser.
    ESSEX: You choose the one thing I must have
And ask me not to ask it! No. Forgive me.
    ELIZABETH: I'll not say it again.
    ESSEX: But if I'm more poet than
General, why poets make better generals
Than generals do, on occasion.
    ELIZABETH: You've proved it so.
On more than one occasion.
    [A clock strikes. She rises]
There's the chime.
The council's waiting, and we shall hear about
    Ireland,
If Cecil has his way. One thing remember,
You must not go to Ireland.
    ESSEX: No. That's a war
I'm content to miss.
    ELIZABETH: Thank God for that much then. I've
    been afraid
Ireland might tempt you. And one more thing re-
    member . . .
I'll have to oppose you in the council on
The Spanish hostages. . . . You'll have your way . . .
But I'll have to oppose you, lest they think it's
    your kingdom. . . .
Will you understand . . . ?
    ESSEX: I'll play my part perfectly.
    [He kisses her hand, then her lips]
    ELIZABETH: Now what can come between us, out
    of heaven or hell,
Or Spain or England?
    ESSEX: Nothing . . . never again.

CURTAIN

SCENE III.

*The same as Scene 1, save that the doors to the
council room have been thrown back, revealing a
chair of state for the* Queen, *and beneath it a table
at which her* Councillors *sit. The* Guards *are placed
at left and right. The* Queen *sits in her chair,* Raleigh,
Cecil, Essex, Burghley, Howard, *and one or two
others are at the table. The queen's* Jester *sits cross-
legged on a mat.* Burghley *is speaking.*

BURGHLEY: It is quite true we shall have an enemy
    in Spain while Philip lives and his state has
    power
To wage war on us, but there is little he can do
Against an island as well walled as ours.
He has tried his best, and failed. My lord of Essex
Says it cost more to fight Spain every year
In this chronic fashion than it would to throw
A challenge down, raid the Escurial
And sack the empire. With this the weight of the
    council
Disagrees, and we may hold it settled
That our tactics continue defensive till the queen
Rule otherwise.

ELIZABETH: You'll wait some time for that.

BURGHLEY: But in the matter
Of the Spanish ransoms it appears to me
Lord Essex has right on his side. The English soldiers
Who brought their prisoners home from the last raid
Deserve their prize money. By immemorial custom
The ransom belongs to the taker of the prisoner
And not to the state.

ELIZABETH: That I intend to change,
That same immemorial custom. I thought you had
    been
Informed, Lord Burghley, that it was my will
That the Spanish ransoms be paid to the treasury.

BURGHLEY: But my lord of Essex . . .

ELIZABETH: My lord of Essex does not speak for
    me.
I was told this expedition into Spain
Would be paid for in booty. The cost, so far,
Has not been made up; and since there are Spanish
    nobles
To be ransomed, I think they should pay it.

ESSEX: Your Majesty,
I do not speak for myself . . . I took no prizes . . .
But only to redeem my word. I assured
My followers that they would have for their own
Whatever ransoms they earned. ·

ELIZABETH: And by what right
Did you make this promise?

ESSEX: By this same ancient custom
Of which Lord Burghley speaks. A custom so well
Established there's not a soldier anywhere
But takes it for granted.

ELIZABETH: Your word is pledged?

ESSEX: It is.

ELIZABETH: [*Smiling*] And if the state should con-
fiscate these ransoms
You would make them good to the captors?

ESSEX: No. To speak frankly . . .
    [*He smiles*]
No.

ELIZABETH: Then the issues lies between the queen
And her soldiers . . . and your lordship need feel no
Concern in the matter.

ESSEX: When I made these promises
I spoke for Your Majesty . . . or believed I did.

ELIZABETH: Master Cecil, advise us; am I as queen
Bound by Lord Essex's promise?

CECIL: No, my liege;
It is well known a regent may repudiate
Treaty or word of a subject officer.
The throne is not bound.

ESSEX: If it comes to repudiation,
The throne can, of course, repudiate what it likes.
But not without breaking faith.

ELIZABETH: I fear we are wrong, Sir Robert;
And what has been promised for me and in my
    name
By my own officer, my delegate in the field,
I must perform. The men may have their ransoms.
The state will take its loss; for this one time
Only, and this the last. In the future a prisoner
Is held in the name of the state, and whatever
    price
Is on his head belongs to the crown. Our action
Here is made no precedent. What further
Business is there before us?

CECIL: There is one perpetual
Subject, Your Majesty, which we take up
Time after time, and always leave unsettled,
But which has come to a place where we must act
One way or another. Tyrone's rebellion in Ulster
Is no longer a smouldering coal, but a running fire
Spreading north to south. We must conquer Ireland
Finally now, or give over what we have won.
Ireland's not Spain.

ELIZABETH: I grant you.

THE FOOL: I also grant you.

ELIZABETH: Be quiet, fool.

THE FOOL: Be quiet, fool.
    [*He slaps his own mouth*]

ELIZABETH: Lord Burghley,
You shall speak first. What's to be done in Ireland?

BURGHLEY: If my son is right, and I believe him
    to be,
We can bide our time no longer there. They have
Some help from Spain, and will have more, no
    doubt,
And the central provinces are rising. We must
Stamp out this fire or lose the island.

ELIZABETH: This means
Men, money, ships?

BURGHLEY: Yes, madam.

CECIL: And more than that . . .
A leader.

ELIZABETH: What leader?

CECIL: A Lord Protector
Of Ireland who can carry sword and fire
From one end of the bogs to the other, and have English law
On Irish rebels till there are no rebels.
We've governed Ireland with our left hand, so far,
And our hold is slipping. The man who goes there now
Must be one fitted to master any field . . .
The best we have.

ELIZABETH: What man? Name one.

CECIL: We should send,
Unless I am wrong, a proved and able general,
Of no less rank, say, than Lord Howard here,
Lord Essex, Sir Walter Raleigh, Knollys, or Mountjoy . . .
This is no slight matter, to keep or lose the island.

ELIZABETH: I grant you that also.

THE FOOL: I also grant you. Be quiet,
Fool! [He slaps his mouth]

ELIZABETH: I ask you for one and you name a dozen, Sir Robert.

RALEIGH: Why should one go alone, if it comes
To that? Why not two expeditions, one
To Dublin, one into Ulster, meeting halfway?

ELIZABETH: Are there two who could work together?

CECIL: Knollys and Mountjoy.
They are friends and of one house.

ESSEX: Yes, of my house.

ELIZABETH: Essex, whom would you name?

ESSEX: Why, since Lord Cecil
Feels free to name my followers, I shall feel free
To name one or two of his. . . .

ELIZABETH: In other words,
You would rather Knollys and Mountjoy did not go?

ESSEX: I would rather they stayed in England, as Sir Robert knows.
I have need of them here. But I will spare one of them
If Lord Cecil will let Sir Francis Vere go with him.

ELIZABETH: Let Vere and Knollys go.

CECIL: Lord Essex names
Sir Francis Vere because he knows full well
I cannot spare him, my liege.

ELIZABETH: Is this appointment
To wait for all our private bickerings?
Can we send no man of worth to Ireland, merely
Because to do so would weaken some house or party
Here at court?

THE FOOL: Your Majesty has said . . .

ELIZABETH: Be quiet. . . .

THE FOOL: Fool!

ELIZABETH: Be quiet!

THE FOOL: Fool!

ELIZABETH: Be quiet!
[The Fool forms the word "fool" with his lips,
but makes no sound]

CECIL: [Rising] I hope I betray no secret, Sir Walter,
If I tell the council that I spoke with you
Before the session, and asked you if you would go
Into Ireland if the queen requested it . . . and that you said
Yes, should the queen desire it.

BURGHLEY: That would answer.

CECIL: But I believe, and Sir Walter believes, there should be
More than one hand in this . . . that if he goes
Lord Essex should go with him.

ELIZABETH: With him?

ESSEX: In what
Capacity?

CECIL: Leading an equal command. Two generals
Of coeval power, landing north and south
And meeting to crush Tyrone.

ESSEX: Would you set up
Two Lord Protectors?

CECIL: It was my thought that we name
Raleigh as Lord Protector.

ESSEX: And I under him?

CECIL: Since the Azores adventure
Which my Lord Essex led, and which came off
A little lamer than could be wished, but in which
Sir Walter showed to very great advantage,
It has seemed to me that Raleigh should receive
First place if he served in this.

ESSEX: [Rising] This is deliberate,
An insult planned!

CECIL: It is no insult, my lord,
But plain truth. I speak for the good of the state.

ESSEX: You lie! You have never spoken here or elsewhere
For any cause but your own!

ELIZABETH: No more of this!

ESSEX: The good of the state! Good God!
Am I to swallow this from a clerk, a pen-pusher . . .
To be told I may have second place, for the good of the state?

CECIL: Were you not wrong at the Azores?

ESSEX: No, by God!
And you know it!

ELIZABETH: Whoever makes you angry has won
Already, Essex!

ESSEX: They have planned this!

CECIL: I say no more.
Raleigh will go to Ireland as Lord Protector
And go alone, if the queen asks it of him,
And since you will not go.

ESSEX: I have not said
I would not go. But if I were to go I would go
Alone, as Lord Protector!

ELIZABETH: That you will not.
I have some word in this.

ESSEX: If this pet rat
Lord Cecil wishes to know my mind about him,
And it seems he does, he shall have it! How he first
crept

Into favor here I know not, but the palace is riddled
With his spying and burrowing and crawling under-
     ground!
He has filled the court with his rat friends, very
     gentle,
White, squeaking, courteous folk, who show their
     teeth
Only when cornered; who smile at you, speak you
     fair
And spend their nights gnawing the floors and chairs
Out from under us all!
     ELIZABETH: My lord!
     ESSEX: I am
Not the gnawing kind, nor will I speak fair
To those who don't mean me well . . . no, nor to
     those
To whom I mean no good! I say frankly here,
Yes, to their faces, that Cecil and Walter Raleigh
Have made themselves my enemies because
They cannot brook greatness or power in any but
Themselves! And I say this to them . . . and to
     the world. . . .
I, too, have been ambitious, as all men are
Who bear a noble mind, but if I rise
It will be by my own effort, and not by dragging
Better men down through intrigue! I admit
Sir Walter Raleigh's skill as a general
And Cecil's statecraft! I could work with them freely
And cheerfully, but every time I turn
My back they draw their knives! When Cecil left
     England
I guarded his interests as I would my own
Because he asked me to . . . but when I left,
And left my affairs in his hands . . . on my return
I found my plans and my friends out in the rain
Along with the London beggars!
     CECIL: I did my best. . . .
     ESSEX: Aye . . . the best for yourself! For the
good of the state!
     RALEIGH: If Lord Essex wishes
To say he is my enemy, very well . . .
He is my enemy.
     ESSEX: But you were mine first. . . .
And I call the gods to witness you would be my
     friend
Still, if I'd had my way! I take it hard
That here, in the queen's council, where there should
     be
Magnanimous minds if anywhere, there is still
No trust or friendship!
     ELIZABETH: I take it hard that you
Should quarrel before me.
     ESSEX: Would you have us quarrel
Behind your back? It suits them all too well
To quarrel in secret and knife men down in the
     dark!
     BURGHLEY: This is fantastic, my lord. There has
     been no knifing.
Let us come to a decision. We were discussing
The Irish protectorate.

     CECIL: And as for Ireland,
I am willing to leave that in Lord Essex' hands
To do as he decides.
     ESSEX: Send your Sir Walter
To Ireland as Protector! And be damned to it!
     CECIL: As the queen wishes.
It is a task both difficult and dangerous.
I cannot blame Lord Essex for refusing
To risk his fame there.
     ESSEX: There speaks the white rat again!
Yet even a rat should know I have never refused
A task out of fear! I said I would not go
As second in command!
     CECIL: Then would you go
As Lord Protector?
     ELIZABETH: You have named your man . . .
Sir Walter Raleigh.
     RALEIGH: I'll go if Essex goes.
     ESSEX: What! Is our Raleigh
Afraid to go alone?
     RALEIGH: I don't care for it . . .
And neither does our Essex!
     ESSEX: Why, what is this
That hangs over Ireland! Is it haunted, this Ireland?
Is it a kind of hell where men are damned
If they set foot on it? I've never seen the place,
But if it's a country like other countries, with peo-
     ple
Like other people in it, it's nothing to be
Afraid of, more than France or Wales or Flanders
Or anywhere else!
     CECIL: We hear you say so.
     ESSEX: If I
Am challenged to go to Ireland, then, Christ, I'll go!
Give me what men and horse I need, and put me
In absolute charge, and if I fail to bring
This Tyrone's head back with me, and put the re-
     bellion
To sleep forever, take my sword from me
And break it . . . I'll never use it again!
     ELIZABETH: Will you listen . . . ?
     ESSEX: They've challenged me!
     ELIZABETH: If you volunteer
To go to Ireland there is none to stop you.
You are first soldier here, first in acclaim
And in achievement, but since the decision lies
With yourself alone, reflect a little.
     ESSEX: My queen,
I can see that Raleigh and Cecil have set themselves
To bait me into Ireland! They know and I know
That Ireland has been deadly to any captain
Who risked his fortunes there; moreover, once
I'm gone they think to strip me here at home,
Ruin me both ways! And I say to them: "Try it!"
There are men who are greater than Ireland or their
     chicane. . . .
Since this is a challenge I go, and go alone,
And return victorious, and, by God, more of a prob-
     lem
To Cecils and Raleighs than when I went!

[*The* Fool *rises and approaches* Essex *from behind*]

BURGHLEY: If Essex
Will go, it solves our problem, Your Majesty.
We could hardly refuse that offer.

ELIZABETH: No.

ESSEX: I will go,
And I will return! Mark me!

THE FOOL: [*Touching* Essex] My lord! my lord!

ESSEX: [*Turning suddenly with an instinctive motion that sweeps the* Fool *to the floor*] Take your
hands off me! You touch me for a fool?

[*He helps the* Fool *up*]
Get up!

THE FOOL: Do not go to Ireland!

ESSEX: [*Impatiently*] You too?

THE FOOL: Because, my lord, I come from Ireland,
All the best fools come from Ireland, but only
A very great fool will go there.

ESSEX: Faugh!

THE FOOL: It's not too late yet!

ELIZABETH: Break up the council, my lords.
We meet tomorrow.

BURGHLEY: And this is decided?

ESSEX: Yes.

ELIZABETH: Yes, if you wish it. Go now.

[*The* Council *rises when the queen does and
files out silently, leaving* Essex *and* Elizabeth]
You should have had
The fool's brain and he yours! You would have bettered
By the exchange.

ESSEX: I thank you kindly, lady.

ELIZABETH: What malicious star
Danced in my sky when you were born, I wonder?

ESSEX: What malicious star danced in the sky
Of Ireland, you should ask.

ELIZABETH: Oh, my dear,
You are a child in council. I saw them start
To draw you into this, and tried to warn you . . .
But it was no use.

ESSEX: They drew me into nothing.
I saw their purpose and topped it with my own.
Let them believe they've sunk me.

ELIZABETH: You will withdraw.
I'll countermand this.

ESSEX: And give them the laugh on me?
I'll have the laugh on them yet.

ELIZABETH: Better they should laugh
A little now than laugh at you forever.

ESSEX: And why not win in Ireland?

ELIZABETH: No man wins there.
You're so dazzled
With the chance to lead an army you'd follow the
devil
In an assault on heaven.

ESSEX: No, but I'd lead him.
Heaven is always taken by storm. That's one thing
The devil doesn't know. Ireland is only

A country, and this is superstition.

ELIZABETH: I know.
You were quite right. I thought so as you said it.
Only somehow here in my breast something constricts . . .
Is it the heart grows heavy? I must let you go . . .
And I'll never see you again.

ESSEX: Mistrust all these
Forebodings. When they prove correct we remember
them,
But when they're wrong we forget them. They mean
nothing.
Remember this when I'm back and all turns out
well . . .
That you felt all would turn out badly.

ELIZABETH: Oh, my love,
Come touch me, tell me all will happen well.

ESSEX: And so it will.

ELIZABETH: Do you want to go?

ESSEX: Why yes . . .
And no. I've said I would and I will.

ELIZABETH: It's not yet
Too late. There are no announcements made, no
orders
Given. If you win, that will divide us . . .
And if you lose, that will divide us too.

ESSEX: I'll win, and it will not divide us. Is it so
hard
To believe in me?

ELIZABETH: No . . . I'll believe in you . . .
And even forgive you if you need it. Here.
My father gave me this ring . . . and told me if
ever
He lost his temper with me, to bring it to him
And he'd forgive me. And so it saved my life . . .
Long after, when he'd forgotten, long after, when
One time he was angry.

ESSEX: Darling, if ever
You're angry rings won't help.

ELIZABETH: Yes, it would.
I'd think of you as you are now, and it would.
Take it.

ESSEX: I have no pledge from you. I'll take it
To remember you in absence.

ELIZABETH: Take it for a better reason. Take it
because
The years are long, and full of sharp, wearing days
That wear out what we are and what we have been
And change us into people we do not know,
Living among strangers. Lest you and I who love
Should wake some morning strangers and enemies
In an alien world, far off; take my ring, my lover.

ESSEX: You fear
You will not always love me?

ELIZABETH: No, that you
Will not love me, and will not let me love you.

[*She puts the ring on his finger*]

CURTAIN

ACT II. SCENE I.

The queen's study. Penelope *is sitting* **reading.**
The Fool *enters. She does not see him.*

THE FOOL: Sh! Make no noise.

PENELOPE: What do you mean?

THE FOOL: Silence! Quiet!

PENELOPE: I am silent, fool.

THE FOOL: You silent? And even as you say it you are talking!

PENELOPE: You began it.

THE FOOL: Began what?

PENELOPE: Talking.

THE FOOL: Oh, no. Talking began long before my time. It was a woman began it.

PENELOPE: Her name?

THE FOOL: Penelope, I should judge.

PENELOPE: Fool.

THE FOOL: [*Looking away*] No, for with this same Penelope began also beauty and courage and tenderness and faith . . . all that a man could desire or a woman offer . . . and all that this early Penelope began has a later Penelope completed.

PENELOPE: [*Rising*] It lacked only this . . . that the court fool should make love to me.

THE FOOL: I am sorry to have been laggard. But truly I have never found you alone before.

PENELOPE: How lucky I've been!

THE FOOL: Are you angered?

PENELOPE: At what?

THE FOOL: At my loving you.

PENELOPE: I've learned to bear nearly everything.

THE FOOL: A lover's absence?

PENELOPE: Among other things.

THE FOOL: The presence of suitors undesired?

PENELOPE: That, too.

THE FOOL: I am not a suitor, my lady. I ask nothing. I know where your heart lies. It is with my Lord Essex in Ireland. I do not love you.

PENELOPE: Good.

THE FOOL: I lied to you. I do love you.

PENELOPE: I am sorry.

THE FOOL: You will not laugh at me?

PENELOPE: No.

THE FOOL: Then there is yet some divinity in the world . . . while a woman can still be sorry for one who loves her without return.

PENELOPE: A woman is sadly aware that when a man loves her it makes a fool of him.

THE FOOL: And if a fool should love a woman . . . would it not make a man of him?

PENELOPE: No, but doubly a fool, I fear.

THE FOOL: And the women . . . how of the women?

PENELOPE: They have been fools, too.

THE FOOL: The more fool I, I tried to save Lord Essex from Ireland . . . but he needs must go . . . the more fool he.

PENELOPE: Let us not talk of that.

THE FOOL: May I kiss you?

PENELOPE: No.

THE FOOL: Your hand?

PENELOPE: Yes. [*He kisses her hand*]

THE FOOL: I thank you.

[*She touches his fool's cap gently with her hand*]

PENELOPE: The more fool you, poor boy.

[Robert Cecil *enters from the left*]

CECIL: This is hardly a seemly pastime, Mistress Gray.

PENELOPE: And are you now the judge of what is seemly, Sir Robert?

CECIL: [*To the* Fool] Be off with you! [*To* Penelope] The queen is expecting Master Bacon here? [*The* Fool *goes*]

PENELOPE: I am set to wait for him.

CECIL: You will not be needed.

PENELOPE: Excellent.

[*She goes out right, passing* Raleigh, *who enters*]

CECIL: This Bacon keeps himself close. I have been unable to speak with him. She has this news?

RALEIGH: Yes.

CECIL: She believes it?

RALEIGH: Burghley himself believes it.

CECIL: Then she does.

RALEIGH: Beyond question.

[*The curtains part at the left and* Bacon *enters*]

CECIL: Good morrow, Master Bacon.

BACON: And to you, my lords.

CECIL: I have sent everywhere for you, sir, this three hours . . . and perhaps it was not altogether by accident that I could not find you.

BACON: I was not at home. You must forgive me.

CECIL: You are here to see the queen?

BACON: [*Bowing*] The queen has also been good enough to send for me.

CECIL: It was my wish to speak with you first . . . and it is my opinion that it will be the better for all of us, if I do so now . . . late as it is.

BACON: I am but barely on time, gentlemen.

CECIL: You need answer one question only. You have been in correspondence with Lord Essex in Ireland?

BACON: Perhaps.

CECIL: The queen has this morning received news warning her that Lord Essex is allied with the Irish rebels and is even now leading his army back to England to usurp her throne. Had you heard this?

BACON: No.

CECIL: Do you credit it?

BACON: It is your own scheme, I believe.

CECIL: That Essex should rebel against the queen?

BACON: Even so.

RALEIGH: You accuse us of treason?

BACON: If the queen were aware of certain matters she would herself accuse you of treason.

CECIL: What matters?

BACON: I prefer that the queen should question me.

CECIL: Look to yourself, Master Bacon. If you intend to accuse any man of the suppression of letters written by Essex to the queen, or of the suppression of letters sent by the queen to Essex, you will be unable to prove these assertions and you will argue yourself very neatly into the Tower.

BACON: My lord . . . I had no such business in mind.

RALEIGH: Then what? . . .

BACON: I hope I can keep my own counsel. The truth is, my lords, you are desperate men. You have overreached yourselves, and if wind of it gets to the royal ears you are done.

RALEIGH: We shall drag a few down with us if we are done, though, and you the first.

CECIL: You have but a poor estimate of me, Master Bacon. If you go in to the queen and reveal to her that her letters to Essex have not reached him . . . as you mean to do . . . the queen will then send for me, and I will send for Lord Essex' last letter to you, containing a plan for the capture of the city of London. It will interest you to know that I have read that letter and you are learned enough in the law to realize in what light you will stand as a witness should the queen see it.

BACON: I think it is true, though, that if I go down I shall also drag a few with me, including those here present.

CECIL: I am not so sure of that either. I am not unready for that contingency. But to be frank with you, it would be easier for both you and us if you were on our side.

BACON: You must expect a man to side with his friends.

CECIL: And a man's friends . . . who are they? Those who can help him to what he wants.

BACON: Not always.

CECIL: When he is wise. You have served Lord Essex well and I believe he has made you promises. But the moment Essex enters England in rebellion, he is doomed, and his friends with him.

BACON: One word from the queen to him . . . one word from him to the queen . . . one word from me, revealing that their letters have been intercepted, and there can be no talk of rebellion. There has been some underhand traffic with the couriers between here and Ireland. Their letters have been lost, you have induced the queen to promulgate arbitrary orders . . . and since they are both proud, you have bred distrust in her and defiance in him. Your machinations have been so direct, so childish, so simple . . . and so simply exposed . . . that I wonder at you!

CECIL: My friend, a child could trip him. Not so simple as your own. I have news this morning that Lord Essex has already landed in England and set up his standard here. He is a rebel, and when a man is once a rebel, do you think there will be any careful inquiry into how he happened to become one?

BACON: Essex in England!

CECIL: In England.

RALEIGH: And has neglected to disband his army.

CECIL: You speak of explanations between the queen and Essex. Unless you betray us there will be no explanations. They are at war and will never meet again.

BACON: That is, if your plan succeed.

CECIL: [Standing aside] Very well, then. Go in. You have chosen your master. I have done with you.

BACON: [Not moving] And if I say nothing?

CECIL: Then . . . whatever you have been promised, whatever you have desired, that you shall have. There is no place in the courts you could not fill. You shall have your choice. If you need excuse, no one should know better than you that this Essex is a danger to the state, a danger to the queen, a danger to liberty.

BACON: If I need excuse I shall find one for myself.

[There is a pause. Then the curtain parts to the right and Penelope enters. She holds the curtain back]

PENELOPE: Yes, Your Majesty; he is here.

ELIZABETH: Why was I not told? [She enters] Is this an ante-chamber, Sir Robert? Am I never to look out of my room without seeing you?

CECIL: Your pardon, Your Majesty. I was just going.

ELIZABETH: Then go. You need not pause to explain why you came. I am weary of your face!

CECIL: Yes, Your Majesty.

[Cecil and Raleigh bow and depart]

ELIZABETH: I have heard that you are a shrewd man, Master Bacon.

BACON: Flattery, Majesty, flattery.

ELIZABETH: I have heard it,
And in a sort I believe it. Tell me one thing . . .
Are you Cecil's friend?

BACON: I have never been.

ELIZABETH: He is a shrewd man; he's
A man to make a friend of if you'd stand well
In the court, sir.

BACON: It may be so.

ELIZABETH: Why are you not
His friend then?

BACON: We are not on the same side.

ELIZABETH: You follow Lord Essex?

BACON: Since I have known him.

ELIZABETH: There's
A dangerous man to follow.

BACON: Lord Essex?

ELIZABETH: Lord Essex.

BACON: I am sorry, madam,
If I have displeased you.

ELIZABETH: You have displeased me.

BACON: I repeat then . . .
I am sorry.

   ELIZABETH: You will change, then? You will forget
This Essex of yours?

   BACON: If you ask it . . . if there is reason . . .

   ELIZABETH: Well, there is reason! He has taken up arms
Against me in Ireland.

   BACON: You are sure of this?

   ELIZABETH: I have reports. Is it so hard to believe?

   BACON: Without proofs, it is.

   ELIZABETH: I have proof.

   BACON: May I ask of what sort?

   ELIZABETH: Proof good enough. You know the punishment
For treason? From what I have heard
Of late both you and Essex should remember
That punishment.

   BACON: Madam, for myself I have
No need to fear, and if Lord Essex has
I am more than mistaken in him.

   ELIZABETH: I am very sorry
That I must do this . . . but all friends of Essex
Go straightway to the Tower. I have sent for you
To give you a last chance to change your mind
Before this blow falls. Are you still his friend?

   BACON: Yes, Majesty.

   ELIZABETH: I am sorry for it.

   BACON: That is all?

   ELIZABETH: Why no. You do not believe me?

   BACON: I do not.

   ELIZABETH: And why?

   BACON: I neither believe our Essex a rebel
Nor that you believe so. If you intended to place me
In the Tower . . . I would be in the Tower . . .
   and no talk about it.

   ELIZABETH: You are shrewd indeed.

   BACON: I am Essex' friend.

   ELIZABETH: If that
Were true . . . if I could speak to you . . . if
   there were only
The sound of one honest voice!
. . . I must rule England,
And they say he is rebel to me . . . and day and
   night,
Waking, sleeping, in council, there is still always
One thing crying out in me over and again . . .
Waking and sleeping I hear it crying: He cannot,
Cannot fail me! But I have written him my love
And he has not answered. What you know of this
Answer me truly, truly . . . bitter or not,
And you shall not lose!

   BACON: He has not answered?

   ELIZABETH: No.

   BACON: If I
Knew why I would know much. Have you angered
   him . . .
Sent arbitrary orders?

   ELIZABETH: I have ordered him to disband
His forces and return. I have cut off
Revenue and supplies.

   BACON: But this was rash . . .
To send a popular leader out with an army
And then check him suddenly, heap disgrace upon
   him . . .
He has great pride.

   ELIZABETH: [Getting up] He has rebelled then?
I wrote him lovingly.

   BACON: And he answered? . . .

   ELIZABETH: Nothing.

   BACON: That could not be excused.

   ELIZABETH: And it cannot be. It's true. It will not
   be!

   BACON: Dear queen, I fear
I have turned you against him!

   ELIZABETH: No, no! I needed that!

   BACON: And if there were something wrong . . .
Some misunderstanding? . . .

   ELIZABETH: No, no . . . don't try comfort now
   . . .
He had my letters. That could not go wrong.
Did he not have my letters?

   BACON: Could it be otherwise?

   ELIZABETH: You would know that. You would
   know if he had not.
You've had word from him?

   BACON: Yes.

   ELIZABETH: He has written you,
But not me! Or are you traitor to him also . . .
I think you are! I think you lie to me! I am
Encompassed by lies! I think you, too, betray him
   . . .
But subtly, with infinite craft, making me believe
First that you would not wrong him! No, no . . .
   I'm gone mad
Pacing my room, pacing the room of my mind.
They say a woman's mind is an airless room,
Sunless and airless, where she must walk alone
Saying he loves me, loves me, loves me not,
And has never loved me. The world goes by, all
   shadows,
And there are voices, all echoes till he speaks . . .
And there's no light till his presence makes a light
There in that room. But I am a queen. Where I walk
Is a hall of torture, where the curious gods bring all
Their racks and gyves, and stretch me there to
   writhe
Till I cry out. They watch me with eyes of iron
Waiting to hear what I cry! I am crying now . . .
Listen, you gods of iron! He never loved me . . .
He wanted my kingdom only . . .
Loose me and let me go! I am yet a queen . . .
That I have! That he will not take from me.
I shall be queen, and walk his room no more.
He thought to break me down by not answering . . .
Break me until I'd say, I'm all yours . . . what I am
And have, all yours! That I will never, never,
Never say. Not broken yet.

BACON: Nor will be, Majesty.

ELIZABETH: We must not follow him.
We must forget him, break him as he would break us,
Bow that bright head . . . I shall be as I was.
See him no more, my friend.
He walks on quicksand. Avoid him.

BACON: Yes, my queen.

ELIZABETH: Go, my friend.
You have done well. I trust you.

BACON: I thank Your Majesty.

[*He goes out. Elizabeth* claps her hands twice. *After a moment* Captain Armin *enters*]

ELIZABETH: Captain Armin, keep a watch on Master Bacon,
On his house and on his correspondence.
I wish to know all he knows.

ARMIN: Yes, Your Majesty.

ELIZABETH: Wait. I have found you true of word,
And sure of hand. Moreover, you can keep counsel—

[Armin *bows. She beckons him to come to her. He does so*]
What we say now is forever secret between us—
Between us two—not one other.

ARMIN: I'll hold it so.

ELIZABETH: It is reported there is an army risen
Against me——

ARMIN: God forbid!

ELIZABETH: It is so reported. The rebellion I speak
of's the force
Lord Essex has brought back with him from Ireland.
I wish to make this preparation for it: Whatever orders
You receive from your superiors, whatever broils
Occur, he is to have free access to my presence.

ARMIN: There would be danger to your person, madam.

ELIZABETH: I will risk that.

ARMIN: You would be hostage if he were in command.

ELIZABETH: Be ready for danger—and if need be, death.

ARMIN: Yes, Majesty.

[*He goes out. Elizabeth* stands motionless for a moment. There is a sudden burst of girls' laughter in an adjoining room, and the *Fool* runs in with a garment in his hand. Three Girls *run after him, the foremost tripping him so that he falls in a corner and is instantly pounced upon by all three*]

MARY: [*Entering*] Thief! Thief! Stop thief!

ELLEN: Kill the slobber thief! Fall on him!

TRESSA: Can a maid not keep a silk smock?

THE FOOL: Help! Salvage! Men-at-arms to the rescue! I am boarded by pirates!

[*They tickle him*]

ELLEN: Tear it from him! He will exhibit it!

TRESSA: No, no! Don't tear it!

THE FOOL: If you sit on me in that fashion, darling, you will regret it. There will be issue!

ELLEN: What issue?

THE FOOL: Twins! Seven or eight!

[Ellen *slaps him*]

MARY: Rise! Rise quickly! The queen is here. Rise!

[*They all get up in confusion*]

TRESSA: We are sorry, Your Majesty.

[Elizabeth *looks at them without seeing them, and goes out to her bedroom*]

ELLEN: What is it? She seemed not to see.

MARY: It's not like her not to strike us.

TRESSA: We'll be whipped.

THE FOOL: No, no. She strikes instantly or not at all.

TRESSA: Give me that.

[*She snatches her smock from the* Fool]

MARY: Come. [*They tiptoe out*]

CURTAIN

SCENE II.

The interior of Essex' *tent on the coast of England. Essex* sits in the light of a candle, reading dispatches. A Guard *stands in the shadow. Marvel, an aide, enters*]

MARVEL: There is a courier from the queen, my lord.

ESSEX: At last, then.

MARVEL: You will see him at once?

ESSEX: Yes . . . Wait. Bring him in and stay here while I read the dispatches. If I give orders to torture or kill him, show no surprise. You understand?

MARVEL: You will not torture him?

ESSEX: Am I not tortured? And you, too, sirrah. You will remember?

THE GUARD: Yes, my lord.

ESSEX: Good.

[Marvel *goes out. Essex* rises and stands out of the light, waiting. Marvel *enters with the* Courier, *who falls on his knee before* Essex]

THE COURIER: My Lord of Essex?

ESSEX: Yes.

COURIER: Dispatches from the queen.

ESSEX: When did you leave London?

COURIER: Four days ago, my lord. We were delayed.

ESSEX: What delayed you?

COURIER: Robbers.

ESSEX: And they took what from you?

COURIER: Our horses and money.

ESSEX: And the letters? . . .

COURIER: Were returned to me untouched.

ESSEX: When did this happen?

COURIER: This side of the ford. There were four armed men against us two.

ESSEX: Give me the letters. [*The* Courier *does so.* Essex *reads briefly*] This is all?

COURIER: Yes, my lord.

ESSEX: You are sure you have lost nothing?

COURIER: Indeed yes, my lord. There was but one missive and the seal was returned unbroken. The cut-throats told us they cared the less about our letters for they could not read.

ESSEX: You are a clever liar, sirrah, and you are the third liar who has come that same road to me from London. You are the third liar to tell this same tale. You shall pay for being the third.

COURIER: My lord, I have not lied to you.

ESSEX: Take his weapons from him, lieutenant. [Marvel *obeys*] Set him against the post there. Not so gently. He shall lose his ears first and then his lying tongue.

COURIER: Your lordship does not mean this?

ESSEX: And why not? We shall then cut him in pieces . . . but gradually, with infinite delicacy.

[Marvel *approaches the* Courier *with a knife. The* Guard *holds him*]

COURIER: No, no, no, no! Oh, God! Oh, my lord! My lord!

ESSEX: What are you waiting for?

MARVEL: We must tie him to the pole first, sir.

ESSEX: Then tie him!

COURIER: No, no . . . oh, God, no! What do you want of me? I swear to you I haven't lied to you! I swear . . . ugh!

[*He is choked*]

ESSEX: Let him speak. What do you swear?

COURIER: My lord, I have not lied . . . I speak truth . . .

ESSEX: Tie him up.

COURIER: Let me speak . . . I can . . . ugh . . .

ESSEX: Silence him. We know too well what you have done, sirrah. We need no evidence of that. What we ask is that you tell us who set you on . . . and your accomplices. Tell us this and I want no more of you. You shall have your freedom . . . and this . . . [*He tosses a clinking bag at his feet*] Speak.

COURIER: My lord, if I knew . . .

ESSEX: Bind him. Truss him up and cut him open. Dispense with these niceties. Have you no knife? [*He is bound*] We have heard enough! Take out his tongue!

[*They approach him. He becomes calm*]

COURIER: My lord, I am not a coward, though it
may seem to you
I am, for I have cried out . . . but I cried out
Not so much for pain or fear of pain
But to know this was Lord Essex, whom I have loved
And who tortures innocent men.

ESSEX: Come, silence him!

COURIER: Come then. I am innocent. If my Lord Essex

Is as I have believed him, he will not hurt me;
If he will hurt me, then he is not as I
And many thousands believe him, who have loved him,
And I shall not mind much dying.

[*A pause*]

ESSEX: Let him go.

[*They unbind the* Courier]
I thought my letters had been tampered with.
You'd tell me if it were so.

COURIER: My honored lord,
By all the faith I have, and most of it's yours,
I'd rather serve you well and lose in doing it
Than serve you badly and gain. If something I've done
Has crossed you or worked you ill I'm enough punished
Only knowing it.

ESSEX: This letter came
From the queen's hands?

COURIER: It is as I received it
From the queen's hands.

ESSEX: There was no other?

COURIER: No other.

ESSEX: Take this and go.

[*He tosses the bag to the* Courier]

COURIER: I have brought misfortune . . .

ESSEX: You bring good news. We break camp tomorrow for London . . . Go . . . take that news with you. They'll welcome you outside. Remain with my guard and return with us.

[*The* Courier *goes out*]

MARVEL: We march tomorrow?

ESSEX: Yes.

MARVEL: Under orders?

ESSEX: No.

[*He reads*]
"Lord Essex is required to disperse his men
And return to the capital straightway on his own
Recognizance, to give himself up."

MARVEL: And nothing with this?

ESSEX: Give out the necessary orders, we shall
Move at daybreak.

MARVEL: Yes, my lord.

ESSEX: And it is
As well it falls out this way! By right of name
And power and popular voice this is my kingdom . . .
This England under my feet, more mine than hers,
As she shall learn. It is quite as well.

MARVEL: There is no man
But will think so. There is victory in your path,
My lord. The London citizens will rise
At the first breath of your name.

ESSEX: Yes . . . that I'm sure of.

MARVEL: And with London in your hands . . .
well . . . it's your world then . . .
As far as you like.

ESSEX: And I am glad for England.
She has lain fallow in fear too long! Her hills

Shall have a spring of victory. Goodnight.

MARVEL: Goodnight.

ESSEX: And for this order, I received it not.

[*He tears the paper*]

CURTAIN

SCENE III.

The council hall of Act I is cleared here for a court assembly. Those who attended the council are present, save for Essex, also the Fool, Ellen, Mary, Tressa, Penelope, Bacon, and other Lords- and Ladies-in-Waiting. Burghley and Cecil are standing to one side in earnest talk. Across from them a group made up of Raleigh, Bacon, the Fool, and a number of others]

BURGHLEY: These players should be put down with an iron hand. They have neither conscience nor morals. They will make any display for money. In my young days they were allowed only interludes and instructive entertainment. The queen has been too lax . . .

CECIL: Have you seen this play of Richard II?

BURGHLEY: I see no plays.

CECIL: It's high treason. Richard is deposed in it. High treason.

BACON: Treason to depose a king? Not if you succeed.

CECIL: No, but treason to teach treason. ·

BACON: What is treason?

RALEIGH: Said jesting Pilate.

CECIL: Is it not treason to depose a king?

RALEIGH: What if it makes a king of you?

THE FOOL: It would then be treason not to have done it.

BACON: The Fool is a Jesuit.

THE FOOL: In truth, he was deposed. It is treason to all his successors to deny it.

BACON: An excellent Jesuit.

THE FOOL: What? I a Jesuit? Jesu!

PENELOPE: And a wit.

BACON: Bad.

PENELOPE: Very bad.

RALEIGH: Unutterably bad. What? Jesuit! Poisonous. Shall we allow this?

PENELOPE: I am guilty. I surrender.

RALEIGH: What did you do with the body?

PENELOPE: There was none. I did eat my words.

RALEIGH: A cannibal, a monster, a word-swallower!

THE FOOL: A man-eater.

PENELOPE: Nay, nay!

BACON: Do you eat your men with butter or salt?

PENELOPE: With salt if they are buttery and with butter if they are salty.

RALEIGH: Ready then. Here comes a salty man to be buttered.

PENELOPE: A butter-in.

THE FOOL: A salt-butter.

BACON: A cheese . . . a whole cheese.

TRESSA: Full of holes, holey.

ELLEN: Pitted.

PENELOPE: What? Am I pitted against a cheese?

RALEIGH: Let but this cheese roll into your pit, Lady . . . and you are answered.

PENELOPE: No . . . you are answered. You are answered no.

BURGHLEY: [*To Cecil*] There can be no doubt the Essex faction sent money to the actors to purchase a performance of Richard. It is an old play; it would draw no public.

CECIL: The actors are then accessory.

BURGHLEY: Think you so?

CECIL: They could hardly be unaware of the purposes of the Essex party.

BACON: It is so certain that Essex has a purpose?

CECIL: He has led his army into London.

BACON: The men live in London. Moreover, the order to disperse on landing may not have been received. Such things have happened.

CECIL: Yes?

BACON: Aye, indeed.

CECIL: [*To Burghley*] You are to see these actors?

BURGHLEY: They are sending spokesmen today.

THE FOOL: Let them put on the play for us.

TRESSA: Yes . . . the deposition scene. It may convince us. We may all turn rebel.

BURGHLEY: Tut!

THE FOOL: Tut? What does this mean . . . this tut?

BURGHLEY: Will you learn manners, sirrah? In my young days there was no such loose speaking about the court.

THE FOOL: There was no tutting, neither.

PENELOPE: You are mistaken. There used to be tutting parties. They all brought their tutting.

THE FOOL: Fie on you! Also pooh on you!

PENELOPE: Yes . . . there were fieing and poohing parties also.

RALEIGH: True, true. Well I remember the old days when all the young people would get together and try which could make the greatest pooh.

TRESSA: There was such laughter and jesting!

RALEIGH: Ah, yes, at the old Tut, Fie and Pooh Tavern! It's torn down now, but what a place it was!

THE FOOL: The game went out of fashion, alas, when it was discovered that a virgin could always pooh farther than anybody else.

TRESSA: Tut!

MARY: Fie!

ELLEN: Pooh!

THE FOOL: I beg pardon. I had forgotten there were virgins present.

PENELOPE: We are all virgins.

RALEIGH: The proof then, quickly. Show me.

PENELOPE: It is nothing that can be seen, my lord.

RALEIGH: They say seeing is believing.

PENELOPE: Virginity is rather a state of mind.

ELLEN: Nay . . . a state of preservation.

THE FOOL: I have seen these preserved virgins.

RALEIGH: You have seen them?

THE FOOL: Seen them? I've been bothered by them. The whole court used to be driven indoors by them regularly on our progress through Middlesex.

RALEIGH: They are worse at night, I believe? Middlesex . . . Middlesex . . .

PENELOPE: Change the subject, gentles. This virginity begins to wear thin.

THE FOOL: It has worn clear through, and a great hole appears in the center.

PENELOPE: A hole in your wit.

RALEIGH: His Jesuit.

PENELOPE: His half-wit.

[*A* Herald *enters and speaks to* Cecil]

THE HERALD: My lord, there are two fellows here who ask for audience with the queen.

CECIL: Who are they?

HERALD: Players, my lord.

CECIL: Tell them to wait. The queen will see them presently.

[*The* Herald *goes out*]

BURGHLEY: To my mind it was one of these same players writ the ballad that was posted up at St. Paul's.

CECIL: No, no . . . the man has been discovered . . . and will have his ears cropped for it.

BURGHLEY: But he could not have written it . . . he was but an instrument. The actors are too devilish ingenious at writing ballads. I cannot put it out of my mind they are all treasonous scoundrels.

RALEIGH: Is this the ballad on the Earl's return?

CECIL: Aye . . . "When England needeth victories
She calleth Essex on . . ."
And more to the same purpose. What I cannot understand is that the queen should take no steps to put the city in a posture of defense. Essex draws near with his army . . . and we swing the gates as usual.

BACON: Is that a symptom of danger . . . that an English general should return with his army to the English capital?

CECIL: Are you not aware that Essex' house in the Strand is a camp brimming full of armed nobles going and coming?

THE FOOL: It is much more likely to be brimming with drunken nobles going and coming brim full.

CECIL: Be quiet!

THE FOOL: Fool. [Cecil *lays a hand on his sword angrily. The* Fool *points to his own breast and repeats:*] Fool.

[Cecil *turns away. There is a rustling among those present. Several rise. At the rear the*

Queen *appears silently, two* Ladies *following her. She comes forward without speaking, her eyes seeking for someone. She fixes on* Lord Burghley]

THE QUEEN: Is it true, then, my dear Burghley, that you have taken to attending the Theatre?

BURGHLEY: No, madam.

THE QUEEN: It was not you, then, who forbade the performances of Richard II without asking my advice?

BURGHLEY: It was, madam.

THE QUEEN: On what ground?

BURGHLEY: Your Majesty, the play is treasonous. It shows the deposition of a king, and its performance was procured by rebels.

THE QUEEN: Rebels? What rebels?

BURGHLEY: I know not, madam. I have sent for the players to discover that.

THE QUEEN: You have sent for them?

BURGHLEY: Aye, madam . . . and they are here.

THE QUEEN: They will laugh at you, dear Burghley.

BURGHLEY: Others have laughed at me, Majesty.

THE QUEEN: They will laugh at you, sir, and you will deserve it. Is my kingdom so shaky that we dare not listen to a true history? Are my people so easily led that the sight of a king deposed in play will send them running hither to pull the queen out of her chair? Have we not passion plays in every little town showing the murder of our Lord? You are nervous, Lord Burghley. Let these children play their plays.

CECIL: Your Majesty, I very much fear they are not children, and that they mean to do harm.

THE QUEEN: Then let them. Let them do all the harm they can. Are we too stupid to see that to prohibit a rebellious play is to proclaim our fear of rebellion? Who is there here who fears a rebellion against me? I do not.

CECIL: It is dangerous to let these mutterings grow, dear queen.

ELIZABETH: It is dangerous to touch them. Let them mutter, if they will. Let them cry out . . . let them run the streets, these children! When they have worn themselves weary running and crying "Up with Essex!" "Down with Elizabeth!" and got themselves drunk on mutual pledges, they will go to bed and sleep soundly and wake up wiser. Let me speak to these players. Bring them to me.

BURGHLEY: Here, madam?

ELIZABETH: Here.

CECIL: Majestas, adsunt legati de curia Galliæ. Placetne eos recipere antequam . . .[1]

THE QUEEN: Cras illos recipiam.

CECIL: Sed maxime præstat . . .

[1] CECIL: Your Majesty, the French ambassadors are here. Would it please you to receive them before . . .
THE QUEEN: I will receive them tomorrow.
CECIL: But it is of the highest importance . . .
THE QUEEN: If it seems well to me, I will receive them when they come back tomorrow.

THE QUEEN: Si bene mihi videbitur, cras redituros recipiam!

Nay, I can bang you in Latin too!

[Cecil *goes out.* Elizabeth *sits and turns to the* Fool]

You, sirrah . . . I hear that you have fallen in love. Do you wish to be whipped?

THE FOOL: I would rather have been whipped, madam; much rather.

ELIZABETH: Why?

THE FOOL: It would hurt less.

ELIZABETH: Good. You shall be whipped.

THE FOOL: Madam, if you can whip it out of me I will give you my lucky shilling.

ELIZABETH: You shall be whipped and keep your shilling.

THE FOOL: You would better take it, madam queen.

ELIZABETH: Your shilling?

THE FOOL: Yes, madam queen, to buy another whip with for yourself. Nay, you had perhaps better buy several. But in truth, dear queen, I have not fallen in love, only a pretty little strumpet has fallen in love with me and I beg leave that we be allowed to marry.

ELIZABETH: Is she of the court?

THE FOOL: Yes, madam.

ELIZABETH: What, are there strumpets at court?

THE FOOL: Oh, they are all strumpets here at court. Some are here because they are strumpets and some are strumpets because they are here, but strumpets they all are.

ELIZABETH: Which is it you wish to marry?

THE FOOL: It is not that I wish to marry her, madam, but she wishes to marry me. [*Walking about to choose, finally pointing to* Tressa] This one, Majesty.

TRESSA: [*Leaping at him*] Scoundrel! . . .

THE FOOL: [*Pointing to* Ellen] No, no . . . I mean this one.

ELLEN: You dog! You . . .

[*The* Fool *passes* Penelope *by*]

THE FOOL: [*Pointing to* Mary] Or that one . . .

MARY: What!

THE FOOL: I feel sure it was one of them, Majesty . . . but it was dark at the time . . . and in truth I gave her my word of honor in the dark that I would make an honest woman of her by daylight. It is thus that most marriages are made.

ELIZABETH: How, fool?

THE FOOL: In the dark, my lady. Quite in the dark.

ELIZABETH: [*To a* Soldier] Take this fool, captain, and put him in the dark for three days with but little bread and water. I have a distaste for this fooling.

THE FOOL: No, no, madam.

ELIZABETH: I am tired of your strumpets! And let him not see his lady Penelope meanwhile. You will be sure of that, mistress?

PENELOPE: I have no desire to see him.

ELIZABETH: Whom do you desire to see?

PENELOPE: No one, your Majesty.

ELIZABETH: You lie! This Mistress Gray, take her too! Let her have bread and water!

[*She looks at* Penelope *with hatred*]

PENELOPE: Your Majesty . . . what is this?

ELIZABETH: I am weary to death of you! I am weary of all men and women, but more of you than any! You have written. You have had letters! I say, take her out of my sight! [*The soldiers start to take out* Penelope *and the* Fool] Whip them first, whip them both! [*The two are taken to the door*] Nay, leave them here, leave them, knaves . . . leave them! Damn you, do you hear me? You are too quick to obey orders! You like this whipping too well, sirrah! You have an itch for laying on! You beef-witted bastards! And now let us have entertainment, gentle lords! Let us be merry! The players are here! Let us have a play!

[*A* Herald *runs in to the* Queen *without ceremony, calling out as he comes:*]

THE HERALD: Your Majesty, Your Majesty! Lord Scroop sends me from the city to tell you there is a rising in London! There is a mob rising in the city!

ELIZABETH: What . . . is this one of the players? Are you playing Richard II for us?

THE HERALD: No, no, Your Majesty! A great number of people came through Fleet Street . . . and they have sacked a grocer's and broken into a wine-merchant's cellar! It is said they will break into Fleet Prison and set all free. . . .

ELIZABETH: Not they. If they've broken into a wine-cellar they'll get no farther. We're a marvellous people, we English, but we cannot hold liquor. Now if they were Scotch one might worry. What are they saying, these wine drinkers?

THE HERALD: I cannot tell you that, Your Majesty.

ELIZABETH: Are they not crying "Up with Essex!" "Down with Elizabeth!"?

THE HERALD: Yes, madam!

ELIZABETH: Why surely. What else would they be crying? "Up with Essex!" Viva! "Down with Elizabeth!" A bas! The queen is dead, long live the king! If I were there I would cry it myself! It has a marvellous ring! "Up with Essex!" "Down with Elizabeth!"

BURGHLEY: What are we to do, madam?

ELIZABETH: [*To the* Herald] What is the Lord Mayor doing about this?

THE HERALD: Nothing, Madam.

ELIZABETH: How like a Lord Mayor and how sensible. That's the first principle of government. Never do anything. Let the others make all the mistakes.

CECIL: But madam . . . there are five hundred of the royal guard at the Tower. . . .

ELIZABETH: Let the mayor of London look out for his people. If he allows them to run up and down breaking into wine-cellars, it's his own affair.

BURGHLEY: But if it spreads to the palace, Majesty?

ELIZABETH: Why yes . . . let them bring their

revolution here to me. I should be amused to see it. They are children, Burghley, drunken children. Would you fire on children?

BURGHLEY: Then let me go into London, madam . . .

ELIZABETH: And call out the guard and put down these traitors with powder and ball? No! They are to be allowed to get quite drunk and then go to sleep. Where are these players?

[Cecil *enters with* Burbage *and* Hemmings]

CECIL: Here, madam.

ELIZABETH: Ah, yes, bold Burbage and handsome Hemmings. Well, my masters, I understand that you have come to me to have your noses slit and your thumbs branded? Is it so?

BURBAGE: Only if unavoidable, Your Majesty.

ELIZABETH: You have put on a play, I believe?

BURBAGE: Many, Your Majesty.

ELIZABETH: You have revived the old play of Richard II, including in it the deposition scene which was censored on its first presentation, and you have done this to foster treasonous projects.

BURBAGE: No, Your Majesty, I swear it.

ELIZABETH: You have not played this play?

BURBAGE: But not to foster treason, that I swear.

ELIZABETH: If you played Richard with that pot-belly it was treason indeed. Then for what purpose?

BURBAGE: To make money.

ELIZABETH: On an old play?

BURBAGE: We were paid in advance . . .

ELIZABETH: By whom?

BURBAGE: By Lord Southampton.

BURGHLEY: You see? A friend of Essex.

ELIZABETH: You have much too handsome a nose for slitting, Master Hemmings, yet you say nothing.

HEMMINGS: There is only this to say, Your Majesty . . . that we knew nothing of any traitorous intent in the matter . . . and that, had we known of such intent, we would not have given the performance.

ELIZABETH: I think you are all traitorous knaves and rascals, as a matter of fact, in league with Essex and Southampton—and the smoothest liars in Christendom. Is there something in this?

HEMMINGS: No, madam.

ELIZABETH: You know Essex and Southampton?

HEMMINGS: We know Lord Southampton.

ELIZABETH: How much were you paid for the revival of Richard?

HEMMINGS: Three pounds, Your Majesty.

ELIZABETH: No more?

HEMMINGS: No more.

ELIZABETH: Play it again this afternoon, masters, play it at my request this afternoon, and you shall have ten pounds for it. Lord Cecil, pay Master Burbage ten pounds from the royal exchequer for one performance of Richard. And let it stand in the record.

CECIL: Yes, madam.

ELIZABETH: [*To* Hemmings] And tell Lord Southampton when you see him that I paid ten to his three. Will you tell him?

HEMMINGS: Yes, Your Majesty.

ELIZABETH: And when you have all this treason out of your systems be ready to play Sir John Falstaff for me at the end of the week. I should like to see your Falstaff again, sir.

BURBAGE: Yes, Your Majesty.

ELIZABETH: You may go.

[Burbage *and* Hemmings *go out*]

CECIL: [*Waiting till they are gone*] You are mad, Your Majesty! This is a rebellion, and you play into their hands. The outer court is thronging with messengers from the city! Half the town is in uprising!

ELIZABETH: I know.

CECIL: Madam . . .

ELIZABETH: Little man, little man, let me alone.

CECIL: This much I must tell you. Lord Essex has been seen with an armed force in the city.

ELIZABETH: Lord Essex?

CECIL: With an army. Where he is now no one can say.

ELIZABETH: And if one were to guess?

CECIL: He is on his way hither.

ELIZABETH: So I think. I shall be glad to see him. Let him bring his revolution here. How long think you it will last after I have looked on it?

BURGHLEY: Madam, the palace is unprotected from the waterside. The guard must be drawn up.

ELIZABETH: With your permission, my lord, I would rather not.

CECIL: I took the liberty of ordering a guard posted along the river.

[*A door is opened without and a sudden snarl of angry voices breaks in on the conference*]

THE VOICES: "Who has given these orders?"
"Back there . . . back!"
"Not the queen, by God!"
"The queen . . . the queen! Defend the queen!"
"An Essex!"
"Hold your mouth!"
"Stand back, fellow!"

ESSEX: [*Outside*] I say the queen will see me! Stand back!

[*There is a clank of armor in the hallway and Essex appears in the doorway,* Soldiers *following him*]

ELIZABETH: You come with a file of soldiers at your back, my lord of Essex.

ESSEX: Do I need them, Your Majesty?

ELIZABETH: No.

ESSEX: Then be off with you. Follow my orders. [Soldiers *go out*] They told me you would not see me.

ELIZABETH: They were wrong. I will see you. It
        seems you are in rebellion,
My good lord. Enter and state your grievance,
If you have grievance. For myself, I have

A great affection for rebels, being one myself
Much of the time.

    ESSEX: I am no rebel, Your Majesty . . .

But, newly arrived from Ireland, and bearing news
Of your subjects there, I venture to come to see you,
No more.

    ELIZABETH: And your army? . . . You have an
army with you?

    ESSEX: I have brought my men home to London.

    ELIZABETH: You received

My orders, no doubt, directing you to disband?

    ESSEX: I believed them to be mistaken. To disband
      on the coast

And leave my expedition there, seemed strange,
And dangerous to the country. An army turned
    loose
Becomes a mob.

    ELIZABETH: And you tell me this! You are in-
      formed in these matters

But I am not!

    ESSEX: Indeed, that is quite true . . .

I do know about armies . . . and you do not.

    ELIZABETH: Oh, yes . . .

Oh, indeed. And who paid them then? I believe
Your supplies were cut off?

    ESSEX: I have paid them.

    ELIZABETH: They are then

In your service?

    ESSEX: In my service and therefore

Devoted yours.

    ELIZABETH: And Ireland? How of Ireland?

    ESSEX: I could have conquered Ireland had you
      given me time.

I left it worse than I found it.

    ELIZABETH: An honest answer,

At any rate.

    ESSEX: Why should I lie? The fault,

If any, was yours. To conquer Ireland requires
More than the months you gave me. Years, perhaps.

    ELIZABETH: You were engaged in subduing the
      rebels, then,

When I summoned you home?

    ESSEX: Just so.

    ELIZABETH: You were not, by chance,

Joined with the rebels?

    ESSEX: Never.

    ELIZABETH: You held no parleys

With our friend Tyrone?

    ESSEX: I did. They were part of my plan.

    ELIZABETH: Your plans! Your plans! Why did you
      write me nothing

Of these your plans? Am I a witch to find out
What happens on the far side of the Irish Sea
Without being told?

    ESSEX: I wrote you . . .

    ELIZABETH: Masterly letters.

Brief, to the point, wasting no words, in short,
Nothing.

    ESSEX: I know not what Your Majesty means

By that. I wrote you fully, and in answer
Received no reply.

    ELIZABETH: You wrote me?

    ESSEX: Many times.

    ELIZABETH: And had no letters from me?

    ESSEX: None.

    ELIZABETH: Before God.

If the couriers were tampered with there shall be
Some necks stretched here! My lords, I wish to
    speak
With Lord Essex here alone! Leave us.

    CECIL: Dear queen,

Do you think it safe . . .

    ELIZABETH: Leave us!

      [Burghley *makes a sign and the stage is silently*
      emptied save for the Queen *and* Essex. *A*
      pause]

What did you write me?

    ESSEX: I wrote you my love—for I thought you
      loved me then—

And then I pled with you not to bring me home
In the midst of my mission—and then at last
    angrily—
For I had not heard—but always to say I loved
    you—
Always.

    ELIZABETH: But is this true?

    ESSEX: Would I lie?

    ELIZABETH: Some one

Has lied and will pay with his life if this is true!—
Before God and hell—some one will pay for this.

    ESSEX: What did you write me?

    ELIZABETH: I wrote—my love——

God keep you safe—I know not—and then, not
    hearing,
I wrote God knows what madness—as to a
    rebel——
Thinking you no longer mine—faithless!
Thinking——

    ESSEX: I would I had known—I was in torment—
I—forgive me——

    ELIZABETH: You should never have gone away.

God, how I've hated you!——

    ESSEX: No!

    ELIZABETH: Planned to put you to torture!

    ESSEX: I have been in torture!

      [*He steps toward her*]

    ELIZABETH: Not yet—I can't breathe yet—I can't
      breathe——

Or think or believe——

    ESSEX: Nor I.

    ELIZABETH: Can we ever——

Believe again? Can it be as it used to be?

    ESSEX: We can make it so.

    ELIZABETH: Come, kill me if you will. Put your
      arms round me——

If you love me. Do you still love me?

    ESSEX: Yes.

    ELIZABETH: Yes, yes——

If this were false, then, then truly—then I should
  die.
I thought because I was older—you see—some one
  else——

ESSEX: No one—never a breath——

ELIZABETH: Is it all, all as before?

ESSEX: We have not changed.

ELIZABETH: No. Yes, a little, perhaps. They have
changed us a little.

ESSEX: Not I. I have not changed.

ELIZABETH: Can I trust you now?

ESSEX: Sweet, think back, all those months,
All those hideous months! No word, no love.
And then word did come, it was to make me
  prisoner!
Christ, I have pride!
And though I came here in defiance, I came truly
  to find you
Who have been lost from me.

ELIZABETH: Do you ask forgiveness?
It is all forgiven.

ESSEX: Then, why then, hell's vanished—
And here's heaven risen out of it, a heaven of years
In the midst of desolate centuries.

ELIZABETH: We have so few years.
Let us make them doubly sweet, these years we have,
Be gracious with each other, sway a little
To left or right if we must to stay together—
Never distrust each other—nay, distrust
All others, when they whisper. Let us make this our
  pact
Now, for the fates are desperate to part us
And the very gods envy this happiness
We pluck out of loss and death.

ESSEX: If two stand shoulder to shoulder against
  the gods,
Happy together, the gods themselves are helpless
Against them, while they stand so.

ELIZABETH: Love, I will be
Your servant. Command me. What would you have?

ESSEX: Why nothing——

ELIZABETH: Take this my world, my present in
  your hands!
You shall stand back of my chair and together we
Shall build an England to make the old world wonder
And the new world worship!—What is this doubt
  in your brow?

ESSEX: I am troubled to be dishonest. I have
  brought my army
Here to the palace—and though it's all true that
  we've said——
No letters—utter agony over long months——
It is something in myself that has made me do this,
Not Cecil—nor anyone. No one but myself.
The rest is all excuse.

ELIZABETH: Speak what you will.

ESSEX: If you had but shown anger I could have
  spoken
Easily. It's not easy now, but speak I must!

Oh, I've thought much about this
On lonely marches and in distant tents,
Thinking of you and me. I say this now
Without rancor—in all friendliness and love——
The throne is yours by right of descent and by
Possession—but if this were a freer time,
And there were election, I should carry the country
  before me,
And this being true, and we being equal in love,
Should we not be equal in power as well?

ELIZABETH: We are equal.
I have made you so.

ESSEX: Yes, but still it's all yours——
Yours to grant me now or take away.

ELIZABETH: How could this well be otherwise?

ESSEX: Am I not—and I say this too in all love—
As worthy to be king as you to be queen?
Must you be sovereign alone?

ELIZABETH: You are young in policy,
My Essex, if you do not see that if I
Should grant high place to you now it would show
  ill to the kingdom——
It would be believed that you had forced this on me,
Would be called a revolution. It would undermine
All confidence. What is built up for years
In people's minds blows away like thistledown
When such things get abroad.

ESSEX: But is this your reason
Or have you another? Would you trust me as king?

ELIZABETH: No.

ESSEX: And are you still reluctant to give up
Your prerogatives?

ELIZABETH: Yes.

ESSEX: Then now, when the country is mine, the
  court in my hands,
You my prisoner, I must send my men away,
Disband my army, give back your kingdom to you,
And know I have been king for a moment only
And never will be again?

ELIZABETH: I am your prisoner?

ESSEX: The palace and the city are in my hands.
This England is mine now for the taking——

ELIZABETH: This is your friendship! This is your
  love!

ESSEX: As water finds its level, so power goes
To him who can use it, and soon or late the name
Of king follows where power is.

ELIZABETH: Oh, my Essex,
You are a child in war as you are in council.
Why all this talk of power? No army opposed you
When your troops came the road from Ireland.
  No guard was set
To stop your entrance with your thousand halberds.
Shall I tell you why? Because I wished to keep
A semblance of peace between us. And for that,
I am your prisoner!

ESSEX: Yes. My dear prisoner.

ELIZABETH: Now I do know at least
What it was you wanted. You wanted my kingdom.
  You have it.

Make the best of it. And so shall I.

What are your plans?

ESSEX: I have none.

ELIZABETH: The Tower, the block——

You could hardly take a queen prisoner and have no thought

Of her destiny. I am my mother's daughter,

I too can walk the path my mother walked.

ESSEX: These are heroics. You know you are free as air.

ELIZABETH: If I do as you ask.

ESSEX: Is it so hard to share your power with your love?

I could have all—and I offer to share with you.

ELIZABETH: Let's have no more pretending.

I'd have given all—but you came with an army, demanding——

In short, you don't love—nor trust me—no—nor want me——

ESSEX: God knows I have wanted you. I have wanted power——

Believed myself fitted to hold it—but not without you.

ELIZABETH: If you had wanted me would you rise and strike

At me with an army? Never, never! You'd have come

To me quietly, and we'd have talked of it together

As lovers should—and we'd both have our way——

And no one the wiser. But now, to take the palace,

Hold me prisoner—no—what you wanted you've taken——

And that is all you shall have. This is your kingdom—

But I—I am not yours.

ESSEX: But I am yours

And have been.

ELIZABETH: Who will believe that? Not the world,

No, and not I. I'd rather go to the Tower

Than share my place on terms like these.

Put me where I

Will do least harm.

ESSEX: I cannot, could not, will not.

ELIZABETH: If I could have given freely—

But not now. Not surrendering. Not to a victor.

ESSEX: I am no victor if I lose you. The only gift

That I could take from you is that we are equals.

ELIZABETH: Yes, but not now.

ESSEX: I ask one word from you.

Give me this word—this one word—and these soldiers

Shall leave, and you shall be free.

ELIZABETH: I'll believe that

When it happens.

ESSEX: I'll believe you when you promise.

ELIZABETH: Then you have my promise.

You shall share the realm with me. As I am queen,

I promise it.

ESSEX: Then this is my answer.

[He kisses her, then calls:]

Marvel!—Marvel!

[Marvel enters]

Carry out the order of release. Dismiss my guard——

Return the palace into the queen's hands.

Retire with all our forces to the Strand.

Release all prisoners. Release the queen's guard

And send them to their stations.

[Marvel goes out]

The palace will be

Returned as quickly as taken. This is our last quarrel.

ELIZABETH: Yes—our last.

MARVEL'S VOICE: [Off-stage] Form for retire!

ANOTHER VOICE: Form for retire!

A MORE DISTANT VOICE: Form for retire!

A VOICE: [In the distance] Ready to march!

ANOTHER VOICE: Ready to march!

ANOTHER: All ready!

ANOTHER: Ready, captain!

[Marvel enters]

MARVEL: The order is obeyed, my lord.

ESSEX: Follow your men.

MARVEL: Yes, my lord. [He goes out]

ESSEX: It is as I planned. They are leaving the palace.

Now let us talk no more of this tonight——

Let us forget this matter of thrones and kingdoms

And be but you and me for a while.

ELIZABETH: [Immobile] Yes—yes——

Let us forget. Have you kept your word indeed?

ESSEX: I have kept my word.

ELIZABETH: If I clapped my hands

Would my guard come now—or yours?

ESSEX: Yours only. Shall I call them?

ELIZABETH: No—I'll call them. [She claps her hands four times. Captain Armin appears in the entrance followed by four Beef-eaters with halberds. They stand at attention in the entrance]

To be sure I have a guard

Once more. [To the Captain]

The palace has been returned? It is in

Our hands?

CAPTAIN: Yes, Majesty.

ELIZABETH: I have ruled England a long time, my Essex,

And I have found that he who would rule must be

Quite friendless, without mercy, without love.

Arrest Lord Essex!

Arrest Lord Essex! Take him to the Tower

And keep him safe.

ESSEX: Is this a jest?

ELIZABETH: I never

Jest when I play for kingdoms, my lord of Essex.

ESSEX: I trusted you.

ELIZABETH: I trusted you,

And learned from you that no one can be trusted.

I will remember that.

ESSEX: Lest that should be all
You ever have to remember, Your Majesty,
Take care what you do.

ELIZABETH: I shall take care.

[Essex *unsheathes his sword, breaks it across
his knee, flings it at the foot of the throne,
turns and walks out between the two files of
guards*]

CURTAIN

ACT III.

*The queen's apartments in the Tower, a square
and heavy room, long and with a raised stone platform, at one end of which stands a regal chair. It is
dawn, the light filtering in coldly.* Ellen *stands in the
doorway at the left, weeping, with one arm before
her face. The* Fool, *who has been sleeping wrapped
in the draperies of the queen's chair, uncoils himself
from among them and rolls over to rub his eyes.*
Tressa *hurries in.*

TRESSA: Come back quickly, dear, quickly! She's
sorry she hurt you. She'll have no one else read to
her.

ELLEN: [*Weeping*] I can't read now. I'm—I don't
mind if she strikes me—only—it wasn't my fault
—— We're all so weary.

TRESSA: She's sorry——

THE FOOL: [*Waking*] One, two—there should be
three.

[Mary *comes to the door*]

MARY: [*Very low*] Ellen——

THE FOOL: Three.

MARY: Ellen! She wants you at once.

[Ellen *runs out*]

THE FOOL: Where am I?

MARY: Yes—and what are you doing there?

THE FOOL: Trying to sleep.

MARY: Sleep? In the Tower?

THE FOOL: Come and help me. I have heard that
you are perfect at lying down. [Mary *and* Tressa
go out. The Fool *looks about him sleepily, then remembers something and hunts for it under a chair.
When he extracts it it proves to be a roasted bird
on a wooden platter, covered with leaves. He examines it, then replaces a large leaf over it.* Penelope,
fully dressed, comes in from the rear] Penelope?

PENELOPE: Yes?

THE FOOL: Have you slept?

PENELOPE: No.

THE FOOL: Then you should break your fast. You
are hungry?

PENELOPE: No. I can't eat.

THE FOOL: [*Showing his capon*] Look.

PENELOPE: What's that?

THE FOOL: Breakfast. I brought it from Whitehall.

PENELOPE: Eat it then.

[*She sits on a step disconsolately*]

THE FOOL: You won't have any?

PENELOPE: No.

THE FOOL: [*Pushing the food away*] I'm not
hungry either.

PENELOPE: Eat it, poor fool.

THE FOOL: I don't want it. I brought it for you.

PENELOPE: I know. But eat it.

[*She wipes her eyes*]

THE FOOL: Why should you weep?

PENELOPE: God knows. He never wept for me.

THE FOOL: The earl's not dead yet, remember.

PENELOPE: No.

THE FOOL: And she'll never let it happen.

PENELOPE: The clock's struck five. He's to die at
six.

THE FOOL: Why has she not sent to him?

PENELOPE: She has. We were awake all night.
She has sent messages but he's not answered. She's
been waiting for word from him. But he's as silent
as if he wanted to die.

THE FOOL: Will she let them kill him if he says
nothing?

PENELOPE: She's a strange woman. She wants him
to beg her pardon . . . or something like that.

THE FOOL: Would you beg her pardon if you were
he?

PENELOPE: No.

THE FOOL: Then he won't. For I think he's as
proud as you.

PENELOPE: He has not said a word or sent a message since his arrest.

THE FOOL: And the queen has not slept?

PENELOPE: No.

THE FOOL: Nor you?

PENELOPE: No.

THE FOOL: God help these women.

PENELOPE: She says she gave him a ring once. If
he ever wanted forgiveness he was to send the ring.
And he sits there stubbornly with the ring on his
finger. Oh, God, will nothing happen?

[*The* Fool *has absent-mindedly pulled the capon
toward him again, and begins to eat.* Elizabeth
emerges from the rear]

ELIZABETH: Penelope?

PENELOPE: Yes.

ELIZABETH: Have the players come?

PENELOPE: Not yet.

[*The* Fool *has pushed the food guiltily behind
him*]

ELIZABETH: These cheating grooms! I'll have them
carbonadoed for this dallying! I shall go mad here!
Bring me the little book of prayers . . . from the
window-sill. No . . . leave it. The gods of men are
sillier than their kings and queens . . . and emptier
and more powerless. There is no god but death,
no god but death! [*She sees the food the* Fool *has
been hiding*] Gnaw your bones somewhere else!

[*The* Fool *goes out left*] Come here, my dear. I heard the clock strike five.

PENELOPE: Yes. I heard it.

[*They sit together on the steps, and* Penelope *puts her arm round* Elizabeth]

ELIZABETH: Do you love him well, my dear?

PENELOPE: Yes, Your Majesty.

[Elizabeth *bows her head wearily on* Penelope]

ELIZABETH: I love him. He has never loved me.

PENELOPE: Yes, yes. He does love you. I've been madly jealous of you.

ELIZABETH: Of me? Poor child.

PENELOPE: But he loved you . . . and never me at all.

ELIZABETH: How do you know?

PENELOPE: He told me.

ELIZABETH: What did he say?

PENELOPE: He said, "I love her dearly." I wanted him for myself, and I warned him against you. He laughed at me. He said, "I love her very dearly."

ELIZABETH: You tell me this because you want to save him.

PENELOPE: No, dear queen. It's true.

ELIZABETH: This is the end of me, dear. This is the end.
It comes late. I've been a long while learning,
But I've learned it now. Life is bitter. Nobody
Dies happy, queen or no. Will he speak, think you?
Will he send to me?

PENELOPE: No. Not now.

ELIZABETH: You see,
This is the end of me. Oh, I shall live.
I shall walk about and give orders . . . a horrible
    while . . .
A horrible old hag.

PENELOPE: You must send for him.
He's proud as you are, and you have the upper hand.
He'll say nothing. You must send for him, bring him
    here.

[*The chimes ring the quarter hour*]

ELIZABETH: Not yet. Not yet. [*She rises*]
Where are the players? I sent
For the players hours ago! They shall pay for this,
The insolent servants! Mary . . . Tressa, God's
    head!
I'm bestially served! Ellen!

[Ellen *looks in, partly dressed*]

Find out if the players
Are here? And be quick.

ELLEN: Yes, madam. [*She disappears*]

ELIZABETH: Where's my fool?

THE FOOL: [*Looking in with a bone in his hand*] Here, madam.

ELIZABETH: Where are you when I need you?
Look at the oaf! Say nothing! You're funny enough
The way you are with your capon in your mouth!
Eat! Eat! Let me see you!

THE FOOL: I don't seem to be hungry!

ELIZABETH: Eat, I say!

THE FOOL: Yes, madam. [*He tries to eat*]

ELIZABETH: Now wipe your fingers.
Here, take my napkin, child. Come here!
You're disgusting!

[*She gives him a kerchief*]

Can you not clean your face?

THE FOOL: With this?

ELIZABETH: Aye, with that.

[*She takes his bone and throws it*]

Why do you make mouths at it? It's clean.

THE FOOL: Yes, madam!

[*He begins to wipe his mouth, then starts to cry; and, sitting down on the steps, sobs heavily, his head in his hands*]

ELIZABETH: What is it now? What good's a fool
    that cries
When you need comfort? What's the matter?

THE FOOL: Please,
I don't know. You aren't like the queen.

ELIZABETH: I am
The queen, though.

TRESSA: [*Looking in*] The players, madam.

ELIZABETH: Bring them here.

PENELOPE: The time's grown short. Will you send
for him?

ELIZABETH: Wait . . . he may come.

PENELOPE: No, no. He won't. You'll let it go too
long
Watching the players.

ELIZABETH: Let them come in.

[Tressa *is seen at the doorway with the* Actors]

PENELOPE: You should eat
A little something first.

ELIZABETH: No, no. Bring them in.

[*The* Actors *enter*]

Come in, my masters, let us have a play . . .
Let us have revels and amusements
    quickly . . .
If ever you played play now. This is my bad
Quarter of an hour.

PENELOPE: Please, please . . .

ELIZABETH: Quick! Quick . . .
You are late, sirs . . . never mind . . . some scene
    from Falstaff . . .
The one where he lies to the prince about running
    away
And the prince catches him . . .

HEMMINGS: Where, Majesty?

ELIZABETH: There, anywhere. Come, sit down. Sit
    down.

[*The* Girls *and the* Fool *group about her*]

Begin, Falstaff! "I call thee coward! I'll see thee
Damned ere I call thee coward!"

FALSTAFF: I call thee coward! I'll see thee damned
ere I call thee coward: but I would give a thousand
pound I could run as fast as thou canst.

PRINCE HENRY: What's the matter?

FALSTAFF: What's the matter! there be four of us
here have ta'en a thousand pound this day morning.

PRINCE HENRY: Where is it, Jack? where is it?

FALSTAFF: Where is it! taken from us it is: a hundred upon poor four of us.

PRINCE HENRY: What, fought ye with them all?

FALSTAFF: All! I know not what ye call all; but if I fought not with fifty of them, I am a bunch of radish: if there were not two or three and fifty upon poor old Jack, then am I no two-legged creature.

ELIZABETH: Come, come . . . this is not to the purpose . . . I had thought this witty . . . [*The* Players *pause*] Play! Play!

PRINCE HENRY: Pray God, you have not murdered some of them.

FALSTAFF: Nay, that's past praying for: I have peppered two of them; two I am sure I have paid, . . . two rogues in buckram suits. I tell thee what, Hal, . . . if I tell thee a lie, spit in my face, call me horse. Thou knowest my old ward . . . here I lay, and thus I bore my point. Four rogues in buckram let drive at me . . .

PRINCE HENRY: What, four? thou saidst but two even now.

FALSTAFF: Four, Hal; I told thee four.

POINS: Ay, ay, he said four.

FALSTAFF: These four came all a-front, and mainly thrust at me. I made me no more ado but took all their seven points in my target, thus.

[*The* Queen *walks from place to place, restlessly*]

PRINCE HENRY: Seven? why, there were but four even now.

FALSTAFF: In buckram?

POINS: Aye, four in buckram suits.

FALSTAFF: Seven, by these hilts, or I am a villain else.

PRINCE HENRY: Pr'ythee, let him alone; we shall have more anon.

FALSTAFF: Dost thou hear me, Hal?

PRINCE HENRY: Ay, and mark thee too, Jack.

ELIZABETH: Aye, aye . . . we are listening . . . Play!

FALSTAFF: Do so, for it is worth the listening to. These nine in buckram that I told thee of . . .

PRINCE HENRY: So, two more already.

FALSTAFF: Began to give me ground: but I followed me close, came in foot and hand; and with a thought seven of the eleven I paid.

PRINCE HENRY: O monstrous! eleven buckram men grown out of two!

FALSTAFF: But, as the devil would have it, three misbegotten knaves in Kendal green came at my back and let drive at me . . . for it was so dark, Hal, that thou couldst not see thy hand.

PRINCE HENRY: These lies are like the father that begets them . . . gross as a mountain, open, palpable. Why, thou clay-brained guts, thou knotty-pated fool, thou whoreson, obscene, greasy tallow-ketch . . .

FALSTAFF: What, art thou mad? art thou mad? is not the truth the truth?

PRINCE HENRY: Why, how couldst thou know these men in Kendal green, when it was so dark thou couldst not see thy hand? come, tell us your reason: what sayest thou to this?

POINS: Come, your reason, Jack . . . your reason.

FALSTAFF: What, upon compulsion? Give you a reason on compulsion! if reasons were as plenty as blackberries I would give no man a reason on compulsion, I.

PRINCE HENRY: I'll be no longer guilty of this sin; this sanguine coward, this bed-presser, this horse back-breaker, this huge hill of flesh . . .

FALSTAFF: Away, you starveling, you elfskin, you dried neat's tongue . . . O for breath to utter what is like thee! . . . you tailor's yard, you sheath, you bowcase, you vile standing-tuck . . .

PRINCE HENRY: Well, breathe awhile, and then to it again: and when thou hast tired thyself in base comparisons, hear me speak but this.

POINS: Mark, Jack.

PRINCE HENRY: We two saw you four set on four; you bound them, and were masters of their wealth. . . . Mark now, how a plain tale shall put you down. . . . Then did we two set on you four; and, with a word, outfaced you from your prize, and have it: yes, and can show it you here in the house: . . . and, Falstaff, you carried your guts away as nimbly, with as quick dexterity, and roared for mercy, and still ran and roared, as ever I heard bull-calf. What a slave art thou, to hack thy sword as thou hast done, and then say it was in fight! What trick, what device, what starting-hole canst thou now find out to hide thee from this open and apparent shame?

POINS: Come, let's hear, Jack; what trick hast thou now?

FALSTAFF: By the Lord, I knew ye as well as He that made ye. Why, hear ye, my masters: was it for me to kill the heir-apparent? Should I turn upon the true prince? Why, thou knowest I am as valiant as Hercules: but beware instinct; the lion will not touch the true prince. Instinct is a great matter; I was a coward on instinct. I shall think the better of myself and thee during my life; I for a valiant lion, and thou for a true prince. But, by the Lord, lads, I am glad you have the money. What, shall we be merry? Shall we have a play extempore?

ELIZABETH: My God, my God . . . can not one forget for a moment?

Who are these strangers? What is this interlude?

Go! Go! It's a vile play and you play it vilely!

Go! By my God, will no one deliver me from this torment? [*The* Players *start out*]

Take your trappings and go!

[*They leave. The chimes strike*]

Again . . . the half-hour . . . [Cecil *enters*]

Yes? [*To* Penelope]

Was I not wise to wait? He has spoken first! Yes?

CECIL: Your Majesty, a citizen rabble has gathered
To protest the execution of Essex. The captain
Begs permission to use your guard. There's no other
Force at hand to disperse them.
    ELIZABETH: It's your day, Cecil.
I daresay you know that. The snake-in-the-grass
Endures, and those who are noble, free of soul,
Valiant and admirable . . . they go down in the
    prime,
Always they go down . . .
    CECIL: Madam, the guard
Is needed at once . . .
    ELIZABETH: Aye . . . the snake-mind is best . . .
One by one you out-last them. To the end
Of time it will be so . . . the rats inherit the earth.
Take my guard. Take it. I thought you brought
    word from . . .
Go, call Lord Essex for me
From his cell . . . and bring him hither! I'll wait
    no longer!
    CECIL: Lord Essex is prepared for execution.
The priest has been sent to him.
    ELIZABETH: Bring him here, I say,
And now . . . at once!
        [Cecil *bows and goes out*]
Go out from me, all of you,
All save Penelope. Go quickly, quickly . . .
All . . . [*They leave*]
Penelope, bring my robe, the one
Laid out . . . [Penelope *goes.* Elizabeth *seats her-*
self in the royal chair. Penelope *returns with the*
robe]
Look here in my face, Penelope. He's so young,
And I'm old, girl, I'm old. It shows in my eyes.
Dear, you're so young. Do not be here when he
    comes . . .
Do you mind? You'll look so young.
    PENELOPE: Yes, madam . . . but you . . .
You're beautiful.
    ELIZABETH: Beautiful still? But I was once . . .
    I was . . .
You'd not believe it now.
    PENELOPE: Oh, yes . . .
You're always beautiful. You've always been.
    ELIZABETH: Thank you,
My dear. Go now. He'll come.
    PENELOPE: Yes.
        [*She goes out to the rear. After a moment*
Essex *enters from the left with a* Guard. *The*
Guard *leaves him and steps out.* Essex *is*
dressed in black and is very pale]
    ESSEX: You sent for me?
Or so they said.
    ELIZABETH: Yes.
    ESSEX: It would have been kinder
To leave me with my thoughts till the axe came
    down
And ended them. You spoil me for death.
    ELIZABETH: Are you
So set on dying?

    ESSEX: I can't say I care for it.
This blood that beats in us has a way of wanting
To keep right on. But if one is to die
It's well to go straight toward it.
    ELIZABETH: You must have known
I never meant you to die.
    ESSEX: I am under sentence
From Your Majesty's courts. There's no appeal that
    I know of.
I am found guilty of treason on good evidence,
And cannot deny it. This treason, I believe,
Is punishable with death.
    ELIZABETH: God knows I am proud . . .
And bitter, too . . . bitter at you with much cause,
But I have sent for you. I've taken the first step
That way. Do not make me take the next!
    ESSEX: The next is to the scaffold. It's only a step
Now, and I've made ready.
    ELIZABETH: Aye, you are bitter,
Too; we have let it go late; we've both
Waited for the other. But it was I who spoke
First . . . Will you make me tell you first how
    much
I've longed for you? It's hard for me.
    ESSEX: My dear,
You can tell me so gracefully, for you
Have nothing to gain or lose by me . . . but I
Have life and love to gain, and I find it less
Than fitting to speak like a lover, lest you suppose
I do it to save my head.
    ELIZABETH: It's true that you never
Loved me, isn't it? You were ambitious, and I
Loved you, and it was the nearest way to power,
And you took the nearest way? No, no . . . one
    moment . . .
This is an hour for truth, if there's ever truth . . .
I'm older than you . . . but a queen; it was natural
You'd flatter me, speak me fair, and I believed you.
I'm sorry I believed you. Sorry for you
More than for me.
    ESSEX: Why, yes . . . that's true enough.
Now may I go? This dying sticks in my mind,
And makes me poor company, I fear.
    ELIZABETH: It was true.
It was true then?
    ESSEX: If you wish to make me tell you
What you well know, how much I used to love you,
How much I have longed for you, very well, I will
    say it.
That's a small victory to win over me now,
But take it with the rest.
    ELIZABETH: You did love me?
    ESSEX: Yes.
    ELIZABETH: And love me still?
    ESSEX: Yes. You should know that, I think.
    ELIZABETH: You kept my ring. You never sent
    my ring.
I've been waiting for it.
    ESSEX: You may have it back.

If you have use for it . . . I had thought to wear it
As far as my grave, but, take it.
    ELIZABETH: I'd have forgiven
All that had passed, at any hour, day or night,
Since I last saw you. I have waited late at night
Thinking, tonight the ring will come, he will never
Hold out against me so long, but the nights went by
Somehow, like the days, and it never came,
Till the last day came, and here it is the last morning
And the chimes beating out the hours.
    ESSEX: Dear, if I'd known . . .
But I could not have sent it.
    ELIZABETH: Why?
    ESSEX: If I'd tried
To hold you to a promise you could not keep
And you had refused me, I should have died much
    more
Unhappy than I am now.
    ELIZABETH: I'd have kept my promise.
I'd keep it now.
    ESSEX: If I offered you this ring?
    ELIZABETH: Yes . . . even now.
    ESSEX: You would pardon me, set me free
Cede back my estates to me, love me as before,
Give me my place in the state?
    ELIZABETH: All as it was.
    ESSEX: And what would happen to your throne?
    ELIZABETH: My throne?
Nothing.
    ESSEX: Yes, for I'd take it from you.
    ELIZABETH: Again? You'd play that game again?
    ESSEX: The games one plays
Are not the games one chooses always. I
Am still a popular idol of a sort.
There are mutterings over my imprisonment,
Even as it is . . . and if you should set me free
And confess your weakness by overlooking treason
And setting me up in power once more, the storm
That broke last time would be nothing to the storm
That would break over you then. As for myself,
I played for power and lost, but if I had
Another chance I think I'd play and win.
    ELIZABETH: Why do you say this?
    ESSEX: I say it because it's true.
I have loved you, love you now, but I know myself.
If I were to win you over and take my place
As it used to be, it would gall me. I have a weakness
For being first wherever I am. I refuse
To take pardon from you without warning you
Of this. And when you know it, pardon becomes
Impossible.
    ELIZABETH: You do this for me?
    ESSEX: Why, yes,
But not altogether. Partly for England, too.
I've lost conceit of myself a little. A life
In prison's very quiet. It leads to thinking.
You govern England better than I should.
I'd lead her into wars, make a great name,
Perhaps, like Henry Fifth and leave a legacy

Of debts and bloodshed after me. You will leave
Peace, happiness, something secure. A woman gov-
    erns
Better than a man, being a natural coward.
A coward rules best.
    ELIZABETH: Still bitter.
    ESSEX: Perhaps a little.
It's a bitter belief to swallow, but I believe it.
You were right all the time.
    [The chimes ring three-quarters]
And now, if you'll pardon me,
I have an appointment near-by with a headsman.
He comes sharp on the hour.
    ELIZABETH: You have an hour yet.
It's but struck five.
    ESSEX: It struck five some time since.
    ELIZABETH: It cannot go this way!
    ESSEX: Aye, but it has.
It has and will. There's no way out. I've thought of
    it
Every way. Speak frankly. Could you forgive me
And keep your throne?
    ELIZABETH: No.
    ESSEX: Are you ready to give
Your crown up to me?
    ELIZABETH: No. It's all I have. [She rises]
Why, who am I
To stand here paltering with a rebel noble!
I am Elizabeth, daughter of a king,
The queen of England, and you are my subject!
What does this mean, you standing here eye to eye
With me, your liege? You whom I made, and gave
All that you have, you, an upstart, defying
Me to grant pardon, lest you should sweep me from
    power
And take my place from me? I tell you if Christ his
    blood
Ran streaming from the heavens for a sign
That I should hold my hand you'd die for this,
You pretender to a throne upon which you have
No claim, you pretender to a heart, who have been
Hollow and heartless and faithless to the end!
    ESSEX: If we'd met some other how we might have
      been happy . . .
But there's been an empire between us! I am to
    die . . .
Let us say that . . . let us begin with that . . .
For then I can tell you that if there'd been no empire
We could have been great lovers. If even now
You were not queen and I were not pretender,
That god who searches heaven and earth and hell
For two who are perfect lovers, could end his search
With you and me. Remember . . . I am to die . . .
And so I can tell you truly, out of all the earth
That I'm to leave, there's nothing I'm very loath
To leave save you. Yet if I live I'll be
Your death or you'll be mine.
    ELIZABETH: Give me the ring.
    ESSEX: No.

ELIZABETH: Give me the ring. I'd rather you
    killed me
Than I killed you.
    ESSEX: It's better for me as it is
Than that I should live and batten my fame and for-
    tune
On the woman I love. I've thought of it all. It's
    better
To die young and unblemished than to live long and
    rule,
And rule not well.
    ELIZABETH: Aye, I should know that.
    ESSEX: Is it not?
    ELIZABETH: Yes.
    ESSEX: Good-by, then.
    ELIZABETH: Oh, then I'm old, I'm old!
I could be young with you, but now I'm old.
I know now how it will be without you. The sun
Will be empty and circle round an empty earth . . .
And I will be queen of emptiness and death. . . .
Why could you not have loved me enough to give me
Your love and let me keep as I was?

    ESSEX: I know not.
I only know I could not. I must go.
    ELIZABETH: [*Frozen*] Yes.
    [*He goes to the door*]
Lord Essex! [*He turns*]
Take my kingdom. It is yours!
    [Essex, *as if not hearing, bows and goes on.*
    Penelope *runs in, meeting him*]
    PENELOPE: My lord! She has forgiven you?
    ESSEX: Good-by, my dear. [*He kisses her*]
    PENELOPE: No, no! She loves you! Go to her.
    [Essex *goes out*]
Run to her! She waits you still! See, if you turn
She waits you still! Dear queen, would you let him
    go?
He goes to his death! Send, send after him!
    [*The queen lifts her head and shows a face so
    stricken that* Penelope, *who has gone to her,
    says no more. The clock strikes six.* Elizabeth
    bows her head on* Penelope's *knees, her hands
    over her ears*]

                  CURTAIN

Marc Connelly

(1890–——)

It would appear that Marc Connelly had to lose one good reputation in order to gain another, greater one. For several years he was well known as George S. Kaufman's collaborator on successful travesties of American life and manners. Connelly, one supposes, could have helped to turn these out indefinitely. Instead, he went his own way and encountered a number of defeats in the theatrical market place. He tasted one victory, however, of the kind that nullifies many reverses and compensates a writer for many disappointments; he wrote a play that is inscribed in the permanent records of the American theatre: *The Green Pastures*. Here he attempted to blend folk imagination with New Testament faith. The results were, not too surprisingly, of a different order of excellence from the results of collaboration with Kaufman.

Connelly was born and spent his boyhood in McKeesport, Pennsylvania. After some higher education, he began writing a daily column of quips for a newspaper in Pittsburgh. His thoughts turned to the theatre, and he inevitably gravitated to New York. He remained there in spite of the failure of his first stage venture, the musical play *The Amber Princess* (1916), to which he contributed the lyrics. After some lean years of free-lancing and play doctoring, he had the good fortune in 1921 to form a partnership with another immigrant from Pennsylvania, George S. Kaufman, then editing the drama page of the *New York Times*. The two men took for their first subject "Dulcinea," a bromidic female celebrated in Franklin P. Adams' famous *New York World* column. The result was the comedy *Dulcy*, about a dull-witted, interfering woman who was to be a symbol of feminine ineptitude for an entire generation. Later in 1921, Kaufman and Connelly won a second hearing on Broadway with the warm comedy of middle-class home life *To the Ladies*, in which the authors were more complimentary to womanhood. A year later, they made theatrical history by turning out the first of Broadway's numerous satires on Hollywood, *Merton of the Movies*, and in 1924, they reached the peak of their partnership with the clever expressionistic satire *Beggar on Horseback*. Connelly must have had a larger share than usual in the writing of the latter play, since it embodies his characteristic qualities of comic fantastication. A devastating dream play based on a young artist's fear that marriage would doom him to the treadmill of big business, *Beggar on Horseback* was one of the best products of the then fashionable Greenwich Village revolt against the machine age. With this play, however, the Kaufman-Connelly partnership ended.

Connelly started the next phase of his career auspiciously enough, when his independent talent for tenderness and fancy asserted itself in *The Wisdom Tooth* (1926). But this comedy was followed by reverses until he had the good fortune to write *The Green Pastures* (1930), a play based on Roark Bradford's collection of more or less genuine Negro folk tales, *Ol' Man Adam an' His Chillun*. The play was brilliantly staged against expressive settings by Robert Edmond Jones with an all-Negro cast, among whom Richard Harrison distinguished himself with a portrayal of "de Lawd" remarkably moving in its simplicity and dignity.

Negro life and manners had interested serious dramatists for a decade, and some of the playwriting inspired by regional literature and theatre was of a high order. The romantic folk drama was already well represented on Broadway by Dorothy and Du Bose Heyward's *Porgy* (1927). For Connelly, however, the regional background was a matter of secondary interest. He sublimated folk drama into religious drama, concluding a play enlivened by scenes such as the celestial fish fry with a mystic vision of the crucifixion.

The Green Pastures is unique: it cannot be placed in any existing classification without some reservations. The Catholic critic Richard Dana Skinner accused Connelly of "sinning against real simplicity," and it is indeed questionable whether the playwright did not veer too far from either folk or religious drama in some details. Is there no discrepancy between the "Harlem" scene and the spirit of the play? Is the play entirely free from a spirit of condescension toward primitive folk and their notions? Yet one cannot overlook the tremendous fascination the play exerted for years after it opened on Broadway. It seemed the culmination of everything we considered a movement toward folk drama for at least a decade, and it was also the only religious drama anyone had succeeded in making tolerable to the American public since the vogue of Charles Rann Kennedy's old-fashioned morality play *The Servant in the House*.

BIBLIOGRAPHY: Burns Mantle, *Contemporary American Playwrights* (pp. 50–53), 1938; Stark Young, *Immortal Shadows* (pp. 119–123), 1948.

THE GREEN PASTURES

By Marc Connelly

CHARACTERS

MR. DESHEE, *the Preacher*	ZEBA	FLATFOOT
MYRTLE	CAIN THE SIXTH	HAM
FIRST BOY	BOY GAMBLER	JAPHETH
SECOND BOY	GENERAL	FIRST CLEANER
FIRST COOK	HEAD MAGICIAN	SECOND CLEANER
A VOICE	FIRST WIZARD	ABRAHAM
SECOND COOK	SECOND WIZARD	ISAAC
FIRST MAN ANGEL	JOSHUA	JACOB
FIRST MAMMY ANGEL	FIRST SCOUT	MOSES
A STOUT ANGEL	MASTER OF CEREMONIES	ZIPPORAH
A SLENDER ANGEL	FIRST GAMBLER	AARON
ARCHANGEL	SECOND GAMBLER	A CANDIDATE MAGICIAN
GABRIEL	VOICE IN SHANTY	PHARAOH
GOD	NOAH	KING OF BABYLON
CHOIR LEADER	NOAH'S WIFE	PROPHET
CUSTARD MAKER	SHEM	HIGH PRIEST
ADAM	FIRST WOMAN	CORPORAL
EVE	SECOND WOMAN	HEZDREL
CAIN	THIRD WOMAN	SECOND OFFICER
CAIN'S GIRL	FIRST MAN	

SCENES

PART I

1. THE SUNDAY SCHOOL
2. A FISH FRY
3. A GARDEN
4. OUTSIDE THE GARDEN
5. A ROADSIDE
6. A PRIVATE OFFICE
7. ANOTHER ROADSIDE AND A HOUSE
8. A HOUSE
9. A HILLSIDE
10. A MOUNTAIN TOP

PART II

1. THE PRIVATE OFFICE
2. THE MOUTH OF A CAVE
3. A THRONE ROOM
4. THE FOOT OF A MOUNTAIN
5. A CABARET
6. THE PRIVATE OFFICE
7. OUTSIDE A TEMPLE
8. ANOTHER FISH FRY

AUTHOR'S NOTE

The Green Pastures is an attempt to present certain aspects of a living religion in the terms of its believers. The religion is that of thousands of Negroes in the deep South. With terrific spiritual hunger and the greatest humility, these untutored black Christians—many of whom cannot even read the book which is the treasure house of their faith—have adapted the contents of the Bible to the consistencies of their everyday lives.

Unburdened by the differences of more educated theologians, they accept the Old Testament as a chronicle of wonders which happened to people like themselves in vague but actual places, and of rules of conduct, true acceptance of which will lead them to a tangible, three-dimensional Heaven. In this Heaven, if one has been born in a district where fish fries are popular, the angels do have magnificent fish fries through an eternity somewhat resembling a series of earthly holidays. The Lord Jehovah will be the promised comforter, a just but compassionate patriarch, the summation of all the virtues. His follower has observed in the human beings about him. The Lord may look like the Reverend Mr.

Dubois, as our Sunday-School teacher speculates in the play, or he may resemble another believer's own grandfather. In any event, His face will be familiar to the one who has come for his reward.

The author is indebted to Mr. Roark Bradford, whose retelling of several of the Old Testament stories in *Ol' Man Adam an' His Chillun* first stimulated his interest in this point of view.

One need not blame a hazy memory of the Bible for the failure to recall the characters of Hezdrel, Zeba and others in the play. They are the author's apocrypha, but he believes persons much like them have figured in the meditations of some of the old Negro preachers, whose simple faith he has tried to translate into a play.

PART I. SCENE I.

A corner in a Negro church.
Ten Children *and an elderly* Preacher.

The costumes are those that might be seen in any lower Louisiana town at Sunday-School time. As the curtain rises, Mr. Deshee, *the preacher, is reading from a Bible. The* Children *are listening with varied degrees of interest. Three or four are wide-eyed in their attention. Two or three are obviously puzzled, but interested, and the smallest ones are engaged in more physical concerns. One is playing with a little doll, and another runs his finger on all angles of his chair.*

DESHEE: "An' Adam lived a hundred and thirty years, an' begat a son in his own likeness, after his image; an' called his name Seth. An' de days of Adam, after he had begotten Seth, were eight hundred years! An' he begat sons an' daughters; an' all de days dat Adam lived were nine hundred an' thirty years; an' he died. An' Seth lived a hundred an' five years an' begat Enos; an' Seth lived after he begat Enos eight hundred an' seven years an' begat sons and daughters. An' all de days of Seth were nine hundred and twelve years; an' he died." An' it go like dat till we come to Enoch an' de Book say: "An' Enoch lived sixty an' five years and begat Methuselah." Den it say: "An' all de days of Methuselah were nine hund'ed an' sixty an' nine years an' he died." An' dat was de oldest man dat ever was. Dat's why we call ol' Mr. Gurney's mammy ol' Mrs. Methuselah, caize she's so ol'. Den a little later it tell about another member of de fam'ly. His name was Noah. Maybe some of you know about him already. I'm gonter tell you all about him next Sunday. Anyway dat's de meat an' substance of de first five chapters of Genesis. Now, how you think you gonter like de Bible?

MYRTLE: I think it's jest wonderful, Mr. Deshee. I cain't understand any of it.

FIRST BOY: Why did dey live so long, Mr. Deshee?

DESHEE: Why? Caize dat was de way God felt.

SECOND BOY: Dat made Adam away back.

DESHEE: Yes, he certainly 'way back by de time Noah come along. Want to ask me any mo' questions?

SECOND BOY: What de worl' look like when de Lawd begin, Mr. Deshee?

DESHEE: How yo' mean what it look like?

MYRTLE: Carlisle mean who was in N'Orleans den.

DESHEE: Dey wasn't nobody in N'Orleans on 'count dey wasn't any N'Orleans. Dat's de whole idea I tol' you at de end of de first Chapter. Yo' got to git yo' minds fixed. Dey wasn't any Rampart Street. Dey wasn't any Canal Street. Dey wasn't any Louisiana. Dey wasn't nothin' on de earth at all caize fo' de reason dey wasn't any earth.

MYRTLE: Yes, but what Carlisle wanter know is—

DESHEE: [*Interrupting and addressing little boy who has been playing with his chair and paying no attention*] Now, Randolph, if you don't listen, how yo' gonter grow up and be a good man? Yo' wanter grow up an' be a transgressor?

LITTE BOY: [*Frightened*] No.

DESHEE: You tell yo' mammy yo' sister got to come wid you next time. She kin git things done in time to bring you to de school. You content yo'self. [*The little boy straightens up in his chair*] Now, what do Carlisle want to know?

SECOND BOY: How He decide He want de worl' to be right yere and how He git de idea He wanted it?

MYRTLE: Caize de Book say, don't it, Mr. Deshee?

DESHEE: De Book say, but at de same time dat's a good question. I remember when I was a little boy de same thing recurred to me. An' ol' Mr. Dubois, he was a wonderful preacher at New Hope Chapel over in East Gretna, he said: "De answer is dat de Book ain't got time to go into all de details." And he was right. You know sometimes I think de Lawd expects us to figure out a few things for ourselves. We know dat at one time dey wasn't anything except Heaven. We don't know jest where it was but we know it was dere. Maybe it was everywhere. Den one day de Lawd got the idea He'd like to make some places. He made de sun and de moon, de stars. An' He made de earth.

MYRTLE: Who was aroun' den, nothin' but angels?

DESHEE: I suppose so.

FIRST BOY: What was de angels doin' up dere?

DESHEE: I suppose dey jest flew aroun' and had a good time. Dey wasn't no sin, so dey musta had a good time.

FIRST BOY: Did dey have picnics?

DESHEE: Sho, dey had the nicest kind of picnics. Dey probably had fish fries, wid b'iled custard and ten-cent seegars for de adults. God gives us humans lotsa ideas about havin' good times. Maybe dey were things he'd seen de angels do. Yes, sir, I bet dey had a fish fry every week.

MYRTLE: Did dey have Sunday School, too?

DESHEE: Yes, dey musta had Sunday School for de cherubs.

MYRTLE: What did God look like, Mr. Deshee?

DESHEE: Well, nobody knows exactly what God looked like. But when I was a little boy I used to imagine dat He looked like de Reverend Dubois. He was de finest-looking ol' man I ever knew. Yes, I used to bet de Lawd looked exactly like Mr. Dubois in de days when He walked de earth in de shape of a natchel man.

MYRTLE: When was dat, Mr. Deshee?

DESHEE: Why, when He was gettin' things started down heah. When he talked to Adam and Eve and Noah and Moses and all dem. He made mighty men in dem days. But aldo dey was awful mighty dey always knew dat He was beyond dem all. Pretty near one o'clock, time fo' you chillun to go home to dinner, but before I let you go I wan' you to go over wid me de main facts of de first lesson. What's de name of de book?

CHILDREN: Genesis.

DESHEE: Dat's right. And what's de other name?

CHILDREN: First Book of Moses.

DESHEE: Da't right. And dis yere's Chapter One. [*The lights begin to dim*] "In de beginnin' God created de heaven and de earth. An' de earth was widout form an' void. An' de darkness was upon de face of de deep."

SCENE II.

In the darkness many voices are heard singing "Rise, Shine, Give God the Glory." They sing it gaily and rapidly. The lights go up as the second verse ends. The chorus is being sung diminuendo by a mixed company of angels. That is, they are angels in that they wear brightly colored robes and have wings protruding from their backs. Otherwise they look and act like a company of happy Negroes at a fish fry. The scene itself is a pre-Creation Heaven with compromises.

In the distance is an unbroken stretch of blue sky. Companionable varicolored clouds billow down to the floor of the stage and roll overhead to the branches of a live oak tree which is up left. The tree is leafy and dripping with Spanish moss, and with the clouds makes a frame for the scene. In the cool shade of the tree are the usual appurtenances of a fish fry; a large kettle of hot fat set on two small parallel logs, with a fire going underneath, and a large rustic table formed by driving four stakes into the ground and placing planks on top of the small connecting boards. On the table are piles of biscuits and corn bread and the cooked fish in dish pans. There are one or two fairly large cedar or crock "churns" containing boiled custard, which looks like milk. There is a gourd dipper beside the churns and several glasses and cups of various sizes and shapes from which the custard is drunk.

The principal singers are marching two by two in a small area at the R. of the stage. Two Mammy Angels are attending to the frying beside the kettle. Behind the table a Man Angel is skinning fish and passing them to the cooks. Another is ladling out the custard. A Mammy Angel is putting fish on bread for a brood of cherubs, and during the first scene they seat themselves on a grassy bank upstage. Another Mammy Angel is clapping her hands disapprovingly and beckoning a laughing Boy Cherub down from a cloud a little out of her reach.

Another Mammy Angel is solicitously slapping the back of a Girl Cherub who has a large fish sandwich in her hand and a bone in her throat. There is much movement about the table, and during the first few minutes several individuals go up to the table to help themselves to the food and drink. Many of the Women Angels wear hats and a few of the Men are smoking cigars. A large boxful is on the table. There is much laughter and chatter as the music softens, but continues during the early part of the action. The following short scenes are played almost simultaneously.

SECOND COOK: [*At kettle, calling off*] Hurry up, Cajey. Dis yere fat's cryin' fo' mo' feesh.

A VOICE: [*Off stage*] We comin', fas' we kin. Dey got to be ketched, ain't dey? We cain't say, "C'm'on, little fish. C'm'on an' git fried," kin we?

SECOND COOK: [*At table*] De trouble is de mens is all worm fishin'.

FIRST MAN ANGEL: [*At table*] Whut dif'runce do it make? Yo' all de time got to make out like somebody's doin' somethin' de wrong way.

SECOND COOK: [*Near table*] I s'pose you got de per'fec' way fo' makin' bait.

FIRST MAN ANGEL: I ain't sayin' dat. I is sayin' whut's wrong wid worm fishin'.

SECOND COOK: Whut's wrong wid worm fishin'? Ever'thing, dat's all. Dey's only one good way fo' catfishin', and dat's minny fishin'. Anybody know dat.

FIRST MAN ANGEL: Well, it jest so happen dat minny fishin' is de doggondest fool way of fishin' dey is. You kin try minny fishin' to de cows come home an' all you catch'll be de backache. De trouble wid you, sister, is you jest got minny fishin' on de brain.

SECOND COOK: Go right on, loud mouf. You tell me de news. My, my! You jest de wisest person in de worl'. First you, den de Lawd God.

FIRST MAN ANGEL: [*To the custard ladler*] You cain't tell dem nothin'. [*Walks away to the custard churn*] Does you try to 'splain some simple fac' dey git man-deaf.

FIRST MAMMY ANGEL: [*To Cherub on the cloud*] Now, you heerd me. [*The Cherub assumes several mocking poses, as she speaks*] You fly down yere. You wanter be put down in de sin book? [*She goes to the table, gets a drink for herself and points out the Cherub to one of the men behind the table*] Dat baby must got imp blood in him he so vexin'. [*She returns to her position under the cloud*] You want me to fly up dere an' slap you down? Now, I tol' you.

[*The Cherub starts to come down*]

STOUT ANGEL: [*To the Cherub with a bone in her throat*] I tol' you you was too little fo' catfish. What you wanter git a bone in yo' froat fo'?

[*She slaps the Cherub's back*]

SLENDER ANGEL: [*Leisurely eating a sandwich as she watches the back-slapping*] What de trouble wid Leonetta?

STOUT ANGEL: She got a catfish bone down her froat. [*To the Cherub*] Doggone, I tol' you to eat grinnel instead.

SLENDER ANGEL: Ef'n she do git all dat et, she gonter have a belly-ache.

STOUT ANGEL: Ain't I tol' her dat? [*To Cherub*]

Come on now; let go dat bone. [*She slaps* Cherub's *back again. The bone is dislodged and the* Cherub *grins her relief*] Dat's good.

SLENDER ANGEL: [*Comfortingly*] Now she all right.

STOUT ANGEL: Go on an' play wid yo' cousins. [*The* Cherub *joins the* Cherubs *sitting on the embankment. The concurrency of scenes ends here*] I ain't see you lately, Lily. How you been?

SLENDER ANGEL: Me, I'm fine. I been visitin' my mammy. She waitin' on de welcome table over by de throne of grace.

STOUT ANGEL: She always was pretty holy.

SLENDER ANGEL: Yes, ma'am. She like it dere. I guess de Lawd's took quite a fancy to her.

STOUT ANGEL: Well, dat's natural. I declare yo' mammy one of de finest lady angels I know.

SLENDER ANGEL: She claim you best one she know.

STOUT ANGEL: Well, when you come right down to it, I suppose we is all pretty near perfec'.

SLENDER ANGEL: Yes, ma'am. Why is dat, Mis' Jenny?

STOUT ANGEL: I s'pose it's caize de Lawd He don' 'low us 'sociatin' wid de devil any mo' so dat dey cain' be no mo' sinnin'.

SLENDER ANGEL: Po' ol' Satan. Whutevah become of him?

STOUT ANGEL: De Lawd put him some place, I s'pose.

SLENDER ANGEL: But dey ain't any place but Heaven, is dey?

STOUT ANGEL: De Lawd could make a place, couldn't He?

SLENDER ANGEL: Dat's de truth. Dey's one thing confuses me though.

STOUT ANGEL: What's dat?

SLENDER ANGEL: I do a great deal of travelin' an' I ain't never come across any place but Heaven anywhere. So if de Lawd kick Satan out of Heaven jest whereat did he go? Dat's my question.

STOUT ANGEL: You bettah let de Lawd keep His own secrets, Lily. De way things is goin' now dey ain't been no sinnin' since dey give dat scamp a kick in de pants. Nowadays Heaven's free of sin an' if a lady wants a little constitutional she kin fly 'til she wing-weary widout gittin' insulted.

SLENDER ANGEL: I was jest a baby when Satan lef'. I don't even 'member what he look like.

STOUT ANGEL: He was jest right fo' a devil. [*An* Archangel *enters. He is older than the others and wears a white beard. His clothing is much darker than that of the others and his wings a trifle more imposing*] Good mo'nin', Archangel.

[*Others say good morning*]

ARCHANGEL: Good mo'nin', folks. I wonder kin I interrup' de fish fry an' give out de Sunday-School cyards? [*Cries of* "Suttingly!" "Mah goodness, yes" —etc. *The marching* Choir *stops*] You kin keep singin' if you want to. Why don' you sing "When de Saints Come Marchin' In"? Seem to me I ain't

heard dat lately. [*The* Choir *begins* "When de Saints Come Marchin' In," *rather softly, but does not resume the marching. The* Archangel *looks off left*] All right, bring 'em yere [*A prim-looking* Woman Teacher-Angel *enters, shepherding ten* Boy *and* Girl Cherubs. *The* Teacher *carries ten beribboned diplomas, which she gives to the* Archangel. *The* Cherubs *are dressed in stiffly starched white suits and dresses, the little girls having enormous ribbons at the backs of their dresses and smaller ones in their hair and on the tips of their wings. They line up in front of the* Archangel *and receive the attention of the rest of the company. The* Choir *sings through the ceremony*] Now den, cherubs, why is you yere?

CHILDREN: Because we so good.

ARCHANGEL: Dat's right. Now who de big boss?

CHILDREN: Our dear Lawd.

ARCHANGEL: Dat's right. When you all grow up what you gonter be?

CHILDREN: Holy angels at de throne of grace.

ARCHANGEL: Dat's right. Now, you passed yo' 'zaminations and it gives me great pleasure to hand out de cyards for de whole class. Gineeva Chaproe. [*The* First Girl Cherub *goes to him and gets her diploma. The* Choir *sings loudly and resumes marching, as the* Archangel *calls out another name—and presents diplomas*] Corey Moulter. [*Second* Girl Cherub *gets her diploma*] Nootzie Winebush. [*Third* Girl Cherub] Harriet Prancy. [*Fourth* Girl Cherub] I guess you is Brozain Stew't. [*He gives the* Fifth Girl Cherub *the paper. Each of the presentations has been accompanied by handclapping from the bystanders*] Now you boys know yo' own names. Suppose you come yere and help me git dese 'sorted right?

[Boy Cherubs *gather about him and receive their diplomas. The little* Girls *have scattered about the stage, joining groups of the* Adult Angels. *The angel* Gabriel *enters. He is bigger and more elaborately winged than even the* Archangel, *but he is also much younger and beardless. His costume is less conventional than that of the other men, resembling more the* Gabriel *of the Doré drawings. His appearance causes a flutter among the others. They stop their chattering with the* Children. *The* Choir *stops as three or four audible whispers of* "Gabriel!" *are heard. In a moment the heavenly company is all attention*]

GABRIEL: [*Lifting his hand*] Gangway! Gangway for de Lawd God Jehovah!

[*There is a reverent hush and* God *enters. He is the tallest and biggest of them all. He wears a white shirt with a white bow tie, a long Prince Albert coat of black alpaca, black trousers and congress gaiters. He looks at the assemblage. There is a pause. He speaks in a rich, bass voice*]

GOD: Is you been baptized?

OTHERS: [*Chanting*] Certainly, Lawd.

GOD: Is you been baptized?

OTHERS: Certainly, Lawd.

GOD: [*With the beginning of musical notation*] Is you been baptized?

OTHERS: [*Now half-singing*] Certainly, Lawd. Certainly, certainly, certainly, Lawd.

> [*They sing the last two verses with equivalent part division*]

Is you been redeemed?

Certainly, Lawd.

Is you been redeemed?

Certainly, Lawd.

Is you been redeemed?

Certainly, Lawd. Certainly, certainly, certainly, Lawd.

Do you bow mighty low?

Certainly, Lawd.

Do you bow mighty low?

Certainly, Lawd.

Do you bow mighty low?

Certainly, Lawd. Certainly, certainly, certainly, Lawd.

> [*As the last response ends all heads are bowed. God looks at them for a moment; then lifts His hand*]

GOD: Let de fish fry proceed.

> [*Everyone rises. The Angels relax and resume their inaudible conversations. The activity behind the table and about the cauldron is resumed. Some of the Choir members cross to the table and get sandwiches and cups of the boiled custard. Three or four of the Children in the Sunday-School class and the girl who had the bone in her throat affectionately group themselves about God as He speaks with the Archangel. He pats their heads, they hang to His coat-tails, etc.*]

ARCHANGEL: Good mo'nin', Lawd.

GOD: Good mo'nin', Deacon. You lookin' pretty spry.

ACHANGEL: I cain' complain. We just been givin' out cyards to de chillun.

GOD: Dat's good.

> [*A small Cherub, his feet braced against one of God's shoes, is using God's coat-tail as a trapeze. One of the Cooks offers a fish sandwich which God politely declines*]

FIRST MAMMY ANGEL: Now, you leave go de Lawd's coat, Herman. You heah me?

GOD: Dat's all right, sister. He jest playin'.

FIRST MAMMY ANGEL: He playin' too rough.

> [*God picks up the Cherub and spanks him good-naturedly. The Cherub squeals with delight and runs to his mother. Gabriel advances to God with a glass of the custard*]

GABRIEL: Little b'iled custud, Lawd?

GOD: Thank you very kindly. Dis looks nice.

CUSTARD MAKER: [*Offering a box*] Ten-cent seegar, Lawd?

GOD: [*Taking it*] Thank you, thank you. How de fish fry goin'? [Ad. lib. *cries of* "O.K., Lawd," "Fine an' dandy, Lawd," "De best one yit, Lawd," etc. *To the* Choir] How you shouters gittin' on?

CHOIR LEADER: We been marchin' and singin' de whole mo'nin'.

GOD: I heerd you. You gittin' better all de time. You gittin' as good as de one at de throne. Why don' you give us one dem ol' time jump-ups?

CHOIR LEADER: Anythin' you say, Lawd. [*To the* Others] "So High!"

> [*The* Choir *begins to sing* "So High You Can't Get Over It." *They sing softly, but do not march. An* Angel *offers his cigar to* God *from which He can light His own*]

GOD: No, thanks. I'm gonter save dis a bit.

> [*He puts His cigar in His pocket and listens to the singers a moment. Then He sips His custard. After the second sip, a look of displeasure comes on His face*]

GABRIEL: What's de matter, Lawd?

GOD: [*Sipping again*] I ain't jest sure, yit. Dey's something 'bout dis custahd.

> [*Takes another sip*]

CUSTARD MAKER: Ain't it all right, Lawd?

GOD: It don't seem seasoned jest right. You make it?

CUSTARD MAKER: Yes, Lawd. I put everythin' in it like I allus do. It's supposed to be perfec'.

GOD: Yeah. I kin taste de eggs and de cream and de sugar. [*Suddenly*] I know what it is. It needs jest a little bit mo' firmament.

CUSTARD MAKER: Dey's firmament in it, Lawd.

GOD: Maybe, but it ain't enough.

CUSTARD MAKER: It's all we had, Lawd. Dey ain't a drap in de jug.

GOD: Dat's all right. I'll jest r'ar back an' pass a miracle. [Choir *stops singing*] Let it be some firmament! An' when I say let it be some firmament, I don't want jest a little bitty dab o' firmament, caize I'm sick an' tired of runnin' out of it when we need it. Let it be a whole mess of firmament! [*The stage has become misty until* God *and the heavenly company are obscured. As He finishes the speech there is a burst of thunder. As the stage grows darker*] Dat's de way I like it.

> [*Murmurs from the others:* "Dat's a lot of firmament!" "Look to me like He created rain," etc.]

FIRST MAMMY ANGEL: [*When the stage is dark*] Now, look, Lawd, dat's too much firmament. De cherubs is gettin' all wet.

SECOND MAMMY ANGEL: Look at my Carlotta, Lawd. She's soaked to de skin. Dat's *plenty* too much firmament.

GOD: Well, 'co'se we don't want the chillun to ketch cold. Can't you dreen it off?

GABRIEL: Dey's no place to dreen it, Lawd.

FIRST MAMMY ANGEL: Why don't we jest take de babies home, Lawd?

GOD: No, I don' wanta bust up de fish fry. You angels keep quiet an I'll pass another miracle. Dat's always de trouble wid miracles. When you pass one you always gotta r'ar back an' pass another. [*There is a hush*] Let dere be a place to dreen off dis firmament. Let dere be mountains and valleys an' let dere be oceans an' lakes. An' let dere be rivers and bayous to dreen it off in, too. As a matter of fac' let dere be de earth. An' when dat's done let dere be de sun, an' let it come out and dry my cherubs' wings.

> [*The lights go up until the stage is bathed in sunlight. On the embankment upstage there is now a waist-high wrought-iron railing such as one sees on the galleries of houses in the French Quarter of New Orleans. The* Cherubs *are being examined by their parents and there is an* ad lib. *murmur of, "You all right, honey?" "You feel better now, Albert?" "Now you all dry, Vangy?" until the* Archangel, *who has been gazing in awe at the railing, drowns them out*]

ARCHANGEL: Look yere!

> [*There is a rush to the embankment accompanied by exclamations, "My goodness!" "What's dis?" "I declah!" etc. Gabriel towers above the group on the middle of the embankment. God is wrapped in thought, facing the audience. The* Choir *resumes singing "So High You Can't Get Over It" softly. The babbling at the balustrade dies away as the people lean over the railing. Gabriel turns and faces God indicating the earth below the railing with his left hand*]

GABRIEL: Do you see it. Lawd?

GOD: [*Quietly, without turning His head upstage*] Yes, Gabriel.

GABRIEL: Looks mighty nice, Lawd.

GOD: Yes.

> [Gabriel *turns and looks over the railing*]

GABRIEL: [*Gazing down*] Yes, suh. Dat'd make mighty nice farming country. Jest look at dat south forty over dere. You ain't going to let dat go to waste is you, Lawd? Dat would be a pity an' a shame.

GOD: [*Not turning*] It's a good earth. [God *turns, room is made for Him beside* Gabriel *on the embankment*] Yes. I ought to have somebody to enjoy it. [*He turns, facing the audience. The others, save for the* Choir *who are lined up in two rows of six on an angle up right, continue to look over the embankment*] Gabriel. [God *steps down from the embankment two paces*]

GABRIEL: [*Joining him*] Yes, Lawd.

GOD: Gabriel, I'm goin' down dere.

GABRIEL: Yes, Lawd.

GOD: I want you to be my working boss yere while I'm gone.

GABRIEL: Yes, Lawd.

GOD: You know dat matter of dem two stars?

GABRIEL: Yes, Lawd.

GOD: Git dat fixed up! You know dat sparrow dat fell a little while ago? Tend to dat, too.

GABRIEL: Yes, Lawd.

GOD: I guess dat's about all. I'll be back Saddy [*To the* Choir] Quiet, angels. [*The* Choir *stops singing. Those on the embankment circle downstage.* God *goes to embankment. Turns and faces the company*] I'm gonter pass one more miracle. You all gonter help me an' not make a soun' caize it's one of the most impo'tant miracles of all. [*Nobody moves.* God *turns, facing the sky, and raises His arms above His head*] Let dere be man.

> [*There is growing roll of thunder as stage grows dark. The* Choir *bursts into "Hallelujah," and continues until the lights go up on the next scene*]

SCENE III.

Enclosing the stage is a heterogeneous cluster of cottonwood, camphor, live oak, and sycamore trees, youpon and turkey berry bushes, with their purple and red berries, sprays of fern-like indigo fiera and splashes of various Louisiana flowers. In the middle of the stage, disclosed when the mistiness at rise grows into warm sunlight, stands Adam.

He is a puzzled man of thirty, of medium height, dressed in the clothing of the average field hand. He is bare-headed. In the distance can be heard the Choir *continuing "Bright Mansions Above." A bird begins to sing.* Adam *smiles and turns to look at the source of this novel sound. He senses his strength and raises his forearms, his fists clenched. With his left hand he carefully touches the muscles of his upper right arm. He smiles again, realizing his power. He looks at his feet which are stretched wide apart. He stamps once or twice and now almost laughs in his enjoyment. Other birds begin trilling and* Adam *glances up joyfully toward the foliage.* God *enters.*

GOD: Good mo'nin', Son.

ADAM: [*With a little awe*] Good mo'nin', Lawd.

GOD: What's yo' name, Son?

ADAM: Adam.

GOD: Adam which?

ADAM: [*Frankly, after a moment's puzzled groping*] Jest Adam, Lawd.

GOD: Well, Adam, how dey treatin' you? How's things goin'?

ADAM: Well, Lawd, you know it's kind of a new line of wukk.

GOD: You'll soon get the hang of it. You know yo' kind of a new style with me.

ADAM: Oh, I guess I'm gonter make out all right soon as I learn de ropes.

GOD: Yes, I guess you will. Yo' a nice job.

ADAM: Yes, Lawd.

GOD: Dey's jest one little thing de matter with you. Did you notice it?

ADAM: Well, now you mentioned it, Lawd, I kind of thought dey was somethin' wrong.

GOD: Yes, suh, you ain't quite right. Adam, you need a family. De reason for dat is in yo' heart you is a family man. [Flicking the ash off His cigar] I'd say dat was de main trouble at de moment.

ADAM: [Smiling] Yes, suh. [His smile fades and he is puzzled again] At de same time—dey's one thing puzzlin' me, Lawd. Could I ask you a question?

GOD: Why certainly, Adam.

ADAM: Lawd, jest what is a family?

GOD: I'm gonter show you. [Indicates a spot] Jest lie down here, Adam. Make out like you was goin' to slumber.

ADAM: [Gently] Yes, Lawd.

[He lies down. God stands beside him and as He raises His arms above His head the lights go down. In the darkness God speaks]

GOD: Eve. [Lights go up. Eve is standing beside Adam. She is about twenty-six, and quite pretty. She is dressed like a country girl. Her gingham dress is quite new and clean. God is now at the other side of the stage, looking at them critically. Eve looks at Adam in timid wonder and slowly turns her head until she meets the glance of God. Adam stands beside Eve. They gaze at each other for a moment. God smiles] Now you all right, Eve. [Adam and Eve face Him] Now I'll tell you what I'm gonter do. I'm gonter put you in charge here. I'm gonter give you de run of dis whole garden. Eve, you take care of dis man, an' Adam, you take care of dis woman. You belong to each other. I don' want you to try to do much caize yo' both kind of experiment wid me an' I ain't sho' whether yo' could make it. You two jest enjoy yo'self. Drink de water from de little brooks an' de wine from de grapes an' de berries, an' eat de food dat's hangin' for you in de trees. [He pauses, startled by a painful thought] Dat is, in all but one tree. [He pauses. Then, not looking at them] You know what I mean, my children?

ADAM and EVE: Yes, Lawd.

[They slowly turn their heads left, toward the branches of an offstage tree. Then they look back at God]

ADAM: Thank you, Lawd.

EVE: Thank you, Lawd.

GOD: I gotter be gittin' along now. I got a hund'ed thousan' things to do 'fo' you take yo' nex' breath. Enjoy yo'selves——

[God exits. Adam and Eve stand looking after Him for a moment, then each looks down and watches their hands meet and clasp. After a moment they lift their heads slowly until they are again gazing at the tree]

EVE: Adam.

ADAM: [Looking at the tree, almost in terror] What?

EVE: [Softly as she too continues to look at the tree] Adam.

[The Choir begins singing "Turn You Round" and as the lights go down the Choir continues until there is blackness. The Choir suddenly stops. The following scene is played in the darkness]

MR. DESHEE'S VOICE: Now, I s'pose you chillun know what happened after God made Adam 'n' Eve. Do you?

FIRST GIRL'S VOICE: I know, Mr. Deshee.

MR. DESHEE'S VOICE: Jest a minute, Randolph. Didn't I tell you you gotta tell yo' mammy let yo' sister bring you? Carlisle, take way dat truck he's eatin'. You sit by him, see kin you keep him quiet. Now, den, Myrtle, what happened?

FIRST GIRL'S VOICE: Why den dey ate de fo'bidden fruit and den dey got driv' out de Garden.

MR. DESHEE'S VOICE: An' den what happened?

FIRST GIRL'S VOICE: Den dey felt ver' bad.

MR. DESHEE'S VOICE: I don' mean how dey feel, I mean how dey do. Do dey have any children or anything like dat?

FIRST GIRL'S VOICE: Oh, yes, suh, dey have Cain 'n' Abel.

MR. DESHEE'S VOICE: Dat's right, dey have Cain 'n' Abel.

BOY'S VOICE: Dat was a long time after dey got married, wasn't it, Mr. Deshee? My mammy say it was a hund'ed years.

MR. DESHEE'S VOICE: Well, nobody kin be so sure. As I tol' you befo' dey was jest beginnin' to be able to tell de time an' nobody was any too sure 'bout anythin' even den. So de bes' thing to do is jest realize dat de thing happened an' don't bother 'bout how many years it was. Jest remember what I told you about it gittin' dark when you go to sleep an' it bein' light when you wake up. Dat's de way time went by in dem days. One thing we do know an' dat was dis boy Cain was a mean rascal.

[The lights go up on the next scene]

SCENE IV.

A Roadside.

Cain, a husky young Negro, stands over the body of the dead Abel. Both are dressed as laborers. Cain is looking at the body in awe, a rock in his right hand. God enters.

GOD: Cain, look what you done to Abel.

CAIN: Lawd, I was min'in' my own business and he come monkeyin' aroun' wit' me. I was wukkin' in de fiel' an' he was sittin' in de shade of de tree. He say "Me, I'd be skeered to git out in dis hot sun. I be 'fraid my brains git cooked. Co'se you ain't got no brains so you ain't in no danger." An' so I up and flang de rock. If it miss 'im all right, an' if it hit 'im all right. Dat's de way I feel.

GOD: All right, but I'm yere to tell you dat's called a crime. When de new Judge is done talkin' to you you'll be draggin' a ball and chain de rest of yo' life.

CAIN: Well, what'd he want to come monkeyin' aroun' me fo' den? I was jest plowin', min'in' my own business, and not payin' him no min', and yere he come makin' me de fool. I'd bust anybody what make me de fool.

GOD: Well, I ain't sayin' you right an' I ain't sayin' you wrong. But I do say was I you I'd jest git myself down de road 'til I was clean out of de county. An' you better take an' git married an' settle down an' raise some chillun. Dey ain't nothin' to make a man fo'git his troubles like raisin' a family. Now, you better git.

CAIN: Yessuh.

[Cain *walks off*. God *watches him from the forestage and as the lights begin to dim looks off. The* Choir *begins* "Run, Sinner, Run"]

GOD: Adam an' Eve, you better try again. You better have Seth an' a lot mo' chillun.

[*There is darkness. The* Choir *continues until the lights go up on the next scene*]

SCENE V.

Cain *is discovered walking on an unseen treadmill. A middle distance of trees, hillsides and shrubbery passes him on an upper treadmill. Behind is the blue sky. He stops under the branches of a tree to look at a sign on a fence railing. Only half the tree is visible on the stage. The sign reads,* "NOD PARISH. COUNTY LINE."

CAIN: [*Sitting down with a sigh of relief under a tree*] At las'! Phew! [*Wipes his forehead with a handkerchief*] Feels like I been walkin' fo'ty years. [*He looks back*] Well, dey cain' git me now. Now I kin raise a fam'ly. [*An idea occurs to him, and suddenly he begins looking right and left*] Well, I'll be hit by a mule! Knock me down for a trustin' baby! Where I gonter git dat family? Dat preacher fooled me. [*He is quite dejected*] Doggone!

CAIN'S GIRL: [*Off stage*] Hello, Country Boy!

[Cain *glances up to the offstage branches of the tree*]

CAIN: Hey-ho, Good-lookin'! Which way is it to town?

CAIN'S GIRL: [*Off stage*] What you tryin' to do? You tryin' to mash me? I be doggone if it ain't gittin' so a gal cain't hardly leave de house 'out some of dese fast men ain' passin' remarks at her.

CAIN: I ain' passin' remarks.

CAIN'S GIRL: [*Off stage*] If I thought you was tryin' to mash me, I'd call de police an' git you tooken to de first precinct.

CAIN: Look yere, gal, I ast you a question, an' if you don' answer me I'm gonter bend you 'cross my pants an' burn you up.

CAIN'S GIRL: [*Off stage*] I'm comin' down.

[Cain *takes his eyes from the tree*]

CAIN: Yes, an' you better hurry.

[Cain's Girl *enters. She is as large as* Cain, *wickedly pretty, and somewhat flashily dressed. She smiles at* Cain]

CAIN'S GIRL: I bet you kin handle a gal mean wid dem big stout arms of your'n. I sho' would hate to git you mad at me, Country Boy.

CAIN: [*Smiling*] Come yere [*She goes a little closer to him*] Don't be 'fraid, I ain' so mean.

CAIN'S GIRL: You got two bad-lookin' eyes. I bet yo' hot coffee 'mong de women folks.

CAIN: I ain' never find out. What was you doin' in dat tree?

CAIN'S GIRL: Jest coolin' myself in de element.

CAIN: Is you a Nod Parish gal?

CAIN'S GIRL: Bo'n an' bred.

CAIN: You know yo' kinda pretty.

CAIN'S GIRL: Who tol' you dat?

CAIN: Dese yere two bad eyes of mine.

CAIN'S GIRL: I bet you say dat to everybody all de way down de road.

CAIN: Comin' down dat road I din't talk to nobody.

CAIN'S GIRL: Where you boun' for, Beautiful?

CAIN: I'm jest seein' de country. I thought I might settle down yere fo' a spell. Yo' live wit' yo' people?

CAIN'S GIRL: Co'se I does.

CAIN: 'Spose dey'd like to take in a boarder?

CAIN'S GIRL: Be nice if dey would, wouldn't it?

CAIN: I think so. You got a beau?

CAIN'S GIRL: Huh-uh!

CAIN: [*Smiling*] You has *now*.

CAIN'S GIRL: I guess—I guess if you wanted to kiss me an' I tried to stop you, you could pretty nearly crush me wit' dem stout arms.

CAIN: You wouldn't try too much, would you?

CAIN'S GIRL: Maybe for a little while.

CAIN: An' den what?

CAIN'S GIRL: Why don' we wait an' see?

CAIN: When would dat be?

CAIN'S GIRL: To-night. After supper. Think you kin walk a little further now, City Boy?

CAIN: Yeh, I ain't so weary now.

[*She takes his hand*]

CAIN'S GIRL: What yo' name?

[*Takes his arm*]

CAIN: Cain.

CAIN'S GIRL: Then I'm Cain's Gal. Come on, honey, an' meet de folks.

[*They go out. The* Choir *is heard singing* "You Better Mind," *as* God *enters.* God *watches the vanishing* Cain *and his girl*]

GOD: [*After shaking His head*] Bad business. I don't like de way things is goin' a-tall.

[*The stage is darkened. The* Choir *continues singing until the lights go up on the next scene*]

SCENE VI.

God's *private office in Heaven. It is a small room, framed by tableau curtains. A large window up center looks out on the sky. There is a battered roll-top desk. On the wall next to the window is a framed religious oleograph with a calendar attached to it underneath. A door is at the left. A hat rack is on the wall above the door. There are two or three cheap pine chairs beside the window, and beyond the door. In front of the desk is an old swivel armchair which creaks every time* God *leans back in it. The desk is open and various papers are stuck in the pigeonholes. Writing implements, etc. are on the desk. On a shelf above the desk is a row of law books. A cuspidor is near the desk, and a waste basket by it. The general atmosphere is that of the office of a Negro lawyer in a Louisiana town. As the lights go up* God *takes a fresh cigar from a box on the desk and begins puffing it without bothering to light it. There is no comment on this minor miracle from* Gabriel *who is sitting in one of the chairs with a pencil and several papers in his hand. The singing becomes pianissimo.*

GABRIEL: [*Looking at the papers*] Well, I guess dat's about all de impo'tant business this mornin', Lawd.

GOD: How 'bout dat cherub over to Archangel Montgomery's house?

GABRIEL: Where do dey live, Lawd?

[*The singing stops*]

GOD: Dat little two-story gold house, over by de pearly gates.

GABRIEL: Oh, dat Montgomery. I thought you was referrin' to de ol' gentleman. Oh, yeh. [*He sorts through the papers and finds one he is looking for*] Yere it 'tis. [*Reads*] "Cherub Christina Montgomery; wings is moltin' out of season an' nobody knows what to do."

GOD: Well, now, take keer of dat. You gotter be more careful, Gabe.

GABRIEL: Yes, Lawd.

[*Folds the papers and puts them in a pocket.* God *turns to His desk, takes another puff or two of the cigar, and with a pencil, begins checking off items on a sheet of paper before Him. His back is turned toward* Gabriel. Gabriel *takes his trumpet from the hat rack and burnishes it with his robe. He then wets his lips and puts the mouthpiece to his mouth*]

GOD: [*Without turning around*] Now, watch yo'self, Gabriel.

GABRIEL: I wasn't goin' to blow, Lawd. I jest do dat every now an' den so I can keep de feel of it.

[*He leans trumpet against the wall.* God *picks up the papers and swings His chair around toward* Gabriel]

GOD: What's dis yere about de moon?

GABRIEL: [*Suddenly remembering*] Oh! De moon people say it's beginnin' to melt a little, on 'count caize de sun's so hot.

GOD: It's goin' 'roun' 'cordin' to schedule, ain't it?

GABRIEL: Yes, Lawd.

GOD: Well, tell 'em to stop groanin'. Dere's nothin' de matter wid dat moon. Trouble is so many angels is flyin' over dere on Saddy night. Dey git to beatin' dere wings when dey dancin' an' dat makes de heat. Tell dem dat from now on dancin' 'roun' de moon is sinnin'. Dey got to stop it. Dat'll cool off de moon. [*He swings back and puts the paper on the desk. He leans back in the chair comfortably, His hands clasped behind His head*] Is dere anythin' else you ought to remin' me of?

GABRIEL: De prayers, Lawd.

GOD: [*Puzzled, slowly swinging chair around again*] De prayers?

GABRIEL: From mankind. You know, down on de earth.

GOD: Oh, yeh, de poor little earth. Bless my soul, I almos' forgot about dat. Mus' be three or four hund'ed years since I been down dere. I wasn't any too pleased wid dat job.

GABRIEL: [*Laughing*] You know you don' make mistakes, Lawd.

GOD: [*Soberly, with introspective detachment*] So dey tell me. [*He looks at* Gabriel, *then through the window again*] So dey tell me. I fin' I kin be displeased though, an' I was displeased wid de mankind I las' seen. Maybe I ought to go down dere agin— I need a little holiday.

GABRIEL: Might do you good, Lawd.

GOD: I think I will. I'll go down an' walk de earth agin an' see how dem poor humans is makin' out. What time is it, by de sun an' de stars?

GABRIEL: [*Glancing out of the window*] Jest exactly half-past, Lawd.

[God *is taking His hat and stick from the hat rack*]

GOD: [*Opening the door*] Well, take keer o' yo'self. I'll be back Saddy.

[*He exits. The stage is darkened. The* Choir *begins "Dere's No Hidin' Place," and continues until the lights go up on the next scene*]

SCENE VII.

God *is walking along a country road. He stops to listen. Church bells are heard in the distance.*

GOD: Dat's nice. Nice an' quiet. Dat's de way I like Sunday to be. [*The sound is broken by a shrill voice of a girl. It is* Zeba *singing a "blues"*] Now, dat ain't so good. [God *resumes His walk and the* upper treadmill brings on a tree stump on which Zeba *is sitting. She is accompanying her song with a ukulele.* God *and the treadmills stop. When the stump reaches the center of the stage, it is seen that* Zeba *is a rouged and extremely flashily dressed chippy of about eighteen*] Stop dat!

ZEBA: What's de matter wid you, Country Boy? Pull up yo' pants.

[*She resumes singing*]

GOD: Stop dat!

ZEBA: [*Stops again*] Say, listen to me, Banjo Eyes. What right you got to stop a lady enjoyin' herself?

GOD: Don't you know dis is de Sabbath? Dat's no kin' o' song to sing on de Lawd's day.

ZEBA: Who care 'bout de Lawd's day any mo'? People jest use Sunday now to git over Saddy.

GOD: You a awful sassy little girl.

ZEBA: I come fum sassy people! We even speak mean of de dead.

GOD: What's yo' name?

ZEBA: [*Flirtatiously*] "What's my name?" Ain't you de ol'-time gal hunter! Fust, "What's my name?" den I s'pose, what would it be like if you tried to kiss me? You preachers is de debbils.

GOD: I ain't aimin' to touch you, daughter. [*A sudden sternness frightens* Zeba. *She looks at him sharply*] What is yo' name?

ZEBA: Zeba.

GOD: Who's yo' fam'ly?

ZEBA: I'm de great-great-gran'daughter of Seth.

GOD: Of Seth? But Seth was a good man.

ZEBA: Yeh, he too good, he die of holiness.

GOD: An' yere's his little gran'daughter reekin' wid cologne. Ain't nobody ever tol' you yo' on de road to Hell?

ZEBA: [*Smiling*] Sho' dat's what de preacher say. Exceptin', of course, I happens to know dat I'm on de road to de picnic groun's, an' at de present time I'm waitin' to keep a engagement wid my sweet papa. He don' like people talkin' to me.

[Cain the Sixth *enters. He is a young buck, wearing a "box" coat and the other flashy garments of a Rampart Street swell*]

CAIN THE SIXTH: Hello, sugah! [*He crosses in front of* God *and faces* Zeba] Hello, mamma! Sorry I'm late, baby, but de gals in de barrel-house jest wouldn't let me go. Doggone, one little wirehead swore she'd tear me down.

[Zeba *smiles and takes his hand*]

GOD: What's yo' name, son?

CAIN THE SIXTH: [*Contemptuously; without turning 'n' water*, Country Boy.

GOD: [*Sternly*] What's yo' name, son?

[Cain *slowly turns and for a moment his manner is civil*]

CAIN THE SIXTH: Cain the Sixth.

GOD: I was afraid so.

CAIN THE SIXTH: [*His impudence returning*] You a new preacher?

GOD: Where you live?

CAIN THE SIXTH: Me, I live mos' any place.

GOD: Yes, an' you gonter see dem all. Is de udder young men all like you?

CAIN THE SIXTH: [*Smiling*] De gals don' think so.

[*He turns towards* Zeba *again, picks her up and sits on the stump with the laughing* Zeba *on his lap*]

ZEBA: Dey ain't nobody in de worl' like my honey-cake.

[Cain *kisses her and she resumes her song.* God *watches them.* Zeba *finishes a verse of the song and begins another softly.* Cain the Sixth's *eyes have been closed during the singing*]

CAIN THE SIXTH: [*His eyes closed*] Is de preacher gone?

[Zeba *looks quickly at* God *without seeing him, and then looks off. She stops the song*]

ZEBA: Yeh, I guess he walks fast.

[Cain *pushes her off his lap and rises*]

CAIN THE SIXTH: [*With acid sweetness*] Dey tell me las' night you was talkin' to a creeper man, baby.

ZEBA: Why, you know dey ain't nobody in de world fo' me but you.

CAIN THE SIXTH: [*Smiling*] I know dey ain't. I even got dat guaranteed. [*Takes a revolver from his pocket*] See dat, baby?

ZEBA: Sho' I see it, honey.

CAIN THE SIXTH: Dat jest makes me positive.

[*Puts the gun back*]

ZEBA: [*Pushing him back on the stump*] You don' wanter believe dem stories, papa.

CAIN THE SIXTH: [*With sinister lightness*] No. I didn't believe dem, baby. Co'se dat big gorilla, Flatfoot, from de other side of de river *is* in town ag'in.

ZEBA: Dat don' mean nothin'. Flatfoot ain't nothin' to me.

CAIN THE SIXTH: [*Sitting again*] Co'se he ain't. Go 'head, sing some mo', baby.

[Zeba *resumes singing*]

GOD: Bad business. [*The treadmills start turning.* God *resumes his walk.* Zeba, *still singing, and* Cain the Sixth *recede with the landscape.* God *is again alone on the country road. There is a twitter of birds.* God *looks up and smiles*] De birds is goin' 'bout deir business, all right. [*A patch of flowers goes by, black-eyed Susans, conspicuously*] How you flowers makin' out? [*Children's voices answer, "We O. K., Lawd."*] Yes, an' you looks very pretty. [*Children's voices: "Thank you, Lawd." The flowers pass out of sight*] It's only de human bein's makes me downhearted. Yere's as nice a Sunday as dey is turnin' out anywhere, an' nobody makin' de right use of it. [*Something ahead of him attracts his attention. His face brightens*] Well, now dis is mo' like it. Now dat's nice to see people prayin'. It's a wonder dey don' do it in de church. But I fin' I don' min' it if dey do it outdoors.

GAMBLER: Oh, Lawd, de smoke-house is empty. Oh, Lawd, lemme git dem groceries. Oh, Lawd, lemme see dat little six. [*He casts the dice*] Wham! Dere she is, frien's.

> [*Exclamations from the others:* "*Well, damn my eyes!*" "*Doggone, dat's de eighth pass he make.*" "*For God's sake, can't you ever crap?*" *etc. The* Boy *is picking up the money*]

GOD: Gamblin'! [*Looks over the group's shoulders*] An' wid frozen dice!

BOY GAMBLER: Dey's a dolla' 'n' a half talkin' fo' me. How much you want of it, Riney?

FIRST GAMBLER: I take fo' bits. Wait a minute. Mebbe I take a little mo.'

> [*He counts some money in his hand*]

SECOND GAMBLER: [*Glancing up at* God] Hello, Liver Lips. [*To the others*] Looka ol' Liver Lips.

> [*The others look up and laugh good-naturedly, repeating "Liver Lips"*]

FIRST GAMBLER: Ain't his pockets high from de groun'? Ol' High Pockets.

> [*The others keep saying "Ole Liver Lips." "Ol' Liver Lips don't like to see people dicin'." "Dat's a good name, 'High Pockets'"*]

BOY GAMBLER: [*To others*] Come on, you gonter fade me or not?

> [God *seizes the* Boy's *ears and drags him to his feet. The others do not move, but watch, amused*]

GOD: Come yere, son. Why, yo' jest a little boy. Gamblin' an' sinnin'. [God *looks at the* Boy's *face*] You been chewin' tobacco, too, like you was yo' daddy. [God *sniffs*] An' you been drinkin' sonny-kick-mammy wine. You oughta be 'shamed. [*To the others*] An' you gamblers oughta be 'shamed, leadin' dis boy to sin.

FIRST GAMBLER: He de bes' crap shooter in town, mister.

GOD: I'm gonter tell his mammy. I bet she don' know 'bout dis.

FIRST GAMBLER: No, she don' know. [*The others laugh*] She don' know anythin'.

SECOND GAMBLER: Dat's de God's truth.

FIRST GAMBLER: See kin you beat 'im, High Pockets. Dey's a dolla' open yere.

GOD: I ain't gonter beat 'im. I'm gonter teach 'im. I may have to teach you all.

> [*He starts walking from them. The* Boy *sticks out his tongue the moment* God's *back is turned*]

BOY GAMBLER: If you fin' my mammy you do mo'n I kin. Come on, gamblers, see kin you gimme a little action. Who wants any part of dat dollar?

> [*The treadmill carries them off. The* First Gambler *is heard saying:* "*I'll take anoder two bits,*" *and the others,* "*Gimme a dime's wo'th,*" "*I ain't only got fifteen cents left,*" *etc., as they disappear*]

GOD: [*Walking*] Where's dat little boy's home? [*The front of a shanty appears and* God *stops in front of the door*] Yere's de place. It ain't any too clean, either.

> [*Knocks on the door with his cane*]

VOICE IN SHANTY: Who dar?

GOD: Never you min' who's yere. Open de door.

VOICE IN SHANTY: You gotta search warrant?

GOD: I don' need one.

VOICE IN SHANTY: Who you wanter see?

GOD: I wanter see de mammy of de little gamblin' boy.

VOICE IN SHANTY: You mean little Johnny Rucker?

GOD: Dat may be his name.

VOICE IN SHANTY: Well, Mrs. Rucker ain't home.

GOD: Where's she at?

VOICE IN SHANTY: Who, Mrs. Rucker?

GOD: You heerd me.

VOICE IN SHANTY: Oh, she run away las' night wid a railroad man. She's eloped.

GOD: Where's Rucker?

VOICE IN SHANTY: He's flat under de table. He so drunk he cain't move.

GOD: Who are you?

VOICE IN SHANTY: I'se jest a frien' an' neighbor. I come in las' night to de party, an' everybody in yere's dead drunk but me. De only reason I kin talk is I drank some new white mule I made myself, an' it burn my throat so I cain't drink no mo'. You got any mo' questions?

GOD: Not for you.

> [*The shanty begins to move off as* God *starts walking again*]

VOICE IN SHANTY: Good riddance, I say.

> [*Shanty disappears*]

GOD: Dis ain't gittin' me nowheres. All I gotta say dis yere mankind I been peoplin' my earth wid sho' ain't much. [*He stops and looks back*] I got good min' to wipe 'em all off an' people de earth wid angels. No. Angels is all right, singin' an' playin' an' flyin' around, but dey ain't much on workin' de crops and buildin' de levees. No, suh, mankind's jest right for my earth, if he wasn't so doggone sinful. I'd rather have my earth peopled wit' a bunch of channel catfish, dan I would mankin' an' his sin. I jest cain't stan' sin.

> [*He is about to resume his walk when* Noah *enters.* Noah *is dressed like a country preacher. His coat is of the "hammer-tail" variety. He carries a prayer book under his arm*]

NOAH: Mo'nin', brother.

GOD: Mo'nin', brother. I declare you look like a good man.

NOAH: I try to be, brother. I'm de preacher yere. I don't think I seen you to de meetin'.

> [*They resume walking*]

GOD: I jest come to town a little while ago an' I been pretty busy.

NOAH: Yeh, mos' everybody say dey's pretty busy dese days. Dey so busy dey cain't come to meetin'. It seem like de mo' I preaches de mo' people ain't got time to come to church. I ain't hardly got enough members to fill up de choir. I gotta do de preachin' an' de bassin' too.

GOD: Is dat a fac'?

NOAH: Yes, suh, brother. Everybody is mighty busy, gamblin', good-timin', and goin' on. You jest wait, though. When Gabriel blow de horn you gonter fin' dey got plenty of time to punch chunks down in Hell. Yes, suh.

GOD: Seems a pity. Dey all perfec'ly healthy?

NOAH: Oh, dey healthy, all right. Dey jest all lazy, and mean, and full of sin. You look like a preacher, too, brother.

GOD: Well, I am, in a way.

NOAH: You jest passin' through de neighborhood?

GOD: Yes. I wanted to see how things was goin' in yo' part of de country, an' I been feelin' jest 'bout de way you do. It's enough to discourage you.

NOAH: Yes, but I gotta keep wres'lin' wid 'em. Where you boun' for right now, brother?

GOD: I was jest walkin' along. I thought I might stroll on to de nex' town.

NOAH: Well, dat's a pretty good distance. I live right yere. [*He stops walking*] Why don' you stop an' give us de pleasure of yo' comp'ny for dinner? I believe my ol' woman has kilt a chicken.

GOD: Why, dat's mighty nice of you, brother. I don't believe I caught yo' name.

NOAH: Noah, jest brother Noah. Dis is my home, brother. Come right in.

[God *and* Noah *start walking towards* Noah's *house which is coming into view on the treadmill. The stage darkens, the* Choir *sings* "Feastin' Table," *and when the lights go up again, the next scene is disclosed*]

SCENE VIII.

Interior of Noah's *house. The ensemble suggests the combination living-dining room in a fairly prosperous Negro's cabin. Clean white curtains hang at the window. A table and chairs are in the center of the room. There is a cheerful checked tablecloth on the table, and on the wall, a framed, highly colored picture reading* "God Bless Our Home." Noah's Wife, *an elderly Negress, simply and neatly dressed,* God *and* Noah *are discovered grouped about the table.*

NOAH: Company, darlin'. [Noah's Wife *takes* Noah's *and* God's *hats*] Dis gemman's a preacher, too. He's jest passin' through de country.

GOD: Good mo'nin', sister.

NOAH'S WIFE: Good mo'nin'. You jest ketch me when I'm gittin' dinner ready. You gonter stay with us?

GOD: If I ain't intrudin'. Brother Noah suggested—

NOAH'S WIFE: You set right down yere. I got a chicken in de pot an' it'll be ready in 'bout five minutes. I'll go out de back an' call Shem, Ham 'n' Japheth. [*To* God] Dey's our sons. Dey live right acrost de way but always have Sunday dinner wid us. You mens make yo'selves comf'table.

GOD: Thank you, thank you very kindly.

NOAH: You run along, we all right.

[God *and* Noah *seat themselves.* Noah's Wife *exits*]

GOD: You got a fine wife, Brother Noah.

NOAH: She pretty good woman.

GOD: Yes, suh, an' you got a nice little home. Have a ten-cent seegar?

[God *offers him one*]

NOAH: Thank you, much obliged.

[*Both men lean back restfully in their chairs*]

GOD: Jest what seems to be the main trouble 'mong mankind, Noah?

NOAH: Well, it seems to me dat de main trouble is dat de whol' distric' is wide open. Now you know dat makes fo' loose livin'. Men folks spen's all deir time fightin', loafin' and gamblin', an' makin' bad likker.

GOD: What about de women?

NOAH: De women is worse dan de men. If dey ain't makin' love powder dey out beg, borrow an' stealin' money for policy tickets. Doggone, I come in de church Sunday 'fo' las' 'bout an' hour befo' de meetin' was to start, and dere was a woman stealin' de altar cloth. She was goin' to hock it. Dey ain't got no moral sense. Now you take dat case las' month, over in East Putney. Case of dat young Willy Roback.

GOD: What about him?

NOAH: Dere is a boy seventeen years old. Doggone, if he didn't elope with his aunt. Now, you know, dat kin' of goin' on is bad fo' a neighborhood.

GOD: Terrible, terrible.

NOAH: Yes, suh. Dis use' to be a nice, decent community. I been doin' my best to preach de Word, but seems like every time I preach de place jest goes a little mo' to de dogs. De good Lawd only knows what's gonter happen.

GOD: Dat's de truth.

[*There is a pause. Each puffs his cigar. Suddenly* Noah *grasps his knee, as if it were paining him, and twists his foot*]

NOAH: Huh!

GOD: What's de matter?

NOAH: I jest got a twitch. My buckaguer I guess. Every now and den I gets a twitch in de knee. Might be a sign of rain.

GOD: That's just what it is. Noah, what's de mos' rain you ever had 'round dese parts?

NOAH: Well, de water come down fo' six days steady last April an' de ribber got so swole it bust down de levee up 'bove Freeport. Raise cain all de way down to de delta.

GOD: What would you say was it to rain for forty days and forty nights?

NOAH: I'd say dat was a *complete* rain!

GOD: Noah, you don't know who I is, do you?

NOAH: [*Puzzled*] Yo' face looks easy, but I don' think I recall de name. [God *rises slowly, and as He reaches His full height there is a crash of lightning, a moment's darkness, and a roll of thunder. It grows light again.* Noah *is on his knees in front of* God] I should have known you. I should have seen de glory.

GOD: Dat's all right, Noah. You didn' know who I was.

NOAH: I'm jes' ol' preacher Noah, Lawd, an' I'm yo' servant. I ain' very much, but I'se all I got.

GOD: Sit down, Noah. Don' let me hear you shamin' you'se'f, caize yo' a good man. [*Timidly* Noah *waits until* God *is seated, and then sits, himself*] I jest wanted to fin' out if you was good, Noah. Dat's why I'm walkin' de earth in de shape of a natchel man. I wish dey was mo' people like you. But, far as I kin see, you and yo' family is de only respectable people in de worl'.

NOAH: Dey jest all poor sinners, Lawd.

GOD: I know. I am your Lawd. I am a god of wrath and vengeance an' dat's why I'm gonter destroy dis worl'.

NOAH: [*Almost in a whisper. Drawing back*] Jest as you say, Lawd.

GOD: I ain't gonter destroy you, Noah. You and yo' family, yo' sheep an' cattle, an' all de udder things dat ain't human I'm gonter preserve. But de rest is gotta go. [*Takes a pencil and a sheet of paper from His pocket*] Look yere, Noah. [Noah *comes over and looks over His shoulder*] I want you to build me a boat. I want you to call it de "Ark," and I want it to look like dis. [*He is drawing on the paper. Continues to write as He speaks*] I want you to take two of every kind of animal and bird dat's in the country. I want you to take seeds an' sprouts an' everything like dat an' put dem on dat Ark, because dere is gonter be all dat rain. Dey's gonter be a deluge, Noah, an' dey's goin' to be a flood. De levees is gonter bust an' everything dat's fastened down is comin' loose, but it ain't gonter float long, caize I'm gonter make a storm dat'll sink everythin' from a hencoop to a barn. Dey ain't a ship on de sea dat'll be able to fight dat tempest. Dey all got to go. Everythin'. Everythin' in dis pretty worl' I made, except one thing, Noah. You an' yo' fam'ly an' de things I said are going to ride dat storm in de Ark. Yere's de way it's to be.

[*He hands* Noah *the paper.* Noah *takes it and reads*]

NOAH: [*Pause. Looks at paper again*] Yes, suh, dis seems to be complete. Now 'bout the animals, Lawd, you say you want everythin'?

GOD: Two of everythin'.

NOAH: Dat would include jayraffes an' hippopotamuses?

GOD: Everythin' dat is.

NOAH: Dey was a circus in town las' week. I guess I kin fin' dem. Co'se I kin git all de rabbits an' possums an' wil' turkeys easy. I'll sen' de boys out. Hum, I'm jest wonderin'—

GOD: 'Bout what?

NOAH: 'Bout snakes. Think you'd like snakes, too?

GOD: Certainly I want snakes.

NOAH: Oh, I kin git snakes, lots of 'em. Co'se some of 'em's a little dangerous. Maybe I better take a kag of likker, too?

GOD: You can have a kag of likker.

NOAH: [*Musingly*] Yes, suh, dey's a awful lot of differ'nt kin's of snakes, come to think about it. Dey's water moccasins, cotton-moufs, rattlers—mus' be a hund'ed kin's of other snakes down in de swamps. Maybe I better take two kags of likker.

GOD: [*Mildly*] I think de one kag's enough.

NOAH: No. I better take two kags. Besides I kin put one on each side of de boat, an' balance de ship wid dem as well as havin' dem fo' medicinal use.

GOD: You kin put one kag in de middle of de ship.

NOAH: [*Buoyantly*] Jest as easy to take de two kags, Lawd.

GOD: I think one kag's enough.

NOAH: Yes, Lawd, but you see forty days an' forty nights——

[*There is a distant roll of thunder*]

GOD: [*Firmly*] One kag, Noah.

NOAH: Yes, Lawd. One kag.

[*The door in the back opens and* Noah's Wife *enters with a tray of dishes and food*]

NOAH'S WIFE: Now, den, gen'lemen, if you'll jest draw up cheers.

[*The stage is darkened. The* Choir *is heard singing "I Want to Be Ready." They continue in the darkness until the lights go up on the next scene*]

SCENE IX.

In the middle of the stage is the Ark. On the hillside, below the Ark, a dozen or more men and women, townspeople, are watching Noah, Shem, Ham, *and* Japheth *on the deck of the Ark. The three sons are busily nailing boards on the cabin.* Noah *is smoking a pipe. He wears a silk hat, captain's uniform and a "slicker."*

NOAH: [*To* Shem] You, Shem, tote up some ol' rough lumber; don' bring up any planed-up lumber, caize dat ain't fo' de main deck.

SHEM: Pretty near supper time, daddy.

NOAH: Maybe 'tis, but I got de feelin' we ought to keep goin'.

FIRST WOMAN: You gonter work all night, Noah, maybe, huh?

NOAH: [*Without looking at her*] If de speerit move me.

SECOND WOMAN: Look yere, Noah, whyn't you give up all dis damn foolishness? Don' you know people sayin' yo' crazy? What you think you doin' anyway?

NOAH: I'se buildin' a Ark. [*Other men and women join those in the foreground*] Ham, you better stop for a while 'n' see whether dey bringin' de animals up all right. [*He looks at his watch*] Dey ought to be pretty near de foot o' de hill by dis time; if dey ain't you wait fo' dem and bring 'em yo'se'f.

[*Ham goes down a ladder at the side of the ship and exits during the following scene. The newcomers in the group have been speaking to some of the early arrivals*]

SECOND WOMAN: [*To Third Woman, one of the newcomers*] No, you don't mean it!

THIRD WOMAN: I do so. Dat's what de talk is in de town.

FIRST MAN: You hear dat, Noah? Dey say yo' ol' lady is tellin' everybody it's gonter rain fo' fo'ty days and fo'ty nights. You know people soon gonter git de idea you *all* crazy.

NOAH: Lot I keer what you think. [*To Japheth*] Straighten up dem boards down dere, Japheth.

[*Indicating floor deck*]

FIRST MAN: [*To Third Woman*] Was I you, I wouldn' go 'round with Mrs. Noah any more, lady. First thing you know you'll be gittin' a hard name, too.

THIRD WOMAN: Don' I know?

SECOND WOMAN: A lady cain't be too partic'lar dese days.

[*Zeba and Flatfoot, a tall, black, wicked-looking buck, enter, their arms around each other's waists*]

ZEBA: Dere it is, baby. Was I lyin'?

FLATFOOT: Well, I'll be split in two!

FIRST MAN: What you think of it, Flatfoot?

FLATFOOT: I must say! Look like a house wit' a warpin' cellar.

NOAH: Dis yere vessel is a boat.

FLATFOOT: When I was a little boy dey used to build boats down near de ribber, where de water was.

[*The others laugh*]

NOAH: Dis time it's been arranged to have de water come up to de boat. [*Japheth looks belligerently over the rail of the Ark at Flatfoot. To Japheth*] Keep yo' shirt on, son.

SECOND WOMAN: [*To Third Woman*] Now, you see de whole fam'ly crazy.

THIRD WOMAN: Listen, dey ain't gonter 'taminate me. It was me dat started resolvin' dem both out o' de buryin' society.

ZEBA: When all dis water due up yere, Noah?

NOAH: You won't know when it gits yere, daughter.

ZEBA: Is she goin' to be a side-wheeler, like de *Bessy-Belle*?

FLATFOOT: No! If she was a side-wheeler she'd get her wheels all clogged wid sharks. She gonter have jus' one great big stern wheel, like de *Commodore*.

Den if dey ain't 'nuf water why de big wheel kin stir some up.

[*General laughter. Two or three of the Gamblers enter and join the group, followed by Cain the Sixth*]

CAIN THE SIXTH: Dere's de fool an' his monument, jest like I said!

[*The Gamblers and Cain the Sixth roar with laughter, slap their legs, etc. The members of the main group talk sotto voce to each other as Cain the Sixth catches Zeba's eye. Flatfoot is on her right and is not aware of Cain the Sixth's presence*]

NOAH: See how dey makin' out inside, son.

[*Stops hammering. Japheth exits into Ark. Noah turns and gazes towards the east*]

CAIN THE SIXTH: Hello, honey.

ZEBA: [*Frightened but smiling*] Hello, sugah.

CAIN THE SIXTH: [*Pleasantly*] Ain't dat my ol' frien' Flatfoot wid you?

ZEBA: Why, so 'tis! [*Flatfoot is now listening. To Flatfoot*] He's got a gun.

CAIN THE SIXTH: No, I ain't.

[*He lifts his hands over his head. Zeba quickly advances and runs her hands lightly over his pockets*]

ZEBA: [*Relieved*] I guess he ain't.

CAIN THE SIXTH: No, I ain't got no gun for my ol' frien', Flatfoot.

[*He walks up to him*]

FLATFOOT: [*Smiling*] Hi, Cain. How's de boy?

[*Cain quickly presses his chest against Flatfoot's, his downstage arm sweeps around Flatfoot's body and his hand goes up to the small of Flatfoot's back*]

CAIN THE SIXTH: [*Quietly, but triumphantly*] I got a little *knife* fo' him.

[*Flatfoot falls dead. The laughter of the others stops and they look at the scene. Zeba for a moment is terrified, her clenched hand pressed to her mouth. She looks at Cain the Sixth, who is smiling at her. He tosses the knife on the ground and holds his hands out to her. She goes to him, smiling*]

ZEBA: You sho' take keer of me, honey.

CAIN THE SIXTH: Dat's caize I think yo' wo'th takin' keer of. [*To the others*] It's all right, folks. I jest had to do a little cleanin' up.

FIRST WOMAN: [*Smiling*] You is de quickes' scoundrel.

FIRST GAMBLER: It was a nice quick killin'. Who was he?

SECOND WOMAN: [*Casually*] Dey called him Flatfoot. From over de river. He wa'n't any good. He owed me for washin' for over a year.

THIRD WOMAN: Used to peddle muggles. Said it had a kick like reg'lar snow. Wasn't no good.

SECOND GAMBLER: Think we ought to bury him?

FIRST MAN: No, just leave him dere. Nobody comes up yere, 'cept ol' Manatee.

[*Indicates* Noah. *Cries of "Ol' Manatee! Ol' Manatee, dat's good!"*]

NOAH: [*Still looking off*] You bettah pray, you po' chillun. [*They all laugh*]

FIRST WOMAN: We bettah pray? You bettah pray, Ol' Manatee?

[*Laughter again*]

NOAH: Dat's what I ain't doin', sinners. Shem! Japheth! [*To others, as he points off. Patter of rain*] Listen!

CAIN THE SIXTH: [*Casually*] Doggone, I believe it *is* gonter shower a little.

FIRST GAMBLER: It do look like rain.

FIRST WOMAN: I think I'll git on home. I got a new dress on.

ZEBA: Me, too. I wants to keep lookin' nice fo' my sweet papa.

[*She pats* Cain the Sixth's *cheek.* Cain the Sixth *hugs her*]

NOAH: [*Almost frantically*] Ham! Is de animals dere?

HAM: [*Off stage*] Yes, suh, dere yere. We're comin'.

NOAH: Den bring 'em on.

[Shem *and* Japheth *come on deck with their hammers. The stage begins to darken*]

THIRD WOMAN: I guess we all might go home 'til de shower's over. Come on, papa.

SECOND GAMBLER: See you after supper, Noah. [*Crowd starts moving off*]

NOAH: God's gittin' ready to start, my sons. Let's git dis plankin' done.

ZEBA: Put a big Texas on it, Noah, an' we'll use it fo' excursions.

[*There is a distant roll of thunder, there are cries of "Good night, Admiral." "See you later." "So long, Manatee," as the crowd goes off. The thunder rumbles again. There is the sound of increasing rain. The hammers of* Shem *and* Japheth *sound louder and are joined by the sounds of other hammerers. There is a flash of lightning. The* Choir *begins "De Ol' Ark's a-Movering," the sounds on the Ark become faster and louder. The rush of rain grows heavier*]

NOAH: Hurry! Hurry! Where are you, Ham!

HAM: [*Just off stage*] Yere I am, Father, wid de animals.

NOAH: God's give us His sign. Send 'em up de gangplank.

[*An inclined plane is thrown against the Ark from the side of the stage by* Ham, *who cracks a whip*]

HAM: Get on, dere.

[*The heads of two elephants are seen*]

NOAH: Bring 'em on board! De Lawd is strikin' down de worl'!

[*The singing and the noises reach fortissimo as* Ham *cracks his whip again, and the rain falls*

on the stage. The stage is darkened. The* Choir *continues singing in the darkness*]

SCENE X

When the lights go up on the scene, the Ark is at sea. Stationary waves run in front of it. The hillside has disappeared. The Ark is in the only lighted area.

Shem *is smoking a pipe on the deck, leaning on the rail. A steamboat whistle blows three short and one long blast.* Shem *is surprised. In a moment* Ham *appears, also with a pipe, and joins* Shem *at the rail.*

SHEM: Who'd you think you was signalin'?

HAM: Dat wasn't me, dat was daddy.

SHEM: He think he gonter git a reply?

HAM: I don't know. He's been gittin' a heap of comfort out of dat likker.

SHEM: De kag's nearly empty, ain't it?

HAM: Pretty nearly almos'. [*They look over the rail. A pause*] Seen anythin'?

SHEM: Dis mornin' I seen somethin' over dere migh'a' been a fish.

HAM: Dat's de big news of de week.

SHEM: How long you think dis trip's gonter las'?

HAM: I don' know! Rain fo'ty days 'n' fo'ty nights an' when dat stop' I thought sho' we'd come up ag'inst a san' bar o' somethin'. Looks now like all dat rain was jest a little incident of de trip. [*The whistle blows again*] Doggone! I wish he wouldn't do dat. Fust thing we know he'll wake up dem animals ag'in.

[Japheth *appears*]

SHEM: What's de matter wit' de ol' man, Jape?

JAPHETH: Doggone, he say he had a dream dat we're nearly dere. Dat's why he pullin' de whistle cord. See kin he git a' answer. [*He looks over the rail*] Look to me like de same ol' territory.

[Mrs. Noah *appears on deck*]

NOAH'S WIFE: You boys go stop yo' paw pullin' dat cord. He so full of likker he think he's in a race.

JAPHETH: He claim he know what he's doin'.

NOAH'S WIFE: I claim he gittin' to be a perfec' nuisance. Me an' yo' wives cain't hardly heah ou'sel'es think. [Noah *appears, his hat rakishly tilted on his head. He goes to the railing and looks out*] You 'spectin' company?

NOAH: Leave me be, woman. De watah don't look so rough to-day. De ol' boat's ridin' easier.

NOAH'S WIFE: Ridin' like a ol' mule!

NOAH: Yes, suh, de air don't feel so wet. Shem! S'pose you sen' out 'nother dove. [Shem *goes into the Ark*] Ham, go git de soundin' line. Jape, keep yo' eye on de East.

[Japheth *goes to the end of the boat*]

NOAH'S WIFE: As fo' you, I s'pose you'll help things along by takin' a little drink.

NOAH: Look yere, who's de pilot of dis vessel?

NOAH'S WIFE: O' Mister Dumb Luck.

NOAH: Well, see dat's where you don' know anythin'.

NOAH'S WIFE: I s'pose you ain't drunk as a fool?

NOAH: [Cordially] I feel congenial.

NOAH'S WIFE: An' you look it. You look jest wonderful. I wonder if you'd feel so congenial if de Lawd was to show up?

NOAH: De Lawd knows what I'm doin', don' you worry 'bout dat.

NOAH'S WIFE: I wouldn't say anythin' ag'inst de Lawd. He suttinly let us know dey'd be a change in de weather. But I bet even the Lawd wonders sometimes why He ever put you in charge.

NOAH: Well, you let de Lawd worry 'bout dat.

[Shem appears with the dove]

SHEM: Will I leave her go, Paw?

NOAH: Leave 'er go. [There's a chorus of "Good Luck, Dove" from the group as the dove flies off stage. Ham appears with the sounding line] Throw 'er over, boy.

[Ham proceeds to do so]

NOAH'S WIFE: An' another thing——

HAM: Hey.

NOAH: [Rushing to his side] What is it?

HAM: Only 'bout a inch! Look!

[They lean over]

JAPHETH: It's gettin' light in de East.

[As Ham works the cord up and down, Noah and Noah's Wife turn toward Japheth. The Choir begins "My Soul Is a Witness for the Lord"]

NOAH: Praise de Lawd, so it is.

NOAH'S WIFE: Oh, dat's pretty.

NOAH: [To Ham] An' de boat's stopped. We've landed. Shem, go down 'n' drag de fires an' dreen de boiler. Yo' go help 'im, Ham.

JAPHETH: Look, Paw.

[The dove wings back to the Ark with an olive branch in its mouth]

NOAH: 'N' yere's de little dove wid greenery in its mouth! Take 'er down, Jape, so she kin tell de animals. [Japheth exits after Shem and Ham carrying the dove. To Mrs. Noah] Now, maybe you feel little different.

NOAH'S WIFE: [Contritely] It was jes' gittin' to be so tiresome. I'm sorry, Noah.

NOAH: Dat's all right, ol' woman. [Noah's Wife exits, Noah looks about him. The lights have changed and the water piece is gone and the Ark is again on the hillside. Two mountains can be seen in the distance and a rainbow slowly appears over the Ark. The singing has grown louder] Thank you, Lawd, thank you very much indeed. Amen.

[The singing stops with the "Amen." God appears on the deck]

GOD: Yo' welcome, Noah.

[Noah turns and sees Him]

NOAH: O, Lawd, it's wonderful.

GOD: [Looking about Him] I sort of like it. I like de way you handled de ship, too, Noah.

NOAH: Was you watchin', Lawd?

GOD: Every minute. [He smiles] Didn't de ol' lady light into you?

NOAH: [Apologetically] She was kinda restless.

GOD: That's right. I ain't blamin' nobody. I don't even min' you cussin' an' drinkin'. I figure a steamboat cap'n on a long trip like you had has a right to a little redeye, jest so he don' go crazy.

NOAH: Thank you, Lawd. What's de orders now?

GOD: All de animals safe?

NOAH: Dey all fin'n' dandy, Lawd.

GOD: Den I want you to open dat starboard door, an' leave 'em all out. Let 'em go down de hill. Den you an' de family take all de seeds 'n' de sprouts an' begin plantin' ag'in. I'm startin' all over, Noah.

[Noah exits. God looks around]

GOD: Well, now we'll see what happens. [God listens with a smile, as noises accompanying the debarking of the animals are heard. They are the cracks of whips, the voices of the men on the Ark, shouting: "Git along dere." "Whoa, take it easy." "Duck yo' head." "Keep in line dere," etc. Over the Ark there is a burst of centrifugal shadows, and the sound of a myriad of wings. God smiles at the shadows] Dat's right, birds, fin' yo' new homes. [Bird twitters are heard again. God listens a moment and rests an arm on the railing. He speaks softly] Gabriel, kin you spare a minute?

GABRIEL: Yes, Lawd?

[The sounds from the other side of the Ark are by now almost hushed. The Lord indicates the new world with a wave of the hand]

GOD: Well, it's did.

GABRIEL: [Respectfully, but with no enthusiasm] So I take notice.

GOD: Yes, suh, startin' all over again.

GABRIEL: So I see.

GOD: [Looking at him suddenly] Don' seem to set you up much.

GABRIEL: Well, Lawd, you see— [He hesitates] 'Tain't none of my business.

GOD: What?

GABRIEL: I say, I don' know very much about it.

GOD: I know you don'. I jest wanted you to see it [A thought strikes Him] Co'se, it ain' yo' business, Gabe. It's my business. 'Twas my idea. De whole thing was my idea. An' every bit of it's my business 'n' nobody else's. De whole thing rests on my shoulders. I declare, I guess dat's why I feel so solemn an' serious, at dis particklar time. You know dis thing's turned into quite a proposition.

GABRIEL: [Tenderly] But it's all right, Lawd, as you say, it's did.

GOD: Yes, suh, it's did. [Sighs deeply. Looks slowly to the right and the left. Then softly] I only hope it's goin' to work out all right.

CURTAIN

PART II. SCENE I.

God's *office again.*

Somewhere the Choir *is singing: "A City Called Heaven." In the office are* Two Women Cleaners. *One is scrubbing the floor, the other dusting the furniture. The one dusting stops and looks out the window. There is a whirr and a distant faint boom. The* Choir *stops.*

FIRST CLEANER: Dat was a long way off.

SECOND CLEANER: [*At window*] Yes, ma'am. An' dat must 'a' been a big one. Doggone, de Lawd mus' be mad fo' sho', dis mo'nin'. Dat's de fo'ty-six' thunde'bolt since breakfast.

FIRST CLEANER: I wonder where at He's pitchin' dem.

SECOND CLEANER: My goodness, don' you know?

FIRST CLEANER: [*A little hurt*] Did I know I wouldn't ask de question.

SECOND CLEANER: Every one of dem's bound fo' de earth.

FIRST CLEANER: De earth? You mean dat little ol' dreenin' place?

SECOND CLEANER: Dat's de planet. [*Another faint whirr and boom*] Dere goes another.

FIRST CLEANER: Well, bless me. *I* didn't know dey was thunde'bolts.

SECOND CLEANER: Wha'd you think dey was?

FIRST CLEANER: [*Above desk*] I wasn't sho', but I thought maybe He might be whittlin' a new star o' two, an' de noise was just de chips fallin'.

SECOND CLEANER: Carrie, where you been? Don' you know de earth is de new scandal? Ever'body's talkin' 'bout it.

FIRST CLEANER: Dey kep' it from me.

SECOND CLEANER: Ain't you noticed de Lawd's been unhappy lately?

FIRST CLEANER: [*Thoughtfully*] Yeah, He ain't been His old self.

SECOND CLEANER: What did you think was de matteh? Lumbago?

FIRST CLEANER: [*Petulantly*] I didn't know. I didn't think it was fo' me t'inquieh.

SECOND CLEANER: Well, it jest so happens dat de Lawd is riled as kin be by dat measly little earth. Or I should say de scum dat's on it.

FIRST CLEANER: Dat's mankind down dere.

SECOND CLEANER: Dey mus' be scum, too, **to git** de Lawd so wukked up.

FIRST CLEANER: I s'pose so. [*Another whirr and boom*] Looks like He's lettin' dem feel de wrath. Ain' dat a shame to plague de Lawd dat way?

SECOND CLEANER: From what I hear dey been beggin' fo' what dey're gittin'. My brother flew down to bring up a saint de other day and he say from what he see mos' of de population down dere has made de debbil king an' dey wukkin' in three shifts fo' him.

FIRST CLEANER: You cain't blame de Lawd.

SECOND CLEANER: Co'se you cain't. Dem human bein's 'd make anybody bile oveh. Ev'rytime de Lawd try to do sompin' fo' dem, doggone if dey don't staht some new ruckus.

FIRST CLEANER: I take notice He's been wukkin' in yere mo' dan usual.

SECOND CLEANER: I wish He'd let us ladies fix it up. Wouldn't take a minute to make dis desk gold-plated.

FIRST CLEANER: I s'pose He likes it dis way. De Lawd's kind o' ol' fashioned in some ways. I s'pose He keeps dis office plain an' simple on purpose.

SECOND CLEANER: [*Finishing her work*] I don't see why.

FIRST CLEANER: [*Looking off*] Well, it's kind of a nice place to come to when He's studyin' somethin' impo'tant. 'Most evahthin' else in heaven's so fin' 'n' gran', maybe ev'ry now an' den He jest gits sick an' tired of de glory.

[*She is also collecting her utensils*]

SECOND CLEANER: Maybe so. Jest de same I'd like to have a free hand wid dis place for a while, so's I could gold it up.

[God *appears in the doorway*]

FIRST AND SECOND CLEANERS: Good mo'nin', Lawd. We was jest finishin'.

GOD: Go ahead den, daughters.

[*Goes to the window*]

FIRST AND SECOND CLEANERS: Yes, Lawd. [*Exeunt. Off stage*] Good mo'nin', Gabriel.

[*Off stage* Gabriel *says, "Good mo'nin', sisters," and enters immediately. He stands in the doorway for a moment watching God—a notebook and pencil in his hand*]

GOD: What's de total?

GABRIEL: [*Consulting the book*] Eighteen thousand nine hund'ed an' sixty for de mo'nin'. Dat's includin' de village wid de fo'tune tellers. Dey certainly kin breed fast.

GOD: [*Solemnly*] Dey displease me. Dey displease me greatly.

GABRIEL: Want some more bolts, Lawd?

GOD: [*Looking through window*] Look at 'em dere. Squirmin' an' fightin' an' bearin' false witness. Listen to dat liar, dere. He don' intend to marry dat little gal. He don' even love her. What did you say?

GABRIEL: Should I git mo' bolts?

GOD: Wait a minute. [*He carefully points His finger down through the window*] I'm goin' to git dat wicked man myself. [*From a great distance comes an agonized cry: "Oh, Lawd!"* God *turns from the window*] No use gittin' mo' thunde'bolts. Dey din' do de trick. [*He goes to the swivel chair and sits*] It's got to be somethin' else.

GABRIEL: How would it be if you was to doom 'em all ag'in, like dat time you sent down de flood? I bet dat would make dem mind.

GOD: You see how much good de flood did. Dere **dey is, jest as bad as ever.**

GABRIEL: How about cleanin' up on de whole mess of 'em and sta'tin' all over ag'in wid some new kind of animal?

GOD: An' admit I'm licked?

GABRIEL: [Ashamedly] No, of co'se not, Lawd.

GOD: No, suh. No, suh. Man is a kind of pet of mine and it ain't right fo' me to give up tryin' to do somethin' wid him. Doggone, mankin' *mus'* be all right at de core or else why did I ever bother wid him in de first place?

[Sits at desk]

GABRIEL: It's jest dat I hates to see you worryin' about it, Lawd.

GOD: Gabe, dere ain't anythin' worth while anywheres dat didn't cause somebody some worryin'. I ain't never tol' you de trouble I had gittin' things started up yere. Dat's a story in itself. No, suh, de more I keep on bein' de Lawd de more I know I got to keep improvin' things. An' dat takes time and worry. De main trouble wid mankin' is he takes up so much of my time. He ought to be able to help hisself a little. [He stops suddenly and cogitates] Hey, dere! I think I got it!

GABRIEL: [Eagerly] What's de news?

GOD: [Still cogitating] Yes, suh, dat seems like an awful good idea.

GABRIEL: Tell me, Lawd.

GOD: Gabriel, have you noticed dat every now an' den, mankin' turns out some pretty good specimens?

GABRIEL: Dat's de truth.

GOD: Yes, suh. Dey's ol' Abraham and Isaac an' Jacob an' all dat family.

GABRIEL: Dat's so, Lawd.

GOD: An' every one of dem boys was a hard wukker an' a good citizen. We got to admit dat.

GABRIEL: Dey wouldn't be up yere flyin' wid us if dey hadn't been.

GOD: No, suh. An' I don' know but what de answer to de whole trouble is right dere.

GABRIEL: How you mean, Lawd?

GOD: Why, doggone it, de good man is de man dat keeps busy. I mean I been goin' along on de principle dat he was something like you angels—dat you ought to be able to give him somethin' an' den jest let him sit back an' enjoy it. Now dat I recollec' I put de first one down dere to take keer o' dat garden an' den I let him go ahead an' do nothin' but git into mischief. [He rises] Sure, *dat's* it. He ain't *built* jest to fool 'roun' an' not do nothin'. Gabe, I'm gonter try a new scheme.

GABRIEL: [Eagerly] What's de scheme, Lawd?

GOD: I'll tell you later. Send in Abraham, Isaac an' Jacob. [A voice outside calls: "Right away, Lawd."] You go tell dem to put dem bolts back in de boxes. I ain' gonter use dem ag'in a while.

GABRIEL: O. K., Lawd.

GOD: Was you goin' anywhere near de Big Pit?

GABRIEL: I could go.

GOD: Lean over de brink and tell Satan he's jest a plain fool if he thinks he kin beat anybody as big as me.

GABRIEL: Yes, suh, Lawd. Den I'll spit right in his eye.

[Gabriel *exits.* God *looks down through the window again to the earth below*]

GOD: Dat new polish on de sun makes it powerful hot. [He "r'ar back"] Let it be jest a little bit cooler. [He feels the air] Dat's nice. [Goes to His desk. A knock on the door] Come in.

[Abraham, Isaac *and* Jacob *enter. All are very old men, but the beard of* Abraham *is the longest and whitest, and they suggest their three generations. They have wings that are not quite so big as those of the native angels*]

ISAAC: Sorry we so long comin', Lawd. But Pappy and me had to take de boy [Pointing to Jacob] over to git him a can of wing ointment.

GOD: What was de matter, son?

JACOB: Dey was chafin' me a little. Dey fine now, thank you, Lawd.

GOD: Dat's good. Sit down an' make yo'selves comf'table. [The three sit. Men: "Thank you, Lawd"] Men, I'm goin' to talk about a little scheme I got. It's one dat's goin' to affec' yo' fam'lies an' dat's why I 'cided I'd talk it over wid you, 'fo it goes into ee-ffect. I don't know whether you boys know it or not, but you is about de three best men of one fam'ly dat's come up yere since I made little apples. Now I tell you what I'm gonter do. Seein' dat you human bein's cain't 'preciate anythin' lessen you fust wukk to git it and den keep strugglin' to hold it, why I'm gonter turn over a very valuable piece of property to yo' fam'ly, and den see what kin dey do with it. De rest of de worl' kin go jump in de river fo' all I keer. I'm gonter be lookin' out fo' yo' descendants only. Now den, seein' dat you boys know de country pretty tho'ly, where at does you think is de choice piece of property in de whole worl'? Think it over for a minute. I'm gonter let you make the s'lection.

ABRAHAM: If you was to ask me, Lawd, I don't think dey come any better dan de Land of Canaan.

GOD: [To Isaac and Jacob] What's yo' feelin' in de matter?

JACOB: [After a nod from Isaac] Pappy an' me think do we get a pick, dat would be it.

GOD: [Goes to window again; looks out] De Land of Canaan. Yes, I guess dat's a likely neighborhood. It's all run over wid Philistines and things right now, but we kin clean dat up. [He turns from the window and resumes His seat] All right. Now who do you boys think is best of yo' men to put in charge down dere? You see I ain't been payin' much attention to anybody in partic'lar lately.

ISAAC: Does you want de brainiest or de holiest, Lawd?

[Men look up]

GOD: I want de holiest. I'll make him brainy.

[Men appreciate the miracle]

ISAAC: [*As* Abraham *and* Jacob *nod to him*] Well, if you want A-Number-One goodness, Lawd, I don't know where you'll git more satisfaction dan in a great-great-great-great-grandson of mine.

GOD: Where's he at?

ISAAC: At de moment I b'lieve he's in de sheep business over in Midian County. He got in a little trouble down in Egypt, but 'twa'n't his doin'. He killed a man dat was abusin' one of our boys in de brick works. Of co'se you know old King Pharaoh's got all our people in bondage.

GOD: I heard of it. [*With some ire*] Who did you think put them dere? [*The visitors lower their heads*] It's all right, boys [*All rise*] I'm gonter take dem out of it. An' I'm gonter turn over de whole Land of Canaan to dem. An' do you know who's gonter lead dem dere? Yo' great, great, great, great-grandson. Moses, ain't it?

ISAAC: Yes, Lawd.

GOD: [*Smiling*] Yes. I been noticin' *him*.

ABRAHAM: It's quite a favor fo' de fam'ly, Lawd.

GOD: Dat's why I tol' you. You see, it so happens I love yo' fam'ly, an' I delight to honor it. Dat's all, gen'lemen. [*The three others rise and cross to the door, murmuring, "Yes, Lawd," "Thank you, Lawd," "Much obliged, Lawd,"* etc. The *Choir begins, "My Lord's A-Writin' All De Time" pianissimo. God stands watching the men leave*] Enjoy yo'selves. [*He goes to the window. The singing grows softer. He speaks through the window to the earth*] I'm comin' down to see you, Moses, an' dis time my scheme's got to wukk.

[*The stage is darkened. The singing grows louder and continues until the lights go up on the next scene*]

SCENE II.

The tableau curtains frame the opening of a cave, which is dimly lighted. A large turkey-berry bush is somewhere near the foreground. Moses *is seated on the grass eating his lunch from a basket in his lap.* Zipporah, *his wife, stands watching him. He is about forty,* Zipporah *somewhat younger. They are dressed inconspicuously.* Moses *stutters slightly when he speaks. He looks up to see* Zipporah *smiling.*

MOSES: What you smilin' at, Zipporah?

ZIPPORAH: Caize you enjoyin' yo'self.

MOSES: You is a good wife, Zipporah.

ZIPPORAH: You is a good husband, Moses. [Moses *wipes his mouth with a handkerchief and begins putting into the basket the various implements of the meal which had been on the ground about him*] Why you suppose it's so dark yere today? Dey's no rain in de air.

MOSES: Seems like it's jest aroun' dis cave. Yo'

father's house is got de sun on it. [*He looks in another direction*] Looks all clear down toward Egypt.

ZIPPORAH: Co'se it *would* be fine weather in Egypt. De sky looks all right. Maybe it's gonter rain jest right yere. Why don't you move de sheep over to de other pasture?

MOSES: [*A bit puzzled*] I don' know. It got dark like dis befo' you come along wid de dinner an' I was gonter stop you on de top of de hill. Den somethin' kep' me yere.

ZIPPORAH: S'pose it could be de Lawd warnin' you dat dey's 'Gyptians hangin' 'roun'?

MOSES: Dey may have fo'gotten all about dat killin' by now. Dey got a new Pharaoh down dere.

ZIPPORAH: An' I hear he's jest as mean to yo' people as his pappy was. I wouldn't put it pas' him to send soljahs all the way up yere fo' you.

MOSES: Dat's all right. De Lawd's looked after me so far. I don't 'spect him to fall down on me now. You better be gittin' home.

ZIPPORAH: [*Taking the basket*] I'll be worryin' about you.

MOSES: [*Kissing her and then smiling*] 'Parently de Lawd ain't. He knows I'm safe as kin be. Lemme see you feel dat way.

ZIPPORAH: You is a good man, Moses.

MOSES: I'se a lucky man [Zipporah *exits with the basket.* Moses *looks up at the sky*] Dat's funny. De sun seems to be shinin' every place but right yere. It's shinin' on sheep. Why ain't dey no clouds dere?

GOD: [*Off stage*] Caize I want it to be like dat, Moses.

MOSES: [*Looking about him*] Who's dat?

GOD: [*Off stage again*] I'm de Lawd, Moses.

MOSES: [*Smiling*] Dat's what you say. Dis yere shadow may be de Lawd's wukk, but dat voice soun' pretty much to me like my ol' brother Aaron.

GOD: [*Off stage*] Den keep yo' eyes open, son. [*The turkey-berry bush begins to glow and then turns completely red.* Moses *looks at it fascinated*] Maybe you notice de bush ain't burnin' up.

MOSES: Dat's de truth.

[Moses *is full of awe but not frightened*]

GOD: [*Off stage*] Now you believe me?

MOSES: Co'se I does. It's wonderful.

[*The light in the bush dies and* God *appears from behind it*]

GOD: No, it ain't, Moses. It was jest a trick.

MOSES: 'Scuse me doubtin' you, Lawd. I always had de feelin' you wuz takin' keer of me, but I never 'spected you'd fin' time to talk wid me pussunly. [*He laughs*] Dat was a good trick, Lawd. I'se seen some good ones, but dat was de beatenest.

GOD: Yo' gonter see lots bigger tricks dan dat, Moses. In fac', yo' gonter perfo'm dem.

MOSES: [*Incredulously*] Me? I'm gonter be a tricker?

GOD: Yes, suh.

MOSES: An' do magic? Lawd, my mouth ain't got de quick talk to go wid it.

GOD: It'll come to you now.

MOSES: [*Now cured of stuttering*] Is I goin' wid a circus?

GOD: [*Slowly and solemnly*] Yo' is goin' down into Egypt, Moses, and lead my people out of bondage. To do dat I'm gonter make you de bes' tricker in de worl'.

MOSES: [*A little frightened*] Egypt! You know I killed a man dere, Lawd. Won't dey kill me?

GOD: Not when dey see yo' tricks. You ain't skeered, is you?

MOSES: [*Simply and bravely*] No, suh, Lawd.

GOD: Den yere's what I'm gonter do. Yo' people is my chillun, Moses. I'm sick and tired o' de way ol' King Pharaoh is treatin' dem, so I'se gonter take dem away, and yo' gonter lead dem. You gonter lead 'em out of Egypt an' across de river Jordan. It's gonter take a long time, and you ain't goin' on no excursion train. Yo' gonter wukk awful hard for somethin' yo' goin' to fin' when de trip's over.

MOSES: What's dat, Lawd?

GOD: It's de Land of Canaan. It's de bes' land I got. I've promised it to yo' people, an' I'm gonter give it to dem.

MOSES: Co'se, ol' King Pharaoh will do everything he kin to stop it.

GOD: Yes, an' dat's where de tricks come in. Dey tell me he's awful fond of tricks.

MOSES: I hear dat's *all* he's fon' of. Dey say if you cain't take a rabbit out of a hat you cain't even git to see him.

GOD: Wait'll you see de tricks you an' me's goin' to show him.

MOSES: [*Delightedly*] Doggone! Huh, Lawd?

GOD: Yes, suh. Now de first trick——

[God *is lifting a stick which He carries*]

MOSES: Jest a minute, Lawd. [God *halts the demonstration*] I'm gonter learn de tricks and do just like you tell me, but I *know* it's gonter take me a little time to learn all dat quick talkin'. Cain't I have my brother Aaron go wid me? He's a good man.

GOD: I was gonter have him help you wid de Exodus. I guess he can watch, too.

MOSES: I'll call 'im.

[*He turns as if to shout*]

GOD: Wait. [Moses *turns and looks at* God] I'll bring him. [*Softly*] Aaron!

[Aaron *appears between* God *and* Moses *in the mouth of the cave. He is a little taller than* Moses *and slightly older. He, too, is dressed like a field hand*]

AARON: [*Blankly*] Hey!

[Moses *goes to him, takes his hand and leads him, bewildered, down to where* Moses *had been standing alone.* Aaron *then sees* God]

MOSES: [*Almost in a whisper*] It's all right.

GOD: Don't worry, son, I'm jest showin' some tricks. Bringin' you yere was one of dem. [Aaron *stares at* God *as if hypnotized*] Now den, you see dis yere rod? Looks like a ordinary walking stick, don' it?

MOSES: Yes, Lawd.

GOD: Well, it ain't no ordinary walkin' stick, caize look. [Moses *leans forward*] When I lays it down on de groun'——

[*The stage is darkened. The* Choir *begins, "Go Down, Moses," and continues until the lights go up on the next scene*]

SCENE III.

The throne room of Pharaoh. *It suggests a Negro lodge room. The plain board walls are colored by several large parade banners of varying sizes, colors and materials, bordered with gold fringe and tassels on them. Some of the inscriptions on them read:*

SUBLIME ORDER OF PRINCES OF THE
HOUSE OF PHARAOH
HOME CHAPTER
MYSTIC BROTHERS OF THE EGYPTIAN
HOME GUARD
LADIES AUXILIARY, NO. I
SUPREME MAGICIANS AND WIZARDS
OF THE UNIVERSE
PRIVATE FLAG OF HIS HONOR
OLD KING PHARAOH
ROYAL YOUNG PEOPLE'S
PLEASURE CLUB
ENCHANTED AND INVISIBLE CADETS
OF EGYPT BOYS' BRIGADE

There is one door up right and a window. The throne, an ordinary armchair with a drapery over its back, is on a dais. Pharaoh *is seated on the throne. His crown and garments might be those worn by a high officer in a Negro lodge during a ritual. About the throne itself are high officials, several of them with plumed hats, clothing that suggests military uniforms, and rather elaborate sword belts, swords and scabbards. A few soldiers carrying spears are also in his neighborhood and one or two bearded ancients in brightly colored robes with the word "Wizard" on their conical hats. In the general group of men and women scattered elsewhere in the room Sunday finery is noticeable everywhere. Most of the civilians have bright "parade" ribbons and wear medals. In a cleared space immediately before the throne a* Candidate Magician *is performing a sleight-of-hand trick with cards.* Pharaoh *watches him apathetically. He is receiving earnest attention from a few of the others, but the majority of the men and women are talking quietly among themselves. Beside the* Candidate Magician *are several paraphernalia of previously demonstrated tricks.*

CANDIDATE MAGICIAN: [*Holding up some cards*] Now den, ol' King Pharaoh, watch dis. [*He completes a trick. There is a murmur of "Not bad," "Pretty good," etc., from a few of the watchers. Pharaoh makes no comment*] Now, I believe de cyard I ast you to keep sittin' on was de trey of diamonds, wasn't it?

PHARAOH: Yeah.

CANDIDATE MAGICIAN: Den kin I trouble you to take a look at it now? [*Pharaoh half rises to pick up a card he has been sitting on, and looks at it*] I believe you'll now notice dat it's de king of clubs? [*Pharaoh nods and shows the card to those nearest him. The Candidate Magician waits for an audible approval and gets practically none*] An' dat, ol' King Pharaoh, completes de puffohmance.

[*An elderly man in a uniform steps forward*]

GENERAL: On behalf of my nephew I beg Yo' Honor to let him jine de ranks of de royal trickers and magicians.

PHARAOH: [*To the two* Wizards] What do de committee think? [*The Wizards shake their heads*] Dat's what I thought. He ain't good enough. I'd like to help you out, General, but you know a man's got to be a awful good tricker to git in de royal society dese days. You better go back an' steddy some mo', son. [*He lifts his voice and directs two* Soldiers *guarding the door*] Is de head magician reached de royal waitin' room yit? [*One of the* Soldiers *opens the door to look out*] If he is, send him in.

[*The* Soldier *beckons to someone off stage, throws the door open, and announces to the court*]

SOLDIER: De Head Magician of de land of Egypt. [*A very old and villainous man enters. His costume is covered with cabalistic and zodiacal signs. He advances to the* King, *the other* Magician *and his uncle making way for him. He bows curtly to* Pharaoh]

HEAD MAGICIAN: Good mo'nin', ol' King Pharaoh.

PHARAOH: Mo'nin', Professor. What's de news?

HEAD MAGICIAN: Evahthing's bein' carried out like you said.

PHARAOH: How's de killin' of de babies 'mongst de Hebrews comin' 'long?

HEAD MAGICIAN: Jes' like you ordered.

PHARAOH: [*Genially*] Dey killed all of 'em, huh?

HEAD MAGICIAN: Do dey see one, dey kill 'em. You teachin' 'em a great lesson. Dey don't like it a-tall.

PHARAOH: [*Smiling*] What do dey say?

HEAD MAGICIAN: [*Pawing the air inarticulately*] I hates to tell in front of de ladies.

PHARAOH: Dey feels pretty bad, huh?

HEAD MAGICIAN: Dat's jest de beginnin' of it. Betwixt de poleece and de soljahs we killed about a thousan' of 'em las' night. Dat's purty good.

PHARAOH: [*Thoughtfully*] Yeh, it's fair. I guess you boys is doin' all you kin. But I fin' I ain't satisfied, though.

HEAD MAGICIAN: How you mean, Yo' Honor?

PHARAOH: I mean I'd like to make dose Hebrew chillun realize dat I kin be even mo' of a pest. I mean I hates dem chillun. An' I'm gonter think of a way of makin' 'em even mo' mizzable.

HEAD MAGICIAN: But dey *ain't* anythin' meaner dan killin' de babies, King.

PHARAOH: Dey must be sump'n. Doggone, you is my head tricker, you put yo' brains on it. [*To the others*] Quiet, whilst de Head Magician go into de silence.

HEAD MAGICIAN: [*After turning completely around twice, and a moment's cogitation*] I tell you what I kin do. All de Hebrews dat ain't out to de buryin' grounds or in de hospitals is laborin' in de brick wukks.

HARAOH: Yeh?

HEAD MAGICIAN: [*After a cackling laugh*] How would it be to take de straw away from 'em and tell 'em dey's got to turn out jest as many bricks as usual? Ain't dat nasty?

PHARAOH: Purty triflin', but I s'pose it'll have to do for de time bein'. Where's de extreme inner guard? [*One of the military* Attendants *comes forward*] Go on out an' tell de sup'intendent to put dat into ee-ffect. [*The* Attendant *bows and starts for the door. He stops as* Pharaoh *calls to him*] Wait a minute! Tell 'im to chop off de hands of anybody dat say he cain't make de bricks dat way. [*The* Attendant *salutes and exits, the door being opened and closed by one of the* Soldiers] Now what's de news in de magic line?

HEAD MAGICIAN: I ain't got very many novelties today, King. I been wukkin' too hard on de killin's. I'm so tired I don' believe I could lift a wand.

[*There are murmurs of protest from the assemblage*]

PHARAOH: Doggone, you was to 'a been de chief feature o' de meetin' dis mo'nin'. Look at de turnout you got account of me tellin' 'em you was comin'.

HEAD MAGICIAN: Well, dat's de way it is, King. Why don' you git de wizards to do some spell castin'?

PHARAOH: Dey say it's in de cyards dat dey cain't wukk till high noon. [*He glances at the* Wizards] Think mebbe you kin cheat a little?

FIRST WIZARD: Oh, dat cain't be done, King.

PHARAOH: Well, we might as well adjourn, den. Looks to me like de whole program's shot to pieces. [*He starts to rise, when there is a furious banging on the door*] What's de idea, dere? See who dat is. [*The* Soldiers *open the door.* Moses *and* Aaron *enter, pushing the two* Soldiers *aside and coming down in front of* Pharaoh. *The* Soldiers *are bewildered and* Pharaoh *is angry*] Say, who tol' you two baboons you could come in yere?

MOSES: Is you ol' King Pharaoh?

PHARAOH: Dat's me. Did you heah what I asked you?

MOSES: My name is Moses, and dis is my brother Aaron.

[*Murmur of "Hebrews" spreads through the room*]

PHARAOH: [*In a rage*] Is you Hebrews?

MOSES: Yes, suh.

PHARAOH: [*Almost screaming*] Put 'em to de sword!

[*As the* Courtiers *approach,* Aaron *suddenly discloses the rod, which he swings once over his head. The* Courtiers *draw back as if their hands had been stung. Cries of "Hey!" "Look out," etc.*]

MOSES: Keep outside dat circle.

[*The* Courtiers *nearest* Moses *and* Aaron *look at each other, exclaiming ad lib., "Did you feel dat?" "What was dat?" "What's goin' on, heah?" "My hands is stingin'!" etc.*]

PHARAOH: [*Puzzled but threatening*] What's de idea yere?

MOSES: We is magicians, ol' King Pharaoh.

PHARAOH: [*To the* Head Magician] Put a spell on 'em. [*The* Head Magician *stands looking at them, bewildered. To* Moses] I got some magicians, too. We'll see who's got de bes' magic. [*Moses and* Aaron *laugh. Most of the* Courtiers *are cowering. To the* Head Magician] Go ahead, give 'em gri-gri.

MOSES: Sure, go ahead.

PHARAOH: Hurry up, dey's laughin' at you. What's de matter?

HEAD MAGICIAN: I cain't think of de right spell.

PHARAOH: [*Now frightened himself*] You mean dey got even *you* whupped?

HEAD MAGICIAN: Dey's got a new kind of magic.

PHARAOH: [*Gazes at* Head Magician *a moment, bewildered. To the* Wizards] I s'pose if de Professor cain't, you cain't.

FIRST WIZARD: Dat's a new trick, King.

HEAD MAGICIAN: [*Rubbing his fingers along his palms*] It's got 'lectricity in it!

PHARAOH: Hm, well dat may make it a little diff'rent. So you boys is magicians, too?

MOSES: Yes, suh.

PHARAOH: Well, we's always glad to see some new trickers in de co't, dat is if dey good. [*He glances about him*] You look like you is O. K.

MOSES: Dat's what we claims, ol' King Pharaoh. We think we's de best in de worl'.

PHARAOH: You certainly kin talk big. Jest what is it you boys would like?

MOSES: We came to show you some tricks. Den we's goin' to ask you to do somethin' for us.

PHARAOH: Well, I s'pose you know I'm a fool for conjurin'. If a man kin show me some tricks I ain't seen, I goes out of my way to do him a favor.

MOSES: Dat's good. Want to see de first trick?

PHARAOH: It ain't goin' to hurt nobody?

MOSES: Dis one won't.

PHARAOH: Go ahead.

MOSES: Dis yere rod my brother has looks jes' like a walkin' stick, don't it?

[*The* Courtiers *now join the* King *in interest*]

PHARAOH: Uh-huh. Le's see.

[Aaron *hands him the rod, which* Pharaoh *inspects and returns*]

MOSES: Well, look what happens when he lays it on de groun'.

[Aaron *places the rod on the second step of the throne. It turns into a life-like snake. There are exclamations from the assemblage*]

PHARAOH: Dat's a good trick! Now turn it back into a walkin' stick again. [Aaron *picks it up and it is again a rod. Exclamations of "Purty good!" "Dat's all right!" "What do you think of that!" etc.*] Say, you is good trickers!

MOSES: You ain't never seen de beat of us. Now I'm goin' to ask de favor.

PHARAOH: Sure, what is it?

MOSES: [*Solemnly*] Let de Hebrew chillun go!

PHARAOH: [*Rises and stares at them. There is a murmur of "Listen to 'im!" "He's got nerve!" "I never in my life!" "My goodness!" etc.*] What did you say?

MOSES: Let de Hebrew chillun go.

[Pharaoh *seats himself again*]

PHARAOH: [*Slowly*] Don' you know de Hebrews is my slaves?

MOSES: Yes, suh.

PHARAOH: Yes, suh, my slaves. [*There is a distant groaning*] Listen, and you kin hear 'em bein' treated like slaves. [*He calls toward the window*] What was dey doin' den?

MAN NEAR THE WINDOW: Dey's jest gettin' de news down in de brickyard.

PHARAOH: I won't let them go. [*He snorts contemptuously*] Let's see another trick.

MOSES: Yes, suh, yere's a better one. [*He lowers his head*] Let's have a plague of de flies.

[Aaron *raises the rod. The room grows dark and a great buzzing of flies is heard. The* Courtiers *break out in cries of "Get away fum me!" "Take 'em away!" "De place is filled with flies!" "Dis is terrible!" "Do sump'n, Pharaoh!"*]

PHARAOH: [*Topping the others*] All right—stop de trick!

MOSES: Will you let de Hebrews go?

PHARAOH: Sho' I will. Go ahead, stop it!

MOSES: [*Also above the others*] Begone!

[*The buzzing stops and the room is filled with light again, as* Aaron *lowers the rod. All except* Moses *and* Aaron *are brushing the flies from their persons*]

PHARAOH: [*Laughing*] Doggone, dat was a good trick! [*The others, seeing they are uninjured, join in the laughter, with exclamations of "Doggone!" "You all right?" "Sho' I'm all right." "Didn't hurt me," etc.*] You is good trickers.

MOSES: Will you let de Hebrew chillun go?

PHARAOH: [Sitting down again] Well, I'll tell you, boys. I'll tell you sump'n you didn' know. You take me, I'm a pretty good tricker, an' I jest outtricked you. So, bein' de bes' tricker, I don' think I will let 'em go. You got any mo' tricks yo'self?

MOSES: Yes, suh. Dis is a little harder one. [Aaron lifts the rod] Gnats in de mill pon', gnats in de clover, gnats in de 'tater patch, stingin' all over.

[The stage grows dark again. There is the humming of gnats and the slapping of hands against faces and arms, and the same protests as were heard with the flies, but with more feeling: "I'm gittin' stung to death!" "I'm all stung!" "Dey're like hornets!" "Dey's on my face!" etc.]

PHARAOH: Take 'em away, Moses!

MOSES: [His voice drowning the others] If I do, will you let 'em go?

PHARAOH: Sho' I will, dis time.

MOSES: Do you mean it?

PHARAOH: Co'se I mean it! Doggone, one just stang me on de nose.

MOSES: Begone! [Lights come up as Aaron lowers the rod. There is a moment of general recovery again. Pharaoh rubs his nose, looks at his hands, etc., as do the others] Now, how about it?

PHARAOH: [Smiling] Well, I'll tell you, Moses. Now dat de trick's over——

[Moses takes a step toward Pharaoh]

MOSES: Listen, Pharaoh. You been lyin' to me, and I'm gittin' tired of it.

PHARAOH: I ain't lyin', I'm trickin', too. You been trickin' me and I been trickin' you.

MOSES: I see. Well, I got one mo' trick up my sleeve which I didn't aim to wukk unless I had to. Caize when I does it, I cain't undo it.

PHARAOH: Wukk it an' I'll trick you right back. I don' say you ain't a good tricker, Moses. You is one of de bes' I ever seen. But I kin outtrick you. Dat's all.

MOSES: It ain't only me dat's goin' to wukk dis trick. It's me an' de Lawd.

PHARAOH: Who?

MOSES: De Lawd God of Israel.

PHARAOH: I kin outtrick you an' de Lawd too!

MOSES: [Angrily] Now you done it, ol' King Pharaoh. You been mean to de Lawd's people, and de Lawd's been easy on you caize you didn' know better. You been givin' me a lot of say-so and no do-so, and I didn' min' dat. But now you've got to braggin' dat you's better dan de Lawd, and dat's too many.

PHARAOH: You talk like a preacher, an' I never did like to hear preachers talk.

MOSES: You ain't goin' to like it any better, when I strikes down de oldes' boy in every one of yo' people's houses.

PHARAOH: Now, you've given up trickin' and is jest lyin'. [He rises] Listen, I'm Pharaoh. I do de strikin' down yere. I strike down my enemies, and dere's no one in all Egypt kin kill who he wants to, 'ceptin' me.

MOSES: I'm sorry, Pharaoh. Will you let de Hebrews go?

PHARAOH: You heard my word. [Aaron is lifting his rod again at a signal from Moses] Now, no more tricks or I'll——

MOSES: Oh, Lawd, you'll have to do it, I guess. Aaron, lift de rod.

[There is a thunderclap, darkness and screams. The lights go up. Several of the younger men on the stage have fallen to the ground or are being held in the arms of the horrified elders]

PHARAOH: What have you done yere? Where's my boy?

[Through the door come four men bearing a young man's body]

FIRST OF THE FOUR MEN: King Pharaoh.

[Pharaoh drops into his chair, stunned, as the dead boy is brought to the throne]

PHARAOH: [Grief-stricken] Oh, my son, my fine son.

[The Courtiers look at him with mute appeal]

MOSES: I'm sorry, Pharaoh, but you cain't fight de Lawd. Will you let his people go?

PHARAOH: Let dem go.

[The lights go out. The Choir begins, "Mary, Don't You Weep," and continues until it is broken by the strains of "I'm Noways Weary and I'm Noways Tired." The latter is sung by many more voices than the former, and the cacophony ends as the latter grows in volume and the lights go up on the next scene]

SCENE IV.

The Children of Israel are marching on the treadmill and now singing fortissimo. They are of all ages and most of them are ragged. The men have packs on their shoulders, one or two have hand carts. The line stretches across the stage. It is nearing twilight, and the faces of the assemblage are illumined by the rays of the late afternoon sun. The upper treadmill carries a gradually rising and falling middle distance past the marchers. The foot of a mountain appears; a trumpet call is heard as the foot of the mountain reaches stage center. The marchers halt. The picture now shows the mountain running up out of sight off right. The singing stops. A babel of "What's de matter?" "Why do we stop?" "'Tain't sundown yet!" "What's happened?" "What's goin' on?" "What are they blowin' for?" etc. Those looking ahead begin to murmur. "It's Moses," "Moses," "What's happened to him?" The others take up the repetition of "Moses," and Moses enters, on the arm of Aaron. He is now an old man, as is his brother, *and he totters toward the center of the stage. Cries of "What's de matter, Moses?" "You ain't hurt, is you?" "Ain't that too bad?" etc. He slowly seats himself on the rock at the foot of the mountain.*

AARON: How you feelin' now, brother?

MOSES: I'm so weary, Aaron. Seems like I was took all of a sudden.

AARON: Do we camp yere?

MOSES: [*Pathetically*] No, you got to keep goin'.

AARON: But you cain't go no further tonight, brother.

MOSES: Dis never happened to me befo'.

A YOUNG WOMAN: But you's a ol' man, now, Father Moses. You cain't expect to go as fas' as we kin.

MOSES: But de Lawd said I'd do it. He said I was to show you de Promised Land. Fo'ty years, I bin leadin' you. I led you out o' Egypt. I led you past Sinai, and through de wilderness. Oh, I cain't fall down on you now.

AARON: Le's res' yere fo' de night. Den we'll see how you feel in de mo'nin'.

MOSES: We tol' de scouts we'd meet 'em three miles further on. I hate fo' 'em to come back all dis way to report. 'Tis gettin' a little dark, ain't it?

AARON: It ain't dark, brother.

MOSES: No, it's my eyes.

AARON: Maybe it's de dust.

MOSES: No, I jest cain't seem to see. Oh, Lawd, dey cain't have a blind man leadin' 'em! Where is you, Aaron?

AARON: I'se right yere, Moses.

MOSES: Do you think— [*Pause*] Oh! Do you think it's de time He said?

AARON: How you mean, Moses?

[*Crowd looks from one to another in wonder*]

MOSES: He said I could lead 'em to de Jordan, dat I'd *see* de Promised Land, and dat's all de further I could go, on account I broke de laws. Little while back I thought I *did* see a river ahead, and a pretty land on de other side. [*Distant shouts "Hooray!" "Yere dey are!" "Dey traveled quick," etc.*] Where's de young leader of de troops? Where's Joshua?

[*The call "Joshua" is taken up by those on the right of the stage, followed almost immediately by "Yere he is!" "Moses wants you!" etc. Joshua enters. He is a fine-looking Negro of about thirty*]

JOSHUA: [*Going to* Moses' *side*] Yes, suh.

MOSES: What's de shoutin' 'bout, Joshua?

JOSHUA: De scouts is back wid de news. De Jordan is right ahead of us, and Jericho is jest on de other side. Moses, we're dere! [*There are cries of "Hallelujah!" "De Lawd be praised!" "Hooray!" "De Kingdom's comin'!" etc. With a considerable stir among the marchers, several new arrivals crowd in from*

right, shouting "Moses, we're dere!" Joshua, *seeing the newcomers*] Yere's de scouts.

[*Three very ragged and dusty young men advance to* Moses]

MOSES: [*As the shouting dies*] So it's de river Jordan?

FIRST SCOUT: Yes, suh.

MOSES: All we got to take is de city of Jericho.

FIRST SCOUT: Yes, suh.

MOSES: Joshua, you got to take charge of de fightin' men, an' Aaron's gotta stay by de priests.

JOSHUA: What about you?

MOSES: You are leavin' me behind. Joshua, you gonter get de fightin' men together and take dat city befo' sundown.

JOSHUA: It's a big city, Moses, wid walls all 'round it. We ain't got enough men.

MOSES: You'll take it, Joshua.

JOSHUA: Yes, suh, but how?

MOSES: Move up to de walls wid our people. Tell de priests to go wid you with de rams' horns. You start marchin' 'roun' dem walls, and den——

JOSHUA: Yes, suh.

MOSES: De Lawd'll take charge, jest as He's took charge ev'y time I've led you against a city. He ain't never failed, has He?

SEVERAL VOICES: No, Moses.

[*All raise their heads*]

MOSES: And He ain't goin' to fail us now. [*He prays. All bow*] Oh, Lawd, I'm turnin' over our brave young men to you, caize I know you don' want me to lead 'em any further. [*Rises*] Jest like you said, I've got to de Jordan but I cain't git over it. An' yere dey goin' now to take de city of Jericho. In a little while dey'll be marchin' 'roun' it. An' would you please be so good as to tell 'em what to do? Amen. [*To* Joshua] Go ahead. Ev'ybody follows Joshua now. Give de signal to move on wid ev'ything. [*A trumpet is heard*] You camp fo' de night in de city of Jericho.

[*Moses seats himself on the rock*]

JOSHUA: Cain't we help you, Moses?

MOSES: You go ahead. De Lawd's got his plans fo' me. Soun' de signal to march. [*Another trumpet call is heard. The company starts marching off.* Aaron *lingers a moment*] Take care of de Ark of de Covenant, Aaron.

AARON: Yes, brother. Goodbye.

MOSES: Goodbye, Aaron. [*The singing is resumed softly and dies away. The last of the marchers has disappeared*] Yere I is, Lawd. De chillun is goin' into de Promised Land. [*God enters from behind the hill. He walks to* Moses, *puts His hands on his shoulders*] You's with me, ain't you, Lawd?

GOD: Co'se I is.

MOSES: Guess I'm through, Lawd. Jest like you said I'd be, when I broke de tablets of de law. De ol' machine broke down.

GOD: Jest what was it I said to you, Moses? Do you remember?

MOSES: You said I couldn't go into de Promised Land.

GOD: Dat's so. But dat ain't all dey was to it.

MOSES: How you mean, Lawd?

GOD: Moses, you been a good man. You been a good leader of my people. You got me angry once, dat's true. And when you anger me I'm a God of Wrath. But I never meant you wasn't gonter have what was comin' to you. An' I ain't goin' to do you out of it, Moses. It's jest de country acrost de river dat you ain't gonter enter. You gonter have a Promised Land. I been gettin' it ready fo' you, fo' a long time. Kin you stand up?

MOSES: [Rising, with God's help] Yes, suh, Lawd.

GOD: Come on, I'm goin' to show it to you. We goin' up this hill to see it. Moses, it's a million times nicer dan de Land of Canaan.

[They start up the hill]

MOSES: I cain't hardly see.

GOD: Don't worry. Dat's jest caize you so old.

[They take a step or two up the hill, when Moses stops suddenly]

MOSES: Oh!

GOD: What's de matter?

MOSES: We cain't be doin' dis!

GOD: Co'se we kin!

MOSES: But I fo'got! I fo'got about Joshua and de fightin' men!

GOD: How about 'em?

MOSES: Dey're marchin' on Jericho. I tol' 'em to march aroun' de walls and den de Lawd would be dere to tell 'em what to do.

GOD: Dat's all right. He's dere.

MOSES: Den who's dis helpin' me up de hill?

GOD: Yo' faith, yo' God.

MOSES: And is you over dere helpin' dem too, Lawd? Is you goin' to tell dem poor chillun what to do?

GOD: Co'se I is. Listen, Moses. I'll show you how I'm helpin' dem.

[From the distance comes the blast of the rams' horns, the sound of crumbling walls, a roar, and a moment's silence. The Choir begins "Joshua Fit de Battle of Jericho" and continues through the rest of the scene]

MOSES: You did it, Lawd! You've tooken it! Listen to de chillun'—dey's in de Land of Canaan at last! You's de only God dey ever was, ain't you, Lawd?

GOD: [Quietly] Come on, ol' man.

[They continue up the hill. The stage is darkened]

MR. DESHEE: [In the dark] But even dat scheme didn' work. Caize after dey got into the Land of Canaan dey went to de dogs again. And dey went into bondage again. Only dis time it was in de city of Babylon.

[The Choir, which has been singing "Cain't Stay Away," stops as the next scene begins]

SCENE V.

Under a low ceiling is a room vaguely resembling a Negro night club in New Orleans. Two or three long tables run across the room, and on the left is a table on a dais with a gaudy canopy above it. The table bears a card marked "Reserved for King and guests."

Flashy young men and women are seated at the tables. About a dozen couples are dancing in the foreground to the tune of a jazz orchestra. The costumes are what would be worn at a Negro masquerade to represent the debauchees of Babylon.

FIRST MAN: When did yuh git to Babylon?

SECOND MAN: I jes' got in yesterday.

THIRD MAN: [Dancing] How do you like dis baby, Joe?

FOURTH MAN: Hot damn! She could be de King's pet!

A WOMAN: Anybody seen my papa?

THIRD MAN: Don' fo'git de dance at de High Priest's home to-morrow.

[The dance stops as a bugle call is heard. Enter Master of Ceremonies]

MASTER OF CEREMONIES: Stop! To-night's guest of honor, de King of Babylon, an' party of five.

[Enter the King and five girls. The King has on an imitation ermine cloak over his conventional clothes and wears a diamond tiara. All rise as the King enters, and sing, "Hail, de King of Bab—Bab—Babylon"]

KING: Wait till you see de swell table I got. [He crosses the stage to his table. The girls are jabbering] Remind me to send you a peck of rubies in de mo'nin'.

MASTER OF CEREMONIES: Ev'nin', King!

KING: Good ev'nin'. How's de party goin'?

MASTER OF CEREMONIES: Bes' one we ever had in Babylon, King.

KING: Any Jew boys yere?

MASTER OF CEREMONIES: [Indicating some of the others] Lot o' dem yere. I kin go git mo' if you want 'em.

KING: I was really referrin' to de High Priest. He's a 'tic'lar frien' o' mine an' he might drop in. You know what he look like?

MASTER OF CEREMONIES: No, suh, but I'll be on de look-out fo' him.

KING: O.K. Now le's have a li'l good time.

MASTER OF CEREMONIES: Yes, suh. [To the orchestra] Let 'er go, boys.

[The music begins, waiters appear with food and great urns painted gold and silver, from which they pour out wine for the guests. The Master of Ceremonies exits. The King's dancing-girls go to the middle of the floor, and start to dance. The King puts his arms about the waists of two girls, and draws them to him]

KING: Hot damn! Da's de way! Let de Jew boys see our gals kin dance better'n deirs. [*There is an ad lib.* babel of *"Da's de truth, King!" "I don't know —we got some good gals, too!"* etc.] Dey ain' nobody in de worl' like Babylon gals.

[*The dancing grows faster, the watchers keep time with handclaps. The door at the left opens suddenly, and the* Prophet, *a patriarchal, ragged figure, enters. He looks belligerently about the room, and is followed almost immediately by the* Master of Ceremonies]

PROPHET: Stop!

[*The music and the dancers halt*]

KING: What's the idea, bustin' up my party?

MASTER OF CEREMONIES: He said he was expected, King. I thought mebbe he was de——

KING: Did you think he was de High Priest of de Hebrews? Why, he's jest an' ol' bum! Throw dis ol' bum out o' yere! De High Priest is a fashion plate. Throw dis ol' bum out o' yere!

PROPHET: Stop!

[*Those who have been advancing to seize him stop, somewhat amused*]

KING: Wait a minute. Don't throw him out. Let's see what he has to say.

PROPHET: Listen to me, King of Babylon! I've been sent yere by de Lawd God Jehovah. Don't you dare lay a hand on de Prophet!

KING: Oh, you're a prophet, is yuh? Well, you know we don't keer much fo' prophets in dis part of de country.

PROPHET: Listen to me, sons and daughters of Babylon! Listen, you children of Israel dat's given yo'selves over to de evil ways of yo' oppressors! You're all wallowin' like hogs in sin, an' de wrath of God ain' goin' to be held back much longer! I'm tellin' you, repent befo' it's too late. Repent befo' Jehovah casts down de same fire dat burned up Sodom and Gomorrah. Repent befo' de——

[*During this scene yells increase as the* Prophet *continues. The* High Priest *enters left. He is a fat voluptuary, elaborately clothed in brightly colored robes. He walks in hand in hand with a gaudily dressed chippy*]

HIGH PRIEST: [*Noise stops*] Whoa, dere! What you botherin' the King fo'?

PROPHET: [*Wheeling*] And you, de High Priest of all Israel, walkin' de town wid a dirty li'l tramp.

KING: Seems to be a frien' o' yours, Jake.

HIGH PRIEST: [*Crossing to the* King *with his girl*] Aw, he's one of dem wild men, like Jeremiah and Isaiah. Don' let him bother you none.

[*Pushes* Prophet *aside and goes to* King's *table*]

PROPHET: You consort with harlots, an' yo' pollution in the sight of the Lawd. De Lawd God's goin' to smite you down, jest as he's goin' to smite down all dis wicked world!

[*Grabs* High Priest *and turns him around*]

KING: [*Angrily against the last part of the pre-ceding speech*] Wait a minute. I'm getting tired of this. Don' throw him out. Jest kill him!

[*There is the sound of a shot. The* Prophet *falls*]

PROPHET: Smite 'em down, Lawd, like you said. Dey ain't a decent person left in de whole world.

[*He dies. The* Master of Ceremonies, *revolver in hand, looks down at the* Prophet]

MASTER OF CEREMONIES: He's dead, King.

KING: Some of you boys take him out.

[*A couple of young men come from the background and walk off with the body*]

HIGH PRIEST: Don' know whether you should'a done that, King.

KING: Why not?

HIGH PRIEST: I don' know whether de Lawd would like it.

KING: Now, listen, Jake. You know yo' Lawd ain't payin' much attention to dis man's town. Except fo' you boys, it's tho'ly protected by de Gods o' Babylon.

HIGH PRIEST: I know, but jest de same——

KING: Look yere, s'pose I give you a couple hund'ed pieces of silver. Don' you s'pose you kin arrange to persuade yo God to keep his hands off?

HIGH PRIEST: [*Oilily*] Well of co'se we could try. I dunno how well it would work.

[*As the* High Priest *speaks, the* King *claps his hands.* Master of Ceremonies *enters with bag of money*]

KING: Yere it is.

HIGH PRIEST: [*Smiling*] I guess we kin square things up. [*He prays—whiningly*] Oh Lawd, please forgive my po' frien' de King o' Babylon. He didn't know what he was doin' an'——

[*There is a clap of thunder, darkness for a second. The lights go up and* God *is standing in the center of the room*]

GOD: [*In a voice of doom*] Dat's about enough. [*The guests are horrified*] I'se stood all I kin from you. I tried to make dis a good earth. I helped Adam, I helped Noah, I helped Moses, an' I helped David. What's de grain dat grew out of de seed? Sin! Nothin' but sin throughout de whole world. I've given you ev'y chance. I sent you warriors and prophets. I've given you laws and commandments, an' you betrayed my trust. Ev'ything I've given you, you've defiled. Ev'y time I've fo'given you, you've mocked me. An' now de High Priest of Israel tries to trifle wid my name. Listen, you chillun of darkness, yo' Lawd is tired. I'm tired of de struggle to make you worthy of de breath I gave you. I put you in bondage ag'in to cure you an' yo' worse dan you was amongst de flesh pots of Egypt. So I renounce you. Listen to the words of yo' Lawd God Jehovah, for dey is de last words yo' ever hear from me. I repent of dese people dat I have made and I will deliver dem no more.

[*There is darkness and cries of "Mercy!" "Have pity, Lawd!" "We didn' mean it, Lawd!"*]

"Forgive us, Lawd!" etc. The Choir *sings "Death's Gwinter Lay His Cold Icy Hands on Me" until the lights go up on the next scene]*

SCENE VI.

God *is writing at His desk. Outside, past the door, goes* Hosea, *a dignified old man, with wings like Jacob's.* God, *sensing his presence, looks up from the paper He is examining, and follows him out of the corner of His eye. Angrily He resumes His work as soon as* Hosea *is out of sight. There is a knock on the door.*

GOD: Who is it?

[Gabriel *enters*]

GABRIEL: It's de delegation, Lawd.

GOD: [*Wearily*] Tell 'em to come in. [Abraham, Isaac, Jacob, *and* Moses *enter*] Good mo'nin', gen'le-men.

THE VISITORS: Good mo'nin', Lawd.

GOD: What kin I do for you?

MOSES: You know, Lawd. Go back to our people.

GOD: [*Shaking His head*] Ev'ry day fo' hund'eds of years you boys have come in to ask dat same thing. De answer is still de same. I repented of de people I made. I said I would deliver dem no more. Good mo'nin', gen'lemen. [*The four visitors rise and exeunt.* Gabriel *remains*] Gabe, why do dey do it?

GABRIEL: I 'spect dey think you gonter change yo' mind.

GOD: [*Sadly*] Dey don' know me. [Hosea *again passes the door. His shadow shows on wall.* Gabriel *is perplexed, as he watches.* God *again looks surreptitiously over His shoulder at the passing figure*] I don' like dat, either.

GABRIEL: What, Lawd?

GOD: Dat man.

GABRIEL: He's just a prophet, Lawd. Dat's jest old Hosea. He jest come up the other day.

GOD: I know. He's one of de few dat's come up yere since I was on de earth last time.

GABRIEL: Ain' been annoyin' you, has he?

GOD: I don' like him walkin' past de door.

GABRIEL: All you got to do is tell him to stop, Lawd.

GOD: Yes, I know. I don' want to tell him. He's got a right up yere or he wouldn' be yere.

GABRIEL: You needn' be bothered by him hangin' aroun' de office all de time. I'll tell 'im. Who's he think he——

GOD: No, Gabe. I find it ain't in me to stop him. I sometimes jest wonder why he don' jest come in an' say hello.

GABRIEL: You want him to do that?

[*He moves as if to go to the door*]

GOD: He never has spoke to me, and if he don't wanta come in, I ain't gonter make him. But dat ain't de worst of it, Gabriel.

GABRIEL: What is, Lawd?

GOD: Ev'y time he goes past de door I hears a voice.

GABRIEL: One of de angels?

GOD: [*Shaking His head*] It's from de earth. It's a man.

GABRIEL: You mean he's prayin'?

GOD: No, he ain't exactly prayin'. He's jest talkin' in such a way dat I got to lissen. His name is Hezdrel.

GABRIEL: Is he on de books?

GOD: No, not yet. But ev'y time dat Hosea goes past I hear dat voice.

GABRIEL: Den tell it to stop.

GOD: I find I don' want to do that, either. Dey's gettin' ready to take Jerusalem down dere. Dat was my big fine city. Dis Hezdrel, he's jest one of de defenders. [*Suddenly and passionately, almost wildly*] I ain't comin' down. You hear me? I ain't comin' down. [*He looks at* Gabriel] Go ahead, Gabriel. 'Tend to yo' chores. I'm gonter keep wukkin' yere.

GABRIEL: I hates to see you feelin' like dis, Lawd.

GOD: Dat's all right. Even bein' God ain't a bed of roses. [Gabriel *exits.* Hosea's *shadow is on the wall. For a second* Hosea *hesitates.* God *looks at the wall. Goes to window*] I hear you. I know yo' fightin' bravely, but I ain't comin' down. Oh, why don' you leave me alone? You know you ain't talkin' to me. *Is* you talkin' to me? I cain't stand yo' talkin' dat way. I kin only hear part of what yo' sayin', and it puzzles me. Don' you know you cain't puzzle God? [*A pause. Then, tenderly*] Do you want me to come down dere ve'y much? You know I said I wouldn't come down? [*Fiercely*] Why don' he answer me a little? [*With clenched fists, looks down through the window*] Listen! I'll tell you what I'll do. I ain't goin' to promise you anythin', and I ain't goin' to do nothin' to help you. I'm jest feelin' a little low, an' I'm only comin down to make myself feel a little better, dat's all.

[*The stage is darkened.* Choir *begins "A Blind Man Stood in de Middle of de Road," and continues until the lights go up on the next scene*]

SCENE VII.

It is a shadowed corner beside the walls of the temple in Jerusalem. The light of camp fires flickers on the figure of Hezdrel, *who was* Adam *in Part I. He stands in the same position* Adam *held when first discovered but in his right hand is a sword, and his left is in a sling. Around him are several prostrate bodies. Pistol and cannon shots, then a trumpet call. Six young men enter from left in command of a* Corporal. *They are all armed.*

CORPORAL: De fightin' stopped fo' de night, Hezdrel.

HEZDREL: Yes?

CORPORAL: Dey're goin' to begin ag'in at cockcrow. [Man *enters, crosses the stage and exits*] Herod say he's goin' to take de temple to-morrow, burn de books and de Ark of de Covenant, and put us all to de sword.

HEZDREL: Yo' ready, ain't you?

EVERYBODY: Yes, Hezdrel.

HEZDREL: Did de food get in through the hole in de city wall?

[*Two* Soldiers *enter, cross the stage and exeunt*]

CORPORAL: Yessuh, we's goin' back to pass it out now.

HEZDREL: Good. Any mo' of our people escape to-day?

CORPORAL: Ol' Herod's got de ol' hole covered up now, but fifteen of our people got out a new one we made.

[*Other* Soldiers *enter, cross the stage and exeunt*]

HEZDREL: Good. Take dese yere wounded men back and git 'em took care of.

CORPORAL: Yes, suh.

[*They pick up the bodies on the ground and carry them off stage as* Hezdrel *speaks*]

HEZDREL: So dey gonter take de temple in de mo'nin'? We'll be waitin' for 'em. Jest remember, boys, when dey kill us we leap out of our skins, right into de lap of God.

[*The* Men *disappear with the wounded; from the deep shadow upstage comes God*]

GOD: Hello, Hezdrel—Adam.

HEZDREL: [*Rubbing his forehead*] Who is you?

GOD: Me? I'm jest an ol' preacher, from back in de hills.

HEZDREL: What you doin' yere?

GOD: I heard you boys was fightin'. I jest wanted to see how it was goin'.

HEZDREL: Well, it ain't goin' so well.

GOD: Dey got you skeered, huh?

HEZDREL: Look yere, who is you, a spy in my brain?

GOD: Cain't you see I'se one of yo' people?

HEZDREL: Listen, Preacher, we ain't skeered. We's gonter be killed, but we ain't skeered.

GOD: I'se glad to hear dat. Kin I ask you a question, Hezdrel?

HEZDREL: What is it?

GOD: How is it you is so brave?

HEZDREL: Caize we got faith, dat's why.

GOD: Faith? In who?

HEZDREL: In our dear Lawd God.

GOD: But God say he abandoned ev'y one down yere.

HEZDREL: Who say dat? Who dare say dat of de Lawd God of Hosea?

GOD: De God of Hosea?

HEZDREL: You heard me. Look yere, you *is* a spy in my brain!

GOD: No, I ain't, Hezdrel, I'm jest puzzled. You ought to know dat.

HEZDREL: How come you so puzzled 'bout de God of Hosea?

GOD: I don't know. Maybe I jest don' hear things. You see, I live 'way back in de hills.

HEZDREL: What you wanter find out?

GOD: Ain't de God of Hosea de same Jehovah dat was de God of Moses?

HEZDREL: [*Contemptuously*] No. Dat ol' God of wrath and vengeance? We have de God dat Hosea preached to us. He's de one God.

GOD: Who's he?

HEZDREL: [*Reverently*] De God of mercy.

GOD: Hezdrel, don' you think dey must be de same God?

HEZDREL: I don' know. I ain't bothered to think much about it. Maybe dey is. Maybe our God is de same ol' God. I guess He jest got tired of His appearance dat ol' way.

GOD: What you mean, Hezdrel?

HEZDREL: Oh, dat ol' God dat walked de earth in de shape of a man. I guess he lived with man so much dat all he seen was de sins in man. Dat's what made him de God of wrath and vengeance. Co'se he made Hosea. An' Hosea never would a found what mercy was unless dere was a little of it in God, too. Anyway, he ain't a fearsome God no mo'. Hosea showed us dat.

GOD: How you s'pose Hosea found dat mercy?

HEZDREL: De only way he could find it. De only way I found it. De only way anyone could find it.

GOD: How's dat?

HEZDREL: Through sufferin'.

GOD: [*After a pause*] What if dey kill you in de mo'nin', Hezdrel?

HEZDREL: If dey do, dey do. Dat's all.

GOD: Herod say he's goin' to burn de temple—

HEZDREL: So he say.

GOD: And burn de Ark an' de books. Den dat's de end of de books, ain't it?

HEZDREL: [*Buoyantly*] What you mean? If he burns dem things in dere? Naw. Dem's jest copies.

GOD: Where is de others?

HEZDREL: [*Tapping his head*] Dey's a set in yere. Fifteen got out through de hole in the city wall to-day. A hundred and fifty got out durin' de week. Each of 'em is a set of de books. Dey's scattered safe all over de countryside now, jest waitin' to git pen and paper fo' to put 'em down ag'in.

GOD: [*Proudly*] Dey cain't lick you, kin dey, Hezdrel?

HEZDREL: [*Smiling*] I know dey cain't. [*Trumpet*] You better get out o' yere, Preacher, if you wanter carry de news to yo' people. It'll soon be daylight.

GOD: I'm goin'. [*He takes a step upstage and stops*] Want me to take any message?

HEZDREL: Tell de people in de hills dey ain't nobody like de Lawd God of Hosea.

GOD: I will; if dey kill you to-morrow I'll bet dat God of Hosea'll be waitin' for you.

HEZDREL: I *know* he will.

GOD: [*Quietly*] Thank you, Hezdrel.

HEZDREL: Fo' what?

GOD: Fo' tellin' me so much. You see, I been so far away, I guess I was jest way behin' de times.

[*He exits. Pause, then trumpet sounds. Hezdrel paces back and forth once or twice. Another young* Soldier *appears. Other men enter and stand grouped about* Hezdrel]

SECOND OFFICER: [*Excitedly*] De cock's jest crowed, Hezdrel. Dey started de fightin' ag'in.

HEZDREL: We's ready for 'em. Come on, boys. [*From the darkness upstage comes another group of soldiers*] Dis is de day dey say dey'll git us. Le's fight till de last man goes. What d'you say?

CORPORAL: Le's go, Hezdrel!

HEZDREL: [*Calling left*] Give 'em ev'ything boys! [*There is a movement toward the left, a bugle call and the sound of distant battle. The lights go out. The Choir is heard singing, "March On," triumphantly. They continue to sing after the lights go up on the next scene*]

SCENE VIII.

It is the same setting as the Fish Fry Scene in Part I. The same angels are present but the Choir, *instead of marching, is standing in a double row on an angle upstage right. God is seated in an armchair near center. He faces the audience. As the* Choir *continues to sing,* Gabriel *enters, unnoticed by the chattering angels. He looks at* God, *who is staring thoughtfully toward the audience.*

GABRIEL: You look a little pensive, Lawd. [*God nods his head*] Have a seegar, Lawd?

GOD: No, thanks, Gabriel.

[Gabriel *goes to the table, accepts a cup of custard; chats with the angel behind the table for a moment as he sips, puts the cup down and returns to the side of* God]

GABRIEL: You look awful pensive, Lawd. You been sittin' yere, lookin' dis way, an awful long time. Is it somethin' serious, Lawd?

GOD: Very serious, Gabriel.

GABRIEL: [*Awed by His tone*] Lawd, is de time come for me to blow?

GOD: Not yet, Gabriel. I'm just thinkin'.

GABRIEL: What about, Lawd?

[*Puts up hand. Singing stops*]

GOD: 'Bout somethin' de boy tol' me. Somethin' 'bout Hosea, and himself. How dey foun' somethin'.

GABRIEL: What, Lawd?

GOD: Mercy. [*A pause*] Through *sufferin'*, he said.

GABRIEL: Yes, Lawd.

GOD: I'm tryin' to find it, too. It's awful impo'tant. It's awful impo'tant to all de people on my earth. Did he mean dat even God must suffer?

[God *continues to look out over the audience for a moment and then a look of surprise comes into His face. He sighs. In the distance a voice cries*]

THE VOICE: Oh, look at him! Oh, look, dey goin' to make him carry it up dat high hill! Dey goin' to nail him to it! Oh, dat's a terrible burden for one man to carry!

[God *rises and murmurs "Yes!" as if in recognition. The heavenly beings have been watching Him closely, and now, seeing Him smile gently, draw back, relieved. All the angels burst into "Hallelujah, King Jesus." God continues to smile as the lights fade away. The singing becomes fortissimo*]

CURTAIN

Thornton Wilder

(1897– ———)

Thornton Niven Wilder has the double distinction of being a successful novelist and an original dramatist. His two important full-length plays—the Pulitzer Prize drama *Our Town* and *The Skin of Our Teeth*—reflect the theme of all Wilder's major writing—man in the universe. He belongs to the select few who have managed to restore the primacy of imagination to the drama in a completely modern idiom.

Born in Madison, Wisconsin, Wilder spent part of his childhood in China, returning to the United States to complete his high-school education. His college studies were interrupted by his service in the Coast Artillery Corps in the First World War, but he returned to complete them and then spent a graduate year studying archaeology at the American Academy in Rome. During and after his further graduate work at Princeton, he taught at the Lawrenceville School. From 1930 to 1936 he was a member of the faculty of the University of Chicago. In the Second World War he served with the Air Forces Intelligence in North Africa and Italy.

Because of his broad knowledge of European culture, Wilder was called upon by producers to adapt to the stage various foreign works, and his literary activities have won awards for him not only in the United States but from other countries as well.

It was as a novelist that Wilder first won recognition. He received high praise for *The Cabala* (1925) and was awarded a Pulitzer Prize for his philosophical novel *The Bridge of San Luis Rey* (1927). Subsequently, he wrote *The Woman of Andros* (1930) and *Heaven's My Destination* (1935). Much later, after winning success in the theatre, he proved that he was still adept at writing noteworthy fiction, with his semi-Shavian story of Julius Caesar, *The Ides of March* (1948).

Wilder's career in the theatre started inauspiciously with a play called *The Trumpet Shall Sound*, which Richard Boleslavsky's Laboratory Theatre produced in New York in 1926. Wilder then brought out two collections of one-act plays, *The Angel That Troubled the Waters* (1928) and *The Long Christmas Dinner* (1931). Some of these one-acters are notable as early examples of Wilder's interest in the everyday events of simple life and of his fondness for nonrealistic styles of play construction. In 1932, he adapted André Obey's *Lucrece* for Katherine Cornell.

It was rather late in his career that Wilder made his special impression on the theatre. In 1938, in addition to adapting a German play, *The Merchant of Yonkers*, which failed on Broadway, he made theatrical history with *Our Town*. This play received a brilliant production on a bare stage from the volatile genius of the American theatre Jed Harris; it had for its chief actor the lovable performer Frank Craven, who played the Narrator. *Our Town* enjoyed a long run on Broadway, toured widely, and has been a favorite production in the little theatres throughout the United States. In 1942, Wilder startled playgoers with a uniquely stylized drama, *The Skin of Our Teeth*, which telescoped human history in the story of a New Jersey suburban family. Although it did not succeed as well as *Our Town*, *The Skin of Our Teeth* made a deep impression. It was the profoundest commentary on the Second World War crisis of which the American theatre proved capable. In 1948, Wilder's adaptation of a play by Sartre, *The Victors*, received an experimental production. But it was not written in Wilder's characteristic vein, and it throws no light on the nonrealistic dramatic art for which he will be remembered.

Our Town is generally regarded as one of the best examples of stylized dramaturgy developed by an American. From a historical point of view, it is, in fact, an example of a style better represented by the artistry of stage designers and directors than by the work of playwrights. From 1910 on, reports of miraculous productions had been drifting to the United States from the Continent. In these productions, the style of the stagecraft called attention to the nonrepresentational or "theatrical" nature of stage art. Theatre was treated frankly as theatre and not as a means of creating an illusion of reality. "Theatricalism" had effective proponents abroad, such as Max Reinhardt before and Eugene Vakhtangov and Vsevolod Meyerhold after the First World War. Vakhtangov, for example, styled his production of the Jewish folk drama *The Dybbuk* for the Habimah troupe with expressive rather than realistic stage settings, with dance rhythms, and with conspicuously theatrical acting. Also, he attracted considerable attention by staging Gozzi's Italian classic *Princess Turandot* in the Chinese convention. Property men appeared in full view of the audience, shifted scenes in front of the playgoer, and discoursed among themselves, even making commentary on the action.

With theatricalism, directors restored the connection between the stage and the auditorium, or between the actor and the spectator, that had existed in the days of the platform and the apron stage, before the realistic, peepshow type of theatre had erected the fourth-wall convention. The play written for theatricalism was so constructed as to present a view of life rather than a literal copy of it, which is what realism tries and pretends to provide. The actor might costume himself in public, frankly set the scene for his demonstration of an idea or situation, address the spectator, and in all respects communicate with the audience. It is for this nonrealistic *presentation,* instead of *representation,* of life that the writer Alexander Bakshy invented the term "presentational" theatre. In America, before *Our Town,* we had had such theatricalist plays as John Howard Lawson's jazz symphony of American life *Processional* (1924) and Eva Le Gallienne's *Alice in Wonderland* (1933).

Our Town is nonillusionistic, presentational drama. The principal actor is the "stage manager." He sets up his demonstration, calling for skeletal or fragmentary stage settings to help the audience visualize a particular situation; he plays the part of a philosophical druggist who has had many occasions to observe the town's characters; and he acts as host, master of ceremonies, commentator, philosopher, and friend to the spectators. He takes them into his confidence and proceeds to communicate to them his knowledge of the little town of Grover's Corners and its people, along with his thoughts about living and dying. In form, *Our Town* achieves, in short, a significant presentation or, as Gordon Craig would have said, "a noble artificiality."

Locating *Our Town* historically and explaining its style is, however, less important than experiencing the play. Once we become acquainted with a dramatic style, it rapidly loses novelty and ceases to have any value apart from the life and feeling it conveys. The formal structure calls to mind the scaffolding on a building in the process of construction. The important question is: what sort of building is arising behind the wooden platforms? The theatricalist form of *Our Town* enables the author to build the kind of play he wants to give us—an informal, intimate, and compellingly human drama. It is a work of love and of wisdom: it pulsates with Wilder's love for the New England environment and way of life and for life itself; and it is pervaded by a wisdom about these things that is as down to earth as the life which the author chronicles.

The content of the play is so simple that it is momentous, for it deals primarily with the *life* in life. Hence Wilder can dismiss all topical issues and situations from his demonstration after briefly noting that they appear in Grover's Corners, as they do everywhere else. Grover's Corners is a little town in New Hampshire, and it can be located by latitude and longitude. But it is all places, and it is located in the universe. Nothing sums up the essence of Wilder's philosophy in *Our Town* better than the address on a letter sent to a Grover's Corners' girl by a humorist who, to Wilder, was probably unknowingly the profoundest person in the world: "June Crofut, the Crofut Farm, Grover's Corners, Sultan County, New Hampshire, United States of America, Continent of North America, Western Hemisphere, the Earth, the Solar System, the Universe, the Mind of God."

Without this comprehensive view, *Our Town* would have to be set down as a broken play, with one part concerned with life and the other with death, or with one part presenting "reality" and the other retailing fantasy, or "metaphysics." For Wilder, however, the two parts are one. The dying gives significance to the living, and the "metaphysical" is included in the "real." "The mind of God" idea may remind us of transcendentalism or Emersonianism so characteristic of New England—the concept that everything is interpenetrated by spirit. But it is homespun philosophy that Wilder's informal presentation gives us, and it serves such simple ends as making us treasure ordinary life just as it is and reminding us to live it to the full before our day is over. "There go all of us," Brooks Atkinson has expressed the meaning of the play, "not 'but for the grace of God,' but 'by the grace of God.' " The play deals ever so unostentatiously, as Atkinson has said, with "the days and deaths of the brotherhood of man." Wilder's cultivated and sophisticated mind reduces our human complexity to its irreducible simplicity.

BIBLIOGRAPHY: Brooks Atkinson, *Broadway Scrapbook* (pp. 85–88, 213–217), 1947; John Mason Brown, *Two on the Aisle* (pp. 187–193), 1938; Edmond M. Gagey, *Revolution in the American Drama* (pp. 107–111), 1947.

OUR TOWN

By Thornton Wilder

ACT I.

No curtain. No scenery. The audience, arriving, sees an empty stage in half-light. Presently the Stage Manager, *hat on and pipe in mouth, enters and begins placing a table and several chairs down stage left, and a table and chairs down stage right. "Left" and "right" are from the point of view of the actor facing the audience. "Up" is towards the back wall. As the house lights go down he has finished setting the stage and leaning against the right proscenium pillar watches the late arrivals in the audience. When the auditorium is in complete darkness he speaks:*

STAGE MANAGER: This play is called "Our Town." It was written by Thornton Wilder, produced and directed by A....; [or: produced by A....; directed by B....]. In it you will see Miss C....; Miss D....; Miss E....; and Mr. F....; Mr. G....; Mr. H....; and many others. The name of the town is Grover's Corners, New Hampshire,—just across the Massachusetts line: longitude 42 degrees 40 minutes; latitude 70 degrees 37 minutes. The First Act shows a day in our town. The day is May 7, 1901. The time is just before dawn. [*A rooster crows*] The sky is beginning to show some streaks of light over in the East there, behind our mount'in. The morning star always gets wonderful bright the minute before it has to go. [*He stares at it for a moment, then goes up stage*] Well, I'd better show you how our town lies. Up here—[*That is: parallel with the back wall*] is Main Street. Way back there is the railway station; tracks go that way. Polish Town's across the tracks and some Canuck families. [*Toward the left*] Over there is the Congregational Church; across the street's the Presbyterian. Methodist and Unitarian are over there. Baptist is down in the holla' by the river. Catholic Church is over beyond the tracks. Here's the Town Hall and Post Office combined; jail's in the basement. Bryan once made a speech from these steps here. Along here's a row of stores. Hitching-posts and horse blocks in front of them. First automobile's going to come along in about five years, belonged to Banker Cartwright, our richest citizen . . . lives in the big white house up on the hill. Here's the grocery store and here's Mr. Morgan's drugstore. Most everybody in town manages to look into those two stores once a day. Public School's over yonder. High School's still farther over. Quarter of nine mornings, noontimes, and three o'clock afternoons, the hull town can hear the yelling and screaming from those schoolyards. [*He approaches the table and chairs down stage right*] This is our doctor's house,—Doc Gibbs'. This is the back door. [*Two arched trellises are pushed out, one by each proscenium pillar*] There's some scenery for those who think they have to have scenery. There's a garden here. Corn . . . peas . . . beans . . . hollyhocks . . . heliotrope . . . and a lot of burdock. [*Crosses the stage*] In those days our newspaper come out twice a week,—the Grover's Corners *Sentinel,*—and this is Editor Webb's house. And this is Mrs. Webb's garden. Just like Mrs. Gibbs's, only it's got a lot of sunflowers, too. Right here,—big butternut tree. [*He returns to his place by the right proscenium pillar and looks at the audience for a minute*] Nice town, y'know what I mean? Nobody very remarkable ever come out of it,—s'far as we know. The earliest tombstones in the cemetery up there on the mountain say 1670-1680—they're Grovers and Cartwrights and Gibbses and Herseys—same names as are around here now. Well, as I said: it's about dawn. The only lights on in town are in a cottage over by the tracks where a Polish mother's just had twins. And in the Joe Crowell house, where Joe Junior's getting up so as to deliver the paper. And in the depot, where Shorty Hawkins is gettin' ready to flag the 5:45 for Boston. [*A train whistle is heard. The* Stage Manager *takes out his watch and nods*] Naturally, out in the country—all around—they've been lights on for some time, what with milkin's and so on. But town people sleep late. So—another day's begun. There's Doc Gibbs comin' down Main Street now, comin' back from that baby case. And here's his wife comin' downstairs to get breakfast. Doc Gibbs died in 1930. The new hospital's named after him. Mrs. Gibbs died first—long time ago in fact. She went out to visit her daughter, Rebecca, who married an insurance man in Canton, Ohio, and died there—pneumonia—but her body was brought back here. She's up in the cemetery there now—in with a whole mess of Gibbses and Herseys —she was Julia Hersey 'fore she married Doc Gibbs in the Congregational Church over there. In our town we like to know the facts about everybody. —That's Doc Gibbs. And there comes Joe Crowell, Jr., delivering Mr. Webb's *Sentinel*.

[Dr. Gibbs *has been coming along Main Street from the left. At the point where he would turn to approach his house, he stops, sets down his—imaginary—black bag, takes off his hat, and rubs his face with fatigue, using an enormous handkerchief. Mrs. Gibbs has entered her kitchen, gone through the motions of put-*

ting wood into a stove, lighting it, and preparing breakfast. Suddenly, Joe Crowell, Jr., *starts down Main Street from the right, hurling imaginary newspapers into doorways]*

JOE CROWELL, JR.: Morning, Doc Gibbs.

DR. GIBBS: Morning, Joe.

JOE CROWELL, JR.: Somebody been sick, Doc?

DR. GIBBS: No. Just some twins born over in Polish Town.

JOE CROWELL, JR.: Do you want your paper now?

DR. GIBBS: Yes, I'll take it.—Anything serious goin' on in the world since Wednesday?

JOE CROWELL, JR.: Yessir. My schoolteacher, Miss Foster, 's getting married to a fella over in Concord.

DR. GIBBS: I declare.—How do you boys feel about that?

JOE CROWELL, JR.: Well, of course, it's none of my business,—but I think if a person starts out to be a teacher, she ought to stay one.

DR. GIBBS: How's your knee, Joe?

JOE CROWELL, JR.: Fine, Doc, I never think about at all. Only like you said, it always tells me when 's going to rain.

DR. GIBBS: What's it telling you today? Goin' to rain?

JOE CROWELL, JR.: No, sir.

DR. GIBBS: Sure?

JOE CROWELL, JR.: Yessir.

DR. GIBBS: Knee ever make a mistake?

JOE CROWELL, JR.: No, sir. [Joe *goes off.* Dr. Gibbs *stands reading his paper]*

STAGE MANAGER: Here comes Howie Newsome delivering the milk.

[Howie Newsome *comes along Main Street, passes* Doctor Gibbs, *comes down the center of the stage, leaves some bottles at* Mrs. Webb's *back door, and crosses the stage to* Mrs. Gibbs's]

HOWIE NEWSOME: Git-ap, Bessie. What's the matter with you?—Morning, Doc.

DR. GIBBS: Morning, Howie.

HOWIE NEWSOME: Somebody sick?

DR. GIBBS: Pair of twins over to Mrs. Goruslawi's.

HOWIE NEWSOME: Twins, eh? This town's gettin' bigger every year.

DR. GIBBS: Going to rain, Howie?

HOWIE NEWSOME: No, no. Fine day—that'll burn through. Come on, Bessie.

DR. GIBBS: Hello Bessie. [*He strokes her*] How old is she, Howie?

HOWIE NEWSOME: Goin' on seventeen. Bessie's all mixed up about the route ever since the Lockharts stopped takin' their quart of milk every day. She wants to leave 'em a quart just the same—keeps holding me the hull trip. [*He reaches* Mrs. Gibbs's back door. *She is waiting for him]*

MRS. GIBBS: Good morning, Howie.

HOWIE NEWSOME: Morning, Mrs. Gibbs. Doc's just comin' down the street.

MRS. GIBBS: Is he? Seems like you're late today?

HOWIE NEWSOME: Yes. Somep'n went wrong with the separator. Don't know what 'twas. [*He goes back to Main Street, clucks for Bessie and goes off right.* Dr. Gibbs *reaches his home and goes in]*

MRS. GIBBS: Everything all right?

DR. GIBBS: Yes. I declare—easy as kittens.

MRS. GIBBS: Bacon'll be ready in a minute. Set down and drink your coffee. Child-*run!* Child-*run!* Time to get up.—George! Rebecca!—You can catch a couple hours' sleep this morning, can't you?

DR. GIBBS: Hm! . . . Mrs. Wentworth's coming at eleven. Guess I know what it's about, too. Her stummick ain't what it ought to be.

MRS. GIBBS: All told, you won't get more'n three hours' sleep. Frank Gibbs, I don't know what's goin' to become of you. I do wish I could get you to go away some place and take a rest. I think it would do you good.

MRS. WEBB: Emileeee! Time to get up! Wally! Seven o'clock!

MRS. GIBBS: I declare, you got to speak to George. Seems like something's come over him lately. He's no help to me at all. I can't even get him to cut me some wood.

DR. GIBBS: Is he sassy to you?

MRS. GIBBS: No. He just whines! All he thinks about is that baseball—George! Rebecca! You'll be late for school.

DR. GIBBS: M-m-m. . . .

MRS. GIBBS: George!

DR. GIBBS: George, look sharp!

GEORGE'S VOICE: Yes, Pa!

DR. GIBBS: [*As he goes off the stage*] Don't you hear your mother calling you?

MRS. WEBB: Walleee! Emileee! You'll be late for school! Walleee! You wash yourself good or I'll come up and do it myself.

REBECCA GIBBS'S VOICE: Ma! What dress shall I wear?

MRS. GIBBS: Don't make a noise. Your father's been out all night and needs his sleep. I washed and ironed the blue gingham for you special.

REBECCA: Ma, I hate that dress.

MRS. GIBBS: Oh, hush-up-with-you.

REBECCA: Every day I go to school dressed like a sick turkey.

MRS. GIBBS: Now, Rebecca, don't be impossible. You always look *very* nice.

REBECCA: Mama, George's throwing soap at me.

MRS. GIBBS: I'll come up and slap the both of you,—that's what I'll do.

[*A factory whistle sounds. The children enter and take their places at the breakfast tables:* Emily *and* Wally Webb; George *and* Rebecca Gibbs]

STAGE MANAGER: We've got a factory in our town too,—hear it? Makes blankets. Cartwrights own it and it brung 'em a fortune.

MRS. WEBB: Children! Now I won't have it. Breakfast is just as good as any other meal and I won't have you gobbling like wolves. It'll stunt your growth,—that's a fact. Put away your book, Wally.

WALLY: Aw, Ma!

MRS. WEBB: You know the rule's well as I do—no books at table. As for me, I'd rather have my children healthy than bright.

EMILY: I'm both, Mama: you know I am. I'm the brightest girl in school for my age. I have a wonderful memory.

MRS. WEBB: Eat your breakfast.

WALLY: I'm bright, too, when I'm looking at my stamp collection.

MRS. GIBBS: I'll speak to your father about it when he's rested. Seems to me twenty-five cents a week's enough for a boy your age. I declare I don't know how you spend it all.

GEORGE: Aw, Ma,—I gotta lotta things to buy.

MRS. GIBBS: Strawberry phosphates—that's what you spend it on.

GEORGE: I don't see how Rebecca comes to have so much money. She has more'n a dollar.

REBECCA: [Spoon in mouth, dreamily] I've been saving it up gradual.

MRS. GIBBS: Well, dear, I think it's a good thing every now and then to spend some.

REBECCA: Mama, do you know what I love most in the world—do you?—Money.

MRS. GIBBS: Eat your breakfast.

[The school bell is heard]

THE CHILDREN: Mama, there's the first bell.—I gotta hurry.—I don't want any more.

MRS. WEBB: Walk fast, but you don't have to run. Wally, pull up your pants at the knee. Stand up straight, Emily.

MRS. GIBBS: Tell Miss Foster I send her my best congratulations—can you remember that?

REBECCA: Yes, Ma.

MRS. GIBBS: You look real nice, Rebecca. Pick up your feet.

ALL: Good-by. [The children from the two houses join at the center of the stage and go up to Main Street, then off left. Mrs. Gibbs fills her apron with food for the chickens and comes down to the footlights]

MRS. GIBBS: Here, chick, chick, chick. No, go away, you. Go away. Here, chick, chick, chick. What's the matter with you? Fight, fight, fight,—that's all you do. Hm . . . you don't belong to me. Where'd you come from? [She shakes her apron] Oh, don't be so scared. Nobody's going to hurt you.

[Mrs. Webb is sitting by her trellis, stringing beans]

MRS. GIBBS: Good morning, Myrtle. How's your cold?

MRS. WEBB: Well, it's better; but I told Charles I didn't know as I'd go to choir practice tonight. Wouldn't be any use.

MRS. GIBBS: Just the same, you come to choir practice, Myrtle, and try it.

MRS. WEBB: Well, if I don't feel any worse than I do now I probably will. While I'm resting myself I thought I'd string some of these beans.

MRS. GIBBS: [Rolling up her sleeves as she crosses the stage for a chat] Let me help you. Beans have been good this year.

MRS. WEBB: I've decided to put up forty quarts if it kills me. The children say they hate 'em but I notice they're able to get 'em down all winter. [Pause]

MRS. GIBBS: Now, Myrtle, I've got to tell you something, because if I don't tell somebody I'll burst.

MRS. WEBB: Why, Julia Gibbs!

MRS. GIBBS: Here, give me some more of those beans. Myrtle, did one of those second-hand furniture men from Boston come to see you last Friday?

MRS. WEBB: No—o.

MRS. GIBBS: Well, he called on me. First I thought he was a patient wantin' to see Dr. Gibbs. 'N he wormed his way into my parlor, and, Myrtle Webb, he offered me three hundred and fifty dollars for Grandmother Wentworth's highboy, as I'm sittin' here!

MRS. WEBB: Why, Julia Gibbs!

MRS. GIBBS: He did! That old thing! Why, it was so big I didn't know where to put it and I almost give it to Cousin Hester Wilcox.

MRS. WEBB: Well, you're going to take it, aren't you?

MRS. GIBBS: I don't know.

MRS. WEBB: You don't know—three hundred and fifty dollars. What's come over you?

MRS. GIBBS: Well, if I could get the Doctor to take the money and go away some place on a real trip, I'd sell it like that.—Myrtle, ever since I was that high I've had the thought that I'd like to see Paris, France. I suppose I'm crazy.

MRS. WEBB: Oh, I know what you mean.—How does the Doctor feel about it?

MRS. GIBBS: Well, I did beat about the bush a little and said that if I got a legacy—that's the way I put it—I'd make him take me somewhere.

MRS. WEBB: M-m-m. . . . What did he say?

MRS. GIBBS: You know how he is. I haven't heard a serious word out of him, ever since I've known him. No, he said, it might make him discontented with Grover's Corners to go traipsin' about Europe; better let well enough alone, he says. Every two years he makes a trip to the battlefields of the Civil War and that's enough treat for anybody, he says.

MRS. WEBB: Well, Mr. Webb just admires the way Dr. Gibbs knows everything about the Civil War. Mr. Webb's a good mind to give up Napoleon and move over to the Civil War, only Dr. Gibbs being one of the greatest experts in the country just makes him despair.

MRS. GIBBS: It's a fact! Doctor Gibbs is never happy as when he's at Antietam or Gettysburg. The times I've walked over those hills, Myrtle, stopping at every bush and pacing it all out, like we was going to buy it.

MRS. WEBB: Well, if that second-hand man's really serious about buyin' it, Julia, you sell it. And then you'll get to see Paris, all right.

MRS. GIBBS: Oh, I'm sorry I mentioned it. Only it seems to me that once in your life before you die you ought to see a country where they don't talk and think in English and don't even want to.

[*The* Stage Manager *returns to the center of the stage*]

STAGE MANAGER: That'll do. That'll do. Thank you very much, ladies. [Mrs. Gibbs *and* Mrs. Webb *gather up their things, return into their homes and disappear*] Now we're going to skip a few hours in the day at Grover's Corners. But before we go on I want you to know some more things about the town,—all kinds of things. So I've asked Prof. Willard of our State University to come down here and sketch in a few details of our past history,—kind of scientific account, you might say. Is Prof. Willard here? [Prof. Willard, *a rural savant, pince-nez on a wide satin ribbon, enters from the right with some notes in his hand*] May I introduce Prof. Willard of our University. A few brief notes, thank you, Professor,—unfortunately our time is limited.

PROF. WILLARD: Grover's Corners . . . let me see . . . Grover's Corners lies on the old Archaeozoic granite of the Appalachian range. I may say it's some of the oldest land in the world. We're very proud of that. A shelf of Devonian basalt crosses it with vestiges of Mesozoic shale, and some sandstone outcroppings; but that's all more recent: two hundred, three hundred million years old. Some highly interesting fossils have been found. . . . I may say: unique fossils . . . two miles out of town, in Silas Peckham's cow pasture. They can be seen at the museum in our University at any time. Did you wish the meteorological conditions?

STAGE MANAGER: Thank you. We would.

PROF. WILLARD: The mean precipitation is 40 inches. The mean annual temperature is 43 degrees, ranging between 102 degrees in the shade, and 38 degrees below zero in winter. The . . . the . . . uh . . .

STAGE MANAGER: Thank you, Professor. And have you Prof. Gruber's notes on the history of human life here?

PROF. WILLARD: Hm . . . yes . . . anthropological data: Early Amerindian stock. Cotahatchee tribes . . . no evidence before the Tenth Century of this era . . . hm . . . now entirely disappeared . . . possible traces in three families. Migration toward the end of the Seventeenth Century of English brachycephalic blue-eyed stock . . . for the most part. Since then some influx of Slav and Mediterranean types. . . .

STAGE MANAGER: And the population, Prof. Willard?

PROF. WILLARD: Within the town limits: 2,640.

The postal district brings in 507 more. Mortality and birth-rates are constant; by MacPherson's gauge: 6.032.

STAGE MANAGER: Thank you *very* much, Professor. We're all very much obliged to you, I'm sure.

PROF. WILLARD: Not at all, sir; not at all.

STAGE MANAGER: This way, Professor, and thank you again. [*Exit* Prof. Willard] Now the political and social report: Editor Webb.—Oh, Mr. Webb?

[Mrs. Webb *appears at her back door*]

MRS. WEBB: He'll be here in a minute. . . . He just cut his hand while he was eatin' an apple.

STAGE MANAGER: Thank you, Mrs. Webb.

MRS. WEBB: Charles! Everybody's waitin'. [*Exit* Mrs. Webb]

STAGE MANAGER: Mr. Webb is Publisher and Editor of The Grover's Corners *Sentinel*. That's our local paper, y'know.

[Mr. Webb *enters from his house, pulling on his coat. His finger is bound in a handkerchief*]

MR. WEBB: Hm. . . . I don't have to tell you that we're run here by a Board of Selectmen.—All males vote at the age of 21. Women vote indirect. We're lower middle-class, sprinkling of professional men . . . 10% illiterate laborers. Politically, we're 86% Republicans; 6% Democrats; 4% Socialists; rest, indifferent. Religiously, we're 85% Protestants; 12% Catholics; rest, indifferent. Do you want the poverty and insanity statistics?

STAGE MANAGER: Thank you, no. Have you any comments, Mr. Webb?

MR. WEBB: Very ordinary town, if you ask me. Little better behaved than most. Probably a lot duller. But our young people here seem to like it well enough: 90% of 'em graduating from High School settle down right here to live—even when they've been away to college.

STAGE MANAGER: Thank you, Mr. Webb. Now, is there anyone in the audience who would like to ask Editor Webb anything about the town?

WOMAN IN THE BALCONY: Is there much drinking in Grover's Corners?

MR. WEBB: Well, ma'am, I wouldn't know what you'd call *much*. Sattidy nights the farmhands meet down in Ellery Greenough's stable and holler some. Fourth of July I've been known to taste a drop myself—and Decoration Day, of course. We've got one or two town drunks, but they're always having remorses every time an evangelist comes to town. No, ma'am, I'd say likker ain't a regular thing in the home here, except in the medicine chest. Right good for snake-bite, y'know—always was.

TALL MAN AT BACK OF AUDITORIUM: Is there no one in town aware of—

STAGE MANAGER: Come forward, will you, where we can all hear you— What were you saying?

TALL MAN: Is there no one in town aware of social injustice and industrial inequality?

MR. WEBB: Oh, yes, everybody is,—somethin' terrible. Seems like they spend most of their time talking about who's rich and who's poor.

TALL MAN: Then why don't they do something about it?

MR. WEBB: Well, we're ready to listen to everybody's suggestion as to how you can see that the diligent and sensible 'll rise to the top and the lazy and quarrelsome sink to the bottom. We'll listen to anybody. Meantime until that's settled, we try to take care of those that can't help themselves, and those that can we leave alone.—Are there any more questions?

LADY IN A BOX: Oh, Mr. Webb? Mr. Webb, is there any culture or love of beauty in Grover's Corners?

MR. WEBB: Well, ma'am, there ain't much—not in the sense you mean. Come to think of it, there's some girls that play the piano at High School Commencement; but they ain't happy about it. Yes, and I see where my daughter's been made to read "The Merchant of Venice" over to the school. Seems all pretty remote to 'em, y'know what I mean. No, ma'am, there isn't much culture; but maybe this is the place to tell you that we've got a lot of pleasures of a kind here: we like the sun comin' up over the mountain in the morning, and we all notice a good deal about the birds. We pay a lot of attention to them, and trees and plants. And we watch the change of the seasons: yes, everybody knows about them. But those other things—you're right, ma'am—there ain't much—"Robinson Crusoe" and the Bible; and Handel's "Largo," we all know that; and Whistler's "Mother"—those are just about as far as we go.

LADY IN A BOX: So I thought. Thank you, Mr. Webb.

STAGE MANAGER: All right! All right! Thank you, everybody. [Mr. Webb *retires*] We'll go back to the town now. It's middle of the afternoon. All 2,642 have had their dinners and all the dishes have been washed. There's an early afternoon calm in our town: a buzzin' and a hummin' from the school buildings; only a few buggies on Main Street—the horses dozing at the hitching-posts; you all remember what it's like. Doc Gibbs is in his office, tapping people and making them say "ah." Mr. Webb's cuttin' his lawn over there; one man in ten thinks it's a privilege to push his own lawn mower. No, sir. It's later than I thought. There are the children coming home from school already.

[Emily Webb *comes sedately down Main Street carrying some school books. There are some signs that she is imagining herself to be a lady of striking elegance. Her father's movements to and fro with the lawn mower bring him into her vicinity*]

EMILY: I *can't*, Lois. I've got to go home and help my mother. I *promised*.

MR. WEBB: Emily, walk simply. Who do you think you are today?

EMILY: Papa, you're terrible. One minute you tell me to stand up straight and the next minute you call me names. I just don't listen to you. [*She gives him an abrupt kiss*]

MR. WEBB: Golly, I never got a kiss from such a great lady before. [*He goes out of sight. Emily leans over and picks some flowers by the gate of her house.* George Gibbs *comes careening down Main Street. He is throwing a ball up to dizzying heights, and waiting to catch it again. This sometimes requires his taking six steps backward*]

GEORGE: Excuse me, Mrs. Forrest.

STAGE MANAGER (*as* MRS. FORREST): Go out and play in the fields, young man. You got no business playing baseball on Main Street.

GEORGE: Awfully sorry, Mrs. Forrest.—Hello, Emily.

EMILY: H'lo.

GEORGE: You made a fine speech in class.

EMILY: Well . . . I was really ready to make a speech about the Monroe Doctrine, but at the last minute Miss Corcoran made me talk about the Louisiana Purchase instead. I worked an awful long time on both of them.

GEORGE: Gee, it's funny, Emily. From my window up there I can just see your head nights when you're doing your homework over in your room.

EMILY: Why, can you?

GEORGE: You certainly do stick to it, Emily. I don't see how you can sit still that long. I guess you like school.

EMILY: Well, I always feel it's something you have to go through.

GEORGE: Yeah.

EMILY: I don't mind it really. It passes the time.

GEORGE: Yeah.—Emily, what do you think? We might work out a kinda telegraph from there to there; and once in a while you could give me a kinda hint or two about one of those Algebra problems. I don't mean the answers, Emily, of course not . . . just some little hint. . . .

EMILY: Oh, I think *hints* are allowed.—So-ah—if you get stuck, George, you whistle to me; and I'll give you some hints.

GEORGE: Emily, you're just naturally bright, I guess.

EMILY: I figure that it's just the way a person's born.

GEORGE: Yeah. But, you see, I want to be a farmer, and my Uncle Luke says whenever I'm ready I can come over and work on his farm and if I'm any good I can just gradually have it.

EMILY: You mean the house and everything?

[*Enter Mrs. Webb*]

GEORGE: Yeah. Well, thanks . . . I better be getting out to the baseball field. Thanks for the talk, Emily.—Good afternoon, Mrs. Webb.

MRS. WEBB: Good afternoon, George.

GEORGE: So-long, Emily.

EMILY: So-long, George.

MRS. WEBB: Emily, come and help me string these beans for the winter. George Gibbs let himself have a real conversation, didn't he? Why, he's growing up. How old would George be?

EMILY: I don't know.

MRS. WEBB: Let's see. He must be almost sixteen.

EMILY: Mama, I made a speech in class today and I was very good.

MRS. WEBB: You must recite it to your father at supper. What was it about?

EMILY: The Louisiana Purchase. It was like silk off a spool. I'm going to make speeches all my life. —Mama, are these big enough?

MRS. WEBB: Try and get them a little bigger if you can.

EMILY: Mama, will you answer me a question, serious?

MRS. WEBB: Seriously, dear—not serious.

EMILY: Seriously,—will you?

MRS. WEBB: Of course, I will.

EMILY: Mama, am I good-looking?

MRS. WEBB: Yes, of course you are. All my children have got good features; I'd be ashamed if they hadn't.

EMILY: Oh, Mama, that's not what I mean. What I mean is: am I *pretty?*

MRS. WEBB: I've already told you, yes. Now that's enough of that. You have a nice young pretty face. I never heard of such foolishness.

EMILY: Oh, Mama, you never tell us the truth about anything.

MRS. WEBB: I *am* telling you the truth.

EMILY: Mama, were *you* pretty?

MRS. WEBB: Yes, I was, if I do say it. I was the prettiest girl in town next to Mamie Cartwright.

EMILY: But, Mama, you've got to say *something* about me. Am I pretty enough . . . to get anybody . . . to get people interested in me?

MRS. WEBB: Emily, you make me tired. Now stop it. You're pretty enough for all normal purposes. Come along now and bring that bowl with you.

EMILY: Oh, Mama, you're no help at all.

STAGE MANAGER: Thank you. Thank you! That'll do. We'll have to interrupt again here. Thank you, Mrs. Webb; thank you, Emily. [Mrs. Webb *and* Emily *withdraw*] There are some more things we've got to explore about this town. This time we're going to go about it in another way: we're going to look back on it from the future. I'm not going to tell you what became of these two families we're seeing most of, because the rest of the play will tell you about them. But take some of these others: Take Joe Crowell, Jr.: Joe was a very bright fellow. He graduated with honors and got a scholarship to Boston Tech.,—M.I.T., that is. But the War broke out and Joe died in France. All that education for nothing. Howie Newsome's still delivering milk at Grover's Corners. He's an old man now, has a lot of help, but he still delivers it himself. Says he gets

the feel of the town that way. Carries all the accounts in his head; never has to write down a word. Mr. Morgan's drug store ain't the same,—it's all citified. Mr. Morgan retired and went out to live in San Diego, California, where his daughter married a real estate man, name of Kerby. Mr. Morgan died there in 1935 and was buried in a lot of palm trees. Kinda lost his religion at the end and took up New Thought or something. They read some new-fangled poetry over him and cre-mated him. The New Hampshire in him sort of broke down in him in that climate, seems like. The Cartwrights got richer and richer. The house is closed most of the year. They're off eating big dinners in hotels now,—in Virginia Hot Springs and Miami Beach. They say the winters are cold here. I see where they've become 'Piscopalians. The Cartwright interests have just begun building a new bank in Grover's Corners —had to go to Vermont for the marble, sorry to say. And they've asked a friend of mine what they should put in the cornerstone for people to dig up a thousand years from now. Of course, they've put in a copy of the New York *Times* and a copy of Mr. Webb's *Sentinel.* We're kind of interested in this because some scientific fellas have found a way of painting all that reading matter with a kind of glue—silicate glue—that'll make it keep a thousand —two thousand years. We're putting in a Bible . . . and the Constitution of the United States and a copy of William Shakespeare's plays. What do you say, folks? What do you think? Y'know—Babylon once had two million people in it, and all we know about 'em is the names of the kings and some copies of wheat contracts and . . . the sales of slaves. Yes, every night all those families sat down to supper, and the father came home from his work, and the smoke went up the chimney,—same as here. And even in Greece and Rome, all we know about the real life of the people is what we can piece together out of the joking poems and the comedies they wrote for the theater back then. So I'm going to have a copy of this play put in the cornerstone and the people a thousand years from now'll know a few simple facts about us—more than the Treaty of Versailles and the Lindbergh flight. See what I mean? Well,—you people a thousand years from now,— in the provinces north of New York at the beginning of the Twentieth Century, people et three times a day: soon after sunrise; at noon; and at sunset. Every seventh day, by law and by religion, was a day of rest and all work come to a stop. The religion at that time was Christianity. I guess you have some other records about Christianity. The domestic set-up was marriage: a binding relation between a male and one female that lasted for life. Christianity strictly forbade killing, but you were allowed to kill animals, and you were allowed to kill human beings in war and government punishings. I guess we don't have to tell you about the government and business forms, because that's the kind of thing people seem to hand down first of all. Let me see now if there's anything else. Oh, yes,—at death people were buried in the ground just as they are. So, friends, this is the way we were in our growing up and in our marrying and in our doctoring and in our living and in our dying. Now we'll return to our day in Grover's Corners. A lot of time has gone by. It's evening. You can hear choir practice going on in the Congregational Church. All the children are at home doing their school work. The day is running down like a tired clock.

[*A choir partially concealed in the orchestra pit has begun singing "Blessed be the tie that binds." Simon Stimson stands directing them. Two ladders have been pushed on to the stage; they serve as indication of the second story in the Gibbs and Webb houses. George and Emily mount them, and apply themselves to their school work. Dr. Gibbs has entered and is seated in his kitchen reading*]

SIMON STIMSON: Now look here, everybody. Music come into the world to give pleasure.— Softer! Softer! Get it out of your heads that music's only good when it's loud. You leave loudness to the Methodists. You couldn't beat 'em, even if you wanted to. Now again. Tenors!

GEORGE: Hssst! Emily!

EMILY: Hello.

GEORGE: Hello!

EMILY: I can't work at all. The moonlight's so *terrible*.

GEORGE: Emily, did you get the third problem?

EMILY: Which?

GEORGE: The *third*?

EMILY: Why, yes, George—that's the easiest of them all.

GEORGE: I don't see it. Emily, can you give me a hint?

EMILY: I'll tell you one thing: the answer's in yards.

GEORGE: ! ! ! In yards? How do you mean?

EMILY: In *square* yards.

GEORGE: Oh . . . in square yards.

EMILY: Yes, George, don't you see?

GEORGE: Yeah.

EMILY: In square yards of *wallpaper*.

GEORGE: Wallpaper,—oh, I see. Thanks a lot, Emily.

EMILY: You're welcome. My, isn't the moonlight *terrible*? And choir practice going on.—I think if you hold your breath you can hear the train all the way to Contookuck. Hear it?

GEORGE: M-m-m—What do you know!

EMILY: Well, I guess I better go back and try to work.

GEORGE: Good night, Emily. And thanks.

EMILY: Good night, George.

SIMON STIMSON: Before I forget it: how many of you will be able to come in Tuesday afternoon and sing at Fred Hersey's wedding,—show your hands.

That'll be fine; that'll be right nice. We'll do the same music we did for Jane Trowbridge's last month. —Now we'll do: "Art thou weary; art thou languid?" It's a question, ladies and gentlemen, make it talk. Ready.

DR. GIBBS: Oh, George, can you come down a minute?

GEORGE: Yes, Pa. [*He descends the ladder*]

DR. GIBBS: Make yourself comfortable, George; I'll only keep you a minute. George, how old are you?

GEORGE: I? I'm sixteen almost seventeen.

DR. GIBBS: What do you want to do after school's over?

GEORGE: Why, you know, Pa, I want to be a farmer on Uncle Luke's farm.

DR. GIBBS: You'll be willing, will you, to get up early and milk and feed the stock . . . and you'll be able to hoe and hay all day?

GEORGE: Sure, I will. What are you . . . what do you mean, Pa?

DR. GIBBS: Well, George, while I was in my office today I heard a funny sound . . . and what do you think it was? It was your mother chopping wood. There you see your mother—getting up early; cooking meals all day long; washing and ironing;—and still she has to go out in the back yard and chop wood. I suppose she just got tired of asking you. She just gave up and decided it was easier to do it herself. And you eat her meals, and put on the clothes she keeps nice for you, and you run off and play baseball,—like she's some hired girl we keep around the house but that we don't like very much. Well, I knew all I had to do was call your attention to it. Here's a handkerchief, son. George, I've decided to raise your spending money twenty-five cents a week. Not, of course, for chopping wood for your mother, because that's a present you give her, but because you're getting older—and I imagine there are lots of things you must find to do with it.

GEORGE: Thanks, Pa.

DR. GIBBS: Let's see—tomorrow's pay day. You can count on it—Hmm. Probably Rebecca'll feel she ought to have some more too. Wonder what could have happened to your mother. Choir practice never was as late as this before.

GEORGE: It's only half-past eight, Pa.

DR. GIBBS: I don't know why she's in that old choir. She hasn't any more voice than an old crow. . . . Traipsin' around the streets at this hour of the night. . . . Just about time you retired, don't you think?

GEORGE: Yes, Pa. [George *mounts to his place on the ladder. Laughter and good nights can be heard on stage left and presently* Mrs. Gibbs, Mrs. Soames *and* Mrs. Webb *come down Main Street. When they arrive at the center of the stage they stop*]

MRS. SOAMES: Good night, Martha. Good night, Mr. Foster.

MRS. WEBB: I'll tell Mr. Webb; I *know* he'll want to put it in the paper.

MRS. GIBBS: My, it's late!

MRS. SOAMES: Good night, Irma.

MRS. GIBBS: Real nice choir practice, wa'n't it? Myrtle Webb! Look at that moon, will you! Tsk-tsk-tsk. Potato weather, for sure.

MRS. SOAMES: Naturally I didn't want to say a word about it in front of those others, but now we're alone—really, it's the worst scandal that ever was in this town!

MRS. GIBBS: What?

MRS. SOAMES: Simon Stimson!

MRS. GIBBS: Now, Louella!

MRS. SOAMES: But, Julia! To have the organist of a church drink and drunk year after year. You know he was drunk tonight.

MRS. GIBBS: Now, Louella! We all know about Mr. Stimson, and we all know about the troubles he's been through, and Dr. Ferguson knows too, and if Dr. Ferguson keeps him on there in his job the only thing the rest of us can do is just not to notice it.

MRS. SOAMES: Not to notice it! But it's getting worse.

MRS. WEBB: No, it isn't, Louella. It's getting better. I've been in that choir twice as long as you have. It doesn't happen anywhere near so often. . . . My, I hate to go to bed on a night like this.—I better hurry. Those children'll be sitting up till all hours. Good night, Louella. [*She hurries down stage, enters her house and disappears*]

MRS. GIBBS: Can you get home safe, Louella?

MRS. SOAMES: It's as bright as day. I can see Mr. Soames scowling at the window now. You'd think we'd been to a dance the way the menfolk carry on.

[*Repeated good nights. Mrs. Gibbs arrives at her home*]

MRS. GIBBS: Well, we had a real good time.

DR. GIBBS: You're late enough.

MRS. GIBBS: Why, Frank, it ain't any later 'n usual.

DR. GIBBS: And you stopping at the corner to gossip with a lot of hens.

MRS. GIBBS: Now, Frank, don't be grouchy. Come out and smell my heliotrope in the moonlight. [*They stroll out arm in arm along the footlights*] Isn't that wonderful? What did you do all the time I was away?

DR. GIBBS: Oh, I read—as usual. What were the girls gossiping about tonight?

MRS. GIBBS: Well, believe me, Frank—there is something to gossip about.

DR. GIBBS: Hmm! Simon Stimson far gone, was he?

MRS. GIBBS: Worst I've ever seen him. How'll that end, Frank? Dr. Ferguson can't forgive him forever.

DR. GIBBS: I guess I know more about Simon Stimson's affairs than anybody in this town. Some people ain't made for small town life. I don't know how that'll end; but there's nothing we can do but just leave it alone. Come, get in.

MRS. GIBBS: No, not yet. . . . Oh, Frank, I'm worried about you.

DR. GIBBS: What are you worried about?

MRS. GIBBS: I think it's my duty to make plans for you to get a real rest and change. And if I get that legacy, well, I'm going to insist on it.

DR. GIBBS: Now, Julia, there's no sense in going over that again.

MRS. GIBBS: Frank, you're just *unreasonable!*

DR. GIBBS: Come on, Julia, it's getting late. First thing you know you'll catch cold. I gave George a piece of my mind tonight. I reckon you'll have your wood chopped for a while anyway. No, no, start getting upstairs.

MRS. GIBBS: Oh, dear. There's always so many things to pick up, seems like. You know, Frank, Mrs. Fairchild always locks her front door every night. All those people up that part of town do.

DR. GIBBS: They're all getting citified, that's the trouble with them. They haven't got nothing fit to burgle and everybody knows it. [*They disappear.* Rebecca *climbs up the ladder beside* George]

GEORGE: Get out, Rebecca. There's only room for one at this window. You're always spoiling everything.

REBECCA: Well, let me look just a minute.

GEORGE: Use your own window.

REBECCA: I did; but there's no moon there. . . . George, do you know what I think, do you? I think maybe the moon's getting nearer and nearer and there'll be a big 'splosion.

GEORGE: Rebecca, you don't know anything. If the moon were getting nearer, the guys that sit up all night with telescopes would see it first and they'd tell about it, and it'd be in all the newspapers.

REBECCA: George, is the moon shining on South America, Canada and half the whole world?

GEORGE: Well—prob'ly is.

[*The Stage Manager strolls on*]

STAGE MANAGER: Nine-thirty. Most of the lights are out. No, there's Constable Warren trying a few doors on Main Street. And here comes Editor Webb, after putting his newspaper to bed.

MR. WEBB: Good evening, Bill.

CONSTABLE WARREN: Evenin', Mr. Webb.

MR. WEBB: Quite a moon!

CONSTABLE WARREN: Yepp.

MR. WEBB: All quiet tonight?

CONSTABLE WARREN: Simon Stimson is rollin' around a little. Just saw his wife movin' out to hunt for him so I looked the other way—there he is now.

[Simon Stimson *comes down Main Street from the left, only a trace of unsteadiness in his walk*]

MR. WEBB: Good evening, Simon. . . . Town seems to have settled down for the night pretty well. . . . [Simon Stimson *comes up to him and pauses a moment*] Good evening. . . . Yes, most of the town's settled down for the night, Simon. . . . I guess we better do the same. Can I walk along a ways with you? [Simon Stimson *continues on his way without a word and disappears at the right*] Good night.

CONSTABLE WARREN: I don't know how that's goin' to end, Mr. Webb.

MR. WEBB: Well, he's seen a peck of trouble, one thing after another. . . . Oh, Bill . . . if you see my boy smoking cigarettes, just give him a word, will you? He thinks a lot of you, Bill.

CONSTABLE WARREN: I don't think he smokes no cigarettes, Mr. Webb. Leastways, not more'n two or three a year. He don't belong to that crowd that hangs out down by the gully.

MR. WEBB: Hm. . . . I hope not.—Well, good night, Bill.

CONSTABLE WARREN: Good night, Mr. Webb. [*Exit*]

MR. WEBB: Who's that up there? Is that you, Myrtle?

EMILY: No, it's me, Papa.

MR. WEBB: Why aren't you in bed?

EMILY: I don't know. I just can't sleep, Papa. The moonlight's so *won*-derful. And the smell of Mrs. Gibbs's heliotrope. Can you smell it?

MR. WEBB: Hm. . . . Yes. Haven't any troubles on your mind, have you, Emily?

EMILY: *Troubles*, Papa. *No*.

MR. WEBB: Well, enjoy yourself, but don't let your mother catch you. Good night, Emily.

EMILY: Good night, Papa.

[Mr. Webb *crosses into the house, whistling "Blessed Be the Tie that Binds" and disappears*]

REBECCA: I never told you about that letter Jane Crofut got from her minister when she was sick. The minister of her church in the town she was in before she came here. He wrote Jane a letter and on the envelope the address was like this: It said: Jane Crofut; The Crofut Farm; Grover's Corners; Sutton County; New Hampshire; United States of America.

GEORGE: What's funny about that?

REBECCA: But listen, it's not finished: the United States of America; Continent of North America; Western Hemisphere; the Earth; the Solar System; the Universe; the Mind of God,—that's what it said on the envelope.

GEORGE: What do you know!

REBECCA: And the postman brought it just the same.

GEORGE: What do you know!

STAGE MANAGER: That's the end of the First Act, friends. You can go and smoke now, those that smoke.

ACT II.

The tables and chairs of the two kitchens are still on the stage. The ladders have been withdrawn. The Stage Manager has been at his accustomed place watching the audience return to its seats.

STAGE MANAGER: Three years have gone by. Yes, the sun's come up over a thousand times. Summers and winters have cracked the mountains a little bit more and the rains have brought down some of the dirt. Some babies that weren't even born before have begun talking regular sentences already; and a number of people who thought they were right young and spry have noticed that they can't bound up a flight of stairs like they used to, without their heart fluttering a little. Some older sons are sitting at the head of the table, and some people I know are having their meat cut up for them.—All that can happen in a thousand days. Nature's been pushing and contriving in other ways, too: a number of young people fell in love and got married. Yes, the mountain got bit away a few fractions of an inch; millions of gallons of water went by the mill; and here and there a new home was set up under a roof. Almost everybody in the world gets married,—you know what I mean? In our town there aren't hardly any exceptions. Most everybody in the world climbs into their graves married. The First Act was called the Daily Life. This Act is called Love and Marriage. There's another Act coming after this: I reckon you can guess what that's about. So: It's three years later. It's 1904. It's July 7th, just after High School Commencement. That's the time most of our young people jump up and get married. Soon as they've passed their last examinations in solid geometry and Cicero's Orations, looks like they suddenly feel themselves fit to be married. It's early morning. Only this time it's been raining. It's been pouring and thundering. Mrs. Gibbs's garden, and Mrs. Webb's here: drenched. All those bean poles and pea vines: drenched. All yesterday over there on Main Street, the rain looked like curtains being blown along. Hm . . . it may begin again any minute. There! You can hear the 5:45 for Boston. And here comes Howie Newsome delivering the milk. And there's Si Crowell delivering the papers like his brother before him.—You remember about his brother?—all that education he's going to get and that'll be wasted. And there's Mrs. Gibbs and Mrs. Webb come down to make breakfast, just as though it were an ordinary day. I don't have to point out to the women in my audience that those ladies they see before them, both those ladies cooked three meals a day,—one of 'em for twenty years, the other for forty,—and no summer vacation. They brought up two children apiece; washed; cleaned the house, —and never a nervous breakdown. Never thought themselves hard-used, either. It's like what one of those Middle West poets said: You've got to love life to have life, and you've got to have life to love life. . . . It's what they call a vicious circle.

[Si Crowell *has entered hurling imaginary news-papers into doorways;* Howie Newsome *has come along Main Street with* Bessie]

HOWIE NEWSOME: Git-ap, Bessie.

SI CROWELL: Morning, Howie.

HOWIE NEWSOME: Morning, Si.—Anything in the papers I ought to know?

SI CROWELL: Nothing much, except we're losing the best baseball pitcher Grover's Corners ever had.

HOWIE NEWSOME: Reckon he was. He's been standing off the whole of South New Hampshire single-handed, looks like.

SI CROWELL: He could hit and run bases, too.

HOWIE NEWSOME: Yep. Mighty fine ball player.—Bessie. I guess I can stop and talk if I've a mind to!

SI CROWELL: I don't see how he could give up a thing like that just to get married. Would you, Howie?

HOWIE NEWSOME: Can't tell, Si. Never had no talent that way. [Constable Warren *enters. They exchange mornings*] You're up early, Bill.

CONSTABLE WARREN: Seein' if there's anything I can do to prevent a flood. River's been risin' all night.

HOWIE NEWSOME: Si Crowell's all worked up here about George Gibbs' retiring from baseball.

CONSTABLE WARREN: Yes, sir; that's the way it goes. Back in '84 we had a player, Si,—even George Gibbs couldn't touch him. Name of Hank Todd. Went down to Maine and become a parson. Wonderful ball player.—Howie, how did the weather look to you?

HOWIE NEWSOME: No, 'tain't bad. Think maybe it'll clear up for good.

[Constable Warren *and* Si Crowell *continue on their way.* Howie Newsome *brings the milk first to* Mrs. Gibbs's *house. She meets him by the trellis*]

MRS. GIBBS: Good morning, Howie. Do you think it's going to rain again?

HOWIE NEWSOME: Morning, Mrs. Gibbs. It rained so heavy, I think maybe it'll clear up.

MRS. GIBBS: Certainly hope it will.

HOWIE NEWSOME: How much did you want to-day?

MRS. GIBBS: I guess I'll need three-a-milk and two-a-cream, Howie. I'm going to have a house full of relations.

HOWIE NEWSOME: My wife says to tell you we both hope they'll be very happy, Mrs. Gibbs. Know they *will*.

MRS. GIBBS: Thanks a lot, Howie. Tell your wife I hope she gits there to the wedding.

HOWIE NEWSOME: Yes, she'll be there; she'll be there if she kin. [Howie Newsome *crosses to* Mrs. Webb's *house*] Morning, Mrs. Webb.

MRS. WEBB: Oh, good morning, Mr. Newsome. I told you four quarts of milk, but I hope you can spare me another.

HOWIE NEWSOME: Yes'm . . . and the two cream.

MRS. WEBB: Will it rain all day, Mr. Newsome?

HOWIE NEWSOME: No'm. Just sayin' to Mrs. Gibbs as how it may lighten up. Mrs. Newsome told me to tell you as how we hope they'll both be very happy, Mrs. Webb. Know they *will*.

MRS. WEBB: Thank you, and thank Mrs. Newsome and we hope to see you all at the wedding.

HOWIE NEWSOME: Yes, Mrs. Webb. We hope to git there. Couldn't miss that. Chck! Bessie! [*Exit* Howie Newsome. Dr. Gibbs *descends in shirt sleeves, and sits down at his breakfast table*]

DR. GIBBS: Well, Ma, the day has come. You're losin' one of your chicks.

MRS. GIBBS: Frank Gibbs, don't you say another word. I feel like crying every minute. Sit down and drink your coffee.

DR. GIBBS: The groom's up shaving himself. Whistling and singing, like he's glad to leave us.— Every now and then he says "I do" to the mirror, but it don't sound convincing to me.

MRS. GIBBS: I declare I don't know how he'll get along. I've arranged his clothes and seen to it he's put warm things on,— Frank! they're too young. Emily won't think of such things. He'll catch his death of cold within a week.—Here's something I made for you.

DR. GIBBS: Why, Julia Hersey! French toast!

MRS. GIBBS: 'Tain't hard to make, and I had to do something.

DR. GIBBS: I remember my wedding morning, Julia.

MRS. GIBBS: Now don't start that, Frank Gibbs. I tell you I can't stand it.

DR. GIBBS: I was the scardest young fella in the State of New Hampshire. I thought I'd made a mistake for sure. And when I saw you comin' down that aisle I thought you were the prettiest girl I'd ever seen, but the only trouble was that I'd never seen you before. There I was in the Congregational Church marryin' a total stranger.

MRS. GIBBS: And how do you think I felt!—Did you hear Rebecca stirring about upstairs?

DR. GIBBS: Only morning in the year she hasn't been managing everybody's business. She's shut up in her room. I got the impression that maybe she's crying.

MRS. GIBBS: Good Lord! This has got to stop.— Rebecca! Rebecca! Everything's getting cold down here. [George *comes rattling down the stairs, very brisk*]

GEORGE: Good morning, everybody. Only five more hours to live. [*Makes the gesture of cutting his throat*]

MRS. GIBBS: Where are you going?

GEORGE: Just stepping across the grass to see my girl.

MRS. GIBBS: Now, George! You take an umbrella or I won't let you out of this house.

GEORGE: Aw, Ma. It's just a *step!*

MRS. GIBBS: From tomorrow on you can kill yourself in all weathers, but while you're in my house you live wisely, thank you. There are your overshoes right there in the hall. And here's an umbrella.

GEORGE: Aw, Ma!

DR. GIBBS: George, do as your mother tells you.

MRS. GIBBS: Maybe Mrs. Webb isn't used to callers at seven in the morning. Take a cup-a coffee first.

GEORGE: Be back in a minute. [*He crosses the stage, leaping over the puddles*] Good morning, Mother Webb.

MRS. WEBB: Goodness! You frightened me!— Now, George, you can come in a minute out of the wet, but you know I can't ask you in.

GEORGE: Why not—?

MRS. WEBB: George, you know's well as I do: the groom can't see his bride on his wedding day, not until he sees her in church.

GEORGE: Aw!—that's just a superstition. [*Enter Mr. Webb*]

MR. WEBB: Good morning, George.

GEORGE: Mr. Webb, you don't believe in that superstition, do you?

MR. WEBB: There's a lot of common sense in some superstitions, George.

MRS. WEBB: Millions have folla'd it, George, and you don't want to be the first to fly in the face of custom.

GEORGE: How is Emily?

MRS. WEBB: She hasn't waked up yet. I haven't heard a sound out of her.

GEORGE: Emily's *asleep!!!*

MRS. WEBB: No wonder! We were up 'til all hours,—sewing and packing. I'll tell you what I'll do; you set down here a minute with Mr. Webb and drink this cup of coffee; and I'll go upstairs and see she doesn't come down and surprise you. There's some bacon, too; but don't be long about it. [*Exit Mrs. Webb. Embarrassed silence*]

MR. WEBB: Well, George, how are you?

GEORGE: Oh, fine. I'm fine. [*Pause*] Mr. Webb, what sense could there be in a superstition like that?

MR. WEBB: Well, you see,—on her wedding morning a girl's head's apt to be full of . . . clothes and things like that. Don't you think that's probably it?

GEORGE: Ye-e-s. I never thought of that.

MR. WEBB: A girl's apt to be a mite nervous on her wedding day. [*Pause*]

GEORGE: I wish a fellow could get married without all that marching up and down.

MR. WEBB: Well, every man that's ever lived has felt that way about it, George; but it hasn't done much good. It's the women that have built up weddings, my boy. From now on they have it pretty much as they like. . . . All those good women standing shoulder to shoulder making sure that the knot's tied in a mighty public way.

GEORGE: But . . . you *believe* in it, don't you, Mr. Webb?

MR. WEBB: Oh, yes; oh, yes. Don't you misunderstand me, my boy. Marriage is a wonderful thing,—wonderful thing. And don't you forget that, George.

GEORGE: No, sir.—Mr. Webb, how old were you when you got married?

MR. WEBB: Well, you see: I'd been to college and I'd taken a little time to get settled. But Mrs. Webb,—she wasn't much older than what Emily is. Oh, age hasn't much to do with it, George,—not compared to other things.

GEORGE: What were you going to say, Mr. Webb?

MR. WEBB: Oh, I don't know,—was I going to say something? [*Pause*] George, I was thinking the other night of some advice my father gave me when I got married. Charles, he said, Charles, start out early showing who's boss, he said. Best thing to do is to give an order, even if it don't make sense; just so she'll learn to obey. And he said: if anything about your wife irritates you,—her conversation, or anything,—just get up and leave the house. That'll make it clear to her, he said. And, oh, yes! he said never *never* let your wife know how much money you have, never.

GEORGE: Well, Mr. Webb . . . I don't think I could . . .

MR. WEBB: So I took the opposite of my father's advice and I've been happy ever since. And let that be a lesson to you, George, never to ask advice on personal matters.—George, are you going to raise chickens on your farm?

GEORGE: What?

MR. WEBB: Are you going to raise chickens on your farm?

GEORGE: Uncle Luke's never been much interested, but I thought—

MR. WEBB: A book came into my office the other day, George, on the Philo System of raising chickens. I want you to read it. I'm thinking of beginning in a small way in the back yard, and I'm going to put an incubator in the cellar—[*Enter Mrs. Webb*]

MRS. WEBB: Charles, are you talking about that old incubator again? I thought you two'd be talking about things worth while.

MR. WEBB: Well, Myrtle, if you want to give the boy some good advice, I'll go upstairs and leave you alone with him.

MRS. WEBB: Now, George, I'm sorry, but I've got to send you away so that Emily can come down and get some breakfast. She told me to tell you that she sends you her love but that she doesn't want to lay eyes on you. So good-by, George. [*George crosses the stage to his own home and disappears*]

MR. WEBB: Myrtle, I guess you don't know about that older superstition.

MRS. WEBB: What do you mean, Charles?

MR. WEBB: Since the cave-men: the groom shouldn't be left alone with his father-in-law on the day of the wedding, or near it. Now don't forget that!

STAGE MANAGER: Thank you. Thank you, everybody. Now I have to interrupt again here. You see, we want to know how all this began,—this wedding, this plan to spend a lifetime together. I'm awfully interested in how big things like that begin. You know how it is: you're twenty-one or twenty-two and you make some decisions; then whisssh! you're seventy: you've been a lawyer for fifty years, and that white-haired lady at your side has eaten over fifty thousand meals with you. How do such things begin? George and Emily are going to show you now the conversation they had when they first knew that . . . that . . . as the saying goes . . . they were meant for one another. But before they do it I want you to try and remember what it was like when you were young, when you were fifteen or sixteen. For some reason it is very hard to do: those days when even the little things in life could be almost too exciting to bear. And particularly the days when you were first in love; when you were like a person sleep-walking, and you didn't quite see the street you were in, and didn't quite hear everything that was said to you. You're just a little bit crazy. Will you remember that, please? Now they'll be coming out of High School at three o'clock. George has just been elected President of the Junior Class, and as it's June, that means he'll be President of the Senior Class all next year. And Emily's just been elected Secretary and Treasurer. I don't have to tell you how important that is. [*He places a board across the backs of two chairs, parallel to the footlights, and places two high stools behind it. This is the counter of* Mr. Morgan's *drugstore*] All ready! [Emily, *carrying an armful of—imaginary—school-books, comes along Main Street from the left*]

EMILY: I can't, Louise. I've got to go home. Goodby. Oh, Earnestine! Earnestine! Can you come over tonight and do Algebra? I did the first and third in Study Hall. No, they're not hard. But, Earnestine, that Caesar's awful hard. I don't see why we have to do a thing like that. Come over about seven. Tell your mother you *have* to. G'by. G'by, Helen. G'by, Fred. [George, *also carrying books, catches up with her*]

GEORGE: Can I carry your books home for you, Emily?

EMILY: [*Coldly*] Thank you. [*She gives them to him*]

GEORGE: Excuse me a minute, Emily.—Say, Bob, get everything ready. I'll be there in a quarter of an hour. If I'm a little late start practice anyway. And give Herb some long high ones. His eye needs a lot of practice. Seeya later.

EMILY: Good-by, Lizzy.

GEORGE: Good-by, Lizzy.—I'm awfully glad you were elected, too, Emily.

EMILY: Thank you.

[*They have been standing on Main Street, almost against the back wall.* George *is about to take the first steps towards the audience when he stops again and says:*]

GEORGE: Emily, why are you mad at me?

EMILY: I'm not mad at you.

GEORGE: You . . . you treat me so funny.

EMILY: Well, I might as well say it right out, George. I don't like the whole change that's come over you in the last year. I'm sorry if that hurts your feelings, but I've just got to tell the truth and shame the devil.

GEORGE: I'm awfully sorry, Emily. Wha-a-what do you mean?

EMILY: Well, up to a year ago I used to like you a lot. And I used to watch you as you did everything . . . because we'd been friends so long . . . and then you began spending all your time at baseball . . . and you never even spoke to anybody any more; not even to your own family you didn't . . . and, George, it's a fact, you've got awful conceited and stuck-up, and all the girls say so. They may not say so to your face, but that's what they say about you behind your back, and it hurts me to hear them say it, but I've got to agree with them a little. I'm sorry if it hurts your feelings . . . but I can't be sorry I said it.

GEORGE: I . . . I'm glad you said it, Emily. I never thought that such a thing was happening to me. I guess it's hard for a fella not to have faults creep into his character. [*They take a step or two in silence, then stand still in misery*]

EMILY: I always expect a man to be perfect and I think he should be.

GEORGE: Oh . . . I don't think it's possible to be perfect, Emily.

EMILY: Well, my father is, and as far as I can see your father is. There's no reason on earth why you shouldn't be, too.

GEORGE: Well, Emily . . . I feel it's the other way round. That men aren't naturally good; but girls are. Like you and your mother and my mother.

EMILY: Well, you might as well know right now that I'm not perfect. It's not as easy for a girl to be perfect as a man, because we girls are more nervous. —Now I'm sorry I said all that about you. I don't know what made me say it.

GEORGE: No, no,—I guess if it's the truth you ought to say it. You stick to it, Emily.

EMILY: I don't know if it's the truth or not. And I suddenly feel that it isn't important at all.

GEORGE: Emily, would you like an ice-cream soda, or something, before you go home?

EMILY: Well, thank you . . . I would. [*They come into the drugstore and seat themselves on the stools*]

STAGE MANAGER: [*As* Mr. Morgan:] Hello, George. Hello, Emily. What'll you have? Why, Emily Webb, what've you been crying about?

GEORGE: [*He gropes for an explanation*] She . . . she just got an awful scare, Mr. Morgan. She almost got run over by that hardware store wagon. Everybody always says that Tom Huckins drives like a crazy man.

STAGE MANAGER: Here, take a drink of water, Emily. You look all shook up. There!—Now, what'll you have?

EMILY: I'll have a strawberry phosphate, thank you, Mr. Morgan.

GEORGE: No, no. You go and have an ice-cream soda with me, Emily.—Two strawberry ice-cream sodas, Mr. Morgan.

STAGE MANAGER: [*Working the faucets*] Yes, sir. I tell you, you've got to look both ways before you cross Main Street these days. Gets worse every year. There are a hundred and twenty-five horses in Grover's Corners this minute I'm talking to you. State Inspector was in here yesterday. And now they're bringing in these auto-mo-biles, the best thing to do is to just stay home. Why, I can remember the time when a dog could lie down all day in the middle of Main Street and nothing would come to disturb him. —Yes, Miss Ellis; be with you in a minute. Here are your sodas. Enjoy 'em. [*He goes off*]

EMILY: They're so expensive.

GEORGE: No, no—don't you think of that. We're celebrating. First, we're celebrating our election. And then do you know what else I'm celebrating?

EMILY: No.

GEORGE: I'm celebrating because I've got a friend who tells me all the things that ought to be told me.

EMILY: George, *please* don't think of that. I don't know why I said it. It's not true. You're—

GEORGE: No, you stick to it, Emily. I'm glad you spoke to me like you did. But you'll see: I'm going to change so quick—you bet I'm going to change. And, Emily, I want to ask you a favor.

EMILY: What?

GEORGE: Emily, if I go away to State Agriculture College next year, will you write me a letter once in a while?

EMILY: I certainly will. I certainly will, George. . . . [*Pause*] It certainly seems like being away three years you'd get out of touch with things.

GEORGE: No, no. I mustn't do that. You see I'm not only going to be just a farmer. After a while maybe I'll run for something to get elected. So your letters'll be very important to me; you know, telling me what's going on here and everything. . . .

EMILY: Just the same, three years is a long time. Maybe letters from Grover's Corners wouldn't be so interesting after a while. Grover's Corners isn't a very important place when you think of all New Hampshire; but I think it's a very nice town.

GEORGE: The day wouldn't come when I wouldn't want to know everything that's happening here. I know *that's* true, Emily.

EMILY: Well, I'll try to make my letters interesting. [*Pause*]

GEORGE: Y'know, Emily, whenever I meet a farmer I ask him if he thinks it's important to go to Agriculture School to be a good farmer.

EMILY: Why, George—

GEORGE: Yeah, and some of them say that it's even a waste of time. You can get all those things, anyway, out of the pamphlets the government sends out. And Uncle Luke's getting old,—he's about ready for me to start in taking over his farm tomorrow, if I could.

EMILY: My!

GEORGE: And, like you say, being gone all that time . . . in other places and meeting other people . . . If anything like that can happen I don't want to go away. I guess new people aren't any better than old ones. I'll bet they almost never are. Emily, . . . I feel that you're as good a friend as I've got. I don't need to go and meet the people in other towns.

EMILY: But, George, maybe it's very important for you to go and learn all that about cattle-judging and soils and those things. And if you're going into politics, maybe you ought to meet people from other parts of the State . . . of course, I don't know.

GEORGE: [*After a pause*] Emily, I'm going to make up my mind right now. I won't go. I'll tell Pa about it tonight.

EMILY: Why, George, I don't see why you have to decide right now. It's a whole year away.

GEORGE: Emily, I'm glad you spoke to me about that . . . that fault in my character. And what you said was right; but there was *one* thing wrong in it, and that was when you said that for a year I wasn't noticing people, and . . . you, for instance. Listen, Emily . . . you say you were watching me when I did everything. . . . Why, I was doing the same about you all the time. Why, sure,—I always thought about you as one of the chief people I thought about. I always made sure where you were sitting on the bleachers, and who you were with. And we've always had lots of talks . . . and joking, in the halls; and they always meant a lot to me. Of course, they weren't as good as the talk we're having now. Lately I'd been noticing that you'd been acting kind of funny to me, and for three days I've been trying to walk home with you, but something's always got in the way. Yesterday I was standing over against the wall waiting for you, and you walked home with Miss Corcoran.

EMILY: George! . . . Life's awful funny! How could I have known that? Why, I thought—

GEORGE: Listen, Emily, I'm going to tell you why I'm not going to Agriculture School. I think that once you've found a person that you're very fond of . . . I mean a person who's fond of you, too,—at least enough to be interested in your character . . . Well, I think that's just as important as college is, and even more so. That's what I think.

EMILY: I think it's awfully important, too.

GEORGE: Emily.

EMILY: Yes, George.

GEORGE: Emily, if I improve and make a big change . . . would you be . . . I mean: *could* you be . . .

EMILY: I . . . I am now; I always have been.

GEORGE: [*Pause*] So I guess this is an important talk we've been having.

EMILY: Yes.

GEORGE: [*Takes a deep breath and straightens his back*] Wait just a minute and I'll take you home. [*He rises and goes to the* Stage Manager *who appears and comes toward him*] Mr. Morgan, I'll have to go home and get the money to pay you for this. It'll only take me a minute.

STAGE MANAGER: What's that? George Gibbs, do you mean to tell me—!

GEORGE: Yes, but I had reasons, Mr. Morgan.— Look, here's my gold watch to keep until I come back with the money.

STAGE MANAGER: That's all right. Keep your watch. I'll trust you.

GEORGE: I'll be back in five minutes.

STAGE MANAGER: I'll trust you ten years, George, —not a day more.—Got all over your shock, Emily?

EMILY: Yes, thank you, Mr. Morgan. It was nothing.

GEORGE: [*Taking up the books from the counter*] I'm ready.

[*They walk in grave silence down the stage, turn, and pass through the trellis at the Webbs' back door and disappear*]

STAGE MANAGER: Thank you, Emily. Thank you, George. Now before we go on to the wedding, there are still some more things we ought to know about this—about this marriage. I want to know some more about how the parents took it; but what I want to know most of all is: oh, you know what I mean,—what Grover's Corners thought about marriage anyway. You know's well as I do: people are never able to say right out what they think of money, or death, or fame, or marriage. You've got to catch it between the lines; you got to *over*-hear it. Oh, Doctor! Mrs. Gibbs!

[*They appear at their side of the stage and exchange a glance of understanding with him. The* Stage Manager *lays the same plank across two chairs that served as a drugstore counter and it has now become* Mrs. Gibbs's *ironing board.* Dr. Gibbs *sits down in a rocker and smokes.* Mrs. Gibbs *irons a moment in silence; then goes to the foot of the stairs and calls:*]

MRS. GIBBS: Rebecca! It's time you turned out your light and went to sleep. George, you'd better get some sleep, too.

REBECCA'S VOICE: Ma, I haven't finished my English.

MRS. GIBBS: What? Well, I bet you haven't been working, Rebecca. You've been reading that Sears, Roebuck catalogue, that's what you've been doing. —All right, I'll give you ten more minutes. If you haven't finished by then you'll just have to fail the course and be a disgrace to your father and me.— George, what are you doing?

GEORGE'S VOICE: [*Hurt*] I'm doing history.

MRS. GIBBS: Well, you'd better go to bed. You're probably sleeping at the desk as it is. [*She casts an amused eye at her husband and returns to her ironing*]

DR. GIBBS: I had a long talk with the boy today.

MRS. GIBBS: Did you?

DR. GIBBS: I tell you, Mrs. G., there's nothing so terrifying in the world as a son. The relation of a father to a son is the damnedest, awkwardest—. I always come away feeling like a soggy sponge of hypocrisy.

MRS. GIBBS: Well, a mother and a daughter's no picnic, let me tell you.

DR. GIBBS: George is set on it: he wants to marry Emily 'soon as school's out and take her right on to the farm. [*Pause*] He says he can sit up nights and learn agriculture from government pamphlets, without going to college for it.

MRS. GIBBS: He always was crazy about farming. Gets that from my people.

DR. GIBBS: At a pinch, I guess he could start in farming;—but I swear I think he's too young to get married. Julia, he's just a green half-grown kid. He isn't ready to be a family man.

MRS. GIBBS: No, he ain't. You're right.—But he's a good boy and I wouldn't like to think of him being alone out there . . . coming into town Satiddy nights, like any old farm hand, tuckered out from work and looking for excitement. He might get into bad ways. It wouldn't be enough fun for him to come and sit by our stove,—and holding hands with Emily, for a year mightn't be enough either. He might lose interest in her.

DR. GIBBS: Hm.

MRS. GIBBS: Frank, I' been watching her. George is a lucky boy when you think of all the silly girls in the world.

DR. GIBBS: But, Julia,—George *married*. That great gangling selfish nincumpoop.

MRS. GIBBS: Yes, I know. [*She takes up a collar and examines it*] Frank, what do you do to your collars? Do you gnaw 'em? I never saw such a man for collars.

DR. GIBBS: Julia, when I married you, do you know what one of my terrors was in getting married?

MRS. GIBBS: Pshaw! Go on with you!

DR. GIBBS: I was afraid we weren't going to have material for conversation more'n 'ld last us a few weeks. I was afraid we'd run out and eat our meals in silence, that's a fact. You and I've been conversing for twenty years now without any noticeable barren spells.

MRS. GIBBS: Well, good weather, bad weather, 'tain't very choice, but I always manage to find something to say. [*Pause*]

DR. GIBBS: What do you think? What do you think,

Julia? Shall we tell the boy he can go ahead and get married?

MRS. GIBBS: Seems like it's up to us to decide. Myrtle and Charles Webb are willing. They think it's a good idea to throw the young people into the sea and let'm sink or swim, as soon as they're ready.

DR. GIBBS: What does that mean? Must we decide right now? This minute?

MRS. GIBBS: There you go putting the responsibility on me!

DR. GIBBS: Here it is, almost April.—I'll go up and say a word to him right now before he goes to bed. [*He rises*] You're sure, Julia? You've nothing more to add?

MRS. GIBBS: [*Stops ironing a moment*] I don't know what to say. Seems like it's too much to ask, for a big outdoor boy like that to go and get shut up in classrooms for three years. And once he's on the farm, he might just as well have a companion, seeing he's found a fine girl like Emily. . . . People are meant to live two by two in this world. . . . Yes, Frank, go up and tell him it's all right.

DR. GIBBS: [*Crosses and is about to call when*]

MRS. GIBBS: [*Her hands on her cheeks, staring into the audience, in sharp alarm*] Wait a minute! Wait a minute!—[*Then resuming her ironing*] No,—go and tell him.

DR. GIBBS: Why did you stop then, Julia?

MRS. GIBBS: Oh, you know: I thought of all those times we went through in the first years when George and Rebecca were babies,—you walking up and down with them at three in the morning; the whooping-cough; the time George fell off the porch. You and I were twenty-five years old, and more. It's wonderful how one forgets one's troubles, like that. —Yes, Frank, go upstairs and tell him. . . . It's worth it.

DR. GIBBS: Yes, they'll have a lot of troubles, but that's none of our business. Let'm. Everybody has a right to his own troubles.—You ought to be present, Julia,—important occasion like that. I'll call him.—George! Oh, George!

GEORGE'S VOICE: Yes, Pa.

DR. GIBBS: Can you come down a minute? Your mother and I want to speak to you.

GEORGE: Yeah, sure.

MRS. GIBBS: [*Putting her arm through her husband's*] Lord, what a fool I am: I'm trembling all over. There's nothing to tremble about.

STAGE MANAGER: Thank you! Thank you! Now we're ready to go on with the wedding. [*While he talks, the actors remove the chair and tables and trellises from the Gibbs and Webb homes. They arrange the pews for the church in the back of the stage. The congregation will sit facing the back wall. The aisle of the church is in the middle of the scene. A small platform is placed against the back wall on which the* Stage Manager *as Minister can stand*] There are a lot of things to be said about a wedding; there are a lot of thoughts that go on during a wedding. We can't get them all into one wedding, naturally, and especially not into a wedding at Grover's Corners where they're awfully plain and short. In this wedding I play the minister. That gives me the right to say a few more things about it. For a while now, the play gets pretty serious. Y'see, some churches say that marriage is a sacrament. I don't quite know what that means, but I can guess. Like Mrs. Gibbs said a few minutes ago: People were made to live two-by-two. This is a good wedding, but people are so put together that even at a good wedding there's a lot of confusion way down deep in people's minds and we thought that that ought to be in our play, too. The real hero of this scene isn't on the stage at all, and you know who that is. It's like what one of those European fellas said: every child born into the world is Nature's attempt to make a perfect human being. Well, we've seen nature pushing and contriving for some time now. We all know that nature's interested in quantity; but I think she's interested in quality, too, —that's why I'm in the ministry.—Maybe she's trying to make another good governor for New Hampshire. And don't forget the other witnesses at this wedding,—the ancestors. Millions of them. Most of them set out to live two-by-two, also. Millions of them. Well, that's all my sermon. 'Twan't very long, anyway.

[*The organ starts playing Handel's "Largo." The congregation streams into the church and sits in silence. Mrs. Webb, on the way to her place, turns back and speaks to the audience*]

MRS. WEBB: I don't know why on earth I should be crying. I suppose there's nothing to cry about. It came over me at breakfast this morning; there was Emily eating her breakfast as she's done for seventeen years and now she's going off to eat it in someone else's house. I suppose that's it. And Emily! She suddenly said: I can't eat another mouthful, and she put her head down on the table and *she* cried. [*She starts toward her seat in the church, but turns back and adds*] Oh, I've got to say it: you know, there's something downright cruel about sending our girls out into marriage this way. I hope some of her girl friends have told her a thing or two. It's cruel, I know, but I couldn't bring myself to say anything. I went into it blind as a bat myself. The whole world's wrong, that's what's the matter. There they come. [*She hurries to her place in the pew. George starts to come down the right aisle of the theater, through the audience. Suddenly three members of his baseball team appear by the right proscenium pillar and start whistling and catcalling to him. They are dressed for the ball field*]

THE BASEBALL PLAYERS: Eh, George, George! Hsst —yaow! If things don't go right, call us in. We know what to do. Eh, fellas? Yaow! George, don't look so innocent, you old geezer. We know what you're thinking. Don't disgrace the team, big boy. Whoo-oo-oo.

STAGE MANAGER: All right! All right! That'll do. That's enough of that. [*Smiling, he pushes them off the stage. They lean back to shout a few more catcalls*] There used to be an awful lot of that kind of thing at weddings in the old days,—Rome, and later. We're more civilized now,—so they say.

[*The choir starts singing "Love divine, all love excelling—." George has reached the stage. He stares at the congregation a moment, then takes a few steps of withdrawal, toward the right proscenium pillar*]

GEORGE: [*Darkly, to himself*] I wish I were back at school. . . . I don't want to get married. [*His mother has left her seat and come toward him. She stops, looking at him anxiously*]

MRS. GIBBS: George, what's the matter?

GEORGE: Ma, I don't want to grow *old*. Why's everybody pushing me so?

MRS. GIBBS: Why, George . . . you wanted it.

GEORGE: Why do I have to get married at all? Listen, Ma, for the last time I ask you—

MRS. GIBBS: No, no, George . . . you're a man now.

GEORGE: Listen, Ma, you never listen to me. All I want to do is to be a fella . . . why do—

MRS. GIBBS: George! If anyone should hear you! Now stop. Why, I'm ashamed of you!

GEORGE: [*Passing his hand over his forehead*] What's the matter? I've been dreaming. Where's Emily?

MRS. GIBBS: Gracious! You gave me such a turn.

GEORGE: Cheer up, Ma. What are you looking so funny for? Cheer up; I'm getting married.

MRS. GIBBS: Let me catch my breath a minute.

GEORGE: Now, Ma, you have Thursday nights. Emily and I are coming over to dinner every Thursday night . . . you'll see. Ma, what are you crying for? Come on; we've got to get ready for this.

[*In the meantime, Emily, in white and wearing her wedding veil, has come through the audience and mounted on to the stage. She too draws back when she sees the congregation in the church. The choir begins: "Blessed be the tie that binds"*]

EMILY: I never felt so alone in my whole life. And George over there, looking so . . . ! I *hate* him. I wish I were dead. Papa! Papa!

MR. WEBB: [*Leaves his seat in the pews and comes toward her anxiously*] Emily! Emily! Now don't get upset. . . .

EMILY: But, Papa,—I don't want to get married. . . .

MR. WEBB: Sh-sh—Emily. Everything's all right.

EMILY: Why can't I stay for a while just as I am? Let's go away.

MR. WEBB: No, no, Emily. Now stop and think.

EMILY: Don't you remember that you used to say,—all the time you used to say that I was *your* girl. There must be lots of places we can go to. Let's go away. I'll work for you. I could keep house.

MR. WEBB: Sh. . . . You mustn't think of such things. You're just nervous, Emily. Now, now,— you're marrying the best young fellow in the world. George is a fine fellow.

EMILY: But, Papa,—

MR. WEBB: George! George! [*Mrs. Gibbs returns to her seat. George hears Mr. Webb and looks up. Mr. Webb beckons to him. They move to the center of the stage*] I'm giving away my daughter, George. Do you think you can take care of her?

GEORGE: Mr. Webb, I want to . . . I want to try. Emily, I'm going to do my best. I love you, Emily. I need you.

EMILY: Well, if you love me, help me. All I want is someone to love me.

GEORGE: I will, Emily.

EMILY: If ever I'm sick or in trouble, that's what I mean.

GEORGE: Emily, I'll try. I'll try.

EMILY: And I mean for *ever*. Do you hear? For ever and ever. [*They fall into each other's arms. The March from "Lohengrin" is heard*]

MR. WEBB: Come, they're waiting for us. Now you know it'll be all right. Come, quick.

[*George slips away and takes his place beside the Stage Manager-Clergyman. Emily proceeds up the aisle on her father's arm*]

STAGE MANAGER: Do you, George, take this woman, Emily, to be your wedded wife, to have . . .

[*Mrs. Soames has been sitting in the last row of the congregation. She now turns to her neighbors and in a shrill voice says*]

MRS. SOAMES: Perfectly lovely wedding! Loveliest wedding I ever saw. Oh, I do love a good wedding, don't you? Doesn't she make a lovely bride?

GEORGE: I do.

STAGE MANAGER: Do you, Emily, take this man, George, to be your wedded husband,—

MRS. SOAMES: Don't know *when* I've seen such a lovely wedding. But I always cry. Don't know why it is, but I always cry. I just like to see young people happy, don't you? Oh, I think it's lovely. [*The ring. The kiss. The stage is suddenly arrested into silent, tableau. The Stage Manager, his eyes on the distance, says to the audience:*] I've married two hundred couples in my day. Do I believe in it? I don't know. M. . . . marries N. . . . millions of them. The cottage, the gocart, the Sunday afternoon drives in the Ford, the first rheumatism, the grandchildren, the second rheumatism, the deathbed, the reading of the will,—Once in a thousand times it's interesting. Well, let's have Mendelssohn's "Wedding March"!

[*The organ picks up the March. The bride and groom come down the aisle, radiant, but trying to be very dignified*]

MRS. SOAMES: Aren't they a lovely couple? Oh, I've never been to such a nice wedding. I'm sure they'll be happy. I always say: *happiness*, that's the great thing! The important thing is to be happy.

[*The bride and groom reach the steps leading*

into the audience. A bright light is thrown upon them. They descend into the auditorium and run up the aisle joyously]

STAGE MANAGER: That's all the Second Act. Ten minutes' intermission, folks.

ACT III.

During the intermission the audience has seen the actors arranging the stage. On the right hand side, a little right of the center, ten or twelve ordinary chairs have been placed in three openly spaced rows facing the audience. These are graves in the cemetery. Towards the end of the intermission the actors enter and take their places. The front row contains: toward the center of the stage, an empty chair; then Mrs. Gibbs, Simon Stimson. *The second row contains, among others,* Mrs. Soames. *The third row has* Wally Webb. *The dead sit in a quiet without stiffness, and in a patience without listlessness. The Stage Manager takes his accustomed place and waits for the house-lights to go down.*

STAGE MANAGER: This time nine years have gone by, friends—summer, 1913. Gradual changes in Grover's Corners. Horses are getting rarer. Farmers coming into town in Fords. Chief difference is in the young people, far as I can see. They want to go to the moving pictures all the time. They want to wear clothes like they see there . . . want to be citified. Everybody locks their house doors now at night. Ain't been any burglars in town yet, but everybody's heard about 'em. But you'd be surprised though—on the whole, things don't change much at Grover's Corners. Guess you want to know what all these chairs are here fur. Smarter ones have guessed it already. I don't know how you feel about such things; but this certainly is a beautiful place. It's on a hilltop—a windy hilltop—lots of sky, lots of clouds, —often lots of sun and moon and stars. You come up here on a fine afternoon and you can see range on range of hills—awful blue they are—up there by Lake Sunapee and Lake Winnapassaukee . . . and way up, if you've got a glass, you can see the White Mountains and Mt. Washington—where North Conway and Conway is. And, of course, our favorite mountain, Mt. Monadnock's, right here—and all around it lie these towns—Jaffrey, 'n East Jaffrey, 'n Peterborough, 'n Dublin and [*Then pointing down in the audience*] there, quite a ways down is Grover's Corners. Yes, beautiful spot up here. Mountain laurel and li-lacks. I often wonder why people like to be buried in Woodlawn and Brooklyn when they might pass the same time up here in New Hampshire. Over in that corner—[*Pointing to stage left*] are the old stones,—1670, 1680. Strong-minded people that come a long way to be independent. Summer people walk around there laughing at the funny words on the tombstones . . . it don't do any harm. And genealogists come up from Boston—get paid by city people for looking up their ancestors. They want to make sure they're Daughters of the American Revolution and of the *Mayflower*. . . . Well, I guess that don't do any harm, either. Wherever you come near the human race, there's layers and layers of nonsense. . . . Over there are some Civil War veterans too. Iron flags on their graves. . . . New Hampshire boys . . . had a notion that the Union ought to be kept together, though they'd never seen more than fifty miles of it themselves. All they knew was the name, friends—the United States of America. The United States of America. And they went and died about it. This here is the new part of the cemetery. Here's your friend, Mrs. Gibbs. 'N let me see— Here's Mr. Stimson, organist at the Congregational Church. And over there's Mrs. Soames who enjoyed the wedding so—you remember? Oh, and a lot of others. And Editor Webb's boy, Wallace, whose appendix burst while he was on a Boy Scout trip to Crawford Notch. Yes, an awful lot of sorrow has sort of quieted down up here. People just wild with grief have brought their relatives up to this hill. We all know how it is . . . and then time . . . and sunny days . . . and rainy days . . . 'n snow . . . tz-tz-tz. We're all glad they're in a beautiful place and we're coming up here ourselves when our fit's over. This certainly is an important part of Grover's Corners. A lot of thoughts come up here, night and day, but there's no post office. Now I'm going to tell you some things you know already. You know'm as well as I do; but you don't take'm out and look at'm very often. I don't care what they say with their mouths—everybody knows that *something* is eternal. And it ain't houses and it ain't names, and it ain't earth, and it ain't even the stars . . . everybody knows in their bones that *something* is eternal, and that something has to do with human beings. All the greatest people ever lived have been telling us that for five thousand years and yet you'd be surprised how people are always losing hold of it. There's something way down deep that's eternal about every human being. [*Pause*] You know as well as I do that the dead don't stay interested in us living people for very long. Gradually, gradually, they let hold of the earth . . . and the ambitions they had . . . and the pleasures they had . . . and the things they suffered . . . and the people they loved. They get weaned away from earth—that's the way I put it,—weaned away. Yes, they stay here while the earth-part of 'em burns away, burns out, and all that time they slowly get indifferent to what's goin' on in Grover's Corners. They're waitin'. They're waitin' for something that they feel is comin'. Something important and great. Aren't they waitin' for the eternal part in them to come out clear? Some of the things they're going to say maybe'll hurt your feelings—but that's the way it is: mother'n daughter . . . husband 'n wife . . . enemy 'n enemy . . . money 'n miser . . . all those terribly important things kind of grow pale around here. And what's left? What's left when memory's gone, and your identity, Mrs. Smith? [*He looks at the audience a minute, then turns to the stage*] Well! There are some *living* people. There's Joe Stoddard, our undertaker, supervising a new-made grave. And here comes a Grover's Corners boy, that left town to go out West.

> [Joe Stoddard *has hovered about in the background. Sam Craig enters left, wiping his forehead from the exertion. He carries an umbrella and strolls front*]

SAM CRAIG: Good afternoon, Joe Stoddard.

JOE STODDARD: Good afternoon, good afternoon. Let me see now: do I know you?

SAM CRAIG: I'm Sam Craig.

JOE STODDARD: Gracious sakes' alive! Of all people! I should'a knowed you'd be back for the funeral. You've been away a long time, Sam.

SAM CRAIG: Yes, I've been away over twelve years. I'm in business out in Buffalo now, Joe. But I was in the East when I got news of my cousin's death, so I thought I'd combine things a little and come and see the old home. You look well.

JOE STODDARD: Yes, yes, can't complain. Very sad, our journey today, Samuel.

SAM CRAIG: Yes.

JOE STODDARD: Yes, yes. I always say, I hate to supervise when a young person is taken. I see you brought your umbrella. It's going to rain and make it sadder still, seems like. They'll be here in a few minutes now. I had to come here early today—my son's supervisin' at the home.

SAM CRAIG: [*Reading stones*] Old Farmer McCarty, I used to do chores for him—after school. He had the lumbago.

JOE STODDARD: Yes, we brought Farmer McCarty here a number of years ago now.

SAM CRAIG: [*Staring at* Mrs. Gibbs' *knees*] Why, this is my Aunt Julia. . . . I'd forgotten that she'd . . . of course, of course.

JOE STODDARD: Yes, Doc Gibbs lost his wife two-three years ago . . . about this time. And today's another pretty bad blow for him, too.

MRS. GIBBS: [*To* Simon Stimson: *in an even voice*] That's my sister Carey's boy, Sam. . . . Sam Craig.

SIMON STIMSON: I'm always uncomfortable when *they're* around.

MRS. GIBBS: Simon.

SIMON STIMSON: They and their nonsense and their damned glee at being alive. . . .

MRS. GIBBS: Simon, be patient. . . .

SAM CRAIG: Do they choose their own verses much, Joe?

JOE STODDARD: No . . . not usual. Mostly the bereaved pick a verse.

SAM CRAIG: Doesn't sound like Aunt Julia. There aren't many of those Hersey sisters left now. Let me

see: where are . . . I wanted to look at my father's and mother's . . .

JOE STODDARD: Over there with the Craigs. . . . Avenue F.

SAM CRAIG: [*Reading* Simon Stimson's *epitaph*] He was organist at church, wasn't he?—Hm, drank a lot, we used to say.

JOE STODDARD: Nobody was supposed to know about it. He'd seen a peck of trouble. Those musical fellas ain't like the rest of us, I reckon. [*Behind his hand*] Took his own life, y' know?

SAM CRAIG: Oh, did he?

JOE STODDARD: Hung himself in the attic. They tried to hush it up, but of course it got around. His wife's just married Senator Barstow. Many a time I've seen her, eleven o'clock at night, goin' around the streets huntin' for her husband. Think o' that! Now she's married to Senator Barstow over at Manchester. He chose his own epy-taph. You can see it there. It ain't a verse exactly.

SAM CRAIG: Why, it's just some notes of music— what is it?

JOE STODDARD: Oh, I wouldn't know. It was wrote up in the Boston papers at the time.

SAM CRAIG: Joe, what did she die of?

JOE STODDARD: Who?

SAM CRAIG: My cousin.

JOE STODDARD: Oh, didn't you know? Had some trouble bringing a baby into the world. Let's see, today's Friday—'twas almost a week ago now.

SAM CRAIG: [*Putting up his umbrella*] Did the baby live?

JOE STODDARD: [*Raising his coat collar*] No. 'Twas her second, though. There's a little boy 'bout four years old.

SAM CRAIG: The grave's going to be over there?

JOE STODDARD: Yes, there ain't much more room over here among the Gibbses, so they're opening up a whole new Gibbs section over by Avenue B. You'll excuse me now. I see they're comin'.

THE DEAD: [*Not lugubrious; and strongly New England in accent*] Rain'll do a lot of good.—Yes, reckon things were gettin' downright parched. Don't look like it's goin' to last long, tho'.—Lemuel, you remember the floods of '79? Carried away all the bridges but one.

> [*From left to right, at the back of the stage, comes a procession. Four men carry a casket, invisible to us. All the rest are under umbrellas. One can vaguely see:* Dr. Gibbs, George, *the* Webbs, *etc. They gather about a grave in the back center of the stage, a little to the left of center*]

MRS. SOAMES: Who is it, Julia?

MRS. GIBBS: [*Without raising her eyes*] My daughter-in-law, Emily Webb.

MRS. SOAMES: [*A little surprised, but no emotion*] Well, I declare! The road up here must have been awful muddy. What did she die of, Julia?

MRS. GIBBS: In childbirth.

MRS. SOAMES: Childbirth. [*Almost with a laugh*] I'd forgotten all about that! My, wasn't life awful— [*With a sigh*] and wonderful.

SIMON STIMSON: [*With a sideways glance*] Wonderful, was it?

MRS. GIBBS: Simon! Now, remember!

MRS. SOAMES: I remember Emily's wedding. Wasn't it a lovely wedding! And I remember her reading the class poem at Graduation Exercises. Emily was one of the brightest girls ever graduated from High School. I've heard Principal Wilkins say so time after time. I called on them at their new farm, just before I died. Perfectly beautiful farm.

A WOMAN FROM AMONG THE DEAD: It's on the same road we lived on.

A MAN AMONG THE DEAD: Yes, just near the Elks' picnic grounds. Remember, Joe? By the lake where we always used to go Fourth of July? Right smart farm.

[*They subside. The group by the grave starts singing "Blessed be the tie that binds"*]

A WOMAN AMONG THE DEAD: I always liked that hymn. I was hopin' they'd sing a hymn.

A MAN AMONG THE DEAD: My wife—my second wife—knows all the verses of about every hymn there is. It just beats the Dutch . . . she can go through them all by heart.

[*Pause. Suddenly Emily appears from among the umbrellas. She is wearing a white dress. Her hair is down her back and tied by a white ribbon like a little girl. She comes slowly, gazing wonderingly at the dead, a little dazed. She stops halfway and smiles faintly*]

EMILY: Hello.

VOICES AMONG THE DEAD: Hello, Emily. H'lo, M's. Gibbs.

EMILY: Hello, Mother Gibbs.

MRS. GIBBS: Emily.

EMILY: Hello. [*The hymn continues. Emily looks back at the funeral. She says dreamily:*] It's raining.

MRS. GIBBS: Yes. . . . They'll be gone soon, dear. Just rest yourself. [*Emily sits down in the empty chair by* Mrs. Gibbs]

EMILY: It seems thousands and thousands of years since I. . . . How stupid they all look. They don't have to look like that!

MRS. GIBBS: Don't look at them now, dear. They'll be gone soon.

EMILY: Oh, I wish I'd been here a long time. I don't like being new here.—How do you do, Mr. Stimson?

SIMON STIMSON: How do you do, Emily.

[*Emily continues to look about her with a wan and wondering smile; but for a moment her eyes do not return to the funeral group. As though to shut out from her mind the thought of that group she starts speaking to* Mrs. Gibbs *with a touch of nervousness*]

EMILY: Mother Gibbs, George and I have made that farm into just the best place you ever saw. We

thought of you all the time. We wanted to show you the new barn and a great long ce-ment drinking fountain for the stock. We bought that out of the money you left us.

MRS. GIBBS: I did?

EMILY: Don't you remember, Mother Gibbs—the legacy you left us? Why, it was over three hundred and fifty dollars.

MRS. GIBBS: Yes, yes, Emily.

EMILY: Well, there's a patent device on this drinking fountain so that it never overflows, Mother Gibbs, and it never sinks below a certain mark they have there. It's fine. [*Her voice trails off and her eyes return to the funeral group*] It won't be the same to George without me, but it's a lovely farm. [*Suddenly she looks directly at* Mrs. Gibbs] Live people don't understand, do they?

MRS. GIBBS: No, dear—not very much.

EMILY: They're sort of shut up in little boxes, aren't they? I feel as though I knew them last a thousand years ago. . . . My boy is spending the day at Mrs. Carter's. [*She sees* Mr. Carter *among the dead*] Oh, Mr. Carter, my little boy is spending the day at your house.

MR. CARTER: Is he?

EMILY: Yes, he loves it there.—Mother Gibbs, we have a Ford, too. Never gives any trouble. I don't drive, though. Mother Gibbs, when does this feeling go away?—Of being . . . one of *them*? How long does it . . . ?

MRS. GIBBS: Sh! dear. Just wait and be patient.

EMILY: [*With a sigh*] I know.—Look, they're finished. They're going.

MRS. GIBBS: Sh—.

[*The umbrellas leave the stage.* Dr. Gibbs *comes over to his wife's grave and stands before it a moment.* Emily *looks up at his face.* Mrs. Gibbs *does not raise her eyes*]

EMILY: Look! Father Gibbs is bringing some of my flowers to you. He looks just like George, doesn't he? Oh, Mother Gibbs, I never realized before how troubled and how . . . how in the dark live persons are. From morning till night, that's all they are— troubled. [Dr. Gibbs *goes off*]

THE DEAD: Little cooler than it was.—Yes, that rain's cooled it off a little. Those North East winds always do the same thing, don't they? If it isn't a rain, it's a three-day blow.—Reckon it may clear up before night; often does.

[*A patient calm falls on the stage. The* Stage Manager *appears at his proscenium pillar, smoking.* Emily *sits up abruptly with an idea*]

EMILY: But, Mother Gibbs, one can go back, one can go back there again . . . into living. I feel it. I know it. Why just then for a moment I was thinking about . . . about the farm . . . and for a minute I *was* there, and my baby was on my lap as plain as day.

MRS. GIBBS: Yes, of course you can.

EMILY: I can go back there and live all those days over again . . . why not?

MRS. GIBBS: All I can say is, Emily, don't.

EMILY: [*Takes a few steps toward the* Stage Manager] But it's true, isn't it? I can go and live . . . back there . . . again.

STAGE MANAGER: Yes, some have tried—but they soon come back here.

MRS. GIBBS: Don't do it, Emily.

MRS. SOAMES: Emily, don't. It's not what you think it'd be.

EMILY: But I won't live over a sad day. I'll choose a happy one—I'll choose the day I first knew that I loved George. Why should that be painful? [*They are silent. Her question turns to the* Stage Manager]

STAGE MANAGER: You not only live it; but you watch yourself living it.

EMILY: Yes?

STAGE MANAGER: And as you watch it, you see the thing that they—down there—never know. You see the future. You know what's going to happen afterwards.

EMILY: But is that—painful? Why?

MRS. GIBBS: That's not the only reason why you shouldn't do it, Emily. When you've been here longer you'll see that our life here is our hope that soon we'll forget all that, and think only of what's ahead, and be ready for what's ahead. When you've been here longer you'll understand.

EMILY: [*Softly*] But, Mother Gibbs, how can I ever forget that life? It's all I know. It's all I had. [Mrs. Gibbs *does not answer*] Mr. Stimson, did you go back?

SIMON STIMSON: [*Sharply*] No.

EMILY: Did you, Mrs. Soames?

MRS. SOAMES: Oh, Emily. It isn't wise. Really, it isn't. All we can do is just warn you. It won't be what you expect.

EMILY: [*Slowly*] But it's a thing I must know for myself. I'll choose a happy day, anyway.

MRS. GIBBS: No. At least, choose an unimportant day. Choose the least important day in your life. It will be important enough.

EMILY: [*To the* Stage Manager] Then it can't be since I was married; or since the baby was born. I can choose a birthday at least, can't I?—I choose my twelfth birthday.

STAGE MANAGER: All right. February 11th, 1899. A Tuesday.—Do you want any special time of day?

EMILY: Oh, I want the whole day.

STAGE MANAGER: We'll begin at dawn. You remember it had been snowing for several days; but it had stopped the night before, and they had begun clearing the roads. The sun's coming up.

EMILY: [*With a cry*] There's Main Street . . . why, that's Mr. Morgan's drugstore before he changed it! . . . And there's the livery stable. [*She walks toward the back of the stage*]

STAGE MANAGER: Yes, it's 1899. This is fourteen years ago.

EMILY: Oh, that's the town I knew as a little girl. And, look, there's the old white fence that used to be around our house. Oh, I'd forgotten that! Oh, I love it so! Are *they* inside?

STAGE MANAGER: Yes, your mother'll be coming downstairs in a minute to make breakfast.

EMILY: [*Softly*] Will she?

STAGE MANAGER: And you remember: your father had been away for several days; he came back on the early morning train.

EMILY: No . . . ?

STAGE MANAGER: He'd been back to his college to make a speech—in Western New York, at Clinton.

EMILY: Look! There's Howie Newsome. There's our policeman. But he's *dead; he died.*

[*The* Stage Manager *retires to his corner. The voices of* Howie Newsome, Constable Warren *and* Joe Crowell, Jr., *are heard at the left of the stage*]

HOWIE NEWSOME: Whoa, Bessie!—Bessie! 'Morning, Bill.

BILL: Morning, Howie.

HOWIE NEWSOME: You're up early.

BILL: Been rescuin' a party; darn near froze to death, down by Polish Town thar. Got drunk and lay out in the snowdrifts. Thought he was in bed when I shook'm.

EMILY: Why, there's Joe Crowell. . . .

JOE CROWELL: Good morning, Mr. Warren. 'Morning, Howie.

[Mrs. Webb *has appeared in her kitchen, but* Emily *does not see her until she calls*]

MRS. WEBB: Chil-*dren!* Wally! Emily! . . . Time to get up.

EMILY: Mama, here I am! Oh! how young Mama looks! I didn't know Mama was ever that young. Oh!

MRS. WEBB: You can come and dress by the kitchen fire, if you like; but hurry. [Howie Newsome *has entered along Main Street and brings the milk to* Mrs. Webb's *door*] Good morning, Mr. Newsome. Whhhh—it's cold.

HOWIE NEWSOME: Ten below by my barn, Mrs. Webb.

MRS. WEBB: Think of it! Keep yourself wrapped up. [*She takes her bottles in, shuddering*]

EMILY: [*With an effort*] Mama, I can't find my blue hair ribbon anywhere.

MRS. WEBB: Just open your eyes, dear, that's all. I laid it out for you special—on the dresser, there. If it were a snake it would bite you.

EMILY: Yes, yes. . . . [*She puts her hand on her heart.* Mr. Webb *comes along Main Street, where he meets* Constable Warren]

MR. WEBB: Good morning, Bill.

BILL: Good morning, Mr. Webb. You're up early.

MR. WEBB: Yes, just been back to my old college in New York State. Been any trouble here?

BILL: Well, I was called up this mornin' to rescue a Polish fella—darn near froze to death he was.

MR. WEBB: We must get it in the paper.

BILL: 'Twan't much.

EMILY: [*Whispers*] Papa. [Mr. Webb *shakes the snow off his feet and enters his house*]

MR. WEBB: Good morning, Mother.

MRS. WEBB: How did it go, Charles?

MR. WEBB: Oh, fine, I guess. I told'm a few things.

MRS. WEBB: Did you sit up on the train all night?

MR. WEBB: Yes. Never could sleep on a Pullman anyway.

MRS. WEBB: Charles, seems to me—we're rich enough so that you could sleep in a train once in a while.

MR. WEBB: Everything all right here?

MRS. WEBB: Yes—can't think of anything that's happened, special. Been right cold. Howie Newsome says it's ten below over to his barn.

MR. WEBB: Yes, well, it's colder than that at Hamilton College. Students' ears are falling off. It ain't Christian.—Paper have any mistakes in it?

MRS. WEBB: None that I noticed. Coffee's ready when you want it. [*He starts upstairs*] Charles! Don't forget; it's Emily's birthday. Did you remember to get her something?

MR. WEBB: [*Patting his pocket*] Yes, I've got something here.

MRS. WEBB: Goodness sakes! I hope she likes what I got for her. I hunted hard enough for it. Children! Hurry up! Hurry up!

MR. WEBB: Where's my girl? Where's my birthday girl? [*He goes off left*]

MRS. WEBB: Don't interrupt her now, Charles. You can see her at breakfast. She's slow enough as it is. Hurry up, children! It's seven o'clock. Now, I don't want to call you again.

EMILY: [*Softly, more in wonder than in grief*] I can't bear it. They're so young and beautiful. Why did they ever have to get old? Mama, I'm here. I'm grown up. I love you all, everything.—I can't look at everything hard enough. There's the butternut tree. [*She wanders up Main Street*] There's Mr. Morgan's drugstore. And there's the High School, forever and ever, and ever. And there's the Congregational Church where I got married. Oh, dear. Oh, dear. Oh, dear! [*The Stage Manager beckons partially to her. He points to the house. She says a breathless "yes" and goes to the house*] Good morning, Mama.

MRS. WEBB: [*At the foot of the stairs, kissing her in a matter-of-fact way*] Well, now, dear, a very happy birthday to my girl and many happy returns. There are some surprises waiting for you on the kitchen table.

EMILY: Oh, Mama, you *shouldn't* have. [*She throws an anguished glance at the Stage Manager*] I can't—I can't.

MRS. WEBB: [*Facing the audience, over her stove*] But birthday or no birthday, I want you to eat your breakfast good and slow. I want you to grow up and be a good strong girl. [*She goes to the stairs and calls*] Wally! Wally, wash yourself good. Everything's getting cold down here. [*She returns to the stove with her back to* Emily. Emily *opens her purcels*] That in the blue paper is from your Aunt Carrie and I reckon you can guess who brought the post card album. I found it on the doorstep when I brought in the milk—George Gibbs . . . must have come over in the cold pretty early . . . right nice of him.

EMILY: [*To herself*] Oh, George; I'd forgotten that. . . .

MRS. WEBB: Chew that bacon slow. It'll help keep you warm on a cold day.

EMILY: [*Beginning softly but urgently*] Oh, Mama, just look at me one minute as though you really saw me. Mama, fourteen years have gone by. I'm dead. You're a grandmother, Mama. I married George Gibbs, Mama. Wally's dead, too. Mama, his appendix burst on a camping trip to North Conway. We felt just terrible about it—don't you remember? But, just for a moment now we're all together. Mama, just for a moment we're happy. Let's look at one another.

MRS. WEBB: That in the yellow paper is something I found in the attic among your grandmother's things. You're old enough to wear it now, and I thought you'd like it.

EMILY: And this is from you. Why, Mama, it's lovely and it's just what I wanted. It's beautiful! [*She flings her arms around her mother's neck. Her mother goes on with her cooking, but is pleased*]

MRS. WEBB: Well, I hoped you'd like it. Hunted all over. Your Aunt Norah couldn't find one in Concord, so I had to send all the way to Boston [*Laughing*] Wally has something for you, too. He made it at Manual Training Class and he's very proud of it. Be sure you make a big fuss about it.— Your father has a surprise for you, too; don't know what it is myself. Sh—here he comes.

MR. WEBB: [*Off stage*] Where's my girl? Where's my birthday girl?

EMILY: [*In a loud voice to the* Stage Manager] I can't. I can't go on. Oh! Oh. It goes so fast. We don't have time to look at one another. [*She breaks down sobbing. At a gesture from the* Stage Manager, Mrs. Webb *disappears*] I didn't realize. So all that was going on and we never noticed. Take me back— up the hill—to my grave. But first: Wait! One more look. Good-by, Good-by, world. Good-by, Grover's Corners . . . Mama and Papa. Good-by to clocks ticking . . . and Mama's sunflowers. And food and coffee. And new-ironed dresses and hot baths . . . and sleeping and waking up. Oh, earth, you're too wonderful for anybody to realize you. [*She looks toward the* Stage Manager *and asks abruptly, through her tears*] Do any human beings ever realize life while they live it?—every, every minute?

STAGE MANAGER: No. [*Pause*] The saints and poets, maybe—they do some.

EMILY: I'm ready to go back. [*She returns to her*

chair beside Mrs. Gibbs] Mother Gibbs, I should have listened to you. Now I want to be quiet for a while.—Oh, Mother Gibbs, I saw it all. I saw your garden.

MRS. GIBBS: Did you, dear?

EMILY: That's all human beings are!—Just blind people.

MRS. GIBBS: Look, it's clearing up. The stars are coming out.

EMILY: Oh, Mr. Stimson, I should have listened to them.

SIMON STIMSON: [*With mounting violence; bitingly*] Yes, now you know. Now you know! That's what it was to be alive. To move about in a cloud of ignorance; to go up and down trampling on the feelings of those . . . of those about you. To spend and waste time as though you had a million years. To be always at the mercy of one self-centered passion, or another. Now you know—that's the happy existence you wanted to go back and see. Did you shout to 'em? Did you call to 'em?

EMILY: Yes, I did.

SIMON STIMSON: Now you know them as they are: in ignorance and blindness.

MRS. GIBBS: [*Spiritedly*] Simon Stimson, that ain't the whole truth and you know it.

[*The dead have begun to stir*]

THE DEAD: Lemuel, wind's coming up, seems like. —Oh, dear,—I keep remembering things tonight.— It's right cold for June, ain't it?

MRS. GIBBS: Look what you've done, you and your rebellious spirit stirring us up here.—Emily, look at that star. I forget its name.

THE DEAD: I'm getting to know them all, but I don't know their names.—My boy Joel was a sailor, —knew 'em all. He'd set on the porch evenings and tell 'em all by name. Yes sir, it was wonderful.—A star's mighty good company.—Yes, yes.—Yes, 'tis.

SIMON STIMSON: Here's one of *them* coming.

THE DEAD: That's funny. 'Taint no time for one of them to be here.—Goodness sakes.

EMILY: Mother Gibbs, it's George.

MRS. GIBBS: Sh, dear. You just rest yourself.

EMILY: It's George. [George *enters from the left, and slowly comes toward them*]

A MAN FROM AMONG THE DEAD: And my boy, Joel, who knew the stars—he used to say it took millions of years for that speck o' light to git to the earth. Don't seem like a body could believe it, but that's what he used to say—millions of years.

ANOTHER: That's what they say.

[George *flings himself on* Emily's *grave*]

THE DEAD: Goodness! That ain't no way to behave!—He ought to be home.

EMILY: Mother Gibbs?

MRS. GIBBS: Yes, Emily?

EMILY: They don't understand much, do they?

MRS. GIBBS: No, dear, not very much.

[*The* Stage Manager *appears at the right, one hand on a dark curtain which he slowly draws across the scene. In the distance a clock is heard striking the hour very faintly*]

STAGE MANAGER: Most everybody's asleep in Grover's Corners. There are a few lights on: Shorty Hawkins, down at the depot, has just watched the Albany train go by. And at the livery stable somebody's setting up late and talking.—Yes, it's clearing up. There are the stars—doing their old, old crisscross journeys in the sky. Scholars haven't settled the matter yet, but they seem to think there are no living beings up there. They're just chalk . . . or fire. Only this one is straining away, straining away all the time to make something of itself. The strain's so bad that every sixteen hours everybody lies down and gets a rest. [*He winds his watch*] Hm. . . . Eleven o'clock in Grover's Corners.—You get a good rest, too. Good night.

THE END

Clifford Odets

(1906– ——)

Clifford Odets was in his early twenties when the depression struck America, during the autumn of 1929. Born in Philadelphia, he was brought up in the mixed proletarian and lower-middle-class life of the Bronx, in New York City, and considered himself, despite the comparative prosperity of his father, a spiritual brother of the restive poor. After graduation from high school, he dabbled in writing and became an actor, but he achieved no particular success. Fortunately, he joined a junior acting company of the Theatre Guild which acquired three very able and progressive leaders: Cheryl Crawford, Lee Strasberg, and Harold Clurman. Under their guidance, this studio company broke off from the parent organization and blossomed forth as the independent Group Theatre, in 1931. Odets was one of the founders of this organization and modestly participated in the Group's effort to adapt to American conditions the famous "Stanislavsky system" of ensemble playing. He also began to write a play with an eye to the capacities of his fellow actors, completing for them a draft of *Awake and Sing!* entitled *I've Got the Blues*. It was a sorrowful account of the misery and restlessness of a poor Bronx family during the depression. Odets' colleagues were interested in the mournful play but not at all confident that it could succeed on the stage.

New developments in the theatrical world combined to give the young playwright a hearing. By 1935 the American theatre was in the throes of insurgency, and the New Theatre League, an outgrowth of numerous social-minded groups, was offering prizes for one-act plays. Odets locked himself in a hotel room for three days and turned out a panoramic treatment of a taxicab strike, *Waiting for Lefty*, which won the first prize for its vivid picture of the depression period. The dramatic form of *Waiting for Lefty*, which presented a strike meeting as a frame for flashbacks into the experience of the speakers, was effectively theatrical, and the dialogue was remarkably colorful and explosive. When the play was produced by the New Theatre League with Group Theatre actors, it was instantly acclaimed as a tour de force even by those who did not subscribe to its advocacy of class conflict.

The success of *Waiting for Lefty* prompted the Group Theatre to give this long one-act play a Broadway production, and, in order to round out the evening, Odets added a stirring short dramatization of the conflict between liberalism and fascism in Germany, *Till the Day I Die*. During the same season, moreover, his fellow players brushed the dust off his full-length family picture, now supplied with a revolutionary varnish and given the new title *Awake and Sing!* The production at once revealed new and even more remarkable facets of Odets' talent. The play concluded, it is true, with vague conversions to radicalism, but it also possessed more noteworthy and less superimposed qualities—namely, humor, insight, and compassion. Drawn with exceptional verisimilitude, the characters revealed themselves as frustrated yet irrepressible human beings, and their separate lives were woven together by Odets with much skill. Critics acclaimed *Awake and Sing!* as a rare, Chekhovian play, and Odets was securely launched on a career which brought him acclaim as the most promising young American playwright since the advent of O'Neill, some fifteen years earlier. Although the claims of some admirers proved extravagant, it is entirely true that Odets was the most talented writer discovered by the theatre of the depression generation.

Each of Odets' plays embodied some basic criticism of a society dominated by individualism and a *laissez-faire* philosophy. *Waiting for Lefty* was as violently anticapitalistic and prolabor as *Till the Day I Die* was passionately antifascist. *Awake and Sing!*, although anything but one-dimensional drama, attacked the middle-class family as a major source of human frustration. *Paradise Lost* (1936) presented the proposition that the middle class was dying, and *Golden Boy* (1937) promoted the thesis that our materialistic society diverted men from humanly satisfying modes of self-realization. *Rocket to the Moon* (1938) propounded the view that economic insecurity inhibits the full flowering of the human personality, and *Night Music* (1940) dramatized the theme of homelessness in modern society. The author of these plays considered himself the chronicler of a dying social order, and the two plays he contributed to the next decade of American theatre—*Clash by Night* (1941) and *The Big Knife* (1949)—also examined manifestations of decay. The former treated a domestic triangle as an effect of unemployment, with the humiliation of the "little man," the husband, culminating in his going berserk; the story implied a parallel to the manner in which common men had managed to translate their frustrations into violence in European fascist movements. *The Big Knife* was not only an exposé of Hollywood but dramatized the problem of artistic integrity in a world which buys and sells talent.

It is plain, then, that the social motivation of Odets' writing cannot be entirely ignored. He wrote with an animus, and his buoyancy as a writer depended largely on his confidence that his criticism was called for, that he was uncovering the source of evil and suffering, and that he was at the same time celebrating the growth of some show of resistance, understanding, or sheer idealism among common people. It is significant, in fact, that his plays succeeded only when he was supported by the social enthusiasms of his youth and by those of the theatre for which he wrote between 1935 and 1940. When, after spending a decade in Hollywood as a writer and producer, Odets severed connections with the film industry, vowing never to have any traffic with it, he found it difficult to re-establish himself in the theatre with *The Big Knife*. The play called attention to weaknesses one had tended to overlook in the early Odets plays because their enthusiasm for life and ideals had been affecting or contagious. Odets had been something more than a writer of routine obituaries on men and capitalism. Even the quietest of his early plays, *Rocket to the Moon,* had been charged with sympathy for those who refuse to be defeated by economic circumstances and personal difficulties.

The two full-length plays with which Odets made himself best known as the exponent of a new, socially charged dramatic style were *Awake and Sing!* and *Golden Boy.* The former is the more spontaneous work; it is more richly characterized, more moving, and also less calculated. It also happens to be less representative of American social reality and more dependent upon local color for its argument. *Golden Boy,* written later, is Odets' best-constructed play. Here Odets selected broadly familiar American material, celebrated in the sporting-news columns and in film stories. He transfigured the material with the help of his metaphorical cast of mind and his vigorous, if often uneven, dialogue. The result was an angular and provocative variant of the success-story theme of fiction and films, a work vividly realistic and at the same time always suggestive of larger experience and of ideas applicable to society as a whole. *Golden Boy* proved to be Odets' most successful play, and it was his only full-length play to be seen by any large segment of the playgoing public outside New York. He had offered it as a sort of American saga, and it was received as such, although with less enthusiasm for his sociological intention than he might have wished.

To insist on the allegory of the "the fiddle and the fist" in *Golden Boy* is to invite argument, since it is easy enough to accept the play as simply an exciting story of the ring, written with more than usual insight. Yet the early draft of *Golden Boy* carried the subtitle "A Modern Allegory," and the play was treated as such by its director, Harold Clurman, and its scene designer, Mordecai Gorelik. It is plain that Odets opposed two ways of life—the creative and the destructive, the socially desirable and the socially undesirable—in the story of Joe Bonaparte, who loved music but became a killer in the ring. As Clurman explained in a preface to the published version, this prize-fight drama was intended as "the picture of a great fight—a fight in which we are all involved, whatever our profession or craft."

To what extent the allegorical intention is supported by the characterization is an interesting question. It is true, for instance, that Odets the social critic showed the "golden boy" becoming a fighter in order to free himself from the scorn attached to "nobodies," especially if they belong to racial minorities. But is it true, as Clurman asserts, that in order to achieve success the boy "must exploit an accidental attribute of his make-up, a mere skill, and abandon the development of his real self"? Is Joe's "real" self one thing and his skill in the ring another? Is it credible that the boy who was a gifted violinist could become a successful boxer? These and other questions we may raise in connection with the story indicate the difficulty of relating allegory to convincing psychological drama. It was a difficulty Odets rarely succeeded in overcoming when he tried to compose social parables.

With or without its allegorical connotations, *Golden Boy* is representative of the charged dramatic realism of the theatre of the nineteen-thirties. But, even more important, the play reveals those qualities of talent that differentiated its author from the ordinary writers of social harangues and blueprints for the noncapitalistic millenium. As Brooks Atkinson noted, "Odets does not discuss the idea in *Golden Boy* so much as he shows it." And Odets "shows it" with the full exercise of his talent for interweaving related themes and situations and, above all, for letting life flow from various directions in a stream often unexpectedly fresh and strangely moving. The characters assert themselves regardless of argument, and we may wonder how it is that they possess so much individuality while their author insists on the theory that they are the product of social pressures. Poor or rich, failures or successes, Odets' characters are irrepressible because they were born alive in their author's memory and imagination. Odets could not have written pat problem plays with such characters, even if he had wanted to do so out of a desire to serve the theatre of "social consciousness." *Golden Boy* arouses interest largely because the thesis drama becomes a fugue again and again, with life providing the variations. And the writing is, characteristically for the young Odets, both concrete and elliptical; it is a poet's kind of writing.

BIBLIOGRAPHY: Brooks Atkinson, *Broadway Scrapbook* (pp. 74–77), 1947; Harold Clurman, Prefaces to *Six Plays of Clifford Odets* (pp. 421–433), 1939; Eleanor Flexner, *American Playwrights 1918–1938* (pp. 290–302, 312–314), 1938; John Gassner, *Masters of the Drama* (pp. 689–693), 1940, 1945; Joseph Wood Krutch, *The American Drama Since 1918* (pp. 263–277), 1939.

GOLDEN BOY

By Clifford Odets

CHARACTERS

SCENES

ACT I. SCENE I.

The small Broadway office of Tom Moody, *the fight manager. The office is scantily furnished, contains desk, chairs, telephone and couch. With* Moody *at present is his girl,* Lorna Moon. *There is a certain quiet glitter about this girl, and if she is sometimes hard, it is more from necessity than choice. Her eyes often hold a soft, sad glance. Likewise,* Moody's *explosiveness covers a soft, boyish quality, and at the same time he possesses a certain vulnerable quality which women find very attractive. The time is eighteen months ago. As the lights fade in, we catch these two at the height of one of their frequent fights.*

MOODY: Pack up your clothes and go! Go! Who the hell's stopping you?
LORNA: You mean it?
MOODY: You brought up the point yourself.

LORNA: No, I didn't!
MOODY: Didn't you say you had a good mind to leave me?
LORNA: No, I said—
MOODY: You said you were going to pack!
LORNA: I said I feel like a tramp and I don't like it. I want to get married, I want—
MOODY: Go home, Lorna, go home! I ain't got time to discuss it. Gimme some air. It's enough I got my wife on my neck.
LORNA: What does she say?
MOODY: Who?
LORNA: Your wife—your sweet goddam Monica!
MOODY: She wants five thousand dollars to give me the divorce. [Lorna *laughs*] I don't see that it's funny.
LORNA: Look, Tom, this means as much to me as it does to you. If she's out of the way, we can get married. Otherwise I'm a tramp from Newark. I don't like the feeling.
MOODY: Lorna, for Pete's sake, use your noodle!

952

When I get rid of Monica, we'll marry. Now, do I have to bang you on the nose to make you understand?

LORNA: Go to hell! . . . But come back tonight. [Moody's *answer is to look at her, then smile, then walk to her. They kiss*]

MOODY: If I had the money, I'd buy you something—I don't know what—a big ostrich feather! If Kaplan wins tonight, I'll take you dancing at the Park.

LORNA: He won't win.

MOODY: How do you know? *I* don't know—how do *you* know?

LORNA: Are you crazy? Do you think your Mr. Kaplan can go ten rounds with the Baltimore Chocolate Drop?

MOODY: How do I know?

LORNA: It's the Twentieth Century, Tom—no more miracles. [Moody's *face turns worried*. Lorna *smiles*] You know what I like about you—you take everything so serious.

MOODY: Who will if I don't? I've been off the gold standard for eight years. This used to be a gorgeous town. New York was hot with money. Kaplan gets four hundred bucks tonight. In the old days, that was nothing. Those were the days when I had Marty Welch, the heavyweight contender—Cy Webster who got himself killed in a big, red Stutz. In '27 and 8 you couldn't go to sleep—the town was crawling with attractions.

LORNA: My mother died in '28.

MOODY: I haven't had a break in years. "Carry me back to old Virginny"—that's how I feel. There isn't much of a future. [*Suddenly despondent*, Moody *goes back to his desk*]

LORNA: I was fooling.

MOODY: What about?

LORNA: Do you think I'd leave you?

MOODY: Why not? I'm an old man. What can I give you?

LORNA: A bang on the nose for a start. But what can I give you?

MOODY: A boy who can fight. Find me a good black boy and I'll show you a mint.

LORNA: Are good boys so hard to find?

MOODY: Honest to God, you make me sick to my stomach! What do you think I took a trip to Philadelphia? What do you think I went to Chicago? Wasn't I up in Boston for a week? You think good boys are laying around like pop-corn? I'd even take a bantamweight, if I found one.

LORNA: How about a nice lady fighter with a beard—[*Preparing to leave*] Well, I'll see you tonight, Moody.

MOODY: [*Thoughtfully*] I'd give me right eye for a good black boy.

LORNA: Let me have your right eye for a minute. [*She kisses his eye*. Moody *begins to embrace her—she eludes his grasp*] That's to keep you hot. But if the truth were known—"yours till hell freezes over."

MOODY: I need you, I need you, Lorna—I need you all the time. I'd like to give you everything you want. Push your mouth over. . . .

[Lorna *holds her face to his; he kisses her. Suddenly a youth is standing at the office door*. Lorna *sees him and breaks away*]

BOY: [*Breathing quickly*] Mr. Moody . . .

MOODY: [*Spinning around*] Don't you knock when you come in an office?

BOY: Sometimes I knock, sometimes I don't.

MOODY: Say your piece and get the hell out!

BOY: I just ran over from the gym . . .

MOODY: What gym?

BOY: Where Kaplan trains. He just broke his hand. . . . [Moody *stiffens to attention*] It's a fact.

MOODY: [*Grasping the phone*] Is Tokio over there? My trainer?

BOY: He's looking after Kaplan.

[Moody *begins to dial the phone but abruptly changes his mind and replaces the phone*]

MOODY: You can put me in the bug-house right now. Moody is the name, folks—step right up and wipe your shoes! Ah, that Kaplan! That phonus bolonus! [*He sits at his desk in despair*] Now I have to call up Roxy Gottlieb and cancel the match. His club's in the red as it is.

BOY: I don't think it's necessary to cancel, Tom.

MOODY: [*Aware of the* Boy *for the first time*] Oh, you don't? Who the hell are you? And who the hell are you to call me Tom? Are we acquainted?

BOY: I wrote you a couple of letters. I can do that stretch.

MOODY: What stretch?

BOY: Why don't you let me take Kaplan's place tonight?

MOODY: [*Sarcastically*] Go slow and tell me again . . . what?

BOY: [*Coolly*] I can take Kaplan's place. . . .

MOODY: You mean you want to fight the Baltimore Chocolate Drop? *You?* [*The* Boy *remains silent*. Moody *comes out from behind his desk and stands face to face with the* Boy. *With sudden discovery*] You're cock-eyed too.

BOY: [*Quietly*] Can't you fix it up with Roxy Gottlieb?

MOODY: [*Suddenly*] Looka, kid, go home, kid, before I blame Kaplan's glass mitts on *you*. Then you won't like it, and I won't like it, and Miss Moon here, she won't like it.

BOY: [*Turning to* Lorna] How do you do, Miss Moon. [Lorna *smiles at the* Boy's *quiet confidence*] I need a good manager, Mr. Moody. You used to be tops around town—everyone says so. I think you can develop me. I can fight. You don't know it, but I can fight. Kaplan's been through for years. He may be the best fighter in your stable, but he's a stumble-bum for the younger boys growing up. Why don't you give me this chance, Tom?

MOODY: I don't want you calling me Tom! [*He*

glares at the Boy *and then returns to the desk and telephone*]

BOY: I'm waiting for your answer. [Moody's *answer is an exasperated glance as he begins to dial the phone. The* Boy *half approaches the desk*] There are forty-three thousand minutes in a month—can't you give me five?

MOODY: I'll give you this phone in the head in a minute! Who are you? What the hell do you want? Where do you fight?

BOY: [*With cool persistence*] We ought to get together, Tom.

MOODY: I don't want you calling me Tom. You're brash, you're fresh, you're callow—and you're cock-eyed! In fact, you're an insult to my whole nature! Now get out! [Moody *turns back to the phone and begins dialing again. The* Boy *stands there, poised on his toes, not sure of his next move. He turns and looks at* Lorna. *She nods her head and gives him a faint smile of encouragement. On phone*] This is Tom Moody . . . is Tokio there? . . . [*He hangs up the phone and holds the instrument thoughtfully*] Tokio's on his way over.

BOY: The Baltimore Chocolate Drop is not as good as you think he is. [Moody *suddenly whirls around and holds the telephone high over his head in a threatening gesture. The* Boy *steps back lightly and continues*] I've studied his style for months; I've perfected the exact punch to quench his thirst. Did you ever watch closely? [*Acting it out*] He likes to pull your lead—he hesitates for a second—he pulls your lead—he slips his face away and then he's in. Suppose you catch that second when he hesitates—he's open for the punch!

MOODY: [*Sarcastically*] And what do you do with his left hook?

BOY: [*Simply*] Avoid it.

MOODY: [*Lowering the phone*] Looka, you idiot, did you ever hear of Phil Mateo?

BOY: I heard of him.

MOODY: The Chocolate Drop marked him lousy in twelve minutes and ten seconds. Was Kid Peters within your ken? And did you ever hear of Eddie Newton? The Chocolate gave him the blues in two rounds. And Frisco Samuels and Mike Mason . . .

BOY: Did you ever hear of me?

MOODY: [*Sarcastically*] No, who are you? I would honestly like to know—who are you?

BOY: [*Quietly*] My name is Bonaparte. [Moody *howls with laughter, and even* Lorna, *sympathetic to the* Boy, *laughs. The* Boy *continues*] I don't think it's funny. . . .

MOODY: Didn't that name used to get you a little giggle in school? Tell the truth, Bonaparte. Didn't it?

BOY: Call me Joe.

MOODY: [*Laughing*] And your eyes . . . Didn't they used to get a little giggle too?

JOE: You don't seem as intelligent as I thought you were.

LORNA: [*To the laughing* Moody, *seeing the* Boy's *pain*] Stop it, Tom.

MOODY: [*Laughing*] You can't blame me, Bonaparte. . . . I haven't laughed for years.

JOE: I don't like it. . . . I don't want you to do it. [*Suddenly* Joe *grabs* Moody *by the coat lapels.* Moody, *surprised, shakes him off. At the same time a small, quiet man enters the office. He is* Tokio, Moody's *trainer*] I'm sorry I did that, Tom. We ought to be together, Tom—not apart.

MOODY: Tokio, did you send this kid here?

TOKIO: No.

MOODY: Take him out before I brain him! [*He storms back to his desk*]

TOKIO: [*After looking at the* Boy] You hear about Kaplan?

MOODY: This idiot told me. It's the end of everything! I'm off my top with the whole thing! Kaplan was our meal-ticket. I'm up to the throat in scandal, blackmail, perjury, alimony and all points west!

TOKIO: [*Turning to* Joe] You oughta be ashamed to show your face in this office.

JOE: If Kaplan's mother fed him milk, he wouldn't have those brittle bones.

MOODY: ? ? ? ?

TOKIO: [*To* Moody] This is the boy who did it to Kaplan.

MOODY: ? ? ?

TOKIO: I went down for an apple and I come back and Kaplan's sparring with this kid—picked him up in the gym. The next thing I know, Kaplan's down on the floor with a busted mitt.

JOE: [*Modestly*] I took it on the elbow.

MOODY: ! ! [*Silence finally*]

LORNA: Where do you come from, Bonaparte?

JOE: Here.

LORNA: How old are you?

JOE: Twenty-one—tomorrow.

MOODY: [*After a look at* Lorna] Fight much?

JOE: Enough.

MOODY: Where?

JOE: [*Fabricating*] Albany, Syracuse . . .

LORNA: Does Roxy Gottlieb know you?

JOE: I never fought at his club.

MOODY: [*Harshly*] Does he know you?

JOE: No. [Tokio *and* Moody *look at each other. The phone rings.*]

MOODY: [*On the phone*] Hello. . . . "What's this you hear?" . . . You hear the truth, Roxy. . . . He bust his mitt again. . . . I can't help it if you got *fifty* judgments on your club. . . . The same to you. . . . Your mother too! [*Keeping his eyes on* Bonaparte] If you tie up your big flabby mouth for a minute, I'll give you some news. I'm in a position to do you a big favor. I got a replacement—*better* than Kaplan . . . Bonaparte. . . . No, Bon-a-parte. [*Holds hand over mouthpiece and asks* Boy] Is that crap?

JOE: No, that's my name.

MOODY: [*Back at phone*] That's right, like in Napoleon. . . . [*Looks the* Boy *over appraisingly*] One hundred and thirty

JOE: Three.

MOODY: Hundred and thirty-three. Your customers'll eat him up. I'll bring him right over . . . you can take my word—the kid's a cock-eyed wonder . . . *your* mother too! [*He hangs up and turns around.* Joe *is the focus of all eyes*] It's revenge on somebody—maybe God.

JOE: [*Quietly*] I think you'll be surprised.

MOODY: [*Sadly*] Do your worst, kid. I've been surprised by experts.

JOE: Don't worry, Tom.

MOODY: Call me Tom again and I'll break your neck!!

QUICK FADEOUT

SCENE II.

Later that night. The combination dining and front room of the Bonaparte home. A round dining-room table, littered with newspapers, is lighted from directly above like a billiard table. Plaster busts of Mozart and Beethoven are on the sideboard. A cage of love birds at the other side of the room. Sitting at the table are two men: Mr. Bonaparte, *the father of* Joe, *and a Jewish friend, a* Mr. Carp, *who owns the local candy and stationery store. As the lights fade in,* Mr. Bonaparte *turns his newspaper.* Mr. Carp *is slowly pouring beer from a bottle. He begins to sip it as* Siggie, Mr. Bonaparte's *son-in-law, enters from the kitchen. He is barefooted, dressed in an undershirt, trousers and hung-down suspenders. He brings his own beer and glass, which he begins to fill with an expert's eye. In the silence,* Mr. Carp *takes a long, cool sip of beer combined with a murmur of relish.*

CARP: [*Finally*] I don't take it easy. That's my trouble—if I could only learn to take it easy. . . .

SIGGIE: What do you call it now, what you're doing?

CARP: Say, it's after business hours.

SIGGIE: That's a business? A man who runs a candy store is an outcast of the world. Don't even sell *nickel* candies—*penny* candies!

CARP: And your taxicab business makes you higher in the social scale?

SIGGIE: So I'm an outcast too. Don't change the subject. Like my father-in-law here—he's always changing the subject when I get a little practical on him. [*Putting his beer on the table and scratching himself under the arms like a monkey*] You—I'm talking about you, Mr. Bonaparte.

MR. BONAPARTE: [*Suddenly shooting out two words*] Ha ha! [*He then resumes his reading*]

SIGGIE: Every time I talk money, he gives me that horse laugh. Suppose you bought me a cab—I could pay it off by the week.

MR. BONAPARTE: [*Who talks with an Italian accent*] I don't go in taxicab business.

SIGGIE: I am married to your daughter and when you do this little thing, you do it for her and me together. A cab in two shifts is a big source of profit. Joe takes the night shift. I'm a married man so you don't expect me to take the night shift. [Anna, Siggie's *wife, in a night-gown, pokes her head in at the door*]

ANNA: Come to bed, Siggie. You'll wake up the whole neighborhood. [Anna *disappears*]

SIGGIE: See? I'm a married man! You don't expect me to take the night shift.

MR. BONAPARTE: [*Having heard this talk for months*] No, Siggie . . . no.

SIGGIE: No, what?

MR. BONAPARTE: No taxicab.

SIGGIE: Don't you wanna help your own family, foolish? After all, Joe's your own son—he's a man, no kid no more—

MR. BONAPARTE: Tomorrow's twenty-one.

SIGGIE: If he don't work he'll turn into a real bum. Look how late he's staying out at night.

MR. BONAPARTE: I don't expects for Joe to drive taxi.

SIGGIE: He's got to do something. He can drive like a fire engine. Why not?

MR. BONAPARTE: He gonna do something.

SIGGIE: What? Play his violinsky in the backyards?

ANNA: [*Looking in at the door again*] Come to bed, Siggie! Poppa, don't talk to him so he'll come to bed! [Anna *disappears again*]

SIGGIE: [*Annoyed*] Women! Always buzzing around. [Mr. Bonaparte's *only answer is to turn over the newspaper on the table before him*]

CARP: [*Reflectively*] Women . . . the less we have to do with women the better. As Schopenhauer says, "Much ado about nothing . . . the comedy of reproduction." [*He wags his head bitterly*] Women . . . !

SIGGIE: I'm hungry, but I ain't got the heart to go in the kitchen again. It reminds me of how my wife slaves for this family of crazy wops! A fine future for an intelligent woman!

MR. BONAPARTE: She'sa your wife, but also my daughter. She'sa not so intelligent as you say. Also, *you* are not so intelligent!

SIGGIE: You can't insult me, I'm too ignorant!

[Anna *now comes fully into the room. She is buxom, energetic, good-natured and adenoidal*]

ANNA: Poppa, why don't you let Siggie come to bed? Looka him, walking around barefooted!

MR. BONAPARTE: I don't stop him. . . .

SIGGIE: Sure he stops me—he stops me every night. I'm worried. I don't sleep. It's my Jewish disposition. He don't wanna help me out, your old man. He wants me to drive a company cab and submit to the brutalities of the foremen all my life. I could be in a healthy little enterprise for myself, but your old man don't wanna help me out.

ANNA: Why don't you buy Siggie a cab, Poppa? You got the cash.

SIGGIE: Buy it for Siggie and Joe.

ANNA: For Siggie and Joe—it don't have to be a new one.

SIGGIE: [*After giving his wife a stabbing glance*] Sure, even an old one—the way they recondition them now-a-days—

MR. BONAPARTE: Children, gone to bed.

SIGGIE: Don't tell a lie—how much you got in the bank?

MR. BONAPARTE: [*With a smile*] Millions.

SIGGIE: Four thousand?

MR. BONAPARTE: No.

SIGGIE: Three? [Mr. Bonaparte *shakes his head*] Three? . . .

ANNA: What's your business how much he's got?

SIGGIE: Shut up, Duchess! Am I asking for my health? If I wanna take you out of the kitchen, is that the gratitude I get? You and your father, you get my goat! I'm sore!

ANNA: Come to bed, Siggie.

SIGGIE: "Come to bed, come to bed!" What the hell's so special in bed. [Anna's *answer is a warm prolonged giggle*] It's a conspiracy around here to put me to bed. I'm warning one thing: if matters go from worse to worse, don't ever expect me to support this family, I'm warning!

MR. BONAPARTE: [*Smiling kindly*] We have-a receive the warning. We are in a conspiracy against you—gone to bed. [*He turns back to his newspaper. Siggie sees he has lost again and now turns on his wife*]

SIGGIE: Who asked you to stick in your two cents about secondhand cabs? As long as I'm not gonna get it, I'll tell you what I want—a first-class job, fresh from the factory. [*He suddenly swats her on the head with a rolled-up newspaper. She hits him back. He returns her blow*]

ANNA: Don't be so free with your hands! [*He hits her again. She hits him back*] You got some nerve, Siggie!

SIGGIE: [*Hitting her again*] The next time I'll break your neck—I'm super-disgusted with you!

MR. BONAPARTE: [*Standing up*] Stop this . . .

SIGGIE: [*Turning to him*] And with you, I'm super-finished! [*Turning back to his wife*] Sit out here with this Unholy Alliance—I'll sleep alone tonight. [*He starts for the door. Mr. Bonaparte puts his arm around Anna who begins to sob*]

MR. BONAPARTE: Hit your wife in private, not in public!

CARP: A man hits his wife and it is the first step to fascism!

SIGGIE: [*To* Carp] What are you talking about, my little prince! I love my wife. You don't stop talking how you hate yours. [*Now to* Mr. Bonaparte] And as for you, don't make believe you care!—Do I have to fall on my knees to you otherwise? We

wanna raise a family—it's a normal instinct. Take your arm off her.

ANNA: [*Suddenly moving over to* Siggie] That's right, poppa. He can hit me any time he likes.

SIGGIE: [*His arm around her*] And we don't want you interfering in our affairs unless you do it the right way!

ANNA: That's right, poppa—you mind your g.d. business! [Mr. Bonaparte *repressing a smile, slowly sits*]

SIGGIE: In the bed, Duchess.

ANNA: [*With a giggle*] Good night.

MR. BONAPARTE *and* MR. CARP: Good night. [*She exits. After a belligerent look at the pair at the table,* Siggie *follows her*]

MR. BONAPARTE: [*Bursting into hushed laughter*] There's a olda remark—never interfere in the laws of nature and you gonna be happy. Love! Ha ha!

CARP: [*Gloomily*] Happy? A famous man remarked in the last century. "Pleasure is negative."

MR. BONAPARTE: I feela good. Like-a to have some music! Hey, where's a my boy Joe? [*Looks at his watch; is surprised*] One o'clock . . . don't come home yet. Hey, he make-a me worry!

CARP: You think you got worries? Wait, you're a young man yet. You got a son, Joe. He practised on his fiddle for ten years? He won a gold medal, the best in the city? They gave him a scholarship in the Erickson Institute? Tomorrow he's twenty-one, yeah?

MR. BONAPARTE: [*Emphatically*] Yeah!

CARP: [*Leaning forward and dramatically making his point*] Suppose a war comes? Before you know it, he's in the army!

MR. BONAPARTE: Naw, naw! Whata you say! Naw!

CARP: [*Wagging his head in imitation*] Look in the papers! On every side the clouds of war—

MR. BONAPARTE: My Joe gotta biga talent. Yesterday I buy-a him present! [*With a dramatic flourish he brings a violin case out of the bottom part of the sideboard*]

CARP: [*As the case is opened*] It looks like a coffin for a baby.

MR. BONAPARTE: [*Looking down at the violin in its case*] His teacher help me to picka him.

CARP: [*The connoisseur*] Fine, fine—beautiful, fine! A cultural thing!

MR. BONAPARTE: [*Touching it fondly*] The mosta golden present for his birthday which I give him tonight.

CARP: How much, if I'm not getting too personal, did such a violin cost you?

MR. BONAPARTE: Twelve hundred dollars.

CARP: [*Shocked*] What?

MR. BONAPARTE: You're surprised of me? Well, I waita for this moment many years.

CARP: [*Sitting*] Ask yourself a pertinent remark: could a boy make a living playing this instrument in our competitive civilization today?

MR. BONAPARTE: Why? Don't expect for Joe to be

a millionaire. He don't need it, to be millionaire. A good life'sa possible—

CARP: For men like us, yes. But nowadays is it possible for a young man to give himself to the Muses? Could the Muses put bread and butter on the table?

MR. BONAPARTE: No millionaire is necessary. Joe love music. Music is the great cheer-up in the language of all countries. I learn that from Joe.

[Carp *sighs as* Mr. Bonaparte *replaces the violin in the buffet*]

CARP: But in the end, as Schopenhauer says, what's the use to try something? For every wish we get, ten remains unsatisfied. Death is playing with us as a cat and her mouse!

MR. BONAPARTE: You make-a me laugh, Mr. Carp. You say life'sa bad. No. life'sa good. Siggie and Anna fight—good! They love—good! You say life'sa bad . . . well, is pleasure for you to say so. No? The streets, winter a' summer—trees, cats—I love-a them all. The gooda boys and girls, they who sing and whistle—[*Bursts into a moment of gay whistling*]—very good! The eating and sleeping, drinking wine—very good! I gone around on my wagon and talk to many people—nice! Howa you like the big buildings of the city?

CARP: Buildings? And suppose it falls? A house fell down last week on Staten Island!

MR. BONAPARTE: Ha ha, you make me laugh, ha ha! [*Now enters* Frank Bonaparte, *oldest son of the family, simple, intelligent, observant*]

MR. BONAPARTE: Hello, Frank.

FRANK: Hello, poppa . . . Mr. Carp . . .

CARP: [*Nodding*] What's new in the world?

FRANK: [*Dropping newspapers to the table, but keeping one for himself*] Read 'em and weep. March first tomorrow—spring on the way. Flowers soon budding, birds twittering—south wind . . . Cannons, bombs and airplane raids! Where's Joe? Did you give him the fiddle yet?

MR. BONAPARTE: No, not in yet. Siggie and Anna sleep. Hungry?

FRANK: [*Beginning to undress—putting his coat on the back of a chair*] No, I'm tired. I'll see you in the morning, before I leave.

CARP: Going away again?

FRANK: South. Tex-tiles. There's hell down there in tex-tiles. [*He sits on the other side of the room and looks at a paper*]

CARP: I don't begin to understand it—tex-tiles! What's it his business if the workers in tex-tiles don't make good wages!

MR. BONAPARTE: Frank, he fight-a for eat, for good life. Why not!

CARP: Foolish!

MR. BONAPARTE: What ever you got ina your nature to do isa not foolish!

CARP: [*Flipping over the newspaper*] For instance —look: playing baseball isn't foolish?

MR. BONAPARTE: No, if you like-a to do.

CARP: Look! Four or five pages—baseball—tennis-ball—it gives you an idea what a civilization! You ever seen a baseball game?

MR. BONAPARTE: No.

CARP: [*Wagging his head*] Hit a ball, catch a ball . . . believe me, my friend—nonsense!

FRANK: Poppa, where did you say Joe was?

MR. BONAPARTE: Don't know—

FRANK: Poppa, you better brace yourself in your chair!

MR. BONAPARTE: What?

[Frank *places the paper before* Mr. Bonaparte. *He reads aloud*]

FRANK: Looka this, Joe's had a fight. "Flash: Chocolate Drop fails to K.O. new cock-eyed wonder." Take a look at the picture.

CARP: What?

MR. BONAPARTE: What?

FRANK: It's my little brother Joie, or I don't know a scab from a picket!

MR. BONAPARTE: Had a fight? That is foolish—not possible.

FRANK: [*Pointing with his finger*] There's his name —Bonaparte.

MR. BONAPARTE: [*Puzzled*] Musta be some other boy.

[Frank *suddenly flips over the newspaper. The others immediately see the reason:* Joe *stands in the entrance, in the shadows*]

JOE: [*In the shadows*] Gee, you're up late. . . .

MR. BONAPARTE: We waita for you.

[Joe *slowly moves into the light. His face is bruised and over one eye is a piece of adhesive tape*]

JOE: [*Seeing their looks*] I had a fight—a boy in the park—

MR. BONAPARTE: He hit you?

JOE: I hit him.

MR. BONAPARTE: You hurt?

JOE: No.

[Mr. Bonaparte *casts a furtive look in the direction of the other men*]

MR. BONAPARTE: Whata you fight him for?

JOE: Didn't like what he said to me.

MR. BONAPARTE: What he said?

JOE: [*Evasively*] It's a long story and I'm tired.

MR. BONAPARTE: [*Trying to break a pause of embarrassment*] I was say to Mr. Carp tomorrow is your birthday. How you like to be so old?

JOE: I forgot about that! I mean I forgot for the last few hours. Where do you think I was? Do you want the truth?

FRANK: Truth is cheap. We bought it for two cents. [*He turns over the paper and shows* Joe *his own face.* Joe *looks at the picture, likes it. General silence*]

JOE: [*Finally, belligerently*] Well, what are you going to do about it?

MR. BONAPARTE: [*Still puzzled*] Abouta what?

JOE: [*Challengingly*] Tomorrow's my birthday!

FRANK: What's that got to do with being a gladiator?

JOE: [*Turning to* Frank, *with sudden vehemence*] Mind your business! You don't know me—I see you once a year; what do you know about me?

FRANK: [*Smiling*] You're a dumb kid!

MR. BONAPARTE: [*Starting to his feet*] Hey, waita one-a minute. What'sa for this excitement?

JOE: [*Hotly*] I don't want to be criticized! Nobody takes me serious here! I want to do what I want. I proved it tonight. I'm good—I went out to earn some money and I earned! I had a professional fight tonight—maybe I'll have some more.

CARP: You honest to God had a fight?

JOE: [*Glaring at* Carp] Why not?

FRANK: [*To* Joe] No one's criticizin'.

MR. BONAPARTE: That's right.

JOE: [*Half sheepishly*] I don't know why I got so sore. . . .

FRANK: You're expecting opposition all the time—

MR. BONAPARTE: Sit down, Joe—resta you'self.

JOE: Don't want to sit. Every birthday I ever had I sat around. Now'sa time for standing. Poppa, I have to tell you—I don't like myself, past, present and future. Do you know there are men who have wonderful things from life? Do you think they're better than me? Do you think I like this feeling of no possessions? Of learning about the world from Carp's encyclopaedia? Frank don't know what it means—he travels around, sees the world! [*Turning to* Frank] You don't know what it means to sit around here and watch the months go ticking by! Do you think that's a life for a boy my age? Tomorrow's my birthday! I change my life!

MR. BONAPARTE: Justa like that?

JOE: Just like that!

FRANK: And what do you do with music?

JOE: Who says I'm married to music? I take a vacation—the notes won't run away!

FRANK: You're a mysterious kid. Where did you learn the fighting game?

JOE: These past two years, all over the city—in the gyms—

MR. BONAPARTE: Hey, Joe, you sounda like crazy! You no gotta nature for fight. You're musician. Whata you say, heh? Whata you do?

JOE: Let's call it a day.

MR. BONAPARTE: Isa no true whata I say?—

JOE: That's all for tonight. [*His lips tightened, he abruptly exits*]

MR. BONAPARTE: [*Calling after him*] Take a gooda sleep, Joe.

FRANK: [*Smiling*] It looks like the gold bug has visited our house.

CARP: [*Sadly*] Fortunes! I used to hear it in my youth—the streets of America is paved with gold. Say, you forgot to give him the present.

MR. BONAPARTE: [*Slowly, puzzled*] I don'ta know . . . he say he gonna fight. . . .

SLOW FADEOUT

SCENE III.

Two months later; Moody's *office as seen before.* Moody *is pacing back and forth in one of his fuming moods. Those present include* Lorna, *stretched out on the couch, blowing cigarette smoke into the air;* Tokio *sitting quietly on the window sill; and* Roxy Gottlieb, *comfortably spread out in the desk chair, wearing a big white panama hat which he seldom removes.*

ROXY: They don't like him. They seen him in five fights already. He's a clever boy, that Bonaparte, and speedy—but he's first-class lousy in the shipping department! I bought a piece of him, so I got a right to say it: a mosquito gives out better! Did you read what he wrote in his column, that Drake? He writes he's a regular "brain trust."

LORNA: What's wrong with that?

ROXY: I'll tell you in a capsule: the people who'll pay to watch a "brain trust" you could fit in a telephone booth! Roxy Gottlieb is telling you!

MOODY: Roxy's right. Joe pulls his punches. Two months already and he don't throw his hands right and he don't throw them enough.

LORNA: Tom, what do you want the boy to do? You surely know by now he's not a slugger. His main asset is his science—he's a student.

ROXY: [*Loftily*] Excuse me, Miss Moon. In the prizefight ring the cash customer don't look for stoodents. Einstein lives in a college—a wonderful man in *his* line! Also, while I think of it, a woman's place is in the hay, not in the office!

MOODY: [*Indignantly*] Where do you come off to make a remark like that?

LORNA: [*Standing up*] At the moment a woman's place is in the bar—see you later. [*She looks at the others with a peculiar smile and exits.* Moody *stares at* Roxy *who realizes he has said the wrong thing*]

MOODY: I'm worried about that boy!

TOKIO: I'd trust him, Tom. Joe knows his own needs, as he says. Don't ask him to change his style. A style is best when it's individual, when it comes out of the inner personality and the lay of the muscles and the set of the bones. That boy stands a chance to make the best lightweight since Benny Simon.

ROXY: On *your* nose!

TOKIO: He's got one of the best defenses I ever seen. And speedy as the wind.

MOODY: But he won't fight!

ROXY: A momma doll gives out better!

TOKIO: He's a peculiar duck—I want him thinking he's the best thing in shoe leather.

MOODY: He thinks so now.

TOKIO: I don't like to contradict you, Tom, but he don't. It's seventy-five percent front. If you want the goods delivered you have to treat him delicate, gentle—like a girl.

ROXY: Like a girl? Why didn't you say so before?

MOODY: No, Roy, not you—you just treat him like a human being.

TOKIO: I think we can begin the build-up now.

MOODY: A road tour?

TOKIO: I'd like to take him around the Middle West, about fifteen bouts.

ROXY: [Answering a look from Moody] I didn't say no. But will he cooperate?

TOKIO: As soon as I find the password.

MOODY: What's the password to make this kid go in and slug—that's the problem. [There is a knock at the door. Moody calls] Yes?

[The door opens and Mr. Bonaparte stands there hesitantly]

MR. BONAPARTE: [Timidly] My name is Joe Bonaparte's father. I come-a to see my son's new friends.

MOODY: [Expansively] Come in, sit down, Mr. Bonaparte.

ROXY: [Sitting comfortably] Take a seat.

MR. BONAPARTE: Am I interrupt?

MOODY: Not at all.

ROXY: What's the matter with your boy?

TOKIO: [To Mr. Bonaparte] This is Mr. Moody and Mr. Gottlieb.

MR. BONAPARTE: [Sitting] Good afternoon.

MOODY: We were just discussing your son.

MR. BONAPARTE: I please to hear. I like find out froma you how's this boxer business for Joe. Whata good in it for him.

MOODY: Your Joe's a very clever fighter.

ROXY: Can you take it? We want to make your boy famous—a millionaire, but he won't let us— won't cooperate. How do you like it?

MR. BONAPARTE: Why? Whatta he do?

ROXY: [Going over and facing the old man in a lecturing position] I'll ask you. What does he do? What does he do that's right? Nothing! We offer him on a gold platter! Wine, women and song, to make a figure of speech. We offer him magnitudes! . . .

MR. BONAPARTE: [Waiting] Yes—?

MOODY: But he won't fight.

MR. BONAPARTE: [Puzzled] He'sa fighta for you, no?

ROXY: You're right—no! Your boy's got unexplored possibilities—unexplored! But you can't make a purse out of somebody's ear.

MOODY: [Trying to counteract Roxy's volubility] My colleague is trying to say that Joe keeps holding back in the ring.

MR. BONAPARTE: Holda back?

TOKIO: He nurses his self—

MOODY: He keeps holding back—

TOKIO: His defense is brilliant—

MOODY: Gorgeous—!

ROXY: But where's the offense? You take but you can't give. Figure it out—where would you be in a traffic jam? You know how to reverse—but to shift in second or high?—nothing!

MR. BONAPARTE: [Quietly to Roxy] Hey, you talka too much—nobody's contradicta you.

ROXY: [After a momentary setback] "Everybody'sa contradicta me!" Even you, and I never met you before. [With a reproachful glance he retires to the desk where he sits and sulks]

MR. BONAPARTE: [Singling out Tokio as a man to whom he can speak] Who are you?

TOKIO: Your son's trainer. . . .

MR. BONAPARTE: You interest to helpa my boy?

TOKIO: [Respectfully] Very much. . . .

MR. BONAPARTE: Me too. Maybe not so as plan by these-a gentleman here. I don't say price fight'sa no good for Joe. Joe like-a to be fame, not feel ashame. . . .

TOKIO: Is Joe afraid of his hands?

MR. BONAPARTE: I don't know. You tella me what'sa what . . . I don't know price fight. His hand coulda get hurt?

MOODY: Every fighter hurts his hands. Sometimes they break—

TOKIO: They heal up in no time.

ROXY: [Flaring out] What's so special about hands? I suppose your kid plays piano!

MR. BONAPARTE: Coulda get hurt? Coulda break?!

ROXY: So what?

MR. BONAPARTE: [Up on his feet] Hey, you! I don't like-a you! You no interest in my boy! [Proudly] My boy'sa besta violin' in New York!

MOODY: [Suddenly sickened] What . . .?

MR. BONAPARTE: Yes, play the violin!

MOODY: That's it! . . .

ROXY: [Anguished by this stupidity] If I had hair I'd tear it out! Five hundred fiddlers stand on Broadway and 48th Street, on the corner, every day, rain or shine, hot or cold. And your boy dares—! [Turning to Moody] How do you like it? [He waves his hands in despair and retires to the desk, where he sits in fuming disgusted silence]

MOODY: [Repressing a feeling of triumph] Your boy's afraid of his hands because he fiddles?

MR. BONAPARTE: Yes, musta be!

TOKIO: Why did you come and tell us this?

MR. BONAPARTE: Because I like-a to help my boy. I like-a for him to try himself out. Maybe thisa better business for him. Maybe not. He mus' try to find out, to see whata he want . . . I don't know. Don't help Joe to tell him I come here. Don't say it. [He slowly walks to the door]

MOODY: That means you won't stand in his way?

MR. BONAPARTE: My boy coulda break his hand? Gentleman, I'ma not so happy as you . . . no! [He slowly exits]

MOODY: [Joyously] I'm beginning to see the light! Joe's mind ain't made up that the fist is mightier than the fiddle.

ROXY: [*Bouncing up and down*] I'll make up his mind. For the money that's involved I'd make Niagara Falls turn around and go back to Canada.

TOKIO: Don't try to bully him into anything

ROXY: In Roxy Gottlieb he met his match.

MOODY: [*Explosively*] What the hell's the matter with you, Roxy! Sit down a minute! [Roxy *sits*] As I see it, the job is to handle him gently, to make him see how much we prize him—to kill his doubts with goodness.

ROXY: I got it: the password is honey! . . .

MOODY: Right! The Middle West tour is on! Tokio goes along to build up a real offensive. I take care of the newspapers here. Chris', I thought it was something serious! I'm getting to feel like 1928 again. Call it intuition: I feel like the Resurrection. [*He gets up and begins to stroll about*] Once we're out of the tunnel, with thirty bouts behind us—

ROXY: If you hear a noise, it's my mouth watering—

[*The telephone rings.* Moody *answers*]

MOODY: Hello? . . . Yeah . . . I think he'll win— [*Hangs up*] Who do you think that was? [*Imitating*] "Fuseli is speaking." Eddie Fuseli!

ROXY: Fuseli? What's he want?

MOODY: Will Joe win against Vincenti Tuesday. Tokio, from now on it's your job.

TOKIO: I got faith in the boy.

MOODY: [*To* Roxy] I have to ask one thing—when Joe comes over from the gym let me do the talking.

TOKIO: And don't mention music! [Lorna *enters*]

LORNA: Shh! Here's Joe.

[Joe Bonaparte *enters the office. Immediately* Moody *and* Roxy *put on their softest kid gloves. Their methods of salesmanship will shortly become so apparent that both* Joe *and* Lorna *become suspicious*]

MOODY: [*Slowly circling around*] Glad to see you, Joe. Joe, you remember in reference to what we were speaking about yesterday? Well . . . we had several friends on the long distance phone. We're booking fifteen out of town bouts for you. Tough ones, too.

ROXY: Tonight I'm calling my Chicago connections.

MOODY: We talked it over with Tokio and he says —well, tell him what you said, Tokio—tell him the truth.

TOKIO: I think you got a wonderful future.

MOODY: [*To* Tokio] Name the names, Tokio.

TOKIO: Well, I said Benny Simon—as good as Simon, I said.

MOODY: Tokio's gonna work with you—help you develop a right—

ROXY: And a left! What'sa right without a left?

MOODY: Tokio thinks that when he brings you back you'll be a contender for Number One.

JOE: [*A little defensively*] Really? . . .

MOODY: But *you* have to help *us* help *you.*

ROXY: Could Webster say it better?

MOODY: [*Softly singing a siren song, his arms around* Joe's *shoulder*] This job needs gorgeous concentration. All your time and thoughts, Joe. No side lines, no side interests—

JOE: [*Defensively*] I don't go out with girls.

MOODY: You're in the fighting game. It's like being a priest—your work comes first. What would you rather do than fight?

JOE: [*Defensively*] I don't know what you mean.

MOODY: [*Carefully picking his words*] Some boys, for instance, like to save their looks. They'd practically throw the fight to keep their nose intact.

JOE: [*Smiling wryly*] My looks don't interest me.

[Lorna *is listening with rapt attention*]

MOODY: [*Still singing the siren song*] Then what's holding you back, Joe? You can tell me, Joe. We've set up housekeeping together, Joe, and I want you to tell me if you can't cook a steak—it don't matter. We're married anyway. . . .

JOE: [*Uneasily*] Who's being put to bed?

MOODY: What do you mean?

JOE: I don't like this seduction scene. [*To* Tokio] What are they after?

TOKIO: They think you're afraid of your hands.

MOODY: Are you?

JOE: Half . . .

TOKIO: Why?

ROXY: [*Bouncing up*] Tell the truth!

JOE: What truth?

MOODY: [*Holding back* Roxy *with a look*] Are you afraid your hands'll bust, Joe? [Joe *remains silent*] What's a busted hand to a *fighter?* You can't go in and do your best if you're scared of your mitts . . . can you? You tell me. . . .

JOE: No. . . .

MOODY: Whyn't you give up outside ideas, Joe?

ROXY: [*Suddenly, in a loud voice to* Tokio] You shoulda seen that bunch of musicians on 48th Street before. Fiddlers, drummers, cornetists—not a dime in a car-load. Bums in the park! Oh, excuse me, Tom, I was just telling Tokio—

[Joe *is now aware that the others know of the violin. Now he is completely closed to them.* Moody *sees this. He says to* Roxy]

MOODY: [*Wrathfully*] What would you like to say, my fine-feathered friend?

ROXY: [*Simulating bewilderment*] What's the matter? What happened? [*Receiving no answer, he looks around several times and adds, with a shrug*] I think I'll run across the street and pick up an eight-cylinder lunch.

MOODY: Sprinkle it with arsenic. Do that for me, for me, sweetheart!!

ROXY: [*Hurt*] That's a fine remark from a friend. [*He haughtily exits*]

JOE: What do you want, Mr. Moody?

MOODY: At the moment, nothing. I'm puffed out. See you tomorrow over the gym.

JOE: Maybe I won't be there. I might give up

fighting as a bad job. I'm not over-convinced it's what I want. I can do other things. . . .

TOKIO: I'll see you tomorrow at the gym, Joe. [Joe *looks at both the men, says nothing, exits*] That Mr. Gottlieb is a case. See you later.

MOODY: [*Not looking up*] Okay. [Tokio *exits*. Lorna *and* Moody *are alone. She blows cigarette smoke to the ceiling.* Moody *puts his feet up on the desk and leans back wearily. Snorting through his nostrils*] The password is honey!

LORNA: What was that all about? [*The telephone rings*]

MOODY: [*Of the ringing bell*] If that's for me, tear it up. I ain't in, not even for God.

LORNA: [*Answering*] Hello? . . . [*Putting her hand on the mouthpiece*] It's Mrs. God—your wife.

[Moody *makes a grimace of distaste but picks up the phone and puts on a sweet voice*]

MOODY: Yes, Monica darling. . . . Yeah . . . you and your support. . . . You're gonna fifty-buck me to death! . . . Monica, if I had fifty bucks I'd buy myself a big juicy coffin—what?—so throw me in jail. [*He hangs up the phone*] Bitch! That'll be time number three. She means it too.

LORNA: What was that scene with Bonaparte?

MOODY: Sweetheart, the jig is up! Believe it or not, Bonaparte's a violinist. Maybe he was on the radio. I don't know what the hell he was. His old man came here and told us. His mitts are on his mind. You can't do a thing with a nut like that.

LORNA: Won't he give up the violin?

MOODY: You heard him stalling. This is the end, Lorna. It's our last chance for a decent life, for getting married—we have to make that kid fight! He's *more* than a meal ticket—he's everything we want and need from life!

[Lorna *goes over and slaps him on the back*]

LORNA: Pick up your chin, little man.

MOODY: Don't Brisbane me, Lorna. I'm licked. I'm tired. Find me a mouse hole to crawl in. . . .

LORNA: Why don't you ask me when you want something? You got the brains of a flea. Do you want Bonaparte to fight?

MOODY: Do I wanna see tomorrow?

LORNA: I'll make him fight.

MOODY: How?

LORNA: How? . . . I'm "a tramp from Newark," Tom. . . . I know a dozen ways. . . .

SLOW FADEOUT

SCENE IV.

A few nights later. Joe *and* Lorna *sit on a bench in the park. It is night. There is carousel music in the distance. Cars ride by in front of the boy and girl in the late spring night. Out of sight a traffic light changes from red to green and back again through-* out the scene and casts its colors on the faces of the boy and girl.

LORNA: Success and fame! Or just a lousy living. You're lucky you won't have to worry about those things. . . .

JOE: Won't I?

LORNA: Unless Tom Moody's a liar.

JOE: You like him, don't you?

LORNA: [*After a pause*] I like him.

JOE: I like how you dress. The girls look nice in the summer time. Did you ever stand at the Fifth Avenue Library and watch those girls go by?

LORNA: No, I never did. [*Switching the subject*] That's the carousel, that music. Did you ever ride on one of those?

JOE: That's for kids.

LORNA: Weren't you ever a kid, for God's sake?

JOE: Not a happy kid.

LORNA: Why?

JOE: Well, I always felt different. Even my name was special—Bonaparte—and my eyes . . .

LORNA: I wouldn't have taken that too serious. . . .

[*There is a silent pause. Joe looks straight ahead*]

JOE: Gee, all those cars.

LORNA: Lots of horses trot around here. The rich know how to live. You'll be rich. . . .

JOE: My brother Frank is an organizer for the C.I.O.

LORNA: What's that?

JOE: If you worked in a factory you'd know. Did you ever work?

LORNA: [*With a smile*] No, when I came out of the cocoon I was a butterfly and butterflies don't work.

JOE: All those cars . . . whizz, whizz. [*Now turning less casual*] Where's Mr. Moody tonight?

LORNA: He goes up to see his kid on Tuesday nights. It's a sick kid, a girl. His wife leaves it at her mother's house.

JOE: That leaves you free, don't it?

LORNA: What are you hinting at?

JOE: I'm thinking about you and Mr. Moody.

LORNA: Why think about it? I don't. Why should you?

JOE: If you belonged to me I wouldn't think about it.

LORNA: Haven't you got a girl?

JOE: No.

LORNA: Why not?

JOE: [*Evasively*] Oh . . .

LORNA: Tokio says you're going far in the fighting game.

JOE: Music means more to me. May I tell you something?

LORNA: Of course.

JOE: If you laugh I'll never speak to you again.

LORNA: I'm not the laughing type.

JOE: With music I'm never alone when I'm

alone— Playing music . . . that's like saying, "I am man. I belong here. How do you do, World—good evening!" When I play music nothing is closed to me. I'm not afraid of people and what they say. There's no war in music. It's not like the streets. Does this sound funny?

LORNA: No.

JOE: But when you leave your room . . . down in the street . . . it's war! Music can't help me there. Understand?

LORNA: Yes.

JOE: People have hurt my feelings for years. I never forget. You can't get even with people by playing the fiddle. If music shot bullets I'd like it better—artists and people like that are freaks today. The world moves fast and they sit around like forgotten dopes.

LORNA: You're loaded with fireworks. Why don't you fight?

JOE: You have to be what you are—!

LORNA: Fight! see what happens—

JOE: Or end up in the bughouse!

LORNA: God's teeth! Who says you have to be one thing?

JOE: My nature isn't fighting!

LORNA: Don't Tokio know what he's talking about? Don't Tom? Joe, listen: be a fighter! Show the world! If you made your fame and fortune—and you can—you'd be anything you want. Do it! Bang your way to the lightweight crown. Get a bank account. Hire a great doctor with a beard—get your eyes fixed—

JOE: What's the matter with my eyes?

LORNA: Excuse me, I stand corrected. [After a pause] You get mad all the time.

JOE: That's from thinking about myself.

LORNA: How old are you, Joe?

JOE: Twenty-one and a half, and the months are going fast.

LORNA: You're very smart for twenty-one and a half "and the months are going fast."

JOE: Why not? I read every page of the Encyclopaedia Britannica. My father's friend, Mr. Carp, has it. A shrimp with glasses had to do something.

LORNA: I'd like to meet your father. Your mother dead?

JOE: Yes.

LORNA: So is mine.

JOE: Where do you come from? The city is full of girls who look as if they never had parents.

LORNA: I'm a girl from over the river. My father is still alive—shucking oysters and bumming drinks somewhere in the wilds of Jersey. I'll tell you a secret: I don't like you.

JOE: [Surprised] Why?

LORNA: You're too sufficient by yourself . . . too inside yourself.

JOE: You like it or you don't.

LORNA: You're on an island—

JOE: Robinson Crusoe . . .

LORNA: That's right—"me, myself, and I." Why not come out and see the world?

JOE: Does it seem that way?

LORNA: Can't you see yourself?

JOE: No. . . .

LORNA: Take a bird's-eye view; you don't know what's right or wrong. You don't know what to pick, but you won't admit it.

JOE: Do you?

LORNA: Leave me out. This is the anatomy of Joe Bonaparte.

JOE: You're dancing on my nose, huh?

LORNA: Shall I stop?

JOE: No.

LORNA: You're a miserable creature. You want your arm in gelt up to the elbow. You'll take fame so people won't laugh or scorn your face. You'd give your soul for those things. But every time you turn your back your little soul kicks you in the teeth. It don't give in so easy.

JOE: And what does your soul do in its perfumed vanity case?

LORNA: Forget about me.

JOE: Don't you want—?

LORNA: [Suddenly nasty] I told you to forget it!

JOE: [Quietly] Moody sent you after me—a decoy! You made a mistake, Lorna, for two reasons. I make up my own mind to fight. Point two, he doesn't know you don't love him—

LORNA: You're a fresh kid.

JOE: In fact he doesn't know anything about you at all.

LORNA: [Challengingly] But you do?

JOE: This is the anatomy of Lorna Moon: she's a lost baby. She doesn't know what's right or wrong. She's a miserable creature who never knew what to pick. But she'd never admit it. And I'll tell you why you picked Moody!

LORNA: You don't know what you're talking about.

JOE: Go home, Lorna. If you stay, I'll know something about you. . . .

LORNA: You don't know anything.

JOE: Now's your chance—go home!

LORNA: Tom loves me.

JOE: [After a long silence, looking ahead] I'm going to buy a car.

LORNA: They make wonderful cars today. Even the lizzies—

JOE: Gary Cooper's got the kind I want. I saw it in the paper, but it costs too much—fourteen thousand. If I found one second-hand—

LORNA: And if you had the cash—

JOE: I'll get it—

LORNA: Sure, if you'd go in and really fight!

JOE: [In a sudden burst] Tell your Mr. Moody I'll dazzle the eyes out of his head!

LORNA: You mean it?

JOE: [Looking out ahead] Those cars are poison in my blood. When you sit in a car and speed you're looking down at the world. Speed, speed, everything is speed—nobody gets me!

LORNA: You mean in the ring?

JOE: In or out, nobody gets me! Gee, I like to stroke that gas!

LORNA: You sound like Jack the Ripper.

JOE: [*Standing up suddenly*] I'll walk you back to your house—your hotel, I mean. [Lorna *stands*. Joe *continues*] Do you have the same room?

LORNA: [*With sneaking admiration*] You're a fresh kid!

JOE: When you're lying in his arms tonight, tell him, for me, that the next World's Champ is feeding in his stable.

LORNA: Did you really read those Britannia books?

JOE: From A to Z.

LORNA: And you're only twenty-one?

JOE: And a half.

LORNA: Something's wrong somewhere.

JOE: I know. . . .

[*They slowly walk out as*]

FADEOUT

SCENE V.

The next week. It is near midnight in the dining room of the Bonaparte home. An open suitcase rests on the table, Siggie *is pouring samples of wine for* Lorna Moon. *He himself drinks appreciatively. To one side sits* Mr. Bonaparte *silently, thoughtfully, watchfully—pretending to read the newspaper.*

SIGGIE: I was fit to be knocked down with a feather when I heard it. I couldn't believe it until I seen him fight over at the Keystone last week. You never know what somebody's got in him—like the man with germs—suddenly he's down in bed with a crisis!

[Joe *enters with an armful of clothes which he begins to pack in the suitcase*]

LORNA: Joe's road tour will do him lots of good.

[Anna *enters and takes off an apron. Silence, in which* Siggie *and* Lorna *sip their wine*]

ANNA: How do you like that wine, Miss Moon? My father makes better wine than any Eyetalian in New York. My father knows everything—don't you, poppa?

[*With a faint smile,* Mr. Bonaparte *shrugs his shoulders*]

SIGGIE: We're thinking of sending the old man to a leper colony. . . .

ANNA: Don't my husband say funny things? Tell her what you told the janitor Tuesday, Siggie.

SIGGIE: Never mind, never mind.

ANNA: You know how I met Siggie? He was a United Cigar Store clerk and I walked in for a pack of Camels and the first thing you know he

said something funny. It was raw, so I can't say it. He had me laughing from the first. Seven years and I haven't stopped laughing yet. [*She laughs loudly, pleasurably*] This will be the first time Joe ever went traveling. Was you ever out of New York, Miss Moon?

LORNA: Oh, many times.

ANNA: That's nice. Far?

LORNA: California, Detroit, Chicago. I was an airplane hostess for two months.

ANNA: That's nice—it's a real adventure. I'd like to fly.

SIGGIE: Stay on the ground! Fly! What for? Who do you know up there? Eagles?

ANNA: It must be a wonderful way to see life.

LORNA: [*Drinking*] I've seen life in all its aspects. [Mr. Bonaparte *stands up with a smile.* Lorna's *eyes follow him as he exits. To* Joe] I think your father left because he don't like me.

JOE: He likes you.

ANNA: My father likes everybody. He's a very deep man. My father has more friends than any man alive. But best of all he likes his horse, Dolly, who drives the fruit wagon. My father can't sit still on Sunday afternoon—he has to go see what that horse is doing. [*Her eyes catch sight of the suitcase*] Joe, you don't know how to pack. [*She starts over to assist him*]

SIGGIE: [*Querulously*] Rest the feet awhile, Duchess.

ANNA: [*Explaining her move*] He don't know how to pack.

[*Beginning to rearrange the suitcase.* Mr. Bonaparte *returns and hands* Joe *a sweater*]

MR. BONAPARTE: You forget your good sweater.

JOE: Thanks. [Mr. Bonaparte *sits.* Joe *looks at him sideways*]

ANNA: When you get out to Chicago, buy yourself some new underwear, Joe. I hear everything's cheaper in Chicago. Is that right, Miss Moon?

LORNA: [*After taking another drink*] Chicago? I don't know. I was there only one night—I got news that night my mother died. As a matter of fact, she killed herself.

ANNA: That's very sad.

LORNA: No, my father's an old drunk son-of-a-bitch. Did you ask me about my father?

MR. BONAPARTE: [*Who has been listening intently*] Yes. . . .

LORNA: Twice a week he kicked my mother's face in. If I let myself go I'd be a drunkard in a year.

ANNA: My father never said one bad word to my mother in her whole lifetime. And she was a big nuisance right up till the day she died. She was more like me, more on the stout side. Take care of your health, Joe, when you're out there. What's better than health?

LORNA: [*Turning to* Mr. Bonaparte, *with whom she is self-conscious*] The question is, do you like me or do you not?

MR. BONAPARTE: [*With a faint smile*] Yes. . . .

LORNA: Your family is very cute— Now do you like me?

MR. BONAPARTE: Yes. . . .

LORNA: Why do you look at me that way?

MR. BONAPARTE: I don't look special. You gonna travel on those train with my son?

LORNA: God's teeth, no! I'm a friend of his manager's, that's all. And a friend of Joe's, too.

MR. BONAPARTE: You are in favor for my son to prizefight?

[Joe *looks at his father sideways and exits*]

LORNA: Certainly. Aren't you?

MR. BONAPARTE: Joe has a dream many year to be superior violin'. Was it boyhood thing? Was it real? Or is this real now? Those are-a my question, Miss Moon. Maybe you are friend to my son. Then I aska you, look out for him. Study him. Help him find what'sa right. Tell me, Miss Moon, when you find out. Help Joe find truthful success. Will you do it for me?

LORNA: I'll be glad to keep my eye on him.

[Joe *enters with slippers, which he puts in bag*]

ANNA: [*To* Joe] You could stand some new shirts, too.

SIGGIE: Listen, pop, I'm a natural man and I don't like wise guys. Joe went in the boxing game 'cause he's ashamed to be poor. That's his way to enter a little enterprise. All other remarks are so much alfalfa!

[Joe *locks the bag*]

ANNA: [*Taking the wine glass from* Siggie's *hand*] Drunk as a horse fly!

JOE: It's getting late and the train won't wait.

SIGGIE: [*Standing up*] My god is success. Need I say more? I'm prouda you, Joe. Come home a champ. Make enough dough to buy your sister's boy friend a new cab. Yes, boys and girls, I'm looking in that old crystal ball and I see strange and wonderful events! Yazoo!

ANNA: [*Giggling*] Drunk as a horse fly!

JOE: [*To* Siggie] You can't drive us down to the station in this condition.

SIGGIE: What condition?

ANNA: You're drunk, stupid.

SIGGIE: Shut the face, foolish! Just because I don't hold in my nerves she thinks I'm drunk. If you hold in your nerves you get ulcers. [*To* Joe] Get your "chapow" and let's go. Or don't you want me to drive you down?

JOE: No.

SIGGIE: I should worry—my cab's in the garage anyway! [*Suddenly he sits*]

JOE: We'd better start. . . .

LORNA: [*To* Mr. Bonaparte] I'd like to have another talk with you some time.

MR. BONAPARTE: Come any time in the evening. You are a very lovely girl. [Mr. Carp *stands in the doorway*] Here is Mr. Carp to say good-bye.

SIGGIE: Come in, my little prince.

CARP: [*Coming in and shaking hands with* Joe] I wish you good luck in every undertaking.

JOE: [*Uneasily, because his father is looking at him*] Thanks.

MR. BONAPARTE: [*Introducing* Carp] Miss Moon, my neighbor, Mr. Carp.

CARP: A pleasure to meet you.

LORNA: Hello.

[Mr. Bonaparte *brings the violin case from its hiding place in the buffet*]

MR. BONAPARTE: Joe, I buy you this some time ago. Don't give cause I don't know whatta you gonna do. Take him with you now. Play for yourself. It gonna remember you your old days of musical life.

[Joe *puts down the suitcase and picks up the violin. He plucks the strings, he tightens one of them. In spite of the tension his face turns soft and tender*]

LORNA: [*Watching intently*] We better not miss the train—Tokio's waiting.

MR. BONAPARTE: [*Of violin*] Take him with you, Joe.

JOE: It's beautiful. . . .

MR. BONAPARTE: Practise on the road.

[Joe *abruptly turns and with the violin exits. The others listen, each standing in his place, as rich violin music comes from the other room.* Joe *returns. There is silence as he places the violin on the table in front of his father*]

JOE: [*In a low voice*] Return it, poppa.

ANNA: [*Hugging* Joe] Have a good trip, Joey.

CARP: Eat in good restaurants. . . .

[*There is silence: the* Father *and* Son *look at each other. The others in the room sense the drama between the two. Finally*]

JOE: I have to do this, poppa.

MR. BONAPARTE: [*To* Joe] Be careful fora your hands.

JOE: Poppa, give me the word—

MR. BONAPARTE: What word?

JOE: Give me the word to go ahead. You're looking at yesterday—I see tomorrow. Maybe you think I ought to spend my whole life here—you and Carp blowing off steam.

MR. BONAPARTE: [*Holding himself back*] Oh, Joe, shut your mouth!

JOE: Give me the word to go ahead!

MR. BONAPARTE: Be careful fora your hands!

JOE: I want you to give me the word!

MR. BONAPARTE: [*Crying out*] No! No word! You gonna fight? All right! Okay! But I don't gonna give no word! No!

JOE: That's how you feel?

MR. BONAPARTE: That'sa how I feel! [Mr. Bonaparte's *voice breaks and there is nothing for father and son to do but to clutch each other in a hasty embrace. Finally* Mr. Bonaparte *disentangles himself and turns away.* Joe *abruptly grabs up his suitcase and exits.* Lorna *follows, stopping at the door to look back at* Mr. Bonaparte. *In the ensuing silence* Anna *looks at her father and shakes her head.* Siggie *suddenly lumbers to his feet and sounds off like a chime]*

SIGGIE: Gong gong gong gong!

ANNA: Gee, poppa . . .

SIGGIE: Come to bed, Anna. . . . Anna-banana . . . [Siggie *exits]*

ANNA: Gee, poppa . . . [*She touches her father sympathetically]*

MR. BONAPARTE: [*Without turning]* Gone to bed, Anna. . . .

   [Anna *slowly exits.* Mr. Bonaparte *now slowly comes back to the table and looks down at the violin]*

CARP: [*Seating him slowly]* Come, my friend . . . we will have a nice talk on a cultural topic. [*Looking at the violin]* You'll work around a number of years before you make it up, the price of that fiddle. . . .

   [Mr. Bonaparte *stands looking down at the violin]*

CARP: [*Sadly]* Yes, my friend, what is man? As Schopenhauer says, and in the last analysis . . .

SLOW FADEOUT

ACT II. SCENE I.

Six months later. Present in the corner of a gymnasium are Roxy, Moody, Lorna *and* Tokio. *They are looking off right, watching* Joe Bonaparte *work out with a partner. From off right come the sounds of typical gym activities: the thud of boxing gloves, the rat-a-tat of the punching bag, and from time to time the general bell which is a signal for rest periods. Tacked on the tin walls are an ad for Everlast boxing equipment, boxing "card" placards, a soiled American flag, some faded exit signs. The group watches silently for several seconds after the lights fade in. A* Boxer, *wiping his perspiring body with a towel, passes from left to right and looks back at* Lorna's *legs. As* Roxy *watches, his head moves to and fro in the rhythm of* Joe's *sparring off stage,* Roxy *nods his head in admiration.*

ROXY: Tokio. I gotta give the devil his dues: in the past six months you done a noble job!

TOKIO: [*Calling off]* With the left! A long left, Joe! . . .

LORNA: [*Looking off]* Joe's a very good-looking boy. I never quite noticed it before.

   [*The general bell sounds; the boxing din off stage stops]*

MOODY: [*Rubbing his hands enthusiastically]* "Let it rain, let it pour! It ain't gonna rain where we're headed for!"

ROXY: I'm tickled to death to see the canary birds left his gloves.

TOKIO: He's the king of all he surveys.

MOODY: Boy, oh, boy, how he surprised them in the Bronx last night! . . . But one thing I can't explain—that knockout he took in Philly five weeks ago.

TOKIO: That night he was off his feed, Tom. Where do you see speed like that? That's style, real style—you can't tag him. And he's giving it with both hands.

MOODY: You don't have to sell me his virtues— I'm sold. Nevertheless, he got tagged in Philly.

TOKIO: Here's what happened there: we run into some man when we're leaving the hotel. Joe goes pale. I ask him what it is. "Nothing," he says. But I see for myself—a man with long hair and a violin case. When we turn the corner, he says, "He's after me," he says. As if it's cops and robbers!

   [*The general bell sounds; the fighting din begins again]*

ROXY: A kidnapper?

LORNA: Don't be a fool. He was reminded . . .

ROXY: Speak when spoken to, Miss Moon!

MOODY: [*Moodily]* And when he got in the ring that night, he kept his hands in his pockets?

TOKIO: Yeah. I didn't mention this before—it's not important.

MOODY: But it's still a danger—

TOKIO: No. No.

MOODY: But anyway, we better get him away from his home. We can't afford no more possible bad showings at this stage of the game. No more apparitions, like suddenly a fiddle flies across the room on wings!

   [*The group again intently watches* Joe *off stage]*

MOODY: Ooh! Did you see that? He's packing a real Sunday punch in that right. [*Calling off]* Hit 'im, Joe, hit 'im! [*As an indistinct answer come back]* Ha ha, looka that, hahaha . . . [*Now turning to* Tokio] What's your idea of a match with Lombardo?

TOKIO: Can you get it?

MOODY: Maybe.

TOKIO: Get it.

MOODY: Sure?

TOKIO: It's an easy win, on points at least.

   [*During the last few lines a thin dark man has entered. His dark hair is grayed at the temples, an inarticulate look in his face. He is* Eddie Fuseli, *a renowned gambler and gunman]*

EDDIE FUSELI: [*Approaching the group]* Hello.

ROXY: [*Nervously]* Hello, Eddie.

MOODY: [*Turning]* I haven't seen you for a dog's age, Fuseli.

EDDIE: [*Pointing off left]* You got this certain boy—Bonaparte. I like his looks. American born?

ROXY: Right from here.

EDDIE: [*Watching* Joe *off]* Like a cat, never off his position. He appeals to me. [*To* Moody] They call you the Brown Fox. What's your opinion of this boy?

MOODY: [*Coolly, on guard*] Possibilities. . . .

EDDIE: [*To* Tokio] What's your idea?

TOKIO: Tom said it.

EDDIE: Could he get on top?

MOODY: [*As above*] I can't see that far ahead. I don't read palms.

EDDIE: Could I buy a piece?

MOODY: No.

EDDIE: [*Coolly*] Could I?

MOODY: No!

EDDIE: [*With a certain tenderness*] I like a good fighter. I like to see you after, Tom. [*Of* Lorna] This your girl?

LORNA: [*Pertly*] I'm my mother's girl.

EDDIE: [*With a small mirthless laugh*] Ha ha— that's a hot one. [*He coolly drifts out of the scene on his cat's feet. The general bell sounds. The din ceases*]

LORNA: What exhaust pipe did he crawl out of?

ROXY: I remember this Eddie Fuseli when he came back from the war with a gun. He's still got the gun and he still gives me goose pimples!

MOODY: That Fuseli's a black mark on my book. Every once in a while he shoots across my quiet existence like a roman candle!

LORNA: Sell or don't sell. But better be careful, that guy's tough.

[*A* Fighter, *robed, hooded with towel, passes across: A* Gambling Type *passes in the opposite direction. Both look at* Lorna's *legs*]

MOODY: Give a rat like that a finger and you lose a hand before you know it!

TOKIO: Did you know Joe bought a car this morning?

ROXY: What kinda car?

TOKIO: A Duesenberg.

MOODY: One of those fancy speed wagons?

TOKIO: [*Agreeing*] It cost him five grand, second-hand.

MOODY: [*Flaring up*] Am I a step-child around here? I'm glad you tell me now, if only outa courtesy!

ROXY: [*Indignantly*] Whatta you keep a thing like that incognito for?

MOODY: He drives like a maniac! That time we drove to Long Beach? I almost lost my scalp! We can't let him drive around like that! Boy, he's getting a bushel of bad habits! We gotta be careful.

[*The general bell sounds again; the fighting din stops*]

MOODY: Here's the truth: our boy can be the champ in three easy lessons—Lombardo, Fulton, the Chocolate Drop. But we gotta be careful!

LORNA: Here he comes. [Joe *enters in bathrobe, taking off his headgear, which* Tokio *takes from him*]

MOODY: [*Completely changing his tone*] You looked very good in there, Joe. You're going swell and I like it. I'd work more with that long left if I were you.

JOE: Yes, I was speaking to Tokio about that. I feel my form's improving. I like to work. I'm getting somewhere—I feel it better every day.

LORNA: Happy?

JOE: [*Looking at her intently*] Every day's Saturday!

ROXY: [*Officiously*] Say, what's this I hear you bought a Duesenberg?

JOE: What's your objection—I might have some fun?

ROXY: I got my wampum on you. I like to know your habits. Ain't I permitted?

[Joe *is about to retort hotly when* Moody *gently takes his arm in an attempt to soothe him*]

MOODY: Wait a minute, Joe. After all we have your welfare at heart. And after all a Duesenberg can go one fifty per—

[Eddie Fuseli *appears above, unseen by the others. He listens*]

JOE: Who'd want to drive that fast?

MOODY: And since we're vitally interested in your future—

JOE: [*Shaking off* Moody's *arm and saying what is really on his mind*] If you're vitally interested in my future, prove it! Get me some fights—fights with contenders, not with dumb-bunny club fighters. Get me some main bouts in the metropolitan area!—

MOODY: [*Losing his temper*] For a kid who got kayoed five weeks ago, your mouth is pretty big! [*The general bell sounds; the din begins*]

JOE: That won't happen again! And how about some mention in the press? Twenty-six bouts—no one knows I'm alive. This isn't vacation for me— it's a profession! I'm staying more than a week. Match me up against real talent. You can't go too fast for me. Don't worry about autos!

MOODY: We can go too fast! You're not so good!

JOE: [*With a boyish grin*] Look at the records! [Joe *abruptly exits.* Tokio *follows him, first giving the others a glance*]

MOODY: Boy, oh, boy, that kid's changing!

ROXY: He goes past my head like a cold wind from the river!

LORNA: But you're gettin' what you want—the contender for the crown!

MOODY: I wish I was sure.

ROXY: Frankenstein! [Eddie Fuseli *saunters down to the others*]

EDDIE: I thought it over, Tom. I like to get a piece of that boy.

MOODY: [*Angrily*] I thought it over, too—not for sale. In fact I had a visitation from Jehovah. He came down on the calm waters and He said, "Let there be unity in the ownership."

EDDIE: [*With a dead face*] I had a visit, too. He

came down in the bar and He ate a pretzel. And He says, "Eddie Fuseli, I like you to buy a piece!"

MOODY: [*Trying to delay the inevitable*] Why not see me in my office tomorrow?

EDDIE: It's a cheap office. I get depressed in that office.

MOODY: [*Finally*] I can't make any guarantees about the boy.

EDDIE: How do you mean it, Tom?

MOODY: I don't know what the hell he'll do in the next six months.

ROXY: Eddie, it's like flap-jacks—up and down—you don't know which side next!

EDDIE: [*With his small mirthless laugh*] Ha ha, that's a good one. You oughta be on the radio.

MOODY: No, it's a fact—

ROXY: We had enough headaches already. He's got a father, but how!

EDDIE: Don't want him to fight?

ROXY: His father sits on the kid's head like a bird's nest! [Roxy *puts his hand on* Eddie's *arm*]

EDDIE: Take your hand off. [Roxy *hastily withdraws*] Let the boy decide. . . .

MOODY: If you buy in?

EDDIE: Let the boy decide.

MOODY: Sure! But if he says no— [*Before* Moody *can finish* Joe *enters.* Eddie *whirls around and faces* Joe, *getting his cue from the others. Curiously,* Eddie *is almost embarrassed before* Joe. *The bell sounds; the din stops*]

MOODY: Joe, this is Eddie Fuseli. He's a man around town—

EDDIE: [*Facing* Joe, *his back to the others*] With good connections—

MOODY: He wantsa buy a piece of you—

EDDIE: [*Whirling around*] I will tell him myself. [*Turning back to* Joe; *with quiet intense dignity*] I'm Eyetalian too—Eyetalian born, but an American citizen. I like to buy a piece of you. I don't care for no profit. I could turn it back to—*you* could take my share. But I like a good fighter; I like a good boy who could win the crown. It's the inter-est of my life. It would be a proud thing for me when Bonaparte could win the crown like I think he can.

MOODY: [*Confidently*] It's up to you, Joe, if he buys in.

EDDIE: [*Wooingly*] Some managers can't give you what you need—

MOODY: Don't say that!

EDDIE: *Some* managers can't! I'll see you get good bouts . . . also press notices . . . I know how. You're a boy who needs that. You decide . . .

[*There is a pause;* Joe's *eyes flit from* Lorna *to the others and back to* Eddie]

JOE: Not my half.

EDDIE: Not your half.

JOE: As long as Mr. Fuseli doesn't mix in my private life . . . cut it up any way you like. Excuse me, I got a date with Miss Duesenberg. [*The others silently watch* Joe *exit*]

EDDIE: A date with who?

MOODY: [*Snorting*] Miss Duesenberg!

ROXY: An automobile. It gives you an idea what a boy—"Miss Duesenberg"!

EDDIE: How do you like it, Tom? Big bills or little bills?

MOODY: Don't think you're buying in for an apple and an egg.

EDDIE: Take big bills—they're new, they feel good. See you in that office tomorrow.

[*The bell clangs off stage.* Eddie *starts off, but abruptly turns and faces* Roxy *whom he inwardly terrifies*]

EDDIE: It's a trick you don't know, Roxy: when a bird sits on your head and interferes with the championship, you shoot him off. All kinds of birds. You be surprised how fast they fall on the ground. Which is my intention in this syndicate. [*He smiles thinly and then moves out of the scene like a cat*]

MOODY: I don't like that!

ROXY: I'm not so happy myself at the present time. How do you like it with our boy for gratitude? He leaves us here standing in our brevities!

LORNA: What makes you think you're worthy of gratitude?

MOODY: [*To* Lorna] For Pete's sake, pipe down! Are you with us or against us?

ROXY: [*Haughtily, to* Moody] Take my advice, Tom. Marry her and the first year give her a baby. Then she'll sit in the corner and get fat and sleepy, and not have such a big mouth! Uncle Roxy's telling you!

LORNA: [*To* Roxy] Couldn't you keep quiet about the father to that gunman? Go home and let your wife give *you* a baby!

ROXY: A woman shouldn't interfere—

MOODY: Peace, for chri' sake, peace! Lorna, we're in a bad spot with Joe. He's getting hard to manage and this is the time when everything's gotta be right. I'm seeing Lombardo's manager tomorrow! Now that gunman's on my tail. You have to help me. You and I wanna do it like the story books, "happy ever after"? Then help me.

LORNA: How?

MOODY: Go after the boy. Keep him away from his folks. Get him away from the buggies—

LORNA: How?

MOODY: [*Impatiently*] You know how.

ROXY: Now you're talking.

LORNA: [*Pointing to* Roxy] You mean the way I see it on his face?

MOODY: For crying out loud! Where do you come off to make a remark like that?

LORNA: You expect me to sleep with that boy?

MOODY: I could tear your ears off for a remark like that!

ROXY: [*Discreetly*] I think I'll go grab a corn-beef sandwich. [*He exits*]

MOODY: [*After silence*] Are you mad?

LORNA: [*Tight-lipped*] No.

MOODY: [*Seductively*] I'm not a bad guy, Lorna. I don't mean anything bad. . . . All right, I'm crude—sometimes I'm worried and I'm crude. [*The bell clangs; the boxing din stops*] But what the hell, my heart's in the right place. . . . [*Coming behind her and putting his arms around her as she looks ahead*] Lorna, don't we both want that sun to come up and shine on us? Don't we? Before you know it the summer'll be here. Then it's the winter again, and it's another year again . . . and we're not married yet. See? . . . See what I mean? . . .

LORNA: [*Quietly*] Yes. . . .

MOODY: [*Beaming, but with uncertainty*] That sounds like the girl I used to know.

LORNA: I see what you mean. . . .

MOODY: [*Worried underneath*] You're not still mad?

LORNA: [*Briefly*] I'm not mad. [*But she abruptly cuts out of the scene, leaving Moody standing there*]

MOODY: [*Shaking his head*] Boy, I still don't know anything about women! . . .

MEDIUM FADEOUT

SCENE II.

A few nights later. Lorna *and* Joe *sit on the same park bench.*

JOE: Some nights I wake up—my heart's beating a mile a minute! Before I open my eyes I know what it is—the feeling that someone's standing at my bed. Then I open my eyes . . . it's gone—ran away!

LORNA: Maybe it's that old fiddle of yours.

JOE: Lorna, maybe it's you. . . .

LORNA: Don't you ever think of it any more—music?

JOE: What're you trying to remind me of? A kid with a Buster Brown collar and a violin case tucked under his arm? Does that sound appetizing to you?

LORNA: Not when you say it that way. You said it different once. . . .

JOE: What's on your mind, Lorna?

LORNA: What's on yours?

JOE: [*Simply*] You. . . . You're real for me—the way music was real.

LORNA: You've got your car, your career—what do you want with me?

JOE: I develop the ability to knock down anyone my weight. But what point have I made? Don't you think I know that? I went off to the wars 'cause someone called me a name—because I wanted to be two other guys. Now it's happening. . . . I'm not sure I like it.

LORNA: Moody's against that car of yours.

JOE: I'm against Moody, so we're even.

LORNA: Why don't you like him?

JOE: He's a manager! He treats me like a possession! I'm just a little silver mine for him—he bangs me around with a shovel!

LORNA: He's helped you—

JOE: No, Tokio's helped me. Why don't you give him up? It's terrible to have just a Tuesday-night girl. Why don't you belong to me every night in the week? Why don't you teach me love? . . . Or am I being a fool?

LORNA: You're not a fool, Joe.

JOE: I want you to be my family, my life—Why don't you do it, Lorna, why?

LORNA: He loves me.

JOE: I love you!

LORNA: [*Treading delicately*] Well . . . Anyway, the early bird got the worm. Anyway, I can't give him anguish. I . . . I know what it's like. You shouldn't kick Moody around. He's poor compared to you. You're alive, you've got yourself—I can't feel sorry for you!

JOE: But you don't love him!

LORNA: I'm not much interested in myself. But the thing I like best about you . . . you still feel like a flop. It's mysterious, Joe. It makes me put my hand out. [*She gives him her hand and he grasps it*]

JOE: I feel very close to you, Lorna.

LORNA: I know. . . .

JOE: And you feel close to me. But you're afraid—

LORNA: Of what?

JOE: To take a chance! Lorna darling, you won't let me wake you up! I feel it all the time—you're half dead, and you don't know it!

LORNA: [*Half smiling*] Maybe I do. . . .

JOE: Don't smile—don't be hard-boiled!

LORNA: [*Sincerely*] I'm not.

JOE: Don't you trust me?

LORNA: [*Evasively*] Why start what we can't finish?

JOE: [*Fiercely*] Oh, Lorna, deep as my voice will reach—*listen!!* Why can't you leave him? Why?

LORNA: Don't pull my dress off—I hear you.

JOE: Why?

LORNA: Because he needs me and you don't—

JOE: That's not true!

LORNA: Because he's a desperate guy who always starts out with two strikes against him. Because he's a kid at forty-two and you're a man at twenty-two.

JOE: You're sorry for him?

LORNA: What's wrong with that?

JOE: But what do *you* get?

LORNA: I told you before I don't care.

JOE: I don't believe it!

LORNA: I can't help that!

JOE: What did he ever do for you?

LORNA: [*With sudden verve*] Would you like to know? He loved me in a world of enemies, of stags and bulls! . . . and I loved him for that. He picked me up in Friskin's hotel on 39th Street. I was nine weeks behind in rent. I hadn't hit the gutter yet, but I was near. He washed my face and combed my hair. He stiffened the space between my shoulder blades. Misery reached out to misery—

JOE: And now you're dead.

LORNA: [Lashing out] I don't know what the hell you're talking about!

JOE: Yes, you do. . . .

LORNA: [Withdrawing] Ho hum. . . .

[There is silence. The soft park music plays in the distance. The traffic lights change. Lorna is trying to appear impassive. Joe begins to whistle softly. Finally Lorna picks up his last note and continues; he stops. He picks up her note, and after he whistles a few phrases she picks him up again. This whistling duet continues for almost a minute. Then the traffic lights change again]

LORNA: [Beginning in a low voice] You make me feel too human, Joe. All I want is peace and quiet, not love. I'm a tired old lady, Joe, and I don't mind being what you call "half dead." In fact it's what I like. [Her voice mounting higher] The twice I was in love I took an awful beating and I don't want it again. [Now half crying] I want you to stop it! Don't devil me, Joe. I beg you, don't devil me . . . let me alone. . . . [She cries softly. Joe reaches out and takes her hand; he gives her a handkerchief which she uses]

LORNA: [Finally] That's the third time I cried in my life. . . .

JOE: Now I know you love me.

LORNA: [Bitterly] Well . . .

JOE: I'll tell Moody.

LORNA: Not yet. Maybe he'd kill you if he knew.

JOE: Maybe.

LORNA: Then Fuseli'd kill him. . . . I guess I'd be left to kill myself. I'll tell him. . . .

JOE: When?

LORNA: Not tonight.

JOE: Swiftly, do it swiftly—

LORNA: Not tonight.

JOE: Everything's easy if you do it swiftly.

LORNA: He went up there tonight with six hundred bucks to bribe her into divorce.

JOE: Oh . . .

LORNA: [Sadly] He's a good guy, neat all over—sweet. I'll tell him tomorrow. I'd like a drink.

JOE: Let's drive over the Washington Bridge.

LORNA: [Standing] No, I'd like a drink.

JOE: [Standing and facing her] Lorna, when I talk to you . . . something moves in my heart. Gee, it's the beginning of a wonderful life! A man and his girl! A warm living girl who shares your room. . . .

LORNA: Take me home with you.

JOE: Yes.

LORNA: But how do I know you love me?

JOE: Lorna . . .

LORNA: How do I know it's true? You'll get to be the champ. They'll all want you, all the girls! But I don't care! I've been undersea a long time! When they'd put their hands on me I used to say, "This isn't it! This isn't what I mean!" It's been a mysterious world for me! But, Joe, I think you're it! I don't know why, I think you're it! Take me home with you.

JOE: Lorna!

LORNA: Poor Tom . . .

JOE: Poor Lorna! [The rest is embrace and kiss and clutching each other]

SLOW FADEOUT

SCENE III.

The next day: the office. Lorna and Moody are present. She has a hangover and is restless.

MOODY: Boy, you certainly double-scotched last night. What's the idea, you making a career of drinking in your old age? Headache?

LORNA: No.

MOODY: I won't let you walk alone in the park any more, if you do that.

LORNA: [Nasty in spite of her best intentions] Well, if you stayed away from your wife for a change . . .

MOODY: It's pretty late to bring that up, isn't it? Tuesday nights—

LORNA: I can't help it—I feel like a tramp. I've felt like a tramp for years.

MOODY: She was pretty friendly last night.

LORNA: Yeah? Did you sleep with her?

MOODY: What the hell's the matter with you, Lorna? [He goes to her. She shrugs away from him]

LORNA: Keep off the grass! [Moody gives her a quizzical look, goes back to his desk and from there gives her another quizzical look]

MOODY: Why do you drink like that?

LORNA: [Pointing to her chest] Right here—there's a hard lump and I drink to dissolve it. Do you mind?

MOODY: I don't mind—as long as you keep your health.

LORNA: Aw, Christ!—you and your health talks!

MOODY: You're looking for a fight, dolly-girl!

LORNA: And you'll give it?

MOODY: [With a grin] No, I'm feeling too good.

LORNA: [Sitting wearily] Who left you a fortune?

MOODY: Better. Monica's seen the light. The truth is she's begun to run around with a retired brewer and now *she* wants the divorce.

LORNA: Good, now she can begin paying *you*.

MOODY: She goes to Reno in a few months.

LORNA: [Moodily] I feel like a tramp. . . .

MOODY: That's what I'm telling you— In a few

months we'll be married! [*He laughs with pleasure*]

LORNA: You still want to marry me? Don't I feel like an old shoe to you?

MOODY: [*Coming to her*] Honest, you're so dumb!

LORNA: [*Touched by his boyishness*] You're so sweet. . . .

MOODY: And flash!—I signed Lombardo today! They meet six weeks from tonight.

LORNA: Goody. . . .

MOODY: [*Disappointed by her flippant reaction, but continuing*] I'm still not sure what he'll show with Lombardo. But my present worry is this: help me get that kid straight. Did you speak to him about the driving last night?

LORNA: I didn't see him. . . .

MOODY: It's very important. A Lombardo win clinches everything. In the fall we ride up to the Chocolate's door and dump him in the gutter! After that . . . I don't like to exaggerate—but the kid's primed! And you and I—Lorna baby, we're set. [*Happily*] What do you think of that?

LORNA: [*Evasively*] You draw beautiful pictures.

[*A knock sounds on the door*]

MOODY: Come in. [Siggie *enters, dressed in cab driver's garb*]

SIGGIE: Hello, Miss Moon.

LORNA: Hello. You know Mr. Moody.

SIGGIE: [*To Moody*] Hello.

MOODY: What can we do for you?

SIGGIE: For me you can't do nothing. I'm sore. I'm here against my better instinct. [*Taking a roll of money from his pocket and slapping it on the desk*] He don't want it—no part of it! My father-in-law don't want it. Joe sent it up—two hundred bucks—enough to choke a horse—but he don't want it!

MOODY: Why?

LORNA: That's nice he remembers his folks.

SIGGIE: Listen, I got a father-in-law nothing's nice to him but feeding his horse and giving a laugh and slicing philosophical salami across the table! He's sore because Joe don't come home half the time. As a matter of fact, ain't he suppose to come to sleep no more? The old man's worried.

MOODY: That's not my concern.

SIGGIE: I can't see what it's such a worry. A boy gets in the higher brackets—what's the worry. He's got enough clothes now to leave three suits home in the closet. [*Turning to Lorna*] It won't hurt if he sends me a few passes—tell him I said so.

LORNA: How's the wife?

SIGGIE: The Duchess? Still laughing.

LORNA: When you getting that cab?

SIGGIE: Do me a favor, Miss Moon—tell him I could use this wad for the first instalment.

LORNA: I'll tell him. Tell Mr. Bonaparte I saw Joe last night. He's fine.

MOODY: I'll see you get some passes.

SIGGIE: Thanks, thanks to both of you. Adios. [*He exits*]

LORNA: He and his wife are crazy for each other. Married . . . they throw each other around, but they're like love birds. Marriage is something special. . . . I guess you have to deserve it.

MOODY: I thought you didn't see Joe last night.

LORNA: I didn't, but why worry his father?

MOODY: The hell with his father.

LORNA: The hell with you!

MOODY: [*After a brooding pause*] I'll tell you something, Lorna. I'm not overjoyed the way Joe looks at you.

LORNA: How's he look?

MOODY: As if he saw the whole island of Manhattan in your face, and I don't like it.

LORNA: You thought of that too late.

MOODY: Too late for what?

LORNA: To bawl me out.

MOODY: Who's bawling you out?

LORNA: You were about to. Or warn me. I don't need warnings. [*Coasting away from the argument*] If you saw Joe's father you'd like him.

MOODY: I saw him.

LORNA: If you knew him you'd like him.

MOODY: Who wantsa like him? What do I need him for? I don't like him and I don't like his son! It's a business—Joe does his work, I do mine. Like this telephone—I pay the bill and I use it!

LORNA: He's human. . . .

MOODY: What're we fighting about?

LORNA: We're fighting about love. I'm trying to tell you how cynical I am. Tell the truth, love doesn't last—

MOODY: [*Suddenly quietly serious*] Everything I said about *Joe*—the opposite goes for you. Love lasts . . . if you want it to. . . . I want it to last. I need it to last. What the hell's all this struggle to make a living for if not for a woman and a home? I don't kid myself. I know what I need. I need you, Lorna.

LORNA: It has to end. . . .

MOODY: What has to end?

LORNA: Everything.

MOODY: What're you talking about?

LORNA: I oughta burn. I'm leaving you. . . .

MOODY: [*With a sick smile*] That's what you think.

LORNA: [*Not looking at him*] I mean it.

MOODY: [*As above*] I mean it too.

LORNA: [*After looking at him for a moment*] You can't take a joke?

MOODY: [*Not knowing where he stands*] It all depends. . . . I don't like a joke that pushes the blood down in my feet.

LORNA: [*Coming to him and putting her arms around his neck*] That's true, you're pale.

MOODY: Who's the man?

LORNA: [*Heartsick, and unable to tell him the truth*] There's no man, Tom . . . even if there was, I couldn't leave you. [*She looks at him, unable to say more*]

MOODY: [*After a pause*] How about some lunch? I'll buy it. . . .

LORNA: [*Wearily*] Where would I put it, Tom?

MOODY: [*Impulsively*] In your hat! [*And suddenly he embraces her roughly and kisses her fully and she allows it.* Joe *walks into the office,* Eddie Fuseli *behind him. They break apart*]

JOE: The first time I walked in here that was going on. It's one long duet around here.

MOODY: Hello.

EDDIE: [*Sardonically*] Hello, Partner. . . .

[Lorna *is silent and avoids* Joe's *looks*]

JOE: How about that fight with Lombardo?

MOODY: Six weeks from tonight.

JOE: He's gonna be surprised.

MOODY: [*Coolly*] No one doubts it.

JOE: [*Sharply*] I didn't say it was doubted!

MOODY: Boy, everyone's off his feed today. It started with the elevator boy—next it's Lorna—now it's you! What are *you* sore about?

LORNA: [*Trying to turn the conversation; to* Joe] Siggie was here looking for you. Your father's worried—

JOE: Not as much as my "manager" worries me.

MOODY: I don't need you to tell me how to run my business. I'll book the matches—

JOE: That doesn't worry me.

MOODY: But you and your speeding worries me! First it's music, then it's motors. Christ, next it'll be girls and booze!

JOE: It's girls already.

LORNA: Joe—

JOE: [*Bitterly*] Certainly! By the dozens!

EDDIE: Haha—that's a hot one. Don't ask me which is worst—women or spiders.

LORNA: Siggie left this money—your father won't take it. Siggie says buy him a cab—

[Joe *takes the money*]

EDDIE: Your relative? I'll get him a cab. [*To* Moody] How about a flock of bouts for Bonaparte over the summer?

MOODY: [*Bitterly*] All he wants—practice fights—to make him a better "artiste."

EDDIE: That is what we like. [Joe *is looking at* Lorna]

MOODY: "We?" Where do *I* come in?

EDDIE: You push the buttons, the *right* buttons. I wanna see Bonaparte with the crown.

MOODY: [*Sarcastically*] Your concern touches me deep in my heart!

EDDIE: What's the matter, Tom? You getting tired?

MOODY: [*Coolly*] I get tired, don't you?

EDDIE: Don't get tired, Tom . . . not in a crucial time.

MOODY: Get him to give up that Duesenberg.

EDDIE: [*After looking at* Joe] That's his fun. . . .

MOODY: His fun might cost your crown.

JOE: [*Suddenly to* Lorna] Why did you kiss him?

MOODY: [*To* Joe] It's about time you shut your mouth and minded your own goddam business. Also, that you took some orders.

JOE: [*Suddenly savage*] Who are you, God?

MOODY: Yes! I'm your maker, you cock-eyed gutter rat! Outa sawdust and spit I made you! I own you—without me you're a blank! Your insolence is gorgeous, but this is the end! I'm a son of a gun! What're you so superior about?

EDDIE: Don't talk so quick, Tom. You don't know . . .

MOODY: I wouldn't take the crap of this last six eight months from the President himself! Cut me up in little pieces, baby—but not me!

EDDIE: [*Quietly*] You could get cut up in little pieces.

MOODY: [*Retiring in disgust*] Sisst!

EDDIE: You hear me?

MOODY: [*From his desk*] You wanna manage this boy? Help yourself—do it! I'll sell my piece for half of what it's worth. You wanna buy?

EDDIE: You are a funny man.

MOODY: Gimme twenty thousand and lemme out. Ten, I'll take ten. I got my girl. I don't need crowns or jewels. I take my girl and we go sit by the river and it's everything.

JOE: What girl?

MOODY: I'm not on speaking terms with you! [*To* Eddie] Well?

EDDIE: It would be funny if your arms got broke.

JOE: Wait a minute! Lorna loves me and I love her.

MOODY: [*After looking from* Joe *to* Lorna *and back*] Crazy as a bat! [*He laughs*]

JOE: [*Frigidly*] Is it so impossible?

MOODY: About as possible as hell freezes over. [*He and* Joe *simultaneously turn to* Lorna]

JOE: Tell him. . . .

LORNA: [*Looking* Joe *in the face*] I love Tom. Tell him what?

[Joe *looks at her intently. Silence.* Joe *then turns and quietly exits from the office.* Moody *shakes his head with a grin*]

MOODY: Eddie, I take everything back. I was a fool to get sore—that boy's a real nutsy-Fagan! [*He offers his hand.* Eddie *looks at it and then viciously slaps it down*]

EDDIE: [*Repressing a trembling voice*] I don't like no one to laugh at that boy. You call a boy like that a rat? An educated boy? What is your idea to call him cock-eyed? When you do it in front of me, I say, "Tom don't like himself" . . . for Bonaparte is a good friend to me . . . you're a clever manager for him. That's the only reason I take your slop. Do your business, Tom. [*To* Lorna] And that goes for you, too! No tricks, Miss Moon! [*He slowly exits.* Moody *stands there thoughtfully.* Lorna *moves to the couch*]

MOODY: I'm a son of a gun!

LORNA: I feel like I'm shot from a cannon.

MOODY: Why?

LORNA: I'm sorry for him.

MOODY: Why? Because he's a queer?

LORNA: I'm not talking of Fuseli. [*Suddenly* Lorna's *eyes flood with tears.* Moody *takes her hand, half sensing the truth*]

MOODY: What's wrong, Lorna? You can tell me. . . .

LORNA: I feel like the wrath of God.

MOODY: You like that boy, don't you?

LORNA: I love him, Tom.

SLOW FADEOUT

SCENE IV.

Six weeks later. A dressing room before the Lombardo fight. There are a couple of rubbing tables in the room. There are some lockers and a few hooks on which hang pieces of clothing. A door to the left leads to the showers; a door to the right leads to the arena. As the lights fade in, Mr. Bonaparte *and* Siggie *are sitting to one side, on a long wooden bench.* Tokio *is fussing around in a locker. A fighter,* Pepper White, *hands already bandaged, is being rubbed down by his trainer-manager,* Mickey. *Throughout the scene is heard the distant* Roar *of* The Crowd *and the clanging of the bell.*

MR. BONAPARTE: [*After a silence of intense listening*] What is that noise?

SIGGIE: That's the roar of the crowd.

MR. BONAPARTE: A thousand people?

SIGGIE: Six thousand.

PEPPER WHITE: [*Turning his head as he lies on his belly*] Nine thousand.

SIGGIE: That's right, nine. You're sitting under nine thousand people. Suppose they fell down on your head? Did you ever think of that?

[*The outside door opens;* Eddie Fuseli *enters. The distant bell clangs.* Eddie *looks around suspiciously, then asks* Tokio]

EDDIE: Where's Bonaparte?

TOKIO: Still with the newspapermen.

EDDIE: [*Unpleasantly surprised*] He's what?

TOKIO: Tom took him upstairs—some sports writers.

EDDIE: A half hour before a fight? What is Moody trying to do?

TOKIO: Tom's the boss.

EDDIE: Looka, Tokio—in the future you are gonna take your orders from me! [*Pointing to* Siggie *and* Mr. Bonaparte] Who is this?

TOKIO: Joe's relatives.

EDDIE: [*Going over to them*] Is that his father?

MR. BONAPARTE: [*Somberly*] Yes, thisa his father.

SIGGIE: And this is his brother-in-law. Joe sent passes up the house. We just got here. I thought it was in Coney Island—it's lucky I looked at the tickets. Believe it or not, the old man never seen a fight in his life! Is it human?

EDDIE: [*Coldly*] Shut your mouth a minute! This is The Arena—Bonaparte is fighting a good man tonight—

SIGGIE: Ahh, that Lombardo's a bag of oats!

EDDIE: When Bonaparte goes in there I like him to have one thing on his mind—fighting! I hope you understand me. An' I don't like to find you here when I return! I hope you understand that. . . . [*After a full glance at them* Eddie *gracefully exits*]

SIGGIE: That's a positive personality!

TOKIO: That's Eddie Fuseli.

SIGGIE: Momma-mia! No wonder I smelled gun powder! [*Turning to* Mr. Bonaparte] Pop, that's a paradox in human behavior: he shoots you for a nickel—then for fifty bucks he sends you flowers!

TOKIO: [*Referring to the distant bell*] That's the next bout.

SIGGIE: [*To* Mr. Bonaparte] Come on, we don't wanna miss the whole show.

MR. BONAPARTE: I waita for Joe.

SIGGIE: You heard what Fuseli said—

MR. BONAPARTE: [*With somber stubbornness*] I gonna wait!

SIGGIE: Listen, pop, you—

MR. BONAPARTE: [*With sudden force*] I say I gonna wait!

SIGGIE: [*Handing* Mr. Bonaparte *a ticket*] Ticket. [*Shrugging*] Good-bye, you're letting flies in! [Siggie *exits jauntily.* Mr. Bonaparte *silently watches* Tokio *work over the fighter's materials. A* Second *comes in, puts a pail under the table where* Tokio *hovers, and exits.* Pepper White, *his head turned, watches* Mr. Bonaparte *as he hums a song*]

PEPPER:
    Oh, Sweet Dardanella, I love your harem eyes,
    Oh, Sweet Dardanella, I'm a lucky fellow to get
        such a prize. . . .

[*To* Mr. Bonaparte] So you're Bonaparte's little boy, Buddy? Why didn't you say so before? Come over here and shake my hand.

[Mr. Bonaparte *does so*]

PEPPER: Tell Bonaparte I like to fight him.

MR. BONAPARTE: Why?

PEPPER: I like to beat him up.

MR. BONAPARTE: [*Naïvely, not amused*] Why? You don't like him?

PEPPER: Don't kid me, Buddy! [*A* Call Boy *looks in at the door*]

CALL BOY: Pepper White! Ready, Pepper White! [Call Boy *exits.* Pepper White *slips off the table and begins to change his shoes*]

PEPPER: [*To* Mr. Bonaparte] When I get back I'll explain you all the ins and outs. [*A* Second *enters, takes a pail from* Mickey *and exits.* Lorna *enters*]

PEPPER: [*Indignantly*] Who told girls to come in here?!

LORNA: Modest? Close your eyes. Is Moody . . . ? [*Suddenly seeing* Mr. Bonaparte] Hello Mr. Bonaparte!

MR. BONAPARTE: [*Glad to see a familiar face*]

Hello, hello, Missa Moon! Howa you feel?

LORNA: What brings you to this part of the world?

MR. BONAPARTE: [Somberly] I come-a to see Joe. . . .

LORNA: Why, what's wrong?

MR. BONAPARTE: [With a slow shrug] He don't come-a to see me. . . .

LORNA: Does he know you're here?

MR. BONAPARTE: No. [Lorna looks at him sympathetically]

LORNA: [Finally] It's a three-ring circus, isn't it?

MR. BONAPARTE: How you mean?

LORNA: Oh, I mean you . . . and him . . . and other people . . .

MR. BONAPARTE: I gonna see how he fight.

LORNA: I owe you a report. I wish I had good news for you, but I haven't.

MR. BONAPARTE: Yes, I know . . . he gotta wild wolf inside—eat him up!

LORNA: You could build a city with his ambition to be somebody.

MR. BONAPARTE: [Sadly, shaking his head] No . . . burn down!

[Now the outside door is thrust open—the distant bell clangs. Joe enters, behind him Moody and Roxy. Joe stops in his tracks when he sees Lorna and his father together—the last two persons in the world he wants to see now. His hands are already bandaged, a bathrobe is thrown around his shoulders]

JOE: Hello, poppa. . . .

MR. BONAPARTE: Hello, Joe. . . .

JOE: [Turning to Tokio] Throw out the girls—this isn't a hotel bedroom!

MOODY: That's no way to talk!

JOE: [Coolly] I talk as I please!

MOODY: [Angrily] The future Mrs. Moody—

JOE: I don't want her here!

LORNA: He's right, Tom. Why fight about it? [She exits]

JOE: [To Moody] Also, I don't want to see writers again before a fight; it makes me nervous!

ROXY: [Softly, for a wonder] They're very important, Joe—

JOE: I'm important! My mind must be clear before I fight. I have to think before I go in. Don't you know that yet?

ROXY: [Suddenly] Yeah, we know—you're a stoodent—you gotta look in your notes.

JOE: What's funny about that? I do, I do!!

ROXY: [Retreating] So I said you do! [Pepper White comes forward, about to exit; to Moody]

PEPPER: How 'bout a bout with Napoleon?

MOODY: On your way, louse!

PEPPER: [With a grin] Pickin' setups?

[Joe suddenly turns and starts for Pepper. Tokio quickly steps in between the two boys]

TOKIO: Save it for the ring!

[The two fighters glare at each other. Joe slowly turns and starts back for the table]

PEPPER: You think he'll be the champ? Where'd you ever read about a cock-eye champ?

[Joe spins around, speeds across the room—Pepper is on the floor! Mickey now starts for Joe. Tokio starts for Mickey. Pepper gets up off the floor and finds himself occupied with Moody. For a moment the fight is general. Eddie Fuseli enters. All see him. The fighting magically stops on the second]

EDDIE: What'sa matter? Cowboys and Indians? [To Pepper] Out!

[Mickey and Pepper sullenly exit]

EDDIE: [To Moody] I'm lookin' for you! You're a manager and a half! You and your fat friend! [Meaning Roxy] You think this boy is a toy?

JOE: Eddie's the only one here who understands me.

MOODY: Who the hell wantsa understand you! I got one wish—for Lombardo to give you the business! The quicker he taps you off tonight, the better! You gotta be took down a dozen pegs! I'm versus you! Completely versus!

EDDIE: [Quietly, to Moody] Moody, your brains is in your feet! This is how you handle a coming champ, to give him the jitters before a bout? Go out and take some air! . . . [Seeing Eddie's quiet deadliness, Moody swallows his wrath and exits; Roxy follows with pursed lips]

EDDIE: Lay down, Joe—take it easy.

[Joe sits on a table]

EDDIE: Who hurt you, Joe? Someone hurt your feelings?

JOE: Everything's all right.

EDDIE: Tokio, I put fifty bucks on Bonaparte's nose for you. It's my appreciation to you. . . .

TOKIO: Thanks.

EDDIE: [Of Mr. Bonaparte] Whatta you want me to do with him?

JOE: Leave him here.

EDDIE: Tell me if you want something. . . .

JOE: Nothing.

EDDIE: Forget that Miss Moon. Stop lookin' down her dress. Go out there and kill Lombardo! Send him out to Woodlawn! Tear his skull off! . . . as I know Bonaparte can do it! [Eddie gives Mr. Bonaparte a sharp look and exits. There is silence intensified by the distant clang of the bell and the muted roar of The Crowd. Tokio looks over at Mr. Bonaparte who has been silently seated on the bench all this time]

JOE: [Not quite knowing what to say] How is Anna, poppa?

MR. BONAPARTE: Fine.

JOE: Siggie watching the fights?

MR. BONAPARTE: Yes. . . .

JOE: You look fine. . . .

MR. BONAPARTE: Yes, feela good. . . .

JOE: Why did you send that money back? [There is no answer] Why did you come here? . . . You sit there like my conscience. . . .

MR. BONAPARTE: Why you say so?

JOE: Poppa, I have to fight, no matter what you say or think! This is my profession! I'm out for fame and fortune, not to be different or artistic! I don't intend to be ashamed of my life!

MR. BONAPARTE: [*Standing up*] Yeah, I understanda you. . . .

JOE: Go out and watch the fights.

MR. BONAPARTE: [*Somberly*] Yeah . . . you fight. Now I know . . . is'a too late for music. The men musta be free an' happy for music . . . not like-a you. Now I see whatta you are . . . I give-a you every word to fight . . . I sorry for you. . . .

[*Silence. The distant roar of* The Crowd *climbs up and falls down; the bell clangs again*]

TOKIO: [*Gently*] I'll have to ask you to leave, Mr. Bonaparte. . . .

MR. BONAPARTE: [*Holding back his tears*] Joe . . . I hope-a you win every fight. [Mr. Bonaparte *slowly exits. As he opens and closes the door the roar of* The Crowd *swells up for an instant*]

TOKIO: Lay down, Joe. There's five minutes left to tune you up.

JOE: [*In a low voice*] That's right, tune me up. . . . [Joe *stretches out on his stomach and* Tokio's *busy hands start up the back of his legs*]

TOKIO: [*Working with steady briskness*] I never worried less about a boy . . . in my life. You're a real sweetheart. . . .

[*Suddenly* Joe *begins to cry in his arms.* Tokio *looks down, momentarily hesitates in his work —then slowly goes ahead with his massaging hands. The* Boy *continues to shake with silent sobs. Again the bell clangs in the distance*]

TOKIO: [*In a soft caressing voice*] You're getting good, honey. Maybe I never told you that before. I seen it happen before. [*Continuing the massaging*] It seems to happen sudden—a fighter gets good. He gets easy and graceful. He learns how to save himself—no energy wasted . . . he slips and slides—he travels with the punch. . . . Oh, sure, I like the way you're shaping up. [Tokio *continues massaging.* Joe *is silent. His sobbing stops. After a moment* Tokio *continues*] What was you saying about Lombardo's trick? I understood you to say he's a bull's-eye for a straight shot from the inside. I think you're right, Joe, but that kind of boy is liable to meet you straight-on in a clinch and give you the back of his head under the chin. Watch out for that.

JOE: He needs a straight punch. . . . [Joe *suddenly sits up on the table, his legs dangling*] Now I'm alone. They're all against me—Moody, the girl . . . you're my family now, Tokio—you and Eddie! I'll show them all—nobody stands in my way! My father's had his hand on me for years. No more. No more for her either—she had her chance! When a bullet sings through the air it has no past—only a future—like me! Nobody, nothing stands in my way! [*In a sudden spurt of feeling* Joe *starts sparring around lightly in a shadow boxing routine.* Tokio

smiles with satisfaction. Now the roar of The Crowd *reaches a frenzied shriek and hangs there. The bell clangs rapidly several times. The roar of* The Crowd *settles down again*]

TOKIO: That sounds like the kill.

[Joe *draws his bathrobe around him and prances on his toes*]

JOE: I'm a new boy tonight! I could take two Lombardos! [*Vigorously shaking out his bandaged hands above his head*] Hallelujah! We're on the Millionaire Express tonight! Nobody gets me!

[*The door is thrust open and a* Call Boy *shouts*]

CALL BOY: Bonaparte, ready. Bonaparte, ready.

[Pepper White *and* Mickey *enter as the* Call Boy *speeds away.* Pepper *is flushed with victory*]

PEPPER: [*To* Joe] Tell me when you want it; you can have it the way I just give it to Pulaski!

[Joe *looks* Pepper *in the face, flexes his hands several times and suddenly breaks out in laughter, to* Pepper's *astonishment.* Joe *and* Tokio *exit.* Pepper *throws off his robe and displays his body*]

PEPPER: Look me over—not a mark. How do you like that for class! I'm in a hurry to grab a cab to Flushing.

MICKEY: [*Impassively*] Keep away from her.

PEPPER: I don't even hear you.

MICKEY: Keep away from her!

PEPPER: I go for her like a bee and the flower.

MICKEY: [*In a droning prophetic voice*] The flower is married. Her husband is an excitable Armenian from the Orient. There will be hell to pay! Keep away from her!

[*Now in the distance is heard the indistinct high voice of the announcer*]

PEPPER: You oughta get me a fight with that cock-eye Napoleon—insteada sticking your nose where it don't belong! I could slaughter him in next to nothing.

MICKEY: [*Impassively*] If you could make his weight and slaughter him, you'd be the next world's champ. But you can't make his weight, you can't slaughter him, and you can't be the champ. Why the hell don't you take a shower?

[*The bell clangs—in the arena,* Joe's *fight is on*]

PEPPER: [*Plaintively, beginning to dress at his locker*] If my girl don't like me without a shower, I'll tell her a thing or two.

MICKEY: If her husband don't tell you first.

[*The roar of* The Crowd *swells up as the door opens and* Mr. Bonaparte *enters. He is unusually agitated. He looks at* Pepper *and* Mickey *and sits on a bench. The roar of* The Crowd *mounts higher than before, then drops*]

PEPPER: [*To* Mr. Bonaparte] What's the matter with you?

MR. BONAPARTE: [*Shaking his head*] Don't like to see . . .

PEPPER: [*Delighted*] Why? Your boy gettin' smeared?

MR. BONAPARTE: They fighta for money, no?

MICKEY: No, they're fighting for a noble cause—

MR. BONAPARTE: If they wasa fight for cause or for woman, woulda not be so bad.

PEPPER: [*Still dressing behind the locker door*] I fight for money and I like it. I don't fight for under a thousand bucks. Do I, Mickey?

MICKEY: Nope.

PEPPER: [*Boasting naïvely*] I didn't fight for under a thousand for five years. Did I, Mickey?

MICKEY: [*Impassively*] Nope.

PEPPER: I get a thousand bucks tonight, don't I?

MICKEY: Nope.

PEPPER: [*Up like a shot*] How much? How much tonight?

MICKEY: Twelve hundred bucks.

PEPPER: What? Mickey, I oughta bust you in the nose. How many times do I have to say I don't fight for under one thousand bucks! [*To Mr. Bonaparte*] Now you see what I'm up against with this manager!

MICKEY: [*Impassively*] Okay, you'll get a thousand.

PEPPER: I better, Buddy! That's all I say—I better! [*To Mr. Bonaparte*] I tell him I want to fight your kid and he don't lift a finger.

[*The roar of* The Crowd *crescendos and drops down again*]

MICKEY: You don't rate no fight with Bonaparte. [*To Mr. Bonaparte, of Pepper*] He's an old man, a fossil!

MR. BONAPARTE: Who?

MICKEY: Him—he's twenty-nine.

MR. BONAPARTE: Old?

MICKEY: In this business, twenty-nine is ancient.

PEPPER: My girl don't think so.

MICKEY: Keep away from her.

[*The roar of* The Crowd *mounts up to a devilish shriek*]

PEPPER: Wow, is your boy getting schlocked!

MR. BONAPARTE: My boy isa win.

PEPPER: Yeah, and that's why you ran away?

MR. BONAPARTE: Whatta the difference who's-a win? Is terrible to see!

PEPPER: [*Grinning*] If I wasn't in a hurry, I'd wait around to help pick up your little Joie's head off the floor. [*He draws on a sport shirt*]

MICKEY: [*To Pepper*] What are you wearing a polo shirt on a winter night for?

PEPPER: For crying out loud, I just bought it! . . . So long, Mr. Bonaparte.

MR. BONAPARTE: I aska you please—whatta happen to a boy's hands when he fight a longa time?

PEPPER: [*Holding up his fists*] Take a look at mine —I got a good pair. See those knuckles? Flat!

MR. BONAPARTE: Broke?

PEPPER: Not broke, flat!—pushed down!

MR. BONAPARTE: Hurt?

PEPPER: You get used to it.

MR. BONAPARTE: Can you use them?

PEPPER: Go down the hall and look at Pulaski.

MR. BONAPARTE: Can you open thees-a hands?

PEPPER: What for?

MR. BONAPARTE: [*Gently touching the fists*] So strong, so hard . . .

PEPPER: You said it, Buddy. So long, Buddy. [*To Mickey*] Take my stuff.

MICKEY: Sam'll take it after. Keep away from her!

[Pepper *looks at* Mickey *with a sardonic grin and exits followed by* Mickey]

MR. BONAPARTE: [*To himself*] So strong . . . so useless . . .

[*The roar of* The Crowd *mounts up and calls for a kill.* Mr. Bonaparte *trembles. For a moment he sits quietly on the bench. Then he goes to the door of the shower room and looks around at the boxing paraphernalia. In the distance the bell begins to clang repeatedly.* Mr. Bonaparte *stares in the direction of the arena. He goes to the exit door. The crowd is cheering and howling.* Mr. Bonaparte *hesitates a moment at the door and then rapidly walks back to the bench, where he sits. Head cocked, he listens for a moment. The roar of* The Crowd *is heated, demanding and hateful. Suddenly* Mr. Bonaparte *jumps to his feet. He is in a murderous mood. He shakes his clenched fist in the direction of the noise—he roars aloud. The roar of* The Crowd *dies down. The door opens,* Pepper's *second,* Sam, *enters softly whistling to himself. Deftly he begins to sling together* Pepper's *paraphernalia*]

MR. BONAPARTE: What'sa happen in the fight?

SAM: Knockout.

MR. BONAPARTE: Who?

SAM: Lombardo's stiff.

[Mr. Bonaparte *slowly sits. Softly whistling,* Sam *exits with the paraphernalia. The outside door is flung open. In come* Joe, Tokio, Moody *and* Roxy, *who is elated beyond sanity.* Joe's *eyes glitter; his face is hard and flushed. He has won by a knockout*]

ROXY: [*Almost dancing*] My boy! My darling boy! My dear darling boy!

[*Silently* Joe *sits on the edge of the table, ignoring his father after a glance. His robe drops from his shoulders.* Roxy *turns to* Moody]

ROXY: How do you like it, Tom? He knocks him out in two rounds!

MOODY: [*Stiffly to* Joe] It's good business to call the sports writers in—

ROXY: That's right, give a statement!

[Moody *gives* Joe *a rapid glance and hurriedly exits*]

ROXY: I'm collecting a bet on you. All my faith and patience is rewarded. [*As he opens the door he almost knocks over* Eddie Fuseli] Haha! How do you like it, Eddie? Haha! [*He exits.* Eddie Fuseli *closes* the door and stands with his back to it. Tokio moves up to Joe and begins to remove a glove]

TOKIO: [Gently] You're a real sweetheart. . . . [Tokio removes the sweaty glove and begins to fumble with the lace of the other one. Joe carefully moves his glove out of Tokio's reach, resting it on his opposite arm]

JOE: [Almost proudly] Better cut it off. . . .
[Mr. Bonaparte is watching tensely. Eddie watches from the door]

TOKIO: . . . Broke? . . .

JOE: [Holding the hand out proudly] Yes, it's broke. . . .
[Tokio slowly reaches for a knife. He begins carefully to cut the glove]

JOE: Hallelujah!! It's the beginning of the world!
[Mr. Bonaparte, lips compressed, slowly turns his head away. Eddie watches with inner excitement and pleasure: Joe has become a fighter. Tokio continues with his work. Joe begins to laugh loudly, victoriously, exultantly—with a deep thrill of satisfaction]

SLOW FADEOUT

ACT III. SCENE I.

Moody's office, six months later. Present are Moody, acting the persuasive salesman with two sports writers, Drake and Lewis; Roxy Gottlieb being helpful in his usual manner; Tokio, to one side, characteristically quiet . . . and Joe Bonaparte. Bonaparte sits on the desk and diffidently swings his legs as he eats a sandwich. His success has added a certain bellicosity to his attitude; it has changed his clothing to silk shirts and custom-made suits.

MOODY: He's got his own style. He won't rush—

ROXY: Nobody claims our boy's Niagra Falls.

DRAKE: [A newspaperman for twenty years] Except himself!

MOODY: You newspaper boys are right.

DRAKE: We newspaper boys are always right!

MOODY: He won't take chances tomorrow night if he can help it. He'll study his man, pick out flaws —then shoot at them.

JOE: [Casually] It won't matter a helluva lot if I win late in the bout or near the opening. The main thing with Bonaparte is to win.

DRAKE: [Dryly] Well, what does Bonaparte expect to do tomorrow night?

JOE: [As dryly] Win.

MOODY: Why shouldn't we have a win from the Chocolate Drop? Look at our record!—

LEWIS: [Good-natured and slow] We just wanna get an impression—

MOODY: Seventeen knockouts? Fulton, Lombardo, Guffey Talbot—?

JOE: Phil Weiner . . .

MOODY: Weiner?

ROXY: That's no powderpuff hitter!

LEWIS: In this fight tomorrow night, can you name the round?

JOE: Which round would you like?

DRAKE: You're either a genius or an idiot!

MOODY: Joe don't mean—

DRAKE: [Sharply] Let him talk for himself.

JOE: [Getting off the desk] Listen, Drake, I'm not the boy I used to be—the honeymoon's over. I don't blush and stammer these days. Bonaparte goes in and slugs with the best. In the bargain his brain is better than the best. That's the truth; why deny it?

DRAKE: The last time you met Chocolate you never even touched him!

JOE: It's almost two years since I "never even touched him." Now I know how!

MOODY: What Joe means to say—

DRAKE: He's the genuine and only modest cock-eyed wonder!

JOE: What good is modesty? I'm a fighter! The whole essence of prizefighting is immodesty! "I'm better than you are—I'll prove it by breaking your face in!" What do you expect? A conscience and a meek smile? I don't believe that bull the meek'll inherit the earth!

DRAKE: Oh, so it's the earth you want!

JOE: I know what I want—that's my business! But I don't want your guff!

DRAKE: I have two sons of my own—I like boys. But I'm a son-of-a-bitch if I can stomach your conceit!

MOODY: [Trying to save the situation] They serve a helluva rum Collins across the street—

DRAKE: Bonaparte, I'll watch for Waterloo with more than interest!

MOODY: Why don't we run across for a drink? How 'bout some drinks?

DRAKE: Tom, you can buy me twenty drinks and I still won't change my mind about him. [He exits]

LEWIS: [Smiling] You're all right, Bonaparte.

JOE: Thanks. . . .

LEWIS: [Clinching a cigarette at the desk] How's that big blonde of yours, Tom?

MOODY: Fine.

LEWIS: How does she feel about the wedding bells? Sunday is it?
[This is news to Joe, and Moody knows it is]

MOODY: [Nervously] Happy, the way I am. Yeah, Sunday.

ROXY: How about the drinks? We'll drink to everybody's health!

LEWIS: [To Joe] Good luck tomorrow.

JOE: Thanks. . . . [They exit, Moody throwing a resentful look at Joe. Joe and Tokio are left. In the silence Joe goes back to the remains of his lunch]

TOKIO: That Drake is a case.

JOE: [Pushing the food away] They don't make cheesecake the way they used to when I was a boy.

Or maybe I don't like it any more. When are they getting married?

TOKIO: Moody? Sunday.

JOE: Those writers hate me.

TOKIO: You give them too much lip.

JOE: [*Looking down at his clenched fists*] I'd rather give than take it. That's one reason I became a fighter. When did Moody get his divorce?

TOKIO: Few weeks ago. . . . [*Cannily*] Why don't you forget Lorna?

JOE: [*As if not understanding*] What?

TOKIO: I'll say it again . . . why not forget her? [*No answer comes*] Joe, you're loaded with love. Find something to give it to. Your heart ain't in fighting . . . your *hate* is. But a man with hate and nothing else . . . he's half a man . . . and half a man . . . is no man. Find something to love, or someone. Am I stepping on your toes?

JOE: [*Coldly*] I won't be unhappy if you mind your business.

TOKIO: Okay. . . . [*Tokio goes to the door, stops there*] Watch your dinner tonight. No girls either.

JOE: Excuse me for saying that—

TOKIO: [*With a faint smile*] Okay. [*Tokio opens the door and* Lorna Moon *enters. Tokio smiles at her and exits. She carries a pack of newspapers under her arm. Joe and she do not know what to say to each other—they wish they had not met here. Lorna crosses and puts the newspapers on the desk. She begins to bang through the desk drawers, looking for the scissors*]

JOE: I hear you're making the leap tomorrow.

LORNA: Sunday. . . .

JOE: Sunday. [*Intense silence*]

LORNA: [*To say anything*] I'm looking for the scissors. . . .

JOE: Who're you cutting up today?

LORNA: [*Bringing out the shears*] Items on Bonaparte, for the press book. [*She turns and begins to unfold and clip a sheet of newspaper. Joe is at a loss for words*]

JOE: [*Finally*] Congratulations. . . .

LORNA: [*Without turning*] Thanks. . .

[*In a sudden irresistible surge* Joe *tears the newspaper out of* Lorna's *hands and hurls them behind the desk. The two stand facing each other*]

JOE: When I speak to you, look at me!

LORNA: What would you like to say? [*They stand face to face, straining. Finally*]

JOE: Marry anyone you like!

LORNA: Thanks for permission!

JOE: Queen Lorna, the tramp of Newark!

LORNA: You haven't spoken to me for months. Why break your silence?

JOE: You're a historical character for me—dead and buried!

LORNA: Then everything's simple; go about your business.

JOE: Moody's right for you—perfect—the mating of zero and zero!

LORNA: I'm not sorry to marry Tom—

JOE: [*Scornfully*] That's from the etiquette book —page twelve: "When you marry a man say you like it!"

LORNA: I know I could do worse when I look at you. When did you look in the mirror last? Getting to be a killer! You're getting to be like Fuseli! You're not the boy I cared about, not you. You murdered that boy with the generous face—God knows where you hid the body! I don't know you.

JOE: I suppose I never kissed your mouth—

LORNA: What do you want from me? Revenge? Sorry—we're all out of revenge today!

JOE: I wouldn't look at you twice if they hung you naked from a Christmas tree!

[*At this moment* Eddie Fuseli *enters with a pair of packages. He looks intently at* Lorna, *then crosses and puts the packages on the desk. He and Joe are dressed almost identically. Lorna exits without a word. Eddie is aware of what has happened but begins to talk casually about the packages*]

EDDIE: This one's your new headgear. This is shirts from Jacobs Brothers. He says the neck bands are gonna shrink, so I had him make sixteens— they'll fit you after one washing. [*Holding up a shirt*] You like that color?

JOE: Thanks.

EDDIE: Your brother-in-law drove me over. Picked him up on 49th. Don't you ever see them no more?

JOE: [*Sharply*] What for?

EDDIE: What'sa matter?

JOE: Why? You see a crowd around here, Eddie?

EDDIE: No.

JOE: That's right, you don't! But I do! I see a crowd of Eddies all around me, suffocating me, burying me in good times and silk shirts!

EDDIE: [*Dialing the telephone*] You wanna go to the Scandals tonight? I got tickets. [*Into the telephone*] Charley? Fuseli is speaking. . . . I'm giving four to five on Bonaparte tomorrow. . . . Four G's worth. . . . Yes. [*Hanging up the phone*] It's gonna be a good fight tomorrow.

JOE: [*Belligerently*] How do you know?

EDDIE: I know Bonaparte. I got eighteen thousand spread out on him tomorrow night.

JOE: Suppose Bonaparte loses?

EDDIE: I look at the proposition from all sides— I know he'll win.

JOE: What the hell do you think I am? A machine? Maybe I'm lonely, maybe—

EDDIE: You wanna walk in a parade? Everybody's lonely. Get the money and you're not so lonely.

JOE: I want some personal life.

EDDIE: I give Bonaparte a good personal life. I got loyalty to his cause. . . .

JOE: You use me like a gun! Your loyalty's to keep me oiled and polished!

EDDIE: A year ago Bonaparte was a rookie with a two-pants suit. Now he wears the best, eats the best, sleeps the best. He walks down the street respected—the golden boy! They howl their heads off when Bonaparte steps in the ring . . . and I done it for him!

JOE: There are other things. . . .

EDDIE: There's no other things! Don't think so much—it could make you very sick! You're in this up to your neck. You owe me a lot—I don't like you to forget. You better be on your toes when you step in that ring tomorrow night. [Eddie *turns and begins to dial the telephone*]

JOE: Your loyalty makes me shiver. [Joe *starts for the door*]

EDDIE: Take the shirts.

JOE: What do I want them for? I can only wear one at a time. . . .

[Eddie *speaks into the phone*]

EDDIE: Meyer? . . . Fuseli is speaking. . . . I'm giving four to five on Bonaparte tomorrow. . . . Two? . . . Yeah. . . .

[*About to exit,* Joe *stands at the door and watches* Eddie *as he calmly begins to dial the phone again*]

MEDIUM FADEOUT

SCENE II.

The next night. The lights fade in on an empty stage. We are in the same dressing room as seen in Act Two. Far in the distance is heard the same roar of The Crowd. *The distant bell clangs menacingly. The room is shadows and patches of light. The silence here has its own ugly dead quality.* Lorna Moon *enters. She looks around nervously; she lights a cigarette; this reminds her to rouge her lips; she puffs the cigarette. The distant bell clangs again.* Eddie Fuseli *enters, pale and tense. He sees* Lorna *and stops short in his tracks. There is an intense silence as they look at each other.*

LORNA: How's the fight?

EDDIE: I like to talk to you.

LORNA: Is Joe still on his feet?

EDDIE: Take a month in the country, Miss Moon.

LORNA: Why?

EDDIE: [*Repressing a murderous mood*] Give the boy . . . or move away.

LORNA: I get married tomorrow. . . .

EDDIE: You heard my request—give him or go!

LORNA: Don't Moody count?

EDDIE: If not for Bonaparte they'd find you in a barrel long ago—in the river or a bush!

LORNA: I'm not afraid of you. . . .

[*The distant bell clangs*]

EDDIE: [*After turning his head and listening*] That's the beginning of the eighth. Bonaparte's un-settled—fighting like a drunken sailor. He can't win no more, unless he knocks the Chocolate out. . . .

LORNA: [*At a complete loss*] Don't look at me . . . what'd you . . . I . . .

EDDIE: Get outa town!

[*The roar of* The Crowd *mounts to a demand for a kill*]

EDDIE: [*Listening intently*] He's like a bum tonight . . . and a bum done it! You! [*The roar grows fuller*] I can't watch him get slaughtered. . . .

LORNA: I couldn't watch it myself. . . . [*The bell clangs loudly several times. The roar of* The Crowd *hangs high in the air*] What's happening now?

EDDIE: Someone's getting murdered. . . .

LORNA: It's me. . . .

EDDIE: [*Quietly, intensely*] That's right . . . if he lost . . . the trees are ready for your coffin. [*The roar of* The Crowd *tones down*] You can go now. I don't wanna make a scandal around his name. . . . I'll find you when I want you. Don't be here when they carry him in.

LORNA: [*At a complete loss*] Where do you want me to go?

EDDIE: [*Suddenly releasing his wrath*] Get outa my sight! You turned down the sweetest boy who ever walked in shoes! You turned him down, the golden boy, that king among the ju-ven-niles! He gave you his hand—you spit in his face! You led him on like Gertie's whoore! You sold him down the river! And now you got the nerve to stand here, to wait and see him bleeding from the mouth!—

LORNA: Fuseli, for God's sake—

EDDIE: Get outa my sight!

LORNA: Fuseli, please—

EDDIE: Outa my sight, you nickel whoore! [*Completely enraged and out of control,* Eddie *half brings his gun out from under his left armpit.* Joe *appears in the doorway. Behind him are* Roxy, Moody *and a Second*]

JOE: Eddie! [Eddie *whirls around. The others enter the room. In the ensuing silence,* Moody, *sensing what has happened, crosses to* Lorna]

LORNA: [*Quietly*] What happened?

ROXY: What happened? [*He darts forward and picks up* Joe's *arm in the sign of victory. The arm drops back limply*] The monarch of the masses!

EDDIE: [*To the* Second] Keep everybody out. Only the newspaper boys.

[*The* Second *exits and closes the door.* Joe *sits on a table. Physically he is a very tired boy. There is a high puff under one eye; the other is completely closed. His body is stained with angry splotches*]

TOKIO: [*Gently*] I have to hand it to you, Joe. . . .

ROXY: [*Explaining to the frigid* Eddie, *elaborately*] The beginning of the eighth: first the bell! Next the Chocolate Drop comes out like a waltz clog, confident. Oh, he was so confident! Haha! The next thing I know the Chocolate's on the floor, the referee lifts our arm, we got on our bathrobe and we're here in the dressing room! How do you like it?

EDDIE: [*Narrowly*] I like it.

TOKIO: [*Taking off* Joe's *gloves*] I'll have you feelin' better in a minute. [*After which he cuts the tapes*]

JOE: I feel all right.

EDDIE: [*To* Tokio] Gimme his gloves.

MOODY: [*Wary of* Joe] That's a bad lump under your eye.

JOE: Not as bad as the Chocolate Drop got when he hit the floor!

ROXY: Darling, how you gave it to him! Not to my enemies!

JOE: 'Twas a straight right—with no trimmings or apologies! Aside from fouling me in the second and fifth—

MOODY: I called them on it—

ROXY: I seen the bastard—

JOE: That second time I nearly went through the floor. I gave him the fury of a lifetime in that final punch! [Eddie *has taken the soggy boxing gloves for his own property.* Tokio *is daubing the bruise under* Joe's *eye*] And did you hear them cheer! [*Bitterly, as if reading a news report*] Flash! As thousands cheer, that veritable whirlwind Bonaparte —that veritable cock-eye wonder, Bonaparte—he comes from behind in the eighth stanza to slaughter the Chocolate Drop and clinch a bout with the champ! Well, how do you like me, boys? Am I good or am I good?

ROXY: Believe *me!*

TOKIO: [*Attempting to settle* Joe] You won the right for a crack at the title. You won it fair and clean. Now lay down. . . .

JOE: [*In a vehement outburst*] I'd like to go outside my weight and beat up the whole damn world!

MOODY: [*Coldly*] Well, the world's your oyster now!

TOKIO: [*Insistently*] Take it easy. Lemme fix that eye, Joe—

[*Now a bustling little Irishman,* Driscoll, *hustles into the room*]

DRISCOLL: Who's got the happy boy's gloves?

EDDIE: Here . . . why?

[Driscoll *rapidly takes the gloves, "breaks" and examines them*]

TOKIO: What's the matter, "Drisc"?

JOE: What's wrong?

DRISCOLL: [*Handing the gloves back to* Eddie] Chocolate's a sick boy. Your hands are clean. [Driscoll *hustles for the door.* Joe *is up and to him*]

JOE: What happened?

DRISCOLL: [*Bustling*] It looks like the Pride of Baltimore is out for good. Change your clothes.

JOE: How do you mean?

DRISCOLL: Just like I said—out! [Driscoll *pats* Joe's *shoulder, hustles out, closing the door in* Joe's *face.* Joe *slowly sits on the nearest bench. Immediately* Tokio *comes to him, as tender as a mother*]

TOKIO: You didn't foul him—you're a clean fighter. You're so honest in the ring it's stupid. If something happened, it's an accident. [*The others stand around stunned, not knowing what to do or say*]

MOODY: [*Very worried*] That's right, there's nothing to worry about.

ROXY: [*Ditto*] That's right. . . .

JOE: Gee. . . . [Joe *stands up, slowly crosses the room and sits on the table, head in his hands, his back to the others. No one knows what to say*]

EDDIE: [*To* Moody] Go out there and size up the situation.

[Moody, *glad of the opportunity to leave the room, turns to the door which is suddenly violently thrust open.* Barker, *the* Chocolate Drop's *manager, pushes* Moody *into the room with him, leaving the door open. From outside a small group of curious people look in.* Barker, *bereft of his senses, grabs* Moody *by the coat lapel*]

BARKER: Do you know it? Do you know it?

MOODY: Now wait a minute, Barker—

[Barker *runs over to* Joe *and screams*]

BARKER: You murdered my boy! He's dead! You killed him!

TOKIO: [*Getting between* Joe *and* Barker] Just a minute!

BARKER: [*Literally wringing his hands*] He's dead! Chocolate's dead!

TOKIO: We're very sorry about it. Now pull yourself together.

[Eddie *crosses the room and slams the door shut as* Barker *points an accusing finger at* Joe *and screams*]

BARKER: This dirty little wop killed my boy!

EDDIE: [*Coming to* Barker] Go back in your room.

BARKER: Yes he did!! [Eddie's *answer is to shove* Barker *roughly toward the door, weeping*] Yes, he did!!

EDDIE: Get out before I slug your teeth apart!

JOE: [*Jumping to his feet*] Eddie, for God sakes, don't hit him! Let him alone!

[Eddie *immediately desists.* Barker *stands there, a weeping idiot*]

MOODY: Accidents can happen.

BARKER: I know . . . I know. . . .

MOODY: Chocolate fouled us twice.

BARKER: I know, I know. . . . [Barker *stammers, gulps and tries to say something more. Suddenly he dashes out of the room. There is a long silent pause during which* Joe *sits down again*]

EDDIE: We'll have to wait for an investigation.

TOKIO: [*To* Joe] Don't blame yourself for nothing. . . .

JOE: That poor guy . . . with those sleepy little eyes. . . .

ROXY: [*Solemnly*] It's in the hands of God, a thing like that.

[Lewis, *the sports writer, tries to enter the room*]

EDDIE: [*Herding him out*] Stay outside. [*To Moody*] See what's happening? [*Moody immediately leaves*] Everybody out—leave Bonaparte to calm hisself. I'll watch the door.

TOKIO: Don't worry, Joe. [*He exits, followed by Roxy. Eddie turns and looks at* Lorna]

EDDIE: You too, Miss Moon—this ain't no cocktail lounge.

LORNA: I'll stay here. [*Eddie looks at her sharply, shifts his glance from her to Joe and back again; he exits*] Joe. . . .

JOE: Gee, that poor boy. . . .

LORNA: [*Holding herself off*] But it wasn't your fault.

JOE: That's right—it wasn't my fault!

LORNA: You didn't mean it!

JOE: That's right—I didn't mean it! I wouldn't want to do that, would I? Everybody knows I wouldn't want to kill a man. Lorna, you know it!

LORNA: Of course!

JOE: But I *did* it! That's the thing—I *did* it! What will my father say when he hears I murdered a man? Lorna, I see what I did. I murdered myself, too! I've been running around in circles. Now I'm smashed! That's the truth. Yes, I was a real sparrow, and I wanted to be a fake eagle! But now I'm hung up by my finger tips—I'm no good—my feet are off the earth!

LORNA: [*In a sudden burst, going to* Joe] Joe, I love you! We love each other. Need each other!

JOE: Lorna darling, I see what's happened!

LORNA: You wanted to conquer the world—

JOE: Yes—

LORNA: But it's not the kings and dictators who do it—it's that kid in the park—

JOE: Yes, that boy who might have said, "I have myself; I am what I want to be!"

LORNA: And now, tonight, here, this minute—finding yourself again—that's what makes you a champ. Don't you see that?

JOE: Yes, Lorna—yes!

LORNA: It isn't too late to tell the world good evening again!

JOE: With what? These fists?

LORNA: Give up the fighting business!

JOE: Tonight!

LORNA: Yes, and go back to your music—

JOE: But my hands are ruined. I'll never play again! What's left, Lorna? Half a man, nothing, useless. . . .

LORNA: No, *we're* left! Two together! We have each other! Somewhere there must be happy boys and girls who can teach us the way of life! We'll find some city where poverty's no shame—where music is no crime!—where there's no war in the streets—where a man is glad to be himself, to live and make his woman herself!

JOE: No more fighting, but where do we go?

LORNA: Tonight? Joe, we ride in your car. We speed through the night, across the park, over the Triboro Bridge—

JOE: [*Taking* Lorna's *arms in his trembling hands*] Ride! That's it, we ride—clear my head. We'll drive through the night. When you mow down the night with headlights, nobody gets you! You're on top of the world then—nobody laughs! That's it—speed! We're off the earth—unconnected! We don't have to think!! That's what speed's for, an easy way to live! Lorna darling, we'll burn up the night! [*He turns and as he begins to throw his street clothes out of his locker*]

MEDIUM FADEOUT

SCENE III.

Late the same night. In the Bonaparte home sit Eddie Fuseli, Moody, Roxy, *and* Siggie, *drinking homemade wine, already half drunk. Mr. Bonaparte stands on the other side of the room, looking out of the window. Frank sits near him, a bandage around his head. Moody is at the telephone as the lights fade in.*

MOODY: [*Impatiently*] . . . 'lo? Hello! . . .

SIGGIE: I'll tell you why we need another drink. . . .

ROXY: No, I'll tell you. . . .

MOODY: [*Turning*] Quiet! For Pete's sake! I can't hear myself think! [*Turning to the phone*] Hello? . . . This is Moody. Any calls for me? Messages? . . . No sign of Miss Moon? . . . Thanks. Call me if she comes in—the number I gave you before. [*Hanging up and returning to his wine glass; to* Mr. Bonaparte] I thought you said Joe was coming up here!

MR. BONAPARTE: I say maybe . . .

MOODY: [*Sitting*] I'll wait another fifteen minutes. [*He drinks*]

SIGGIE: Here's why we need another drink; it's a night of success! Joe's in those lofty brackets from now on! We're gonna move to a better neighborhood, have a buncha kids! [*To* Mr. Bonaparte] Hey, pop, I wish we had a mortgage so we could pay it off! To the next champ of the world! [*Siggie lifts his glass; the others join him*]

ROXY: Bonaparte.

EDDIE: Don't you drink, Mr. Bonaparte?

SIGGIE: You, too, Frank—it's all in the family.

[Mr. Bonaparte *shrugs and comes down, accepting a glass*]

ROXY: It's in the nature of a celebration!

MR. BONAPARTE: My son'sa kill a man tonight—what'sa celebrate? What'sa gonna be, heh?

SIGGIE: Ahh, don't worry—they can't do him nothing for that! An accident!

EDDIE: [*Coldly, to* Mr. Bonaparte] Listen, it's old

news. It's been out on the front page two-three hours.

MR. BONAPARTE: Poor color' boy . . .

MOODY: Nobody's fault. Everybody's sorry—we give the mother a few bucks. But we got the next champ! Bottoms up. [All drink, Frank included]

ROXY: [To Mr. Bonaparte] You see how a boy can make a success nowadays?

MR. BONAPARTE: Yeah . . . I see.

EDDIE: [Resenting Mr. Bonaparte's attitude] Do we bother you? If I didn't think Joe was here I don't come up. I don't like nobody to gimme a boycott!

MR. BONAPARTE: [Going back to the window] Helpa you'self to more wine.

SIGGIE: [To Eddie] leave him alone—he don't feel social tonight.

MOODY: Don't worry, Mr. Bonaparte. Looka me —take a lesson from me—I'm not worried. I'm getting married tomorrow—this afternoon!—I don't know where my girl is, but I'm not worried! What for? We're all in clover up to our necks!

SIGGIE: Shh . . . don't wake up my wife.

[Moody suddenly sits heavily; jealousy begins to gnaw at him despite his optimism. Roxy takes another drink. Eddie asks Frank, apropos of his bandaged head]

EDDIE: What's that "Spirit of '76" outfit for?

SIGGIE: [Grinning to Eddie] Didn't you hear what he said before? They gave it to him in a strike—

EDDIE: [To Frank] You got a good build—you could be a fighter.

FRANK: I fight. . . .

EDDIE: Yeah? For what?

FRANK: A lotta things I believe in. . . .

[Eddie looks at Frank and appreciates his quality]

EDDIE: Whatta you get for it?

ROXY: [Laughing] Can't you see? A busted head!

FRANK: I'm not fooled by a lotta things Joe's fooled by. I don't get autos and custom-made suits. But I get what Joe don't.

EDDIE: What don't he get?

[Mr. Bonaparte comes in and listens intently]

FRANK: [Modestly] The pleasure of acting as you think! The satisfaction of staying where you belong, being what you are . . . at harmony with millions of others!

ROXY: [Pricking up his ears] Harmony? That's music! the family's starting up music again!

FRANK: [Smiling] That's right, that's music—

[Now Moody emphatically stamps his glass down on the table and stands]

MOODY: What's the use waiting around! They won't be back. [Bitterly] Lorna's got a helluva lotta nerve, riding around in Long Island with him! Without even asking me!

SIGGIE: Long Island's famous for the best eating ducks.

EDDIE: [To Moody] You got the champ—you can't have everything.

MOODY: What's that supposed to mean?

EDDIE: [Coldly] That girl belongs to Bonaparte. They're together now, in some roadhouse . . . ana they ain't eating duck!

MOODY: [Finally, unsteadily] You don't know what you're talking about!

EDDIE: Moody, what do you figger your interest is worth in Bonaparte?

MOODY: Why?

EDDIE: [Without turning] Roxy . . . are you listening?

ROXY: Yeah. . . .

EDDIE: 'Cause after tonight I'd like to handle Bonaparte myself.

MOODY: . . . Your gall is gorgeous! But I got a contract. . . .

ROXY: Eddie, have a heart—I'm holding a little twenty percent. . . . [Out of sheer rage Moody drinks more wine; Roxy follows his example]

FRANK: [To Eddie] How much does Joe own oi himself?

EDDIE: Thirty percent. After tonight I own the rest.

MOODY: Oh, no! No, sir-ee!!

EDDIE: You're drunk tonight! Tomorrow!

MR. BONAPARTE: [Coming forward] Maybe Joe don't gonna fight no more, after tonight. . . .

EDDIE: Listen, you creep! Why don't you change your tune for a minute!

ROXY: [To Mr. Bonaparte] What're you worried about?

MR. BONAPARTE: My boy usta coulda be great for all men. Whatta he got now, heh? Pardon me fora nota to feel so confident in Joe'sa future! Pardon me fora to be anxious. . . .

EDDIE: [Standing up] I don't like this talk!

SIGGIE: Sit down, pop—you're rocking the boat! Shh! Shh! [He slips out of the room]

ROXY: Does anyone here know what he's talking about?

FRANK: He's trying to say he's worried for Joe.

ROXY: But why? Why? Don't he realize this kid's worth a fortune from tonight on? [After giving Eddie a quick glance] Ain't he got brains enough to see two feet ahead? Tell him in Italian—he don't understand our language—this is a festive occasion! To Bonaparte, the Monarch of the Masses! [The telephone rings]

MOODY: [Triumphantly, to Eddie] That's my hotel! You see, you were all wrong! That's Lorna! [Speaking into the telephone] Hello? . . . No. . . . [Turning to Mr. Bonaparte] It's for you. [Moody extends the telephone in Mr. Bonaparte's direction, but the latter stands in his place, unable to move. After a few seconds Frank sees this and briskly moves to the telephone, taking it from Moody. In the meantime Moody has begun to address Eddie with drunken eloquence. Wavering on his feet] There's a constitution in this country, Eddie

Fuseli. Every man here enjoys life, liberty and the pursuit of happiness!

FRANK: [*Speaking into the telephone*] Yes? . . . No, this is his son . . .

[*Mr. Bonaparte watches Frank mutely as he listens at the telephone*]

MOODY: There's laws in this country, Fuseli— contracts! We live in a civilized world—!

FRANK: [*Loudly, to the others*] Keep quiet! [*Resumes listening*] Yes . . . yes. . . .

ROXY: [*To* Eddie] And there's a God in heaven —don't forget it!

FRANK: [*On the telephone*] Say it again. . . . [*He listens*] Yes.

MOODY: [*To* Eddie] You're a killer! A man tries to do his best—but you're a killer!

[Frank *lowers the telephone and comes down to the others*]

FRANK: *You're all killers!*

[Mr. Bonaparte *advances a step toward* Frank]

MR. BONAPARTE: Frank . . . is it . . . ?

FRANK: I don't know how to tell you, poppa. . . .

MR. BONAPARTE: [*Hopefully*] Yes? . . .

FRANK: We'll have to go there—

EDDIE: Go where?

FRANK: Both of them . . . they were killed in a crash—

EDDIE: Who?! What?!

FRANK: They're waiting for identification—Long Island, Babylon.

EDDIE: [*Moving to* Frank] What are you handing me?! [Eddie, *suddenly knowing the truth, stops in his tracks. The telephone operator signals for the telephone to be replaced. The mechanical clicks call* Frank *to attention; he slowly replaces the instrument*]

MOODY: I don't believe that! Do you hear me? I don't believe it—

FRANK: What waste! . . .

MOODY: It's a goddam lie!!

MR. BONAPARTE: What have-a you expect? . . .

MOODY: [*Suddenly weeping*] Lorna!

MR. BONAPARTE: [*Standing, his head high*] Joe. . . . Come, we bring-a him home . . . where he belong. . . .

SLOW FADEOUT

N STANDARDS

l emission standards in this Section
n average daily emissions. These
do not preclude a requirement to
trol equipment that incorporates best
able and reasonable methods of emission

shall be unlawful for any person to
llow the emission of TRS from all recovery
cks in excess of one-half pound of sulfur
equivalent air-dried kraft pulp, or
recovery furnace stack, in excess of
and one-half ppm, expressed as hydrogen
a dry gas basis, or such other limit of
the Agency that proves to be reasonably
utilizing the latest in design of recovery
uipment, controls, and procedures, which-
re restrictive.

t shall be unlawful for any person to
llow the emission of noncondensibles
sters and/or multiple-effect evaporators
reating them to reduce the emission of TRS
the reduction that would be achieved by
xidation in a lime kiln.

It shall be unlawful for any person to cause
the emission of particulate matter from all
furnace stacks in excess of four pounds per

nan

-4-

who reluctantly hires strikebreakers. Pro-
936, *Days to Come* revealed new evidence
Hellman's vigor, although the play was
thdrawn from Broadway. Later that year,
used her royalties from *The Children's*
iden her knowledge of the contemporary
aveling to Russia, France, and Spain. In
witnessed the Civil War, experienced
nt, and was profoundly stirred by the
r sympathies entirely on the side of the
publicans, she came back to the United
combative frame of mind and henceforth
us support to all efforts to check the
sm. She became a radical in politics and
en in her approach to social problems.
ess, Miss Hellman's convictions did not
write the kind of political harangues that
playwriting of the radical wing in the
ough her animus was plain enough in
y, *The Little Foxes* (1939), her pro-
nalytical and aloof in this story of un-
oguery associated with the rise of
tunes on the ruins of the old South.
flare in her work when she turned to
resistance against German fascism, in
e Rhine. This play was produced in
1941, when the Second World War was in full swing
and when it was only a matter of months before the
United States would become embroiled. Melodramatic in action but conceived with much humanity,
Watch on the Rhine instantly won acclaim. It was
considered beyond doubt the best of the anti-Nazi
plays written for the American stage. Miss Hellman
followed this exciting drama with a panoramic investigation of the errors that had brought us into the
war. This inquisition, suitably entitled *The Searching
Wind,* appeared in 1944, when the fortunes of war
still hung in the balance. Snarled somewhat by a
love plot, the chronicle recapitulated our appease-
ment of fascism in its early stages. Still in a prosecuting frame of mind in 1946, Miss Hellman exhumed
the villains of *The Little Foxes* and wrote a second
satire on acquisitiveness, *Another Part of the
Forest*. Her last play, at the midpoint of the century
of social conflict, was an adaptation from the
French, *Montserrat,* in which an idealist faces the
necessity of sending innocent people to their death
in order to save the cause of freedom in South
America.

Miss Hellman acquired a formidable reputation
as a moralist, a strong hater, and a driving dramatist who never lost control of a situation **or an**

plays
producers, and acted as a press agent for
the theatre. In 1930, she went to Hollywood as a
script reader, or "story analyst," acquiring more
preparation for the stage and the screen. In 1932,
on returning to New York, she began working as a
play reader for Herman Shumlin, a meticulous and
clear-headed New York producer and director. It was
at this time that she read a famous early-nineteenth-
century Scottish law report, "The Great Drumsheugh
Case." Having already developed a taste for playwriting by collaborating on a farce with Louis Kro-
nenberger, she proceeded to dramatize this lawsuit,
although advised against it by her employer. Changing the background to a small Connecticut town and
creating full-sized characters, she wrote an impressive original play, *The Children's Hour*. Shumlin
produced and directed it, and it ran for 691 performances in New York. It also toured widely,
attracting much attention and running into difficulties in Boston and Chicago because its story of a
fiendish child's machinations against two school-
teachers involved the subject of sexual abnormality.

As a partisan of labor, Miss Hellman next wrote
Days to Come, a somewhat muddled treatment of
the demoralizing effect of a labor conflict on a manu-

argument. To critics who found her dramaturgy altogether too melodramatic and violent she could offer the partial defense that there was evil in the world and that it was her business to expose it. Never having much use for bumbling, she did not propose to write panegyrics on good intentions, and she showed no inclination to wallow in congenial but futile sentiment. Critics who found her mode of attack quite rasping sometimes voiced the suspicion that Miss Hellman simply did not like people. This was, however, an indictment easily dismissed on the evidence of the plays. The young Birdie in *Another Part of the Forest* and the middle-aged wreck of Birdie in *The Little Foxes,* Regina's husband and daughter in the latter play, and all but one of the major characters in *Watch on the Rhine* were conceived with sympathy and understanding.

Although Miss Hellman never overlooked the social framework within which her subjects functioned, characterization was primary in her procedure as a playwright. She worked slowly and tried to develop a full life for her characters in the ample notes she collected before writing each of her plays. If her stage pieces generally fall into the allegedly outmoded category of the well-made play, they are "well made" with the substance of reality, which consists of people as well as of situations and ideas. If they do not give us much of the wayward flow and happy surprise of writings which convey the "feel" of life more than they demonstrate a point, Miss Hellman's plays also avoid the amorphousness of this kind of "organic" or "protoplasmic" kind of composition. In any case, it must be conceded that, although Miss Hellman forced her dramatic action a little too much, piling evil upon evil and grief upon grief, she carried on the tradition of Ibsen and the social realists with due consideration for both the logic of character and the logic of situations.

The Little Foxes, considered the strongest and most closely knit of Miss Hellman's plays, is also her most interesting contribution to the modern theatre. Its obvious virtues of compactness and firmly drawn characterization are supported by a crackling style. And here her indictment of the predatory life leaves room for an understanding attitude toward those who are broken by it and those who try to resist it. The play exists, indeed, on many levels— as character drama, melodrama, and comedy. This is so decidedly the case that it is less easy than one

would imagine to define the nature and ultimate effect of the play. It belongs to an intermediate genre of playwriting, troubling to precisians in criticism, that came into vogue in modern times with such dramatists as Ibsen, Strindberg, Becque (whose comedy *The Vultures* provides interesting possibilities for a comparison), and Shaw. For an equivalent type of writing in the older drama one may have to go back to the "dark comedies" of Shakespeare, although there is hardly a glimmer of poetry in Miss Hellman's work.

Much has also been made of the sociological aspects of *The Little Foxes,* such as the historical picture of the coming of industrialism to the South and the implication that the modern capitalistic world is full of Hubbards, great and small. Although these elements are certainly present, the argument against capitalism is actually peripheral to the story and not perfectly sustained. (One may wonder whether the Hubbards would not be Hubbards in any kind of society and whether modern big business does operate in the crude ways that the Hubbards favor. Then, too, Miss Hellman has included such capitalists as Regina's husband and William Marshall, who show no affinity for Regina's brothers. Miss Hellman concerns herself generally with damnation as a state of the soul, and a case might be made out for saying that her real theme, whether she knew it or not, is "original sin" in a modern context, which brings her closer to such contemporary Catholic writers as Mauriac than to Bernard Shaw or Karl Marx.) Ultimately, however, the most considered judgment on *The Little Foxes* will be that it is fundamentally an effective work for the stage. Within the strict confines of the theatre, the life in the play holds no insoluble questions and presents no ramifications requiring debate. It is in the theatrical completeness of this and other plays that Miss Hellman proves her mettle as a playwright.

BIBLIOGRAPHY: Brooks Atkinson, *Broadway Scrapbook* (pp. 107–110, 192–195, 255–257), 1947; John Mason Brown, *Broadway in Review* (pp. 116–120), 1940; Margaret Case Harriman, "Miss Lily of New Orleans," in *The New Yorker,* Vol. XVII, No. 39, November 8, 1941; Lillian Hellman, Introduction to *Four Plays,* 1942; Joseph Wood Krutch, *The American Drama Since 1918* (pp. 130–133), 1939.

THE LITTLE FOXES

By Lillian Hellman

CHARACTERS

ADDIE
CAL
BIRDIE HUBBARD

OSCAR HUBBARD
LEO HUBBARD
REGINA GIDDENS
WILLIAM MARSHALL

ALEXANDRA GIDDENS
BENJAMIN HUBBARD
HORACE GIDDENS

SCENE

SCENE: *The living room of the Giddens house in a small town of the Deep South.*

TIME: *The Spring of 1900.*
ACT I: *Evening, after supper.*

ACT II: *Morning, a week later.*
ACT III: *Late afternoon, two weeks later.*

ACT I.

SCENE: *The living room of the Giddens house, a small town in the Deep South, the spring of 1900. Upstage is a staircase leading to the second story. U.R. are double doors to the dining room. When these doors are open we see a section of the dining room and the furniture. U.L. is an entrance hall with a coat-rack and umbrella stand. There are large lace-curtained windows on the L. wall. The room is lit by a center gas chandelier and painted china oil lamps on the tables. Against the wall is a large piano. D.R. are a high couch, a large table, several chairs. Against the L. backwall are a table and several chairs. Near the window there are a smaller couch and tables. The room is good-looking, the furniture expensive; but it reflects no particular taste. Everything is of the best, and that is all.*

AT RISE: *Addie, a tall, nice-looking Negro woman of about fifty-five, is closing the U.S. windows. From behind the closed dining-room doors there is the sound of voices. After a second Cal, a middle-aged Negro, comes in from the entrance L. hall, carrying a tray with 10 glasses and a bottle of port wine. Addie crosses, takes the tray from him, puts it on table, begins to arrange it.*

ADDIE: [*Pointing to the bottle*] You gone stark out of your head?

CAL: No, smart lady, I ain't. Miss Regina told me to get out that bottle, [*Points to bottle*] that very bottle for the mighty honored guest. When Miss Regina changes orders like that you can bet your dime she got her reason.

ADDIE: [*Points to dining room—not looking*] Go on. You'll be needed. [*She arranges glasses and pours wine*]

CAL: [*Looking at Addie while wiping glasses*] Miss

Zan she had two helpings frozen fruit cream and she tell that honored guest, she tell him that you make the [*Steps down to* Addie] best frozen fruit cream in all the South.

ADDIE: [*Smiles, pleased*] Did she? Well, see that Belle saves a little for her. She like it right before she go to bed. Save a few little cakes, too, she like——

[*The dining-room doors are opened and quickly closed again by* Birdie Hubbard. Birdie *is a woman of about forty, with a pretty, well-bred, faded face. Her movements are usually nervous and timid, but now, as she comes running into the room, she is gay and excited. Cal turns to* Birdie]

BIRDIE: Oh, Cal. [*Closes door*] I want you to get one of the kitchen boys to run home for me. He's to look in my desk drawer and—— [*Crosses D. to back of chair* R.C. *to* Addie] My, Addie. What a good supper. Just as good as good can be.

ADDIE: You look pretty this evening, Miss Birdie, and young.

BIRDIE: [*Laughing*] Me, young? [*Turns back to* Cal] Maybe you better find Simon and tell him to do it himself. He's to look in my desk, the left drawer, and bring my music album right away. Mr. Marshall is very anxious to see it because of his father and the opera in Chicago. [*To* Addie] Mr. Marshall is such a polite man with his manners, and very educated and cultured, and I've told him all about how my Mama and Papa used to go to Europe for the music—— [*Laughs. To* Addie] Imagine going all the way to Europe just to listen to music. Wouldn't that be nice, Addie? Just to sit there and listen and—— [*Turns and takes step to* Cal] Left drawer, Cal. Tell him that twice because he forgets. And tell him not to let any of the things drop out of the album and to bring it right in here when he comes back.

935

[*The dining-room doors are opened and quickly closed by* Oscar Hubbard. *He is a man in his late forties*]

CAL: Yes'm. But Simon he won't get it right. [*Crossing to door* L.] But I'll tell him.

BIRDIE: Left drawer, Cal, and tell him to bring the blue book and——

OSCAR: [*Sharply*] Birdie.

BIRDIE: [*Turning nervously*] Oh, Oscar. I was just sending Simon for my music album.

OSCAR: [*To* Cal *who has stopped at door* L. *to listen*] Never mind about the album. Miss Birdie has changed her mind.

BIRDIE: But, really, Oscar. Really I promised Mr. Marshall. I——

[Cal *looks at them, exits* L.]

OSCAR: Why do you leave the dinner table and go running about like a child?

[Addie *crosses around sofa to* D.S. *window, closes windows*]

BIRDIE: [*Trying to be gay*] But Oscar, Mr. Marshall said most specially he *wanted* to see my album. I told him about the time Mama met Wagner and Mrs. Wagner gave her the signed program and the big picture. [Oscar *moves away* D.C.] Mr. Marshall wants to see that. [Birdie *moves to him*] Very, very much. We had such a nice talk and——

OSCAR: [*Taking step to her*] You have been chattering to him like a magpie. You haven't let him be for a second. I can't think he came South to be bored with you. [*He turns away, crosses* D.R.]

BIRDIE: [*Quickly, hurt*] He wasn't bored. I don't believe he was bored. He's a very educated, cultured gentleman. [*Her voice rises*] I just don't believe it. [Addie *moves up to back of sofa*] You always talk like that when I'm having a nice time.

OSCAR: [*Turning to her, sharply*] You have had too much wine. Get yourself in hand now.

BIRDIE: [*Drawing back, about to cry, shrilly*] What am I doing? I am not doing anything. [Addie *crosses* U. *back of sofa*] What am I doing?

OSCAR: [*Taking a step to her, tensely*] I said get yourself in hand. Stop acting like a fool. [Addie *crosses to* U.S. *windows, closes them*]

BIRDIE: [*Moves up, then turns to him, quietly*] I don't believe he was bored. I just don't believe it. Some people like music and like to talk about it. [Leo *enters from dining room*. Regina *in dining room rings bell*] That's all I was doing.

[Leo Hubbard *comes hurrying through the door. He is a young man of twenty, with a weak kind of good looks.*]

LEO: Mama! [Birdie *turns sharply to him*] Papa. They are coming in now.

OSCAR: [*Softly, stepping up to* Birdie] Sit down, Birdie. Sit down now.

[Oscar *crosses* D.R. Leo *crosses* D.L. *to piano.* Birdie *sits down in chair* L.C., *bows her head as if to hide her face. The dining-room doors are opened by* Cal. *We see people beginning to*

rise from the table. Regina Giddens *comes in with* William Marshall. Regina *is a handsome woman of forty.* Marshall *is forty-five, pleasant looking, self-possessed. Behind them comes* Alexandra Giddens, *a very pretty, rather delicate looking girl of seventeen. She is followed by* Benjamin Hubbard, *fifty-five, with a large jovial face and the light graceful movements that one often finds in large men.* Regina, *after a sharp look at* Birdie *and* Oscar, *crosses to sofa* R. Marshall *crosses* C. *to chair* R.C. Alexandra *crosses* D.L. *to settee and sits*]

REGINA: Mr. Marshall, I think you're trying to console me. Chicago may be the noisiest, dirtiest city in the world but I should still prefer it to the sound of our horses and the smell of our azaleas. I should like crowds of people, and theaters, and lovely women—— [Regina *sits on sofa, smiles at* Marshall *and indicates for him to sit next to her*] Very lovely women, Mr. Marshall? [Ben *crosses to back of settee* L.]

MARSHALL: [*Crossing to sofa* R.] In Chicago? Oh, I suppose so. But I can tell you this: I've never dined there with three *such* lovely ladies.

[*He sits on sofa to* R. *of* Regina. Addie *comes down to table, takes bottle off tray and serves wine*]

BEN: [*Crossing to* C. *nods*] Our Southern women are well favored.

LEO: [*Stepping in, laughs*] But one must go to Mobile for the ladies, sir. Very elegant worldly ladies, too.

[Addie *is serving* Regina, *who hands a glass to* Marshall, *then takes one for herself*]

BEN: [*Looks at him very deliberately*] Worldly, eh? *Worldly,* did you say?

[Addie *serves* Ben]

OSCAR: [*Hastily, to* Leo] Your Uncle Ben means that worldliness is not a mark of beauty in any woman.

LEO: [*Steps up to above settee* L. *Quickly*] Of course, Uncle Ben. I didn't mean——

[Ben *cross* R. *to chair* R.C., *sits*]

MARSHALL: Your port is excellent, Mrs. Giddens.

[Addie *serves* Birdie, *who catches* Oscar's *look at her, and refuses the drink*]

REGINA: Thank you, Mr. Marshall. We had been saving that bottle, hoping we could open it just for you.

ALEXANDRA: [*As* Addie *comes to her with tray*] Oh. May I *really,* Addie?

ADDIE: Better ask Mama.

ALEXANDRA: May I, Mama?

REGINA: [*Nods, smiles*] In Mr. Marshall's honor.

ALEXANDRA: [*Smiles*] Mr. Marshall, this will be the first taste of port I've ever had.

[Addie *serves* Leo]

MARSHALL: [*Leaning forward*] No one ever had their first taste of a better port. [*He lifts his glass in a toast, she lifts hers, they both drink. Sits back.*

Looks around the room, smiles. Addie *crosses to* Oscar U.R., *serves him*] Well, I suppose it is all true, Mrs. Giddens. [Oscar *crosses* D.R.]

REGINA: What is true?

[Addie *crosses to table for bottle, takes the tray to table* U.C., *places it there, then exits* L.]

MARSHALL: That you Southerners occupy a unique position in America. You live better than the rest of us, you eat better, you drink better. I wonder you find time, or want to find time, to do business.

BEN: [*Laughs*] A great many Southerners don't.

MARSHALL: Do all of you live here together?

REGINA: Here with me? [*Laughs*] Oh, no. My brother Ben lives next door. My brother Oscar and his family live in the next square.

BEN: [*Sitting forward*] But we are a very close family. We've always *wanted* it that way.

MARSHALL: That is very pleasant. Keeping your family together to share each other's lives. My family moves around too much. My children seem never to come home. Away at school in the winter; in the summer, Europe with their mother——

[Ben *sits back*]

REGINA: [*Eagerly*] Oh, yes. Even down here we read about Mrs. Marshall in the society pages.

MARSHALL: I dare say. She moves about a great deal. And all of you are part of the same business? Hubbard Sons?

BEN: [*Motions to* Oscar] Oscar and me. [*Motions to* Regina] My sister's good husband is a banker.

MARSHALL: [*Looks at* Regina, *surprised*] Oh.

REGINA: I am so sorry that my husband isn't here to meet you. He's been very ill. He is at Johns Hopkins. But he will he home soon. We think he is getting better now.

LEO: [*Crosses to above chair* L.C.] I work for Uncle Horace. [Regina *looks at him*] I mean I work for Uncle Horace at his bank. I keep an eye on things while he's away.

REGINA: [*Smiles*] Really, Leo?

BEN: [*Looks at him, then to* Marshall] Modesty in the young is as excellent as it is rare. [*Looks at* Leo *again*]

OSCAR: [*To* Leo] Your Uncle means that a young man should speak more modestly.

LEO: [*Hastily, taking a step to* Ben] Oh, I didn't mean, sir——

MARSHALL: Oh, Mrs. Hubbard. Where's that Wagner autograph you promised to let me see? My train will be leaving soon and——

[Leo *crosses* U. *to table* U.C., *pours himself a drink*]

BIRDIE: The autograph? Oh. Well. Really, Mr. Marshall, I didn't mean to chatter so about it. Really I—— [*Nervously, looking at* Oscar] You must excuse me. I didn't get it because, well, because I had—I—I had a little headache and——

OSCAR: My wife is a miserable victim of headaches. [*Crosses* U.R. *to above sofa* R.]

REGINA: [*Quickly*] Mr. Marshall said at supper that he would like you to play for him, Alexandra.

ALEXANDRA: [*Who has been looking at* Birdie] It's not I who play well, sir. It's my aunt. She plays just wonderfully. She's my teacher. [*Rises; eagerly*] May we play a duet? May we, Mama?

BIRDIE: [*Taking* Alexandra's *hand*] Thank you, dear. But I have my headache now. I——

OSCAR: [*Sharply*] Don't be stubborn, Birdie. Mr. Marshall wants you to play.

MARSHALL: Indeed I do. If your headache isn't——

BIRDIE: [*Hesitates, then gets up, pleased*] But I'd like to, sir. Very much.

[She and Alexandra *go to piano.* Alexandra *brings chair from* U.L. *corner to piano for herself.* Birdie *moves stool* D.S., *then takes some music from top of piano. They talk about the music for a second, then study it.* Oscar *slowly crosses* L. *to chair* L.C.]

MARSHALL: It's very remarkable how you Southern aristocrats have kept together. Kept together and kept what belonged to you.

BEN: You misunderstand, sir. Southern aristocrats have *not kept* together and have *not* kept what belonged to them.

MARSHALL: [*Laughs, indicates room*] You don't call this keeping what belongs to you?

[Oscar *sits chair* L.C.]

BEN: But we are not aristocrats. [Leo *slowly crosses* R. *to* D.R.—*listening. Points to* Birdie *at piano*] Our brother's wife is the only one of us who belongs to the Southern aristocracy.

[Birdie *selects a book of music. She opens it as* Alexandra *sits down. She is stopped by "our brother's wife," looks toward* Ben. Alexandra *looks up at her*]

MARSHALL: [*Smiles*] My information is that you people have been here, and solidly here, for a long time.

[Birdie *turns back and goes through the pages*]

OSCAR: And so we have. Since our great-grandfather.

BEN: [*Smiles*] Who was *not* an aristocrat, like Birdie's.

MARSHALL: [*A little sharply*] You make great distinctions.

[Birdie *has found the page, and looks up again on "like* Birdie's." Alexandra *turns head a little to them.* Birdie *turns back to music.* Leo *is* D.R.]

BEN: Oh, they have been made for us. And maybe they are important distinctions. [*Leans forward, intimately*] Now you take Birdie's family. When my great-grandfather came here they were the highest tone plantation owners in this state.

[Birdie *looks at them.* Alexandra *looks back to her, takes her hand, pats it*]

LEO: [*Steps to* Marshall. *Proudly*] My mother's

grandfather was *governor* of the state before the war.

[Birdie *turns back to* Alexandra]

OSCAR: They owned the plantation, Lionnet. You may have heard of it, sir?

MARSHALL: [*Laughs*] No, I've never heard of anything but brick houses on a lake, and *cotton mills*.

BEN: Lionnet in its day was the best cotton land in the South. It still brings us in a fair crop. [*Sits back*] Ah, they were great days for those people— even when I can remember. They had the best of everything. [Birdie *turns to them*] Cloth from Paris, trips to Europe, horses you can't raise any more, niggers to lift their fingers——

BIRDIE: [*Suddenly*] We were good to our people. Everybody knew that. We were better to them than——

[Marshall *looks up at* Birdie]

REGINA: [*A quick look at* Marshall, *then to* Birdie] Why, Birdie. You aren't playing.

[Marshall *has been looking curiously at* Birdie]

BEN: But when the war comes these fine gentlemen ride off and leave the cotton, *and* the women, to rot.

BIRDIE: My father was killed in the war. He was a fine soldier, Mr. Marshall. A fine man.

REGINA: Oh, certainly, Birdie. A famous soldier.

BEN: [*To* Birdie] But that isn't the tale I am telling Mr. Marshall. [*To* Marshall] Well, sir, the war ends. [Birdie *goes back to piano, puts down music, sits and is ready to play*] Lionnet is almost ruined, and the sons finish ruining it. And there were thousands like them. Why? [*Leans forward*] Because the Southern aristocrat can adapt himself to nothing. Too high-toned to try.

MARSHALL: Sometimes it is difficult to learn new ways.

[Birdie *and* Alexandra *begin to play*. Marshall *leans forward, listening*]

BEN: Perhaps, perhaps. [*All listen to music. He sees that* Marshall *is paying attention to music. Irritated, he turns to* Birdie *and* Alexandra *at piano, then back to* Marshall] You're right, Mr. Marshall. It is difficult to learn new ways. But maybe that's why it's profitable. *Our* grandfather and *our* father learned the new ways and learned how to make them pay. They work. [*Smiles nastily*] *They* are in trade. Hubbard Sons, Merchandise. Others, Birdie's family for example, look down on them. [*Settles back in chair*] To make a long story short, Lionnet now belongs to *us*. [Birdie *stops playing and turns to them*] Twenty years ago we took over their land, their cotton, and their daughter.

[Birdie *rises and stands stiffly by piano*. Marshall, *who has been watching her, rises*]

MARSHALL: May I bring you a glass of port, Mrs. Hubbard?

BIRDIE: [*Softly*] No thank you, sir. You are most polite.

[*She turns away and sits*. Alexandra *tries to soothe her and asks her to play again. She pantomimes that she cannot, and for* Alexandra *to play alone*]

REGINA: [*Sharply, to* Ben] You are boring Mr. Marshall with these ancient family tales.

BEN: I hope not. I hope not. I am trying to make an important point—— [*Bows to* Marshall] for our future business partner.

[Marshall *sits*]

OSCAR: [*To* Marshall] My brother always says that it's folks like us who have struggled and fought to bring to our land some of the prosperity of your land.

BEN: Some people call that patriotism.

REGINA: [*Laughs gaily*] I hope you don't find my brothers too obvious, Mr. Marshall. I'm afraid they mean that this is the time for the ladies to leave the gentlemen to talk business.

MARSHALL: [*Hastily*] Not at all. We settled everything this afternoon. [Alexandra *starts to play, alone*. Marshall *looks at his watch*] I have only a few minutes before I must leave for the train. [*Smiles at her*] And I insist they be spent with you.

REGINA: And with another glass of port.

MARSHALL: Thank you.

[Regina *looks at him, smiles, gets up, takes his glass and crosses to table* U.C. Marshall *rises when she does, then sits*]

BEN: [*To* Regina *as she passes him*] My sister is right. [*To* Marshall] I am a plain man and I am trying to say a plain thing. [*Sitting forward*] A man ain't only in business for what he can get out of it. It's got to give him something here. [*Puts hand to his breast*. Regina *pours* Marshall's *drink*] That's every bit as true for the nigger picking cotton for a silver quarter, as it is for you and me. [Regina *hands* Marshall *glass, then sits*] If it don't give him something here, then he don't pick the cotton right. [*Sits back*. Regina *crosses* D. *to sofa*] Money isn't all. Not by three shots.

MARSHALL: Really? Well, I always thought it was a great deal. [*Drinks*]

REGINA: And so did I, Mr. Marshall.

MARSHALL: [*Leans forward. Pleasantly, but with meaning*] Now you don't have to convince me that you are the right people for the deal. I wouldn't be here if you hadn't convinced me six months ago. You want the mill here, and I want it here. It isn't my business to find out *why* you want it.

BEN: To bring the machine to the cotton, and not the cotton to the machine.

MARSHALL: [*Amused*] You have a turn for neat phrases, Hubbard. Well, however grand your reasons are, mine are simple: [Leo *crosses* U.C. *to table —pours drink*] I want to make money and I believe I'll make it on you. [*As* Ben *starts to speak, he smiles*] Mind you, I have no objections to more high minded reasons. They are mighty valuable in business. It's fine to have partners who so closely follow the teachings of Christ. [*Gets up*] And now I must leave for my train.

> [*Puts his glass on table. All except* Birdie *rise.* Alexandra *stops playing*]

REGINA: I'm sorry you won't stay over with us, Mr. Marshall, but you'll come again, any time you like.

BEN: [*Motions to* Leo, *indicating bottle*] Fill them up, boy, fill them up. [Leo *moves around, filling glasses as* Ben *speaks*] Down here, sir, we have a strange custom. We drink the *last* drink for a toast. That's to prove that the Southerner is always still on his feet for the last drink. [*Picks up his glass*] It was Henry Frick, your Mr. Henry Frick, who said, "Railroads are the Rembrandts of investments." Well, *I* say "Southern cotton mills *will* be the Rembrandts of investments." So I give you the firm of Hubbard Sons and Marshall, Cotton Mills, and to it a long and prosperous life.

> [*They all pick up their glasses.* Marshall *looks at them, amused. Then he, too, lifts his glass, smiles*]

OSCAR: The children will drive you to the depot. [*Crosses to table* U.C.—*puts down glass*] Leo! Alexandra! You will drive Mr. Marshall down.

LEO: [*Eagerly, looks at* Ben *who nods*] Yes, sir. [*To* Marshall] Not often Uncle Ben lets *me* drive the horses. And a beautiful pair they are. [*Starts for hall*] Come on Zan. [*Exits*]

ALEXANDRA: [*Crosses to* Ben] May I drive tonight, Uncle Ben, please? I'd like to and——

BEN: [*Shakes his head, laughs*] In your evening clothes? Oh, no, my dear.

ALEXANDRA: But Leo, always——

> [*Stops, exits quickly*]

REGINA: I don't like to say goodbye to you, Mr. Marshall.

MARSHALL: Then we won't say goodbye. You have promised that you would come and let me show you Chicago. Do I have to make you promise again?

REGINA: [*Looks at him as he presses her hand*] I promise again.

> [Ben *crosses to hall*]

MARSHALL: [*Touches her hand again, then moves to* Birdie] Goodbye, Mrs. Hubbard.

> [Birdie *rises, crosses* C.]

BIRDIE: [*Shyly, with sweetness and dignity*] Goodbye, sir.

> [*He bows, starts toward entrance hall.* Regina *crosses to* C.]

MARSHALL: [*As he passes* Regina] Remember.

REGINA: I will.

OSCAR: We'll see you to the carriage.

> [Marshall *exits followed by* Oscar. *For a second* Regina *and* Birdie *stand looking after them. Then* Regina *throws up her arms, laughs happily*]

REGINA: And there, Birdie, goes the man who has opened the door to our future.

BIRDIE: [*Surprised at the unaccustomed friendliness*] What?

REGINA: [*Turning to her*] Our future. Yours and mine, Ben's and Oscar's, the children's——[*Looks at* Birdie's *puzzled face, laughs*] Our future! [*After a second crosses* D.L. *to* Birdie] You were charming at supper, Birdie. Mr. Marshall certainly thought so.

BIRDIE: [*Pleased*] Why, Regina. Do you think he did?

REGINA: Can't you tell when you're being admired?

BIRDIE: Oscar said I bored Mr. Marshall. [*Then quietly*] But he admired *you.* He told me so.

REGINA: What did he say?

BIRDIE: He said to me, "I hope your sister-in-law will come to Chicago. Chicago will be at her feet." He said the ladies would bow to your manner and the gentlemen to your looks.

REGINA: [*Crossing* R. *to sofa*] Did he? He seems a lonely man. Imagine being lonely with all that money. I don't think he likes his wife.

BIRDIE: Not like his wife? What a thing to say.

REGINA: [*Sits sofa* R.] She's away a great deal. He said that several times. And once he made fun of her being so social and hightoned. But that fits in all right. [*Sits back, arms on back of sofa, stretches*] Her being social, I mean. She can introduce me. It won't take long with an introduction from her.

BIRDIE: [*Bewildered*] Introduce you? In Chicago? You mean you really might go? [*Crosses* R. *to table*] Oh, Regina, you can't leave here. What about Horace?

REGINA: Don't look so scared about everything, Birdie. I'm going to live in Chicago. I've always wanted to. And now there'll be plenty of money to go with.

BIRDIE: [*Sits chair* R.C.] But Horace won't be able to move around. You know what the doctor wrote.

REGINA: There'll be millions, Birdie, millions. You know what I've always said when people told me we were rich? I said I think you should either be a nigger or a millionaire. In between, like us, what for? [*Laughs. Looks at* Birdie] But I'm not going away tomorrow, Birdie. [*Takes her arms down*] There's plenty of time to worry about Horace when he comes home. If he ever decides to come home.

BIRDIE: Will we be going to Chicago? I mean, Oscar and Leo and me?

REGINA: You? I shouldn't think so. [*Laughs. Leaning forward*] Well, we must remember tonight. It's a very important night and we mustn't forget it. We shall plan all the things we'd like to have and then we'll really have them. Make a wish, Birdie, any wish. It's bound to come true now.

> [Ben *and* Oscar *enter*]

BIRDIE: [*Laughs*] Well. Well, I don't know. Maybe. [Regina *turns to look at* Ben] Well, I guess I'd know right off what I wanted.

> [Ben *crosses to above* Regina. Oscar *stands by*

the upper window, waves to the departing carriage]

REGINA: [*Looks up at Ben, smiles. He smiles back at her*] Well, you did it. [*Grasps his hand*]

BEN: Looks like it might be we did.

REGINA: [*Springs up, laughs*] Looks like it! Don't pretend. [*Rises, crossing* U.C.] You're like a cat who's been licking the cream. [*Crosses to wine bottle on table* U.C.] Now we must all have a drink to celebrate.

[Ben *crosses to table* U.C.]

OSCAR: [*From window*] The children, Alexandra and Leo, make a very handsome couple, Regina. [Regina *does not look at him. Ben and* Regina *drink.* Oscar *steps in*] Marshall remarked himself what fine young folks they were. How well they looked together.

REGINA: [*Sharply*] Yes. You said that before, Oscar. [*She puts drink down, crosses* D. *to chair* L.C. *—sits*]

BEN: Yes, sir. [*Crossing* D.R.] It's beginning to look as if the deal's all set. I may not be a subtle man—but—— [*Turns to them. After a second*] Now somebody ask me how I know the deal is set.

OSCAR: What do you mean, Ben?

BEN: You remember I told him that down here we drink the *last* drink for a toast?

OSCAR: [*Thoughtfully*] Yes. I never heard that before.

BEN: Nobody's ever heard it before. [*Turns chair* D.R. *to face room. Stands in front of it*] God forgives those who invent what they need. [*Holding up his glass*] I already had his signature. But we've all done business with men whose word over a glass is better than a bond. Anyway it don't hurt to have both. [*He sits*]

OSCAR: [*Turns to* Regina. *Crosses* L. *to above sofa*] You understand what Ben means?

REGINA: [*Smiles*] Yes, Oscar. I understand. I understood immediately.

BEN: [*Looks at her admiringly*] Did you, Regina? Well, when he lifted his glass to drink, I closed my eyes and saw the bricks going into place.

REGINA: And *I* saw a lot more than that. [Oscar *sits sofa* R., *lights cigar, sits back to relax*]

BEN: Slowly, slowly. As yet we have only our hopes.

REGINA: Birdie and I have just been planning what we want. I know what I want. What will you want, Ben?

BEN: Caution. Don't count the chickens. [*Leans back, laughs.* Regina *laughs*] Well, God would allow us a little day dreaming. Good for the soul when you've worked hard enough to deserve it. [*Pauses*] I think I'll have a stable. For a long time I've had my good eye on Carter's in Savannah. A rich man's pleasure, the sport of kings, why not the sport of Hubbards? Why not?

REGINA: [*Smiles*] Why not? What will you have, Oscar?

OSCAR: I don't know. [*Thoughtfully—leaning forward on table*] The pleasure of seeing the bricks grow will be enough for me.

BEN: Oh, of course. Our *greatest* pleasure will be to see the bricks grow. But we are all entitled to a little side indulgence.

OSCAR: [*Looking front*] Yes, I suppose so. Well, then, I think we might take a few trips here and there, [*To* Birdie] eh, Birdie?

BIRDIE: [*Surprised at being consulted*] Yes, Oscar. I'd like that.

OSCAR: [*Looking front*] We might even make a regular trip to Jekyll Island. I've heard the Cornelly place is for sale. We might think about buying it. Make a nice change. [*To* Birdie] Do you good, Birdie, a change of climate. [*Front*] Fine shooting, on Jekyll, the best.

BIRDIE: I'd like——

OSCAR: [*Indulgently—front*] What would you like?

BIRDIE: *Two* things. Two things I'd like most.

REGINA: Two! I should like a thousand. You are modest, Birdie.

BIRDIE: [*Warmly, delighted with the unexpected interest*] I should like to have Lionnet back. I know you own it now, but I'd like to see it fixed up again, the way Mama and Papa had it. Every year it used to get a nice coat of paint—Papa was very particular about the paint—and the lawn was so smooth all the way down to the river, with the trims of zinnias and red-feather plush. And the figs and blue little plums and the scuppernongs——[*Smiles. Turns to* Regina] The organ is still there and it wouldn't cost much to fix. We could have parties for Zan, [*rises, crosses to* Regina] the way Mama used to have for me. [*Crosses* U.C., *moving about, dreamily*]

BEN: That's a pretty picture, Birdie. Might be a most pleasant way to live. [*Dismissing* Birdie] What do you want, Regina?

BIRDIE: [*Very happily, not noticing that they are no longer listening to her; crosses* D.S.] I could have a cutting garden. Just where Mama's used to be. Oh, I do think we could be happier there. Papa used to say that *nobody* had ever lost their temper at Lionnet, and *nobody* ever would. Papa would never let anybody be nasty spoken, or mean. No, sir. [*Moving about* U.C.] He just didn't like it.

BEN: What do you want, Regina?

REGINA: I'm going to Chicago. And when I'm settled there and know the right people and the right things to buy—because I certainly don't now—I shall go to *Paris* and buy them. [*Laughs*] I'm going to leave you and Oscar to count the bricks.

BIRDIE: [*Turning to* Oscar, *crosses to chair* R.C.] Oscar. Please let me have Lionnet back.

OSCAR: [*To* Regina] You are serious about moving to Chicago?

[Birdie *crosses* U. *to table* U.C., *pours drink, drinks it fast*]

BEN: She is going to see the great world and leave us in the little one. Well, we'll come and visit you and meet all the great and be proud to think you are our sister.

REGINA: [*Gaily*] Certainly. And you won't even have to learn to be subtle, Ben. Stay as you are. You will be rich and the rich don't have to be subtle.

OSCAR: But what about Alexandra? She's seventeen. Old enough to be thinking about marrying.

BIRDIE: [*Crosses D. to* Oscar] And, Oscar, I have one more wish. Just one more wish.

OSCAR: [*Turns*] What is it, Birdie? What are you saying?

BIRDIE: I want you to stop shooting. I mean, so much. I don't like to see animals and birds killed just for the killing. You only throw them away——

BEN: [*To* Regina] It'll take a great deal of money to live as you're planning, Regina.

REGINA: Certainly. But there'll be plenty of money. You have estimated the profits very high.

BEN: I have——

BIRDIE: [*Does not notice that* Oscar *is looking at her furiously*] And you never let anybody else shoot, and the niggers need it so much to keep from starving. It's wicked to shoot food just because you like to shoot, when poor people need it so——

BEN: [*Laughs*] I have estimated the profits very high—for myself.

REGINA: What did you say?

BIRDIE: I've always wanted to speak about it, Oscar.

OSCAR: [*Slowly, carefully*] What are you chattering about?

BIRDIE: [*Finally catches his tone, nervously*] I was talking about Lionnet and—and about your shooting——

OSCAR: You are exciting yourself.

REGINA: [*To* Ben] I didn't hear you. There was so much talking.

OSCAR: [*To* Birdie] You have been acting very childish, very excited, all evening.

BIRDIE: Regina asked me what I'd like——

REGINA: What did you say, Ben?

BIRDIE: ——now that we'll be so rich. Everybody was saying what they would like, so *I* said what *I* would like, too.

BEN: I said——[*He is interrupted by* Oscar]

OSCAR: [*To* Birdie] Very well. We've all heard you. That's enough now.

BEN: I am waiting! [*They stop. Irritated, to* Oscar] I am waiting for you to finish. You and Birdie. Four conversations are three too many. [Birdie *crosses U.C. slowly, sits chair R. of table.* Oscar *nods,* Ben *waits, sees that everything is quiet. Smiles, to* Regina] I said that I had, and I do, estimate the profits very high—for myself, and Oscar, of course.

REGINA: [*Slowly*] And what does that mean? [Ben *shrugs, looks toward* Oscar]

OSCAR: [*Looks at* Ben, *clears throat*] Well, Regina, it's like this. For forty-nine per cent Marshall will put up four hundred thousand dollars. For fifty-one

per cent—— [*Smiles archly*] a controlling interest, mind you, we will put up two hundred and twenty-five thousand dollars besides offering him certain benefits that our [*Looks at* Ben *to include him*] local position allows us to manage. Ben means that two hundred and twenty-five thousand dollars is a lot of money.

REGINA: I know the terms and I know it's a lot of money.

BEN: [*Nodding*] It is.

OSCAR: Ben means that we are ready with our two-thirds of the money. Your third, Horace's, I mean, doesn't seem to be ready. [*Raises his hand as* Regina *starts to speak*] Ben has written to Horace, I have written, and you have written. He answers. But he never mentions this business. Yet we have explained it to him in great detail, and told him the urgency. Still he never mentions it. Ben has been very patient, Regina. [*Sits back*] Naturally, you are our sister and we want you to benefit from anything we do. [*Looks at* Ben]

REGINA: [*Rises. To* Oscar] And in addition to your concern for me, you do not want control to go out of the family. [*To* Ben] That right, Ben?

BEN: That's cynical. [*Smiles*] Cynicism is only an unpleasant way of saying the truth.

OSCAR: [*Rises. Crosses L. to* C.] No need to be cynical. We'd have no trouble raising the third share, the share that you want to take.

REGINA: I am sure you could get the third share, the share you were saving for me. But that would give you a strange partner. [*Crosses R. to sofa*] And strange partners sometimes want a great deal. [*Smiles unpleasantly*] But perhaps it would be wise for you to find him.

OSCAR: [*Turns, step* C.] Now, now. Nobody says we *want* to do that. We would like to have you in and you would like to come in.

REGINA: Yes. I certainly would.

BEN: [*Laughs, puts up his hand*] But we haven't heard from Horace.

REGINA: I've given my word that Horace will put up the money. That should be enough.

[Oscar *crosses to table* D.L.—*flicks ash off cigar*]

BEN: Oh, it was enough. I took your word. But I've got to have more than your word now. The contracts will be signed this week, and Marshall will want to see our money soon after. Regina, Horace has been in Baltimore for five months. I know that you've written him to come home, and that he hasn't come.

OSCAR: It's beginning to look as if he doesn't want to come home.

REGINA: Of course he wants to come home. [*Crossing* C.] You can't move around with heart trouble at any moment you choose. You know what doctors are like once they get their hands on a case like this——

OSCAR: They can't very well keep him from answering letters, can they? [Regina *turns to* Ben] They couldn't keep him from arranging for the money if he wanted to——

REGINA: [*Crossing* R.] Has it occurred to you that Horace is also a good business man?

BEN: Certainly. He is a shrewd trader. Always has been. The bank is proof of that.

REGINA: Then, possibly, he may be keeping silent because he doesn't think he is getting enough for his money. [*Looks at* Oscar] Seventy-five thousand he has to put up. That's a lot of money, too. [*Sits sofa*]

OSCAR: Nonsense. He knows a good thing when he hears it. [*Crosses* R. *to table*] He knows that we can make *twice* the profit on cotton goods manufactured *here* than can be made in the North.

BEN: That isn't what Regina means. [*Smiles*] May I interpret you, Regina? [*To* Oscar] Regina is saying that Horace wants *more* than a third of our share.

OSCAR: [*Amazed, playing along*] But he's only putting up a third of the money. You put up a third and you get a third. What else *could* he expect?

REGINA: Well, *I* don't know. I don't know about these things. It would seem that if you put up a third you should only get a third. But then again, there's no law about it, is there? [Oscar *turns—crosses to chair* L.C.] I should think that if you knew your money was very badly needed, well, you just might say, I want more, I want a bigger share. [Oscar *turns—crosses* U. *back of sofa* L.] You *boys* have done that. I've heard you say so.

BEN: [*After a pause, laughs*] So you believe he has deliberately held out? [Oscar *crosses* D. *to chair* L.C.] For a larger share? [*Leaning forward*] Well, I *don't* believe it. But I *do* believe that's what *you* want. Am I right, Regina?

REGINA: Oh, I shouldn't like to be too definite. [Oscar *sits chair* L.C. *To* Ben] But I *could* say that I wouldn't like to persuade Horace unless he did get a larger share. I must look after his interests. It seems only natural——

OSCAR: And where would the larger share come from?

REGINA: I don't know. That's not my business. [*Giggles*] But perhaps it could come off your share, Oscar.

[Regina *and* Ben *laugh*]

OSCAR: [*Rises and wheels furiously on both of them as they laugh*] What kind of talk is this?

BEN: I haven't said a thing.

OSCAR: [*Crosses to table* R. *To* Regina] You are talking very big tonight.

REGINA: [*Stops laughing*] Am I? Well, you should know me well enough to know that I wouldn't be asking for things I didn't think I could get.

OSCAR: Listen. I don't believe you can even get Horace to come home, much less get money from him or talk quite so big about what you want.

REGINA: Oh, I can get him home.

OSCAR: Then why haven't you?

REGINA: I thought I should fight his battles for him, before he came home. Horace is a very sick man. And even if *you* don't care how sick he is, I do.

BEN: Stop this foolish squabbling. [Oscar *turns, crosses* L.C.] How *can* you get him home?

REGINA: I will send Alexandra to Baltimore. She will ask him to come home. She will say that she *wants* him to come home, and that *I* want him to come home.

BIRDIE: [*Suddenly*] Well, of course she wants him here, but he's sick and maybe he's happy where he is.

REGINA: [*As if she had not heard* Birdie, *to* Ben] You agree that he will come home if she asks him to, if she says that I miss him and want him——

BEN: [*Looks at her, smiles*] I admire you, Regina. And I agree. That's settled now, and——[*Starts to rise*]

REGINA: [*Quickly stopping him*] But before she brings him home, I want to know what he's going to get.

BEN: What do you want?

REGINA: Twice what you offered.

BEN: Well, you won't get it.

OSCAR: [*To* Regina] I think you've gone crazy.

REGINA: I don't want to fight, Ben——

BEN: I don't either. You won't get it. There isn't any chance of that. [*Roguishly*] You're holding us up, and that's not pretty, Regina, not pretty. [*Holds up his hand as he sees she is about to speak*] But we need you, and I don't want to fight. Here's what I'll do: I'll give Horace forty per cent, instead of the thirty-three and a third he really should get. I'll do that provided he is home and his money is up within two weeks. How's that?

REGINA: All right.

OSCAR: [*Crossing* C. *to* Ben] I've asked before: Where is this extra share coming from?

BEN: [*Pleasantly*] From you. From your share.

OSCAR: [*Furiously. Crosses* R. *to table* R.] From me, is it? That's just fine and dandy. That's my reward. For thirty-five years I've worked my hands to the bone for you. For thirty-five years I've done all the things you didn't want to do. And this is what I——

BEN: [*Turns slowly to look at* Oscar. Oscar *breaks off*] My, my. I am being attacked tonight on all sides. First by my sister, then by my brother. And I ain't a man who likes being attacked. I can't believe that God wants the strong to parade their strength, but I don't mind doing it, if it's got to be done. [Oscar *turns, crosses to above chair* L.C., *facing* L. *Leans back in his chair*] You ought to take these things better, Oscar. I've made you money in the past. I'm going to make you more money now. You'll be a very rich man. What's the difference to any of us if a little more goes here, a little less goes there—it's all in the family. And it will stay in the family. [Addie *enters, begins to gather the glasses from table* U.C. Oscar *turns to* Ben] So my money will go to Alexandra and Leo. They may even marry some day and——

[Addie *looks at* Ben, *then crosses to table* R., *picks up glasses, then crosses to table* U.C., *picks up tray and exits* L.]

BIRDIE: [*Rising*] Marry—Zan and Leo——

OSCAR: [*Carefully—crossing* D. *to chair* L.C.] That would make a great difference in my feelings. If they married. [*Sits chair* L.C. Birdie *sits chair* U.C.]

BEN: Yes, that's what I mean. Of course it would make a difference.

OSCAR: [*Carefully*] Is that what you mean, Regina?

REGINA: Oh, it's too far away. We'll talk about it in a few years.

OSCAR: I want to talk about it now.

BEN: [*Nods*] Naturally.

REGINA: There's a lot of things to consider. They are first cousins, and——

OSCAR: That isn't unusual. Our grandmother and grandfather were first cousins.

REGINA: [*Giggles*] And look at us.

[Ben *giggles*]

OSCAR: [*Angrily—rises, crosses* D.L.] You're both being very gay with my money.

[Oscar *pacing front piano*]

BEN: [*Sighs*] These quarrels. I dislike them so. [*Leans forward to* Regina. Oscar *stops walking at table* L. *Listens*] A marriage might be a very wise arrangement, for several reasons. And then, Oscar has given up something for you. You should try to manage something for him.

REGINA: I haven't said I was opposed to it. But Leo is a wild boy. There were those times when he took a little money from the bank and——

OSCAR: [*A step in*] That's all past history—

REGINA: Oh, I know. And I know all young men are wild. I'm only mentioning it to show you that there are considerations——

BEN: [*Irritated that she does not understand he is trying to keep* Oscar *quiet*] All right, so there are. But please assure Oscar that you will think about it very seriously.

REGINA: [*Smiles, nods*] Very well. I assure Oscar that I will think about it seriously.

OSCAR: [*Sharply*] That is not an answer.

REGINA: My, [*Rises*] you're in a bad humor and you shall put me in one. [*Crossing to* C.] I have said all that I am willing to say now. After all, Horace has to give his consent, too.

OSCAR: Horace will do what you tell him to.

REGINA: Yes, I think he will.

OSCAR: [*A step to her*] And I have your word that you will try to——

REGINA: [*Patiently. Crosses to him*] Yes, Oscar. You have my word that I will think about it. Now do leave me alone.

[*There is the sound of* Alexandra *and* Leo *opening and closing the front door*]

BIRDIE: [*Rising*] I—Alexandra is only seventeen. She——

REGINA: [*Calling. Crossing in to hall*] Alexandra? Are you back? [Birdie *sits*]

ALEXANDRA: Yes, Mama.

LEO: [*Comes into room. Crossing* D.L.] Mr. Marshall got off safe and sound. Weren't those fine clothes he had? You can always spot clothes made in a good place. Look like maybe they were done in England. [Regina *and* Alexandra *enter room*] Lots of men in the North send all the way to England for their stuff.

BEN: [*To* Leo] Were you careful driving the horses?

LEO: [*Turns to* Ben] Oh, yes sir. I was.

[Alexandra *has come in on* Ben's *question, hears the answer, looks angrily at* Leo]

ALEXANDRA: [*Crosses to* Birdie] It's a lovely night. You should have come, Aunt Birdie.

REGINA: Were you gracious to Mr. Marshall?

ALEXANDRA: I think so, Mama. I liked him. [Leo *crosses to settee* L.—*sits*]

REGINA: Good. And now I have great news for you. [Addie *enters* L. *with tray with water pitcher and glasses. Crosses to table* U.C. Alexandra *crosses to* Regina] You are going to Baltimore in the morning to bring your father home.

ALEXANDRA: [*Gasps, then delighted*] Me? Papa said I should come? That must mean—— [*Turns to* Addie] Addie, he must be well. [*Crosses to* Addie] Think of it, he'll be back home again. We'll *bring* him home.

REGINA: You are going alone, Alexandra. [*Sits sofa* R.]

ADDIE: [Alexandra *has turned in surprise*] Going alone? Going by herself? [*Crosses to above table* R.] A child that age! Mr. Horace ain't going to like Zan traipsing up there by herself.

REGINA: [*Sharply*] Go upstairs and lay out Alexandra's things.

ADDIE: He'd expect me to be along——

REGINA: I'll be up in a few minutes to tell you what to pack. [Addie *slowly begins to climb steps. To* Alexandra] I should think you'd like going alone. At your age it certainly would have delighted me. You're a strange girl, Alexandra. Addie has babied you so much.

ALEXANDRA: I only thought it would be more fun if Addie and I went together.

BIRDIE: [*Timidly*] Maybe I could go with her, Regina. I'd really like to.

REGINA: She is going alone. She is getting old enough to take some responsibilities.

OSCAR: She'd better learn now. She's almost old enough to get married. [*Jovially, to* Leo, *slapping him on shoulder*] Eh, son?

LEO: Huh?

OSCAR: [*Annoyed with* Leo *for not understanding*] Old enough to get married, you're thinking, eh?

LEO: Oh, yes, sir. [*Feebly*] Lots of girls get married at Zan's age. Look at Mary Prester and Johanna and——

REGINA: Well, she's not getting married tomorrow. But she is going to Baltimore tomorrow, so let's talk about *that*. [Oscar *turns away—crosses* U.L. *To* Alexandra] You'll be glad to have Papa home again.

ALEXANDRA: I wanted to go before, Mama. You remember that. [*Crosses* R.C.] But you said *you* couldn't go, and that *I* couldn't go alone.

REGINA: I've changed my mind. [*Too casually*] You're to tell Papa how much you missed him, and that he must come home now—for your sake. Tell him that you *need him* home.

ALEXANDRA: [*Crosses to above table* R.] Need him home? I don't understand.

REGINA: There is nothing for you to understand. You are simply to say what I have told you.

BIRDIE: [*Rises, a step* D. *to* Regina] He may be too sick. She couldn't do that——

ALEXANDRA: Yes. He may be too sick to travel. I couldn't make him think he had to come home for me, if he is too sick to——

REGINA: [*Looks at her, sharply, challengingly*] You *couldn't* do what I tell you to do, Alexandra?

ALEXANDRA: [*Looks at her quietly*] No. I couldn't. If I thought it would hurt him.

REGINA: [*After a second's silence, smiles pleasantly*] But you are doing this for Papa's own good. [*Takes* Alexandra's *hand*] You must let me be the judge of his condition. It's the best possible cure for him to come home and be taken care of here. He mustn't stay there any longer and listen to those alarmist doctors. You are doing this entirely for his sake. Tell your Papa that I want him to come home, that I miss him very much.

ALEXANDRA: [*Slowly*] Yes, Mama.

REGINA: [*To the rest. Rises*] I must go and start getting Alexandra ready now. [*Crosses* U.C. *to stairs*] Why don't you all go home?

BEN: [*Rises*] I'll attend to the railroad ticket. One of the boys will bring it over. [*Crosses* U.R. *back of sofa*] Good night, everybody. Have a nice trip, Alexandra. The food on the train is very good. The celery is so crisp. Have a good time and act like a little lady. [*He exits*]

REGINA: [*On landing*] Good night, Ben. Good night, Oscar——[*Playfully*] Don't be so glum, Oscar. It makes you look as if you had chronic indigestion. [*He does not answer*]

BIRDIE: Good night, Regina.

REGINA: Good night, Birdie. [*Exit upstairs*]

OSCAR: [*Starts for hall, to* Birdie *and* Leo] Come along.

LEO: [*As he crosses* U.R. *to* Alexandra] Imagine your not wanting to go! What a little fool you are. [Alexandra *crosses* D.L.] Wish it were me. What I could do in a place like Baltimore!

ALEXANDRA: [*Angrily, looking away from him*] Mind your business. I can guess the kind of things you could do.

LEO: [*Laughs*] Oh, no, you couldn't. [*He exits*]

REGINA: [*Calling from top of stairs*] Come on, Alexandra.

BIRDIE: [*Quickly, crossing* D.L. *to* Alexandra, *softly*] Zan.

ALEXANDRA: [*Quietly*] I don't understand about my going, Aunt Birdie. [*Shrugs*] But anyway, Papa will be home again. [*Pats* Birdie's *arm*] Don't worry about me. I can take care of myself. Really I can.

BIRDIE: [*Shakes her head, softly*] That's not what I'm worried about, Zan——

ALEXANDRA: [*Comes close to her*] What's the matter?

BIRDIE: It's about Leo——

ALEXANDRA: [*Whispering*] He beat the horses. That's why we were late getting back. We had to wait until they cooled off. He always beats the horses as if——

BIRDIE: [*Whispering frantically, holding* Alexandra's *hands*] He's my son. My own son. But you are more to me—more to me than my own child. I love you more than anybody else——

ALEXANDRA: Don't worry about the horses. I'm sorry I told you.

BIRDIE: [*Her voice rising*] I am not worrying about the horses. I am worrying about you. You are *not* going to marry Leo. I am not going to let them do that to you——

ALEXANDRA: Marry? To Leo? [*Laughs*] I wouldn't marry, Aunt Birdie. I've never even thought about it——

BIRDIE: Hush! But they have thought about it. [*Wildly*] Zan, I couldn't stand to think about such a thing. You and——

[Oscar *has come into doorway on* Alexandra's *speech. He is standing quietly, listening*]

ALEXANDRA: [*Laughs*] But I'm not going to marry. And I'm certainly not going to marry Leo.

[Oscar *takes one step into the room*]

BIRDIE: Don't you understand? They'll make you. They'll make you——

ALEXANDRA: [*Takes* Birdie's *hands, quietly, firmly*] That's foolish, Aunt Birdie. I'm grown now. Nobody can make me do anything——

BIRDIE: I just couldn't stand——

OSCAR: [*Sharply*] Birdie. [Birdie *looks up, draws quickly away from* Alexandra. *She stands rigid, fearful. Quietly*] Birdie, get your hat and coat.

ADDIE: [*Unseen calls from upstairs hallway*] Come on, baby. Your Mama's waiting for you, and she ain't nobody to keep waiting.

ALEXANDRA: All right. [*Then softly, embracing* Birdie] Good night, Aunt Birdie. [*Crosses upstairs. As she passes* Oscar] Good night, Uncle Oscar. [Birdie *begins to move slowly towards door as* Alexandra *climbs the stairs.* Alexandra *is almost out of view when* Birdie *reaches* Oscar *in doorway. As* Birdie *quickly attempts to pass him, he slaps her hard, across the face.* Birdie *cries out, puts her hand to her face. On the cry,* Alexandra *turns, begins to run down the stairs*] Aunt Birdie! What happened? What happened? I——

BIRDIE: [*Softly, without turning*] Nothing, darling. Nothing happened. [*Quickly, as if anxious to keep* Alexandra *from coming close*] Now go to bed. [Oscar *exits*] Nothing happened. [*Turns to* Alexandra, *who is holding her hand*] I only—I only twisted my ankle.

[*She goes out.* Alexandra *stands on stairs looking after her as if she were puzzled and frightened*]

MEDIUM CURTAIN

ACT II.

SCENE: *Same as* ACT I. *A week later, morning.*

AT RISE: *The light comes from the open shutter of the* R. *window; the other shutters are tightly closed.* Addie *is standing at window, looking out. Near the dining-room doors are brooms, mops, rags, etc. After a second* Oscar *comes into entrance hall, looks in the room, shivers, decides not to take his hat and coat off, comes into the room. At the sound of the door,* Addie *turns to see who has come in.*

ADDIE: [*Without interest*] Oh, it's you, Mr. Oscar.

[Addie *turns back to window, closes windows*]

OSCAR: What is this? It's not night. [*Crosses to above sofa* R.] What's the matter here? [*Shivers.* Addie *crosses to* U.W. *windows*] Fine thing at this time of the morning. Blinds all closed. [Addie *begins to open shutters. The room lights up*] Where's Miss Regina? It's cold in here. [*He crosses* C.]

ADDIE: Miss Regina ain't down yet.

OSCAR: She had any word?

ADDIE: [*Wearily, crossing* D. *to chair* D.R. *picks up feather duster*] No sir.

OSCAR: [*Crossing to settee* L.] Wouldn't you think a girl that age could get on a train at one place and have sense enough to get off at another? [*He sits settee*]

ADDIE: [*At chair* D.R.] Something must have happened. [*Crosses to sofa* R. *for broom*] If Zan say she was coming last night, she's coming last night. Unless something happened. [*Crosses* U.L.] Sure fire disgrace to let a baby like that go all that way alone to bring home a sick man without——

OSCAR: You do a lot of judging around here, Addie, eh? Judging of your white folks, I mean.

ADDIE: [*Looks at him, sighs*] I'm tired. I been up all night watching for them.

REGINA: [*Who cannot be seen. Speaking from upstairs hall*] Who's downstairs, Addie? [*She appears in a dressing gown, peers down from landing.* Addie *picks up carpet sweeper, dustpan and brush, standing* R. *of dining-room door, exits* L.] Oh, it's you,

Oscar. What are you doing here so early? I haven't been down yet. I'm not finished dressing.

OSCAR: [*Speaking up to her*] You had any word from them?

REGINA: No.

OSCAR: Then something certainly has happened. People don't just say they are arriving on Thursday night, and they haven't come by Friday morning.

REGINA: Oh, nothing has happened. Alexandra just hasn't got sense enough to send a message.

OSCAR: [*Rises, crosses* U.C.] If nothing's happened, then why aren't they here?

REGINA: You asked me that ten times last night. My, you do fret so, Oscar. Anything might have happened. They may have missed connections in Atlanta, the train may have been delayed—oh, a hundred things could have kept them.

OSCAR: [*Crosses* R.] Where's Ben?

REGINA: [*As she disappears up stairs*] Where should he be? At home, probably. Really, Oscar, I don't tuck him in his bed and I don't take him out of it. Have some coffee and don't worry so much.

OSCAR: Have some coffee? [*Crosses* U.C.] There isn't any coffee. [*Looks at his watch, shakes his head. After a second* Cal *enters with a large silver tray, coffee urn, 6 small cups, newspaper. He puts tray on table* U.C., *begins to set out cups*] Oh, there you are. [*Crosses* D.C.] Is everything in this house always late?

[*Takes off coat and hat*]

CAL: [*Looks at him surprised*] You ain't out shooting this morning, Mr. Oscar?

OSCAR: [*Places coat and hat on chair* U.C.] First day I missed since I had a head cold. First day I missed in eight years. [*Crosses* D.L., *sits on settee*]

CAL: Yes, sir. I bet you. Simon he say you had a mighty good day yesterday morning. That's what Simon say. [*Brings* Oscar *small coffee and newspaper*]

OSCAR: Pretty good, pretty good. [*Opens newspaper*]

CAL: [*Laughs, slyly, puts coffee cup on table* L. *of settee, moves table toward* Oscar] Bet you got enough bob-white and squirrel to give every nigger in town a Jesus-party. Most of 'em ain't had no meat since the cotton picking was over. Bet they'd give anything for a little piece of that meat——

OSCAR: [*Turns his head to look at* Cal] Cal, if I catch a nigger in this town going shooting, you know what's going to happen.

[Leo *enters*]

CAL: [*Hastily steps back*] Yes sir, Mr. Oscar. I didn't say nothing about nothing. It was Simon who told me and—Morning, Mr. Leo. You gentlemen having your breakfast with us here?

LEO: [*Comes immediately to* Oscar] The boys in the bank don't know a thing. They haven't had any message.

[Cal *waits for an answer, gets none, shrugs, moves to door* L., *looks back at them, exits*]

OSCAR: [*Peers at* Leo] What you doing here, son?

LEO: You told me to find out if the boys at the bank had any message from Uncle Horace or Zan——

OSCAR: I told you if they had a message to bring it here. I told you that if they didn't have a message to stay at the bank and do your work.

LEO: Oh, I guess I misunderstood.

OSCAR: You didn't misunderstand. You just were looking for any excuse to take an hour off. [*Leo crosses to table* U.C., *pours coffee*] You got to stop that kind of thing. You got to start settling down. You going to be a married man one of these days.

LEO: Yes, sir.

OSCAR: You also got to stop with that woman in Mobile. [*As* Leo *is about to speak he puts up a hand.* Leo *turns back for sugar*] You're young and I haven't got no objections to outside women. That is, I haven't got no objections so long as they don't interfere with serious things. Outside women are all right in their place, but *now* isn't their place! You got to realize that.

LEO: [*Nods*] Yes, sir. I'll tell her. She'll act all right about it. [*He drinks his coffee*]

OSCAR: Also, you got to start working harder at the bank. You got to convince your Uncle Horace you going to make a fit husband for Alexandra.

LEO: [*Crossing* D. *to back of settee* L.] What do you think has happened to them? Supposed to be here last night——[*Laughs—crosses to* C.] Bet you Uncle Ben's mighty worried. Seventy-five thousand dollars worried.

OSCAR: [*Smiles happily*] Ought to be worried. Damn well ought to be. First he don't answer the letters, then he don't come home—— [*Giggles*]

LEO: [*Crosses* L. *to chair* L.C.] What will happen if Uncle Horace don't come home or don't——?

OSCAR: Or don't put up the money? Oh, we'll get it from outside. Easy enough.

LEO: [*Surprised*] But *you* don't want outsiders. [*Sits chair* L.C.]

OSCAR: What do I care who gets my share? I been shaved already. Serve Ben right if he had to give away some of his.

LEO: Damn shame what they did to you.

[*Picks up cup to drink*]

OSCAR: [*Looking up the stairs*] Don't talk so loud. [*Leo starts to speak*] Don't you worry. When I die, you'll have as much as the rest. You might have yours *and* Alexandra's. I'm not so easily licked.

LEO: [*Smoothly*] I wasn't thinking of myself, Papa——

OSCAR: Well, you should be, you should be. It's every man's duty to think of himself.

LEO: [*Turns to* Oscar] You think Uncle Horace don't want to go in on this?

OSCAR: [*Giggles*] That's my hunch. [*Leo drinks*] He hasn't showed any signs of *loving* it yet.

[*Leo looks at empty cup*]

LEO: [*Laughs—turns front*] But he hasn't listened to Aunt Regina yet, either. Oh, he'll go along. It's

too good a thing. [*Rises*] Why wouldn't he want to? [*Crosses* U.C. *to pour another coffee*] He's got plenty and plenty to invest with. He don't even have to sell anything. Eighty-eight thousand worth of Union Pacific bonds sitting right in his safe deposit box. All he's got to do is open the box. [*Turns front*]

OSCAR: [*After a pause. Looks at his watch*] Mighty late breakfast in this fancy house. [*Leo drinks*] Yes, he's had those bonds for fifteen years. Bought them when they were low and just locked them up.

LEO: [*Nods—steps* D.C.] Yeah. Just has to open the box and take them out. That's all. Easy as easy can be. [*Laughs*] The things in that box! There's all those bonds, looking mighty fine. [*Oscar slowly puts down his newspaper and turns to* Leo] Then right next to them is a baby shoe of Zan's and a cheap old cameo on a string, and, *and*—nobody'd believe this—a piece of an old violin. Not even a whole violin. Just a piece of an old thing, a piece of a violin.

OSCAR: [*Very softly, as if he were trying to control his voice—looking at* Leo] A piece of a violin! What do you think of that!

LEO: Yes, siree. [*Crossing* R. *to table, puts cup down*] A lot of other crazy things, too. [*Turns to* Oscar *who is staring at him*] A poem, I guess it is, signed with his mother's name, and two old school books with notes and——

[Leo *catches* Oscar's *look. His voice trails off. He turns his head away*]

OSCAR: [*Very softly*] How do you know what's in the box, son?

LEO: [*Stops, draws back, frightened, realizing what he has said. Then after a second, he manages to speak*] Oh, well, well—er. [*Crossing* L. *to chair* L.C.] Well, one of the boys, sir. It was one of the boys at the bank. He took old Mander's keys. It was Joe Horns. He just up and took Mander's keys and, and—well, took the box out. [*Quickly*] Then they all asked me if I wanted to see, too. So I looked a little, I guess, but then I made them close up the box quick and I told them never——

OSCAR: [*Looks at him*] Joe Horns, you say? He opened it?

LEO: Yes, sir, yes he did. My word of honor. [*Very nervously looking away*] I suppose that don't excuse *me* for looking,— [*Looking at* Oscar] but I did make him close it up and put the keys back in Mander's drawer——

OSCAR: [*Leans forward, very softly*] Tell me the truth, Leo. I am not going to be angry with you. Did you open the box yourself?

LEO: *No sir,* I *didn't.* I told you I didn't. No, I——

OSCAR: [*Irritated, patient*] I am *not* going to be angry with you. [*Leo turns—crosses to table* R. *Watching* Leo *carefully*] Sometimes a young fellow deserves credit for looking round him to see what's going on. Sometimes that's a good sign in a fellow your age. [*Leo turns head to listen. Oscar rises*]

Many great men have made their fortune with their eyes. [*Crosses to* C.] Did you open the box?

LEO: [*Very puzzled*] No. I——

OSCAR: [*Taking a step to him*] Did you open the box? It may have been——[*Moving to* Leo] well, it may have been a good thing if you had.

LEO: [*After a long pause*] I opened it.

OSCAR: [*Quickly*] Is that the truth? [Leo *nods*] Does anybody else know that you opened it? Come, Leo, don't be afraid of speaking the truth to me.

LEO: No. Nobody knew. Nobody was in the bank when I did it. But——

OSCAR: Did your Uncle Horace ever know you opened it?

LEO: [*Shakes his head*] He only looks in it once every six months when he cuts the coupons, and sometimes Mander even does that for him. Uncle Horace don't even have the keys. Mander keeps them for him. Imagine not looking at all that. You can bet if I had the bonds, I'd watch 'em like——

OSCAR: If you had them. [*Turns front, crossing* R. *to sofa.* Leo *watches him*] If you had them. Then you could have the share in the mill, you and me. [*Turns to* Leo] A fine, big share, too. [*Pauses—shrugs*] Well, a man can't be shot for wanting to see his son get on in the world, can he, boy?

[Oscar *sits on sofa* R.]

LEO: [*Looks up, begins to understand*] No, he can't! Natural enough. [*Laughs*] But I haven't got the bonds and Uncle Horace has. And now we can just sit back and wait to be a millionaire.

OSCAR: [*Innocently*] You think your Uncle Horace likes you well enough to lend *you* the bonds if he decides not to use them himself?

LEO: Papa, it must be that you haven't had your breakfast! [*Laughs loudly*] Lend me the bonds! My God——

OSCAR: [*Disappointed*] No, I suppose not. Just a fancy of mine. A loan for three months, maybe four, easy enough for us to pay it back then. Anyway, this is only April—— [*Slowly counting the months on his fingers*] and if he doesn't look at them until Fall, he wouldn't even *miss* them out of the box.

LEO: That's it. He wouldn't even miss them. Ah, well——

OSCAR: No, sir. Wouldn't even miss them. How could he miss them if he never looks at them? [*Sighs as* Leo *stares at him*] Well, here we are sitting around waiting for him to come home and invest his money in something he hasn't lifted his hand to get. [Leo *crosses* L.C.] But I can't help thinking he's acting strange. You laugh when I say he could lend you the bonds if he's not going to use them himself. But would it hurt him?

LEO: [*Slowly looking at* Oscar] No. No, it wouldn't.

OSCAR: People *ought* to help other people. But that's not always the way it happens. [Ben *enters, hangs his coat and hat on hall tree. Very carefully*] And so sometimes you got to think of yourself. [*As*

Leo *stares at him,* Ben *appears in doorway*] Morning, Ben.

BEN: [*Coming in, carrying his newspaper. Crosses to chair* R.C.] Fine, sunny morning, Any news from the runaways?

[Ben *sits chair* R.C.]

REGINA: [*On landing*] There's no news or you would have heard it. [*Coming down stairs*] Quite a convention so early in the morning, aren't you all? [*Goes to coffee urn*]

OSCAR: You rising mighty late these days. Is that the way they do things in Chicago society?

BEN: [*Looking at his paper*] Old Carter died up in Senateville. Eighty-one is a good time for us all, eh? What do you think has really happened to Horace, Regina?

REGINA: Nothing.

BEN: [*Too casually, still reading*] You don't think maybe he never started from Baltimore and never intends to start?

REGINA: [*Irritated—steps* D.] Of course they've started. Didn't I have a letter from Alexandra? What is so strange about people arriving late? [*Crosses* U. *to table—pours coffee*] He has that cousin in Savannah he's so fond of. He may have stopped to see him. They'll be along today some time, very flattered that you and Oscar are so worried about them. [*Steps* D.]

BEN: I'm a natural worrier. Especially when I am getting ready to close a business deal and one of my partners remains silent *and* invisible.

REGINA: [*Laughs*] Oh, is that it? I thought you were worried about Horace's *health.*

OSCAR: Oh, that too. Who could help but worry? *I'm* worried. This is the first day I haven't shot since my head cold.

REGINA: [*Starts toward dining room*] Then you haven't had your breakfast. Come along.

[Oscar *and* Leo *follow her.* Ben *remains seated*]

BEN: Regina. [*She turns at dining-room door*] That cousin of Horace's has been dead for years and, in any case, the train does not go through Savannah.

REGINA: [*Laughs. Then continues into dining room, seats herself, motions to* Leo *and* Oscar] Did he die? You're always remembering about people dying. [Ben *rises, leaves newspaper on table, crosses* U.L. *to dining room*] Now I intend to eat my breakfast in peace, and read my newspaper. [*Rings bell*]

BEN: [*Goes toward dining room as he talks*] This is second breakfast for me. My first was bad. Celia ain't the cook she used to be. Too old to have taste any more. If she hadn't belonged to Mama, I'd send her off to the country.

[Cal *is putting two silver serving dishes on table.* Oscar *and* Leo *start to eat.* Ben *seats himself*]

LEO: Uncle Horace will have some tales to tell, I bet. Baltimore is a lively town.

REGINA: [*To* Cal] The grits isn't hot enough. Take it back.

CAL: Oh, yes'm. [*Calling into kitchen as he exits off dining room*] Grits didn't hold the heat. Grits didn't hold the heat.

LEO: When I was at school three of the boys and myself took a train once and went over to Baltimore. It was so big we thought we were in Europe. I was just a kid then——

REGINA: [*Looks up, helps herself from a dish*] I find it very pleasant—— [*Addie enters from* L.] to have breakfast alone. I hate chattering before I've had something hot. [*Cal has come back, closes dining-room doors*] Do be still, Leo.

[*Addie comes into the room, begins gathering up cups, carries them to the large tray, then quickly she runs into the hall. Outside there are the sounds of* Voices *and* People *moving about. A few seconds later* Addie *appears again in doorway, her arm around the shoulders of* Horace Giddens, *supporting him.* Horace *is a tall man of about forty-five. He has been good-looking, but now his face is tired and ill. He walks stiffly, as if it were an enormous effort, and carefully, as if he were unsure of his balance.* Addie *takes off his overcoat and hangs it on hall tree. She then helps him across to the chair* L.C.]

HORACE: [*As they are crossing*] How are you, Addie? How have you been?

ADDIE: I'm all right, Mr. Horace. I've just been worried about you.

[*Horace sits in chair.* Alexandra *enters. She is flushed and excited, her hat awry, her face dirty. Her arms are full of packages, but she comes quickly to* Addie]

ALEXANDRA: Now don't tell me how worried you were. We couldn't help it and there was no way to send a message.

ADDIE: [*To* Horace, *begins to take packages from* Alexandra] Yes, sir, I was mighty worried.

ALEXANDRA: We had to stop in Mobile over night. Papa—— [*Looks at him*] Papa didn't feel well. The trip was too much for him, and I made him stop and rest—— [*As* Addie *takes last package*] No, don't take that. That's Father's medicine. [*Crosses* D. *to table* R.C. Addie *puts the packages on the chair* L. *of table* U.C., *then crosses to* Alexandra] I'll hold it. It mustn't break. Now, about the stuff outside. Papa must have his wheel chair. I'll get that and the valises——

[*Alexandra starts to go, but* Addie *stops her*]

ADDIE: [*Very happy, holding* Alexandra's *arms*] Since when you got to carry your own valises? Since when I ain't old enough to hold a bottle of medicine? [*Horace coughs. Turns and steps to* Horace. Alexandra *looks at* Horace] You feel all right, Mr. Horace?

HORACE: [*Nods*] Glad to be sitting down.

ALEXANDRA: [*Opening package of medicine on table* R.C.] He doesn't feel all right. [*Addie looks at her, then at* Horace] He just says that. The trip was very hard on him, and now he must go right to bed.

ADDIE: [*Looking at him carefully*] Them fancy doctors, they give you help?

HORACE: They did their best.

LEO: [*In dining room*] Papa, can I have your part of the paper?

ALEXANDRA: [*Has become conscious of the voices in dining room*] I bet Mama was worried. I better tell her we're here now. [*She starts for door*]

HORACE: Zan. [*She stops, steps* D. *to above settee* L.] Not for a minute, dear.

ALEXANDRA: Oh, Papa, you feel bad again. I knew you did. Do you want your medicine?

HORACE: No, I don't feel that way. I'm just tired, darling. Let me rest a little.

ALEXANDRA: Yes, but Mama will be mad if I don't tell her we're here.

ADDIE: They're all in there eating breakfast.

ALEXANDRA: Oh, are they all here? [*Crosses to* Addie] Why do they *always* have to be here? I was hoping Papa wouldn't have to see anybody, that it would be nice for him and quiet.

ADDIE: [*Patting* Alexandra's *arm*] Then let your Papa rest for a minute.

HORACE: Addie, I bet your coffee's as good as ever. They don't have such good coffee up North. [*Looks hungrily at urn*] Is it as good, Addie?

[*Addie starts for coffee urn*]

ALEXANDRA: No. [*Step to* Addie—*stops her*] Dr. Reeves said not much coffee. Just now and then. [*Proudly to* Addie] I'm the nurse now, Addie.

ADDIE: You'd be a better one if you didn't look so dirty. [*Taking* Alexandra *to stairs*] Now go and take a bath, Miss Grownup. Change your linens, get out a fresh dress and give your hair a good brushing—go on—

ALEXANDRA: Will you be all right, Papa?

ADDIE: [*Slapping her backside*] Go on.

ALEXANDRA: [*On stairs, talks as she goes up*] The pills Papa must take once every four hours. [*Addie steps into room*] And the bottle only when—only if he feels very bad. [*On landing*] Now don't move until I come back and don't talk much and remember about his medicine, Addie——

ADDIE: Ring for Belle and have her help you and then I'll make you a fresh breakfast.

ALEXANDRA: [*As she disappears up stairs*] How's Aunt Birdie? Is she here?

ADDIE: [*Crosses* D.R. *of* Horace] It ain't right for you to have coffee? It will hurt you?

HORACE: [*Slowly*] Nothing can make much difference now. Get me a cup, Addie. [*She looks at him, crosses to urn, pours a cup*] Funny. They can't make coffee up North. [*Addie brings him a cup*] They don't like red pepper, either. [*He takes cup and gulps it greedily*] God, that's good. You remember how I used to drink it? Ten, twelve cups a day. [*Slight laugh as he picks up cup again. He speaks more slowly*] Addie, before I see anybody else, I want to know why *Zan* came to fetch me home.

She's tried to tell me, but she doesn't seem to know herself. [*Drinks*]

ADDIE: [*Turns away*] I don't know. [*Crosses* R. *to table*] All I know is big things are going on. [*To* Horace] Everybody going to be high-tone rich. Big rich. You too. [*Looks away—at table*] All because smoke's going to start out of a building that ain't even up yet. [*She angrily creases the medicine bottle paper on the table*]

HORACE: I've heard about it.

ADDIE: And, er—— [*Hesitates—steps to him*] And —well, Zan, she going to marry Mr. Leo in a little while.

HORACE: [*Looks at her, then very slowly*] What are you talking about?

ADDIE: [*Crossing to* R. *of* Horace] That's right. That's the talk, God help us.

HORACE: [*Angrily*] *What's* the talk?

ADDIE: I'm telling you. There's going to be a wedding—— [*Angrily clenches paper in her hand, turns head away*] Over my dead body there is.

HORACE: [*He hands cup to* Addie, *not looking at her. After a second, quietly*] Go and tell them I'm home.

ADDIE: [*Hesitates*] Now you ain't to get excited. You're to be in your bed——

HORACE: Go on, Addie. Go and say I'm back.

[Addie *takes cup and paper to tray, looking at him as he is rising, then crosses* L. *and opens dining-room doors. He rises with difficulty, stands stiff as if he were in pain facing the dining room*]

ADDIE: [*Opens doors, then stands in corner* U.L.] Miss Regina. They're home. They got here——

[*Everybody turns to look at her*]

BEN: They are?

OSCAR: Good.

LEO: Just now?

REGINA: Horace.

[Regina *quickly rises, runs into the room. Others follow her*]

REGINA: [*Warmly*] Horace! You've finally arrived. [*As she kisses him, the others come forward, all talking together*]

BEN: [*In doorway, carrying a napkin*] Well, sir, you had us all mighty worried.

[*He steps forward. They shake hands. Addie watches them, then exits* L.]

OSCAR: [*Crossing to above settee*] You're a sight for sore eyes.

HORACE: Hello Ben.

[Ben *crosses* R.C. Leo *enters eating biscuit*]

OSCAR: And how you feel? Tip-top, I bet, because that's the way you're looking.

HORACE: [*Coldly, irritated with* Oscar's *lie*] Hello, Oscar. Hello Leo, [Leo *steps* D. *extends hand*] how are you?

LEO: [*Shaking hands*] I'm fine, sir. But a lot better now that you're back.

REGINA: [*Steps to* Horace] Now sit down. [Leo

backs away D.L. *as* Horace *sits*] What did happen to you and where's Alexandra? I am so excited about seeing you that I almost forgot about her.

HORACE: I didn't feel good, a little weak, I guess, and we stopped overnight to rest. Zan's upstairs washing off the train dirt.

REGINA: [*Crossing above* Horace, *to his* L.] Oh, I am so sorry the trip was hard on you. I didn't think that——

HORACE: [*Sarcastically, looking around at them*] Well, it's just as if I had never been away. All of you here——

BEN: Waiting to welcome you home.

[Birdie *bursts in. She is wearing a flannel kimono and her face is flushed and excited.* Ben *crosses* D.R. *to mantel*]

BIRDIE: [*Runs to him, kisses him*] Horace!

HORACE: [*Warmly pressing her arm*] I was just wondering where you were, Birdie.

BIRDIE: [*Excited*] Oh, I would have been here. I didn't know you were back until Simon said he saw the buggy—— [*She draws back to look at him. Her face sobers*] Oh, you don't look well, Horace. No you don't.

REGINA: [*Laughs*] Birdie, what a thing to say——

HORACE: [*Looking at* Oscar] Oscar thinks I look very well.

OSCAR: [*Annoyed. Turns on* Leo] Don't stand there holding that biscuit in your hand.

[*Crosses* R. *to above chair* R.C.]

LEO: Oh. Well. I'll just finish my breakfast, Uncle Horace, and then I'll give you all the news about the bank——

[*He exits into dining room, taking newspaper from settee*]

OSCAR: [*Comes to* R. *of* Birdie] And what is that costume you have on?

BIRDIE: [*Is looking at* Horace] Now that you're home, you'll feel better. Plenty of good rest and we'll take such fine care of you—— [*Stops*] But where is Zan? [Horace *motions to staircase*] I missed her so much.

OSCAR: I asked you what is that strange costume you're parading around in?

BIRDIE: [*Nervously, backing toward stairs*] Me? [*Looks at costume—drops* Horace's *hand.* Oscar *crosses* U.R.] Oh! It's my wrapper. I was so excited about Horace I just rushed out of the house——

OSCAR: Did you come across the square dressed that way? My dear Birdie, I——

HORACE: [*To* Regina, *wearily*] Yes, it's just like old times.

REGINA: [*Quickly to* Oscar] Now no fights. This is a holiday.

BIRDIE: [*Runs quickly up stairs*] Zan! Zannie!

OSCAR: Birdie! [*She stops*]

BIRDIE: Tell Zan I'll be back in a little while. [*Exits door* R.]

REGINA: [*To* Oscar *and* Ben] Why don't you go finish your breakfast—— [*Looks at* Oscar. *He looks* at Ben, *then crosses into dining room.* Regina *crosses* D.C.] and let Horace rest for a minute?

BEN: [*Crossing to dining room.* Regina *crosses* D.R.] Never leave a meal unfinished. There are too many poor people who need the food. Mighty glad to see you home, Horace. Fine to have you back. Fine to have you back.

OSCAR: [*To* Leo *as* Ben *is closing dining-room doors*] Your mother has gone crazy. Running around the streets like a woman——

[*The moment* Regina *and* Horace *are alone, they become awkward and self-conscious*]

REGINA: [*Laughs awkwardly*] Well. Here we are. It's been a long time. [Horace *smiles*] Five months. You know, Horace, I wanted to come and be with you in the hospital, but I didn't know where my duty was. Here, or with you. But you know how much I *wanted* to come.

HORACE: That's kind of you, Regina. There was no need to come.

REGINA: Oh, but there was. Five months lying there all by yourself, no kin-folk, no friends. Don't try to tell me you didn't have a bad time of it.

HORACE: I didn't have a bad time. [*As she shakes her head, he becomes insistent*] No, I didn't, Regina. Oh, at first when I—when I heard the news about myself—but after I got used to that, I liked it there.

REGINA: You *liked* it? [*Coldly*] Isn't that strange! You liked it so well you didn't want to come home?

HORACE: That's not the way to put it. [*Then, kindly, as he sees her turn her head away*] But there I was and I got kind of used to it, kind of to like lying there and thinking. [*Smiles*] I never had much time to think before. And time's become valuable to me.

REGINA: It sounds almost like a holiday. [*Takes a step* R.]

HORACE: [*Laughs*] It was, sort of. The first holiday I've had since I was a little kid.

REGINA: And here I was thinking you were in pain and——

HORACE: [*Quietly*] I was in pain.

REGINA: And instead you were having a holiday! [*She sits chair* R.C.] A holiday of thinking. Couldn't you have done that here?

HORACE: I wanted to do it before I came here. I was thinking about us.

REGINA: About us? About you and me? Thinking about you and me after all these years? [*Unpleasantly. Rises, crosses* D.R.] You shall tell me everything you thought—some day.

HORACE: [*There is silence for a minute*] Regina. [*She turns to him*] Why did you send Zan to Baltimore?

REGINA: Why? Because I wanted you home. [*Crossing to him*] You can't make anything suspicious out of that, can you?

HORACE: I didn't mean to make anything suspicious about it. [*Hesitantly, taking her hand*] Zan

said you wanted me to come home. I was so pleased at that and touched, it made me feel good.

REGINA: [*Taking away her hand, turns*] Touched that I should want you home?

HORACE: [*Sighs*] I'm saying all the wrong things, as usual. Let's try to get along better. There isn't so much more time. Regina, what's all this crazy talk I've been hearing about Zan and Leo? [*Slight laugh*] Zan and Leo marrying?

REGINA: [*Turning to him, sharply*] Who gossips so much around here?

HORACE: [*Shocked*] Regina!

REGINA: [*Annoyed, anxious to quiet him, steps to him*] It's some foolishness that Oscar thought up. I'll explain later. I have no intention of allowing any such arrangement. It was simply a way of keeping Oscar quiet in all this business I've been writing you about——

HORACE: [*Carefully*] What has Zan to do with any business of Oscar's? Whatever it is, you had better put it out of Oscar's head immediately. You know what I think of Leo.

REGINA: But there's no need to talk about it now.

HORACE: There is no need to talk about it ever. Not as long as I live. [Regina *turns crosses* R. Horace *stops, slowly, turns to look at her*] As long as I live. I've been in a hospital for five months. Yet since I've been here you have not once asked me about—about my health. [*Then gently*] Well, I suppose they've written you. I can't live very long.

REGINA: [*Coldly*] I've never understood why people have to talk about this kind of thing. [*Crosses* U.R.]

HORACE: [*There is a silence. Then he looks up at her, his face cold*] You misunderstand. [Regina *pacing* U.R.C.] I don't intend to gossip about my sickness. I thought it was only fair to tell you. I was not asking for your sympathy.

REGINA: [*Sharply, turns to him*] What do the doctors think caused your bad heart?

HORACE: What do you mean?

REGINA: [R. *of* Horace] They didn't think it possible, did they, that your fancy women may have——?

HORACE: [*Smiles, unpleasantly*] Caused my heart to be bad? I don't think that's the best scientific theory. You don't catch heart trouble in bed.

REGINA: [*Angrily*] I didn't think you did. I only thought you might catch a bad conscience—in bed, as you say. [*Crosses* D.R.]

HORACE: I didn't tell them about my bad conscience. Or about my *fancy women.* Nor did I tell them that my wife has not wanted me in bed with her for—— [*Sharply*] How long is it, Regina? [Regina *turns to him*] Ten years? Did you bring me home for this, to make me feel guilty again? That means you want something. But you'll not make me feel guilty any more. My "thinking" has made a difference.

REGINA: I see that it has.

BEN: [*In dining room*] Put down that paper, Leo.

REGINA: [*She looks toward dining-room door. Then comes to him, her manner warm and friendly*] It's foolish for us to fight this way. I didn't mean to be unpleasant. I was stupid.

HORACE: [*Wearily*] God knows I didn't either. I came home wanting so much not to fight, and then all of a sudden there we were. I got hurt and——

REGINA: [*Hastily*] It's all my fault. I didn't ask about——your illness because I didn't want to remind you of it. Anyway I never believe doctors when they talk about——[*Brightly*] when they talk like that.

HORACE: [*Not looking at her*] Well, we'll try our best with each other. [*He rises, starts for stairs. He gets as far as chair* R.C., *when* Regina *stops him*]

REGINA: [*Quickly, crossing with him*] I'll try. Honestly, I will. Horace, [*He stops, turns to her*] Horace, I know you're tired out, but—couldn't you stay down here a few minutes longer? I want Ben to tell you something.

HORACE: Tomorrow.

REGINA: I'd like to now. It's very important to me. It's very important to all of us. [*Gaily, as she moves toward dining room*] Important to your beloved daughter. She'll be a very great heiress——

HORACE: Will she? That's nice.

REGINA: [*Opens doors*] Ben, are you finished breakfast?

HORACE: Is this the mill business I've had so many letters about?

REGINA: [*To Ben*] Horace would like to talk to you now.

HORACE: Horace would not like to talk to you now. I am very tired, Regina—— [*He starts*]

REGINA: [*Comes to him and stops him*] Please. You've said we'll try our best with each other. I'll try. Really, I will. But please do this for me now. [*Urging him into chair* R.C.] You will see what I've done while you've been away. How I watched your interests. [*Laughs gaily*] And I've done very well, too. But things can't be delayed any longer. Everything must be settled this week——[Horace *crosses —sits chair* R.C. Regina *crosses to* Ben, *who is entering. Brings him* C. Oscar *has stayed in the dining room, his head turned to watch them.* Leo *is pretending to read newspaper*] Now you must tell Horace all about it. Only be quick because he is very tired and must go to bed. [Horace *is looking up at her as if he finally understood. His face hardens as she speaks*] But I think your news will be better for him than all the medicine in the world.

BEN: [*Who is looking at* Horace] It could wait. Horace may not feel like talking today.

REGINA: What an old faker you are! You know it can't wait. You know it must be finished this week. [*Crosses* D.R.] You've been just as anxious for Horace to get here as I've been.

BEN: [*Very jovial*] I suppose I have been. And why not? Horace has done Hubbard Sons many a good turn. Why shouldn't I be anxious to help him now?

REGINA: [*Laughs*] Help him! Help him when you need him, that's what you mean. [*Sits sofa* R.]

BEN: What a woman you married, Horace! [*Laughs awkwardly when* Horace *does not answer*] Well, then I'll make it quick. You know what I've been telling you for years. How I've always said that every one of us little Southern business men had great things—— [*Extends his arm, moves his fingers*] —right beyond our finger-tips. It's been my dream: my dream to make those fingers grow longer. I'm a lucky man, Horace, a lucky man. To dream and to live to get what you've dreamed of. That's *my* idea of a lucky man. [*Looks at his fingers as his arm drops slowly*] For thirty years I've cried, bring the cotton mills to the cotton! [Horace *opens medicine bottle, pours dose into spoon*] Well, finally I got up nerve to go to the Marshall Company in Chicago.

HORACE: [*Has finally taken his eyes from* Regina] I know all this.

[*He takes medicine.* Regina *rises, steps to him*]

BEN: Can I get you something?

HORACE: Some water, please.

REGINA: [*Turns quickly*] Oh, I'm sorry. Let me. [*Crosses to tray on table* U.C. *brings him glass. He drinks as they wait in silence*] You feel all right now?

HORACE: Yes. You wrote me. I know all that. [Oscar *rises—crosses to dining-room doors*]

REGINA: [*Triumphantly*] But you don't know that in the last few days Ben has agreed to give us—— you, I mean—a much larger share.

HORACE: Really? That's very generous of him. [Oscar *crosses* D. *to above settee* L.]

BEN: [*Laughs*] It wasn't so generous of me; it was smart of Regina.

REGINA: [*As if she were signalling* Horace] I explained to Ben that perhaps you hadn't answered his letters because you didn't think he was offering you enough, and that the time was getting short and you could guess how much he needed you——

HORACE: [*Smiles at her—nods*] And I could guess that he wants to keep control in the family?

REGINA: [*To Ben, triumphantly*] Exactly. [*To Horace*] So I did a little bargaining for you and convinced my brothers they weren't the only Hubbards who had a business sense. [*Crosses* D. *to front sofa*]

HORACE: Did you have to convince them of that? How little people know about each other! [Oscar *crosses* D.L. *slowly. Laughs*] But you'll know better about Regina next time, eh, Ben? [Ben, Regina, Horace *laugh together.* Oscar's *face is angry*] Now let's see. We're getting a bigger share. [*Looking at* Oscar] Who's getting less?

BEN: Oscar.

HORACE: Well, Oscar, you've grown very unselfish. What's happened to you?

[Leo *rises, crosses to dining-room doors*]

BEN: [*Quickly, before* Oscar *can answer*] Oscar doesn't mind. [*Crossing* U.L.] Not worth fighting about now, eh, Oscar?

OSCAR: [*Angrily*] I'll get mine in the end. You can be sure of that. I've got my son's future to think about.

HORACE: [*Sharply*] Leo? Oh, I see. [*Puts his head back, laughs.* Regina *looks at him nervously*] I am beginning to see. Everybody will get theirs.

BEN: [*Crossing* R. *to* L. *of* Horace] I knew you'd see it. Seventy-five thousand, and that seventy-five thousand will make you a million.

REGINA: [*Steps to table, leaning forward*] It will, Horace, it will.

HORACE: I believe you. [Regina *steps back, sits sofa. After a second*] Now I can understand Oscar's self-sacrifice, but what did you have to promise Marshall Company besides the money you're putting up?

[Leo *crosses* D. *to back of settee* L.]

BEN: They wouldn't take promises. They wanted guarantees.

HORACE: Of what?

BEN: [*Nods*] Water power. Free and plenty of it.

HORACE: You got them that, of course?

BEN: Cheap. You'd think the governor of a great State would make his price a little higher. [*Crossing to chair* L.C.] From pride, you know. [Horace *smiles.* Ben *smiles*] Cheap wages. [*Sits chair*] What do you mean by cheap wages, I say to Marshall? Less than Massachusetts, he says to me, and that averages eight a week. [*Leans back*] Eight a week! By God, I tell him, *I'd* work for eight a week myself. Why, there ain't a mountain white or a town nigger but wouldn't give his right arm for three silver dollars every week, eh Horace?

HORACE: Sure. And they'll take less than that when you get around to playing them off against each other. You can save a little money *that* way, Ben. [*Angrily*] And make them hate each other just a little more than they do now.

REGINA: What's all this about?

BEN: [*Laughs*] There'll be no trouble from anybody, white or black, Marshall said that to me. "What about strikes? That's all we've had in Massachusetts for the last three years." I say to him, "What's a strike? I never heard of one. Come South, Marshall. We got good folks and we don't stand for any fancy fooling."

HORACE: You're right. [*Slowly*] Well, it looks like you made a good deal for yourselves, and for Marshall, too. [Cal *has come into dining room and closes doors. To* Ben] Your father used to say he made the thousands and you boys would make the millions. I think he was right. [*Rises*]

REGINA: [*They are all looking at* Horace. *She laughs, nervously, leans forward*] Millions for *us*, too.

HORACE: Us? You and me? I don't think so. We've got enough money, Regina. We'll just sit by and watch the boys grow rich. [*Steps* U.C., *holding on to chair.* Oscar *sits on piano stool. They watch him tensely, as he begins to move toward staircase. He passes* Leo, *looks at him for a second. Brightly*] How's everything at the bank, Leo?

LEO: Fine, sir. Everything is fine.

HORACE: How are all the ladies in Mobile? [Leo *draws back.* Horace *turns, a step to* Regina, *sharply*] Whatever made you think I'd let Zan marry——?

REGINA: [*Crosses above table* R.] Do you mean that you are turning this down? Is it possible that's what you mean?

BEN: [*Nervously, but speaking with good nature—gesturing* Regina *to be quiet*] No, that's not what he means. Turning down a fortune! Horace is tired. He'd rather talk about it tomorrow——

REGINA: We can't keep putting it off this way. Oscar must be in Chicago by the end of the week with the money and contracts. [*Crosses to* Horace]

OSCAR: [*Giggles, pleased*] Yes, sir. Got to be there end of the week. [Horace *crosses* R.] No sense going without the money.

REGINA: [*Tensely*] I've waited long enough for your answer. I'm not going to wait any longer.

HORACE: [*Crossing to stairs, above* Regina, *very deliberately*] I'm very tired now, Regina.

BEN: [*Hastily*] Now Horace probably has his reasons. Things he'd like explained. Tomorrow will do. I can——

REGINA: [*Turns to* Ben, *sharply*] I want to know his reasons now.

[*Turns back to* Horace]

HORACE: [*As he climbs the steps*] I don't know them all myself. Let's leave it at that.

REGINA: [*Crosses* U. *to foot of stairs*] We shall not leave it at that. We have waited for you here like children. Waited for you to come home.

HORACE: So that you could invest my money. So this is why you wanted me home? Well, I had hoped —— [*Quietly*] If you are disappointed, Regina, I'm sorry. But I must do what I think best. We'll talk about it another day.

REGINA: We'll talk about it now. Just you and me.

HORACE: [*Stops on landing, looks down at her. His voice is tense*] Please, Regina. It's been a hard trip. I don't feel well. Please leave me alone now.

REGINA: [*Quietly*] I want to talk to you. Horace, I'm coming up.

[*He looks at her for a moment, then moves on again out of sight. She begins to climb stairs*]

BEN: [*Softly.* Regina *turns to him as he speaks*] Sometimes it is better to wait for the sun to rise again. [*She does not answer*] And sometimes, as our mother used to tell you, [Regina *starts up stairs*] it's unwise for a good-looking woman to frown. [Ben *rises, crosses* U. *to landing*] Softness and a smile do more to the heart of men——

[*She disappears.* Ben *stands looking up the*

stairs. *A long silence. Then, suddenly,* Oscar *giggles*]

OSCAR: Let us hope she'll change his mind. Let us hope.

[*After a second* Ben *crosses to table* R., *picks up his newspaper, continues to sofa* R., *sits— begins to read.* Oscar *looks at* Ben. *The silence makes* Leo *uncomfortable*]

LEO: [*Steps* R. *to* C.] The paper says twenty-seven cases of Yellow Fever in New Orleans. Guess the flood waters caused it. [*Nobody pays attention*] Thought they were building levees high enough. Like the niggers always say: a man born of woman can't build nothing high enough for the Mississippi.

[*Gets no answer. Gives an embarrassed laugh. Upstairs there is the sound of* Voices. *The* Voices *are not loud, but* Ben, Oscar, Leo *become conscious of them.* Leo *crosses* U. *to landing, looks up, listens*]

REGINA: I can't understand what you mean. I can't believe that you mean to turn this down. This is what you've been waiting for, what all of us have been waiting for. You must be going crazy or you must have reasons that you are not telling us.

HORACE: I don't know my reasons. I just don't want it.

REGINA: You don't want it. But I do want it.

OSCAR: [*Pointing up*] Now just suppose she don't change his mind? Just suppose he keeps on refusing?

[Leo *turns back to them, listens*]

BEN: [*Without conviction*] He's tired. It was a mistake to talk to him today. He's a sick man but he isn't a crazy one.

OSCAR: [*Giggles*] But just suppose he is crazy. What then?

[Leo *crosses slowly to back of sofa* L.]

BEN: [*Puts down his paper, peers at* Oscar] Then we'll go outside for the money. There's plenty who would give it.

OSCAR: And plenty who will want a lot for what they give. The ones who are rich enough to give, will be smart enough to want. That means we'd be working for them, don't it, Ben?

BEN: You don't have to tell me the things I told you six months ago.

OSCAR: Oh, you're right not to worry. She'll change his mind. She always has.

[*There is a silence. Suddenly* Regina's *voice becomes louder and sharper. All of them begin to listen now. Slowly* Ben *rises, goes to listen by the staircase.* Oscar, *watching him, smiles. As they listen* Regina's *voice becomes very loud.* Horace's *voice is no longer heard*]

REGINA: People don't pass up chances like this. I won't let you pass up chances like this. I won't let you pass up this one just because you've gone crazy!

OSCAR: Maybe.

REGINA: And if you change your mind in a week, it will be too late. It's got to be done now.

HORACE: I won't change my mind. I don't want it.

REGINA: You don't want it but I do want it. I'm your wife. I have a right to expect that you will take care of my future. Of your child's future.

OSCAR: But I don't believe it. I never did believe he was going in with us.

BEN: [*Turning to him—crosses* D.C.] What the hell do you expect me to do?

OSCAR: [*Mildly*] Nothing. You done your almighty best. Nobody could blame you if the whole thing just dripped away right through our fingers. [Ben *crosses* R. *to sofa for paper*] You can't do a thing. But there may be something I could do for us. [Oscar *rises.* Ben *starts to pick up paper but is stopped by* Oscar's *words*] Or, I might better say, [*Crossing to* C.] Leo could do for us. [Ben *stops, turns, looks at* Oscar. Leo *is staring at* Oscar. *Turns to* Leo] Ain't that true, son? [Leo *crosses* D.L.] Ain't it true you might be able to help your own kin-folks?

LEO: [*Nervously taking a step to him*] Papa, I——

BEN: [*Slowly*] How would he help us, Oscar?

OSCAR: Leo's got a friend. [*Crosses to* Ben] Leo's friend owns eighty-eight thousand dollars in Union Pacific Bonds. [Ben *turns to look at* Leo] Leo's friend don't look at the bonds much, not for five or six months at a time.

BEN: [*After a pause*] Union Pacific. Uh, huh. Let me understand. Leo's friend would—would lend him these bonds and he——?

OSCAR: [*Nods*] Would be kind enough to lend them to us.

BEN: [*Crossing to* C.] Leo.

LEO: [*Excited, comes to him*] Yes, sir?

BEN: When would your friend be wanting the bonds back?

LEO: [*Very nervous*] I don't know. I—well, I——

OSCAR: [*Sharply—step to him*] You told me he won't look at them until fall——

LEO: Oh. That's right. But I—not till fall. Uncle Horace never——

BEN: [*Sharply*] Be still.

OSCAR: [*Smiles at* Leo—*crosses to* C.] Your Uncle doesn't wish to know your friend's name.

LEO: [*Starts to laugh*] That's a good one. Not know his name——

OSCAR: Shut up, Leo! [Leo *turns away slowly, moves to table* L. Ben *turns to* Oscar] He won't look at them again until September. That gives us five months. Leo will return the bonds in three months. And we'll have no trouble raising the money once the mills are going up. Will Marshall accept bonds?

[Ben *stops to listen to sudden sharp voices from above. The voices are now very angry and very loud*]

REGINA: I have a right to expect that.

HORACE: Please go away and leave me alone.

REGINA: I won't leave you alone. I demand that you put up this money and I demand that you do it immediately.

BEN: [*Then smiling*] Why not? Why not? [*Laughs —to* Oscar] Good. We are lucky. We'll take the loan from Leo's friend—I think he will make a safer partner than our sister. [*Nods toward stairs. Turns to* Leo] How soon can you get them?

LEO: Today. Right now. [*Steps to* Ben] They're in the safe deposit box and——

BEN: [*Sharply*] I don't want to know where they are.

OSCAR: [*Laughs*] We will keep it secret from you. [*Pats Ben's arm*]

BEN: [*Smiles*] Good. Draw a check for our part. You can take the night train for Chicago. [*To* Oscar] Well, Oscar, [*Holds out his hand—Oscar takes it, they shake hands*] good luck to us. [*Crosses R. to table*]

OSCAR: [*Turns to* Ben] Leo will be taken care of?

LEO: I'm entitled to Uncle Horace's share. I'd enjoy being a partner——

BEN: [*Turns to stare at him*] You would? You can go to hell, you little——[*Starts toward* Leo]

OSCAR: [*Nervously, stopping* Ben] Now, now. He didn't mean that. I only want to be sure he'll get something out of all this.

BEN: Of course. We'll take care of him. We won't have any trouble about that. I'll see you at the store.

OSCAR: [*Nods*] That's settled then. Come on, son. [*Starts for door*]

LEO: [*Puts out his hand—crosses to* Ben] I didn't mean just that. I was only going to say what a great day this was for me and——

[Ben *ignores his hand*]

BEN: Go on. [*Crosses R. to front of table.* Leo *looks at him, turns, follows* Oscar *out.* Ben *stands where he is, thinking. Again the* Voices *upstairs can be heard.* Regina's *is high and furious.* Ben *looks up, smiles, winces at the noise*]

REGINA: Nobody would turn this down. You must have your reasons. You must have reasons you won't talk about.

[*The noise of fists pounding against a door is heard, and* Alexandra's *voice*]

ALEXANDRA: Mama—Mama—don't——

[*The noise of running footsteps is heard, and* Alexandra *comes running down the steps, speaking as she comes, together with the voices upstairs*]

REGINA: What are they? What possible reasons could there be? I demand to know. All my life I've had to force you to make something out of yourself.

HORACE: Let me alone.

REGINA: I won't let you alone. If I'd let you alone you'd still be working for somebody else.

HORACE: So that's why you wanted me home?

REGINA: Yes, that's the reason.

HORACE: Then it's a bad one. Because it won't work.

REGINA: Did you think I wanted you home for yourself? Is that what you thought?

ALEXANDRA: [*Almost crying. On landing*] Uncle Ben! [*Coming down stairs*] Uncle Ben! [Ben *crosses* U.C.] Please go up. Please make Mama stop. Uncle Ben, he's sick, he's so sick. How can Mama talk to him like that—please, make her stop. She'll——

BEN: Alexandra, you have a tender heart.

ALEXANDRA: Go on up, Uncle Ben, please——

[*Suddenly the noise from above stops, and a second later there is the sound of a door opening and then being slammed*]

BEN: Now you see. Everything is over. Don't worry. [*He starts for door.* Alexandra *crosses* D. *to above chair* L.C.] Alexandra, I want you to tell your mother how sorry I am that I had to leave. [*Crosses to hall*] And don't worry so, my dear. Married folk frequently raise their voices, unfortunately.

[*He starts to put on his hat and coat as* Regina *appears on stairs. When she speaks to* Ben, *her voice is cold and calm*]

ALEXANDRA: [*Furiously—turns, crosses* U. *to landing*] How can you treat Papa like this! He's sick. He's very sick. Don't you know that! I won't let you.

REGINA: Mind your business, Alexandra. [Alexandra *turns down to above settee* L., *facing* L. *To* Ben *on landing*] How much longer can you wait for the money?

BEN: [*Putting on his coat—steps in*] He has refused? My, that's too bad.

REGINA: He will change his mind. I'll find a way to make him. What's the longest you can wait now?

BEN: I could wait until next week. [*Steps in*] But I can't wait until next week. [*He giggles, pleased at the joke*] I could but I can't. Could and can't. Well, I must go now. I'm very late——[*He starts*]

REGINA: [*Coming downstairs toward him*] You're not going. I want to talk to you.

[*She crosses into room*]

BEN: [*Looks at her, crosses* D. *to her*] Oh, I was about to give Alexandra a message for you. I wanted to tell you that Oscar is going to Chicago tonight, so we can't be here for our usual Friday supper.

REGINA: [*Tensely*] Oscar is going to Chi—— [*Softly*] What do you mean?

BEN: Just that. Everything is settled. He's going on to deliver to Marshall——

REGINA: [*Taking a step to him*] I demand to know what—you are lying. You are trying to scare me. *You haven't got the money.* How could you have it? You can't have——[Ben *laughs*] you will wait until I——

[Horace *comes into view on landing*]

BEN: You are getting out of hand. Since when do I take orders from you? [*He turns*]

REGINA: Wait, you—— [Ben *stops.* Regina *steps to him*] How *can* he go to Chicago? Did a ghost arrive with the money? [Ben *starts for hall*] I don't believe you. Come back here. [Regina *starts after him*] Come back here, you——

[*The door slams. She stops in the doorway, staring, her fists clenched. After a pause she turns slowly and steps into the room*]

HORACE: [*Standing on landing of the stairs, very quietly*] It's a great day when you and Ben cross swords. I've been waiting for it for years.

ALEXANDRA: Papa, Papa, [*Crosses* U. *to below landing*] please go back! You will——

HORACE: And so they don't need you, and so you will not have your millions, after all?

REGINA: [*Turns slowly*] You hate to see anybody live now, don't you? You hate to think that I'm going to be alive and have what I want.

[*Comes toward stairs, looking up at him*]

HORACE: I should have known you'd think that was the reason.

REGINA: Because you're going to die and you know you're going to die.

ALEXANDRA: [*Shrilly*] Mama! Don't—Don't listen, Papa. Just don't listen. Go away——

HORACE: Not to keep you from getting what you want. Not even partly that. [*Steps down one step, holding on to rail, leaning over to look down at her*] I'm sick of you, sick of this house, sick of my life here. I'm sick of your brothers and their dirty tricks to make a dime. [*Alexandra turns away, crosses* D. *to back of settee*] There must be better ways of getting rich than cheating niggers on a pound of bacon. Why should I give you the money? [*Very angrily*] To pound the bones of this town to make dividends for you to spend? You wreck the town, you and your brothers, *you* wreck the town and live on it. Not me. Maybe it's easy for the dying to be honest. But it's not my fault I'm dying. [*Addie enters* L., *stands at door quietly*] I'll do no more harm now. I've done enough. I'll die my own way. And I'll do it without making the world any worse. I leave that to you.

REGINA: [*Looks up at him slowly, calmly*] I hope you die. I hope you die soon. [*Smiles*] I'll be waiting for you to die.

ALEXANDRA: [*Shrieking*] Papa! Don't—don't listen —don't——

ADDIE: Come here, Zan. Come out of this room.

[*Alexandra runs quickly to Addie, who holds her in her arms. Horace turns slowly and starts upstairs*]

MEDIUM CURTAIN

ACT III.

SCENE: *Same as* ACT I. *Two weeks later. It is late afternoon and it is raining.*

AT RISE: *Horace is sitting near the window in a wheel chair. On the table next to him is a safe deposit box, and one small bottle of medicine and spoon. Birdie and Alexandra are playing the piano. On the chair* R. *of table* U.C. *is a large sewing-basket.*

A phrase of the song is played before the curtain rises. As the curtain is going up the song is reaching its conclusion.

BIRDIE: [*Counting for* Alexandra] One and two and three and four. One and two and three and four. [*They finish song and laugh.* Alexandra *repeats a phrase. Nods—turns to* Horace] We used to play together, Horace. Remember?

HORACE: [*Has been looking out of window*] What, Birdie?

BIRDIE: We played together. You and me.

ALEXANDRA: [*Stops playing, looks to* Horace, *then* Birdie] Papa used to play?

BIRDIE: Indeed he did. [*Addie appears at door* L. *in a large kitchen apron. She is wiping her hands on a towel*] He played the fiddle and very well, too. [*Turns to piano and starts playing*]

ALEXANDRA: [*Turns to smile at* Horace] I never knew——

ADDIE: Where's your Mama?

ALEXANDRA: Gone to Miss Safronia's to fit her dresses.

[*Addie nods, starts to exit*]

HORACE: Addie.

ADDIE: [*Crossing to* C.] Yes, Mr. Horace.

HORACE: [*Speaks as if he had made a sudden decision*] Tell Cal to get his things. I want him to go an errand.

[*Addie nods, exits* L. Horace *moves nervously in his chair, looks out of window*]

ALEXANDRA: [*Who has been watching him*] It's too bad it's been raining all day, Papa. But you can go out in the yard tomorrow. Don't be restless.

HORACE: I'm not restless, darling.

[*Alexandra turns to piano and joins* Birdie *in playing; after playing one measure together* Birdie *stops and turns to* Horace. Alexandra *continues playing alone*]

BIRDIE: I remember so well the time we played together. [*To* Alexandra] Your Papa and me. [*To* Horace] It was the first time Oscar brought me here to supper. I had never seen all the Hubbards together before, [*To* Alexandra] and you know what a ninny I am and how shy. [*Turns to look at* Horace] You said you could play the fiddle. [*Rises, crosses to table* U.C.] and you'd be much obliged if I'd play with you. [*Pouring glass of water*] *I* was obliged to *you*, all right, all right. [*Laughs when he does not answer her*] Horace, [*Steps to him, holding glass*] you haven't heard a word I've said.

HORACE: Birdie, when did Oscar get back from Chicago?

BIRDIE: Yesterday. Hasn't he been here yet?

ALEXANDRA: [*Stops playing*] No. Neither has Uncle Ben since—since that day.

BIRDIE: Oh, [*To* Alexandra] I didn't know it was that bad. [*Turns to* Horace] Oscar never tells *me* anything——

HORACE: [*Smiles, nods*] The Hubbards have had their great quarrel. I knew it would come some day. [*Laughs*] It came.

ALEXANDRA: It came. It certainly came all right.

BIRDIE: [*Amazed*] But Oscar was in such a good humor when he got home, [Addie *enters*] I didn't—

HORACE: Yes, I can understand that.

[Addie *is carrying a large tray with three water glasses, a carafe of elderberry wine, and a plate of cookies, which she puts on the table* D.L. *Birdie hurries to Addie, leaving water glass on table* U.C.]

ALEXANDRA: Addie! A party! What for?

ADDIE: [*Pouring wine into the three glasses*] Nothing for, I had the fresh butter so I made the cakes, and a little elderberry does the stomach good in the rain.

[Addie *looks at* Horace, *then crosses to* C., *moves chair* R.C. *upstage, then crosses to him, moves him to* C., L. *of table* R.]

BIRDIE: [*Takes her glass and puts* Alexandra's *on piano*] Isn't this nice! A party just for us. Let's play party music, Zan.

[Alexandra *begins to play a gay piece*]

ADDIE: [*To* Horace, *wheeling his chair to* C.] Come over here, Mr. Horace, and don't be thinking so much. [*She crosses to table* L. *for* Horace's *glass, brings it to him.* Alexandra *stops playing, turns and watches him*] A glass of elderberry will do more good.

[Alexandra *reaches for another cake,* Birdie *pours herself another glass of wine*]

ALEXANDRA: [*Her mouth full*] Good cakes, Addie. It's nice here. Just us. Be nice if it could always be this way.

BIRDIE: [*Nods, happily*] Quiet and restful. [*Drinks, then crosses to piano stool, sits*]

ADDIE: [*Crossing to table* U.C., *lights lamp*] Well, it won't be that way long. Little while now, even sitting here, you'll hear the red bricks going into place. The next day the smoke'll be pushing out the chimneys [Alexandra *crosses to chair at piano, sits*] and by church time that Sunday every human born of woman will be living on chicken. [*Crossing* R. *to mantel*] That's how Mr. Ben's been telling the story.

HORACE: [*Looks at her*] They believe it that way?

ADDIE: Believe it? [*Placing footstool so that she can reach upstage lamp on mantel.* Birdie *crosses to table, pours another drink*] They use to believing what Mr. Ben orders. There ain't been so much talk around here since Sherman's army didn't come near. [*Lights upper mantel lamp*]

HORACE: [*Softly*] They are fools.

ADDIE: [*Nods*] You ain't born in the South unless you're a fool.

[Addie *moves footstool to downstage end of mantel, and lights lower mantel lamp*]

BIRDIE: [*Has drunk another glass. She has been listening to the others*] But we didn't play together after that night. [*Crosses to front settee* L.] Oscar said he didn't like me to play on the piano. [*Turns to* Alexandra] You know what he said that night?

[Addie *crosses to chair* U.C., *gets sewing-basket,*

crosses to chair D.R., *turns it to face them, sits*]

ALEXANDRA: Who?

BIRDIE: Oscar. He said that music made him nervous. He said he just sat and waited for the next note. [Alexandra *laughs*] He wasn't poking fun. He meant it. Ah, well——[*She finishes her glass, shakes her head.* Horace *looks at her, smiles. Crossing to* Horace] Your Papa don't like to admit it, but he's been mighty kind to me all these years. [*Running the back of her hand along his sleeve*] Often he'd step in when somebody said something and once——[*She stops, turns away, her face still*] Once he stopped Oscar from——[*She stops, turns steps* U.S. *Quickly*] I'm sorry I said that. [*Crossing* L. *back of settee*] Why, here I am so happy and yet I think about bad things. [*Laughs nervously*] That's not right, now is it?

[*Crosses to table* L., *pours drink, crosses to upper end piano.* Cal *appears in the door* L. *He has on an old coat and is carrying a torn umbrella*]

ALEXANDRA: Have a cake, Cal.

CAL: [*Comes in, takes a cake*] Yes'm. You want me, Mr. Horace? [*Crosses* C. *to* L. *of* Horace]

HORACE: What time is it, Cal? [*Puts glass on table*]

CAL: Bout ten minutes before it's five.

HORACE: All right. Now you walk yourself down to the bank.

[Alexandra *starts to play softly*]

CAL: It'll be closed. Nobody'll be there but Mr. Mander, Mr. Joe Horns, Mr. Leo——

HORACE: Go in the back way. They'll be at the table, going over the day's business. [*Points to deposit box*] See that box?

CAL: [*Nods*] Yes, sir.

HORACE: You tell Mander that Mr. Horace says he's much obliged to him for bringing the box, it arrived all right.

CAL: [*Bewildered*] He know you got the box. He bring it hisself Wednesday. I opened the door to him and he say, "Hello, Cal, coming on to summer weather"——

HORACE: You say just what I tell you. Understand?

[Birdie *crosses to table* L. *pours drink, stands at table*]

CAL: No, sir. I ain't going to say I understand. I'm going down and tell a man he give you something he already know he give you, and you say "understand."

HORACE: Now, Cal——

CAL: Yes, sir. I just going to say you obliged for the box coming all right. I ain't going to understand it, but I'm going to say it——

HORACE: And tell him I want him to come over here after supper, and to bring Mr. Sol Fowler with him.

[Alexandra *playing*]

CAL: [*Nods*] He's to come after supper and bring Mr. Sol Fowler, your attorney-at-law, with him.

HORACE: [*Smiles*] That's right. Just walk right in the back room and say your piece. [*Slowly*] In front of everybody.

CAL: [*Takes step to* Horace, *then turns away* L.] Yes, sir. [*Mumbles to himself as he exits* L.]

ALEXANDRA: [*Who has been watching* Horace] Is anything the matter, Papa?

HORACE: Oh, no. Nothing.

ADDIE: [*Watching* Birdie *take another glass of wine*] Miss Birdie, that elderberry going to give you a headache spell.

BIRDIE: [*Beginning to be drunk. Gaily*] Oh, I don't think so. I don't think it will. [*Drinks*]

ALEXANDRA: [*As* Horace *puts his hand to his throat. Rises, crosses to his* L.] Do you want your medicine, Papa?

HORACE: No, no. I'm all right, darling.

BIRDIE: [*At* L. *of table* L.] Mama used to give me elderberry wine when I was a little girl. For hiccoughs. [*Laughs*] You know, I don't think people get hiccoughs anymore. Isn't that funny? [Birdie *laughs.* Horace *and* Alexandra *laugh, too*] I used to get hiccoughs just when I shouldn't have. [*Crosses to piano, sits, starts playing, drinks*]

ADDIE: [*Nods*] And nobody get growing pains no more. That is funny. Just as if there was some style in what you get. One year an ailment's stylish [Birdie *stops playing*] and the next year, it ain't.

BIRDIE: [*Turns to them*] I remember. It was my first big party, at Lionnet I mean, and I was so excited, [*Rises, crosses to table* L.] and there I was with hiccoughs and Mama laughing. [*Softly, looking at carafe*] Mama always laughed. [*Picks up carafe*] A big party, a lovely dress from Mr. Worth in Paris, France, and hiccoughs. [*Pours drink*] My brother pounding me on the back and Mama with the elderberry bottle, laughing at me. Everybody was on their way to come, and I was such a ninny, hiccoughing away. [*Drinks. Pauses*] You know, that was the first day I ever saw Oscar Hubbard. [*Crosses to* C.] The Ballongs were selling their horses and he was going there to buy. He passed and lifted his hat—we could see him from the window—and my brother, to tease Mama, said maybe we should have invited the Hubbards to the party. He said Mama didn't like them because they kept a store, and he said that was old-fashioned of her. [*Her face lights up—looking out*] And then, and *then*, I saw Mama angry for the first time in my life. She said that wasn't the reason. She said she was old-fashioned, but not that way. She said she was old-fashioned enough not to like people who killed animals they couldn't use, and who made their money charging awful interest to poor, ignorant niggers and cheating them on what they bought. She was very angry, Mama was. I had never seen her face like that. And then suddenly she laughed and said, "Look, I've frightened Birdie out of the hiccoughs." [*Her head drops, then softly*] And so she

had. They were all gone. [*Moves up to sofa* L., *sits.* Alexandra *crosses* L. *to chair* L.C.]

ADDIE: [*To her sewing*] Yeah, they got mighty well off cheating niggers. [*To them*] Well, there are people who eat the earth and eat all the people on it like in the Bible with the locusts. Then, there are people who stand around and watch them eat it. [*Softly*] Sometimes I think it ain't right to stand and watch them do it.

BIRDIE: [*Thoughtfully*] Like I say, if we could only go back to Lionnet. Everybody'd be better there. They'd be good and kind. I like people to be kind. [*Pours drink*] Don't you, Horace, don't you like people to be kind?

HORACE: Yes, Birdie.

BIRDIE: [*Very drunk now*] Yes, that was the first day I ever saw Oscar. Who would have thought——? [*Drinks. Quickly—caressing the glass*] You all want to know something? Well, I don't like Leo. My very own son, and I don't like him. [*Laughs, gaily*] My, I guess, I even like Oscar more. [*Drinks*]

ALEXANDRA: [*A step to* Birdie] Why did you marry Uncle Oscar?

ADDIE: [*Sharply*] That's no question for you to be asking.

HORACE: [*Sharply*] Why not? She's heard enough around here to ask anything.

ALEXANDRA: Aunt Birdie, why did you marry Uncle Oscar?

BIRDIE: [*Places glass on table. Pleasantly*] I don't know. I thought I liked him. He was so kind to me and I thought it was because he liked me, too. But that wasn't the reason——[*Wheels on* Alexandra] Ask why *he* married *me!* I can tell you that; he's told it to me often enough.

ADDIE: [*Leaning forward*] Miss Birdie, don't——

BIRDIE: [*Speaking very rapidly, tensely*] My family was good and the cotton on Lionnet's fields was better. Ben Hubbard wanted the cotton and [*Rises*] Oscar Hubbard married it for him. [Alexandra *crosses to* Horace] He was kind to me, then. He used to smile at me. He hasn't smiled at me since. Everybody knew that's what he married me for. [Addie *rises*] Everybody but me. [*Turns away, crosses* D.L.] Stupid, stupid me.

[Addie *puts sewing basket on chair, takes step to* Horace]

ALEXANDRA: [*To* Horace, *holding his hand, softly*] I see. [*Hesitates*] Papa, I mean—when you feel better couldn't we go away? I mean, by ourselves. Couldn't we find a way to go——

HORACE: [*Placing his hand over hers*] Yes, I know what you mean. We'll try to find a way. I promise you, darling.

ADDIE: [*Looks at them for a second, then goes* L. *to* Birdie] Rest a bit, Miss Birdie. You get talking like this you'll get a headache and——

BIRDIE: [*Sharply turning to her*] I've never had a headache in my life. [*Crosses* U.L. *Begins to cry; hysterically*] You know it as well as I do. [*Turns to

Alexandra. *Crossing to her back of settee. Addie crosses* U.L.] I never had a headache, Zan. That's a lie they tell for me. *I drink.* All by myself, in my own room, by myself, *I drink.* Then, when they want to hide it, they say "Birdie's got a headache again"——

ALEXANDRA: [*Comes to her, quickly*] Aunt Birdie.
[Addie *turns to look at them*]

BIRDIE: [*Turning away*] Even you won't like me now. You won't like me, any more.

ALEXANDRA: I love you. I'll always love you.

BIRDIE: [*Furiously*] Well, don't. [*Turns to Alexandra*] Don't love me. Because in twenty years you'll just be like me. They'll do all the same things to you. [*Begins to laugh, hysterically*] You know what? In twenty-two years I haven't had a whole day of happiness. Oh, a little, like today with you all. But never a single, whole day. I say to myself, if only I had one more *whole* day, then——[*The laugh stops*] And that's the way you'll be. And you'll trail after them, just like me, hoping they won't be so mean that day or say something to make you feel so bad —only you'll be worse off because you haven't got my Mama to remember——

[*Turns away, her head drops. She stands quietly, swaying a little, holding onto sofa. Alexandra leans down, puts her cheek on Birdie's arm*]

ALEXANDRA: [*To Birdie*] I guess we were all trying to make a happy day. You know, we sit around and try to pretend nothing's happened. We try to pretend we are not here. We make believe we are just by ourselves, some place else, and it doesn't seem to work. [*Kisses Birdie's hand, which she has been holding*] Come now, Aunt Birdie, I'll walk you home. You and me.

[*She takes Birdie's arm, they move slowly out. In the hallway Alexandra places a raincoat over Birdie's shoulders. They exit. Addie and Horace are silent*]

ADDIE: Well. [*Sighs*] First time I ever heard Miss Birdie say a word. [*Crossing R. to table R. Horace looks at her*] Maybe it's good for her. [*Picks up glass from table R.*] I'm just sorry Zan had to hear it. [*Takes glass to table U.C. Horace moves his head as if he were uncomfortable*] You feel bad, don't you? [*He shrugs*]

HORACE: So you didn't want Zan to hear? It would be nice to let her stay innocent, like Birdie at her age. Let her listen now. Let her see everything. How else is she going to know that she's got to get away? I'm trying to show her that. I'm trying, but I've only got a little time left. She can even hate me when I'm dead, if she'll only learn to hate and fear this.

ADDIE: Mr. Horace——

HORACE: Pretty soon there'll be nobody to help her but you.

ADDIE: [*Crossing to him*] What can I do?

HORACE: Take her away.

ADDIE: How can I do that? Do you think they'd let me just go away with her——?

HORACE: I'll fix it so they can't stop you when you're ready to go. You'll go, Addie?

ADDIE: [*After a second, softly*] Yes sir, I promise.
[*He touches her arm, nods*]

HORACE: [*After a second, quietly*] I'm going to have Sol Fowler make me a new will. They'll make trouble, but you make Zan stand firm and Fowler'll do the rest. [*She looks at him, nods, crosses R., front table*] Addie, [*She turns to Horace*] I'd like to leave you something for yourself. I always wanted to.

ADDIE: [*Laughs*] Don't you do that, Mr. Horace. A nigger woman in a white man's will! I'd never get it nohow.

HORACE: I know. But upstairs in the armoire drawer there's seventeen hundred-dollar bills. It's money left from my trip. It's in an envelope with your name. It's for you.

ADDIE: Seventeen hundred-dollar bills! My God, Mr. Horace, I won't know how to count up that high. [*Shyly*] It's mighty kind and good of you. I don't know what to *say* for thanks——

CAL: [*Appears in doorway*] I'm back. [*Stands umbrella in* U.L. *corner. No answer. Crossing to* C.] I'm back.

ADDIE: [*Crossing R. to chair* D.R., *picks up basket, sits*] So we see.

HORACE: Well?

CAL: Nothing. I just went down and spoke my piece. Just like you told me, I say Mr. Horace he thank you mightily for the safe box arriving in good shape and he say you come right after supper to his house and bring Mr. Attorney-at-law Sol Fowler with you. Then I wipe my hands on my coat. Every time I ever told a lie in my whole life, I wipe my hands right after. Can't help doing it. Well, while I'm wiping my hands, Mr. Leo jump up and say to me "What box! What you talking about?"

HORACE: [*Smiles*] Did he?

CAL: And Mr. Leo say he got to leave a little early 'cause he got something to do. And then Mr. Mander say Mr. Leo should sit right down and finish up his work and stop acting like somebody made him Mr. President. So he sit down. Now, just like I told you, Mr. Mander was mighty surprised with the message because he knows right well he brought the box——[*Pointing to box. Sighs*] But he took it all right. Some men take everything easy and some do not.

HORACE: [*Puts his head back, laughs*] Mr. Leo was telling the truth: he *has* got something to do. I hope Mander don't keep him too long. [*Outside there is the sound of voices. Cal exits* R. *Addie crosses quickly to Horace, puts basket on table* R., *begins to wheel his chair toward the stairs. Sharply*] No. Leave me where I am.

ADDIE: [*Step* D. *to his* L.] But that's Miss Regina coming back.

HORACE: [*Nods, looking at door*] Go away, Addie.

ADDIE: [*Hesitates*] Mr. Horace. Don't talk no more today. You don't feel well and it won't do you no good——

HORACE: [*As he hears footsteps in the hall*] Go on. [*She looks at him for a second, then picks up her sewing from table* R. *and exits* L. *as Regina comes in from hall. Horace's chair is now so placed that he is in front of table with the medicine. Regina stands in the hall, shakes umbrella, stands it in* U.R. *corner, takes off her cloak and throws it over bannister. She stares at* Horace]

REGINA: [*As she takes off her gloves, crossing to* C.] We had agreed that you were to stay in your part of this house and I in mine. This room is *my* part of the house. Please don't come down here again.

HORACE: I won't.

REGINA: [*Crosses* D.R. *toward bell-cord below mantel*] I'll get Cal to take you upstairs.

HORACE: [*Smiles*] Before you do I want to tell you that after all, we have invested our money in Hubbard, Sons and Marshall, Cotton Manufacturers.

REGINA: [*Stops, turns, stares at him*] What are you talking about? You haven't seen Ben—When did you change your mind?

HORACE: I didn't change my mind. *I* didn't invest the money. [*Smiles at the expression on her face*] It was invested for me.

REGINA: [*Angrily*] What——?

HORACE: I had eighty-eight thousand dollars' worth of Union Pacific bonds in that safe deposit box. They are not there now. Go and look. [*As she stares at him. Points to box*] Go and look, Regina. [*She crosses quickly to box, opens it. He speaks when she is at table*] Those bonds are as negotiable as money. [*She closes box*]

REGINA: [*Turns back to him*] What kind of joke are you playing now? Is this for my benefit?

HORACE: I don't look in that box very often, but three days ago, on Wednesday it was, because I had made a decision——

REGINA: I want to know what you are talking about.

HORACE: [*Sharply*] Don't interrupt me again. [*Regina stiffens*] Because I had made a decision, I sent for the box. The bonds were gone. Eighty-eight thousand dollars gone. [*He smiles at her*]

REGINA: [*After a moment's silence, quietly crossing* U.C.] Do you think I'm crazy enough to believe what you're saying?

HORACE: [*Shrugs*] Believe anything you like.

REGINA: [*Stares at him, slowly*] Where did they go to?

HORACE: They are in Chicago. With Mr. Marshall, I should guess.

REGINA: [*Crossing* D. *to chair* L.C.] What did they do? Walk to Chicago? Have you really gone crazy?

HORACE: Leo took the bonds.

REGINA: [*Turns sharply, then speaks softly, without conviction*] I don't believe it.

HORACE: [*Leans forward*] I wasn't there but I can guess what happened. [*Regina sits chair* L.C.] This fine gentleman, to whom you were willing to marry your daughter, took the keys and opened the box. You remember that the day of the fight, Oscar went to Chicago? Well, he went with my bonds that his son Leo had stolen for him. [*Pleasantly*] And for Ben, of course, too.

REGINA: [*Slowly, nods*] When did you find out the bonds were gone?

HORACE: Wednesday night.

REGINA: I thought that's what you said. Why have you waited three days to do anything? [*Suddenly laughs*] This *will* make a fine story.

HORACE: [*Nods*] Couldn't it?

REGINA: [*Still laughing. Rises, crosses* U.L.—*takes off hat*] A fine story to hold over their heads. How could they be such fools? [*Turns to him back of settee*]

HORACE: But I'm not going to hold it over their heads.

REGINA: [*The laugh stops*] What?

HORACE: [*Turns his chair to face* L.] I'm going to let them keep the bonds—as a loan from you. An eighty-eight thousand dollar loan; they should be grateful to you. They will be, I think.

REGINA: [*Slowly, smiles*] I see. You are punishing me. But I won't let you punish me. If you won't do anything, I will. Now. [*She starts for door*]

HORACE: You won't do anything. Because you can't. [*Regina stops above chair* R.C.] It won't do you any good to make trouble because I shall simply say that I lent them the bonds.

REGINA: [*Slowly*] You would do that?

HORACE: Yes. [*Regina crosses* D. *to chair* L.C.] For once in your life I am tying your hands. There is nothing for you to do.

[*There is silence. Then she sits down*]

REGINA: I see. You are going to lend them the bonds and let them keep all the profit they make on them, and there is nothing I can do about it. Is that right?

HORACE: Yes.

REGINA: [*Softly*] Why did you say that I was making this gift?

HORACE: I was coming to that. I am going to make a new will, Regina, leaving you eighty-eight thousand dollars in Union Pacific bonds. The rest will go to Zan. It's true that your brothers have borrowed your share for a little while. After my death I advise you to talk to Ben and Oscar. They won't admit anything and Ben, I think, will be smart enough to see that he's *safe*. Because I knew about the theft and said nothing. Nor *will* I say anything as long as I live. Is that clear to you?

REGINA: [*Nods, softly, without looking at him*] You will not say anything as long as you live.

HORACE: That's right. And by that time they will probably have replaced your bonds, and then they'll belong to you and nobody but us will ever know what happened. [*Stops, smiles*] They'll be around any minute to see what I am going to do. I took good care to see that word reached Leo. They'll be mighty relieved to know I'm going to do nothing and Ben will think it all a capital joke on you. And that will be the end of that. There's nothing you can do to them, nothing you can do to me.

REGINA: You hate me very much.

HORACE: No.

REGINA: Oh, I think you do. [*Puts her head back, sighs*] Well, we haven't been very good together. Anyway, I don't hate you either. I have only contempt for you. I've always had.

HORACE: From the very first?

REGINA: I think so.

HORACE: I was in love with *you*. But why did *you* marry *me*?

REGINA: I was lonely when I was young.

HORACE: *You* were lonely?

REGINA: Not the way people usually mean. Lonely for all the things I wasn't going to get. Everybody in this house was so busy and there was so little place for what I wanted. I wanted the world. Then, and then—— [*Smiles*] Papa died and left the money to Ben and Oscar.

HORACE: And you married me?

REGINA: Yes, I thought—but I was wrong. You were a small-town clerk then. You haven't changed.

HORACE: [*Nods, smiles*] And that wasn't what you wanted.

REGINA: No. No, it wasn't what I wanted. [*Pauses, leans back, pleasantly*] It took me a little while to find out I had made a mistake. As for you—I don't know. It was almost as if I couldn't stand the kind of man you were. [*Smiles, softly*] I used to lie there at night, praying you wouldn't come near—

HORACE: Really? It was as bad as that?

REGINA: [*Nods*] Remember when I went to Doctor Sloan and I told you he said there was something the matter with me and that you shouldn't touch me any more?

HORACE: I remember.

REGINA: But you believed it? I couldn't understand that. I couldn't understand that anybody could be such a soft fool. That was when I began to despise you.

HORACE: [*Puts his hand to his throat, glances around at bottle of medicine on table, then to her*] Why didn't you leave me?

REGINA: I told you I married you *for* something. It turned out it was only for this. [*Carefully*] This wasn't what I wanted, but it was something. I never thought about it much, but if I had, [Horace *puts his hand to his throat*] I'd have known that you would die before I would. But I couldn't have known that you would get heart trouble so early and so bad. I'm lucky, Horace. I've always been lucky. [Horace *turns slowly to medicine*] I'll be lucky again.

[Horace *looks at her. Then he puts his hand to his throat. Because he cannot reach the bottle*

he moves the chair closer. He reaches for medicine, takes out cork, picks up spoon, tries to pour some in the spoon, the bottle slips out of his shaking fingers and crashes on the table. He draws in his breath, gasps*]

HORACE: Please. Tell Addie—the other bottle is upstairs. [*She has not moved. She does not move now. He stares at her. Then, suddenly as if he understood, he raises his voice. It is a panic-stricken whisper, too small to be heard outside the room*] Addie! Addie! Come——

[*Stops as he hears the softness of his voice. He makes a sudden, furious spring from the chair to the stairs, taking the first few steps as if he were a desperate runner. On the fourth step he slips, gasps, grasps the rail, makes a great effort to reach the landing. When he reaches the landing, he is on his knees. His knees give way, he falls on the landing, out of view. Regina has not turned during his climb up the stairs. Now she waits a second. Then she goes below the landing, speaks up*]

REGINA: Horace. [*When there is no answer, she turns, crosses to door L., opens door, calls*] Addie! Cal! Come in here. [*Crosses R. Starts up the steps. When she is on first step, Addie appears, followed by Cal. Both run toward stairs*] He's had an attack. Come up here.

[*They run up steps quickly, passing Regina*]

CAL: My God! Mr. Horace——

REGINA: [*They cannot be seen now. Her voice comes from the head of the stairs*] Be still, Cal. Bring him in here.

[*Before the footsteps and voices have completely died away, Alexandra appears in hall door, in her raincloak and hood. She comes into the room, begins to unfasten the cloak, suddenly looks around, sees the empty wheelchair, stares, begins to move swiftly as if to look in the dining room. At the same moment, Addie runs down the stairs. She turns and stares up at Addie*]

ALEXANDRA: Addie! What?

ADDIE: [*Takes Alexandra by the shoulders*] I'm going for the doctor. Go upstairs.

[Alexandra *looks at her, then quickly breaks away and runs up the steps. Addie exits L. The stage is empty for a minute. Then the front door bell begins to ring. When there is no answer it rings again. A second later Leo appears in the hall, talking as he comes in*]

LEO: [*Very nervous*] Hello. [*Irritably*] Never saw any use ringing a bell when a door was open. If you are going to ring a bell, then somebody should answer it. [*Gets in the room, looks around, puzzled, listens, hears no sound*] Aunt Regina. [*Puts hat on sofa R. No answer. He moves around restlessly, crossing L.*] Addie. [*Waits, turns crossing C.*] Where the hell——? [*Crosses D.R. to bell cord, rings it im-*

patiently, twice, waits and gets no answer; calls] Cal! [*Rings again, then calls*] Cal——

[*After a second* Cal *appears on stair landing*]

CAL: [*His voice is soft, shaken*] Mr. Leo. Miss Regina says you stop that screaming noise.

LEO: [*Angrily crosses to table* R.] Where is everybody?

CAL: Mr. Horace he got an attack. He's bad. Miss Regina says you stop that noise.

LEO: Uncle Horace—What—— [*Crosses* U.C.]— What happened? [*Cal starts down stairs. Cal shakes his head, begins to move swiftly* L. *off.* Leo *looks around wildly*] But when—You seen Mr. Oscar or Mr. Ben? [*Cal shakes his head. Moves on.* Leo *grabs him by the arm*] Answer me, will you?

CAL: No ain't seen 'em. I ain't got time to answer you. [*Cal breaks* Leo's *hold, crosses* L.] I got to get things. [*Cal exits*]

LEO: But what's the matter with him? When did this happen——? [*Crossing to door* L., *calling after* Cal] You'd think Papa'd be some place where you could find him. I been chasing him all afternoon.

[Oscar *and* Ben *come swiftly into the room, talking excitedly*]

OSCAR: I hope it's not a bad attack.

BEN: It's the first one he's had since he come home.

[Leo *crosses to* Oscar, *excitedly*]

LEO: Papa, I've been looking all over town for you and Uncle Ben——

BEN: Where is he?

OSCAR: Addie said it was sudden.

BEN: [*To* Leo] Where is he? When did it happen?

LEO: Upstairs. Will you listen to me, please? I been looking for you for——

OSCAR: [*To* Ben] You think we should go up?

[Ben, *looking up the steps, shakes his head*]

BEN: I don't know. I don't know.

OSCAR: [*Shakes his head*] But he was all right——

LEO: [*Almost yelling—turns, crosses* D. *to front chair* L.C.] Will you listen to me?

OSCAR: [*Sharply—crossing* D. *to* Leo] What is the matter with you?

LEO: [*Coming to him*] I been trying to tell you. I been trying to find you for an hour——

OSCAR: Tell me what?

LEO: Uncle Horace knows about the bonds. He knows about them. He's had the box since Wednesday——

BEN: [*Sharply*] Stop shouting! [*Crosses* D.C. *to him*] What the hell are you talking about?

LEO: [*Furiously. Crossing to* Ben] I'm telling you he knows about the bonds. Ain't that clear enough——?

OSCAR: [*Grabbing* Leo's *arm*] You God damn fool! Stop screaming!

BEN: Now what happened? Talk quietly.

LEO: [*Closes his eyes, angrily attempted patience*] You heard me. Uncle Horace knows about the bonds. He's known since Wednesday.

BEN: [*After a second.* Oscar *draws close to them*] How do you know that?

LEO: Because Cal comes down to Mander and says the box came O. K. and——

OSCAR: [*Trembling, crosses to* Ben, *pushing* Leo *away* L.] That might not mean a thing——

LEO: [*Angrily steps* D. *to* L. *of* Oscar] No? It might not, huh? [*Takes* Oscar's *arm.* Oscar *turns to him*] Then he says Mander should come here tonight and bring Sol Fowler with him. [Ben *crosses* R. *to* R. *of table*] I guess that don't mean a thing either. [Leo *turns—crosses* D.L.]

OSCAR: [*Panicky, to* Ben] Ben—What—Do you think he's seen the——

BEN: [*Motions to box*] There's the box. [*Both* Oscar *and* Leo *turn sharply.* Leo *makes a leap to the box, crossing* R. *back of* Oscar, *picks up box*] You ass. Put it down. What are you going to do with it, eat it?

LEO: I'm going to—— [*Starts*]

BEN: [*Furiously*] Put it down. Don't touch it again. Now sit down and shut up for a minute.

[Leo *puts box down on table*]

OSCAR: [*Crossing to* Leo] Since Wednesday. [*To* Leo] You said he had it since Wednesday. Why didn't he say something——[*To* Ben] I don't understand——

LEO: [*Taking a step* R.] I can put it back. I can put it back before anybody knows.

BEN: [*Who is standing at the table* R., *softly*] He's had it since Wednesday. Yet he hasn't said a word to us.

OSCAR: *Why? Why?*

LEO: What's the difference why? He was getting ready to say plenty. He was going to say it to Fowler tonight——

OSCAR: [*Angrily*] Be still. [*Turns to* Ben, *looks at him, waits*]

BEN: [*After a moment*] I don't believe that.

LEO: [*Wildly, leaning toward* Ben *over table*] *You* don't believe it? What do I care what *you* believe? I do the dirty work and then——

BEN: [*Turning his head sharply to* Leo] I'm remembering that. I'm remembering that, Leo.

OSCAR: [*A step* D.] What do you mean?

LEO: You——

BEN: [*To* Oscar] If you don't shut that little fool up, I'll show you what I mean. [Oscar *makes a gesture at* Leo. Leo *crosses* U.C.] For some reason he knows, but he don't say a word.

OSCAR: [*Crossing to* Ben] Maybe he didn't know that we——

BEN: [*Quickly*] That *Leo*——? [*Crosses* C.] He's no fool. [*Crossing up to* Leo] Does Mander know the bonds are missing?

LEO: How could I tell? I was half crazy. I don't think so. Because Mander seemed kind of puzzled and——

OSCAR: But we got to find out——

[*He breaks off as* Cal *comes into the room*

carrying a kettle of hot water and clean cloths, leaving door open. They turn to Cal. Leo, *startled, crosses* U.L. *to buck settee*]

BEN: [*Crosses to above chair* L.] How is he, Cal?

CAL: I don't know, Mr. Ben. He was bad. [*Going toward stairs*]

OSCAR: [*Crosses* L. *to chair* L.] But when did it happen?

CAL: [*Shrugs*] He wasn't feeling so bad early. [Addie *comes in quickly from hall*] Then there he is next thing on the landing, fallen over, his eyes tight ——[*He hurries toward stairs*]

ADDIE: [*To* Cal] Dr. Sloan's over at the Ballongs. Hitch the buggy and go get him. [*She takes kettle and cloths from him, pushes him, runs up stairs*] Go on. [*She disappears*]

[Cal *exits* L., *picking up his umbrella as he goes.* Oscar *crosses* D.R.]

BEN: [*Takes off coat and hat, places them on chair* U.C.] Never seen Sloan anywhere when you need him.

OSCAR: [*Softly*] Sounds bad.

LEO: [*Taking a step to* Ben] He would have told *her* about it. Aunt Regina. He would have told his own wife——

BEN: [*Turning to* Leo] Yes, he might have told her. [*Crossing, to front wheel-chair*] But they weren't on such pretty terms and maybe he didn't. Maybe he didn't. [*Goes quickly to* Leo] Now, listen to me. If she doesn't know, it may work out all right. [*Holding* Leo's *lapel*] If she does know, you're to say he lent you the bonds.

LEO: Lent them to me! Who's going to believe that?

BEN: Nobody.

OSCAR: [*To* Leo, *crossing to* Ben] Don't you understand? It can't do no harm to say it—— [Ben *releases grip on* Leo's *lapel*]

LEO: Why should I say he lent them to me? Why not to you? [*Carefully*] Why not to Uncle Ben?

BEN: [*Smiles*] Just because he didn't lend them to me. Remember that.

LEO: But all he has to do is say he didn't lend them to me——

BEN: [*Furiously*] But for some reason, he doesn't seem to be talking, does he?

[*There are footsteps above. They all stand looking at the stairs.* Regina *begins to come slowly down*]

BEN: [*Crosses* U.R., *to* Regina] What happened?

REGINA: He's had a bad attack. [*Crosses* D.C.]

OSCAR: Too bad. I'm so sorry we weren't here when—when Horace needed us.

BEN: [*Crosses* D.C.] When *you* needed us.

REGINA: [*At chair* L.C. *Looks at him*] Yes.

BEN: How is he? Can we—can we go up?

REGINA: [*Shakes her head*] He's not conscious.

OSCAR: [*Pacing around*] It's that—it's that bad? [*Turns, crosses* D.R.] Wouldn't you think Sloan could be found quickly, just once, just once?

REGINA: I don't think there is much for him to do.

BEN: [*Crossing to* Regina] Oh, don't talk like that. He's come through attacks before. He will now.

[Regina *sits down, chair* L.C. *After a second she speaks softly.* Leo *crosses* R. *to above table* R.]

REGINA: Well. We haven't seen each other since the day of our fight.

BEN: [*Tenderly*] That was nothing. Why, you and Oscar and I used to fight when we were kids.

OSCAR: [*Hurriedly taking a step* L.] Don't you think we should go up? Is there anything we can do for Horace——

BEN: You don't feel well. Ah——

REGINA: [*Without looking at them*] No, I don't. [*Slight pause*] Horace told me about the bonds this afternoon.

[*There is an immediate shocked silence*]

LEO: [*Taking several short steps to* L. *of table* R.] The bonds. What do you mean? What bonds? What——?

OSCAR: [*Looks at him furiously. Then to* Regina] The Union Pacific bonds? *Horace's* Union Pacific Bonds?

REGINA: Yes.

OSCAR: [*Steps to her, very nervously*] Well. Well what—what about them? What—what could he say?

REGINA: He said that Leo had stolen the bonds and given them to you.

OSCAR: [*Aghast, very loudly*] That's ridiculous, Regina, absolutely——

LEO: I don't know what you're talking about. What would I—why——

REGINA: [*Wearily to* Ben] Isn't it enough that he stole them from me? Do I have to listen to this in the bargain?

OSCAR: You are talking——

LEO: I didn't steal anything. I don't know why——

REGINA: [*To* Ben] Would you ask them to stop that, please?

[*There is silence for a minute.* Ben *glowers at* Oscar *and* Leo, Leo *looks at* Oscar]

BEN: Aren't we starting at the wrong end, Regina? What did Horace tell you?

REGINA: [*Smiles at him*] He told me that Leo had stolen the bonds.

LEO: [*To* Ben] I didn't steal——

REGINA: Please. Let me finish. [Leo *crosses* R. *slowly*] Then he told me that he was going to pretend that he had lent them to you [Leo *turns sharply to* Regina, *then looks at* Oscar, *then looks back at* Regina] as a present from me to my brothers. He said there was nothing I could do about it. He said the rest of his money would go to Alexandra. That is all.

[*There is a silence.* Oscar *coughs,* Leo *smiles slyly*]

LEO: [*Taking a step to her*] I told you he had lent them—I could have told you——

REGINA: [*Ignores him, smiles sadly at* Ben] So I'm

very badly off, you see. [*Carefully*] But Horace said there was nothing I could do about it as long as he was alive to say he had lent you the bonds.

BEN: You shouldn't feel that way. It can all be explained, all be adjusted. It isn't as bad——

REGINA: So you, at least, are willing to admit that the bonds were stolen?

BEN: [Oscar *laughs nervously*] I admit no such thing. It's possible that Horace made up that part of the story to tease you—— [*Looks at her*] Or perhaps to punish you. Punish you.

REGINA: [*Sadly*] It's not a pleasant story. I feel bad, Ben, naturally. I hadn't thought——

BEN: Now you shall have the bonds safely back. That was the understanding, wasn't it, Oscar?

OSCAR: [*Crossing to* C.] Yes.

REGINA: I'm glad to know that. [*Smiles*] Ah, I had greater hopes——

BEN: Don't talk that way. That's foolish. [*Looks at his watch*] I think we ought to drive out for Sloan ourselves. [*Looks at* Oscar] If we can't find him we'll go over to Senateville for Doctor Morris. [*Looks at her.* Oscar *crosses* U. *to chair* R.C. *for hat,* Leo *crosses* U. *back of sofa to hall, picking up hat*] And don't think I'm dismissing this other business. I'm not. We'll have it all out on a more appropriate day.

[Ben *crosses* U. *to chair* U.C. *for coat and hat*]

REGINA: [*Waits until they are near the door. Looks up, quietly*] I don't think you had better go yet. I think you had better stay and sit down. [Oscar *crosses to hall*]

BEN: [*Picking up coat and hat*] We'll be back with Sloan.

REGINA: Cal has gone for him. I don't want you to go.

[Oscar *turns, looks at them*]

BEN: [*Crossing* U.C.] Now don't worry and——

REGINA: You will come back in this room and sit down. I have something more to say.

[Leo *steps back into view*]

BEN: [*Turns, comes toward her to* C.] Since when do I take orders from you?

REGINA: [*Smiles*] You don't—yet. [Oscar *takes a step in. Sharply*] Come back, Oscar. You too, Leo.

OSCAR: [*Takes another step in. Sure of himself, laughs*] My dear Regina——

BEN: [*Crosses to her. Softly, pats her hand*] Horace has already clipped your wings and very wittily. Do I have to clip them, too? [*Smiles at her*] You'd get farther with a smile, Regina. I'm a soft man for a woman's smile.

REGINA: I'm smiling, Ben. I'm smiling because you are quite safe while Horace lives. But I don't think Horace will live. [Leo *looks at* Oscar. *To* Ben] And if he doesn't live I shall want seventy-five per cent in exchange for the bonds.

BEN: [*Steps back. Whistles, laughs*] Greedy! What a greedy girl you are! You want so much of everything.

REGINA: Yes. And if I don't get what I want I am going to put all three of you in jail.

OSCAR: [*Crosses* L. *to* R. *of* Regina, *furiously*] You're mighty crazy. Having just admitted—— [Leo *steps* D.]

BEN: And on what evidence would you put Oscar and Leo in jail?

REGINA: [*Laughs, gaily*] Oscar, listen to him. He's getting ready to swear that it was you and Leo! What do you say to that? [*As* Oscar *turns furiously toward* Ben] Oh, don't be angry, Oscar. I'm going to see that he goes in with you.

[Oscar *turns, steps* U.C.]

BEN: Try anything you like, Regina. [*Steps to* Regina. Oscar *crosses* U.R. *Sharply*] And now we can stop all this and say goodbye to you. [Alexandra *comes into view on landing, moving slowly down steps*] It's his money and he's obviously willing to let us borrow it. [*More pleasantly.* Leo *slowly crosses* U. *to hall*] Learn to make threats when you can carry them through: for how many years have I told you a good-looking woman gets more by being soft and appealing? Mama used to tell you that. [*Looks at his watch*] Where the hell is Sloan? [*To* Oscar] Take the buggy and——

[*As* Ben *turns to* Oscar, *he sees* Alexandra *and stops.* Oscar *turns to her.* Alexandra *has come slowly down the steps. She walks stiffly. She comes down as if she did not see any of them. She goes slowly to lower window, her head bent. They all turn to look at her*]

OSCAR: [*After a second, moving toward her above sofa*] What? Alexandra——

[*She does not answer. After a second* Addie *comes slowly down the stairs, moving as if she were very tired. At foot of steps, she looks at* Alexandra, *then turns and slowly crosses to door* L. *and exits.* Regina *rises. She sees* Addie. Ben *looks nervously at* Alexandra, *at* Regina]

OSCAR: [*As* Addie *passes him, irritably to* Alexandra] Well, what is—— [*Turns into room—sees* Addie *at foot of steps*] what's?—[Ben *puts up a hand, shakes his head. His movements become nervous and fidgety, as if he were anxious to get out.* Oscar *clears his throat, looks at* Regina, *tries to fill the silence.* Leo *steps* D.] My God, I didn't know—who *could* have known—I didn't know he was that sick. Well, well—I——

[Regina *stands quietly, her back to them*]

BEN: [*Softly, sincerely*] Seems like yesterday when he first came here.

[*Places coat and hat on chair above wheelchair*]

OSCAR: [*Sincerely, nervously*] Yes, that's true. [*Turns to* Ben] The whole town loved him and respected him.

ALEXANDRA: [*Turns and crosses to below sofa* R.] Did you love him, Uncle Oscar?

OSCAR: [*Turns to* Alexandra] Certainly, I—What a strange thing to ask? I——

ALEXANDRA: [*Turns to look at* Ben] Did you love him, Uncle Ben?

BEN: [*Simply*] He had——

ALEXANDRA: [*Suddenly starts to laugh very loudly*] And you, Mama, did you love him, too?

REGINA: I know what you feel, Alexandra, but please try to control yourself.

ALEXANDRA: [*Still laughing*] I'm trying, Mama. I'm trying very hard.

BEN: Grief makes some people laugh and some people cry. It's better to cry, Alexandra.

ALEXANDRA: [*The laugh has stopped. Tensely. Moves toward* Regina, *crossing to front sofa*] What was Papa doing on the staircase?

REGINA: [*Crossing* R. *to* Alexandra. Ben *turns to look at* Alexandra *with interest*] Please go and lie down, my dear. We all need time to get over shocks like this. [Alexandra *does not move.* Regina's *voice becomes softer, more insistent*] Please go, Alexandra.

ALEXANDRA: No, Mama. I'll wait. I've got to talk to you.

REGINA: Later. Go and rest now.

ALEXANDRA: [*Quietly*] I'll wait, Mama. I've plenty of time. [*Sits down on sofa*] All my life.

REGINA: [*Hesitates, stares, makes a half shrug, turns back to* Ben, *crossing* L. *to* C.] As I was saying. Tomorrow morning I am going up to Judge Simmes. I shall tell him about Leo.

BEN: [*Motioning toward* Alexandra, *steps* D. *to chair* L.C.] Not in front of the child, Regina. I——

REGINA: [*Turns to him. Sharply*] I didn't ask her to stay. [*Turns away, crossing* L.] Tomorrow morning I go to Judge Simmes——

OSCAR: And what proof? What proof of all this——

REGINA: [*Turns, crosses to* C. *between* Ben *and* Oscar. *To* Oscar *sharply*] None. I won't need any. The bonds are missing and they are with Marshall. That will be enough. If it isn't, I'll add what's necessary.

BEN: I'm sure of that.

REGINA: [*Turns to* Ben] You can be quite sure.

OSCAR: We'll deny——

REGINA: Deny your heads off. You couldn't find a jury that wouldn't weep for a woman whose brothers steal from her. *And* you couldn't find twelve men in this State you haven't cheated and hate you for it.

OSCAR: What kind of talk is this? You couldn't do anything like that! We're your own brothers. How can you talk that way when upstairs not five minutes ago—— [*Points up stairs*]

REGINA: [*Slowly*] There are people who can never go back, who must finish what they start. I am one of those people, Oscar. [*After a slight pause, turns back to* Ben, *almost teasingly*] Where was I? [*Smiles at* Ben] Well, they'll convict you. But I won't care much if they don't. [*Leans forward, pleasantly*] Because by that time you'll be ruined. [*Crosses* D.L.] I shall also tell my story to Mr. Marshall, who likes me, I think, and who will not want to be involved

in your scandal. A respectable firm like Marshall & Company! The deal would be off in an hour. [*Turns to them angrily*] And you know it. Now I don't want to hear any more from any of you. *You'll do no more bargaining in this house.* I'll take my seventy-five per cent and we'll forget the story forever. That's one way of doing it, and the way I prefer. [*Crosses to settee* L.] You know me well enough to know that I don't mind taking the other way. [*Sits down on settee*]

BEN: [*After a second, slowly, at chair* L.C.] None of us have ever known you well enough, Regina.

REGINA: You're getting old, Ben. Your tricks aren't as smart as they used to be. [*There is no answer. She waits, then smiles*] All right. I take it that's settled and I get what I asked for.

OSCAR: [*Furiously to* Ben] Are you going to let her do this——?

BEN: [*Turns to look at him, slowly*] You have a suggestion?

REGINA: [*Puts her arms above her head, stretches, laughs*] No, he hasn't. All right. Now, Leo, I have forgotten that you ever saw the bonds. [*Archly, to* Ben *and* Oscar] And as long as you boys both behave yourselves, I've forgotten that we ever talked about them. You can draw up the necessary papers tomorrow.

[Ben *laughs.* Leo *stares at him, starts for door. Exits.* Oscar *moves toward door, angrily.* Regina *looks at* Ben, *nods, laughs with him. For a second,* Oscar *stands in the door, looking back at them. Then he exits*]

REGINA: You're a good loser, Ben. I like that.

BEN: [*He picks up his coat, then turns to her*] Well, I say to myself, what's the good? You and I aren't like Oscar. We're not sour people. I think that comes from a good digestion. [*Putting on coat*] Then, too, one loses today and wins tomorrow. I say to myself, years of planning and I get what I want. Then I don't get it. But I'm not discouraged. The century's turning, the world is open. Open for people like you and me. Ready for us, waiting for us. After all, this is just the beginning. [*Crosses* L. *to above chair* L.C.] There are hundreds of Hubbards sitting in rooms like this throughout the country. All their names aren't Hubbard, but they are all Hubbards and they will own this country some day. We'll get along.

REGINA: [*Smiles*] I think so.

BEN: [*Crosses to chair, picks up hat*] Then, too, I say to myself, things may change. [*Looks at* Alexandra] I agree with Alexandra. [*Looks up at landing*] What is a man in a wheel chair doing on a staircase? I ask myself that.

REGINA: [*Looks up at him*] And what do you answer?

BEN: I have no answer. [*Crosses* L. *to back of settee*] But maybe some day I will. Maybe never, but maybe some day. [*Smiles. Patting her arm*] When I do, I'll let you know. [*Crosses to* C., *toward hall*]

REGINA: [*As he turns for door*] When you do, write me. I will be in Chicago. [*Gaily*] Ah, Ben, if Papa had only left me his money.

BEN: I'll see you tomorrow. [*Crosses R. to above wheel chair*]

REGINA: Oh, yes. Certainly. You'll be sort of working for me now.

BEN: [*Turns, crosses to above sofa R., looks at* Alexandra, *smiles at her*] Alexandra, you're turning out to be a right interesting girl. [*Looks at* Regina] Well, goodnight, all. [*He exits*]

REGINA: [*Sits quietly for a second, stretches, turns to look at* Alexandra] What do you want to talk to me about, Alexandra?

ALEXANDRA: [*Slowly*] I've changed my mind. I don't want to talk. There's nothing to talk about now.

REGINA: You're acting very strange. Not like yourself. You've had a bad shock today. I know that. And you loved Papa, but you must have expected this to come someday. You knew how sick he was.

ALEXANDRA: I knew. We all knew.

REGINA: It will be good for you to get away from here. Good for me, too. Time heals most wounds, Alexandra. You're young, you shall have all the things I wanted. I'll make the world for you the way I wanted it to be for me. [*Uncomfortably*] Don't sit there staring. You've been around Birdie so much you're getting just like her.

ALEXANDRA: [*Nods*] Funny. That's what Aunt Birdie said today.

REGINA: [*Nods*] Be good for you to get away from all this.

[Addie *enters*]

ADDIE: Cal is back, Miss Regina. He says Dr. Sloan will be coming in a few minutes.

REGINA: We'll go in a few weeks. A few weeks! That means two or three Saturdays, two or three Sundays. [*Sighs*] Well, I'm very tired. I shall go to bed. I don't want any supper. Put the lights out and lock up. [Addie *moves to the piano lamp, turns it out*] You go to your room, Alexandra. Addie will bring you something hot. You look very tired. [*Rises, crosses U.C. To* Addie] Call me when Dr. Sloan gets here. I don't want to see anybody else. I don't want any condolence calls tonight. The whole town will be over.

ALEXANDRA: Mama, I'm not coming with you. I'm not going to Chicago.

REGINA: [*Turns, to her*] You're very upset, Alexandra.

ALEXANDRA: [*Quietly*] I mean what I say. With all my heart.

REGINA: [*Quietly*] We'll talk about it tomorrow. The morning will make a difference.

ALEXANDRA: It won't make any difference. And there isn't anything to talk about. I am going away from you. Because I want to. Because I know Papa would want me to.

REGINA: [*Puzzled, careful, polite*] You *know* your Papa wanted you to go away from me?

ALEXANDRA: Yes.

REGINA: [*Softly*] And if I say no?

ALEXANDRA: [*Looks at her, firmly*] Say it, Mama, say it. And see what happens.

REGINA: [*Softly, after a pause*] And if I make you stay?

ALEXANDRA: That would be foolish. It wouldn't work in the end.

REGINA: You're very serious about it, aren't you? [*Crosses to steps—up two steps*] Well, you'll change your mind in a few days.

ALEXANDRA: You only change your mind when you want to. And I won't want to.

REGINA: [*Going up steps*] Alexandra, I've come to the end of my rope. [*On 5th step*] Somewhere there has to be what I want, too. Life goes too fast. Do what you want; think what you want; go where you want. I'd like to keep you with me, but I won't make you stay. Too many people used to make me do too many things. No. [*Going up to landing*] I won't make you stay.

ALEXANDRA: You couldn't, Mama, because I want to leave here. As I've never wanted anything in my life before. Because I understand what Papa was trying to tell me. [*Pause*] All in one day: Addie said there were people who ate the earth and other people who stood around and watched them do it. And just now Uncle Ben said the same thing. Really, he said the same thing. [*Tensely*] Well, tell him for me, Mama, I'm not going to stand around and watch you do it. Tell him I'll be fighting as hard as he'll be fighting [*Rises, steps U. to table*] someplace where people don't just stand around and watch.

REGINA: Well, you have spirit, after all. I used to think you were all sugar water. We don't have to be bad friends. I don't want us to be bad friends, Alexandra. [*Starts off, stops, turns to* Alexandra] Would you like to come and talk to me, Alexandra? Would you—would you like to sleep in my room tonight?

ALEXANDRA: [*Takes a step toward her*] Are you afraid, Mama?

[Regina *does not answer, but moves slowly out of sight.* Addie *then comes to* Alexandra, *squeezes her arm with affection and pride, then starts for the other lamp, as*

THE CURTAIN FALLS]

William Saroyan

(1908– ——)

When William Saroyan made his strange debut as a playwright, in the spring of 1939, he was already well known as an original short-story writer. He had brought out five collections of stories, had expressed notably uninhibited opinions on art and life, and had announced himself as the only original genius in the land. Since the appearance of his first collection, *The Daring Young Man on the Flying Trapeze and Other Stories* (1934), moreover, a number of critics had been willing to accept him at his own high estimation.

Saroyan was born of Armenian parentage in Fresno, California, and was educated at a Fresno grammar school, where he was anything but a model pupil. He started knocking about at an early age, with scant preparation for success other than a buoyant disposition and a vast amount of curiosity about everything except intellectual matters. For a time he worked as a Western Union messenger boy, a roving occupation that evidently pleased him a good deal, for he was fond of returning to this experience in his reminiscences. He also performed odd chores in the neighborhood and worked for a while in his uncle's vineyard. Then, at the age of seventeen, he left Fresno "for some of the rest of the world," as he declared, and simply decided that he was a writer. Taking as his subjects himself and the people he knew, he began to produce generally disorganized but surprisingly fresh stories. *The Daring Young Man on the Flying Trapeze,* a tale of a young writer's starvation-induced delirium, was published in the February 1934 issue of *Story* magazine and received instant acclaim. Since this was all the encouragement Saroyan needed, he proceeded to turn out enough stories at lightning speed to have a volume ready for publication later that year.

For Saroyan, who had not studied writing but had read voluminously and indiscriminately, literary composition (and later on, playwriting) held no mysteries. His rules, the first of which he claimed to have discovered at the age of eleven, were: "Do not pay attention to the rules other people make. . . . Forget everybody who ever wrote anything. . . . Learn to typewrite, so you can turn out stories as fast as Zane Grey." As for playwriting, his considered advice to the young was not to take George Pierce Baker's course at Harvard but to look at the world, to write a great deal without ever being careful, and never to try to achieve a style, "because style is something which is there from the beginning and doesn't have to be achieved." A playwright's sole aim should be "to uncover the magnificent and unending drama in the most ordinary environments, events, and people."

The theatre had attracted Saroyan from his earliest years, but it was the theatricality of the dramatic arts, the showmanship and the excitements of the stage, that absorbed him. "I take pride," he wrote later, "in my having sneaked into every theatre in my home town . . . ; into every circus that came to town; into the County Fairs; into the Summer stock company shows." Vaudeville fascinated him especially, and it had a decisive influence on his playwriting. What effort he made to acquaint himself with the literary drama left him unimpressed. *Lady Windermere's Fan,* read when he was fourteen, had worldly and brilliant style, but "didn't seem right" for him. His world, he realized early, "was a world of plain and poor people, broken-down houses, casualness, good health, poverty, and uproarious laughter." Copies of Ibsen's *Ghosts* and of other plays by "that great and magnificently dull dramatist" were apparently available to the boy. But Ibsen drama had no effect on him, because it was "too cagey, crafty, and calculating." He liked vaudeville much better. It was "easygoing and didn't try for too much and as a result very often achieved things Ibsen himself couldn't achieve. Vaudeville was American, too, which made a great difference."

Like vaudeville, Saroyan's plays were briskly spontaneous, disjointed, and improvisatory. He did not actually cultivate "surrealism." A freedom from the reins of practical reality and normal logic characterized most of his work; a madcap fancy, combined with indefinable intimations, ran riot in it; and the plays, composed at incredible speed, sometimes gave the impression of having come from their author almost automatically. (The French surrealists, we may recall, stressed "automatic writing.") In these respects, Saroyan's plays can be called "surrealist" and they are, indeed, the best representation of this modern style in English-language drama. But Saroyan's writing was native and impulsive rather than borrowed and learned; it was definitely not patterned after the subjective style of the French cult. Vaudeville exerted the most considerable influence in his work. For Saroyan, his kind of sketchy writing was "realistic," in the sense that he did not contrive it but set down what he saw or impulsively felt.

Saroyan's first play was *Subway Circus* (1935); it was a collection of scenes conveying people's daydreams, connected only by the circumstance that the characters happen to be riding in the subway.

Next, in 1938, he dramatized his short story *The Man with the Heart in the Highlands* for William Kozlenko's *One-Act Play Magazine,* under the title *My Heart's in the Highlands.* Kozlenko scheduled it for production by his short-lived One-Act Play Theatre. Subsequently, the author enlarged the then very short play and the Group Theatre produced it on April 13, 1939, with an excellent score by Paul Bowles, an enchanting semisurrealistic setting by Herbert Andrews, and superb direction by Robert Lewis. The newspaper critics were violently divided in their opinion, but Saroyan found powerful champions in Brooks Atkinson, John Mason Brown, and George Jean Nathan. The play, which had originally been scheduled by the Group for four experimental performances, was thereupon taken over by the Theatre Guild and presented to its membership.

Encouraged to continue playwriting, Saroyan completed his first full-length play, *The Time of Your Life,* in six days of furious writing. It was produced in the fall of 1939 by Eddie Dowling and the Theatre Guild, ran the greater part of the season in New York, toured extensively, and won both the Drama Critics Circle award and the Pulitzer Prize. In the spring of 1940, Dowling and the Theatre Guild produced a second full-length play by Saroyan, *Love's Old Sweet Song,* a somewhat more conventional drama that proved less successful. In 1941, using the income he had earned from *The Time of Your Life,* Saroyan acted as his own producer, as well as director, and gave New York the strangely beautiful, if somewhat chaotic, fantasy *The Beautiful People.* In 1941 too, the National Theatre Conference released his wildly fantastic *Jim Dandy* to sixty of its college and community-theatre affiliates. Eddie Dowling used the remarkable one-act play *Hello, Out There* as a curtain raiser in 1942, and in 1943 George Abbott staged Saroyan's travesty on Hollywood, *Get Away Old Man,* written out of the author's experience on the Metro-Goldwyn-Mayer lot. A number of other, rather loosely written and confusing plays of his also managed to be produced. Among these were *Sweeney in the Trees,* which the author described as "anything you like, whatever you please," and *Across the Board on Tomorrow Morning,* a mystical piece which he arranged to have played twice in the same evening at the Pasadena Playhouse, for any playgoers who wanted to see it a second time!

After 1943, Saroyan plays had few productions, none of them on Broadway; but the prolific writer continued to turn out script after script. Two of these (*Afton Water* and the war play *A Decent Birth, a Happy Funeral*) were singularly touching, although faulty. A few plays written after the war, especially the depressing *Don't Go Away Mad,* continued to reveal an original talent, although they showed plainly that their author had never bothered to learn the craft of playwriting. War service as a private had exerted an unfortunate effect on Saroyan's individualistic personality, inspiring a bitter novel, *The Adventures of Wesley Jackson* (he had previously written a charming autobiography, *My Name Is Aram,* and a loose novel, *The Human Comedy*), and depressing his playwriting, which had depended hitherto on buoyancy for success in the theatre.

My Heart's in the Highlands is the simplest and perhaps the best example of Saroyan's style of playwriting. It is free from the excesses of much of his later work. Moreover, it retains an undivided effect, whereas some of the best of his other plays, such as *The Time of Your Life* and *Love's Old Sweet Song,* demand constant adjustment on our part to an alternation of probabilities and improbabilities. Except for a few maladroit passages, *My Heart's in the Highlands* is written in a single vein as a work of inviolable innocence. Although the author's innocence does not exclude the realities of poverty and of old age, the play is a paean to man's impulsive love of beauty, to kindliness and dignity among the obscure, and to the wondering faith that children reveal. The play is sentimental without apology and optimistic without reason—attributes which, incidentally, Saroyan would claim for the greater part of the human race. "The fable of a tenth-rate poet whose protective little boy worships him as a genius," as George Jean Nathan called it, appeals more readily to the heart than to the mind. "There is more human pressure per square foot in it," another reviewer declared, "than in acres of sensible drama."

Perhaps the entire question of sense or nonsense in *My Heart's in the Highlands* is, indeed, altogether irrelevant beside Saroyan's feeling for people and for sheer existence. The play expresses a diffuse Whitmanesque spirit, a poetic caprice that requires no more explanations than does the taste of food and drink. Nothing and everything is in this play. And this is also true of the writing, which has no particular distinction other than that of being alive. The thoughts uttered by the characters are less important than those they do not or are unable to put into words. For all its simplicity, *My Heart's in the Highlands* therefore demands considerable empathy and theatrical imagination, and argument about it leads nowhere. We like the play insofar as we experience it; we dislike it insofar as we do not experience it.

BIBLIOGRAPHY: Brooks Atkinson, *Broadway Scrapbook* (pp. 115–120, 129–132), 1947; Harold Clurman, *The Fervent Years* (pp. 250–252, 263–264), 1945; Edmond M. Gagey, *Revolution in the American Drama* (pp. 111–119), 1947; George Jean Nathan, *The Entertainment of a Nation* (pp. 42–54), 1942; William Saroyan, Introductions to *Three Plays* (see also quotations of critical comment), 1940; Stark Young, *Immortal Shadows* (pp. 215–217), 1948.

MY HEART'S IN THE HIGHLANDS

By William Saroyan

THE PEOPLE

JOHNNY
HIS FATHER, BEN ALEXANDER, *the poet*
JOHNNY'S GRANDMOTHER
JASPER MAC GREGOR, *the man with the heart in the highlands*
MR. KOSAK, *the grocer*

ESTHER, *his beautiful daughter*
RUFE APLEY, *the carpenter*
PHILIP CARMICHAEL, *the young man from the Old People's Home*
HENRY, *the morning paper route carrier*
MR. WILEY, *the mailman*

MR. CUNNINGHAM, *the real estate agent*
THE YOUNG HUSBAND AND WIFE, AND THEIR BABY
GOOD FRIENDS AND NEIGHBORS
A DOG

THE PLACE

A house on San Benito Avenue in Fresno, California. Mr. Kosak's grocery store.

THE TIME

August and November, 1914

An old white, broken-down, frame house with a front porch, on San Benito Avenue in Fresno, California. There are no other houses near by, only a desolation of bleak land and red sky. It is late afternoon of a day in August, 1914. The evening sun is going down.

Johnny, aged nine, but essentially ageless, is sitting, dynamic and acrobatic, on the steps of the porch, dead to the world and deep in thought of a high and holy order. Far away a train whistle cries mournfully. He listens eagerly, cocking his head on one side like a chicken, trying to understand the meaning of the cry and at the same time to figure out everything. He doesn't quite make it and when the cry ends he stops being eager. A fourteen-year-old boy on a bicycle, eating an ice-cream cone and carrying newspaper bags, goes by on the sidewalk in silence, oblivious of the weight on his shoulders and of the contraption on which he is seated, because of the delight and glory of ice cream in the world. Johnny leaps to his feet and waves to the boy, smiling in a big humanitarian way, but is ignored. He sits down again and listens to a small overjoyed but angry bird. After making a brief forceful speech of no meaning, the bird flies away.

From inside the house is heard the somber voice of Johnny's Father *reciting poetry of his own composition.*

JOHNNY'S FATHER: The long silent day journeys through the sore solemn heart, and——[*Bitter pause*] And——[*Quickly*] The long silent day journeys

through the sore solemn heart, and——[*Pause*] No. [*He roars and begins again*] Crippled and weeping, time stumbles through the lone lorn heart.

[*A table or chair is pushed over in anger. A groan. Silence. The boy listens. He gets up and tries to stand on his head, fails, tries again, fails, tries again, and succeeds. While he is standing on his head he hears the loveliest and most amazing music in the world: a solo on a bugle. The music is "My Heart's in the Highlands." The bugler, a very old man, finishes the solo in front of the house. The boy leaps to his feet and runs up to the old man, amazed, delighted and bewildered*]

JOHNNY: I sure would like to hear you play another song.

MAC GREGOR: Young man, could you get a glass of water for an old man whose heart is not here, but in the highlands?

JOHNNY: What highlands?

MAC GREGOR: The Scotch Highlands. Could you?

JOHNNY: What's your heart doing in the Scotch Highlands?

MAC GREGOR: My heart's grieving there. Could you get me a glass of cool water?

JOHNNY: Where's your *mother*?

MAC GREGOR: [*Inventing for the boy*] My mother's in Tulsa, Oklahoma, but her heart isn't.

JOHNNY: Where *is* her heart?

MAC GREGOR: [*Loud*] In the Scotch Highlands. [*Soft*] I'm very thirsty, young man.

1018

JOHNNY: How come the members of your family are always leaving their hearts in the highlands?

MAC GREGOR: [*In the Shakespearean manner*] That's the way we are. Here today and gone tomorrow.

JOHNNY: [*Aside*] Here today and gone tomorrow? [*To MacGregor*] How do you figure?

MAC GREGOR: [*The philosopher*] Alive one minute and dead the next.

JOHNNY: Where's your *mother's* mother?

MAC GREGOR: [*Inventing, but angry*] She's up in Vermont, in a little town called White River, but her heart isn't.

JOHNNY: Is her poor old withered heart in the highlands, too?

MAC GREGOR: Right smack in the highlands. Son, I'm dying of thirst.

[Johnny's Father *comes out of the house in a fury, as if he has just broken out of a cage, and roars at the boy like a tiger that has just awakened from evil dreams*]

JOHNNY'S FATHER: Johnny, get the hell away from that poor old man. Get him a pitcher of water before he falls down and dies. Where the hell are your manners?

JOHNNY: Can't a fellow try to find out something from a traveler once in a while?

JOHNNY'S FATHER: Get the old man some water, God damn it. Don't stand there like a dummy. Get him a drink, I tell you, before he falls down and dies.

JOHNNY: *You* get him a drink. You're not doing anything.

JOHNNY'S FATHER: Not doing anything? Why, Johnny, you *know* I'm getting a new poem arranged in my mind.

JOHNNY: How do you figure I know? You're just standing there on the porch with your sleeves rolled up.

JOHNNY'S FATHER: [*Angry*] Well, you ought to know. [*Roaring*] You're my son. [*Amazed*] If you shouldn't know, who should?

MAC GREGOR: [*Blithely*] Good afternoon. Your son has been telling me how clear and cool the climate is in these parts.

JOHNNY: [*Bewildered, but eager to learn. Aside*] Holy Moses, I didn't say anything about the climate. Where's he getting that stuff from?

JOHNNY'S FATHER: [*The aristocrat, grandly*] How do you do? Won't you come in for a little rest? We should be honored to have you at our table for a bit of supper.

MAC GREGOR: [*The realist*] Sir, I'm starving. I shall come right in. [*He moves to enter the house.* Johnny *gets in his way, looking up at him*]

JOHNNY: [*The romantic*] Can you play "Drink to Me Only with Thine Eyes"? I sure would like to hear you play that song on the bugle. That song is my favorite. I guess I like that song better than any song in the world.

MAC GREGOR: [*The disillusioned*] Son, when you get to be my age you'll know songs aren't important, bread's the thing.

JOHNNY: [*The faithful*] Anyway, I sure would like to hear you play that song.

[MacGregor *goes up on the porch and shakes hands with* Johnny's Father]

MAC GREGOR: [*History in the making*] My name is Jasper MacGregor. I am an actor.

JOHNNY'S FATHER: [*Delighted*] I'm mighty glad to make your acquaintance. [*The imperial giver of orders*] Johnny, get Mr. MacGregor a pitcher of water. [Johnny *runs around the house*]

MAC GREGOR: [*Dying of thirst, sighing, but telling the truth nevertheless*] Charming boy.

JOHNNY'S FATHER: [*Ordinary statement*] Like myself, he's a genius.

MAC GREGOR: [*Roaring from fatigue*] I suppose you're very fond of him?

JOHNNY'S FATHER: [*Delighted to be alive*] We are the same person— He is the heart of my youth— Have you noticed his eagerness?

MAC GREGOR: [*Delighted to be still alive*] I should say I have.

JOHNNY'S FATHER: [*Proudly and with anger*] I'm the same way myself, although older and less brilliant.

[Johnny, *running, returns with a pitcher of water which he hands to the old man. The old man throws back his shoulders, lifts his head, his nostrils expand, he snorts, his eyes widen, he lifts the pitcher of water to his lips and drinks all the water in one long swig, while* Johnny *and his* Father *watch with amazement and admiration. The old man breathes deeply, looks around at the landscape and up at the sky and to the end of San Benito Avenue where the evening sun is going down*]

MAC GREGOR: [*Reflection, sadly; weariness, softly*] I reckon I'm five thousand miles from home. Do you think we could eat a little bread and cheese to keep my body and spirit together?

JOHNNY'S FATHER: [*Napoleon*] Johnny, run down to the grocer's and get a loaf of French bread and a pound of cheese.

JOHNNY: [*The voice of doom*] Give me the money.

JOHNNY'S FATHER: [*Statistics, poetic, with pride*] You know I haven't got a *penny*, Johnny. Tell Mr. Kosak to give us credit.

JOHNNY: [*The unwilling dutiful son*] He won't do it. He's tired of giving us credit. He says we don't work and never pay our bills. We owe him forty cents.

JOHNNY'S FATHER: [*Impatient, irritated*] Go on down there and argue it out with him. You know that's your job.

JOHNNY: [*Defending his rights*] He won't listen to reason. He says he doesn't know anything about anything. All he wants is the forty cents.

JOHNNY'S FATHER: [*Napoleon*] Go on down there and make him give you a loaf of bread and a pound of cheese. [*Gently, pleading, flattering*] You can do it, Johnny.

MAC GREGOR: [*Impatient and hungry*] Go on down there and tell Mr. Kosak to give you a loaf of bread and a pound of cheese, son.

JOHNNY'S FATHER: Go ahead, Johnny. You've never failed to leave that store with something or other. You'll be back here in ten minutes with food fit for a King. [*For his own amusement*] Or at least a Duke of some kind.

JOHNNY: I don't know. Mr. Kosak says we are trying to give him the merry run-around. He wants to know what kind of work you do.

JOHNNY'S FATHER: [*Furiously*] Well, go ahead and tell him. [*The hero*] I have nothing to conceal. I write poetry, night and day.

JOHNNY: [*Giving in at last*] All right, but I don't think he'll be impressed. He says you never go out and look for work. He says you're lazy and no good.

JOHNNY'S FATHER: [*Roaring*] You go down there and tell that great-hearted Slovak he's crazy, Johnny. You go on down there and tell that splendid scholar and gentleman your father is one of the greatest unknown poets living.

JOHNNY: He won't care, Pa, but I'll go. I'll do my best. Haven't we got anything in the house?

JOHNNY'S FATHER: [*Mock-tragically, roaring*] Only popcorn. [*To* MacGregor] We've been eating popcorn four days in a row now. Johnny, you've got to get bread and cheese if you expect me to finish that long poem.

JOHNNY: I'll do my best.

MAC GREGOR: Don't take too long, Johnny. I'm five thousand miles from home.

JOHNNY: I'll run all the way, Mr. MacGregor.

JOHNNY'S FATHER: [*For the amusement of the good Lord*] If you find any money on the way, remember we go fifty-fifty.

JOHNNY: [*Delighted with the comedy*] All right, Pa. [Johnny *runs down the street*]

The inside of Mr. Kosak's Grocery Store. Mr. Kosak *is sleeping on his folded arms when* Johnny *runs into the store.* Mr. Kosak *lifts his head. He is a fine, gentle, serious man with a big, blond, old-fashioned mustache. He shakes his head trying to waken.*

JOHNNY: [*The diplomat, as it were*] Mr. Kosak, if you were in China and didn't have a friend in the world and no money, you'd expect somebody over there to give you a pound of rice, wouldn't you?

MR. KOSAK: What do you want?

JOHNNY: I just want to talk a little. You'd expect some member of the Aryan race to help you out a little, wouldn't you, Mr. Kosak?

MR. KOSAK: How much money you got?

JOHNNY: It's not a question of money, Mr. Kosak. I'm talking about being in China.

MR. KOSAK: I don't know nothing about nothing.

JOHNNY: How would you feel in China that way, Mr. Kosak?

MR. KOSAK: I don't know, Johnny. What would I be doing in China?

JOHNNY: Well, you'd be visiting there. You'd be hungry and five thousand miles from home and not a friend in the world. You wouldn't expect *everybody* to turn you away without even a pound of rice, would you, Mr. Kosak?

MR. KOSAK: I guess not, but you ain't in China, Johnny, and neither is your Pa. You or your Pa's got to go out and work sometime in your lives, so you might as well start now. I ain't going to give you no more groceries on credit because I know you won't pay me.

JOHNNY: Mr. Kosak, you misunderstand me. This is 1914, not 1913. I'm not talking about a few groceries. I'm talking about all them heathen people around you in China and you hungry and dying.

MR. KOSAK: This ain't China. You got to go out and make your living in this country. Everybody's got to work in America.

JOHNNY: Mr. Kosak, suppose it was a loaf of bread and a pound of cheese you needed to keep you alive in the world, would you hesitate to ask a Christian *missionary* for these things?

MR. KOSAK: Yes, I would. I would be ashamed to ask.

JOHNNY: Even if you knew you would give him back *two* loaves of bread and *two* pounds of cheese instead of one loaf and one pound? Even then, Mr. Kosak?

MR. KOSAK: Even then.

JOHNNY: Don't be that way, Mr. Kosak. That's defeatist talk, and you know it. Why, the only thing that would happen to you would be death. You'd *die* out there in China, Mr. Kosak.

MR. KOSAK: I wouldn't care if I would. You and your Pa have got to pay for bread and cheese. Why don't your Pa go out and get a job?

JOHNNY: [*Swift abandonment of the intellectual attack for the human one*] Mr. Kosak, how are you?

MR. KOSAK: I'm fine, Johnny. How are *you*?

JOHNNY: Couldn't be better, Mr. Kosak. How are the children?

MR. KOSAK: They're all fine, Johnny. Stephan is beginning to walk now.

JOHNNY: That's great. How's Angela?

MR. KOSAK: Angela's beginning to sing. How's your Grandmother?

JOHNNY: She's fine. She's beginning to sing too. She says she'd rather be an opera singer than Queen of England. How's your wife Martha, Mr. Kosak?

MR. KOSAK: Oh, swell.

JOHNNY: I can't tell you how glad I am to hear that everything is fine at your house. I know Stephan is going to be a great man some day.

MR. KOSAK: I hope so. I'm going to send him to high school and see that he gets every chance I didn't get. I don't want *him* to have trouble all *his* life, too.

JOHNNY: I have great faith in Stephan, Mr. Kosak.

MR. KOSAK: What do you want, Johnny, and how much money you got?

JOHNNY: Mr. Kosak, you know I didn't come here to buy anything. You know I enjoy a quiet philosophical chat with you every now and then. [*Quickly, pleading*] Let me have a loaf of French bread and a pound of cheese.

MR. KOSAK: You got to pay cash, Johnny.

JOHNNY: And Esther? How is your beautiful daughter Esther?

MR. KOSAK: She's all right, Johnny, but you got to pay cash. You and your Pa are the worst citizens in this county.

JOHNNY: I'm glad Esther's all right, Mr. Kosak. Jasper MacGregor is visiting our house. He's a great actor.

MR. KOSAK: Never heard of him.

JOHNNY: And a bottle of beer for Mr. MacGregor.

MR. KOSAK: I can't give you a bottle of beer.

JOHNNY: Sure, you can.

MR. KOSAK: I can't. I'll let you have one loaf of French bread and a pound of cheese, but that's all. What kind of work does your Pa do *when* he works, Johnny?

JOHNNY: My father writes poetry, Mr. Kosak. That's the only work my father does. He's one of the greatest writers of poetry in the world.

MR. KOSAK: When does he get any money?

JOHNNY: He *never* gets any money. You can't have your cake and eat it too.

MR. KOSAK: I don't like that kind of work. Why doesn't your Pa work like everybody else, Johnny?

JOHNNY: He works harder than everybody else. My father works twice as hard as the average man.

[*Mr. Kosak hands Johnny a loaf of French bread and a pound of cheese*]

MR. KOSAK: Well, that's fifty-five cents you owe me, Johnny. I'll let you have some stuff this time, but never again.

JOHNNY: [*At the door*] Tell Esther I love her. [*Johnny runs out of the store. Mr. Kosak swings at a fly, misses, swings again, misses, and, objecting to the world in this manner, he chases the fly all around the store, swinging with all his might*]

The house. Johnny's Father and the old man are looking down the street to see if Johnny is coming back with food. His Grandmother is standing on the porch also eager to know if there is to be food.

MAC GREGOR: I think he's got some food with him.

JOHNNY'S FATHER: [*With pride*] Of course he has. [*He waves at the old lady on the porch who runs into the house to set the table.* Johnny *runs to his* Father *and* MacGregor] I knew you'd do it.

MAC GREGOR: So did I.

JOHNNY: He says we got to pay him fifty-five cents. He says he's not going to give us any more stuff on credit.

JOHNNY'S FATHER: That's *his* opinion. What did you talk about?

JOHNNY: First I talked about being hungry and at death's door in China. Then I inquired about the family.

JOHNNY'S FATHER: How is everyone?

JOHNNY: Fine. I didn't find any money, though. Not even a *penny*.

JOHNNY'S FATHER: Oh, that's all right. Money isn't everything. [*They go into the house*]

The living room. They are all at the table after supper. MacGregor *finds crumbs here and there which he places delicately in his mouth. He looks around the room to see if there isn't something more to eat.*

MAC GREGOR: That green can up there, Johnny. What's in there?

JOHNNY: Marbles.

MAC GREGOR: That cupboard, Johnny. Anything *edible* in there?

JOHNNY: Crickets.

MAC GREGOR: That big jar in the corner there, Johnny. What's delectable in there?

JOHNNY: I got a gopher snake in that jar.

MAC GREGOR: Well, I could go for a bit of boiled gopher snake in a big way, Johnny.

JOHNNY: [*Defiantly, protector of animals*] Nothing doing, Mr. MacGregor.

MAC GREGOR: Why not, Johnny? Why the hell not, son? I hear of fine Borneo natives eating snakes and grasshoppers. You haven't got a half dozen fat grasshoppers around, have you, Johnny?

JOHNNY: Only four.

MAC GREGOR: Well, trot them out, son, and after we've had our fill, I'll play "Drink to Me Only with Thine Eyes" for you. I'm mighty hungry, Johnny.

JOHNNY: So am I, but I don't want anybody killing them innocent animals. They got rights the same as anybody else.

JOHNNY'S FATHER: [*To MacGregor*] How about a little music? I think the boy would be delighted.

JOHNNY: [*Leaping to his feet*] I sure would, Mr. MacGregor.

MAC GREGOR: All right, Johnny. Bread. Bread. My God, how savagely it quarrels with the heart. [*MacGregor gets up and begins to blow into the bugle. He blows louder and more beautifully and mournfully than anybody ever blew into a bugle. Eighteen Neighbors gather in front of the house and cheer when he finishes the solo: "Drink to Me Only with Thine Eyes"*]

JOHNNY'S FATHER: [*Delighted, for amusement*] I want you to meet your public. [*They go out on the porch*]

The house. The crowd is looking up at Johnny's Father, MacGregor *and* Johnny.

JOHNNY'S FATHER: Good neighbors, and friends, I want you to meet Jasper MacGregor, the greatest Shakespearean actor of our day. [*Pause*] I believe.

MAC GREGOR: [*The actor*] I remember my first appearance in London in 1851 as if it was yesterday. I was a boy of fourteen from the slums of Glasgow. My first part was a courier in a play, the title of which I have unfortunately forgotten. I had no lines to speak, but moved about a good deal, running from officer to officer, and from lover to his beloved, and back again, over and over again.

RUFE APLEY, THE CARPENTER: [*Regretfully interrupting the great speech*] How about another song, Mr. MacGregor?

MAC GREGOR: Have you got an egg at your house?

RUFE APLEY: I sure have. I've got a *dozen* eggs at my house.

MAC GREGOR: Would it be convenient for you to go and get one of them dozen eggs? When you return I'll play a song that will make your heart leap with joy and grief.

RUFE APLEY: I'm on my way already. [*He goes*]

MAC GREGOR: [*To the crowd*] My friends, I should be delighted to play another song for you on this golden-throated bugle, but time and distance from home find me weary. If you will be so good as to go, each of you to his home, and return in a moment with some morsel of food, I shall be proud to gather my spirit together and play a song I know will change the course of each of your lives, and change it, mind you, for the better. [*The people go. The last to go is Esther Kosak, who hears the speech out, then runs. MacGregor, Johnny's father, and Johnny sit on the steps and remain in silence, and one by one the people return, bringing food to MacGregor: an egg, a sausage, a dozen green onions, two kinds of cheese, butter, two kinds of bread, boiled potatoes, fresh tomatoes, a melon, tea, and many other good things to eat*] Thank you, my friends, thank you. [*He stands solemnly, waiting for absolute silence, straightens himself, looks about him furiously, lifts the bugle to his lips and is irritated by the swift and noisy return of Esther Kosak, bringing an eggplant. When there is silence, he plays "My Heart's in the Highlands, My Heart is not Here." The* People *weep, kneel, sing the chorus, and go away.* MacGregor *turns to the father and son. Grandly*] Sir, if it is all the same to you I should like to dwell in your house for a long time to come.

JOHNNY'S FATHER: [*Delighted and amazed*] Sir, my house is your house. [*They go into the house*]

The living room. Eighteen days later, MacGregor *is lying on the floor, face up, asleep.* Johnny *is walking about quietly in the room, looking at everybody. His* Father *is at the table, writing poetry. His Grandmother is sitting in the rocking chair, rocking. There is a knock on the door. Everybody but MacGregor jumps up and runs to it.*

JOHNNY'S FATHER: [*At the door*] Yes?

YOUNG MAN: I am looking for Jasper MacGregor, the actor.

JOHNNY'S FATHER: What do you want?

JOHNNY: Well, ask him in anyway, Pa.

JOHNNY'S FATHER: Yes, of course. Excuse me. Won't you please come in? [*The* Young Man *enters*]

YOUNG MAN: My name is Philip Carmichael. I am from the Old People's Home. I have been sent to bring Mr. MacGregor home.

MAC GREGOR: [*Wakening and sitting up*] Home? Did someone mention home? [*Roaring*] I'm five thousand miles from home, always have been, and always will be. Who is this young man?

YOUNG MAN: Mr. MacGregor, I'm Philip Carmichael, from the Old People's Home. They've sent me to bring you back. We are putting on our annual show in two weeks and need you for the leading role.

MAC GREGOR: [*Getting up with the help of* Johnny's Father *and* Johnny] What kind of a part is it? I can't be playing young adventurers any longer.

YOUNG MAN: The part is King Lear, Mr. MacGregor. It is perfect for you.

MAC GREGOR: [*The actor, with a job again*] Goodby, my beloved friends. [*He returns from the porch*] In all the hours of my life, in all the places I have visited, never and nowhere have I had the honor and pleasure to commune with souls loftier, purer, or more delightful than yours. Good-by. [*The Old Man and the Young Man leave the house. There is a moment of silence, full of regret and loneliness*]

JOHNNY'S FATHER: [*Hungry, loudly*] Johnny, go on down to Mr. Kosak's store and get a little something to eat. I know you can do it, Johnny. Get ANYTHING.

JOHNNY: [*Hungry, loudly, and angry*] Mr. Kosak wants eighty-five cents. He won't give us anything more without money.

JOHNNY'S FATHER: Go on down there, Johnny. You know you can get that fine Slovak gentleman to give us a little something to eat.

JOHNNY: [*With despair*] Aw, Pa.

JOHNNY'S FATHER: [*Amazed, roaring*] What? You, my son, in a mood like that. Come on. I fought the world this way before you were born. After you were born we fought it together, and we're going to go on fighting it. The people love poetry but don't know it, that's all. Nothing is going to stop us, Johnny. Go on down there now and get us something to eat.

JOHNNY: All right, Pa. I'll do my best. [*He runs to the door*]

*The house. It now has a large sign: "For Rent."
It is a moment before daybreak of a day early in
November, 1914. There is a suggestion of Winter
coming. High in the sky a flock of geese flying south
make their call. Johnny is sitting on the steps of the
front porch with his chin in his hand. He hears the
geese, listening carefully, leaps to his feet and looks
into the sky for them. The sound decreases, then
ends. Johnny goes back to the steps of the porch
and sits down. As the sun rises, a big solemn smile
comes over his face. He looks out of the corner of
his eye at the morning's light as if it were a quiet
friend with whom he was on terms of perfect understanding. As the light increases, this play between
Johnny and the sun grows, like a theme of music,
bringing him to his feet, turning his face to the light.
He lifts his arms, and very solemnly begins turning
somersaults. He then runs around the house lickety-
split and returns on the other side, almost dancing.*

*A freight train goes by not far enough away not to
make the earth tremble. The light of morning increases.*

*A newspaper route carrier arrives on foot, whis-
tling. He is the typical small-town morning route
carrier: about thirteen years old. He is in that somber
and dignified state which comes over men who have
done their work. His paper bags are empty. Night is
over. His daily wage has been earned. The papers
have been left at the doors of the readers. Another
day has come to the world. He has walked two hours
through dark streets to morning. The song he is
whistling is soft and full of understanding. It is a
song of his own composition, a morning song.*

JOHNNY: [*Running down the steps*] Hello.

THE BOY: [*Stopping*] Hello.

JOHNNY: What was that song?

THE BOY: What song?

JOHNNY: That you were whistling?

THE BOY: Was I whistling?

JOHNNY: Sure. Didn't you know?

THE BOY: I guess I'm always whistling.

JOHNNY: What was it?

THE BOY: I don't know.

JOHNNY: I wish I could whistle.

THE BOY: Anybody can whistle.

JOHNNY: I can't. How do you do it?

THE BOY: There's no *how* to it. You just whistle.

JOHNNY: How?

THE BOY: Like this. [*He whistles a moment, obviously improvising a tour de force of technique*]

JOHNNY: [*With admiration*] I wish I could do that.

THE BOY: [*Pleased and eager to make an even
better impression*] That was nothing. Listen to this.
[*He gives the melody a sort of counterpoint, two
tones, and a bit of syncopation*]

JOHNNY: Can't you teach me to do that?

THE BOY: You can't teach whistling. You just do
it. This is another way. [*He whistles a little melody,
the loud newsboy's style, but keeps it soft*]

JOHNNY: [*Trying to whistle*] Like that?

THE BOY: That's the way to start. Keep it up and
after a while your mouth'll take the right shape and
you'll be whistling before you know it.

JOHNNY: Honest?

THE BOY: Sure.

JOHNNY: Is your mother dead?

THE BOY: How did you know?

JOHNNY: My mother's dead too.

THE BOY: Yeah?

JOHNNY: [*With a sigh*] Yeah. She died.

THE BOY: I don't remember my mother. Do you
remember your mother?

JOHNNY: I don't exactly remember her. Sometimes I dream about her, though.

THE BOY: I used to, too.

JOHNNY: Don't you any more?

THE BOY: [*Disillusioned*] Naaaah. What good does
that do you?

JOHNNY: My mother sure is beautiful.

THE BOY: Yeah, I know. I remember. You got a
father?

JOHNNY: [*Proudly*] Oh, sure. He's in the house
now, sleeping.

THE BOY: My *father's* dead, too.

JOHNNY: Your *father*, too?

THE BOY: [*Matter-of-fact*] Yeah. [*They begin
bouncing an old tennis ball back and forth to each
other*]

JOHNNY: Haven't you got anybody?

THE BOY: I got an aunt, but she ain't really my
aunt. I was brought up in an orphanage. I'm adopted.

JOHNNY: What's an orphanage?

THE BOY: That's a kind of a place where kids that
ain't got any mothers and fathers live until somebody adopts them.

JOHNNY: What do you mean, adopts?

THE BOY: Somebody who wants a boy or girl
comes to the orphanage and looks everybody over
and goes away with whoever they like. If they pick
you, you go and stay with them.

JOHNNY: Do you like that?

THE BOY: It's all right. [*The Boy puts away the
ball*]

JOHNNY: What's your name?

THE BOY: Henry. What's yours?

JOHNNY: Johnny.

THE BOY: Do you want a paper? There's a War
in Europe.

JOHNNY: I haven't got any money. We aren't rich.
We don't work. My father writes poetry.

THE BOY: [*Giving Johnny the extra*] Oh, that's all
right. Don't you *ever* have any money?

JOHNNY: Sometimes. I found a quarter once. It
was lying on the sidewalk, right in front of me.
Once my father got a check for ten dollars from
New York, too. We bought a chicken and a lot of

stamps and paper and envelopes. The chicken wouldn't lay eggs, though, so my grandmother killed it and cooked it for us. Did you ever eat chicken?

THE BOY: Sure. I guess I've eaten chicken six or seven times.

JOHNNY: What are you going to do when you grow up?

THE BOY: Shucks. I don't know. I don't know what I'll do.

JOHNNY: [*Proudly*] I'm going to be a poet, like my father. He said so.

THE BOY: I guess I'll carry a paper route for a while. [*He moves to go*] Well. So long.

JOHNNY: Won't you come here again?

THE BOY: I go by here every morning about this time. I ain't never seen you up before, though.

JOHNNY: [*Smiling*] I had a dream and then I woke up and didn't want to sleep any more. I wanted to get up and come out here. I saw my mother.

THE BOY: Maybe I'll see you again some morning when you can't sleep.

JOHNNY: I hope so. So long.

THE BOY: So long. Just keep trying and you'll be whistling before you know it.

JOHNNY: Thanks. [*The Boy goes, whistling. Johnny tosses the folded paper up on the porch, and sits down again on the steps. His Grandmother comes out on the porch with a broom and begins to sweep*]

JOHNNY'S GRANDMOTHER: [*In Armenian, which is the only language she speaks, with the exception of Turkish, Kurdish, and a little Arabic, which nobody around seems to know*] How are you, my heart?

JOHNNY: [*Who understands Armenian, but hardly ever speaks it; in English*] Fine.

JOHNNY'S GRANDMOTHER: How's your Papa?

JOHNNY: I don't know. [*Calling loudly to his Father*] Oh, Pa. How are you? [*Pause. Louder*] Pa. [*Pause. Silence*] I guess he's sleeping.

JOHNNY'S GRANDMOTHER: Is there any money?

JOHNNY: Money? [*Shaking his head*] No.

JOHNNY'S FATHER: [*From inside the house*] Johnny?

JOHNNY: [*Jumping to his feet*] Pa?

JOHNNY'S FATHER: Did you call?

JOHNNY: Yeah. How are you?

JOHNNY'S FATHER: Fine, Johnny. How are you?

JOHNNY: Fine, Pa.

JOHNNY'S FATHER: Is that all you woke me up for?

JOHNNY: [*To his Grandmother*] He's fine. [*Louder to his Father*] The old lady wanted to know.

JOHNNY'S FATHER: [*In Armenian, to the old lady*] Good night, Ma. [*To Johnny, in English*] What do you mean, old? She's not so old.

JOHNNY: I don't mean old. You know what I mean.

[*Johnny's Father comes out on the porch, buttoning his shirt, nods to the old lady, looks out of the corner of his eye at the sun, exactly the same way Johnny did, smiling the same way, stretches all over, faces the sun, leaps down the steps and turns one somersault, not so good. The somersault leaves him flat on his back*]

JOHNNY: You ought to get a little more exercise, Pa. You're always sitting down.

JOHNNY'S FATHER: [*On his back*] Johnny, your father is a great poet. I may not be able to turn a somersault as well as you, but if you want to know what kind of an athlete I am, just read the poetry I wrote yesterday.

JOHNNY: Is it really good, Pa?

JOHNNY'S FATHER: Good? [*He leaps to his feet, like an acrobat*] It's great. I'm going to send it to *The Atlantic Monthly*, too.

JOHNNY: Oh, I forgot, Pa. There's a paper on the porch.

JOHNNY'S FATHER: [*Going up to the porch*] You mean a morning paper, Johnny?

JOHNNY: Yeah.

JOHNNY'S FATHER: Well, that's a pleasant surprise. Where in the world did you get it?

JOHNNY: Henry gave it to me.

JOHNNY'S FATHER: Henry? Who's Henry?

JOHNNY: He's a boy who hasn't got a mother or a father, either. He sure can whistle, too.

JOHNNY'S FATHER: [*Picking up the paper, opening it*] That was certainly nice of him. [*He loses himself in the headlines*]

JOHNNY'S GRANDMOTHER: [*To both of them, to herself, and to the world*] Where's that man?

JOHNNY'S FATHER: [*Deep in the news*] Hmmm?

JOHNNY: Who?

JOHNNY'S GRANDMOTHER: You know. That old man who blew the horn. [*She pantomimes the blowing of a horn*]

JOHNNY: Oh. Mr. MacGregor? They took him back to the Old People's Home.

JOHNNY'S FATHER: [*Reading the paper*] Austria. Germany. France. England. Russia. Zeppelins. Submarines. Tanks. Machine guns. Bombs. [*Shaking his head*] They've gone crazy again.

JOHNNY'S GRANDMOTHER: [*To Johnny, reproachfully*] Why don't you speak Armenian, boy?

JOHNNY: I can't talk Armenian.

JOHNNY'S FATHER: [*To Johnny*] What's the matter?

JOHNNY: She wants to know about Mr. MacGregor.

JOHNNY'S GRANDMOTHER: [*To Johnny's Father*] Where is he?

JOHNNY'S FATHER: [*In Armenian*] He's back in the Old People's Home.

JOHNNY'S GRANDMOTHER: [*Shaking her head sadly*] Ahkh, ahkh, the poor old prisoner.

JOHNNY: Is it like a prison, Pa?

JOHNNY'S FATHER: I don't know for sure, Johnny.

JOHNNY'S GRANDMOTHER: [*Furiously, the way her son and grandson speak when they are irritated*]

Why doesn't he come back and stay here where he belongs? [*She goes into the house*]

JOHNNY: That's right, Pa. Why doesn't Mr. Mac-Gregor come back and stay here? Does he have to stay in that place?

JOHNNY'S FATHER: If you're an old, old man, Johnny, and haven't got any people, and no money, I guess you do.

JOHNNY: I sure get lonesome for him sometimes. Don't you, Pa?

JOHNNY'S FATHER: To tell you the truth, Johnny, I do.

JOHNNY: I'm always remembering him, especially the music. And the way he drinks water.

JOHNNY'S FATHER: He's a great man.

JOHNNY: Is his heart really in the highlands like he said, Pa?

JOHNNY'S FATHER: Not exactly.

JOHNNY: Is he really five thousand miles from home, too?

JOHNNY'S FATHER: At least that many.

JOHNNY: Do you think he'll ever get home again some day?

JOHNNY'S FATHER: He's an old man, Johnny. He will.

JOHNNY: You mean he'll take a train and a boat and get back where the highlands are?

JOHNNY'S FATHER: Not that, Johnny. It's a little different from that. He'll *die*.

JOHNNY: Is that the only way a man gets home?

JOHNNY'S FATHER: That's the only way.

[*All this time, of course,* Johnny's Father *has been turning the pages of the morning paper, and* Johnny *has been going through various kinds of acrobatics, walking on the porch railing, leaping down, turning somersaults, standing on his head, and so forth. Some of his questions have been asked while he has been standing on his head. A sharp whistle is heard in the distance*]

JOHNNY: [*Eagerly*] It's Mr. Wiley, the mailman, Pa. [Johnny's Father *jumps to his feet, dropping the paper*]

JOHNNY: Do you think maybe we'll get a letter from New York with a check in it maybe?

JOHNNY'S FATHER: I don't know, Johnny.

[Mr. Wiley, *riding a bicycle, arrives. He is almost knocked off the bicycle by* Johnny *and* Johnny's Father]

MR. WILEY: [*Getting off the bicycle as if it were a horse*] Good morning, Mr. Alexander.

JOHNNY'S FATHER: Good morning, Mr. Wiley.

JOHNNY: Any mail for us, Mr. Wiley?

MR. WILEY: [*Bringing a packet of letters from his bag, loosening the strap, and looking them over*] Well, now, let me see, Johnny. I think I've got something here for your father.

JOHNNY: Is it from New York?

MR. WILEY: [*Holding a flat envelope*] Yes, it is,

Johnny. Well, Mr. Alexander, it looks like Winter's coming again. The geese were flying this morning.

JOHNNY'S FATHER: [*Excited, tense, yet eager to be casual*] Yes, I know. [*To himself*] I know. I know.

JOHNNY: If *I* ever get a letter from New York I'm going to save it up.

MR. WILEY: [*He wants to talk*] How are things, Mr. Alexander?

JOHNNY'S FATHER: I've been lucky in my work, thank you, Mr. Wiley.

JOHNNY: My father was in New York once. Weren't you, Pa?

JOHNNY'S FATHER: Yes, I was, Johnny. How is your family, Mr. Wiley?

MR. WILEY: All fine, except the littlest one, Joe. He's always crying. That's one thing I can't stand either, a baby crying all the time. I don't know what it does to me, but it makes me lose all faith in everything. When Joe cries I say to myself, Aw, what's the use?

JOHNNY: I guess I'll reach New York some day before I die.

JOHNNY'S FATHER: It's nothing, Mr. Wiley. He'll stop crying after a while.

MR. WILEY: Well, I hope so, and the sooner the better. [*He goes off with the envelope*] Good-by, Mr. Alexander. Good-by, Johnny.

JOHNNY'S FATHER: Mr. Wiley.

[Mr. Wiley *hands over the envelope. They say good-by, and* Mr. Wiley *rides off.* Johnny's Father *holds the envelope before him, obviously eager to open it, yet fearful to do so*]

JOHNNY: [*Impatient*] All right, Pa. Go ahead; open it. What are you waiting for?

JOHNNY'S FATHER: [*Angry; roaring*] Johnny, I'm scared. I can't understand how I, your father, can be so scared.

JOHNNY: You don't sound scared, Pa. Who's it from?

JOHNNY'S FATHER: It's from *The Atlantic Monthly* all right. You remember them poems I wrote after Mr. MacGregor was here?

JOHNNY: Maybe they've bought the poems.

JOHNNY'S FATHER: Bought them, my eye. They don't buy *poetry*, Johnny. They *scare* you to death. [*Reading his name and address with great solemnity, awful fearfulness and terrible rage*] Ben Alexander, 2226 San Benito Avenue, Fresno, California.

JOHNNY: It's for you all right, Pa. Why don't you open it?

JOHNNY'S FATHER: [*Roaring*] I'm scared, I tell you. I'm scared and ashamed. *Those poems were great.* How can it be that I'm scared?

JOHNNY: [*Also defiant*] Don't be scared, Pa.

JOHNNY'S FATHER: [*Angry*] Why do they clamor for all things but the best? Why do they destroy themselves running after things of death, and thrust aside all things of life? I can't understand it. There's no hope for *anybody*.

JOHNNY: Sure there is, Pa. [*Furiously*] Who the hell is *The Atlantic Monthly*?

JOHNNY'S FATHER: [*Angry*] Johnny, go away. Go away. Please go away.

JOHNNY: [*Angry, too*] All right, Pa. [Johnny *goes around the house, reappears, looks at his father a moment, and then knows he must stay out of the way*]

[*It is obvious that* Johnny's Father *knows* The Atlantic Monthly *has sent back the poems. It is equally obvious that he can't believe the poems have come back. It is obvious too that the poems are great, because the man is. He paces about like a tiger. He seems to be speaking to the world, even though his lips are set. At last he tears the envelope open, in a fury. The envelope falls. He unfolds the manuscript of poems. A slip of white, heavy paper falls to the floor of the porch. He stands, very tall, and very proud, and reads the poems to himself, turning the pages swiftly*]

JOHNNY'S FATHER: [*Furiously*] Ah, you crazy, miserable fools. [*He sits on the steps of the porch and buries his face in his hands. The manuscript of poems is on the steps. After several minutes he kicks the poems off the steps of the porch onto the ground and takes up the morning paper again, looking at the headlines. Quietly, with deep fury, his voice mounting in intensity*] Go ahead, kill *everybody*. Declare *War* on one another. Take the people by the thousands and mangle them. Their poor hearts and their poor spirits and their poor bodies. Give them ugliness. Pollute their dreams. Horrify them. Distort them with hatred for one another. Befoul the legend of the living, you maniacs whose greatness is measured by the number you destroy. [Johnny *appears at the side of the house, unseen. He stands in a trance, listening to his father. The sky begins to darken*] You frauds of the world. You wretched and ungodly. [*He stands and points a finger, as if across the world*] Go ahead. *Fire* your feeble guns. You won't kill *anything*. [*Quietly, smiling*] There will always be poets in the world.

[*Lightning flashes silently*]

The house. The sky is dark, as at the beginning of a storm. An occasional deep and faraway roar of thunder is heard, and a flash of lightning is seen. Johnny's Father is on the steps of the porch, smiling: a foolish, tragic, desolate, lonely smile. Everything is the same; the manuscript of poems is on the ground; the envelope is on the porch. The newspaper too. It is several hours later.

JOHNNY'S FATHER: [*Shaking his head foolishly, unable to accept the truth*] Johnny. [*Pause. A little louder*] Johnny. [*Pause, softer this time*] Johnny. [*Roaring*] Johnny. [*The boy comes around the house shyly and stands before his father. His father looks up, fire in his eye, defiant, bitter, stubborn, powerful*]

JOHNNY'S FATHER: [*Tenderly, but with tremendous power*] Have you had your breakfast?

JOHNNY: [*Shyly*] I'm not hungry, Pa.

JOHNNY'S FATHER: You go inside now and eat.

JOHNNY: I'm not hungry.

JOHNNY'S FATHER: You do what I tell you.

JOHNNY: I won't eat unless you do.

JOHNNY'S FATHER: You do what I *tell* you.

JOHNNY: I won't eat unless you do.

JOHNNY'S FATHER: I'm not hungry.

JOHNNY: I'll go down to Mr. Kosak's and see if I can get something.

JOHNNY'S FATHER: [*Humiliated. Taking the boy's arm*] No, Johnny. [*He pauses, obviously trying to find words with which to explain about themselves and the grocer*] Johnny? I thought we'd be getting some money. I didn't think it would be this way. Now, go on inside and eat.

JOHNNY: [*Going up the stairs*] You got to eat, too. [*He goes into the house*]

[*There is a silent flash of lightning. A Man in a business suit, and a young Husband and Wife with a Baby in the mother's arms, come up*]

THE REAL ESTATE MAN: This is the house. The rent's six dollars a month. It's not exactly fancy, but it'll keep out the rain and cold.

[Johnny's Father *has been staring at the people, his vision frozen*]

THE REAL ESTATE MAN: [*Coming up to* Johnny's Father, *extending his hand, while the others stand back in a group*] Remember me? I put up the "For Rent" sign.

JOHNNY'S FATHER: [*Rising*] I remember. How do you do.

THE REAL ESTATE MAN: [*Embarrassed*] Well. Mr. Corey, the owner of the house, is out of town, and these people are looking for a house. *Right away*.

JOHNNY'S FATHER: Of course. I can leave any time. Have they furniture?

THE REAL ESTATE MAN: [*Turning to the poor family*] Have you furniture?

THE HUSBAND: No.

JOHNNY'S FATHER: [*To the family*] You can have my furniture. There isn't much of it, but it'll do. There's a pretty good stove.

THE WIFE: [*With the dignity of the poor*] We wouldn't want to take *your* furniture.

JOHNNY'S FATHER: That's all right. I haven't paid rent for three months. I'll leave the furniture for the rent. [The Real Estate Man *tries to speak*]

JOHNNY'S FATHER: It's all right. I'm sorry I haven't the $18. The furniture's worth about that much. You can let these people have it till Mr. Corey gets back. [*To the family*] Do you want to go through the house?

THE HUSBAND: It looks all right.

THE REAL ESTATE MAN: [*Going*] Then that's settled. [*To the people*] The rent's six dollars a month. We pay the water.

JOHNNY'S FATHER: [*To the people*] You can move in any time.

THE HUSBAND: Thank you very much. We'll be back this afternoon or tomorrow. [*They are going* as Johnny *comes out with a plate containing two slices of bread and a small bunch of grapes*]

JOHNNY: Who were those people?

JOHNNY'S FATHER: Just some people walking by.

JOHNNY: What were you talking about?

JOHNNY'S FATHER: Just talking, Johnny.

JOHNNY: [*Shouting; very angry*] Don't feel bad, Pa.

JOHNNY'S FATHER: [*Turning and looking at the boy with love, amazement, admiration, and delight, laughing suddenly*] I don't feel bad, Johnny. Let the world be the world, and God love everyone.

JOHNNY: [*Bantering*] All right then. Let's eat. [*He puts the plate on the top step and they sit down together and begin to eat. They eat in silence, looking at one another, the boy looking at his father out of the corner of his eye as he had looked at the sun; the father looking at the boy the same way. The boy begins to smile. The father begins to smile too*]

JOHNNY: Do you like grapes, Pa?

JOHNNY'S FATHER: Of course I like grapes.

JOHNNY: Pa?

JOHNNY'S FATHER: Yes?

JOHNNY: Is it really like a prison?

JOHNNY'S FATHER: Sometimes I'm *sure* it is. Sometimes I *know* it never can be.

JOHNNY: What, Pa?

JOHNNY'S FATHER: I guess it's fifty-fifty, Johnny. You know. It's both.

JOHNNY: I mean, do you think he gets homesick sometimes?

JOHNNY'S FATHER: I'm sure he does.

JOHNNY: I wish he'd come back.

JOHNNY'S FATHER: I'd like to see him again.

JOHNNY: I remember him all the time.

JOHNNY'S FATHER: I do too. I'll always remember him.

JOHNNY: So will I. Did he *have* to go back, Pa?

JOHNNY'S FATHER: I guess he did.

JOHNNY: He seemed like a nice young man.

JOHNNY'S FATHER: You mean the young man who came and got him?

JOHNNY: Yeah, you know. That young man who talked so sharp, like he was speaking in front of an audience.

JOHNNY'S FATHER: He was all right. [*There is one more grape on the plate*]

JOHNNY: Go ahead, Pa. Take it.

JOHNNY'S FATHER: [*Blithely*] No, that's yours, Johnny. I counted.

JOHNNY: All right, Pa. [*He takes the last grape and eats it*] Is it stealing, Pa?

JOHNNY'S FATHER: [*Comically*] Well, some say it is and some say it isn't. [*Dramatically*] *I* say it isn't. [*Shouting*] You took them off the vines, didn't you?

JOHNNY: I took them off the vines all right, Pa.

JOHNNY'S FATHER: [*Comically*] Then it couldn't very well be stealing.

JOHNNY: When would it be stealing?

JOHNNY'S FATHER: [*Tossing it off like nothing*] The way I see it, Johnny, stealing is where there's unnecessary damage or cruelty to an innocent one, so that there may be undeserved profit or power to one who is not innocent.

JOHNNY: Oh. [*Pause*] Well, if it isn't stealing, Pa, I guess I'll go get some more. [*He gets up*] They'll all be gone pretty soon. [*Goes off*]

JOHNNY'S FATHER: [*When the boy is gone, laughing*] My son John. My God, how fortunate I have been. How grateful I am. [*He picks up the manuscript of poems, puts it in his coat pocket, and walks down the street*]

The inside of Mr. Kosak's Grocery Store. Again Mr. Kosak is sleeping on his folded arms. The store looks more poverty-stricken than before. The family apparently has been eating the stock. Johnny's father comes into the store quietly, almost shyly. Mr. Kosak lifts his head, blinks his eyes, stands.

JOHNNY'S FATHER: [*Almost guiltily*] I'm Johnny's father.

[*The two men stand staring at one another a moment, each of them delighted, embarrassed, impressed, pleased, and angry about the same things in the world: greed, deceit, unkindliness, disproportion. They each begin to smile, then shake hands warmly*]

MR. KOSAK: I recognize you. Johnny has told me about you. It is an honor.

JOHNNY'S FATHER: You are a kind man.

MR. KOSAK: I do not know.

JOHNNY'S FATHER: [*Slowly*] I have come to say good-by. To apologize. To thank you.

MR. KOSAK: [*Swiftly*] You're not going away?

JOHNNY'S FATHER: I'm sorry, yes.

MR. KOSAK: We shall all miss Johnny.

JOHNNY'S FATHER: I have no money. I am in debt to you.

MR. KOSAK: It is nothing.

JOHNNY'S FATHER: I may not see you again. [*He brings the manuscript of poems from his pocket. Powerfully*] I am a poet. *These* are some of my poems. [*Swiftly*] I am not offering them to you in place of the money I owe you. Money is another thing. [*Pleading*] Will you keep them for your kindness?

MR. KOSAK: [*Sincerely*] I cannot take your poems. [*Pause*]

JOHNNY'S FATHER: I hope you have been prospering.

MR. KOSAK: The people have no money. I do not know how I am going to put in new stock.

JOHNNY'S FATHER: I'm sorry.

MR. KOSAK: In the Winter it is worse. The packing-houses are closed. There are no jobs. I would give them something if I could, but this Winter I have no money for new stock. I may have to close the store. There is hardly enough for my family.

JOHNNY'S FATHER: [*Touched and angry*] These poems. Let me tell you they are the finest I have ever written. I want to leave them with you.

[*Mr. Kosak's daughter,* Esther, *a beautiful girl of seven, comes into the store, from the back*]

MR. KOSAK: This is my daughter Esther. Esther, this is Johnny's father.

JOHNNY'S FATHER: Johnny's told me about you.

ESTHER: [*Really pleased, but shy*] How do you do.

MR. KOSAK: They're going away.

ESTHER: [*Shocked*] Oh.

JOHNNY'S FATHER: Johnny will miss you.

[*The girl's lips tremble, tears come to her eyes. She turns and runs out of the store*]

MR. KOSAK: Everything is like that.

JOHNNY'S FATHER: They are children.

MR. KOSAK: Yes, but it's that way from the beginning and it never changes. Only women never learn to believe it.

JOHNNY'S FATHER: Won't you give *her* these poems?

MR. KOSAK: Please. It's nothing. She will cry for a while, but it is nothing.

JOHNNY'S FATHER: Here. [*Giving* Mr. Kosak *the poems*] You will be doing me a kindness by keeping them. [*Loudly, to God and the world*] Don't you see, poetry must be *read* to be poetry. It may be that one reader is all that I deserve. If this is so, I want that reader to be you.

MR. KOSAK: Thank you. I am unworthy.

JOHNNY'S FATHER: [*Smiling*] Good-by.

MR. KOSAK: Good-by.

[*Johnny's Father goes out of the store. The grocer takes his glasses out of his pocket, puts them on, unfolds the manuscript, and standing in the middle of the store, begins to read, softly, to himself, moving his lips. The expression of his face begins to change. Rain begins to fall. His daughter* Esther *comes back into the store*]

MR. KOSAK: [*Reading from one of the poems, in a quiet voice*] Deep in the bowels of the earth, and far dispersed into the green waters of the sea, and held tight within the hardness of rock, I thee remember, love, remember me. [*The girl begins to sob aloud, and the father turns and goes to her*]

The living room of the house. Some time later. Johnny's Father *is at his table, looking over a stack of manuscripts. It is still raining. Every once in a while he gets up and goes to the window.*

JOHNNY'S FATHER: What the hell's happened to him? [*He goes back to his manuscripts and looks over some poems, grows irritated with them, throws them down, and goes to the window again. Then begins to walk back and forth, waiting. At last* Johnny *tears up the front porch stairs, bursts into the house, closes the door quickly, and bolts it. He*

is breathless and scared. You know he is one who has been pursued. He has four medium-sized bunches of purple-red Emperors; a half dozen black figs, and two pomegranates]

JOHNNY: [*Excited and breathless*] Where shall I hide them, Pa?

JOHNNY'S FATHER: What's the matter, Johnny?

JOHNNY: You said it wasn't stealing, Pa.

JOHNNY'S FATHER: [*With furious irritation*] Well, it isn't.

JOHNNY: What about the farmer's dog, then?

JOHNNY'S FATHER: What are you talking about? What farmer's dog?

JOHNNY: The farmer's dog that chased me all the way here.

JOHNNY'S FATHER: Dog? Do you mean to tell me a dog chased you? What kind of a dog?

JOHNNY: I didn't get a chance to take a good look, but I guess it's a great big one.

JOHNNY'S FATHER: [*Very angry at this awful humiliation*] Did the God damn thing try to bite you or anything, Johnny?

JOHNNY: I don't think so, Pa, but I thought it was going to any minute.

JOHNNY'S FATHER: Did it growl at you?

JOHNNY: It wasn't exactly a growl.

JOHNNY'S FATHER: What happened?

JOHNNY: I just ran all the way, with the dog right behind me.

JOHNNY'S FATHER: Where is it now?

JOHNNY: It's *outside,* I think, Pa. Are you sure it isn't stealing?

JOHNNY'S FATHER: [*Very angry, eating three or four grapes*] Of course it isn't stealing. I'll take care of the dog. No man or beast can scare your father, Johnny. Always remember that. [*He goes cautiously to the window and peeks out*]

JOHNNY: Is it out there, Pa?

JOHNNY'S FATHER: There's a little dog out there, Johnny. It's asleep, I think.

JOHNNY: [*Jumping bitterly*] *I knew it.* It's the farmer's dog, waiting for me.

JOHNNY'S FATHER: It's not a very big dog, Johnny.

JOHNNY: Yeah, but if it's stealing—if it's the *farmer's* dog—what about that?

JOHNNY'S FATHER: Why, that little bitty dog doesn't belong to anybody, Johnny. That little dog is looking for a friend, I bet.

JOHNNY: It chased me all the way. Are you sure, Pa?

JOHNNY'S FATHER: Sure I'm sure, Johnny. I'm no poet for nothing. I understand things. [*The dog begins to growl and bark.* Johnny's Father *jumps back from the window, frightened.* Johnny *jumps tense and speechless*]

JOHNNY: [*Whispering*] What is it, Pa?

JOHNNY'S FATHER: Somebody's coming, I think.

JOHNNY: You see, Pa? *It is stealing.* It's the farmer. [*He runs to the table and gathers the fruit* into his arms. *His* Grandmother *comes running into the room*]

JOHNNY'S GRANDMOTHER: [*In Armenian*] What's all the hullabaloo, in the rain?

JOHNNY'S FATHER: Shhhh. [Johnny *takes the fruit out of the living room; returns, scared to death. The dog is still growling and barking.* Johnny's Father *is even more scared than* Johnny]

JOHNNY: [*Sore, and now defiant*] God damn it, Pa. Now look at the mess we're in.

JOHNNY'S FATHER: I wish I had a cigarette.

JOHNNY: [*Now worrying about his father; to his grandmother, in Armenian*] Are there cigarettes? [Johnny's Grandmother *runs into the next room. The dog stops growling*]

JOHNNY: You see, Pa? It's the farmer. Where shall I hide? Don't open the door.

JOHNNY'S FATHER: *Open the door?* Help me with this table. [*They push the table up against the door, and tiptoe back to the center of the room.* Johnny's Grandmother *runs back with one cigarette and one match which she hands to* Johnny's Father, *who lights the cigarette, inhales deeply, and straightens up*]

JOHNNY'S FATHER: [*Dramatically*] *I* am the one who took the fruit, understand, Johnny?

JOHNNY: Don't open the door, Pa. [Johnny's Father *picks up a small stool, takes it quietly to the table up against the door, places it on the table, to make it heavier.* Johnny *picks up a chair and puts it on the table. The Old Lady puts a vase on the table.* Johnny's Father *adds three books to the barricade. In fact, as the knocks continue, the family little by little puts all the household goods up against the door*]

JOHNNY'S FATHER: Don't be afraid, Johnny.

JOHNNY: He can't get in, can he, Pa?

JOHNNY'S FATHER: I don't think so.

[*The* Grandmother, *the* Father *and the* Son *stand together in the bare room, defying the world. There is a long pause, full of mingling of awful fear and furious defiance. After half a minute the silence is broken. It is a solo on the bugle: "My Heart's in the Highlands." The sun comes out*]

JOHNNY: [*Shouting*] It's Mr. MacGregor.

JOHNNY'S FATHER: [*Running to the window, lifting it, and shouting out to* MacGregor] Welcome, Mr. MacGregor. Johnny, rearrange the furniture. [Johnny's Father *returns to the barricade and helps* Johnny *and his* Grandmother *rearrange the furniture. At last everything is out of the way.* Johnny's Father *swings open the door. Jasper MacGregor, still playing the solo, preceded by the dog, which is a very small street dog, comes in. The dog runs around playfully, all excited. MacGregor's eyes are full of grief and joy.* Johnny *begins making trips to the kitchen, returning with the fruit, on a plate, and a pitcher of water.* MacGregor *finishes the solo. There is a moment when everybody stands stock-*

still, including the dog. Johnny *offers* MacGregor *the pitcher of water*]

MAC GREGOR: [*Weary*] Not this time, Johnny.

JOHNNY'S FATHER: Welcome, my friend.

MAC GREGOR: I've run away. They're after me now, but I won't go back. They stole my bugle. They tried to keep me in bed. They said I was sick. I'm not sick; I'm old. I know my days on earth are numbered. I want them to be with you. Don't let them take me back.

JOHNNY'S FATHER: I won't. [*He draws out a chair for the old man*] Please sit down. [*They all sit down.* MacGregor *looks around at everybody*]

MAC GREGOR: It's good to see you again.

JOHNNY: Is your heart still in the highlands?

MAC GREGOR: [*Nodding*] In the highlands, son.

JOHNNY'S FATHER: [*Angry*] Johnny.

JOHNNY: [*Sore, too*] What?

JOHNNY'S FATHER: Shut up.

JOHNNY: Why?

JOHNNY'S FATHER: *Why?* What do you get so dumb for every once in a while? Can't you see Mr. MacGregor is weary?

JOHNNY: [*To* MacGregor] Are you?

MAC GREGOR: [*Nods*] But where's your mother, son?

JOHNNY: She's dead.

MAC GREGOR: [*Almost to himself*] Not dead, Johnny. [*He shakes his head*] In the highlands.

JOHNNY'S GRANDMOTHER: [*To his father*] What's he saying?

JOHNNY'S FATHER: [*Shaking his head*] Nothing. [*To* MAC GREGOR] Won't you eat?

MAC GREGOR: [*Looking at the plate*] One grape. No more. [*He plucks a grape off a bunch, puts it in his mouth. Suddenly turns, startled*] Are they coming?

JOHNNY'S FATHER: Don't be afraid, my friend. Lie down and rest. [Johnny's Father *takes the* Old Man *to the couch. The* Old Man *stretches out, face up.* Johnny's Father *returns to the table. Nobody is eating. The* Old Man *jumps up suddenly. It's nothing again. He gets up and returns to the table*]

MAC GREGOR: You won't let them take me back, will you?

JOHNNY'S FATHER: No. [*He breaks open a pomegranate and hands* MacGregor *half*] Try to eat something.

MAC GREGOR: Thank you, my friend. [*He eats some of the pomegranate. There is a knock on the door,* MacGregor *leaps to his feet, furiously*]

MAC GREGOR: [*Roaring*] You'll not take me back. I warn you. I'll fall down and die. I belong here, with these people.

JOHNNY'S FATHER: [*Scared*] Shall we open the door?

JOHNNY: [*Also scared*] Shall we?

MAC GREGOR: [*Powerfully*] Of course we'll open the door. [*He goes to the door, opens it. It is* Rufe

Apley, *the carpenter, who is a little shaken up by* MacGregor's *fury*]

RUFE APLEY: Hello, Mr. MacGregor.

JOHNNY: Who is it?

RUFE APLEY: It's Rufe Apley.

MAC GREGOR: How do you do, Rufe.

JOHNNY'S FATHER: [*At the door*] Come in, Rufe. [Rufe *comes in. He has a loaf of bread, a sausage and two eggs in his hands*]

RUFE: I was sitting home doing nothing when I heard that song again. I was sure it was Mr. Mac-Gregor.

MAC GREGOR: I'm delighted you remembered.

RUFE: Nobody could ever forget that song, Mr. MacGregor. I brought these few things.

MAC GREGOR: [*Taking them and putting them on the table*] Thank you, my friend, thank you.

[*There is another knock at the door. It is* Sam Wallace; *he is a lineman, in full regalia: overalls, tools hanging all over him, tape, straps around his calves, spikes, everything. He has cheese and tomatoes and radishes with him*]

WALLACE: I *knew* it was Mr. MacGregor. I said to myself, I'll go over with a few little things to eat.

MAC GREGOR: This is indeed a pleasant surprise.

RUFE: [*Obviously trying hard to say something*] Ah, Mr. MacGregor?

MAC GREGOR: Yes, my friend? Speak up. I'm a plain man, no different in any way from yourself.

RUFE: My wife's sister and her family are outside. I know they'd like to hear you play again. There are some other people.

MAC GREGOR: [*Flattered*] Of course I'll play. I'm over eighty and not long for this world. Before I go I'd like to become a part of you who shall live after I am dead. Are there children out there too?

RUFE: Seven. My wife's sister's kids.

[*Three or four more neighbors come in, bringing food.* MacGregor *takes up his bugle. Everybody follows him out of the room to the porch, except* Johnny's Father. MacGregor *begins to play the solo again. This time he's too old and weak to really play, but he finishes the solo as well as he is able to.* Johnny's Father *paces about the room, smiling, frowning, loving the place. The door to the kitchen opens quietly and* Esther Kosak *stands in the doorway.* Johnny's Father *turns and sees her. She is no longer crying. She has something clutched in her fist*]

JOHNNY'S FATHER: [*Quietly*] Hello, Esther.

ESTHER: Where's Johnny?

JOHNNY'S FATHER: I'll go get him. [*He goes out on the porch. The Girl stands alone in terrible sadness and loneliness. After a moment* Johnny *comes rushing in, all excited, but calms down quickly when he begins to feel the mood of the girl*]

JOHNNY: Hello, Esther.

ESTHER: Hello, Johnny.

JOHNNY: What's the matter?

ESTHER: My father read me the poems.

JOHNNY: What?

ESTHER: [*Holding out her hand*] Here. This is all I've got. [Johnny *takes a handful of coins*] I've been saving up for Christmas. [*She begins to cry, turns, and runs out of the house*]

JOHNNY: [*Deeply touched and furious, sensing something profound and beautiful and terrible*] Holy Moses. [*His face takes on boyhood's tragic expression of grief, and he begins to cry. He throws the coins against the wall and falls down, sobbing*] Who the hell wants that stuff? [Johnny's Father *comes back*]

JOHNNY'S FATHER: Johnny. [*Going closer*] Johnny?

JOHNNY: [*Sobbing and angry*] She brought me money.

JOHNNY'S FATHER: It's no use crying, Johnny.

JOHNNY: [*Jumping up*] Who's crying? [*He cries harder than ever*]

JOHNNY'S FATHER: Go wash your face. It's nothing.

JOHNNY: [*Going*] Something's wrong somewhere. [MacGregor *finishes the solo, the people are silent with awe and the knowledge that something is wrong.* MacGregor's Voice *is heard for a moment in a speech*]

MAC GREGOR: [*Wearily*] The years, my friends. I have walked to the end of them. I'm sorry I can no longer play for you. Thank you. Thank you.

[Johnny's Father *walks back and forth in the room. He sits down at the table and looks at the food.* MacGregor *and* Johnny's Grandmother *return and sit at the table. The dog lies down in a corner*]

MAC GREGOR: [*He lifts the water pitcher, drinks a little*] They wouldn't let me play. [*He drinks a little more*] They stole my bugle. [*He drinks a little more*] They said I was sick. [*He drinks a little more*] I'm strong as a bull. If they come to take me back, I shall pretend that I am dying. I shall play the death scene from "King Lear." I shall play *all* the death scenes.

[Johnny *returns solemnly. They are all at the table. Nobody can eat but the* Old Lady. *There is a long silence. The* Old Lady *stops eating*]

JOHNNY'S GRANDMOTHER: What's the matter? Why this terrible gloom? [MacGregor *rises*]

MAC GREGOR: [*Reciting, remembering lines from Shakespeare, and inventing a few of his own*] Blow, winds, and crack your cheeks! Rage! blow! You cataracts and hurricanes, spout till you have drenched our steeples, drowned the cocks! You sulphurous and thought-executing fires, singe my white head! Humble thy belly-full, spit fire, spout rain! I never gave you kingdom, call'd you children. Here I stand, your slave, a poor infirm, weak and despised old man. To be or not to be . . . [*Tragically*] To be— To be— What? A fool? A man mocked by destiny? Turned away from home and fire and love? I am a man more sinned against than sinning. Arms! Arms! Sword! Fire! Corruption in the place! The little dogs and all, Tray, Blanche, Sweetheart. See? They bark at me. O, that way madness lies— no more of that—let me shun that. My wits begin to turn. [Johnny *goes to him and kneels*] Come on, my boy, how dost my boy? Art cold? let me alone! Wilt break my heart? And my poor fool is hang'd. No, no, no life! Why should a dog, a horse, a rat have life and thou no life at all? Thou'lt come no more, never, never, never, never! Pray you undo this button—thank you, sir— [*Holds the bugle before him*] Do you see this? Look on her. Look. Look there, look there!!

[*While* MacGregor *is acting* Johnny *returns to the coins on the floor and picks them up one by one and looks at them. The room is in absolute silence. A horse and wagon in the street is heard; then steps on the front porch; then a knock at the door.* Johnny's Father *goes to the door. It is* Philip Carmichael *and two guards from the Old People's Home. The guards stand at attention at the door*]

CARMICHAEL: We heard him playing. He's very sick. We've come to take him back.

JOHNNY'S FATHER: Please come in. [*He enters. To* MacGregor] Mr. MacGregor. [*There is no answer*]

JOHNNY'S FATHER: [*Louder*] Mr. MacGregor. [*Goes closer*] Mr. MacGregor, Mr. Mac—

[Carmichael *hurries over to* MacGregor *and examines him*]

CARMICHAEL: He's dead.

JOHNNY: No, he isn't. He was acting.

JOHNNY'S FATHER: By God, he *was* the greatest Shakespearean actor of our day.

CARMICHAEL: I'm sorry this had to happen here.

JOHNNY'S FATHER: Why not? Why not here? This is where he wanted it to be.

JOHNNY: He was acting, Pa. He isn't dead. [*He goes to* MacGregor] Are you, Mr. MacGregor? [*There is no answer, of course*]

CARMICHAEL: We'll take him back.

JOHNNY'S FATHER: Here's his bugle. Keep it with him. [Johnny's Father *lifts* MacGregor *and carries him out. The guards carry him up the street. The light of the afternoon sun increases to the same intensity as at the beginning of the play. The horse and wagon goes off. There is a moment of strange silence, and the faint far-away sound of the bugle solo. A knock at the door.* Johnny's Father *opens the door. It's the young* Husband *and* Wife. *The* Baby *is crying. They come in*]

THE WIFE: The kid is tired and sleepy.

JOHNNY'S FATHER: The house is ready. [*To* Johnny] Get your stuff. [*To the* Old Lady, *in Armenian*] We're going. [*He gets a straw suitcase from under the couch and throws his poems, books, envelopes, one loaf of bread, and a few of the other items of food into it. The* Old Lady *puts a shawl around her head and shoulders.* Johnny *leaves all his junk; takes only the handful of coins. The* Baby *stops crying. The dog follows* Johnny *around. The music increases in intensity*]

THE HUSBAND: Thank you very much.

THE WIFE: Have you some place to go?

JOHNNY'S FATHER: Yes, we have. Good-by.

THE HUSBAND AND WIFE: Good-by. [*They go out of the house to the street*]

JOHNNY: Where the hell do we think we're going, Pa?

JOHNNY'S FATHER: Never mind, Johnny. You just follow me.

JOHNNY: I'm not mentioning any names, Pa, but something's wrong somewhere.

[*The music grows louder. They walk up the street*]

Tennessee Williams

(1914– ———)

Nothing is so characteristic of Tennessee Williams as his ability to adapt extreme subjectivity to the most objective of the arts. An individualist and a man of wayward impulse, he learned to discipline a volatile temperament for the purpose of calculating dramatic effects and developing a point to relentless conclusion. It was by no means easy for him to work himself out of the tunnel of subjective artistry into the light of orderly judgment and clear vistas.

Although a cosmopolitan by taste and literary interest, Williams is a Southern artist. He is that not merely because he has given us pictures of the South and dealt with its products, chiefly with the overdelicate girls and futile middle-aged women whom Southern writers have so often portrayed, but in his awareness of decadence. A "Southern Gothic" imagination appears in his world of oppressive half-lights, anxieties, and outbursts of desperation. There is, it is true, something of D. H. Lawrence in Williams' concern with suppressed sexuality and in his search for liberation through uninhibited animality. Williams is an admirer of Lawrence, and the English writer's influence may be traced in some of the plays. But there is a good deal more of Faulkner in Williams' clinical presentation of warped souls and crass conduct. Only one play, The Glass Menagerie, and one adaptation, of a story by D. H. Lawrence, have more light than darkness.

We may feel, indeed, that Williams would have been quite lost if he had not made a dramatist of himself. He might have become a minor poet and prose writer for a small coterie. That he should have come to write plays for large audiences and so move out of the confines of esoteric art is evidence of a certain quantity of iron in his constitution. He is an artist to his fingertips, yet he has knocked about in the world instead of living in refined seclusion; he has exquisite tastes, yet he has lived and worked in environments where indulgence of those tastes was an unlikely possibility.

Thomas Lanier ("Tennessee") Williams was born of pioneering, Indian-fighting Tennessee ancestry in Columbus, Mississippi. His father was a shoe salesman; his mother was of the Southern aristocracy. Her father, an Episcopalian clergyman who had much to do with the shaping of the boy's mind, was a gentleman with a taste for poetry and literature, as well as for bridge and cocktails. It was in his grandfather's rectory that Williams first observed the Southern women who fill his plays with their genteel anguish. It would be more accurate to say, however, that Williams grew up in a world divided between the cultured life of the rectory and a not particularly prosperous home environment.

The future playwright attended high school in St. Louis and went on to the University of Missouri in 1931. He found it necessary after his sophomore year to take a job in the shoe factory where his father was employed, and he spent two years there, gaining, as he reported later, "valuable insight into the monotony of the white collar worker's life." But the writing fever that made him stay up late at night brought on a nervous collapse. He returned to college in 1936, studying at Washington University in St. Louis, and then went to the University of Iowa to take a Bachelor of Arts degree. Restlessness seizing him, he began to travel across the land, sustaining himself with odd jobs. He was a bellhop in a New Orleans hotel, a teletypist in Jacksonville, Florida, a seventeen-dollar-a-week usher in a New York motion picture theatre, and a waiter and reciter of verses in a Bohemian Greenwich Village night club. Throughout this apprenticeship he wrote continually, experimenting with poetry, stories, and plays.

Williams' interest in the theatre began when he saw a performance of Ghosts, with which Alla Nazimova was touring the country. He was then an undergraduate at the University of Missouri. "It was," he recalled later, "one of the things that made me want to write for the theatre." Numerous one-acters and ten full-length plays by the time he wrote his greatest success, A Streetcar Named Desire (1947), testify to his energetic pursuit of a dramatic career. The early full-length plays made no impression and were discarded by the author, but his one-acters, in which the themes of his later long plays are prefigured, attracted attention by 1939. He found an agent, Audrey Wood, who fought hopefully for him, and he won a small cash prize from the Group Theatre for four short pieces, American Blues, dealing with victims of the depression. In January 1940, Theresa Helburn and John Gassner, of the Theatre Guild, gave him a scholarship to their advanced playwrights' seminar and brought the play he wrote that semester to the Guild. Entitled Battle of Angels, it received a production that autumn under the direction of Margaret Webster and the supervision of the Guild's Lawrence Langner. It closed in Boston for repairs after affronting Bostonians with its somewhat lurid story of decadence in a Southern town and of the affair of a D. H. Lawrence hero and a sexually starved woman. But this defeat on the brink of professional success was salved somewhat by American Academy and Rockefeller Fellowship awards, and in 1945, Eddie Dowling, in association with Louis J. Singer, produced *The Glass Menagerie* in New York after a long tryout period in Chicago. It was a difficult play with which to attract the average playgoer, seemingly too tenuous and depressing as well as too unconventionally constructed. But the magic of the play, movingly conveyed by Laurette Taylor and Julie Haydon in the respective roles of the mother and the daughter, prevailed, and *The Glass Menagerie*, which won the Drama Critics Circle award, became a notable success.

Subsequently, in 1946, Williams had a disappointing production with *You Touched Me,* a collaborative adaptation of a D. H. Lawrence story of frustration in an English home. But a year later, he won an ecstatic reception in New York (and later throughout the country and abroad) with *A Streetcar Named Desire.* It was an unsavory tragedy of a woman's frustration, but its sordid matter of sexual depravity and madness in the New Orleans Latin Quarter was transfigured by poetic dramaturgy and overwhelming compassion. In 1948, Williams faced another disappointment when his next drama of a Southern woman's deterioration, *Summer and Smoke,* failed to live up to the expectations it had aroused when tried out by Margo Jones in her small arena theatre in Dallas. But the play again proved him a master of sensitive characterization and an able observer of town life in the South. Not at all daunted by critics who feared he was repeating himself and exhausting the theme of Southern decadence, Williams went ahead with the composition of a number of plays with which he hoped to extend the range of his playwriting. But even if these plays prove unsatisfactory, Williams will retain a high place in the American theatre. Several of his one-act plays (such as *Portrait of a Madonna* and *The Lady of Larkspur Lotion*) possess much power; his failures (*Battle of Angels* and *Summer and Smoke*) contain distinguished writing; and both *The Glass Menagerie* and *A Streetcar Named Desire* are among the noteworthy creations of the American drama.

Of the latter two plays, *The Glass Menagerie* is the more lyrical, if also more tenuous, example of their author's artistry. But it is plain enough that even in this delicate work Williams retains a highly objective attitude toward his picture of a life of failure. He locates his story in the context of the larger world, which demands a wide-awake attitude toward a society that, ailing and torn with the conflict of a Second World War, challenges our intelligence and capacity for action. The narrations that frame the story of the mother, the daughter, and the son form another dimension and supply a measure of objective reality. The "lives of quiet desperation" seem all the more defeated because they are lived in a world that no longer affords them shelter. A mighty wind has arisen and nobody seems to temper it to the shorn lamb, whether it be an aging Southern belle abandoned by her husband or a girl too painfully shy for the coarse-grained world. Although the play is written in a mood of tenderly rueful reminiscence, Williams exhibits here much strength of mind and objectivity. Sympathize though he does with his failures, he recognizes that one cannot accept their quiescence and bumbling. The son pays a tribute of compassion to his mother and sister, but acknowledges the validity of the instinct of self-preservation that made him leave them; he knows, too, that in the great struggle of the times their plight is, in a sense, of minor consequence. *The Glass Menagerie* is, as had been claimed, a "mood." But it is a mood not mistaken by either the author or the Narrator (and they are actually the same person, since the play is largely autobiographical) for the whole of reality. The author was attached to his characters to such a degree that he could make them move us deeply, but he was also detached enough to locate them in time, place, and necessity. He created *The Glass Menagerie* as both poet and dramatist, as subjective writer and realist.

Fortunately, Williams found an effective form for this mixed kind of playwriting. He did not, it is true, entirely control his medium, mistaking theatrical virtuosity for effective emphases out of an apparent desire to depart as far as possible from realistic technique. This may be seen in the stage directions he insisted on retaining for the published version—directions which were moderated in Eddie Dowling's excellent production. Yet Williams' feeling for form was essentially right. He used narrations and scenes with emphatic alternation, envisioned the action in the manner of vignettes that soon become alive and charged, and called for the expressive use of visual and musical effects. His work represents a poet who is thoroughly at home in the theatre. *The Glass Menagerie* exists on several levels; it is a work in which imaginative and realistic elements stand in sound relation to each other. It is not a shattering drama, but it is a notable example of exquisite playwriting that is more tensile than it appears to be on the surface.

THE AUTHOR'S PRODUCTION NOTES

Being a "memory play," *The Glass Menagerie* can be presented with unusual freedom of convention. Because of its considerably delicate or tenuous material, atmospheric touches and subtleties of direction play a particularly important part. Expressionism and all other unconventional techniques in drama have only one valid aim, and that is a closer approach to truth. When a play employs unconventional techniques, it is not, or certainly shouldn't be, trying to escape its responsibility of dealing with reality, or interpreting experience, but is actually or should be attempting to find a closer approach, a more penetrating and vivid expression of things as they are. The straight realistic play with its genuine frigidaire and authentic ice-cubes, its characters that speak exactly as its audience speaks, corresponds to the academic landscape and has the same virtue of a photographic likeness. Everyone should know nowadays the unimportance of the photographic in art: that truth, life, or reality is an organic thing which the poetic imagination can represent or suggest, in essence, only through transformation, through changing into other forms than those which were merely present in appearance.

These remarks are not meant as a preface only to this particular play. They have to do with a conception of a new, plastic theatre which must take the place of the exhausted theatre of realistic conventions if the theatre is to resume vitality as a part of our culture.

THE SCREEN DEVICE. There is *only one important difference between the original and acting version of the play* and that is the *omission* in the latter of the device which I tentatively included in my *original* script. This device was the use of a screen on which were projected magic-lantern slides bearing images or titles. I do not regret the omission of this device from the present Broadway production. The extraordinary power of Miss Taylor's performance made it suitable to have the utmost simplicity in the physical production. But I think it may be interesting to some readers to see how this device was conceived. So I am putting it into the published manuscript. These images and legends, projected from behind, were cast on a section of wall between the front-room and dining-room areas, which should be indistinguishable from the rest when not in use.

The purpose of this will probably be apparent. It is to give accent to certain values in each scene. Each scene contains a particular point (or several) which is structurally the most important. In an episodic play, such as this, the basic structure or narrative line may be obscured from the audience; the effect may seem fragmentary rather than architectural. This may not be the fault of the play so much as a lack of attention in the audience. The legend or image upon the screen will strengthen the effect of what is merely allusion in the writing and allow the primary point to be made more simply and lightly than if the entire responsibility were on the spoken lines. Aside from this structural value, I think the screen will have a definite emotional appeal, less definable but just as important. An imaginative producer or director may invent many other uses for this device than those indicated in the present script. In fact the possibilities of the device seem much larger to me than the instance of this play can possibly utilize.

THE MUSIC. Another extra-literary accent in this play is provided by the use of music. A single re-curring tune, "The Glass Menagerie," is used to give emotional emphasis to suitable passages. This tune is like circus music, not when you are on the grounds or in the immediate vicinity of the parade, but when you are at some distance and very likely thinking of something else. It seems under those circumstances to continue almost interminably and it weaves in and out of your preoccupied consciousness; then it is the lightest, most delicate music in the world and perhaps the saddest. It expresses the surface vivacity of life with the underlying strain of immutable and inexpressible sorrow. When you look at a piece of delicately spun glass you think of two things: how beautiful it is and how easily it can be broken. Both of those ideas should be woven into the recurring tune, which dips in and out of the play as if it were carried on a wind that changes. It serves as a thread of connection and allusion between the narrator with his separate point in time and space and the subject of his story. Between each episode it returns as reference to the emotion, nostalgia, which is the first condition of the play. It is primarily Laura's music and therefore comes out most clearly when the play focuses upon her and the lovely fragility of glass which is her image.

THE LIGHTING. The lighting in the play is not realistic. In keeping with the atmosphere of memory, the stage is dim. Shafts of light are focused on selected areas or actors, sometimes in contradistinction to what is the apparent center. For instance, in the quarrel scene between Tom and Amanda, in which Laura has no active part, the clearest pool of light is on her figure. This is also true of the supper scene, when her silent figure on the sofa should remain the visual center. The light upon Laura should be distinct from the others, having a peculiar pristine clarity such as light used in early religious portraits of female saints or madonnas. A certain correspondence to light in religious paintings, such as El Greco's, where the figures are radiant in atmosphere that is relatively dusky, could be effectively used throughout the play. (It will also permit a more effective use of the screen.) A free, imaginative use of light can be of enormous value in giving a mobile, plastic quality to plays of a more or less static nature.

BIBLIOGRAPHY: John Mason Brown, *Seeing Things* (pp. 224–230), 1946; Brown, *Seeing More Things* (pp. 266–272), 1948; John Gassner, "Tennessee Williams: Dramatist of Frustration," in *College English*, Vol. 10, No. 1, October 1948; Paul Moor, "A Mississippian Named Tennessee," in *Harper's*, July 1948; George Jean Nathan, *Theatre Book of the Year 1944–1945; 1947–1948; 1948–1949;* Tennessee Williams, "The Catastrophe of Success," in *The Glass Menagerie* (New Classics edition), 1945; Stark Young, *Immortal Shadows* (pp. 249–253), 1948.

THE GLASS MENAGERIE

By Tennessee Williams

THE CHARACTERS

AMANDA WINGFIELD, *the mother*

A little woman of great but confused vitality clinging frantically to another time and place. Her characterization must be carefully created, not copied from type. She is not paranoiac, but her life is paranoia. There is much to admire in Amanda, and as much to love and pity as there is to laugh at. Certainly she has endurance and a kind of heroism, and though her foolishness makes her unwittingly cruel at times, there is tenderness in her slight person.

LAURA WINGFIELD, *her daughter*

Amanda, having failed to establish contact with reality, continues to live vitally in her illusions, but Laura's situation is even graver. A childhood illness has left her crippled, one leg slightly shorter than the other, and held in a brace. This defect need not be more than suggested on the stage. Stemming from this, Laura's separation increases till she is like a piece of her own glass collection, too exquisitely fragile to move from the shelf.

TOM WINGFIELD, *her son*

And the narrator of the play. A poet with a job in a warehouse. His nature is not remorseless, but to escape from a trap he has to act without pity.

JIM O'CONNOR, *the gentleman caller*

A nice, ordinary, young man.

SCENE

AN ALLEY IN ST. LOUIS

PART I. Preparation for a Gentleman Caller.
PART II. The Gentleman calls.

Time: Now and the Past.

SCENE I.

The Wingfield apartment is in the rear of the building, one of those vast hive-like conglomerations of cellular living-units that flower as warty growths in overcrowded urban centers of lower middle-class population and are symptomatic of the impulse of this largest and fundamentally enslaved section of American society to avoid fluidity and differentiation and to exist and function as one interfused mass of automatism.

The apartment faces an alley and is entered by a fire-escape, a structure whose name is a touch of accidental poetic truth, for all of these huge buildings are always burning with the slow and implacable fires of human desperation. The fire-escape is included in the set—that is, the landing of it and steps descending from it.

The scene is memory and is therefore nonrealistic. Memory takes a lot of poetic license. It omits some details; others are exaggerated, according to the emotional value of the articles it touches, for memory is seated predominantly in the heart. The interior is therefore rather dim and poetic.

At the rise of the curtain, the audience is faced with the dark, grim rear wall of the Wingfield tene-ment. This building, which runs parallel to the footlights, is flanked on both sides by dark, narrow alleys which run into murky canyons of tangled clothes-lines, garbage cans and the sinister lattice-work of neighboring fire-escapes. It is up and down these side alleys that exterior entrances and exits are made, during the play. At the end of Tom's opening commentary, the dark tenement wall slowly reveals (by means of a transparency) the interior of the ground floor Wingfield apartment.

Downstage is the living room, which also serves as a sleeping room for Laura, the sofa unfolding to make her bed. Upstage, center, and divided by a wide arch or second proscenium with transparent faded portieres (or second curtain), is the dining room. In an old-fashioned what-not in the living room are seen scores of transparent glass animals. A blown-up photograph of the father hangs on the wall of the living room, facing the audience, to the left of the archway. It is the face of a very handsome young man in a doughboy's First World War cap. He is gallantly smiling, ineluctably smiling, as if to say, "I will be smiling forever."

The audience hears and sees the opening scene in the dining room through both the transparent fourth wall of the building and the transparent gauze portieres of the dining-room arch. It is during this revealing scene that the fourth wall slowly ascends, out of sight. This transparent exterior wall is not brought down again until the very end of the play, during Tom's *final speech.*

The narrator is an undisguised convention of the play. He takes whatever license with dramatic convention as is convenient to his purposes.

Tom *enters dressed as a merchant sailor from alley, stage left, and strolls across the front of the stage to the fire-escape. There he stops and lights a cigarette. He addresses the audience.*

TOM: Yes, I have tricks in my pocket, I have things up my sleeve. But I am the opposite of a stage magician. He gives you illusion that has the appearance of truth. I give you truth in the pleasant disguise of illusion.

To begin with, I turn back time. I reverse it to that quaint period, the thirties, when the huge middle class of America was matriculating in a school for the blind. Their eyes had failed them, or they had failed their eyes, and so they were having their fingers pressed forcibly down on the fiery Braille alphabet of a dissolving economy.

In Spain there was revolution. Here there was only shouting and confusion.

In Spain there was Guernica. Here there were disturbances of labor, sometimes pretty violent, in otherwise peaceful cities such as Chicago, Cleveland, Saint Louis . . .

This is the social background of the play.

[MUSIC]

The play is memory.

Being a memory play, it is dimly lighted, it is sentimental, it is not realistic.

In memory everything seems to happen to music. That explains the fiddle in the wings.

I am the narrator of the play, and also a character in it.

The other characters are my mother, Amanda, my sister, Laura, and a gentleman caller who appears in the final scenes.

He is the most realistic character in the play, being an emissary from a world of reality that we were somehow set apart from.

But since I have a poet's weakness for symbols, I am using this character also as a symbol; he is the long delayed but always expected something that we live for.

There is a fifth character in the play who doesn't appear except in this larger-than-life-size photograph over the mantel.

This is our father who left us a long time ago.

He was a telephone man who fell in love with long distances; he gave up his job with the telephone company and skipped the light fantastic out of town . . .

The last we heard of him was a picture post-card from Mazatlan, on the Pacific coast of Mexico, containing a message of two words—

"Hello— Good-bye!" and no address.

I think the rest of the play will explain itself. . . .

[Amanda's *voice becomes audible through the portieres*]

[LEGEND ON SCREEN: "OÙ SONT LES NEIGES"]

He divides the portieres and enters the upstage area. Amanda *and* Laura *are seated at a drop-leaf table. Eating is indicated by gestures without food or utensils.* Amanda *faces the audience.* Tom *and* Laura *are seated in profile. The interior has lit up softly and through the scrim we see* Amanda *and* Laura *seated at the table in the upstage area.*

AMANDA: [*Calling*] Tom?

TOM: Yes, Mother.

AMANDA: We can't say grace until you come to the table!

TOM: Coming, Mother. [*He bows slightly and withdraws, reappearing a few moments later in his place at the table*]

AMANDA: [*To her son*] Honey, don't *push* with your *fingers.* If you have to push with something, the thing to push with is a crust of bread. And chew —chew! Animals have sections in their stomachs which enable them to digest food without mastication, but human beings are supposed to chew their food before they swallow it down. Eat food leisurely, son, and really enjoy it. A well-cooked meal has lots of delicate flavors that have to be held in the mouth for appreciation. So chew your food and give your salivary glands a chance to function!

[Tom *deliberately lays his imaginary fork down and pushes his chair back from the table*]

TOM: I haven't enjoyed one bite of this dinner because of your constant directions on how to eat it. It's you that make me rush through meals with your hawk-like attention to every bite I take. Sickening— spoils my appetite—all this discussion of—animals' secretion—salivary glands—mastication!

AMANDA: [*Lightly*] Temperament like a Metropolitan star! [*He rises and crosses downstage*] You're not excused from the table.

TOM: I'm getting a cigarette.

AMANDA: You smoke too much. [Laura *rises*]

LAURA: I'll bring in the blanc mange. [*He remains standing with his cigarette by the portieres during the following*]

AMANDA: [*Rising*] No, sister, no, sister—you be the lady this time and I'll be the darky.

LAURA: I'm already up.

AMANDA: Resume your seat, little sister—I want you to stay fresh and pretty—for gentlemen callers!

LAURA: I'm not expecting any gentlemen callers.

AMANDA: [*Crossing out to kitchenette. Airily*] Sometimes they come when they are least expected! Why, I remember one Sunday afternoon in Blue Mountain—[*Enters kitchenette*]

TOM: I know what's coming!

LAURA: Yes. But let her tell it.

TOM: Again?

LAURA: She loves to tell it.

[Amanda *returns with bowl of dessert*]

AMANDA: One Sunday afternoon in Blue Mountain—your mother received—*seventeen*—gentlemen callers! Why, sometimes there weren't chairs enough to accommodate them all. We had to send the nigger over to bring in folding chairs from the parish house.

TOM: [*Remaining at portieres*] How did you entertain those gentlemen callers?

AMANDA: I understood the art of conversation!

TOM: I bet you could talk.

AMANDA: Girls in those days *knew* how to talk, I can tell you.

TOM: Yes?

[IMAGE: Amanda AS A GIRL ON A PORCH, GREETING CALLERS]

AMANDA: They knew how to entertain their gentlemen callers. It wasn't enough for a girl to be possessed of a pretty face and a graceful figure—although I wasn't slighted in either respect. She also needed to have a nimble wit and a tongue to meet all occasions.

TOM: What did you talk about?

AMANDA: Things of importance going on in the world! Never anything coarse or common or vulgar. [*She addresses* Tom *as though he were seated in the vacant chair at the table though he remains by portieres. He plays this scene as though he held the book*] My callers were gentlemen—all! Among my callers were some of the most prominent young planters of the Mississippi Delta—planters and sons of planters!

[Tom *motions for music and a spot of light on* Amanda. *Her eyes lift, her face glows, her voice becomes rich and elegiac*]

[SCREEN LEGEND: "OÙ SONT LES NEIGES"]

There was young Champ Laughlin who later became vice-president of the Delta Planters Bank.

Hadley Stevenson who was drowned in Moon Lake and left his widow one hundred and fifty thousand in Government bonds.

There were the Cutrere brothers, Wesley and Bates. Bates was one of my bright particular beaux! He got in a quarrel with that wild Wainwright boy. They shot it out on the floor of Moon Lake Casino. Bates was shot through the stomach. Died in the ambulance on his way to Memphis. His widow was also well-provided for, came into eight or ten thousand acres, that's all. She married him on the rebound—never loved her—carried my picture on him the night he died!

And there was that boy that every girl in the Delta had set her cap for! That beautiful, brilliant young Fitzhugh boy from Greene County!

TOM: What did he leave his widow?

AMANDA: He never married! Gracious, you talk as though all of my old admirers had turned up their toes to the daisies!

TOM: Isn't this the first you've mentioned that still survives?

AMANDA: That Fitzhugh boy went North and made a fortune—came to be known as the Wolf of Wall Street! He had the Midas touch, whatever he touched turned to gold!

And I could have been Mrs. Duncan J. Fitzhugh, mind you! But—I picked your *father*!

LAURA: [*Rising*] Mother, let me clear the table.

AMANDA: No, dear, you go in front and study your typewriter chart. Or practice your shorthand a little. Stay fresh and pretty!—It's almost time for our gentlemen callers to start arriving. [*She flounces girlishly toward the kitchenette*] How many do you suppose we're going to entertain this afternoon?

[Tom *throws down the paper and jumps up with a groan*]

LAURA: [*Alone in the dining room*] I don't believe we're going to receive any, Mother.

AMANDA: [*Reappearing, airily*] What? No one—not one? You must be joking! [Laura *nervously echoes her laugh. She slips in a fugitive manner through the half-open portieres and draws them gently behind her. A shaft of very clear light is thrown on her face against the faded tapestry of the curtains.* MUSIC: "THE GLASS MENAGERIE" UNDER FAINTLY. *Lightly*] Not one gentleman caller? It can't be true! There must be a flood, there must have been a tornado!

LAURA: It isn't a flood, it's not a tornado, Mother. I'm just not popular like you were in Blue Mountain. . . . [Tom *utters another groan.* Laura *glances at him with a faint, apologetic smile. Her voice catching a little*] Mother's afraid I'm going to be an old maid.

THE SCENE DIMS OUT WITH "GLASS MENAGERIE"

MUSIC

SCENE II.

"Laura, Haven't You Ever Liked Some Boy?"

On the dark stage the screen is lighted with the image of blue roses. Gradually Laura's *figure becomes apparent and the screen goes out. The music subsides.*

Laura *is seated in the delicate ivory chair at the small clawfoot table. She wears a dress of soft violet material for a kimono—her hair tied back from her forehead with a ribbon. She is washing and polishing her collection of glass.*

Amanda *appears on the fire-escape steps. At the sound of her ascent,* Laura *catches her breath, thrusts the bowl of ornaments away and seats herself stiffly before the diagram of the typewriter keyboard as though it held her spellbound. Something has happened to* Amanda. *It is written in her face as she climbs to the landing: a look that is grim and hopeless and a little absurd. She has on one of those cheap or imitation velvety-looking cloth coats with imitation fur collar. Her hat is five or six years old, one of those dreadful cloche hats that were worn in the late twenties and she is clasping an enormous black patent-leather pocketbook with nickel clasps and initials. This is her full-dress outfit, the one she usually wears to the D.A.R. Before entering she looks through the door. She purses her lips, opens her eyes very wide, rolls them upward and shakes her head. Then she slowly lets herself in the door. Seeing her mother's expression Laura touches her lips with a nervous gesture.*

LAURA: Hello, Mother, I was— [*She makes a nervous gesture toward the chart on the wall.* Amanda *leans against the shut door and stares at* Laura *with a martyred look*]

AMANDA: Deception? Deception? [*She slowly removes her hat and gloves, continuing the sweet suffering stare. She lets the hat and gloves fall on the floor—a bit of acting*]

LAURA: [*Shakily*] How was the D.A.R. meeting? [Amanda *slowly opens her purse and removes a dainty white handkerchief which she shakes out delicately and delicately touches to her lips and nostrils*] Didn't you go to the D.A.R. meeting, Mother?

AMANDA: [*Faintly, almost inaudibly*]—No.—No. [*Then more forcibly*] I did not have the strength— to go to the D.A.R. In fact, I did not have the courage! I wanted to find a hole in the ground and hide myself in it forever! [*She crosses slowly to the wall and removes the diagram of the typewriter keyboard. She holds it in front of her for a second, staring at it sweetly and sorrowfully—then bites her lips and tears it in two pieces*]

LAURA: [*Faintly*] Why did you do that, Mother? [Amanda *repeats the same procedure with the chart of the Gregg Alphabet*] Why are you—

AMANDA: Why? Why? How old are you, Laura?

LAURA: Mother, you know my age.

AMANDA: I thought that you were an adult; it seems that I was mistaken. [*She crosses slowly to the sofa and sinks down and stares at* Laura]

LAURA: Please don't stare at me, Mother.

[Amanda *closes her eyes and lowers her head. Count ten*]

AMANDA: What are we going to do, what is going to become of us, what is the future? [*Count ten*]

LAURA: Has something happened, Mother? [Amanda *draws a long breath and takes out the handkerchief again. Dabbing process*] Mother, has —something happened?

AMANDA: I'll be all right in a minute, I'm just bewildered—[*Count five*]—by life. . . .

LAURA: Mother, I wish that you would tell me what's happened!

AMANDA: As you know, I was supposed to be inducted into my office at the D.A.R. this afternoon. [IMAGE: A SWARM OF TYPEWRITERS] But I stopped off at Rubicam's Business College to speak to your teachers about your having a cold and ask them what progress they thought you were making down there.

LAURA: Oh. . . .

AMANDA: I went to the typing instructor and introduced myself as your mother. She didn't know who you were. Wingfield, she said. We don't have any such student enrolled at the school!

I assured her she did, that you have been going to classes since early in January.

"I wonder," she said, "if you could be talking about that terribly shy little girl who dropped out of school after only a few days' attendance?"

"No," I said, "Laura, my daughter, has been going to school every day for the past six weeks!"

"Excuse me," she said. She took the attendance book out and there was your name, unmistakably printed, and all the dates you were absent until they decided that you had dropped out of school.

I still said, "No, there must have been some mistake! There must have been some mix-up in the records!"

And she said, "No—I remember her perfectly now. Her hands shook so that she couldn't hit the right keys! The first time we gave a speed-test, she broke down completely—was sick at the stomach and almost had to be carried into the wash-room! After that morning she never showed up any more. We phoned the house but never got any answer— while I was working at Famous and Barr, I suppose, demonstrating those— Oh!"

I felt so weak I could barely keep on my feet!

I had to sit down while they got me a glass of water!

Fifty dollars' tuition, all of our plans—my hopes and ambitions for you—just gone up the spout, just gone up the spout like that. [Laura *draws a long breath and gets awkwardly to her feet. She crosses to the victrola and winds it up*] What are you doing?

LAURA: Oh! [*She releases the handle and returns to her seat*]

AMANDA: Laura, where have you been going when you've gone out pretending that you were going to business college?

LAURA: I've just been going out walking.

AMANDA: That's not true.

LAURA: It is. I just went walking.

AMANDA: Walking? Walking? In winter? Deliberately courting pneumonia in that light coat? Where did you walk to, Laura?

LAURA: All sorts of places—mostly in the park.

AMANDA: Even after you'd started catching that cold?

LAURA: It was the lesser of two evils, Mother. [IMAGE: WINTER SCENE IN PARK] I couldn't go back up. I—threw up—on the floor!

AMANDA: From half past seven till after five every day you mean to tell me you walked around in the park, because you wanted to make me think that you were still going to Rubicam's Business College?

LAURA: It wasn't as bad as it sounds. I went inside places to get warmed up.

AMANDA: Inside where?

LAURA: I went in the art museum and the bird-houses at the Zoo. I visited the penguins every day! Sometimes I did without lunch and went to the movies. Lately I've been spending most of my afternoons in the Jewel-box, that big glass house where they raise the tropical flowers.

AMANDA: You did all this to deceive me, just for deception? [Laura *looks down*] Why?

LAURA: Mother, when you're disappointed, you get that awful suffering look on your face, like the picture of Jesus' mother in the museum!

AMANDA: Hush!

LAURA: I couldn't face it.

[*Pause. A whisper of strings*]

[LEGEND: "THE CRUST OF HUMILITY"]

AMANDA: [*Hopelessly fingering the huge pocket-book*] So what are we going to do the rest of our lives? Stay home and watch the parades go by? Amuse ourselves with the glass menagerie, darling? Eternally play those worn-out phonograph records your father left as a painful reminder of him?

We won't have a business career—we've given that up because it gave us nervous indigestion! [*Laughs wearily*] What is there left but dependency all our lives? I know so well what becomes of unmarried women who aren't prepared to occupy a position. I've seen such pitiful cases in the South—barely tolerated spinsters living upon the grudging patronage of sister's husband or brother's wife!—stuck away in some little mouse-trap of a room—encouraged by one in-law to visit another—little birdlike women without any nest—eating the crust of humility all their life!

Is that the future that we've mapped out for ourselves?

I swear it's the only alternative I can think of!

It isn't a very pleasant alternative, is it?

Of course—some girls *do marry*.

[Laura *twists her hands nervously*]

Haven't you ever liked some boy?

LAURA: Yes. I liked one once. [*Rises*] I came across his picture a while ago.

AMANDA: [*With some interest*] He gave you his picture?

LAURA: No, it's in the year-book.

AMANDA: [*Disappointed*] Oh—a high-school boy.

[SCREEN IMAGE: JIM AS HIGH-SCHOOL HERO BEARING A SILVER CUP]

LAURA: Yes. His name was Jim. [Laura *lifts the heavy annual from the claw-foot table*] Here he is in *The Pirates of Penzance*.

AMANDA: [*Absently*] The what?

LAURA: The operetta the senior class put on. He had a wonderful voice and we sat across the aisle from each other Mondays, Wednesdays and Fridays in the Aud. Here he is with the silver cup for debating! See his grin?

AMANDA: [*Absently*] He must have had a jolly disposition.

LAURA: He used to call me—Blue Roses.

[IMAGE: BLUE ROSES]

AMANDA: Why did he call you such a name as that?

LAURA: When I had that attack of pleurosis—he asked me what was the matter when I came back. I said pleurosis—he thought that I said Blue Roses! So that's what he always called me after that. Whenever he saw me, he'd holler, "Hello, Blue Roses!" I didn't care for the girl that he went out with. Emily Meisenbach. Emily was the best-dressed girl at Soldan. She never struck me, though, as being sincere . . . It says in the Personal Section—they're engaged. That's—six years ago! They must be married by now.

AMANDA: Girls that aren't cut out for business careers usually wind up married to some nice man. [*Gets up with a spark of revival*] Sister, that's what you'll do!

[Laura *utters a startled, doubtful laugh. She reaches quickly for a piece of glass*]

LAURA: But, Mother—

AMANDA: Yes? [*Crossing to photograph*]

LAURA: [*In a tone of frightened apology*] I'm—crippled!

[IMAGE: SCREEN]

AMANDA: Nonsense! Laura, I've told you never, never to use that word. Why, you're not crippled, you just have a little defect—hardly noticeable, even! When people have some slight disadvantage like that, they cultivate other things to make up for it—develop charm—and vivacity—and—*charm!* That's all you have to do! [*She turns again to the photograph*] One thing your father had *plenty of*—was *charm!*

[Tom *motions to the fiddle in the wings*]

THE SCENE FADES OUT WITH MUSIC

SCENE III.

LEGEND ON SCREEN: "AFTER THE FIASCO—"
TOM *speaks from the fire-escape landing.*

TOM: After the fiasco at Rubicam's Business College, the idea of getting a gentleman caller for Laura began to play a more and more important part in Mother's calculations.

It became an obsession. Like some archetype of the universal unconscious, the image of the gentleman caller haunted our small apartment. . . .

[IMAGE: YOUNG MAN AT DOOR WITH FLOWERS]

An evening at home rarely passed without some allusion to this image, this spectre, this hope. . . .

Even when he wasn't mentioned, his presence hung in Mother's preoccupied look and in my sister's frightened, apologetic manner—hung like a sentence passed upon the Wingfields!

Mother was a woman of action as well as words. She began to take logical steps in the planned direction.

Late that winter and in the early spring—realizing that extra money would be needed to properly feather the nest and plume the bird—she conducted a vigorous campaign on the telephone, roping in subscribers to one of those magazines for matrons called *The Home-maker's Companion,* the type of journal that features the serialized sublimations of ladies of letters who think in terms of delicate cup-like breasts, slim, tapering waists, rich, creamy thighs, eyes like wood-smoke in autumn, fingers that soothe and caress like strains of music, bodies as powerful as Etruscan sculpture.

[SCREEN IMAGE: GLAMOR MAGAZINE COVER]

[Amanda *enters with phone on long extension cord. She is spotted in the dim stage*]

AMANDA: Ida Scott? This is Amanda Wingfield! We *missed* you at the D.A.R. last Monday!

I said to myself: She's probably suffering with that sinus condition! How is that sinus condition?

Horrors! Heaven have mercy!—You're a Christian martyr, yes, that's what you are, a Christian martyr!

Well, I just now happened to notice that your subscription to the *Companion's* about to expire! Yes, it expires with the next issue, honey!—just when that wonderful new serial by Bessie Mae Hopper is getting off to such an exciting start. Oh, honey, it's something that you can't miss! You remember how *Gone With the Wind* took everybody by storm? You simply couldn't go out if you hadn't read it. All everybody *talked* was Scarlett O'Hara. Well, this is a book that critics already compare to *Gone With the Wind.* It's the *Gone With the Wind* of the post-World War generation!—What?—Burning?—Oh, honey, don't let them burn, go take a look in the oven and I'll hold the wire! Heavens—I think she's hung up!

DIM OUT

[LEGEND ON SCREEN: "YOU THINK I'M IN LOVE WITH CONTINENTAL SHOEMAKERS?"]

[*Before the stage is lighted, the violent voices of* Tom *and* Amanda *are heard. They are quarreling behind the portieres. In front of them stands* Laura *with clenched hands and panicky expression. A clear pool of light on her figure throughout this scene*]

TOM: What in Christ's name am I—

AMANDA: [*Shrilly*] Don't you use that—

TOM: Supposed to do!

AMANDA: Expression! Not in my—

TOM: Ohhh!

AMANDA: Presence! Have you gone out of your senses?

TOM: I have, that's true, *driven* out!

AMANDA: What is the matter with you, you—big—big—IDIOT!

TOM: Look!—I've got *no thing,* no single thing—

AMANDA: Lower your voice!

TOM: In my life here that I can call my OWN! Everything is—

AMANDA: Stop that shouting!

TOM: Yesterday you confiscated my books! You had the nerve to—

AMANDA: I took that horrible novel back to the library—yes! That hideous book by that insane Mr. Lawrence. [Tom *laughs wildly*] I cannot control the output of diseased minds or people who cater to them—[Tom *laughs still more wildly*] BUT I WON'T ALLOW SUCH FILTH BROUGHT INTO MY HOUSE! No, no, no, no, no!

TOM: House, house! Who pays rent on it, who makes a slave of himself to—

AMANDA: [*Fairly screeching*] Don't you DARE to—

TOM: No, no, *I* mustn't say things! *I've* got to just—

AMANDA: Let me tell you—

TOM: I don't want to hear any more! [*He tears the portieres open. The upstage area is lit with a turgid smoky red glow*]

[Amanda's *hair is in metal curlers and she wears a very old bathrobe, much too large for her slight figure, a relic of the faithless Mr. Wingfield. An upright typewriter and a wild disarray of manuscripts is on the drop-leaf table. The quarrel was probably precipitated by Amanda's interruption of his creative labor. A chair lying overthrown on the floor. Their gesticulating shadows are cast on the ceiling by the fiery glow*]

AMANDA: You *will* hear more, you—

TOM: No, I won't hear more, I'm going out!

AMANDA: You come right back in—

TOM: Out, out, out! Because I'm—

AMANDA: Come back here, Tom Wingfield! I'm not through talking to you!

TOM: Oh, go—

LAURA: [*Desperately*]—Tom!

AMANDA: You're going to listen, and no more insolence from you! I'm at the end of my patience!

[*He comes back toward her*]

TOM: What do you think I'm at? Aren't I supposed to have any patience to reach the end of, Mother? I know, I know. It seems unimportant to you, what I'm *doing*—what I *want* to do—having a little *difference* between them! You don't think that—

AMANDA: I think you've been doing things that you're ashamed of. That's why you act like this. I don't believe that you go every night to the movies. Nobody goes to the movies night after night. Nobody in their right minds goes to the movies as often as you pretend to. People don't go to the movies at

nearly midnight, and movies don't let out at two
A.M. Come in stumbling. Muttering to yourself like
a maniac! You get three hours' sleep and then go
to work. Oh, I can picture the way you're doing
down there. Moping, doping, because you're in no
condition.

TOM: [*Wildly*] No, I'm in no condition!

AMANDA: What right have you got to jeopardize
your job? Jeopardize the security of us all? How
do you think we'd manage if you were—

TOM: Listen! You think I'm crazy *about* the
warehouse? [*He bends fiercely toward her slight
figure*] You think I'm in love with the Continental
Shoemakers? You think I want to spend fifty-five
years down there in that—*celotex interior!* with—
fluorescent—tubes! Look! I'd rather somebody
picked up a crowbar and battered out my brains—
than go back mornings! I *go!* Every time you come
in yelling that God damn *"Rise and Shine!" "Rise
and Shine!"* I say to myself, "How *lucky dead* people
are!" But I get up. I *go!* For sixty-five dollars a
month I give up all that I dream of doing and being
ever! And you say self—*self's* all I ever think of.
Why, listen, if self is what I thought of, Mother, I'd
be where he is—GONE! [*Pointing to father's picture*] As far as the system of transportation reaches!
[*He starts past her. She grabs his arm*] Don't grab
at me, Mother!

AMANDA: Where are you going?

TOM: I'm going to the *movies!*

AMANDA: I don't believe that lie!

TOM: [*Crouching toward her, overtowering her
tiny figure. She backs away, gasping*] I'm going to
opium dens! Yes, opium dens, dens of vice and
criminals' hang-outs, Mother. I've joined the Hogan
gang, I'm a hired assassin, I carry a tommy-gun in a
violin case! I run a string of cat-houses in the
Valley! They call me Killer, Killer Wingfield, I'm
leading a double-life, a simple, honest warehouse
worker by day, by night a dynamic *czar* of the
underworld, Mother. I go to gambling casinos, I
spin away fortunes on the roulette table! I wear a
patch over one eye and a false mustache, sometimes
I put on green whiskers. On those occasions they
call me—*El Diablo!* Oh, I could tell you things to
make you sleepless! My enemies plan to dynamite
this place. They're going to blow us all sky-high
some night! I'll be glad, very happy, and so will
you! You'll go up, up on a broomstick, over Blue
Mountain with seventeen gentlemen callers! You
ugly—babbling old—witch. . . . [*He goes through
a series of violent, clumsy movements, seizing his
overcoat, lunging to the door, pulling it fiercely
open. The women watch him, aghast. His arm
catches in the sleeve of the coat as he struggles to
pull it on. For a moment he is pinioned by the
bulky garment. With an outraged groan he tears
the coat off again, splitting the shoulder of it, and
hurls it across the room. It strikes against the shelf*

of Laura's *glass collection, there is a tinkle of shattering glass.* Laura *cries out as if wounded*]
[MUSIC. LEGEND: "THE GLASS MENAGERIE"]

LAURA: [*Shrilly*] My glass!—menagerie. . . .
[*She covers her face and turns away*]
[*But Amanda is still stunned and stupefied by
the "ugly witch" so that she barely notices this
occurrence. Now she recovers her speech*]

AMANDA: [*In an awful voice*] I won't speak to you
—until you apologize! [*She crosses through portieres and draws them together behind her. Tom
is left with Laura. Laura clings weakly to the mantel
with her face averted. Tom stares at her stupidly for
a moment. Then he crosses to shelf. Drops awkwardly on his knees to collect the fallen glass, glancing at Laura as if he would speak but couldn't*]
"The Glass Menagerie" steals in as

THE SCENE DIMS OUT

SCENE IV.

*The interior is dark. Faint light in the alley. A
deep-voiced bell in a church is tolling the hour of
five as the scene commences.*

Tom *appears at the top of the alley. After each
solemn boom of the bell in the tower, he shakes a
little noise-maker or rattle as if to express the tiny
spasm of man in contrast to the sustained power
and dignity of the Almighty. This and the unsteadiness of his advance make it evident that he has been
drinking. As he climbs the few steps to the fire-
escape landing light steals up inside. Laura appears
in night-dress, observing Tom's empty bed in the
front room. Tom fishes in his pockets for door-key,
removing a motley assortment of articles in the
search, including a perfect shower of movie-ticket
stubs and an empty bottle. At last he finds the key,
but just as he is about to insert it, it slips from his
fingers. He strikes a match and crouches below the
door.*

TOM: [*Bitterly*] One crack—and it falls through!
[Laura *opens the door*]

LAURA: Tom! Tom, what are you doing?

TOM: Looking for a door-key.

LAURA: Where have you been all this time?

TOM: I have been to the movies.

LAURA: All this time at the movies?

TOM: There was a very long program. There was
a Garbo picture and a Mickey Mouse and a trav-
elogue and a newsreel and a preview of coming
attractions. And there was an organ solo and a collection for the milk-fund—simultaneously—which
ended up in a terrible fight between a fat lady and an
usher!

LAURA: [*Innocently*] Did you have to stay through
everything?

TOM: Of course! And, oh, I forgot! There was a big stage show! The headliner on this stage show was Malvolio the Magician. He performed wonderful tricks, many of them, such as pouring water back and forth between pitchers. First it turned to wine and then it turned to beer and then it turned to whiskey. I know it was whiskey it finally turned into because he needed somebody to come up out of the audience to help him, and I came up—both shows! It was Kentucky Straight Bourbon. A very generous fellow, he gave souvenirs. [*He pulls from his back pocket a shimmering rainbow-colored scarf*] He gave me this. This is his magic scarf. You can have it, Laura. You wave it over a canary cage and you get a bowl of gold-fish. You wave it over the gold-fish bowl and they fly away canaries. . . . But the wonderfullest trick of all was the coffin trick. We nailed him into a coffin and he got out of the coffin without removing one nail. [*He has come inside*] There is a trick that would come in handy for me—get me out of this 2 by 4 situation. [*Flops onto bed and starts removing shoes*]

LAURA: Tom—Shhh!

TOM: What're you shushing me for?

LAURA: You'll wake up Mother.

TOM: Goody, goody! Pay 'er back for all those "Rise an' Shines." [*Lies down, groaning*] You know it don't take much intelligence to get yourself into a nailed-up coffin, Laura. But who in hell ever got himself out of one without removing one nail?

[*As if in answer, the father's grinning photograph lights up*]

SCENE DIMS OUT

[*Immediately following: The church bell is heard striking six. At the sixth stroke the alarm clock goes off in* Amanda's *room, and after a few moments we hear her calling: "Rise and Shine! Rise and Shine! Laura, go tell your brother to rise and shine!"*]

TOM: [*Sitting up slowly*] I'll rise—but I won't shine.

[*The light increases*]

AMANDA: Laura, tell your brother his coffee is ready.

[Laura *slips into front room*]

LAURA: Tom!—It's nearly seven. Don't make Mother nervous. [*He stares at her stupidly. Beseechingly*] Tom, speak to Mother this morning. Make up with her, apologize, speak to her!

TOM: She won't to me. It's her that started not speaking.

LAURA: If you just say you're sorry she'll start speaking.

TOM: Her not speaking—is that such a tragedy?

LAURA: Please—please!

AMANDA: [*Calling from kitchenette*] Laura, are you going to do what I asked you to do, or do I have to get dressed and go out myself?

LAURA: Going, going—soon as I get on my coat!

[*She pulls on a shapeless felt hat with nervous,* jerky movement, pleadingly glancing at Tom. *Rushes awkwardly for coat. The coat is one of* Amanda's, *inaccurately made-over, the sleeves too short for* Laura] Butter and what else?

AMANDA: [*Entering upstage*] Just butter. Tell them to charge it.

LAURA: Mother, they make such faces when I do that.

AMANDA: Sticks and stones can break our bones, but the expression on Mr. Garfinkel's face won't harm us! Tell your brother his coffee is getting cold.

LAURA: [*At door*] Do what I asked you, will you, will you, Tom?

[*He looks sullenly away*]

AMANDA: Laura, go now or just don't go at all!

LAURA: [*Rushing out*] Going—going! [*A second later she cries out.* Tom *springs up and crosses to door.* Amanda *rushes anxiously in.* Tom *opens the door*]

TOM: Laura?

LAURA: I'm all right. I slipped, but I'm all right.

AMANDA: [*Peering anxiously after her*] If anyone breaks a leg on those fire-escape steps, the landlord ought to be sued for every cent he possesses! [*She shuts door. Remembers she isn't speaking and returns to other room*]

[*As* Tom *enters listlessly for his coffee, she turns her back to him and stands rigidly facing the window on the gloomy gray vault of the areaway. Its light on her face with its aged but childish features is cruelly sharp, satirical as a Daumier print*]

[MUSIC UNDER: "AVE MARIA"]

[Tom *glances sheepishly but sullenly at her averted figure and slumps at the table. The coffee is scalding hot; he sips it and gasps and spits it back in the cup. At his gasp,* Amanda *catches her breath and half turns. Then catches herself and turns back to window.* Tom *blows on his coffee, glancing sidewise at his mother. She clears her throat.* Tom *clears his. He starts to rise. Sinks back down again, scratches his head, clears his throat again.* Amanda *coughs.* Tom *raises his cup in both hands to blow on it, his eyes staring over the rim of it at his mother for several moments. Then he slowly sets the cup down and awkwardly and hesitantly rises from the chair*]

TOM: [*Hoarsely*] Mother. I—I apologize, Mother. [Amanda *draws a quick, shuddering breath. Her face works grotesquely. She breaks into childlike tears*] I'm sorry for what I said, for everything that I said, I didn't mean it.

AMANDA: [*Sobbingly*] My devotion has made me a witch and so I make myself hateful to my children!

TOM: *No, you don't.*

AMANDA: I worry so much, don't sleep, it makes me nervous!

TOM: [*Gently*] I understand that.

AMANDA: I've had to put up a solitary battle all

these years. But you're my right-hand bower! Don't fall down, don't fail!

TOM: [*Gently*] I try, Mother.

AMANDA: [*With great enthusiasm*] Try and you will SUCCEED! [*The notion makes her breathless*] Why, you—you're just *full* of natural endowments! Both of my children—they're *unusual* children! Don't you think I know it? I'm so—*proud!* Happy and—feel I've—so much to be thankful for but—— Promise me one thing, Son!

TOM: What, Mother?

AMANDA: Promise, son, you'll—never be a drunkard!

TOM: [*Turns to her grinning*] I will never be a drunkard, Mother.

AMANDA: That's what frightened me so, that you'd be drinking! Eat a bowl of Purina!

TOM: Just coffee, Mother.

AMANDA: Shredded wheat biscuit?

TOM: No. No, Mother, just coffee.

AMANDA: You can't put in a day's work on an empty stomach. You've got ten minutes—don't gulp! Drinking too-hot liquids makes cancer of the stomach. . . . Put cream in.

TOM: No, thank you.

AMANDA: To cool it.

TOM: No! No, thank you, I want it black.

AMANDA: I know, but it's not good for you. We have to do all that we can to build ourselves up. In these trying times we live in, all that we have to cling to is—each other. . . . That's why it's so important to—— Tom, I—— I sent out your sister so I could discuss something with you. If you hadn't spoken I would have spoken to you. [*Sits down*]

TOM: [*Gently*] What is it, Mother, that you want to discuss?

AMANDA: *Laura!*

[Tom *puts his cup down slowly*]

[LEGEND ON SCREEN: "LAURA"]

[MUSIC: "THE GLASS MENAGERIE"]

TOM: —Oh.—Laura . . .

AMANDA: [*Touching his sleeve*] You know how Laura is. So quiet but—still water runs deep! She notices things and I think she—broods about them. [Tom *looks up*] A few days ago I came in and she was crying.

TOM: What about?

AMANDA: You.

TOM: Me?

AMANDA: She has an idea that you're not happy here.

TOM: What gave her that idea?

AMANDA: What gives her any idea? However, you do act strangely. I—I'm not criticizing, understand *that!* I know your ambitions do not lie in the warehouse, that like everybody in the whole wide world —you've had to—make sacrifices, but—Tom—Tom —life's not easy, it calls for—Spartan endurance! There's so many things in my heart that I cannot

describe to you! I've never told you but I—*loved* your father. . . .

TOM: [*Gently*] I know that, Mother.

AMANDA: And you—when I see you taking after his ways! Staying out late—and—well, you *had* been drinking the night you were in that—terrifying condition! Laura says that you hate the apartment and that you go out nights to get away from it! Is that true, Tom?

TOM: No. You say there's so much in your heart that you can't describe to me. That's true of me, too. There's so much in my heart that I can't describe to *you!* So let's respect each other's—

AMANDA: But, why—*why*, Tom—are you always so *restless?* Where do you *go* to, nights?

TOM: I—go to the movies.

AMANDA: Why do you go to the movies so much, Tom?

TOM: I go to the movies because—I like adventure. Adventure is something I don't have much of at work, so I go to the movies.

AMANDA: But, Tom, you go to the movies *entirely too much!*

TOM: I like a lot of adventure.

[Amanda *looks baffled, then hurt. As the familiar inquisition resumes he becomes hard and impatient again.* Amanda *slips back into her querulous attitude toward him*]

[IMAGE ON SCREEN: SAILING VESSEL WITH JOLLY ROGER]

AMANDA: Most young men find adventure in their careers.

TOM: Then most young men are not employed in a warehouse.

AMANDA: The world is full of young men employed in warehouses and offices and factories.

TOM: Do all of them find adventure in their careers?

AMANDA: They do or they do without it! Not everybody has a craze for adventure.

TOM: Man is by instinct a lover, a hunter, a fighter, and none of those instincts are given much play at the warehouse!

AMANDA: Man is by instinct! Don't quote instinct to me! Instinct is something that people have got away from! It belongs to animals! Christian adults don't want it!

TOM: What do Christian adults want, then, Mother?

AMANDA: Superior things! Things of the mind and the spirit! Only animals have to satisfy instincts! Surely your aims are somewhat higher than theirs! Than monkeys—pigs—

TOM: I reckon they're not.

AMANDA: You're joking. However, that isn't what I wanted to discuss.

TOM: [*Rising*] I haven't much time.

AMANDA: [*Pushing his shoulders*] Sit down.

TOM: You want me to punch in red at the warehouse, Mother?

AMANDA: You have five minutes. I want to talk about Laura.

[LEGEND: "PLANS AND PROVISIONS"]

TOM: All right! What about Laura?

AMANDA: We have to be making some plans and provisions for her. She's older than you, two years, and nothing has happened. She just drifts along doing nothing. It frightens me terribly how she just drifts along.

TOM: I guess she's the type that people call home girls.

AMANDA: There's no such type, and if there is, it's a pity! That is unless the home is hers, with a husband!

TOM: What?

AMANDA: Oh, I can see the handwriting on the wall as plain as I see the nose in front of my face! It's terrifying! More and more you remind me of your father! He was out all hours without explanation!—Then *left! Good-bye!* And me with the bag to hold. I saw that letter you got from the Merchant Marine. I know what you're dreaming of. I'm not standing here blindfolded. Very well, then. Then *do* it! But not till there's somebody to take your place.

TOM: What do you mean?

AMANDA: I mean that as soon as Laura has got somebody to take care of her, married, a home of her own, independent—why, then you'll be free to go wherever you please, on land, on sea, whichever way the wind blows you! But until that time you've got to look out for your sister. I don't say me because I'm old and don't matter! I say for your sister because she's young and dependent. I put her in business college—a dismal failure! Frightened her so it made her sick at the stomach. I took her over to the Young People's League at the church. Another fiasco. She spoke to nobody, nobody spoke to her. Now all she does is fool with those pieces of glass and play those worn-out records. What kind of a life is that for a girl to lead?

TOM: What can I do about it?

AMANDA: Overcome selfishness! Self, self, self is all that you ever think of! [Tom *springs up and crosses to get his coat. It is ugly and bulky. He pulls on a cap with earmuffs*] Where is your muffler? Put your wool muffler on! [*He snatches it angrily from the closet and tosses it around his neck and pulls both ends tight*] Tom! I haven't said what I had in mind to ask you.

TOM: I'm too late to—

AMANDA: [*Catching his arm—very importunately. Then shyly*] Down at the warehouse, aren't there some—nice young men?

TOM: No!

AMANDA: There *must* be—*some* . . .

TOM: Mother—[*Gesture*]

AMANDA: Find out one that's clean-living—doesn't drink and—ask him out for sister!

TOM: What?

AMANDA: For *sister!* To *meet!* Get *acquainted!*

TOM: [*Stamping to door*] Oh, my *go-osh!*

AMANDA: Will you? [*He opens door. Imploringly*] Will you? [*He starts down*] Will you? *Will* you, dear?

TOM: [*Calling back*] YES!

[Amanda *closes the door hesitantly and with a troubled but faintly hopeful expression*]

[SCREEN IMAGE: GLAMOR MAGAZINE COVER]

[*Spot* Amanda *at phone*]

AMANDA: Ella Cartwright? This is Amanda Wingfield! How are you, honey? How is that kidney condition? [*Count five*] Horrors! [*Count five*] You're a Christian martyr, yes, honey, that's what you are, a Christian martyr! Well, I just now happened to notice in my little red book that your subscription to the *Companion* has just run out! I knew that you wouldn't want to miss out on the wonderful serial starting in this new issue. It's by Bessie Mae Hopper, the first thing she's written since *Honeymoon for Three*. Wasn't that a strange and interesting story? Well, this one is even lovelier, I believe. It has a sophisticated, society background. It's all about the horsey set on Long Island!

FADE OUT

SCENE V.

LEGEND ON SCREEN: "ANNUNCIATION." *Fade with music.*

*It is early dusk of a spring evening. Supper has just been finished in the Wingfield apartment. * Amanda *and* Laura *in light-colored dresses are removing dishes from the table, in the upstage area, which is shadowy, their movements formalized almost as a dance or ritual, their moving forms as pale and silent as moths.* Tom, *in white shirt and trousers, rises from the table and crosses toward the fire-escape.*

AMANDA: [*As he passes her*] Son, will you do me a favor?

TOM: What?

AMANDA: Comb your hair! You look so pretty when your hair is combed! [Tom *slouches on sofa with evening paper. Enormous caption "Franco Triumphs"*] There is only one respect in which I would like you to emulate your father.

TOM: What respect is that?

AMANDA: The care he always took of his appearance. He never allowed himself to look untidy. [*He throws down the paper and crosses to fire-escape*] Where are you going?

TOM: I'm going out to smoke.

AMANDA: You smoke too much. A pack a day at fifteen cents a pack. How much would that amount to in a month? Thirty times fifteen is how much, Tom? Figure it out and you will be astounded at what you could save. Enough to give you a night-school course in accounting at Washington U! Just think what a wonderful thing that would be for you, Son!

[Tom *is unmoved by the thought*]

TOM: I'd rather smoke. [*He steps out on landing, letting the screen door slam*]

AMANDA: [*Sharply*] I know! That's the tragedy of it. . . . [*Alone, she turns to look at her husband's picture*]

[DANCE MUSIC: "ALL THE WORLD IS WAITING FOR THE SUNRISE!"]

TOM: [*To the audience*] Across the alley from us was the Paradise Dance Hall. On evenings in spring the windows and doors were open and the music came outdoors. Sometimes the lights were turned out except for a large glass sphere that hung from the ceiling. It would turn slowly about and filter the dusk with delicate rainbow colors. Then the orchestra played a waltz or a tango, something that had a slow and sensuous rhythm. Couples would come outside, to the relative privacy of the alley. You could see them kissing behind ash-pits and telephone poles. This was the compensation for lives that passed like mine, without any change or adventure. Adventure and change were imminent in this year. They were waiting around the corner for all these kids. Suspended in the mist over Berchtesgaden, caught in the folds of Chamberlain's umbrella—In Spain there was Guernica! But here there was only hot swing music and liquor, dance halls, bars, and movies, and sex that hung in the gloom like a chandelier and flooded the world with brief, deceptive rainbows. . . . All the world was waiting for bombardments!

[Amanda *turns from the picture and comes outside*]

AMANDA: [*Sighing*] A fire-escape landing's a poor excuse for a porch. [*She spreads a newspaper on a step and sits down, gracefully and demurely as if she were settling into a swing on a Mississippi veranda*] What are you looking at?

TOM: The moon.

AMANDA: Is there a moon this evening?

TOM: It's rising over Garfinkel's Delicatessen.

AMANDA: So it is! A little silver slipper of a moon. Have you made a wish on it yet?

TOM: Um-hum.

AMANDA: What did you wish for?

TOM: That's a secret.

AMANDA: A secret, huh? Well, I won't tell mine either. I will be just as mysterious as you.

TOM: I bet I can guess what yours is.

AMANDA: Is my head so transparent?

TOM: You're not a sphinx.

AMANDA: No, I don't have secrets. I'll tell you what I wished for on the moon. Success and happiness for my precious children! I wish for that whenever there's a moon, and when there isn't a moon, I wish for it, too.

TOM: I thought perhaps you wished for a gentleman caller.

AMANDA: Why do you say that?

TOM: Don't you remember asking me to fetch one?

AMANDA: I remember suggesting that it would be nice for your sister if you brought home some nice young man from the warehouse. I think that I've made that suggestion more than once.

TOM: Yes, you have made it repeatedly.

AMANDA: Well?

TOM: We are going to have one.

AMANDA: *What?*

TOM: A gentleman caller!

[THE ANNUNCIATION IS CELEBRATED WITH MUSIC]

[Amanda *rises*]

[IMAGE ON SCREEN: CALLER WITH BOUQUET]

AMANDA: You mean you have asked some nice young man to come over?

TOM: Yep. I've asked him to dinner.

AMANDA: You really did?

TOM: I did!

AMANDA: You did, and did he—*accept?*

TOM: He did!

AMANDA: Well, well—well, well! That's—lovely!

TOM: I thought that you would be pleased.

AMANDA: It's definite, then?

TOM: Very definite.

AMANDA: Soon?

TOM: Very soon.

AMANDA: For heaven's sake, stop putting on and tell me some things, will you?

TOM: What things do you want me to tell you?

AMANDA: *Naturally* I would like to know when he's *coming!*

TOM: He's coming tomorrow.

AMANDA: *Tomorrow?*

TOM: Yep. Tomorrow.

AMANDA: But, Tom!

TOM: Yes, Mother?

AMANDA: Tomorrow gives me no time!

TOM: Time for what?

AMANDA: Preparations! Why didn't you phone me at once, as soon as you asked him, the minute that he accepted? Then, don't you see, I could have been getting ready!

TOM: You don't have to make any fuss.

AMANDA: Oh, Tom, Tom, Tom, of course I have to make a fuss! I want things nice, not sloppy! Not thrown together. I'll certainly have to do some fast thinking, won't I?

TOM: I don't see why you have to think at all.

AMANDA: You just don't know. We can't have a gentleman caller in a pig-sty. All my wedding silver has to be polished, the monogrammed table linen ought to be laundered! The windows have to be washed and fresh curtains put up. And how about clothes? We have to *wear* something, don't we?

TOM: Mother, this boy is no one to make a fuss over!

AMANDA: Do you **realize** he's the first young man

we've introduced to your sister? It's terrible, dreadful, disgraceful that poor little sister has never received a single gentleman caller! Tom, come inside! [*She opens the screen door*]

TOM: What for?

AMANDA: I want to ask you some things.

TOM: If you're going to make such a fuss, I'll call it off, I'll tell him not to come!

AMANDA: You certainly won't do anything of the kind. Nothing offends people worse than broken engagements. It simply means I'll have to work like a Turk! We won't be brilliant, but we will pass inspection. Come on inside. [Tom *follows, groaning*] Sit down.

TOM: Any particular place you would like me to sit?

AMANDA: Thank heavens I've got that new sofa! I'm also making payments on a floor lamp I'll have sent out! And put the chintz covers on, they'll brighten things up! Of course I'd hoped to have these walls re-papered. . . . What is the young man's name?

TOM: His name is O'Connor.

AMANDA: That, of course, means fish—tomorrow is Friday! I'll have that salmon loaf—with Durkee's dressing! What does he do? He works at the warehouse?

TOM: Of course! How else would I—

AMANDA: Tom, he—doesn't drink?

TOM: Why do you ask me that?

AMANDA: Your father *did*!

TOM: Don't get started on that!

AMANDA: He *does* drink, then?

TOM: Not that I know of!

AMANDA: Make sure, be certain! The last thing I want for my daughter's a boy who drinks!

TOM: Aren't you being a little bit premature? Mr. O'Connor has not yet appeared on the scene!

AMANDA: But will tomorrow. To meet your sister, and what do I know about his character? Nothing! Old maids are better off than wives of drunkards!

TOM: Oh, my God!

AMANDA: Be still!

TOM: [*Leaning forward to whisper*] Lots of fellows meet girls whom they don't marry!

AMANDA: Oh, talk sensibly, Tom—and don't be sarcastic! [*She has gotten a hairbrush*]

TOM: What are you doing?

AMANDA: I'm brushing that cow-lick down! What is this young man's position at the warehouse?

TOM: [*Submitting grimly to the brush and the interrogation*] This young man's position is that of a shipping clerk, Mother.

AMANDA: Sounds to me like a fairly responsible job, the sort of a job *you* would be in if you just had more *get-up*.

What is his salary? Have you any idea?

TOM: I would judge it to be approximately eighty-five dollars a month.

AMANDA: Well—not princely, but—

TOM: Twenty more than I make.

AMANDA: Yes, how well I know! But for a family man, eighty-five dollars a month is not much more than you can just get by on. . . .

TOM: Yes, but Mr. O'Connor is not a family man.

AMANDA: He might be, mightn't he? Some time in the future?

TOM: I see. Plans and provisions.

AMANDA: You are the only young man that I know of who ignores the fact that the future becomes the present, the present the past, and the past turns into everlasting regret if you don't plan for it!

TOM: I will think that over and see what I can make of it.

AMANDA: Don't be supercilious with your mother! Tell me some more about this—what do you call him?

TOM: James D. O'Connor. The D. is for Delaney.

AMANDA: Irish on *both* sides! *Gracious!* And doesn't drink?

TOM: Shall I call him up and ask him right this minute?

AMANDA: The only way to find out about those things is to make discreet inquiries at the proper moment. When I was a girl in Blue Mountain and it was suspected that a young man drank, the girl whose attentions he had been receiving, if any girl *was*, would sometimes speak to the minister of his church, or rather her father would if her father was living, and sort of feel him out on the young man's character. That is the way such things are discreetly handled to keep a young woman from making a tragic mistake!

TOM: Then how did you happen to make a tragic mistake?

AMANDA: That innocent look of your father's had everyone fooled! He *smiled*—the world was *enchanted*! No girl can do worse than put herself at the mercy of a handsome appearance! I hope that Mr. O'Connor is not too good-looking.

TOM: No, he's not too good-looking. He's covered with freckles and hasn't too much of a nose.

AMANDA: He's not right-down homely, though?

TOM: Not right-down homely. Just medium homely, I'd say.

AMANDA: Character's what to look for in a man.

TOM: That's what I've always said, Mother.

AMANDA: You've never said anything of the kind and I suspect you would never give it a thought.

TOM: Don't be so suspicious of me.

AMANDA: At least I hope he's the type that's up and coming.

TOM: I think he really goes in for self-improvement.

AMANDA: What reason have you to think so?

TOM: He goes to night school.

AMANDA: [*Beaming*] Splendid! What does he do, I mean study?

TOM: Radio engineering and public speaking!

AMANDA: Then he has visions of being advanced

in the world! Any young man who studies public speaking is aiming to have an executive job some day! And radio engineering? A thing for the future! Both of these facts are very illuminating. Those are the sort of things that a mother should know concerning any young man who comes to call on her daughter. Seriously or—not.

TOM: One little warning. He doesn't know about Laura. I didn't let on that we had dark ulterior motives. I just said, why don't you come and have dinner with us? He said okay and that was the whole conversation.

AMANDA: I bet it was! You're eloquent as an oyster. However, he'll know about Laura when he gets here. When he sees how lovely and sweet and pretty she is, he'll thank his lucky stars he was asked to dinner.

TOM: Mother, you mustn't expect too much of Laura.

AMANDA: What do you mean?

TOM: Laura seems all those things to you and me because she's ours and we love her. We don't even notice she's crippled any more.

AMANDA: Don't say crippled. You know that I never allow that word to be used!

TOM: But face facts, Mother. She is and—that's not all—

AMANDA: What do you mean "not all"?

TOM: Laura is very different from other girls.

AMANDA: I think the difference is all to her advantage.

TOM: Not quite all—in the eyes of others—strangers—she's terribly shy and lives in a world of her own and those things make her seem a little peculiar to people outside the house.

AMANDA: Don't say peculiar.

TOM: Face the facts. She is.

[THE DANCE-HALL MUSIC CHANGES TO A TANGO THAT HAS A MINOR AND SOMEWHAT OMINOUS TONE]

AMANDA: In what way is she peculiar—may I ask?

TOM: [Gently] She lives in a world of her own—a world of—little glass ornaments, Mother. . . . [Gets up. Amanda remains holding brush, looking at him, troubled] She plays old phonograph records and—that's about all— [He glances at himself in the mirror and crosses to door]

AMANDA: [Sharply] Where are you going?

TOM: I'm going to the movies. [Out screen door]

AMANDA: Not to the movies, every night to the movies! [Follows quickly to screen door] I don't believe you always go to the movies! [He is gone. Amanda looks worriedly after him for a moment. Then vitality and optimism return and she turns from the door. Crossing to portieres] Laura! Laura! [Laura answers from kitchenette]

LAURA: Yes, Mother.

AMANDA: Let those dishes go and come in front! [Laura appears with dish towel. Gaily] Laura, come here and make a wish on the moon!

[SCREEN IMAGE: MOON]

LAURA: [Entering] Moon—moon?

AMANDA: A little silver slipper of a moon. Look over your left shoulder, Laura, and make a wish! [Laura looks faintly puzzled as if called out of sleep. Amanda seizes her shoulders and turns her at an angle by the door] Now! Now, darling, wish!

LAURA: What shall I wish for, Mother?

AMANDA: [Her voice trembling and her eyes suddenly filling with tears] Happiness, Good fortune!

[The violin rises and the stage dims out]

CURTAIN

SCENE VI.

[IMAGE: HIGH SCHOOL HERO]

And so the following evening I brought Jim home to dinner. I had known Jim slightly in high school. In high school Jim was a hero. He had tremendous Irish good nature and vitality with the scrubbed and polished look of white chinaware. He seemed to move in a continual spotlight. He was a star in basketball, captain of the debating club, president of the senior class and the glee club and he sang the male lead in the annual light operas. He was always running or bounding, never just walking. He seemed always at the point of defeating the law of gravity. He was shooting with such velocity through his adolescence that you would logically expect him to arrive at nothing short of the White House by the time he was thirty. But Jim apparently ran into more interference after his graduation from Soldan. His speed had definitely slowed. Six years after he left high school he was holding a job that wasn't much better than mine.

[IMAGE: CLERK]

He was the only one at the warehouse with whom I was on friendly terms. I was valuable to him as someone who could remember his former glory, who had seen him win basketball games and the silver cup in debating. He knew of my secret practice of retiring to a cabinet of the wash-room to work on poems when business was slack in the warehouse. He called me Shakespeare. And while the other boys in the warehouse regarded me with suspicious hostility, Jim took a humorous attitude toward me. Gradually his attitude affected the others, their hostility wore off and they also began to smile at me as people smile at an oddly fashioned dog who trots across their path as some distance.

I knew that Jim and Laura had known each other at Soldan, and I had heard Laura speak admiringly of his voice. I didn't know if Jim remembered her or not. In high school Laura had been as unobtrusive as Jim had been astonishing. If he did remember Laura, it was not as my sister, for when I asked him to dinner, he grinned and said, "You know, Shakespeare, I never thought of you as having folks!"

He was about to discover that I did. . . .

[*Light up stage*]

[LEGEND ON SCREEN: "THE ACCENT OF A COMING FOOT"]

[*Friday evening. It is about five o'clock of a late spring evening which comes "scattering poems in the sky." A delicate lemony light is in the Wingfield apartment. Amanda has worked like a Turk in preparation for the gentleman caller. The results are astonishing. The new floor lamp with its rose-silk shade is in place, a colored paper lantern conceals the broken light-fixture in the ceiling, new billowing white curtains are at the windows, chintz covers are on chairs and sofa, a pair of new sofa pillows make their initial appearance. Open boxes and tissue paper are scattered on the floor.* Laura *stands in the middle with lifted arms while* Amanda *crouches before her, adjusting the hem of the new dress, devout and ritualistic. The dress is colored and designed by memory. The arrangement of* Laura's *hair is changed; it is softer and more becoming. A fragile, unearthly prettiness has come out in* Laura: *she is like a piece of translucent glass touched by light, given a momentary radiance, not actual, not lasting*]

AMANDA: [*Impatiently*] Why are you trembling?

LAURA: Mother, you've made me so nervous!

AMANDA: How have I made you nervous?

LAURA: By all this fuss! You make it seem so important!

AMANDA: I don't understand you, Laura. You couldn't be satisfied with just sitting home, and yet whenever I try to arrange something for you, you seem to resist it. [*She gets up*] Now take a look at yourself. No, wait! Wait just a moment—I have an idea!

LAURA: What is it now?

[Amanda *produces two powder puffs which she wraps in handkerchiefs and stuffs in* Laura's *bosom*]

LAURA: Mother, what are you doing?

AMANDA: They call them "Gay Deceivers"!

LAURA: I won't wear them!

AMANDA: You will!

LAURA: Why should I?

AMANDA: Because, to be painfully honest, your chest is flat.

LAURA: You make it seem like we were setting a trap.

AMANDA: All pretty girls are a trap, a pretty trap, and men expect them to be. [LEGEND: "A PRETTY TRAP"] Now look at yourself, young lady. This is the prettiest you will ever be! I've got to fix myself now! You're going to be surprised by your mother's appearance! [*She crosses through portieres, humming gaily.* Laura *moves slowly to the long mirror*

and stares solemnly at herself. A wind blows the white curtains inward in a slow, graceful motion and with a faint, sorrowful sighing]

AMANDA: [*Off stage*] It isn't dark enough yet. [*She turns slowly before the mirror with a troubled look*]

[LEGEND ON SCREEN: "THIS IS MY SISTER: CELEBRATE HER WITH STRINGS!" MUSIC]

AMANDA: [*Laughing, off*] I'm going to show you something. I'm going to make a spectacular appearance!

LAURA: What is it, Mother?

AMANDA: Possess your soul in patience—you will see! Something I've resurrected from that old trunk! Styles haven't changed so terribly much after all. . . . [*She parts the portieres*] Now just look at your mother! [*She wears a girlish frock of yellowed voile with a blue silk sash. She carries a bunch of jonquils—the legend of her youth is nearly revived. Feverishly*] This is the dress in which I led the cotillion. Won the cakewalk twice at Sunset Hill, wore one spring to the Governor's ball in Jackson! See how I sashayed around the ballroom, Laura? [*She raises her skirt and does a mincing step around the room*] I wore it on Sundays for my gentlemen callers! I had it on the day I met your father—I had malaria fever all that spring. The change of climate from East Tennessee to the Delta—weakened resistance—I had a little temperature all the time—not enough to be serious—just enough to make me restless and giddy!—Invitations poured in—parties all over the Delta!—"Stay in bed," said Mother, "you have fever!"—but I just wouldn't.—I took quinine but kept on going, going!—Evenings, dances!—Afternoons, long, long rides! Picnics—lovely!—So lovely, that country in May.—All lacy with dogwood, literally flooded with jonquils!—That was the spring I had the craze for jonquils. Jonquils became an absolute obsession. Mother said "Honey, there's no more room for jonquils." And still I kept on bringing in more jonquils. Whenever, wherever I saw them, I'd say, "Stop! Stop! I see jonquils!" I made the young men help me gather the jonquils! It was a joke, Amanda and her jonquils! Finally there were no more vases to hold them, every available space was filled with jonquils. No vases to hold them? All right, I'll hold them myself! And then I—[*She stops in front of the picture.* MUSIC] met your father! Malaria fever and jonquils and then—this—boy. . . . [*She switches on the rose-colored lamp*] I hope they get here before it starts to rain. [*She crosses upstage and places the jonquils in bowl on table*] I gave your brother a little extra change so he and Mr. O'Connor could take the service car home.

LAURA: [*With altered look*] What did you say his name was?

AMANDA: O'Connor.

LAURA: What is his first name?

AMANDA: I don't remember. Oh, yes, I do. It was —Jim!

[Laura *sways slightly and catches hold of a chair*]

[LEGEND ON SCREEN: "NOT JIM!"]

LAURA: [*Faintly*] Not—Jim!

AMANDA: Yes, that was it, it was Jim! I've never known a Jim that wasn't nice!

[MUSIC: OMINOUS]

LAURA: Are you sure his name is Jim O'Connor?

AMANDA: Yes. Why?

LAURA: Is he the one that Tom used to know in high school?

AMANDA: He didn't say so. I think he just got to know him at the warehouse.

LAURA: There was a Jim O'Connor we both knew in high school—[*Then, with effort*] If that is the one that Tom is bringing to dinner—you'll have to excuse me, I won't come to the table.

AMANDA: What sort of nonsense is this?

LAURA: You asked me once if I'd ever liked a boy. Don't you remember I showed you this boy's picture?

AMANDA: You mean the boy you showed me in the year book?

LAURA: Yes, that boy.

AMANDA: Laura, Laura, were you in love with that boy?

LAURA: I don't know, Mother. All I know is I couldn't sit at the table if it was him!

AMANDA: It won't be him! It isn't the least bit likely. But whether it is or not, you will come to the table. You will not be excused.

LAURA: I'll have to be, Mother.

AMANDA: I don't intend to humor your silliness, Laura. I've had too much from you and your brother, both! So just sit down and compose yourself till they come. Tom has forgotten his key so you'll have to let them in, when they arrive.

LAURA: [*Panicky*] Oh, Mother—*you* answer the door!

AMANDA: [*Lightly*] I'll be in the kitchen—busy!

LAURA: Oh, Mother, please answer the door, don't make me do it!

AMANDA: [*Crossing into kitchenette*] I've got to fix the dressing for the salmon. Fuss, fuss—silliness!—over a gentleman caller!

[*Door swings shut. Laura is left alone*]

[LEGEND: "TERROR!"]

[*She utters a low moan and turns off the lamp—sits stiffly on the edge of the sofa, knotting her fingers together*]

[LEGEND ON SCREEN: "THE OPENING OF A DOOR!"]

[*Tom and Jim appear on the fire-escape steps and climb to landing. Hearing their approach, Laura rises with a panicky gesture. She retreats to the portieres. The doorbell. Laura catches her breath and touches her throat. Low drums*]

AMANDA: [*Calling*] Laura, sweetheart! The door!

[*Laura stares at it without moving*]

JIM: I think we just beat the rain.

TOM: Uh-huh. [*He rings again, nervously. Jim whistles and fishes for a cigarette*]

AMANDA: [*Very, very gaily*] Laura, that is your brother and Mr. O'Connor! Will you let them in, darling?

[*Laura crosses toward kitchenette door*]

LAURA: [*Breathlessly*] Mother—you go to the door!

[*Amanda steps out of kitchenette and stares furiously at Laura. She points imperiously at the door*]

LAURA: Please, please!

AMANDA: [*In a fierce whisper*] What is the matter with you, you silly thing?

LAURA: [*Desperately*] Please, you answer it, *please!*

AMANDA: I told you I wasn't going to humor you, Laura. Why have you chosen this moment to lose your mind?

LAURA: Please, please, please, you go!

AMANDA: You'll have to go to the door because I can't!

LAURA: [*Despairingly*] I can't either!

AMANDA: *Why?*

LAURA: I'm *sick!*

AMANDA: I'm sick, too—of your nonsense! Why can't you and your brother be normal people? Fantastic whims and behavior! [*Tom gives a long ring*] Preposterous goings on! Can you give me one reason—[*Calls out lyrically*] Coming! Just one second!—why you should be afraid to open a door? Now you answer it, Laura!

LAURA: Oh, oh, oh . . . [*She returns through the portieres. Darts to the victrola and winds it frantically and turns it on*]

AMANDA: Laura Wingfield, you march right to that door!

LAURA: Yes—yes, Mother!

[*A faraway, scratchy rendition of "Dardanella" softens the air and gives her strength to move through it. She slips to the door and draws it cautiously open. Tom enters with the caller, Jim O'Connor*]

TOM: Laura, this is Jim. Jim, this is my sister, Laura.

JIM: [*Stepping inside*] I didn't know that Shakespeare had a sister!

LAURA: [*Retreating stiff and trembling from the door*] How—how do you do?

JIM: [*Heartily extending his hand*] Okay! [*Laura touches it hesitantly with hers*]

JIM: Your hand's *cold*, Laura!

LAURA: Yes, well—I've been playing the victrola. . . .

JIM: Must have been playing classical music on it! You ought to play a little hot swing music to warm you up!

LAURA: Excuse me—I haven't finished playing the victrola. . . . [*She turns awkwardly and hurries into the front room. She pauses a second by the victrola.*

Then catches her breath and darts through the portieres like a frightened deer]

JIM: [*Grinning*] What was the matter?

TOM: Oh—with Laura? Laura is—terribly shy.

JIM: Shy, huh? It's unusual to meet a shy girl nowadays. I don't believe you ever mentioned you had a sister.

TOM: Well, now you know. I have one. Here is the *Post Dispatch.* You want a piece of it?

JIM: Uh-huh.

TOM: What piece? The comics?

JIM: Sports! [*Glances at it*] Ole Dizzy Dean is on his bad behavior.

TOM: [*Disinterest*] Yeah? [*Lights cigarette and crosses back to fire-escape door*]

JIM: Where are *you* going?

TOM: I'm going out on the terrace.

JIM: [*Goes after him*] You know, Shakespeare—I'm going to sell you a bill of goods!

TOM: What goods?

JIM: A course I'm taking.

TOM: Huh?

JIM: In public speaking! You and me, we're not the warehouse type.

TOM: Thanks—that's good news. But what has public speaking got to do with it?

JIM: It fits you for—executive positions!

TOM: Awww.

JIM: I tell you it's done a helluva lot for me.

[IMAGE: EXECUTIVE AT DESK]

TOM: In what respect?

JIM: In every! Ask yourself what is the difference between you an' me and men in the office down front? Brains?—No!—Ability?—No! Then what? Just one little thing—

TOM: What is that one little thing?

JIM: Primarily it amounts to—social poise! Being able to square up to people and hold your own on any social level!

AMANDA: [*Off stage*] Tom?

TOM: Yes, Mother?

AMANDA: Is that you and Mr. O'Connor?

TOM: Yes, Mother.

AMANDA: Well, you just make yourselves comfortable in there.

TOM: Yes, Mother.

AMANDA: Ask Mr. O'Connor if he would like to wash his hands.

JIM: Aw, no—no—thank you—I took care of that at the warehouse. Tom—

TOM: Yes?

JIM: Mr. Mendoza was speaking to me about you.

TOM: Favorably?

JIM: What do you think?

TOM: Well—

JIM: You're going to be out of a job if you don't wake up.

TOM: I am waking up—

JIM: You show no signs.

TOM: The signs are interior.

[IMAGE ON SCREEN: THE SAILING VESSEL WITH JOLLY ROGER AGAIN]

TOM: I'm planning to change. [*He leans over the rail speaking with quiet exhilaration. The incandescent marquees and signs of the first-run movie houses light his face from across the alley. He looks like a voyager*] I'm right at the point of committing myself to a future that doesn't include the warehouse and Mr. Mendoza or even a night-school course in public speaking.

JIM: What are you gassing about?

TOM: I'm tired of the movies.

JIM: Movies!

TOM: Yes, movies! Look at them—[*A wave toward the marvels of Grand Avenue*] All of those glamorous people—having adventures—hogging it all, gobbling the whole thing up! You know what happens? People go to the *movies* instead of *moving!* Hollywood characters are supposed to have all the adventures for everybody in America, while everybody in America sits in a dark room and watches them have them! Yes, until there's a war. That's when adventure becomes available to the masses! *Everyone's* dish, not only Gable's! Then the people in the dark room come out of the dark room to have some adventures themselves—Goody, goody! —It's our turn now, to go to the South Sea Island —to make a safari—to be exotic, far-off!—but I'm not patient. I don't want to wait till then. I'm tired of the *movies* and I am *about* to *move!*

JIM: [*Incredulously*] Move?

TOM: Yes.

JIM: When?

TOM: Soon!

JIM: Where? Where?

[*Theme three music seems to answer the question, while* Tom *thinks it over. He searches among his pockets*]

TOM: I'm starting to boil inside. I know I seem dreamy, but inside—well, I'm boiling!—Whenever I pick up a shoe, I shudder a little thinking how short life is and what I am doing!— Whatever that means, I know it doesn't mean shoes—except as something to wear on a traveler's feet! [*Finds paper*] Look—

JIM: What?

TOM: I'm a member.

JIM: [*Reading*] The Union of Merchant Seamen.

TOM: I paid my dues this month, instead of the light bill.

JIM: You will regret it when they turn the lights off.

TOM: I won't be here.

JIM: How about your mother?

TOM: I'm like my father. The bastard son of a bastard! See how he grins? And he's been absent going on sixteen years!

JIM: You're just talking, you drip. How does your mother feel about it?

TOM: Shhh!—Here comes Mother! Mother is not acquainted with my plans!

AMANDA: [*Enters portieres*] Where are you all?

TOM: On the terrace, Mother.

[*They start inside. She advances to them. Tom is distinctly shocked at her appearance. Even Jim blinks a little. He is making his first contact with girlish Southern vivacity and in spite of the night-school course in public speaking is somewhat thrown off the beam by the unexpected outlay of social charm. Certain responses are attempted by Jim but are swept aside by Amanda's gay laughter and chatter. Tom is embarrassed but after the first shock Jim reacts very warmly. Grins and chuckles, is altogether won over.*]

[IMAGE: AMANDA AS A GIRL]

AMANDA: [*Coyly smiling, shaking her girlish ringlets*] Well, well, well, so this is Mr. O'Connor. Introductions entirely unnecessary. I've heard so much about you from my boy. I finally said to him, Tom—good gracious!—why don't you bring this paragon to supper? I'd like to meet this nice young man at the warehouse!—Instead of just hearing him sing your praises so much!

I don't know why my son is so stand-offish—that's not Southern behavior!

Let's sit down and—I think we could stand a little more air in here! Tom, leave the door open. I felt a nice fresh breeze a moment ago. Where has it gone to?

Mmm, so warm already! And not quite summer, even. We're going to burn up when summer really gets started.

However, we're having—we're having a very light supper. I think light things are better fo' this time of year. The same as light clothes are. Light clothes an' light food are what warm weather calls fo'. You know our blood gets so thick during th' winter—it takes a while fo' us to *adjust* ou'selves!—when the season changes . . .

It's come so quick this year. I wasn't prepared. All of a sudden—heavens! Already summer!—I ran to the trunk an' pulled out this light dress— Terribly old! Historical almost! But feels so good—so good an' co-ol, y'know. . . .

TOM: Mother—

AMANDA: Yes, honey?

TOM: How about—supper?

AMANDA: Honey, you go ask Sister if supper is ready! You know that Sister is in full charge of supper!

Tell her you hungry boys are waiting for it. [*To Jim*] Have you met Laura?

JIM: She—

AMANDA: Let you in? Oh, good, you've met already! It's rare for a girl as sweet an' pretty as Laura to be domestic! But Laura is, thank heavens, not only pretty but also very domestic. I'm not at all. I never was a bit. I never could make a thing but angel-food cake. Well, in the South we had so many servants. Gone, gone, gone. All vestige of gracious living! Gone completely! I wasn't prepared for what the future brought me. All of my gentlemen callers were sons of planters and so of course I assumed that I would be married to one and raise my family on a large piece of land with plenty of servants. But man proposes—and woman accepts the proposal!—To vary that old, old saying a little bit— I married no planter! I married a man who worked for the telephone company!—That gallantly smiling gentleman over there! [*Points to the picture*] A telephone man who—fell in love with long-distance!— Now he travels and I don't even know where!— But what am I going on for about my tribulations? Tell me yours—I hope you don't have any! Tom?

TOM: [*Returning*] Yes, Mother?

AMANDA: Is supper nearly ready?

TOM: It looks to me like supper is on the table.

AMANDA: Let me look— [*She rises prettily and looks through portieres*] Oh, lovely!—But where is Sister?

TOM: Laura is not feeling well and she says that she thinks she'd better not come to the table.

AMANDA: What?—Nonsense!—Laura? Oh, Laura!

LAURA: [*Off stage, faintly*] Yes, Mother.

AMANDA: You really must come to the table. We won't be seated until you come to the table! Come in, Mr. O'Connor. You sit over there, and I'll— Laura? Laura Wingfield! You're keeping us waiting, honey! We can't say grace until you come to the table!

[*The back door is pushed weakly open and Laura comes in. She is obviously quite faint, her lips trembling, her eyes wide and staring. She moves unsteadily toward the table*]

[LEGEND: "TERROR!"]

[*Outside a summer storm is coming abruptly. The white curtains billow inward at the windows and there is a sorrowful murmur and deep blue dusk. Laura suddenly stumbles—she catches at a chair with a faint moan*]

TOM: Laura!

AMANDA: Laura!

[*There is a clap of thunder*]

[LEGEND: "AH!"]

[*Despairingly*]

Why, Laura, you *are* sick, darling! Tom, help your sister into the living room, dear! Sit in the living room, Laura—rest on the sofa. Well! [*To the gentleman caller*] Standing over the hot stove made her ill!—I told her that it was just too warm this evening, but— [*Tom comes back in. Laura is on the sofa*] Is Laura all right now?

TOM: Yes.

AMANDA: What *is* that? Rain? A nice cool rain has come up! [*She gives the gentleman caller a frightened look*] I think we may—have grace—now . . . [*Tom looks at her stupidly*] Tom, honey—you say grace!

TOM: Oh . . . "For these and all thy mercies—" [*They bow their heads*, Amanda *stealing a nervous glance at* Jim. *In the living room* Laura, *stretched on the sofa, clenches her hand to her lips, to hold back a shuddering sob*] God's Holy Name be praised—

THE SCENE DIMS OUT

SCENE VII

A Souvenir.

Half an hour later. Dinner is just being finished in the upstage area which is concealed by the drawn portieres. As the curtain rises Laura *is still huddled upon the sofa, her feet drawn under her, her head resting on a pale blue pillow, her eyes wide and mysteriously watchful. The new floor lamp with its shade of rose-colored silk gives a soft, becoming light to her face, bringing out the fragile, unearthly prettiness which usually escapes attention. There is a steady murmur of rain, but it is slackening and stops soon after the scene begins; the air outside becomes pale and luminous as the moon breaks out. A moment after the curtain rises, the lights in both rooms flicker and go out.*

JIM: Hey, there, Mr. Light Bulb!
    [Amanda *laughs nervously*]
    [LEGEND: "SUSPENSION OF A PUBLIC SERVICE"]
AMANDA: Where was Moses when the lights went out? Ha-ha. Do you know the answer to that one, Mr. O'Connor?
JIM: No, Ma'am, what's the answer?
AMANDA: In the dark! [Jim *laughs appreciatively*] Everybody sit still. I'll light the candles. Isn't it lucky we have them on the table? Where's a match? Which of you gentlemen can provide a match?
JIM: Here.
AMANDA: Thank you, sir.
JIM: Not at all, Ma'am!
AMANDA: I guess the fuse has burnt out. Mr. O'Connor, can you tell a burnt-out fuse? I know I can't and Tom is a total loss when it comes to mechanics.
    [*Sound: Getting up: Voices recede a little to kitchenette*]
    Oh, be careful you don't bump into something. We don't want our gentleman caller to break his neck. Now wouldn't that be a fine howdy-do?
JIM: Ha-ha! Where is the fuse-box?
AMANDA: Right here next to the stove. Can you see anything?
JIM: Just a minute.
AMANDA: Isn't electricity a mysterious thing? Wasn't it Benjamin Franklin who tied a key to a kite? We live in such a mysterious universe, don't we? Some people say that science clears up all the mysteries for us. In my opinion it only creates more! Have you found it yet?
JIM: No, Ma'am. All these fuses look okay to me.
AMANDA: Tom!
TOM: Yes, Mother?
AMANDA: That light bill I gave you several days ago. The one I told you we got the notices about?
    [LEGEND: "HA!"]
TOM: Oh.—Yeah.
AMANDA: You didn't neglect to pay it by any chance?
TOM: Why, I—
AMANDA: Didn't! I might have known it!
JIM: Shakespeare probably wrote a poem on that light bill, Mrs. Wingfield.
AMANDA: I might have known better than to trust him with it! There's such a high price for negligence in this world!
JIM: Maybe the poem will win a ten-dollar prize.
AMANDA: We'll just have to spend the remainder of the evening in the nineteenth century, before Mr. Edison made the Mazda lamp!
JIM: Candlelight is my favorite kind of light.
AMANDA: That shows you're romantic! But that's no excuse for Tom. Well, we got through dinner. Very considerate of them to let us get through dinner before they plunged us into everlasting darkness, wasn't it, Mr. O'Connor?
JIM: Ha-ha!
AMANDA: Tom, as a penalty for your carelessness you can help me with the dishes.
JIM: Let me give you a hand.
AMANDA: Indeed you will not!
JIM: I ought to be good for something.
AMANDA: Good for something? [*Her tone is rhapsodic*] You? Why, Mr. O'Connor, nobody, *nobody's* given me this much entertainment in years—as you have!
JIM: Aw, now, Mrs. Wingfield!
AMANDA: I'm not exaggerating, not one bit! But Sister is all by her lonesome. You go keep her company in the parlor!
    I'll give you this lovely old candelabrum that used to be on the altar at the church of the Heavenly Rest. It was melted a little out of shape when the church burnt down. Lightning struck it one spring. Gypsy Jones was holding a revival at the time and he intimated that the church was destroyed because the Episcopalians gave card parties.
JIM: Ha-ha.
AMANDA: And how about you coaxing Sister to drink a little wine? I think it would be good for her! Can you carry both at once?
JIM: Sure. I'm Superman!
AMANDA: Now, Thomas, get into this apron!
    [*The door of the kitchenette swings closed on* Amanda's *gay laughter; the flickering light approaches the portieres.* Laura *sits up nervously as he enters. Her speech at first is low and*

breathless from the almost intolerable strain of being alone with a stranger]

[THE LEGEND: "I DON'T SUPPOSE YOU REMEMBER ME AT ALL!"]

[*In her first speeches in this scene, before* Jim's *warmth overcomes her paralyzing shyness,* Laura's *voice is thin and breathless as though she has just run up a steep flight of stairs.* Jim's *attitude is gently humorous. In playing this scene it should be stressed that while the incident is apparently unimportant, it is to* Laura *the climax of her secret life*]

JIM: Hello, there, Laura.

LAURA: [*Faintly*] Hello. [*She clears her throat*]

JIM: How are you feeling now? Better?

LAURA: Yes. Yes, thank you.

JIM: This is for you. A little dandelion wine. [*He extends it toward her with extravagant gallantry*]

LAURA: Thank you.

JIM: Drink it—but don't get drunk! [*He laughs heartily.* Laura *takes the glass uncertainly; laughs shyly*] Where shall I set the candles?

LAURA: Oh—oh, anywhere . . .

JIM: How about here on the floor? Any objections?

LAURA: No.

JIM: I'll spread a newspaper under to catch the drippings. I like to sit on the floor. Mind if I do?

LAURA: Oh, no.

JIM: Give me a pillow?

LAURA: What?

JIM: A pillow!

LAURA: Oh . . . [*Hands him one quickly*]

JIM: How about you? Don't you like to sit on the floor?

LAURA: Oh—yes.

JIM: Why don't you then?

LAURA: I—will.

JIM: Take a pillow! [Laura *does. Sits on the other side of the candelabrum.* Jim *crosses his legs and smiles engagingly at her*] I can't hardly see you sitting way over there.

LAURA: I can—see you.

JIM: I know, but that's not fair, I'm in the limelight. [Laura *moves her pillow closer*] Good! Now I can see you! Comfortable?

LAURA: Yes.

JIM: So am I. Comfortable as a cow! Will you have some gum?

LAURA: No, thank you.

JIM: I think that I will indulge, with your permission. [*Musingly unwraps it and holds it up*] Think of the fortune made by the guy that invented the first piece of chewing gum. Amazing, huh? The Wrigley Building is one of the sights of Chicago. —I saw it summer before last when I went up to the Century of Progress. Did you take in the Century of Progress?

LAURA: No, I didn't.

JIM: Well, it was quite a wonderful exposition. What impressed me most was the Hall of Science. Gives you an idea of what the future will be in America, even more wonderful than the present time is! [*Pause. Smiling at her*] Your brother tells me you're shy. Is that right, Laura?

LAURA: I—don't know.

JIM: I judge you to be an old-fashioned type of girl. Well, I think that's a pretty good type to be. Hope you don't think I'm being too personal—do you?

LAURA: [*Hastily, out of embarrassment*] I believe I *will* take a piece of gum, if you—don't mind. [*Clearing her throat*] Mr. O'Connor, have you—kept up with your singing?

JIM: Singing? Me?

LAURA: Yes. I remember what a beautiful voice you had.

JIM: When did you hear me sing?

[VOICE OFF STAGE IN THE PAUSE]

VOICE: [*Off stage*]

O blow, ye winds, heigh-ho,
A-roving I will go!
I'm off to my love
With a boxing glove—
Ten thousand miles away!

JIM: You say you've heard me sing?

LAURA: Oh, yes! Yes, very often . . . I—don't suppose—you remember me—at all?

JIM: [*Smiling doubtfully*] You know I have an idea I've seen you before. I had that idea as soon as you opened the door. It seemed almost like I was about to remember your name. But the name I started to call you—wasn't a name! And so I stopped myself before I said it.

LAURA: Wasn't it—Blue Roses?

JIM: [*Springs up. Grinning*] Blue Roses!—My gosh, yes—Blue Roses! That's what I had on my tongue when you opened the door! Isn't it funny what tricks your memory plays? I didn't connect you with high school somehow or other. But that's where it was; it was high school. I didn't even know you were Shakespeare's sister! Gosh, I'm sorry.

LAURA: I didn't expect you to. You—barely knew me!

JIM: But we did have a speaking acquaintance, huh?

LAURA: Yes, we—spoke to each other.

JIM: When did you recognize me?

LAURA: Oh, right away!

JIM: Soon as I came in the door?

LAURA: When I heard your name I thought it was probably you. I knew that Tom used to know you a little in high school. So when you came in the door—Well, then I was—sure.

JIM: Why didn't you *say* something, then?

LAURA: [*Breathlessly*] I didn't know what to say, I was—too surprised!

JIM: For goodness' sakes! You know, this sure is funny!

LAURA: Yes! Yes, isn't it, though . . .

JIM: Didn't we have a class in something together?

LAURA: Yes, we did.

JIM: What class was that?

LAURA: It was—singing—Chorus!

JIM: Aw!

LAURA: I sat across the aisle from you in the Aud.

JIM: Aw.

LAURA: Mondays, Wednesdays and Fridays.

JIM: Now I remember—you always came in late.

LAURA: Yes, it was so hard for me, getting upstairs. I had that brace on my leg—it clumped so loud!

JIM: I never heard any clumping.

LAURA: [Wincing at the recollection] To me it sounded like—thunder!

JIM: Well, well, well, I never even noticed.

LAURA: And everybody was seated before I came in. I had to walk in front of all those people. My seat was in the back row. I had to go clumping all the way up the aisle with everyone watching!

JIM: You shouldn't have been self-conscious.

LAURA: I know, but I was. It was always such a relief when the singing started.

JIM: Aw, yes, I've placed you now! I used to call you Blue Roses. How was it that I got started calling you that?

LAURA: I was out of school a little while with pleurosis. When I came back you asked me what was the matter. I said I had pleurosis—you thought I said Blue Roses. That's what you always called me after that!

JIM: I hope you didn't mind.

LAURA: Oh, no—I liked it. You see, I wasn't acquainted with many—people. . . .

JIM: As I remember you sort of stuck by yourself.

LAURA: I—I—never have had much luck at—making friends.

JIM: I don't see why you wouldn't.

LAURA: Well, I—started out badly.

JIM: You mean being—

LAURA: Yes, it sort of—stood between me—

JIM: You shouldn't have let it!

LAURA: I know, but it did, and—

JIM: You were shy with people!

LAURA: I tried not to be but never could—

JIM: Overcome it?

LAURA: No, I—I never could!

JIM: I guess being shy is something you have to work out of kind of gradually.

LAURA: [Sorrowfully] Yes—I guess it—

JIM: Takes time!

LAURA: Yes—

JIM: People are not so dreadful when you know them. That's what you have to remember! And everybody has problems, not just you, but practically everybody has got some problems. You think of yourself as having the only problems, as being the only one who is disappointed. But just look around

you and you will see lots of people as disappointed as you are. For instance, I hoped when I was going to high school that I would be further along at this time, six years later, than I am now— You remember that wonderful write-up I had in *The Torch*?

LAURA: Yes! [*She rises and crosses to table*]

JIM: It said I was bound to succeed in anything I went into! [Laura *returns with the annual*] Holy Jeez! *The Torch!* [*He accepts it reverently. They smile across it with mutual wonder. Laura crouches beside him and they begin to turn through it. Laura's shyness is dissolving in his warmth*]

LAURA: Here you are in *The Pirates of Penzance!*

JIM: [*Wistfully*] I sang the baritone lead in that operetta.

LAURA: [*Raptly*] So—beautifully!

JIM: [*Protesting*] Aw—

LAURA: Yes, yes—beautifully—beautifully!

JIM: You heard me?

LAURA: All three times!

JIM: No!

LAURA: Yes!

JIM: All three performances?

LAURA: [*Looking down*] Yes.

JIM: Why?

LAURA: I—wanted to ask you to—autograph my program.

JIM: Why didn't you ask me to?

LAURA: You were always surrounded by your own friends so much that I never had a chance to.

JIM: You should have just—

LAURA: Well, I—thought you might think I was—

JIM: Thought I might think you was—what?

LAURA: Oh—

JIM: [*With reflective relish*] I was beleaguered by females in those days.

LAURA: You were terribly popular!

JIM: Yeah—

LAURA: You had such a—friendly way—

JIM: I was spoiled in high school.

LAURA: Everybody—liked you!

JIM: Including you?

LAURA: I—yes, I—I did, too— [*She gently closes the book in her lap*]

JIM: Well, well, well!—Give me that program, Laura. [*She hands it to him. He signs it with a flourish*] There you are—better late than never!

LAURA: Oh, I—what a—surprise!

JIM: My signature isn't worth very much right now. But some day—maybe—it will increase in value! Being disappointed is one thing and being discouraged is something else. I am disappointed but I am not discouraged. I'm twenty-three years old. How old are you?

LAURA: I'll be twenty-four in June.

JIM: That's not old age!

LAURA: No, but—

JIM: You finished high school?

LAURA: [*With difficulty*] I didn't go back.

JIM: You mean you dropped out?

LAURA: I made bad grades in my final examinations. [*She rises and replaces the book and the program. Her voice strained*] How is—Emily Meisenbach getting along?

JIM: Oh, that kraut-head!

LAURA: Why do you call her that?

JIM: That's what she was.

LAURA: You're not still—going with her?

JIM: I never see her.

LAURA: It said in the Personal Section that you were—engaged!

JIM: I know, but I wasn't impressed by that—propaganda!

LAURA: It wasn't—the truth?

JIM: Only in Emily's optimistic opinion!

LAURA: Oh—

[LEGEND: "WHAT HAVE YOU DONE SINCE HIGH SCHOOL?"]

[Jim *lights a cigarette and leans indolently back on his elbows smiling at* Laura *with a warmth and charm which lights her inwardly with altar candles. She remains by the table and turns in her hands a piece of glass to cover her tumult*]

JIM: [*After several reflective puffs on a cigarette*] What have you done since high school? [*She seems not to hear him*] Huh? [Laura *looks up*] I said what have you done since high school, Laura?

LAURA: Nothing much.

JIM: You must have been doing something these six long years.

LAURA: Yes.

JIM: Well, then, such as what?

LAURA: I took a business course at business college—

JIM: How did that work out?

LAURA: Well, not very—well—I had to drop out, it gave me—indigestion—

[Jim *laughs gently*]

JIM: What are you doing now?

LAURA: I don't do anything—much. Oh, please don't think I sit around doing nothing! My glass collection takes up a good deal of time. Glass is something you have to take good care of.

JIM: What did you say—about glass?

LAURA: Collection I said—I have one— [*She clears her throat and turns away again, acutely shy*]

JIM: [*Abruptly*] You know what I judge to be the trouble with you? Inferiority complex! Know what that is? That's what they call it when someone lowrates himself! I understand it because I had it, too. Although my case was not so aggravated as yours seems to be. I had it until I took up public speaking, developed my voice, and learned that I had an aptitude for science. Before that time I never thought of myself as being outstanding in any way whatsoever! Now I've never made a regular study of it, but I have a friend who says I can analyze people better than doctors that make a profession of it. I don't claim that to be necessarily true, but I can sure guess a person's psychology, Laura! [*Takes out his gum*] Excuse me, Laura. I always take it out when the flavor is gone. I'll use this scrap of paper to wrap it in. I know how it is to get it stuck on a shoe. Yep—that's what I judge to be your principal trouble. A lack of confidence in yourself as a person. You don't have the proper amount of faith in yourself. I'm basing that fact on a number of your remarks and also on certain observations I've made. For instance that clumping you thought was so awful in high school. You say you even dreaded to walk into class. You see what you did? You dropped out of school, you gave up an education because of a clump, which as far as I know was practically non-existent! A little physical defect is what you have. Hardly noticeable even! Magnified thousands of times by imagination! You know what my strong advice to you is? Think of yourself as *superior* in some way!

LAURA: In what way would I think?

JIM: Why, man alive, Laura! Just look about you a little. What do you see? A world full of common people! All of 'em born and all of 'em going to die! Which of them has one-tenth of your good points! Or mine! Or anyone else's, as far as that goes— Gosh! Everybody excels in some one thing. Some in many! [*Unconsciously glances at himself in the mirror*] All you've got to do is discover in *what*! Take me, for instance. [*He adjusts his tie at the mirror*] My interest happens to lie in electro-dynamics. I'm taking a course in radio engineering at night school, Laura, on top of a fairly responsible job at the warehouse. I'm taking that course and studying public speaking.

LAURA: Ohhhh.

JIM: Because I believe in the future of television! [*Turning back to her*] I wish to be ready to go up right along with it. Therefore I'm planning to get in on the ground floor. In fact I've already made the right connections and all that remains is for the industry to get under way! Full steam— [*His eyes are starry*] Knowledge—Zzzzzp! Money—Zzzzzzp! —Power! That's the cycle democracy is built on! [*His attitude is convincingly dynamic.* Laura *stares at him, even her shyness eclipsed in her absolute wonder. He suddenly grins*] I guess you think I think a lot of myself!

LAURA: No—o-o-o, I—

JIM: Now how about you? Isn't there something you take more interest in than anything else?

LAURA: Well, I do—as I said—have my—glass collection—

[*A peal of girlish laughter from the kitchen*]

JIM: I'm not right sure I know what you're talking about. What kind of glass is it?

LAURA: Little articles of it, they're ornaments mostly! Most of them are little animals made out of glass, the tiniest little animals in the world. Mother calls them a glass menagerie! Here's an example of one, if you'd like to see it! This is one of the oldest. It's nearly thirteen.

[*Music: "The Glass Menagerie"*]

[*He stretches out his hand*]

Oh, be careful—if you breathe, it breaks!

JIM: I'd better not take it. I'm pretty clumsy with things.

LAURA: Go on, I trust you with him! [*Places it in his palm*] There now—you're holding him gently! Hold him over the light, he loves the light! You see how the light shines through him?

JIM: It sure does shine!

LAURA: I shouldn't be partial, but he is my favorite one.

JIM: What kind of a thing is this one supposed to be?

LAURA: Haven't you noticed the single horn on his forehead?

JIM: A unicorn, huh?

LAURA: Mmm-hmmm!

JIM: Unicorns, aren't they extinct in the modern world?

LAURA: I know!

JIM: Poor little fellow, he must feel sort of lonesome.

LAURA: [*Smiling*] Well, if he does he doesn't complain about it. He stays on a shelf with some horses that don't have horns and all of them seem to get along nicely together.

JIM: How do you know?

LAURA: [*Lightly*] I haven't heard any arguments among them!

JIM: [*Grinning*] No arguments, huh? Well, that's a pretty good sign! Where shall I set him?

LAURA: Put him on the table. They all like a change of scenery once in a while!

JIM: [*Stretching*] Well, well, well, well—Look how big my shadow is when I stretch!

LAURA: Oh, oh, yes—it stretches across the ceiling!

JIM: [*Crossing to door*] I think it's stopped raining. [*Opens fire-escape door*] Where does the music come from?

LAURA: From the Paradise Dance Hall across the alley.

JIM: How about cutting the rug a little, Miss Wingfield?

LAURA: Oh, I—

JIM: Or is your program filled up? Let me have a look at it. [*Grasps imaginary card*] Why, every dance is taken! I'll just have to scratch some out. [*Waltz music: "La Golondrina"*] Ahhh, a waltz! [*He executes some sweeping turns by himself then holds his arms toward* Laura]

LAURA: [*Breathlessly*] I—can't dance!

JIM: There you go, that inferiority stuff!

LAURA: I've never danced in my life!

JIM: Come on, try!

LAURA: Oh, but I'd step on you!

JIM: I'm not made out of glass.

LAURA: How—how—how do we start?

JIM: Just leave it to me. You hold your arms out a little.

LAURA: Like this?

JIM: A little bit higher. Right. Now don't tighten up, that's the main thing about it—relax.

LAURA: [*Laughing breathlessly*] It's hard not to.

JIM: Okay.

LAURA: I'm afraid you can't budge me.

JIM: What do you bet I can't? [*He swings her into motion*]

LAURA: Goodness, yes, you can!

JIM: Let yourself go, now, Laura, just let yourself go.

LAURA: I'm—

JIM: Come on!

LAURA: Trying!

JIM: Not so stiff— Easy does it!

LAURA: I know but I'm—

JIM: Loosen th' backbone! There now, that's a lot better.

LAURA: Am I?

JIM: Lots, lots better! [*He moves her about the room in a clumsy waltz*]

LAURA: Oh, my!

JIM: Ha-ha!

LAURA: Oh, my goodness!

JIM: Ha-ha-ha! [*They suddenly bump into the table.* Jim *stops*] What did we hit on?

LAURA: Table.

JIM: Did something fall off it? I think—

LAURA: Yes.

JIM: I hope that it wasn't the little glass horse with the horn!

LAURA: Yes.

JIM: Aw, aw, aw. Is it broken?

LAURA: Now it is just like all the other horses.

JIM: It's lost its—

LAURA: Horn! It doesn't matter. Maybe it's a blessing in disguise.

JIM: You'll never forgive me. I bet that that was your favorite piece of glass.

LAURA: I don't have favorites much. It's no tragedy, Freckles. Glass breaks so easily. No matter how careful you are. The traffic jars the shelves and things fall off them.

JIM: Still I'm awfully sorry that I was the cause.

LAURA: [*Smiling*] I'll just imagine he had an operation. The horn was removed to make him feel less —freakish! [*They both laugh*] Now he will feel more at home with the other horses, the ones that don't have horns . . .

JIM: Ha-ha, that's very funny! [*Suddenly serious*] I'm glad to see that you have a sense of humor. You know—you're—well—very different! Surprisingly different from anyone else I know! [*His voice becomes soft and hesitant with a genuine feeling*] Do you mind me telling you that? [Laura *is abashed beyond speech*] I mean it in a nice way . . . [Laura *nods shyly, looking away*] You make me feel sort of—I don't know how to put it! I'm usually pretty good at expressing things, but—This is something that I don't know how to say! [*Laura touches her throat and clears it—turns the broken unicorn in her hands. Even softer*] Has anyone ever told you that you were pretty?

    [PAUSE: MUSIC]

    [*Laura looks up slowly, with wonder, and shakes her head*]

Well, you are! In a very different way from anyone else. And all the nicer because of the difference too. [*His voice becomes low and husky. Laura turns away, nearly faint with the novelty of her emotions*] I wish that you were my sister. I'd teach you to have some confidence in yourself. The different people are not like other people, but being different is nothing to be ashamed of. Because other people are not such wonderful people. They're one hundred times one thousand. You're one times one! They walk all over the earth. You just stay here. They're common as—weeds, but—you—well, you're—*Blue Roses!*

    [IMAGE ON SCREEN: BLUE ROSES]

    [MUSIC CHANGES]

LAURA: But blue is wrong for—roses . . .

JIM: It's right for you!—You're—pretty!

LAURA: In what respect am I pretty?

JIM: In all respects—believe me! Your eyes—your hair—are pretty! Your hands are pretty! [*He catches hold of her hand*] You think I'm making this up because I'm invited to dinner and have to be nice. Oh, I could do that! I could put on an act for you, Laura, and say lots of things without being very sincere. But this time I am. I'm talking to you sincerely. I happened to notice you had this inferiority complex that keeps you from feeling comfortable with people. Somebody needs to build your confidence up and make you proud instead of shy and turning away and—blushing—Somebody—ought to—ought to—*kiss* you, Laura! [*His hand slips slowly up her arm to her shoulder*]

    [MUSIC SWELLS TUMULTUOUSLY]

    [*He suddenly turns her about and kisses her on the lips. When he releases her, Laura sinks on the sofa with a bright, dazed look. Jim backs away and fishes in his pocket for a cigarette*]

    [LEGEND ON SCREEN: "SOUVENIR"]

Stumble-john! [*He lights the cigarette, avoiding her look. There is a peal of girlish laughter from Amanda in the kitchen. Laura slowly raises and opens her hand. It still contains the little broken glass animal. She looks at it with a tender, bewildered expression*] Stumble-john! I shouldn't have done that — That was way off the beam. You don't smoke, do you? [*She looks up, smiling, not hearing the question. He sits beside her a little gingerly. She looks at him speechlessly—waiting. He coughs decorously and moves a little farther aside as he considers the situation and senses her feelings, dimly, with perturbation. Gently*] Would you—care for a—mint? [*She doesn't seem to hear him but her look grows brighter even*] Peppermint—Life-Saver? My pocket's a regular drug store—wherever I go . . . [*He pops a mint in his mouth. Then gulps and decides to make a clean breast of it. He speaks slowly and gingerly*] Laura, you know, if I had a sister like you, I'd do the same thing as Tom. I'd bring out fellows and—introduce her to them. The right type of boys of a type to—appreciate her. Only—well—he made a mistake about me. Maybe I've got no call to be saying this. That may not have been the idea in having me over. But what if it was? There's nothing wrong about that. The only trouble is that in my case—I'm not in a situation to—do the right thing.

I can't take down your number and say I'll phone. I can't call up next week and—ask for a date. I thought I had better explain the situation in case you—misunderstood it and—hurt your feelings. . . .

    [*Pause. Slowly, very slowly, Laura's look changes, her eyes returning slowly from his to the ornament in her palm. Amanda utters another gay laugh in the kitchen*]

LAURA: [*Faintly*] You—won't—call again?

JIM: No, Laura, I can't. [*He rises from the sofa*] As I was just explaining, I've—got strings on me. Laura, I've—been going steady! I go out all of the time with a girl named Betty. She's a home-girl like you, and Catholic, and Irish, and in a great many ways we—get along fine. I met her last summer on a moonlight boat trip up the river to Alton, on the *Majestic*. Well—right away from the start it was—love!

    [LEGEND: LOVE!]

    [*Laura sways slightly forward and grips the arm of the sofa. He fails to notice, now enrapt in his own comfortable being*]

Being in love has made a new man of me! [*Leaning stiffly forward, clutching the arm of the sofa, Laura struggles visibly with her storm. But Jim is oblivious, she is a long way off*] The power of love is really pretty tremendous! Love is something that—changes the whole world, Laura! [*The storm abates a little and Laura leans back. He notices her again*] It happened that Betty's aunt took sick, she got a wire and had to go to Centralia. So Tom—when he asked me to dinner—I naturally just accepted the invitation, not knowing that you—that he—that I—[*He stops awkwardly*] Huh—I'm a stumble-john! [*He flops back on the sofa. The holy candles in the altar of Laura's face have been snuffed out. There is a look of almost infinite desolation. Jim glances at her uneasily*] I wish that you would—say something. [*She bites her lip which was trembling and then bravely smiles. She opens her hand again on the broken glass ornament. Then she gently takes his hand and raises it level with her own. She carefully places the unicorn in the palm of his hand, then pushes his fingers closed upon it*] What are you—doing that for? You want me to have him?—Laura? [*She nods*] What for?

LAURA: A—souvenir . . . [*She rises unsteadily and crouches beside the victrola to wind it up*]

[LEGEND ON SCREEN: "THINGS HAVE A WAY OF TURNING OUT SO BADLY!"]

[OR IMAGE: "GENTLEMAN CALLER WAVING GOOD-BYE!—GAILY"]

[*At this moment Amanda rushes brightly back in the front room. She bears a pitcher of fruit punch in an old-fashioned cut-glass pitcher and a plate of macaroons. The plate has a gold border and poppies painted on it*]

AMANDA: Well, well, well! Isn't the air delightful after the shower? I've made you children a little liquid refreshment. [*Turns gaily to the gentleman caller*] Jim, do you know that song about lemonade?

"Lemonade, lemonade

Made in the shade and stirred with a spade—

Good enough for any old maid!"

JIM: [*Uneasily*] Ha-ha! No—I never heard it.

AMANDA: Why, Laura! You look so serious!

JIM: We were having a serious conversation.

AMANDA: Good! Now you're better acquainted!

JIM: [*Uncertainly*] Ha-ha! Yes.

AMANDA: You modern young people are much more serious-minded than my generation. I was so gay as a girl!

JIM: You haven't changed, Mrs. Wingfield.

AMANDA: Tonight I'm rejuvenated! The gaiety of the occasion, Mr. O'Connor! [*She tosses her head with a peal of laughter. Spills lemonade*] Oooo! I'm baptizing myself!

JIM: Here—let me—

AMANDA: [*Setting the pitcher down*] There now. I discovered we had some maraschino cherries. I dumped them in, juice and all!

JIM: You shouldn't have gone to that trouble, Mrs. Wingfield.

AMANDA: Trouble, trouble? Why, it was loads of fun! Didn't you hear me cutting up in the kitchen? I bet your ears were burning! I told Tom how outdone with him I was for keeping you to himself so long a time! He should have brought you over much, much sooner! Well, now that you've found your way, I want you to be a very frequent caller! Not just occasional but all the time. Oh, we're going to have a lot of gay times together! I see them coming! Mmmm, just breathe that air! So fresh, and the moon's so pretty! I'll skip back out—I know where my place is when young folks are having a—serious conversation!

JIM: Oh, don't go out, Mrs. Wingfield. The fact of the matter is I've got to be going.

AMANDA: Going, now? You're joking! Why, it's only the shank of the evening, Mr. O'Connor!

JIM: Well, you know how it is.

AMANDA: You mean you're a young workingman and have to keep workingmen's hours. We'll let you off early tonight. But only on the condition that next time you stay later. What's the best night for you? Isn't Saturday night the best night for you workingmen?

JIM: I have a couple of time-clocks to punch, Mrs. Wingfield. One at morning, another one at night!

AMANDA: My, but you *are* ambitious! You work at night, too?

JIM: No, Ma'am, not work but—Betty! [*He crosses deliberately to pick up his hat. The band at the Paradise Dance Hall goes into a tender waltz*]

AMANDA: Betty? Betty? Who's—Betty! [*There is an ominous cracking sound in the sky*]

JIM: Oh, just a girl. The girl I go steady with! [*He smiles charmingly. The sky falls*]

[LEGEND: "THE SKY FALLS"]

AMANDA: [*A long-drawn exhalation*] Ohhhh . . . Is it a serious romance, Mr. O'Connor?

JIM: We're going to be married the second Sunday in June.

AMANDA: Ohhhh—how nice! Tom didn't mention that you were engaged to be married.

JIM: The cat's not out of the bag at the warehouse yet. You know how they are. They call you Romeo and stuff like that. [*He stops at the oval mirror to put on his hat. He carefully shapes the brim and the crown to give a discreetly dashing effect*] It's been a wonderful evening, Mrs. Wingfield. I guess this is what they mean by Southern hospitality.

AMANDA: It really wasn't anything at all.

JIM: I hope it don't seem like I'm rushing off. But I promised Betty I'd pick her up at the Wabash depot, an' by the time I get my jalopy down there her train'll be in. Some women are pretty upset if you keep 'em waiting.

AMANDA: Yes, I know— The tyranny of women! [*Extends her hand*] Good-bye, Mr. O'Connor. I wish you luck—and happiness—and success! All three of them, and so does Laura!—Don't you, Laura?

LAURA: Yes!

JIM: [*Taking her hand*] Good-bye, Laura. I'm certainly going to treasure that souvenir. And don't you forget the good advice I gave you. [*Raises his voice to a cheery shout*] So long, Shakespeare! Thanks again, ladies— Good night! [*He grins and ducks jauntily out. Still bravely grimacing, Amanda closes the door on the gentleman caller. Then she turns back to the room with a puzzled expression. She and Laura don't dare to face each other. Laura crouches beside the victrola to wind it*]

AMANDA: [*Faintly*] Things have a way of turning out so badly. I don't believe that I would play the victrola. Well, well—well—Our gentleman caller was engaged to be married! Tom!

TOM: [*From back*] Yes, Mother?

AMANDA: Come in here a minute. I want to tell you something awfully funny.

TOM: [*Enters with macaroon and a glass of the*

lemonade] Has the gentleman caller gotten away already?

AMANDA: The gentleman caller has made an early departure. What a wonderful joke you played on us!

TOM: How do you mean?

AMANDA: You didn't mention that he was engaged to be married.

TOM: Jim? Engaged?

AMANDA: That's what he just informed us.

TOM: I'll be jiggered! I didn't know about that.

AMANDA: That seems very peculiar.

TOM: What's peculiar about it?

AMANDA: Didn't you call him your best friend down at the warehouse?

TOM: He is, but how did I know?

AMANDA: It seems extremely peculiar that you wouldn't know your best friend was going to be married!

TOM: The warehouse is where I work, not where I know things about people!

AMANDA: You don't know things anywhere! You live in a dream; you manufacture illusions! [*He crosses to door*] Where are you going?

TOM: I'm going to the movies.

AMANDA: That's right, now that you've had us make such fools of ourselves. The effort, the preparations, all the expense! The new floor lamp, the rug, the clothes for Laura! All for what? To entertain some other girl's fiancé! Go to the movies, go! Don't think about us, a mother deserted, an unmarried sister who's crippled and has no job! Don't let anything interfere with your selfish pleasure! Just go, go, go—to the movies!

TOM: All right, I will! The more you shout about my selfishness to me the quicker I'll go, and I won't go to the movies!

AMANDA: Go, then! Then go to the moon—you selfish dreamer!

[Tom *smashes his glass on the floor. He plunges out on the fire-escape, slamming the door. Laura screams—cut by door. Dance-hall music up. Tom goes to the rail and grips it desperately, lifting his face in the chill white moonlight penetrating the narrow abyss of the alley*]
[LEGEND ON SCREEN: "AND SO GOOD-BYE . . ."]
[Tom's *closing speech is timed with the interior pantomime. The interior scene is played as though viewed through soundproof glass.* Amanda *appears to be making a comforting speech to Laura who is huddled upon the sofa. Now that we cannot hear the mother's speech, her silliness is gone and she has dignity and tragic beauty. Laura's dark hair hides her face until at the end of the speech she lifts it to smile at her mother. Amanda's gestures are slow and graceful, almost dance-like, as she comforts the daughter. At the end of her speech she glances a moment at the father's picture—then withdraws through the portieres. At close of* Tom's *speech,* Laura *blows out the candles, ending the play*]

TOM: I didn't go to the moon, I went much further—for time is the longest distance between two places—Not long after that I was fired for writing a poem on the lid of a shoe-box. I left Saint Louis. I descended the steps of this fire-escape for a last time and followed, from then on, in my father's footsteps, attempting to find in motion what was lost in space—I traveled around a great deal. The cities swept about me like dead leaves, leaves that were brightly colored but torn away from the branches. I would have stopped, but I was pursued by something. It always came upon me unawares, taking me altogether by surprise. Perhaps it was a familiar bit of music. Perhaps it was only a piece of transparent glass—Perhaps I am walking along a street at night, in some strange city, before I have found companions. I pass the lighted window of a shop where perfume is sold. The window is filled with pieces of colored glass, tiny transparent bottles in delicate colors, like bits of a shattered rainbow. Then all at once my sister touches my shoulder. I turn around and look into her eyes . . . Oh, Laura, Laura, I tried to leave you behind me, but I am more faithful than I intended to be! I reach for a cigarette, I cross the street, I run into the movies or a bar, I buy a drink, I speak to the nearest stranger—anything that can blow your candles out! [*Laura bends over the candles*]—for nowadays the world is lit by lightning! Blow out your candles, Laura—and so good-bye. . . . [*She blows the candles out*]

THE SCENE DISSOLVES

Arthur Miller

(1916– ——)

On February 10, 1949, Arthur Miller became famous overnight in a manner that would make most American success stories seem comparatively modest; ironically the occasion was the *première* of *Death of a Salesman,* which tells the story of a failure caused by its hero's worship of the wrong kind of success. The merits of *Death of a Salesman* were conceded even by stern critics and officially signalized by five awards, including the Drama Critics Circle award and the Pulitzer Prize. Miller's victory was quick and decisive on Broadway, and in time it spread to England and the Continent. (After an enthusiastically received production in Vienna in March 1950, the play was quickly scheduled for production in Zurich, Munich, and Berlin.) Unlike the heroes of the success stories he viewed with skepticism, Miller amply deserved the good fortune that came to him. He had been working steadily toward excellence and had already distinguished himself with much thoughtful writing in his thirty-three years.

Miller was born to a lower-middle-class Jewish family in New York's Harlem district and was reared in a suburban section of Brooklyn. He grew into a tall, raw-boned lad with a remarkable resemblance to the young Abraham Lincoln. In high school he became a football player. He went on to the University of Michigan, found an able guide in Professor Kenneth E. Rowe of the English department, and discovered an aptitude for playwriting that helped to support him through college. He won the Avery Hopwood award of $500 two successive years and received a $1,250 prize from the Hollywood-financed Bureau of New Plays, directed by the Theatre Guild's Theresa Helburn and John Gassner. After graduation from college, in 1938, he found employment on the Federal Theatre's WPA playwriting project during the last four months of its existence. He then supported himself by writing radio plays, chiefly for the Columbia Workshop of the Columbia Broadcasting System and for the Cavalcade of America program. He married a University of Michigan classmate, Mary Grace Slattery, became the father of two children, and settled down to a plain life in Brooklyn remote from Bohemian and fashionable intellectual circles. These details are in Miller's case more than usually important because his strength comes from his ability to wring significance out of common reality. He is an artist and intellectual who identifies himself with average life, understands it well, and defends it with demo-cratic fervor. He likes manual work and neighborliness. He might be described as owning a kinship to Walt Whitman but maintaining a critical rather than rhapsodic attitude toward the life of our democracy.

In 1942, he was chosen, at the recommendation of the producer Herman Shumlin, to collect material for the scenario of Ernie Pyle's *The Story of G.I. Joe.* To get the background for the film, Miller, who was incapacitated for war service by a football injury, spent six months in ground-forces camps throughout the country, going on maneuvers with the infantry and the tank crews. A diary of his experiences was published in 1944 under the title of *Situation Normal.* During the war Miller also worked for a while as a steamfitter in the Brooklyn Navy Yard and wrote radio scripts and one-act plays designed to promote civilian morale.

In 1944, Miller had his first production on Broadway: a novelistic and short-lived play, *The Man Who Had All the Luck.* Although unskillfully made, it was rich with human detail, and its rueful story of people who tried to succeed with an insufficient understanding of reality prefigured *Death of a Salesman.* A year later, Miller tasted literary success for the first time, with his novel *Focus,* an account of anti-Semitism in an American community, which he had originally planned as a three-act play.

Encouraged by the success of his novel, Miller spent two years writing another study of American life, this time for the stage. The play, *All My Sons,* revolved around a small industrialist, Joe Keller, who is saved from bankruptcy by the wartime demand for machine products and who, under pressure, sells defective parts to the air force, thus becoming responsible for the death of twenty-one pilots. He is able to shift the burden of guilt to the shoulders of a little man less rugged than himself, and he wins acquittal. But the conscience of his son indicts him, and before this tribunal there can be no acquittal. Joe Keller's defense is that his motives were the best in the world; a deeply affectionate parent, he wanted to preserve his business for his sons. It was the author's contention that no individual's actions can be self-contained, not even within the compass of a family. Miller, who wrote *All My Sons* with humane understanding but moral sinew as well as taut dramaturgy, summarized his theme as "the responsibility of man to society" or "the responsibility of a man for his actions, a recognition of his ethical responsibility to the world outside his home as well as in his own home."

More than a drama about war profiteering, *All My Sons* made a strong impression and won the Drama Critics Circle award for the best play of the season. Its limitations, an overweaving of plot threads and the use of the old-fashioned device of decisive revelations by means of a letter, made it less than the masterpiece some critics thought it to be. But the play was a culmination of technical prowess for Miller in the Ibsen-influenced social-problem type of drama. It also represented a command of plot structure that was to serve the dramatist extremely well when he turned to his next project, the writing of a play in a free dramatic form. *Death of a Salesman* would not be so successful a drama of time present and time past, of present action and reminiscence, but for its author's skill in pulling threads together and keeping a tight rein on scenes that would otherwise fly apart.

On the occasion of the *première* of *All My Sons*, Miller declared in a press interview: "In all my plays and books I try to take settings and dramatic situations from life which involve real questions of right and wrong. Then I set out, rather implacably and in the most realistic situations I can find, the moral dilemma and try to point a real, though hard, path out. I don't see how you can write anything decent without using the question of right and wrong as the basis." How well this statement applies to *Death of a Salesman* is readily apparent. The "way out" is not found for its hero, Willy Loman, for the play is an elegy on a life that has failed and has come to its end. It is too late for reformation or for him to take on a new set of values. (Only his son Biff arrives at an understanding of different objectives and a different way of life.) But it is not too late for the spiritual redemption or the burst of heroic determination in defeat which constitutes the essence of the austere art of tragedy.

Willy Loman's story plainly involves a failure of values in the world around him. Willy accepts the denatured ideals of American society—not the values considered the highest but those that were overpublicized in America. He naïvely succumbs to success-worship, to the belief that a jolly locker-room personality which makes one not only liked but "well liked" is a substitute for solid accomplishment, and to "the wrong dream" of material success. At the age of sixty-three, he is faced with the failure of this way of life, as an unwanted employee and a parent disappointed in the sons to whom he has imparted his own values. Insofar as mistaken ideas have deluded Willy Loman, the play is social criticism. But it is more than that. It is a character drama so firmly drawn that many Americans, from all walks of life, have identified themselves or their relatives with Willy and have been moved by his pathos and his very human qualities.

Miller rejected the notion that the common world is "below tragedy," and in an essay intended for the published version of *Death of a Salesman* he wrote that "in essence the tragic hero is intent upon claiming his whole due as a personality," that the commonest man may take on tragic stature "to the extent of his willingness to throw all he has into the contest," and that tragedy springs from "the underlying fear of being displaced, the disaster inherent in being torn away from our chosen image of what and who we are in this world." And by these standards the commonest of men may exhibit man's heroic spirit. Miller believed that his Willy Loman was a character of heroic dimensions and that, for all his pathos, he made *Death of a Salesman* a tragedy rather than a lament.

Both Miller's theory of tragedy and its applicability to the play are subject to debate. Is "our chosen image of what and who we are" always acceptable, and is it, in Willy's case, worthy of the respect that alone can give us tragic exaltation? Since Miller refused to accept the validity of his hero's factitious view of himself, did the author waste compassion and respect on him? It is possible to contend that he did. Yet most playgoers were willing to accept *Death of a Salesman* as a tragedy, for Miller supplied his loud-mouthed little man with some magnificence of spirit. Willy fights for his family all his life, carries on a difficult struggle for sales long after he has ceased to be welcome in the market place, and holds on to an impossible dream for his son. If in nothing else, moreover, he is tragically impassioned as a father. Perhaps it is well to make here an old distinction between high tragedy and bourgeois tragedy—that is, tragedy of commonplace life in commonplace circumstances. Willy may be called a suburban King Lear, with sons instead of daughters breaking his heart. Although obviously devoid of the splendor of Shakespeare's old man, limited as Willy is by a small mind and by unelevated language, he is not conceived in merely pathetic terms. He is, for example, more passionate and active than Balzac's Lear, the hero of *Père Goriot,* who accepts his fate passively. Willy engages in an intense conflict with his son and dies in order to effectuate his hopes for him, refusing to concede defeat for the ideal of success he has set up for him. Since he makes his sacrifice after discovering his own responsibility for Biff's failure, he ennobles himself; his act is a sort of expiation. Since he kills himself in order to leave the boy his insurance immediately after learning that Biff still loves him, it is also plain that the deluded man's inmost desire has been directed at something greater than a salesman's success; he dies as a father, not as a salesman. This transfiguration of a man who would otherwise have to be dismissed as a cheat and dolt endows him with some of the magnitude we expect to find in tragedy.

The tragic quality of *Death of a Salesman* is more than an academic achievement for the American theatre. In several respects, it represents a culmination of American playwrights' efforts to create a significant American drama. The play carries forward the struggle to create a realistically critical expression of American life, to present the common man as the center of dramatic interest, to find more expressive dramatic forms than the realistic technique permits, and to develop a poetic drama rooted in American speech and manners.

Miller's dramatic approach to the American scene reflects some thirty years of playwriting. Insofar as it exposes the hollowness of materialistic values, *Death of a Salesman* carries on the cultural rebellion staged by the playwrights, novelists, critics, and artists of the nineteen-twenties. Insofar as it relates the fate of a little man who is worn out with the economic struggle to make a home for his family and is discarded by his employer in old age, *Death of a Salesman* continues the social discontent of the theatre of the nineteen-thirties. Willy's story is another variant of the treatment of lower-middle-class life developed by Odets and the Group Theatre as part of an analysis of the social system. And the play possesses the tender regard for the average man that American writers have favored when they have gone beyond satirization of the commonplaceness of suburban and small-town life.

Willy's story, however, does not yield the usual realistic chronicle, but is transfigured by the imagination. To tell this tale of a dispossessed and defeated commoner, Miller has retained all the verisimilitude of realistic description. The dialogue is colloquial, the manners are familiar, the background is authentically suburban. But the author has also availed himself of the expressionistic dream or memory sequence that appeared impressively in American drama as early as 1920, when *The Emperor Jones* was produced at the Provincetown Playhouse. He has even used symbolism for expressive purposes, notably in the treatment of Willy's successful brother, Ben, who went into the jungle and came out a wealthy man. Miller has, in short, succeeded in projecting his social realism, his "humanistic jurisprudence" (as the critic Harold Clurman called it), by imaginative means that tell the story of Willy's errors and failures with dramatic economy and suggestive emphasis. Here, in other words, the expressionistic and realistic styles exist in a fused state.

From this theatrical treatment, finally, emerges a poetic drama not of the first order but rare in the American theatre. Many efforts to create a poetic drama had previously been made in America. O'Neill had developed a mystique of the soul and pitted man against his private demons and inscrutable, often malicious, fate. Maxwell Anderson had chosen a derivative procedure in patterning his historical plays after the older style of tragedy. He had selected high-spirited historical characters, allowed them to speak in more or less formal verse, and permitted them to universalize their emotions and thoughts in time-honored generalizations. He did not depart radically from this approach in *Winterset*, when he tried to write tragedy on a contemporary theme, with the result that his gangsters seemed to belong to the Elizabethan theatre and his lovers frequently bore an odd resemblance to Romeo and Juliet or Hamlet and Ophelia. Saroyan had given free rein to his fancy and depended upon his intuitions and improvisations to create an overgrown child's view of the world, fresh and naïve but at a considerable remove from the realities of the American scene. He created a poetry of flight. Tennessee Williams was able to develop a poetic drama on the basis of psychological deterioration of sensitive characters who do not belong to the mainstream of American realities. He made drama largely out of private sensibility. Miller's poetic drama is of a different order from all these efforts. It is rooted in everyday reality and employs the general idiom of American speech. It has none of the mystique of O'Neill and none of the formality and generalized rhetoric of Anderson; it never leaves the actual world, it does not cultivate naïveté, and it takes a responsible view of life in our society—and it deals with the men and women who struggle with the everyday reality of the average American rather than with a more or less private world. Miller's poetry of theatre is completely rooted in the world we know. It consists of reality rather than of dreams.

BIBLIOGRAPHY: Brooks Atkinson, *Broadway Scrapbook* (pp. 277–279), 1947; John Mason Brown, "Even as You and I," in *The Saturday Review of Literature,* February 26, 1949; George Jean Nathan, *Theatre Book of the Year 1948–1949* (pp. 279–285), 1949.

DEATH OF A SALESMAN[1]

By Arthur Miller

CHARACTERS

WILLY LOMAN	BERNARD	JENNY
LINDA	THE WOMAN	STANLEY
BIFF	CHARLEY	MISS FORSYTHE
HAPPY	UNCLE BEN	LETTA
	HOWARD WAGNER	

ACT I.

A melody is heard, played upon a flute. It is small and fine, telling of grass and trees and the horizon. The curtain rises.

Before us is the Salesman's house. We are aware of towering, angular shapes behind it, surrounding it on all sides. Only the blue light of the sky falls upon the house and forestage; the surrounding area shows an angry glow of orange. As more light appears, we see a solid vault of apartment houses around the small, fragile-seeming home. An air of the dream clings to the place, a dream rising out of reality. The kitchen at center seems actual enough, for there is a kitchen table with three chairs, and a refrigerator. But no other fixtures are seen. At the back of the kitchen there is a draped entrance, which leads to the living-room. To the right of the kitchen, on a level raised two feet, is a bedroom furnished only with a brass bedstead and a straight chair. On a shelf over the bed a silver athletic trophy stands. A window opens onto the apartment house at the side.

Behind the kitchen, on a level raised six and a half feet, is the boys' bedroom, at present barely visible. Two beds are dimly seen, and at the back of the room a dormer window. (This bedroom is above the unseen living-room.) At the left a stairway curves up to it from the kitchen.

The entire setting is wholly or, in some places, partially transparent. The roof-line of the house is one-dimensional; under and over it we see the apartment buildings. Before the house lies an apron, curving beyond the forestage into the orchestra. This forward area serves as the back yard as well as the locale of all Willy's imaginings and of his city scenes. Whenever the action is in the present the actors observe the imaginary wall-lines, entering the house only through its door at the left. But in the scenes of the past these boundaries are broken, and characters enter or leave a room by stepping "through" a wall onto the forestage.

[1] Copyright 1949 by Arthur Miller. See p. v for caution notice.

From the right, Willy Loman, *the Salesman, enters, carrying two large sample cases. The flute plays on. He hears but is not aware of it. He is past sixty years of age, dressed quietly. Even as he crosses the stage to the doorway of the house, his exhaustion is apparent. He unlocks the door, comes into the kitchen, and thankfully lets his burden down, feeling the soreness of his palms. A word-sigh escapes his lips—it might be "Oh, boy, oh, boy." He closes the door, then carries his cases out into the living-room, through the draped kitchen doorway.*

Linda, *his wife, has stirred in her bed at the right. She gets out and puts on a robe, listening. Most often jovial, she has developed an iron repression of her exceptions to* Willy's *behavior—she more than loves him, she admires him, as though his mercurial nature, his temper, his massive dreams and little cruelties, served her only as sharp reminders of the turbulent longings within him, longings which she shares but lacks the temperament to utter and follow to their end.*

LINDA: [*Hearing* Willy *outside the bedroom, calls with trepidation*] Willy!

WILLY: It's all right. I came back.

LINDA: Why? What happened? [*Slight pause*] Did something happen, Willy?

WILLY: No, nothing happened.

LINDA: You didn't smash the car, did you?

WILLY: [*With casual irritation*] I said nothing happened. Didn't you hear me?

LINDA: Don't you feel well?

WILLY: I'm tired to the death. [*The flute has faded away. He sits on the bed beside her, a little numb*] I couldn't make it. I just couldn't make it, Linda.

LINDA: [*Very carefully, delicately*] Where were you all day? You look terrible.

WILLY: I got as far as a little above Yonkers. I stopped for a cup of coffee. Maybe it was the coffee.

LINDA: What?

WILLY: [*After a pause*] I suddenly couldn't drive any more. The car kept going off onto the shoulder, y'know?

LINDA: [*Helpfully*] Oh. Maybe it was the steering again. I don't think Angelo knows the Studebaker.

WILLY: No, it's me, it's me. Suddenly I realize I'm goin' sixty miles an hour and I don't remember the last five minutes. I'm—I can't seem to—keep my mind to it.

LINDA: Maybe it's your glasses. You never went for your new glasses.

WILLY: No, I see everything. I came back ten miles an hour. It took me nearly four hours from Yonkers.

LINDA: [*Resigned*] Well, you'll just have to take a rest, Willy, you can't continue this way.

WILLY: I just got back from Florida.

LINDA: But you didn't rest your mind. Your mind is overactive, and the mind is what counts, dear.

WILLY: I'll start out in the morning. Maybe I'll feel better in the morning. [*She is taking off his shoes*] These goddam arch supports are killing me.

LINDA: Take an aspirin. Should I get you an aspirin? It'll soothe you.

WILLY: [*With wonder*] I was driving along, you understand? And I was fine. I was even observing the scenery. You can imagine, me looking at scenery, on the road every week of my life. But it's so beautiful up there, Linda, the trees are so thick, and the sun is warm. I opened the windshield and just let the warm air bathe over me. And then all of a sudden I'm goin' off the road! I'm tellin' ya, I absolutely forgot I was driving. If I'd've gone the other way over the white line I might've killed somebody. So I went on again—and five minutes later I'm dreamin' again, and I nearly—[*He presses two fingers against his eyes*] I have such thoughts, I have such strange thoughts.

LINDA: Willy, dear. Talk to them again. There's no reason why you can't work in New York.

WILLY: They don't need me in New York. I'm the New England man. I'm vital in New England.

LINDA: But you're sixty years old. They can't expect you to keep traveling every week.

WILLY: I'll have to send a wire to Portland. I'm supposed to see Brown and Morrison tomorrow morning at ten o'clock to show the line. Goddammit, I could sell them! [*He starts putting on his jacket*]

LINDA: [*Taking the jacket from him*] Why don't you go down to the place tomorrow and tell Howard you've simply got to work in New York? You're too accommodating, dear.

WILLY: If old man Wagner was alive I'd a been in charge of New York now! That man was a prince, he was a masterful man. But that boy of his, that Howard, he don't appreciate. When I went north first time, the Wagner Company didn't know where New England was!

LINDA: Why don't you tell those things to Howard, dear?

WILLY: [*Encouraged*] I will, I definitely will. Is there any cheese?

LINDA: I'll make you a sandwich.

WILLY: No, go to sleep. I'll take some milk. I'll be up right away. The boys in?

LINDA: They're sleeping. Happy took Biff on a date tonight.

WILLY: [*Interested*] That so?

LINDA: It was so nice to see them shaving together, one behind the other, in the bathroom. And going out together. You notice? The whole house smells of shaving lotion.

WILLY: Figure it out. Work a lifetime to pay off a house. You finally own it, and there's nobody to live in it.

LINDA: Well, dear, life is a casting off. It's always that way.

WILLY: No, no, some people—some people accomplish something. Did Biff say anything after I went this morning?

LINDA: You shouldn't have criticized him, Willy, especially after he just got off the train. You mustn't lose your temper with him.

WILLY: When the hell did I lose my temper? I simply asked him if he was making any money. Is that a criticism?

LINDA: But, dear, how could he make any money?

WILLY: [*Worried and angered*] There's such an undercurrent in him. He became a moody man. Did he apologize when I left this morning?

LINDA: He was crestfallen, Willy. You know how he admires you. I think if he finds himself, then you'll both be happier and not fight any more.

WILLY: How can he find himself on a farm? Is that a life? A farmhand? In the beginning, when he was young, I thought, well, a young man, it's good for him to tramp around, take a lot of different jobs. But it's more than ten years now and he has yet to make thirty-five dollars a week!

LINDA: He's finding himself, Willy.

WILLY: Not finding yourself at the age of thirty-four is a disgrace!

LINDA: Shh!

WILLY: The trouble is he's lazy, goddammit!

LINDA: Willy, please!

WILLY: Biff is a lazy bum!

LINDA: They're sleeping. Get something to eat. Go on down.

WILLY: Why did he come home? I would like to know what brought him home.

LINDA: I don't know. I think he's still lost, Willy. I think he's very lost.

WILLY: Biff Loman is lost. In the greatest country in the world a young man with such—personal attractiveness, gets lost. And such a hard worker. There's one thing about Biff—he's not lazy.

LINDA: Never.

WILLY: [*With pity and resolve*] I'll see him in the morning; I'll have a nice talk with him. I'll get him a job selling. He could be big in no time. My God! Remember how they used to follow him around in high school? When he smiled at one of them their faces lit up. When he walked down the street . . . [*He loses himself in reminiscences*]

LINDA: [*Trying to bring him out of it*] Willy, dear, I got a new kind of American-type cheese today. It's whipped.

WILLY: Why do you get American when I like Swiss?

LINDA: I just thought you'd like a change—

WILLY: I don't want a change! I want Swiss cheese. Why am I always being contradicted?

LINDA: [*With a covering laugh*] I thought it would be a surprise.

WILLY: Why don't you open a window in here, for God's sake?

LINDA: [*With infinite patience*] They're all open, dear.

WILLY: The way they boxed us in here. Bricks and windows, windows and bricks.

LINDA: We should've bought the land next door.

WILLY: The street is lined with cars. There's not a breath of fresh air in the neighborhood. The grass don't grow any more, you can't raise a carrot in the back yard. They should've had a law against apartment houses. Remember those two beautiful elm trees out there? When I and Biff hung the swing between them?

LINDA: Yeah, like being a million miles from the city.

WILLY: They should've arrested the builder for cutting those down. They massacred the neighborhood. [*Lost*] More and more I think of those days, Linda. This time of year it was lilac and wisteria. And then the peonies would come out, and the daffodils. What fragrance in this room!

LINDA: Well, after all, people had to move somewhere.

WILLY: No, there's more people now.

LINDA: I don't think there's more people. I think—

WILLY: There's more people! That's what ruining this country! Population is getting out of control. The competition is maddening! Smell the stink from that apartment house! And another one on the other side . . . How can they whip cheese?

[*On Willy's last line, Biff and Happy raise themselves up in their beds, listening*]

LINDA: Go down, try it. And be quiet.

WILLY: [*Turning to Linda, guiltily*] You're not worried about me, are you, sweetheart?

BIFF: What's the matter?

HAPPY: Listen!

LINDA: You've got too much on the ball to worry about.

WILLY: You're my foundation and my support, Linda.

LINDA: Just try to relax, dear. You make mountains out of molehills.

WILLY: I won't fight with him any more. If he wants to go back to Texas, let him go.

LINDA: He'll find his way.

WILLY: Sure. Certain men just don't get started till later in life. Like Thomas Edison, I think. Or B. F. Goodrich. One of them was deaf. [*He starts for the bedroom doorway*] I'll put my money on Biff.

LINDA: And Willy—if it's warm Sunday we'll drive in the country. And we'll open the windshield, and take lunch.

WILLY: No, the windshields don't open on the new cars.

LINDA: But you opened it today.

WILLY: Me? I didn't. [*He stops*] Now isn't that peculiar! Isn't that a remarkable—[*He breaks off in amazement and fright as the flute is heard distantly*]

LINDA: What, darling?

WILLY: That is the most remarkable thing.

LINDA: What, dear?

WILLY: I was thinking of the Chevvy. [*Slight pause*] Nineteen twenty-eight . . . when I had that red Chevvy—[*Breaks off*] That funny? I coulda sworn I was driving that Chevvy today.

LINDA: Well, that's nothing. Something must've reminded you.

WILLY: Remarkable. Ts. Remember those days? The way Biff used to simonize that car? The dealer refused to believe there was eighty thousand miles on it. [*He shakes his head*] Heh! [*To Linda*] Close your eyes, I'll be right up. [*He walks out of the bedroom*]

HAPPY: [*To Biff*] Jesus, maybe he smashed up the car again!

LINDA: [*Calling after Willy*] Be careful on the stairs, dear! The cheese is on the middle shelf! [*She turns, goes over to the bed, takes his jacket, and goes out of the bedroom*]

[*Light has risen on the boys' room. Unseen, Willy is heard talking to himself, "Eighty thousand miles," and a little laugh. Biff gets out of bed, comes downstage a bit, and stands attentively. Biff is two years older than his brother Happy, well built, but in these days bears a worn air and seems less self-assured. He has succeeded less, and his dreams are stronger and less acceptable than Happy's. Happy is tall, powerfully made. Sexuality is like a visible color on him, or a scent that many women have discovered. He, like his brother, is lost, but in a different way, for he has never allowed himself to turn his face toward defeat and is thus more confused and hard-skinned, although seemingly more content*]

HAPPY: [*Getting out of bed*] He's going to get his license taken away if he keeps that up. I'm getting nervous about him, y'know, Biff?

BIFF: His eyes are going.

HAPPY: No, I've driven with him. He sees all right. He just doesn't keep his mind on it. I drove into the city with him last week. He stops at a green light and then it turns red and he goes. [*He laughs*]

BIFF: Maybe he's color-blind.

HAPPY: Pop? Why he's got the finest eye for color in the business. You know that.

BIFF: [*Sitting down on his bed*] I'm going to sleep.

HAPPY: You're not still sour on Dad, are you, Biff?

BIFF: He's all right, I guess.

WILLY: [*Underneath them, in the living-room*] Yes, sir, eighty thousand miles—eighty-two thousand!

BIFF: You smoking?

HAPPY: [*Holding out a pack of cigarettes*] Want one?

BIFF: [*Taking a cigarette*] I can never sleep when I smell it.

WILLY: What a simonizing job, heh!

HAPPY: [*With deep sentiment*] Funny, Biff, y'know? Us sleeping in here again? The old beds. [*He pats his bed affectionately*] All the talk that went across those two beds, huh? Our whole lives.

BIFF: Yeah. Lotta dreams and plans.

HAPPY: [*With a deep and masculine laugh*] About five hundred women would like to know what was said in this room.

[*They share a soft laugh*]

BIFF: Remember that big Betsy something—what the hell was her name—over on Bushwick Avenue?

HAPPY: [*Combing his hair*] With the collie dog!

BIFF: That's the one. I got you in there, remember?

HAPPY: Yeah, that was my first time—I think. Boy, there was a pig! [*They laugh, almost crudely*] You taught me everything I know about women. Don't forget that.

BIFF: I bet you forgot how bashful you used to be. Especially with girls.

HAPPY: Oh, I still am, Biff.

BIFF: Oh, go on.

HAPPY: I just control it, that's all. I think I got less bashful and you got more so. What happened, Biff? Where's the old humor, the old confidence? [*He shakes* Biff's *knee*. Biff *gets up and moves restlessly about the room*] What's the matter?

BIFF: Why does Dad mock me all the time?

HAPPY: He's not mocking you, he—

BIFF: Everything I say there's a twist of mockery on his face. I can't get near him.

HAPPY: He just wants you to make good, that's all. I wanted to talk to you about Dad for a long time, Biff. Something's—happening to him. He—talks to himself.

BIFF: I noticed that this morning. But he always mumbled.

HAPPY: But not so noticeable. It got so embarrassing I sent him to Florida. And you know something? Most of the time he's talking to you.

BIFF: What's he say about me?

HAPPY: I can't make it out.

BIFF: What's he say about me?

HAPPY: I think the fact that you're not settled, that you're still kind of up in the air . . .

BIFF: There's one or two other things depressing him, Happy.

HAPPY: What do you mean?

BIFF: Never mind. Just don't lay it all to me.

HAPPY: But I think if you just got started—I mean—is there any future for you out there?

BIFF: I tell ya, Hap, I don't know what the future is. I don't know—what I'm supposed to want.

HAPPY: What do you mean?

BIFF: Well, I spent six or seven years after high school trying to work myself up. Shipping clerk, salesman, business of one kind or another. And it's a measly manner of existence. To get on that subway on the hot mornings in summer. To devote your whole life to keeping stock, or making phone calls, or selling or buying. To suffer fifty weeks of the year for the sake of a two-week vacation, when all you really desire is to be outdoors, with your shirt off. And always to have to get ahead of the next fella. And still—that's how you build a future.

HAPPY: Well, you really enjoy it on a farm? Are you content out there?

BIFF: [*With rising agitation*] Hap, I've had twenty or thirty different kinds of jobs since I left home before the war, and it always turns out the same. I just realized it lately. In Nebraska when I herded cattle, and the Dakotas, and Arizona, and now in Texas. It's why I came home now, I guess, because I realized it. This farm I work on, it's spring there now, see? And they've got about fifteen new colts. There's nothing more inspiring or—beautiful than the sight of a mare and a new colt. And it's cool there now, see? Texas is cool now, and it's spring. And whenever spring comes to where I am, I suddenly get the feeling, my God, I'm not gettin' anywhere! What the hell am I doing, playing around with horses, twenty-eight dollars a week! I'm thirty-four years old, I oughta be makin' my future. That's when I come running home. And now, I get here, and I don't know what to do with myself. [*After a pause*] I've always made a point of not wasting my life, and everytime I come back here I know that all I've done is to waste my life.

HAPPY: You're a poet, you know that, Biff? You're a—you're an idealist!

BIFF: No, I'm mixed up very bad. Maybe I oughta get married. Maybe I oughta get stuck into something. Maybe that's my trouble. I'm like a boy. I'm not married, I'm not in business, I just—I'm like a boy. Are you content, Hap? You're a success, aren't you? Are you content?

HAPPY: Hell, no!

BIFF: Why? You're making money, aren't you?

HAPPY: [*Moving about with energy, expressiveness*] All I can do now is wait for the merchandise manager to die. And suppose I get to be merchandise manager? He's a good friend of mine, and he just built a terrific estate on Long Island. And he lived there about two months and sold it, and now he's building another one. He can't enjoy it once it's finished. And I know that's just what I would do. I don't know what the hell I'm workin' for. Sometimes I sit in my apartment—all alone. And I think of the rent I'm paying. And it's crazy. But then, it's what I always wanted. My own apartment, a car, and plenty of women. And still, goddammit, I'm lonely.

BIFF: [*With enthusiasm*] Listen, why don't you come out West with me?

HAPPY: You and I, heh?

BIFF: Sure, maybe we could buy a ranch. Raise cattle, use our muscles. Men built like we are should be working out in the open.

HAPPY: [*Avidly*] The Loman Brothers, heh?

BIFF: [*With vast affection*] Sure, we'd be known all over the counties!

HAPPY: [*Enthralled*] That's what I dream about, Biff. Sometimes I want to just rip my clothes off in the middle of the store and outbox that goddam merchandise manager. I mean I can outbox, outrun, and outlift anybody in that store, and I have to take orders from those common, petty sons-of-bitches till I can't stand it any more.

BIFF: I'm tellin' you, kid, if you were with me I'd be happy out there.

HAPPY: [*Filled with enthusiasm*] See, Biff, everybody around me is so false that I'm constantly lowering my ideals . . .

BIFF: Baby, together we'd stand up for one another, we'd have someone to trust.

HAPPY: If I were around you—

BIFF: Hap, the trouble is we weren't brought up to grub for money. I don't know how to do it.

HAPPY: Neither can I!

BIFF: Then let's go!

HAPPY: The only thing is—what can you make out there?

BIFF: But look at your friend. Builds an estate and then hasn't the peace of mind to live in it.

HAPPY: Yeah, but when he walks into the store the waves part in front of him. That's fifty-two thousand dollars a year coming through the revolving door, and I got more in my pinky finger than he's got in his head.

BIFF: Yeah, but you just said—

HAPPY: I gotta show some of those pompous, self-important executives over there that Hap Loman can make the grade. I want to walk into the store the way he walks in. Then I'll go with you, Biff. We'll be together yet, I swear. But take those two we had tonight. Now weren't they gorgeous creatures?

BIFF: Yeah, yeah, most gorgeous I've had in years.

HAPPY: I get that any time I want, Biff. Whenever I feel disgusted. The only trouble is, it gets like bowling or something. I just keep knockin' them over and it doesn't mean anything. You still run around a lot?

BIFF: Naa. I'd like to find a girl—steady, somebody with substance.

HAPPY: That's what I long for.

BIFF: Go on! You'd never come home.

HAPPY: I would! Somebody with character, with resistance! Like Mom, y'know? You're gonna call me a bastard when I tell you this. That girl Charlotte I was with tonight is engaged to be married in five weeks. [*He tries on his new hat*]

BIFF: No kiddin'!

HAPPY: Sure, the guy's in line for the vice-presidency of the store. I don't know what gets into me, maybe I just have an overdeveloped sense of competition or something, but I went and ruined her, and furthermore I can't get rid of her. And he's the third executive I've done that to. Isn't that a crummy characteristic? And to top it all, I go to their weddings! [*Indignantly, but laughing*] Like I'm not supposed to take bribes. Manufacturers offer me a hundred-dollar bill now and then to throw an order their way. You know how honest I am, but it's like this girl, see. I hate myself for it. Because I don't want the girl, and, still, I take it and—I love it!

BIFF: Let's go to sleep.

HAPPY: I guess we didn't settle anything, heh?

BIFF: I just got one idea that I think I'm going to try.

HAPPY: What's that?

BIFF: Remember Bill Oliver?

HAPPY: Sure, Oliver is very big now. You want to work for him again?

BIFF: No, but when I quit he said something to me. He put his arm on my shoulder, and he said, "Biff, if you ever need anything, come to me."

HAPPY: I remember that. That sounds good.

BIFF: I think I'll go to see him. If I could get ten thousand or even seven or eight thousand dollars I could buy a beautiful ranch.

HAPPY: I bet he'd back you. 'Cause he thought highly of you, Biff. I mean, they all do. You're well liked, Biff. That's why I say to come back here, and we both have the apartment. And I'm tellin' you, Biff, any babe you want . . .

BIFF: No, with a ranch I could do the work I like and still be something. I just wonder though. I wonder if Oliver still thinks I stole that carton of basketballs.

HAPPY: Oh, he probably forgot that long ago. It's almost ten years. You're too sensitive. Anyway, he didn't really fire you.

BIFF: Well, I think he was going to. I think that's why I quit. I was never sure whether he knew or not. I know he thought the world of me, though. I was the only one he'd let lock up the place.

WILLY: [*Below*] You gonna wash the engine, Biff?

HAPPY: Shh!

[Biff *looks at* Happy, *who is gazing down, listening.* Willy *is mumbling in the parlor*]

HAPPY: You hear that?

[*They listen.* Willy *laughs warmly*]

BIFF: [*Growing angry*] Doesn't he know Mom can hear that?

WILLY: Don't get your sweater dirty, Biff!

[*A look of pain crosses Biff's face*]

HAPPY: Isn't that terrible? Don't leave again, will you? You'll find a job here. You gotta stick around. I don't know what to do about him, it's getting embarrassing.

WILLY: What a simonizing job!

BIFF: Mom's hearing that!

WILLY: No kiddin', Biff, you got a date? Wonderful!

HAPPY: Go on to sleep. But talk to him in the morning, will you?

BIFF: [*Reluctantly getting into bed*] With her in the house. Brother!

HAPPY: [*Getting into bed*] I wish you'd have a good talk with him.

[*The light on their room begins to fade*]

BIFF: [*To himself in bed*] That selfish, stupid . . .

HAPPY: Sh . . . Sleep, Biff.

[*Their light is out. Well before they have finished speaking, Willy's form is dimly seen below in the darkened kitchen. He opens the refrigerator, searches in there, and takes out a bottle of milk. The apartment houses are fading out, and the entire house and surroundings become covered with leaves. Music insinuates itself as the leaves appear*]

WILLY: Just wanna be careful with those girls, Biff, that's all. Don't make any promises. No promises of any kind. Because a girl, y'know, they always believe what you tell 'em, and you're very young, Biff, you're too young to be talking seriously to girls.

[*Light rises on the kitchen. Willy, talking, shuts the refrigerator door and comes downstage to the kitchen table. He pours milk into a glass. He is totally immersed in himself, smiling faintly*]

WILLY: Too young entirely, Biff. You want to watch your schooling first. Then when you're all set, there'll be plenty of girls for a boy like you. [*He smiles broadly at a kitchen chair*] That so? The girls pay for you? [*He laughs.*] Boy, you must really be makin' a hit.

[*Willy is gradually addressing—physically—a point off stage, speaking through the wall of the kitchen, and his voice has been rising in volume to that of a normal conversation*]

WILLY: I been wondering why you polish the car so careful. Ha! Don't leave the hubcaps, boys. Get the chamois to the hubcaps. Happy, use newspaper on the windows, it's the easiest thing. Show him how to do it, Biff! You see, Happy? Pad it up, use it like a pad. That's it, that's it, good work. You're doin' all right, Hap. [*He pauses, then nods in approbation for a few seconds, then looks upward*] Biff, first thing we gotta do when we get time is clip that big branch over the house. Afraid it's gonna fall in a storm and hit the roof. Tell you what. We get a rope and sling her around, and then we climb up there with a couple of saws and take her down. Soon as you finish the car, boys, I wanna see ya. I got a surprise for you, boys.

BIFF: [*Offstage*] Whatta ya got, Dad?

WILLY: No, you finish first. Never leave a job till you're finished—remember that. [*Looking toward the "big trees"*] Biff, up in Albany I saw a beautiful hammock. I think I'll buy it next trip, and we'll hang it right between those two elms. Wouldn't that be something? Just swingin' there under those branches. Boy, that would be . . .

[*Young Biff and Young Happy appear from the direction Willy was addressing. Happy carries rags and a pail of water. Biff, wearing a sweater with a block "S," carries a football*]

BIFF: [*Pointing in the direction of the car offstage*] How's that, Pop, professional?

WILLY: Terrific. Terrific job, boys. Good work, Biff.

HAPPY: Where's the surprise, Pop?

WILLY: In the back seat of the car.

HAPPY: Boy! [*He runs off*]

BIFF: What is it, Dad? Tell me, what'd you buy?

WILLY: [*Laughing, cuffs him*] Never mind, something I want you to have.

BIFF: [*Turns and starts off*] What is it, Hap?

HAPPY: [*Offstage*] It's a punching bag!

BIFF: Oh, Pop!

WILLY: It's got Gene Tunney's signature on it!

[*Happy runs onstage with a punching bag*]

BIFF: Gee, how'd you know we wanted a punching bag?

WILLY: Well, it's the finest thing for the timing.

HAPPY: [*Lies down on his back and pedals with his feet*] I'm losing weight, you notice, Pop?

WILLY: [*To Happy*] Jumping rope is good too.

BIFF: Did you see the new football I got?

WILLY: [*Examining the ball*] Where'd you get a new ball?

BIFF: The coach told me to practice my passing.

WILLY: That so? And he gave you the ball, heh?

BIFF: Well, I borrowed it from the locker room. [*He laughs confidentially*]

WILLY: [*Laughing with him at the theft*] I want you to return that.

HAPPY: I told you he wouldn't like it!

BIFF: [*Angrily*] Well, I'm bringing it back!

WILLY: [*Stopping the incipient argument, to Happy*] Sure, he's gotta practice with a regulation ball, doesn't he? [*To Biff*] Coach'll probably congratulate you on your initiative!

BIFF: Oh, he keeps congratulating my initiative all the time, Pop.

WILLY: That's because he likes you. If somebody else took that ball there'd be an uproar. So what's the report, boys, what's the report?

BIFF: Where'd you go this time, Dad? Gee we were lonesome for you.

WILLY: [*Pleased, puts an arm around each boy and they come down to the apron*] Lonesome, heh?

BIFF: Missed you every minute.

WILLY: Don't say? Tell you a secret, boys. Don't breathe it to a soul. Someday I'll have my own business, and I'll never have to leave home any more.

HAPPY: Like Uncle Charley, heh?

WILLY: Bigger than Uncle Charley! Because Charley is not—liked. He's liked, but he's not—well liked.

BIFF: Where'd you go this time, Dad?

WILLY: Well, I got on the road, and I went north to Providence. Met the Mayor.

BIFF: The Mayor of Providence!

WILLY: He was sitting in the hotel lobby.

BIFF: What'd he say?

WILLY: He said, "Morning!" And I said, "You got a fine city here, Mayor." And then he had coffee with me. And then I went to Waterbury. Waterbury is a fine city. Big clock city, the famous Waterbury clock. Sold a nice bill there. And then Boston—Boston is the cradle of the Revolution. A fine city. And a couple of other towns in Mass., and on to Portland and Bangor and straight home!

BIFF: Gee, I'd love to go with you sometime, Dad.

WILLY: Soon as summer comes.

HAPPY: Promise?

WILLY: You and Hap and I, and I'll show you all the towns. America is full of beautiful towns and fine, upstanding people. And they know me, boys, they know me up and down New England. The finest people. And when I bring you fellas up, there'll be open sesame for all of us, 'cause one thing, boys: I have friends. I can park my car in any street in New England, and the cops protect it like their own. This summer, heh?

BIFF AND HAPPY: [*Together*] Yeah! You bet!

WILLY: We'll take our bathing suits.

HAPPY: We'll carry your bags, Pop!

WILLY: Oh, won't that be something! Me comin' into the Boston stores with you boys carryin' my bags. What a sensation!

[Biff *is prancing around, practicing passing the ball*]

WILLY: You nervous, Biff, about the game?

BIFF: Not if you're gonna be there.

WILLY: What do they say about you in school, now that they made you captain?

HAPPY: There's a crowd of girls behind him everytime the classes change.

BIFF: [*Taking* Willy's *hand*] This Saturday, Pop, this Saturday—just for you, I'm going to break through for a touchdown.

HAPPY: You're supposed to pass.

BIFF: I'm takin' one play for Pop. You watch me, Pop, and when I take off my helmet, that means I'm breakin' out. Then you watch me crash through that line!

WILLY: [*Kisses* Biff] Oh, wait'll I tell this in Boston!

[Bernard *enters in knickers. He is younger than* Biff, *earnest and loyal, a worried boy*]

BERNARD: Biff, where are you? You're supposed to study with me today.

WILLY: Hey, looka Bernard. What're you lookin' so anemic about, Bernard?

BERNARD: He's gotta study, Uncle Willy. He's got Regents next week.

HAPPY: [*Tauntingly, spinning* Bernard *around*] Let's box, Bernard!

BERNARD: Biff! [*He gets away from* Happy] Listen, Biff, I heard Mr. Birnbaum say that if you don't start studyin' math he's gonna flunk you, and you won't graduate. I heard him!

WILLY: You better study with him, Biff. Go ahead now.

BERNARD: I heard him!

BIFF: Oh, Pop, you didn't see my sneakers! [*He holds up a foot for* Willy *to look at*]

WILLY: Hey, that's a beautiful job of printing!

BERNARD: [*Wiping his glasses*] Just because he printed University of Virginia on his sneakers doesn't mean they've got to graduate him, Uncle Willy!

WILLY: [*Angrily*] What're you talking about? With scholarships to three universities they're gonna flunk him?

BERNARD: But I heard Mr. Birnbaum say—

WILLY: Don't be a pest, Bernard! [*To his boys*] What an anemic!

BERNARD: Okay, I'm waiting for you in my house, Biff.

[Bernard *goes off. The* Lomans *laugh*]

WILLY: Bernard is not well liked, is he?

BIFF: He's liked, but he's not well liked.

HAPPY: That's right, Pop.

WILLY: That's just what I mean. Bernard can get the best marks in school, y'understand, but when he gets out in the business world, y'understand, you are going to be five times ahead of him. That's why I thank Almighty God you're both built like Adonises. Because the man who makes an appearance in the business world, the man who creates personal interest, is the man who gets ahead. Be liked and you will never want. You take me, for instance. I never have to wait in line to see a buyer. "Willy Loman is here!" That's all they have to know, and I go right through.

BIFF: Did you knock them dead, Pop?

WILLY: Knocked 'em cold in Providence, slaughtered 'em in Boston.

HAPPY: [*On his back, pedaling again*] I'm losing weight, you notice, Pop?

[Linda *enters, as of old, a ribbon in her hair, carrying a basket of washing*]

LINDA: [*With youthful energy*] Hello, dear!

WILLY: Sweetheart!

LINDA: How'd the Chevvy run?

WILLY: Chevrolet, Linda, is the greatest car ever built. [*To the boys*] Since when do you let your mother carry wash up the stairs?

BIFF: Grab hold there, boy!

HAPPY: Where to, Mom?

LINDA: Hang them up on the line. And you better go down to your friends, Biff. The cellar is full of boys. They don't know what to do with themselves.

BIFF: Ah, when Pop comes home they can wait!

WILLY: [*Laughs appreciatively*] You better go down and tell them what to do, Biff.

BIFF: I think I'll have them sweep out the furnace room.

WILLY: Good work, Biff.

BIFF: [*Goes through wall-line of kitchen to doorway at back and calls down*] Fellas! Everybody sweep out the furnace room! I'll be right down!

VOICES: All right! Okay, Biff.

BIFF: George and Sam and Frank, come out back! We're hangin' up the wash! Come on, Hap, on the double! [*He and* Happy *carry out the basket*]

LINDA: The way they obey him!

WILLY: Well, that's training, the training. I'm tellin' you, I was sellin' thousands and thousands, but I had to come home.

LINDA: Oh, the whole block'll be at that game. Did you sell anything?

WILLY: I did five hundred gross in Providence and seven hundred gross in Boston.

LINDA: No! Wait a minute, I've got a pencil. [*She pulls pencil and paper out of her apron pocket*] That makes your commission . . . Two hundred—my God! Two hundred and twelve dollars!

WILLY: Well, I didn't figure it yet, but . . .

LINDA: How much did you do?

WILLY: Well, I—I did—about a hundred and eighty gross in Providence. Well, no—it came to—roughly two hundred gross on the whole trip.

LINDA: [*Without hesitation*] Two hundred gross. That's . . . [*She figures*]

WILLY: The trouble was that three of the stores were half closed for inventory in Boston. Otherwise I woulda broke records.

LINDA: Well, it makes seventy dollars and some pennies. That's very good.

WILLY: What do we owe?

LINDA: Well, on the first there's sixteen dollars on the refrigerator—

WILLY: Why sixteen?

LINDA: Well, the fan belt broke, so it was a dollar eighty.

WILLY: But it's brand new.

LINDA: Well, the man said that's the way it is. Till they work themselves in, y'know.

[*They move through the wall-line into the kitchen*]

WILLY: I hope we didn't get stuck on that machine.

LINDA: They got the biggest ads of any of them!

WILLY: I know, it's a fine machine. What else?

LINDA: Well, there's nine-sixty for the washing machine. And for the vacuum cleaner there's three and a half due on the fifteenth. Then the roof, you got twenty-one dollars remaining.

WILLY: It don't leak, does it?

LINDA: No, they did a wonderful job. Then you owe Frank for the carburetor.

WILLY: I'm not going to pay that man! That goddam Chevrolet, they ought to prohibit the manufacture of that car!

LINDA: Well, you owe him three and a half. And odds and ends, comes to around a hundred and twenty dollars by the fifteenth.

WILLY: A hundred and twenty dollars! My God, if business don't pick up I don't know what I'm gonna do!

LINDA: Well, next week you'll do better.

WILLY: Oh, I'll knock 'em dead next week. I'll go to Hartford. I'm very well liked in Hartford. You know, the trouble is, Linda, people don't seem to take to me.

[*They move onto the forestage*]

LINDA: Oh, don't be foolish.

WILLY: I know it when I walk in. They seem to laugh at me.

LINDA: Why? Why would they laugh at you? Don't talk that way, Willy.

[Willy *moves to the edge of the stage.* Linda *goes into the kitchen and starts to darn stockings*]

WILLY: I don't know the reason for it, but they just pass me by. I'm not noticed.

LINDA: But you're doing wonderful, dear. You're making seventy to a hundred dollars a week.

WILLY: But I gotta be at it ten, twelve hours a day. Other men—I don't know—they do it easier. I don't know why—I can't stop myself—I talk too much. A man oughta come in with a few words. One thing about Charley. He's a man of few words, and they respect him.

LINDA: You don't talk too much, you're just lively.

WILLY: [*Smiling*] Well, I figure, what the hell, life is short, a couple of jokes. [*To himself*] I joke too much! [*The smile goes*]

LINDA: Why? You're—

WILLY: I'm fat. I'm very—foolish to look at, Linda. I didn't tell you, but Christmas time I happened to be calling on F. H. Stewarts, and a salesman I know, as I was going in to see the buyer I heard him say something about—walrus. And I—I cracked him right across the face. I won't take that. I simply will not take that. But they do laugh at me. I know that.

LINDA: Darling . . .

WILLY: I gotta overcome it. I know I gotta overcome it. I'm not dressing to advantage, maybe.

LINDA: Willy, darling, you're the handsomest man in the world—

WILLY: Oh, no, Linda.

LINDA: To me you are. [*Slight pause*] The handsomest.

[*From the darkness is heard the laughter of a woman. Willy doesn't turn to it, but it continues through Linda's lines*]

LINDA: And the boys, Willy. Few men are idolized by their children the way you are.

[*Music is heard as behind a scrim, to the left of the house,* The Woman, *dimly seen, is dressing*]

WILLY: [*With great feeling*] You're the best there is, Linda, you're a pal, you know that? On the road —on the road I want to grab you sometimes and just kiss the life outa you.

[*The laughter is loud now, and he moves into a brightening area at the left, where* The Woman *has come from behind the scrim and is standing, putting on her hat, looking into a "mirror" and laughing*]

WILLY: 'Cause I get so lonely—especially when business is bad and there's nobody to talk to. I get the feeling that I'll never sell anything again, that I won't make a living for you, or a business, a business for the boys. [*He talks through* The Woman's *subsiding laughter;* The Woman *primps at the "mirror"*] There's so much I want to make for—

THE WOMAN: Me? You didn't make me, Willy. I picked you.

WILLY: [*Pleased*] You picked me?

THE WOMAN: [*Who is quite proper-looking, Willy's age*] I did. I've been sitting at that desk watching all the salesmen go by, day in, day out. But you've got such a sense of humor, and we do have such a good time together, don't we?

WILLY: Sure, sure. [*He takes her in his arms*] Why do you have to go now?

THE WOMAN: It's two o'clock . . .

WILLY: No, come on in! [*He pulls her*]

THE WOMAN: . . . my sisters'll be scandalized. When'll you be back?

WILLY: Oh, two weeks about. Will you come up again?

THE WOMAN: Sure thing. You do make me laugh. It's good for me. [*She squeezes his arm, kisses him*] And I think you're a wonderful man.

WILLY: You picked me, heh?

THE WOMAN: Sure. Because you're so sweet. And such a kidder.

WILLY: Well, I'll see you next time I'm in Boston.

THE WOMAN: I'll put you right through to the buyers.

WILLY: [*Slapping her bottom*] Right. Well, bottoms up!

THE WOMAN: [*Slaps him gently and laughs*] You just kill me, Willy. [*He suddenly grabs her and kisses her roughly*] You kill me. And thanks for the stockings. I love a lot of stockings. Well, good night.

WILLY: Good night. And keep your pores open!

THE WOMAN: Oh, Willy!

[*The Woman bursts out laughing, and* Linda's laughter blends in. *The Woman disappears into the dark. Now the area at the kitchen table brightens.* Linda *is sitting where she was at the kitchen table, but now is mending a pair of her silk stockings*]

LINDA: You are, Willy. The handsomest man. You've got no reason to feel that—

WILLY: [*Coming out of* The Woman's *dimming area and going over to* Linda] I'll make it all up to you, Linda, I'll—

LINDA: There's nothing to make up, dear. You're doing fine, better than—

WILLY: [*Noticing her mending*] What's that?

LINDA: Just mending my stockings. They're so expensive—

WILLY: [*Angrily, taking them from her*] I won't have you mending stockings in this house! Now throw them out!

[Linda *puts the stockings in her pocket*]

BERNARD: [*Entering on the run*] Where is he? If he doesn't study!

WILLY: [*Moving to the forestage, with great agitation*] You'll give him the answers!

BERNARD: I do, but I can't on a Regents! That's a state exam! They're liable to arrest me!

WILLY: Where is he? I'll whip him, I'll whip him!

LINDA: And he'd better give back that football, Willy, it's not nice.

WILLY: Biff! Where is he? Why is he taking everything?

LINDA: He's too rough with the girls, Willy. All the mothers are afraid of him!

WILLY: I'll whip him!

BERNARD: He's driving the car without a license!

[*The Woman's laugh is heard*]

WILLY: Shut up!

LINDA: All the mothers—

WILLY: Shut up!

BERNARD: [*Backing quietly away and out*] Mr. Birnbaum says he's stuck up.

WILLY: Get outa here!

BERNARD: If he doesn't buckle down he'll flunk math! [*He goes off*]

LINDA: He's right, Willy, you've gotta—

WILLY: [*Exploding at her*] There's nothing the matter with him! You want him to be a worm like Bernard? He's got spirit, personality . . .

[*As he speaks,* Linda, *almost in tears, exits into the living-room.* Willy *is alone in the kitchen, wilting and staring. The leaves are gone. It is night again, and the apartment houses look down from behind*]

WILLY: Loaded with it. Loaded! What is he stealing? He's giving it back, isn't he? Why is he stealing? What did I tell him? I never in my life told him anything but decent things.

[Happy *in pajamas has come down the stairs;* Willy *suddenly becomes aware of* Happy's *presence*]

HAPPY: Let's go now, come on.

WILLY: [*Sitting down at the kitchen table*] Huh! Why did she have to wax the floors herself? Everytime she waxes the floors she keels over. She knows that!

HAPPY: Sh! Take it easy. What brought you back tonight?

WILLY: I got an awful scare. Nearly hit a kid in Yonkers. God! Why didn't I go to Alaska with my brother Ben that time! Ben! That man was a genius, that man was success incarnate! What a mistake! He begged me to go.

HAPPY: Well, there's no use in—

WILLY: You guys! There was a man started with the clothes on his back and ended up with diamond mines!

HAPPY: Boy, someday I'd like to know how he did it.

WILLY: What's the mystery? The man knew what he wanted and went out and got it! Walked into a jungle, and comes out, the age of twenty-one, and he's rich! The world is an oyster, but you don't crack it open on a mattress!

HAPPY: Pop, I told you I'm gonna retire you for life.

WILLY: You'll retire me for life on seventy goddam dollars a week? And your women and your car and your apartment, and you'll retire me for life! Christ's sake, I couldn't get past Yonkers today! Where are you guys, where are you? The woods are burning! I can't drive a car!

[Charley *has appeared in the doorway. He is a large man, slow of speech, laconic, immovable. In all he says, despite what he says, there is pity, and now, trepidation. He has a robe over pajamas, slippers on his feet. He enters the kitchen*]

CHARLEY: Everything all right?

HAPPY: Yeah, Charley, everything's . . .

WILLY: What's the matter?

CHARLEY: I heard some noise. I thought something happened. Can't we do something about the walls? You sneeze in here, and in my house hats blow off.

HAPPY: Let's go to bed, Dad. Come on.

[Charley *signals to* Happy *to go*]

WILLY: You go ahead, I'm not tired at the moment.

HAPPY: [*To* Willy] Take it easy, huh? [*He exits*]

WILLY: What're you doin' up?

CHARLEY: [*Sitting down at the kitchen table opposite* Willy] Couldn't sleep good. I had a heartburn.

WILLY: Well, you don't know how to eat.

CHARLEY: I eat with my mouth.

WILLY: No, you're ignorant. You gotta know about vitamins and things like that.

CHARLEY: Come on, let's shoot. Tire you out a little.

WILLY: [*Hesitantly*] All right. You got cards?

CHARLEY: [*Taking a deck from his pocket*] Yeah, I got them. Someplace. What is it with those vitamins?

WILLY: [*Dealing*] They build up your bones. Chemistry.

CHARLEY: Yeah, but there's no bones in a heartburn.

WILLY: What are you talkin' about? Do you know the first thing about it?

CHARLEY: Don't get insulted.

WILLY: Don't talk about something you don't know anything about.

[*They are playing. Pause*]

CHARLEY: What're you doin' home?

WILLY: A little trouble with the car.

CHARLEY: Oh. [*Pause*] I'd like to take a trip to California.

WILLY: Don't say.

CHARLEY: You want a job?

WILLY: I got a job, I told you that. [*After a slight pause*] What the hell are you offering me a job for?

CHARLEY: Don't get insulted.

WILLY: Don't insult me.

CHARLEY: I don't see no sense in it. You don't have to go on this way.

WILLY: I got a good job. [*Slight pause*] What do you keep comin' in here for?

CHARLEY: You want me to go?

WILLY: [*After a pause, withering*] I can't understand it. He's going back to Texas again. What the hell is that?

CHARLEY: Let him go.

WILLY: I got nothin' to give him, Charley, I'm clean, I'm clean.

CHARLEY: He won't starve. None a them starve. Forget about him.

WILLY: Then what have I got to remember?

CHARLEY: You take it too hard. To hell with it. When a deposit bottle is broken you don't get your nickel back.

WILLY: That's easy enough for you to say.

CHARLEY: That ain't easy for me to say.

WILLY: Did you see the ceiling I put up in the living-room?

CHARLEY: Yeah, that's a piece of work. To put up a ceiling is a mystery to me. How do you do it?

WILLY: What's the difference?

CHARLEY: Well, talk about it.

WILLY: You gonna put up a ceiling?

CHARLEY: How could I put up a ceiling?

WILLY: Then what the hell are you bothering me for?

CHARLEY: You're insulted again.

WILLY: A man who can't handle tools is not a man. You're disgusting.

CHARLEY: Don't call me disgusting, Willy.

[Uncle Ben, *carrying a valise and an umbrella, enters the forestage from around the right corner of the house. He is a stolid man, in his sixties, with a mustache and an authoritative air. He is utterly certain of his destiny, and there is an aura of far places about him. He enters exactly as Willy speaks]*

WILLY: I'm getting awfully tired, Ben.

[*Ben's music is heard.* Ben *looks around at everything*]

CHARLEY: Good, keep playing; you'll sleep better. Did you call me Ben?

[Ben *looks at his watch*]

WILLY: That's funny. For a second there you reminded me of my brother Ben.

BEN: I only have a few minutes. [*He strolls, inspecting the place.* Willy *and* Charley *continue playing*]

CHARLEY: You never heard from him again, heh? Since that time?

WILLY: Didn't Linda tell you? Couple of weeks ago we got a letter from his wife in Africa. He died.

CHARLEY: That so.

BEN: [*Chuckling*] So this is Brooklyn, eh?

CHARLEY: Maybe you're in for some of his money.

WILLY: Naa, he had seven sons. There's just one opportunity I had with that man . . .

BEN: I must make a train, William. There are several properties I'm looking at in Alaska.

WILLY: Sure, sure! If I'd gone with him to Alaska that time, everything would've been totally different.

CHARLEY: Go on, you'd froze to death up there.

WILLY: What're you talking about?

BEN: Opportunity is tremendous in Alaska, William. Surprised you're not up there.

WILLY: Sure, tremendous.

CHARLEY: Heh?

WILLY: There was the only man I ever met who knew the answers.

CHARLEY: Who?

BEN: How are you all?

WILLY: [*Taking a pot, smiling*] Fine, fine.

CHARLEY: Pretty sharp tonight.

BEN: Is Mother living with you?

WILLY: No, she died a long time ago.

CHARLEY: Who?

BEN: That's too bad. Fine specimen of a lady, Mother.

WILLY: [*To* Charley] Heh?

BEN: I'd hoped to see the old girl.

CHARLEY: Who died?

BEN: Heard anything from Father, have you?

WILLY: [*Unnerved*] What do you mean, who died?

CHARLEY: [*Taking a pot*] What're you talkin' about?

BEN: [*Looking at his watch*] William, it's half-past eight!

WILLY: [*As though to dispel his confusion he angrily stops* Charley's *hand*] That's my build!

CHARLEY: I put the ace—

WILLY: If you don't know how to play the game I'm not gonna throw my money away on you!

CHARLEY: [*Rising*] It was my ace, for God's sake!

WILLY: I'm through, I'm through!

BEN: When did Mother die?

WILLY: Long ago. Since the beginning you never knew how to play cards.

CHARLEY: [*Picks up the cards and goes to the door*] All right! Next time I'll bring a deck with five aces.

WILLY: I don't play that kind of game!

CHARLEY: [*Turning to him*] You ought to be ashamed of yourself!

WILLY: Yeah?

CHARLEY: Yeah! [*He goes out*]

WILLY: [*Slamming the door after him*] Ignoramus!

BEN: [*As Willy comes toward him through the wall-line of the kitchen*] So you're William.

WILLY: [*Shaking* Ben's *hand*] Ben! I've been waiting for you so long! What's the answer? How did you do it?

BEN: Oh, there's a story in that.

[Linda *enters the forestage, as of old, carrying the wash basket*]

LINDA: Is this Ben?

BEN: [*Gallantly*] How do you do, my dear.

LINDA: Where've you been all these years? Willy's always wondered why you—

WILLY: [*Pulling* Ben *away from her impatiently*] Where is Dad? Didn't you follow him? How did you get started?

BEN: Well, I don't know how much you remember.

WILLY: Well, I was just a baby, of course, only three or four years old—

BEN: Three years and eleven months.

WILLY: What a memory, Ben!

BEN: I have many enterprises, William, and I have never kept books.

WILLY: I remember I was sitting under the wagon in—was it Nebraska?

BEN: It was South Dakota, and I gave you a bunch of wild flowers.

WILLY: I remember you walking away down some open road.

BEN: [*Laughing*] I was going to find Father in Alaska.

WILLY: Where is he?

BEN: At that age I had a very faulty view of geography, William. I discovered after a few days that I was heading due south, so instead of Alaska, I ended up in Africa.

LINDA: Africa!

WILLY: The Gold Coast!

BEN: Principally diamond mines.

LINDA: Diamond mines!

BEN: Yes, my dear. But I've only a few minutes—

WILLY: No! Boys! Boys! [*Young* Biff *and* Happy *appear*] Listen to this. This is your Uncle Ben, a great man! Tell my boys, Ben!

BEN: Why, boys, when I was seventeen I walked into the jungle, and when I was twenty-one I walked out. [*He laughs*] And by God I was rich.

WILLY: [*To the boys*] You see what I been talking about? The greatest things can happen!

BEN: [*Glancing at his watch*] I have an appointment in Ketchikan Tuesday week.

WILLY: No, Ben! Please tell about Dad. I want my boys to hear. I want them to know the kind of stock they spring from. All I remember is a man with a big beard, and I was in Mamma's lap, sitting around a fire, and some kind of high music.

BEN: His flute. He played the flute.

WILLY: Sure, the flute, that's right!

[*New music is heard, a high, rollicking tune*]

BEN: Father was a very great and a very wild-hearted man. We would start in Boston, and he'd toss the whole family into the wagon, and then he'd drive the team right across the country; through Ohio, and Indiana, Michigan, Illinois, and all the Western states. And we'd stop in the towns and sell the flutes that he'd made on the way. Great inventor, Father. With one gadget he made more in a week than a man like you could make in a lifetime.

WILLY: That's just the way I'm bringing them up, Ben—rugged, well liked, all-around.

BEN: Yeah? [*To Biff*] Hit that, boy—hard as you can. [*He pounds his stomach*]

BIFF: Oh, no, sir!

BEN: [*Taking boxing stance*] Come on, get to me! [*He laughs*]

WILLY: Go to it, Biff! Go ahead, show him!

BIFF: Okay! [*He cocks his fists and starts in*]

LINDA: [*To Willy*] Why must he fight, dear?

BEN: [*Sparring with Biff*] Good boy! Good boy!

WILLY: How's that, Ben, heh?

HAPPY: Give him the left, Biff!

LINDA: Why are you fighting?

BEN: Good boy! [*Suddenly comes in, trips Biff, and stands over him, the point of his umbrella poised over Biff's eye*]

LINDA: Look out, Biff!

BIFF: Gee!

BEN: [*Patting Biff's knee*] Never fight fair with a stranger, boy. You'll never get out of the jungle that way. [*Taking Linda's hand and bowing*] It was an honor and a pleasure to meet you, Linda.

LINDA: [*Withdrawing her hand coldly, frightened*] Have a nice—trip.

BEN: [*To Willy*] And good luck with your—what do you do?

WILLY: Selling.

BEN: Yes. Well . . . [*He raises his hand in farewell to all*]

WILLY: No, Ben, I don't want you to think . . . [*He takes Ben's arm to show him*] It's Brooklyn, I know, but we hunt too.

BEN: Really, now.

WILLY: Oh, sure, there's snakes and rabbits and —that's why I moved out here. Why, Biff can fell any one of these trees in no time! Boys! Go right over to where they're building the apartment house and get some sand. We're gonna rebuild the entire front stoop right now! Watch this, Ben!

BIFF: Yes, sir! On the double, Hap!

HAPPY: [*As he and Biff run off*] I lost weight, Pop, you notice?

[*Charley enters in knickers, even before the boys are gone*]

CHARLEY: Listen, if they steal any more from that building the watchman'll put the cops on them!

LINDA: [*To Willy*] Don't let Biff . . .

[*Ben laughs lustily*]

WILLY: You shoulda seen the lumber they brought home last week. At least a dozen six-by-tens worth all kinds a money.

CHARLEY: Listen, if that watchman—

WILLY: I gave them hell, understand. But I got a couple of fearless characters there.

CHARLEY: Willy, the jails are full of fearless characters.

BEN: [*Clapping Willy on the back, with a laugh at Charley*] And the stock exchange, friend!

WILLY: [*Joining in Ben's laughter*] Where are the rest of your pants?

CHARLEY: My wife bought them.

WILLY: Now all you need is a golf club and you can go upstairs and go to sleep. [*To Ben*] Great athlete! Between him and his son Bernard they can't hammer a nail!

BERNARD: [*Rushing in*] The watchman's chasing Biff!

WILLY: [*Angrily*] Shut up! He's not stealing anything!

LINDA: [*Alarmed, hurrying off left*] Where is he? Biff, dear! [*She exits.*]

WILLY: [*Moving toward the left, away from Ben*] There's nothing wrong. What's the matter with you?

BEN: Nervy boy. Good!

WILLY: [*Laughing*] Oh, nerves of iron, that Biff!

CHARLEY: Don't know what it is. My New England man comes back and he's bleedin', they murdered him up there.

WILLY: It's contacts, Charley, I got important contacts!

CHARLEY: [*Sarcastically*] Glad to hear it, Willy. Come in later, we'll shoot a little casino. I'll take some of your Portland money. [*He laughs at Willy and exits*]

WILLY: [*Turning to Ben*] Business is bad, it's murderous. But not for me, of course.

BEN: I'll stop by on my way back to Africa.

WILLY: [*Longingly*] Can't you stay a few days? You're just what I need, Ben, because I—I have a fine position here, but I—well, Dad left when I was such a baby and I never had a chance to talk to him and I still feel—kind of temporay about myself.

BEN: I'll be late for my train.

[*They are at opposite ends of the stage*]

WILLY: Ben—my boys—can't we talk? They'd go into the jaws of hell for me, see, but I—

BEN: William, you're being first-rate with your boys. Outstanding, manly chaps!

WILLY: [*Hanging on to his words*] Oh, Ben, that's good to hear! Because sometimes I'm afraid that I'm not teaching them the right kind of— Ben, how should I teach them?

BEN: [*Giving great weight to each word, and with a certain vicious audacity*] William, when I walked into the jungle, I was seventeen. When I walked out I was twenty-one. And, by God, I was rich! [*He goes off into darkness around the right corner of the house*]

WILLY: . . . was rich! That's just the spirit I want to imbue them with! To walk into a jungle! I was right! I was right! I was right!

[Ben *is gone, but* Willy *is still speaking to him as* Linda, *in nightgown and robe, enters the kitchen, glances around for* Willy, *then goes to the door of the house, looks out and sees him. Comes down to his left. He looks at her*]

LINDA: Willy, dear? Willy?

WILLY: I was right!

LINDA: Did you have some cheese? [*He can't answer*] It's very late, darling. Come to bed, heh?

WILLY: [*Looking straight up*] Gotta break your neck to see a star in this yard.

LINDA: You coming in?

WILLY: Whatever happened to that diamond watch fob? Remember? When Ben came from Africa that time? Didn't he give me a watch fob with a diamond in it?

LINDA: You pawned it, dear. Twelve, thirteen years ago. For Biff's radio correspondence course.

WILLY: Gee, that was a beautiful thing. I'll take a walk.

LINDA: But you're in your slippers.

WILLY: [*Starting to go around the house at the left*] I was right! I was! [*Half to* Linda, *as he goes, shaking his head*] What a man! There was a man worth talking to. I was right!

LINDA: [*Calling after* Willy] But in your slippers, Willy!

[Willy *is almost gone when* Biff, *in his pajamas, comes down the stairs and enters the kitchen*]

BIFF: What is he doing out there?

LINDA: Sh!

BIFF: God Almighty, Mom, how long has he been doing this?

LINDA: Don't, he'll hear you.

BIFF: What the hell is the matter with him?

LINDA: It'll pass by morning.

BIFF: Shouldn't we do anything?

LINDA: Oh, my dear, you should do a lot of things, but there's nothing to do, so go to sleep.

[Happy *comes down the stair and sits on the steps*]

HAPPY: I never heard him so loud, Mom.

LINDA: Well, come around more often; you'll hear him. [*She sits down at the table and mends the lining of* Willy's *jacket*]

BIFF: Why didn't you ever write me about this, Mom?

LINDA: How would I write to you? For over three months you had no address.

BIFF: I was on the move. But you know I thought of you all the time. You know that, don't you, pal?

LINDA: I know, dear, I know. But he likes to have a letter. Just to know that there's still a possibility for better things.

BIFF: He's not like this all the time, is he?

LINDA: It's when you come home he's always the worst.

BIFF: When I come home?

LINDA: When you write you're coming, he's all smiles, and talks about the future, and—he's just wonderful. And then the closer you seem to come, the more shaky he gets, and then, by the time you get here, he's arguing, and he seems angry at you. I think it's just that maybe he can't bring himself to —to open up to you. Why are you so hateful to each other? Why is that?

BIFF: [*Evasively*] I'm not hateful, Mom.

LINDA: But you no sooner come in the door than you're fighting!

BIFF: I don't know why. I mean to change. I'm tryin', Mom, you understand?

LINDA: Are you home to stay now?

BIFF: I don't know. I want to look around, see what's doin'.

LINDA: Biff, you can't look around all your life, can you?

BIFF: I just can't take hold, Mom. I can't take hold of some kind of a life.

LINDA: Biff, a man is not a bird, to come and go with the springtime.

BIFF: Your hair . . . [*He touches her hair*] Your hair got so gray.

LINDA: Oh, it's been gray since you were in high school. I just stopped dyeing it, that's all.

BIFF: Dye it again, will ya? I don't want my pal looking old. [*He smiles*]

LINDA: You're such a boy! You think you can go away for a year and . . . You've got to get it into your head now that one day you'll knock on this door and there'll be strange people here—

BIFF: What are you talking about? You're not even sixty, Mom.

LINDA: But what about your father?

BIFF: [*Lamely*] Well, I meant him too.

HAPPY: He admires Pop.

LINDA: Biff, dear, if you don't have any feeling for him, then you can't have any feeling for me.

BIFF: Sure I can, Mom.

LINDA: No. You can't just come to see me, because I love him. [*With a threat, but only a threat, of tears*] He's the dearest man in the world to me, and I won't have anyone making him feel unwanted and low and blue. You've got to make up your mind now, darling, there's no leeway any more. Either he's your father and you pay him that respect, or else you're not to come here. I know he's not easy to get along with—nobody knows that better than me—but . . .

WILLY: [*From the left, with a laugh*] Hey, hey, Biffo!

BIFF: [*Starting to go out after* Willy] What the hell is the matter with him? [Happy *stops him*]

LINDA: Don't—don't go near him!

BIFF: Stop making excuses for him! He always, always wiped the floor with you. Never had an ounce of respect for you.

HAPPY: He's always had respect for—

BIFF: What the hell do you know about it?

HAPPY: [*Surlily*] Just don't call him crazy!

BIFF: He's got no character— Charley wouldn't do this. Not in his own house—spewing out that vomit from his mind.

HAPPY: Charley never had to cope with what he's got to.

BIFF: People are worse off than Willy Loman. Believe me, I've seen them!

LINDA: Then make Charley your father, Biff. You can't do that, can you? I don't say he's a great man. Willy Loman never made a lot of money. His name was never in the paper. He's not the finest character that ever lived. But he's a human being, and a terrible thing is happening to him. So attention must be paid. He's not to be allowed to fall into his grave like an old dog. Attention, attention must be finally paid to such a person. You called him crazy—

BIFF: I didn't mean—

LINDA: No, a lot of people think he's lost his—balance. But you don't have to be very smart to know what his trouble is. The man is exhausted.

HAPPY: Sure!

LINDA: A small man can be just as exhausted as a great man. He works for a company thirty-six years this March, opens up unheard-of territories to their trademark, and now in his old age they take his salary away.

HAPPY: [*Indignantly*] I didn't know that, Mom.

LINDA: You never asked, my dear! Now that you get your spending money someplace else you don't trouble your mind with him.

HAPPY: But I gave you money last—

LINDA: Christmas time, fifty dollars! To fix the hot water it cost ninety-seven fifty! For five weeks he's been on straight commission, like a beginner, an unknown!

BIFF: Those ungrateful bastards!

LINDA: Are they any worse than his sons? When he brought them business, when he was young, they were glad to see him. But now his old friends, the old buyers that loved him so and always found some order to hand him in a pinch—they're all dead, retired. He used to be able to make six, seven calls a day in Boston. Now he takes his valises out of the car and puts them back and takes them out again and he's exhausted. Instead of walking he talks now. He drives seven hundred miles, and when he gets there no one knows him any more, no one welcomes him. And what goes through a man's mind, driving seven hundred miles home without having earned a cent? Why shouldn't he talk to himself? Why? When he has to go to Charley and borrow fifty dollars a week and pretend to me that it's his pay? How long can that go on? How long? You see what I'm sitting here and waiting for? And you tell me he has no character? The man who never worked a day but for your benefit? When does he get the medal for that? Is this his reward—to turn around at the age of sixty-three and find his sons, who he loved better than his life, one a philandering bum—

HAPPY: Mom!

LINDA: That's all you are, my baby! [*To* Biff] And you! What happened to the love you had for him? You were such pals! How you used to talk to him on the phone every night! How lonely he was till he could come home to you!

BIFF: All right, Mom. I'll live here in my room, and I'll get a job. I'll keep away from him, that's all.

LINDA: No, Biff. You can't stay here and fight all the time.

BIFF: He threw me out of this house, remember that.

LINDA: Why did he do that? I never knew why.

BIFF: Because I know he's a fake and he doesn't like anybody around who knows!

LINDA: Why a fake? In what way? What do you mean?

BIFF: Just don't lay it all at my feet. It's between me and him—that's all I have to say. I'll chip in from now on. He'll settle for half my pay check. He'll be all right. I'm going to bed. [*He starts for the stairs*]

LINDA: He won't be all right.

BIFF: [*Turning on the stairs, furiously*] I hate this city and I'll stay here. Now what do you want?

LINDA: He's dying, Biff.

[Happy *turns quickly to her, shocked*]

BIFF: [*After a pause*] Why is he dying?

LINDA: He's been trying to kill himself.

BIFF: [*With great horror*] How?

LINDA: I live from day to day.

BIFF: What're you talking about?

LINDA: Remember I wrote you that he smashed up the car again? In February?

BIFF: Well?

LINDA: The insurance inspector came. He said that they have evidence. That all these accidents in the last year—weren't—weren't—accidents.

HAPPY: How can they tell that? That's a lie.

LINDA: It seems there's a woman . . . [*She takes a breath as*

⎧BIFF: [*Sharply but contained*] What woman?

⎩LINDA: [*Simultaneously*] . . . and this woman . . .

LINDA: What?

BIFF: Nothing. Go ahead.

LINDA: What did you say?

BIFF: Nothing. I just said what woman?

HAPPY: What about her?

LINDA: Well, it seems she was walking down the road and saw his car. She says that he wasn't driving fast at all, and that he didn't skid. She says he came to that little bridge, and then deliberately smashed into the railing, and it was only the shallowness of the water that saved him.

BIFF: Oh, no, he probably just fell asleep again.

LINDA: I don't think he fell asleep.

BIFF: Why not?

LINDA: Last month . . . [*With great difficulty*] Oh, boys, it's so hard to say a thing like this! He's just a big stupid man to you, but I tell you there's more good in him than in many other people. [*She chokes, wipes her eyes*] I was looking for a fuse. The lights blew out, and I went down the cellar. And behind the fuse box—it happened to fall out—was a length of rubber pipe—just short.

HAPPY: No kidding?

LINDA: There's a little attachment on the end of it. I knew right away. And sure enough, on the bottom of the water heater there's a new little nipple on the gas pipe.

HAPPY: [*Angrily*] That—jerk.

BIFF: Did you have it taken off?

LINDA: I'm—I'm ashamed to. How can I mention it to him? Every day I go down and take away that little rubber pipe. But, when he comes home, I put it back where it was. How can I insult him that way? I don't know what to do. I live from day to day, boys. I tell you, I know every thought in his mind. It sounds so old-fashioned and silly, but I tell you he put his whole life into you and you've turned your backs on him. [*She is bent over in the chair, weeping, her face in her hands*] Biff, I swear to God! Biff, his life is in your hands!

HAPPY: [*To Biff*] How do you like that damned fool!

BIFF: [*Kissing her*] All right, pal, all right. It's all settled now. I've been remiss. I know that, Mom. But now I'll stay, and I swear to you, I'll apply myself. [*Kneeling in front of her, in a fever of self-reproach*] It's just—you see, Mom, I don't fit in business. Not that I won't try. I'll try, and I'll make good.

HAPPY: Sure you will. The trouble with you in business was you never tried to please people.

BIFF: I know, I—

HAPPY: Like when you worked for Harrison's. Bob Harrison said you were tops, and then you go and do some damn fool thing like whistling whole songs in the elevator like a comedian.

BIFF: [*Against* Happy] So what? I like to whistle sometimes.

HAPPY: You don't raise a guy to a responsible job who whistles in the elevator!

LINDA: Well, don't argue about it now.

HAPPY: Like when you'd go off and swim in the middle of the day instead of taking the line around.

BIFF: [*His resentment rising*] Well, don't you run

off? You take off sometimes, don't you? On a nice summer day?

HAPPY: Yeah, but I cover myself!

LINDA: Boys!

HAPPY: If I'm going to take a fade the boss can call any number where I'm supposed to be and they'll swear to him that I just left. I'll tell you something that I hate to say, Biff, but in the business world some of them think you're crazy.

BIFF: [*Angered*] Screw the business world!

HAPPY: All right, screw it! Great, but cover yourself!

LINDA: Hap, Hap!

BIFF: I don't care what they think! They've laughed at Dad for years, and you know why? Because we don't belong in this nuthouse of a city! We should be mixing cement on some open plain, or—or carpenters. A carpenter is allowed to whistle!

[Willy *walks in from the entrance of the house, at left*]

WILLY: Even your grandfather was better than a carpenter. [*Pause. They watch him*] You never grew up. Bernard does not whistle in the elevator, I assure you.

BIFF: [*As though to laugh* Willy *out of it*] Yeah, but you do, Pop.

WILLY: I never in my life whistled in an elevator! And who in the business world thinks I'm crazy?

BIFF: I didn't mean it like that, Pop. Now don't make a whole thing out of it, will ya?

WILLY: Go back to the West! Be a carpenter, a cowboy, enjoy yourself!

LINDA: Willy, he was just saying—

WILLY: I heard what he said!

HAPPY: [*Trying to quiet* Willy] Hey, Pop, come on now . . .

WILLY: [*Continuing over* Happy's *line*] They laugh at me, heh? Go to Filene's, go to the Hub, go to Slattery's, Boston. Call out the name Willy Loman and see what happens! Big shot!

BIFF: All right, Pop.

WILLY: Big!

BIFF: All right!

WILLY: Why do you always insult me?

BIFF: I didn't say a word. [*To* Linda] Did I say a word?

LINDA: He didn't say anything, Willy.

WILLY: [*Going to the doorway of the living-room*] All right, good night, good night.

LINDA: Willy, dear, he just decided . . .

WILLY: [*To* Biff] If you get tired hanging around tomorrow, paint the ceiling I put up in the living-room.

BIFF: I'm leaving early tomorrow.

HAPPY: He's going to see Bill Oliver, Pop.

WILLY: [*Interestedly*] Oliver? For what?

BIFF: [*With reserve, but trying, trying*] He always said he'd stake me. I'd like to go into business, so maybe I can take him up on it.

LINDA: Isn't that wonderful?

WILLY: Don't interrupt. What's wonderful about it? There's fifty men in the City of New York who'd stake him. [*To* Biff] Sporting goods?

BIFF: I guess so. I know something about it and—

WILLY: He knows something about it! You know sporting goods better than Spalding, for God's sake! How much is he giving you?

BIFF: I don't know, I didn't even see him yet, but—

WILLY: Then what're you talkin' about?

BIFF: [*Getting angry*] Well, all I said was I'm gonna see him, that's all!

WILLY: [*Turning away*] Ah, you're counting your chickens again.

BIFF: [*Starting left for the stairs*] Oh, Jesus, I'm going to sleep!

WILLY: [*Calling after him*] Don't curse in this house!

BIFF: [*Turning*] Since when did you get so clean?

HAPPY: [*Trying to stop them*] Wait a . . .

WILLY: Don't use that language to me! I won't have it!

HAPPY: [*Grabbing* Biff, *shouts*] Wait a minute! I got an idea. I got a feasible idea. Come here, Biff, let's talk this over now, let's talk some sense here. When I was down in Florida last time, I thought of a great idea to sell sporting goods. It just came back to me. You and I, Biff—we have a line, the Loman Line. We train a couple of weeks, and put on a couple of exhibitions, see?

WILLY: That's an idea!

HAPPY: Wait! We form two basketball teams, see? Two water-polo teams. We play each other. It's a million dollars' worth of publicity. Two brothers, see? The Loman Brothers. Displays in the Royal Palms—all the hotels. And banners over the ring and the basketball court: "Loman Brothers." Baby, we could sell sporting goods!

WILLY: That is a one-million-dollar idea!

LINDA: Marvelous!

BIFF: I'm in great shape as far as that's concerned.

HAPPY: And the beauty of it is, Biff, it wouldn't be like a business. We'd be out playin' ball again . . .

BIFF: [*Filled with enthusiasm*] Yeah, that's . . .

WILLY: Million-dollar . . .

HAPPY: And you wouldn't get fed up with it, Biff. It'd be the family again. There'd be the old honor, and comradeship, and if you wanted to go off for a swim or somethin'—well, you'd do it! Without some smart cooky gettin' up ahead of you!

WILLY: Lick the world! You guys together could absolutely lick the civilized world.

BIFF: I'll see Oliver tomorrow. Hap, if we could work that out . . .

LINDA: Maybe things are beginning to—

WILLY: [*Wildly enthusiastic, to* Linda] Stop interrupting! [*To* Biff:] But don't wear sport jacket and slacks when you see Oliver.

BIFF: No, I'll—

WILLY: A business suit, and talk as little as possible, and don't crack any jokes.

BIFF: He did like me. Always liked me.

LINDA: He loved you!

WILLY: [*To* Linda] Will you stop! [*To* Biff] Walk in very serious. You are not applying for a boy's job. Money is to pass. Be quiet, fine, and serious. Everybody likes a kidder, but nobody lends him money.

HAPPY: I'll try to get some myself, Biff. I'm sure I can.

WILLY: I see great things for you kids, I think your troubles are over. But remember, start big and you'll end big. Ask for fifteen. How much you gonna ask for?

BIFF: Gee, I don't know—

WILLY: And don't say "Gee." "Gee" is a boy's word. A man walking in for fifteen thousand dollars does not say "Gee!"

BIFF: Ten, I think, would be top though.

WILLY: Don't be so modest. You always started too low. Walk in with a big laugh. Don't look worried. Start off with a couple of your good stories to lighten things up. It's not what you say, it's how you say it—because personality always wins the day.

LINDA: Oliver always thought the highest of him—

WILLY: Will you let me talk?

BIFF: Don't yell at her, Pop, will ya?

WILLY: [*Angrily*] I was talking, wasn't I?

BIFF: I don't like you yelling at her all the time, and I'm tellin' you, that's all.

WILLY: What're you, takin' over this house?

LINDA: Willy—

WILLY: [*Turning on her*] Don't take his side all the time, god-dammit!

BIFF: [*Furiously*] Stop yelling at her!

WILLY: [*Suddenly pulling on his cheek, beaten down, guilt ridden*] Give my best to Bill Oliver—he may remember me. [*He exits through the living-room doorway*]

LINDA: [*Her voice subdued*] What'd you have to start that for? [Biff *turns away*] You see how sweet he was as soon as you talked hopefully? [*She goes over to* Biff] Come up and say good night to him. Don't let him go to bed that way.

HAPPY: Come on, Biff, let's buck him up.

LINDA: Please, dear. Just say good night. It takes so little to make him happy. Come. [*She goes through the living-room doorway, calling upstairs from within the living-room*] Your pajamas are hanging in the bathroom, Willy!

HAPPY: [*Looking toward where Linda went out*] What a woman! They broke the mold when they made her. You know that, Biff?

BIFF: He's off salary. My God, working on commission!

HAPPY: Well, let's face it: he's no hot-shot selling man. Except that sometimes, you have to admit, he's a sweet personality.

BIFF: [*Deciding*] Lend me ten bucks, will ya? I want to buy some new ties.

HAPPY: I'll take you to a place I know. Beautiful stuff. Wear one of my striped shirts tomorrow.

BIFF: She got gray. Mom got awful old. Gee, I'm gonna go in to Oliver tomorrow and knock him for a——

HAPPY: Come on up. Tell that to Dad. Let's give him a whirl. Come on.

BIFF: [*Steamed up*] You know, with ten thousand bucks, boy!

HAPPY: [*As they go into the living-room*] That's the talk, Biff, that's the first time I've heard the old confidence out of you! [*From within the living-room, fading off*] You're gonna live with me, kid, and any babe you want just say the word . . . [*The last lines are hardly heard. They are mounting the stairs to their parents' bedroom*]

LINDA: [*Entering her bedroom and addressing Willy, who is in the bathroom. She is straightening the bed for him*] Can you do anything about the shower? It drips.

WILLY: [*From the bathroom*] All of a sudden everything falls to pieces! Goddam plumbing, oughta be sued, those people. I hardly finished putting it in and the thing . . . [*His words rumble off*]

LINDA: I'm just wondering if Oliver will remember him. You think he might?

WILLY: [*Coming out of the bathroom in his pajamas*] Remember him? What's the matter with you, you crazy? If he'd've stayed with Oliver he'd be on top by now! Wait'll Oliver gets a look at him. You don't know the average caliber any more. The average young man today—[*He is getting into bed*]—is got a caliber of zero. Greatest thing in the world for him was to bum around.

[*Biff and Happy enter the bedroom. Slight pause*]

WILLY: [*Stops short, looking at Biff*] Glad to hear it, boy.

HAPPY: We wanted to say good night to you, sport.

WILLY: [*To Biff*] Yeah. Knock him dead, boy. What'd you want to tell me?

BIFF: Just take it easy, Pop. Good night. [*He turns to go*].

WILLY: [*Unable to resist*] And if anything falls off the desk while you're talking to him—like a package or something—don't you pick it up. They have office boys for that.

LINDA: I'll make a big breakfast——

WILLY: Will you let me finish? [*To Biff*] Tell him you were in the business in the West. Not farm work.

BIFF: All right, Dad.

LINDA: I think everything—

WILLY: [*Going right through her speech*] And don't undersell yourself. No less than fifteen thousand dollars.

BIFF: [*Unable to bear him*] Okay. Good night, Mom. [*He starts moving*]

WILLY: Because you got a greatness in you, Biff, remember that. You got all kinds a greatness. . . . [*He lies back, exhausted. Biff walks out*]

LINDA: [*Calling after Biff*] Sleep well, darling!

HAPPY: I'm gonna get married, Mom. I wanted to tell you.

LINDA: Go to sleep, dear.

HAPPY: [*Going*] I just wanted to tell you.

WILLY: Keep up the good work. [*Happy exits*] God . . . remember that Ebbets Field game? The championship of the city?

LINDA: Just rest. Should I sing to you?

WILLY: Yeah. Sing to me. [*Linda hums a soft lullaby*] When that team came out—he was the tallest, remember?

LINDA: Oh, yes. And in gold.

[*Biff enters the darkened kitchen, takes a cigarette, and leaves the house. He comes downstage into a golden pool of light. He smokes, staring at the night*]

WILLY: Like a young god. Hercules—something like that. And the sun, the sun all around him. Remember how he waved to me? Right up from the field, with the representatives of three colleges standing by? And the buyers I brought, and the cheers when he came out—Loman, Loman, Loman! God Almighty, he'll be great yet. A star like that, magnificent, can never really fade away!

[*The light on Willy is fading. The gas heater begins to glow through the kitchen wall, near the stairs, a blue flame beneath red coils*]

LINDA: [*Timidly*] Willy dear, what has he got against you?

WILLY: I'm so tired. Don't talk any more.

[*Biff slowly returns to the kitchen. He stops, stares toward the heater*]

LINDA: Will you ask Howard to let you work in New York?

WILLY: First thing in the morning. Everything'll be all right.

[*Biff reaches behind the heater and draws out a length of rubber tubing. He is horrified and turns his head toward Willy's room, still dimly lit, from which the strains of Linda's desperate but monotonous humming rise*]

WILLY: [*Staring through the window into the moonlight*] Gee, look at the moon moving between the buildings!

[*Biff wraps the tubing around his hand and quickly goes up the stairs*]

CURTAIN

ACT II.

Music is heard, gay and bright. The curtain rises as the music fades away. Willy, in shirt sleeves, is sitting at the kitchen table, sipping coffee, his hat in his lap. Linda is filling his cup when she can.

WILLY: Wonderful coffee. Meal in itself.

LINDA: Can I make you some eggs?

WILLY: No. Take a breath.

LINDA: You look so rested, dear.

WILLY: I slept like a dead one. First time in months. Imagine, sleeping till ten on a Tuesday morning. Boys left nice and early, heh?

LINDA: They were out of here by eight o'clock.

WILLY: Good work!

LINDA: It was so thrilling to see them leaving together. I can't get over the shaving lotion in this house!

WILLY: [Smiling] Mmm—

LINDA: Biff was very changed this morning. His whole attitude seemed to be hopeful. He couldn't wait to get downtown to see Oliver.

WILLY: He's heading for a change. There's no question, there simply are certain men that take longer to get—solidified. How did he dress?

LINDA: His blue suit. He's so handsome in that suit. He could be a—anything in that suit!

[Willy gets up from the table. Linda holds his jacket for him]

WILLY: There's no question, no question at all. Gee, on the way home tonight I'd like to buy some seeds.

LINDA: [Laughing] That'd be wonderful. But not enough sun gets back there. Nothing'll grow any more.

WILLY: You wait, kid, before it's all over we're gonna get a little place out in the country, and I'll raise some vegetables, a couple of chickens . . .

LINDA: You'll do it yet, dear.

[Willy walks out of his jacket. Linda follows him]

WILLY: And they'll get married, and come for a weekend. I'd build a little guest house. 'Cause I got so many fine tools, all I'd need would be a little lumber and some peace of mind.

LINDA: [Joyfully] I sewed the lining . . .

WILLY: I could build two guest houses, so they'd both come. Did he decide how much he's going to ask Oliver for?

LINDA: [Getting him into the jacket] He didn't mention it, but I imagine ten or fifteen thousand. You going to talk to Howard today?

WILLY: Yeah. I'll put it to him straight and simple. He'll just have to take me off the road.

LINDA: And Willy, don't forget to ask for a little advance, because we've got the insurance premium. It's the grace period now.

WILLY: That's a hundred . . . ?

LINDA: A hundred and eight, sixty-eight. Because we're a little short again.

WILLY: Why are we short?

LINDA: Well, you had the motor job on the car . . .

WILLY: That goddam Studebaker!

LINDA: And you got one more payment on the refrigerator . . .

WILLY: But it just broke again!

LINDA: Well, it's old, dear.

WILLY: I told you we should've bought a well-advertised machine. Charley bought a General Electric and it's twenty years old and it's still good, that son-of-a-bitch.

LINDA: But, Willy—

WILLY: Whoever heard of a Hastings refrigerator? Once in my life I would like to own something outright before it's broken! I'm always in a race with the junkyard! I just finished paying for the car and it's on its last legs. The refrigerator consumes belts like a goddam maniac. They time those things. They time them so when you finally paid for them, they're used up.

LINDA: [Buttoning up his jacket as he unbuttons it] All told, about two hundred dollars would carry us, dear. But that includes the last payment on the mortgage. After this payment, Willy, the house belongs to us.

WILLY: It's twenty-five years!

LINDA: Biff was nine years old when we bought it.

WILLY: Well, that's a great thing. To weather a twenty-five year mortgage is—

LINDA: It's an accomplishment.

WILLY: All the cement, the lumber, the reconstruction I put in this house! There ain't a crack to be found in it any more.

LINDA: Well, it served its purpose.

WILLY: What purpose? Some stranger'll come along, move in, and that's that. If only Biff would take this house, and raise a family . . . [He starts to go] Good-by, I'm late.

LINDA: [Suddenly remembering] Oh, I forgot! You're supposed to meet them for dinner.

WILLY: Me?

LINDA: At Frank's Chop House on Forty-eighth near Sixth Avenue.

WILLY: Is that so! How about you?

LINDA: No, just the three of you. They're gonna blow you to a big meal!

WILLY: Don't say! Who thought of that?

LINDA: Biff came to me this morning, Willy, and he said, "Tell Dad, we want to blow him to a big meal." Be there six o'clock. You and your two boys are going to have dinner.

WILLY: Gee whiz! That's really somethin'. I'm gonna knock Howard for a loop, kid. I'll get an advance, and I'll come home with a New York job. Goddammit, now I'm gonna do it!

LINDA: Oh, that's the spirit, Willy!

WILLY: I will never get behind a wheel the rest of my life!

LINDA: It's changing, Willy, I can feel it changing!

WILLY: Beyond a question. G'by, I'm late. [He starts to go again]

LINDA: [Calling after him as she runs to the kitchen table for a handkerchief] You got your glasses?

WILLY: [Feels for them, then comes back in] Yeah, yeah, got my glasses.

LINDA: [*Giving him the handkerchief*] And a handkerchief.

WILLY: Yeah, handkerchief.

LINDA: And your saccharine?

WILLY: Yeah, my saccharine.

LINDA: Be careful on the subway stairs.

[*She kisses him, and a silk stocking is seen hanging from her hand.* Willy *notices it*]

WILLY: Will you stop mending stockings? At least while I'm in the house. It gets me nervous. I can't tell you. Please.

[Linda *hides the stocking in her hand as she follows* Willy *across the forestage in front of the house*]

LINDA: Remember, Frank's Chop House.

WILLY: [*Passing the apron*] Maybe beets would grow out there.

LINDA: [*Laughing*] But you tried so many times.

WILLY: Yeah. Well, don't work hard today. [*He disappears around the right corner of the house*]

LINDA: Be careful.

[*As* Willy *vanishes,* Linda *waves to him. Suddenly the phone rings. She runs across the stage and into the kitchen and lifts it*]

LINDA: Hello? Oh, Biff! I'm so glad you called, I just . . . Yes, sure, I just told him. Yes, he'll be there for dinner at six o'clock. I didn't forget. Listen, I was just dying to tell you. You know that little rubber pipe I told you about? That he connected to the gas heater? I finally decided to go down the cellar this morning and take it away and destroy it. But it's gone! Imagine? He took it away himself, it isn't there! [*She listens*] When? Oh, then you took it. Oh—nothing, it's just that I'd hoped he'd taken it away himself. Oh, I'm not worried, darling, because this morning he left in such high spirits, it was like the old days! I'm not afraid any more. Did Mr. Oliver see you? . . . Well, you wait there then. And make a nice impression on him, darling. Just don't perspire too much before you see him. And have a nice time with Dad. He may have big news too! . . . That's right, a New York job. And be sweet to him tonight, dear. Be loving to him. Because he's only a little boat looking for a harbor. [*She is trembling with sorrow and joy*] Oh, that's wonderful, Biff, you'll save his life. Thanks, darling. Just put your arm around him when he comes into the restaurant. Give him a smile. That's the boy . . . Good-by, dear . . . You got your comb? . . . That's fine. Good-by, Biff dear.

[*In the middle of her speech,* Howard Wagner, *thirty-six, wheels on a small typewriter table on which is a wire-recording machine and proceeds to plug it in. This is on the left forestage. Light slowly fades on* Linda *as it rises on* Howard. Howard *is intent on threading the machine and only glances over his shoulder as* Willy *appears*]

WILLY: Pst! Pst!

HOWARD: Hello, Willy, come in.

WILLY: Like to have a little talk with you, Howard.

HOWARD: Sorry to keep you waiting. I'll be with you in a minute.

WILLY: What's that, Howard?

HOWARD: Didn't you ever see one of these? Wire recorder.

WILLY: Oh. Can we talk a minute?

HOWARD: Records things. Just got delivery yesterday. Been driving me crazy, the most terrific machine I ever saw in my life. I was up all night with it.

WILLY: What do you do with it?

HOWARD: I bought it for dictation, but you can do anything with it. Listen to this. I had it home last night. Listen to what I picked up. The first one is my daughter. Get this. [*He flicks the switch and "Roll out the Barrel!" is heard being whistled*] Listen to that kid whistle.

WILLY: That is lifelike, isn't it?

HOWARD: Seven years old. Get that tone.

WILLY: Ts, ts. Like to ask a little favor of you . . .

[*The whistling breaks off, and the voice of* Howard's *daughter is heard*]

HIS DAUGHTER: "Now you, Daddy."

HOWARD: She's crazy for me! [*Again the same song is whistled*] That's me! Ha! [*He winks*]

WILLY: You're very good!

[*The whistling breaks off again. The machine runs silent for a moment*]

HOWARD: Sh! Get this now, this is my son.

HIS SON: "The capital of Alabama is Montgomery; the capital of Arizona is Phoenix; the capital of Arkansas is Little Rock; the capital of California is Sacramento . . ." [*and on, and on*]

HOWARD: [*Holding up five fingers*] Five years old, Willy.

WILLY: He'll make an announcer some day!

HIS SON: [*Continuing*] "The capital . . ."

HOWARD: Get that—alphabetical order! [*The machine breaks off suddenly*] Wait a minute. The maid kicked the plug out.

WILLY: It certainly is a—

HOWARD: Sh, for God's sake.

HIS SON: "It's nine o'clock, Bulova watch time. So I have to go to sleep."

WILLY: That really is—

HOWARD: Wait a minute! The next is my wife.

[*They wait*]

HOWARD'S VOICE: "Go on, say something." [*Pause*] "Well, you gonna talk?"

HIS WIFE: "I can't think of anything."

HOWARD'S VOICE: "Well, talk—it's turning."

HIS WIFE: [*Shyly, beaten*] "Hello." [*Silence*] "Oh, Howard, I can't talk into this . . ."

HOWARD: [*Snapping the machine off*] That was my wife.

WILLY: That is a wonderful machine. Can we—

HOWARD: I tell you, Willy, I'm gonna take my camera, and my bandsaw, and all my hobbies, and out they go. This is the most fascinating relaxation I ever found.

WILLY: I think I'll get one myself.

HOWARD: Sure, they're only a hundred and a half. You can't do without it. Supposing you wanna hear Jack Benny, see? But you can't be at home at that hour. So you tell the maid to turn the radio on when Jack Benny comes on, and this automatically goes on with the radio . . .

WILLY: And when you come home you . . .

HOWARD: You can come home twelve o'clock, one o'clock, any time you like, and you get yourself a Coke and sit yourself down, throw the switch, and there's Jack Benny's program in the middle of the night!

WILLY: I'm definitely going to get one. Because lots of time I'm on the road, and I think to myself, what I must be missing on the radio!

HOWARD: Don't you have a radio in the car?

WILLY: Well, yeah, but who ever thinks of turning it on?

HOWARD: Say, aren't you supposed to be in Boston?

WILLY: That's what I want to talk to you about, Howard. You got a minute? [He draws a chair in from the wing]

HOWARD: What happened? What're you doing here?

WILLY: Well . . .

HOWARD: You didn't crack up again, did you?

WILLY: Oh, no. No . . .

HOWARD: Geez, you had me worried there for a minute. What's the trouble?

WILLY: Well, tell you the truth, Howard. I've come to the decision that I'd rather not travel any more.

HOWARD: Not travel! Well, what'll you do?

WILLY: Remember, Christmas time, when you had the party here? You said you'd try to think of some spot for me here in town.

HOWARD: With us?

WILLY: Well, sure.

HOWARD: Oh, yeah, yeah. I remember. Well, I couldn't think of anything for you, Willy.

WILLY: I tell ya, Howard. The kids are all grown up, y'know. I don't need much any more. If I could take home—well, sixty-five dollars a week, I could swing it.

HOWARD: Yeah, but Willy, see I—

WILLY: I tell ya why, Howard. Speaking frankly and between the two of us, y'know—I'm just a little tired.

HOWARD: Oh, I could understand that, Willy. But you're a road man, Willy, and we do a road business. We've only got a half-dozen salesmen on the floor here.

WILLY: God knows, Howard, I never asked a favor of any man. But I was with the firm when your father used to carry you in here in his arms.

HOWARD: I know that, Willy, but—

WILLY: Your father came to me the day you were born and asked me what I thought of the name of Howard, may he rest in peace.

HOWARD: I appreciate that, Willy, but there just is no spot here for you. If I had a spot I'd slam you right in, but I just don't have a single solitary spot.

[He looks for his lighter. Willy has picked it up and gives it to him. Pause]

WILLY: [With increasing anger] Howard, all I need to set my table is fifty dollars a week.

HOWARD: But where am I going to put you, kid?

WILLY: Look, it isn't a question of whether I can sell merchandise, is it?

HOWARD: No, but it's a business, kid, and everybody's gotta pull his own weight.

WILLY: [Desperately] Just let me tell you a story, Howard—

HOWARD: 'Cause you gotta admit, business is business.

WILLY: [Angrily] Business is definitely business, but just listen for a minute. You don't understand this. When I was a boy—eighteen, nineteen—I was already on the road. And there was a question in my mind as to whether selling had a future for me. Because in those days I had a yearning to go to Alaska. See, there were three gold strikes in one month in Alaska, and I felt like going out. Just for the ride, you might say.

HOWARD: [Barely interested] Don't say.

WILLY: Oh, yeah, my father lived many years in Alaska. He was an adventurous man. We've got quite a little streak of self-reliance in our family. I thought I'd go out with my older brother and try to locate him, and maybe settle in the North with the old man. And I was almost decided to go, when I met a salesman in the Parker House. His name was Dave Singleman. And he was eighty-four years old, and he'd drummed merchandise in thirty-one states. And old Dave, he'd go up to his room, y'understand, put on his green velvet slippers—I'll never forget—and pick up his phone and call the buyers, and without ever leaving his room, at the age of eighty-four, he made his living. And when I saw that, I realized that selling was the greatest career a man could want. 'Cause what could be more satisfying than to be able to go, at the age of eighty-four, into twenty or thirty different cities, and pick up a phone, and be remembered and loved and helped by so many different people? Do you know? when he died—and by the way he died the death of a salesman, in his green velvet slippers in the smoker of the New York, New Haven and Hartford, going into Boston—when he died, hundreds of salesmen and buyers were at his funeral. Things were sad on a lotta trains for months after that. [He stands up. Howard has not looked at him] In those days there was personality in it, Howard. There was respect, and comradeship, and gratitude in it. Today, it's all cut and dried, and there's no chance for bringing friendship to bear—or personality. You see what I mean? They don't know me any more.

HOWARD: [*Moving away, to the right*] That's just the thing, Willy.

WILLY: If I had forty dollars a week—that's all I'd need. Forty dollars, Howard.

HOWARD: Kid, I can't take blood from a stone, I—

WILLY: [*Desperation is on him now*] Howard, the year Al Smith was nominated, your father came to me and—

HOWARD: [*Starting to go off*] I've got to see some people, kid.

WILLY: [*Stopping him*] I'm talking about your father! There were promises made across this desk! You mustn't tell me you've got people to see—I put thirty-four years into this firm, Howard, and now I can't pay my insurance! You can't eat the orange and throw the peel away—a man is not a piece of fruit! [*After a pause*] Now pay attention. Your father—in 1928 I had a big year. I averaged a hundred and seventy dollars a week in commissions.

HOWARD: [*Impatiently*] Now, Willy, you never averaged—

WILLY: [*Banging his hand on the desk*] I averaged a hundred and seventy dollars a week in the year of 1928! And your father came to me—or rather, I was in the office here—it was right over this desk—and he put his hand on my shoulder—

HOWARD: [*Getting up*] You'll have to excuse me, Willy, I gotta see some people. Pull yourself together. [*Going out*] I'll be back in a little while.

[*On Howard's exit, the light on his chair grows very bright and strange.*]

WILLY: Pull myself together! What the hell did I say to him? My God, I was yelling at him! How could I! [*Willy breaks off, staring at the light, which occupies the chair, animating it. He approaches this chair, standing across the desk from it*] Frank, Frank, don't you remember what you told me that time? How you put your hand on my shoulder, and Frank . . . [*He leans on the desk and as he speaks the dead man's name he accidentally switches on the recorder, and instantly*]

HOWARD'S SON: ". . . of New York is Albany. The capital of Ohio is Cincinnati, the capital of Rhode Island is . . ." [*The recitation continues*]

WILLY: [*Leaping away with fright, shouting*] Ha! Howard! Howard! Howard!

HOWARD: [*Rushing in*] What happened?

WILLY: [*Pointing at the machine, which continues nasally, childishly, with the capital cities*] Shut it off! Shut it off!

HOWARD: [*Pulling the plug out*] Look, Willy . . .

WILLY: [*Pressing his hands to his eyes*] I gotta get myself some coffee. I'll get some coffee . . .

[*Willy starts to walk out. Howard stops him*]

HOWARD: [*Rolling up the cord*] Willy, look . . .

WILLY: I'll go to Boston.

HOWARD: Willy, you can't go to Boston for us.

WILLY: Why can't I go?

HOWARD: I don't want you to represent us. I've been meaning to tell you for a long time now.

WILLY: Howard, are you firing me?

HOWARD: I think you need a good long rest, Willy.

WILLY: Howard—

HOWARD: And when you feel better, come back, and we'll see if we can work something out.

WILLY: But I gotta earn money, Howard. I'm in no position to—

HOWARD: Where are your sons? Why don't your sons give you a hand?

WILLY: They're working on a very big deal.

HOWARD: This is no time for false pride, Willy. You go to your sons and you tell them that you're tired. You've got two great boys, haven't you?

WILLY: Oh, no question, no question, but in the meantime . . .

HOWARD: Then that's that, heh?

WILLY: All right, I'll go to Boston tomorrow.

HOWARD: No, no.

WILLY: I can't throw myself on my sons. I'm not a cripple!

HOWARD: Look, kid, I'm busy this morning.

WILLY: [*Grasping Howard's arm*] Howard, you've got to let me go to Boston!

HOWARD: [*Hard, keeping himself under control*] I've got a line of people to see this morning. Sit down, take five minutes, and pull yourself together, and then go home, will ya? I need the office, Willy. [*He starts to go, turns, remembering the recorder, starts to push off the table holding the recorder*] Oh, yeah. Whenever you can this week, stop by and drop off the samples. You'll feel better, Willy, and then come back and we'll talk. Pull yourself together, kid, there's people outside.

[*Howard exits, pushing the table off left. Willy stares into space, exhausted. Now the music is heard—Ben's music—first distantly, then closer, closer. As Willy speaks, Ben enters from the right. He carries valise and umbrella*]

WILLY: Oh, Ben, how did you do it? What is the answer? Did you wind up the Alaska deal already?

BEN: Doesn't take much time if you know what you're doing. Just a short business trip. Boarding ship in an hour. Wanted to say good-by.

WILLY: Ben, I've got to talk to you.

BEN: [*Glancing at his watch*] Haven't the time, William.

WILLY: [*Crossing the apron to Ben*] Ben, nothing's working out. I don't know what to do.

BEN: Now, look here, William. I've bought timberland in Alaska and I need a man to look after things for me.

WILLY: God, timberland! Me and my boys in those grand outdoors!

BEN: You've a new continent at your doorstep, William. Get out of these cities, they're full of talk and time payments and courts of law. Screw on your fists and you can fight for a fortune up there.

WILLY: Yes, yes! Linda, Linda!

[Linda *enters as of old, with the wash*]

LINDA: Oh, you're back?

BEN: I haven't much time.

WILLY: No, wait! Linda, he's got a proposition for me in Alaska.

LINDA: But you've got—[*To* Ben] He's got a beautiful job here.

WILLY: But in Alaska, kid, I could—

LINDA: You're doing well enough, Willy!

BEN: [*To* Linda] Enough for what, my dear?

LINDA: [*Frightened of* Ben *and angry at him*] Don't say those things to him! Enough to be happy right here, right now. [*To* Willy, *while* Ben *laughs*] Why must everybody conquer the world? You're well liked, and the boys love you, and someday—[*To* Ben]—why, old man Wagner told him just the other day that if he keeps it up he'll be a member of the firm, didn't he, Willy?

WILLY: Sure, sure. I am building something with this firm, Ben, and if a man is building something he must be on the right track, mustn't he?

BEN: What are you building? Lay your hand on it. Where is it?

WILLY: [*Hesitantly*] That's true, Linda, there's nothing.

LINDA: Why? [*To* Ben] There's a man eighty-four years old—

WILLY: That's right, Ben, that's right. When I look at that man I say, what is there to worry about?

BEN: Bah!

WILLY: It's true, Ben. All he has to do is go into any city, pick up the phone, and he's making his living and you know why?

BEN: [*Picking up his valise*] I've got to go.

WILLY: [*Holding* Ben *back*] Look at this boy!

[Biff, *in his high school sweater, enters carrying suitcase.* Happy *carries* Biff's *shoulder guards, gold helmet, and football pants*]

WILLY: Without a penny to his name, three great universities are begging for him, and from there the sky's the limit, because it's not what you do, Ben. It's who you know and the smile on your face! It's contacts, Ben, contacts! The whole wealth of Alaska passes over the lunch table at the Commodore Hotel, and that's the wonder, the wonder of this country, that a man can end with diamonds here on the basis of being liked! [*He turns to* Biff] And that's why when you get out on that field today it's important. Because thousands of people will be rooting for you and loving you. [*To* Ben, *who has again begun to leave*] And Ben! when he walks into a business office his name will sound out like a bell and all the doors will open to him! I've seen it, Ben, I've seen it a thousand times! You can't feel it with your hand like timber, but it's there!

BEN: Good-by, William.

WILLY: Ben, am I right? Don't you think I'm right? I value your advice.

BEN: There's a new continent at your doorstep, William. You could walk out rich. Rich! [*He is gone*]

WILLY: We'll do it here, Ben! You hear me? We're gonna do it here!

[*Young* Bernard *rushes in. The gay music of the* Boys *is heard*]

BERNARD: Oh, gee, I was afraid you left already!

WILLY: Why? What time is it?

BERNARD: It's half-past one!

WILLY: Well, come on, everybody! Ebbets Field next stop! Where's the pennants? [*He rushes through the wall-line of the kitchen and out into the living-room*]

LINDA: [*To* Biff] Did you pack fresh underwear?

BIFF: [*Who has been limbering up*] I want to go!

BERNARD: Biff, I'm carrying your helmet, ain't I?

HAPPY: No, I'm carrying the helmet.

BERNARD: Oh, Biff, you promised me.

HAPPY: I'm carrying the helmet.

BERNARD: How am I going to get in the locker room?

LINDA: Let him carry the shoulder guards. [*She puts her coat and hat on in the kitchen*]

BERNARD: Can I, Biff? 'Cause I told everybody I'm going to be in the locker room.

HAPPY: In Ebbets Field it's the clubhouse.

BERNARD: I meant the clubhouse. Biff.

HAPPY: Biff!

BIFF: [*Grandly, after a slight pause*] Let him carry the shoulder guards.

HAPPY: [*As he gives* Bernard *the shoulder guards*] Stay close to us now.

[Willy *rushes in with the pennants*]

WILLY: [*Handing them out*] Everybody wave when Biff comes out on the field. [Happy *and* Bernard *run off*] You set now, boy?

[*The music has died away*]

BIFF: Ready to go, Pop. Every muscle is ready.

WILLY: [*At the edge of the apron*] You realize what this means?

BIFF: That's right, Pop.

WILLY: [*Feeling* Biff's *muscles*] You're comin' home this afternoon captain of the All-Scholastic Championship Team of the City of New York.

BIFF: I got it, Pop. And remember, pal, when I take off my helmet, that touchdown is for you.

WILLY: Let's go! [*He is starting out, with his arm around* Biff, *when* Charley *enters, as of old, in knickers*] I got no room for you, Charley.

CHARLEY: Room? For what?

WILLY: In the car.

CHARLEY: You goin' for a ride? I wanted to shoot some casino.

WILLY: [*Furiously*] Casino! [*Incredulously*] Don't you realize what today is?

LINDA: Oh, he knows, Willy. He's just kidding you.

WILLY: That's nothing to kid about!

CHARLEY: No, Linda, what's goin' on?

LINDA: He's playing in Ebbets Field.

CHARLEY: Baseball in this weather?

WILLY: Don't talk to him. Come on, come on! [*He is pushing them out*]

CHARLEY: Wait a minute, didn't you hear the news?

WILLY: What?

CHARLEY: Don't you listen to the radio? Ebbets Field just blew up.

WILLY: You go to hell! [Charley *laughs. Pushing them out*] Come on, come on! We're late.

CHARLEY: [*As they go*] Knock a homer, Biff, knock a homer!

WILLY: [*The last to leave, turning to* Charley] I don't think that was funny, Charley. This is the greatest day of his life.

CHARLEY: Willy, when are you going to grow up?

WILLY: Yeah, heh? When this game is over, Charley, you'll be laughing out of the other side of your face. They'll be calling him another Red Grange. Twenty-five thousand a year.

CHARLEY: [*Kidding*] Is that so?

WILLY: Yeah, that's so.

CHARLEY: Well, then, I'm sorry, Willy. But tell me something.

WILLY: What?

CHARLEY: Who is Red Grange?

WILLY: Put up your hands. Goddam you, put up your hands!

[Charley, *chuckling, shakes his head and walks away, around the left corner of the stage.* Willy *follows him. The music rises to a mocking frenzy*]

WILLY: Who the hell do you think you are, better than everybody else? You don't know everything, you big, ignorant, stupid . . . Put up your hands!

[*Light rises, on the right side of the forestage, on a small table in the reception room of* Charley's *office. Traffic sounds are heard.* Bernard, *now mature, sits whistling to himself. A pair of tennis rackets and an overnight bag are on the floor beside him*]

WILLY: [*Offstage*] What are you walking away for? Don't walk away! If you're going to say something say it to my face! I know you laugh at me behind my back. You'll laugh out of the other side of your goddam face after this game. Touchdown! Eighty thousand people! Touchdown! Right between the goal posts.

[Bernard *is a quiet, earnest, but self-assured young man.* Willy's *voice is coming from right upstage now.* Bernard *lowers his feet off the table and listens.* Jenny, *his father's secretary, enters*]

JENNY: [*Distressed*] Say, Bernard, will you go out in the hall?

BERNARD: What is that noise? Who is it?

JENNY: Mr. Loman. He just got off the elevator.

BERNARD: [*Getting up*] Who's he arguing with?

JENNY: Nobody. There's nobody with him. I can't deal with him any more, and your father gets all upset everytime he comes. I've got a lot of typing to do, and your father's waiting to sign it. Will you see him?

WILLY: [*Entering*] Touchdown! Touch—[*He sees* Jenny] Jenny, Jenny, good to see you. How're ya? Workin'? Or still honest?

JENNY: Fine. How've you been feeling?

WILLY: Not much any more, Jenny. Ha, ha! [*He is surprised to see the rackets*]

BERNARD: Hello, Uncle Willy.

WILLY: [*Almost shocked*] Bernard! Well, look who's here! [*He comes quickly, guiltily, to* Bernard *and warmly shakes his hand*]

BERNARD: How are you? Good to see you.

WILLY: What are you doing here?

BERNARD: Oh, just stopped by to see Pop. Get off my feet till my train leaves. I'm going to Washington in a few minutes.

WILLY: Is he in?

BERNARD: Yes, he's in his office with the accountant. Sit down.

WILLY: [*Sitting down*] What're you going to do in Washington?

BERNARD: Oh, just a case I've got there, Willy.

WILLY: That so? [*Indicating the rackets*] You going to play tennis there?

BERNARD: I'm staying with a friend who's got a court.

WILLY: Don't say. His own tennis court. Must be fine people, I bet.

BERNARD: They are, very nice. Dad tells me Biff's in town.

WILLY: [*With a big smile*] Yeah, Biff's in. Working on a very big deal, Bernard.

BERNARD: What's Biff doing?

WILLY: Well, he's been doing very big things in the West. But he decided to establish himself here. Very big. We're having dinner. Did I hear your wife had a boy?

BERNARD: That's right. Our second.

WILLY: Two boys! What do you know!

BERNARD: What kind of a deal has Biff got?

WILLY: Well, Bill Oliver—very big sporting-goods man—he wants Biff very badly. Called him in from the West. Long distance, carte blanche, special deliveries. Your friends have their own private tennis court?

BERNARD: You still with the old firm, Willy?

WILLY: [*After a pause*] I'm—I'm overjoyed to see how you made the grade, Bernard, overjoyed. It's an encouraging thing to see a young man really— really— Looks very good for Biff—very—[*He breaks off, then*] Bernard— [*He is so full of emotion, he breaks off again*]

BERNARD: What is it, Willy?

WILLY: [*Small and alone*] What—what's the secret?

BERNARD: What secret?

WILLY: How—how did you? Why didn't he ever catch on?

BERNARD: I wouldn't know that, Willy.

WILLY: [*Confidentially, desperately*] You were his friend, his boyhood friend. There's something I don't understand about it. His life ended after that Ebbets Field game. From the age of seventeen nothing good ever happened to him.

BERNARD: He never trained himself for anything.

WILLY: But he did, he did. After high school he took so many correspondence courses. Radio mechanics; television; God knows what, and never made the slightest mark.

BERNARD: [*Taking off his glasses*] Willy, do you want to talk candidly?

WILLY: [*Rising, faces* Bernard] I regard you as a very brilliant man, Bernard. I value your advice.

BERNARD: Oh, the hell with the advice, Willy. I couldn't advise you. There's just one thing I've always wanted to ask you. When he was supposed to graduate, and the math teacher flunked him—

WILLY: Oh, that son-of-a-bitch ruined his life.

BERNARD: Yeah, but, Willy, all he had to do was go to summer school and make up that subject.

WILLY: That's right, that's right.

BERNARD: Did you tell him not to go to summer school?

WILLY: Me? I begged him to go. I ordered him to go!

BERNARD: Then why wouldn't he go?

WILLY: Why? Why! Bernard, that question has been trailing me like a ghost for the last fifteen years. He flunked the subject, and laid down and died like a hammer hit him!

BERNARD: Take it easy, kid.

WILLY: Let me talk to you—I got nobody to talk to. Bernard, Bernard, was it my fault? Y'see? It keeps going around in my mind, maybe I did something to him. I got nothing to give him.

BERNARD: Don't take it so hard.

WILLY: Why did he lay down? What is the story there? You were his friend!

BERNARD: Willy, I remember, it was June, and our grades came out. And he'd flunked math.

WILLY: That son-of-a-bitch!

BERNARD: No, it wasn't right then. Biff just got very angry, I remember, and he was ready to enroll in summer school.

WILLY: [*Surprised*] He was?

BERNARD: He wasn't beaten by it at all. But then, Willy, he disappeared from the block for almost a month. And I got the idea that he'd gone up to New England to see you. Did he have a talk with you then?

[Willy *stares in silence*]

BERNARD: Willy?

WILLY: [*With a stronge edge of resentment in his voice*] Yeah, he came to Boston. What about it?

BERNARD: Well, just that when he came back— I'll never forget this, it always mystifies me. Because I'd thought so well of Biff, even though he'd always taken advantage of me. I loved him, Willy, y'know?

And he came back after that month and took his sneakers—remember those sneakers with "University of Virginia" printed on them? He was so proud of those, wore them every day. And he took them down in the cellar, and burned them up in the furnace. We had a fist fight. It lasted at least half an hour. Just the two of us, punching each other down the cellar, and crying right through it. I've often thought of how strange it was that I knew he'd given up his life. What happened in Boston, Willy?

[Willy *looks at him as at an intruder*]

BERNARD: I just bring it up because you asked me.

WILLY: [*Angrily*] Nothing. What do you mean, "What happened?" What's that got to do with anything?

BERNARD: Well, don't get sore.

WILLY: What are you trying to do, blame it on me? If a boy lays down is that my fault?

BERNARD: Now, Willy, don't get—

WILLY: Well, don't—don't talk to me that way! What does that mean, "What happened?"

[Charley *enters. He is in his vest, and he carries a bottle of bourbon*]

CHARLEY: Hey, you're going to miss that train. [*He waves the bottle*]

BERNARD: Yeah, I'm going. [*He takes the bottle*] Thanks, Pop. [*He picks up his rackets and bag*] Good-by, Willy, and don't worry about it. You know, "If at first you don't succeed . . ."

WILLY: Yes, I believe in that.

BERNARD: But sometimes, Willy, it's better for a man just to walk away.

WILLY: Walk away?

BERNARD: That's right.

WILLY: But if you can't walk away?

BERNARD: [*After a slight pause*] I guess that's when it's tough. [*Extending his hand*] Good-by, Willy.

WILLY: [*Shaking* Bernard's *hand*] Good-by, boy.

CHARLEY: [*An arm on* Bernard's *shoulder*] How do you like this kid? Gonna argue a case in front of the Supreme Court.

BERNARD: [*Protesting*] Pop!

WILLY: [*Genuinely shocked, pained, and happy*] No! The Supreme Court!

BERNARD: I gotta run. 'By, Dad!

CHARLEY: Knock 'em dead, Bernard!

[Bernard *goes off*]

WILLY: [*As* Charley *takes out his wallet*] The Supreme Court! And he didn't even mention it!

CHARLEY: [*Counting out money on the desk*] He don't have to—he's gonna do it.

WILLY: And you never told him what to do, did you? You never took any interest in him.

CHARLEY: My salvation is that I never took any interest in anything. There's some money—fifty dollars. I got an accountant inside.

WILLY: Charley, look . . . [*With difficulty*] I got

my insurance to pay. If you can manage it—I need a hundred and ten dollars.

[Charley *doesn't reply for a moment; merely stops moving*]

WILLY: I'd draw it from my bank but Linda would know, and I . . .

CHARLEY: Sit down, Willy.

WILLY: [*Moving toward the chair*] I'm keeping an account of everything, remember. I'll pay every penny back. [*He sits*]

CHARLEY: Now listen to me, Willy.

WILLY: I want you to know I appreciate . . .

CHARLEY: [*Sitting down on the table*] Willy, what're you doin'? What the hell is goin' on in your head?

WILLY: Why? I'm simply . . .

CHARLEY: I offered you a job. You can make fifty dollars a week. And I won't send you on the road.

WILLY: I've got a job.

CHARLEY: Without pay? What kind of a job is a job without pay? [*He rises*] Now, look, kid, enough is enough. I'm no genius but I know when I'm being insulted.

WILLY: Insulted!

CHARLEY: Why don't you want to work for me?

WILLY: What's the matter with you? I've got a job.

CHARLEY: Then what're you walkin' in here every week for?

WILLY: [*Getting up*] Well, if you don't want me to walk in here—

CHARLEY: I am offering you a job.

WILLY: I don't want your goddam job!

CHARLEY: When the hell are you going to grow up?

WILLY: [*Furiously*] You big ignoramus, if you say that to me again I'll rap you one! I don't care how big you are! [*He's ready to fight*]

[*Pause*]

CHARLEY: [*Kindly, going to him*] How much do you need, Willy?

WILLY: Charley, I'm strapped, I'm strapped. I don't know what to do. I was just fired.

CHARLEY: Howard fired you?

WILLY: That snotnose. Imagine that? I named him. I named him Howard.

CHARLEY: Willy, when're you gonna realize that them things don't mean anything? You named him Howard, but you can't sell that. The only thing you got in this world is what you can sell. And the funny thing is that you're a salesman, and you don't know that.

WILLY: I've always tried to think otherwise, I guess. I always felt that if a man was impressive, and well liked, that nothing—

CHARLEY: Why must everybody like you? Who liked J. P. Morgan? Was he impressive? In a Turkish bath he'd look like a butcher. But with his pockets on he was very well liked. Now listen, Willy, I know you don't like me, and nobody can say I'm in love with you, but I'll give you a job because—just

for the hell of it, put it that way. Now what do you say?

WILLY: I—I just can't work for you, Charley.

CHARLEY: What're you, jealous of me?

WILLY: I can't work for you, that's all, don't ask me why.

CHARLEY: [*Angered, takes out more bills*] You been jealous of me all your life, you damned fool! Here, pay your insurance. [*He puts the money in Willy's hand*]

WILLY: I'm keeping strict accounts.

CHARLEY: I've got some work to do. Take care of yourself. And pay your insurance.

WILLY: [*Moving to the right*] Funny, y'know? After all the highways, and the trains, and the appointments, and the years, you end up worth more dead than alive.

CHARLEY: Willy, nobody's worth nothin' dead. [*After a slight pause*] Did you hear what I said?

[Willy *stands still, dreaming*]

CHARLEY: Willy!

WILLY: Apologize to Bernard for me when you see him. I didn't mean to argue with him. He's a fine boy. They're all fine boys, and they'll end up big—all of them. Someday they'll all play tennis together. Wish me luck, Charley. He saw Bill Oliver today.

CHARLEY: Good luck.

WILLY: [*On the verge of tears*] Charley, you're the only friend I got. Isn't that a remarkable thing? [*He goes out*]

CHARLEY: Jesus!

[Charley *stares after him a moment and follows. All light blacks out. Suddenly raucous music is heard, and a red glow rises behind the screen at right. Stanley, a young waiter, appears, carrying a table, followed by* Happy, *who is carrying two chairs*]

STANLEY: [*Putting the table down*] That's all right, Mr. Loman, I can handle it myself. [*He turns and takes the chairs from* Happy *and places them at the table*]

HAPPY: [*Glancing around*] Oh, this is better.

STANLEY: Sure, in front there you're in the middle of all kinds a noise. Whenever you got a party, Mr. Loman, you just tell me and I'll put you back here. Y'know, there's a lotta people they don't like it private, because when they go out they like to see a lotta action around them because they're sick and tired to stay in the house by theirself. But I know you, you ain't from Hackensack. You know what I mean?

HAPPY: [*Sitting down*] So how's it coming, Stanley?

STANLEY: Ah, it's a dog's life. I only wish during the war they'd a took me in the Army. I coulda been dead by now.

HAPPY: My brother's back, Stanley.

STANLEY: Oh, he come back, heh? From the Far West.

HAPPY: Yeah, big cattle man, my brother, so treat him right. And my father's coming too.

STANLEY: Oh, your father too!

HAPPY: You got a couple of nice lobsters?

STANLEY: Hundred per cent, big.

HAPPY: I want them with the claws.

STANLEY: Don't worry, I don't give you no mice. [Happy laughs] How about some wine? It'll put a head on the meal.

HAPPY: No. You remember, Stanley, that recipe I brought you from overseas? With the champagne in it?

STANLEY: Oh, yeah, sure. I still got it tacked up yet in the kitchen. But that'll have to cost a buck apiece anyways.

HAPPY: That's all right.

STANLEY: What'd you, hit a number or somethin'?

HAPPY: No, it's a little celebration. My brother is —I think he pulled off a big deal today. I think we're going into business together.

STANLEY: Great! That's the best for you. Because a family business, you know what I mean?—that's the best.

HAPPY: That's what I think.

STANLEY: 'Cause what's the difference? Somebody steals? It's in the family. Know what I mean? [Sotto voce] Like this bartender here. The boss is goin' crazy what kinda leak he's got in the cash register. You put it in but it don't come out.

HAPPY: [Raising his head] Sh!

STANLEY: What?

HAPPY: You notice I wasn't lookin' right or left, was I?

STANLEY: No.

HAPPY: And my eyes are closed.

STANLEY: So what's the—?

HAPPY: Strudel's comin'.

STANLEY: [Catching on, looks around] Ah, no, there's no—

[He breaks off as a furred, lavishly dressed girl enters and sits at the next table. Both follow her with their eyes]

STANLEY: Geez, how'd ya know?

HAPPY: I got radar or something. [Staring directly at her profile] Oooooooo . . . Stanley.

STANLEY: I think that's for you, Mr. Loman.

HAPPY: Look at that mouth. Oh, God. And the binoculars.

STANLEY: Geez, you got a life, Mr. Loman.

HAPPY: Wait on her.

STANLEY: [Going to the Girl's table] Would you like a menu, ma'am?

GIRL: I'm expecting someone, but I'd like a—

HAPPY: Why don't you bring her—excuse me, miss, do you mind? I sell champagne, and I'd like you to try my brand. Bring her a champagne, Stanley.

GIRL: That's awfully nice of you.

HAPPY: Don't mention it. It's all company money. [He laughs]

GIRL: That's a charming product to be selling, isn't it?

HAPPY: Oh, gets to be like everything else. Selling is selling, y'know.

GIRL: I suppose.

HAPPY: You don't happen to sell, do you?

GIRL: No, I don't sell.

HAPPY: Would you object to a compliment from a stranger? You ought to be on a magazine cover.

GIRL: [Looking at him a little archly] I have been.

[Stanley comes in with a glass of champagne]

HAPPY: What'd I say before, Stanley? You see? She's a cover girl.

STANLEY: Oh, I could see, I could see.

HAPPY: [To the Girl] What magazine?

GIRL: Oh, a lot of them. [She takes the drink] Thank you.

HAPPY: You know what they say in France, don't you? "Champagne is the drink of the complexion" —Hya, Biff!

[Biff has entered and sits with Happy]

BIFF: Hello, kid. Sorry I'm late.

HAPPY: I just got here. Uh, Miss—?

GIRL: Forsythe.

HAPPY: Miss Forsythe, this is my brother.

BIFF: Is Dad here?

HAPPY: His name is Biff. You might've heard of him. Great football player.

GIRL: Really? What team?

HAPPY: Are you familiar with football?

GIRL: No, I'm afraid I'm not.

HAPPY: Biff is quarterback with the New York Giants.

GIRL: Well, that is nice, isn't it? [She drinks]

HAPPY: Good health.

GIRL: I'm happy to meet you.

HAPPY: That's my name. Hap. It's really Harold, but at West Point they called me Happy.

GIRL: [Now really impressed] Oh, I see. How do you do? [She turns her profile]

BIFF: Isn't Dad coming?

HAPPY: You want her?

BIFF: Oh, I could never make that.

HAPPY: I remember the time that idea would never come into your head. Where's the old confidence, Biff?

BIFF: I just saw Oliver—

HAPPY: Wait a minute. I've got to see that old confidence again. Do you want her? She's on call.

BIFF: Oh, no. [He turns to look at the Girl]

HAPPY: I'm telling you. Watch this. [Turning to the Girl] Honey? [She turns to him] Are you busy?

GIRL: Well, I am . . . but I could make a phone call.

HAPPY: Do that, will you, honey? And see if you can get a friend. We'll be here for a while. Biff is one of the greatest football players in the country.

GIRL: [*Standing up*] Well, I'm certainly happy to meet you.

HAPPY: Come back soon.

GIRL: I'll try.

HAPPY: Don't try, honey, try hard.

[*The Girl exits. Stanley follows, shaking his head in bewildered admiration*]

HAPPY: Isn't that a shame now? A beautiful girl like that? That's why I can't get married. There's not a good woman in a thousand. New York is loaded with them, kid!

BIFF: Hap, look—

HAPPY: I told you she was on call!

BIFF: [*Strangely unnerved*] Cut it out, will ya? I want to say something to you.

HAPPY: Did you see Oliver?

BIFF: I saw him all right. Now look, I want to tell Dad a couple of things and I want you to help me.

HAPPY: What? Is he going to back you?

BIFF: Are you crazy? You're out of your goddam head, you know that?

HAPPY: Why? What happened?

BIFF: [*Breathlessly*] I did a terrible thing today, Hap. It's been the strangest day I ever went through. I'm all numb, I swear.

HAPPY: You mean he wouldn't see you?

BIFF: Well, I waited six hours for him, see? All day. Kept sending my name in. Even tried to date his secretary so she'd get me to him, but no soap.

HAPPY: Because you're not showin' the old confidence, Biff. He remembered you, didn't he?

BIFF: [*Stopping Happy with a gesture*] Finally, about five o'clock, he comes out. Didn't remember who I was or anything. I felt like such an idiot, Hap.

HAPPY: Did you tell him my Florida idea?

BIFF: He walked away. I saw him for one minute. I got so mad I could've torn the walls down! How the hell did I ever get the idea I was a salesman there? I even believed myself that I'd been a salesman for him! And then he gave me one look and— I realized what a ridiculous lie my whole life has been! We've been talking in a dream for fifteen years. I was a shipping clerk.

HAPPY: What'd you do?

BIFF: [*With great tension and wonder*] Well, he left, see. And the secretary went out. I was all alone in the waiting-room. I don't know what came over me, Hap. The next thing I know I'm in his office— paneled walls, everything. I can't explain it. I—Hap, I took his fountain pen.

HAPPY: Geez, did he catch you?

BIFF: I ran out. I ran down all eleven flights. I ran and ran and ran.

HAPPY: That was an awful dumb—what'd you do that for?

BIFF: [*Agonized*] I don't know, I just—wanted to take something, I don't know. You gotta help me, Hap, I'm gonna tell Pop.

HAPPY: You crazy? What for?

BIFF: Hap, he's got to understand that I'm not the man somebody lends that kind of money to. He thinks I've been spiting him all these years and it's eating him up.

HAPPY: That's just it. You tell him something nice.

BIFF: I can't.

HAPPY: Say you got a lunch date with Oliver tomorrow.

BIFF: So what do I do tomorrow?

HAPPY: You leave the house tomorrow and come back at night and say Oliver is thinking it over. And he thinks it over for a couple of weeks, and gradually it fades away and nobody's the worse.

BIFF: But it'll go on forever!

HAPPY: Dad is never so happy as when he's looking forward to something!

[*Willy enters*]

HAPPY: Hello, scout!

WILLY: Gee, I haven't been here in years!

[*Stanley has followed Willy in and sets a chair for him. Stanley starts off but Happy stops him*]

HAPPY: Stanley!

[*Stanley stands by, waiting for an order*]

BIFF: [*Going to Willy with guilt, as to an invalid*] Sit down, Pop. You want a drink?

WILLY: Sure, I don't mind.

BIFF: Let's get a load on.

WILLY: You look worried.

BIFF: N-no. [*To Stanley*] Scotch all around. Make it doubles.

STANLEY: Doubles, right. [*He goes*]

WILLY: You had a couple already, didn't you?

BIFF: Just a couple, yeah.

WILLY: Well, what happened, boy? [*Nodding affirmatively, with a smile*] Everything go all right?

BIFF: [*Takes a breath, then reaches out and grasps Willy's hand*] Pal . . . [*He is smiling bravely, and Willy is smiling too*] I had an experience today.

HAPPY: Terrific, Pop.

WILLY: That so? What happened?

BIFF: [*High, slightly alcoholic, above the earth*] I'm going to tell you everything from first to last. It's been a strange day. [*Silence. He looks around, composes himself as best he can, but his breath keeps breaking the rhythm of his voice*] I had to wait quite a while for him, and—

WILLY: Oliver?

BIFF: Yeah, Oliver. All day, as a matter of cold fact. And a lot of—instances—facts, Pop, facts about my life came back to me. Who was it, Pop? Who ever said I was a salesman with Oliver?

WILLY: Well, you were.

BIFF: No, Dad, I was a shipping clerk.

WILLY: But you were practically—

BIFF: [*With determination*] Dad, I don't know who said it first, but I was never a salesman for Bill Oliver.

WILLY: What're you talking about?

BIFF: Let's hold on to the facts tonight, Pop.

We're not going to get anywhere bullin' around. I was a shipping clerk.

WILLY: [*Angrily*] All right, now listen to me—

BIFF: Why don't you let me finish?

WILLY: I'm not interested in stories about the past or any crap of that kind because the woods are burning, boys, you understand? There's a big blaze going on all around. I was fired today.

BIFF: [*Shocked*] How could you be?

WILLY: I was fired, and I'm looking for a little good news to tell your mother, because the woman has waited and the woman has suffered. The gist of it is that I haven't got a story left in my head, Biff. So don't give me a lecture about facts and aspects. I am not interested. Now what've you got to say to me?

[*Stanley enters with three drinks. They wait until he leaves*]

WILLY: Did you see Oliver?

BIFF: Jesus, Dad!

WILLY: You mean you didn't go up there?

HAPPY: Sure he went up there.

BIFF: I did. I saw him. How could they fire you?

WILLY: [*On the edge of his chair*] What kind of a welcome did he give you?

BIFF: He won't even let you work on commission?

WILLY: I'm out! [*Driving*] So tell me, he gave you a warm welcome?

HAPPY: Sure, Pop, sure!

BIFF: [*Driven*] Well, it was kind of—

WILLY: I was wondering if he'd remember you. [*To* Happy] Imagine, man doesn't see him for ten, twelve years and gives him that kind of a welcome!

HAPPY: Damn right!

BIFF: [*Trying to return to the offensive*] Pop, look—

WILLY: You know why he remembered you, don't you? Because you impressed him in those days.

BIFF: Let's talk quietly and get this down to the facts, huh?

WILLY: [*As though* Biff *had been interrupting*] Well, what happened? It's great news, Biff. Did he take you into his office or'd you talk in the waiting-room?

BIFF: Well, he came in, see, and—

WILLY: [*With a big smile*] What'd he say? Betcha he threw his arm around you.

BIFF: Well, he kinda—

WILLY: He's a fine man. [*To* Happy] Very hard man to see, y'know.

HAPPY: [*Agreeing*] Oh, I know.

WILLY: [*To* Biff] Is that where you had the drinks?

BIFF: Yeah, he gave me a couple of—no, no!

HAPPY: [*Cutting in*] He told him my Florida idea.

WILLY: Don't interrupt. [*To* Biff] How'd he react to the Florida idea?

BIFF: Dad, will you give me a minute to explain?

WILLY: I've been waiting for you to explain since I sat down here! What happened? He took you into his office and what?

BIFF: Well—I talked. And—and he listened, see.

WILLY: Famous for the way he listens, y'know. What was his answer?

BIFF: His answer was— [*He breaks off, suddenly angry*] Dad, you're not letting me tell you what I want to tell you!

WILLY: [*Accusing, angered*] You didn't see him, did you?

BIFF: I did see him!

WILLY: What'd you insult him or something? You insulted him, didn't you?

BIFF: Listen, will you let me out of it, will you just let me out of it!

HAPPY: What the hell!

WILLY: Tell me what happened!

BIFF: [*To* Happy] I can't talk to him!

[*A single trumpet note jars the ear. The light of green leaves stains the house, which holds the air of night and a dream. Young Bernard enters and knocks on the door of the house*]

YOUNG BERNARD: [*Frantically*] Mrs. Loman, Mrs. Loman!

HAPPY: Tell him what happened!

BIFF: [*To* Happy] Shut up and leave me alone!

WILLY: No, no! You had to go and flunk math!

BIFF: What math? What're you talking about?

YOUNG BERNARD: Mrs. Loman, Mrs. Loman!

[*Linda appears in the house, as of old*]

WILLY: [*Wildly*] Math, math, math!

BIFF: Take it easy, Pop!

YOUNG BERNARD: Mrs. Loman!

WILLY: [*Furiously*] If you hadn't flunked you'd've been set by now!

BIFF: Now, look, I'm gonna tell you what happened, and you're going to listen to me.

YOUNG BERNARD: Mrs. Loman!

BIFF: I waited six hours—

HAPPY: What the hell are you saying?

BIFF: I kept sending in my name but he wouldn't see me. So finally he . . . [*He continues unheard as light fades low on the restaurant*]

YOUNG BERNARD: Biff flunked math!

LINDA: No!

YOUNG BERNARD: Birnbaum flunked him! They won't graduate him!

LINDA: But they have to. He's gotta go to the university. Where is he? Biff! Biff!

YOUNG BERNARD: No, he left. He went to Grand Central.

LINDA: Grand— You mean he went to Boston!

YOUNG BERNARD: Is Uncle Willy in Boston?

LINDA: Oh, maybe Willy can talk to the teacher. Oh, the poor, poor boy!

[*Light on house area snaps out*]

BIFF: [*At the table, now audible, holding up a gold fountain pen*] . . . so I'm washed up with Oliver, you understand? Are you listening to me?

WILLY: [*At a loss*] Yeah, sure. If you hadn't flunked—

BIFF: Flunked what? What're you talking about?

WILLY: Don't blame everything on me! I didn't flunk math—you did! What pen?

HAPPY: That was awful dumb, Biff, a pen like that is worth—

WILLY: [*Seeing the pen for the first time*] You took Oliver's pen?

BIFF: [*Weakening*] Dad, I just explained it to you.

WILLY: You stole Bill Oliver's fountain pen!

BIFF: I didn't exactly steal it! That's just what I've been explaining to you!

HAPPY: He had it in his hand and just then Oliver walked in, so he got nervous and stuck it in his pocket!

WILLY: My God, Biff!

BIFF: I never intended to do it, Dad!

OPERATOR'S VOICE: Standish Arms, good evening!

WILLY: [*Shouting*] I'm not in my room!

BIFF: [*Frightened*] Dad, what's the matter? [*He and Happy stand up*]

OPERATOR: Ringing Mr. Loman for you!

WILLY: I'm not there, stop it!

BIFF: [*Horrified, gets down on one knee before Willy*] Dad, I'll make good, I'll make good. [*Willy tries to get to his feet. Biff holds him down*] Sit down now.

WILLY: No, you're no good, you're no good for anything.

BIFF: I am, Dad, I'll find something else, you understand? Now don't worry about anything. [*He holds up Willy's face*] Talk to me, Dad.

OPERATOR: Mr. Loman does not answer. Shall I page him?

WILLY: [*Attempting to stand, as though to rush and silence the Operator*] No, no, no!

HAPPY: He'll strike something, Pop.

WILLY: No, no . . .

BIFF: [*Desperately, standing over Willy*] Pop, listen! Listen to me! I'm telling you something good. Oliver talked to his partner about the Florida idea. You listening? He—he talked to his partner, and he came to me . . . I'm going to be all right, you hear? Dad, listen to me, he said it was just a question of the amount!

WILLY: Then you . . . got it?

HAPPY: He's gonna be terrific, Pop!

WILLY: [*Trying to stand*] Then you got it, haven't you? You got it! You got it!

BIFF: [*Agonized, holds Willy down*] No, no. Look, Pop. I'm supposed to have lunch with them tomorrow. I'm just telling you this so you'll know that I can still make an impression, Pop. And I'll make good somewhere, but I can't go tomorrow, see?

WILLY: Why not? You simply—

BIFF: But the pen, Pop!

WILLY: You give it to him and tell him it was an oversight!

HAPPY: Sure, have lunch tomorrow!

BIFF: I can't say that—

WILLY: You were doing a crossword puzzle and accidentally used his pen!

BIFF: Listen, kid, I took those balls years ago, now I walk in with his fountain pen? That clinches it, don't you see? I can't face him like that! I'll try elsewhere.

PAGE'S VOICE: Paging Mr. Loman!

WILLY: Don't you want to be anything?

BIFF: Pop, how can I go back?

WILLY: You don't want to be anything, is that what's behind it?

BIFF: [*Now angry at Willy for not crediting his sympathy*] Don't take it that way! You think it was easy walking into that office after what I'd done to him? A team of horses couldn't have dragged me back to Bill Oliver!

WILLY: Then why'd you go?

BIFF: Why did I go? Why did I go! Look at you! Look at what's become of you!

[*Off left, The Woman laughs*]

WILLY: Biff, you're going to go to that lunch tomorrow, or—

BIFF: I can't go. I've got no appointment!

HAPPY: Biff, for . . . !

WILLY: Are you spiting me?

BIFF: Don't take it that way! Goddammit!

WILLY: [*Strikes Biff and falters away from the table*] You rotten little louse! Are you spiting me?

THE WOMAN: Someone's at the door, Willy!

BIFF: I'm no good, can't you see what I am?

HAPPY: [*Separating them*] Hey, you're in a restaurant! Now cut it out, both of you! [*The girls enter*] Hello, girls, sit down.

[*The Woman laughs, off left*]

MISS FORSYTHE: I guess we might as well. This is Letta.

THE WOMAN: Willy, are you going to wake up?

BIFF: [*Ignoring Willy*] How're ya, miss, sit down. What do you drink?

MISS FORSYTHE: Letta might not be able to stay long.

LETTA: I gotta get up very early tomorrow. I got jury duty. I'm so excited! Were you fellows ever on a jury?

BIFF: No, but I been in front of them! [*The girls laugh*] This is my father.

LETTA: Isn't he cute? Sit down with us, Pop.

HAPPY: Sit him down, Biff!

BIFF: [*Going to him*] Come on, slugger, drink us under the table. To hell with it! Come on, sit down, pal.

[*On Biff's last insistence, Willy is about to sit*]

THE WOMAN: [*Now urgently*] Willy, are you going to answer the door!

[*The Woman's call pulls Willy back. He starts right, befuddled*]

BIFF: Hey, where are you going?

WILLY: Open the door.

BIFF: The door?

WILLY: The washroom . . . the door . . . where's the door?

BIFF: [*Leading* Willy *to the left*] Just go straight down.

[Willy *moves left*]

THE WOMAN: Willy, Willy, are you going to get up, get up, get up, get up?

[Willy *exits left*]

LETTA: I think it's sweet you bring your daddy along.

MISS FORSYTHE: Oh, he isn't really your father!

BIFF: [*At left to her resentfully*] Miss Forsythe, you've just seen a prince walk by. A fine, troubled prince. A hard-working, unappreciated prince. A pal, you understand? A good companion. Always for his boys.

LETTA: That's so sweet.

HAPPY: Well, girls, what's the program? We're wasting time. Come on, Biff. Gather round. Where would you like to go?

BIFF: Why don't you do something for him?

HAPPY: Me!

BIFF: Don't you give a damn for him, Hap?

HAPPY: What're you talking about? I'm the one who—

BIFF: I sense it, you don't give a good goddam about him. [*He takes the rolled-up hose from his pocket and puts it on the table in front of* Happy] Look what I found in the cellar, for Christ's sake. How can you bear to let it go on?

HAPPY: Me? Who goes away? Who runs off and—

BIFF: Yeah, but he doesn't mean anything to you. You could help him—I can't! Don't you understand what I'm talking about? He's going to kill himself, don't you know that?

HAPPY: Don't I know it! Me!

BIFF: Hap, help him! Jesus . . . help him . . . Help me, help me, I can't bear to look at his face! [*Ready to weep, he hurries out, up right*]

HAPPY: [*Starting after him*] Where are you going?

MISS FORSYTHE: What's he so mad about?

HAPPY: Come on, girls, we'll catch up with him.

MISS FORSYTHE: [*As* Happy *pushes her out*] Say, I don't like that temper of his!

HAPPY: He's just a little overstrung, he'll be all right!

WILLY: [*Off left, as* The Woman *laughs*] Don't answer! Don't answer!

LETTA: Don't you want to tell your father—

HAPPY: No, that's not my father. He's just a guy. Come on, we'll catch Biff, and, honey, we're going to paint this town! Stanley, where's the check! Hey, Stanley!

[*They exit.* Stanley *looks toward left*]

STANLEY: [*Calling to* Happy *indignantly*] Mr. Loman! Mr. Loman!

[Stanley *picks up a chair and follows them off. Knocking is heard off left. The Woman enters, laughing.* Willy *follows her. She is in a black slip; he is buttoning his shirt. Raw, sensuous music accompanies their speech.*]

WILLY: Will you stop laughing? Will you stop?

THE WOMAN: Aren't you going to answer the door? He'll wake the whole hotel.

WILLY: I'm not expecting anybody.

THE WOMAN: Whyn't you have another drink, honey, and stop being so damn self-centered?

WILLY: I'm so lonely.

THE WOMAN: You know you ruined me, Willy? From now on, whenever you come to the office, I'll see that you go right through to the buyers. No waiting at my desk any more, Willy. You ruined me.

WILLY: That's nice of you to say that.

THE WOMAN: Gee, you are self-centered! Why so sad? You are the saddest, self-centeredest soul I ever did see-saw. [*She laughs. He kisses her*] Come on inside, drummer boy. It's silly to be dressing in the middle of the night. [*As knocking is heard*] Aren't you going to answer the door?

WILLY: They're knocking on the wrong door.

THE WOMAN: But I felt the knocking. And he heard us talking in here. Maybe the hotel's on fire!

WILLY: [*His terror rising*] It's a mistake.

THE WOMAN: Then tell him to go away!

WILLY: There's nobody there.

THE WOMAN: It's getting on my nerves, Willy. There's somebody standing out there and it's getting on my nerves!

WILLY: [*Pushing her away from him*] All right, stay in the bathroom here, and don't come out. I think there's a law in Massachusetts about it, so don't come out. It may be that new room clerk. He looked very mean. So don't come out. It's a mistake, there's no fire.

[*The knocking is heard again. He takes a few steps away from her, and vanishes into the wing. The light follows him, and now he is facing* Young Biff, *who carries a suitcase.* Biff *steps toward him. The music is gone*]

BIFF: Why didn't you answer?

WILLY: Biff! What are you doing in Boston?

BIFF: Why didn't you answer? I've been knocking for five minutes, I called you on the phone—

WILLY: I just heard you. I was in the bathroom and had the door shut. Did anything happen home?

BIFF: Dad—I let you down.

WILLY: What do you mean?

BIFF: Dad . . .

WILLY: Biffo, what's this about? [*Putting his arm around* Biff] Come on, let's go downstairs and get you a malted.

BIFF: Dad, I flunked math.

WILLY: Not for the term?

BIFF: The term. I haven't got enough credits to graduate.

WILLY: You mean to say Bernard wouldn't give you the answers?

BIFF: He did, he tried, but I only got a sixty-one.

WILLY: And they wouldn't give you four points?

BIFF: Birnbaum refused absolutely. I begged him, Pop, but he won't give me those points. You gotta talk to him before they close the school. Because if he saw the kind of man you are, and you just talked to him in your way, I'm sure he'd come through for me. The class came right before practice, see, and I didn't go enough. Would you talk to him? He'd like you, Pop. You know the way you could talk.

WILLY: You're on. We'll drive right back.

BIFF: Oh, Dad, good work! I'm sure he'll change it for you!

WILLY: Go downstairs and tell the clerk I'm checkin' out. Go right down.

BIFF: Yes, sir! See, the reason he hates me, Pop— one day he was late for class so I got up at the blackboard and imitated him. I crossed my eyes and talked with a lithp.

WILLY: [*Laughing*] You did? The kids like it?

BIFF: They nearly died laughing!

WILLY: Yeah? What'd you do?

BIFF: The thquare root of thixty twee is . . . [Willy *bursts out laughing*; Biff *joins him*] And in the middle of it he walked in!

[Willy *laughs and* The Woman *joins in offstage*]

WILLY: [*Without hesitation*] Hurry downstairs and—

BIFF: Somebody in there?

WILLY: No, that was next door.

[The Woman *laughs offstage*]

BIFF: Somebody got in your bathroom!

WILLY: No, it's the next room, there's a party—

THE WOMAN: [*Enters, laughing. She lisps this*] Can I come in? There's something in the bathtub, Willy, and it's moving!

[Willy *looks at* Biff, *who is staring open-mouthed and horrified at* The Woman]

WILLY: Ah—you better go back to your room. They must be finished painting by now. They're painting her room so I let her take a shower here. Go back, go back . . . [*He pushes her*]

THE WOMAN: [*Resisting*] But I've got to get dressed, Willy, I can't—

WILLY: Get out of here! Go back, go back . . . [*Suddenly striving for the ordinary*] This is Miss Francis, Biff, she's a buyer. They're painting her room. Go back, Miss Francis, go back . . .

THE WOMAN: But my clothes, I can't go out naked in the hall!

WILLY: [*Pushing her offstage*] Get outa here! Go back, go back!

[Biff *slowly sits down on his suitcase as the argument continues offstage*]

THE WOMAN: Where's my stockings? You promised me stockings, Willy!

WILLY: I have no stockings here!

THE WOMAN: You had two boxes of size nine sheers for me, and I want them!

WILLY: Here, for God's sake, will you get outa here!

THE WOMAN: [*Enters holding a box of stockings*] I just hope there's nobody in the hall. That's all I hope. [*To* Biff] Are you football or baseball?

BIFF: Football.

THE WOMAN: [*Angry, humiliated*] That's me too. G'night. [*She snatches her clothes from* Willy, *and walks out*]

WILLY: [*After a pause*] Well, better get going. I want to get to the school first thing in the morning. Get my suits out of the closet. I'll get my valise. [Biff *doesn't move*] What's the matter? [Biff *remains motionless, tears falling*] She's a buyer. Buys for J. H. Simmons. She lives down the hall—they're painting. You don't imagine—[*He breaks off. After a pause*] Now listen, pal, she's just a buyer. She sees merchandise in her room and they have to keep it looking just so . . . [*Pause. Assuming command*] All right, get my suits. [Biff *doesn't move*] Now stop crying and do as I say. I gave you an order. Biff, I gave you an order! Is that what you do when I give you an order? How dare you cry! [*Putting his arm around* Biff] Now look, Biff, when you grow up you'll understand about these things. You mustn't— you mustn't overemphasize a thing like this. I'll see Birnbaum first thing in the morning.

BIFF: Never mind.

WILLY: [*Getting down beside* Biff] Never mind! He's going to give you those points. I'll see to it.

BIFF: He wouldn't listen to you.

WILLY: He certainly will listen to me. You need those points for the U. of Virginia.

BIFF: I'm not going there.

WILLY: Heh? If I can't get him to change that mark you'll make it up in summer school. You've got all summer to—

BIFF: [*His weeping breaking from him*] Dad . . .

WILLY: [*Infected by it*] Oh, my boy . . .

BIFF: Dad . . .

WILLY: She's nothing to me, Biff. I was lonely, I was terribly lonely.

BIFF: You—you gave her Mama's stockings! [*His tears break through and he rises to go*]

WILLY: [*Grabbing for* Biff] I gave you an order!

BIFF: Don't touch me, you—liar!

WILLY: Apologize for that!

BIFF: You fake! You phony little fake! You fake! [*Overcome, he turns quickly and weeping fully goes out with his suitcase. Willy is left on the floor on his knees*]

WILLY: I gave you an order! Biff, come back here or I'll beat you! Come back here! I'll whip you!

[Stanley *comes quickly from the right and stands in front of* Willy]

WILLY: [*Shouts at* Stanley] I gave you an order . . .

STANLEY: Hey, let's pick it up, pick it up, Mr. Loman. [*He helps* Willy *to his feet*] Your boys left with the chippies. They said they'll see you home.

[*A second waiter watches some distance away*]

WILLY: But we were supposed to have dinner together.

[*Music is heard,* Willy's *theme*]

STANLEY: Can you make it?

WILLY: I'll—sure, I can make it. [*Suddenly concerned about his clothes*] Do I—I look all right?

STANLEY: Sure, you look all right. [*He flicks a speck off* Willy's *lapel*]

WILLY: Here—here's a dollar.

STANLEY: Oh, your son paid me. It's all right.

WILLY: [*Putting it in* Stanley's *hand*] No, take it. You're a good boy.

STANLEY: Oh, no, you don't have to . . .

WILLY: Here—here's some more, I don't need it any more. [*After a slight pause*] Tell me—is there a seed store in the neighborhood?

STANLEY: Seeds? You mean like to plant?

[*As* Willy *turns,* Stanley *slips the money back into his jacket pocket*]

WILLY: Yes. Carrots, peas . . .

STANLEY: Well, there's hardware stores on Sixth Avenue, but it may be too late now.

WILLY: [*Anxiously*] Oh, I'd better hurry. I've got to get some seeds. [*He starts off to the right*] I've got to get some seeds, right away. Nothing's planted. I don't have a thing in the ground.

[Willy *hurries out as the light goes down.* Stanley *moves over to the right after him, watches him off. The other waiter has been staring at* Willy]

STANLEY: [*To the waiter*] Well, whatta you looking at?

[*The waiter picks up the chairs and moves off right.* Stanley *takes the table and follows him. The light fades on this area. There is a long pause, the sound of the flute coming over. The light gradually rises on the kitchen, which is empty.* Happy *appears at the door of the house, followed by* Biff. Happy *is carrying a large bunch of long-stemmed roses. He enters the kitchen, looks around for* Linda. *Not seeing her, he turns to* Biff, *who is just outside the house door, and makes a gesture with his hands, indicating "Not here, I guess." He looks into the living-room and freezes. Inside,* Linda, *unseen, is seated,* Willy's *coat on her lap. She rises ominously and quietly and moves toward* Happy, *who backs up into the kitchen, afraid*]

HAPPY: Hey, what're you doing up? [Linda *says nothing but moves toward him implacably*] Where's Pop? [*He keeps backing to the right, and now* Linda *is in full view in the doorway to the living-room*] Is he sleeping?

LINDA: Where were you?

HAPPY: [*Trying to laugh it off*] We met two girls, Mom, very fine types. Here, we brought you some flowers. [*Offering them to her*] Put them in your room, Ma.

[*She knocks them to the floor at* Biff's *feet. He has now come inside and closed the door behind him. She stares at* Biff, *silent*]

HAPPY: Now what'd you do that for? Mom, I want you to have some flowers—

LINDA: [*Cutting* Happy *off, violently to* Biff] Don't you care whether he lives or dies?

HAPPY: [*Going to the stairs*] Come upstairs, Biff.

BIFF: [*With a flare of disgust, to* Happy] Go away from me! [*To* Linda] What do you mean, lives or dies? Nobody's dying around here, pal.

LINDA: Get out of my sight! Get out of here!

BIFF: I wanna see the boss.

LINDA: You're not going near him!

BIFF: Where is he? [*He moves into the living-room and* Linda *follows*]

LINDA: [*Shouting after* Biff] You invite him for dinner. He looks forward to it all day—[Biff *appears in his parents' bedroom, looks around, and exits*]—and then you desert him there. There's no stranger you'd do that to!

HAPPY: Why? He had a swell time with us. Listen, when I—[Linda *comes back into the kitchen*]—desert him I hope I don't outlive the day!

LINDA: Get out of here!

HAPPY: Now look, Mom . . .

LINDA: Did you have to go to women tonight? You and your lousy rotten whores!

[Biff *re-enters the kitchen*]

HAPPY: Mom, all we did was follow Biff around trying to cheer him up! [*To* Biff] Boy, what a night you gave me!

LINDA: Get out of here, both of you, and don't come back! I don't want you tormenting him any more. Go on now, get your things together! [*To* Biff] You can sleep in his apartment. [*She starts to pick up the flowers and stops herself*] Pick up this stuff, I'm not your maid any more. Pick it up, you bum, you!

[Happy *turns his back to her in refusal.* Biff *slowly moves over and gets down on his knees, picking up the flowers*]

LINDA: You're a pair of animals! Not one, not another living soul would have had the cruelty to walk out on that man in a restaurant!

BIFF: [*Not looking at her*] Is that what he said?

LINDA: He didn't have to say anything. He was so humiliated he nearly limped when he came in.

HAPPY: But, Mom, he had a great time with us—

BIFF: [*Cutting him off violently*] Shut up!

[*Without another word,* Happy *goes upstairs*]

LINDA: You! You didn't even go in to see if he was all right!

BIFF: [*Still on the floor in front of* Linda, *the flowers in his hand, with self-loathing*] No. Didn't. Didn't do a damned thing. How do you like that, heh? Left him babbling in a toilet.

LINDA: You louse. You . . .

BIFF: Now you hit it on the nose! [*He gets up, throws the flowers in the wastebasket*] The scum of the earth, and you're looking at him!

LINDA: Get out of here!

BIFF: I gotta talk to the boss, Mom. Where is he?

LINDA: You're not going near him. Get out of this house!

BIFF: [*With absolute assurance, determination*] No. We're gonna have an abrupt conversation, him and me.

LINDA: You're not talking to him!

[*Hammering is heard from outside the house, off right. Biff turns toward the noise*]

LINDA: [*Suddenly pleading*] Will you please leave him alone?

BIFF: What's he doing out there?

LINDA: He's planting the garden!

BIFF: [*Quietly*] Now? Oh, my God!

[Biff *moves outside, Linda following. The light dies down on them and comes up on the center of the apron as* Willy *walks into it. He is carrying a flashlight, a hoe, and a handful of seed packets. He raps the top of the hoe sharply to fix it firmly, and then moves to the left, measuring off the distance with his foot. He holds the flashlight to look at the seed packets, reading off the instructions. He is in the blue of night*]

WILLY: Carrots . . . quarter-inch apart. Rows . . . one-foot rows. [*He measures it off*] One foot. [*He puts down a package and measures off*] Beets. [*He puts down another package and measures again*] Lettuce. [*He reads the package, puts it down*] One foot— [*He breaks off as* Ben *appears at the right and moves slowly down to him*] What a proposition, ts, ts. Terrific, terrific. 'Cause she's suffered, Ben, the woman has suffered. You understand me? A man can't go out the way he came in, Ben, a man has got to add up to something. You can't, you can't— [Ben *moves toward him as though to interrupt*] You gotta consider, now. Don't answer so quick. Remember, it's a guaranteed twenty-thousand dollar proposition. Now look, Ben, I want you to go through the ins and outs of this thing with me. I've got nobody to talk to, Ben, and the woman has suffered, you hear me?

BEN: [*Standing still, considering*] What's the proposition?

WILLY: It's twenty thousand dollars on the barrelhead. Guaranteed, gilt-edged, you understand?

BEN: You don't want to make a fool of yourself. They might not honor the policy.

WILLY: How can they dare refuse? Didn't I work like a coolie to meet every premium on the nose? And now they don't pay off? Impossible!

BEN: It's called a cowardly thing, William.

WILLY: Why? Does it take more guts to stand here the rest of my life ringing up a zero?

BEN: [*Yielding*] That's a point, William. [*He moves, thinking, turns*] And twenty thousand—that *is* something one can feel with the hand, it is there.

WILLY: [*Now assured, with rising power*] Oh, Ben, that's the whole beauty of it! I see it like a diamond,

shining in the dark, hard and rough, that I can pick up and touch in my hand. Not like—like an appointment! This would not be another damned-fool appointment, Ben, and it changes all the aspects. Because he thinks I'm nothing, see, and so he spites me. But the funeral— [*Straightening up*] Ben, that funeral will be massive! They'll come from Maine, Massachusetts, Vermont, New Hampshire! All the old-timers with the strange license plates—that boy will be thunder-struck, Ben, because he never realized—I am known! Rhode Island, New York, New Jersey—I am known, Ben, and he'll see it with his eyes once and for all. He'll see what I am, Ben! He's in for a shock, that boy!

BEN: [*Coming down to the edge of the garden*] He'll call you a coward.

WILLY: [*Suddenly fearful*] No, that would be terrible.

BEN: Yes. And a damned fool.

WILLY: No, no, he mustn't, I won't have that! [*He is broken and desperate*]

BEN: He'll hate you, William.

[*The gay music of the* Boys *is heard*]

WILLY: Oh, Ben, how do we get back to all the great times? Used to be so full of light, and comradeship, the sleigh-riding in winter, and the ruddiness on his cheeks. And always some kind of good news coming up, always something nice coming up ahead. And never even let me carry the valises in the house, and simonizing, simonizing that little red car! Why, why can't I give him something and not have him hate me?

BEN: Let me think about it. [*He glances at his watch*] I still have a little time. Remarkable proposition, but you've got to be sure you're not making a fool of yourself.

[Ben *drifts off upstage and goes out of sight.* Biff *comes down from the left*]

WILLY: [*Suddenly conscious of* Biff, *turns and looks up at him, then begins picking up the packages of seeds in confusion*] Where the hell is that seed? [*Indignantly*] You can't see nothing out here! They boxed in the whole goddam neighborhood!

BIFF: There are people all around here. Don't you realize that?

WILLY: I'm busy. Don't bother me.

BIFF: [*Taking the hoe from* Willy] I'm saying good-by to you, Pop. [Willy *looks at him, silent, unable to move*] I'm not coming back any more.

WILLY: You're not going to see Oliver tomorrow?

BIFF: I've got no appointment, Dad.

WILLY: He put his arm around you, and you've got no appointment?

BIFF: Pop, get this now, will you? Everytime I've left it's been a fight that sent me out of here. Today I realized something about myself and I tried to explain it to you and I—I think I'm just not smart enough to make any sense out of it for you. To hell with whose fault it is or anything like that. [*He takes*

Willy's *arm*] Let's just wrap it up, heh? Come on in, we'll tell Mom. [*He gently tries to pull* Willy *to left*]

WILLY: [*Frozen, immobile, with guilt in his voice*] No, I don't want to see her.

BIFF: Come on! [*He pulls again, and* Willy *tries to pull away*]

WILLY: [*Highly nervous*] No, no, I don't want to see her.

BIFF: [*Tries to look into* Willy's *face, as if to find the answer there*] Why don't you want to see her?

WILLY: [*More harshly now*] Don't bother me, will you?

BIFF: What do you mean, you don't want to see her? You don't want them calling you yellow, do you? This isn't your fault; it's me, I'm a bum. Now come inside! [Willy *strains to get away*] Did you hear what I said to you?

[Willy *pulls away and quickly goes by himself into the house.* Biff *follows*]

LINDA: [*To* Willy] Did you plant, dear?

BIFF: [*At the door, to* Linda] All right, we had it out. I'm going and I'm not writing any more.

LINDA: [*Going to* Willy *in the kitchen*] I think that's the best way, dear. 'Cause there's no use drawing it out, you'll just never get along.

[Willy *doesn't respond*]

BIFF: People ask where I am and what I'm doing, you don't know, and you don't care. That way it'll be off your mind and you can start brightening up again. All right? That clears it, doesn't it? [Willy *is silent, and* Biff *goes to him*] You gonna wish me luck, scout? [*He extends his hand*] What do you say?

LINDA: Shake his hand, Willy.

WILLY: [*Turning to her, seething with hurt*] There's no necessity to mention the pen at all, y'know.

BIFF: [*Gently*] I've got no appointment, Dad.

WILLY: [*Erupting fiercely*] He put his arm around . . . ?

BIFF: Dad, you're never going to see what I am, so what's the use of arguing? If I strike oil I'll send you a check. Meantime forget I'm alive.

WILLY: [*To* Linda] Spite, see?

BIFF: Shake hands, Dad.

WILLY: Not my hand.

BIFF: I was hoping not to go this way.

WILLY: Well, this is the way you're going. Goodby.

[Biff *looks at him a moment, then turns sharply and goes to the stairs*]

WILLY: [*Stops him with*] May you rot in hell if you leave this house!

BIFF: [*Turning*] Exactly what is it that you want from me?

WILLY: I want you to know, on the train, in the mountains, in the valleys, wherever you go, that you cut down your life for spite!

BIFF: No, no.

WILLY: Spite, spite, is the word of your undoing!

And when you're down and out, remember what did it. When you're rotting somewhere beside the railroad tracks, remember, and don't you dare blame it on me!

BIFF: I'm not blaming it on you!

WILLY: I won't take the rap for this, you hear?

[Happy *comes down the stairs and stands on the bottom step, watching*]

BIFF: That's just what I'm telling you!

WILLY: [*Sinking into a chair at the table, with full accusation*] You're trying to put a knife in me—don't think I don't know what you're doing!

BIFF: All right, phony! Then let's lay it on the line. [*He whips the rubber tube out of his pocket and puts it on the table*]

HAPPY: You crazy—

LINDA: Biff! [*She moves to grab the hose, but* Biff *holds it down with his hand*]

BIFF: Leave it there! Don't move it!

WILLY: [*Not looking at it*] What is that?

BIFF: You know goddam well what that is.

WILLY: [*Caged, wanting to escape*] I never saw that.

BIFF: You saw it. The mice didn't bring it into the cellar! What is this supposed to do, make a hero out of you? This supposed to make me sorry for you?

WILLY: Never heard of it.

BIFF: There'll be no pity for you, you hear it? No pity!

WILLY: [*To* Linda] You hear the spite!

BIFF: No, you're going to hear the truth—what you are and what I am!

LINDA: Stop it!

WILLY: Spite!

HAPPY: [*Coming down toward* Biff] You cut it now!

BIFF: [*To* Happy] The man don't know who we are! The man is gonna know! [*To* Willy] We never told the truth for ten minutes in this house!

HAPPY: We always told the truth!

BIFF: [*Turning on him*] You big blow, are you the assistant buyer? You're one of the two assistants to the assistant, aren't you?

HAPPY: Well, I'm practically—

BIFF: You're practically full of it! We all are! And I'm through with it. [*To* Willy] Now hear this, Willy, this is me.

WILLY: I know you!

BIFF: You know why I had no address for three months? I stole a suit in Kansas City and I was in jail. [*To* Linda, *who is sobbing*] Stop crying. I'm through with it.

[Linda *turns away from them, her hands covering her face*]

WILLY: I suppose that's my fault!

BIFF: I stole myself out of every good job since high school!

WILLY: And whose fault is that?

BIFF: And I never got anywhere because you blew

me so full of hot air I could never stand taking orders from anybody! That's whose fault it is!

WILLY: I hear that!

LINDA: Don't, Biff!

BIFF: It's goddam time you heard that! I had to be boss big shot in two weeks, and I'm through with it!

WILLY: Then hang yourself! For spite, hang yourself!

BIFF: No! Nobody's hanging himself, Willy! I ran down eleven flights with a pen in my hand today. And suddenly I stopped, you hear me? And in the middle of that office building, do you hear me? I stopped in the middle of that building and I saw—the sky. I saw the things that I love in this world. The work and the food and time to sit and smoke. And I looked at the pen and said to myself, what the hell am I grabbing this for? Why am I trying to become what I don't want to be? What am I doing in an office, making a contemptuous, begging fool of myself, when all I want is out there, waiting for me the minute I say I know who I am! Why can't I say that, Willy? [*He tries to make* Willy *face him, but* Willy *pulls away and moves to the left*]

WILLY: [*With hatred, threateningly*] The door of your life is wide open!

BIFF: Pop! I'm a dime a dozen, and so are you!

WILLY: [*Turning on him now in an uncontrolled outburst*] I am not a dime a dozen! I am Willy Loman, and you are Biff Loman!

[Biff *starts for* Willy, *but is blocked by* Happy. *In his fury,* Biff *seems on the verge of attacking his father*]

BIFF: I am not a leader of men, Willy, and neither are you. You were never anything but a hard-working drummer who landed in the ash can like all the rest of them! I'm one dollar an hour, Willy! I tried seven states and couldn't raise it. A buck an hour! Do you gather my meaning! I'm not bringing home any prizes any more, and you're going to stop waiting for me to bring them home!

WILLY: [*Directly to* Biff] You vengeful, spiteful mut!

[Biff *breaks from* Happy. Willy, *in fright, starts up the stairs.* Biff *grabs him*]

BIFF: [*At the peak of his fury*] Pop, I'm nothing! I'm nothing, Pop. Can't you understand that? There's no spite in it any more. I'm just what I am, that's all.

[Biff's *fury has spent itself, and he breaks down, sobbing, holding on to* Willy, *who dumbly fumbles for* Biff's *face*]

WILLY: [*Astonished*] What're you doing? What're you doing? [*To* Linda] Why is he crying?

BIFF: [*Crying, broken*] Will you let me go, for Christ's sake? Will you take that phony dream and burn it before something happens? [*Struggling to contain himself, he pulls away and moves to the stairs*] I'll go in the morning. Put him—put him to bed. [*Exhausted,* Biff *moves up the stairs to his room*]

WILLY: [*After a long pause, astonished, elevated*] Isn't that—isn't that remarkable? Biff—he likes me!

LINDA: He loves you, Willy!

HAPPY: [*Deeply moved*] Always did, Pop.

WILLY: Oh, Biff! [*Staring wildly*] He cried! Cried to me. [*He is choking with his love, and now cries out his promise*] That boy—that boy is going to be magnificent!

[Ben *appears in the light just outside the kitchen*]

BEN: Yes, outstanding, with twenty thousand behind him.

LINDA: [*Sensing the racing of his mind, fearfully, carefully*] Now come to bed, Willy. It's all settled now.

WILLY: [*Finding it difficult not to rush out of the house*] Yes, we'll sleep. Come on. Go to sleep, Hap.

BEN: And it does take a great kind of a man to crack the jungle.

[*In accents of dread,* Ben's *idyllic music starts up*]

HAPPY: [*His arm around* Linda] I'm getting married, Pop, don't forget it. I'm changing everything. I'm gonna run that department before the year is up. You'll see, Mom. [*He kisses her*]

BEN: The jungle is dark but full of diamonds, Willy.

[Willy *turns, moves, listening to* Ben]

LINDA: Be good. You're both good boys, just act that way, that's all.

HAPPY: 'Night, Pop. [*He goes upstairs*]

LINDA: [*To* Willy] Come, dear.

BEN: [*With greater force*] One must go in to fetch a diamond out.

WILLY: [*To* Linda, *as he moves slowly along the edge of the kitchen, toward the door*] I just want to get settled down, Linda. Let me sit alone for a little.

LINDA: [*Almost uttering her fear*] I want you upstairs.

WILLY: [*Taking her in his arms*] In a few minutes, Linda. I couldn't sleep right now. Go on, you look awful tired. [*He kisses her*]

BEN: Not like an appointment at all. A diamond is rough and hard to the touch.

WILLY: Go on now. I'll be right up.

LINDA: I think this is the only way, Willy.

WILLY: Sure, it's the best thing.

BEN: Best thing!

WILLY: The only way. Everything is gonna be—go on, kid, get to bed. You look so tired.

LINDA: Come right up.

WILLY: Two minutes.

[Linda *goes into the living-room, then reappears in her bedroom.* Willy *moves just outside the kitchen door*]

WILLY: Loves me. [*Wonderingly*] Always loved me. Isn't that a remarkable thing? Ben, he'll worship me for it!

BEN: [*With promise*] It's dark there, but full of diamonds.

WILLY: Can you imagine that magnificence with twenty thousand dollars in his pocket?

LINDA: [*Calling from her room*] Willy! Come up!

WILLY: [*Calling into the kitchen*] Yes! Yes. Coming! It's very smart, you realize that, don't you, sweetheart? Even Ben sees it. I gotta go, baby. 'By! 'By! [*Going over to Ben, almost dancing*] Imagine? When the mail comes he'll be ahead of Bernard again!

BEN: A perfect proposition all around.

WILLY: Did you see how he cried to me? Oh, if I could kiss him, Ben!

BEN: Time, William, time!

WILLY: Oh, Ben, I always knew one way or another we were gonna make it, Biff and I!

BEN: [*Looking at his watch*] The boat. We'll be late. [*He moves slowly off into the darkness*]

WILLY: [*Elegiacally, turning to the house*] Now when you kick off, boy, I want a seventy-yard boot, and get right down the field under the ball, and when you hit, hit low and hit hard, because it's important, boy. [*He swings around and faces the audience*] There's all kinds of important people in the stands, and the first thing you know . . . [*Suddenly realizing he is alone*] Ben! Ben, where do I . . . ? [*He makes a sudden movement of search*] Ben, how do I . . . ?

LINDA: [*Calling*] Willy, you coming up?

WILLY: [*Uttering a gasp of fear, whirling about as if to quiet her*] Sh! [*He turns around as if to find his way; sounds, faces, voices, seem to be swarming in upon him and he flicks at them, crying*] Sh! Sh! [*Suddenly music, faint and high, stops him. It rises in intensity, almost to an unbearable scream. He goes up and down on his toes, and rushes off around the house*] Shhh!

LINDA: Willy?

[*There is no answer. Linda waits. Biff gets up off his bed. He is still in his clothes. Happy sits up. Biff stands listening*]

LINDA: [*With real fear*] Willy, answer me! Willy!

[*There is the sound of a car starting and moving away at full speed*]

LINDA: No!

BIFF: [*Rushing down the stairs*] Pop!

[*As the car speeds off, the music crashes down in a frenzy of sound, which becomes the soft pulsation of a single cello string. Biff slowly returns to his bedroom. He and Happy gravely don their jackets. Linda slowly walks out of her room. The music has developed into a dead march. The leaves of day are appearing over everything. Charley and Bernard, somberly dressed, appear and knock on the kitchen door. Biff and Happy slowly descend the stairs to the kitchen as Charley and Bernard enter. All stop a moment when Linda, in clothes of mourning, bearing a little bunch of roses, comes through the draped doorway into the kitchen. She goes to Charley and takes his arm. Now all move toward the audience, through the wall-line of the kitchen. At the limit of the apron, Linda lays down the flowers, kneels, and sits back on her heels. All stare down at the grave*]

REQUIEM

CHARLEY: It's getting dark, Linda.

[*Linda doesn't react. She stares at the grave*]

BIFF: How about it, Mom? Better get some rest, heh? They'll be closing the gate soon.

[*Linda makes no move. Pause*]

HAPPY: [*Deeply angered*] He had no right to do that. There was no necessity for it. We would've helped him.

CHARLEY: [*Grunting*] Hmmm.

BIFF: Come along, Mom.

LINDA: Why didn't anybody come?

CHARLEY: It was a very nice funeral.

LINDA: But where are all the people he knew? Maybe they blame him.

CHARLEY: Naa. It's a rough world, Linda. They wouldn't blame him.

LINDA: I can't understand it. At this time especially. First time in thirty-five years we were just about free and clear. He only needed a little salary. He was even finished with the dentist.

CHARLEY: No man only needs a little salary.

LINDA: I can't understand it.

BIFF: There were a lot of nice days. When he'd come home from a trip; or on Sundays, making the stoop; finishing the cellar; putting on the new porch; when he built the extra bathroom; and put up the garage. You know something, Charley, there's more of him in that front stoop than in all the sales he ever made.

CHARLEY: Yeah. He was a happy man with a batch of cement.

LINDA: He was so wonderful with his hands.

BIFF: He had the wrong dreams. All, all, wrong.

HAPPY: [*Almost ready to fight Biff*] Don't say that!

BIFF: He never knew who he was.

CHARLEY: [*Stopping Happy's movement and reply. To Biff*] Nobody dast blame this man. You don't understand: Willy was a salesman. And for a salesman, there is no rock bottom to the life. He don't put a bolt to a nut, he don't tell you the law or give you medicine. He's a man way out there in the blue, riding on a smile and a shoeshine. And when they start not smiling back—that's an earthquake. And then you get yourself a couple of spots on your hat, and you're finished. Nobody dast blame this man. A salesman is got to dream, boy. It comes with the territory.

BIFF: Charley, the man didn't know who he was.

HAPPY: [*Infuriated*] Don't say that!

BIFF: Why don't you come with me, Happy?

HAPPY: I'm not licked that easily. I'm staying right in this city, and I'm gonna beat this racket! [*He looks at* Biff, *his chin set*] The Loman Brothers!

BIFF: I know who I am, kid.

HAPPY: All right, boy. I'm gonna show you and everybody else that Willy Loman did not die in vain. He had a good dream. It's the only dream you can have—to come out number-one man. He fought it out here, and this is where I'm gonna win it for him.

BIFF: [*With a hopeless glance at* Happy, *bends toward his mother*] Let's go, Mom.

LINDA: I'll be with you in a minute. Go on, Charley. [*He hesitates*] I want to, just for a minute. I never had a chance to say good-by.

[Charley *moves away, followed by* Happy. Biff *remains a slight distance up and left of* Linda. *She sits there, summoning herself. The flute begins, not far away, playing behind her speech*]

LINDA: Forgive me, dear. I can't cry. I don't know what it is, but I can't cry. I don't understand it. Why did you ever do that? Help me, Willy, I can't cry. It seems to me that you're just on another trip. I keep expecting you. Willy, dear. I can't cry. Why did you do it? I search and search and I search, and I can't understand it, Willy. I made the last payment on the house today. Today, dear. And there'll be nobody home. [*A sob rises in her throat*] We're free and clear. [*Sobbing more fully, released*] We're free. [Biff *comes slowly toward her*] We're free . . . We're free . . .

[Biff *lifts her to her feet and moves out up right with her in his arms.* Linda *sobs quietly.* Bernard *and* Charley *come together and follow them, followed by* Happy. *Only the music of the flute is left on the darkening stage as over the house the hard towers of the apartment buildings rise into sharp focus, and*

THE CURTAIN FALLS]

A REPRESENTATIVE LIST OF MODERN PLAYS

The following appendix is intended to supplement this anthology with a selected list of historically important plays. Many of these titles have already been mentioned or discussed in the introductions, but they are repeated here for the convenience of the reader. The editor makes no claim of completeness for this list. The informed reader, the student, and his instructor will undoubtedly want to add their own preferences. The starting date for this volume of *A Treasury of the Theatre* is more or less arbitrarily taken to be 1875. The forerunners of the modern playwrights are represented in the first two volumes of the anthology.

ENGLISH DRAMA

OSCAR WILDE: *Lady Windermere's Fan* (1892). The first notable English comedy after Sheridan's *School for Scandal*. Combines comedy of manners with problem drama and the fallen-woman theme of early realism.

The Importance of Being Earnest (1895). See page 512.

BRANDON THOMAS: *Charley's Aunt* (1892). The best of the late Victorian farces. Revolves around an Oxford undergraduate's impersonation of a classmate's unknown aunt from Brazil, "where the nuts come from."

ARTHUR WING PINERO: *The Second Mrs. Tanqueray* (1893). Important as one of the earliest realistic problem plays of the English stage. Deals with a fallen woman's struggle for respectability.

The Thunderbolt (1908). A comedy exposing middle-class cupidity and hypocrisy. Revolves around the conventional device of a destroyed will.

Mid-Channel (1909). A realistic study of a wrecked marriage.

HENRY ARTHUR JONES: *Michael and His Lost Angel* (1896). An early example of social tragedy, dealing with a clergyman's illicit passion and struggle with conscience.

The Liars (1897). A comedy of manners. Shows the author at his best.

GEORGE BERNARD SHAW: *Widowers' Houses* (1892). The first of Shaw's social satires.

Mrs. Warren's Profession (1902; written in 1893; published in 1898). An onslaught on complacent respectability, an analysis of the economic sources of prostitution, and a backhanded slap at the profit system.

Arms and the Man (1894). Shaw's spoof on romanticism and military vainglory.

Candida (1897; published in 1898). See page 538.

Caesar and Cleopatra (1899; published in 1900). Shaw's first antiromantic treatment of a historical subject; a character study of a Shavian "superman."

Man and Superman (1905; published in 1903). An antiromantic treatment of the problem of sex; emphasizes the role of the "Life Force" and maintains that woman, not man, is the pursuer.

John Bull's Other Island (1903). Shaw's only play about the Irish question, later produced by the Abbey Theatre. A satirical inversion of Irish and English national characteristics.

Major Barbara (1905). An attack on conventional philanthropy and meliorism, a challenge to the social system which makes charity necessary, and a comedy which presents a munitions magnate as more beneficial to society than conventional philanthropists and reformers.

The Doctor's Dilemma (1906). A satire on medicine and medical ethics, but also an investigation of the relative value of the artist and the commonplace man to society, with a memorable characterization of the man whose integrity is confined to his art.

Getting Married (1908). Shaw's discussion piece on marriage. Technically interesting as a play without a plot.

Androcles and the Lion (1912). A Shavian treatment of martyrdom and of nascent Christianity in the Roman Empire.

Pygmalion (1912; produced in English in 1914; screen version in 1938). A comedy on the superficiality of class distinctions.

Heartbreak House (1920; written in 1913–1916). A comedy of social disintegration, written rather broadly in the manner of Chekhov, concerning upper-class decadence during the First World War.

Back to Methuselah (1922). An oversized philosophical comedy concerning the importance of longevity as a factor in human progress. Contends that only a life counted in centuries rather than in decades can make human beings wise enough to order society rationally.

Saint Joan (1923). A sympathetic treatment of Joan of Arc as a superior person in advance of her times—an instinctive Protestant before the Protestant Reformation and a nationalist before feudalism made way for progressive nationalism.

The Apple Cart (1929). A political comedy about the problems of governing England—where the Labour party may be voted into office but the corporations still rule the nation—and the efforts of a benevolent monarch to govern better than the cabinet.

Too True to Be Good (1932). An extravaganza on the collapse of European society on the eve of Hitler's National Socialist revolution.

On the Rocks (1933). A political comedy about the failure of the British government to cope with economic problems and the failure of a well-intentioned statesman to take the ship of state "off the rocks."

In Good King Charles's Golden Days (1939). Shaw's discursive comedy about Charles II's political acumen and Newton's genius.

C. HADDON CHAMBERS: *The Tyranny of Tears* (1899). A Pinero-Jones type of comedy of character, showing how a husband may be dominated by his wife through sentiment.

JAMES M. BARRIE: *The Admirable Crichton* (1903). See page 566.

Peter Pan (1904). The fantasy play of childhood which best exemplifies Barrie's whimsy and charm. The outstanding fantastic play of the modern English stage.

What Every Woman Knows (1908). A shrewd treatment of marriage, in which a wife promotes her husband's career without his realizing it.

The Twelve-Pound Look (1910). Barrie's famous one-act comedy about a successful stuffed shirt who is deflated by his former wife, who left him and became a typist because he bored her.

HARLEY GRANVILLE-BARKER: *The Voysey Inheritance* (1905). A comedy of business practices and social responsibility, written in the Shavian manner.

Waste (1907). A drama about the deplorable waste of personal talent and loss to society caused by a scandalous romance.

The Madras House (1910). A disquisition on the problem of sexuality in the modern world; a unique drama of ideas. Shows Shaw's influence.

ST. JOHN HANKIN: *The Cassilis Engagement* (1907). A comedy about a clever mother's successful elimination of her son's unsuitable fiancée.

The Last of the De Mullins (1908). A treatment of the problem of the emancipation of woman. Reflects the influence of Ibsen.

JOHN MASEFIELD: *The Tragedy of Nan* (1908). A powerful peasant tragedy, remarkable for its picture of human bestiality and pathos. Deals with the persecution of a girl whose father was unjustly hanged for sheepstealing.

ELIZABETH BAKER: *Chains* (1909). A drama of humdrum suburban life and of the failure of a man to win his freedom when his wife is with child.

STANLEY HOUGHTON: *Hindle Wakes* (1912). An Ibsensite comedy about the double standard. A poor girl refuses to let a rich weakling make a respectable woman of her by marrying her at the insistence of a righteous father.

GITHA SOWERBY: *Rutherford and Son* (1912). A grim drama of conflict in the home of a righteous and unbending industrialist.

JOHN GALSWORTHY: *The Silver Box* (1906). A drama of social inequality and injustice.

Strife (1909). A treatment of the clash between labor and capital; the first notable British play about a strike.

Justice (1910). A drama of legal injustice. Deals with a weakling's misfortunes in the grip of circumstances and the law.

The Pigeon (1912). An ironic comedy about the problem of society's misfits and about the complications of philanthropy.

Loyalties (1922). A drama of class loyalties and racial prejudice, in which a thieving "gentleman" is supported by members of good society, with disastrous results.

Escape (1926). See page 597.

W. SOMERSET MAUGHAM: *Our Betters* (1917). A satire on snobbishness; especially caustic in its picture of socially aspiring Americans in England.

The Circle (1921). See page 665.

The Constant Wife (1923). A comedy about the double standard and its elimination by a woman who wins economic independence and therefore moral freedom after her husband's infidelity.

For Services Rendered (1932). A grim picture of the effect of war on an English family.

JOHN DRINKWATER: *Abraham Lincoln* (1918). A poetic chronicle play about Lincoln during the Civil War.

CLEMENCE DANE: *A Bill of Divorcement* (1921). A moving drama of postwar misery. Deals with a shell-shocked veteran, his divorced wife, and their daughter.

Come of Age (1934). A poetic drama in which the tragedy of the eighteenth-century poet Thomas Chatterton is translated into modern terms.

C. K. MUNRO: *At Mrs. Beam's* (1921). A comedy of London boarding-house life.

A. A. MILNE: *The Truth About Blayds* (1922). A satiric comedy about a literary charlatan and his family's readiness to profit by his dishonesty.

SUTTON VANE: *Outward Bound* (1923). A drama revolving around death and the afterlife. Notable for restrained fantasy and sympathy.

NOEL COWARD: *The Vortex* (1923). A study of a mother and son suffering defeat through character disintegration in postwar society.

Private Lives (1930). Coward's ultrasophisticated farce about an exchange of husbands and wives.

Fumed Oak (1935). A one-act comedy about the revolt of a middle-class Englishman against his unbearable family.

Blithe Spirit (1941). See page 730.

ASHLEY DUKES: *The Man with a Load of Mischief* (1924). A poetic fantasy play set in England during the French Revolution, satirizing aristocratic arrogance and championing the common man.

JOHN VAN DRUTEN: *Young Woodley* (1925). A drama of public-school (that is, private-school) life and adolescence in England.

ROBERT NICHOLS and MAURICE BROWNE: *Wings over Europe* (1928). The first atom-bomb play, revolving around the conflict between war-making statesmanship and humanitarian science, with the proponents of the latter attempting to force governments to renounce war.

R. C. SHERRIFF: *Journey's End* (1929). See page 693.

RUDOLPH BESIER: *The Barretts of Wimpole Street* (1931). The biographical romance of Elizabeth and Robert Browning; presented with psychological overtones.

DODIE SMITH: *Autumn Crocus* (1931). A romantic comedy revolving around the thawing out of an English schoolteacher on vacation in Switzerland.

Call It a Day (1935). A genteel comedy of an English family and its confusions on a more or less typical day.

BENN W. LEVY: *Springtime for Henry* (1931). A farce about the attempted reformation of a clever scapegrace.

MORDAUNT SHAIRP: *The Green Bay Tree* (1932). An incisive treatment of sybaritism and sexual inversion from a Freudian standpoint.

JAMES BRIDIE: *Tobias and the Angel* (1932). A biblical comedy, written with canny Scottish humor and wisdom.

A Sleeping Clergyman (1933). An anti-eugenics chronicle showing how humanity would have been cheated by a narrow and obtuse application of eugenics.

J. B. PRIESTLEY: *Dangerous Corner* (1932). An original psychological melodrama.

Laburnum Grove (1933). A comedy of middle-class suburban life.

An Inspector Calls (1946). A morality play on the subject of social responsibility, in which members of the upper class are exposed as callous and irresponsible.

RONALD GOW and WALTER GREENWOOD: *Love on the Dole* (1935). A study of the British depression of the nineteen-thirties,

LAURENCE HOUSMAN: *Victoria Regina* (1935). A biographical chronicle of Queen Victoria, compounded of a number of Housman's one-act plays. Perhaps chiefly memorable for Helen Hayes's impersonation of the Queen in the New York production.

PATRICK HAMILTON: *Gaslight* (1938) (*Angel Street* in the American production, 1941). A superior melodrama, dealing with a husband's effort to remove his wife by driving her insane.

EMLYN WILLIAMS: *The Corn Is Green* (1938). A drama of the Welsh mining districts. Revolves around the education of a miner's son by a resolutely idealistic woman.

TERENCE RATTIGAN: *The Winslow Boy* (1945). A dramatization of the famous old Archer-Shee case. Justice is secured for an inconsequential victim of officialdom—a tribute to England's regard for civil liberties.

W. H. AUDEN and CHRISTOPHER ISHERWOOD: *The Dog Beneath the Skin* (1935). A satirical, poetic revue on the deterioration of Europe and the collapse of society. Critical of capitalism and fascism.

The Ascent of F 6 (1936). A poetic indictment of British imperialism, profit-seeking exploitation, and the sentimentality of the easily deluded common people, presented in the story of the exploration of a mountain.

T. S. ELIOT: *Murder in the Cathedral* (1935). Eliot's poetic, liturgical drama of the martyrdom of St. Thomas à Becket; a treatment of the conflict between church and state and between spiritual and worldly values.

The Cocktail Party (1949; first commercial production in 1950 in America). A verse drama of spiritual failure and redemption largely in terms of British comedy of manners (but with mystical touches). An essentially shallow couple is brought back together by a "psychiatrist" by being faced with the truth about their shallowness, and a girl with deeper capacity for love is directed into social service and eventual martyrdom.

DOROTHY L. SAYERS: *The Zeal of Thy House* (1937). A poetic religious drama on the building of a cathedral by a famous medieval architect who learns to mediate between his ego and his faith.

ROBERT MORLEY and NOEL LANGLEY: *Edward, My Son* (1947). A theatrically ingenious chronicle of an egotist whose career of ruthlessness begins with his desire to cure his son of a limp.

CHRISTOPHER FRY: *The Lady's Not for Burning* (1948). A poetic comedy in which a soldier saves a woman from being burned as a witch in medieval England by diverting suspicion to himself as a murderer.

IRISH DRAMA

WILLIAM BUTLER YEATS: *Kathleen ni Houlihan* (1902). A symbolic patriotic drama in which an old woman (Ireland) claims a young man's devotion and turns out to be beautiful and have "the walk of a Queen" when he follows her. With *The Countess Cathleen* (1892), *The Land of Heart's Desire* (1894), and *The Shadowy Waters* (1900), representative of Yeats's early dramatic work.

Four Plays for Dancers (1920). Short poetic treatments of Irish legend in the style of Japanese Noh drama. Remarkable for their extreme concentration and poetic power.

EDWARD MARTYN: *The Heather-Field* (1899). An Ibsenite semisymbolist drama of a land-owner's effort to reclaim a wind-swept heather field for use as pasture land. Symbolic of Ireland's struggle.

JOHN MILLINGTON SYNGE: *In the Shadow of the*

Glen (1903). A one-act play dealing with the revolt of a frustrated young wife and her departure from her home in the company of a carefree tramp.

Riders to the Sea (1904). See page 626.

The Well of the Saints (1905). A drama of disenchantment and dissatisfaction with reality, in which two beggars, cured of blindness by a miracle-working saint, are glad to become blind again.

The Tinker's Wedding (published in 1909). A robust farce of Irish tramp life.

The Playboy of the Western World (1907). A comedy of Irish peasantry. Concerns the misadventures of a youth who thinks he slew his father, is lionized in the remote village to which he flees, and is ultimately disenchanted. Synge's most important full-length play.

Deirdre of the Sorrows (1910). A poetic love tragedy based on Irish legend.

LADY GREGORY: *Hyacinth Halvey* (1906). A long one-act farce dealing with the burdens of an unearned reputation and the effort of a youth to divest himself of it.

The Gaol Gate (1906). A one-act tragedy of a patriot's execution for refusing to betray his neighbors to the police.

The Workhouse Ward (1908). See page 620.

PADRAIC COLUM: *The Fiddler's House* (1907). A drama about the restlessness of a natural-born fiddler and the struggle to keep him tethered to his farm.

The Land (1905). A treatment of the conflict between the old generation, which tries to make the best of the impoverished land, and the younger generation, which wants to leave home and find a new way of life.

T. C. MURRAY: *Maurice Hart* (1912). A realistic drama of peasant family life and of a favorite son's difficulty in accepting the call to the priesthood, for which the family prepares him at great sacrifice.

Autumn Fire (1924). A somber drama of a young man's passion for his father's second wife. May be compared with O'Neill's *Desire Under the Elms*.

ST. JOHN ERVINE: *Jane Clegg* (1913). A realistic drama of a woman's marriage to a weakling and struggle to make a decent life for her family against heavy odds.

John Ferguson (1915). A tragedy of middle-class Protestant life in Ulster. Revolves around the strong character of an upright, religious man.

The First Mrs. Frazer (1928). A high comedy in which a man gets rid of an unfaithful second wife with the help of his sensible and clever first wife.

LENNOX ROBINSON: *The White-headed Boy* (1916). A light comedy about a high-spirited Irish lad whose family makes many sacrifices for him, while he seemingly behaves with great indiscretion. It is finally discovered that he is married to the girl he was believed to be seducing.

The Far-off Hills (1928). A comedy revolving around a domineering elder daughter who manages her father's life until he escapes her ministrations by remarrying. She marries a "go-getting" young man who will provide fresh opportunities for her to manage affairs.

SEAN O'CASEY: *The Shadow of a Gunman* (1923). A tragedy of Irish political strife and a bitter excoriation of pseudo patriotism.

Juno and the Paycock (1924). A drama of Irish life, part comedy and part tragedy. Revolves around the confused and unhappy family of a boastful idler who intoxicates himself with drink and windy words while his daughter is betrayed, his son is executed by Irish patriots for treachery to their cause, and his wife, Juno, struggles in vain to keep the impoverished family intact.

The Plough and the Stars (1926). See page 633.

The Silver Tassie (1929; written in 1927). A half-realistic, half-expressionistic antiwar drama.

Within the Gates (1933). A poetic and symbolic play laid in Hyde Park. Constitutes an allegory on modern life and a protest of the "down-and-outers" against the privileged classes.

The Purple Dust (1940). An exuberant satire on Englishmen in Ireland.

The Star Turns Red (1940). A poetic drama of class conflict in Ireland.

Red Roses for Me (1943). A poetic strike drama, half realistic and half symbolic.

GEORGE SHIELS: *The New Gossoon* (1930). A peasant comedy about a young wastrel and a roguish poacher who is an Irish Autolycus.

DENIS JOHNSTON: *The Old Lady Says 'No'* (1929). An expressionistic play about the tawdriness of Irish society and the contrast between what Ireland has become and the ideals represented by Robert Emmet. Presented as the delirium of an actor who is knocked unconscious while acting the role of Emmet.

The Moon in the Yellow River (1931). A Chekhovian drama of Irish life, of ignorant and bumbling conservatism, of failure to improve conditions in Ireland, and of an intelligent, sensitive man who succumbs to depression and nihilism.

PAUL VINCENT CARROLL: *Shadow and Substance* (1934). A tragedy of the conflict between cold, formal faith and simple Christianity. Notable for its characterization of an intellectual priest.

The White Steed (1938). A social comedy concerning the political ambitions of an Irish priest and the effects of intolerance and vigilantism, which are opposed by another clerical character, a lovable old priest.

AMERICAN DRAMA

JAMES A. HERNE: *Margaret Fleming* (1890). The first American realistic drama; revolves around a husband's infidelity and his wife's understanding attitude.

CLYDE FITCH: *The Climbers* (1901). A satire on social climbing.

The Truth (1907). A high comedy revolving around a woman's chronic prevarications.

The City (1910). An exposure of a respectable career as founded on corruption. Watered-down social criticism by comparison with Ibsen's work (*Pillars of Society, An Enemy of the People*), but marks an advance in American comedy.

WILLIAM VAUGHN MOODY: *The Great Divide* (1906). A realistic drama in which a woman overcomes her conventional training and loves the rough man who forced her to marry him.

AUGUSTUS THOMAS: *The Witching Hour* (1907). A primitive attempt to inject "ideas" into American drama by dealing with the subject of mental telepathy.

EUGENE WALTER: *The Easiest Way* (1908). A realistic portrait of a rich man's mistress who falls in love with a reporter but fails to redeem herself.

PERCY MACKAYE: *The Scarecrow* (1908). A fantastic play about witchcraft in New England.

This Fine-Pretty World (1924). A folk play of native types and dialect in the Kentucky mountains.

EDWARD SHELDON: *The Nigger* (1910). An early study of the Negro problem.

GEORGE C. HAZELTON and J. HARRY BENRIMO: *The Yellow Jacket* (1912). A comedy written in the style of Chinese drama; marked by whimsical humor and technical ingenuity.

EUGENE O'NEILL: *The Long Voyage Home* (1917). A realistic one-acter about the fate of a Swedish sailor who is shanghaied in spite of his resolve to stay sober and return to his homeland.

The Moon of the Caribbees (1918). A notable atmospheric one-act sea play filled with a sense of defeat and fate. An early example of O'Neill's poetic naturalism.

Beyond the Horizon (1920). A realistic tragedy of frustration and defeat.

The Emperor Jones (1920). An expressionistic drama of fear and atavism in the jungle. A Negro dictator tries to flee from a revolt of the natives he has oppressed, but he is destroyed by his obsessive fantasies.

Anna Christie (1921). See page 786.

The Hairy Ape (1922). See page 817.

Desire Under the Elms (1924). A tragedy of life on the soil. Revolves around a son's passion for his father's second wife.

Marco Millions (1927). A social satire exposing the materialism and narrow-mindedness of a Babbitt of Western civilization (Marco Polo), who is impervious to romantic love and ancient Chinese culture.

Strange Interlude (1928). The psychological drama of a woman who finds fulfillment of her multifaceted love in three men who for her supplement one another. A play in nine acts, notable for its use of stream-of-consciousness monologues and asides.

Mourning Becomes Electra (1931). A modern variant of the classic Oresteian story, given a New England setting and treated as a tragedy of the Oedipus complex in psychoanalytical terms.

Ah, Wilderness! (1933). A nostalgic comedy of adolescence and of an understanding father at the beginning of the century.

The Iceman Cometh (1946; written in 1939). A tragedy dealing with men's need for illusions to make the failure of their lives endurable.

JOHN COLTON and CLEMENCE RANDOLPH: *Rain* (1922). A psychological melodrama of religious fanaticism, hypocrisy, and sexual repression. Revolves around the conflict between a missionary and a prostitute. Based on a short story, *Miss Thompson*, by W. Somerset Maugham.

OWEN DAVIS: *Icebound* (1923). A drama of New England frustration.

ELMER RICE: *The Adding Machine* (1923). An expressionistic treatment of the commonplaceness and mediocrity caused by the routinized life of the modern world.

Street Scene (1929). A tragedy of a woman driven into adultery by a dreary life. Notable for its realistic picture of tenement life.

The Left Bank (1931). A comedy of American expatriates in Paris who fail to appreciate America.

Counsellor-at-Law (1931). A character comedy of a successful lawyer with a poor Jewish background and of his conflict with snobbery.

JOHN HOWARD LAWSON: *Roger Bloomer* (1923). A satirical, expressionistic account of a young man's difficulties in a money-minded world and a clever exposure of that world.

Processional (1925). A humorous and imaginative "jazz symphony" of the confusions and conflicts of American life in the "jazz age"; presented through a vaudevillian but socially critical picture of a labor strike in a West Virginia town.

HATCHER HUGHES: *Hell-Bent fer Heaven* (1923). A drama of American mountaineer life, notable for its use of folk elements.

GEORGE KELLY: *The Show-Off* (1924). A satirical comedy of egotism and high-pressure salesmanship.

Craig's Wife (1925). A character study of a middle-class woman who substitutes possessiveness and homemaking for love and ultimately exposes her selfishness to her long-suffering husband.

The Deep Mrs. Sykes (1945). A comedy of a self-centered woman who relies on intuitions that always fail her.

The Fatal Weakness (1946). A comedy of a foolishly romantic woman; deals with her love of weddings and her loss of her husband to a refugee woman.

LAURENCE STALLINGS and MAXWELL ANDERSON: *What Price Glory?* (1924). See page 837.

MAXWELL ANDERSON: *Saturday's Children* (1927). A comedy of marriage of young people whose romance founders on economic problems.

Elizabeth the Queen (1930). See page 864.

Both Your Houses (1933). A political satire on Congressional logrolling; the story of a young legislator's struggle to purify politics.

Mary of Scotland (1933). A romantic verse tragedy about Mary Stuart's destruction by her designing rival, Elizabeth of England.

Winterset (1935). A poetic tragedy of modern life, in which the son of a wronged man foregoes for the sake of love his chance to vindicate his father and to save his own life.

High Tor (1937). A poetic fantasy about a young man's rebellion against the machine age; a satire on the mercenary world of materialists.

Anne of the Thousand Days (1948). A verse tragedy of Anne Boleyn, Elizabeth's mother, and her violent romance with Henry VIII. Notable for the conflict of high-spirited characters.

DAN TOTHEROH: *Wild Birds* (1925). A sensitive farm tragedy ending in a brutal murder.

SIDNEY HOWARD: *The Silver Cord* (1926). A psychological drama of overpossessive and destructive mother love.

Yellow Jack (1933). A semidocumentary treatment of the battle against yellow fever, reflecting the modern interest in science.

SIDNEY HOWARD and SINCLAIR LEWIS: *Dodsworth* (1933). A comedy of a wife's infatuation with European pseudo culture and of a Midwestern husband's awakening.

GEORGE S. KAUFMAN and MARC CONNELLY: *Beggar on Horseback* (1924). An expressionistic, satirical comedy of big business and its threat to individuality.

GEORGE S. KAUFMAN and RING LARDNER: *June Moon* (1929). A broad comedy of the popular-music-publishing business and a satire on commercialized "culture."

GEORGE S. KAUFMAN and MOSS HART: *Once in a Lifetime* (1930). A broad comedy of Hollywood life and manners.

You Can't Take It With You (1936). A comedy of carefree family life during the economic depression.

The Man Who Came to Dinner (1939). A high comedy of egotism on the part of a literary figure (Alexander Woollcott), ending in a farcical solution of the problem of his secretary's love affair.

GEORGE S. KAUFMAN and MORRIE RYSKIND: *Of Thee I Sing* (1931). A musical-comedy satire on American presidential campaigns and politics.

PAUL GREEN: *In Abraham's Bosom* (1926). A chronicle of a Negro's tragic struggle for education and dignity.

The House of Connelly (1932). A drama of

decadent Southern culture and of its dissolution.

Hymn to the Rising Sun (1936). A one-act drama of the chain gang in which social protest is fused with character study and poetic power.

Johnny Johnson (1937). The tragicomic history of a homespun American idealist, his disillusionment with Wilsonian democracy, and his vain attempt to oppose war, resulting in his ending his life in an insane asylum.

DU BOSE and DOROTHY HEYWARD: *Porgy* (1927). A Negro folk play. The basis of George Gershwin's folk opera, *Porgy and Bess* (1935).

E. P. CONKLE: *Crick Bottom Plays* (1928). A series of Midwestern one-act plays, among which is the grim *Minnie Field*.

JOHN BALDERSTON: *Berkeley Square* (1928). A fantasy in which an American, transported into eighteenth-century England, observes the manners of his English ancestors and returns to modern life.

S. N. BEHRMAN: *The Second Man* (1927). A high comedy of the difficulties of a sophisticated man in extricating himself from the situation of having an idealistic young woman in love with him when he prefers a life that makes fewer demands. A "second man" in him inclines him to a life of ease with a wealthy mistress.

Meteor (1929). A study of an American business tycoon, his will to power, and his delusions of grandeur.

Biography (1932). A high comedy contrasting two dispositions or outlooks—a too-relaxed tolerance and a too-insistent sense of righteousness. A comparison with *The Misanthrope* reveals parallels to Molière's comedy.

Rain from Heaven (1934). A study of an aloof esthete's realization that he must join the struggle against social evil as represented by fascism.

End of Summer (1936). A high comedy of the futility and distress of an idle rich woman and of her daughter's search for a life with more meaning and purpose.

JOHN WEXLEY: *The Last Mile* (1929). A realistic melodrama of prison life and of the electrocution of a convict.

They Shall Not Die (1934). An indictment of legal injustice to the Negro. Based on the famous Scottsboro case.

PHILIP BARRY: *Holiday* (1928). A comedy of the rebellion of an upper-class girl against the conservative standards of her family.

Hotel Universe (1930). A philosophical and psychological study of warped lives that are enlightened by an uncanny character.

Here Come the Clowns (1938). A fantasy of the conflict between good and evil in the world.

The Philadelphia Story (1939). A comedy of a too-righteous daughter of the social set who learns to make allowances for human frailty and remarries her former husband.

LYNN RIGGS: *Green Grow the Lilacs* (1931). A folk play of life on the Oklahoma frontier. The basis of the Rodgers and Hammerstein musical comedy *Oklahoma!* (1943).

LAWRENCE LANGNER and ARMINA MARSHALL: *The Pursuit of Happiness* (1933). A comedy of democratic ardor and "bundling" in New England during the Revolutionary War.

PAUL PETERS and GEORGE SKLAR: *Stevedore* (1934). A realistic melodrama and thesis drama of racial conflict in the South, showing white and Negro labor uniting to oppose a lynching.

SIDNEY KINGSLEY: *Dead End* (1934). A sociological picture of slum life and of the making of criminals in the environment of the underprivileged.

The World We Make (1939). A dramatization of Millen Brand's novel *The Outward Room*. A neurotic rich girl is cured of her anxieties by the kindness and courage of the common people among whom she finds shelter and love.

The Patriots (1943). A historical play presenting the conflict of Jefferson and Hamilton over social and political matters; concludes with Hamilton's support of Jefferson against Aaron Burr for the presidency.

Detective Story (1949). A naturalistic study of night-court life and a drama in which too much righteousness on the part of an idealistic detective backfires; a plea for tolerance and the tempering of righteousness with some consideration for the frailty of the human race.

LILLIAN HELLMAN: *The Children's Hour* (1934). A psychological drama of the maliciousness of a neurotic child who destroys two of her teachers with insinuations of homosexual relations between them.

The Little Foxes (1939). See page 983. See also *Another Part of the Forest,* treating the early history of the characters.

Watch on the Rhine (1941). A drama in which the struggle against fascism invades an American household that has tried to remain aloof from the social conflicts of the day and to lead a civilized life in a world torn by momentous issues.

CLIFFORD ODETS: *Waiting for Lefty* (1935). A semiexpressionistic one-act strike drama. Uses flashbacks into the lives of the underprivileged to explain their revolt against the social system of capitalism.

Till the Day I Die (1935). A one-act drama of the anti-Nazi underground in Germany.

Awake and Sing! (1935). A Chekhovian picture of disintegrating lower-middle-class life and of the rebellion of the young against the seedy respectability and timorousness of that life.

Paradise Lost (1936). An allegorical treatment of the failure of false middle-class hopes and dreams in a world of economic collapse and social conflict.

Golden Boy (1937). See page 950.

Rocket to the Moon (1938). A study of failure of nerve in middle-class society.

MARK REED: *Yes, My Darling Daughter* (1937). A comedy of a former "new woman" of the Greenwich Village period of Bohemianism, now conventionally married and the mother of a grown daughter, who is faced with the unconventional behavior of her daughter.

IRWIN SHAW: *Bury the Dead* (1936). A one-act fantasy of the revolt of the dead against the society that cheated them of a full life and then sent them to die in a new world war. May be compared with Hans Chlumberg's *The Miracle at Verdun.*

CLARE BOOTH: *The Women* (1936). A comedy of scandalmongering upper-class women and of their destruction of a woman's marriage.

THORNTON WILDER: *Our Town* (1938). See page 926.

JOHN STEINBECK: *Of Mice and Men* (1937). A drama of itinerant life, revolving around the friendship of a keen-witted youth for a pathetic imbecile endowed with too much physical strength.

ROBERT E. SHERWOOD: *The Road to Rome* (1926). An antiwar comedy about a Roman woman who breaks Hannibal's resolve to conquer Rome by awakening him to normal sexual appetites.

The Petrified Forest (1935). A symbolic drama, told in the form of a Western melodrama. Represents the failure of nerve in society and the suicidal impulse in civilization, which enable the barbarians to take over the world.

Idiots' Delight (1936). An augury of the coming of a second world war and a description of an outbreak of instinctive chauvinism among advocates of international-mindedness while the munitions magnates thrive.

There Shall Be No Night (1940). The drama of a Nobel Prize scientist and man of peace who arrives at the conclusion that, although war is madness, it is necessary to fight in behalf of freedom. First set in Finland, the action of the play was transferred to Greece for the British production in 1941.

ARTHUR ARENT and FEDERAL THEATRE STAFF: *The Living Newspaper: Power* (1937). A documentary drama of the utilities problem in the United States.

One-Third of a Nation (1938). A documentary "living newspaper" on the problem of housing and slum clearance in America.

PAUL OSBORN: *On Borrowed Time* (1938). A fantasy on death. Adapted from the novel by Lawrence Edward Watkin.

A Bell for Adano (1945). A dramatization of John Hersey's novel of the same title, dealing with the struggle of an American officer of Italian extraction to bring the democratic way of life to Italy under the Allied occupation.

JAMES THURBER and ELLIOTT NUGENT: *The Male Animal* (1939). A comic treatment of a college professor's domestic difficulties and effort to maintain a liberal point of view as a teacher.

HOWARD LINDSAY and RUSSEL CROUSE: *Life With Father* (1939). The famous period piece. A dramatization of Clarence Day's book of the same title.

State of the Union (1945). A "liberal comedy" about a presidential candidate's revolt against the politicians and reactionaries who use him to promote their interests and about his return to a wife who always deflates his ego but represents his better self.

Life With Mother (1949). A sequel to *Life With Father*.

WILLIAM SAROYAN: *My Heart's in the Highlands* (1939). See page 1016.

The Time of Your Life (1939). A bizarre comedy of life in a San Francisco water-front honky-tonk, where a wealthy idler encourages the marriage of his dull-witted but good-natured protégé to an unhappy young prostitute who tries to escape the miserable life she has been leading.

Love's Old Sweet Song (1940). A broad and romantic comedy of the love of a retiring old maid and a "pitchman," or vendor of quack medicines.

The Beautiful People (1941). A poetic fantasy about an oversensitive girl who succors mice and her philosophical father who tries to lead a carefree life.

Hello, Out There (West coast production, 1941; Broadway production, 1942). A realistic one-act play in which a tramp is imprisoned and killed when charged with rape by an immoral woman.

JOSEPH KESSELRING: *Arsenic and Old Lace* (1941). A farcical melodrama about kind old ladies who specialize in poison in order to put old men out of their misery.

SAMSON RAPHAELSON: *Jason* (1942). A high comedy dealing with the conflict of a hyper-esthetic drama critic and a rugged playwright of the people for the affections of an upstart girl.

JOHN VAN DRUTEN: *The Voice of the Turtle* (1943). A three-character comedy of love in wartime between two people who, when they take a seemingly passing affair seriously, discover that they are still capable of genuine love.

I Remember Mama (1944). A dramatization of Kathryn Forbes's *Mama's Bank Account*. Deals with a Norwegian immigrant family and an understanding mother who gives her children courage to face the world.

JAMES GOW and ARNAUD D'USSEAU: *Tomorrow the World* (1943). The reconditioning of the little son of a German liberal by understanding Americans who have taken charge of him after his education under National Socialism.

Deep Are the Roots (1945). A drama purporting to show that racial prejudice is so ingrained that it breaks out even in a Southern woman of liberal persuasion.

ARTHUR GOETZ and RUTH GOODMAN: *One-Man Show* (1944). A drama of the art dealers' world. Revolves around a father's effort to wean his daughter from himself and his reluctance to let her go when she falls in love.

The Heiress (1947). A notably successful dramatization of Henry James's short novel *Washington Square*.

MARY COYLE CHASE: *Harvey* (1944). A comedy of an alcoholic and his imaginary man-sized rabbit.

TENNESSEE WILLIAMS: *The Glass Menagerie* (1944 in Chicago; 1945 in New York). See page 1032.

A Streetcar Named Desire (1947). The drama of a mentally ailing woman who becomes a prostitute after the suicide of her homosexual husband. She seeks shelter in the home of her sister after coming to the end of her resources, but arouses the antagonism of her brother-in-law, is stripped of her defenses by him, and loses her mind after he sadistically violates her.

Summer and Smoke (1948). A novelistic drama of the love of an unworldly girl for a high-spirited young physician whose advances repel her and of her desperation on being rejected by him when she is at last ready for physical love.

JOHN PATRICK: *The Hasty Heart* (1945). A war drama set in the convalescent ward of a British general hospital.

ARTHUR LAURENTS: *Home of the Brave* (1945). A drama of racial tensions that cause the psychopathological condition of an American Jewish soldier of the Second World War; his condition is uncovered and cured by narcosynthesis.

EMMET LAVERY: *The Magnificent Yankee* (1946). A biography of Justice Oliver Wendell Holmes and a representation of his family life and championship of liberal principles.

GARSON KANIN: *Born Yesterday* (1946). A comedy of the awakening of the naïve mistress of a racketeer by a crusading reporter; an example of the liberal farce or comedy.

WILLIAM WISTER HAINES: *Command Decision* (1947). A notable war play dealing with an air-force officer's anguish over having to sacrifice his men in raids over Germany.

ARTHUR MILLER: *All My Sons* (1947). A social drama dealing with the discovery that loyalty to family cannot serve as an excuse for socially irresponsible conduct. An example of realistic thesis drama.

Death of a Salesman (1949). See page 1060.

THOMAS HEGGEN and JOSHUA LOGAN: *Mister Roberts* (1948). A dramatization of Heggen's novel of the same title, dealing with naval life and with a young lieutenant's efforts to badger his superiors into allowing him to see active duty.

CARSON MCCULLERS: *The Member of the Wedding* (1950). A dramatization by Miss McCullers of her novel of the same title. A sensitive study of the adolescence of a girl emerging from the tomboy stage.

WILLIAM ARCHIBALD: *The Innocents* (1950). A successful dramatization of Henry James's famous ghost novel *The Turn of the Screw*.

BIBLIOGRAPHY

This is a selective bibliography and is limited to general studies in the English language. Special studies are listed after the introductions to the plays included in this volume.

ENGLISH AND IRISH DRAMA AND THEATRE

BEERBOHM, MAX, *Around the Theatres*. New York: Knopf, 1930.

BYRNE, DAWSON: *The Story of Ireland's National Theatre*. Dublin: Talbot, 1929.

CUNLIFFE, J. W.: *Modern English Playwrights*. New York: Harper, 1927.

DICKINSON, THOMAS H.: *The Contemporary Drama of England*. Boston: Little, Brown, 1931.

GASSNER, JOHN: *Masters of the Drama*. New York: Random House, 1940; Dover Publications, 1945. (See pages 542–628.)

GREGORY, LADY AUGUSTA: *Our Irish Theatre*. New York: Putnam, 1913.

MacCARTHY, DESMOND: *Drama*. London: Putnam, 1940. (See especially pages 194–354.)

MALONE, ANDREW E.: *The Irish Drama*. New York: Scribner, 1929.

MARSHALL, NORMAN: *The Other Theatre*. London: John Lehman, 1947. (A history of British repertory companies.)

MORGAN, A. E.: *Tendencies of Modern English Drama*. New York: Scribner, 1924.

NICOLL, ALLARDYCE: *World Drama*. New York: Harcourt, 1950. (See pages 664–668, 689–699, 729–733, 741–770, 864–874, 880–903.)

PEACOCK, RONALD: *The Poet in the Theatre*. New York: Harcourt, 1946. (See especially pages 3–25, 86–93, 105–128.)

SHAW, G. B.: *Dramatic Opinions and Essays*. New York: Brentano's, 1906.

SPEAIGHT, ROBERT: *Drama Since 1939*. London: Longmans, 1947.

SHORT, ERNEST: *Theatrical Cavalcade*. London: Eyre and Spottiswoode, 1942.

WALKLEY, A. B.: *Drama and Life*. New York: Brentano's, 1908. (See pages 170–250, 309–315.)

WEYGANDT, CORNELIUS: *Irish Plays and Playwrights*. Boston: Houghton, 1913.

AMERICAN DRAMA AND THEATRE

ANDERSON, JOHN: *The American Theatre*. New York: Dial, 1938.

ATKINSON, BROOKS: *Broadway Scrapbook*. New York: Theatre Arts, 1947. (All but a few chapters deal with modern American drama.)

BROWN, JOHN MASON: *Two on the Aisle*. New York: Norton, 1938. (All but a few essays deal with the modern American theatre.)

Broadway Review. New York: Norton, 1940. (All but a few essays deal with the modern American theatre.)

Seeing Things. New York: Whittlesey House, 1946. (See reviews of American plays.)

Seeing More Things. New York: Whittlesey House, 1948. (See reviews of American plays.)

CARTER, JEAN, and JESSE OGDEN: *Everyman's Drama: A Study of the Non-Commercial Theatre in the United States*. New York: American Association for Adult Education, 1938.

CLURMAN, HAROLD: *The Fervent Years: The Story of the Group Theatre and the Thirties*. New York: Knopf, 1945.

DEUTSCH, HELEN, and STELLA HANAN: *The Provincetown*. New York: Farrar, 1931.

EATON, WALTER PRICHARD: *The Theatre Guild: The First Ten Years*. New York: Brentano's, 1929. (See also supplements published by the Theatre Guild at various times.)

FLANAGAN, HALLIE: *Arena*. New York: Duell, 1940. (The history of the Federal Theatre.)

Dynamo. New York: Duell, 1943. (A history of the Vassar Theatre; important for an understanding of the function of experimental theatre in America.)

FLEXNER, ELEANOR: *American Playwrights 1918–1938*. New York: Simon & Schuster, 1938.

GAGEY, EDMOND M.: *Revolution in the American Drama*. New York: Columbia University Press, 1947.

GASSNER, JOHN: *Masters of the Drama*. New York: Random House, 1940; Dover Publications, 1945. (See pages 629–694.)

Twenty-five Best Plays of the Modern American Theatre: Early Series (1919–1929). New York: Crown Publishers, 1949. (See Introduction, pages vii–xxviii.)

Twenty Best Plays of the Modern American Theatre (1929–1939). New York: Crown Publishers, 1939. (See Introduction, pages vii–xxii.)

Best Plays of the Modern American Theatre: Second Series (1939–1945). New York: Crown Publishers, 1945. (See Introduction, pages ix–xxx.)

HOUGHTON, NORRIS: *Advance from Broadway*. New York: Harcourt, 1941. (An account of the community-theatre production.)

HUGHES, GLENN: *The Penthouse Theatre*. New York: French, 1924. (A history of Professor Hughes's experimental theatre at the University of Washington.)

KRUTCH, JOSEPH WOOD: *The American Drama Since 1918*. New York: Random House, 1939. (The best critical study available.)

MANTLE, BURNS: *The Best Plays of 1909* (edited with Garrison Sherwood); *The Best Plays of 1919* and annual volumes thereafter until Mr. Mantle's death; *The Burns Mantle Best Plays of 1947–1948* (edited by John Chapman) and annual volumes thereafter. New York: Dodd, Mead. (These volumes provide a record of the American theatre.)

American Playwrights of Today. New York: Dodd, Mead, 1938.

MOREHOUSE, WARD: *Matinee Tomorrow: Fifty Years of Our Theatre*. New York: Whittlesey House, 1949.

NATHAN, GEORGE JEAN: *The Theatre Book of the Year 1942–1943* and annual volumes thereafter, New York: Knopf.

The Entertainment of a Nation. New York: Knopf, 1942.

QUINN, ARTHUR HOBSON: *A History of the American Drama*. New York: Crofts, 1936.

YOUNG, STARK: *Immortal Shadows*. New York: Scribner, 1948. (A large part of the volume deals with American drama.)

ABOUT THE EDITOR

JOHN GASSNER *has been acclaimed as "the greatest authority on the drama living in America" by* Commonweal *and as "the American theatre's official anthologist-in-chief" by* Theatre Arts. *He has also been well known as a drama critic, having written play reviews for a number of periodicals, and been a member of the New York Drama Critics Circle since 1936. His articles have been translated into many languages and his books have been used all over the world. As a practical man of the theatre, Mr. Gassner was chairman of the Theatre Guild's Play Department for more than a dozen years and executive head of Columbia Pictures' Play Department, in addition to operating more recently as an independent Broadway producer. Throughout an extraordinarily busy career, he has also found time to be a lecturer, radio commentator, and teacher; and many of the best-known younger playwrights have been at one time or another his students or protégés. He is at present an Associate Professor of English at Queens College and a Lecturer in Dramatic Arts in the Graduate School and the School of Dramatic Arts of Columbia University. In addition to having had several play adaptations produced, Mr. Gassner has published more than a dozen books on drama, theatrical art, motion pictures, and comparative literature. Among the best known of these are his* Masters of the Drama, Producing the Play, *and* Our Heritage of World Literature. *Mr. Gassner was educated at Columbia University and has been awarded university and Guggenheim Fellowships.*